On the Trail
of the
Buffalo Soldier

Biographies of African Americans in the U.S. Army, 1866–1917

Compiled and Edited by
Frank N. Schubert

 *Scholarly Resources Inc.*
Wilmington, Delaware

© 1995 by Scholarly Resources Inc.
All rights reserved
First published 1995
Printed and bound in the United States of America

Scholarly Resources Inc.
104 Greenhill Avenue
Wilmington, DE 19805-1897

Library of Congress Cataloging-in-Publication Data

On the trail of the buffalo soldier : biographies of African Americans in the U.S. Army, 1866–1917 / compiled and edited by Frank N. Schubert.
    p.   cm.
  Includes bibliographical references.
  ISBN 0-8420-2482-4 (alk. paper)
  1. Afro-American soldiers—Biography. 2. United States. Army—Biography.
3. United States. Army—Afro-Americans—History—20th century. 4. United States.
Army—Afro-Americans—History—19th century. I. Schubert, Frank N.
U52.05   1994
355'.0092'273—dc20
[B]
                                         93-46408
                                             CIP

dedicated to the memory of Max,

my father (1907–1964),

and to Max, my son

FRANK SCHUBERT has been conducting biographical research on buffalo soldiers for over twenty-five years. During that time his writings on the black regulars have appeared in several scholarly journals and in the *Dictionary of American Negro Biography* (1982). His latest book, *Buffalo Soldiers, Braves, and Brass: The Story of Fort Robinson, Nebraska* (1993), deals extensively with the experience of the Ninth and Tenth Cavalry in the decades around the turn of the twentieth century.

Employed for nearly twenty years as a historian in the U.S. Department of Defense, Dr. Schubert has also written on other topics. His books include *Vanguard of Expansion: Army Engineers in the Trans-Mississippi West, 1819–1879* (1980) and *Building Air Bases in Negev: The U.S. Army Corps of Engineers in Israel* (1992). Dr. Schubert is a graduate of Howard University and a Vietnam veteran. He holds a doctorate in history from the University of Toledo.

Contents

Acknowledgments

IN THE LAST FEW YEARS, as it became clear that my biographical files might develop into a book, a number of people helped me complete the transition. They include Nuala Barry of the U.S. Army Institute of Heraldry; Constance Potter of the National Archives; Margaret Vining of the Smithsonian Institution; Anthony Powell of San José, California, who may know as much about the buffalo soldiers as anyone; Gordon L. Olson, the Grand Rapids, Michigan, city historian; and Romana Danysh of the U.S. Army Center of Military History. Arthur S. Hardyman and John Birmingham, also of the Center of Military History, offered valuable suggestions regarding the design of the book.

I was also fortunate enough to work with the very able and dedicated group of professionals at Scholarly Resources. I especially appreciate the efforts of Laura Huey Cunningham, with whom I started this project, and managing editor Carolyn Travers, with whom it was finished. Both always strove to produce the finest possible book, and it was a pleasure to work with them. I also would like to thank Ann M. Aydelotte, Linda Pote Musumeci, Barbara Frechette, Sharon L. Beck, production manager James L. Preston, editorial director Richard M. Hopper, and president Daniel C. Helmstadter.

Because this project was started about twenty-five years ago, some of my debts go back a long way. I was particularly fortunate to have had the opportunity to learn from the late James D. Walker of the National Archives, who was always willing to take the time to teach and encourage a young historian. I also had the good fortune to work with Michael C. Robinson, now with the U.S. Army Corps of Engineers, as we studied together the few black soldiers who had defected in the Philippines. My wife Irene tolerated my compulsive behavior while I chased biographical data for my files. In addition, she realized that there was a book here and convinced me to pursue this project after I had turned my back on it. She and our son Max also helped me correct the problems created by some of my earlier note-taking. For their help and so much more, I thank them both.

Introduction

The Regiments

THE MILITARY CONTRIBUTIONS of black soldiers in the war for the Union and subsequent conflicts are generally well covered in the literature that has emerged since the 1960s.[1] The small regular Army that remained after the Civil War set important precedents for black soldiers. Most important, the post-Civil War Army included six regiments set aside for black enlisted men. For the first time, blacks had a permanent place in the peacetime military establishment of the United States. Their officers were all white and, with only a handful of exceptions, remained so for almost a century. Moreover, the establishment of regiments exclusively for blacks introduced de jure segregation to the military service long before President Woodrow Wilson imposed it on the civilian branches of government. Nevertheless, the creation of the 9th and 10th Cavalry regiments and the 38th, 39th, 40th, and 41st Infantry units was generally considered a positive step taken in recognition of the major contributions that black soldiers had made to preserving the Union during the Civil War.

Congress created the six black regiments as part of the reorganization act of July 28, 1866.[2] In the spring of 1869 the six became four, as the Army was reduced once more. The two cavalry units remained intact, but the four infantry regiments were reduced to two. The 38th and 41st were combined to make up the 24th Infantry regiment; the 39th and 40th became the 25th.[3] In the fifty-year period that is covered in this book, until the American entry in the great European war, the troops in these regiments served in all of the nation's battles.[4] They chased and fought plains and desert tribes during the decades immediately following the Civil War and stayed in the West to garrison scattered posts and provide assurance for nervous settlers. They also participated in the Cuban battles against Spain and in the ensuing guerrilla war in the Philippines and fought in skirmishes along the Mexican border.[5]

In the course of the 10th Cavalry's early clashes with the tribes of the southern plains, the men of the regiment came to be called buffalo soldiers. The name apparently originated with the Indians, who may have seen a similarity between the hair and the skin of the soldiers and those of the buffalo. Most writers on the subject contend that the name reflected the respect that the Indian warriors had for the African-American soldiers, and the buffalo became a prominent element of the 10th's regimental crest.[6] Before long, the 9th's troopers also became known as buffalo soldiers, as did ultimately the infantrymen. The name still has resonance, and General Colin Powell, the first African-American chairman of the Joint Chiefs of Staff, has referred to himself as a descendant of the buffalo soldier.[7]

A handful of volunteer regiments also served at the turn of the century. They consisted of black enlisted men and gave some black veterans the opportunity to serve briefly as commissioned officers. During the war with Spain, these units included the 7th, 8th, 9th, and 10th U.S. Volunteer Infantry regiments. In addition, the 48th and 49th U.S. Volunteer Infantry regiments were created late in 1898, and their members fought in the Philippine Insurrection. A few state units also included blacks. However, only the four regular regiments remained part of the active Army continuously through almost the entire period of the segregated Army, the 9th and 10th until 1944 and the 24th and 25th until 1951 and 1949, respectively.[8]

The Research

As a graduate student in the late 1960s, I started research on the buffalo soldiers. Frustrated that the growing literature on the soldiers, as well as the official records of regiments and posts, did little to illuminate the men as individuals, I began to assemble scraps of biographical data into what I called my Name File. At first, these bits of information came from government records and reports and local newspapers. Later, I began to look at collective biographies, black newspapers, pension files, and a variety of other sources. My ultimate goal was to learn about these men—who they were, where they came from, what marked their experiences in the Army, what they found there that made them stay in the service, and what became of them after their terms were over or they retired.

The biographical research inevitably followed my other research interests. The focus initially fell on black soldiers in Wyoming and then moved to Fort Robinson, Nebraska, where black cavalrymen served from 1885 to 1898 and from 1902 to 1907. Later the emphasis shifted to the Philippine Insurrection and to the career of Private David Fagen of the 24th Infantry, who defected to the Filipino insurgents in 1899 and became an officer among them.

The long-range goal was to create a comprehensive record of the lives of black soldiers. As the project progressed, the research became more systematic, and my notes began to represent an index to major sources of information. My files and the entries in this book therefore contain all references to black soldiers from a number of key components of the literature. These include the annual reports of the secretary of war (for the entire period from 1867 to 1917), the weekly *Army and Navy Journal*, and the Manila (Philippines) *Times*, an English-language daily that closely covered the activities of the Army during the insurrection. The entries provide similar coverage for three major black weeklies, as well as for *Winners of the West*, *Crisis*, and other periodicals, in addition to a number of books and articles.

Another important class of documentation involves occasional comprehensive lists of personnel. The earliest of these in terms of the period covered is Anita McMiller's work on the formation of the 10th Cavalry. Later publications include a roster of 10th Cavalry contributors to an 1890 testimonial to General Benjamin H. Grierson, an 1893 roster of 9th Cavalry noncommissioned officers, and a similar list for the 10th Cavalry in 1897. Herschel Cashin and his coauthors listed all 10th Cavalry soldiers who served in 1898 during the war with Spain, and a private publisher produced a comprehensive illustrated review of the 9th Cavalry in 1910.[9]

The entries also draw from military records, a vast and largely untapped resource for biographical research, but in many cases only to the extent that these records were used in other projects. For example, entries based on bimonthly muster rolls identify and provide data on every man who served during 1898 and 1899 in H and I companies of the 24th Infantry, David Fagen's units before he defected, but make no mention of the regiment's other elements. Muster rolls for the entire period from the Civil War to World War I (actually from 1784 to 1912) are among the many records preserved in Record Group 94 in the National Archives, and they constitute a massive collection.

Exceptions to this selectivity involve the unit records in the National Archives' Record Group 391 and the Veterans Administration pension files that are cited in the bibliography. With those records I tried to create a comprehensive index, similar to that devised for the newspapers and annual reports mentioned above. Various obligations and imperatives ultimately forced me to curtail the entire research, but the result remains an introduction to the literature and a basic source of biographical information on about eight thousand of the soldiers.

The Name File grew over the years, as did the sense that something was still lacking in this field of scholarship. In fact, the observations of others who studied the black regulars reinforced this impression. Anita McMiller, also a student of the buffalo soldiers, once complained that much of what has been written concentrates on the white officers who led black troops. She observed that if you changed the names of the units in some narratives to, say, the 3rd Infantry or the 7th Cavalry, instead of the 24th Infantry or the 9th Cavalry, the story would read approximately the same way. She wanted to know about the black enlisted soldiers, namely, what set them apart, what characterized their experiences, what were their origins, and what had happened to them after their periods of service. Monroe Billington, in his book on black soldiers in New Mexico, raised a similar question when he reflected on the potential value of a biographical directory of enlisted men, white and black, along the lines of Francis Heitman's compilation of officers.[10]

Even if the scope were limited to include only black soldiers, such a volume would have significant ground to cover. African Americans served as volunteers in all of the nation's wars, and nearly two hundred thousand bore arms for the Union during the Civil War. This book is the closest approximation available to a biographical directory of the blacks who served their nation in the fifty years between the Civil War and World War I.

The Entries

On the Trail of the Buffalo Soldier represents a starting point for biographical research on a little-known group that contributed significantly to the nation's development. The alphabetically arranged entries range from virtually complete life histories to individual fragments of data, with the more substantial entries including a wide range of personal information, such as date and place of birth, civilian occupation, and names of family members, as well as details of military service. Sometimes the information from one source differs from that taken from another, but the entries ordinarily present what was found and make no judgment regarding the accuracy of the material. (NOTE: The data used to compile the tables in the Appendix also were taken from various sources; therefore, the same approach was followed, and discrepancies may exist between this information and that in the entries.) The main exception to this rule occurs in cases in which a soldier's name was obviously misspelled. The entries also illuminate the range of sources available to historians and genealogists, so that a researcher who does not locate the name of a particular soldier in this volume should find ample suggestions about the kinds of sources to examine.

Each entry starts with the name, rank, and unit (usually company and regiment) of the individual, or as much of that information as possible. The rank and unit cited within the bold headings reflect the latest period of the soldier's career on which such data were available. In some cases, neither his highest rank attained is shown nor the unit in which he served the longest. Moreover, while the men included all served between the Civil War and World War I, data are provided for later years when it is reasonably clear that the information pertains to men who had served earlier. For example, one listing gives a report of a sergeant's retirement in 1932 because he probably served for thirty years previously.

Within each entry the biographical information is organized chronologically to the extent possible, starting with the source relating to the first phase of a soldier's career. All of the sources available for each man are presented together. In some cases, material from individual sources covers long periods of a soldier's life. Generally, the information is followed by a shortened reference to the source. For some of the entries, gathered about twenty-five years ago before I knew what I intended to do with the data I was amassing, sources were not documented; therefore, a few of the entries lack citations.

One of the most useful sources, the unit descriptive book, regrettably exists only for a few units and for brief periods. Six are in the National Archives in Record Group 391, and a complete set for the volunteer 49th Infantry is in Record Group 94. These books contain information on a soldier's place of birth, family, and occupation before enlistment, as well as on his military record. They show, for instance, whether he was inclined to put away part of his pay, whether he managed to save any of his clothing allowance or had to reimburse the government for supplies lost or damaged, and how much pay had been retained as a hedge against desertion pending his discharge. They also indicate his court martial record and the character assigned to him, which functioned as an early version of an efficiency rating—fair, good, very good, or excellent if he served acceptably, or no character if he did not. In addition, these records show the number of enlistments and where service took place.

Most of the anecdotal evidence indicates that black soldiers in the fifty years following the Civil War tended to reenlist much more regularly than whites. But they did not necessarily stay in one regiment. Monthly reports, known as regimental returns, which reveal changes in personnel strengths, frequently mention men transferring into or out of the black regiments. Descriptive books and pension files also show soldiers who had served in more than one regiment. In some cases, in order to build biographical sketches, I used bits of data from different periods concerning various regiments. However, care was taken in doing so because of the danger of possibly creating life stories that did not exist.

It is probable that the entries in this work represent fewer than the approximately eight thousand men listed. Genealogists making connections across the decades should exercise great caution, particularly when considering the careers of men with names that are not distinctive. For example, this volume contains almost two pages of William Johnsons; seven served in the 10th Cavalry in 1898, and they may or may not be the same William Johnsons who served at other times.

Although the entries cover fifty years, the number of black soldiers who served and are listed here peaked at about the turn of the century. Black service increased because of the recruitment of volunteer regiments for duty in Cuba and the Philippines. The regular regiments expanded for the war years as well, as shown in the table of black enlisted men for the years from 1867 to 1916 (see Appendix). The concentration of entries around the period of the Cuban and Philippine wars is due partly to this expansion but also to the concentration of my early research on that particular time and on the years immediately before and after.

Overall, this compilation of biographical material focuses on buffalo soldiers as individuals. But the sum is at least as important as the parts. Taken together, the entries demonstrate the variety of the experience of African-American soldiers in and out of the Army and the wide range of sources available for the study of their lives and times.

Notes

1. For overviews see Bernard C. Nalty, *Strength for the Fight: A History of Black Americans in the Military* (New York: Free Press, 1986); Jack D. Foner, *Blacks and the Military in American History: A New Perspective* (New York: Praeger, 1974); and Morris J. MacGregor and Bernard C. Nalty, eds., *Blacks in the United States Armed Forces: Basic Documents*, 13 vols. (Wilmington, DE: Scholarly Resources, 1977). On the Civil War service of blacks there is a large body of scholarship. See especially Dudley T. Cornish, *The Sable Arm: Negro Troops in the Union Army, 1861–1865* (New York: W. W. Norton and Co., 1966); and Joseph T. Glathaar, *Forged in Battle: The Civil War Alliance of Black Soldiers and White Officers* (New York: Free Press, 1990).

2. The establishment of the six regiments was announced to the Army in General Order (GO) 56, published by the Adjutant General's Office (AGO) on August 1, 1866.

3. GO 17, AGO, 15 March 1869.

4. The recent literature starts with William H. Leckie's *The Buffalo Soldiers: A Narrative of the Negro Cavalry in the West* (Norman: University of Oklahoma Press, 1967). See also Arlen L. Fowler, *The Black Infantry in the West, 1869–1891* (Westport, CT: Greenwood Publishing Corp., 1971); Marvin E. Fletcher, *The Black Soldier and Officer in the United States Army, 1891–1917* (Columbia: University of Missouri Press, 1974); Monroe L. Billington, *New Mexico's Buffalo Soldiers, 1866–1900* (Nitow, CO: University of Colorado Press, 1991); and Frank N. Schubert, *Buffalo Soldiers, Braves, and the Brass: The Story of Fort Robinson, Nebraska* (Shippensburg, PA: White Mane Publishing Co., 1993).

5. Official campaign credits for the 9th and 10th Cavalry are in Mary Lee Stubbs and Stanley Russell Connor, *Armor-Cavalry*, Part 1: *Regular Army and Army Reserve* (Washington, DC: Office of the Chief of Military History, 1969), 191–209. For the infantry regiments see *The Army Lineage Book*, vol. 2: *Infantry* (Washington, DC: Government Printing Office, 1953), 132–41.

6. For the majority view see Leckie, *The Buffalo Soldiers*, 26. For a native American view see Vernon Bellecourt, "The Glorification of Buffalo Soldiers Raises Racial Divisions between Blacks, Whites," *Indian Country Today* (formerly *Lakota Times*), May 4, 1994.

7. *New York Times*, May 15, 1994.

8. Stubbs and Connor, *Armor-Cavalry*, 192, 201; *Army Lineage Book*, 132, 135.

9. All of the works mentioned here are cited in the bibliography at the end of this volume.

10. Billington, *New Mexico's Buffalo Soldiers*, 246; Francis B. Heitman, *Historical Register and Dictionary of the United States Army, from Its Organization, September 29, 1789, to March 2, 1903*, 2 vols. (Washington, DC: Government Printing Office, 1903; reprinted by University of Illinois Press, 1965).

Abbreviations

AAAG	Acting Assistant Adjutant General	Kans Inf	Kansas Infantry
AAG	Assistant Adjutant General	KSHS	Kansas State Historical Society
ACP	Appointment, commission, and personal	LR	Letters Received
Adj	Adjutant	LS	Letters Sent
AG	Adjutant General	LTC	Lieutenant Colonel
AGO	Adjutant General's Office	Mass Inf	Massachusetts Infantry
Ala Inf	Alabama Infantry	MG	Major General
ANJ	*Army and Navy Journal*	MHI	Military History Institute
ANR	*Army and Navy Register*	Misc	Miscellaneous
AR	*Annual Report*	NCO	Noncommissioned Officer
Bde	Brigade	NCS	Noncommissioned Staff
Bks	Barracks	NSHS	Nebraska State Historical Society
Bn	Battalion	Ord Sgt	Ordnance Sergeant
Cav	Cavalry	PMG	Paymaster General
CG	Commanding General	QM	Quartermaster
CO	Commanding Officer	QM Sgt	Quartermaster Sergeant
Comsy Sgt	Commissary Sergeant	RBHL	Rutherford B. Hayes Library
DeptColo	Department of Colorado	Regt	Regiment
DeptMo	Department of the Missouri	RO	Regimental Order
DeptPlatte	Department of the Platte	SD	Special Duty
Det	Detachment	SecWar	Secretary of War
DivMo	Division of the Missouri	SG	Surgeon General
DivPI	Division of the Philippines	SO	Special Order
DP	Department of the Platte	Sqdn	Squadron
ES	Endorsements Sent	Sup Sgt	Supply Sergeant
Ft	Fort	Tech Sgt	Technical Sergeant
GCM	General Court Martial	TS	Telegrams Sent
GCMO	General Court Martial Order	USA	United States Army
GO	General Order	USMA	United States Military Academy
HQ	Headquarters	USV	United States Volunteers
Ill Inf	Illinois Infantry	VA	Veterans Administration
Inf	Infantry	Vol	Volunteer

We made the West; defeated the hostile tribes of Indians;
and made the country safe to live in.
PRIVATE HENRY McCOMBS, E/10TH CAVALRY—*WINNERS OF THE WEST*, 1927

~

We did our duty in Cuba, and we don't think we should be insulted because we are black.
CORPORAL STEPHEN PATTERSON, H/24TH INFANTRY—SAN FRANCISCO *CHRONICLE*, 1899

~

We glory in the prestige won by our regiments.
CHAPLAIN GEORGE W. PRIOLEAU, 9TH CAVALRY—*ARMY AND NAVY JOURNAL*, 1899

~

If there is any doubt on the part of any citizen as to our valor, courage, and obedience in
the Army, I simply refer him to the records of the War Department, in Washington, DC.
SERGEANT MAJOR EUGENE FRIERSON, 10TH CAVALRY—CURTIS, *THE BLACK SOLDIER*, 1918

A

ABBOTT, James W.; Ord Sgt; U.S. Army. Born Hendricks County, KY, 1860; occupation soldier; regimental clerk, 24 Mar 1884; discharged 29 Jul 1886; character excellent; Ht 5'8", complexion brown; reenlisted and joined regiment at Ft Sill, Indian Territory, 2 Aug 1886; marksman, 1883–87; made corporal, E/24th Infantry, 9 Dec 1886; reduced to ranks at own request, 6 Feb 1888; promoted to regimental sergeant major, 17 Feb 1889; extra duty as schoolteacher, Ft Bayard, NM, 13 Jun 1886–17 Feb 1889; detached service with Band/24th Infantry, Deming, NM, 18–22 Apr 1891, to receive president of the United States; discharged from Ft Bayard, 1 Aug 1891, character good; single; additional pay $2 per month, retained $60, clothing $7.19, deduction for subsistence stores $16.83. SOURCE: Descriptive Book, 24 Inf NCS & Band.

Mentioned as schoolteacher, Ft Bayard, temporarily reassigned from San Carlos, AZ, 1888. SOURCE: Billington, *New Mexico's Buffalo Soldiers*, 162.

Enlisted and joined regiment, Ft Bayard, 7 Aug 1891; detached service, Washington, DC, conducting insane soldier to asylum, 4–19 Apr 1893; detached service, Trinidad, CO, with four companies and regiment headquarters protecting railroads from strikers; discharged from Ft Bayard, 6 Aug 1896, character excellent; single; additional pay $3 per month, retained $55.30, clothing $7.43. SOURCE: Descriptive Book, 24 Inf NCS & Band.

Author of neat roster of noncommissioned officers, correct to Apr 1890. SOURCE: *ANJ* 27 (3 May 1890): 679.

At Ft Bayard, 1890. *See* HENDRICKS, Lewis, 24th Infantry

Mentioned, at Ft Bayard, 1892. SOURCE: *ANJ* 29 (26 Mar 1892): 537.

Appointed ordnance sergeant; with 24th Infantry since initial enlistment on 29 Jul 1881; now at Ft Douglas, UT. SOURCE: *ANJ* 34 (7 Aug 1897): 907.

ABBOTT, John W.; Recruit; 24th Inf. Tried by general court martial, Columbus Barracks, OH, for desertion, 9 Oct 1881; pleaded not guilty but found guilty of absence without leave and fined $10 per month for six months and six months' confinement. SOURCE: GCMO 7, AGO, 18 Jan 1882.

ABERNATHY, Wooten R.; Sgt Maj; 48th Inf. Promoted from corporal. SOURCE: Richmond *Planet*, 14 Apr 1900.

Died in the Philippines, 19 Dec 1900. SOURCE: *ANJ* 38 (29 Dec 1900): 431.

ACKLIN, John R.; Private; M/10th Cav. Served in 10th Cavalry, 1898; remained in U.S. during war with Spain. SOURCE: Cashin, *Under Fire with the Tenth Cavalry*, 351.

ACRE, Henry; F/10th Cav. Original member of 10th Cavalry; in troop when organized, Ft Leavenworth, KS, 21 Jun 1867. SOURCE: McMiller, "Buffalo Soldiers," 73.

ADAIR, Clifford J.; Private; C/25th Inf. His silver pen confiscated by U.S. customs officer, Brownsville, on his return from Mexico, 8 Aug 1906. SOURCE: Haynes, *A Night of Violence*, 55.

Dishonorable discharge, Brownsville. SOURCE: SO 266, AGO, 9 Nov 1906.

One of fourteen cleared of involvement in Brownsville raid by court in 1910 and authorized to reenlist. SOURCE: Weaver, *The Brownsville Raid*, 248.

ADAMS, Alex; Private; 10th Cav. Not yet received at Ft Leavenworth, KS, from Jefferson Barracks, MO. SOURCE: Adj, Ft Leavenworth, to HQ, Jefferson Bks, 9 Oct 1866.

ADAMS, Alexander H.; Corporal; H/9th Cav. Born Woodville, MS; occupation schoolteacher; enlisted Xenia, OH, 13 Oct 1895, at age 24; Ht 5'7 1/2"; joined at Ft Robinson, NE, 18 Oct 1895; promoted to corporal, 13 Sep 1898; discharged, expiration of service, Ft Sill, OK, 13 Oct 1898. SOURCE: Descriptive Book, H/9 Cav.

Qualified but not teaching, Ft Duchesne, UT, schools, 1 Nov 1895–29 Feb 1896. SOURCE: Reports of Schools, Ft Duchesne.

ADAMS, Earnest E.; Private; 24th Inf. Served in Houston, TX, 1917; convinced court martial that he hid behind icebox behind company kitchen during riot. SOURCE: Haynes, *A Night of Violence*, 86, 268.

ADAMS, Henry; Recruit; E/10th Cav. Original member of 10th Cavalry; in troop when organized, Ft Leavenworth, KS, 15 Jun 1867. SOURCE: McMiller, "Buffalo Soldiers," 72.

Enlisted spring 1867. SOURCE: LS, 10 Cav, 1866–67.

ADAMS, Howard; Cook; F/9th Cav. At Ft D. A. Russell, WY, in 1910; resident of Macon, GA. SOURCE: *Illustrated Review: Ninth Cavalry*, with picture.

ADAMS, John; B/10th Cav. Original member of 10th Cavalry; in troop when organized, Ft Leavenworth, KS, 1 Apr 1867. SOURCE: McMiller, "Buffalo Soldiers," 69.

ADAMS, John; L/10th Cav. Original member of 10th Cavalry; in troop when organized, Ft Riley, KS, 21 Sep 1867. SOURCE: McMiller, "Buffalo Soldiers," 78.

ADAMS, John; Private; C/9th Cav. Commended for bravery against Apaches, Florida Mountains, NM, 24 Jan 1877. SOURCE: Leckie, *The Buffalo Soldiers*, 179.

Commendation mentioned. SOURCE: Billington, *New Mexico's Buffalo Soldiers*, 51.

ADAMS, Joseph; Trumpeter; A/10th Cav. At Ft Apache, AZ, 1890, subscribed $.50 to testimonial to General Grierson. SOURCE: List of subscriptions, 23 Apr 1890, 10th Cavalry papers, MHI.

ADAMS, Nimrod; 1st Sgt; A/10th Cav. As saddler sergeant, A/10th Cavalry, Ft Apache, AZ, 1890, subscribed $.50 to testimonial to General Grierson. SOURCE: List of subscriptions, 23 Apr 1890, 10th Cavalry papers, MHI.

Served in 10th Cavalry in Cuba, 1898. SOURCE: Cashin, *Under Fire with the Tenth Cavalry*, 336.

Retired as first sergeant, A/10th Cavalry. SOURCE: SO 296, AGO, 7 Dec 1903.

No Veterans Administration pension file.

ADAMS, P. F.; Private; A/9th Cav. At Ft Stanton, NM, 1881. SOURCE: Regt Returns, 9 Cav, Jan 1881.

ADAMS, Percy; Corporal; A/25th Inf. Promoted from private. SOURCE: *ANR* 38 (28 Oct 1905): 21.

ADAMS, Singleton; F/10th Cav. Served 1875–80; member, Camp 11, National Indian War Veterans, St. Joseph, MO; died Waco, TX. SOURCE: *Winners of the West* 14 (Apr 1937): 4.

ADAMS, William; Sergeant; D/10th Cav. At Ft Apache, AZ, 1890, sergeant, subscribed $.50 to testimonial to General Grierson. SOURCE: List of subscriptions, 23 Apr 1890, 10th Cavalry papers, MHI.

ADAMS, William; Private; B/10th Cav. Served in 10th Cavalry, 1898; remained in U.S. during war with Spain. SOURCE: Cashin, *Under Fire with the Tenth Cavalry*, 339.

ADINGS, John; G/24th Inf. Age 31, admitted to Soldiers Home for disability, 21 Aug 1888; six years and eight months' service. SOURCE: SecWar, *AR 1888*, 904.

ADKERSON, Charlie; Private; B/9th Cav. At Ft D. A. Russell, WY, in 1910. SOURCE: *Illustrated Review: Ninth Cavalry.*

ADKINS, William; Private; B/10th Cav. Served in 10th Cavalry, 1898; remained in U.S. during war with Spain. SOURCE: Cashin, *Under Fire with the Tenth Cavalry*, 339.

AHREN, Irwin; Private; A/9th Cav. Discharged, certificate of disability, Ft Stanton, NM, 11 Jan 1881. SOURCE: Regt Returns, 9 Cav, Jan 1881.

AIKEN, Flex; B/10th Cav. Original member of 10th Cavalry; in troop when organized, Ft Leavenworth, KS, 1 Apr 1867. SOURCE: McMiller, "Buffalo Soldiers," 69.

AIKEN, John H.; L/10th Cav. Original member of 10th Cavalry; in troop when organized, Ft Riley, KS, 21 Sep 1867. SOURCE: McMiller, "Buffalo Soldiers," 78.

AIKIN, John P.; Private; L/10th Cav. Died Ft Arbuckle, KS, 27 Apr 1870. SOURCE: CO, L/10 Cav, to CO, 10 Cav, Apr 1870, LS, 10 Cav, 1868–71.

ALBERT, John; E/10th Cav. Original member of 10th Cavalry; in troop when organized, Ft Leavenworth, KS, 15 Jun 1867. SOURCE: McMiller, "Buffalo Soldiers," 72.

ALBERT, Stewart; Sergeant; D/9th Cav. Participated in Victorio campaign, 1881. SOURCE: Billington, *New Mexico's Buffalo Soldiers*, 102.

ALBRIGHT; Private; B/10th Cav. At Ft Apache, AZ, 1890, subscribed $.50 to testimonial to General Grierson. SOURCE: List of subscriptions, 23 Apr 1890, 10th Cavalry papers, MHI.

ALDNGE, George; A/10th Cav. Original member of 10th Cavalry; in A Troop when organized, Ft Leavenworth, KS, 18 Feb 1867. SOURCE: McMiller, "Buffalo Soldiers," 68.

ALDRICH, G. B.; Private; G/10th Cav. On extra duty as schoolteacher. SOURCE: *ANJ* 35 (18 Dec 1897): 292.

ALDRIDGE, George; Private; 10th Cav. Arrived at Ft Leavenworth, KS, from Jefferson Barracks, MO. SOURCE: Adj, Ft Leavenworth, to HQ, Jefferson Bks, 9 Oct 1866.

ALDRIDGE, J. E.; Private; A/9th Cav. At Ft Stanton, NM, 1881. SOURCE: Regt Returns, 9 Cav, Jan 1881.

Discharged, certificate of disability, Ft Stanton, 23 Feb 1881. SOURCE: Regt Returns, 9 Cav, Feb 1881.

ALEXANDER; Corporal; F/9th Cav. With detachment scouting vicinity of Ft Lewis, CO, Jun 1883. SOURCE: Regt Returns, 9 Cav, Jun 1883.

ALEXANDER; Private; A/10th Cav. At Ft Apache, AZ, 1890, subscribed $.50 to testimonial to General Grierson. SOURCE: List of subscriptions, 23 Apr 1890, 10th Cavalry papers, MHI.

ALEXANDER; Private; B/10th Cav. At Ft Apache, AZ, 1890, subscribed $.50 to testimonial to General Grierson. SOURCE: List of subscriptions, 23 Apr 1890, 10th Cavalry papers, MHI.

ALEXANDER; 1st Sgt; D/10th Cav. Directed 10th Cavalry's Wild West show, at the riding hall, Ft Ethan Allen, VT, Thanksgiving 1911. SOURCE: Fletcher, *The Black Soldier*, 80.

ALEXANDER, Alphonso; Private; I/10th Cav. Served in 10th Cavalry, 1898; remained in U.S. during war with Spain. SOURCE: Cashin, *Under Fire with the Tenth Cavalry*, 348.

ALEXANDER, Andrew; C/10th Cav. Original member of 10th Cavalry; in troop when organized, Ft Leavenworth, KS, 14 May 1867. SOURCE: McMiller, "Buffalo Soldiers," 70.

ALEXANDER, Benjamin F.; Private; K/10th Cav. Served in 10th Cavalry, 1898; remained in U.S. during war with Spain. SOURCE: Cashin, *Under Fire with the Tenth Cavalry*, 349.

ALEXANDER, Cook; Private; Band/24th Inf. Born Columbia, TN; Ht 5'9", black eyes, hair, and complexion; first enlisted in D/9th Cavalry, 5 Jan 1878–4 Jan 1883, character good; second enlistment: K/24th Infantry, 15 Jan 1883–14 Jan 1888, character excellent; third enlistment: 25 Jan 1888, Ft Leavenworth, KS, transferred from K/24th Infantry, 4 Oct 1888; married, character fair, age 31 in 1888. SOURCE: Entry dated 4 Oct 1888, Ft Bayard, NM, Descriptive Book, 24 Inf NCS & Band.

At Ft Supply, Indian Territory, 1883, wife's travel expenses from East paid by Lt. J. B. Batchelor, 24th Infantry, with understanding that she would work for him as maid. SOURCE: Fowler, *The Black Infantry*, 78.

ALEXANDER, Edward; Private; D/24th Inf. Transferred to Hospital Corps, Jun 1894. SOURCE: *ANJ* 31 (30 Jun 1894): 771.

ALEXANDER, Fred; F/9th Cav. Enlisted for Spanish War, was in Tampa, FL, and with his troop for the duration, then Montauk, NY, and Ft Huachuca, AZ; honorable discharge, character good; lynched, Leavenworth, KS, for murder of Minnie Forbes. SOURCE: Cleveland *Gazette*, 26 Jan and 9 Feb 1901.

ALEXANDER, Henry; Private; C/25th Inf. At San Antonio, TX, 1878, best marksman in his company, tied for fourth in regiment. SOURCE: Scrapbook, 25 Inf, I, 145.

ALEXANDER, Henry; Private; F/24th Inf. Died of dysentery in the Philippines, 8 Dec 1899. SOURCE: *ANJ* 37 (10 Mar 1900): 659.

ALEXANDER, Henry E.; Farrier; K/9th Cav. Veteran of Philippine Insurrection; at Ft D. A. Russell, WY, in 1910; resident of Berkeville, KY. SOURCE: *Illustrated Review: Ninth Cavalry*, with picture.

ALEXANDER, James H.; Sergeant; 10th Cav. A pair of his gloves was stolen by Pvt. Charles Waters, when both were in L/10th Cavalry, Ft Bayard, NM, 1889. SOURCE: Billington, *New Mexico's Buffalo Soldiers*, 168.

At Ft Apache, AZ, 1890, sergeant, D/10th Cavalry, subscribed $.50 to testimonial to General Grierson. SOURCE: List of subscriptions, 23 Apr 1890, 10th Cavalry papers, MHI.

An excellent noncommissioned officer who should command, according to John E. Lewis, H/10th Cavalry, in letter, Lakeland, FL, 5 Jun 1898. SOURCE: Gatewood, *"Smoked Yankees,"* 36.

Served in 10th Cavalry, 1898; remained in U.S. during war with Spain. SOURCE: Cashin, *Under Fire with the Tenth Cavalry*, 346.

Was visited at Thanksgiving 1898, Camp Forse, AL, by his wife and family from Ft Assiniboine, MT. SOURCE: Richmond *Planet*, 3 Dec 1898.

Promoted from corporal. SOURCE: *ANJ* 35 (22 Jan 1898): 382.

ALEXANDER, John Hanks; 2nd Lt; 9th Cav. Born Helena, AR, 6 Jan 1864; father had purchased mother and first three children from slavery by 1850; John H. was the fourth of seven; father was dry-goods merchant, first black justice of the peace in Arkansas, in state legislature from Phillips Co., died 1871. Went to Helena High School for blacks, was only graduate before abolition, worked selling papers, riding mail, other odd jobs; fall 1880 attended Oberlin after six months as teacher in Mississippi; worked summer in Cleveland hotel. Other United States Military Academy cadets were "very gentlemanly, friendly, and kind. The boys in my class treat me as well as could be desired, even some of them from the South acting very good-naturedly toward me. Today one of the gentlemen of the Senior class came home and expressed himself as glad to have me here. He gave me some good advice, and told me he would always be ready to help me if I needed assistance." SOURCE: Cleveland *Gazette*, 29 Nov 1884.

Second black officer in regular Army, graduated from United States Military Academy in 1887; was "an inconspicuous second lieutenant for seven years with the Ninth Cavalry," and died in 1894 of natural causes. SOURCE: Thompson, "The Negro Regiments."

Recent graduate of USMA. SOURCE: Cleveland *Gazette*, 18 Jun 1887, with picture.

Arrived at Ft Niobrara, NE, and tentatively assigned to A/9th Cavalry, according to Omaha *Excelsior*, 4 Aug 1887. SOURCE: *ANJ* 25 (6 Aug 1887): 23.

Reported for duty at Ft Robinson, NE, today: he is "quite small but very bright and pleasant." SOURCE: Corliss diary, vol. 2, entry for 1 Oct 1887, DPL.

Relieved from duty at Ft Robinson; to go to Ft Washakie, WY, for duty with M/9th Cavalry. SOURCE: *ANJ* 26 (24 Mar 1888), 694.

Mentioned. SOURCE: *ANJ* 27 (16 Nov 1889): 229; *ANJ* 27 (18 Jan 1890): 402.

To conduct horses and men transferred from C/9th Cavalry, Ft Duchesne, UT, to Ft Washakie. SOURCE: *ANJ* 28 (30 Aug 1890): 5.

Mentioned as first black officer at Ft Duchesne. SOURCE: Clark, "Twenty-fourth Infantry," 12.

To visit camp of Charlotte Light Infantry at Raleigh, NC, as instructor, 2–7 Nov 1891. SOURCE: Cleveland *Gazette*, 31 Oct 1891.

Acting adjutant, Ft Robinson, in absence of Lt. Grote Hutcheson. SOURCE: Cleveland *Gazette*, 18 Feb 1893.

Recently passed examination for first lieutenant at Ft Leavenworth, KS. SOURCE: Cleveland *Gazette*, 11 Nov 1893.

Died of apoplexy, in barbershop, Springfield, OH, 11 A.M., 26 Mar 1894. SOURCE: Cleveland *Gazette*, 31 Mar 1894.

When died, serving as military instructor, Wilberforce University, OH. SOURCE: Work, *The Negro Year Book, 1912*, 76.

Orders 20, 9th Cavalry, Ft Robinson, 30 Mar 1894, mourned him and praised his "ability and energy" and his appreciation of "the delicate distinctions of social intercourse." SOURCE: Cleveland *Gazette*, 7 Apr 1894.

Drawing. SOURCE: Lynk, *The Black Troopers*, 145.

Camp Alexander, Newport News, VA, named for him. SOURCE: Cleveland *Gazette*, 26 Oct 1918.

Mentioned as United States Military Academy graduate. SOURCE: Billington, *New Mexico's Buffalo Soldiers*, 190.

ALEXANDER, Joseph; Sergeant; G/10th Cav. Original member of 10th Cavalry; in B troop when organized, Ft Leavenworth, KS, 1 Apr 1867. SOURCE: McMiller, "Buffalo Soldiers," 69.

Honorable mention for bravery against Comanches, Double Mountain Fork, Brazos River, TX, 5 Feb 1874. SOURCE: Baker, Roster.

ALEXANDER, Joseph; Private; I/24th Inf. Mutineer, Houston, TX, 1917, who had second thoughts. SOURCE: Haynes, *A Night of Violence*, 147.

ALEXANDER, Julius; Private; G/9th Cav. Three-month furlough authorized. SOURCE: AGO to CO, Ft Robinson, 15 Aug 1894, Register of Correspondence, Ft Robinson.

Transferred to Hospital Corps. SOURCE: SO 40, AGO, 17 Feb 1898.

Reenlistment authorized. SOURCE: TWX, AGO, 24 Aug 1900.

ALEXANDER, Nicholas; Recruit; 10th Cav. At St. Louis, MO, depot, May 1875, awaiting assignment to the regiment. SOURCE: LS, 10 Cav, 1873–77.

ALEXANDER, Samuel; Farrier; A/10th Cav. Served in 10th Cavalry, 1898; remained in U.S. during war with Spain. SOURCE: Cashin, *Under Fire with the Tenth Cavalry*, 337.

ALEXANDER, Samuel H.; 1st Sgt; E/10th Cav. Sergeant, F/10th Cavalry; served in 10th Cavalry in Cuba, 1898. SOURCE: Cashin, *Under Fire with the Tenth Cavalry*, 343.

Sergeant, B/10th Cavalry, on furlough at Cook's Ranch, NE, starting 22 Jul 1904, from Ft Robinson, NE. SOURCE: Regt Returns, 10 Cav, Jul 1904.

As first sergeant, E/10th Cavalry, participated in 9 Jan 1918 fight against Yaquis, Atasco Canyon, AZ. SOURCE: Wharfield, *10th Cavalry and Border Fights*, 7.

ALEXANDER, Thomas; D/10th Cav. Original member of 10th Cavalry; in troop when organized, Ft Leavenworth, KS, 1 Jun 1867. SOURCE: McMiller, "Buffalo Soldiers," 71.

ALEXANDER, Wesley; Principal Musician; Band/24th Inf. Born Maury Co., TN; Ht 5'8", brown complexion; enlisted 22 Jan 1891, at Louisville, KY; age 42; with previous service in 10th Cavalry band. Assigned to F/24th Infantry, 16 Apr 1891. Discharged on expiration of service, Ft Bayard, NM, 21 Jan 1896, character excellent, married, no children; additional pay $4 per month, retained $60, clothing $104. SOURCE: Entry, 21 Jan 1896, Descriptive Book, 24 Inf NCS & Band.

At Ft Apache, AZ, 1890, private, Band/10th Cavalry, subscribed $.50 to testimonial to General Grierson. SOURCE: List of subscriptions, 23 Apr 1890, 10th Cavalry papers, MHI.

Retired as principal musician, 24th Infantry, from Ft Douglas, UT. SOURCE: *ANJ* 35 (11 Dec 1897): 273.

ALEXANDER, Will; Private; 25th Inf. Died of diarrhea, Maslinoc, Luzon, Philippines, 9 Jun 1901. SOURCE: *ANJ* 38 (3 Aug 1901): 1187.

ALEXANDER, William; Private; D/10th Cav. Sentenced to ten days on head of barrel (9 A.M. to 4 P.M.) and $14 fine in 1867 for selling overcoat, buying jug of whiskey, and going on spree. SOURCE: Leckie, *The Buffalo Soldiers*, 29.

ALEXANDER, William; Private; D/10th Cav. Served in 10th Cavalry in Cuba, 1898. SOURCE: Cashin, *Under Fire with the Tenth Cavalry*, 341.

President McKinley congratulated him and shook his hand on trip from New York City to Long Island City. SOURCE: Cleveland *Gazette*, 17 Sep 1898.

ALEXANDER, William; Sergeant; L/9th Cav. Sergeant; ranks as thirty-third among rifle experts in the Army, 1905, with 77.00 percent. SOURCE: GO 101, AGO, 31 May 1906.

Private; expert rifleman, at Ft D. A. Russell, WY, in 1910; resident of Culpepper Court House, VA. SOURCE: *Illustrated Review: Ninth Cavalry*, with picture.

ALEXANDER, William; Private; G/10th Cav. Served in 10th Cavalry in Cuba, 1898. SOURCE: Cashin, *Under Fire with the Tenth Cavalry*, 345.

ALEXANDER, William C.; L/10th Cav. Original member of 10th Cavalry; in troop when organized, Ft Riley, KS, 21 Sep 1867. SOURCE: McMiller, "Buffalo Soldiers," 78.

ALEXANDER, Willis; Sergeant; F/24th Inf. En route from San Antonio, TX, to Ft Jackson, LA, with prisoner; then authorized furlough. SOURCE: CO, Post of San Antonio, 19 Dec 1870, to CO, Ft Jackson, Name File, 24 Inf.

ALLAN; Private; 25th Inf. Transferred from L/10th Cavalry. SOURCE: SO 224, AGO, 23 Sep 1902.

ALLEN, Charles; Cook; B/9th Cav. At Ft D. A. Russell, WY, in 1910. SOURCE: *Illustrated Review: Ninth Cavalry.*

ALLEN, Charles; Private; D/24th Inf. At Cabanatuan, Philippines, 1901. *See* **HALE**, Moses, Private, K/24th Infantry

ALLEN, Charles S.; Private; H/10th Cav. Served in 10th Cavalry in Cuba, 1898. SOURCE: Cashin, *Under Fire with the Tenth Cavalry*, 356.

ALLEN, Charley; Private; K/10th Cav. *See* **BRANSFORD**, Wesley, Private, K/10th Cavalry

ALLEN, David M.; Private; Band/9th Cav. Son Winslow Fillmore, second child, born at Ft Robinson, NE, 27 May 1898, to wife, maiden name Leona M. Howard. SOURCE: Medical History, Ft Robinson.

ALLEN, Frank; Private; G/9th Cav. Veteran of Indian wars, Spanish-American War, and Philippine Insurrection; at Ft D. A. Russell, WY, in 1910. SOURCE: *Illustrated Review: Ninth Cavalry.*

ALLEN, Frank; Private; D/10th Cav. On furlough at Buffalo, WY, 13 Mar–21 May 1891. SOURCE: Regt Returns, 9 Cav, Mar–May 1881.

Discharged. SOURCE: SO 198, AGO, 23 Aug 1894.

ALLEN, George; Corporal; C/10th Cav. In post hospital, Ft Riley, KS, 21 Apr 1868. SOURCE: LR, Det 10 Cav, 1868–69.

ALLEN, George; Private; C/9th Cav. At Ft D. A. Russell, WY, in 1910; sharpshooter; resident of R.F.D. 2, Cave Springs, GA. SOURCE: *Illustrated Review: Ninth Cavalry*, with picture.

ALLEN, George; Private; K/10th Cav. Served in 10th Cavalry, 1898; remained in U.S. during war with Spain. SOURCE: Cashin, *Under Fire with the Tenth Cavalry*, 349.

ALLEN, Henry; Private; B/10th Cav. Original member of 10th Cavalry; in troop when organized, Ft Leaven-worth, KS, 1 Apr 1867. SOURCE: McMiller, "Buffalo Soldiers," 69.

Adjutant has not received descriptive roll for Allen yet. SOURCE: Adj, 10 Cav to Capt. Henry Davis, Recruiting Officer, 10 Cav, Memphis, 17 Apr 1867, LS, 10 Cav.

ALLEN, Henry; Sergeant; D/10th Cav. Born in Virginia; private, F/20th U.S. Colored Troops, 15 Oct 1864–7 Oct 1865; private and sergeant, H/10th Cavalry, 24 Aug 1869; private, D/10th Cavalry, 23 Aug 1882; corporal, 12 October 1892; sergeant, 15 Apr 1893; stationed at Ft Assiniboine, MT, in 1897. SOURCE: Baker, Roster.

Retired from Ft Assiniboine. SOURCE: *ANJ* 35 (30 Oct 1897): 156.

Retired from Ft Assiniboine, residing in Helena, MT, "and is doing well." SOURCE: Indianapolis *Freeman*, 11 Dec 1897.

ALLEN, Hubert F.; A/10th Cav. Original member of 10th Cavalry; in A Troop when organized, Ft Leavenworth, KS, 18 Feb 1867. SOURCE: McMiller, "Buffalo Soldiers," 68.

ALLEN, J.; Private; A/9th Cav. At Ft Stanton, NM, 1881. SOURCE: Regt Returns, 9 Cav, Jan 1881.

ALLEN, James; Corporal; F/10th Cav. Promoted from private, Jun 1902. SOURCE: *ANJ* 39 (2 Aug 1902): 1218.

Best in standing high jump, Department of Colorado, 1903, while stationed at Ft Washakie, WY: 4'5". SOURCE: SecWar, *AR 1903*, I, 430.

ALLEN, James; Private; B/25th Inf. Dishonorable discharge, Brownsville. SOURCE: SO 266, AGO, 9 Nov 1906.

ALLEN, John; Private; D/9th Cav. At Ft D. A. Russell, WY, in 1910; resident of Iola, KS. SOURCE: *Illustrated Review: Ninth Cavalry*, with picture.

ALLEN, Joseph. Adjutant, Col. Charles Young Camp, No. 24, Washington, DC, National Indian War Veterans. SOURCE: *Winners of the West* 6 (Jun 1929): 4.

ALLEN, Joseph S.; Private; E/10th Cav. Served in 10th Cavalry in Cuba, 1898. SOURCE: Cashin, *Under Fire with the Tenth Cavalry*, 342.

ALLEN, Kendrick; Sergeant; C/9th Cav. Sergeant, C/9th Cavalry, since 4 Aug 1883. SOURCE: Roster, 9 Cav, 1893.

Retired from Ft Robinson, NE. SOURCE: *ANJ* 35 (20 Nov 1897): 213; SO 267, AGO, 13 Nov 1897.

ALLEN, Lee; Recruit; Colored Detachment/ Mounted Service. Tried by general court martial, Jefferson Barracks, MO, for violating Article 62, theft from Recruit Frederick Weinheimer, Company D of Instruction, Mounted

Service, of silver watch worth $18, and bartering it to Recruit Edward Williams, Colored Detachment/Mounted Service, at Jefferson Barracks, 19 Apr 1888; and for violation of Article 32, absence without leave, from taps on 25 Apr 1888, to 4 A.M., 26 Apr 1888; pleaded guilty; found guilty; sentenced to dishonorable discharge and eighteen months at hard labor. SOURCE: GCMO 40, AGO, 19 Mar 1888.

ALLEN, Loyd D.; Private; H/24th Inf. At Ft Huachuca, AZ, 1894. *See* **FOX**, William, Private, B/24th Infantry

ALLEN, Luther; 10th Cav. Fined $5 plus costs for being drunk and disorderly but paid only $1 of fine and $4.80 of costs, Crawford, NE, 30 Jun 1902. SOURCE: Police Court Docket, Crawford, NE.

ALLEN, Samuel; Sergeant; A/38th Inf. At Ft Cummings, NM, autumn 1867; acquitted of involvement in revolt but convicted of stealing greatcoat belonging to Pvt. John Hughes, A/38th Infantry, reduced to ranks, and fined $8 per month for three months. SOURCE: Billington, *New Mexico's Buffalo Soldiers*, 39, 41.

ALLEN, T. H.; 1st Sgt; D/10th Cav. Will retire around 15 Dec 1897; "The members of Troop D look forward to his retirement with much regret, as he is a model soldier"; ten years as sergeant, A/10th Cavalry; twenty years as sergeant, D/10th Cavalry; with A/10th Cavalry on expedition of Aug 1877, when troop was lost on Staked Plains and several died of hunger and thirst. SOURCE: Indianapolis *Freeman*, 11 Dec 1897.

ALLEN, Thomas F.; K/10th Cav. Original member of 10th Cavalry; in troop when organized, Ft Riley, KS, 1 Sep 1867. SOURCE: McMiller, "Buffalo Soldiers," 77.

ALLEN, William H.; 1st Lt; B/48th Inf. As sergeant, B/10th Cavalry, Ft Apache, AZ, 1890, subscribed $.50 to testimonial to General Grierson. SOURCE: List of subscriptions, 23 Apr 1890, 10th Cavalry papers, MHI.

Transferred from B/10th Cavalry, San Carlos, AZ, to regimental band, Ft Grant, AZ. SOURCE: *ANJ* 29 (14 Nov 1891): 198.

Was sergeant in 9th Cavalry when commissioned as first lieutenant in 48th Infantry, U.S. Volunteers, as of 12 Sep 1899. SOURCE: *ANJ* 37 (6 Jan 1900): 436.

Mentioned as first lieutenant, B/48th Infantry. SOURCE: Beasley, *Negro Trailblazers*, 248.

ALLEN, Willie; Private; M/49th Inf. Engaged against enemy, Tuao, Cagayan, Philippines, 18 Oct 1900. SOURCE: *ANJ* 38 (11 May 1901): 901.

ALLENSWORTH, Allen; Chaplain; 24th Inf. Born 1842; escaped slavery to fight with Union in Civil War and

stayed in Army; founder of black community in San Joaquin Valley, CA, called Allensworth, halfway between San Francisco and Los Angeles, 1908. SOURCE: *New York Times*, 22 Oct 1972.

His predecessor as teacher, in Hopkinsville, KY, was Charles Spencer Smith, later African Methodist Episcopal bishop and doctor of divinity, who worked there Nov 1869-Jun 1870. SOURCE: Wright, *Centennial Encyclopedia of the AME Church*, 205.

Honorary Master's degree from Roger Williams University; superintendent of Sunday Schools, Kentucky State Baptist Convention and missionary, American Baptist Publication Society, for four years before taking Cincinnati congregation. SOURCE: Simmons, *Men of Mark*, 843–46.

"Mr. President: The bearer hereof, Rev. Mr. Allensworth, a Baptist Minister of Kentucky, desires to pay his respects to you, and if your time will permit, hold some conversation in reference to his people. I take pleasure in presenting him to you. Yr. obt servt, John M. Harlan." SOURCE: Harlan to Rutherford B. Hayes, Washington, DC, 31 Jan 1881, Hayes papers, RBHL.

Appointed chaplain, 24th Infantry, from Mound Street Church, Cincinnati, at $1,800 per year. SOURCE: Cleveland *Gazette*, 24 Apr 1886.

Reported for duty as chaplain, Ft Supply, Indian Territory, 2 Jul 1886, vice retired J. C. Laverty; Baptist ex-slave and navy veteran; former teacher with Freedmen's Bureau; endorsed on application for chaplaincy by former owner, Mrs. A. P. Starbird. SOURCE: Fowler, *The Black Infantry*, 104–5.

Stationed at Ft Supply; during leave in Louisville, KY, interviewed by Louisville *Commercial*, to which he spoke very highly of Army men: "There are several colored commissioned officers now in the Army—Chaplain Plummer, 9th Cav.; Lieut. Alexander, 9th Cav.; and myself and one cadet at West Point. As to how I am treated by the white officers, prudence suggests that I have not been in the service long enough to determine my status, from the fact that an officer's social status is governed by the time it takes him to become identified with his regiment or post. However, my social relations so far have been pleasant and considerate. This is one of the things I patiently allow to take its natural course." SOURCE: *ANJ* 25 (13 Aug 1887): 39.

Began in 1888 to train selected enlisted men as teachers; when War Department made elementary education compulsory for enlisted men, he was staffed and ready for influx of students; 118 men enrolled in his Ft Bayard, NM, school, 1889. SOURCE: Fowler, *The Black Infantry*, 105.

Supervised schoolchildren's viewing of amusements and fireworks, Ft Bayard, 4 Jul 1888. SOURCE: Cleveland *Gazette*, 14 Jul 1888.

"The pioneer colored chaplain of the army" spent week hunting in mountains and is reported as good there as he is as evangelist, "which is saying not a little." SOURCE: *ANJ* 26 (8 Dec 1888): 287.

His booklet *Outline of Course of Study and the Rules Governing Post Schools of Ft Bayard, N.M.* (Mar 1889) detailed graded levels of his program and reviewed content of each subject taught at every level. SOURCE: Fowler, *The Black Infantry*, 105.

Sponsored Literary and Debating Society, which met weekly in Ft Bayard school after duty hours, 1890. SOURCE: Fowler, *The Black Infantry*, 85.

His letter to Army chaplains, Ft Bayard, 18 Apr 1890, calls attention to National Education Association meeting in St. Paul, MN; chaplains should attend; could fill need for chaplains to convene; will show our interest in educational work and help overcome stereotype as placemen without concern for our men. SOURCE: *ANJ* 27 (3 May 1890): 680.

Recently delivered address in St. Paul on temperance in Army and spoke highly of canteen system; thought whole moral tone of Army was advancing and ascribed it to wise policy of War Department, aided by efforts of chaplains and line officers. SOURCE: *ANJ* 27 (9 Aug 1890): 922.

Asked by National Education Association to prepare paper on "The History and Progress of Education in the U.S. Army": "The reverend gentleman is, to our knowledge, fully capable of handling the matter satisfactorily." SOURCE: *ANJ* 28 (25 Apr 1891): 590.

"The efficient superintendent of post schools" at Ft Bayard was asked by president of National Education Association to read paper on education at Toronto convention, 14–17 Jul; War Department refused his request to be ordered there. SOURCE: *ANJ* 28 (30 May 1891): 674.

Took leave to attend Toronto meeting of National Education Association and deliver paper on "Education in the United States Army." SOURCE: Fowler, *The Black Infantry*, 106.

Expects to leave Ft Bayard this week to spend until next Aug on leave. SOURCE: *ANJ* 28 (20 Jun 1891): 730.

Mentioned as second Afro-American chaplain. SOURCE: Cleveland *Gazette*, 29 Aug 1891.

Conducted public installation and dedication of Soldiers Home Lodge No. 3491, Grand United Order of Odd Fellows, Ft Grant, AZ, 4 Mar 1892; gave "very intelligent and interesting sermon" 6 Mar, then returned to post at Ft Bayard, 7 Mar. SOURCE: Cleveland *Gazette*, 19 Mar 1892.

Rejoined regiment at Ft Bayard after leave. SOURCE: *ANJ* 29 (12 Mar 1892): 502.

Detailed for duty pertaining to World's Columbian Exposition, Chicago. SOURCE: *ANJ* 30 (18 Feb 1893): 427.

Has opened cooking school at Ft Bayard, where chemistry of food is explained and cooking taught as science and art; kitchen of his quarters fitted up as model kitchen, where instructions are practically demonstrated. SOURCE: *ANJ* 31 (26 May 1894): 676.

Will be on leave from Ft Bayard for the summer "for the benefit of his health." SOURCE: *ANJ* 32 (11 May 1895): 604.

Daughter Eva at Ft Bayard appointed notary public by governor of New Mexico, according to St. Paul *Appeal*. SOURCE: Cleveland *Gazette*, 10 Oct 1896.

Post school, Ft Douglas, UT, "in a flourishing condition" under him, with 120 students and classes in grammar, arithmetic, history, printing, telegraphy, clerkship, signaling; graduates in clerkship readily detailed as clerks to commander, adjutant, quartermaster, and commissary. "There are few schools in the Army that are run on the plan of the one at Fort Douglas, at least if there is they are very seldom heard of. A school of this kind is very useful, and should be encouraged on every post of the United States." SOURCE: *ANJ* 34 (6 Feb 1897): 409.

His efforts as teacher discussed. SOURCE: Billington, *New Mexico's Buffalo Soldiers*, 161–63, with picture at 160.

Arrived at Ft Douglas with 24th Infantry in 1896. SOURCE: Clark, "Twenty-fourth Infantry," 58–60.

Quoted in Salt Lake City *Broadax* as saying that preachers should not hold political office. SOURCE: Cleveland *Gazette*, 13 Feb 1897.

At Ft Douglas, hosted Salt Lake City Ministers Association; doing remarkable job with post garden, with ten acres under cultivation and "great variety of vegetables." SOURCE: *ANJ* 34 (19 Jun 1897): 776.

Successfully recruited college graduates for 24th Infantry. SOURCE: Clark, "Twenty-fourth Infantry," 83.

His attitude regarding vice mentioned. SOURCE: Clark, "Twenty-fourth Infantry," 63.

His relations with Mormon leaders while at Ft Douglas mentioned. SOURCE: Clark, "Twenty-fourth Infantry," 65.

Daughter Nella spoke on "Confidence" to 24th Infantry's Christian Endeavor Society, Ft Douglas, Mar 1897. SOURCE: Clark, "Twenty-fourth Infantry," 68.

Went to Ogden, UT, from Ft Douglas, on 27 Nov 1897 to deliver three lectures on 28 Nov 1897. SOURCE: *ANJ* 35 (4 Dec 1897): 253.

View of Spanish-American War. SOURCE: Stover, *Up from Handymen*, 109–10.

Authorized five-day leave on 26 Aug 1898. SOURCE: *ANJ* 36 (3 Sep 1898): 11.

With his wife at Presidio of San Francisco, entertained Rev. and Mrs. J. Ford of Los Angeles. SOURCE: *ANJ* 36 (17 Jun 1899): 1004.

"The Misses Allensworth" are visiting in Oakland from the Presidio. SOURCE: *ANJ* 36 (15 Jul 1899): 1100.

"The Misses Maryatt" of Oakland are guests of "The Misses Allensworth," at the Presidio. SOURCE: *ANJ* 36 (29 Jul 1899): 1148.

On Thursday, 24 Aug 1899, 6:30 P.M. at Soldiers Institute, Manila, Allensworth will give "Scoptoconical Projection"; "in simple language this is a new up to date limelight magic lantern with lots of slides"; all invited. SOURCE: Manila *Times*, 23 Aug 1899.

To preach on Sunday at 9:30 A.M. at Soldiers Institute, and marry Filipino couple. SOURCE: Manila *Times*, 2 Dec 1899.

Will deliver his humorous lecture "Humbugs" this evening at 6:30, Soldiers Institute. SOURCE: Manila *Times*, 8 Feb 1900.

To deliver his lecture on "Gems from the Life of Napoleon" tonight at YMCA, 7 P.M.; all invited. SOURCE: Manila *Times*, 16 Feb 1900.

"Chaplain Allensworth's lecture at the YMCA last night was given to a crowded room and proved not only interesting but amusing. The lecture presented certain phases of the life of the Famous General and Emperor . . . which he held up as examples to the American soldier." SOURCE: Manila *Times*, 17 Feb 1900.

Tomorrow to give sermon at YMCA, 10 A.M. SOURCE: Manila *Times*, 24 Feb 1900.

Lectured at Soldiers Institute, Manila, 28 Apr 1900, on "Rise and Fall of the Kiss"; "it might be suggested that it would be difficult to select a subject better fitted to develop homesickness in men thousands of miles from their home." SOURCE: *ANJ* 37 (16 Jun 1900): 985.

Experience in the Philippines discussed. SOURCE: Stover, *Up from Handymen*, 127–28.

His letter from Ft Harrison, MT, dated 4 Oct 1902, discusses accomplishments of 24th Infantry band and possibilities for men in it to advance and develop; praises regimental Sgt. Maj. Walter B. Williams, "one of the most efficient sergeant-majors of the Army." SOURCE: Indianapolis *Freeman*, 18 Oct 1902.

Promoted to major, 14 Jun 1904; one of four promoted out of fourteen who were eligible. SOURCE: Stover, *Up from Handymen*, 151.

Conducted church service for 174 men, Sunday, 10 Jul 1904, at Ft Robinson, NE; he "has a powerful influence among the enlisted men." SOURCE: Monthly Report, Chaplain Anderson, 1 Aug 1904, AGO File 53910.

Daughter Nella performed solo "Estella" at Christian Endeavor Society program, Ft Harrison, Nov 1904. SOURCE: Indianapolis *Freeman*, 17 Dec 1904.

At Ft Harrison, with his wife, entertained at dinner, Mr. and Mrs. Clark of Helena, now "in the East on business." SOURCE: Indianapolis *Freeman*, 17 Dec 1904.

Relieved from duty with regiment and ordered home to retire. SOURCE: *ANR* 38 (1 Jul 1905): 21.

Reassigned to Los Angeles, CA, where he and his family will go on 17 Jul; address there at 1851 30th Place. SOURCE: Indianapolis *Freeman*, 15 Jul 1905.

Senior Army chaplain, now stationed in Los Angeles. SOURCE: Indianapolis *Freeman*, 19 Aug 1905.

Resignation offers opportunity for some aspiring young minister; place "is very desirable." SOURCE: Cleveland *Gazette*, 4 Oct 1905.

Retires as lieutenant colonel. SOURCE: Indianapolis *Freeman*, 14 Apr 1906.

Retires as lieutenant colonel, "the highest honor ever given an Afro-American in the army." SOURCE: Cleveland *Gazette*, 21 Apr 1906.

Lives in Los Angeles; replaced by Rev. Washington E. Gladden, Baptist minister of Denver. SOURCE: Cleveland *Gazette*, 12 May 1906, with picture of Allensworth.

"Lieutenant Colonel Allensworth, U.S.A., colored, has a movement on foot for the establishment of a Negro commonwealth in the United States. (It would be the worst mistake that the race could make.)" SOURCE: Washington *Bee*, 2 Nov 1907.

Mentioned. SOURCE: Work, *The Negro Year Book, 1912*, 76.

Mrs. Payne of Allensworth, CA, was guest of her uncle W. B. Wright of West 85th St. for some weeks, also visited her former home in Rendville, OH. SOURCE: Cleveland *Gazette*, 7 Sep 1912.

"Citizens of Allensworth, Cal., the Race town founded in the San Joaquin Valley by Col. Allensworth, backed by the Pacific Farming Co., is having its time, and the courts have been called upon to settle differences between the colonists and the Pacific Farming Co. The citizens have organized, raised funds, have a legal committee and have retained an irrigation attorney to force the farming co. to give what they declare due them.—Los Angeles (Cal.) *Liberator*." SOURCE: Cleveland *Gazette*, 16 Aug 1913.

Resided in Los Angeles; retired lieutenant colonel; killed in motorcycle accident, 1914. SOURCE: *Crisis* 9 (Nov 1914): 8.

Funeral 18 Sep 1914 was "much curtailed and simple" out of respect for wishes of his widow and daughters; memorial service conducted 27 Sep 1914 "when due tribute to our beloved leader was paid." SOURCE: Cleveland *Gazette*, 3 Oct 1914.

Mentioned as retired and deceased. SOURCE: Work, *The Negro Yearbook, 1918–1919*, 228.

Picture, "Col. Allen Allensworth, Reg'tal Chaplain, Died September 14, 1914." SOURCE: Muller, *The Twenty Fourth Infantry*, 285.

2nd Lt. Oscar Overr, 23rd Kansas Volunteer Infantry, resided in Allensworth. SOURCE: Beasley, *Negro Trailblazers*, 285.

Daughters Eva (Mrs. Harrie Skanks) and Nella (Mrs. L. M. Blodgett) "genuine gentlewomen of the old school of aristocracy." SOURCE: Beasley, *Negro Trailblazers*, 226.

Organized company for colonization of Negroes in California; subscription and purchase of lots; town site named for him. SOURCE: Beasley, *Negro Trailblazers*, 287.

Born a slave; educated at Baptist Roger Williams University, Nashville; appointed by American Baptist Association to travel and lecture to children; in Civil War, Spanish-American War, and Philippine Insurrection; retired to Los Angeles as lieutenant colonel. SOURCE: Beasley, *Negro Trailblazers*, 287.

Tragically died at hands of careless motorcyclist on streets of Monrovia, CA, near Los Angeles, Sunday morning, Sep 1914; while en route to preach at small Monrovia church, was run over when he stepped from Pacific Electric streetcar, "loved and respected by all who knew him." SOURCE: Beasley, *Negro Trailblazers*, 288.

Mrs. Josephine Leavell Allensworth stayed in San Francisco while he was in the Philippines and acted as treasurer for men of 24th Infantry; received their money and distributed it to their wives. When he retired, men of 24th presented him and his daughters with "handsome carved silver tray" and candelabra. She organized "Women's Improvement Club" of Allensworth, which established children's playground and other improvements; established public reading room named for her mother, Mary Dickson; was president of School Board. "A sincere club worker." SOURCE: Beasley, *Negro Trailblazers*, 226, 287.

Biography. SOURCE: Charles Alexander, *Battles and Victories of Allen Allensworth* (Boston, 1914), 435 pp.

Biographical sketches. SOURCE: Logan and Winston, eds., *Dictionary of American Negro Biography*, 13–14; Stover, *Up from Handymen*, 53–57.

Biographical sketch of Josephine L. Allensworth. SOURCE: Hine, ed., *Black Women in America*, 22–23.

ALLEY, John; H/10th Cav. Original member of 10th Cavalry; in troop when organized, Ft Leavenworth, KS, 21 Jul 1867. SOURCE: McMiller, "Buffalo Soldiers," 75.

ALLISON, Walter; Private; B/48th Inf. Died of tuberculosis in the Philippines, 5 Jun 1900. SOURCE: *ANJ* 37 (6 Jun 1900): 999.

ALLSBERRY, William; 24th Inf. While at Ft Douglas, UT, in 1898 he lived at 1321 East 4th Street South, Salt Lake City. SOURCE: Clark, "Twenty-fourth Infantry," appendix E.

ALLSUP, Thomas H.; 1st Sgt; D/10th Cav. Born in Maryland; stationed at Ft Assiniboine, MT, in 1897; private, A/10th Cavalry, 25 Nov 1867; trumpeter, 10 Apr 1868; corporal, 1 Feb 1871; sergeant, 6 Feb 1872; first sergeant, 1 Aug 1877; transferred to D/10th Cavalry, 1 Jan 1882; in many engagements against Indians and border ruffians, including with Captain Nolan on Staked Plains in 1877 and from Ft Concho, TX. SOURCE: Baker, Roster.

At San Carlos, AZ, sharpshooter. SOURCE: *ANJ* 25 (13 Aug 1887): 42.

Authorized three-month furlough from station at San Carlos. SOURCE: *ANJ* 25 (17 Dec 1887): 402.

At Ft Apache, AZ, 1890, subscribed $.50 to testimonial to General Grierson. SOURCE: List of subscriptions, 23 Apr 1890, 10th Cavalry papers, MHI.

Retires from Ft Assiniboine. SOURCE: *ANJ* 35 (18 Dec 1897): 293.

Letter from his widow, Mrs. Sadie H. Allsup, who gets pension of $30 per month. SOURCE: *Winners of the West* 6 (Nov 1930): 2.

Widow lived at 1235 E. 25th, Los Angeles; pension of $12 per month, 17 Mar 1922, increased to $30 per month, 19 Sep 1927; died 6 Mar 1936. Allsup retired 1897 and died 16 Mar 1922 at Patton State (mental) Hospital, San Bernardino, CA. Son James A. born Havre, MT, Jan 1914, to Sadie Johnson Allsup, born in Mississippi, address 620 3rd St., Havre. SOURCE: VA File XC 2659797, Thomas H. Allsup.

Sadie Johnson Allsup born 7 May 1873, Topeka, KS, to Angeline Young and Absalom Johnson, who deserted them; mother married Frank McKinney, who died Deming, NM, then Silas Johnson of Winooski, VT, farrier, D/10th Cavalry; Sadie lived with him and mother at Ft Bayard until married; mother died Ft Benton, MT, over twenty years ago; Allsup born Talbot Co., MD, 1846; his father, cook on boat, drowned when pushed overboard; Sadie and Thomas H. married 23 May 1891, Central City, NM; Thomas H. lost his mind three weeks before he died; Sadie brought him to Los Angeles, Feb 1922, from Havre; he divorced first wife, Apache Co., AZ; seven children died as infants; the survivors: Margaret, born Ft Bayard, 1891, married Paul Redd, pipefitter, Los

Angeles; Thomas, Jr., clerk, roundhouse, Havre, MT; Ina May, married David Walton, car washer, with whom Sadie lives; Elenora, divorced Robert Johnson and now at home; George A., died at age of 7; Bertha Louise died at 16; James died at 12. SOURCE: Affidavit, Sadie Allsup, 7 Apr 1926, VA File XC 2659797, Thomas H. Allsup.

See **BELDEN**, James H., D/10th Cavalry; **BOOKER**, James F., 10th Cavalry; **DENNY**, Elbiron, Saddler, F/10th Cavalry; **GRAVES**, Johnson, Sergeant, A/10th Cavalry; **HOUSTON**, Adam, Quartermaster Sergeant, 10th Cavalry; **LIVINGSTON**, James, Farrier, D/10th Cavalry; **MILLER**, Cooper, Artificer, E/25th Infantry; **MURPHY**, Israel B., First Sergeant, B/9th Cavalry; **POTTER**, Thomas, 10th Cavalry; **ROSS**, Milton, Sergeant, D/10th Cavalry; **SMITH**, Jacob Clay, Sergeant, 10th Cavalry; **SMITH**, Lewis M., First Sergeant, M/10th Cavalry; **SNOTEN**, Peter, Sergeant, G/9th Cavalry; **STRONG**, Christopher, A/10th Cavalry; **TAYLOR**, Belford, Private, D/10th Cavalry; **WILLIAMS**, James H., Corporal, A/10th Cavalry

ALSTON, Douglas; Private; C/49th Inf. Died in the Philippines, 17 Oct 1900. SOURCE: *ANJ* 38 (3 Nov 1900): 235.

AMBER, Wiley; Private; K/10th Cav. Mentioned. SOURCE: ES, 10 Cav, 1873–81.

AMMONS, William; Private; K/49th Inf. In the Philippines, 1900. *See* **BLUNT**, Hamilton H., Captain, K/49th Infantry

Died of alcoholism in the Philippines, 19 Oct 1900. SOURCE: *ANJ* 38 (1 Dec 1900): 331.

ANCRUM, William; Sergeant; C/10th Cav. Born in South Carolina; private, A/10th Cavalry, 5 Jan 1888–4 Jan 1893; C/10th Cavalry, 9 Jan 1893; corporal, 1 Oct 1894; sergeant, 15 Jun 1895; at Ft Assiniboine, MT, 1897. SOURCE: Baker, Roster.

At Ft Apache, AZ, 1890, private, A/10th Cavalry, subscribed $.50 to testimonial to General Grierson. SOURCE: List of subscriptions, 23 Apr 1890, 10th Cavalry papers, MHI.

Served in 10th Cavalry in Cuba, 1898; narrates San Juan Hill experience. SOURCE: Cashin, *Under Fire with the Tenth Cavalry*, 339, 189–90.

ANDERS, J. C.; 2nd Lt; C/48th Inf.

ANDERSON; Band/10th Cav. At Ft Concho, TX, in 1877; "a gay darkey" who lived in tent on grounds of Colonel Grierson's quarters to look after his carriage and livestock. SOURCE: Miles, "Fort Concho in 1877," 31.

ANDERSON; Sergeant; H/9th Cav. Displayed extraordinary leadership against Nana, Gavilan Canyon, NM, Aug 1881. SOURCE: Billington, *New Mexico's Buffalo Soldiers*, 106–7.

ANDERSON; Private; H/9th Cav. To be tried by summary court martial. SOURCE: Letter, DP, 5 Dec 1895, LS, DP.

ANDERSON, Abby; Private; A/9th Cav. Veteran of Philippine Insurrection; at Ft D. A. Russell, WY, in 1910; marksman. SOURCE: *Illustrated Review: Ninth Cavalry*, with picture.

ANDERSON, Andrew; I/10th Cav. Original member of 10th Cavalry; in troop when organized, Ft Riley, KS, 15 Aug 1867. SOURCE: McMiller, "Buffalo Soldiers," 76.

ANDERSON, Anthony; Corporal; I/24th Inf. Enlisted 11 Feb 1899, at Ft D. A. Russell, WY, with six years' continuous service; appointed corporal, Ft Douglas, UT, 11 Feb 1899. SOURCE: Muster Roll, I/24 Inf, Feb 1899.

Reduced to private and fined one month's pay by general court martial, 31 Mar 1899. SOURCE: Muster Roll, I/24 Inf, Apr 1899.

Appointed corporal, 20 May 1899. SOURCE: Muster Roll, I/24 Inf, Jun 1899.

On detached service at Arayat, Philippines, since 31 Oct 1899. SOURCE: Muster Roll, I/24 Inf, Oct 1899.

ANDERSON, Benjamin A.; QM Sgt; U.S. Army. Born Bethel, OH, 1875; Ht 5'9", light complexion; in H/10th Cavalry, 5 Jul 1889–4 Oct 1892 and 20 May 1893–19 Aug 1896; in A, B, & Noncommissioned Staff/10th Cavalry, 28 Dec 1896–27 Dec 1899; married; character excellent; appointed regimental quartermaster sergeant 28 Dec 1899; in Cuba, 22 Jun–14 Aug 1898, 7 May 1899–20 Nov 1901, 27 Feb–27 May 1902; deposits $100, Jan–Sep 1901; clothing not drawn $88.99, 1901. Reenlisted Ft Robinson, NE, 28 Dec 1902; regimental quartermaster sergeant until 21 Sep 1904 appointment as post quartermaster sergeant, Ft Robinson; records transferred to Post Noncommissioned Staff Descriptive Book; married, resides with wife at Ft Robinson; deposits $25, Feb–Mar 1903. SOURCE: Descriptive Book, 10 Cav Officers & NCOs.

As private, H/10th Cavalry, at Ft Apache, AZ, 1890, subscribed $.50 to testimonial to General Grierson. SOURCE: List of subscriptions, 23 Apr 1890, 10th Cavalry papers, MHI.

As sergeant, H/10th Cavalry, in 1893, placed fifth with carbine, in competition for Departments of Dakota and Columbia at Ft Keogh, MT, won bronze medal; in 1894, fourth with carbine, same departments, silver medal. SOURCE: Baker, Roster.

Placed fourth, carbine competition, Departments of Columbia and Dakota, Ft Keogh, 18–27 Sep 1894. SOURCE: GO 62, AGO, 15 Nov 1894.

At Ft Robinson for cavalry competition as private, B/10th Cavalry, in Sep 1897.

Relieved from extra duty as schoolteacher and transferred to extra duty as clerk, Quartermaster Department, while serving as private, B/10th Cavalry. SOURCE: *ANJ* 35 (18 Dec 1897): 292.

Served in 10th Cavalry in Cuba, 1898. SOURCE: Cashin, *Under Fire with the Tenth Cavalry*, 352.

Distinguished marksman, as sergeant, H/10th Cavalry, 1893; as sergeant, H/10th Cavalry, 1894; and as regimental quartermaster sergeant in 1903. SOURCE: GO 52, AGO, 19 Mar 1904.

Eighth best marksman, Departments of Texas and the Missouri, 1903; best marksman in Army, 1904. SOURCE: Glass, *History of the Tenth Cavalry*, 43, 44.

Member of fourth-place team, U.S. Army Cavalry, in national marksmanship matches, Ft Riley, KS; won $150 and medal (money split with team). SOURCE: GO 172, AGO, 10 Nov 1904.

Won recent cavalry marksmanship competition, Ft Riley. SOURCE: Cleveland *Gazette*, 3 Sep 1904.

Second Army cavalry competition, Ft Riley, 1905, distinguished marksman and gold medalist. SOURCE: GO 173, AGO, 20 Oct 1905.

Served as post quartermaster sergeant, Ft Robinson, 26 Sep 1904–16 Dec 1908, then moved to Ft Terry, NY.

Honored with smoker, 13 Dec 1908, by Chief Musician William Brinsmead and Sgt. 1st Class A. S. Donnan, Hospital Corps, before departing Ft Robinson for assignment at Ft Terry. SOURCE: Crawford *Tribune*, 18 Dec 1908.

ANDERSON, Charles; D/10th Cav. Original member of 10th Cavalry; in troop when organized, Ft Leavenworth, KS, 1 Jun 1867. SOURCE: McMiller, "Buffalo Soldiers," 71.

ANDERSON, Charles; Private; K/10th Cav. Mentioned 1873. SOURCE: ES, 10 Cav, 1873–81.

ANDERSON, Charles L.; Private; D/24th Inf. Engaged in fistfight with Private George Tilman, D/24th Infantry, Ft Bayard, NM, Aug 1890; afterward Tilman got a shotgun and threatened to kill Anderson. SOURCE: Billington, *New Mexico's Buffalo Soldiers*, 164.

ANDERSON, Charles N.; Recruit; Colored Detachment/Mounted Service. Tried by general court-martial, Jefferson Barracks, MO, for violating Article 47, desertion, 8–12 Aug 1883; pleaded guilty and found guilty; sentenced to dishonorable discharge and two years' hard labor. SOURCE: GCMO 41, AGO, 8 Sep 1883.

ANDERSON, Cornelius; L/10th Cav. Original member of 10th Cavalry; in troop when organized, Ft Riley, KS, 21 Sep 1867. SOURCE: McMiller, "Buffalo Soldiers," 78.

ANDERSON, Dudley; Private; H/10th Cav. Served in 10th Cavalry, 1898; remained in U.S. during war with Spain. SOURCE: Cashin, *Under Fire with the Tenth Cavalry*, 346.

ANDERSON, Fred; Private; Band/9th Cav. At Ft D. A. Russell, WY, in 1910; resident of Little Rock, AR. SOURCE: *Illustrated Review: Ninth Cavalry*, with picture.

ANDERSON, George; Private; A/10th Cav. Released to duty from treatment for gonorrhea, Ft Robinson, NE, 23 Oct 1903. SOURCE: Post Surgeon to CO, Det 10 Cav, 23 Oct 1903, LS, Post Surgeon, Ft Robinson.

ANDERSON, George; C/10th Cav. Original member of 10th Cavalry; in troop when organized, Ft Leavenworth, KS, 14 May 1867. SOURCE: McMiller, "Buffalo Soldiers," 70.

ANDERSON, George; Private; I/25th Inf. Fined $3 by summary court, San Isidro, Philippines, for violating Article 31, lying out of quarters, 15 Apr 1902, first conviction; fined $3 for violating Article 33, failure to attend drill, 9 May 1902. SOURCE: Register of Summary Court, San Isidro.

ANDERSON, George G.; Sergeant; K/25th Inf. Served as private and corporal, 8th Illinois Infantry, 1899; private and corporal, K/25th Infantry, 1899–1902; served in Cuba in 1899 and in the Philippines, 1899–1903; home: Paducah, KY. SOURCE: *Colored American Magazine* 4 (Apr 1902): 400–401.

Sergeant, K/25th Infantry, FT Niobrara, NE, 1904. SOURCE: Wilson, "History of Fort Niobrara."

ANDERSON, George W.; B/10th Cav. Original member of 10th Cavalry; in troop when organized, Ft Leavenworth, KS, 1 Apr 1867. SOURCE: McMiller, "Buffalo Soldiers," 69.

ANDERSON, Henry; Private; L/10th Cav. Born 6 Feb 1848, Desoto Co. (now Tate Co.), MS; at enlistment lived at Lewellens Crossroads, MS; enlisted at Memphis, TN, 28 Aug 1867; occupation farmer; Ht 5'7"; honorable discharge from Ft Sill, Indian Territory, 28 Aug 1872; pension based on paralysis of left arm, kicked by horse while shoeing it, Apr 1870, Ft Sill, bladder affected since; farmer and minister, Byars, OK, 1910; living at Rural Route 1, Byars, McClain Co., OK; pensioned with $20 per month, 4 Mar 1917, increased to $50 per month, 4 Apr 1927; lived at 129 E 11th St., Newton, KS, 1930; at son's address, 22 Frisco St., Oklahoma City, OK, 1933; married Louisa Payton Johnson Taylor, 14 Apr 1907, Pauls Valley, OK; previous marriages to Caldonia Tentoby, 18 May 1873 (died 28 Dec 1902), Byars, OK; and to Isabell Gillespee, 1903, divorced 1906, Pauls Valley; children: Minicha, born 1874; Richard, 1876; Minnie, 1879; Lotta, 1880; Wister Homer, 1882; Lillie, 1881; parents Carter Anderson and Betsy Givan. SOURCE: VA File SO 1388939, Henry Anderson.

Original member of 10th Cavalry; in L Troop when organized, Ft Riley, KS, 21 Sep 1867. SOURCE: McMiller, "Buffalo Soldiers," 78.

Served five years; 84 years old; subscribes to *Winners of the West.* SOURCE: *Winners of the West* 9 (Apr 1932): 2.

Former comrades mentioned in Veterans Administration pension file:

Blackburn, Joseph A., 951 Magnolia, Ft Worth, TX
Carter, Isaac, Box 18, Accotink, VA
Ford, George W., Riverton, IL
Silvey, Jerry, Rear 611 San Jacinto, El Paso, TX
SOURCE: VA File SO 1388939, Henry Anderson.

Died of pulmonary tuberculosis, 1 Apr 1933; buried in Rosedale, OK. SOURCE: VA File SO 1388939, Henry Anderson.

Served with Anderson at Ft Sill in 1870. SOURCE: Affidavit, J. Goldsmith, McClain Co., OK, 7 Nov 1910, VA File SO 1388939, Henry Anderson.

Served with Anderson at Ft Sill; Anderson was company blacksmith in 1870; aware of Anderson's injury. SOURCE: Affidavit, George Ford, Riverton, IL, 29 Aug 1910, VA File SO 1388939, Henry Anderson.

ANDERSON, Isaac; Private; G/9th Cav. Farrier, Ft Robinson, NE, 1893. *See* **GILLENWATER**, Walter, Corporal, Band/25th Infantry

Private, relieved from extra duty with Quartermaster Department, Ft Robinson, as laborer. SOURCE: SO 86, Ft Robinson, 8 Aug 1896, Post Orders, Ft Robinson.

Authorized to reenlist as married soldier. SOURCE: Letter, AGO, 19 Aug 1896.

Family resides at Ft Robinson, claims indigence, dependent on charity of garrison for subsistence. SOURCE: CO, Ft Robinson, to CO, 9 Cav, 25 Jul 1898, LS, Ft Robinson.

ANDERSON, J. B.; Private; D/10th Cav. Served in 10th Cavalry, 1898; remained in U.S. during war with Spain. SOURCE: Cashin, *Under Fire with the Tenth Cavalry*, 341.

ANDERSON, James; Private; F/10th Cav. Original member of 10th Cavalry; in troop when organized, Ft Leavenworth, KS, 21 Jun 1867. SOURCE: McMiller, "Buffalo Soldiers," 73.

Wounded in action, Kansas, 21 Aug 1867. SOURCE: Armes, *Ups and Downs*, 247.

ANDERSON, James; Corporal; M/10th Cav. Original member of 10th Cavalry; in troop when organized, Ft Leavenworth, KS, 15 Oct 1867. SOURCE: McMiller, "Buffalo Soldiers," 79.

Commanding officer, M/10th Cavalry, reports in Dec 1869 that his company records are incomplete so he cannot furnish final statements regarding casualties Sergeant Jefferson and Corporal Anderson. SOURCE: ES, 10 Cav, 1866–77.

ANDERSON, John; Private; D/10th Cav. Honorable mention for bravery against Comanches, Double Mountain Fork, Brazos River, TX, 5 Feb 1874. SOURCE: Baker, Roster.

ANDERSON, John; Trumpeter; M/10th Cav. At Ft Apache, AZ, 1890, subscribed $.50 to testimonial to General Grierson. SOURCE: List of subscriptions, 23 Apr 1890, 10th Cavalry papers, MHI.

ANDERSON, John; Corporal; A/10th Cav. Served in 10th Cavalry in Cuba, 1898. SOURCE: Cashin, *Under Fire with the Tenth Cavalry*, 339.

ANDERSON, John A.; Private; K/10th Cav. Served in 10th Cavalry, 1898; remained in U.S. during war with Spain. SOURCE: Cashin, *Under Fire with the Tenth Cavalry*, 349.

ANDERSON, John B.; Private; B/25th Inf. Dishonorable discharge, Brownsville. SOURCE: SO 266, AGO, 9 Nov 1906.

ANDERSON, John B.; Private; G/10th Cav. Born a slave near Covington, Newton Co., GA, 14 Sep 1860; remained in vicinity until several years after 1870; father reportedly was white, Dr. Cay Anderson; mother was slave, Patience Baker; enlisted Atlanta, GA, 30 Oct 1876; discharged San Antonio, TX, 30 Oct 1881. Lived at 424 Pine St., Chattanooga, TN, and barbered in Reed House, 1890–96; lived at 993 Florida Ave., NW, Washington, DC, 1896–1900; worked for Post Office Department, Washington, DC, 1897–1907; lived at 1 Main St., Butte, MT, with chiropody offices in 64 and 65 Owsley Building, 1910–20; lived at 1937 13th St., NW, Washington, DC, 1922; lived in Aquasco, MD, 1929. SOURCE: VA File C 2579187, John B. Anderson.

First wife Dora Hammond born in Georgia, died of typhoid in Chattanooga, 22 May 1890, at age 27; married Bessie Sublett, 3 Jul 1899, Washington, DC, widow of Prof. DeLorenzo Sublett, who died at home, Chapel Hill, TX, 1892. Bessie lived at 505 Rhode Island Ave., NW, Washington, DC, when Anderson died of heart disease on 6 Mar 1939, at Soldiers Home, Washington, DC, where he lived from 1 Sep 1937; buried at Arlington; widow died 18 Jan 1952, while residing (since 1945) at 1937 13th St., NW, Apt. 2, Washington, DC. Son Clifton C. Anderson, lived at 1430 Morris Road, SE, Washington, DC, in 1939, and had served in 63rd Pioneer Infantry, rising to first sergeant, 24 Sep–10 Dec 1918. SOURCE: VA File C 2579187, John B. Anderson.

Pensions: $20 per month, 4 Sep 1922; $30 per month, 5 May 1927; $40 per month, 15 Feb 1929; $50 per month, 22 Aug 1929; $30 per month, 23 Mar 1939; $40 per month, 23 Mar 1944. SOURCE: VA File C 2579187, John B. Anderson.

Renews subscription; wants to hear from old troopers of G/10th Cavalry. SOURCE: *Winners of the West* 6 (Sep 1929): 8.

ANDERSON, John H.; 1st Lt; D/48th Inf. Private, A/9th Cavalry, and schoolteacher although not teaching, Ft Robinson, NE, 1 Nov 1893–30 Apr 1894. SOURCE: Reports of Schools, Ft Robinson, 1892–96.

On extra duty as schoolteacher, Ft Robinson. SOURCE: Order 8, 29 Jan 1894, Post Orders, Ft Robinson.

Appointed saddler sergeant, 9th Cavalry, Ft Robinson, May 1896. SOURCE: *ANJ* 33 (9 May 1896): 652.

Promoted to sergeant major, 9th Cavalry, Ft Robinson, 6 Jul 1897, vice Jeremiah Jones, promoted to ordnance sergeant. SOURCE: *ANJ* 34 (17 Jul 1897): 854.

Sent to Hemingford, NE, to conduct deserter Frank H. Bosley, 8th Cavalry, to Ft Robinson. SOURCE: SO 42, 9 Mar 1898, Post Orders, Ft Robinson.

Served in Cuba as regimental sergeant major; commissioned second lieutenant, 10th Volunteer Infantry, 1898; first lieutenant, 10th U.S. Volunteer Infantry, 1898; second lieu-

tenant, 48th U.S. Volunteer Infantry, 1899. SOURCE: Cashin, *Under Fire with the Tenth Cavalry*, 360.

Served as squadron sergeant major, 9th Cavalry. SOURCE: *ANJ* 37 (9 Dec 1899): 344.

Mentioned as first lieutenant, D/48th Infantry. SOURCE: Beasley, *Negro Trailblazers*, 284.

ANDERSON, John H.; Corporal; F/10th Cav. Served in 10th Cavalry in Cuba, 1898. SOURCE: Cashin, *Under Fire with the Tenth Cavalry*, 343.

ANDERSON, John L.; Private; E/10th Cav. Served in 10th Cavalry in Cuba, 1898. SOURCE: Cashin, *Under Fire with the Tenth Cavalry*, 354.

ANDERSON, John R.; Private; H/24th Inf. Enlisted 18 Sep 1898, Camp Wikoff, Long Island, with four years' continuous service; on furlough until 18 Oct 1898, due to illness; on detached service en route to duty station, 18–22 Oct 1898; sick in quarters since 24 Oct 1898. SOURCE: Muster Roll, H/24 Inf, Sep–Oct 1898.

Sick in quarters to 12 Nov 1898; on special duty as teamster, Quartermaster Department, since 19 Nov. SOURCE: Muster Roll, H/24 Inf, Nov–Dec 1898.

On special duty as teamster from 19 Nov 1898; discharged 29 Jan 1899, character excellent, single; due soldier for clothing $31.36; reenlisted, Ft Douglas, UT, 30 Jan 1899. SOURCE: Muster Roll, H/24 Inf, Jan–Feb 1899.

Picture. SOURCE: Indianapolis *Freeman*, 18 Mar 1899.

ANDERSON, John W.; Private; A/9th Cav. Died in the Philippines, 28 Nov 1900. SOURCE: *ANJ* 38 (29 Dec 1900): 431.

Died of disease in Nueva Caceres, Philippines. SOURCE: Hamilton, "History of the Ninth Cavalry," 103.

ANDERSON, John W.; Corporal; H/9th Cav. Private, 1896; corporal, 1897; deposits with paymaster: $10, Nov–Dec 1896; $27, 1897; $10, Jan–May 1898.

ANDERSON, Joe B.; Private; E/10th Cav. Served in 10th Cavalry in Cuba, 1898. SOURCE: Cashin, *Under Fire with the Tenth Cavalry*, 342.

ANDERSON, Joseph; Sergeant; M/24th Inf. Served in Houston, TX, 1917. SOURCE: Haynes, *A Night of Violence*, 121.

ANDERSON, Levi; Private; D/10th Cav. Born Williamsburg, SC; resided at enlistment in Allegheny, PA; awarded distinguished service medal in lieu of certificate of merit for rescue of drowning comrade, 6 Jul 1911, Mallets Bay, near Ft Ethan Allen, VT. SOURCE: *Decorations US Army. Supplement I*, 35; AGO, Bulletin 9, 1912.

Served as officer, 368th Infantry, World War I; retired as private, D/10th Cavalry. SOURCE: *Crisis* 42 (Oct 1931): 346.

ANDERSON, Lewis L.; Sergeant; B/9th Cav. Veteran of Spanish-American War and Philippine Insurrection; at Ft D. A. Russell, WY, in 1910; marksman. SOURCE: *Illustrated Review: Ninth Cavalry*, with picture.

ANDERSON, Lewis S.; Blacksmith; E/10th Cav. Served in 10th Cavalry in Cuba, 1898. SOURCE: Cashin, *Under Fire with the Tenth Cavalry*, 342.

Wounded in action, Santiago, 1 Jul 1898. SOURCE: SecWar, *AR 1898*, 324.

ANDERSON, Louis; Private; 10th Cav. Born a slave, Moss Lake, GA, 4 Jul 1850; enlisted St. Louis, MO; occupation laborer; Ht 5'8", dark complexion; served 2 Mar 1876–1 Mar 1881; teamster after service; pensioned by private law, 8 Dec 1924; pension $20 per month, 12 Jan 1925 and $50 per month, 23 Sep 1927; died 23 Mar 1928, address 162 Cebada, El Paso, TX; lived at 712 E. Third, El Paso, in 1919. SOURCE: VA File SC 12244, Louis Anderson.

Mentioned Jun 1876 as enlisted 2 Mar 1876. SOURCE: ES, 10 Cav, 1873–81.

Served in 1876–81; recent subscriber to *Winners of the West*. SOURCE: *Winners of the West* 4 (Mar 1927): 8.

Letter, Mr. and Mrs. Alonzo Miller, El Paso, TX: Louis Anderson died at age 81, after seven days in bed, 23 Mar 1928; lived in our house eleven years. SOURCE: *Winners of the West* 5 (Apr 1928): 2.

ANDERSON, Louis; Private; K/10th Cav. Served in 10th Cavalry, 1898; remained in U.S. during war with Spain. SOURCE: Cashin, *Under Fire with the Tenth Cavalry*, 349.

ANDERSON, Louis; Private; G/25thInf. Died of typhoid in the Philippines, 3 Oct 1901. SOURCE: *ANJ* 39 (7 Dec 1901): 339.

ANDERSON, Luke; Private; I/25th Inf. Fined $.50 by summary court for violating Article 33, missing reveille, San Isidro, Philippines, 29 Mar 1902, fourth conviction; fined $5 for violating Article 31, lying out of quarters, 6 Apr 1902; sentenced to one month and forfeiture of one month's pay for violating Article 62, assaulting civilian with brick, 9 May 1902; fined $5 for violating Article 31, lying out of quarters, 24 Mar 1902. SOURCE: Register of Summary Court, San Isidro.

ANDERSON, R.; 1st Sgt; B/9th Cav. On detached service, Ft Bayard, NM, 16 Jan–9 Feb 1881. SOURCE: Regt Returns, 9 Cav.

ANDERSON, Richard; Comsy Sgt; U.S. Army. Appointed post quartermaster sergeant from regimental quartermaster sergeant, 9th Cavalry, 5 Feb 1885. SOURCE: Roster, 9 Cav, 1893.

Retired as commissary sergeant; narrates Victorio campaign. SOURCE: Steward, *The Colored Regulars*, 318–20.

ANDERSON, Robert; B/10th Cav. Original member of 10th Cavalry; in troop when organized, Ft Leavenworth, KS, 1 Apr 1867. SOURCE: McMiller, "Buffalo Soldiers," 69.

ANDERSON, Robert; Saddler Sgt; 10th Cav. Private, L/10th Cavalry, 1867; sergeant, L/10th Cavalry, honorable mention for gallantry against Kiowas and Comanches, Wichita Agency, Indian Territory, 22–23 Aug 1874. SOURCE: Baker, Roster.

As saddler sergeant, 10th Cavalry, Ft Apache, AZ, 1890, subscribed $.50 to testimonial to General Grierson. SOURCE: List of subscriptions, 23 Apr 1890, 10th Cavalry papers, MHI.

Retires as saddler sergeant, 10th Cavalry, Ft Custer, MT. SOURCE: *ANJ* 30 (24 Jun 1893): 727; Baker, Roster.

ANDERSON, Robert; Private; Band/10th Cav. Mentioned Mar 1874, as playing bass drum and cymbals. SOURCE: ES, 10 Cav.

Deposited $30 with paymaster, Ft Concho, TX, 29 Jan 1877. SOURCE: Adj, 10 Cav, to PMG, 30 Jan 1877, LS, 10 Cav, 1873–83.

Deposited $25 with paymaster, Ft Concho, 12 Mar 1877. SOURCE: Adj, 10 Cav, to PMG, 12 Mar 1877, LS, 10 Cav, 1873–83.

Deposited $80 with paymaster, Ft Concho, 7 May 1877. SOURCE: Adj, 10 Cav, to PMG, 7 May 1877, LS, 10 Cav, 1873–83.

ANDERSON, Robert; Private; I/9th Cav. At Ft Robinson, NE, from Ft Washakie, WY, as witness in court martial of Pvt. Lewis Jones, 4 Nov–7 Dec 1895. SOURCE: Regt Returns, 9 Cav, Nov–Dec 1895.

ANDERSON, Robert; Corporal; H/10th Cav. Died in Cuba, 14 Aug 1898. SOURCE: *ANJ* 36 (11 Feb 1899): 567.

Cause of death, yellow fever. SOURCE: AG, *Correspondence Regarding the War with Spain*, I, 228.

Died of yellow fever at Siboney, 14 Aug 1898. SOURCE: Hospital Papers, Spanish-American War.

ANDERSON, Robert; Sergeant; B/10th Cav. Affidavit, Ft Custer, MT, 14 Sep 1893: saw John Howerton thrown from horse while herd guard. SOURCE: VA File XC 896871, John C. Howerton.

ANDERSON, Roudie; Private; F/9th Cav. At Ft D. A. Russell, WY, in 1910; resident of Green Co., MO. SOURCE: *Illustrated Review: Ninth Cavalry*, with picture.

ANDERSON, Thomas; Private; B/9th Cav. At Ft D. A. Russell, WY, in 1910; marksman. SOURCE: *Illustrated Review: Ninth Cavalry*.

ANDERSON, Walker; Private; A/10th Cav. At Ft Apache, AZ, 1890, private, Band/10th Cavalry, subscribed $.50 to testimonial to General Grierson. SOURCE: List of subscriptions, 23 Apr 1890, 10th Cavalry papers, MHI.

ANDERSON, William; Private; B/25th Inf.
Dishonorable discharge, Brownsville. SOURCE: SO 266, AGO, 9 Nov 1906.

ANDERSON, William; Recruit; Colored Detachment/Mounted Service. Tried by general court martial, Jefferson Barracks, MO, for violating Article 32, absence without leave, from 9 P.M., 9 Oct 1888 to 4 P.M., 15 Oct 1888; pleaded guilty; found guilty; sentenced to six months at hard labor and loss of $10 per month for six months. SOURCE: GCMO 56, AGO, 6 Nov 1888.

ANDERSON, William; Private; G/10th Cav. On daily duty with Quartermaster Department. SOURCE: SO 6, Det 10 Cav, Camp near Ft Lyon, CO, 17 Mar 1869, Orders, Det 10 Cav, 1868–69.

ANDERSON, William; Corporal; G/10th Cav. At Ft Apache, AZ, 1890, subscribed $.50 to testimonial to General Grierson. SOURCE: List of subscriptions, 23 Apr 1890, 10th Cavalry papers, MHI.

ANDERSON, William; Private; A/10th Cav. Served in 10th Cavalry in Cuba, 1898. SOURCE: Cashin, *Under Fire with the Tenth Cavalry*, 336.

ANDERSON, William H.; G/10th Cav. Original member of 10th Cavalry; in troop when organized, Ft Leavenworth, KS, 5 Jul 1867. SOURCE: McMiller, "Buffalo Soldiers," 74.

ANDERSON, William T.; Chaplain; 10th Cav. Born a slave; mother led him to escape to Galveston, TX, to father, who was prominent merchant; worked five years as messenger for railroad and superintended African Methodist Episcopal Sunday School, Galveston; Texas Conference of African Methodist Episcopal Church sent him to Wilberforce University for three years, after which he supported himself with odd jobs; Mr. and Mrs. Stephen Watson (vice president, London Exchange Bank, Madison Co., OH) sent him to Howard University, where he graduated with honors, then to Homeopathic Medical College, Cleveland, OH, 1885; graduated 12 Mar 1888 with honors; superintendent, St. John's AME Sabbath School, Cleveland, going to Washington, DC, to practice medicine. SOURCE: Cleveland *Gazette*, 31 Mar 1888.
    Born Saguin, TX, 20 Aug 1859. SOURCE: Cashin, *Under Fire with the Tenth Cavalry*, 290.
    Educated at Wilberforce, Howard, Cleveland Homeopathic Medical College; AME minister; chaplain since 1897 with 10th Cavalry, Ft Assiniboine, MT; major, Aug 1907; commander, U.S. Morgue, Manila, and chaplain, Ft Wm McKinley, 1909. SOURCE: *Colored American Magazine* 16 (Apr 1909): 223.
    Arrived with bride at Urbana, OH. SOURCE: Cleveland *Gazette*, 28 Jul 1890.

Appointed to African Methodist Episcopal Church, Lima, OH. SOURCE: Cleveland *Gazette*, 13 Oct 1893.
    Pastor, St. John's African Methodist Episcopal Church, Cleveland, May 1896–May 1897. SOURCE: *Encyclopedia of African Methodism* (1947), 357.
    Ordered to duty by 1 Nov 1897, Ft Assiniboine. SOURCE: *ANJ* 35 (9 Oct 1897): 96.
    Orders directing him to report amended to 11 Nov 1897. SOURCE: *ANJ* 35 (16 Oct 1897): 116.
    Confirmed as chaplain by Senate, 16 Dec 1897. SOURCE: *ANJ* 35 (25 Dec 1897): 311.
    Left Cleveland for 10th Cavalry and Ft Assiniboine, as new chaplain; reception in his honor at Forest City National Guard Armory, Forest Street. SOURCE: Cleveland *Gazette*, 6 Nov 1897.
    En route to Ft Assiniboine 11 Nov and has conducted services twice per week since. SOURCE: Indianapolis *Freeman*, 11 Dec 1897.
    Chastened for saying that he prefers the chaplaincy to "the best church in the country." SOURCE: Cleveland *Gazette*, 15 Jan 1898.
    Defended as competent against attacks in *Gazette*; Mrs. Anderson "a lady of rare accomplishments" who plays organ and sings at his well-attended services. SOURCE: Indianapolis *Freeman*, 12 Feb 1898.
    10th Cavalry to depart, with Chaplain Anderson staying at Ft Assiniboine as post commander. SOURCE: *ANJ* 35 (23 Apr 1898): 648.
    As commander of Ft Assiniboine, first black officer to command military post. SOURCE: Stover, *Up from Handymen*, 111.
    On arrival of Maj. Joseph M. Kelley at Ft Assiniboine, Anderson is to join his regiment. SOURCE: *ANJ* 35 (4 Jun 1898): 792.
    In Cuba with regiment; physician by profession; commander Ft Assiniboine, 19 Apr–28 Jun 1898; at Ft MacIntosh, TX, 1899. SOURCE: Cashin, *Under Fire with the Tenth Cavalry*, 105, 290–91, picture on 290.
    As one of several authors of *Under Fire with the Tenth Cavalry*. SOURCE: Cashin, *Under Fire with the Tenth Cavalry*.
    Only black chaplain to serve with regiment in Cuba during war with Spain, 1898. SOURCE: Stover, *Up from Handymen*, 111.
    On duty with regiment in Cuba, transferred from Gibara to Manzanillo. SOURCE: *ANJ* 36 (1 Jul 1899): 1047.
    Anderson's letter from Manzanillo, 30 Jul 1899, gives biography of Signal Sgt. James A. Richards. SOURCE: Cleveland *Gazette*, 28 Oct 1899.
    Post treasurer, Manzanillo, 12 Jan 1900; sanitary officer, 25 Jan 1900; exchange officer, 18 Jul 1901; on detached service at Holguin, Cuba, 20–30 Apr 1901; inspector of schools, Municipality of Manzanillo, May 1901–Apr 1902; two months' sick leave, from 22 Apr 1902; joined regiment at Ft Robinson, NE, 7 Jul 1902; post treasurer and in charge of library, 8 Jul 1902; on detached service on post, with regiment on practice march, 6–16 Sep 1902; in charge of post schools, 23 Sep 1903; on detached service on post, while

regiment at Ft Riley, KS, 4 Oct–11 Nov 1903; absent with leave hunting 17–22 Oct 1904; left U.S. with regiment 3 Apr 1907 and took station at Ft Wm McKinley, Philippines; in charge of schools, 22 May 1907; post treasurer, 7 Aug 1907. SOURCE: Descriptive Book, 10 Cav Officers & NCOs.

His monthly reports from Ft Robinson, 1902–1906. SOURCE: AGO File 53910.

Played large part in development and success of 10th Cavalry YMCA. SOURCE: Indianapolis *Freeman*, 19 Jul 1902.

Ordered before retiring board: "President Taft seems determined to oust from office every Negro holding a decent position with the federal service. This is in accordance with his infamous 'new Southern policy.' " SOURCE: Cleveland *Gazette*, 7 Aug 1901.

Letter, Ft Robinson, 17 Jan 1903, to commander, Ft Robinson, asks that railroads of department grant furloughed soldiers half-rates; forwarded to Adjutant, Department of the Missouri, and returned, not approved by railroads. Letter to commander, Ft Robinson, 29 May 1903, reports departure on leave and address, "Finlay, Ohio." SOURCE: Register, LR, Ft Robinson, 1903.

Will preach at Congregational Church, Crawford, NE, next Sunday morning: "Be sure to hear him." SOURCE: Crawford *Bulletin*, 23 Oct 1903.

On Thanksgiving, Ft Robinson, 1904, sang duet "In Thy Love" with his wife at church service. SOURCE: Indianapolis *Freeman*, 3 Dec 1904.

Will preach at Crawford Methodist Church, Sunday, 12 Feb 1905. SOURCE: Crawford *Tribune*, 10 Feb 1905.

Biography with picture: a permanent trustee, Wilberforce University, and delegate to last General Conference, African Methodist Episcopal Church. SOURCE: Talbert, *The Sons of Allen*, 240.

"Among the many [Wilberforce graduates] who have reached eminence." SOURCE: Hartshorn, *An Era of Progress and Promise*, 281.

Promoted to major. SOURCE: Cleveland *Gazette*, 21 Sep 1907.

Sent Auditor Ralph W. Tyler "a handsome leather-trimmed Morris chair," of Philippine mahogany with brass fixtures and plate for engraving. SOURCE: Washington *Bee*, 25 Jun 1908.

Visited here ten days. SOURCE: Cleveland *Gazette*, 12 Jun 1909.

Granted leave until 16 Dec, date to be retired. SOURCE: Cleveland *Gazette*, 4 Dec 1909.

Retired with physical disability and replaced by white Roman Catholic priest, Rev. Joseph Kennedy, from Oregon; regiment practically all Protestant. SOURCE: Cleveland *Gazette*, 18 Dec 1909.

Retired for disability 10 Jan 1910, after treatment at Walter Reed Army Medical Center and at Hot Springs, AR, for "tropical fever" contracted in Cuba. SOURCE: Cleveland *Gazette*, 25 Aug 1934.

Lectured on travels in Palestine, Egypt, Japan at Northern District of Northern Ohio Conference, AME meeting at Sandusky. SOURCE: Cleveland *Gazette*, 27 May 1911.

Mrs. George Myers and daughter of Cleveland as guests of "Ex-chaplain and Mrs. W. T. Anderson" of Wilberforce. SOURCE: Cleveland *Gazette*, 8 Jul 1911.

Ex-chaplain Anderson, former pastor of St. John's, preached excellent sermon there on Sunday; now lives on "Bishop Arnett" homestead, which he bought and beautified; left here Tuesday for annual AME conference, Youngstown; while in Cleveland, guest of George A. Myers. SOURCE: Cleveland *Gazette*, 23 Sep 1911.

At Northern Ohio Conference, AME, "delivered a fine lecture on the Holy Land." SOURCE: Cleveland *Gazette*, 30 Sep 1911.

A trustee of Wilberforce, visited from there with Mr. and Mrs. George Myers last week; on way home from conference meetings at Lima and Columbus. SOURCE: Cleveland *Gazette*, 3 Oct 1914.

Was here last week as guest of George A. Myers. SOURCE: Cleveland *Gazette*, 10 Apr 1915.

Mrs. Anderson joined him here from Washington, DC; considering leaving Wilberforce to locate here or Chicago. SOURCE: Cleveland *Gazette*, 17 Apr 1915.

Left 5 May with his wife for Chicago, Denver, San Francisco; will visit Panama-Pacific Exposition, San Francisco, as special representative of *Gazette*. SOURCE: Cleveland *Gazette*, 8 May 1915.

Back as guests of Mrs. Della Eubanks and her mother, Mrs. Harmon, 1202 Lakewood Ave.; may locate here. SOURCE: Cleveland *Gazette*, 3 Jul 1915.

Resident of Washington, DC; was in Cleveland last week and in Akron to see Sen. Charles Dick. SOURCE: Cleveland *Gazette*, 6 May 1916.

Was here last week en route home from Wilberforce to Washington, DC. SOURCE: Cleveland *Gazette*, 24 Jun 1916.

Moving to Toledo, as pastor of Warren Chapel, replacing Rev. Charles A. Bundy. SOURCE: Cleveland *Gazette*, 2 Oct 1916.

In Toledo. SOURCE: Cleveland *Gazette*, 16 Oct 1919.

Speaker in crowded city hall auditorium, Wellsville, OH, on "Man to Man," 300th anniversary celebration of Negroes in America; Rev. Mr. Mason, Wellsville African Methodist Episcopal Church, presided. SOURCE: Cleveland *Gazette*, 11 Jan 1919.

Pastor of Warren AME church will retire at fall conference in Dayton, 13 Sep; Toledo congregation will hold farewell reception 16 Sep, at which time portrait by Frederick D. Allen will be presented to church; previously in Toledo, 1896–97; returned Sep 1916. "Has an enviable Army record," including letter of recommendation for promotion from General Pershing; only colored officer in battle at Santiago; only black member of Military Order of Foreign Wars; wife organized missionary group of Warren church; they are great travelers, having been to Japan, China, India, Egypt, Palestine, elsewhere; will leave Toledo 1 Oct for Washington, DC, where he has applied for reinstatement in service with Quartermaster Department. SOURCE: Toledo *Blade*, 7 Sep 1918, with picture.

Attended Bishop Shaffer funeral, Chicago, with Mrs. Anderson. SOURCE: Cleveland *Gazette*, 19 Apr 1919.

Letter, 2215 E. 89th St., Cleveland, appeals for funds for defense of Dr. Leroy N. Bundy, East St. Louis, IL; treasurer of local Bundy fund. SOURCE: Cleveland *Gazette*, 3 May 1919.

Cleveland resident; will preach at St. John's African Methodist Episcopal Church, Cadiz, OH, on Sunday. SOURCE: Cleveland *Gazette*, 19 July 1919.

Picture of Anderson residence. SOURCE: Joiner, *A Half Century of Freedom*, 122.

Mentioned. SOURCE: Work, *The Negro Year Book, 1912*, 76.

Died 21 Aug 1934, Cleveland. SOURCE: *Official Army Register*, January 1, 1935.

Died this Tuesday at his E. 95th St. residence, age 75; found dead in his room, 9:30 A.M.; widow survives. SOURCE: Cleveland *Gazette*, 25 Aug 1934.

Funeral tomorrow, 2 P.M. Secretary to bishop and accountant, Third Episcopal District, African Methodist Episcopal Church, since retirement from Army; William T. Anderson Post, American Legion, bears his name; wife Sada J. survives and is statistician, Women's Parent Mite Missionary Society, African Methodist Episcopal Church, and president, North Ohio Conference Branch, Third Episcopal District. SOURCE: Cleveland *Plain Dealer*, 23 Aug 1934.

Ladies Auxiliary, Maj. William T. Anderson Camp, United Spanish War Veterans, No. 70, appeared in uniform at his funeral, St. James African Methodist Episcopal Church. SOURCE: Chicago *Defender*, 15 Sep 1934.

Funeral on 24 Aug with eulogy by Bishop R. C. Ransom, African Methodist Episcopal Church; many prominent churchmen attended. SOURCE: Cleveland *Gazette*, 1 Sep 1934.

Front-page banner headline, "Major Anderson dies in Sleep," with current picture; body in state at St. James African Methodist Episcopal Church, East 84th and Cedar, 12:30 to 2 P.M., Friday; survived by Mrs. Sada J. Anderson, statistician, Women's Parent Mite Missionary Society, African Methodist Episcopal Church, and president, Northern Ohio Branch, Third Episcopal District; was secretary and accountant to bishop, Third Episcopal District, African Methodist Episcopal Church; 33rd degree Mason. SOURCE: Cleveland *Call & Post*, 25 Aug 1934.

Biographical sketch. SOURCE: Logan and Winston, *Dictionary of American Negro Biography*, 15–16.

ANDREWS; Private; E/10th Cav. At Ft Apache, AZ, 1890, subscribed $.50 to testimonial to General Grierson. SOURCE: List of subscriptions, 23 Apr 1890, 10th Cavalry papers, MHI.

ANDREWS; Private; H/10th Cav. Tied for second-best time, 220-yard run, Department of Colorado, 1904, at 25.0 seconds, during competition at Ft Mackenzie, WY. SOURCE: SecWar, *AR 1903*, I, 429.

ANDREWS, Clyde O.; Private; Band/9th Cav. At Ft D. A. Russell, WY, in 1910; resident of St. Louis, MO. SOURCE: *Illustrated Review: Ninth Cavalry*, with picture.

ANDREWS, George; G/24th Inf. Remained in the Philippines at Bautista after discharge; died 1903. SOURCE: Funston papers, KSHS.

ANDREWS, Joseph C.; 2nd Lt; 48th Inf. One of nineteen officers of 48th Infantry recommended as regular Army second lieutenants. SOURCE: CG, DivPI, Manila, 8 Feb 1901, to AGO, AGO File 355163.

ANDREWS, Lazaras; Private; A/9th Cav. At Ft D. A. Russell, WY, in 1910. SOURCE: *Illustrated Review: Ninth Cavalry*, with picture.

ANDREWS, William; Private; K/25th Inf. At Ft Niobrara, NE, 1904. SOURCE: Wilson, "History of Fort Niobrara."

ANKIN, Edward; M/10th Cav. Original member of 10th Cavalry; in troop when organized, Ft Riley, KS, 15 Oct 1867. SOURCE: McMiller, "Buffalo Soldiers," 79.

ANSIL, Jeremiah; C/10th Cav. Original member of 10th Cavalry; in troop when organized, Ft Leavenworth, KS, 14 May 1867. SOURCE: McMiller, "Buffalo Soldiers," 70.

ANTHONY; Wagoner; F/9th Cav. Absent from post school for two weeks, Mar 1889. SOURCE: CO, Ft Robinson, to CO, F/9 Cav, 30 Mar 1889, LS, Ft Robinson.

ANTHONY, Dark; Private; K/24th Inf. Fined $5 for violating Article 62, entering and refusing to leave native's house, 14 Feb 1901, Talavera, Philippines. SOURCE: Summary Court Register, 24 Inf.

ANTONIO, Joseph; Private; B/10th Cav. At Ft Thomas, AZ, transferred to Hospital Corps. SOURCE: *ANJ* 25 (18 Dec 1888): 586.

APPLEBY, Frayer; Private; A/24th Inf. Died at Santiago, Cuba, 2 Sep 1898. SOURCE: *ANJ* 36 (10 Sep 1898): 43; *ANJ*, 36 (11 Feb 1899): 567.

Pvt. Frazier [*sic*] Appleby, sick with yellow fever since 19 Jul 1898, transferred to Reserve Divisional Hospital, Siboney, around 22 Jul 1898, as convalescent. SOURCE: Hospital Papers, Spanish-American War.

APPLEWHITE, Richard; 25th Inf. Convicted of rape in the Philippines and sentenced to twenty years, 21 Jan 1901.

ARCH, William; Private; H/25th Inf. Transferred from Reserve Divisional Hospital, Siboney, Cuba to Fortress Monroe, VA, on U.S. Army Transport *Concho*, 23 Jul 1898, with remittent malarial fever. SOURCE: Hospital Papers, Spanish-American War.

ARCHER; Private; F/9th Cav. Absent from post school for two weeks, Mar 1889. SOURCE: CO, Ft Robinson, to CO, F/9 Cav, 30 Mar 1889, LS, Ft Robinson.

ARCHER, Aaron; Private; H/10th Cav. *See* **BARD**, Benjamin, Private, H/10th Cavalry

ARCHRY, John; Recruit; 10th Cav. Commander, 7th Cavalry, to Commander, 10th Cavalry, Apr 1870, forwards descriptive list of Recruit Archry. SOURCE: ES, 10 Cav, 1866–71.

ARMFIELD, John; Corporal; M/10th Cav. Corporal, M/10th Cavalry; at Ft Apache, AZ, 1890, subscribed $.50 to testimonial to General Grierson. SOURCE: List of subscriptions, 23 Apr 1890, 10th Cavalry papers, MHI.

Private, G/10th Cavalry; qualified as sharpshooter with carbine, 1892, his first qualification. SOURCE: GO 1, AGO, 3 Jan 1893.

Private, G/10th Cavalry; served in 10th Cavalry, 1898; remained in U.S. during war with Spain. SOURCE: Cashin, *Under Fire with the Tenth Cavalry*, 345.

ARMS, Benjamin; 1st Sgt; A/24th Inf. Born McIntosh, GA, 1845; black; enlisted in A/38th Infantry, 14 May 1867; discharged Ft Bliss, TX; reenlisted A/24th Infantry, 17 May 1870–17 May 1875; discharged Ft Ringgold, TX; reenlisted 17 May 1875–16 May 1880; discharged Ft Duncan, TX; reenlisted 17 May 1880–16 May 1885; discharged Ft Reno, Indian Territory; reenlisted Ft Reno, 17 May 1885; noncommissioned staff, Ft Supply, Indian Territory, 18 Jan 1887; promoted to sergeant, A/38th Infantry, 24 Nov 1868; sergeant, A/24th Infantry, until promoted to quartermaster sergeant, 3 Jan 1887, and first sergeant, 8 Apr 1875–16 May 1885; sergeant, A/24th Infantry, 25 Feb 1890. "An excellent soldier and man, sober, intelligent and trustworthy." Each discharge with character excellent; married, no children; deposits $300 ($100 in each year, 1885, 1887, 1888); additional pay $5 per month. SOURCE: Entry dated 25 Feb 1890, Ft Bayard, NM, Descriptive Book, 24 Inf NCS & Band.

To report from Ft Reno to Ft Supply, as quartermaster sergeant. SOURCE: *ANJ* 24 (15 Jan 1887): 490.

Senior sergeant, 24th Infantry, with warrant dating from 28 Nov 1868, now stationed at Ft Bayard, sergeant, A/24th Infantry. SOURCE: *ANJ* 27 (3 May 1890): 679.

Retires as first sergeant, A/24th Infantry, from Ft Douglas, UT. SOURCE: Cleveland *Gazette*, 26 Jun 1897; *ANJ* 34 (22 May 1897): 705.

ARMSTEAD; Private; 9th Cav. With Lt. John McBlain escaped Apache raid to Mason's Ranch, NM, Jan 1881. SOURCE: Billington, *New Mexico's Buffalo Soldiers*, 101.

ARMSTRONG, Allen; A/10th Cav. Original member of 10th Cavalry; in troop when organized, Ft Leavenworth, KS, 18 Feb 1867. SOURCE: McMiller, "Buffalo Soldiers," 68.

ARMSTRONG, Fred; Private; E/25th Inf. Died of typhoid in the Philippines, 16 Jan 1900. SOURCE: *ANJ* 37 (3 Mar 1900): 635.

ARMSTRONG, James E.; Musician; C/25th Inf. Dishonorable discharge, Brownsville. SOURCE: SO 266, AGO, 9 Nov 1906.

ARMSTRONG, Walter; Private; H/10th Cav. Honorable mention for services rendered in capture of the Apache Mangas and his band, Rio Bonito, AZ, 18 Oct 1886. SOURCE: Baker, Roster.

ARMSTRONG, William; F/10th Cav. Original member of 10th Cavalry; in troop when organized, Ft Leavenworth, KS, 21 Jun 1867. SOURCE: McMiller, "Buffalo Soldiers," 73.

ARMSTRONG, Wilson, H.; Sergeant; A/9th Cav. Promoted corporal, A/9th Cavalry, 24 Jul 1893. SOURCE: Roster, 9 Cav, Jul 1893.

Corporal, Ft Robinson, NE, 1894. SOURCE: Investigation of Charges against Chaplain Plummer.

Promoted to sergeant. SOURCE: *ANJ* 34 (17 Jul 1897): 854.

Sergeant, on special duty instructing recruits, as of 9 May 1902. SOURCE: SD Lists, A/9 Cav, 24 May 1902, Nueva Caceres, Philippines.

ARNEL, William; Private; C/25th Inf. Fined $60 and confined six months for altering target scores, Ft Snelling, MN. SOURCE: *ANJ* 25 (3 Sep 1887): 103.

ARNETT, Alexander; 1st Sgt; E/24th Inf. Commended for voluntarily nursing fever-stricken officers of his regiment for weeks, under particularly trying conditions, "in the most faithful and self-sacrificing manner," Cuban campaign, Jul 1898. SOURCE: GO 15, AGO, 13 Feb 1900.

Cited for distinguished service in Jul 1898. SOURCE: *ANJ* 37 (24 Feb 1900): 611.

ARNETT, Budd; Private; D/10th Cav. Served in 10th Cavalry, 1898; remained in U.S. during war with Spain. SOURCE: Cashin, *Under Fire with the Tenth Cavalry*, 341.

Letter, 2nd Lt. Seth W. Cook, 10th Cavalry, Ft Robinson, NE, 15 Mar 1903, submits charges against Arnett; forwarded to Adjutant General, Department of the Missouri, 16 Mar 1903, with recommendation for general court martial. SOURCE: Register, LR, Ft Robinson.

Dishonorable discharge and jail, Ft Robinson, Mar 1904. SOURCE: SO 48, DeptMo, 12 Mar 1904.

Released Jun 1904.

ARNOLD, Charles; Private; D/10th Cav. Served in 10th Cavalry in Cuba, 1898. SOURCE: Cashin, *Under Fire with the Tenth Cavalry*, 354.

ARNOLD, John; Private; G/10th Cav. Served in 10th Cavalry in Cuba, 1898. SOURCE: Cashin, *Under Fire with the Tenth Cavalry*, 345.

Wounded in action, Santiago, Cuba, 3 Jul 1898. SOURCE: SecWar, *AR 1898*, 324.

ARNOLD, Joseph; C/10th Cav. Original member of 10th Cavalry; in troop when organized, Ft Leavenworth, KS, 14 May 1867. SOURCE: McMiller, "Buffalo Soldiers," 70.

ARNOLD, Julius; Musician; M/25th Inf. Convicted of murder, 15 Jan 1900. SOURCE: GO 9, HQ PMG, Manila, 25 Apr 1900.

On his killing native woman in self-defense. SOURCE: Manila *Times*, 17 Jan 1900.

"Musician Julius Arnold of Company M, 25th U.S. Infantry (colored) has been sentenced by a general court martial to be dishonorably discharged from the service of the United States and to be confined at hard labor for . . . life. . . . The man was tried for the brutal murder of a virtuous married native woman, leaving a nursing infant motherless after offering her the grossest insult that a man can offer a chaste woman." SOURCE: Manila *Times*, 22 May 1900.

Killed woman who attacked him with bolo; he "is a quite unassuming fellow." SOURCE: Richmond *Planet*, 17 Mar 1900.

Reported to have received life sentence. SOURCE: Richmond *Planet*, 28 Jul 1900.

ARNOLD, Meredith; Corporal; D/10th Cav. Served in 10th Cavalry in Cuba, 1898. SOURCE: Cashin, *Under Fire with the Tenth Cavalry*, 341.

ARNOLD, Walter; Private; C/10th Cav. Served in 10th Cavalry, 1898; remained in U.S. during war with Spain. SOURCE: Cashin, *Under Fire with the Tenth Cavalry*, 340.

ARRILIEN, Wiley M.; K/10th Cav. Original member of 10th Cavalry; in troop when organized, Ft Riley, KS, 1 Sep 1867. SOURCE: McMiller, "Buffalo Soldiers," 77.

ARRINGTON, George; C/24th Inf. Mentioned as among men who recently distinguished themselves; awarded certificate of merit for gallant and meritorious service while escorting Maj. Joseph W. Wham, paymaster, when attacked by robbers between Fts Grant and Thomas, AZ; now out of service. SOURCE: GO 18, AGO, 1891.

Born Halifax, NC, resided Charleston, SC, when enlisted; Distinguished Service Cross awarded in lieu of certificate of merit for gallant and meritorious conduct while escorting Paymaster Wham, 11 May 1889. SOURCE: *Decorations. US Army, Supplement I*, 28.

Admitted to Soldiers Home, with disability, on 22 Jul 1890, after serving one year and ten months. SOURCE: SecWar, *AR 1890*, 1043.

Mentioned. SOURCE: *Winners of the West* 13 (Jan 1936): 3.

His certificate of merit mentioned. SOURCE: *Winners of the West* 14 (Feb 1937).

ARRINGTON, John H.; Private; K/9th Cav. At Ft D. A. Russell, WY, in 1910; sharpshooter; resident of Colbert Co., AL. SOURCE: *Illustrated Review: Ninth Cavalry*, with picture.

ARTER, Charles; Corporal; I/25th Inf. Promoted from private. SOURCE: *ANJ* 38 (28 Oct 1905): 21.

ARTHUR, Charles; Private; G/10th Cav. Served in 10th Cavalry in Cuba, 1898. SOURCE: Cashin, *Under Fire with the Tenth Cavalry*, 354.

Wounded in action, Santiago, Cuba, 1 Jul 1898. SOURCE: SecWar, *AR 1898*, 324.

ARTHUR, Joseph; Private; 9th Cav. To be tried by general court martial, Ft Duchesne, UT. SOURCE: *ANJ* 35 (25 Dec 1897): 310.

Convicted at Ft Duchesne of stabbing another soldier; conviction disapproved by reviewing authority, Colonel Huntt, Commander, Department of Colorado; accused only had opportunity to challenge one member of court; court record a shambles; reconvening is impractical and costly. SOURCE: *ANJ* 35 (5 Feb 1898): 423.

ARVIN, Henry W.; Private; C/25th Inf. Dishonorable discharge, Brownsville. SOURCE: SO 266, AGO, 9 Nov 1906.

One of fourteen cleared of involvement in Brownsville raid by court, 1910, and authorized to reenlist. SOURCE: Weaver, *The Brownsville Raid*, 248.

ASBURRY, Samuel H.; Private; Band/9th Cav. With band on detached service at headquarters, District of New Mexico, Santa Fe, 1880; played E-flat tuba. SOURCE: Billington, *New Mexico's Buffalo Soldiers*, 226.

ASH, Alexander; Private; 9th Cav. At Ft Riley, KS; with 25th Infantry at Ft Brown, TX, during Brownsville raid; discharged without honor. SOURCE: Cleveland *Gazette*, 1 Dec 1906.

ASH, John; QM Sgt; E/24th Inf. Awarded certificate of merit 11 Jan 1907 for conspicuous gallantry against Pulahanes while sergeant, E/24th Infantry; fine example and cool bravery in command of ten soldiers and detachment of constabulary; was surrounded and brought engagement to successful conclusion, at Tabon-Tabon, Leyte, Philippines, 24 Jul 1906. SOURCE: GO 143, AGO, 1 Jul 1907.

In the Philippines, 1906, as sergeant, E/24th Infantry. *See* **HARRIS**, William C., Sergeant, E/24th Infantry

ASH, Joseph; F/10th Cav. Original member of 10th Cavalry; in troop when organized, Ft Leavenworth, KS, 21 Jun 1867. SOURCE: McMiller, "Buffalo Soldiers," 73.

ASH, Robert; Private; E/10th Cav. Served in 10th Cavalry, 1898; remained in U.S. during war with Spain. SOURCE: Cashin, *Under Fire with the Tenth Cavalry*, 343.

ASH, Robert H.; Private; K/9th Cav. Veteran of Philippine Insurrection; at Ft D. A. Russell, WY, in 1910; sharpshooter; resident of Baltimore. SOURCE: *Illustrated Review: Ninth Cavalry*, with picture.

ASH, Ruben; D/10th Cav. Original member of 10th Cavalry; in troop when organized, Ft Leavenworth, KS, 1 Jun 1867. SOURCE: McMiller, "Buffalo Soldiers," 71.

ASHBRIDGE, George; Private; L/9th Cav. Discharged on expiration of service, Ft Bliss, TX, 19 Jan 1881. SOURCE: Regt Returns, 9 Cav, Jan 1881.

ASHBY, Leo; Private; I/24th Inf. Enlisted 28 Jul 1898, Chicago, with one year continuous service; sick 9 Nov 1898–16 Jan 1899, in line of duty. SOURCE: Muster Roll, I/24 Inf, Jan–Feb 1899.

Confined at hard labor under guard for thirty days and fined $15 by general court martial, 16 Mar 1899. SOURCE: Muster Roll, I/24 Inf, Mar–Apr 1899.

Discharged 31 Dec 1899, with $11.62 due him for clothing, $45 due him for deposits, $5 due U.S. per special court martial, Dec 1899, character good. SOURCE: Muster Roll, I/24 Inf, Nov–Dec 1899.

ASHE, Stephen; Private; E/10th Cav. Served in 10th Cavalry, 1898; remained in U.S. during war with Spain. SOURCE: Cashin, *Under Fire with the Tenth Cavalry*, 343.

ASKEW, Charles W.; Private; C/25th Inf. Dishonorable discharge, Brownsville. SOURCE: SO 266, AGO, 9 Nov 1906.

ASKEW, Preston; 1st Sgt; E/24th Inf. Awarded certificate of merit on 11 Jan 1907 for conspicuous gallantry as corporal against Pulahanes at Tabon-Tabon, Leyte, Philippines. SOURCE: GO 143, AGO, 1 Jul 1907.

In the Philippines, 1906. *See* **HARRIS**, William C., Sergeant, E/24th Infantry

At Ft Ontario, NY, 24th Infantry band played at presentation of certificate of merit to 1st Sgt. Preston Askew, E/24th Infantry. SOURCE: *ANJ* (23 May 1908), cited in Fletcher, *"The Negro Soldier and the United States Army."*

ATKINS, Jackson; Private; D/9th Cav. At Ft D. A. Russell, WY, in 1910; resident of East St. Louis, IL. SOURCE: *Illustrated Review: Ninth Cavalry.*

ATKINSON, Russell; Artificer; B/24th Inf. Sergeant, I/24th Infantry, at Ft Apache, AZ, authorized three-month furlough. SOURCE: *ANJ* 25 (28 Jul 1888), 1055.

Retires as artificer, B/24th Infantry, Apr 1901. SOURCE: *ANJ* 38 (27 Apr 1901): 843.

ATKISON, Willis; Private; G/9th Cav. Veteran of Philippine Insurrection; at Ft D. A. Russell, WY, in 1910; sharpshooter. SOURCE: *Illustrated Review: Ninth Cavalry*, with picture.

ATUS, George; Private; H/9th Cav. Relieved from extra duty as laborer, Quartermaster Department, Ft Robinson, NE. SOURCE: SO 90, 20 Aug 1896, Post Orders, Ft Robinson.

AUGUSTIN, Frank E.; Private; C/9th Cav. At Ft D. A. Russell, WY, in 1910; resident of 3224 Dryades St., New Orleans. SOURCE: *Illustrated Review: Ninth Cavalry*, with picture.

AUGUSTUS, George; I/10th Cav. Original member of 10th Cavalry; in troop when organized, Ft Riley, KS, 15 Aug 1867. SOURCE: McMiller, "Buffalo Soldiers," 76.

AUSTIN; Private; G/10th Cav. At Ft Apache, AZ, 1890, subscribed $.50 to testimonial to General Grierson. SOURCE: List of subscriptions, 23 Apr 1890, 10th Cavalry papers, MHI.

AUSTIN, Charles; Sergeant; C/25th Inf. Died Ft Sam Houston, TX, hospital, after critical abdominal operation; Spanish-American War veteran; wife and family in Virginia; "a brave man, a valiant soldier, and a kind husband." SOURCE: *ANJ* 37 (19 May 1900): 904.

AUSTIN, David; Corporal; C/25th Inf. Died of gunshot wound inflicted by Pvt. James Stein, at Ft George Wright, Spokane, WA. SOURCE: Cleveland *Gazette*, 24 Aug 1912.

AUSTIN, Edward S.; Private; I/25th Inf. In affidavit, from 267 W. Commerce St., San Antonio, TX, 25 Aug 1890, he claims he was at Ft Sill, Indian Territory, and saw William Branch in hospital after 1874 accident. SOURCE: VA File 2581520, William Branch.

AUSTIN, James H.; Private; B/10th Cav. Served in 10th Cavalry in Cuba, 1898. SOURCE: Cashin, *Under Fire with the Tenth Cavalry*, 338.

AUSTIN, John; Private; I/25th Inf. Died of variola in the Philippines. SOURCE: *ANJ* 37 (24 Mar 1900): 707.

AUSTIN, John T.; Private; E/9th Cav. Veteran of Philippine Insurrection; at Ft D. A. Russell, WY, in 1910; resident of St. Louis, MO. SOURCE: *Illustrated Review: Ninth Cavalry*, with picture.

AVERY, Fred; Private; A/9th Cav. At Ft D. A. Russell, WY, in 1910. SOURCE: *Illustrated Review: Ninth Cavalry.*

AVERY, Stephen; C/10th Cav. Original member of 10th Cavalry; in troop when organized, Ft Leavenworth, KS, 14 May 1867. SOURCE: McMiller, "Buffalo Soldiers," 70.

AXOM, Ned; Farrier; I/10th Cav. Served in 10th Cavalry, 1898; remained in U.S. during war with Spain. SOURCE: Cashin, *Under Fire with the Tenth Cavalry*, 349.

AYERS, Alexander; Private; E/9th Cav. At Ft D. A. Russell, WY, in 1910. SOURCE: *Illustrated Review: Ninth Cavalry*, with picture.

AYERS, Robert; Private; A/10th Cav. Served in 10th Cavalry, 1898; remained in U.S. during war with Spain. SOURCE: Cashin, *Under Fire with the Tenth Cavalry*, 337.

AYRES, John; Private; B/10th Cav. Served in 10th Cavalry in Cuba, 1898. SOURCE: Cashin, *Under Fire with the Tenth Cavalry*, 338.

B

BACKERS, William; Corporal; E/10th Cav. Killed in action, by Comanches, Ojo Caliente, TX, 28 Oct 1880; Backers Road, Ft Huachuca, AZ, named for him. SOURCE: Orville A. Cochran to H. B. Wharfield, 5 Apr 1965, 10th Cavalry papers, MHI.

BACKMAN, Harrison; H/10th Cav. In 1912 lived in National Military Home, Kansas. *See* **BARD**, Benjamin, Private, H/10th Cavalry

BACKUS, William; Corporal; K/10th Cav. Killed in action, Ojo Caliente, TX, 29 Oct 1880. SOURCE: Baker, Roster.

Killed in action, Ojo Caliente, 28 Oct 1880. SOURCE: Leckie, *The Buffalo Soldiers*, 230.

BACON, Henry; Private; H/24th Inf. Enlisted in Louisville, KY, by Chaplain Allensworth, 1898; later regimental clerk. SOURCE: Alexander, *Battles and Victories*, 358.

Transferred from F/24th Infantry to H/24th Infantry, 20 Sep 1898; on special duty as clerk in adjutant's office since 10 Oct 1898. SOURCE: Muster Roll, H/24 Inf, Sep–Oct 1898.

On special duty as clerk in adjutant's office. SOURCE: Muster Roll, H/24 Inf, Nov–Dec 1898.

Discharged, single, character excellent, 28 Jan 1899; reenlisted Ft Douglas, UT, 29 Jan 1899; continued on special duty as clerk in adjutant's office. SOURCE: Muster Roll, H/24 Inf, Jan–Feb 1899.

Died of heart disease in the Philippines, 3 Feb 1900. SOURCE: *ANJ* 37 (3 Mar 1900): 635.

BACON, Martin; Corporal; G/9th Cav. Private, E/9th Cavalry; wounded (foot) in action, Camalig, Philippines, 24 Nov 1900. SOURCE: *ANJ* 38 (5 Jan 1901): 455; *Illustrated Review: Ninth Cavalry*.

Corporal, G/9th Cavalry, at Ft D. A. Russell, WY, in 1910. SOURCE: *Illustrated Review: Ninth Cavalry*.

BADGETT, Green; Private; 25th Inf. Born Marysville, TN; 30 years old, Ht 5'4", brown eyes, black hair, brown complexion; enlisted Band/25th Infantry, at Iba, Zambales, Philippines, 23 Apr 1900; ninth year of continuous service, character very good. SOURCE: Descriptive & Assignment Cards of Recruits, 25 Inf.

In Band/25th Infantry, fined $3.00 for insubordination to noncommissioned officer, Ft Logan, CO, 3 Jun 1900. SOURCE: Record of Summary Court, 25 Inf.

In H/25th Infantry when he died in the Philippines, 17 Apr 1901. SOURCE: *ANJ* 38 (4 Mar 1901): 876.

BADIE, David; 1st Sgt; 9th Cav. Sergeant, B/9th Cavalry; praised for bravery against Victorio, Nov 1879, by Maj. Albert P. Morrow. SOURCE: Billington, "Black Cavalrymen," 68; Billington, *New Mexico's Buffalo Soldiers*, 93.

As sergeant, B/9th Cavalry, 16 Aug 1881, led detachment of fourteen against Indians in Nogal Canyon, NM. SOURCE: Hamilton, "History of the Ninth Cavalry," 57; Billington, *New Mexico's Buffalo Soldiers*, 105.

First sergeant, B/9th Cavalry, Ft Duchesne, UT, authorized four-month furlough. SOURCE: *ANJ* 25 (15 Oct 1887): 222.

Ranked number 53 among sharpshooters over 90 percent with 91.00 percent, 1887. SOURCE: GO 79, AGO, 31 Dec 1887.

First sergeant, B/9th Cavalry, Ft Robinson, NE, 1888. *See* **HOCKINS**, Benjamin, Corporal, G/9th Cavalry

First sergeant, I/9th Cavalry as of 25 Jun 1891; sergeant since 1 Oct 1873. SOURCE: Roster, 9 Cav, Jul 1893.

Died Ft Robinson, 24 Jan 1894. SOURCE: List of Interments, Ft Robinson.

Funeral service at post hall, Ft Robinson, 26 Jan 1894. SOURCE: Order 7, 25 Jan 1894, Post Orders, Ft Robinson.

BADIE, M. V.; 9th Cav. Herald, Crispus Attucks Lodge No. 3, Knights of Pythias, Ft Robinson, NE. SOURCE: Richmond *Planet*, 18 Dec 1897.

BADIE, William E.; Sergeant; C/9th Cav. Veteran of Philippine Insurrection; at Ft D. A. Russell, WY, in 1910; sharpshooter. SOURCE: *Illustrated Review: Ninth Cavalry* with picture.

BADY, George; L/10th Cav. Original member of 10th Cavalry; in troop when organized, Ft Riley, KS, 21 Sep 1867. SOURCE: McMiller, "Buffalo Soldiers," 78.

BADY, Robert; Sergeant; 10th Cav. Retired Ft Leavenworth, KS, with thirty years' service. SOURCE: *Cavalry Journal* 41 (Jul 1932): 61.

BAFFIT, E. J.; Private; G/24th Inf. Died Santiago, Cuba, early Sep 1898. SOURCE: *ANJ* 36 (10 Sep 1898): 43.

BAGBY; Private; B/10th Cav. At Ft Apache, AZ, 1890, subscribed $.50 to testimonial to General Grierson.

SOURCE: List of subscriptions, 23 Apr 1890, 10th Cavalry papers, MHI.

BAILEY; Cook; K/10th Cav. Discharged. SOURCE: SO 169, AGO, 19 Jul 1902.

BAILEY, A.; Private; H/24th Inf. At Ft Grant, AZ, 1890. *See* **BERRY**, Edward, Sergeant, H/24th Infantry

BAILEY, Albert; Private; E/9th Cav. 1st Lt. Edward Heyle charged with superintending tying Bailey up by hands, 9 Apr 1867, at Camp near San Antonio, TX.

BAILEY, Battier; Private; B/25th Inf. Dishonorable discharge, Brownsville. SOURCE: SO 266, AGO, 9 Nov 1906.

BAILEY, Charles; Private; E/10th Cav. Served in 10th Cavalry, 1898; remained in U.S. during war with Spain. SOURCE: Cashin, *Under Fire with the Tenth Cavalry*, 343.

BAILEY, George; Private; 10th Cav. Released to duty with C/10th Cavalry from treatment for acute gonorrhea, Ft Robinson, NE, 18 Sep 1903. SOURCE: Post Surgeon to CO, C/10, 18 Sep 1903, LS, Post Surgeon, Ft Robinson.

Released to duty with I/10th Cavalry from treatment for gonorrhea, Ft Robinson, 5 Dec 1903. SOURCE: Post Surgeon to CO, I/10, 5 Dec 1903, LS, Post Surgeon, Ft Robinson.

BAILEY, Gus; Corporal; B/9th Cav. At Ft Robinson, NE, 1884. *See* **HERBERT**, Thomas H., Private, K/9th Cavalry

At Ft Robinson, 1889. *See* **WATERS**, George, Private, B/9th Cavalry

BAILEY, Isaac; 1st Sgt; B/10th Cav. Born Parker Co., TX, 1860; enlisted 10 Jul 1883; commended for gallantry in Apache campaign, 28 Aug 1886 and 11 Jun 1887; at Ft Robinson, NE, 1902–06; participated in Ute campaign, 1906. SOURCE: Bailey Collection, NSHS.

Born in Texas; private, B/10th Cavalry, 10 Jul 1883; corporal, 1 Nov 1887; sergeant, 15 Feb 1888; first sergeant, 2 Dec 1892; at Ft Custer, MT, 1897. SOURCE: Baker, Roster.

"Military Record of Isaac Bailey," dateline Omaha, NE, with picture. SOURCE: Cleveland *Gazette*, 24 Apr 1915.

Marksman, 1884–85, 1889–90, 1893; sharpshooter, 1894, 1896, 1900, 1903–04; expert, 1905–07. SOURCE: Bailey Collection, NSHS.

Honorable mention for daring effort to capture Indian outlaw, San Carlos, AZ, 28 Aug 1886, and for gallant and meritorious service in pursuit of hostile Indians, Arizona, 1888. SOURCE: Baker, Roster.

At Ft Apache, AZ, 1890, sergeant, B/10th Cavalry, subscribed $.50 to testimonial to General Grierson. SOURCE: List of subscriptions, 23 Apr 1890, 10th Cavalry papers, MHI.

Recommended for Medal of Honor, for heroism in assault on San Juan Hill, Cuba, 1 Jul 1898. SOURCE: Cashin, *Under Fire with the Tenth Cavalry*, 186, 336.

Ranked number 120 among rifle experts in 1905 with 73.33 percent. SOURCE: GO 101, AGO, 31 May 1905.

Ranked number 23 in Northern Division·rifle competition, Ft Sheridan, IL, 1906. SOURCE: GO 198, AGO, 6 Dec 1906.

Ranked number 23 in Northern Division cavalry marksmanship, 1906. SOURCE: Glass, *History of the Tenth Cavalry*, 45.

Retired, 1 Mar 1909. SOURCE: SO 48, AGO, 1 Mar 1909.

Boxed Penski of 8th Cavalry, at Ft Robinson, 30 Mar 1909; knocked out in second round. SOURCE: Crawford *Tribune*, 2 Apr 1909.

Awarded Silver Star for 1898 heroism, San Juan Hill, in 1924; died Omaha, NE, 1946, where he lived from time of retirement. SOURCE: Bailey Collection, NSHS.

BAILEY, Isaac W.; Private; L/9th Cav. Born in Delaware; private, A/10th Cavalry, 18 Oct 1892; corporal, 6 Nov 1895; sergeant, 13 Apr 1896, stationed at Ft Custer, MT, 1897. SOURCE: Baker, Roster.

Contributed $.50 of $3.25 sent by men of A/10th Cavalry to Richmond *Planet* for defense fund of three black women accused of murder, Lunenburg Co., VA, according to letter, A/10th Cavalry, Ft Keogh, MT, 9 Sep 1895. SOURCE: Richmond *Planet*, 21 Sep 1895.

Served in 10th Cavalry in Cuba, 1898. SOURCE: Cashin, *Under Fire with the Tenth Cavalry*, 336.

Reduced to ranks from corporal at his own request. SOURCE: *ANJ* 37 (23 Sep 1899): 80.

Veteran of Spanish-American War and Philippine Insurrection; private, L/9th Cavalry, at Ft D. A. Russell, WY, in 1910; resident of Moore Station, PA. SOURCE: *Illustrated Review: Ninth Cavalry*.

BAILEY, James; Private; B/25th Inf. Dishonorable discharge, Brownsville. SOURCE: SO 266, AGO, 9 Nov 1906.

BAILEY, John; Private; A/9th Cav. Veteran of Philippine Insurrection; at Ft D. A. Russell, WY, in 1910. SOURCE: *Illustrated Review: Ninth Cavalry*, with picture.

BAILEY, John H.; Corporal; D/25th Inf. Retires as private from Ft Custer, MT, Mar 1894. SOURCE: *ANJ* 31 (17 Mar 1894): 496.

Retires as corporal from Ft Custer, after career that dates to 1863, with praise of commander, Capt. Owen J. Sweet. SOURCE: *ANJ* 31 (7 Apr 1894): 553.

Affidavit, Ft Custer, 31 Mar 1891: now age 47, served ten years with George D. Crockett. SOURCE: VA File XC 2624113, George D. Crockett.

BAILEY, Mack; Private; A/9th Cav. Veteran of Philippine Insurrection; at Ft D. A. Russell, WY, in 1910; marksman. SOURCE: *Illustrated Review: Ninth Cavalry,* with picture.

BAILEY, Matthew; Private; F/25th Inf. Died of enterocolitis in the Philippines, 3 Jan 1902. SOURCE: *ANJ* 39 (1 Mar 1902): 645.

BAILEY, Richard; Private; E/10th Cav. Served in 10th Cavalry, 1898; remained in U.S. during war with Spain. SOURCE: Cashin, *Under Fire with the Tenth Cavalry*, 343.

BAILEY, W. H.; Sergeant; D/10th Cav. Served in 10th Cavalry in Cuba, 1898. SOURCE: Cashin, *Under Fire with the Tenth Cavalry*, 341.

BAILEY, William; L Corp; E/25th Inf. Picture, at Ft Buford, ND, 1893. SOURCE: Nankivell, *History of the Twenty-fifth Infantry*, 50.

BAILEY, Willis; Private; C/10th Cav. Letter, Adjutant, 10th Cavalry, to Lt. M. Amick, 10th Cavalry, Recruiting Officer, 10 Apr 1867, forwards his enlistment papers and correspondence reporting his occupation, which was listed variously as laborer and boatman. SOURCE: LS, 10 Cav, 1866–67.

On extra duty at Ft Leavenworth, KS, but commander of his company, C/10th Cavalry, asks that he be immediately relieved because the company is ready to march west without delay. SOURCE: CO, 10 Cav, to Lt. S. W. Bonsall, Adj, Ft Leavenworth, 15 May 1867, LS, 10 Cav, 1866–67.

Private, F/24th Infantry; recruited to teach in Chaplain Allensworth's post school, Ft Bayard, NM, 1888; retained as teacher after promoted to corporal. SOURCE: Billington, *New Mexico's Buffalo Soldiers*, 162.

BAILY, William; C/10th Cav. Original member of 10th Cavalry; in troop when organized, Ft Leavenworth, KS, 14 May 1867. SOURCE: McMiller, "Buffalo Soldiers," 70.

BAINES, Arthur; Private; F/10th Cav. Original member of 10th Cavalry; in troop when organized, Ft Leavenworth, KS, 21 Jun 1867. SOURCE: McMiller, "Buffalo Soldiers," 73.

On extra duty as teamster. SOURCE: SO 58, HQ, Camp Supply, IT, 13 Aug 1869, Orders, Detachment of 10th Cav, 1868–69.

BAIRD, J. H.; Private; F/9th Cav. Discharged, expiration of service, Ft Robinson, NE, Aug 1885. SOURCE: Post Returns, Fort Robinson.

BAKER, B.; Private; H/24th Inf. At Ft Grant, AZ, 1890. *See* **BERRY**, Edward, Sergeant, H/24th Infantry

BAKER, Bird; Sergeant; K/24th Inf. Acquitted, Ft Grant, AZ, of permitting an Indian prisoner to escape; General Grierson, reviewing authority, disapproves and considers Baker an unfit noncommissioned officer. SOURCE: *ANJ* 26 (16 Mar 1889): 377–78.

BAKER, Charles; 1st Sgt; C/10th Cav. Killed in action, 4 May 1877, Lake Quemado, TX, by Comanches.

SOURCE: Leckie, *The Buffalo Soldiers*, 156. *See* **BUTLER**, Charles, First Sergeant, G/10th Cavalry

BAKER, Charles H.; Private; F/24th Inf. Wounded in action, Cuba, 1898. SOURCE: Muller, *The Twenty Fourth Infantry*, 18.

BAKER, Charles W.; Corporal; 10th Cav. Born in South Carolina; private and corporal, K/10th Cavalry, 11 Oct 1889–10 Oct 1894; private, A/10th Cavalry, 13 Dec 1894; corporal, 8 Sep 1896; at Ft Custer, MT, 1897. SOURCE: Baker, Roster.

At Ft Apache, AZ, 1890, private, K/10th Cavalry, subscribed $.50 to testimonial to General Grierson. SOURCE: List of subscriptions, 23 Apr 1890, 10th Cavalry papers, MHI.

BAKER, Douglas; Private; I/9th Cav. At Ft D. A. Russell, WY, in 1910; resident of Knoxville, TN. SOURCE: *Illustrated Review: Ninth Cavalry*, with picture.

BAKER, Edward L., Jr.; QM Sgt; U.S. Army. Born on Platte River, Laramie Co., WY, 28 Dec 1865; enlisted at Cincinnati, OH, in D/9th Cavalry, 27 Jul 1882; trumpeter, 2 Jul 1883; discharged, 26 Jul 1887; enlisted B/10th Cavalry, 25 Aug 1887; regimental clerk, 4 May 1888; chief trumpeter, 10th Cavalry, 9 Feb 1890; quartermaster sergeant, 10th Cavalry, 28 Jan 1891; enlisted 25 Aug 1892; promoted to sergeant major, 10th Cavalry, 25 Aug 1892; attended cavalry school, Saumar, France, Nov 1896–May 1897; enlisted 25 Aug 1897; appointed first lieutenant, 10th U.S. Volunteer Infantry, 2 August 1898; mustered out and reverted to sergeant major, 10th Cavalry, 8 Mar 1899; appointed captain, 49th Infantry, 9 Sep 1899; mustered out, 30 Jun 1901; discharged from 10th Cavalry, 5 Sep 1901; appointed second lieutenant, Philippine Scouts, 7 Feb 1902; promoted to first lieutenant, 10 Sep 1906; promoted to captain, 12 Sep 1908; resigned, 31 Oct 1909; enlisted, Ft McDowell, CA, post quartermaster sergeant, 7 Nov 1909; retired 12 Jan 1910, in accordance with Special Order 41, War Department, 6 Jan 1910. SOURCE: VA File XC 2715800, Edward L. Baker.

"He served in Arizona, New Mexico, Texas, Colorado, Kansas, Indian Territory, Nebraska, Wyoming, Montana. He took part in numerous scouts, arduous marches, and expeditions against isolated bands of Indians and other marauders from 1882 to 1898 on our western frontier." SOURCE: Widow's declaration for pension, 1916, VA File XC 2715800, Edward L. Baker.

As chief trumpeter, 10th Cavalry, at Ft Apache, AZ, 1890, subscribed $.50 to testimonial to General Grierson. SOURCE: List of subscriptions, 23 Apr 1890, 10th Cavalry papers, MHI.

Married Mary Elizabeth Hawley, born Mary E. Prince and widow of Heber Hawley, Santa Fe, NM, 31 Jul 1887; no previous marriages. SOURCE: VA File XC 2715800, Edward L. Baker.

Medical history: typhoid, 1875; kicked by horse, 5 Oct 1882; "constipation in line of duty, cured," 8–9 Mar 1884;

dysentery, 1890; gunshot wound, 1898; dysentery, 30 Aug–15 Sep 1898; bronchitis, 1909; "alcoholism acute, not in line of duty," 18–19 Jun 1909. SOURCE: VA File XC 2715800, Edward L. Baker.

Stationed at Ft Assiniboine, MT, 1897, with wife and five children: Edward Lee Baker, Eugenia Sheridan Baker, Myrtle Mary Baker, Gwenderlyn James Baker, Dexter Murat Baker; father French; mother American, colored. SOURCE: AGO, Carded Records, Voluntary Organizations, Spanish-American War.

Served in 10th Cavalry in Cuba, 1898. SOURCE: Cashin, *Under Fire with the Tenth Cavalry*, 352.

Participated in battles at Las Guasimas and San Juan Hill, Cuba; wounded slightly by shrapnel, left side and arm, at San Juan. SOURCE: Regt Returns, 10 Cav, Jun–Jul 1898.

Awarded Medal of Honor for heroism, San Juan Hill, 1898. SOURCE: Logan and Winston, *Dictionary of American Negro Biography*, 21.

Diary of Cuban campaign of 1898. SOURCE: Steward, *The Colored Regulars*, 255–79.

First lieutenant, M/10th U.S. Volunteer Infantry, 1898; captain, L/49th Infantry, 1899; second lieutenant to captain, Philippine Scouts, 1902–09.

Organized, equipped, commanded L/49th Infantry "and conducted same to the Philippines, and returned to U.S. with every man in excellent health, and every man in the company having deposits with the paymaster." SOURCE: Widow's declaration for pension, 1916, VA File XC 2715800, Edward L. Baker.

Died 1914.

Biographical sketch. SOURCE: Logan and Winston, *Dictionary of American Negro Biography*, 21.

BAKER, George; Private; 10th Cav. Arrived Ft Leavenworth, KS, from Jefferson Barracks, MO. SOURCE: Adj, Ft Leavenworth, to HQ, Jefferson Bks, 9 Oct 1866.

BAKER, Hiram, Jr.; Private; I/24th Inf. Enlisted Dayton, OH, 27 Mar 1899; joined company 8 Apr 1899. SOURCE: Muster Roll, I/24 Inf, Mar–Apr 1899.

On detached service, Three Rivers, CA, 3 May–21 Jun 1899; on detached service, Presidio of San Francisco, CA, since 22 Jun 1899. SOURCE: Muster Roll, I/24 Inf, May–Jun 1899.

Rejoined company, 26 Jul 1899. SOURCE: Muster Roll, I/24 Inf, Jul–Aug 1899.

On detached service at Cabanatuan, Philippines. SOURCE: Muster Roll, I/24 Inf, Nov–Dec 1899.

BAKER, Ishmael; K/25th Inf. Admitted to Soldiers Home, age 49, 28 Oct 1889; twenty-three years and nine months' service. SOURCE: SecWar, *AR 1890*, 1040.

BAKER, J.; Private; L/9th Cav. On detached service in the field, New Mexico, 21 Jan–4 Feb 1881. SOURCE: Regt Returns, 9 Cav, Feb 1881.

BAKER, Jesse; Sergeant; H/10th Cav. Born in Tennessee; enlisted in H/10th Cavalry, 23 Sep 1892; promoted to corporal, 1 Jul 1896; at Ft Assiniboine, MT, 1897. SOURCE: Baker, Roster.

Distinguished marksman, as corporal, H/9th Cavalry, Department of Colorado, bronze medal, 1903; Northern Division bronze medal, 1904; ranked number ten, Northern Division cavalry competition, Ft Riley, KS, bronze medal, 1905. SOURCE: GO 173, AGO, 20 Oct 1905.

Ranked number twelve, competition of Northern Division Cavalry Team, Ft Riley, 1904. SOURCE: GO 167, AGO, 28 Oct 1904.

Twelfth best marksman, Northern Division, Cavalry, 1904; tenth best marksman, Northern Division, Cavalry, 1905. SOURCE: Glass, *History of the Tenth Cavalry*, 44–45.

Ranked number 284 among rifle experts, 1905, with 70.33 percent. SOURCE: GO 101, AGO, 31 May 1906.

BAKER, John; D/10th Cav. Original member of 10th Cavalry; in troop when organized, Ft Leavenworth, KS, 1 Jun 1867. SOURCE: McMiller, "Buffalo Soldiers," 71.

BAKER, Lewis J.; Cook; C/25th Inf. Dishonorable discharge, Brownsville. SOURCE: SO 266, AGO, 9 Nov 1906.

One of fourteen cleared of involvement in Brownsville raid, 1910, and authorized to reenlist. SOURCE: Weaver, *The Brownsville Raid*, 248.

BAKER, Robert L.; Private; A/49th Inf. Died of malaria in the Philippines, 22 Oct 1900. SOURCE: *ANJ* 38 (3 Nov 1900): 235.

BAKER, W. A.; Corporal; 3rd Ala Inf. Letter from Camp Shipp, AL, n.d. SOURCE: Gatewood, "*Smoked Yankees*," 177.

BAKER, William; A/10th Cav. Original member of 10th Cavalry; in troop when organized, Ft Leavenworth, KS, 18 Feb 1867. SOURCE: McMiller, "Buffalo Soldiers," 68.

BAKER, William; Recruit; B/10th Cav. Enlisted at Memphis, TN, spring 1867. SOURCE: LS, 10 Cav, 1866–67.

Original member of 10th Cavalry; in troop when organized, Ft Leavenworth, KS, 1 Apr 1867. SOURCE: McMiller, "Buffalo Soldiers," 698.

BAKER, William; Sergeant; H/9th Cav. At Ft Cummings, NM, 1876. SOURCE: Billington, *New Mexico's Buffalo Soldiers*, 113.

On detached service from Ft Bliss, TX, 9 Jan–10 Feb 1881. SOURCE: Regt Returns, 9 Cav, Feb 1881.

BALDOCK, Thomas; Corporal; F/10th Cav. Original member of 10th Cavalry; in troop when organized, Ft Leavenworth, KS, 21 Jun 1867. SOURCE: McMiller, "Buffalo Soldiers," 73.

Corporal; with three privates to escort Captain Armes tomorrow to Ft Hays, KS, rest one day, and return. SOURCE:

SO 29, Det 10 Cav, Ft Dodge, KS, 19 May 1869, Orders, Det 10 Cav, 1868–69.

BALDRIDGE, John; I/10th Cav. Original member of 10th Cavalry; in troop when organized, Ft Riley, KS, 15 Aug 1867. SOURCE: McMiller, "Buffalo Soldiers," 76.

BALDWELL, Nathaniel; Corporal; A/10th Cav. Discharged. SOURCE: SO 38, AGO, 14 Feb 1903.

BALDWIN; Private; 10th Cav. First casualty at San Juan Hill, Cuba, "a young volunteer." SOURCE: Johnson, *History of Negro Soldiers*, 64.

BALDWIN, Andrew; A/10th Cav. Original member of 10th Cavalry; in troop when organized, Ft Leavenworth, KS, 18 Feb 1867. SOURCE: McMiller, "Buffalo Soldiers," 68.

BALDWIN, Charles; K/49th Inf. Released from five-year sentence at Alcatraz for disobedience of orders, based on Supreme Court's Deming decision. SOURCE: San Francisco *Chronicle*, 4 Jun 1902.

Convicted of larceny and striking victim on head with revolver, Philippines, Mar 1900; sentenced to five years. Released from Alcatraz in accordance with Supreme Court's Deming decision, 19 Mar 1902. SOURCE: *ANJ* 39 (7 Jun 1902): 1005.

BALDWIN, James R.; Private; D/9th Cav. On special duty, as assistant, post canteen, Fort Robinson, NE. SOURCE: Order 61, 31 Mar 1891, Post Orders, Ft Robinson.

Relieved from special duty, post canteen, Ft Robinson. SOURCE: Order 98, 12 May 1891, Post Orders, Ft Robinson.

BALDWIN, Jessie; Private; C/9th Cav. At Ft McKinney, WY, granted three-day pass to Sheridan, WY, Aug 1894.

BALDWIN, Lewis; Corporal; A/25th Inf. Retires from Ft Custer, MT. SOURCE: *ANJ* 28 (1 Aug 1891): 833.

BALL, G.; Corporal; D/9th Cav. With detachment under 1st Lt. John Guilfoyle scouting in Utah Territory, Sep–Oct 1883.

BALL, John F.; Private; F/25th Inf. At Ft Stockton, TX, 1878, best marksman in his company and second best in regiment. SOURCE: Scrapbook, 25 Inf, I, 145.

BALLANTYNE, H. B.; 24th Inf. Fined for drunkenness by Salt Lake City, UT, police court, 1896. SOURCE: Clark, "A History of the Twenty-fourth," 84.

BALLARD, James H.; Corporal; D/25th Inf. Dishonorable discharge, Brownsville. SOURCE: SO 266, AGO, 9 Nov 1906.

BALLARD, Wilson C.; 1st Lt; 48th Inf. Born Concordia Parish, LA, to Isaiah Ballard and Patsy Beverly, both of Louisiana, 17 Jun 1877; enlisted in B/9th Ohio Infantry, 14 May 1898, promoted to corporal, sergeant, and second lieutenant, mustered out 28 Jan 1899; appointed first lieutenant, 48th Infantry, 9 Sep 1899; served to 30 Jun 1901; still a student when mustered out; became dentist, with private practice in Louisville, KY, that paid around $100 per month and $50 per month from part-time work for City Health Department; lived in Columbus and Dayton, OH, and Louisville; first wife Pearl Ballard born Zanesville, OH, to William H. Penn of Virginia and Mary E. Hicks of Knox Co., OH; married 10 Feb 1912, Louisville, and lived at 2123 West Chestnut, Louisville; first wife born 19 Aug 1883; died 11 Aug 1929; second wife Mary D. Taylor, of Zanesville, married Jan 1940; lived at 601 Walnut, Louisville, in 1943, then 2417 West Walnut. Pension: $12 per month in 1920; $20 per month in 1928; $25 per month in 1935; $50 per month in 1938; $60 per month in 1941; died in Louisville and buried in Zachary Taylor National Cemetery; widow moved to 64 Miami Ave., Columbus. SOURCE: VA File C 2366152, Wilson C. Ballard.

Mentioned as second lieutenant, K/48th Infantry. SOURCE: Beasley, *Negro Trailblazers*, 284.

One of nineteen officers of 48th Infantry recommended for regular Army commissions. SOURCE: CG, Div PI, Manila, 8 Feb 1901, to AGO, AGO File 355163.

Joined Liberian Frontier Police as major, 1913, and should get credit, instead of Charles Young, for ending Kroo War; isolated with 82 men against 2,000 without communication with Young or Monrovia; after service with 48th Infantry, was commandant of cadets, Wilberforce University, OH; all according to unsigned letter, Nayaaha Frontier Stations, Harper, Cape Palmas, Liberia, 29 Apr 1913. SOURCE: Cleveland *Gazette*, 25 Dec 1915.

Was major, Liberian Defense Force, for five years. SOURCE: *Crisis* 13 (Apr 1917).

"Aided in the pacification of the Liberians." SOURCE: Fletcher, *The Black Soldier*, 172, 178.

BALLENGER, George, Trumpeter; M/9th Cav. Veteran of Philippine Insurrection; expert rifleman at Ft D. A. Russell, WY, in 1910. SOURCE: *Illustrated Review: Ninth Cavalry*.

BALLEW, John; Private; Band/9th Cav. Veteran of Philippine Insurrection; at Ft D. A. Russell, WY, in 1910; resident of Richmond, KY. SOURCE: *Illustrated Review: Ninth Cavalry*, with picture.

BALMAN, John; C/10th Cav. Original member of 10th Cavalry; in troop when organized, Ft Leavenworth, KS, 14 May 1867. SOURCE: McMiller, "Buffalo Soldiers," 70.

BALSER, Linsey; Private; C/24th Inf. Deserted at San Francisco, CA, 25 Jul 1902. SOURCE: Regt Returns, 24 Inf, Aug 1902.

BALTIMORE, Charles W.; Corporal; I/24th Inf. "Model soldier," beaten and jailed by Houston police when he tried to intervene in jailing of Pvt. Alonzo Edwards; rumored to have been killed; one of Sergeant Henry's "most dedicated disciples," Houston riot; sentenced to death; wrote farewell letter to his family, 11 Dec 1917, just before his execution. SOURCE: Haynes, *A Night of Violence*, 96–99, 101–3, 128, 271.

Hanged, Ft Sam Houston, TX, 13 Dec 1917, for part in Houston riot. SOURCE: Cleveland *Gazette*, 15 Dec 1917.

BALTINGER, Henry; Private; D/48th Inf. Died of variola in the Philippines, 27 Jun 1900. SOURCE: *ANJ* 37 (14 Jul 1900): 1083.

BANDY, Elmer; Private; M/24th Inf. Served in Houston, age 23, four-year veteran, 1917; testified at court martial under grant of immunity. SOURCE: Haynes, *A Night of Violence*, 137.

BANKS; Private; B/10th Cav. At Ft Apache, AZ, 1890, subscribed $.50 to testimonial to General Grierson. SOURCE: List of subscriptions, 23 Apr 1890, 10th Cavalry papers, MHI.

BANKS; Private; E/10th Cav. At Ft Apache, AZ, 1890, private, E/10th Cavalry, subscribed $.50 to testimonial to General Grierson. SOURCE: List of subscriptions, 23 Apr 1890, 10th Cavalry papers, MHI.

BANKS; Private; K/24th Inf. At Cabanatuan, Philippines, 1901. *See* **NICKLE**, Elijah, Private, K/24th Infantry

BANKS, Charles; Private; 24th Inf. Served in Houston, 1917. SOURCE: Haynes, *A Night of Violence*, 122.

BANKS, Frank; Sergeant; A/24th Inf. Enlisted 1884. *See* **JONES**, Stephen, Recruit, 25th Infantry

At Ft Huachuca, AZ, 1896, contributed $2 to defense fund of three black women accused of murder, Lunenburg Co., VA. *See* **GREEN**, John R., Sergeant, A/24th Infantry

Killed in action, Cuba, 1898. SOURCE: Scipio, *Last of the Black Regulars*, 29.

Died in Cuba, 3 Jul 1898. SOURCE: *ANJ* 36 (11 Feb 1899): 567.

When died in Cuba, was sergeant, 24th Infantry, and recently married in Salt Lake City. SOURCE: Clark, "A History of the Twenty-fourth," 100.

BANKS, Gabriel H.; 24th Inf. Served 1867–79, first in C/41st Infantry, then 24th Infantry; member of Camp 11, National Indian War Veterans, St. Joseph, MO. SOURCE: *Winners of the West* 20 (Feb 1937): 7.

BANKS, Isaac; I/10th Cav. Original member of 10th Cavalry; in troop when organized, Ft Riley, KS, 15 Aug 1867. SOURCE: McMiller, "Buffalo Soldiers," 76.

BANKS, Munroe H.; Private; A/10th Cav. Mentioned Jan 1873. SOURCE: LS, 10 Cav, 1873–77.

BANKS, Plum; Sergeant; B/9th Cav. Veteran of Indian wars, Spanish-American War, and Philippine Insurrection; at Ft D. A. Russell, WY, in 1910; marksman. SOURCE: *Illustrated Review: Ninth Cavalry,* with picture.

BANKS, Robert; H/10th Cav. Original member of 10th Cavalry; in troop when organized, Ft Leavenworth, KS, 21 Jul 1867. SOURCE: McMiller, "Buffalo Soldiers," 75.

BANKS, Robert; Private; F/49th Inf. Died in the Philippines, 6 Oct 1900. SOURCE: *ANJ* 38 (27 Oct 1900): 211.

BANKS, Walter; Musician; C/25th Inf. Dishonorable discharge, Brownsville. SOURCE: SO 266, AGO, 9 Nov 1906.

BANKS, William; Private; B/49th Inf. Died of dysentery in the Philippines, 27 Feb 1900. SOURCE: *ANJ* 37 (10 Mar 1900): 659.

BARBER, Jones; Private; 9th Cav. Deserted 1867. *See* **MYERS**, Thomas C., Sergeant, D/25th Infantry

BARBER, William; Private; K/10th Cav. Buried at Ft Sill, Indian Territory. SOURCE: CO, 10 Cav, to AG, USA, 30 Jun 1873, ES, 10 Cav, 1873–81.

BARBOUR, Charles H.; Sergeant; A/25th Inf. Ranked number 420 among rifle experts with 69.00 percent in 1905. SOURCE: GO 101, AGO, 31 May 1906.

Picture. SOURCE: Curtis, *The Black Soldiers*, opposite 47.

BARCLAY, Henry; Private; D/25th Inf. Dishonorable discharge, Brownsville. SOURCE: SO 266, AGO, 9 Nov 1906.

BARD, Benjamin; Private; H/10th Cav. Born around 1853; Ht 5'5", black complexion; occupation farmer; parents William and Sallie Ann Bard; worked as laborer for five years at Philadelphia brickyards, then enlisted 1 Dec 1873; fought in 1874–75 war against Kiowas, Comanches, and Cheyennes; discharged with 50 percent disability 4 Feb 1876, Ft Davis, TX, due to frostbite received 16 Nov 1874 while scouting against hostile Indians in Indian Territory; returned to Philadelphia until he went to Winston, VA, in 1894. Pension $6 per month in 1912; $20 per month in 1917; $18 per month in 1920; $40 per month in 1927; $50 a month on 4 May 1927; died at home, Crestmont, Montgomery Co., PA, of nephritis, age about 75, 19 Aug 1927. SOURCE: VA File XC 2625176, Benjamin Bard.

Married second wife Nellie Wilson Bard in Philadelphia, 26 Mar 1890; son Benjamin Edward Bard born Philadelphia, 2

Aug 1892; son Clifton Wilson Bard born Winston, 11 Mar 1894; daughter Josephine Bard born Winston, 11 Oct 1897, and died 12 May 1908; son Theophilus Wesley Bard born Winston, 18 Dec 1899. SOURCE: VA File XC 2625176, Benjamin Bard.

Married third wife Edmonia Bard, born Edmonia Roy as slave, Caroline Co., VA, 15 Mar 1863; her pension claim was rejected because she was not married before 4 Mar 1917; married 18 Aug 1918 as Edmonia Nalls, widow of John Nalls; she moved from Culpepper, VA, to 30 Edgar Court, Newport, RI, 7 Dec 1933. SOURCE: VA File XC 2625176, Benjamin Bard.

Department of the Interior, Bureau of Pensions, Record Division, Names and Addresses of Comrades of H/10th Cavalry, 11 Sep 1912:

Harrison Backman, National Military Home, KS
Robert Daniell, 914 North 8th St., Richmond, VA
Robert Miller, 1430 South 13th St., Terre Haute, IN
Andrew Howard, Purcell, McClain Co., OK
Charles Woods (alias George Brown), Ardmore, Carter Co., OK
SOURCE: VA File XC 2625176, Benjamin Bard.

Foot frostbitten after Christmas 1874 on sixty-day scout from Ft Davis, TX, with H/10th Cavalry; Captain Carpenter put him in wagon train, where he rode until he arrived at Ft Davis; then on guard duty on "a cold sleety night with rain freezing as fast as it fell," and feet froze; spent three to four months in post hospital. SOURCE: Affidavit, Bard, Winston, VA, farmer, 14 May 1913, VA File XC 2625176, Benjamin Bard.

Aaron Archer, H/10th Cavalry, 2 Jan 1873–26 Mar 1876 when discharged with disability; enlisted and returned to Philadelphia after discharge; knew Bard casually after service. His feet frostbitten, Camp Sweetwater, Indian Territory, winter 1874–75, and in hospital; Archer had minor frostbite at same time. SOURCE: Affidavit, Aaron Archer, 927 Locust St., Philadelphia, laborer, age 58, 29 Apr 1913, VA File XC 2625176, Benjamin Bard.

George Thompson, E/9th Cavalry, Sep 1872–late 1874 when discharged during reduction of Army; met Bard in St. Louis, MO, when he came as recruit and later in Philadelphia; when Thompson saw him, he was lame and limped but Thompson did not know why. SOURCE: Affidavit, George Thompson, 1112 Locust St., Philadelphia, junk dealer, age 58, 1913, VA File XC 2625176, Benjamin Bard.

Special Examiner to Commissioner of Pensions, 14 May 1913: George Thompson, alleged comrade, served E/9th Cavalry and repudiates former affidavit, admits no knowledge of disability; Aaron Archer did serve with Bard and recalls freezing feet but repudiates testimony supporting claim to rheumatism in service; Bard first married Annie Bard, 1880; deserted her for Nellie Wilson; Annie says that Bard worked as car sweeper for Pennsylvania Railroad and Baltimore & Ohio Railroad before leaving her. SOURCE: VA File XC 2625176, Benjamin Bard.

Recent subscriber; three years in the Army. SOURCE: *Winners of the West* 4 (Mar 1927): 8.

BARDISON, George; Private; E/10th Cav. Served in 10th Cavalry, 1898; remained in U.S. during war with Spain. SOURCE: Cashin, *Under Fire with the Tenth Cavalry*, 343.

BARKLEY, William H.; Sergeant; E/24th Inf. In K/24th Infantry, San Carlos, AZ, 1890. *See* **HARDEE**, James A., Private, K/24th Infantry

Directed to join his company, E/24th Infantry, at San Carlos. SOURCE: *ANJ* 28 (7 Feb 1891): 401.

BARKS, William; Private; K/10th Cav. Private, C/10th Cavalry; served in 10th Cavalry, 1898; remained in U.S. during war with Spain. SOURCE: Cashin, *Under Fire with the Tenth Cavalry*, 340.

Transferred from M/25th Infantry to K/10th Cavalry, Ft Robinson, NE. SOURCE: SO 195, AGO, 19 Aug 1904.

BARNER, George; Corporal; H/9th Cav. Corporal, F/24th Infantry; ranked number nine, Northern Infantry Team Competition, Ft Sheridan, IL, 1904. SOURCE: GO 167, AGO, 28 Oct 1904.

Ranked number 25 among expert riflemen, 1904. SOURCE: GO 79, AGO, 1 Jun 1905.

Corporal, H/9th Cavalry, veteran of Philippine Insurrection; at Ft D. A. Russell, WY, in 1910; sharpshooter; resident of Andersonville, KY. SOURCE: *Illustrated Review: Ninth Cavalry*, with picture.

BARNER, Moses; Private; H/9th Cav. Private, E/25th Infantry; ranked number 76 among expert riflemen, 1905, with 72.33 percent. SOURCE: GO 79, AGO, 1 Jun 1905.

At Ft D. A. Russell, WY, in 1910; resident of Fayetteville, TN. SOURCE: *Illustrated Review: Ninth Cavalry*, with picture.

BARNES, Andrew; I/10th Cav. Original member of 10th Cavalry; in troop when organized, Ft Riley, KS, 15 Aug 1867. SOURCE: McMiller, "Buffalo Soldiers," 76.

BARNES, C. H.; Private; H/10th Cav. In hands of civil authorities, Sheridan, WY, 27 Jun–2 Jul 1904. SOURCE: Regt Returns, 10 Cav.

BARNES, Edward; C/25th Inf. Sends best regards to friends. SOURCE: Richmond *Planet*, 8 Dec 1900.

BARNES, Francis I.; Private; D/25th Inf. Retires from Ft Custer, MT, Jun 1896. SOURCE: *ANJ* 33 (20 Jun 1896): 765.

BARNES, Henry S.; I/10th Cav. Original member of 10th Cavalry; in troop when organized, Ft Riley, KS, 15 Aug 1867. SOURCE: McMiller, "Buffalo Soldiers," 76.

BARNES, James; Private; I/10th Cav. Served in 10th Cavalry, 1898; remained in U.S. during war with Spain. SOURCE: Cashin, *Under Fire with the Tenth Cavalry*, 348.

BARNES, James H.; L/10th Cav. Original member of 10th Cavalry; in troop when organized, Ft Riley, KS, 21 Sep 1867. SOURCE: McMiller, "Buffalo Soldiers," 78.

BARNES, James S.; Private; H/10th Cav. Served in 10th Cavalry, 1898; remained in U.S. during war with Spain. SOURCE: Cashin, *Under Fire with the Tenth Cavalry*, 346.

BARNES, Martin; Private; L/10th Cav. Served in 10th Cavalry, 1898; remained in U.S. during war with Spain. SOURCE: Cashin, *Under Fire with the Tenth Cavalry*, 350.

BARNES, Napoleon; Private; B/9th Cav. At Ft D. A. Russell, WY, in 1910. SOURCE: *Illustrated Review: Ninth Cavalry,* with picture.

BARNES, Samuel; Sergeant; A/25th Inf. Retires from Ft Custer, MT, Nov 1895. SOURCE: *ANJ* 33 (2 Nov 1895): 139.

BARNES, Samuel G.; Sergeant; M/25th Inf. Private, on special duty with headquarters, 2nd Brigade, Camp Sanger, KY. SOURCE: SO 2, 2nd Brigade, 18 Oct 1903, Misc Records, 25 Inf.

Promoted from corporal to sergeant. SOURCE: *ANR* 38 (29 Jul 1905): 21.

BARNES, Walter; Sergeant; I/24th Inf. Enlisted Ft Douglas, UT, 3 Feb 1897, with seven years' continuous service. SOURCE: Muster Roll, I/24 Inf, Jan–Feb 1899.

Reduced to private and fined one month's pay by a general court martial, 23 Mar 1899. SOURCE: Muster Roll, I/24 Inf, Mar–Apr 1899.

Appointed corporal, 9 Sep 1899. SOURCE: Muster Roll, I/24 Inf, Sep–Oct 1899.

BARNES, William; Private; F/10th Cav. Born Carter Co., KY, 1856; enlisted 24th Infantry, 1872; participated in Victorio campaign; transferred to 10th Cavalry, 1883; participated in Geronimo campaign, 1885; promoted to sergeant, 1892; served in Cuba, 1899–1900; promoted to first sergeant, 26 Jun 1899; assigned to Samar, Philippines, Apr 1901. SOURCE: *Colored American Magazine* 6 (Feb 1903): 295–97.

Born in Kentucky; private, C/24th Infantry, 5 Mar 1878–4 Mar 1883; private, A/10th Cavalry, 4 Apr 1883–3 Apr 1888; transferred to B/10th Cavalry, 19 Apr 1888; corporal, 1 Aug 1888; transferred to F/10th Cavalry, 18 Apr 1892; promoted to sergeant, 21 May 1892. SOURCE: Baker, Roster.

At Ft Apache, AZ, 1890, corporal, B/10th Cavalry, subscribed $.50 to testimonial to General Grierson. SOURCE: List of subscriptions, 23 Apr 1890, 10th Cavalry papers, MHI.

Served in 10th Cavalry in Cuba, 1898. SOURCE: Cashin, *Under Fire with the Tenth Cavalry*, 343.

Sergeant, F/10th Cavalry, reduced to ranks. SOURCE: SO 91, 10 Cav, 9 Dec 1909, Ft Ethan Allen.

BARNETT, A. K.; 1st Lt; 23rd Kans Inf. Mentioned. SOURCE: Beasley, *Negro Trailblazers*, 285.

BARNETT, Charles; Band/25th Inf. Born Winchester, VA; Ht 5'7", black hair, eyes and complexion; enlisted at age 28, 22 Apr 1898, Lytle, GA; in eleventh year of continuous service; character excellent. SOURCE: Descriptive & Assignment Cards of Recruits, 25 Inf.

BARNETT, Grant; B/9th Cav. Applicant for membership, Camp 11, National Indian War Veterans, St. Joseph, MO. SOURCE: *Winners of the West* 11 (Jun 1928): 3.

BARNETT, John; Private; 25th Inf. Born Old Town, SC; Ht 5'7", black hair and eyes, dark complexion; occupation laborer, enlisted at age 25, Charleston, SC, 16 Jul 1881. SOURCE: Descriptive & Assignment Rolls of Recruits, 25 Inf.

BARNETT, Peter W.; L/24th Inf. Born Livingston Co., KY; educated in Kentucky and Indiana; taught in Kentucky; moved to Indianapolis, 1891, attended high school and two years at State Normal, Terre Haute; worked as general and soliciting agent, Union Publishing Co., Indianapolis, and reporter for Indianapolis *Freeman*; with J. T. V. Hill published Colored Business Directory of Indianapolis, 1898; studied law with Hill when enlisted; regular correspondent of Indianapolis *Recorder* while at Chickamauga as corporal, A/1st Indiana; will continue as such if he goes to West Indies. With picture. From Indianapolis *Recorder*, 14 Jan 1899. SOURCE: Gatewood, "Indiana Negroes," 135.

Letter to editor from Ft Wrangel, AK, 4 Dec 1899, wishes Merry Christmas and Happy New Year; Indiana native and ex-employee of *Freeman*. SOURCE: Indianapolis *Freeman*, 30 Dec 1899.

BARNS, Benjamin R.; Corporal; B/9th Cav. Promoted from saddler, Ft Robinson, NE, Dec 1894. SOURCE: *ANJ* 32 (15 Dec 1894): 262.

BARNSWELL, John; F/10th Cav. Original member of 10th Cavalry; in troop when organized, Ft Leavenworth, KS, 21 Jun 1867. SOURCE: McMiller, "Buffalo Soldiers," 73.

BARR, Edward; Saddler; E/10th Cav. At Ft Apache, AZ, 1890, subscribed $.50 to testimonial to General Grierson. SOURCE: List of subscriptions, 23 Apr 1890, 10th Cavalry papers, MHI.

Served in 10th Cavalry in Cuba, 1898. SOURCE: Cashin, *Under Fire with the Tenth Cavalry*, 342.

BARROW, Stephen B.; Sergeant; 10th Cav. Stationed at Ft Robinson, NE, 1904–05.

Author of "Christmas in the United States Army," 1905, *Colored American Magazine*. SOURCE: *Colored American Magazine* 8 (Feb 1905): 95–97.

"Some knowledge of table arrangement [acquired] in civil life." SOURCE: Barrow, "Christmas in the United States Army," 96.

Sergeant, B/10th Cavalry, commissioned second lieutenant, Camp Des Moines, IA, 15 Oct 1917. SOURCE: Glass, *History of the Tenth Cavalry*, appendix M; Sweeney, *History of the American Negro*, 120.

Serving as warrant officer, at Camp Mara, TX. SOURCE: Work, *The Negro Yearbook, 1925-1926*, 254.

Retired as warrant officer, resides at 1668 Harvard Ave., Columbus, OH. SOURCE: Work, *The Negro Yearbook, 1931-1932*, 334.

BARRY, Edgar S.; H/25th Inf. Letter, 1900, in Manila *Times*. SOURCE: Manila *Times*, 22 Jul 1900.

BARTON; I/9th Cav. Wife Suzie Barton, laundress, not of good character, has been ordered off post at Ft Robinson, NE, previously. SOURCE: CO, Ft Robinson, to CO, I/9 Cav, 23 Jul 1890, LS, Ft Robinson.

Wife Suzie Barton, servant to wife of 1st Lt. E. Hubert, 8th Infantry, Ft Robinson, to be dismissed when Mrs. Hubert regains her health. SOURCE: CO, Ft Robinson, to 1st Lt. E. Hubert, 8 Inf, 25 Jul 1890, LS, Ft Robinson.

BARTON, Hardy; B/10th Cav. Original member of 10th Cavalry; in troop when organized, Ft Leavenworth, KS, 1 Apr 1867. SOURCE: McMiller, "Buffalo Soldiers," 69.

BARTON, Henry; B/10th Cav. Original member of 10th Cavalry; in troop when organized, Ft Leavenworth, KS, 1 Apr 1867. SOURCE: McMiller, "Buffalo Soldiers," 69.

BARTON, Ignatius; Farrier; C/9th Cav. Veteran of Philippine Insurrection; at Ft D. A. Russell, WY, in 1910. SOURCE: *Illustrated Review: Ninth Cavalry*, with picture.

BARTS, David W.; Private; C/10th Cav. Served in 10th Cavalry in Cuba, 1898. SOURCE: Cashin, *Under Fire with the Tenth Cavalry*, 340.

BASEY, Rodney S.; Wagoner; E/9th Cav. At Ft D. A. Russell, WY, in 1910; resident of Springfield, OH. SOURCE: *Illustrated Review: Ninth Cavalry*, with picture.

BASKERVILLE, E. S.; 1st Sgt; H/25th Inf. "As fine a specimen of manhood as we found in any race, intelligent, brave and absolutely trustworthy," according to Col. Andrew S. Burt in 11 Sep 1902 Chicago speech. SOURCE: Cleveland *Gazette*, 11 Oct 1902.

Rumored to have commission in Filipino regiment. SOURCE: Richmond *Planet*, 22 Jun 1901.

Accompanied Chaplain Steward on recruiting duty as corporal in 1898; rose to first sergeant; now Rev. E. S. Baskerville, PE Church, Charleston, SC, "a natural leader"; native of Virginia, over 6' tall, devout Christian, now archdeacon in Episcopal Church, Charleston. SOURCE: Steward, *Fifty Years in the Gospel Ministry*, 303, 322, 351.

BASS, Emanuel D.; Captain; E/49th Inf. Transferred from F/9th Cavalry to K/10th Cavalry in Sep 1876. SOURCE: LS, 10 Cav, 1873-83.

Second lieutenant and adjutant, 9th Ohio Infantry Battalion, 14 May 1898; first lieutenant, 19 Aug 1898; mustered out, 28 Jan 1899; captain, 49th Infantry, 9 Sep 1899, in the Philippines; engaged against insurgents between Las Oinas and Paranaque, 25 Sep 1900; commanded battalion, 13 Aug-13 Sep 1900, 4-30 Dec 1900, 24 Jan-20 May 1901; commanded Las Pinas, 4 Mar-23 Apr 1900; commanded Paranaque, 13 Aug-13 Sep 1900; commanded Abaminos, 15 Oct 1900-9 Apr 1901; commanded San Pablo, 10 Apr-11 May 1901. SOURCE: Descriptive Book, E/49 Inf.

In letter from Las Pinas, 8 Feb 1900, he requests that *Gazette* be mailed to him at Manila. SOURCE: Cleveland *Gazette*, 24 Mar 1900.

One of twenty-three 49th Infantry officers recommended for commissions as second lieutenants in regular Army. SOURCE: CG, Div PI, Manila, to AG, 8 Feb 1901, AGO File 355163.

BASS, Walter; Corporal; I/24th Inf. Enlisted Nashville, TN, 26 Jul 1898; relieved as wagoner, 17 Jan 1899. SOURCE: Muster Roll, I/24 Inf, Jan-Feb 1899.

On special duty as assistant cook since 15 Feb 1899. SOURCE: Muster Roll, I/24 Inf, Mar-Apr 1899.

Appointed corporal, 3 May 1899. SOURCE: Muster Roll, I/24 Inf, May-Jun 1899.

Discharged in the Philippines, n.d. SOURCE: Muster Roll, I/24 Inf, Nov-Dec 1899.

BASSETT, Effie J.; Private; G/24th Inf. Died Cuba, 6 Sep 1898. SOURCE: *ANJ* 36 (11 Feb 1899): 567.

BASSETT, George; Private; A/10th Cav. Served in 10th Cavalry, 1898; remained in U.S. during war with Spain. SOURCE: Cashin, *Under Fire with the Tenth Cavalry*, 337.

BATES; Corporal; G/24th Inf. Seriously wounded in leg, near Anibongan, Philippines, against Pulahanes, 10 Sep 1906. SOURCE: Muller, *The Twenty Fourth Infantry*, 46.

BATES; Private; H/10th Cav. Jailed for attempted assault on prostitute. SOURCE: Cheyenne *Daily Leader*, 22 Feb 1907.

BATES, Anchor; H/10th Cav. Original member of 10th Cavalry; in troop when organized, Ft Leavenworth, KS, 21 Jul 1867. SOURCE: McMiller, "Buffalo Soldiers," 75.

BATES, George; Private; M/10th Cav. Served in 10th Cavalry, 1898; remained in U.S. during war with Spain. SOURCE: Cashin, *Under Fire with the Tenth Cavalry*, 351.

BATES, Henry; Private; M/9th Cav. At Ft D. A. Russell, WY, in 1910; resident of Milledgeville, GA. SOURCE: *Illustrated Review: Ninth Cavalry*.

BATES, James; Private; H/9th Cav. Cited for gallantry against enemy, 1 Jul 1898. SOURCE: SecWar, *AR 1898*, 708.

Commended for gallantry, 1 Jul 1898, and awarded certificate of merit. SOURCE: GO 15, AGO, 13 Feb 1900.

Certificate of merit noted. SOURCE: Steward, *The Colored Regulars*, 280.

BATES, Milton F.; Private; I/25th Inf. Died of malaria in the Philippines, 9 Aug 1900. SOURCE: *ANJ* 37 (18 Aug 1900): 1214.

Died of chronic dysentery in hospital, Castillejos, Philippines, early Aug 1900; native of Kentucky. SOURCE: Richmond *Planet*, 20 Oct 1900.

BATES, Richard; L/10th Cav. Original member of 10th Cavalry; in troop when organized, Ft Riley, KS, 21 Sep 1867. SOURCE: McMiller, "Buffalo Soldiers," 78.

BATES, William; Private; I/24th Inf. Enlisted Chicago, IL, 29 Jul 1898; sick, in line of duty, since 20 Oct 1898. SOURCE: Muster Roll, I/24 Inf, Jan–Feb 1899.

Deserted from Ft D. A. Russell, WY, 7 Mar 1899. SOURCE: Muster Roll, I/24 Inf, Mar–Apr 1899.

BATIE, Henry; QM Sgt; L/24th Inf. Born Grayson Co., TX; served in Spanish-American War; musician, corporal, sergeant, and quartermaster sergeant, L/24th Infantry; discharged at Skagway, AK, May 1899; in Alaska through 1899; returned to Los Angeles to marry Mrs. Roberta Johnson of San Diego; daughter Katherine "grew to be very patriotic" and was Red Cross worker until she died 30 May 1918, age 15; active worker for benefit of Negro race; active in Afro-American Council and officer of General Harrison Gray Otis Marching Club; died 29 Oct 1917, "a beautiful Christian gentleman," less than year before death of his daughter. SOURCE: Beasley, *Negro Trailblazers*, 299.

At San Carlos, AZ, private, K/24th Infantry, 1890. *See* HARDEE, James A., Private, K/24th Infantry

Wife came from old California family; active worker in Sojourner Truth Home for Working Girls; first colored woman to study and master art of chiropody in California and enjoyed long practice "among the exclusive rich." SOURCE: Beasley, *Negro Trailblazers*, 234–35.

BATIE, John; Private; L/10th Cav. Convicted of mutiny by general court martial, Bayamo, Cuba, 12 Oct 1899, and sentenced to ten years. SOURCE: *ANJ* 37 (24 Feb 1900): 602.

BATSON; Private; E/10th Cav. At Ft Apache, AZ, 1890, subscribed $.50 to testimonial to General Grierson. SOURCE: List of subscriptions, 23 Apr 1890, 10th Cavalry papers, MHI.

BATTER; Corporal; F/10th Cav. Commended for heroism in battle, Kansas, 21 Aug 1867. SOURCE: Armes, *Ups and Downs*, 247.

BATTER, Henry; Private; I/9th Cav. Fined $3 by summary court, 13 Apr 1891, for having liquor in barracks. SOURCE: Summary Court Record, Ft Robinson.

BATTIAS, Edward; G/10th Cav. Original member of 10th Cavalry; in troop when organized, Ft Leavenworth, KS, 5 Jul 1867. SOURCE: McMiller, "Buffalo Soldiers," 74.

BATTISE, Joseph; Private; K/9th Cav. At Ft D. A. Russell, WY, in 1910; resident of Mobile, AL. SOURCE: *Illustrated Review: Ninth Cavalry.*

BATTLE, Arthur; Corporal; G/10th Cav. Born in North Carolina; private and corporal, B/10th Cavalry, 5 Jun 1882–9 Oct 1894; private, A/10th Cavalry, 13 Dec 1894; corporal, 23 Apr 1895; private, G/10th Cavalry, 12 Jan 1896; corporal, 1 Jan 1897; stationed at Ft Assiniboine, MT, 1897. SOURCE: Baker, Roster.

At Ft Apache, AZ, 1890, private, B/10th Cavalry, subscribed $.50 to testimonial to General Grierson. SOURCE: List of subscriptions, 23 Apr 1890, 10th Cavalry papers, MHI.

Discharged. SOURCE: *ANJ* 35 (9 Apr 1898): 602.

BATTLE, Sam M.; Private; D/25th Inf. Dishonorable discharge, Brownsville. SOURCE: SO 266, AGO, 9 Nov 1906.

BATTLE, William P.; Private; H/10th Cav. Honorable mention for services rendered in capture of Mangas and his band, Rio Bonito, AZ, 18 Oct 1886. SOURCE: Baker, Roster.

BATTLES; Private; H/10th Cav. Shot in quarrel with Privates Downs and Young (all hit), in brothel, Cheyenne, WY. SOURCE: Cheyenne *Daily Leader*, 24 Feb 1907.

BATTLES, Henry; Private; F/24th Inf. Wounded in action, Cuba, 1898. SOURCE: Muller, *The Twenty Fourth Infantry*, 18.

BATTON, Henry; Private; A/49th Inf. Died of malaria in the Philippines, 22 Aug 1900. SOURCE: *ANJ* 38 (8 Sep 1900): 43.

BAUSBRY, Arthur; I/10th Cav. Original member of 10th Cavalry; in troop when organized, Ft Riley, KS, 15 Aug 1867. SOURCE: McMiller, "Buffalo Soldiers," 76.

BAXTER, Llewellyn B.; Private; K/25th Inf. At Ft Niobrara, NE, 1904. SOURCE: Wilson, "History of Fort Niobrara."

BAXTER, Reuben W.; Bugler; 24th Inf. Served in Houston, 1917; tried unsuccessfully at court martial to establish alibi for being off post during riot. SOURCE: Haynes, *A Night of Violence*, 268.

BAYER, Jacob; Private; H/10th Cav. Acted as witness at court martial of Private Andy Clayton, Ft Concho, TX, 21 May 1874. SOURCE: Stallard, *Glittering Misery*, 100.

See **CLAYTON**, Andy, Private, H/9th Cavalry

BAYLESS, John M.; Private; H/24th Inf. Enlisted Chicago, IL; six years' continuous service; special duty as cook, 19 May–25 Jun 1898. SOURCE: Muster Roll, H/24 Inf, May–Jun 1898.

Transferred from Reserve Divisional Hospital, Siboney, Cuba, to Fortress Monroe, VA, via U.S. Army Transport *Concho*, 24 Jul 1898, with yellow fever. SOURCE: Hospital Papers, Spanish-American War.

Sick in U.S., in line of duty; appointed artificer, 14 Sep 1898; rejoined company from sick, 2 Oct 1898; on special duty as laborer, Subsistence Department, Ft Douglas, UT, since then. SOURCE: Muster Roll, H/24 Inf, Jul–Aug 1898.

Discharged, expiration of enlistment, character excellent, single, Ft Douglas, 15 Dec 1898, with $45 deposits and $13.77 clothing; reenlisted in company; on four-month furlough since 16 Dec 1898. SOURCE: Muster Roll, H/24 Inf, Jan–Feb 1899.

BAYLOR, George; Private; A/24th Inf. Wounded in action, Santiago, Cuba, Jul 1898. SOURCE: SecWar, *AR 1898*, 43; Muller, *The Twenty Fourth Infantry*, 16; Clark, "A History of the Twenty-fourth," 100.

BAYLOR, Robert H.; 9th Cav. Escaped post guard, Ft Bayard, NM, after confinement for assault with intent to kill; in I/10th Cavalry. SOURCE: Cleveland *Gazette*, 9 May 1891.

Baylor, deserter from your troop, awaiting trial at Ft Robinson, NE; taken up as deserter this date; please forward descriptive list and charges. SOURCE: CO, Ft Robinson, to CO, A/10, Ft Grant, 4 Mar 1892, LS, Ft Robinson.

Commander, Ft Robinson, believes charges can be proved but recommends that Baylor be returned to duty, transferred to 9th Cavalry, and be allowed to make up time; he is "a mere boy in appearance" and eager to continue in service; offense due to potential trouble in his troop; behavior here excellent. SOURCE: CO, Ft Robinson, to AAG, DP, 13 Mar 1892, LS, Ft Robinson.

Awaiting trial for desertion at Ft Robinson 4 Mar–28 May 1892. SOURCE: Post Returns, Ft Robinson.

Transferred to 9th Cavalry. SOURCE: SO 145, AGO, 21 Jun 1892.

President, Oak and Ivy Dancing Club of Ft Robinson, which gives dancing schools on post. SOURCE: Ft Robinson Weekly Bulletin, 5 Apr 1893, Court Martial Records, McKay.

BEACHEM, Will; Private; F/9th Cav. At Ft D. A. Russell, WY, in 1910; marksman; resident of Lee Co., MS. SOURCE: *Illustrated Review: Ninth Cavalry*, with picture.

BEACOAT, William D.; Private; 24th Inf. Served in Houston, 1917; convinced court martial that he remained in camp during riot. SOURCE: Haynes, *A Night of Violence*, 269.

BEAIRD, Otis; Private; A/10th Cav. Served in 10th Cavalry, 1898; remained in U.S. during war with Spain. SOURCE: Cashin, *Under Fire with the Tenth Cavalry*, 337.

BEAMON, William Henry; Private; 10th Cav. Not yet arrived at Ft Leavenworth, KS, from Jefferson Barracks, MO. SOURCE: Adj, Ft Leavenworth, to HQ, Jefferson Bks, 9 Oct 1866.

In hospital, Jefferson Barracks. SOURCE: Grierson, Ft Leavenworth, to Recruiting Officer, n.d., ES, 10 Cav, 1866–71.

BEAND, Harrison; Private; F/9th Cav. Wounded in action, Florida Mountains, NM, 15 Sep 1876. SOURCE: *Illustrated Review: Ninth Cavalry*.

BEARD, Allen; Private; M/9th Cav. At Ft D. A. Russell, WY, in 1910; sharpshooter; resident of Louisville. SOURCE: *Illustrated Review: Ninth Cavalry*, with picture.

BEARD, Charley; Private; E/10th Cav. Served in 10th Cavalry, 1898; remained in U.S. during war with Spain. SOURCE: Cashin, *Under Fire with the Tenth Cavalry*, 343.

BEARD, George J.; Corporal; H/8th Ill Inf. Typesetter, Springfield, IL, as civilian; letter from San Luis, Cuba, 21 Oct 1898. SOURCE: Gatewood, *"Smoked Yankees"*, 202.

BEARD, James E.; Sergeant; Machine Gun Troop/ 10th Cav. Commissioned first lieutenant, Camp Des Moines, IA, 15 Oct 1917. SOURCE: Glass, *History of the Tenth Cavalry*, appendix M.

BEASLEY, Arnie; G/10th Cav. Original member of 10th Cavalry; in troop when organized, Ft Leavenworth, KS, 5 Jul 1867. SOURCE: McMiller, "Buffalo Soldiers," 74.

BEASLEY, David E.; Private; A/24th Inf. Schoolteacher, Ft Huachuca, AZ, since 6 Dec 1892. SOURCE: Report of Schools, Ft Huachuca, 1 Dec 1892–1 Feb 1893, Name File, 24 Inf.

On extra duty as schoolteacher. SOURCE: Order 162, Ft Huachuca, 1 Nov 1893, Letters & Orders Received, 24 Inf.

Relieved from extra duty as schoolteacher. SOURCE: Order 177, Ft Huachuca, 30 Nov 1893, Letters & Orders Received, 24 Inf.

BEASON, Roy; Private; M/9th Cav. At Ft D. A. Russell, WY, in 1910; resident of Fort Payne, AL. SOURCE: *Illustrated Review: Ninth Cavalry*, with picture.

BEATTIE, Ether; Private; C/10th Cav. Served in 10th Cavalry, 1898; remained in U.S. during war with Spain. SOURCE: Cashin, *Under Fire with the Tenth Cavalry*, 340.

BEATY, George; Corporal; E/10th Cav. Promoted from private, Sep 1899. SOURCE: *ANJ* 37 (7 Oct 1899): 122.

BEAUMAN, William H.; 10th Cav. Recruit for regiment, hospitalized, Jefferson Barracks, MO, 29 Sep 1866; deserted from hospital. SOURCE: McMiller, "Buffalo Soldiers," 45–46.

BECHERES, Jesse; Private; M/10th Cav. Original member of 10th Cavalry; in troop when organized, Ft Riley, KS, 15 Oct 1867. SOURCE: McMiller, "Buffalo Soldiers," 79.

Mentioned, Jan 1873, as having enlisted in Sep 1867. SOURCE: LS, 10 Cav, 1873–77.

BECK, Howard; Private; Band/24th Inf. Played trombone, mandolin, tambourine; harassed and arrested by Manila Police, 19 Jun 1902. SOURCE: Letter, CO, 24 Inf, to Chief of Police, Manila, 21 Jun 1902.

BECK, James, Jr.; Private; I/24th Inf. *See* AG File 439153.

Deserted from Rosales, Philippines, 3 Feb 1902. SOURCE: Regt Returns, 24 Inf, Feb 1902.

BECKETT, William C.; Sergeant; E/10th Cav. Born in Virginia; private, E/10th Cavalry, 21 Dec 1887–20 Dec 1892; in G/10th Cavalry, 10 Apr 1893; in E/10th Cavalry, 5 Jun 1893; corporal, 16 Jan 1896; stationed at Ft Custer, MT, 1897. SOURCE: Baker, Roster.

At Ft Apache, AZ, 1890, private, E/10th Cavalry, subscribed $.50 to testimonial to General Grierson. SOURCE: List of subscriptions, 23 Apr 1890, 10th Cavalry papers, MHI.

Sergeant, E/10th Cavalry; served in 10th Cavalry in Cuba, 1898. SOURCE: Cashin, *Under Fire with the Tenth Cavalry*, 342.

Lived in Crawford, NE, age 48, in 1919; was in A/10th Cavalry, when Henry McClain was in B Troop; stationed at Ft Robinson, NE, 1902–07, and since then well acquainted with McClain. SOURCE: Affidavit, Beckett, 24 Mar 1919, VA File XC 2705872, Henry McClain.

No Veterans Administration pension file.

BECKHAM, John G.; Sergeant; F/24th Inf. Commissioned first lieutenant, 9th U.S. Volunteer Infantry. SOURCE: Cashin, *Under Fire with the Tenth Cavalry*, 360.

BEELER, George; Private; G/10th Cav. Served in 10th Cavalry, 1898; remained in U.S. during war with Spain. SOURCE: Cashin, *Under Fire with the Tenth Cavalry*, 345.

BELDEN, James H.; D/10th Cav. Served with 1st Sgt. Thomas Allsup, D/10th Cavalry; in 1926 resided at 196 Austin, Worcester, MA. SOURCE: Affidavit, Belden, VA File XC 2659797, Thomas H. Allsup.

BELL; Private; A/10th Cav. At Ft Apache, AZ, 1890, subscribed $.50 to testimonial to General Grierson. SOURCE: List of subscriptions, 23 Apr 1890, 10th Cavalry papers, MHI.

BELL; Private; B/10th Cav. At Ft Apache, AZ, 1890, subscribed $.50 to testimonial to General Grierson. SOURCE: List of subscriptions, 23 Apr 1890, 10th Cavalry papers, MHI.

BELL, Andrew; M/10th Cav. Original member of 10th Cavalry; in troop when organized, Ft Riley, KS, 15 Oct 1867. SOURCE: McMiller, "Buffalo Soldiers," 79.

BELL, Andrew; I/10th Cav. Original member of 10th Cavalry; in troop when organized, Ft Riley, KS, 15 Aug 1867. SOURCE: McMiller, "Buffalo Soldiers," 76.

BELL, Andrew; Private; D/24th Inf. Retired Jan 1901. SOURCE: *ANJ* 38 (2 Feb 1901): 547.

BELL, Arthur; Private; H/10th Cav. Served in 10th Cavalry, 1898; remained in U.S. during war with Spain. SOURCE: Cashin, *Under Fire with the Tenth Cavalry*, 347.

BELL, Benjamin; L/10th Cav. Original member of 10th Cavalry; in troop when organized, Ft Riley, KS, 21 Sep 1867. SOURCE: McMiller, "Buffalo Soldiers," 78.

BELL, David; Private; K/10th Cav. Served in 10th Cavalry, 1898; remained in U.S. during war with Spain. SOURCE: Cashin, *Under Fire with the Tenth Cavalry*, 349.

BELL, Dennis; Private; H/10th Cav. Served in 10th Cavalry in Cuba, 1898. SOURCE: Cashin, *Under Fire with the Tenth Cavalry*, 347.

Awarded Medal of Honor for heroism in Cuba, 1898. *See* **THOMPKINS**, William H., Sergeant, H/25th Infantry

Medal of Honor mentioned. SOURCE: Steward, *The Colored Regulars*, 205.

Born Washington, DC; received medal while in hospital, Ft Bliss, TX. SOURCE: Lee, *Negro Medal of Honor Men*, 92, 98.

Now out of service; holder of Medal of Honor. SOURCE: *ANJ* 37 (24 Feb 1900): 611.

BELL, Ernie; K/10th Cav. Original member of 10th Cavalry; in troop when organized, Ft Riley, KS, 1 Sep 1867. SOURCE: McMiller, "Buffalo Soldiers," 77.

BELL, Henry; 24th Inf. Born Gallatin, TN; age 26 in 1891; Ht 5'3"; black complexion; first enlisted in K/24th Infantry; private, Band/24th Infantry, joined 30 Aug 1886, Ft Reno, Indian Territory; discharged Aug 1891, Ft Bayard, NM, character excellent, married, one child; due U.S. for subsistence $2, summary court $3, additional pay $5, retained $60, clothing $27. SOURCE: Entry, 29 Aug 1891, Ft Bayard. Descriptive Book, 24 Inf NCS & Band.

Sergeant, K/24th Infantry, Ft Reno, authorized four-month furlough. SOURCE: *ANJ* 24 (7 Aug 1886): 28.

Enlisted and joined, Ft Bayard, 31 Aug 1891; E/24th Infantry, 3 May 1892; character good, married, one child; additional pay $3, clothing $26. SOURCE: Entry, 3 May 1892, Ft Bayard, Descriptive Book, 24 Inf NCS & Band.

BELL, Henry; Private; D/10th Cav. Served in 10th Cavalry, 1898; remained in U.S. during war with Spain. SOURCE: Cashin, *Under Fire with the Tenth Cavalry*, 341.

BELL, Henry C.; Trumpeter; A/25th Inf. Ranked number 78 among expert riflemen in 1904, with 72.33 percent. SOURCE: GO 79, AGO, 1 Jun 1905.

Ranked number 208 among expert riflemen in 1905, with 71.67 percent. SOURCE: GO 101, AGO, 31 May 1906.

BELL, Hezerial; Private; 25th Inf. Died of dysentery, Camp Wikoff, NY, 4 Sep 1898. SOURCE: Hospital Papers, Spanish-American War.

BELL, Howard; Private; A/9th Cav. At Ft D. A. Russell, WY, in 1910. SOURCE: *Illustrated Review: Ninth Cavalry.*

BELL, James; Private; 38th Inf. Died of chronic diarrhea at Ft Cummings, NM, Dec 1867. SOURCE: Billington, *New Mexico's Buffalo Soldiers*, 34.

BELL, James; Private; G/10th Cav. Served in 10th Cavalry in Cuba, 1898. SOURCE: Cashin, *Under Fire with the Tenth Cavalry*, 345.

BELL, John; K/10th Cav. Original member of 10th Cavalry; in troop when organized, Ft Riley, KS, 1 Sep 1867. SOURCE: McMiller, "Buffalo Soldiers," 77.

BELL, John; Private; E/25th Inf. Died in the Philippines, 10 Sep 1900. SOURCE: *ANJ* 38 (8 Dec 1900): 355.

BELL, John A.; 1st Lt; 48th Inf. To report to Ft Thomas, KY, for duty. SOURCE: *ANJ* 37 (30 Sep 1899): 101.

BELL, Lewis; Corporal; D/10th Cav. Original member of 10th Cavalry; in troop when organized, Ft Leavenworth, KS, 1 Jun 1867. SOURCE: McMiller, "Buffalo Soldiers," 71.

Appointed corporal, Aug 1867. SOURCE: Adj, 10 Cav, to CO, D/10, Ft Arbuckle, Indian Territory, 20 Aug 1867, LS, 10 Cav, 1866–67.

BELL, Lloyd; Private; I/10th Cav. Served in 10th Cavalry, 1898; remained in U.S. during war with Spain. SOURCE: Cashin, *Under Fire with the Tenth Cavalry*, 348.

BELL, Mark; Private; C/9th Cav. At Ft Robinson, NE, 1885–86; $35 on deposit with paymaster.

Sick at Ft Robinson, Jun 1888, awaiting transportation to Ft Duchesne, UT.

BELL, Mat; Private; D/10th Cav. Served in 10th Cavalry, 1898; remained in U.S. during war with Spain. SOURCE: Cashin, *Under Fire with the Tenth Cavalry*, 341.

BELL, Matthew; Principal Musician; 24th Inf. Born Warren Co., TN; joined at Ft Supply, Indian Territory, 1 Jan 1885; occupation soldier; Ht 5'7", yellow complexion; first enlisted in Band/24th Infantry, discharged 14 Nov 1884; reenlisted 21 Nov 1884, Ft Leavenworth, KS; principal musi-

cian, 3 Apr 1889; discharged, expiration of term, 20 Nov 1889, character excellent; married, no children; additional pay $2 per month; retained $60; clothing $71.15. SOURCE: Entry, 20 Nov 1889, Ft Bayard, NM, Descriptive Book, 24 Inf NCS & Band.

Born Warren Co., TN; age 31; enlisted and joined, Ft Bayard, 21 Nov 1889, third enlistment; discharged, expiration of service, Ft Bayard, 20 Nov 1894; character excellent; married with two children; additional pay $3 per month; retained $60; clothing $16.77; owes government $5.02 for subsistence stores. SOURCE: Entry, 20 Nov 1894, Ft Bayard, Descriptive Book, 24 Inf NCS & Band.

BELL, Riley; Blacksmith; D/9th Cav. Recruit from depot, arrived at Ft Craig, NM, 12 Jan 1881. SOURCE: Regt Returns, 9 Cav, Jan 1881.

BELL, Robert; Private; F/9th Cav. At Ft D. A. Russell, WY, in 1910; resident of Indianapolis. SOURCE: *Illustrated Review: Ninth Cavalry*, with picture.

BELL, Thomas; Corporal; A/9th Cav. Private, C/9th Cavalry; sick at Ft Robinson, NE, Jun 1888, awaiting transportation to Ft Duchesne, UT.

Veteran of Philippine Insurrection; at Ft D. A. Russell, WY, in 1910; sharpshooter. SOURCE: *Illustrated Review: Ninth Cavalry*, with picture.

BELL, Thomas; Private; A/24th Inf. Died of acute dysentery in the Philippines, 19 Nov 1899. SOURCE: *ANJ* 37 (2 Dec 1899): 327.

BELL, Wade; G/9th Cav. Enlisted in K Troop, 6 Dec 1888, then assigned to G Troop; remembers difficulties experienced by Cpl. James F. Jackson of G/9th Cavalry, in raising his arm, May 1891, Ft Robinson, NE; applied liniment to Jackson's arm in quarters; Jackson claimed he was beset by rheumatism; was age 27 and residing at 223 N. 11th St., Omaha, in 1898. SOURCE: Affidavit, Bell, 1898, VA File C 2555351, James F. Jackson.

BELL, William; 1st Sgt; G/10th Cav. At Ft Apache, AZ, 1890, subscribed $.50 to testimonial to General Grierson. SOURCE: List of subscriptions, 23 Apr 1890, 10th Cavalry papers, MHI.

BELL, William; QM Sgt; B/10th Cav. Bell's deposition attests to heroism of Pvt. Arthur G. Wheeler, B/10th Cavalry, Las Guasimas, Cuba, 24 Jun 1898; sergeant, recommended for Medal of Honor, for heroism in assault on San Juan Hill, 1 Jul 1898. SOURCE: Cashin, *Under Fire with the Tenth Cavalry*, 180, 186, 337.

Shot twice by wife with pistol at Ft Robinson, NE, dance in honor of Sergeant Perry, L/10th Cavalry; died 26 Jul 1904. SOURCE: Crawford *Tribune*, 29 Jul 1904.

Quartermaster sergeant, died Ft Robinson, 26 Jul 1904; twenty-three-year veteran. SOURCE: Monthly Report, Chaplain William T. Anderson, Ft Robinson, 1 Aug 1904, AGO File 53910.

Shot and killed by wife at Ft Robinson dance, 24 July 1904; had resided in southwest part of Crawford, NE. SOURCE: Crawford *Bulletin*, 29 Jul 1904.

Buried, Ft Robinson, 27 Jul 1904. SOURCE: List of Interments, Ft Robinson.

BELL, William; Private; I/24th Inf. Enlisted Louisville, KY, 20 Feb 1899; joined company 23 Feb 1899. SOURCE: Muster Roll, I/24 Inf, Jan–Feb 1899.

On detached service at Benicia Barracks, CA, since 8 Apr 1899. SOURCE: Muster Roll, I/24 Inf, Mar–Apr 1899.

BENJAMIN, Gordon; D/10th Cav. Original member of 10th Cavalry; in troop when organized, Ft Leavenworth, KS, 1 Jun 1867. SOURCE: McMiller, "Buffalo Soldiers," 71.

BENJAMIN, James; Private; 25th Inf. Sends love to parents and friends. SOURCE: Richmond *Planet*, 20 Jun 1900.

BENJAMIN, James H.; Private; C/24th Inf. Missing in action, Manicling, Philippines, 13 Sep 1900; accidentally killed by 22nd Infantry while a prisoner trying to escape insurgents. SOURCE: Muller, *The Twenty Fourth Infantry*, 38–39.

Killed in action, Jean, Saragossa, Luzon, Philippines, while captive of insurgents, in fight with Lieutenant Hannay and K/22nd Infantry, 15 Oct 1900. SOURCE: *ANJ* 38 (27 Oct 1900): 211; Manila *Times*, 17 Oct 1900.

BENJAMIN, Robert A.; Ord Sgt; U.S. Army. Born Kingston, Jamaica; enlisted at age 21; occupation waiter; Ht 5'6", brown complexion; enlisted, M/9th Cavalry, 2 Jun 1873; continuous service until retirement, 2 Feb 1905; saddler sergeant, 9th Cavalry, 1 Apr 1883; ordnance sergeant, U.S. Army, 9 Oct 1894; at marriage a resident of Orangeburg, SC, married in Columbia, SC; father Isaac Alfred Augustus Benjamin of England; mother Sarah Anne Miller of Jamaica; wife's father James L. Thompson and mother Malinda Simons, both of Richland Co., SC; died 30 Jan 1916, Columbia; first wife, Mary G. Young Benjamin, died 6 Feb 1907, and buried in Highland Cemetery, Geary Co., KS; second wife, Syrene E. Benjamin, widow, address 2506 Taylor St., Columbia, in 1918; had $20 per month in 1922 and lived at 1913 Bambridge St., Philadelphia; pension granted 1917 as Comanche War widow; pension stopped at 2506 Taylor St., Columbia, when she died 14 Nov 1929. SOURCE: VA File WC 927337, Robert A. Benjamin.

Born Kingston, Jamaica; arrived New York, 1869, stayed to 1873; enlisted, Philadelphia, 1873; six months at St. Louis, MO, arsenal; then Fts McKavett and Stockton, TX; married eleven years in 1894, with one daughter, Clara. SOURCE: Court Martial Records, Plummer.

At Ft Robinson, NE, authorized four-month furlough. SOURCE: *ANJ* 25 (31 Mar 1888): 714.

Sergeant, Ft Robinson; wife expected back at post soon. SOURCE: Cleveland *Gazette*, 12 Jan 1889.

With Pvt. John W. Nicholls, I/8th Infantry, ordered to conduct insane Pvt. Lewellen Young, F/9th Cavalry, to asylum, Washington, DC, from Ft Robinson, 14 Jan 1889. SOURCE: Order 10, 12 Jan 1889, Post Orders, Ft Robinson.

Recommended by Commander, Ft Robinson, for ordnance sergeant: "sober and reliable and an excellent clerk." SOURCE: Letter to AG, through CO, 9 Cav, Ft Robinson, 18 Mar 1891, LS, Ft Robinson.

Promoted to regimental quartermaster sergeant, in accordance with 9th Cavalry Order 27, Ft Robinson, 23 Apr 1891. SOURCE: Cleveland *Gazette*, 16 May 1891.

Discharge revoked; returned to regimental saddler sergeant. SOURCE: TWX, AGO, 7 Jan 1892.

Assists with regimental clerical work. SOURCE: CO, Ft Robinson, to AAG, DP, 5 May 1892, LS, Ft Robinson.

Saddler sergeant since 28 Jun 1888. SOURCE: Roster, 9 Cav, 1893.

Examined for ordnance sergeant, Ft Robinson. SOURCE: *ANJ* 30 (1 Jul 1893): 745.

Resides at Ft Robinson with wife and child. SOURCE: Medical History, Ft Robinson, Aug 1893.

His daughter is student at post Sunday School, 1894; has organ in quarters. SOURCE: Investigation of Charges against Chaplain Plummer.

Involved in argument at Ft Robinson, 11 Sep 1894, for which general court martial dishonorably discharged Sgt. David R. Dillon, 24 Sep 1894; at the time lived with wife and mother-in-law, Mrs. Young. SOURCE: Court Martial Records, Dillon.

Promoted to ordnance sergeant. SOURCE: *ANJ* 32 (27 Oct 1894): 141.

On promotion to ordnance sergeant, Commander, 9th Cavalry, "desires to give expression to the worth of Sgt Benjamin's long and faithful service in the regiment and in the position he now relinquishes." SOURCE: *ANJ* 32 (3 Nov 1894): 154.

See **JEFFERDS**, Wesley, Sergeant A/9th Cavalry; **DAVIS**, Benjamin F., Quartermaster Sergeant, U.S. Army

Inquired from retirement in 1910 whether War Department objected to his becoming commandant, Claflin College, Orangeburg. SOURCE: AGO File 1607790.

BENN, Jesse; Private; K/10th Cav. Served in 10th Cavalry, 1898; remained in U.S. during war with Spain. SOURCE: Cashin, *Under Fire with the Tenth Cavalry*, 349.

BENN, Simon; Private; E/10th Cav. Served in 10th Cavalry, 1898; remained in U.S. during war with Spain. SOURCE: Cashin, *Under Fire with the Tenth Cavalry*, 343.

BENNARD, Bert; Horseshoer; D/9th Cav. At Ft D. A. Russell, WY, in 1910; marksman; resident of Muskogee, Indian Territory. SOURCE: *Illustrated Review: Ninth Cavalry,* with picture.

BENNETT; Private; E/10th Cav. At Ft Apache, AZ, 1890, private, subscribed $.50 to testimonial to General Grierson. SOURCE: List of subscriptions, 23 Apr 1890, 10th Cavalry papers, MHI.

BENNETT, Alexander; Sergeant; E/9th Cav. Sergeant, E/9th Cavalry, since 3 Apr 1893. SOURCE: Roster, 9 Cav, 1893.

BENNETT, Bert; Private; I/25th Inf. Fined $1 by summary court, San Isidro, Philippines; for charges *see* **BRYAN**, John S., Private, I/25th Infantry

BENNETT, Frank D.; Private; I/10th Cav. Served in 10th Cavalry in Cuba, 1898. SOURCE: Cashin, *Under Fire with the Tenth Cavalry*, 347.

Wounded in action, Santiago, Cuba, 1 Jul 1898. SOURCE: SecWar, *AR 1898*, 324.

BENNETT, Henry Clay; Sergeant; Supply Troop/ 10th Cav. Commissioned second lieutenant of cavalry, 1918. SOURCE: Glass, *History of the Tenth Cavalry*, appendix M.

BENNETT, John W.; Private; L/10th Cav. Original member of 10th Cavalry; in troop when organized, Ft Riley, KS, 21 Sep 1867. SOURCE: McMiller, "Buffalo Soldiers," 78.

Mentioned Jan 1873 as having enlisted Sep 1867. SOURCE: LS, 10 Cav, 1873–77.

BENNETT, William; A/10th Cav. Original member of 10th Cavalry; in troop when organized, Ft Leavenworth, KS, 18 Feb 1867. SOURCE: McMiller, "Buffalo Soldiers," 68.

BENNIN, Thomas; A/10th Cav. Original member of 10th Cavalry; in troop when organized, Ft Leavenworth, KS, 18 Feb 1867. SOURCE: McMiller, "Buffalo Soldiers," 68.

BENSON, Abram; Private; E/24th Inf. Born Burlington, NJ; enlisted Philadelphia, PA, 3 Dec 1891; two previous enlistments in Band/10th Cavalry, discharged 3 Nov 1891; joined Band/24th Infantry, Ft Bayard, NM, 1 Nov 1892, age 37, Ht 5'3", brown complexion, single; transferred to G/24th Infantry, 28 Sep 1896; additional pay $2 per month; retained $51. SOURCE: Entry, Ft Bayard, 28 Sep 1896, Descriptive Book, 24 Inf NCS & Band.

Died of yellow fever in Cuba, 12 Aug 1898, as private, E/24th Infantry. SOURCE: AG, *Correspondence Regarding the War with Spain*, I, 223.

BENSON, Caleb; Sergeant; K/10th Cav. Born Jacksonville, FL, 25 Jun 1859; enlisted 2 Feb 1875; private, 9th Cavalry, 1875–80; private, B and K/10th Cavalry, 1885–1904; in K/10th Cavalry 1907–08; retired as sergeant from K/10th Cavalry, 29 Sep 1908; married Percilla Smith of Dawes Co., NE, age 27, 26 Mar 1909; died 19 Nov 1937, Crawford, NE, of coronary thrombosis, with B. F. Richards as attending physician; civilian occupation waiter; buried Ft Robinson, NE. SOURCE: VA File XC 2499129, Caleb Benson.

Attacked by Indians in Colorado, mouth of Navcos River, Sep 1878. SOURCE: Hamilton, "History of the Ninth Cavalry," 8.

At Ft Apache, AZ, 1890, private, B/10th Cavalry, subscribed $.50 to testimonial to General Grierson. SOURCE: List of subscriptions, 23 Apr 1890, 10th Cavalry papers, MHI.

Private, served in 10th Cavalry, 1898; remained in U.S. during war with Spain. SOURCE: Cashin, *Under Fire with the Tenth Cavalry*, 349.

Retired to Crawford after tour in Philippines, 1909; married Percilla at Crawford in 1909; homesteaded to 1914 when moved to Ft Robinson, where employed first by Captain and Mrs. Whitehead, then Colonel Calvert; then traveled before returning permanently to Crawford. SOURCE: *Souvenir Book: Crawford*, 59.

Unable to earn living and "dependent largely upon the good will of my former troop, K 10th Cavalry, for my support"; rejected to finish my thirty years due to disability "after having put in the best years of my life [27] as a soldier in the U.S. Army, and I therefore beg you to hasten the assistance which of right I should have from my Government." SOURCE: Benson, Letter to Commissioner of Pensions, Washington, DC, 22 Aug 1905, VA File XC 2499129, Caleb Benson.

See **GAINES**, George W., First Sergeant, A/10th Cavalry; **CLARK**, W. F., Saddler, 10th Cavalry; **LETCHER**, Philip E., Sergeant, K/10th Cavalry; **THORNTON**, Beverly F., Cook, K/10th Cavalry

Buried Ft Robinson, 16 Nov 1937. SOURCE: List of Interments, Ft Robinson.

Career summary. SOURCE: Omaha *World-Herald*, 6 Dec 1992.

BENSON, Harice; Private; B/9th Cav. At Ft D. A. Russell, WY, in 1910. SOURCE: *Illustrated Review: Ninth Cavalry*.

BENTLEY, George; Private; K/9th Cav. Born Danville, KY; Ht 5'8", mulatto; occupation laborer; character on discharge good; received $147.15 on honorable discharge, completion of enlistment, Ft Davis, TX, 1871, at age 26. SOURCE: Carroll, *The Black Military Experience*, 438–40.

BENTLEY, James; Private; H/24th Inf. Wounded slightly in the scalp, Naguilian, Philippines, 7 Dec 1899. SOURCE: *ANJ* 37 (10 Mar 1900): 657; Muller, *The Twenty Fourth Infantry*, 35.

Fined $6 by summary court, San Isidro, Philippines, for violating Article 32, absent without leave from formation without authorization, 17 Nov 1901, fifth conviction; fined $5 for failure to perform duty as member of fatigue party, 11 Dec 1901; fined $5 for violating Article 62, disorderly in streets, talking and making threatening gestures to natives, 22 Dec 1901. SOURCE: Register of Summary Court, San Isidro.

BENTLEY, James B.; G/10th Cav. Appointed national aide-de-camp, National Indian War Veterans; lives at Gulfport, MS. SOURCE: *Winners of the West* 9 (Dec 1931): 3.

Served 1886–91; member, Camp 11, National Indian War Veterans, St. Joseph, MO; died Tucson, AZ. SOURCE: *Winners of the West* 13 (Apr 1936): 3.

BENTON, Willie; Cook; D/10th Cav. Benton to post surgeon, Ft Robinson, NE, 6 Sep 1906, submits bill from dentist O. K. Ivins, Crawford, NE, and requests to be paid in accordance with Paragraph 96, Army Regulations; endorsement, post surgeon to surgeon general, 8 Oct 1906, notes that Benton was referred to Ivins by Capt. J. R. Church before surgeon arrived. SOURCE: Register of Correspondence, Post Surgeon, Ft Robinson.

BERGEON, Samuel; Private; H/10th Cav. Served in 10th Cavalry, 1898; remained in U.S. during war with Spain. SOURCE: Cashin, *Under Fire with the Tenth Cavalry*, 347.

BERHANAN, Smith; Private; M/25th Inf. Died of heart ailment in the Philippines, 10 Oct 1900. SOURCE: *ANJ* 38 (20 Oct 1900): 187.

BERKLEY, Alex B.; Private; H/9th Cav. Transferred to C/9th Cavalry and attached to Band/9th Cavalry for instruction in music. SOURCE: Order 16, 9 Cav, 26 May 1887.

Discharged, certificate of disability, Ft Robinson, NE, for secondary syphilis, 1887. SOURCE: Certificates of Disability, Ft Robinson.

BERNARD, John; I/9th Cav. Enlistment authorized. SOURCE: Letter, AGO, 8 Aug 1894.

BERNHARD, Robert; F/10th Cav. Original member of 10th Cavalry; in troop when organized, Ft Leavenworth, KS, 21 Jun 1867. SOURCE: McMiller, "Buffalo Soldiers," 73.

BERRY, A. M.; Private; D/10th Cav. Served in 10th Cavalry, 1898; remained in U.S. during war with Spain. SOURCE: Cashin, *Under Fire with the Tenth Cavalry*, 341.

BERRY, Butler; H/10th Cav. Resided at 1808 11th St., NW, Washington DC, in 1912; could not recall disability of Webb Chatmoun, who was "my bunkie friend," and now lives at 1712 G St., NW, Washington, DC. SOURCE: Affidavit, Butler, 1922, VA File C 2360629, Webb Chatmoun.

BERRY, Charles; Private; L/10th Cav. Served in 10th Cavalry, 1898; remained in U.S. during war with Spain. SOURCE: Cashin, *Under Fire with the Tenth Cavalry*, 350.

BERRY, Charles; Private; C/10th Cav. Convicted of mutiny by general court martial, Bayamo, Cuba, 12 Oct 1899, and sentenced to ten years. SOURCE: *ANJ* 37 (24 Feb 1900): 602.

BERRY, Edward; Sergeant; H/24th Inf. Born in Virginia, 1830; volunteered 1863, served with F/26th New York Colored Infantry as first sergeant until 7 Oct 1865; enlisted in regular Army at Cleveland, OH, 10 Jan 1868; served

in H/41st Infantry and H/24th Infantry; participated in Victorio campaign; quartermaster sergeant of his company for nineteen years; also post commissary sergeant and quartermaster sergeant; died Ft Grant, AZ, of Bright's disease, age 60, 23 Apr 1890. Funeral conducted by Chaplain Weaver; Musician Rounds blew taps; pallbearers commanded by Sgt. William Henson, H/24th Infantry, and included Sgts. John Johnson, H/24th Infantry, G. D. Powell, C/24th Infantry, W. Pearcall, E/24th Infantry, J. W. Wright and O. Brown, G/10th Cavalry, Pvts. B. Baker, Benjamin Webb, W. Williams, L. Varnes, A. Bailey, and W. H. Booker, H/24th Infantry. SOURCE: Cleveland *Gazette*, 26 Apr 1890.

BERRY, Edward; Private; L/10th Cav. Served in 10th Cavalry, 1898; remained in U.S. during war with Spain. SOURCE: Cashin, *Under Fire with the Tenth Cavalry*, 350.

BERRY, George; K/10th Cav. Original member of 10th Cavalry; in troop when organized, Ft Riley, KS, 1 Sep 1867. SOURCE: McMiller, "Buffalo Soldiers," 77.

BERRY, George; Sergeant; G/10th Cav. Sergeant, D/10th Cavalry; at Ft Apache, AZ, 1890, subscribed $.50 to testimonial to General Grierson. SOURCE: List of subscriptions, 23 Apr 1890, 10th Cavalry papers, MHI.

Sergeant, G/10th Cavalry; served in 10th Cavalry in Cuba, 1898. SOURCE: Cashin, *Under Fire with the Tenth Cavalry*, 344.

BERRY, George; L/24th Inf. Killed in action in the Philippines. SOURCE: Cleveland *Gazette*, 29 Dec 1906.

BERRY, Harvey; Corporal; L/10th Cav. Served in 10th Cavalry, 1898; remained in U.S. during war with Spain. SOURCE: Cashin, *Under Fire with the Tenth Cavalry*, 350.

BERRY, Henry; Private; B/9th Cav. Died of cholera in the Philippines. SOURCE: *ANJ* 39 (9 Aug 1902): 1248.

BERRY, James; Corporal; B/9th Cav. Appointed corporal, 9 Jul 1892. SOURCE: Roster, 9 Cav, 1893.

Teaching school at Ft Duchesne, UT, 20 Dec 1892–30 Apr 1893. SOURCE: Report of Schools, Ft Duchesne.

BERRY, Robert; Private; F/38th Inf. At Ft Cummings, NM, 1868. *See* **TOWNSEND**, Allen, Private, F/38th Infantry

BERRY, Thomas; Private; B/10th Cav. Served in 10th Cavalry in Cuba, 1898; wounded in action. SOURCE: Cashin, *Under Fire with the Tenth Cavalry*, 338.

BERRY, William; Private; I/10th Cav. Served in 10th Cavalry, 1898; remained in U.S. during war with Spain. SOURCE: Cashin, *Under Fire with the Tenth Cavalry*, 348.

BERRY, William H.; Private; D/24th Inf. Fined $1 for wasting two rounds of ammunition in violation of Article

16, Cabanatuan, Philippines, 16 Nov 1900; witness: 1st Sgt. M. H. Ellis, D/24th Infantry. SOURCE: Name File, 24 Inf.

In Cabanatuan, 1901. *See* **BROWN**, Philip, Private, D/24th Infantry

BERRYMAN, Eddie J.; Private; H/10th Cav. Served in 10th Cavalry, 1898; remained in U.S. during war with Spain. SOURCE: Cashin, *Under Fire with the Tenth Cavalry*, 347.

BERRYMAN, Henry; Private; D/10th Cav. Born Fayette Co., KY, to James and Caroline Berryman, Mar 1851; four brothers and sisters; lived on Fayette Co. farm of Mrs. Polley Halley with his parents, who were servants, 1870–72; served 27 Jul 1872–31 May 1877, including against Comanches, Kiowas, Cheyennes, at Washita, Elk Horn Creek, Ft Sill, Indian Territory, 1874–75; worked in coalyard, Lexington, KY, 1877–80; only marriage to Emma Christopher, born Scott Co., KY, and divorced from Mark Whitney, 1882; neither could sign name. SOURCE: VA File C 2580814, Henry Berryman.

BERTS, Willie; Private; D/24th Inf. At Cabanatuan, Philippines, 1900. *See* **LEAVELL**, William, Private, D/24th Infantry

BEST; Private; E/10th Cav. At Ft Apache, AZ, 1890, subscribed $.50 to testimonial to General Grierson. SOURCE: List of subscriptions, 23 Apr 1890, 10th Cavalry papers, MHI.

BETHEL, Elijah; Private; I/24th Inf. Enlisted Baltimore, MD, 6 Feb 1899; joined company 23 Feb 1899. SOURCE: Muster Roll, I/24 Inf, Jan–Feb 1899.

On detached service at Benicia Barracks, CA, since 8 Apr 1899. SOURCE: Muster Roll, I/24 Inf, Mar–Apr 1899.

On detached service at Tarlac, Philippines, since 2 Dec 1899. SOURCE: Muster Roll, I/24 Inf, Nov–Dec 1899.

Killed in action in the Philippines, 31 Jul 1900. *See* **SMITH**, C. H., Sergeant, I/24th Infantry

BETHEL, James; Corporal; C/9th Cav. Veteran of eleven years, death in 1877 caused by accidental discharge of his carbine in Mogollon Mountains; buried at Ft Bayard, NM. SOURCE: Leckie, *The Buffalo Soldiers*, 186-87.

BETTERS, James; Corporal; C/9th Cav. Mortally wounded in Mogollon Mountains, NM, 1876, when his carbine discharged accidentally; buried without ceremony, Ft Bayard, NM. SOURCE: Billington, *New Mexico's Buffalo Soldiers*, 53–54.

BETTIS, Benjamin; Sergeant; A/10th Cav. Trumpeter, ranked number 347 among rifle experts with 60.67 percent in 1905. SOURCE: GO 101, AGO, 31 May 1906.

Sergeant, ranked number 14 at Northern Division rifle competition, Ft Sheridan, IL, 1906. SOURCE: GO 198, AGO, 6 Dec 1906.

Commissioned second lieutenant, Camp Des Moines, IA, Oct 1917. SOURCE: Sweeney, *History of the American Negro*, 120.

Sergeant, A/10th Cavalry, when commissioned, 15 Oct 1917. SOURCE: Glass, *History of the Tenth Cavalry*, appendix M.

BETTIS, W. H.; 1st Lt; 23rd Kans Inf. Mentioned. SOURCE: Beasley, *Negro Trailblazers*, 285.

BEVERLY, William; G/10th Cav. Original member of 10th Cavalry; in troop when organized, Ft Leavenworth, KS, 5 Jul 1867. SOURCE: McMiller, "Buffalo Soldiers," 74.

BEVILL, James; Private; H/25th Inf. Wounded in action, El Caney, Cuba, 1 Jul 1898. SOURCE: Nankivell, *History of the Twenty-fifth Infantry*, 83.

BIBBY, Charles W.; Private; B/9th Cav. At Ft D. A. Russell, WY, in 1910. SOURCE: *Illustrated Review: Ninth Cavalry,* with picture.

BIDDLE, George; M/10th Cav. Original member of 10th Cavalry; in troop when organized, Ft Riley, KS, 15 Oct 1867. SOURCE: McMiller, "Buffalo Soldiers," 79.

BIGGS, David; Private; D/9th Cav. His sentence for desertion, which began 4 Feb 1876, reduced to eighteen months. SOURCE: GCMO 22, AGO, 23 Feb 1877.

BIGGS, John; Corporal; E/10th Cav. Served in 10th Cavalry in Cuba, 1898. SOURCE: Cashin, *Under Fire with the Tenth Cavalry*, 342.

BIGSTAFF, Peter; Sergeant; C/10th Cav. Private, served in 10th Cavalry, 1898; remained in U.S. during war with Spain. SOURCE: Cashin, *Under Fire with the Tenth Cavalry*, 340.

Served as Captain Boyd's horseholder during negotiations with Mexicans outside Carrizal before 1916 fight. SOURCE: Clendenen, *Blood on the Border*, 307.

BILL, I.; Private; G/9th Cav. On detached service, Ft Stanton, NM, 29 Jan–5 Feb 1881. SOURCE: Regt Returns, 9 Cav, Feb 1881.

BILL, James; Private; A/24th Inf. Died late Aug 1898. SOURCE: *ANJ* 36 (3 Sep 1898): 19.

BILL, John B.; Private; K/25th Inf. At Ft Niobrara, NE, 1904. SOURCE: Wilson, "History of Fort Niobrara."

BILLINGS, John; H/10th Cav. Original member of 10th Cavalry; in troop when organized, Ft Leavenworth, KS, 21 Jul 1867. SOURCE: McMiller, "Buffalo Soldiers," 75.

See **PRENDERGAST**, Julian, Private, H/10th Cavalry

BILLIONS, James; Corporal; C/9th Cav. Killed accidentally by Sgt. John Pearm [Prear?], C/9th Cavalry, while together on detached service from Ft Bayard, NM, Oct 1877. SOURCE: Billington, *New Mexico's Buffalo Soldiers*, 128.

BILLS, Thomas; Sergeant; 9th Cav. Commanded detachment from Ft Cummings, NM, that garrisoned Mason's Ranch, Oct 1880. SOURCE: Billington, *New Mexico's Buffalo Soldiers*, 98.

BINNER, L.; Private; H/9th Cav. On detached service, Ft Bayard, NM, 16 Jan–10 Feb 1881. SOURCE: Regt Returns, 9 Cav, Feb 1881.

BINNS, Robert; C/10th Cav. Original member of 10th Cavalry; in troop when organized, Ft Leavenworth, KS, 14 May 1867. SOURCE: McMiller, "Buffalo Soldiers," 70.

BIRCH, William A.; Hospital Corps. Well-known Indianapolis dentist, sends letter to editor from aboard U.S. Army Transport *Grant*, en route to the Philippines after training at Angel Island, CA, 21 Oct 1900. SOURCE: Indianapolis *Freeman*, 1 Dec 1900.

BIRD; Private; A/10th Cav. At Ft Apache, AZ, 1890, subscribed $.50 to testimonial to General Grierson. SOURCE: List of subscriptions, 23 Apr 1890, 10th Cavalry papers, MHI.

BIRD; Private; K/10th Cav. At Ft Apache, AZ, 1890, subscribed $.50 to testimonial to General Grierson. SOURCE: List of subscriptions, 23 Apr 1890, 10th Cavalry papers, MHI.

BIRD, Andrew; Private; F/10th Cav. Discharged without character, Feb 1877. SOURCE: ES 10 Cav, 1873–81.

BIRD, Joseph; Private; G/10th Cav. Served in 10th Cavalry in Cuba, 1898. SOURCE: Cashin, *Under Fire with the Tenth Cavalry*, 345.

BIRD, Matthew; L Corp; I/10th Cav. Lance corporal, in hands of civil authorities, Omaha, NE, 4 Feb–May 1892, and Florence, AZ, May 1892–May 1893. SOURCE: Regt Returns, 9 Cav.

Private, convicted by garrison court martial, Ft Robinson, NE, of violating Article 62, failure to clean saddle after being warned regarding same; then going to quarters of commander, I/9th Cavalry, Capt. John Guilfoyle, without permission or invitation and behaving in insubordinate, disrespectful, and unsoldierly way; sentenced to five days' confinement. SOURCE: Order 12, 17 Feb 1894, Post Orders, Ft Robinson.

BIRD, Robert; Private; A/10th Cav. Deserter from Ft Robinson, NE, Oct 1902. SOURCE: Certificate, Capt. W. H. Hay, 10th Cav, 15 Jan 1903, 10th Cavalry papers, MHI.

BIRD, Savage; Trumpeter; B/10th Cav. Private, A/9th Cavalry, discharged, expiration of service, from Ft Robinson, NE, 1 Apr 1893; will visit his people in Maryland and not reenlist. SOURCE: Ft Robinson Weekly Bulletin, 15 Apr 1893, in Court Martial Records, McKay.

Trumpeter, D/25th Infantry, arraigned for highway robbery and acquitted. SOURCE: *ANJ* 34 (19 Dec 1896): 272.

Transferred from 25th Infantry to B/10th Cavalry. SOURCE: SO 395, AGO, 17 Dec 1903.

Left halfback, B/10th Cavalry football team, Ft Robinson, 1904. SOURCE: Clement, "Athletics in the American Army," 28, with picture.

BIRD, Solomon J.; Cook; I/9th Cav. At Ft D. A. Russell, WY, in 1910; resident of Luray, VA. SOURCE: *Illustrated Review: Ninth Cavalry*, with picture.

BIRDSON, D.; Private; E/9th Cav. On detached service in the field, New Mexico, 26 Jan–1 Feb 1881. SOURCE: Regt Returns, 9 Cav, Feb 1881.

BIRDSONG, Eugene; Private; C/9th Cav. At Ft D. A. Russell, WY, in 1910; sharpshooter; resident of Conway, AR. SOURCE: *Illustrated Review: Ninth Cavalry*.

BIRGE, Henry; Private; D/24th Cav. Ranked number 116 among expert riflemen with 70.33 percent, 1904. SOURCE: GO 79, AGO, 1 June 1905.

BIRT, Henry; Private; B/10th Cav. Served in 10th Cavalry, 1898; remained in U.S. during war with Spain. SOURCE: Cashin, *Under Fire with the Tenth Cavalry*, 339.

BISHOP, Alexander; C/10th Cav. Original member of 10th Cavalry; in troop when organized, Ft Leavenworth, KS, 14 May 1867. SOURCE: McMiller, "Buffalo Soldiers," 70.

BISMUCKES, Samuel; Cook; E/9th Cav. Veteran of Indian wars, Spanish-American War, and Philippine Insurrection; at Ft D. A. Russell, WY, in 1910. SOURCE: *Illustrated Review: Ninth Cavalry*, with picture.

BISSELL, Richard H.; Private; A/24th Cav. Killed in action, Santiago, Cuba, 2 Jul 1898. SOURCE: *ANJ* 36 (11 Feb 1899): 567; SecWar, *AR 1898*, 437.

Killed in action, Cuba, 1898. SOURCE: Scipio, *Last of the Black Regulars*, 29.

BIVANS, George E.; Private; I/24th Inf. Name also spelled **BIVENS** and **BIVINS**

Enlisted in I/24 Infantry, Baltimore, MD, 18 Feb 1899. SOURCE: Muster Roll, I/24 Inf, Jan–Feb 1899.

On detached service, Three Rivers, CA, 3 May–21 June 1899; on detached service, Presidio of San Francisco, since 22 Jun 1899. SOURCE: Muster Roll, I/24 Inf, May–Jun 1899.

Rejoined company 26 Jul 1899. SOURCE: Muster Roll, I/24 Inf, Jul–Aug 1899.

Allotted $5 per month for three months to Emma Buey. SOURCE: Muster Roll, I/24 Inf, Sep–Oct 1899.

Wounded in action, 31 Jul 1900. *See* **SMITH**, C. H., Sergeant, I/24th Infantry

Forced to accompany mutineers, Houston, 1917; died of wounds inflicted by whites. SOURCE: Haynes, *A Night of Violence*, 126, 170.

BIVINS, Horace W.; Ord Sgt; U.S. Army. Born Pungoteague, Accomack Co., VA, son of Severn S. and Elizabeth Bivins, farmers; at age 15 put in charge of eight-horse farm, one mile from Keller Station, VA; first military training at Hampton Institute, 1885; enlisted Washington, DC, 7 Nov 1887; assigned to E/10th Cavalry and joined troop at Ft Grant, AZ, 19 Oct 1888; transferred to Ft Apache, AZ, Oct 1889; appointed corporal, 15 Jun 1890; an author of *Under Fire with the Tenth Cavalry*; stationed at Ft Sam Houston, TX, 1899. SOURCE: Cashin, *Under Fire with the Tenth Cavalry*, 56–58 (with picture), 344.

"A distinguished member of the Tenth U.S. Cavalry—a character worthy of the emulation of every young man of the Negro race"; entered Hampton as work student at age 17; one year later entered Wayland Seminary, Washington, DC; six months later enlisted in Army; joined 10th Cavalry, 19 Jun 1888, and immediately assigned to adjutant as clerk; many marksmanship prizes; offered $75 per week to travel with Buffalo Bill's Wild West show; returned to Hampton on furlough to attend, 3 Dec 1897, and remained until war; "a sober, sensible, industrious Negro, who, in his daily life evinces that kind of race pride that is beautifully commendable and who would have all men thoroughly convinced that the Negro can learn, if given the opportunity, all the arts and cunning performed by any race of men." SOURCE: Indianapolis *Freeman*, 25 Feb 1899.

In E/10th Cavalry, 7 Nov 1887–6 Nov 1892; in G/10th Cavalry, 7 Nov 1892–6 Nov 1897; in G/10th Cavalry and on regimental noncommissioned staff, 7 Nov 1897–10 Jul 1901; in Ordnance Department, 11 Jul 1901–15 Jul 1913; foreign service in Cuba, 22 Jun–13 Aug 1898, 7 May 1899–5 Jan 1900; in the Philippines, 14 May 1901–6 Oct 1902, 8 Jun 1906–2 Oct 1907, 3 Feb–15 Nov 1908. SOURCE: Bivins to AG, USA, 1 Jul 1913, AGO File 137634.

At Ft Apache, 1890, private, E/10th Cavalry, subscribed $.50 to testimonial to General Grierson. SOURCE: List of subscriptions, 23 Apr 1890, 10th Cavalry papers, MHI.

Sharpshooter, as private, E/10th Cavalry, Ft Apache. SOURCE: *ANJ* 28 (4 Jul 1891): 765.

Ranked number six with revolver, bronze medal, Departments of Dakota and Columbia, Ft Keogh, MT, 15–23 Aug 1892. SOURCE: Baker, Roster; GO 75, AGO, 3 Nov 1892.

Second with revolver, silver medal, Departments of Dakota and Columbia, Ft Keogh, 14–22 Aug 1893. SOURCE: Baker, Roster; GO 82, AGO, 24 Oct 1893.

First with carbine and revolver, gold medal, Departments of Dakota and Columbia, and Army, distinguished marksman, 1894. SOURCE: Baker, Roster.

Won Army gold medal in carbine competition, Ft Sheridan, IL, 16 Oct 1894, with 589 points. SOURCE: Cleveland *Gazette*, 3 Nov 1894; GO 62, AGO, 15 Nov 1894.

Highest carbine score in Army, 1894. SOURCE: *ANJ* 32 (20 Oct 1894): 119.

Ranked number 24 among carbine sharpshooters. SOURCE: GO 1, AGO, 2 Jan 1895.

Appointed corporal, G/10th Cavalry, 5 Mar 1893; sergeant, 5 Dec 1895; at Ft Assiniboine, MT, 1897. SOURCE: Baker, Roster.

Only man ever to win three marksmanship gold medals in one year. SOURCE: Indianapolis *Freeman*, 10 Jul 1897.

Ht 5'9", black complexion; distinguished marksman, 1894; served with Hotchkiss Gun battery, San Juan, Cuba, 1–3 Jul 1898; promoted from quartermaster sergeant to sergeant major, 2nd Squadron, 10th Cavalry, and on detached service at Bayamo, Cuba, with squadron, 28 Sep–14 Dec 1899; in U.S. with squadron, 2 Jan 1900; married, character excellent; $3 per month additional pay for ten years' continuous service; reenlisted 16 Nov 1900, beginning fourteenth year; ordnance sergeant, U.S. Army, 1 Jul 1901. SOURCE: Descriptive Book, 10 Cav Officers & NCOs.

Cited for conspicuous gallantry with Hotchkiss Guns, Cuba, 1 Jul 1898. SOURCE: SecWar, *AR 1898*, 335; *ANJ* 37 (24 Feb 1900): 611; GO 15, AGO, 13 Feb 1900.

Recommended for commission by William H. Heard, late minister resident and consul general to Liberia, as "a brave man and worthy in every way of promotion." SOURCE: Heard to President McKinley, 11 Sep 1899, AGO File 137634.

Appointed in colored U.S. volunteers. SOURCE: AGO File 277172, 16 Sep 1899.

Regarding commission in regular Army. SOURCE: AGO File 280745, 26 Sep 1899.

Appointed in U.S. volunteers. SOURCE: AGO File 295452, 24 Oct 1899.

On detached service at Ft Clark, TX, 31 Jan 1899–30 Jul 1900, at Ft Brown, TX, 30 Jul–Dec 1900. SOURCE: Muster Roll, Det, Regt NCS, 10 Cav, 31 Dec 1899–31 Dec 1900.

On detached service at Pena Colorado, TX, superintending disinterment of bodies of deceased soldiers, 3–7 May 1900. SOURCE: Muster Roll, Det, Regt NCS, 10 Cav, 30 Apr–30 Jun 1900.

Discharged end of term, character excellent, with $22.62 clothing allowance; reenlisted, married, 7 Nov 1900. SOURCE: Muster Roll, Det, Regt NCS, 10 Cav, 31 Oct–31 Dec 1900.

In charge of detachment, La Granga, Samar, Philippines, 2 Jul–2 Aug 1901, scouting and reconnoitering in northwest corner of island and cleaning out vicinity of insurgents and supplies; marched 655 miles on foot. SOURCE: Bivins to AG, USA, 5 Jul 1916, AGO File 137634.

Appointed ordnance sergeant. SOURCE: AGO File 387233, 6 Jul 1901.

Ordered to report from residence, 721 5th St., Oakland, CA, to Commander, Presidio of San Francisco, at end of furlough, for transportation to Ft Missoula, MT, for duty. SOURCE: SO 304, AGO, 29 Dec 1902.

Reassigned from Ft Missoula to the Philippines. SOURCE: AGO File 1112753, Mar 1906.

Expert marksman, 1908, 1909, 1910. SOURCE: AGO File 137634.

Stationed at Camp Overton, Philippines. SOURCE: AGO File 1317273, 21 Apr 1908.

On arrival at San Francisco, to be sent to Depot of Recruits and Casuals, Ft McDowell, AZ. SOURCE: AGO File 1437874, 21 Apr 1908.

Recommended to try out for Cavalry National Rifle Team by Capt. W. H. Hay, 10th Cavalry. SOURCE: AGO File 1511426, 12 Apr 1909.

Requests transfer from station at Ft McDowell to Ft Missoula or Ft Mackenzie, WY, preferably latter; mother is aged and unable to travel from Billings, MT, home; Bivins suffering from chronic constipation and would like to serve in cold climate. SOURCE: Bivins to AG, USA, 21 Feb 1909, AGO File 137634.

Transferred to Ft Mackenzie. SOURCE: SO 66, AGO, 23 Mar 1909.

Ordered from Ft Mackenzie to Ft Ontario, NY. SOURCE: SO 199, AGO, 25 Aug 1910.

Ordered to Ft Ethan Allen, VT. SOURCE: AGO File 1728451, 24 Dec 1910.

Requests transfer to Ft Mackenzie due to ill health; wife and three children in Billings since 23 Apr 1911 due to poor health in this climate, on advice of doctor. SOURCE: Bivins to AG, USA, 19 Mar 1913, AGO File 137634.

On temporary duty at Ft Mackenzie until eligible to retire. SOURCE: SO 85, AGO, 12 Apr 1913.

Retired as of 19 Jul 1913. SOURCE: TWX, CO, Ft Mackenzie to AG, USA, 23 Jul 1913, AGO File 137634.

Offers his services as captain in event of call for colored volunteers or guard; outlines his service and states that he was never tried by court martial and that his physical condition is good. SOURCE: Bivins to AG, USA, 5 Jul 1916, AGO File 137634.

Repeats 1916 offer: "Refering to letter your office last July I tender you my services to help organize a regiment in my home Virginia." SOURCE: TWX, Bivins to AG, USA, 4 Feb 1917, AGO File 137634.

Retired 1930, with thirty-two years' service; was lieutenant of volunteers, 1899; captain, Camp Dix, NJ, 1918; resides at Billings. SOURCE: *Crisis* 40 (May 1930): 168.

Mrs. Claudia Bivins raised most money for scholarship loan fund of Colored Women's Clubs of Montana, 1930; fund was named for her. SOURCE: Davis, *Lifting as They Climb*, 357.

Captain, retired, in accordance with Act of 7 May 1932; captain, Infantry, U.S. Army, 18 Sep 1918; active duty, 12 May–18 Sep 1918; died 1937. SOURCE: *Official Army Register, 1937*, 1254.

Drawing. SOURCE: Lynk, *The Black Troopers*, 31.

Biographical sketch. SOURCE: Logan and Winston, *Dictionary of American Negro Biography*, 45–46.

BIZZELLE, John; Private; I/24th Inf. Enlisted Mobile, AL, 11 Jan 1899; joined company, 12 Jan 1899. SOURCE: Muster Roll, I/24 Inf, Jan–Feb 1899.

On detached service, Benicia Barracks, CA, since 8 Apr 1899. SOURCE: Muster Roll, I/24 Inf, Mar–Apr 1899.

Allotted $5 per month to Addie Bizzelle. SOURCE: Muster Roll, I/24 Inf, Sep–Oct 1899.

BLACK, Aaron; Corporal; A/24th Inf. Killed in action, San Juan River, Cuba, 1 Jul 1898. SOURCE: SecWar, *AR 1898*, 437; Muller, *The Twenty Fourth Infantry*, 16.

BLACK, Allen; D/10th Cav. Original member of 10th Cavalry; in troop when organized, Ft Leavenworth, KS, 1 Jun 1867. SOURCE: McMiller, "Buffalo Soldiers," 71.

BLACK, Charles; H/10th Cav. Original member of 10th Cavalry; in troop when organized, Ft Leavenworth, KS, 21 Jul 1867. SOURCE: McMiller, "Buffalo Soldiers," 75.

BLACK, Edward; Private; I/25th Inf. Acquitted by summary court, San Isidro, Philippines, of violating Article 62, leaving rifle standing in door of quarters, 14 Apr 1902, no previous convictions. SOURCE: Register of Summary Court, San Isidro.

BLACK, Henry; Private; K/24th Inf. Fined $5 for violating Article 62, being drunk and absent from quarters after taps, Cabanatuan, Philippines, 12 May 1901; witnesses: Private Christon, K/24th Infantry; Sgt. William H. Brice, D/24th Infantry; Cpl. Philip Chestnut, D/24th Infantry; Pvt. Alston Morrow, D/24th Infantry. SOURCE: Charges and Specifications against Henry Black, Name File, 24 Inf.

BLACK, James; Private; H/10th Cav. Served in 10th Cavalry, 1898; remained in U.S. during war with Spain. SOURCE: Cashin, *Under Fire with the Tenth Cavalry*, 347.

BLACK, Jefferson; Sergeant; F/10th Cav. In charge of detachment patrolling Shoshoni Reservation, to prevent trespass, Jun 1906.

BLACK, Schuyler C.; Corporal; I/9th Cav. Deserted, San Francisco, CA, 9 Nov 1902. SOURCE: Regt Returns, 9 Cav, Nov 1902.

BLACK, Solomon; Musician; G/24th Inf. Born Rome, GA, 10 Aug 1854; enlisted in E/44th U.S. Colored Troops, 5 Jun 1864; saw action at Dalton, GA, 15 Aug 1864; discharged 30 Apr 1866; claimed to have been youngest soldier in Civil War; married first wife Virginia at Ft Bayard, NM; married second wife Emily Drake at Bexar Co., TX, Mar 1901; no children; died at 78. SOURCE: Clark, "A History of the Twenty-fourth," 74–76.

Born Rome, GA; age 36 in 1891; Ht 5'6", dark complexion; served in H/24th Infantry, 10 Dec 1870–10 Dec 1875, character good; in Band/24th Infantry, 10 Dec 1875–9 Dec 1880, character excellent; in D/10th Cavalry, 4 Jun 1881–3 Jan 1886, "a good mus."; joined Band/24th Infantry, 9 Feb 1886; fined $5 by garrison court martial, 1889; discharged Ft Bayard, end of term, character excellent, married, no children,

10 Jun 1891; additional pay $5 per month; retained $36; clothing $10.36; owes for subsistence stores $5.48. SOURCE: Descriptive Book, 24 Inf NCS & Band.

Retires as musician, G/24th Infantry, Ft Douglas, UT. SOURCE: *ANJ* 34 (1 May 1897), 645.

BLACK, William; H/10th Cav. Original member of 10th Cavalry; in troop when organized, Ft Leavenworth, KS, 21 Jul 1867. SOURCE: McMiller, "Buffalo Soldiers," 75.

BLACKBURN; D/10th Cav. Original member of 10th Cavalry; in troop when organized, Ft Leavenworth, KS, 1 Jun 1867. SOURCE: McMiller, "Buffalo Soldiers," 71.

BLACKBURN, Charles; Saddler; C/9th Cav. Deposited $50 with paymaster, Ft Robinson, NE, 1885–86; discharged, end of term, Ft Robinson, 8 Aug 1886.

BLACKBURN, George W.; Private; K/9th Cav. On special duty as assistant post librarian, Fort Robinson, NE. SOURCE: Order 30, 16 May 1895, Post Orders, Ft Robinson.

Relieved from special duty as assistant post librarian, Fort Robinson. SOURCE: Order 67, 24 Sep 1895, Post Orders, Ft Robinson.

On special duty as assistant post librarian, Fort Robinson. SOURCE: Order 74, 9 Oct 1895, Post Orders, Ft Robinson.

BLACKBURN, John; 2nd Lt; 49th Inf. Born Xenia, OH, age 22 in 1899; occupation student; enlisted Chicago, IL, for A/49th Infantry, 2 Oct 1899, single. SOURCE: Descriptive Book, 49 Inf NCS.

Mentioned. SOURCE: *ANJ* 37 (14 Jul 1900): 1087; *ANJ* 38 (15 Dec 1900): 371.

In battalion of Indiana Volunteers, 7 Jul 1898–20 Jan 1899; regimental commissary sergeant and sergeant major, 49th Infantry, 3 Oct 1899–Jun 1900; appointed second lieutenant from regimental sergeant major, 15 Jun 1900; commanded detachment scouting Ranches Managas, Philippines, Dec 1900; commanded detachment of twenty men of 16th Infantry, 10–18 Mar 1900. SOURCE: Descriptive Book, I/49 Inf.

One of twenty-three officers of 49th Infantry recommended for regular Army commissions. SOURCE: CG, DivPI, to AG, USA, 8 Feb 1901, AGO File 355163.

BLACKBURN, Joseph A.; Sergeant; L/10th Cav. Born Fairfax Co., VA; enlisted Washington, DC, age 21, farmer, Ht 5'5", yellow complexion, 10 Sep 1867; served until 11 Sep 1877; filed pension request from Lewisville, Denton Co., TX, based on wound in right arm, at Wichita Agency, Indian Territory, 22 Aug 1874, witnessed by Lt. Charles R. Ward, few feet away; married Lizzie A. Blackburn, Jacksboro, TX, 10 Jan 1875; daughter Grace Ella born 5 Jul 1875 and married Frazier; daughter Helen S. born 30 Sep 1877 and died 11 Apr 1878; pension $2 per month, 20 Apr 1883; $50 per month, 4 Apr 1927; lived at 915 Magnolia, Ft Worth, TX, 1899–1917; died Marlin, TX, 18 May 1934,

buried Ft Worth. SOURCE: VA File SC 258952, Joseph A. Blackburn.

Original member of 10th Cavalry; in troop when organized, Ft Riley, KS, 21 Sep 1867. SOURCE: McMiller, "Buffalo Soldiers," 78.

Was first sergeant at Ft Sill, Indian Territory, 1871; lived in Ft Worth, 1892. *See* **FORD**, George W., Quartermaster Sergeant, 10th Cavalry

Mentioned as Indian war survivor. SOURCE: *Winners of the West* 3 (Jun 1926): 7.

See **ANDERSON**, Henry, Private, L/10th Cavalry

BLACKBURN, Walter; Band/10th Cav. Worked as houseboy for Colonel Grierson, Ft Concho, TX, 1877. SOURCE: Miles, "Fort Concho in 1877," 31.

BLACKBURNE, Leonard R.; Private; B/10th Cav. Served in 10th Cavalry in Cuba, 1898. SOURCE: Cashin, *Under Fire with the Tenth Cavalry*, 338.

BLACKMAN, Andrew M.; Private; E/24th Inf. In the Philippines, 1906. *See* **HARRIS**, William C., Sergeant, E/24th Infantry

BLACKSTON, J.; Private; B/9th Cav. Returned to duty, Dec 1889.

BLACKSTONE, Charley; Private; G/9th Cav. With Troutman patrol, Jan 1875; killed Pvt. John Fredericks, Ft Stockton, TX, in dispute over borrowed attorney's fees, Apr 1876. SOURCE: Leckie, *The Buffalo Soldiers*, 108–9.

BLACKWELL; Private; B/10th Cav. At Ft Apache, AZ, 1890, subscribed $.50 to testimonial to General Grierson. SOURCE: List of subscriptions, 23 Apr 1890, 10th Cavalry papers, MHI.

BLAINE, George; Private; M/9th Cav. At Ft D. A. Russell, WY, in 1910; resident of Georgetown, SC. SOURCE: *Illustrated Review: Ninth Cavalry.*

BLAIR, Jacob; Private; F/9th Cav. Fined $2.50 for absence without leave and disturbance in barracks, same day, by garrison court martial, Ft Robinson, NE, 1887. SOURCE: Order 238, 2 Dec 1887, Post Orders, Fort Robinson.

BLAKE, Henry E.; Private; G/9th Cav. Veteran of Indian wars, Spanish-American War, and Philippine Insurrection; at Ft D. A. Russell, WY, in 1910; resident of Charlotte. SOURCE: *Illustrated Review: Ninth Cavalry,* with picture.

BLAKE, Isaac; Private; K/9th Cav. Born Philadelphia, PA, parents unknown, 1 Aug 1855; enlisted Baltimore, MD, 6 Jan 1880, single, occupation hostler, Ht 5'6", mulatto complexion; joined regiment Feb 1880; in the field, South Dakota, Nov 1890–Feb 1891; until 1927 lived in Omaha, NE; worked as laborer; resided at 1013 Capitol Ave., Omaha, in 1925; resided at 2041 Charles St., Omaha, in 1926; resided at

2204 54th St., Leavenworth, KS, in 1934, with $50 per month pension; died of cardiac asthma in Soldiers Home, Leavenworth, 2 Mar 1934. SOURCE: VA File XC 876498, Isaac Blake.

As private, I/9th Cavalry, persuaded other enlisted men to sign petition to transfer Capt. John Guilfoyle, commander, I/9th Cavalry. SOURCE: CO, Ft Robinson, NE, to AAG, DP, 26 Jun 1891, LS, Ft Robinson.

Transferred to K/9th Cavalry. SOURCE: SO 44, AGO, 23 Feb 1892.

Serving six-month sentence, Ft Robinson, as of 29 Feb 1892.

Discharged without character. SOURCE: SO 239, AGO, 11 Oct 1892.

Request for pension rejected in 1925; pension established by Private Law 169 at $20 per month, 17 Jul 1929. SOURCE: VA File 876498, Isaac Blake.

Passage of private law mentioned. SOURCE: *Winners of the West* 9 (Apr 1926): 2.

BLAKE, William H.; Sergeant; Band/9th Cav. Private, on furlough between enlistments in Baltimore, MD, and apparently followed by fourteen-year-old local white tramp; Blake could not have abducted and transported her two thousand miles by railroad; she could have obtained help anywhere. SOURCE: CO, Ft Robinson, NE, to AG, USA, 26 June 1897, LS, Ft Robinson.

At Ft D. A. Russell, WY, in 1910; resident of Chestertown, MD. SOURCE: *Illustrated Review: Ninth Cavalry*, with picture.

BLAKEMAN, John; Private; E/10th Cav. Mentioned in 1873 as enlisting in Aug 1872. SOURCE: ES, 10 Cav, 1873–81.

BLAKEMAN, Robert; 1st Lt; K/49th Inf. Born Haskinsville, Green Co., KY, 10 Dec 1870; graduated from Springfield, IL, high school, 1890; commissioned in 8th Illinois Volunteer Infantry. SOURCE: *ANJ* 37 (4 Nov 1899): 219.

Private, first sergeant, H/8th Illinois, 21 Jul 1898–3 Apr 1899; first lieutenant, 49th Infantry, 9 Sep 1899; commanded K Company, 26 Mar–23 Jul, 31 Aug–14 Sep 1900; died of hepatitis, 3 Oct 1900, and buried at Aparri, Philippines. SOURCE: Descriptive Book, K/49 Inf.

BLAKEMORE, John; Private; M/9th Cav. At Ft D. A. Russell, WY, in 1910. SOURCE: *Illustrated Review: Ninth Cavalry*.

BLAKENY, William F.; K/25th Inf. Letter from Castillejos, Philippines, 24 Jan 1902. SOURCE: Gatewood, *"Smoked Yankees"*, 311.

Letter, Malabon, Rizal, Philippines, notes great record of 25th Infantry, states that large number of men went intending to stay there. SOURCE: Indianapolis *Freeman*, 2 Aug 1902.

BLAKEY, Gabriel; Private; A/9th Cav. At Ft D. A. Russell, WY, in 1910; sharpshooter. SOURCE: *Illustrated Review: Ninth Cavalry,* with picture.

BLAND, Robert C.; Trumpeter; 9th Cav. At Ft Niobrara, NE, 1889. *See* **CARTER**, William H., Trumpeter, A/9th Cavalry

BLAND, William; Corporal; C/10th Cav. Original member of 10th Cavalry; in troop when organized, Ft Leavenworth, KS, 14 May 1867. SOURCE: McMiller, "Buffalo Soldiers," 70.

Mentioned 19 Jul 1867. SOURCE: Adj, 10 Cav, to CO, C/10, 19 Jul 1867, LS, 10 Cav, 1866–67.

Mentioned, as corporal, C/10th Cavalry, Oct 1870. SOURCE: ES, 10 Cav, 1866–71.

BLANEY, William; Corporal; H/24th Inf. Enlisted, Pittsburgh, PA, 23 May 1893; discharged as corporal, H/24th Infantry, Camp Tampa, FL, end of enlistment, character excellent, single, 22 May 1898; $57.73 retained pay and $100 deposits due soldier; $4.45 for clothing due government. SOURCE: Muster Roll, H/24 Inf, May–Jun 1898.

BLANEY, William F.; QM Sgt; B/25th Inf. Enlisted D/10th Cavalry, 31 Oct 1888; transferred to F/24th Infantry; reenlisted in F/24th Infantry, 8 Nov 1897; then assigned to L/24th Infantry and noncommissioned staff; discharged 18 Jun 1899; appointed second lieutenant, 10th U.S. Volunteer Infantry, 30 Jul 1898–8 Mar 1899; second lieutenant, F/49th Infantry, 9 Sep 1899; first lieutenant, 7 Nov 1899; transferred to B/49th Infantry, 13 Nov 1899; engagements in the Philippines, at Las Pinas, 24–26 Sep 1900, Dolores, 26 Nov 1900, San Ignacio and Santa Nino, 18 Dec 1900; on detached service at Manila, in charge of prisoners, 11–20 Jan 1901. SOURCE: Descriptive Books, B/49 Inf and F/49 Inf.

Letter from Ft Huachuca, AZ, 13 Sep 1895, sends $1.50 for one-year subscription and requests picture of battle at Ft Wagner, NC, as premium. SOURCE: Richmond *Planet*, 28 Sep 1895.

Served as second lieutenant of B/10th U.S. Volunteer Infantry, Camp Haskell, GA, with Capt. Crandall Mackay and 1st Lt. Edward L. Baker. SOURCE: Regt Returns, 10 Inf USV.

Commissioned in 49th Infantry as of 9 Sep 1899. SOURCE: *ANJ* 37 (4 Nov 1899): 228.

Promoted to first lieutenant. SOURCE: *ANJ* 37 (23 Dec 1899): 392.

Commended by regimental commander for leadership against insurgents, Zapote Bridge, Philippines, 24 Sep 1900. SOURCE: GO 20, 49 Inf, 11 Oct 1900.

Mentioned as first lieutenant, B/49th Infantry. SOURCE: Beasley, *Negro Trailblazers*, 284.

One of twenty-three officers of 49th Infantry recommended for commissions in the regular Army. SOURCE: CG, Division of the Philippines, to AG, USA, 8 Feb 1901, AGO File 355163.

Acquitted by general court martial of violating Article 62. SOURCE: GO 22, Department of Northern Luzon, 31 May 1901.

Quartermaster sergeant, B/25th Infantry, and crack shot, on leave during Brownsville incident, 1906. SOURCE: Weaver, *The Brownsville Raid*, 177.

Stationed in Mindanao, Philippines, 1908. SOURCE: Nankivell, *History of the Twenty-fifth Infantry*, 130.

Commissioned first lieutenant, U.S. Army, at Des Moines, IA, Oct 1917. SOURCE: Sweeney, *History of the American Negro*, 120.

BLASTON, Francis M.; E/10th Cav. Original member of 10th Cavalry; in troop when organized, Ft Leavenworth, KS, 15 Jun 1867. SOURCE: McMiller, "Buffalo Soldiers," 72.

BLEADSAW, James; Private; E/25th Inf. Convicted of assault with rifle, Santa Cruz, Philippines, 11 Oct 1901, and sentenced to six months' confinement and forfeiture of pay.

BLEADSOE, Robert, Sergeant; C/9th Cav. Veteran of Spanish-American War and Philippine Insurrection; expert rifleman at Ft D. A. Russell, WY, in 1910. SOURCE: *Illustrated Review: Ninth Cavalry,* with picture.

BLEDSOE, Wade; Private; D/10th Cav. Served in 10th Cavalry in Cuba, 1898. SOURCE: Cashin, *Under Fire with the Tenth Cavalry*, 341.

Wounded in thigh by Spanish sniper, Santiago, Cuba. SOURCE: SecWar, *AR 1898*, 710.

Wounded by bullet that killed Private Stovall, passing through latter's heart before hitting Bledsoe. SOURCE: Bigelow, *Reminiscences of Santiago*, 114.

BLENKINSHIP, William; Corporal; C/10th Cav. Drowned, Manzanillo, Cuba, 11 Oct 1900. SOURCE: *ANJ* 38 (24 Nov 1900): 307.

BLEW, Joseph; Sergeant; G/9th Cav. Born Pulaski Co., KY, 31 Jan 1858; lived with parents Dave and Celia, brother George, sisters Malinda and Viola, on farm ten miles south of Summerset, Pulaski Co., until 1870; tattoo of girl on right arm; enlisted Louisville, KY, Ht 5'11", Aug 1873; in G/9th Cavalry, Aug 1873–Oct 1889; in A/9th Cavalry, Nov 1889–92; sergeant, 1 Oct 1876; corporal, 26 Mar 1880; sergeant, 17 Sep 1881; private, 16 Sep 1888; corporal, 10 Feb 1889; sergeant, 1 Nov 1891; stationed at Ft Sill, Indian Territory, Oct 1884–Aug 1885, at Ft Niobrara, NE, Aug 1885-Nov 1890, on Sioux campaign, Nov 1890–Mar 1891; and Ft Robinson, NE, Mar 1891 until discharge, Camp Bettens, WY, Jun 1892; police officer, Omaha, NE, from discharge to death. Married Dora Green (nee Hammett) of Macon Co., MO, 12 Jan 1896, with service performed by Rev. J. W. Braxton, African Methodist Episcopal Church, Omaha. SOURCE: VA File XC 970422, Joseph Blew.

Sergeant, G/9th Cavalry; one of six enlisted men of G/9th Cavalry to testify against Lt. John Conline at his 1877 court martial for misconduct, including drunkenness, sexual misconduct, misappropriation of funds belonging to men of his troop, Ft Garland, CO. SOURCE: Billington, *New Mexico's Buffalo Soldiers*, 121–23.

Saw Pvt. James F. Jackson, "always a sober quiet peaceable soldier," at Ft Niobrara shortly before Jackson was shot by Moseby of G/9th Cavalry, "a very dangerous man," 12 May 1886. SOURCE: Affidavit, Blew, Omaha, 1899, VA File C 2555351, James F. Jackson.

Resided at 6514 21st St., Omaha, with pension of $10 per month in 1896, $17 per month in 1898, $20 per month in 1917. SOURCE: VA File XC 970422, Joseph Blew.

Mentioned as surviving veteran of Indian wars. SOURCE: *Winners of the West* 3 (Jun 1926): 7.

Wife was loyal follower of Father Divine, resided with daughter Mrs. Alberta Broyles Jackson, who owned "a large old home in the colored section of Oakland," CA, at 1022 Filbert, until 1948; resided at 2328 23rd St., Oakland, until her death, 31 Jan 1958; daughter worked in cafeteria, Montgomery Ward store, Oakland; pension $12 per month in 1923, $30 per month in 1938, $40 per month in 1944, $48 per month in 1948. SOURCE: VA File XC 970422, Joseph Blew.

See **JOHNSON**, Robert, Sergeant, G/9th Cavalry; **SHEAFF**, Joseph E., Corporal, G/9th Cavalry; **TUCKER**, George C., G/9th Cavalry

BLOODGOOD; Sergeant; 10th Cav. Fatally wounded Lieutenant Adair fell into Bloodgood's arms at Carrizal, Mexico, 21 Jun 1916. SOURCE: Wharfield, *10th Cavalry and Border Fights*, 36.

BLOOM; Private; A/10th Cav. At Ft Apache, AZ, 1890, subscribed $.50 to testimonial to General Grierson. SOURCE: List of subscriptions, 23 Apr 1890, 10th Cavalry papers, MHI.

BLUE, Daniel; Corporal; A/10th Cav. Private, A/10th Cavalry; served in 10th Cavalry in Cuba, 1898. SOURCE: Cashin, *Under Fire with the Tenth Cavalry*, 354.

Sergeant, ordered to station. SOURCE: SO 44, AGO, 23 Feb 1904.

Private, promoted to corporal, Ft Ethan Allen, VT. SOURCE: SO 88, 10 Cav, 23 Nov 1909.

BLUE, John; Sergeant; F/9th Cav. Died of dysentery at First Reserve Hospital, Manila, 12 Aug 1901. SOURCE: *ANJ* 39 (12 Oct 1901): 140.

BLUE, Joseph; Sergeant; I/9th Cav. At Ft Niobrara, NE, 1886.

BLUFORD, Clarence L.; Private; G/10th Cav. Served in 10th Cavalry in Cuba, 1898. SOURCE: Cashin, *Under Fire with the Tenth Cavalry*, 345.

BLUFORD, Emmitt L.; Private; G/10th Cav. Served in 10th Cavalry in Cuba, 1898. SOURCE: Cashin, *Under Fire with the Tenth Cavalry*, 345.

BLUFORD, J.; Corporal; H/9th Cav. Sharpshooter with carbine, 75.57 percent, second award, 1892. SOURCE: GO 1, AGO, 3 Jan 1893.

BLUNT, Hamilton H.; Captain; K/49th Inf. First lieutenant, 9th U.S. Volunteer Infantry, 25 Jul 1898–25 May 1899; first lieutenant, B/49th Infantry, 28 Oct 1899; captain, K/49th Infantry, 13 Nov 1899. SOURCE: Descriptive Book, B/49 Inf.

Only colored officer to command a military post, Cristo, Cuba, as commander of E and H Companies, 9th U.S. Volunteer Infantry; described as "cool, suave, courageous and discreet." SOURCE: Coston, *The Spanish-American War Volunteer*, 57.

Resident of Louisiana; only colored delegate at recent meeting of Spanish-American War Veterans, Washington, DC; elected to council alongside Col. William Jennings Bryan. SOURCE: Indianapolis *Freeman*, 7 Oct 1899.

Beaten and arrested because he refused to show ticket at Memphis depot gates; carried to lock-up and fined $10; his attorney telegraphed President McKinley and got no answer. SOURCE: Richmond *Planet*, 25 Nov 1899.

Tried to keep Daniel Jackson from testifying in the case of Andrew Jackson of San Francisco; admonished by Judge Conlan: "This man needs to be taught a lesson in regard to the respect he owes to the civil authorities." SOURCE: San Francisco *Chronicle*, 6 Dec 1899.

Promoted to captain vice McNabb, deceased. SOURCE: *ANJ* 37 (23 Dec 1899): 392.

Addressed 49th Infantry troops aboard transport en route to the Philippines as part of variety show. SOURCE: Fletcher, *The Black Soldier*, 291.

Relieved of command, 7 Mar 1900; restored to duty, 9 Mar 1900; relieved, 26 Mar 1900; arrested, 2 Jun 1900; sentenced to suspension from rank and command and fined $100, 5 Jul 1900; dismissed from service, 2 Jan 1901. SOURCE: Descriptive Book, K/49 Inf.

Convicted of eleven violations of Article 61, conduct unbecoming an officer and gentleman, mainly involving abusive treatment of his men: Privates William Ammons, Benjamin Hailey, Thomas Jackson, Robert Kidd, David Knight, General Light, Zack Odom, and Frank Taylor, all of K/49th Infantry; dismissed from service. SOURCE: GO 139, AGO, 13 Dec 1900.

Story regarding his court martial, with biographical data and picture. SOURCE: Washington *Colored American*, 16 Nov 1901.

BOADLEY, Levi; D/10th Cav. Original member of 10th Cavalry; in troop when organized, Ft Leavenworth, KS, 1 Jun 1867. SOURCE: McMiller, "Buffalo Soldiers," 71.

BOARD, Homer; Private; B/9th Cav. At Ft D. A. Russell, WY, in 1910. SOURCE: *Illustrated Review: Ninth Cavalry*, with picture.

BOARD, Walter W.; Private; F/10th Cav. Served in 10th Cavalry in Cuba, 1898; narrates Spanish-American War experiences. SOURCE: Cashin, *Under Fire with the Tenth Cavalry*, 343, 252–57.

Drowned in the Philippines, 13 May 1901; body not recovered. SOURCE: *ANJ* 38 (25 May 1901): 948.

Body recovered. SOURCE: TWX, MG MacArthur, Manila, to AG, USA, 3 Jun 1901.

BOARMAN, Lewis; Private; D/10th Cav. Served in 10th Cavalry in Cuba, 1898. SOURCE: Cashin, *Under Fire with the Tenth Cavalry*, 341.

Sent by First Sergeant Givens to look after wounded Capt. John Bigelow, Santiago, Cuba; on return to unit, had three ribs broken when roof of bombproof fell on him; requested discharge for disability. SOURCE: Bigelow, *Reminiscences of Santiago*, 135, 139, 163.

BOCK, Henry; K/9th Cav. Served in 1876–81; died in Omaha, NE. SOURCE: *Winners of the West* 12 (May 1935): 3.

BOGGS, Carter; Private; H/24th Inf. Private, C/24th Infantry; on extra duty as janitor, post hall. SOURCE: Order 115, Ft Huachuca, AZ, 4 Aug 1893, Name File, 24 Inf.

Enlisted Ft Huachuca, AZ, 17 Sep 1896; seventeen years' continuous service in 1898. SOURCE: Muster Roll, H/24 Inf, May–Jun 1898.

Died at field hospital, Siboney, Cuba, of disease contracted in line of duty, 3 Aug 1898; due government for clothing, overdrawn $14.62. SOURCE: Muster Roll, H/24 Inf, Jul–Aug 1898.

BOGGS, Jesse; Recruit; Colored Detachment/Mounted Service. At Jefferson Barracks, MO, 1889. *See* **HUNTER**, Ellis, Recruit, Colored Detachment/Mounted Service

BOHON, Robert O.; Private; K/9th Cav. At Ft D. A. Russell, WY, in 1910; sharpshooter; resident of Hannibal, MO. SOURCE: *Illustrated Review: Ninth Cavalry*, with picture.

BOLAND; Private; A/10th Cav. At Ft Apache, AZ, 1890, subscribed $.50 to testimonial to General Grierson. SOURCE: List of subscriptions, 23 Apr 1890, 10th Cavalry papers, MHI.

BOLAND, John; Wagoner; I/10th Cav. Cited for "coolness in action," Cuba, 24 Jun 1898. SOURCE: SecWar, *AR 1898*, 349.

Distinguished service at Las Guasimas, Cuba, mentioned. SOURCE: Steward, *The Colored Regulars*, 137.

Citation for distinguished service noted. SOURCE: *ANJ* 37 (24 Feb 1900): 611.

Heroism mentioned. SOURCE: Cashin, *Under Fire with the Tenth Cavalry*, 185, 347.

Commended for conspicuous courage while wagoner, I/10th Cavalry, in exposing himself to heavy fire and killing Spaniard standing on stone entrenchments and directing fire, thus materially assisting in causing end of Spanish fire at Las Guasimas, 24 Jun 1898. SOURCE: GO 15, AGO, 13 Feb 1900.

BOLDEN; Private; E/10th Cav. At Ft Apache, AZ, 1890, subscribed $.50 to testimonial to General Grierson. SOURCE: List of subscriptions, 23 Apr 1890, 10th Cavalry papers, MHI.

BOLDEN, Douglas T.; Private; I/24th Inf. Served in Houston, 1917; threatened with jail term by military investigators after riot; failed to convince court martial he remained in camp during riot. SOURCE: Haynes, *A Night of Violence*, 247, 269.

BOLDEN, Henry; Private; K/10th Cav. Served in 10th Cavalry, 1898; remained in U.S. during war with Spain. SOURCE: Cashin, *Under Fire with the Tenth Cavalry*, 349.

BOLDEN, I. G.; Private; B/10th Cav. Dishonorable discharge and two months in prison, Ft Robinson, NE, 2 Jul–1 Sep 1902. SOURCE: SO 122, DeptMo.
    Released from sentence, 23 Aug 1902.

BOLES, Lewis; Private; K/9th Cav. Deserted "while in confinement," 27 Aug 1902. SOURCE: Regt Returns, 9 Cav, Sep 1902.

BOLIN, Robert; Private; D/9th Cav. Convicted by general court martial, Jefferson Barracks, MO, of desertion, 12 Feb 1882–23 Feb 1884; sentenced to three years' confinement. SOURCE: GCMO 32, AGO, 2 Aug 1884.

BOLLEN, William H.; K/10th Cav. Original member of 10th Cavalry; in troop when organized, Ft Riley, KS, 1 Sep 1867. SOURCE: McMiller, "Buffalo Soldiers," 77.

BOLLER, Solomon; Blacksmith; H/10th Cav. Honorable mention for service in capture of Mangas and his band, Rio Bonito, AZ, 18 Oct 1886. SOURCE: Baker, Roster.

BOLLING, William; Corporal; F/10th Cav. Served in 10th Cavalry in Cuba, 1898. SOURCE: Cashin, *Under Fire with the Tenth Cavalry*, 343.

BOLT; Private; M/9th Cav. Wounded in action, 17 Jan 1880. *See* **STOUT**, Albert, Ordnance Sergeant, U.S. Army

BOMEN, Austin; A/10th Cav. Original member of 10th Cavalry; in troop when organized, Ft Leavenworth, KS, 18 Feb 1867. SOURCE: McMiller, "Buffalo Soldiers," 68.

BOMEN, Samuel; A/10th Cav. Original member of 10th Cavalry; in troop when organized, Ft Leavenworth, KS, 18 Feb 1867. SOURCE: McMiller, "Buffalo Soldiers," 68.

BONAPARTE, Frank W.; Private 1st Cl; 24th Inf. Usually partner of Cpl. Charles Baltimore on provost guard. SOURCE: Haynes, *A Night of Violence*, 110.

BOND, Howard G.; Private; B/9th Cav. At Ft D. A. Russell, WY, in 1910. SOURCE: *Illustrated Review: Ninth Cavalry,* with picture.

BOND, Howard H.; Private; L/10th Cav. Found crushed by Chicago & Northwestern train; buried at Ft Robinson, NE, 5 Jul 1906. SOURCE: List of Interments, Ft Robinson.

BOND, James Oliver; C/10th Cav. Original member of 10th Cavalry; in troop when organized, Ft Leavenworth, KS, 14 May 1867. SOURCE: McMiller, "Buffalo Soldiers," 70.

BOND, John; Private; A/10th Cav. Died on Staked Plains expedition, Aug 1877. SOURCE: Leckie, *The Buffalo Soldiers*, 162.

BOND, Rhoden; Sup Sgt; I/24th Inf. Private, K/25th Infantry, Ft Niobrara, NE, 1904. SOURCE: Wilson, "History of Fort Niobrara."
    Ranked number 27 in Division of the Philippines rifle competition, Ft William McKinley, Rizal, Philippines, 1907. SOURCE: GO 213, AGO, 19 Oct 1907.
    Lance corporal, ranked twenty-sixth best marksman, bronze medal, Division of the Philippines, 1908. SOURCE: Muller, *The Twenty Fourth Infantry*, 48.
    Corporal, C/24th Infantry, second among eighty-seven competitors to QM Sgt. Emmett Hawkins, K/24th Infantry, in rifle competition, Departments of the East and Gulf, Ft Niagara, NY. SOURCE: Cleveland *Gazette*, 14 Aug 1909.
    Supply sergeant, I/24th Infantry, served in Houston, 1917; old buddy of Sgt. Vida Henry, at Houston, 1917. SOURCE: Haynes, *A Night of Violence*, 111, 127.

BONDLEY, Richard; Sergeant; 10th Cav. Appointed first lieutenant, 8th Illinois Infantry, 1915.

BONDS, George; Private; 10th Cav. At Ft Bayard, NM, Jul 1888; selected for Department of Arizona rifle competition, Ft Wingate, NM. SOURCE: Billington, *New Mexico's Buffalo Soldiers*, 154.

BONE, Walter W.; Private; I/9th Cav. Discharged on surgeon's certificate, 25 May 1896.

BONEPART, Clarence; Private; K/25th Inf. Drowned, Rio Grande, Philippines, 27 Oct 1899. SOURCE: *ANJ* 37 (9 Dec 1899): 354.

BONN, William D.; Private; I/24th Inf. Hanged 24 Sep 1918 for part in Houston riot. SOURCE: Cleveland *Gazette*, 28 Sep 1918.

BONNER, Tillman; Private; K/10th Cav. Served in 10th Cavalry, 1898; remained in U.S. during war with Spain. SOURCE: Cashin, *Under Fire with the Tenth Cavalry*, 349.

BONNSELOR, Pearl; Private; A/24th Inf. Wounded in leg at San Juan River, Cuba, 1 Jul 1898. SOURCE: SecWar, *AR 1898*, 437.
    See **BOUNCLER**, Pearl, Private, A/24th Infantry

BOODSON, Frank; H/10th Cav. Original member of 10th Cavalry; in troop when organized, Ft Leavenworth, KS, 21 Jul 1867. SOURCE: McMiller, "Buffalo Soldiers," 75.

BOOKER, A. M.; 2nd Lt; 23rd Kans Inf. Mentioned. SOURCE: Beasley, *Negro Trailblazers*, 285.

BOOKER, Andrew J.; Sergeant; K/25th Inf. In the Philippines; recovered from "slight tropical ailment." SOURCE: Richmond *Planet*, 16 Dec 1899.
Guest at wedding of Pvt. Willie Redding, K/25th Infantry, 15 Apr 1900. SOURCE: Richmond *Planet*, 16 Jun 1900.
At Ft Niobrara, NE, 1904. SOURCE: Wilson, "History of Fort Niobrara."

BOOKER, Edward; Cook; I/24th Inf. Enlisted Louisville, KY, 7 Feb 1899; joined company, 11 Feb 1899; appointed cook, 7 April 1899. SOURCE: Muster Rolls, I/24 Inf, Jan–Feb and Mar–Apr 1899.

BOOKER, Fred; Corporal; B/9th Cav. Died of dysentery, Nueva Caceres, Luzon, Philippines, 15 Aug 1901. SOURCE: *ANJ* 39 (12 Oct 1901): 140.

BOOKER, James; Private; 38th Inf. Jailed for six months, Ft Cummings, NM, 1869. SOURCE: Billington, *New Mexico's Buffalo Soldiers*, 37.

BOOKER, James; Private; K/24th Inf. Died of malaria in the Philippines, 12 Dec 1899. SOURCE: *ANJ* 37 (30 Dec 1899): 412.

BOOKER, James; H/25th Inf. Letter from Masinloc, Zambales, Philippines, 22 Sep 1900. SOURCE: Richmond *Planet*, 18 Sep 1900.
Letter from Masinloc, 22 Dec 1900. SOURCE: Gatewood, *"Smoked Yankees"*, 284.

BOOKER, James F.; 10th Cav. His former wife (separated) Venia, age 59 in 1926, resided at 1518 South Street, Los Angeles, worked as cook, since 1920; at Ft Custer, MT, she knew Louisa Allsup, wife of Sgt. Thomas Allsup, who worked for Colonel Perry; saw her again at Huntsville, AL, 1898, took train to Texas together, Allsup to Ft Clark and Booker to Ft Sam Houston. SOURCE: VA File XC 2659797, Thomas H. Allsup.

BOOKER, James W.; Sqdn Sgt Maj; 10th Cav. Commissioned captain, Camp Des Moines, IA, 15 Oct 1917. SOURCE: Glass, *History of the Tenth Cavalry*, appendix M.

BOOKER, John; Private; B/9th Cav. At Ft D. A. Russell, WY, in 1910. SOURCE: *Illustrated Review: Ninth Cavalry,* with picture.

BOOKER, John D.; Private; K/24th Inf. Wounded in the head near Payug, Philippines, 24 Feb 1900. SOURCE: Richmond *Planet*, 14 Apr 1900.

BOOKER, O. H.; Private; A/9th Cav. On special duty at post canteen, Ft Robinson, NE. SOURCE: Order 74, 10 Apr 1891, Post Orders, Ft Robinson.

BOOKER, Powhattan E.; Private; 9th Cav. At Ft Niobrara, NE, 1889. *See* CARTER, William H., Trumpeter, A/9th Cavalry

BOOKER, Robert; Musician; H/24th Inf. Enlisted Chicago, IL, 24 Jan 1896; eighteen years' continuous service; died of disease contracted in line of duty, in field hospital, Siboney, Cuba, 23 Aug 1898; $1.70 retained pay and $11.59 for clothing due him. SOURCE: Muster Roll, H/24 Inf, Jul–Aug 1898.
Died in Cuba, 24 Aug 1898. SOURCE: *ANJ* 36 (11 Feb 1899): 567.

BOOKER, William; Private; I/24th Inf. Enlisted Cleveland, OH, 20 Feb 1899. SOURCE: Muster Roll, I/24 Inf, Jan–Feb 1899.

BOOKER, William H.; Sergeant; H/24th Inf. Private, H/24th Infantry, Ft Grant, AZ, 1890. *See* BERRY, Edward, Sergeant, H/24th Infantry
At Ft Huachuca, AZ, 1893. SOURCE: Name File, 24 Inf.
Ranked number 425 among rifle experts with 69.00 percent, 1905. SOURCE: GO 101, AGO, 31 May 1906.

BOOKES, Albert; D/10th Cav. Original member of 10th Cavalry; in troop when organized, Ft Leavenworth, KS, 1 Jun 1867. SOURCE: McMiller, "Buffalo Soldiers," 71.

BOOKRUM, Edward; Sergeant; E/24th Inf. First sergeant, G/25th Infantry, San Antonio, TX, 1878; best marksman in company and tied for sixth in regiment. SOURCE: Scrapbook, 25 Inf, I, 145.
Promoted from private to corporal, E/24th Infantry, Ft Bayard, NM, May 1891. SOURCE: Cleveland *Gazette*, 9 May 1891.
Retires as sergeant, E/24th Infantry, from Ft Douglas, UT. SOURCE: *ANJ* 35 (11 Sep 1897): 23.

BOOKS, Robert; G/10th Cav. Original member of 10th Cavalry; in troop when organized, Ft Leavenworth, KS, 5 Jul 1867. SOURCE: McMiller, "Buffalo Soldiers," 74.

BOON, Andrew; Recruit; B/10th Cav. Enlisted Memphis, TN, spring 1867. SOURCE: LS, 10 Cav, 1866–67.
Original member of 10th Cavalry; in troop when organized, Ft Leavenworth, KS, 1 Apr 1867. SOURCE: McMiller, "Buffalo Soldiers," 69.

BOON, Arthur; Private; A/10th Cav. Served in 10th Cavalry, 1898; remained in U.S. during war with Spain. SOURCE: Cashin, *Under Fire with the Tenth Cavalry*, 337.

BOONE; Private; L/25th Inf. Killed in ambush, Philippines, 29 Jan 1900; "a jolly fellow" and "faithful to duty." SOURCE: Richmond *Planet*, 17 Mar 1900.

BOONE, Adrick; Private; F/9th Cav. Listing on Ft Robinson, NE, post returns changed from deserted to on furlough as of 8 Dec 1886; leave had been extended by Adjutant General without knowledge of post commander.

Transferred from 9th Cavalry to Hospital Corps, Ft Robinson, Oct 1887.

Formerly of Crawford, NE; adjudged insane and taken to asylum at Norfolk, NE, 4 Jun 1900; had been riding horse through town and threatening people with loaded rifle. SOURCE: Crawford *Tribune*, 8 Jun 1900.

No Veterans Administration pension file.

BOONE, William; Private; H/9th Cav. Charges against Boone amended. SOURCE: Letter, DP, 5 Mar 1897.

Dishonorable discharge and three months' confinement, Ft Robinson, NE. SOURCE: SO 36, DP, 28 Mar 1897.

Released, 28 May 1897. SOURCE: Post Returns, Ft Robinson, May 1897.

BOONE, William; Private; 24th Inf. Sentenced to death for role in Houston riot, 1917. SOURCE: Haynes, *A Night of Violence*, 289–90.

BOOTHE, Virgil; Private; B/49th Inf. Deserted at Zapote Bridge, Philippines, 11 Apr 1900; apprehended, Manila, 17 Apr 1900; dishonorable discharge and eighteen months at Bilibid Prison, 30 May 1900. SOURCE: Descriptive Book, B/49 Inf.

BOOZE, Richard; Private; I/24th Inf. Enlisted Baltimore, MD, 9 Feb 1899; joined company, 13 Feb 1899. SOURCE: Muster Roll, I/24 Inf, Jan–Feb 1899.

On detached service, Benicia Barracks, CA, from 5 Apr 1899; left post, 8 Apr 1899. SOURCE: Muster Roll, I/24 Inf, Mar–Apr 1899.

Fined $3.50 by garrison court martial, 15 May 1899. SOURCE: Muster Roll, I/24 Inf, May–Jun 1899.

Died of malaria in the Philippines, 9 Aug 1900. SOURCE: *ANJ* 37 (18 Aug 1900): 1214.

BORBON, J. H.; Corporal; K/9th Cav. On detached service in field, New Mexico, 21 Jan–8 Feb 1881. SOURCE: Regt Returns, 9 Cav, Feb 1881.

BORDEN, Frank F.; Private; F/9th Cav. Recruit from depot, arrived at Ft Robinson, NE, 1 Mar 1887. SOURCE: Regt Returns, 9 Cav, Mar 1887.

BORDINGHAMMER, Edward D.; Musician; C/24th Inf. Sergeant, K/24th Infantry, at San Carlos, AZ, 1890. *See* HARDEE, James A., Private, K/24th Infantry

Retired as musician, C/24th Infantry, from Skagway, AK, Jul 1900. SOURCE: *ANJ* 37 (21 Jul 1900): 1119.

BOROLER, William; F/10th Cav. Original member of 10th Cavalry; in troop when organized, Ft Leavenworth, KS, 21 Jun 1867. SOURCE: McMiller, "Buffalo Soldiers," 73.

BORZOTRA, James; Private; H/24th Inf. Fined $10 by summary court, for violating Article 62, carelessly discharging weapon on guard duty, San Isidro, Philippines, 29 Mar 1902. SOURCE: Register of Summary Court, San Isidro.

BOSSLEY, Robert; Private; G/24th Inf. Transferred from Reserve Divisional Hospital, Siboney, Cuba, to U.S. on U.S. Army Transport *Santiago*, with yellow fever, 25 Jul 1898. SOURCE: Hospital Papers, Spanish-American War.

BOSWELL, John T.; Private; H/24th Inf. Sentenced to five months and $50 fine for conduct to prejudice of good order and discipline, being drunk and disorderly, failure to cease disturbing public meeting when so ordered by chaplain, resistance, and abuse of noncommissioned officer. SOURCE: *ANJ* 35 (13 Nov 1897): 192.

BOTHWELL, William H.; Private; K/48th Inf. Died of variola in the Philippines, 2 Aug 1900. SOURCE: *ANJ* 37 (11 Aug 1901): 1191.

BOUDOW, John; D/10th Cav. Original member of 10th Cavalry; in troop when organized, Ft Leavenworth, KS, 1 Jun 1867.

BOUNCLER, Pearl; Private; A/24th Inf. Wounded in action, Cuba, 1898. SOURCE: Muller, *The Twenty Fourth Infantry*, 16.

See **BONNSELOR**, Pearl, Private, A/24th Infantry

BOUNCLER, Willis S.; Private; Band/24th Inf. Private, K/24th Infantry, San Carlos, AZ, 1890. *See* HARDEE, James A., Private, K/24th Infantry

Private, Band/24th Infantry, transferred from Reserve Divisional Hospital, Siboney, Cuba, to U.S. Army transport *Vigilancia*, with yellow fever, 6 Sep 1898. SOURCE: Hospital Papers, Spanish-American War.

BOUNSLER, Frank; Private; C/25th Inf. Dishonorable discharge, Brownsville. SOURCE: SO 266, AGO, 9 Nov 1906.

BOURROUGHS, Ossie O.; Trumpeter; A/10th Cav. Served in 10th Cavalry in Cuba, 1898. SOURCE: Cashin, *Under Fire with the Tenth Cavalry*, 336.

BOWEN; Corporal; H/25th Inf. Best running broad jump in Department of the Missouri competition, Ft Reno, OK, and the entire Army, 22'5", 1903. SOURCE: SecWar, *AR 1903*, I, 430.

BOWEN, Austin; Private; 10th Cav. Arrived Ft Leavenworth, KS, from Jefferson Barracks, MO. SOURCE: Adj, Ft Leavenworth, to HQ, Jefferson Bks, 9 Oct 1866.

BOWENS, Alonzo; Corporal; F/10th Cav. Private, H/9th Cavalry; relieved from extra duty as laborer, Quartermaster Department, Ft Robinson, NE. SOURCE: SO 90, 20 Aug 1896, Post Orders, Ft Robinson.

To be discharged at expiration of term, with $72.92 retained pay and $8.12 clothing due him. SOURCE: CO, H/9, to Chief Paymaster, DP, 26 Aug 1897, LS, H/9.

Corporal, F/10th Cavalry; served in 10th Cavalry in Cuba, 1898. SOURCE: Cashin, *Under Fire with the Tenth Cavalry*, 343.

BOWENS, Major; Sergeant; G/9th Cav. Sergeant, E/9th Cavalry; with detachment of nineteen that skirmished with insurgents at Tagitay, Philippines, 22 Feb 1901. SOURCE: Hamilton, "History of the Ninth Cavalry," 106; *Illustrated Review: Ninth Cavalry.*

Veteran of Indian wars, Spanish-American War, and Philippine Insurrection; at Ft D. A. Russell, WY, in 1910; marksman; resident of Fort Leavenworth, KS. SOURCE: *Illustrated Review: Ninth Cavalry,* with picture.

BOWENS, Marcellus; Private; I/9th Cav. At Ft D. A. Russell, WY, in 1910; resident of Rolla, MO. SOURCE: *Illustrated Review: Ninth Cavalry,* with picture.

BOWERS, Charles; F/10th Cav. Original member of 10th Cavalry; in troop when organized, Ft Leavenworth, KS, 21 Jun 1867. SOURCE: McMiller, "Buffalo Soldiers," 68.

BOWERS, Edward; Private; K/9th Cav. Killed in action against force of nine hundred Kickapoos, Navahos, Mexicans, and white renegades, Ft Lancaster, TX, along with Pvts. William Sharpe and Anderson Trimble, K/9th Cavalry, 26 Dec 1867. SOURCE: Hamilton, "History of the Ninth Cavalry," 7; *Illustrated Review: Ninth Cavalry. See* **TRIMBLE**, Anderson, Private, K/9th Cavalry

BOWLEY, Samuel T.; I/25th Inf. Admitted to Soldiers Home with disability, age 36, sixteen years' service. SOURCE: SecWar, *AR 1889,* 1013.

BOWMAN; Private; B/10th Cav. At Ft Apache, AZ, 1890, subscribed $.50 to testimonial to General Grierson. SOURCE: List of subscriptions, 23 Apr 1890, 10th Cavalry papers, MHI.

BOWMAN, Ashton J.; 10th Cav. Born Knoxville, TN; resided with father, W. S. Bowman, Clinton, TN; enlisted for colored cavalry, Harriman, TN, 22 Aug 1907, age 20, Ht 5'7"; brown complexion. SOURCE: 1st Lt. Henry J. Terrell, Recruiting Officer, Descriptive Book of Recruits, 1907–08.

BOWMAN, John; 1st Sgt; 9th Cav. Retired from Ft Riley, KS. SOURCE: *Cavalry Journal* 41 (Nov 1932): 60.

BOWMAN, John H.; Sergeant; B/10th Cav. Served in 10th Cavalry, 1898; remained in U.S. during war with Spain. SOURCE: Cashin, *Under Fire with the Tenth Cavalry,* 339.

Retired. SOURCE: SO 250, AGO, 24 Oct 1902.

BOWMAN, Lewis; Private; 10th Cav. Broke two ribs at San Juan, Cuba, 1898; narrative of 10th Cavalry's role in battle. SOURCE: Johnson, *History of Negro Soldiers,* 69–71; Young, *Reminiscences,* 232–33.

BOWMAN, Willie; Private; K/49th Inf. Died of tuberculosis in the Philippines, 4 May 1900. SOURCE: *ANJ* 37 (19 May 1900): 903.

BOWSER, Frank T.; Private; F/9th Cav. Sentenced to twenty days' confinement by garrison court martial for conduct to prejudice of good order and discipline for disobeying Sgt. Robert Harris, F/9th Cavalry; escorted to quarters by Pvt. George Gates, F/9th Cavalry. SOURCE: Order 23, 20 Jun 1887, Post Orders, Ft Robinson.

Discharged from Ft Robinson, NE, on surgeon's certificate, due to gunshot wound, 19 Jan 1888.

BOXBRY, W. H.; Private; E/9th Cav. On detached service in field, New Mexico, 26 Jan–1 Feb 1881. SOURCE: Regt Returns, 9 Cav, Feb 1881.

BOYCE, Alex; Private; G/9th Cav. On detached service, South Fork, NM, 17 Nov 1880–12 Jan 1881. SOURCE: Regt Returns, 9 Cav, Jan 1881.

BOYD; Private; A/10th Cav. At Ft Apache, AZ, 1890, subscribed $.50 to testimonial to General Grierson. SOURCE: List of subscriptions, 23 Apr 1890, 10th Cavalry papers, MHI.

BOYD, Benjamin; 9th and 10th Cav. Ten-year veteran and recent subscriber. SOURCE: *Winners of the West* 4 (Mar 1927): 8.

BOYD, Charles; Private; D/10th Cav. Served in 10th Cavalry in Cuba, 1898. SOURCE: Cashin, *Under Fire with the Tenth Cavalry,* 341.

BOYD, Daniel; Sergeant; L/10th Cav. Original member of 10th Cavalry; in troop when organized, Ft Riley, KS, 21 Sep 1867. SOURCE: McMiller, "Buffalo Soldiers," 78.

Commander, 10th Cavalry, forwards inventory of Sergeant Boyd's personal effects and final statement to Adjutant General. SOURCE: Letter, CO, 10 Cav, to AG, 24 Jul 1870, ES, 10 Cav, 1866–71.

BOYD, David; Private; 9th Cav. Accidentally killed by comrade, Ft Davis, TX, Jul 1876. SOURCE: Carroll, *The Black Military Experience,* 273.

BOYD, Frederick D.; Corporal; G/10th Cav. Served in 10th Cavalry in Cuba, 1898. SOURCE: Cashin, *Under Fire with the Tenth Cavalry,* 345.

BOYD, George; Private; 9th Cav. Wounded in the left thigh, Naco, AZ, 28 Nov 1914. SOURCE: Cleveland *Gazette,* 13 May 1916.

BOYD, James; Corporal; A/24th Inf. Deserted from Honolulu, HI, 23 Jul 1899. SOURCE: Regt Returns, 24 Inf, Aug 1899.

BOYD, John; D/10th Cav. Original member of 10th Cavalry; in troop when organized, Ft Leavenworth, KS, 1 Jun 1867. SOURCE: McMiller, "Buffalo Soldiers," 71.

BOYD, John; Private; C/25th Inf. Wounded in action, El Caney, Cuba, 1 Jul 1898. SOURCE: Nankivell, *History of the Twenty-fifth Infantry*, 83.

BOYD, Peter; Private; K/10th Cav. At Ft Robinson, NE, 1904.

BOYD, Thomas; Saddler; K/10th Cav. Served in 10th Cavalry in Cuba, 1898. SOURCE: Cashin, *Under Fire with the Tenth Cavalry*, 352.

BOYD, Thomas A.; Corporal; L/9th Cav. Promoted from lance corporal, Apr 1900. SOURCE: *ANJ* 37 (5 May 1900): 843.

BOYER, A.; Private; G/9th Cav. On detached service, Ft Stanton, NM, 29 Jan–5 Feb 1881. SOURCE: Regt Returns, 9 Cav, Feb 1881.

BOYER, Carl D.; Private; C/9th Cav. At Ft D. A. Russell, WY, in 1910; resident of 6638 Carpenter St., Chicago. SOURCE: *Illustrated Review: Ninth Cavalry*, with picture.

BOYER, Eli; Private; K/9th Cav. Killed in action, 1867. SOURCE: Leckie, *The Buffalo Soldiers*, 85.

BOYKIN, King C.; Private; K/10th Cav. Served in 10th Cavalry, 1898; remained in U.S. during war with Spain. SOURCE: Cashin, *Under Fire with the Tenth Cavalry*, 349.

BOYLE, Frank; Sergeant; B/10th Cav. Served in 10th Cavalry, 1898; remained in U.S. during war with Spain. SOURCE: Cashin, *Under Fire with the Tenth Cavalry*, 347.

Private, H/10th Cavalry, stationed at Camp Forse, AL, Nov 1898. SOURCE: Richmond *Planet*, 3 Dec 1898.

Promoted to corporal from lance corporal, B/10th Cavalry, Aug 1902. SOURCE: *ANJ* 39 (30 Aug 1902): 1315.

Sergeant, B/10th Cavalry, released to duty from treatment for gonorrhea, Ft Robinson, NE, 16 Jul 1906. SOURCE: Post Surgeon to CO, B/10, 16 Jul 1903, LS, Post Surgeon, Ft Robinson.

BOYNE, Thomas; H/25th Inf. Native of Prince George's Co., MD; won Medal of Honor for two actions against Victorio, Mimbres Mountains, NM, 29 May 1879, and Cuchillo Negro, NM, 27 Sep 1879, while sergeant, C/9th Cavalry. SOURCE: Carroll, *The Black Military Experience*, 411; Koger, *The Maryland Negro in Our Wars*, 23; Lee, *Negro Medal of Honor Men*, 63, 66; Billington, *New Mexico's Buffalo Soldiers*, 88–89.

Corporal, L/9th Cavalry, on detached service in the field, New Mexico, 21 Jan–24 Feb 1881. SOURCE: Regt Returns, 9 Cav, Feb 1881.

Admitted to Soldiers Home, from H/25th Infantry, age 43, with twenty-three years and seven months' service. SOURCE: SecWar, *AR 1889*, 1013.

Died of consumption at Soldiers Home, age 50, 21 Apr 1896. SOURCE: SecWar, *AR 1896*, 640.

BOZIER, Charles; A/10th Cav. Original member of 10th Cavalry; in troop when organized, Ft Leavenworth, KS, 18 Feb 1867. SOURCE: McMiller, "Buffalo Soldiers," 68.

BRABHAM, Jeremiah; Private; D/24th Inf. Born Barnwell, SC; occupation drayman; Ht 5'8", dark complexion; enlisted Charleston, SC, age 17, 14 May 1881; assigned to A/24th Infantry; attached to band learning to play, 12 Sep 1883–4 Sep 1884; joined band, Ft Sill, Indian Territory, 4 Nov 1884; garrison court martial fines of $5 and $10 in 1884; discharged, character excellent, with $72 retained pay and $48.14 clothing, 13 May 1886; enlisted Ft Leavenworth, KS, 22 May 1886; joined band, Ft Supply, Indian Territory, 8 Jul 1886; transferred to E/24th Infantry, Ft Sill, character "fair, but disinclined to pay his just debts," single, additional pay $2 per month, clothing $ 37.27, 17 Jan 1888; transferred to Band/24th Infantry, Ft Bayard, NM, character very good, 18 Nov 1890; first class marksman, 1889, and marksman, 1890; discharged, Ft Bayard, character generally good, single, additional pay $5 per month, retained $60.57, clothing $54.24, 7 Jun 1891; enlisted, Ft Leavenworth, 23 Jun 1891; joined, Ft Bayard, 13 Sep 1891; transferred to D/24th Infantry, character good, single, additional pay $3 per month, retained pay $33.33, clothing $52.44, owes $1.08 for subsistence, 2 Apr 1894. SOURCE: Descriptive Book, 24 Inf NCS & Band.

BRACHER, Albert; Private; H/9th Cav. Died of pneumonia at Ft McKinney, WY, 10 Nov 1887.

BRADDEN, Alfred; Sergeant; Band/9th Cav. Born in Alabama; Ht 5'9", brown complexion; served in 17th U.S. Colored Troops until 25 Apr 1866; served in C/38th Infantry, discharged as sergeant, 17 Nov 1869; in H/24th Infantry, discharged as sergeant, 16 Aug 1875; in B/24th Infantry, discharged as sergeant, 18 Feb 1881; enlisted in Band/24th Infantry, Ft Supply, Indian Territory, 19 Feb 1881; principal musician, 1 Oct 1881; resigned 24 Jun 1884; discharged, expiration of service, character excellent, "a good E flat cornet player," married, five children, additional pay $2 per month, retained $60, clothing $59.53, 18 Feb 1886. SOURCE: Descriptive Book, 24 Inf NCS & Band.

Sergeant, Band/9th Cavalry, since 11 Aug 1892. SOURCE: Roster, 9 Cav, 1893.

Resides with wife at Ft Robinson, NE. SOURCE: Medical History, Ft Robinson.

Retires from Ft Robinson, Nov 1893. SOURCE: *ANJ* 31 (4 Nov 1893): 172.

Retired post exchange bartender, Ft Robinson, 1894. SOURCE: Investigation of Charges against Chaplain Plummer.

Worked as attendant, post exchange billiard room, for $10.85 per month. SOURCE: Report of Inspection, Ft Robinson, 3 Sep 1894, Reports of Inspection, Dept Platte, II.

Lives retired at Ft Robinson, one of six retirees there, four of whom are black. SOURCE: Soldiers on the Retired List Paid in the Department of the Platte by Mail, Misc Records, Dept Platte, 1894–98.

Wife Laura died at Ft Robinson, 9 Jun 1910. SOURCE: List of Interments, Ft Robinson.

Lives in Crawford, NE, with personal property assessed at $30 and tax of $2 in 1912. SOURCE: Dawes County tax records.

No Veterans Administration pension file.

BRADFORD, Caesar; K/10th Cav. Original member of 10th Cavalry; in troop when organized, Ft Riley, KS, 1 Sep 1867. SOURCE: McMiller, "Buffalo Soldiers," 77.

BRADFORD, Harrison; Sergeant; E/9th Cav. Led mutiny near San Antonio, TX, spring 1867; shot and killed while resisting arrest, 9 Apr 1867. SOURCE: Hamilton, "History of the Ninth Cavalry," 5; Ninth Cavalry, *Historical and Pictorial Review*, 44.

Shot by Lieutenant Smith, while leading mutiny, 9 Apr 1867. SOURCE: *Illustrated Review: Ninth Cavalry.*

BRADFORD, Leroy; Private; 10th Cav. Wounded, shot through body, Naco, AZ, 4 Oct 1914. SOURCE: Cleveland *Gazette*, 13 May 1916.

BRADFORD, Rudolph; Private; F/9th Cav. Sentenced to fifteen days and $10 retained by summary court, Ft Robinson, NE, for conduct prejudicial to good order: answered "because I wanted to" in insubordinate manner to query of First Sgt. Edward Fletcher regarding why he had saddle and equipment of another man at horse exercise. SOURCE: Summary Court Record, Ft Robinson, I.

BRADLEY; Private; 9th Cav. At Ft Cummings, NM, 1881. SOURCE: Billington, *New Mexico's Buffalo Soldiers*, 130.

BRADLEY, Levi; Sergeant; E/10th Cav. Born in South Carolina; private, D/10th Cavalry, 20 Apr 1867–20 Apr 1872; in E/10th Cavalry, 10 Sep 1892; corporal, 1 Sep 1877; sergeant, 1 Jan 1878; first sergeant, 1 Jan 1891–31 Mar 1894; sergeant, 1 Apr 1894. SOURCE: Baker, Roster.

Stationed at San Felipe, TX; marched one hundred miles in command of detachment of eight scouting vicinity of Rio Grande, for murderers of Colson family, 6–13 Jun 1879. SOURCE: SecWar, *AR 1879*, 112.

At Ft Apache, AZ, 1890, subscribed $.50 to testimonial to General Grierson. SOURCE: List of subscriptions, 23 Apr 1890, 10th Cavalry papers, MHI.

Retires from Ft Custer, MT. SOURCE: *ANJ* 35 (16 Oct 1897): 1117.

BRADLEY, Taylor; Farrier; C/9th Cav. Discharged, expiration of service, Ft Robinson, NE, 31 Aug 1885. SOURCE: Regt Returns, 9 Cav, Aug 1885.

BRADLEY, William; L/10th Cav. Original member of 10th Cavalry; in troop when organized, Ft Riley, KS, 21 Sep 1867. SOURCE: McMiller, "Buffalo Soldiers," 78.

BRADSHAW, Samuel; Private; G/24th Inf. At Siboney, Cuba, 1898. *See* **WOODS**, Robert Gordon, Captain, I/49th Infantry

BRADSHAW, William; H/10th Cav. Original member of 10th Cavalry; in troop when organized, Ft Leavenworth, KS, 21 Jul 1867. SOURCE: McMiller, "Buffalo Soldiers," 75.

BRAGGS, Bishop; Private; M/9th Cav. At Ft D. A. Russell, WY, in 1910. SOURCE: *Illustrated Review: Ninth Cavalry*, with picture.

BRAHAM, Josiah; I/10th Cav. Original member of 10th Cavalry; in troop when organized, Ft Riley, KS, 15 Aug 1867. SOURCE: McMiller, "Buffalo Soldiers," 76.

BRAIN, Norman; G/10th Cav. Original member of 10th Cavalry; in troop when organized, Ft Leavenworth, KS, 5 Jul 1867. SOURCE: McMiller, "Buffalo Soldiers," 74.

BRANCH, James; Corporal; H/10th Cav. Served in 10th Cavalry, 1898; remained in U.S. during war with Spain. SOURCE: Cashin, *Under Fire with the Tenth Cavalry*, 346.

At Camp Forse, AL, Nov 1898. SOURCE: Richmond *Planet*, 3 Dec 1898.

BRANCH, Norwood; Private; C/10th Cav. Served in 10th Cavalry in Cuba, 1898. SOURCE: Cashin, *Under Fire with the Tenth Cavalry*, 340.

BRANCH, William; Private; I/25th Inf. Born Lunenburg Co., VA; occupation laborer; Ht 5'6", enlisted Baltimore, MD, 4 Jun 1870; discharged 6 Jun 1875; enlisted 28 Jul 1875; discharged 27 Jul 1880; participated in war against Cheyennes, Kiowas, Comanches, 1874–75. SOURCE: VA File C 2581520, William Branch.

Rheumatism caused by accident ten miles from Ft Sill, Indian Territory; coming down steep hill, as rear teamster was locking wagon wheels, mules ran down hill and wheels passed over toes of his right foot; when he got to camp, his right leg numb and his boot half full of blood; sent to hospital in wagon; spent twenty-eight days there and been lame ever since. SOURCE: Branch to Commissioner of Pensions, 11 Apr 1892, VA File C 2581520, William Branch.

Married Rebecca Bryand, 1882, who died in 1886; then Ella Scott, who died 11 Jan 1899; then Ada Livingston, later divorced; then Julia Nelson, married to William Scott, private, D/9th Cavalry, 1894 and divorced 21 May 1908. SOURCE: VA File C 2581520, William Branch.

Pension increased from $8 to $20 per month, 4 Mar 1917; addresses in San Antonio, TX: 312 North San Saba, 1903; 905 Castro, 1904; 725 North Laredo, 1905; 409 South Trio, 1906; 101 National, 1909; 129 DeVilbiss, 1915; 740 Barrera, 1918. Died 27 Feb 1941, Station Hospital, Ft Sam

Houston, TX; at death mentally incompetent, lived with guardian, Mrs. Willie Young Richardson, 1014 Iowa St., as of 9 May 1940, with pension of $72 per month. SOURCE: VA File C 2581520, William Branch.

Served 1870–80; now 80 years old, gets $50 per month pension, belongs to Abraham Lincoln Chapter, No. 30, National Indian War Veterans, San Antonio. SOURCE: *Winners of the West* 7 (Jul 1930): 4.

Subscriber, now age 82. SOURCE: *Winners of the West* 10 (Jan 1933): 1.

Renews subscription; was born Lunenburg Co., 13 May 1850; discharged Ft Sill. SOURCE: *Winners of the West* 11 (Aug 1934): 3.

See **AUSTIN**, Edward S., Private, I/25th Infantry; **McKAY**, George, Private, K/24th Infantry; **REDDICK**, Charles, First Sergeant, I/25th Infantry; **ROE**, John W., I/25th Infantry; **WILLIAMS**, William H., Private, I/25th Infantry

BRANDT; Private; B/10th Cav. Released to duty from treatment for acute gonorrhea, Ft Robinson, NE, 16 Jul 1906. SOURCE: Post Surgeon to CO, Det 10 Cav, 9 Oct 1903, LS, Post Surgeon, Ft Robinson.

BRANNER, George; Private; I/24th Inf. Enlisted Louisville, KY, 29 Jul 1898. SOURCE: Muster Roll, I/24 Inf, Jan–Feb 1899.

Sentenced to forfeit $.75 by garrison court martial, 19 Apr 1899. SOURCE: Muster Roll, I/24 Inf, Mar–Apr 1899.

Sentenced to forfeit $1 by garrison court martial, 14 Jun 1899. SOURCE: Muster Roll, I/24 Inf, May–Jun 1899.

Sentenced to forfeit $1 by summary court martial; sick in hospital, El Deposito, Philippines, since 30 Aug 1899. SOURCE: Muster Roll, I/24 Inf, Jul–Aug 1899.

Discharged, end of term, 31 Dec 1899. SOURCE: Muster Roll, I/24 Inf, Nov–Dec 1899.

BRANSFORD, Wesley; Private; K/10th Cav. Born Meadowville, TN; lived with mother Margaret Bransford, in home of Wilson Meadows, Meadowville, Macon Co., TN, 1860; lived on Mr. Bowman's farm, Sumner Co., TN, between Gallatin and Castilian Springs, with parents Archie and Margaret, brother Archie, sister Martha, 1870; enlisted Indianapolis, IN, Ht 5'5", dark complexion, 5 Oct 1882; discharged 4 Oct 1885; laborer since discharge; contracted rheumatism from severe cold contracted in rainstorm, Ft Davis, TX, 1884; after service lived in El Paso, TX; Clifton, Phoenix, and Globe, AZ; Kansas City, MO; Tulsa, OK; at time of death, resided at 149 Winchester St., Gallatin, with sister Martha Wilson; died of gangrene, pneumonia, and diabetes, 11 Jan 1929; never married. SOURCE: VA File SC 11242, Wesley Bransford.

Stations: Ft Davis, 1 Jan–1 Apr 1885; Bowie Station, AZ, 1 Apr–1 May 1885; Ft Grant, AZ, 1 May–26 Jul 1885; in field scouting against Indians, 26–31 Jul 1885; Ft Grant, 31 Jul–1 Aug 1885; in field scouting against Indians, Aug–Oct 1885. SOURCE: VA File SC 11242, Wesley Bransford.

First sergeant was William H. Givens; other enlisted men of company were John Magruder, Charley Allen, William

Young, Charley Howard, Sam Cropper, Richmond Bridges (employed by Phelps-Dodge, Morenci, AZ, 1907–08), John Patterson, John Hall, Henry Brooks (now in penitentiary, Santa Fe, NM, for murder). SOURCE: VA File SC 11242, Wesley Bransford.

Served 1882–85; recent subscriber. SOURCE: *Winners of the West* 4 (Mar 1927): 8.

BRANSOME, Junior; Sergeant; 24th Inf. In charge of quarters, regimental headquarters, on night of Houston riot, 1917. SOURCE: Haynes, *A Night of Violence*, 277.

BRANTLEY, Dennis; Sergeant; L/49th Inf. Led detachment against marauders southeast of Paranaque, Philippines, 26 Jan 1900; no casualties; several captured. SOURCE: Muster Roll, L/49 Inf, Jan–Feb 1900.

BRANTLEY, Sim D.; Private; G/10th Cav. Served in 10th Cavalry, 1898; remained in U.S. during war with Spain. SOURCE: Cashin, *Under Fire with the Tenth Cavalry*, 345.

BRANTLY, James; Private; G/10th Cav. Served in 10th Cavalry in Cuba, 1898. SOURCE: Cashin, *Under Fire with the Tenth Cavalry*, 345.

BRATCHER, James B.; Private; B/10th Cav. Served in 10th Cavalry, 1898; remained in U.S. during war with Spain. SOURCE: Cashin, *Under Fire with the Tenth Cavalry*, 339.

BRATTON, James; Corporal; C/24th Inf. Transferred from Reserve Divisional Hospital, Siboney, Cuba, to U.S., aboard U.S. Army Transport *Santiago*, with yellow fever, 25 Jul 1898. SOURCE: Hospital Papers, Spanish-American War.

BRAWNER, Darby W. O.; Sergeant; C/25th Inf. Enlisted spring 1893; character excellent on each reenlistment. SOURCE: Weaver, *The Brownsville Raid*, 71.

Dishonorable discharge, Brownsville. SOURCE: SO 266, AGO, 9 Nov 1906.

BRAWNER, Jeadah; Private; C/9th Cav. At Ft D. A. Russell, WY, in 1910; resident of 167 Park Ave., Delaware, OH. SOURCE: *Illustrated Review: Ninth Cavalry,* with picture.

BRAWNER, Lisbon; Private; H/24th Inf. Fined $5 by summary court, San Isidro, Philippines, for violating article 33, absent from roll call, 10 Jan 1902, second conviction. SOURCE: Register of Summary Court, San Isidro.

BRAXTON, Edward H.; Corporal; H/10th Cav. Promoted corporal from private, 15 Nov 1897. SOURCE: *ANJ* 35 (4 Dec 1897): 252.

Sergeant, served in 10th Cavalry, 1898; remained in U.S. during war with Spain. SOURCE: Cashin, *Under Fire with the Tenth Cavalry*, 346.

BRAXTON, George E.; Private; B/10th Cav. Served in 10th Cavalry in Cuba, 1898; wounded in action. SOURCE: Cashin, *Under Fire With the Tenth Cavalry*, 338.

BRECKENRIDGE, William; Private; L/9th Cav. Robbed and killed William and Emmett Maxwell, Cimarron, NM, Apr 1876; convicted and hanged publicly in Cimarron, May 1877. SOURCE: Billington, *New Mexico's Buffalo Soldiers*, 67.

BRECKINRIDGE, William; Corporal; I/24th Inf. Involved in Houston riot, 1917; sentenced to death. SOURCE: Haynes, *A Night of Violence*, 167, 271.

Hanged, Ft Sam Houston, TX, 13 Dec 1917, for part in Houston riot. SOURCE: Cleveland *Gazette*, 15 Dec 1917.

BREGES, John; Private; K/25th Inf. At Ft Niobrara, NE, 1904. SOURCE: Wilson, "History of Fort Niobrara."

BRENSTON, Tevis; Private; K/25th Inf. Killed in action in ambush, Philippines, 29 Jan 1900; age 25 and "a good soldier." SOURCE: Richmond *Planet*, 17 Mar 1900.

BRENT; Private; A/24th Inf. At Ft Huachuca, AZ, 1893. *See* **HAM**, James, Sergeant, B/24th Infantry

BRENT, Daniel; Recruit; Mounted Service. Sentenced to one year, including seven days' solitary on bread and water, for desertion, by general court martial; solitary on bread and water remitted. SOURCE: GCMO 7, AGO, 22 Jan 1874.

BRENT, William; Musician; H/24th Inf. Enlisted Ft Huachuca, AZ, 9 Jan 1896; eight years' continuous service. SOURCE: Muster Roll, H/24 Inf, May–Jun 1898.

Died, field hospital, Siboney, Cuba, of disease contracted in line of duty, 28 Jul 1898; due soldier $5.80 clothing, $53.75 deposits, $2.27 retained. SOURCE: Muster Roll, H/24 Inf, Jul–Aug 1898.

Died in Cuba, 29 Jul 1898. SOURCE: Cashin, *Under Fire with the Tenth Cavalry*, 125; *ANJ* 37 (11 Feb 1899): 567; AG, *Correspondence Regarding the War with Spain*, I, 192.

BREWER, John; Private; M/10th Cav. Served in 10th Cavalry, 1898; remained in U.S. during war with Spain. SOURCE: Cashin, *Under Fire with the Tenth Cavalry*, 351.

BREWER, John W.; Private; D/9th Cav. His sentence for desertion, as of 4 Feb 1876, reduced to eighteen months. SOURCE: GCMO 22, AGO, 23 Feb 1877.

BREWER, Llewellyn; F/10th Cav. Served 1881–86; age 75. SOURCE: *Winners of the West* 12 (Nov 1935): 3.

BREWSTER, William; M/10th Cav. Original member of 10th Cavalry; in troop when organized, Ft Riley, KS, 15 Oct 1867. SOURCE: McMiller, "Buffalo Soldiers," 79.

BRICE, Walter H.; K/10th Cav. Original member of 10th Cavalry; in troop when organized, Ft Riley, KS, 1 Sep 1867. SOURCE: McMiller, "Buffalo Soldiers," 77.

BRICE, William; Corporal; H/10th Cav. At Ft Apache, AZ, 1890, subscribed $.50 to testimonial to General Grierson. SOURCE: List of subscriptions, 23 Apr 1890, 10th Cavalry papers, MHI.

BRICE, William H.; 1st Sgt; D/24th Inf. At Cabanatuan, Philippines, 1901. *See* **BLACK**, Henry, Private, K/24th Infantry; **BUFORD**, James J., Private, D/24th Infantry; **LEAVELL**, William, Private, D/24th Infantry; **STEVENS**, Samuel, Private, D/24th Infantry; **TAYLOR**, Albert B., Private, K/24th Infantry

Retired with twenty-six years' service, as first sergeant, 1914. SOURCE: *Crisis* 7 (Feb 1914): 165.

Recently retired from 24th Infantry with twenty-five years' service. SOURCE: Curtis, *The Black Soldier*, 42.

BRICK, William; Private; D/9th Cav. At Ft D. A. Russell, WY, in 1910; marksman. SOURCE: *Illustrated Review: Ninth Cavalry.*

BRIDGES, Randell; D/10th Cav. Original member of 10th Cavalry; in troop when organized, Ft Leavenworth, KS, 1 Jun 1867. SOURCE: McMiller, "Buffalo Soldiers," 71.

BRIDGES, Richmond; Private; K/10th Cav. *See* **BRANSFORD**, Wesley, Private, K/10th Cavalry

BRIDGEWATER, Samuel; Private; A/24th Inf. Relieved from special duty at post exchange. SOURCE: Order 60, Ft Huachuca, AZ, 28 Apr 1893, Name File, 24 Inf.

Wounded in foot, San Juan River, Cuba, 1 Jul 1898. SOURCE: SecWar, *AR 1898*, 437; Muller, *The Twenty Fourth Infantry*, 16.

BRIDGEWATER, Scott; Private; I/10th Cav. Original member of 10th Cavalry; in troop when organized, Ft Riley, KS, 15 Aug 1867. SOURCE: McMiller, "Buffalo Soldiers," 76.

Detailed as teamster. SOURCE: SO 54, HQ, Camp Supply, Indian Territory, 31 Jul 1869, Orders, Detachment of 10 Cav, 1868–69.

BRIGS, Tazwell; Private; I/10th Cav. At Ft Apache, AZ, 1890, subscribed $.50 to testimonial to General Grierson. SOURCE: List of subscriptions, 23 Apr 1890, 10th Cavalry papers, MHI.

Served in 10th Cavalry in Cuba, 1898. SOURCE: Cashin, *Under Fire with the Tenth Cavalry*, 347.

BRIGGS, Albert J.; Private; L/9th Cav. Veteran of Philippine Insurrection; at Ft D. A. Russell, WY, in 1910; sharpshooter; resident of Augusta, GA. SOURCE: *Illustrated Review: Ninth Cavalry*, with picture.

BRIGGS, Allen; Sergeant; H/9th Cav. Sergeant, H/9th Cavalry, since 19 Mar 1881. SOURCE: Roster, 9 Cav, 1893.

At Ft Robinson, NE, 1895; sergeant since 1881. SOURCE: *ANJ* 32 (20 Jul 1895): 774.

Detailed as regimental standard-bearer, Mar 1896. SOURCE: *ANJ* 33 (28 Mar 1896): 540.

Retires from Ft Robinson in accordance with Special Order 170, Adjutant General's Office, 27 Jul 1897. SOURCE: *ANJ* 34 (7 Aug 1897): 909.

Retired with $8.30 retained, $60.07 clothing, $100 deposits due him. SOURCE: CO, H/9, to Chief QM, DP, 3 Aug 1897, Descriptive Book, H/9 Cav.

Died of consumption, Crawford, NE, 11 Oct 1901; buried, Ft Robinson, 12 Oct 1901. SOURCE: Crawford *Tribune*, 18 Oct 1901.

No Veterans Administration pension file.

BRIGGS, James; Sergeant; C/9th Cav. Veteran of Philippine Insurrection; at Ft D. A. Russell, WY, in 1910; sharpshooter. SOURCE: *Illustrated Review: Ninth Cavalry*, with picture.

BRIGGS, Moses; D/10th Cav. Original member of 10th Cavalry; in troop when organized, Ft Leavenworth, KS, 1 Jun 1867. SOURCE: McMiller, "Buffalo Soldiers," 71.

BRIGHT; Corporal; D/9th Cav. Discharged. SOURCE: SO 84, AGO, 16 Apr 1891.

BRIGHT, Aaron D.; Captain; 48th Inf. Date of rank 9 Sep 1899. SOURCE: *ANJ* 37 (4 Nov 1899): 228.

One of nineteen officers of 48th Infantry recommended for regular Army commissions. SOURCE: CG, Div PI, Manila, 8 Feb 1901, to AGO, AGO File 355163.

BRIGHT, Grandvill W.; Private; G/25th Inf. In regiment 1910. *See* **JAMES**, John, Sergeant, G/25th Infantry

BRIGHT, Isaac; Private; C/10th Cav. Served in 10th Cavalry, 1898; remained in U.S. during war with Spain. SOURCE: Cashin, *Under Fire with the Tenth Cavalry*, 340.

BRIGHT, Perry; F/10th Cav. Original member of 10th Cavalry; in troop when organized, Ft Leavenworth, KS, 21 Jun 1867. SOURCE: McMiller, "Buffalo Soldiers," 73.

BRIGHT, Robert; Private; B/10th Cav. Discharged. SOURCE: SO 241, AGO, 14 Oct 1902.

BRIGHT, Spencer; Private; M/10th Cav. Served as nurse, post hospital, Ft McDowell, AZ, Mar 1887.

BRIGHTWELL, Charley; Private; K/25th Inf. At Ft Niobrara, NE, 1904. SOURCE: Wilson, "History of Fort Niobrara."

BRIGHTWELL, Henry; Private; G/25th Inf. Wounded in action, El Caney, Cuba, 1 Jul 1898. SOURCE: Nankivell, *History of the Twenty-fifth Infantry*, 83.

BRINGHAM, George; H/10th Cav. Original member of 10th Cavalry; in troop when organized, Ft Leavenworth, KS, 21 Jul 1867. SOURCE: McMiller, "Buffalo Soldiers," 75.

BRINKLEY, Frank; Private; A/10th Cav. Served in 10th Cavalry in Cuba, 1898. SOURCE: Cashin, *Under Fire with the Tenth Cavalry*, 336.

BRINKLEY, Jackson; Private; B/10th Cav. Transferred to Hospital Corps. SOURCE: SO 140, DeptMo, 29 Jul 1904.

BRINSON, Theodore M.; Private; E/9th Cav. Qualified as schoolteacher but not teaching, Ft Robinson, NE, 1 Nov 1895–29 Feb 1896. SOURCE: Reports of Schools, Ft Robinson, 1892–96.

On extra duty as schoolteacher, Ft Robinson. SOURCE: SO 125, 6 Nov 1896, Post Orders, Ft Robinson.

Relieved from extra duty as schoolteacher, Ft Robinson. SOURCE: SO 34, 30 Mar 1897, Post Orders, Ft Robinson.

BRISCO, Harry; Private; I/25th Inf. Fined $10 by summary court, San Isidro, Philippines, for violation of Article 62, loaded and fired rifle while on guard duty contrary to post orders, 19 Mar 1902, second conviction. SOURCE: Register of Summary Court, San Isidro.

BRISCOE, Edward; Sergeant; B/10th Cav. Born St. Mary's, MD; brown complexion; first enlisted 15 May 1875; corporal, 1 Jul 1876; sergeant, 1 Jul 1878; reenlisted Chinati Mountain, TX, 15 May 1880, age 28; private, 27 Aug 1881; corporal, 10 Mar 1882; farrier, 1 Sep 1882; private, 16 Feb 1883; farrier, 28 Jul 1884; corporal, 1 Nov 1884; marksman, 1884; discharged, Whipple Barracks, AZ, character excellent, unmarried, with $60 retained pay, $51 clothing, $160 deposits, 22 May 1885. Reenlisted Baltimore, MD, 18 Jun 1885; joined, Whipple Barracks, 19 Aug 1885; corporal, 15 Mar 1887; sergeant, 2 Mar 1888; campaigns against Geronimo and Kid; discharged, Ft Apache, AZ, character excellent, retained pay $60, clothing $37, 17 Jun 1889. SOURCE: Descriptive Book, B/10 Cav, 1880–96.

At Ft Apache, 1890, subscribed $.50 to testimonial to General Grierson. SOURCE: List of subscriptions, 23 Apr 1890, 10th Cavalry papers, MHI.

BRISCOE, Henry; C/9th Cav. Born in Kentucky, date unknown; resided Georgetown, Woodford Co., KY, when enlisted; parents George and Ellen, brother Alex, sister Mary; served 21 May 1879–10 Jul 1882; discharged on surgeon's certificate with constitutional syphilis, disease not contracted in line of duty; one son, Roy, by first wife Jane; pension: $30 per month 17 Nov 1928, $40 per month 23 Jan 1930, $50 per month 31 Oct 1931, $55 per month 1 Sep 1937, $100 per month 20 Dec 1946; hospitalized, Wadsworth Veterans Administration Hospital, KS, 5 Jan 1948; died 29 Jan 1948; widow Callie Briscoe, 2740 Highland, Kansas City, MO, died 8 Mar 1948. SOURCE: VA File C 2349975, Henry Briscoe.

Letter to editor: served 1879–82. SOURCE: *Winners of the West* 8 (May 1931): 7.

Letter to editor: now age 68; enlisted at Cincinnati, OH, 1 May 1879; served at Jefferson Barracks, MO, Ft Hays, KS, Fts Stanton and Bayard, NM; in fight against Victorio, 25 Nov 1879, then pursuit to Rio Grande; discharged with disability, 10 Jul 1882. SOURCE: *Winners of the West* 8 (Oct 1931): 2.

See **LYMAN**, George, Color Sergeant, 9th Cavalry

BRISCOE, Thomas; Private; K/10th Cav. Inquiry of Jennie Briscoe regarding facts of her brother's death referred by Adjutant General to Commander, K/10th Cavalry. SOURCE: ES, 10 Cav, 1866–71.

BRISTOL, Charlie; Private; H/9th Cav. At Ft D. A. Russell, WY, in 1910; resident of Roanoke, VA. SOURCE: *Illustrated Review: Ninth Cavalry*, with picture.

BRITTON, Samuel; Private; K/10th Cav. Served in 10th Cavalry, 1898; remained in U.S. during war with Spain. SOURCE: Cashin, *Under Fire with the Tenth Cavalry*, 350.

BRITTON, William H.; Recruit; Mounted Service. Convicted by general court martial, St. Louis Barracks, MO, for theft of overcoats from colored recruits George Reed and Lindsay Kendrick; sentenced to dishonorable discharge and one year's confinement. SOURCE: GCMO 69, AGO, 31 May 1876.

BROADEN, William; Sergeant; H/9th Cav. Corporal, B/10th Cavalry; served in 10th Cavalry in Cuba, 1898. SOURCE: Cashin, *Under Fire with the Tenth Cavalry*, 337.

Ranked number 529 among rifle experts, with 68 percent in 1905. SOURCE: GO 101, AGO, 31 May 1906.

BROADEY, Farleigh; Private; K/10th Cav. Served in 10th Cavalry, 1898; remained in U.S. during war with Spain. SOURCE: Cashin, *Under Fire with the Tenth Cavalry*, 349.

BROADNAX, Van; Corporal; G/9th Cav. Veteran of Philippine Insurrection; at Ft D. A. Russell, WY, in 1910; marksman. SOURCE: *Illustrated Review: Ninth Cavalry*, with picture.

BROADUS, E. B.; Private; 24th Inf. Served in Houston, 1917; did not participate in riot. SOURCE: Haynes, *A Night of Violence*, 185.

BROADUS, Joseph; 1st Sgt; G/9th Cav. Sergeant, one of six enlisted men of G/9th Cavalry to testify against Lt. John Conline at his 1877 court martial for misconduct, including drunkenness, sexual misconduct, misappropriation of funds belonging to men of his troop, Ft Garland, CO. SOURCE: Billington, *New Mexico's Buffalo Soldiers*, 121–23.

On detached service, Ft Craig, NM, 26 Jan–6 Feb 1881. SOURCE: Regt Returns, 9 Cav, Feb 1881.

BROADUS, Lewis; 1st Sgt; M/25th Inf. Born Richmond, VA; resided there at enlistment; awarded Distinguished Service Cross in lieu of certificate of merit for coolness, presence of mind, bravery in saving lives, Ft Niobrara, NE, 3 Jul 1906. SOURCE: *Decorations. US Army. Supplement 1*, 28.

Mentioned as extremely efficient noncommissioned officer. SOURCE: Steward, *Fifty Years in the Gospel Ministry*, 352.

Ranked number 177 among rifle experts, with 68.67 percent in 1904. SOURCE: GO 79, AGO, 1 Jun 1905.

Ranked number 390 among rifle experts, with 69.33 percent in 1905. SOURCE: GO 101, AGO, 31 May 1906.

Twenty-six-year veteran; served in Cuba and the Philippines; prepared ordnance returns, Hartford, CT, armory, at request of state adjutant general, 1917. SOURCE: *Crisis* 14 (June 1917): 84.

Commissioned captain, Camp Des Moines, IA, Oct 1917. SOURCE: Sweeney, *History of the American Negro*, 120.

BROCK, William H.; M/10th Cav. Original member of 10th Cavalry; in troop when organized, Ft Riley, KS, 15 Oct 1867. SOURCE: McMiller, "Buffalo Soldiers," 79.

BROCKINGTON, Harry; C/24th Inf. Subscriber, served 1888–93, now age 68. SOURCE: *Winners of the West* 12 (Mar 1935): 2.

BRODEN, John; Private; K/9th Cav. Deserted from Ft Duchesne, UT, 20 Nov 1900. SOURCE: Regt Returns, 9 Cav, Nov 1900.

BRODNAX, John; Private; H/9th Cav. At Ft D. A. Russell, WY, in 1910; sharpshooter; resident of Reidsville, SC. SOURCE: *Illustrated Review: Ninth Cavalry*.

BROKER, Powell H.; 9th Cav. Body transferred from Montauk, NY, to National Cemetery, Cypress Hills, NY. SOURCE: *ANJ* 36 (21 Jan 1899): 480.

BRON, William; Private; H/9th Cav. At Ft Robinson, NE, deposited $10 with paymaster, Jan–May 1898.

BRONTZ, Elijah; Lance Cpl; Mounted Service. Convicted by general court martial, Jefferson Barracks, MO, for violation of Article 62, as noncommissioned officer of post guard and in temporary charge of guard, failed to notice and prevent escape of Recruit Lester Weber, Company D of Instruction, Mounted Service, then prisoner in post guardhouse, 14 Dec 1883; fined $10, with clemency because of good character. SOURCE: GCMO 5, AGO, 26 Jan 1884.

BROOK, Robert B.; Corporal; Band/9th Cav. At Ft D. A. Russell, WY, in 1910; resident of Fredericksburg, VA. SOURCE: *Illustrated Review: Ninth Cavalry*, with picture.

BROOKINGS, George W.; E/10th Cav. Original member of 10th Cavalry; in troop when organized, Ft Leavenworth, KS, 15 Jun 1867. SOURCE: McMiller, "Buffalo Soldiers," 72.

BROOKINS, George; Private; D/10th Cav. Served in 10th Cavalry, 1898; remained in U.S. during war with Spain. SOURCE: Cashin, *Under Fire with the Tenth Cavalry*, 341.

BROOKS, Benjamin; Saddler; D/10th Cav. Served in 10th Cavalry in Cuba, 1898. SOURCE: Cashin, *Under Fire with the Tenth Cavalry*, 341.

BROOKS, Charles H.; Private; C/9th Cav. Arrived Ft Robinson, NE, from depot, 1 Mar 1887.

Discharged from Ft Robinson, on surgeon's certificate of disability, 21 Jun 1887.

BROOKS, Edward; Private; A/9th Cav. In hands of civil authorities, Valentine, NE, 27 Jul–Oct 1888. SOURCE: Regt Returns, 9 Cav.

BROOKS, George; Private; 10th Cav. Deserted; surrendered to civil authorities, Ft Smith, AR; reward of $30 paid Jan 1873. SOURCE: ES, 10 Cav, 1873–81.

BROOKS, Harry; Private; D/10th Cav. Served in 10th Cavalry in Cuba, 1898. SOURCE: Cashin, *Under Fire with the Tenth Cavalry*, 341.

Died of acute gastritis, Holguin, Cuba, 21 Oct 1900. SOURCE: *ANJ* 38 (3 Nov 1900): 235.

BROOKS, Henry; G/10th Cav. Original member of 10th Cavalry; in troop when organized, Ft Leavenworth, KS, 5 Jul 1867. SOURCE: McMiller, "Buffalo Soldiers," 74.

BROOKS, Henry; Private; K/10th Cav. *See* **BRANSFORD**, Wesley, Private, K/10th Cavalry

BROOKS, Isaiah; Private; K/49th Inf. Died in the Philippines. SOURCE: *ANJ* 38 (18 May 1901): 925.

BROOKS, James; L/10th Cav. Original member of 10th Cavalry; in troop when organized, Ft Riley, KS, 21 Sep 1867. SOURCE: McMiller, "Buffalo Soldiers," 78.

BROOKS, James; Private; A/10th Cav. Retires from Ft Keogh, MT. SOURCE: *ANJ* 35 (19 Feb 1898): 459.

BROOKS, John; Private; G/10th Cav. Served in 10th Cavalry in Cuba, 1898. SOURCE: Cashin, *Under Fire with the Tenth Cavalry*, 345.

Wounded in action, Santiago, Cuba, 1 Jul 1898. SOURCE: SecWar, *AR 1898*, 324.

BROOKS, John R.; Private; H/10th Cav. Served in 10th Cavalry, 1898; remained in U.S. during war with Spain. SOURCE: Cashin, *Under Fire with the Tenth Cavalry*, 347.

Killed by black civilian outside Camp Forse, AL, 11 Nov 1898, along with Cpl. Daniel Garrett, H/10th Cavalry; killer in pay of local white conspiracy. SOURCE: Richmond *Planet*, 19 Nov 1898.

Born Richmond, VA; father "in the Pullman service"; graduate of Richmond public schools; apprentice to Richmond *Planet*, 1890; enlisted 1896; died at age 21, survived by mother, father, two brothers, three sisters. SOURCE: Richmond *Planet*, 26 Nov 1898.

BROOKS, Norman H.; Private; E/9th Cav. At Ft D. A. Russell, WY, in 1910; resident of Parsons, KS. SOURCE: *Illustrated Review: Ninth Cavalry.*

BROOKS, Preston; Corporal; D/9th Cav. Stationed at Ft Riley, KS, 1 Jan–19 Jul 1884; at camp on Chicaskia River, Indian Territory, 21 Jul–19 Oct 1884; at Ft Riley, Oct 1884–27 Feb 1885; at camp on Chilicco Creek, Indian Territory, Mar–May 1885; at Ft Riley to 14 Jun 1885; at Ft McKinney, WY, 19 Aug 1885–21 Aug 1887; served as artificer, Quartermaster Department, Ft McKinney, 30 Apr–31 Dec 1886. SOURCE: VA Invalid Claim 1061386, Preston Brooks.

Original pension application based on injury to right hip, ankle, back; injured when he fell twenty-eight feet off scaffold while weatherboarding building, Ft McKinney, 16 Dec 1885; then sprained right ankle mounting horse, in line of duty, 10 May 1887; discharged Ft McKinney, 21 Aug 1887; resided Junction City, Geary Co., KS, age 36, yellow complexion, 1891; previously carpenter but now cannot work. SOURCE: VA Invalid Claim 1061386, Preston Brooks.

Married to Anna Griffin, Ft Riley; children: Preston Jr., born 4 Jun 1884; Harriet, born Dec 1886, Mary Anna, born Sep 1890. SOURCE: Affidavit, Brooks, 2 May 1902, VA Invalid Claim 1061386, Preston Brooks.

Post engineer, Ft Robinson, NE, admonished to guard against fire by wetting down ashes in barrels as required by post orders. SOURCE: Commander, Ft Robinson, to Mr. Preston Brooks, 12 Apr 1893, LS, Ft Robinson.

Died 10 Aug 1905; buried at Ft Robinson with Masonic rites and 10th Cavalry band; managed Ft Robinson waterworks and sawmill about fifteen years. SOURCE: Crawford *Tribune*, 15 Aug 1905.

Buried, Ft Robinson, 11 Aug 1905. SOURCE: List of Interments, Ft Robinson.

Widow Anna resides in Crawford, NE, 1912, with personal property assessed at $49 and taxed at $4. SOURCE: Dawes County tax records.

Widow inquired about obtaining pension in 1931. SOURCE: VA Invalid Claim 1061386, Preston Brooks.

BROOKS, Robert F.; Private; D/24th Inf. Fined $4 for violating Article 62, while on sick report and restricted to quarters failed to appear at sick call, Cabanatuan, Philippines, 15 Dec 1900. SOURCE: Name File, 24 Inf.

BROOKS, Robert H.; Private; I/24th Inf. Enlisted Baltimore, MD, 17 Feb 1899; joined company 20 Feb 1899. SOURCE: Muster Roll, I/24 Inf, Jan–Feb 1899.

On detached service at Three Rivers, CA, 3 May–21 Jun 1899; on detached service at Presidio of San Francisco, 22 Jun 1899. SOURCE: Muster Roll, I/24 Inf, May–Jun 1899.

Rejoined company, 26 Jul 1899. SOURCE: Muster Roll, I/24 Inf, Jul–Aug 1899.

Fined $1 by summary court, 13 Oct 1899. SOURCE: Muster Roll, I/24 Inf, Sep–Oct 1899.

Captured in the Philippines, 31 Jul 1900. *See* **SMITH**, C. H., Sergeant, I/24th Infantry

BROOKS, W.; Private; A/9th Cav. At Ft Stanton, NM, 1881. SOURCE: Regt Returns, 9 Cav, Jan 1881.

BROOKS, William C.; Corporal; B/10th Cav. At Ft Apache, AZ, 1890, subscribed $.50 to testimonial to General Grierson. SOURCE: List of subscriptions, 23 Apr 1890, 10th Cavalry papers, MHI.

BROOKS, William W.; Recruit; C/9th Cav. Arrived from Jefferson Barracks, MO, 1 Sep 1885. SOURCE: Post Returns, Ft Robinson.

Highly regarded and considered noncommissioned officer material by commander, C/9th Cavalry, who knew him as soldier for number of years. SOURCE: CO, C/9, to AG, USA, 22 Oct 1885, LS, C/9 Cav.

BROOM, Swain P.; Private; I/24th Inf. Enlisted Mobile, AL, 8 Apr 1899; joined company 26 Apr 1899. SOURCE: Muster Roll, I/24 Inf, Mar–Apr 1899.

Allotted $6 per month for six months to Susan Broom. SOURCE: Muster Roll, I/24 Inf, Sep–Oct 1899.

Captured by insurgents in the Philippines, 10 Oct 1900. *See* **BURNS**, William J., Corporal, I/24th Infantry

BROOMFIELD, George; C/10th Cav. Original member of 10th Cavalry; in troop when organized, Ft Leavenworth, KS, 14 May 1867. SOURCE: McMiller, "Buffalo Soldiers," 70.

BROWN; Private; A/10th Cav. At Ft Apache, AZ, 1890, subscribed $.50 to testimonial to General Grierson. SOURCE: List of subscriptions, 23 Apr 1890, 10th Cavalry papers, MHI.

BROWN; Corporal; 10th Cav. Killed while operating Hotchkiss Gun during shelling of San Juan, Cuba, blockhouse, Jul 1898. SOURCE: Johnson, *History of Negro Soldiers*, 28, with picture opposite.

BROWN, Albert; Private; F/9th Cav. At Ft McKinney, WY, studying music, Oct 1886–Apr 1887. SOURCE: Post Returns, Ft Robinson, Feb 1887.

Absent from post school for two weeks, Ft Robinson, NE, Mar 1889. SOURCE: CO, Ft Robinson, to CO, F/9, 30 Mar 1889, LS, Ft Robinson.

BROWN, Albert; Private; Band/24th Inf. Born Murray Co., TN; enlisted E/24th Infantry, age 22, Ht 5'2", black eyes, hair, and complexion, 18 Feb 1876; reenlisted Ft Supply, Indian Territory, 18 Feb 1881; two garrison court martial convictions: fined $1, 17 Jan 1882, and fined one month's pay, 1884; discharged, expiration of term, single, character excellent, "fair alto player," with additional pay $2 per month, retained pay $60, deposits $5, and clothing $86.42, 20 Feb 1886. SOURCE: Descriptive Book, 24 Inf NCS & Band.

BROWN, Albert; Private; D/10th Cav. Enlisted Memphis, TN, 22 Apr 1867. SOURCE: LS, 10 Cav, 1866–67.

BROWN, Alfred; Private; 10th Cav. Enlisted Ft Smith, AR, 16 Apr 1867. SOURCE: LS, 10 Cav, 1866–67.

BROWN, Alfred; 1st Sgt; H/24th Inf. Sergeant, H/24th Infantry, authorized to obey summons to appear at civil court, Tombstone, AZ, with Cpl. James Davis, Pvt. Solomon Scott, Pvt. James H. Williams, all in B/24th Infantry, 26 Oct 1893; authorized to appear again with same men at same court, 17 Nov 1893. SOURCE: Order 159, Ft Huachuca, AZ, 25 Oct 1893, and Order 168, Ft Huachuca, 16 Nov 1893, Letters & Orders Received, 24 Inf, 1893.

Enlisted Ft Huachuca, 22 Sep 1895. SOURCE: Muster Roll, H/24 Inf, May–Jun 1898.

Wounded, San Juan, Cuba, 1 Jul 1898; returned to U.S. for treatment. SOURCE: Muster Roll, H/24 Inf, Jul–Aug 1898.

First sergeant, H/24th Infantry, wounded in action, Cuba, 1898. SOURCE: Muller, *The Twenty Fourth Infantry*, 19.

Discharged, Camp Wikoff, Long Island, character excellent, with $5.76 retained, $46.44 clothing, and $203.50 deposits; enlisted Camp Wikoff, 22 Sep 1898; warrant as sergeant continuous from original appointment, Oct 1892; first sergeant since 5 May 1897; present, sick, wounded in action, since 23 Oct 1898. SOURCE: Muster Roll, H/24 Inf, Sep–Oct 1898.

Sick in quarters, 23 Sep–4 Nov 1898. SOURCE: Muster Roll, H/24 Inf, Nov–Dec 1898.

Discharged, Ft Douglas, UT, character excellent, single, with $37.38 clothing and $416.58 deposits, 29 Jan 1899; enlisted Ft Douglas, beginning twenty-ninth year, 30 Jan 1899. SOURCE: Muster Roll, H/24 Inf, Jan–Feb 1899.

Retired as sergeant, H/24th Infantry, Ft Bayard, NM, Jul 1900. SOURCE: *ANJ* 37 (28 Jul 1900): 1143.

BROWN, Andrew J.; Sergeant; K/9th Cav. Veteran of Philippine Insurrection; at Ft D. A. Russell, WY, in 1910; sharpshooter; resident of Macon, GA. SOURCE: *Illustrated Review: Ninth Cavalry,* with picture.

BROWN, Arthur M.; Acting Assistant Surgeon; 10th Cav. Born Raleigh, NC; graduated from Lincoln University, 1888; graduated from University of Michigan Medical School with high honors, 1891; medical practice and drug business, Birmingham, AL; only black surgeon with regular Army regiment; commander, 10th Cavalry, 12 Aug–8 Oct 1898. SOURCE: Lynk, *The Black Troopers*, 37–39, with drawing on 39; Cashin, *Under Fire with the Tenth Cavalry*, 317–21.

Son of Winfield Scott Brown and Jane M. Brown; first practice at Bessemer, AL, then Chicago, IL, and Cleveland, OH; in Birmingham, 1894, and after Spanish-American War; now surgeon to Home Hospital, Birmingham, and member, surgical staff, Andrew Memorial Hospital, Tuskegee, AL; past president, National Medical Association; married first wife Mamie Lou Coleman of Atlanta, GA, 5 Jun 1895; married present wife Mamie Nellie Adams of Birmingham, 27 Sep 1905; four children: Arthur, Herald, Walter, Marjorie. SOURCE: Richardson, *National Cyclopedia*, 65.

Volunteer for Spanish-American War. SOURCE: Indianapolis *Freeman*, 18 Feb 1899.

An author of *Under Fire with the Tenth Cavalry*, stationed Ft MacIntosh, TX, 1899. SOURCE: Cashin, *Under Fire with the Tenth Cavalry*.

Chairman, surgical section, National Medical Association; attended thirteenth annual convention, Hampton, VA. SOURCE: Cleveland *Gazette*, 30 Sep 1911.

Member of Charles Young mission to Liberia to organize constabulary; title of captain conferred by Liberian government; paid $1,600 per year with quarters. SOURCE: Cleveland *Gazette*, 10 Feb 1912.

BROWN, Augustus; Private; C/10th Cav. Served in 10th Cavalry, 1898; remained in U.S. during war with Spain. SOURCE: Cashin, *Under Fire with the Tenth Cavalry*, 340.

BROWN, Benjamin; Drum Major; 24th Inf. Born Platte City, MO; occupation packer; Ht 5'8", dark complexion; enlisted, age 25, Ft Leavenworth, KS, 14 Oct 1881, G/24th Infantry, transferred to band; discharged, expiration of service, character excellent, Ft Supply, Indian Territory, with $72 retained, $21 clothing, 13 Jul 1886; reenlisted Ft Supply, 16 Jul 1886; discharged, married, character good, Ft Bayard, NM, with additional pay of $2 per month, $65 retained, $11 clothing, 15 Jul 1891; reenlisted Ft Leavenworth, 5 Aug 1891; discharged, married, no children, character very good, Ft Bayard, with additional pay of $3 per month, $53 retained, $7 clothing, 4 Aug 1896. SOURCE: Descriptive Book, 24 Inf NCS & Band.

Sergeant, C/24th Infantry, and sharpshooter, stationed at Ft Sill, Indian Territory. SOURCE: *ANJ* 24 (22 Jan 1887): 510.

Mentioned among men who distinguished themselves in 1889; Medal of Honor awarded for gallant and meritorious conduct while escorting Maj. Joseph W. Wham, paymaster, when attacked by band of robbers between Fts Grant and Thomas, AZ. SOURCE: GO 18, AGO, 1891.

Awarded Medal of Honor for role in Paymaster Wham fight, AZ, 1889. SOURCE: Carroll, *The Black Military Experience*, 279; Thompson, "The Negro Regiments."

Distinguished marksman, 1889 and 1990. SOURCE: GO 112, AGO, 2 Oct 1890.

Sergeant, C/24th Infantry, and one of best marksmen in Army, as he proved at Department of Arizona competition last August. SOURCE: Cleveland *Gazette*, 18 Feb 1893.

His six-month furlough rescinded as of 10 Apr 1893 because he loafed around post most of time since 1 Nov 1892,

stopped at house of ill fame on north border of military reserve on 8 Apr 1893, and was present when enlisted man of the command was killed there. SOURCE: LTC Henry E. Noyes, 2 Cav, Commander, Ft Huachuca, AZ, to AAG, Department of Arizona, 18 Apr 1893, Letters & Orders Received, 24 Inf, 1893.

Distinguished marksman who deserves to compete for place on department rifle team. SOURCE: Commander, C/24, to Adj, Ft Huachuca, 13 Jul 1893, Name File, 24 Inf.

Distinguished marksman, eligible for Army team; designated to participate in Department of Arizona rifle meet. SOURCE: Order 119, Ft Huachuca, 10 Aug 1893, Letters & Orders Received, 24 Inf, 1893.

Authorized to obey summons to appear before civil court, Tombstone, AZ, with Cpl. Thornton Jackson, C/24th Infantry, and Pvt. Alonzo Warnzer, C/24th Infantry. SOURCE: Order 172, Ft Huachuca, Nov 1893, Letters & Orders Received, 24 Inf, 1893.

Succeeds Abbott, appointed ordnance sergeant, as sergeant major, 24th Infantry; Medal of Honor as Wham escort; wounded against Indians; seventeen-year veteran. SOURCE: *ANJ* 34 (7 Aug 1897): 907.

Enlisted Ft Douglas, UT, 24 Mar 1898; sick en route to U.S. since 25 Jul 1898; reduced from regimental sergeant major to private, H/24th Infantry. SOURCE: Muster Roll, H/24 Inf, Jul–Aug 1898.

Furlough authorized by surgeon's certificate, 12 Sep–11 Oct 1898; on special duty, clerk, Quartermaster Department, 5 Oct 1898; promoted to corporal, 8 Oct 1898. SOURCE: Muster Roll, H/24 Inf, Sep–Oct 1898.

Clerk, Quartermaster Department, 5 Oct–24 Dec 1898; sick in hospital since 24 Dec 1898, disease contracted in line of duty. SOURCE: Muster Roll, H/24 Inf, Nov–Dec 1898.

Sick in hospital until 7 Jan 1899; clerk, Quartermaster Department since 5 Oct 1898. SOURCE: Muster Roll, H/24 Inf, Jan–Feb 1899.

Drum major, 24th Infantry, and ranked number 54 among expert riflemen with 68 percent in 1903. SOURCE: GO 52, AGO, 19 Mar 1904.

BROWN, Caesar B.; Private; A/10th Cav. Private, E/10th Cavalry; served in 10th Cavalry, 1898; remained in U.S. during war with Spain. SOURCE: Cashin, *Under Fire with the Tenth Cavalry*, 343.

Daughter Lillian born to wife, maiden name Catherine Rebecca Hill, Ft Robinson, NE, 8 Oct 1904; second child. SOURCE: Medical History, Ft Robinson; Monthly Report, Chaplain Anderson, Ft Robinson, 1 Nov 1904.

BROWN, Charles R.; Corporal; F/9th Cav. Promoted from private, Apr 1902. SOURCE: *ANJ* 39 (10 May 1902): 904.

BROWN, Charles S.; Private; K/25th Inf. Deserted from San Marcelino, Philippines, "cause unknown," 13 Oct 1900. SOURCE: Regt Returns, 25 Inf, Nov 1900.

Apprehended from desertion, 10 Apr 1901. SOURCE: Regt Returns, 25 Inf, Apr 1901.

See Adjutant General Files 432374, 919935, 928208, 932231, 932308, 937305, 942093, 946531

Brown's commander, Col. Andrew Burt, reports delivery of deserters Brown and Pvt. Benjamin Edwards, L/25th Infantry, by surrendering insurgent forces commanded by Col. Ruperto A. Arce, who claims he had captured the two soldiers, that neither took part in operations against U.S., and that both had been treated by him as prisoners of war; Burt believes they are deserters from Army, although he does not think he can prove charges before general court martial. Brown disappeared from his station at San Marcelino, Zambales, 4 Oct 1900, having shown "a peculiar disposition, having very little intercourse with the other men of the company," after assaulting with ax Pvt. Walter Lewis, I/25th Infantry, sentinel on post, intending to rob Lewis, known to carry considerable sum of money on his person; Edwards was captured by insurgents, between Subig and Castillejos, while member of mail escort, 10 Nov 1900; Cpl. Arthur R. D. Smith, L/25th Infantry, also member of detail, was wounded and captured at same time, was freed by insurgents within day or two after capture, has since died; Edwards presumably was offered same privilege but did not accept it; in best interests of service and particularly 25th Infantry, both men should be discharged without honor. SOURCE: Letter, A. S. Burt, Headquarters, 25th Infantry, Iba, Zambales, to Adjutant General, 3rd District, Dagupan, 29 Apr 1901, LS, 25 Inf, 1899–1902.

Brown "made a cowardly assault with intent to kill" on Pvt. Walter Lewis, I/25th Infantry, San Marcelino, 12 Oct 1900, broken up by Corporal Scarce. SOURCE: Staff correspondent [Rienzi B. Lemus, K/25th Infantry], Castillejos, 10 Dec 1900, Richmond *Planet*, 12 Jan 1901.

Deserter Brown returned by insurgent General Arsi [*sic*], when Arsi surrendered to K/25th Infantry, Castillejos, 10 Apr 1901, according to staff correspondent [Rienzi B. Lemus, K/25th Infantry], Castillejos, 23 Apr 1901. SOURCE: Richmond *Planet*, 8 Jun 1901.

BROWN, Charles W.; Sergeant; K/10th Cav. Original member of 10th Cavalry; in troop when organized, Ft Riley, KS, 1 Sep 1867. SOURCE: McMiller, "Buffalo Soldiers," 77.

Sergeant, mentioned, Mar 1869. SOURCE: LR, Det 10 Cav, 1868–69.

BROWN, Clayton L.; Sergeant; 10th Cav. Stationed at Naco, AZ; only African American to pass examination for ordnance sergeant. SOURCE: Cleveland *Gazette*, 2 Oct 1915.

BROWN, Daniel; Cook; D/9th Cav. Veteran of Philippine Insurrection; at Ft D. A. Russell, WY, in 1910; resident of Richmond, VA. SOURCE: *Illustrated Review: Ninth Cavalry.*

BROWN, Daniel; Sergeant; I/10th Cav. Born in Maryland; private, I/10th Cavalry, 26 Jul 1867; corporal, 1 Jan 1871; sergeant, 14 Aug 1872. SOURCE: Baker, Roster.

Original member of 10th Cavalry; in troop when organized, Ft Riley, KS, 15 Aug 1867. SOURCE: McMiller, "Buffalo Soldiers," 76.

Retires from Ft Assiniboine, MT. SOURCE: *ANJ* 35 (11 Sep 1897): 23.

BROWN, Daniel; Sergeant; I/9th Cav. At Ft Niobrara, NE, authorized six-month furlough. SOURCE: *ANJ* 25 (7 Aug 1887): 80.

BROWN, Darrell; K/10th Cav. Original member of 10th Cavalry; in troop when organized, Ft Riley, KS, 1 Sep 1867. SOURCE: McMiller, "Buffalo Soldiers," 77.

BROWN, David; Sergeant; C/24th Inf. At San Carlos, AZ, 1890; awarded Medal of Honor for role in affair (Paymaster Wham robbery) near Cedar Springs, AZ, 11 May 1889. SOURCE: SecWar, *AR 1890*, 290.

BROWN, David; Private; B/9th Cav. Retires from Ft Duchesne, UT, Oct 1893. SOURCE: *ANJ* 31 (28 Oct 1893): 151.

BROWN, David S.; H/10th Cav. Served with Webb Chatmoun, 1880s; lived in Scranton, PA, 1913. SOURCE: VA File C 2360629, Webb Chatmoun.

BROWN, David T.; Sergeant; H/10th Cav. Born in Pennsylvania; private and corporal, H/10th Cav, 17 Nov 1888–16 Nov 1893; private, 18 Nov 1893; corporal, 11 Dec 1893; sergeant, 23 Oct 1895; stationed at Ft Assiniboine, MT, 1897. SOURCE: Baker, Roster.

Stationed in recruiting office, Atlanta, GA, with Lt. Carter P. Johnson, during Cuban campaign, 1898. SOURCE: Cashin, *Under Fire with the Tenth Cavalry*, 220, 346.

BROWN, Edmond; Private; A/10th Cav. Died 11 Mar 1870. SOURCE: ES, 10 Cav, 1866–71.

BROWN, Edward; Private; D/10th Cav. Served in 10th Cavalry, 1898; remained in U.S. during war with Spain. SOURCE: Cashin, *Under Fire with the Tenth Cavalry*, 341.

BROWN, Edward; 24th Inf. Letter from Cranglen, Philippines, 14 Apr 1900, published in Indianapolis *Recorder*, 9 Jun 1900. SOURCE: Gatewood, *"Smoked Yankees"*, 276–77.

BROWN, Elmer; Private; B/25th Inf. Dishonorable discharge, Brownsville. SOURCE: SO 266, AGO, 9 Nov 1906.

Pallbearer for Col. Andrew S. Burt, who had requested that men of 25th Infantry carry his coffin. SOURCE: Curtis, *The Black Soldier*, 49.

BROWN, Elwin; Private; L/10th Cav. Sentenced by general court martial. SOURCE: SO 56, DeptMo, 24 Mar 1904.

BROWN, Francis M.; E/10th Cav. Original member of 10th Cavalry; in troop when organized, Ft Leavenworth, KS, 15 Jun 1867. SOURCE: McMiller, "Buffalo Soldiers," 72.

BROWN, Frank; Private; B/9th Cav. At Ft D. A. Russell, WY, in 1910. SOURCE: *Illustrated Review: Ninth Cavalry.*

BROWN, Frank A. D.; Private; C/10th Cav. Drowned, Bayamo, Cuba, 3 Apr 1901. SOURCE: *ANJ* 38 (13 Apr 1901): 803.

BROWN, Frank B.; Corporal; L/24th Inf. Enlisted Boston, MA, 14 Nov 1897, with fourteen years' service. SOURCE: Muster Roll, H/24 Inf, May–Jun 1898.

On special duty as cook since 27 Aug 1898. SOURCE: Muster Roll, H/24 Inf, Jul–Aug 1898.

Absent, whereabouts unknown; sick since 23 Sep 1898, line of duty. SOURCE: Muster Roll, H/24 Inf, Sep–Oct 1898.

Sick, in line of duty, 23 Sep–1 Dec 1898; fifteenth year began 11 Nov 1898. SOURCE: Muster Roll, H/24 Inf, Nov–Dec 1898.

On special duty as laborer, Quartermaster Department, since 27 Jan 1899. SOURCE: Muster Roll, H/24 Inf, Jan–Feb 1899.

Ranked number 21 among rifle experts with 78.33 percent in 1905. SOURCE: GO 101, AGO, 31 May 1906.

BROWN, Frederic; Private; F/10th Cav. Transferred to Hospital Corps at Ft Grant, AZ. SOURCE: *ANJ* 25 (25 Aug 1888): 1132.

BROWN, Garfield; Trumpeter; G/9th Cav. Served as private, G/10th Cavalry, in Cuba, 1898. SOURCE: Cashin, *Under Fire with the Tenth Cavalry*, 343.

Trumpeter, G/9th Cavalry, at Ft D. A. Russell, WY, in 1910; resident of New York City. SOURCE: *Illustrated Review: Ninth Cavalry*, with picture.

BROWN, George; Private; M/9th Cav. At Ft Cummings, NM, 1881. *See* **WHITE**, Thomas, Private, M/9th Cavalry

BROWN, George; Private; G/10th Cav. Honorable mention for bravery against Indians, Lake Quemado, TX, 3 Aug 1880. SOURCE: Baker, Roster.

Died Somerton, AZ. SOURCE: *Winners of the West* 6 (Jun 1929): 7.

BROWN, George; B/9th Cav. Admitted to Soldiers Home, with twenty years and seven months' service, age 42. SOURCE: SecWar, *AR 1890*, 1041.

BROWN, George; Private; K/25th Inf. At Ft Niobrara, NE, 1904. SOURCE: Wilson, "History of Fort Niobrara."

BROWN, George A.; Wagoner; K/24th Inf. Died in Cuba, 1 Jul 1898. SOURCE: *ANJ* 36 (11 Feb 1899): 567.

Killed in action, Cuba, 1898. SOURCE: Scipio, *Last of the Black Regulars*, 29.

BROWN, George F.; Private; H/9th Cav. At Ft D. A. Russell, WY, in 1910; sharpshooter; resident of Gallipolis, OH. SOURCE: *Illustrated Review: Ninth Cavalry.*

BROWN, George H.; M/10th Cav. Original member of 10th Cavalry; in troop when organized, Ft Riley, KS, 15 Oct 1867. SOURCE: McMiller, "Buffalo Soldiers," 79.

BROWN, George H.; Private; B/10th Cav. Commander of 10th Cavalry asks that Brown, Ft Griffin, TX, be returned to duty without trial for desertion; while at Dennison, TX, Brown was left behind by his detachment, went to Ft Gibson, nearest post, and surrendered; eight years in regiment, seven as sergeant, five as quartermaster sergeant, until now "a good and efficient soldier." SOURCE: Commander, 10 Cav, to AAG, Department of Texas, 19 Sep 1875, LS,10 Cav, 1873–83.

BROWN, George L.; Corporal; D/9th Cav. Veteran of Spanish-American War and Philippine Insurrection; at Ft D. A. Russell, WY, in 1910; sharpshooter. SOURCE: *Illustrated Review: Ninth Cavalry*, with picture.

BROWN, George W.; E/10th Cav. Original member of 10th Cavalry; in troop when organized, Ft Leavenworth, KS, 15 Jun 1867. SOURCE: McMiller, "Buffalo Soldiers," 72.

Admitted to Soldiers Home, for disability, with one and one-half year's service, age 46, 18 Feb 1890. SOURCE: SecWar, *AR 1890*, 1041.

Died, Soldiers Home, chronic pneumonia, 20 Aug 1894. SOURCE: SecWar, *AR 1894*, 526.

BROWN, George W.; Private; I/10th Cav. Ranked number nine with revolver, Department of the Missouri, bronze medal, 1894. SOURCE: Baker, Roster.

BROWN, George W.; Private; B/10th Cav. Released to duty from treatment for acute gonorrhea, Ft Robinson, NE, 18 Jan 1903. SOURCE: Post Surgeon to CO, B/10, 18 Jan 1903, LS, Post Surgeon, Ft Robinson.

Sentenced to dishonorable discharge and confinement, Ft Robinson, Dec 1903. SOURCE: SO 242, DeptMo, 14 Dec 1903.

Released Jun 1904.

BROWN, George W.; QM Sgt; M/9th Cav. Veteran of Philippine Insurrection; at Ft D. A. Russell, WY, in 1910; resident of Macon, GA. SOURCE: *Illustrated Review: Ninth Cavalry*, with picture.

BROWN, Griggs; A/10th Cav. Original member of 10th Cavalry; in troop when organized, Ft Leavenworth, KS, 18 Feb 1867. SOURCE: McMiller, "Buffalo Soldiers," 68.

BROWN, Harvey; Private; F/9th Cav. At Ft D. A. Russell, WY, in 1910; resident of Dallas. SOURCE: *Illustrated Review: Ninth Cavalry.*

BROWN, Hays; Private; E/10th Cav. Served in 10th Cavalry, 1898; remained in U.S. during war with Spain. SOURCE: Cashin, *Under Fire with the Tenth Cavalry*, 343.

BROWN, Henry R.; Private; K/25th Inf. At Ft Niobrara, NE, 1904. SOURCE: Wilson, "History of Fort Niobrara."

BROWN, Henry T. W.; Private; D/25th Inf. Dishonorable discharge, Brownsville. SOURCE: SO 266, AGO, 9 Nov 1906.

BROWN, Hillery; Private; E/10th Cav. Served in 10th Cavalry in Cuba, 1898. SOURCE: Cashin, *Under Fire with the Tenth Cavalry*, 342.

Wounded in action, Santiago, Cuba, 1 Jul 1898. SOURCE: SecWar, *AR 1898*, 324.

BROWN, Isaac; Private; C/9th Cav. Recruit, arrived at Ft Robinson, NE, from depot, 1 Mar 1887.

BROWN, J.; Private; F/10th Cav. Wounded in action, Kansas, 21 Aug 1867. SOURCE: Armes, *Ups and Downs*, 247.

BROWN, J. F.; Private; K/9th Cav. Deserted, Ft Cummings, NM, 14 Jan 1881. SOURCE: Regt Returns, 9 Cav, Jan 1881.

BROWN, J. M.; Private; B/10th Cav. Discharged. SOURCE: SO 128, DeptMo, 12 Jul 1904.

BROWN, James; F/10th Cav. Original member of 10th Cavalry; in troop when organized, Ft Leavenworth, KS, 21 Jun 1867. SOURCE: McMiller, "Buffalo Soldiers," 73.

BROWN, James; K/10th Cav. Original member of 10th Cavalry; in troop when organized, Ft Riley, KS, 1 Sep 1867. SOURCE: McMiller, "Buffalo Soldiers," 77.

BROWN, James; 1st Sgt; I/10th Cav. "Displayed rare courage and judgment," severely wounded by arrow in running fight with Cheyennes, Kansas, Jun 1867; honorable mention for conspicuous bravery against Cheyennes, Beaver Creek, KS, where he was severely wounded by arrow which pinned his legs together, 18 Oct 1868. SOURCE: Baker, Roster.

Original member of 10th Cavalry; in troop when organized, Ft Riley, KS, 15 Aug 1867. SOURCE: McMiller, "Buffalo Soldiers," 76.

Reenlisted as first sergeant, I/10th Cavalry, Jul 1877. SOURCE: ES, 10 Cav, 1873–81.

At Ft Apache, AZ, 1890, subscribed $.50 to testimonial to General Grierson. SOURCE: List of subscriptions, 23 Apr 1890, 10th Cavalry papers, MHI.

See **LOVELACE**, Scott, Corporal, I/10th Cavalry

In 10th Cavalry since Jul 1867 and I Troop since Aug 1867; promoted first sergeant, 1 Aug 1872; probably senior first sergeant in Army; recommended for Medal of Honor for

heroism, 18 Oct 1868; froze to death in storm, en route from Havre, MT, to Ft Assiniboine, MT, 5 Feb 1895. Capt. S. L. Woodward, I/10th Cavalry, called him "in every sense a gallant and efficient soldier. He knew no fear and there were no difficulties too great for him to attempt to surmount. His untimely death has deprived the regiment and the Army of a model soldier." SOURCE: *ANJ* 32 (23 Feb 1895): 422.

His widow of one year taken care of by 10th Cavalry; according to a sergeant, "that woman ain't going to want for bread while the 10th Cav. has a ration left." SOURCE: *ANJ* 33 (7 Dec 1895): 29.

BROWN, James; Private; B/9th Cav. On detached service, Ft Bayard, NM, 16 Jan–9 Feb 1881. SOURCE: Regt Returns, 9 Cav, Feb 1881.

Killed in action against Apaches, Gabaldon Canyon, NM, Aug 1881. SOURCE: Billington, *New Mexico's Buffalo Soldiers*, 105.

Killed in action, 19 Aug 1881. *See* **GOLDEN**, Thomas, Saddler, B/9th Cavalry

BROWN, James; Private; E/10th Cav. Served in 10th Cavalry, 1898; remained in U.S. during war with Spain. SOURCE: Cashin, *Under Fire with the Tenth Cavalry*, 343.

BROWN, James E.; Private; Band/24th Inf. Born York, PA; brown eyes, brown hair, mulatto; served in F/9th Cavalry, character good, 27 Jun 1878–26 Jun 1883; enlisted, E/24th Infantry, Ft Leavenworth, KS, 11 Aug 1884; joined Band/24th Infantry, Ft Sill, Indian Territory, 6 Feb 1888; returned to E/24th Infantry, 1 Oct 1888. SOURCE: Entry, Ft Bayard, NM, 6 Oct 1888, Descriptive Book, 24 Inf NCS & Band.

BROWN, James M.; D/10th Cav. Original member of 10th Cavalry; in troop when organized, Ft Leavenworth, KS, 1 Jun 1867. SOURCE: McMiller, "Buffalo Soldiers," 71.

BROWN, John; A/10th Cav. Original member of 10th Cavalry; in troop when organized, Ft Leavenworth, KS, 18 Feb 1867. SOURCE: McMiller, "Buffalo Soldiers," 68.

BROWN, John; E/10th Cav. Original member of 10th Cavalry; in troop when organized, Ft Leavenworth, KS, 15 Jun 1867. SOURCE: McMiller, "Buffalo Soldiers," 68.

BROWN, John; H/10th Cav. Original member of 10th Cavalry; in troop when organized, Ft Leavenworth, KS, 21 Jul 1867. SOURCE: McMiller, "Buffalo Soldiers," 75.

BROWN, John; I/10th Cav. Original member of 10th Cavalry; in troop when organized, Ft Riley, KS, 15 Aug 1867. SOURCE: McMiller, "Buffalo Soldiers," 76.

BROWN, John; Private; M/10th Cav. Enlisted Buffalo, NY, Aug 1876; belongs with B Troop, Ft Duncan, TX, not M Troop, Ft Clark, TX. SOURCE: ES, 10 Cav, 1873–81.

BROWN, John; Recruit; Colored Detachment/ Mounted Service. Convicted by general court martial, Jefferson Barracks, MO, of desertion, 13–14 Jan 1884; pled not guilty; sentenced to dishonorable discharge and two years' confinement. SOURCE: GCMO 12, AGO, 26 Feb 1885.

BROWN, John; Private; C/9th Cav. At Ft D. A. Russell, WY, in 1910; resident of Makersville, MO. SOURCE: *Illustrated Review: Ninth Cavalry*, with picture.

BROWN, John; Private; C/9th Cav. Died of typhoid, post hospital, Ft Robinson, NE, 26 Jun 1887. SOURCE: Medical History, Ft Robinson.

Funeral, Ft Robinson, 27 Jun 1887. SOURCE: Order 127, 26 Jun 1887, Post Orders, Ft Robinson; List of Interments, Ft Robinson.

Post commander replies to letter from Mrs. Laura V. Brown of Los Angeles, CA, informing her that Private Brown died on 26 Jun 1887, and that his troop is now at Ft Duchesne, UT. SOURCE: CO, Ft Robinson, to Mrs. Laura V. Brown, 2 Jul 1890, LS, Ft Robinson.

BROWN, John; Private; C/10th Cav. Served in 10th Cavalry in Cuba, 1898. SOURCE: Cashin, *Under Fire with the Tenth Cavalry*, 340.

Wounded in action, Santiago, Cuba, 1 July 1898. SOURCE: SecWar, *AR 1898*, 324.

BROWN, John; Trumpeter; K/10th Cav. Served in 10th Cavalry, 1898; remained in U.S. during war with Spain. SOURCE: Cashin, *Under Fire with the Tenth Cavalry*, 349.

BROWN, John; Private; B/25th Inf. Dishonorable discharge, Brownsville. SOURCE: SO 266, AGO, 9 Nov 1906.

BROWN, John H.; Sergeant; 9th Cav. On detached recruiting service. SOURCE: SO 91, AGO, 18 Apr 1892.

BROWN, John H.; Private; E/10th Cav. Served in 10th Cavalry in Cuba, 1898. SOURCE: Cashin, *Under Fire with the Tenth Cavalry*, 342.

Appointed cook. SOURCE: SO 35, 10 Cav, Ft Sam Houston, TX, 1 Apr 1899.

BROWN, John H.; Private; K/10th Cav. At Ft Robinson, NE, 1904.

BROWN, John H.; Private; H/24th Inf. Convicted by summary court martial of being drunk and disorderly in quarters and using abusive language to first sergeant, San Isidro, Philippines, 19 Dec 1901, sentenced to twenty days and fined one month's pay, second conviction; fined $3 for allowing prisoners to gamble while prison guard, 19 Jan 1902; fined one month's pay for absence from 10 P.M. inspection and lying out of quarters without leave, 12 Feb 1902. SOURCE: Register of Summary Court, San Isidro.

BROWN, John L.; Private; G/10th Cav. "A letter just received at these Hdqrs signed the Enlisted men of Company G 10 Cavalry states that 'Pvt. John L. Brown on the night of 28th was taken out and tied up, and remained there until he died, and then he was cut down and put in a box, thrown in the ground just as if he was a dog, and that is not all, they put great logs on men and make them carry it until they can't walk and we call on you for protection' "; commander unwilling to credit this statement and wants full report. SOURCE: Adj, 10 Cav, to CO, G/10, 7 Dec 1876, LS, 10 Cav, 1873–83.

Follow-up letter calls attention to 7 Dec 1876 letter, again asks for full report. SOURCE: Adj, 10 Cav, to CO, G/10, 11 Feb 1877, LS, 10 Cav, 1873–83.

Adjutant forwards statement of enlisted men of G/10th Cavalry and two earlier requests for full report of commander, G/10th Cavalry; asks for investigation and report without delay. SOURCE: Adj, 10 Cav, to AAG, Department of Texas, 19 Mar 1877, LS, 10 Cav, 1873–83.

Commander of Tenth Cavalry forwards additional complaints from G/10th Cavalry, Ft Griffin, TX; contends interests of service require further action; writes that commander, G/10th Cavalry, reports Brown a suicide; wants full investigation. SOURCE: CO, 10 Cav, to AAG, Department of Texas, 27 Apr 1877, LS, 10 Cav, 1873–83.

Letter from enlisted men, 10th Cavalry, Ft Concho, TX, who "respectfully request that investigations be made in the case of the murder of John L. Brown, late private of Company G 10th Cavalry," forwarded to Department of the Missouri. SOURCE: CO, 10 Cav, to HQ, Department of the Missouri, 27 Apr 1877, LS, 10 Cav, 1873–83.

BROWN, John L.; Private; D/10th Cav. Killed by civilian, San Angelo, TX, 1877. SOURCE: Leckie, *The Buffalo Soldiers*, 164.

BROWN, John M.; Major; 23rd Kans Inf. Commanded first battalion. SOURCE: Beasley, *Negro Trailblazers*, 284.

BROWN, John W.; Private; C/9th Cav. Enlisted Baltimore, MD; discharged, Ft Robinson, NE, expiration of term, 19 May 1886. SOURCE: CO, C/9, to Chief Paymaster, DP, 22 Apr 1886, LS, C/9 Cav.

BROWN, John W.; Comsy Sgt; 9th Cav. Born Falmouth, Stafford Co., VA, 5 May 1856; enlisted 24 Apr 1876; assigned to D/24th Infantry; discharged as sergeant, 23 Apr 1881; reenlisted, C/9th Cavalry, May 1881; corporal, sergeant, first sergeant, saddler sergeant; commissioned second lieutenant, 9th U.S. Volunteer Infantry, 24 Oct 1898, and joined regiment at San Luis, Cuba, 6 Dec 1898. SOURCE: Coston, *The Spanish-American War Volunteer*, 27.

Sergeant, A/9th Cavalry, since 8 Aug 1886. SOURCE: Roster, 9 Cav, 1893.

Sergeant, A/9th Cavalry, promoted to saddler sergeant, 9th Cavalry, 7 Jul 1897. SOURCE: *ANJ* 34 (17 Jul 1897): 854.

Saddler sergeant, 9th Cavalry, commissioned second lieutenant, 9th Volunteer Infantry, 1898. SOURCE: Cashin, *Under Fire with the Tenth Cavalry* 360; San Francisco *Chronicle*, 15 Nov 1899.

Appointed regimental commissary sergeant, Apr 1902. SOURCE: *ANJ* 39 (10 May 1902): 904.

Son of John B. and Julia Miner, Falmouth, VA; excellent marksman and former regimental clerk; commissioned in 9th U.S. Volunteer Infantry and served in Cuba; first lieutenant, G/48th Infantry, Philippines; returned to 9th Cavalry after insurrection; retired with twenty-seven years as commissary sergeant. SOURCE: Beasley, *Negro Trailblazers*, 298.

BROWN, Joseph; Private; A/9th Cav. Relieved from extra duty as teamster, Quartermaster Department, Ft Robinson, NE. SOURCE: SO 86, 8 Aug 1896, Post Orders, Ft Robinson.

BROWN, Larson J.; Private; L/24th Inf. A leader of Houston mutiny, had trouble persuading men of his company to join rebels; sentenced to death. SOURCE: Haynes, *A Night of Violence*, 128, 271.

Hanged, Ft Sam Houston, TX, 13 Dec 1917, for part in Houston riot. SOURCE: Cleveland *Gazette*, 15 Dec 1917.

BROWN, Lee; Private; C/24th Inf. Missing in action, Manicling, Philippines, 13 Sep 1900. SOURCE: Muller, *The Twenty Fourth Infantry*, 38.

Died of tuberculosis in the Philippines. SOURCE: *ANJ* 38 (16 Mar 1901): 703.

BROWN, Louis; Corporal; K/49th Inf. Died of appendicitis at Aparri, Luzon, Philippines, 24 May 1901.

BROWN, Milton M.; Corporal; 49th Inf. In the Philippines, 1899–1901; reports that white troops did easier garrison duty than blacks. SOURCE: Cleveland *Gazette*, 14 Nov 1908.

BROWN, Morris; Sergeant; Band/9th Cav. Veteran of Philippine Insurrection; at Ft D. A. Russell, WY, in 1910; resident of Baltimore. SOURCE: *Illustrated Review: Ninth Cavalry,* with picture.

BROWN, Oscar S.; Corporal; F/24th Inf. Sergeant, M/10th Cavalry, 1890, subscribed $.50 to testimonial to General Grierson. SOURCE: List of subscriptions, 23 Apr 1890, 10th Cavalry papers, MHI.

Sergeant, G/10th Cavalry, Ft Grant, AZ, 1890. *See* **BERRY**, Edward, Sergeant, H/24th Infantry

Sergeant, C/10th Cavalry, reduced to ranks, Ft Bayard, NM, for disobeying orders. SOURCE: *ANJ* 29 (6 Feb 1892): 411.

As corporal, F/24th Infantry, ranked number 152 among rifle experts with 69 percent, 1904. SOURCE: GO 79, AGO, 1 Jun 1905.

BROWN, Philip; Private; D/24th Inf. Fined $10 for violating Article 62, insubordination to Cpl. Thomas Johnson, refusal to accompany him to 1st Sgt. M. H. Ellis before he finished his breakfast, and saying to Sergeant Ellis, "You can put charges against me, I don't give a damn, you have been trying to get me into the guardhouse for over a year," Cabanatuan, Philippines, 14 Jan 1901; witnesses: 1st Sgt. M. H. Ellis, Cpl. Thomas Johnson, Pvt. J. D. Davis, Pvt. C. F. Mitchell, all D/24th Infantry; confined for one month and fined one month's pay for violating Article 62, insubordination to Cpl. Thomas Johnson's order to clean up his bunk, Cabanatuan, 14 Jun 1901; witnesses: Cpl. Thomas Johnson, Pvt. Wheeler Pride, Pvt. William Berry, all D/24th Infantry. SOURCE: Name File, 24 Inf.

BROWN, R. H.; Private; F/24th Inf. Died of "gastro-duo" at Camp Wikoff, NY, 14 Sep 1898. SOURCE: Hospital Papers, Spanish-American War.

BROWN, Richard; Recruit; G/Colored Inf General Service Recruits. Convicted by general court martial, Columbus Barracks, OH, for desertion, 8 Nov–29 Dec 1879; sentenced to dishonorable discharge and four years' confinement. SOURCE: GCMO 3, AGO, 9 Jan 1880.

BROWN, Richard; Private; 24th Inf. Served in Houston, 1917. SOURCE: Haynes, *A Night of Violence*, 87.

BROWN, Robert; L/10th Cav. Original member of 10th Cavalry; in troop when organized, Ft Riley, KS, 21 Sep 1867. SOURCE: McMiller, "Buffalo Soldiers," 78.

BROWN, Robert; Private; H/24th Inf. Enlisted Louisville, KY, 3 Aug 1893; five years' continuous service; due U.S. for lost ordnance (one spoon), two cents. SOURCE: Muster Roll, H/24 Inf, May–Jun 1898.

Honorably discharged, expiration of term, character excellent, single, Siboney, Cuba, 10 Aug 1898; due for clothing $6.80, retained $7.53. SOURCE: Muster Roll, H/24 Inf, Jul–Aug 1898.

BROWN, Robert C., Jr.; Private; D/10th Cav. Served in 10th Cavalry, 1898; remained in U.S. during war with Spain. SOURCE: Cashin, *Under Fire with the Tenth Cavalry*, 341.

BROWN, Rosen T.; 1st Sgt; Machine Gun Troop/ 10th Cav. Private, K/9th Cavalry, expert rifleman at Ft D. A. Russell, WY, in 1910; resident of Whiteside, TN. SOURCE: *Illustrated Review: Ninth Cavalry,* with picture.

Sergeant, D/10th Cavalry, commissioned first lieutenant, Camp Des Moines, IA, 15 Oct 1917. SOURCE: Glass, *History of the Tenth Cavalry*, appendix M.

Won Shipp Cup as outstanding soldier in 10th Cavalry, Organization Day, 28 Jul 1928. SOURCE: *Cavalry Journal* 37 (Oct 1928): 594.

Picture, as first sergeant, Machine Gun Troop, 10th Cavalry. SOURCE: *Cavalry Journal* 40 (Sep–Oct 1931): 59.

BROWN, Samuel; Private; F/9th Cav. At Ft D. A. Russell, WY, in 1910; resident of Eufaula, AL. SOURCE: *Illustrated Review: Ninth Cavalry,* with picture.

BROWN, Samuel, Jr.; Private; A/10th Cav. Served in 10th Cavalry, 1898; remained in U.S. during war with Spain. SOURCE: Cashin, *Under Fire with the Tenth Cavalry,* 337.

BROWN, Simon; Private; 23rd Kans Inf. Letter from San Luis, Cuba, 12 Sep 1898. SOURCE: Gatewood, *"Smoked Yankees",* 193–96.

BROWN, Smith; Private; C/10th Cav. Dishonorably discharged and confined, Ft Robinson, NE, Dec 1903. SOURCE: SO 241, DeptMo, 11 Dec 1903.

General prisoner, Ft Robinson; application for clemency disapproved by officer in charge of prisoners, with concurrence of post commander and Department of the Missouri headquarters. SOURCE: Register, LR, Ft Robinson.

BROWN, Sterling Price; 1st Lt; 9th Inf USV. Born Atlanta, GA, 23 Dec 1863; attended public schools until age 14; completed academic course at Central Tennessee College, Nashville, TN; graduated Meharry Medical College with honors, 1884; practiced medicine in New Orleans, LA. SOURCE: Coston, *The Spanish-American War Volunteer,* 29.

BROWN, Thaddeus W.; E/25th Inf and E/9th Cav. Subscriber, age 70. SOURCE: *Winners of the West* 9 (Apr 1932): 2.

BROWN, Thomas; Private; F/9th Cav. Convicted by general court martial, David's Island, NY, of desertion, 10 Jul 1880–26 May 1885; sentenced to dishonorable discharge and three years' confinement. SOURCE: GCMO 68, AGO, 24 Jun 1885.

BROWN, Thomas; Sergeant; A/24th Inf. Retires from Ft Huachuca, AZ, Oct 1895. SOURCE: *ANJ* 33 (12 Oct 1895): 87.

BROWN, Thomas; Private; H/24th Inf. Enlisted Versailles, KY, 7 Oct 1898; joined company 17 Nov 1898. SOURCE: Muster Roll, H/24 Inf, Nov–Dec 1898.

Discharged, Ft Douglas, UT, character good, single, deposits $6, 28 Jan 1899. SOURCE: Muster Roll, H/24 Inf, Jan–Feb 1899.

BROWN, Thomas C.; Private; C/24th Inf. Wounded in action, Manicling, Luzon, Philippines, northeast of San Isidro, 24 Jul 1900; missing in action, Manicling, 13 Sep 1900. SOURCE: Muller, *The Twenty Fourth Infantry,* 38.

Captured by insurgents south of Saragossa, Luzon; released by Lieutenant Hannay and K/22nd Infantry. SOURCE: Manila *Times,* 17 and 19 Oct 1900.

Wounded in shoulder, Manicling, 4 Jul 1901. SOURCE: *ANJ* 37 (14 Jul 1901): 1083.

BROWN, Thomas Hatcher; E/24th Inf. Served 1893–96. SOURCE: *Winners of the West* 13 (Sep 1936): 16.

Has had ten months' work in last four years: "in a city like Chicago with its high costs of living it is only by the mercies of others I am able to get by"; served at Ft Bayard, NM, with Jack Haines, who is in Chicago; got $30 per month pension in Jun 1932. SOURCE: *Winners of the West* 9 (Mar 1932): 7.

BROWN, Tom; Private; B/25th Inf. Born in Tennessee; private and corporal, K/24th Infantry, 14 Nov 1879–13 Nov 1889; private, corporal, sergeant, B/9th Cavalry, 14 Nov 1889–13 Nov 1894; private, C/10th Cavalry, 6 Dec 1894; corporal, 21 Mar 1895; sergeant, 20 Sep 1895. SOURCE: Baker, Roster.

Sergeant, B/9th Cavalry, since 18 Jun 1891. SOURCE: Roster, 9 Cav, 1893.

As private, B/25th Infantry, wounded, El Caney, Cuba, 1 Jul 1898. SOURCE: Nankivell, *History of the Twenty-fifth Infantry,* 83.

BROWN, Tracy F.; Private; F/10th Cav. Served in 10th Cavalry in Cuba, 1898. SOURCE: Cashin, *Under Fire with the Tenth Cavalry,* 343.

BROWN, W.; Private; L/9th Cav. On detached service, Santa Fe, NM, 7 Sep 1880–22 Feb 1881. SOURCE: Regt Returns, 9 Cav, Feb 1881.

BROWN, W. A.; Private; K/9th Cav. On detached service in field, New Mexico, 21 Jan–8 Feb 1881. SOURCE: Regt Returns, 9 Cav, Feb 1881.

BROWN, W. H.; Private; D/9th Cav. Discharged, Ft Cummings, NM, 31 Jan 1881, in accordance with General Court Martial Order 9, Department of the Missouri. SOURCE: Regt Returns, 9 Cav, Feb 1881.

BROWN, Walker; G/25th Inf. Recent suicide by shooting, Ft Missoula, MT. SOURCE: *ANJ* 30 (11 Mar 1893): 479.

BROWN, Washington; Sergeant; K/10th Cav. Born in Maryland; enlisted E/40th Infantry, 6 Nov 1866; discharged 6 Nov 1869; reenlisted G/10th Cavalry, 22 Nov 1869; private, corporal, sergeant, first sergeant; transferred to K/10th Cavalry as private, 10 Apr 1885; sergeant, 7 Aug 1885; stationed at Ft Custer, MT, 1897; cited for heroism against Apaches in General Field Order 12, Department of Arizona, 1886. SOURCE: Baker, Roster.

At Ft Apache, AZ, 1890, subscribed $.50 to testimonial to General Grierson. SOURCE: List of subscriptions, 23 Apr 1890, 10th Cavalry papers, MHI.

Will be sent from San Carlos, AZ, to Hot Springs, AR, Army and Navy Hospital for admission. SOURCE: *ANJ* 28 (28 Mar 1891): 528.

Retires from Ft Custer. SOURCE: *ANJ* 34 (8 May 1897): 665.

BROWN, William; F/41st Inf. Served 1867–70; now 84 years old. SOURCE: *Winners of the West* 12 (Nov 1935): 3.

BROWN, William; Private; F/10th Cav. Original member of 10th Cavalry; in troop when organized, Ft Leavenworth, KS, 21 Jun 1867. SOURCE: McMiller, "Buffalo Soldiers," 73.

Detailed as teamster. SOURCE: SO 54, HQ, Camp Supply, Indian Territory, 31 Jul 1869, Orders, Det 10 Cav, 1868–69.

BROWN, William; Private; B/24th Inf. At Ft Mac-Intosh, TX, 1877. *See* **GRAYSON**, Charles H., Private, G/24th Infantry

BROWN, William; Private; K/9th Cav. Deserted, Ft Cummings, NM, 14 Jan 1881. SOURCE: Regt Returns, 9 Cav, Jan 1881.

BROWN, William; Private; A/9th Cav. Transferred to Hospital Corps, Ft Niobrara, NE. SOURCE: *ANJ* 26 (1 Sep 1888): 6.

BROWN, William; Private; E/9th Cav. Relieved from extra duty as teamster, Quartermaster Department, Ft Robinson, NE. SOURCE: SO 90, 20 Aug 1896, Post Orders, Ft Robinson.

Authorized to reenlist as married. SOURCE: Regt Returns, 9 Cav, Nov 1896.

BROWN, William; Sergeant; H/10th Cav. Born in Maryland; private, F/10th Cavalry, 9 Dec 1881–8 Dec 1886; private and corporal, B/10th Cavalry, 30 Dec 1886–29 Dec 1891; private, H/10th Cavalry, 11 Jan 1892; corporal, 11 Aug 1893; sergeant, 6 Feb 1895; stationed at Ft Assiniboine, MT, 1897. SOURCE: Baker, Roster.

At Ft Apache, AZ, corporal, B/10th Cavalry, 1890, subscribed $.50 to testimonial to General Grierson. SOURCE: List of subscriptions, 23 Apr 1890, 10th Cavalry papers, MHI.

At Ft Apache, corporal, B/10th Cavalry, 1891; sharpshooter. SOURCE: *ANJ* 28 (4 Jul 1891): 765.

At Ft Robinson, NE, Sep 1897, for cavalry competition.

Served in 10th Cavalry, 1898; remained in U.S. during war with Spain. SOURCE: Cashin, *Under Fire with the Tenth Cavalry*, 347.

Visited by wife from Washington, DC, at Camp Forse, AL, Thanksgiving 1898. SOURCE: Richmond *Planet*, 3 Dec 1898.

BROWN, William; Private; D/10th Cav. Served in 10th Cavalry in Cuba, 1898. SOURCE: Cashin, *Under Fire with the Tenth Cavalry*, 341.

BROWN, William (1); Private; G/10th Cav. Served in 10th Cavalry in Cuba, 1898. SOURCE: Cashin, *Under Fire with the Tenth Cavalry*, 345.

BROWN, William (2); Private; G/10th Cav. Served in 10th Cavalry, 1898; remained in U.S. during war with Spain. SOURCE: Cashin, *Under Fire with the Tenth Cavalry*, 345.

BROWN, William; Private; G/10th Cav. Appointed cook. SOURCE: SO 35, 10 Cav, Ft Sam Houston, TX, 1 Apr 1899.

BROWN, William; Sergeant; L/10th Cav. Ranked number 29 among expert riflemen with 77.33 percent in 1904. SOURCE: GO 79, AGO, 1 Jun 1905.

BROWN, William; Private; B/25th Inf. Dishonorable discharge, Brownsville. SOURCE: SO 266, AGO, 9 Nov 1906.

BROWN, William; Private; C/9th Cav. Veteran of Philippine Insurrection; at Ft D. A. Russell, WY, in 1910; resident of Topeka, KS. SOURCE: *Illustrated Review: Ninth Cavalry,* with picture.

Deserter, caught at Cheyenne, WY, railroad depot. SOURCE: Cheyenne *State Leader*, 14 Mar 1911.

BROWN, William A.; Private; I/10th Cav. Confined at Ft Robinson, NE, Oct–Nov 1902.

BROWN, William H.; Private; D/9th Cav. At Ft Robinson, NE, awaiting trial for desertion, Oct 1889–22 Jan 1890, when returned to station, Ft McKinney, WY.

BROWN, William H.; Private; A/10th Cav. Served in 10th Cavalry in Cuba, 1898. SOURCE: Cashin, *Under Fire with the Tenth Cavalry*, 336.

Wounded in action, Santiago, Cuba, 3 Jul 1898. SOURCE: SecWar, *AR 1898*, 324.

Narrative of participation in San Juan campaign. SOURCE: Johnson, *History of Negro Soldiers*, 64; Young, *Reminiscences*.

BROWN, William H.; Private; C/10th Cav. Served in 10th Cavalry in Cuba, 1898. SOURCE: Cashin, *Under Fire with the Tenth Cavalry*, 340.

BROWN, William H.; Captain; G/48th Inf. Born Blue Ridge Mountains, VA; educated in Pittsburgh, PA; in 10th Cavalry, 1886–91, and participated in Lt. Carter P. Johnson's expedition against the Apache leader Kid; in 9th Cavalry, 1882–99, private, sergeant, and sergeant major. SOURCE: *ANJ* 37 (18 Nov 1899): 278.

Private, 9th Cavalry, at Ft Robinson, NE, awaiting assignment, Jul 1892.

Private, A/9th Cavalry, on extra duty as schoolteacher, Ft Robinson, 1 Nov 1893–12 Sep 1894.

Typist, post headquarters, Ft Robinson, 1894; with troops to Butte, MT, summer 1894. SOURCE: Court Martial Records, Plummer.

Teacher, Ft Robinson school, 1 Feb–30 Apr 1895. SOURCE: Reports of Schools, Ft Robinson.

Sergeant, L/9th Cavalry, commissioned second lieutenant, 7th Volunteer Infantry, 1898. SOURCE: Cashin, *Under Fire with the Tenth Cavalry*, 359.

Mentioned. SOURCE: San Francisco *Chronicle*, 15 Nov 1899.

Discharged at Ft Grant, AZ, to accept commission in 48th Infantry. SOURCE: *ANJ* 37 (9 Dec 1899): 344.

Mentioned as captain, G/48th Infantry. SOURCE: Beasley, *Negro Trailblazers*, 284.

BROWN, William H., Jr.; Corporal; D/10th Cav. Commissioned first lieutenant, Camp Des Moines, IA, 15 Oct 1917. SOURCE: Glass, *History of the Tenth Cavalry*, appendix M.

BROWN, William M.; Private; E/25th Inf. Drowned in the Philippines, 6 Mar 1900. SOURCE: *ANJ* 37 (24 Mar 1900): 707.

BROWN, William W.; Private; C/9th Cav. At Ft D. A. Russell, WY, in 1910; resident of 12 Dakota St., Dayton, OH. SOURCE: *Illustrated Review: Ninth Cavalry*.

BROWN, William W.; 24th and 25th Inf. Alice A. Brown, age 49, 1126 E. 53rd Street, Los Angeles, CA, widow of William W. Brown, veteran of Spanish-American War, who served in A Company and Band/24th Infantry and 25th Infantry, is pensioned, File C 1243461; married to first husband, William H. Oliver, Band/9th Cavalry, by Chaplain George Prioleau, Ft Walla Walla, WA, 1904; Oliver died in Honolulu, HI, before she married Brown. SOURCE: VA File C 1392575, George W. Prioleau.

BROWNE, Stephen A.; Sergeant; A/25th Inf. Wounded in action, El Caney, Cuba, 1 Jul 1898. SOURCE: Nankivell, *History of the Twenty-fifth Infantry*, 83.

BROWNE, Sylvanus; Private; B/9th Cav. At Ft D. A. Russell, WY, in 1910. SOURCE: *Illustrated Review: Ninth Cavalry*, with picture.

BROWNIE, George; Private; D/24th Inf. At Cabanatuan, Philippines, 1901. *See* **MOORE**, Cato, Private, D/24th Infantry

BROWNING, Andrew; Sergeant; C/9th Cav. Sergeant, C/9th Cavalry since 2 Jun 1882. SOURCE: Roster, 9 Cav, 1893.

At Ft McKinney, WY, granted hunting pass to Big Horn Mountains, 12–18 Sep 1894.

Authorized to reenlist as married, Dec 1896.

Retired Jul 1901. SOURCE: *ANJ* 38 (27 Jul 1901): 1163.

BROYLES, William; Corporal; M/25th Inf. Promoted from private. SOURCE: *ANR* 38 (22 Jul 1905): 21.

BRUCE, Henry; Private; H/25th Inf. In A Company, convicted of assault on young Filipino girl, Aug 1901.

Deserted from H Company, San Francisco, CA, 19 Aug 1902. SOURCE: Regt Returns, 25 Inf, Aug 1902.

BRUDEN, Samuel; Private; D/10th Cav. Served in 10th Cavalry, 1898; remained in U.S. during war with Spain. SOURCE: Cashin, *Under Fire with the Tenth Cavalry*, 341.

BRUFF, Thomas; Private; Band/10th Cav. Honorable mention as private, H/10th Cavalry, in capture of Mangas and his band, Rio Bonito, AZ, 18 Oct 1886. SOURCE: Baker, Roster.

Corporal, K/9th Cavalry, since 25 Mar 1892. SOURCE: Roster, 9 Cav, 1893.

Private, Band/10th Cavalry, served in 10th Cavalry in Cuba, 1898; died of Cuban fever. SOURCE: Cashin, *Under Fire with the Tenth Cavalry*, 352, 359.

BRUIN, Albert; Private; I/10th Cav. Served in 10th Cavalry, 1898; remained in U.S. during war with Spain. SOURCE: Cashin, *Under Fire with the Tenth Cavalry*, 348.

BRUINS, Robert B.; Private; G/9th Cav. At Ft D. A. Russell, WY, in 1910. SOURCE: *Illustrated Review: Ninth Cavalry*.

BRUNSON, Charles S.; Private; C/10th Cav. Enlisted Charleston, SC, 22 Dec 1887; at Ft Union, NM, with measles and pneumonia. SOURCE: Muster Roll, Det 10 Cav, 22 Dec 1887–29 Feb 1888.

BRUXTON, Isaiah; Private; E/49th Inf. Died in the Philippines, Dec 1900. SOURCE: *ANJ* 38 (29 Dec 1900): 431.

BRYAN, Edward; Private; B/9th Cav. At Ft D. A. Russell, WY, in 1910. SOURCE: *Illustrated Review: Ninth Cavalry*, with picture.

BRYAN, John S.; Private; I/25th Inf. Fined $1 by summary court, San Isidro, Philippines, for violating Article 31, lying out of quarters, 31 Mar 1902; acquitted of violating Article 62, entering native house without permission, same date, third conviction. SOURCE: Register of Summary Court, San Isidro.

BRYAN, William; Private; G/9th Cav. Witness for defense, Barney McKay court martial, Ft Robinson, NE, 1893. SOURCE: Court Martial Records, McKay.

BRYANT, Benjamin F.; Corporal; G/10th Cav. Served in 10th Cavalry in Cuba, 1898. SOURCE: Cashin, *Under Fire with the Tenth Cavalry*, 340.

Promoted from lance corporal, Jun 1902. SOURCE: *ANJ* 39 (7 Jun 1902): 1004.

BRYANT, David A.; Private; B/9th Cav. At Ft D. A. Russell, WY, in 1910; marksman. SOURCE: *Illustrated Review: Ninth Cavalry.*

BRYANT, Ferdinand; 24th Inf. Lives at 579 63rd Street, Oakland, CA, in 1931; has known Archy Wall and his wife since 1886. SOURCE: Affidavit, Bryant, 28 Oct 1931, VA File C 2643745, Archy Wall.

BRYANT, George; M/10th Cav. Original member of 10th Cavalry; in troop when organized, Ft Riley, KS, 15 Oct 1867. SOURCE: McMiller, "Buffalo Soldiers," 79.

BRYANT, Gilbert; Private; I/10th Cav. Served in 10th Cavalry, 1898; remained in U.S. during war with Spain. SOURCE: Cashin, *Under Fire with the Tenth Cavalry*, 348.

BRYANT, James A.; Corporal; I/9th Cav. At Ft D. A. Russell, WY, in 1910; resident of Henderson, KY. SOURCE: *Illustrated Review: Ninth Cavalry,* with picture.

BRYANT, Jessey H.; K/10th Cav. Original member of 10th Cavalry; in troop when organized, Ft Riley, KS, 1 Sep 1867. SOURCE: McMiller, "Buffalo Soldiers," 77.

BRYANT, Lounie; C/48th Inf. Convicted of attempted rape in the Philippines, Jan 1901; sentenced to ten years.

BRYANT, M. C.; Private; 25th Inf. Enlisted Wichita, KS, and left for California, en route to the Philippines, 13 Nov 1900. SOURCE: Wichita *Searchlight*, 17 Nov 1900.

BRYANT, Major; Private; B/10th Cav. Served in 10th Cavalry, 1898; remained in U.S. during war with Spain. SOURCE: Cashin, *Under Fire with the Tenth Cavalry*, 339.

BRYANT, William; Private; C/10th Cav. Served in 10th Cavalry, 1898; remained in U.S. during war with Spain. SOURCE: Cashin, *Under Fire with the Tenth Cavalry*, 340.

BRYANT, William H.; Private; 25th Inf. Born Conwayboro, SC; Ht 5'11"; black eyes and hair, dark complexion, occupation miner, age 23, enlisted Charleston, SC, 20 Jun 1881. SOURCE: Descriptive & Assignment Roll, 25 Inf.

BUCHANAN, Clarence; Private; M/10th Cav. Dishonorable discharge and confinement, Ft Robinson, NE, Jun 1903. SOURCE: SO 120, DeptMo, 23 Jun 1903.

Escaped, Oct 1903.

BUCHANAN, James; Private; A/10th Cav. Served in 10th Cavalry in Cuba, 1898. SOURCE: Cashin, *Under Fire with the Tenth Cavalry*, 336.

President, YMCA, Ft Robinson, NE. SOURCE: Cleveland *Gazette*, 24 Jul 1903.

BUCHANAN, Lawrence; Private; I/24th Inf. Enlisted Louisville, KY, 4 Feb 1899; joined company 7 Feb 1899. SOURCE: Muster Roll, I/24 Inf, Jan–Feb 1899.

Fined $2 by garrison court martial, 19 May 1899. SOURCE: Muster Roll, I/24 Inf, May–Jun 1899.

Wounded in action in the Philippines, 31 Jul 1900. *See* **SMITH**, C. H., Sergeant, I/24th Infantry

BUCK, John; QM Sgt; 10th Cav. Born Chapel Hill, TX, 1861; enlisted in 10th Cavalry, 1880; "a man of strong character, an experienced horseman and packer." SOURCE: Steward, *The Colored Regulars*, 149.

Private, corporal, sergeant, F/10th Cavalry, from 6 Nov 1880; private, B/10th Cavalry, 22 Oct 1889; corporal, 19 Aug 1890; sergeant, 2 Apr 1893; stationed at Ft Custer, MT, 1897. SOURCE: Baker, Roster.

Private, B/10th Cavalry, at Ft Apache, AZ, 1890, subscribed $.50 to testimonial to General Grierson. SOURCE: List of subscriptions, 23 Apr 1890, 10th Cavalry papers, MHI.

Authorized four-month furlough from station at Ft Apache. SOURCE: *ANJ* 28 (15 Nov 1890): 188.

Ranked fifth with carbine, bronze medal, Departments of Dakota and Columbia, 1892. SOURCE: Baker, Roster.

Ranked fifth with revolver, Departments of Dakota and Columbia, at competition, Ft Keogh, MT, 15–23 Aug 1892. SOURCE: GO 75, AGO, 3 Nov 1892.

Ranked third with carbine, silver medal, Departments of Dakota and Columbia, 1894. SOURCE: Baker, Roster.

Ranked third with revolver, Departments of Dakota and Columbia, at competition, Ft Keogh, 18–27 Sep 1894. SOURCE: GO 62, AGO, 15 Nov 1894.

Cited for highly meritorious service leading pack train in severe weather from station at Ft Missoula, MT, across Bitterroot Mountains, ID, Nov 1893, in search of lost party of gentlemen. SOURCE: Steward, *The Colored Regulars*, 237; Baker, Roster.

First sergeant, B/10th Cavalry, cited for heroism at Las Guasimas, Cuba, 24 Jun 1898; recommended for Medal of Honor by Capt. J. W. Watson; commissioned second lieutenant, 7th Volunteer Infantry, 1898. SOURCE: Cashin, *Under Fire with the Tenth Cavalry*, 179, 186, 337, 354, 359.

Pictures. SOURCE: Cashin, *Under Fire with the Tenth Cavalry*, 353; Indianapolis *Freeman*, 4 Nov 1899.

Directed to report to Ft Thomas, KY, as captain, 48th Infantry. SOURCE: *ANJ* 37 (7 Oct 1899): 123.

Captain, 48th Infantry, one of nineteen 48th Infantry officers recommended for commissions as second lieutenants in the regular Army. SOURCE: CG, Div PI, Manila, to AG, 8 Feb 1901, AGO File 355163.

Drum major, 10th Cavalry, and "an old soldier of long service, has done good work as an officer and enlisted man, in Indian wars, at Santiago, and in the Philippines, and in my opinion is qualified for the position he seeks." SOURCE: Endorsement, CO, 10 Cav, Ft Robinson, NE, 11 Feb 1903, LS, Ft Robinson.

Drum major, 10th Cavalry band, and manager, regimental baseball team, Ft Robinson, NE, 1904. SOURCE: Lowe, "Camp Life," 205.

Mentioned as retired quartermaster sergeant in acknowledgments. SOURCE: Curtis, *The Black Soldier*, with picture opposite 15.

BUCKHALTER, James; Private; A/48th Inf. Died in the Philippines, 28 Mar 1901. SOURCE: *ANJ* 38 (13 Apr 1901): 803.

BUCKNER, Benjamin; Sergeant; C/10th Cav. Farrier, C/10th Cavalry, at Ft Apache, AZ, 1890, subscribed $.50 to testimonial to General Grierson. SOURCE: List of subscriptions, 23 Apr 1890, 10th Cavalry papers, MHI.

Tried and acquitted of "marrying a notorious strumpet to the scandal and disgrace of the service," Ft Assinniboine, MT. SOURCE: *ANJ* 31 (28 Jul 1894): 842.

BUCKNER, David; Private; G/25th Inf. Wounded in action, El Caney, Cuba, 1 Jul 1898. SOURCE: Nankivell, *History of the Twenty-fifth Infantry*, 83.

BUCKNER, Dock; Corporal; C/9th Cav. Veteran of Philippine Insurrection; at Ft D. A. Russell, WY, in 1910. SOURCE: *Illustrated Review: Ninth Cavalry,* with picture.

BUCKNER, Earnest; Private; M/9th Cav. At Ft D. A. Russell, WY, in 1910; resident of Macon, GA. SOURCE: *Illustrated Review: Ninth Cavalry,* with picture.

BUCKNER, Henry; Private; G/10th Cav. Served in 10th Cavalry, 1898; remained in U.S. during war with Spain. SOURCE: Cashin, *Under Fire with the Tenth Cavalry*, 345.

BUCKNER, Richard; Private; L/10th Cav. Served in 10th Cavalry, 1898; remained in U.S. during war with Spain. SOURCE: Cashin, *Under Fire with the Tenth Cavalry*, 350.

BUCKNER, Robert; Private; M/10th Cav. Served in 10th Cavalry, 1898; remained in U.S. during war with Spain. SOURCE: Cashin, *Under Fire with the Tenth Cavalry*, 351.

BUCKNER, Robert; Corporal; C/9th Cav. At Ft D. A. Russell, WY, in 1910. SOURCE: *Illustrated Review: Ninth Cavalry,* with picture.

BUCKNER, Robert D.; Private; G/9th Cav. At Ft D. A. Russell, WY, in 1910; resident of El Paso, TX. SOURCE: *Illustrated Review: Ninth Cavalry,* with picture.

BUDELL; Private; K/9th Cav. Discharged from confinement, Ft Robinson, NE. SOURCE: SO 110, AGO, 10 May 1890.

BUDERIS, W.; QM Sgt; 10th Cav. Memorial service over his grave held by noncommissioned staff at Ft Grant, AZ, held 30 May 1891. SOURCE: *ANJ* 28 (28 Jun 1891): 713.

BUEFORD, John; Private; H/10th Cav. Served in 10th Cavalry, 1898; remained in U.S. during war with Spain. SOURCE: Cashin, *Under Fire with the Tenth Cavalry*, 347.

BUFORD, James J.; Private; 24th Inf. Born 1869, son of Parker Buford, 24th Infantry; enlisted San Carlos, AZ, 31 Mar 1891; died 1898. SOURCE: Clark, "A History of the Twenty-fourth," 77.

BUFORD, James J.; Private; D/24th Inf. Fined $10 for violating Article 16, losing accoutrements (fifteen rounds of ammunition), and for violating Article 33, failure to repair for guard mount, Cabanatuan, Philippines, 28 Nov 1900; witnesses: 1st Sgt. M. H. Ellis, D/24th Infantry, and Quartermaster Sergeant Duvall, D/24th Infantry. SOURCE: Summary Court Register, 24 Inf.

Fined $5 for violating Article 62, failure to obey lawful order of Sgt. Wilson Prear to police around quarters, Cabanatuan, 10 Feb 1901. SOURCE: Summary Court Register, 24 Inf.

Fined $5 for violating Article 33, failure to repair for reveille, Cabanatuan, 20 Feb 1901, and again on 26 May 1901; witnesses: 1st Sgt. M. H. Ellis and Sgt. William Brice, D/24th Infantry. SOURCE: Summary Court Register, 24 Inf.

BUFORD, John; Private; K/10th Cav. Discharged on certificate of disability with syphilis, Ft Robinson, NE, 6 Feb 1904. SOURCE: Certificates of Disability, Ft Robinson.

BUFORD, Parker; 24th Inf. Born Pulaski, TN, around 1849; occupation laborer; married Eliza Reynolds, of Giles Co., TN, 8 Aug 1867; son James J. Buford born 1869; enlisted 1869; retired from Ft Douglas, UT, 20 Sep 1900, and stayed in Salt Lake City at 333 South 13th East; died 1911; widow lived at 1333 East 7th South, in 1911; moved to Pasadena, CA, 1920, to live with grandson Alonzo Wooley; died 17 Sep 1932. SOURCE: Clark, "A History of the Twenty-fourth," 77.

Died 19 Feb 1911; buried at Ft Douglas. SOURCE: Clark, "A History of the Twenty-fourth," appendix A.

BULGER, William; Private; D/10th Cav. Honorable mention for bravery against Comanches, Double Mountain Fork, Brazos River, TX, 5 Feb 1874. SOURCE: Baker, Roster.

BULLET, William; Private; B/10th Cav. Served in 10th Cavalry, 1898; remained in U.S. during war with Spain. SOURCE: Cashin, *Under Fire with the Tenth Cavalry*, 339.

BULLOCK; Private; C/9th Cav. Wounded in action at San Juan, Cuba, 1 Jul 1898. SOURCE: *Illustrated Review: Ninth Cavalry.*

BULLOCK, B. H.; Private; D/9th Cav. At Ft Robinson, NE, 1892. SOURCE: Order 181, 26 Oct 1892, Post Orders, Ft Robinson.

BULLOCK, Ezekiel; Private; I/24th Inf. Involved in Houston riot, 1917; testified in exchange for immunity. SOURCE: Haynes, *A Night of Violence*, 215–16.

BULLOCK, Nathaniel; Private; H/10th Cav. Served in 10th Cavalry in Cuba, 1898. SOURCE: Cashin, *Under Fire with the Tenth Cavalry*, 347.

BUMSIDE, Robert; B/10th Cav. Original member of 10th Cavalry; in troop when organized, Ft Leavenworth, KS, 1 Apr 1867. SOURCE: McMiller, "Buffalo Soldiers," 69.

BUNCH, Joseph; F/24th Inf. Remained at San Quentin, Philippines, after service. SOURCE: Funston papers, KSHS.

BUNCH, Richard; Farrier; H/9th Cav. Born in North Carolina, 16 Feb 1852; parents unknown, died of pneumonia; enlisted Cincinnati, OH, 1 Sep 1869, Ht 5'9", light complexion, occupation laborer, discharged 1 Sep 1874; worked as laborer and coachman afterward. Married Virginia Kyte (born 1 Oct 1863), 22 Aug 1885; children: Richard born 1886, twins John and Joseph born 1888, Virginia born 1891, Margaret born 1893, Herbert born 1897, Eliza born 1899, Clifford born 1903, Rose born 1905; resided at 11 Willow Street, Cincinnati; suffered totally disabling paralytic stroke, died 16 Nov 1933. Widow moved from 117 Taft Lane, Cincinnati, to 2536 Center, Pittsburgh, PA, in 1936; moved to 511 Carlisle Avenue, Cincinnati, in 1937; moved to 1076 Flint, Cincinnati, in 1941; widow's pension $20 per month, 1 Apr 1935, and $40 per month, 7 Apr 1944; died 3 Jul 1944. SOURCE: VA File XC 2658566, Richard Bunch.
Died in Cincinnati. SOURCE: *Winners of the West* 11 (Apr 1934): 4.

BUNCH, Thomas; Trumpeter; H/10th Cav. Served in 10th Cavalry, 1898; remained in U.S. during war with Spain. SOURCE: Cashin, *Under Fire with the Tenth Cavalry*, 346.

BUNDY, Arthur S.; Farrier; M/10th Cav. At Ft Apache, AZ, 1890, subscribed $.50 to testimonial to General Grierson. SOURCE: List of subscriptions, 23 Apr 1890, 10th Cavalry papers, MHI.

BUNDY, H.; Private; C/10th Cav. Mentioned Oct 1870. SOURCE: ES, 10 Cav, 1866–71.

BUNION, Thomas; D/24th Inf. Served 1875–80; age 85; subscriber. SOURCE: *Winners of the West* 12 (Mar 1935): 2.
Member, Camp 11, National Indian War Veterans, St. Joseph, MO; died Nashville, TN. SOURCE: *Winners of the West* 15 (Apr 1938): 5.

BUNN, James W.; Corporal; I/49th Inf. Killed in action, Ilagan, Luzon, Philippines, 31 Dec 1900. SOURCE: *ANJ* 38 (12 Jan 1901): 479.

Attacked and killed by insurgents near Ilagan, 31 Dec 1900; body not recovered. SOURCE: *ANJ* 38 (13 Apr 1901): 801.

BUNN, William N.; Private; B/10th Cav. Served in 10th Cavalry in Cuba, 1898; Sgt. James W. Ford, B/10th Cavalry, and Pvt. Marion W. Murphy, B/10th Cavalry, Camp Forse, AL, 4 Dec 1898, attest to Bunn's heroism at Las Guasimas, Cuba, 24 Jun 1898. SOURCE: Cashin, *Under Fire with the Tenth Cavalry*, 338, 180–81.
Recommended for certificate of merit for heroism in assault on Las Guasimas.

BURBE, Lester; Private; H/24th Inf. Enlisted Ft McPherson, GA, 31 Jan 1899; assigned to and joined company, 6 Feb 1899; died of disease contracted in line of duty, in hospital, Ft Douglas, UT, 13 Feb 1899; due U.S. for clothing $65.88. SOURCE: Muster Roll, H/24 Inf, Jan–Feb 1899.

BURBRIDGE, Clarence; Private; E/10th Cav. Served in 10th Cavalry, 1898; remained in U.S. during war with Spain. SOURCE: Cashin, *Under Fire with the Tenth Cavalry*, 343.

BURCH, Roy; Staff Sgt; E/9th Cav. Private, at Ft D. A. Russell, WY, in 1910. SOURCE: *Illustrated Review: Ninth Cavalry*, with picture.
Retires as staff sergeant from second squadron, at U.S. Military Academy, West Point, 30 Nov 1931. SOURCE: *Cavalry Journal* 40 (Nov–Dec 1931): 61.
Retirement mentioned. SOURCE: *Cavalry Journal* 41 (Jul 1932): 62.

BURDEN, Henry; Corporal; F/25th Inf. Transferred to Hospital Corps, Ft Missoula, MT. SOURCE: *ANJ* 34 (10 Apr 1897): 585.

BURDEN, James; F/10th Cav. Served 1877–82; writes from Soddy, TN, expressing sincere thanks for work of magazine on behalf of old soldiers; pension now $30 per month; got back pay of $202; "troopers of F Troop, 10th U.S. Cavalry, 1877–1882, write to me." SOURCE: *Winners of the West* 5 (May 1928): 5.
Letter encloses dues. SOURCE: *Winners of the West* 5 (Aug 1928): 5.
Renews subscription; "in our Army days we fought and bled together, and now again we are united to fight for better pension laws in our behalf." SOURCE: *Winners of the West* 6 (May 1929): 5.
Now 78 years old. SOURCE: *Winners of the West* 9 (Aug 1932): 8.
Died at Soddy, TN. SOURCE: *Winners of the West* 13 (Apr 1936): 3.

BURDES, William; Private; L/25th Inf. Died in the Philippines, 30 Oct 1900. SOURCE: *ANJ* 38 (8 Dec 1900): 355.

BURDETTE, Bernard M.; Recruit; Colored Detachment/Mounted Service. Convicted by general court martial of violating Article 62, refusing order of sergeant, refusing to go to guardhouse, and resisting sergeant, 23 Aug 1899; sentenced to three months and fined $10 per month for three months. SOURCE: GCMO 56, AGO, 12 Sep 1889.

BURDETTE, Nelson; I/10th Cav. Original member of 10th Cavalry; in troop when organized, Ft Riley, KS, 15 Aug 1867. SOURCE: McMiller, "Buffalo Soldiers," 76.

BURDETTE, Ray; Corporal; B/25th Inf. Dishonorable discharge, Brownsville. SOURCE: SO 266, AGO, 9 Nov 1906.

BURGE, Benjamin; Private; E/24th Inf. Mentioned among men who distinguished themselves in 1889; awarded certificate of merit for gallant and meritorious conduct while escorting Maj. Joseph W. Wham, paymaster, when attacked by robbers between Fts Grant and Thomas, AZ. SOURCE: GO 18, AGO, 1891.

Private, K/24th Infantry, Ft Grant, 1890. SOURCE: SecWar, *AR 1890*, 289.

BURGESS, Ed P.; Private; B/10th Cav. Letter, Commander, Chickamauga, GA, to Commander, Ft Robinson, NE, 6 Aug 1904, reports apprehension of Burgess; Commander, Ft Robinson, forwards charges and descriptive list, 10 Aug 1904. SOURCE: Register, LR, Ft Robinson.

BURGESS, Harry. Graduate of Washington Colored High School and one of finest lieutenants in Spanish-American War. SOURCE: *The Voice of the Negro* 1 (Jun 1904): 222.

BURGESS, Lewis; Sergeant; G/24th Inf. At San Carlos, AZ, granted six-month furlough. SOURCE: *ANJ* 28 (14 Feb 1891): 422.

BURK, W. A.; Private; L/10th Cav. Sentenced by general court martial to three years for mutiny, Bayamo, Cuba, 12 Oct 1899. SOURCE: *ANJ* 37 (24 Feb 1900): 602.

BURKE, James; QM Sgt; H/24th Inf. Enlisted Washington Barracks, 7 Dec 1897; eleventh year continuous service; sergeant. SOURCE: Muster Roll, H/24 Inf, May–Jun 1898.

Promoted quartermaster sergeant, 14 Jan 1899. SOURCE: Muster Roll, H/24 Inf, Jan–Feb 1899.

BURKE, Lester; 24th Inf. Died 13 Feb 1899; buried Ft Douglas, UT. SOURCE: Clark, "A History of the Twenty-fourth," appendix A.

BURKE, Louis; Private; 24th Inf. Died 17 Jan 1899; buried Ft Douglas, UT. SOURCE: Clark, "A History of the Twenty-fourth," appendix A. *See* **BURKS**, Lewis, Private, K/24th Infantry

BURKE, William A.; Private; 24th Inf. Enlisted three months ago; resided at 6 Miami Alley, Cleveland, OH; en route to Ft D. A. Russell, WY. SOURCE: Cleveland *Gazette*, 1 Oct 1898.

BURKE, William H.; Private; E/9th Cav. At Ft D. A. Russell, WY, in 1910; resident of Washington, DC. SOURCE: *Illustrated Review: Ninth Cavalry*, with picture.

BURKLEY, Monroe; Private; D/10th Cav. Transferred to Hospital Corps. SOURCE: SO 1, DeptMo, 2 Jan 1904.

BURKLEY, Thornton; Private; I/10th Cav. Served in 10th Cavalry in Cuba, 1898. SOURCE: Cashin, *Under Fire with the Tenth Cavalry*, 347.

Wounded in action, Santiago, Cuba, 1 Jul 1898. SOURCE: SecWar, *AR 1898*, 324.

BURKS, Alonzo J.; Private; B/24th Inf. At Ft D. A. Russell, WY; in hands of civil authorities, Cheyenne, 30 Oct–11 Nov 1898.

BURKS, Dock; QM Sgt; I/10th Cav. Original member of 10th Cavalry; in troop when organized, Ft Riley, KS, 15 Aug 1867. SOURCE: McMiller, "Buffalo Soldiers," 76.

As private, assisted in capture of two 10th Cavalry deserters, Pvts. James Reed, B Troop, and Frank Wilson, H Troop, Hays City, KS, 25 May 1868. SOURCE: Maj. J. E. Yard, CO, Ft Hays, KS, to Adj, Det 10 Cav, Camp near Ft Wallace, 28 May 1868, LR, Det 10 Cav, 1868–69.

Applied for discharge to enable him to contribute to support of his mother, from Ft Hays, 16 Jun 1868; commander disapproved: "Dock Burks is the Q.M. Sergt. of my company. He is an excellent soldier and I consider it detrimental to the service and the efficiency of my Company in having him discharged. I think his pay as Q.M. Sergt. is ample to support his mother and he is quite economical." SOURCE: ES, 10 Cav, 1866–71.

BURKS, George; Private; H/9th Cav. At Ft D. A. Russell, WY, in 1910; resident of Oklahoma City. SOURCE: *Illustrated Review: Ninth Cavalry.*

BURKS, Henry; Private; 9th Cav. Deserted with Pvts. William Burns and James Nelson, 9th Cavalry, late 1880, after one of them killed commander, K/9th Cavalry; apprehended at Trinidad, CO, and returned to Ft Marcy, NM, for trial. SOURCE: Billington, *New Mexico's Buffalo Soldiers*, 131.

BURKS, Lewis; Private; K/24th Inf. Died at Camp Pilot Butte, WY, 16 Jan 1899; body shipped to Ft Douglas, UT, for burial; originally from Louisville, KY. SOURCE: Rock Springs *Miner*, 19 Jan 1899. *See* **BURKE**, Louis, Private, 24th Infantry

BURLES, Charles; Private; Band/9th Cav. Born Charleston, WV; first enlistment in B/24th Infantry, until 29

Aug 1886; enlisted, age 26, Ht 5'7", Ft Supply, Indian Territory, 21 Sep 1886; transferred to F/24th Infantry, 20 Nov 1888, single, character very good; transferred to Band, single, character excellent, 16 Nov 1890; discharged, expiration of service, character good, retained pay $60, owes government $4 for clothing, $4 for subsistence, $1 fine. SOURCE: Descriptive Book, 24 Inf NCS & Band.

Private, Band/9th Cavalry, charged in U.S. court with cutting another soldier with razor. SOURCE: CO, Ft Robinson, NE, to AAG, DP, 25 Nov 1893, LS, Ft Robinson.

In hands of civil authorities, Omaha, NE, 22 Sep–18 Dec 1893.

BURLEY, Robert; Sergeant; I/9th Cav. Private, G/9th Cavalry, on detached service, Ft Stanton, NM, 29 Jan–5 Feb 1881. SOURCE: Regt Returns, 9 Cav, Feb 1881.

Sergeant since 10 Nov 1888. SOURCE: Roster, 9 Cav, 1893.

Sergeant, I/9th Cavalry, Ft Robinson, NE. SOURCE: *ANJ* 31 (9 Dec 1893): 254.

Sergeant, I/9th Cavalry, retires from Ft Robinson, Sep 1895. SOURCE: *ANJ* 33 (14 Sep 1895): 231.

No Veterans Administration pension file.

BURLEY, William; Private; F/10th Cav. Corporal, at Camp Supply, Indian Territory, 1870. *See* **TAYLOR**, John, Private, F/10th Cavalry

Private, recruit from depot, 1873. SOURCE: ES, 10 Cav, 1873–81.

BURNELL, George; Private; M/9th Cav. Veteran of Philippine Insurrection; at Ft D. A. Russell, WY, 1910. SOURCE: *Illustrated Review: Ninth Cavalry.*

BURNES, William T.; Corporal; D/10th Cav. Commissioned first lieutenant, Camp Des Moines, IA, 15 Oct 1917. SOURCE: Glass, *History of the Tenth Cavalry*, appendix M.

BURNETT, John; Private; 10th Cav. Killed by civilian Pablo Fernandez while member of guard, Ft Stockton, TX, quelling disturbance in neighboring settlement. SOURCE: CO, 10 Cav, to AG, USA, 6 Jul 1875, ES, 10 Cav, 1873–81.

BURNETT, Ripling; Private; H/24th Inf. Enlisted Camp Tampa, FL, 30 May 1898; absent sick, disease contracted in line of duty, at Tampa since 7 Jun 1898. SOURCE: Muster Roll, H/24 Inf, May–Jun 1898.

Still sick, Tampa. SOURCE: Muster Roll, H/24 Inf, Jul–Aug 1898.

Transferred to K/24th Infantry, 16 Dec 1898; due U.S. for clothing $20.06. SOURCE: Muster Roll, H/24 Inf, Sep–Oct 1898.

BURNHAM, Charles; Private; H/24th Inf. Mentioned Jun 1867. SOURCE: LS, 10 Cav, 1866–67.

BURNHAM, William; C/10th Cav. Original member of 10th Cavalry; in troop when organized, Ft Leavenworth,

KS, 14 May 1867. SOURCE: McMiller, "Buffalo Soldiers," 70.

BURNOM, Robert S.; Private; H/24th Inf. Fined $10 by summary court for violating Article 62, carelessly discharging weapon while sentry, San Isidro, Philippines, 25 Mar 1902, first conviction. SOURCE: Register of Summary Court, San Isidro.

BURNS, Calvin C.; Private; I/10th Cav. At Ft Apache, AZ, 1890, subscribed $.25 to testimonial to General Grierson. SOURCE: List of subscriptions, 23 Apr 1890, 10th Cavalry papers, MHI.

Served in 10th Cavalry in Cuba, 1898. SOURCE: Cashin, *Under Fire with the Tenth Cavalry*, 347.

BURNS, Carter; Private; B/10th Cav. Killed in action, by Comanches, Ojo Caliente, TX, 28 Oct 1880. SOURCE: Orville A. Cochran to H. B. Wharfield, 5 Apr 1965, 10th Cavalry papers, MHI; Leckie, *The Buffalo Soldiers*, 230; Baker, Roster.

Burns Street, FT Huachuca, AZ, named for him. SOURCE: Orville A. Cochran to H. B. Wharfield, 5 Apr 1965, 10th Cavalry papers, MHI.

BURNS, Charles; H/10th Cav. Original member of 10th Cavalry; in troop when organized, Ft Leavenworth, KS, 21 Jul 1867. SOURCE: McMiller, "Buffalo Soldiers," 75.

BURNS, Doc; K/10th Cav. Original member of 10th Cavalry; in troop when organized, Ft Riley, KS, 1 Sep 1867. SOURCE: McMiller, "Buffalo Soldiers," 77.

BURNS, Frank; H/8th Ill Inf. Letter from San Luis, Cuba, n.d. SOURCE: Gatewood, *"Smoked Yankees"*, 205.

BURNS, Grover; Private; I/24th Inf. Served in Houston riot, 1917; threatened with jail term by military investigators after riot; convinced court martial that he remained in camp during riot; acquitted. SOURCE: Haynes, *A Night of Violence*, 247, 269, 271.

BURNS, Lee; Private; H/9th Cav. Born Georgetown, KY; laborer, Ht 5'8", mulatto; enlisted Lexington, KY, 9 Jan 1895; joined company, Ft Robinson, NE, 12 Jan 1895; four summary court martial convictions with fines totaling $13.50, 1895–97; discharged, end of enlistment, character very good, single, retained pay $4.40, clothing $9.28, deposits $25, 10 Jun 1898. SOURCE: Descriptive Book, H/9 Cav.

BURNS, William; Private; 9th Cav. Deserted 1880. *See* **BURKS**, Henry, Private, 9th Cavalry

BURNS, William J.; Corporal; I/24th Inf. Enlisted Dayton, OH, 27 Mar 1899; joined company 8 Apr 1899. SOURCE: Muster Roll, I/24 Inf, Mar–Apr 1899.

Promoted to corporal, 31 Oct 1899. SOURCE: Muster Roll, I/24, Nov–Dec 1899.

Ambushed with detachment of twelve men while repairing telegraph line, Minoz, Philippines, 10 Oct 1900; captured with eleven others, one missing in action. Members of detachment, all in I/24th Infantry: Pvt. William H. James, captured, killed trying to escape; Cpl. Cash Henry, captured, died of sunstroke; Pvt. Edward Skinner, wounded and captured; Pvt. George W. Jackson, captured; Pvt. Henry Clay, captured; Pvt. Henry Jackson, captured; Pvt. Thomas H. Morris, captured; Pvt. Claude Washington, captured; Pvt. William H. Watson, captured; Pvt. Joseph B. Turner, captured; Pvt. Swain P. Broom, captured; Pvt. Eugene Toung, missing in action, probably killed. SOURCE: Muller, *The Twenty Fourth Infantry*, 39.

BURNS, Willie; Private; I/24th Inf. Enlisted Raleigh, NC, 24 Mar 1899; joined company 8 Apr 1899. SOURCE: Muster Roll, I/24 Inf, Mar–Apr 1899.

Two garrison court martial convictions, fined total of $6. SOURCE: Muster Roll, I/24 Inf, May–Jun 1899.

Fined $5 by summary court martial, 22 Jul 1899; fined one month's pay by summary court martial, 8 Aug 1899; on detached service as messenger to regimental headquarters, 25 Aug 1899. SOURCE: Muster Roll, I/24 Inf, Jul–Aug 1899.

On detached service at Arayat, Philippines, since 31 Oct 1899. SOURCE: Muster Roll, I/24 Inf, Sep–Oct 1899.

BURNSIDE, Fairfax W.; Sergeant; A/9th Cav. Private, on special duty as assistant baker since 2 Apr 1902. SOURCE: Special Duty List, A/9 Cav, 24 May 1902, Nueva Caceres, Philippines.

Veteran of Spanish-American War and Philippine Insurrection; sergeant, at Ft D. A. Russell, WY, in 1910; sharpshooter. SOURCE: *Illustrated Review: Ninth Cavalry*, with picture.

BURNSIDE, Richard; C/24th Inf. Died in Seattle, WA, age 91; member, Camp 33, National Indian War Veterans, Portland, OR. SOURCE: *Winners of the West* 9 (Mar 1932): 7.

BURR, John L.; Private; G/10th Cav. Commander, 10th Cavalry, to AG, USA, 16 Dec 1876, forwards final statement in Burr case. SOURCE: ES, 10 Cav, 1873–81.

BURRELL, Cornelius; Blacksmith; G/9th Cav. Convicted by general court martial, Jefferson Barracks, MO, of desertion, 11 Jul 1886–9 Jul 1887; sentenced to dishonorable discharge and four years. SOURCE: GCMO 76, AGO, 29 Oct 1887.

BURRELL, James H.; Sergeant. Born in Virginia; served in Spanish-American War; died in Minnesota, 23 Jul 1948. SOURCE: Taylor, "Minnesota Black Spanish-American War Veterans."

BURRUS, Grant; Corporal; F/10th Cav. Private, M/10th Cavalry, served in 10th Cavalry in Cuba, 1898. SOURCE: Cashin, *Under Fire with the Tenth Cavalry*, 352.

Promoted from private. SOURCE: *ANJ* 35 (4 Dec 1897): 252.

BURSE, Jet; Recruit; Colored Detachment/ General Service. Convicted by general court martial, Columbus Barracks, OH, of two violations of Article 62: (1) in Company C of Instruction General Service, maliciously assaulted Recruit James Perry, Colored Detachment, same company, and tried to cut him with razor, 11 Jan 1890; (2) while prisoner under charge of Recruit Charles Matthews, Company A of Instruction, sentinel of guard, refused to work and on order of Matthews to go to guardhouse tried to take his weapon until forced to desist by outside assistance; sentenced to dishonorable discharge and two years; sentence reduced by reviewing authority to six months and $10 per month fine for six months, because evidence did not support charge. SOURCE: GCMO 12, AGO, 24 Feb 1890.

BURTON, Columbus E.; Private; M/9th Cav. At Ft D. A. Russell, WY, in 1910. SOURCE: *Illustrated Review: Ninth Cavalry*, with picture.

BURTON, Dock; Private; D/24th Inf. Transferred from Reserve Divisional Hospital, Siboney, Cuba, to Fortress Monroe, VA, on U.S. Army Transport *Concho*, 23 Jul 1898. SOURCE: Hospital Papers, Spanish-American War.

BURTON, Eugene; Private; D/9th Cav. At Ft D. A. Russell, WY, in 1910; resident of Homestead, PA. SOURCE: *Illustrated Review: Ninth Cavalry*.

BURTON, Hardy; Private; B/10th Cav. To be brought under guard to Ft Hays, KS, for trial by general court martial, 29 Apr 1868. SOURCE: LR, Det 10 Cav, 1868–69.

Reenlisted as private, B/10th Cavalry, Apr 1877. SOURCE: LS, 10 Cav, 1873–77.

BURTON, Hayes; Private; F/9th Cav. At Ft D. A. Russell, WY, in 1910; resident of Madison, MO. SOURCE: *Illustrated Review: Ninth Cavalry*, with picture.

BURTON, James; Private; I/9th Cav. Deserted from Ft Wingate, NM, 11 Jan 1881. SOURCE: Regt Returns, 9 Cav, Jan 1881.

BURTON, John; L/10th Cav. Original member of 10th Cavalry; in troop when organized, Ft Riley, KS, 21 Sep 1867. SOURCE: McMiller, "Buffalo Soldiers," 78.

BURTON, John; Saddler; A/9th Cav. Veteran of Indian wars and Philippine Insurrection; at Ft D. A. Russell, WY, in 1910; sharpshooter. SOURCE: *Illustrated Review: Ninth Cavalry*, with picture.

BURTON, John; Sergeant; E/24th Inf. Private, I/24th Infantry, at San Carlos, AZ, 1890. *See* **HARDEE**, James A., Private, K/24th Infantry

Retires as sergeant, E/24th Infantry, from Ft Douglas, UT. SOURCE: *ANJ* 35 (23 Oct 1897): 137.

BURTON, William E.; Corporal; I/10th Cav. Ranked number 457 among rifle experts with 68.67 percent, 1905. SOURCE: GO 101, AGO, 31 May 1906.

Born Northampton, VA; died, Fort Robinson, NE, age 33, 23 Nov 1906; buried 24 Nov 1906. SOURCE: Monthly Report, Chaplain Anderson, Nov 1906, Ft Robinson; List of Interments, Ft Robinson.

BUSH; Private; C/10th Cav. At Ft Apache, AZ, 1890, subscribed $.50 to testimonial to General Grierson. SOURCE: List of subscriptions, 23 Apr 1890, 10th Cavalry papers, MHI.

BUSH, Emanuel; Private; K/9th Cav. At Ft D. A. Russell, WY, in 1910; sharpshooter; resident of Mt. Sterling, KY. SOURCE: *Illustrated Review: Ninth Cavalry,* with picture.

BUSH, J. W.; Private; H/9th Cav. On detached service, Ft Bayard, NM, 29 Jan–10 Feb 1881. SOURCE: Regt Returns, 9 Cav, Feb 1881.

BUSH, Robert; Private; C/10th Cav. Served in 10th Cavalry in Cuba, 1898. SOURCE: Cashin, *Under Fire with the Tenth Cavalry,* 340.

BUSH, William Henry; Private; C/9th Cav. Born Amherstburg, Ontario, Canada; enlisted Cincinnati, OH; occupation cook; served 11 Jun 1878–10 Jun 1883; married Gertrude Henrietta Smith (1859–1944), Sandusky, OH, 6 Aug 1890; after service lived in Amherstburg and worked as cook "on the lakes"; pensioned by Private Law 68, 8 Dec 1924, at $20 per month, $50 per month 1928, $30 per month in 1937; died 3 Mar 1937. Widow's pension $40 per month in 1944. SOURCE: VA File C 2577213, William H. Bush.

"My company was continuously on scouting service which subjected us to great exposure, such as sleeping in rains and snows in the mountains unprotected from the elements, sometimes no sleep for two days, sometimes subsisting on the most meager diet, sometimes marches of ninety miles across the prairies of New Mexico and Texas in a hot scorching sun, sometimes marching through blinding sand storms and beating rains, sometimes wet wearing apparel for days and other exposures which soldiers are naturally subject to while in the field." SOURCE: Bush to Commissioner of Pensions, 3 May 1915, VA File C 2577213, William H. Bush.

Served five years; recent subscriber. SOURCE: *Winners of the West* 20 (30 Mar 1927): 8.

Served 1878–83; member, Camp 11, National Indian War Veterans, St. Joseph, MO; died Ontario, Canada. SOURCE: *Winners of the West* 30 (30 Aug 1937): 5.

BUTCHER, A. F.; Private; K/24th Inf. At San Carlos, AZ, 1890. *See* **HARDEE**, James A., Private, K/24th Infantry

BUTCHER, George N.; Private; C/10th Cav. Convicted by general court martial, Ft Robinson, NE; dishonorably discharged and confined. SOURCE: SO 173, DeptMo, 13 Sep 1902.

Released from confinement, Nov 1902.

BUTCHER, Joseph; Private; F/24th Inf. Wounded in action, Cuba, 1898. SOURCE: Muller, *The Twenty Fourth Infantry,* 18.

BUTLER; Private; C/10th Cav. At Ft Apache, AZ, 1890, subscribed $.25 to testimonial to General Grierson. SOURCE: List of subscriptions, 23 Apr 1890, 10th Cavalry papers, MHI.

BUTLER, Abram; Private; K/10th Cav. At Ft Robinson, NE, 1904.

BUTLER, Arthur B.; A/25th Inf. Convicted of assault with intent to rape, fined $45 and confined five months, Philippines, Mar 1901.

BUTLER, Benjamin G. W.; L/10th Cav. Original member of 10th Cavalry; in troop when organized, Ft Riley, KS, 21 Sep 1867. SOURCE: McMiller, "Buffalo Soldiers," 78.

BUTLER, Charles; 1st Sgt; G/10th Cav. Honorable mention for bravery against Comanches, Double Mountain Fork, Brazos River, TX, 5 Feb 1874. SOURCE: Baker, Roster.

Killed in action, by Comanches, Lake Quemado, TX, 4 May 1877; Butler Street, Ft Huachuca, AZ, named for him. SOURCE: Orville A. Cochran to H. B. Wharfield, 5 Apr 1965, 10th Cavalry papers, MHI.

Stationed at Ft Griffin, TX, at time of death. SOURCE: SecWar, *AR 1877,* 82.

Final statement, inventory of effects, certificates of deposit forwarded by regimental commander. SOURCE: CO, 10 Cav, to AG, USA, 10 Jun 1877, ES, 10 Cav, 1873–81.

BUTLER, Charles (1); Private; L/10th Cav. Served in 10th Cavalry, 1898; remained in U.S. during war with Spain. SOURCE: Cashin, *Under Fire with the Tenth Cavalry,* 350.

BUTLER, Charles (2); Private; L/10th Cav. Served in 10th Cavalry, 1898; remained in U.S. during war with Spain. SOURCE: Cashin, *Under Fire with the Tenth Cavalry,* 350.

BUTLER, Garland; Private; D/9th Cav. At Ft D. A. Russell, WY, in 1910; marksman; resident of Birmingham, AL. SOURCE: *Illustrated Review: Ninth Cavalry.*

BUTLER, George H.; Sergeant; L/9th Cav. At Ft D. A. Russell, WY, in 1910; sharpshooter; resident of Atlanta. SOURCE: *Illustrated Review: Ninth Cavalry,* with picture.

BUTLER, Harry; Private; B/10th Cav. Served in 10th Cavalry in Cuba, 1898. SOURCE: Cashin, *Under Fire with the Tenth Cavalry*, 338.

BUTLER, Henry; Saddler; G/9th Cav. As private, I/9th Cavalry, on special duty at post canteen, Ft Robinson, NE. SOURCE: Order 186, 23 Sep 1891, Post Orders, Ft Robinson.
  Retired, Apr 1902. SOURCE: *ANJ* 39 (19 Apr 1902): 827.

BUTLER, James H.; Musician; 25th Inf. Organized brass band at Ft Meade, SD, with Pvt. John H. Cansby, D/25th Infantry, for Christmas, 1887. SOURCE: Cleveland *Gazette*, 7 Jan 1888.

BUTLER, James H.; Private; G/9th Cav. On special duty as assistant post librarian, Ft Robinson, NE. SOURCE: Order 92, 15 Dec 1894, Post Orders, Ft Robinson.
  Relieved of duty as assistant post librarian. SOURCE: Order 16, 16 Mar 1895, Post Orders, Ft Robinson.

BUTLER, John; Private; Band/9th Cav. With band on detached service at headquarters, District of New Mexico, Santa Fe, 1880; played E-flat tuba. SOURCE: Billington, *New Mexico's Buffalo Soldiers*, 226.

BUTLER, John; Private; D/25th Inf. Dishonorable discharge, Brownsville. SOURCE: SO 266, AGO, 9 Nov 1906.

BUTLER, John H.; M/10th Cav. Original member of 10th Cavalry; in troop when organized, Ft Riley, KS, 15 Oct 1867. SOURCE: McMiller, "Buffalo Soldiers," 79.

BUTLER, Lewis; F/10th Cav. Original member of 10th Cavalry; in troop when organized, Ft Leavenworth, KS, 21 Jun 1867. SOURCE: McMiller, "Buffalo Soldiers," 73.

BUTLER, Louis; Private; F/10th Cav. Corporal, at Camp Supply, Indian Territory, 1870. *See* **TAYLOR**, John, Private, F/10th Cavalry
  Private in 1873. SOURCE: ES, 10 Cav, 1873–81.

BUTLER, Nathaniel; E/10th Cav. Original member of 10th Cavalry; in troop when organized, Ft Leavenworth, KS, 15 Jun 1867. SOURCE: McMiller, "Buffalo Soldiers," 72.

BUTLER, Patrick; Private; K/10th Cav. Original member of 10th Cavalry; in troop when organized, Ft Riley, KS, 1 Sep 1867. SOURCE: McMiller, "Buffalo Soldiers," 77.
  His commander asks that he be transferred to Ft Dodge, KS; he is encumbrance to the command. SOURCE: CO, Det 10 Cav, to AAG, District of the Upper Arkansas, 3 October 1868, LR, Det 10 Cav, 1868–69.

BUTLER, Rasche; Private; E/9th Cav. At Ft D. A. Russell, WY, in 1910; resident of Houston. SOURCE: *Illustrated Review: Ninth Cavalry*, with picture.

BUTLER, Thomas C.; 1st Lt; F/49th Inf. Born Baltimore, MD; left home when young to study for priesthood, St. Mary's College (Jesuit), Annapolis, MD; sailor until shipwrecked off Cape Hatteras, NC, 1887, when joined 9th Cavalry; "speaks with undisguised but pardonable pride of the part his regiment took in the Sioux campaign of 1890–91. He was then a non-commissioned officer of D Troop of that regiment, which company was 'rear guard' during the night the regiment made the forced march from Harney Springs to Pine Ridge Agency, to be engaged next morning, December 30, 1890, and had not brought in their lost, when on the same day in the evening they were ordered to rescue from annihilation the gallant but unlucky 7th U.S. Regular Cavalry." SOURCE: Coston, *The Spanish-American War Volunteer*, 31.
  Enlisted New York City, 1 Apr 1887, age 21 and 11 months; occupation sailor; Ht 5'6", yellow; discharged Ft Robinson, NE, as corporal, character excellent, 31 Mar 1892. SOURCE: Register of Enlistments.
  Letter, DeptPlatte, 27 May 1891, restores Corporal Butler to duty.
  Enlisted Ft Robinson, 1 Apr 1892; discharged Ft Robinson, as corporal, character very good, 30 Jun 1895. SOURCE: Register of Enlistments.
  See **MARTIN**, Jerry, Private, D/9th Cavalry
  Corporal, D/9th Cavalry, since 28 Jul 1890. SOURCE: Roster, 9 Cav, 1893.
  Desires to enlist in H/25th Infantry. SOURCE: AG File 25332.
  Performed solo at Easter service, Ft Missoula, MT, 1898. SOURCE: Steward, *The Colored Regulars*, 93.
  First to enter Spanish blockhouse at El Caney, Cuba, 1898, where he seized Spanish flag. SOURCE: Johnson, *History of Negro Soldiers*, 30; SecWar, *AR 1898*, 387.
  Took piece of El Caney flag and gave it to 1st Lt. Vernon A. Caldwell: "I went ahead of the company and when the artillery blew that hole in the wall I went in and got the flag, and along come a white man dressed something like an officer and made me give it to him, but I tore a corner off the flag anyway." SOURCE: Nankivell, *History of the Twenty-fifth Infantry*, 82.
  Cited for bravery in general orders, 11 Aug 1898. SOURCE: Cashin, *Under Fire with the Tenth Cavalry*, 144, 360.
  Accepts commission as second lieutenant, 9th Infantry, U.S. Volunteers, 1 Nov 1898. SOURCE: AGO File 147420.
  Accepts commission and encloses oath of office, 11 Feb 1899. SOURCE: AGO File 199435.
  Recommended as second lieutenant of volunteers by Brig. Gen. G. D. Ruggles, Ret., 29 Mar 1899. SOURCE: AGO File 216687.
  Requests commission in volunteers, 8 Sep 1899. SOURCE: AGO File 274484.

Recommended by Gen. Nelson Miles for appointment as captain in colored volunteers, 10 Sep 1899. SOURCE: AGO File 288998.

Appointed in colored volunteers, 15 Sep 1899. SOURCE: AGO File 277042.

Before joining 49th Infantry, served eight years and three months in D/9th Cavalry, private and corporal, 1 Apr 1887–30 Jun 1895; in H/25th Infantry, 6 Sep 1896–8 Sep 1898; second lieutenant, 9th Infantry, U.S. Volunteers, 29 Oct 1898–5 May 1899; recruiting duty, Baltimore, MD, 17–28 Sep 1899; appointed first lieutenant, 49th Infantry, 9 Sep 1899, and joined 21 Sep 1899; in arrest, 27 Nov–2 Dec 1899; released in accordance with General Orders 38 and 45; on special duty as police officer, U.S. Army Transport *Warren*, 3 Dec 1899–3 Jan 1900; sick on *Warren*, 13–15 Dec 1899, disease contracted in line of duty; sick, Honolulu, HI, 15–30 Dec 1899, disease contracted in line of duty; joined regiment 1 Feb 1900; on detached service, Cabayan Nuevo, Philippines, 28 Mar–15 Jun 1900; on detached service, Gamu, Luzon, Philippines, 13 Aug 1900–16 Apr 1901. SOURCE: Descriptive Book, F/49 Inf.

Ordered to report for recruiting duty at Baltimore, with ten enlisted men, 20 Sep 1899. SOURCE: AGO File 277287.

Accepts commission and encloses oath of office as first lieutenant, 49th Infantry, 23 Sep 1899. SOURCE: AGO File 279616.

Ordered under close arrest. SOURCE: SO 35, 49 Inf, 27 Nov 1899, Order Book, F/49 Inf.

Released to duty. SOURCE: SO 37, 49 Inf, 29 Nov 1899, Order Book, F/49 Inf.

With five men, stood off, then charged and scattered 250 insurgents, killing twenty, Cabayan Nuevo, 29 May 1900. SOURCE: Cleveland *Gazette*, 14 Nov 1908.

Commander, 49th Infantry, takes pleasure in announcing facts regarding engagement of detachment of seventeen enlisted men under Lieutenant Butler, Cabayan Nuevo, midnight, 30 May 1900; subpost attacked by large number of insurgents, estimated with fifty guns and seventy-five bolos; Butler with "great courage" repulsed attack after "hot and continuous fight" of over two hours; enemy had twenty killed. SOURCE: GO 10, 49 Inf, 15 Jun 1900, Order Book, F/49 Inf.

Butler at Cabayan Nuevo was attacked last night; he is "thoroughly competent" to cope with situation. SOURCE: TWX, Adj, 49th Inf, to AAG, Aparri, 30 May 1900, LS, 49 Inf.

Letter, Commander, 49th Infantry, 16 Jun 1900, Tuguegarao, Philippines, transmits copy of General Order 10, 49th Infantry, to Butler, Tumauni, Philippines, "and it affords me great pleasure to do so." SOURCE: LS, 49 Inf.

Commended by commander, 49th Infantry, for bravery leading detachment of scouts, Gamu, 12 Aug 1900; in dark night he went alone on porch of native house, disarmed an insurgent by snatching his rifle from him, returned fire of another with pistol and killed him; detachment killed four others; Butler and his men "rendered valuable service to the government besides making an honorable name for themselves and history for the regiment." SOURCE: GO 20, 49 Inf, 11 Oct 1900.

Wife inquires about his whereabouts, 14 Aug 1900. SOURCE: AGO File 338801.

Bill presented for $25 by Dr. Charles West; Butler charged with failure to support his wife and child, 20 Sep 1900. SOURCE: AGO File 343528.

His sister, Ida M. Carter, asks that he be compelled to support his wife and child, 21 Sep 1900. SOURCE: AGO File 343600.

Regarding allotment of pay to his wife, 24 Oct 1900. SOURCE: AGO File 343528.

Claim against him by Jesse Savage, 9 Jan 1901. SOURCE: AGO File 356743.

One of twenty-three officers of 49th Infantry recommended for regular Army commissions. SOURCE: CG, DivPI, to AG, USA, 8 Feb 1901, AGO File 355163.

Wife requests transportation to Manila through Hon. William H. Calderhead, member of Congress, 8 Mar 1901. SOURCE: AGO File 367084.

Bill of indebtedness to Dr. Charles West, 6 Jun 1901. SOURCE: AGO File 343528.

Regarding transportation for himself and his family from San Francisco to Manila, 22 Aug 1901. SOURCE: AGO File 395288.

Captured flag at El Caney; commissioned in 49th Infantry, with two complimentary regimental orders for gallantry, according to Col. Andrew Burt in Chicago speech, 11 Sep 1902. SOURCE: Cleveland *Gazette*, 11 Oct 1902.

Chaplain, U.S. Morgue, Manila, regarding his death, 17 June 1905. SOURCE: AGO File 1026919.

Capt. A. W. Butt, firing party, and trumpeter, to fire salute at funeral, 22 Aug 1905. SOURCE: AGO File 1047081.

Remains of Lt. Thomas C. Butler, 49th Infantry, who died in Manila, to be buried tomorrow, eleven A.M., Arlington, VA, with military honors. SOURCE: Washington *Star*, 22 Aug 1905.

Burial, Arlington Cemetery, 23 Aug 1905. SOURCE: AGO File 1047081.

BUTLER, William H.; Private; M/9th Cav. At Ft D. A. Russell, WY, in 1910; resident of Chicago. SOURCE: *Illustrated Review: Ninth Cavalry.*

BUTLER, William H.; Captain; K/49th Inf. Violinist and leader of Ft Meade, SD, orchestra, member of 25th Infantry, 1887. SOURCE: Cleveland *Gazette*, 7 Jan 1888.

First lieutenant, 7th Infantry, U.S. Volunteers, 13 Jul 1898–28 Feb 1899; second lieutenant, 49th Infantry, 9 Sep 1899; first lieutenant, 21 Sep 1899; captain, Company K, 20 Jun 1901. SOURCE: Descriptive Book, K/49 Inf.

One of twenty-three officers of 49th Infantry recommended for regular Army commissions. SOURCE: CG, DivPI, to AG, USA, 8 Feb 1901, AGO File 355163.

Mentioned as first lieutenant, C/49th Infantry. SOURCE: Beasley, *Negro Trailblazers*, 284.

BUTTON, F.; 25th Inf. Authorized to reenlist. SOURCE: TWX, DeptPlatte, 21 May 1895, Post Returns, Ft Robinson.

BYERS, George; Wagoner; H/9th Cav. Born Newville, PA, 1872; teamster; transferred from 6th Cavalry to H/9th Cavalry, 10 Apr 1896; wagoner, 11 Jan 1897; private, 1 Mar 1898; served at Ft Sill, Indian Territory, 19 Oct–22 Nov 1898; married Sarah Bell (Richardson) Byers, Newville, 7 Dec 1898, by Methodist Reverend Taylor. SOURCE: VA File C 2441072, George Byers.

With A/6th Cavalry, Ft Myers, VA; with H/9th Cavalry, Ft Robinson, NE; on hunting trips of Brigadier General Coppinger and Seward Webb, 1896 and 1897, the second time by request: "I always seemed to get along with the men. Officers seemed to like me." Worked as laborer four years after discharge, then three years for state, twelve years for knitting mill as fireman and engineer; trustee of church since 1904 and superintendent of Sunday School. SOURCE: Affidavit, 2 Apr 1928, VA File C 2441072, George Byers.

"My trouble began in Florida: The bread had hair 1 inch long and would not go down while reaching for water the meat would crawl off my plate this upset my stomach when I landed in Cuba I was sick." SOURCE: Statement, 8 May 1933, VA File C 2441072, George Byers.

Received Spanish-American War pension of $37.50 per month, 1934; lived at Soldiers Home, 1950–51; clinical record, Veterans Administration Hospital, Lebanon, PA, refers to him as "this 88 year old white man," 14 Jul 1959; lived with daughter at 1823 Boas St., Harrisburg, PA, just before death; died 26 Apr 1962; buried Carlisle, PA. SOURCE: VA File C 2441072, George Byers.

Application for certificate as veteran, 2 Oct 1934, reports his complexion as yellow; enlisted A/6th Cavalry, Harrisburg, PA, 1895; married Sarah Byers, 429 Northwest St., Carlisle. SOURCE: VA File C 2441072, George Byers.

Report, Veterans Administration Hospital, 23 Feb 1955, refers to him as "a protestant, negro veteran of the Spanish American War," born 6 Aug 1872. SOURCE: VA File C 2441072, George Byers.

BYRD, Allen; Private; Band/9th Cav. At Ft D. A. Russell, WY, in 1910; resident of Quincy, FL. SOURCE: *Illustrated Review: Ninth Cavalry*, with picture.

BYRD, Anderson; Private; 25th Inf. Arrested as suspect in beating of man who said "all niggers will steal"; private, K/25th Infantry. SOURCE: Richmond *Planet*, 28 Jul 1900.

Formerly of D/25th Infantry; retired and bought five acres at Allensworth, CA; raises sugar beets. SOURCE: Beasley, *Negro Trailblazers*, 156.

BYRD, Clarence; Private; K/24th Inf. Died of variola in the Philippines, 29 Jul 1900. SOURCE: *ANJ* 37 (11 Aug 1900): 1191.

BYRD, J. C.; Captain; USV. Writes letter to Manila *Times*. SOURCE: Manila *Times*, 15 Aug 1900.

BYRON, Thomas H.; Private; G/9th Cav. Appears as witness for prosecution in general court martial of Barney McKay, Ft Robinson, NE, 1893. SOURCE: Court Martial Records, McKay.

Convicted of four specifications of one charge of lying, to prejudice of good order and discipline, all to commander, Capt. Walter L. Finley, 9th Cavalry, Ft Robinson, 19 Aug 1893; sentenced to one month's hard labor in post guardhouse. SOURCE: GCMO 51, DeptPlatte, 4 Sep 1893; Court Martial Records, McKay.

c

CAGER, John T.; QM Sgt; G/9th Cav. Veteran of Spanish-American War and Philippine Insurrection; at Ft D. A. Russell, WY, in 1910. SOURCE: *Illustrated Review: Ninth Cavalry*, with picture.

CAGLE, Walter W.; Sergeant; F/9th Cav. Veteran of Philippine Insurrection; at Ft D. A. Russell, WY, in 1910; sharpshooter; resident of Harrisburg, NC. SOURCE: *Illustrated Review: Ninth Cavalry*, with picture.

CAIN, Allen; Private; 9th Cav. Wounded in head, Naco, AZ, 30 Nov 1914.

CAINE, George; Private; F/9th Cav. Discharged, end of term, Ft Robinson, NE, 26 Feb 1887.

CAINE, W. H.; Private; F/24th Inf. Qualified as sharpshooter, Ft Bayard, NM, 26 Feb 1887. SOURCE: *ANJ* 28 (27 Sep 1890): 70.

CALDWELL, Arthur; A/10th Cav. Original member of 10th Cavalry; in troop when organized, Ft Leavenworth, KS, 18 Feb 1867. SOURCE: McMiller, "Buffalo Soldiers," 68.

CALDWELL, Charles; Private; H/24th Inf. Acquitted by summary court martial of theft of silver-mounted bolo knife worth $6 from Contract Dental Surgeon Hugo C. Reitz, San Isidro, Philippines, late Dec 1901. SOURCE: Register of Summary Court, San Isidro.

CALDWELL, Charles C.; 1st Lt; F/48th Inf. Mentioned. SOURCE: Beasley, *Negro Trailblazers*, 284.

One of nineteen officers of 48th Infantry recommended as regular Army second lieutenants. SOURCE: CG, DivPI, Manila, 8 Feb 1901, to AGO, AGO File 355163.

CALDWELL, Eugene; Corporal; A/9th Cav. Born in South Carolina; private, I/10th Cavalry, 12 Dec 1892; corporal, 1 Sep 1895; sergeant, 9 Feb 1897. SOURCE: Baker, Roster.

Corporal, A/9th Cavalry, on recruiting duty, early 1898. SOURCE: Cashin, *Under Fire with the Tenth Cavalry*, 112.

CALDWELL, Frank; A/10th Cav. Original member of 10th Cavalry; in troop when organized, Ft Leavenworth, KS, 18 Feb 1867. SOURCE: McMiller, "Buffalo Soldiers," 68.

CALDWELL, Henry; L/10th Cav. Original member of 10th Cavalry; in troop when organized, Ft Riley, KS, 21 Sep 1867. SOURCE: McMiller, "Buffalo Soldiers," 78.

CALDWELL, John D.; Private; B/9th Cav. At Ft D. A. Russell, WY, in 1910. SOURCE: *Illustrated Review: Ninth Cavalry*.

CALDWELL, Lewis A.; M/10th Cav. Original member of 10th Cavalry; in troop when organized, Ft Riley, KS, 15 Oct 1867. SOURCE: McMiller, "Buffalo Soldiers," 79.

CALDWELL, Walter; Private; G/9th Cav. At Ft D. A. Russell, WY, in 1910; resident of Houston. SOURCE: *Illustrated Review: Ninth Cavalry*, with picture.

CALDWELL, William; Private; H/9th Cav. Best athlete, Department of the Philippines, after athletic meet, Manila, 9–14 Dec 1907. SOURCE: Hamilton, "History of the Ninth Cavalry," 116.

Veteran of Philippine Insurrection; at Ft D. A. Russell, WY, in 1910; sharpshooter; resident of Cynthiania, KY. SOURCE: *Illustrated Review: Ninth Cavalry*, with picture.

CALHOUN, Frank; Private; L/10th Cav. Served in 10th Cavalry, 1898; remained in U.S. during war with Spain. SOURCE: Cashin, *Under Fire with the Tenth Cavalry*, 350.

CALLEY, Elmwood; L/10th Cav. Original member of 10th Cavalry; in troop when organized, Ft Riley, KS, 21 Sep 1867. SOURCE: McMiller, "Buffalo Soldiers," 78.

CALLEY, John; Private; K/24th Inf. Absent without leave, Cuartel de Espana, Manila, Philippines, 17 June 1902; carried on return until 2 Aug 1902, under assumption that he joined another company en route to U.S. but failed to report. SOURCE: Regt Returns, 24 Inf.

CALLOWAY, Albert G.; Private; M/10th Cav. Served in 10th Cavalry, 1898; remained in U.S. during war with Spain. SOURCE: Cashin, *Under Fire with the Tenth Cavalry*, 351.

CALLOWAY, H. T.; Private; H/10th Cav. At Camp Forse, AL, Nov 1898. SOURCE: Richmond *Planet*, 3 Dec 1898.

CALLOWAY, John W.; Sergeant; 24th Inf. Enlisted Chicago, IL, 7 Mar 1894; promoted to corporal, Tampa, FL, 10 May 1898. SOURCE: Muster Roll, H/24 Inf, May–Jun 1898.

Occupation printer; age 23; Ht 5'7", complexion mulatto, hair black, eyes brown. SOURCE: Register of Enlistments, 1894.

Reduced from regimental quartermaster sergeant to private for disobedience of orders and conduct prejudicial to good order and military discipline. SOURCE: *ANJ* 35 (2 Oct 1897): 77.

Reminiscence of San Juan, Cuba. SOURCE: Lynk, *The Black Troopers*, 55–64.

Sick, disease contracted in line of duty, Siboney, Cuba, 10–25 Aug 1898; sick, en route to U.S. since 25 Aug 1898. SOURCE: Muster Roll, H/24 Inf, Jul–Aug 1898.

On furlough authorized by surgeon's certificate, 11 Sep–10 Oct 1898; relieved from special duty as regimental clerk, 2 Oct 1898; present, sick, since 26 Oct 1898. SOURCE: Muster Roll, H/24 Inf, Sep–Oct 1898.

On special duty as regimental clerk, 6 Nov 1898–28 Feb 1899. SOURCE: Muster Rolls, H/24 Inf, Nov–Dec 1898, Jan–Feb 1899.

Enlisted 7 Mar 1899; previous service, F/25th Infantry, 1 Jun 1891–30 Nov 1893; discharge, character excellent, Ft Missoula, MT, 30 Nov 1893; served in H/24th Infantry 7 Mar 1894–6 Mar 1899, discharged Ft Douglas, UT, character excellent, married; one-month furlough, Salt Lake City, UT, 11 Sep 1898. SOURCE: Register of Enlistments.

Virginian and nephew of late T. J. Bannister of Danville, VA; "we black men are so much between the 'Devil and the deep sea' on the Philippine question." SOURCE: Richmond *Planet*, 30 Sep 1899.

Letter from San Isidro, Philippines, 10 Nov 1899. SOURCE: Gatewood, *"Smoked Yankees"*, 251.

After military officials confiscated letter from Calloway to suspected Manila insurgent, Calloway was imprisoned, reduced to private, returned to U.S., and dishonorably discharged. SOURCE: Robinson and Schubert, "David Fagen," 79.

Adjudged to be menace to American interests in the Philippines in letter, 1st Lt. Arthur R. Kerwin, 13th Infantry, Acting Assistant Adjutant General, Manila, to Superintendent of Police, Manila, with five endorsements. SOURCE: Press copies of letters sent, Jul–Dec 1901, 24 Inf.

"On August 25, pursuant to writ of habeas corpus, case Calloway ordered deported, I declined to produce prisoner Court of First Instance, making return that prisoner was held by authority United States, that Court had no jurisdiction in such case, Court decided no jurisdiction, man was deported": MG Adna R. Chaffee to AG, USA, 2 Oct 1901. SOURCE: Carter, *The Life of Lt. General Chaffee*, 247.

"Request for Permission to Reenlist," 19 Jan 1918, denied; previous discharge without honor, "by reason of his own misconduct," 22 Feb 1901. SOURCE: Register of Enlistments.

See AGO Files 17043, 39492, 58153, 192847, 196933, 236467, 356799, 401746, 472919, 1702878, 2333974.

CALVERT, Frank; Private; I/10th Cav. At Ft Richardson, TX, 1873. SOURCE: ES, 10 Cav, 1873–81.

CAMIL, William; C/10th Cav. Original member of 10th Cavalry; in troop when organized, Ft Leavenworth, KS, 14 May 1867. SOURCE: McMiller, "Buffalo Soldiers," 70.

CAMMEL, Joseph; Private; H/10th Cav. Honorable mention for services rendered in capture of Mangas and his Apache band, Rio Bonito, AZ, 18 Oct 1886. SOURCE: Baker, Roster.

CAMP; Corporal; K/24th Inf. At Cabanatuan, Philippines, 1901. *See* **STEVENS**, Samuel, Private, D/24th Infantry

CAMPBELL, Guilford E.; 2nd Lt; G/49th Inf. Private and sergeant, E/8th Illinois Infantry, 28 Jun 1898–16 Mar 1899; commanded troops in engagements in the Philippines at Zapote Bridge, 24 Sep, and at San Nicolas, 25 Sep 1900; in engagement at Dalano, Tayabas, 25 Nov 1900; commended in General Order 20, Headquarters, 49th Infantry, 11 Oct 1900, for bravery in action at Zapote Bridge, 24 Sep 1900. SOURCE: Descriptive Book, F/49 Inf.

One of twenty-three officers of 49th Infantry recommended as regular Army second lieutenants. SOURCE: CG, DivPI, Manila, 8 Feb 1901, to AGO, AGO File 355163.

CAMPBELL, Henry; L/10th Cav. Original member of 10th Cavalry; in troop when organized, Ft Riley, KS, 21 Sep 1867. SOURCE: McMiller, "Buffalo Soldiers," 78.

CAMPBELL, J. H.; Private; D/10th Cav. Served in 10th Cavalry in Cuba, 1898. SOURCE: Cashin, *Under Fire with the Tenth Cavalry*, 341.

Wounded in action, Santiago, Cuba, Jul 1898. SOURCE: SecWar, *AR 1898*, 711; Bigelow, *Reminiscences of Santiago*, 133.

CAMPBELL, James; B/10th Cav. Original member of 10th Cavalry; in troop when organized, Ft Leavenworth, KS, 1 Apr 1867. SOURCE: McMiller, "Buffalo Soldiers," 69.

CAMPBELL, James; D/10th Cav. Original member of 10th Cavalry; in troop when organized, Ft Leavenworth, KS, 1 Jun 1867. SOURCE: McMiller, "Buffalo Soldiers," 71.

CAMPBELL, James; Sergeant; H/10th Cav. Reduced to private by general court martial, Jan 1877. SOURCE: ES, 10 Cav, 1873–81.

Deceased. SOURCE: CO, 10 Cav, to AG, USA, 3 Sep 1877, ES, 10 Cav, 1873–81.

CAMPBELL, James; Sergeant; A/24th Inf. At Ft Reno, Indian Territory, 1887. *See* **HAMILTON**, J. H., 24th Infantry

Retires from Ft Huachuca, AZ, Sep 1892. SOURCE: *ANJ* 30 (8 Oct 1892): 100.

CAMPBELL, James W.; Private; K/10th Cav. Served in 10th Cavalry, 1898; remained in U.S. during war with Spain. SOURCE: Cashin, *Under Fire with the Tenth Cavalry*, 349.

CAMPBELL, John B.; Master Sgt; 10th Cav. Enlisted 9th Cavalry, 1911; transferred to 10th Cavalry and served many years at Ft Huachuca, AZ; retired as master sergeant; resided at 4452 South 21st, Phoenix, AZ, 1972. SOURCE: *9th and 10th Cavalry Association Bulletin* (Jan–Mar 1972).

CAMPBELL, John M.; Recruit; Colored Detachment/Mounted Service. Convicted by Jefferson Barracks, MO, general court martial of desertion, 9–11 Nov 1888. SOURCE: GCMO 63, AGO, 13 Dec 1888.

CAMPBELL, John W.; Chief Trumpeter; Band/10th Cav. Served in 10th Cavalry in Cuba, 1898; cited for heroic care of wounded, San Juan, Cuba, Jul 1898. SOURCE: Cashin, *Under Fire with the Tenth Cavalry*, 352, 272.

CAMPBELL, John W.; Private; L/9th Cav. At Ft D. A. Russell, WY, in 1910; marksman; resident of Hopkinsville, AL. SOURCE: *Illustrated Review: Ninth Cavalry,* with picture.

CAMPBELL, Matt; Private; I/10th Cav. Served in 10th Cavalry, 1898; remained in U.S. during war with Spain. SOURCE: Cashin, *Under Fire with the Tenth Cavalry*, 348.

CAMPBELL, Robert; Private; B/25th Inf. Born Martinsburg, VA; enlisted, Pittsburgh, PA, 15 Aug 1896, occupation butcher, Ht 5'7", mulatto; marksman, 1897; character good; stationed at Ft Missoula, MT. SOURCE: Descriptive & Assignment Cards, 25 Inf.

CAMPBELL, Thomas; Sergeant; K/9th Cav. On detached service in field, New Mexico, 21 Jan–8 Feb 1881. SOURCE: Regt Returns, 9 Cav.

Discharged, end of term, Ft Cummings, NM, 22 Feb 1881. SOURCE: Regt Returns, 9 Cav.

CAMPBELL, Thomas C.; Captain; C/49th Inf. Appointed to 49th Infantry, 9 Sep 1899; formerly first lieutenant, 7th Volunteer Infantry. SOURCE: Descriptive Book, C/49 Inf.

Commanded detachment that captured Tomas Aguinaldo, brother of Emilio, 28 Feb 1900. SOURCE: Regt Returns, 49 Inf.

One of twenty-three officers of 49th Infantry recommended as regular Army second lieutenants. SOURCE: CG, DivPI, Manila, 8 Feb 1901, to AGO, AGO File 355163.

St. Louis, MO, resident since 1898; graduate of Howard University law school, 1893; delegate at large to Missouri state Republican convention, 1902; former clerk, U.S. General Land Office, Washington, DC; practiced in Muskogee, Creek Nation, OK; captured Col. Tomas Aguinaldo; married to Lizzie Anderson of Wilberforce, OH, Wilberforce graduate and formerly lady principal, Wilberforce University. SOURCE: Indianapolis *Freeman*, 2 Aug 1902, with picture.

Mentioned. SOURCE: Beasley, *Negro Trailblazers*, 284.

CAMPBELL, Wash C.; Private; M/49th Inf. Engaged against enemy, Tuao, Cagayan, Philippines, 18 Oct 1900. SOURCE: *ANJ* 38 (11 May 1901): 901.

CAMPBELL, William; Private; G/9th Cav. Dishonorable discharge, Ft Robinson, NE, Apr 1891; sent to Ft Leavenworth, KS, to serve two-year sentence, 2 May 1891.

CAMPBELL, William; Private; D/10th Cav. Served in 10th Cavalry in Cuba, 1898. SOURCE: Cashin, *Under Fire with the Tenth Cavalry*, 341.

CAMPER, James H.; Private; C/10th Cav. Served in 10th Cavalry in Cuba, 1898. SOURCE: Cashin, *Under Fire with the Tenth Cavalry*, 340.

CAMPHOR, George; Private; Band/9th Cav. With band on detached service at headquarters, District of New Mexico, Santa Fe, 1880; played small drum. SOURCE: Billington, *New Mexico's Buffalo Soldiers*, 226.

Soldier's dread of horses and riding makes his usefulness doubtful; should be discharged by way of favor because of excellent character and seventeen years of service; enlisted Baltimore, MD, 1873 and 1883; enlisted Chicago, IL, 1887; always faithful. SOURCE: CO, Ft Robinson, to AG, USA, 5 Sep 1894, LS, Ft Robinson.

CAMPLE, Sandy; Private; I/24th Inf. Enlisted Anniston, AL, 25 Mar 1899; joined company 8 Apr 1899. SOURCE: Muster Roll, I/24 Inf, Mar–Apr 1899.

Fined $2 by garrison court martial, 10 May 1899. SOURCE: Muster Roll, I/24 Inf, May–Jun 1899.

On detached service at Arayat, Philippines, since 31 Oct 1899. SOURCE: Muster Roll, I/24 Inf, Sep–Oct 1899.

CANADA, A.; Private; G/9th Cav. On detached service, Ft Craig, NM, 12 Jan–6 Feb 1881. SOURCE: Regt Returns, 9 Cav.

CANDY; Private; C/9th Cav. Wounded in action, San Juan, Cuba, 1 Jul 1898. SOURCE: *Illustrated Review: Ninth Cavalry*.

CANDY, George; Private; B/25th Inf. Died of dysentery, First Reserve Hospital, Manila, Philippines, 7 Jul 1901. SOURCE: *ANJ* 38 (24 Aug 1901): 1256.

CANIE, Alexander; A/10th Cav. Original member of 10th Cavalry; in troop when organized, Ft Leavenworth, KS, 18 Feb 1867. SOURCE: McMiller, "Buffalo Soldiers," 68.

CANNON, Henry; Private; I/9th Cav. On special duty as janitor at post library, reading room, chapel, school room, Ft Robinson, NE. SOURCE: Order 130, 23 Jun 1891, Post Orders, Ft Robinson.

At Ft Robinson, 9 Sep–4 Oct 1895, awaiting transportation to his unit, Ft Washakie, WY.

Discharged, certificate of disability, 2 Apr 1896.

CANNON, Horace; Corporal; K/48th Inf. Wounded in shoulder, Philippines, 6 May 1900. SOURCE: *ANJ* 37 (9 Jun 1900): 975.

CANNON, William; Private; D/10th Cav. Served in 10th Cavalry in Cuba, 1898. SOURCE: Cashin, *Under Fire with the Tenth Cavalry*, 341.

CANSBY, John H.; Private; Band/25th Inf. In D Company, Ft Meade, SD, 1887. *See* **BUTLER**, James H., Musician, 25th Infantry

Born Calloway Co., MO; fourth enlistment, Ft Missoula, MT, 12 Mar 1896; age 39, Ht 5'10", dark brown complexion, single. SOURCE: Descriptive Cards, 25 Inf.

CANTS, Henry; Corporal; E/9th Cav. Served in 1867. *See* **DOUGLAS**, Joseph, First Sergeant, E/9th Cavalry

CANTY, Henry; Farrier; A/10th Cav. At Ft Apache, AZ, 1890, subscribed $.50 to testimonial to General Grierson. SOURCE: List of subscriptions, 23 Apr 1890, 10th Cavalry papers, MHI.

Admitted to Soldiers Home with disability, with fourteen years and one month's service, age 38, 26 May 1891. SOURCE: SecWar, *AR 1891*, 753.

CAPERS, Harrison; Private; I/24th Inf. Involved in Houston riot, 1917. SOURCE: Haynes, *A Night of Violence*, 155.

CAPITE, Charles; Saddler; G/10th Cav. At Ft Robinson, NE, for cavalry competition, Sep 1897.

CARDOZA, William; Lieutenant. Graduate of Washington Colored High School; one of finest lieutenants in Spanish-American War. SOURCE: *The Voice of the Negro* 1 (Jun 1904): 222.

CAREY, Wilson; Private; K/10th Cav. Served in 10th Cavalry, 1898; remained in U.S. during war with Spain. SOURCE: Cashin, *Under Fire with the Tenth Cavalry*, 349.

CARLISLE, Newton; Sergeant; C/25th Inf. Dishonorable discharge, Brownsville. SOURCE: SO 266, AGO, 9 Nov 1906.

CARLTON, William J.; Private; B/25th Inf. Dishonorable discharge, Brownsville. SOURCE: SO 266, AGO, 9 Nov 1906.

CARMICHAEL, Harry; Private; B/25th Inf. Dishonorable discharge, Brownsville. SOURCE: SO 266, AGO, 9 Nov 1906.

CARMICHAEL, Joseph C.; 24th Inf. Died 2 Jan 1899; buried, Ft Douglas, UT. SOURCE: Clark, "A History of the Twenty-fourth," appendix A.

CARMOUCHE, Pierre L.; 1st Lt; L/9th Inf USV. Born Donaldsville, Ascension Parish, LA, 20 Nov 1862; common school education; barber at age 14, then dentist, later blacksmith and farrier, with own smith business; offered

services of 250 colored men to War Department, 25 Feb 1898; furnished company for 9th Infantry, 8 Jul 1898; well-liked strict disciplinarian. SOURCE: Coston, *The Spanish-American War Volunteer*, 77–79.

CARNEY, Lewis G.; Private; H/24th Inf. Enlisted Nashville, TN, 19 Apr 1898. SOURCE: Muster Roll, H/24 Inf, Mar–Apr 1898.

Sick, disease contracted in line of duty; at Siboney, Cuba, since 23 Aug 1898. SOURCE: Muster Roll, H/24 Inf, Jul–Aug 1898.

Rejoined company 10 Sep 1898; due U.S. for canteen and strap $.85. SOURCE: Muster Roll, H/24 Inf, Sep–Oct 1898.

On special duty as schoolteacher, since 4 Dec 1898. SOURCE: Muster Rolls, H/24 Inf, Nov–Dec 1898 and Jan–Feb 1899.

See **WILLIAMS**, Walter B., Sergeant Major, 24th Infantry

CARPENTAR, Kenny; H/10th Cav. Original member of 10th Cavalry; in troop when organized, Ft Leavenworth, KS, 21 Jul 1867. SOURCE: McMiller, "Buffalo Soldiers," 75.

CARPENTER, Allen; Private; M/9th Cav. Killed by Indians while hunting on North Llano River, TX, 21 Dec 1870. SOURCE: Hamilton, "History of the Ninth Cavalry," 12; *Historical and Pictorial Review*, 45; *Illustrated Review: Ninth Cavalry*.

CARPENTER, John; E/10th Cav. Original member of 10th Cavalry; in troop when organized, Ft Leavenworth, KS, 15 Jun 1867. SOURCE: McMiller, "Buffalo Soldiers," 72.

CARPENTER, Thomas W.; Private; H/24th Inf. Fined $3 by summary court, San Isidro, Philippines, for violating Article 32, absent without orders overnight, 25–26 Nov 1901, fourth conviction; fined $5 for violating Article 32, absent without leave, 9–9:45 A.M., 9 Feb 1902, while patient at hospital. SOURCE: Register of Summary Court, San Isidro.

CARR, Charles; Sergeant; B/9th Cav. Corporal, promoted from private, Ft Duchesne, UT, Jan 1895. SOURCE: *ANJ* 32 (26 Jan 1895): 358.

Promoted to sergeant, Ft Duchesne, Jun 1895. SOURCE: *ANJ* 32 (22 Jun 1895): 706.

Retires from Ft Duchesne, Nov 1895. SOURCE: *ANJ* 33 (16 Nov 1895): 179.

CARR, David; Trumpeter; K/9th Cav. At Ft D. A. Russell, WY, in 1910; sharpshooter; resident of Whitehall, KY. SOURCE: *Illustrated Review: Ninth Cavalry*, with picture.

CARR, Hayes; Private; M/49th Inf. Engaged against enemy, Tuao, Cagayan, Philippines, 18 Oct 1900. SOURCE: *ANJ* 38 (11 May 1901): 901.

CARR, Henry; Corporal; F/9th Cav. Veteran of Philippine Insurrection; at Ft D. A. Russell, WY, in 1910; resident of Goldsboro, NC. SOURCE: *Illustrated Review: Ninth Cavalry,* with picture.

CARR, James; Private; F/10th Cav. In post hospital, Ft Riley, KS, Apr 1868. SOURCE: LR, Det 10 Cav, 1868–69.

CARR, John M.; F/10th Cav. Original member of 10th Cavalry; in troop when organized, Ft Leavenworth, KS, 21 Jun 1867. SOURCE: McMiller, "Buffalo Soldiers," 73.

CARR, Louis; Private; C/10th Cav. Served in 10th Cavalry, 1898; remained in U.S. during war with Spain. SOURCE: Cashin, *Under Fire with the Tenth Cavalry,* 340.

CARR, Thomas; Private; 24th Inf. Harassed and arrested by police, Manila, Philippines, 19 Jun 1902. SOURCE: CO, 24 Inf, to Chief of Police, Manila, 21 Jun 1902.

CARRICO; Private; B/10th Cav. At Ft Apache, AZ, 1890, subscribed $.50 to testimonial to General Grierson. SOURCE: List of subscriptions, 23 Apr 1890, 10th Cavalry papers, MHI.

CARROLL, Benjamin F.; Private; L/9th Cav. At Ft D. A. Russell, WY, in 1910; resident of Ninety-Six, SC. SOURCE: *Illustrated Review: Ninth Cavalry,* with picture.

CARROLL, F.; Private; A/9th Cav. At Ft Stanton, NM, 1881. SOURCE: Regt Returns, 9 Cav.

CARROLL, Frank; Private; H/10th Cav. Served in 10th Cavalry, 1898; remained in U.S. during war with Spain. SOURCE: Cashin, *Under Fire with the Tenth Cavalry,* 346.

CARROLL, George; D/10th Cav. Mentioned as surviving Indian war veteran. SOURCE: *Winners of the West* 3 (Jun 1926): 7.

Kansan, died, age 83, on 24 Jul 1939; favorite literature was Bible and *Winners of the West.* SOURCE: *Winners of the West* 16 (Aug 1939): 2.

CARROLL, Joseph H.; 1st Lt; 49th Inf. Born Cleveland, OH, 30 Jan 1870; local education; worked two years as collector, National Bank of Commerce; graduated second in class of thirty-seven, Western Reserve Medical School, 1895; practiced four years, Frankfort, KY, then fifteen months, Columbus, OH; runs sixty-two-bed hospital, San Pablo, Philippines, 100 miles north of Manila. SOURCE: Cleveland *Gazette,* 30 Mar 1900, with picture.

Resided at 179 North Cleveland Ave., Columbus, in 1905. SOURCE: Affidavit, Carroll, 14 Dec 1905, VA File 2624105, Floyd H. Crumbly.

One of twenty-three officers of 49th Infantry recommended as regular Army second lieutenants. SOURCE: CG, DivPI, Manila, 8 Feb 1901, to AGO, AGO File 355163.

Mentioned. SOURCE: Beasley, *Negro Trailblazers,* 284.

CARROLL, Lawn; Private; D/10th Cav. Served in 10th Cavalry, 1898; remained in U.S. during war with Spain. SOURCE: Cashin, *Under Fire with the Tenth Cavalry,* 341.

CARROLL, W. H.; Sergeant; G/24th Inf. At Siboney, Cuba, 1898. *See* **WOODS,** Robert Gordon, Captain, I/49th Infantry

CARROLL, Walker; Private; H/10th Cav. Sentenced to ten years in Wyoming state penitentiary for attempted criminal assault on eleven-year-old girl in Cheyenne. SOURCE: Cheyenne *Daily Leader,* 14 Feb and 21, 25 Dec 1906.

CARSON; 25th Inf. Ex-soldier tried for larceny and acquitted in Manila. SOURCE: Manila *Times,* 12 Apr 1901.

CARSON, Hiram; B/10th Cav. Original member of 10th Cavalry; in troop when organized, Ft Leavenworth, KS, 1 Apr 1867. SOURCE: McMiller, "Buffalo Soldiers," 69.

On daily duty with Quartermaster Department. SOURCE: SO 14, Det 10 Cav, in field near Ft Dodge, KS, 9 Apr 1869, Orders, Det 10 Cav, 1868–69.

Relieved. SOURCE: SO 20, Det 10 Cav, 16 Apr 1869.

CARSON, James R.; Sergeant; B/9th Cav. Corporal since 18 Jun 1892. SOURCE: Roster, 9 Cav, Jul 1893.

Promoted sergeant, Ft Duchesne, UT, Apr 1895. SOURCE: *ANJ* 32 (4 May 1895): 590.

CARSON, Willie; Private; M/10th Cav. Died Ft Robinson, NE, Jun 1902. SOURCE: Medical History, Ft Robinson.

Buried Ft Robinson, 27 Jun 1902. SOURCE: List of Interments, Ft Robinson.

CARTER; Private; A/9th Cav. Reenlistment, married, authorized. SOURCE: Letter, AG, USA, 12 May 1897, Post Returns, Ft Robinson.

CARTER; Sergeant; 9th Cav. Wife Helen buried at Ft Robinson, NE, 10 Jan 1898. SOURCE: List of Interments, Ft Robinson.

CARTER, Alfred; 10th Cav. Served ten years, in C and H/10th Cavalry; recent subscriber. SOURCE: *Winners of the West* 4 (Mar 1927): 8.

Served 1884–89; member, Camp 11, National Indian War Veterans, St. Joseph, MO; died Weems, VA. SOURCE: *Winners of the West* 8 (Sep 1931): 8.

CARTER, Amos A.; Sgt 1st Cl; Hospital Corps. Surgeon, Ft Robinson, NE, seeks Carter's transfer from post; Carter does not have good control over men, has confessed to theft from liquor supply, has failed to keep promises to refrain from use and replenish stock; Hospital Corps detachment has lost confidence and respect for him; previously commissioned officer, 48th Infantry; returned from the Philippines depressed, despondent, in debt; used pay to cover debts and stole liquor, replacing with other fluids; in Army since 1896, with excellent character on discharges, no court martials, wishes assignment to Ft Harrison, MT. SOURCE: Post Surgeon to SG, USA, 20 Nov 1903, LS, Post Surgeon, Ft Robinson.

CARTER, Andrew; I/9th Cav. Admitted to Soldiers Home, with twenty years and ten months' service, age 46, 18 Feb 1887. SOURCE: SecWar, *AR 1887*, 746.

CARTER, Andrew; B/10th Cav. Admitted to Soldiers Home, with disability, after six years and eight months' service, age 28, 21 Jan 1888. SOURCE: SecWar, *AR 1889*, 1012.

CARTER, Charles; Private; M/10th Cav. Served in 10th Cavalry, 1898; remained in U.S. during war with Spain. SOURCE: Cashin, *Under Fire with the Tenth Cavalry*, 351.

CARTER, Charles McD.; Sergeant; A/9th Cav. Commander, 10th Cavalry, forwards Carter's application for remission of sentence to commander, E/10th Cavalry, for comment, then forwards application to Adjutant General, approved, late Dec 1876. SOURCE: ES, 10 Cav, 1873–81.

Prisoner, late private, E/10th Cavalry, released from Ft Leavenworth, KS. SOURCE: GCMO 22, AGO, 23 Feb 1877.

Appointed sergeant 2 May 1893. SOURCE: Roster, 9 Cav, Jul 1893.

CARTER, Cornelius E.; Private; E/24th Inf. Died of dysentery in the Philippines. SOURCE: *ANJ* 37 (31 Mar 1900): 731.

CARTER, Fletcher; Private; K/10th Cav. Served in 10th Cavalry, 1898; remained in U.S. during war with Spain. SOURCE: Cashin, *Under Fire with the Tenth Cavalry*, 349.

CARTER, Frederick; D/10th Cav. Original member of 10th Cavalry; in troop when organized, Ft Leavenworth, KS, 1 Jun 1867. SOURCE: McMiller, "Buffalo Soldiers," 71.

CARTER, George W.; Private; A/9th Cav. On special duty as orderly to general court martial since 27 Jan 1902. SOURCE: Special Duty List, A/9 Cav, 24 May 1902, Nueva Caceres, Philippines.

CARTER, H.; Private; B/9th Cav. On detached service, Ft Bayard, NM, 16 Jan–9 Feb 1881. SOURCE: Regt Returns, 9 Cav, Feb 1881.

CARTER, Henry; Corporal; F/24th Inf. Retires from Ft Bayard, NM, Apr 1893. SOURCE: *ANJ* 30 (22 Apr 1893): 575.

CARTER, Henry; Private; D/48th Inf. Convicted by general court martial, Angel Island, CA, of willful disobedience and resisting noncommissioned officer making arrest;

sentenced to dishonorable discharge and two months' confinement. SOURCE: *ANJ* 37 (23 Dec 1899): 394.

CARTER, Henry H. B.; Sergeant; G/9th Cav. Corporal, one of six enlisted men of G/9th Cavalry to testify against Lt. John Conline at his 1877 court martial for misconduct, including drunkenness, sexual misconduct, misappropriation of funds belonging to men of his troop, Ft Garland, CO. SOURCE: Billington, *New Mexico's Buffalo Soldiers*, 121–23.

Led detachment on scout from Ft Bayard, NM, Nov 1878. SOURCE: Billington, *New Mexico's Buffalo Soldiers*, 58.

Sergeant, scouted 475 miles with detachment, autumn 1878. SOURCE: Hamilton, "History of the Ninth Cavalry," 37; *Illustrated Review: Ninth Cavalry*.

CARTER, Isaac; L/10th Cav. Original member of 10th Cavalry; in troop when organized, Ft Riley, KS, 21 Sep 1867. SOURCE: McMiller, "Buffalo Soldiers," 78.

See **ANDERSON**, Henry, Private, L/10th Cavalry

CARTER, Isaac; Private; A/38th Inf. On extra duty with Quartermaster Department, Ft Cummings, NM, 1868, and considered "trustworthy, reliable, and faithful." SOURCE: Billington, *New Mexico's Buffalo Soldiers*, 191–92.

CARTER, J. T.; Corporal; C/9th Cav. While herd guard, lost four horses; admonished and threatened with trial and pay of rewards for return, which amounts to $100; a good man. SOURCE: 1LT B. D. Humphrey, CO, C/9, to Adj, Ft Robinson, 14 Sep 1886, LS, Ft Robinson.

Dropped as deserter; recommend his return to duty without trial and payment of reward for horses. SOURCE: CO, Ft Robinson, to AAG, DP, 15 Sep 1886, LS, Ft Robinson.

Recommend approval of Carter's application for restoration to duty; he states why he was frightened away. SOURCE: CO, Ft Robinson, to AAG, DP, 24 Sep 1886, LS, Ft Robinson.

CARTER, James; B/10th Cav. Original member of 10th Cavalry; in troop when organized, Ft Leavenworth, KS, 1 Apr 1867. SOURCE: McMiller, "Buffalo Soldiers," 69.

At Ft Lyon, CO, Mar 1869. SOURCE: LR, Det 10 Cav, 1868–69.

CARTER, James; C/10th Cav. Original member of 10th Cavalry; in troop when organized, Ft Leavenworth, KS, 14 May 1867. SOURCE: McMiller, "Buffalo Soldiers," 70.

In post hospital, Ft Riley, KS, Apr 1868. SOURCE: LR, Det 10 Cav, 1868–69.

CARTER, Joe; Private; M/9th Cav. At Ft D. A. Russell, WY, in 1910; resident of Mobile, AL. SOURCE: *Illustrated Review: Ninth Cavalry*, with picture.

CARTER, John F.; Private; C/9th Cav. Buried Ft Robinson, NE, 23 Aug 1888. SOURCE: List of Interments, Ft Robinson.

CARTER, John T.; Private; H/9th Cav. At Ft Robinson, NE, awaiting transportation to Hot Springs, AR, since 17 Nov 1887.

Died of pulmonary consumption, Ft Robinson hospital, 23 Mar 1888.

Funeral 24 Mar 1888. SOURCE: Order 56, 23 Mar 1888, Post Orders, Ft Robinson.

CARTER, Lewis; E/10th Cav. Original member of 10th Cavalry; in troop when organized, Ft Leavenworth, KS, 15 Jun 1867. SOURCE: McMiller, "Buffalo Soldiers," 72.

CARTER, Louis A.; Chaplain; 25th Inf. Successful pastor of large Knoxville, TN, congregation, before joining Army. SOURCE: Stover, *Up from Handymen*, 149.

Managed 10th Cavalry Wild West show, Ft Ethan Allen, VT, riding hall, Thanksgiving 1911. SOURCE: Fletcher, *The Black Soldier*, 80.

First lieutenant, 10th Cavalry. SOURCE: Work, *The Negro Year Book, 1912*, 77.

When 10th Cavalry soldier killed a cowboy in response to racial slurs and was accused of murder, Ft Douglas, AZ, 1913, Chaplain Carter led effort to get him a lawyer; soldier was acquitted on basis of self-defense; served with 9th Cavalry in the Philippines, 1915; helped married men provide their own housing, Camp Stotsenburg, to keep them from town. SOURCE: Stover, *Up from Handymen*, 162, 164.

Major, 9th Cavalry. SOURCE: Work, *The Negro Yearbook, 1918–1919*, 228.

Captain, 25th Infantry, stationed at Camp Henry J. Jones, AZ. SOURCE: Work, *The Negro Yearbook, 1925–1926*, 253.

Biographical sketch. SOURCE: Logan and Winston, *Dictionary of American Negro Biography*, 91–92.

CARTER, Nelson; Private; K/25th Inf. At Ft Niobrara, NE, 1904. SOURCE: Wilson, "History of Fort Niobrara."

CARTER, Pat; E/25th Inf. Ex-solder who operates his own sailing launch between Manila and Santa Cruz, Philippines; does business with both natives and Americans. SOURCE: Richmond *Planet*, 16 Mar 1901.

CARTER, Richard; Private; C/9th Cav. Buried Ft Robinson, NE, Dec 1896. SOURCE: SO 138, 15 Dec 1896, Post Orders, Ft Robinson; List of Interments, Ft Robinson.

CARTER, Robert; Private; A/10th Cav. At Ft Apache, AZ, 1890, subscribed $.50 to testimonial to General Grierson. SOURCE: List of subscriptions, 23 Apr 1890, 10th Cavalry papers, MHI.

Served in 10th Cavalry in Cuba, 1898. SOURCE: Cashin, *Under Fire with the Tenth Cavalry*, 336.

CARTER, Thomas; Corporal; K/9th Cav. At Ft D. A. Russell, WY, in 1910; sharpshooter; resident of Birmingham, AL. SOURCE: *Illustrated Review: Ninth Cavalry*, with picture.

CARTER, William; A/10th Cav. Recruit, arrested by civil authorities, Nov 1866; original member of 10th Cavalry; in troop when organized, Ft Leavenworth, KS, 18 Feb 1867. SOURCE: McMiller, "Buffalo Soldiers," 46, 68.

CARTER, William; H/10th Cav. Served with Webb Chatmoun, 1880s; resided at 314 E. Larau, Pensacola, FL, in 1913. SOURCE: VA File C 2360629, Webb Chatmoun.

CARTER, William; Private; F/9th Cav. At Ft D. A. Russell, WY, in 1910; resident of Dallas. SOURCE: *Illustrated Review: Ninth Cavalry*, with picture.

CARTER, William; Private; E/10th Cav. Served in 10th Cavalry, 1898; remained in U.S. during war with Spain. SOURCE: Cashin, *Under Fire with the Tenth Cavalry*, 343.

CARTER, William; Private; 24th Inf. Drowned crossing San Mateo River, Philippines, 21 Aug 1899. SOURCE: Richmond *Planet*, 2 Sep 1899.

CARTER, William H.; Trumpeter; A/9th Cav. Shot and killed by carbine in hands of friends, near A Troop barracks, Ft Niobrara, NE, 16 Jun 1889. Committee that drafted resolution of sympathy for ten-year veteran Carter included 1st Sgt. Solomon Holloman, Sgt. Charles H. Dowd, Trumpeter Robert C. Bland, Blacksmith Nathan Ward, Cpl. Henry Coker, Pvt. James T. Cotton, Pvt. Powhattan E. Booker, Pvt. John Henderson, Jr. SOURCE: *ANJ* 26 (29 Jun 1889): 900.

CARTER, William H.; Private; C/9th Cav. At Ft Douglas, UT, 1899. *See* **JACKSON**, John J., First Sergeant, C/9th Cavalry

Died 8 Aug 1899; buried Ft Douglas. SOURCE: Clark, "A History of the Twenty-fourth," appendix A.

CARTER, William L.; Private; C/10th Cav. Served in 10th Cavalry, 1898; remained in U.S. during war with Spain. SOURCE: Cashin, *Under Fire with the Tenth Cavalry*, 340.

CARTHIN, William; Private; C/9th Cav. At Ft D. A. Russell, WY, in 1910; sharpshooter; resident of 1716 W. Herman St., Nashville. SOURCE: *Illustrated Review: Ninth Cavalry*, with picture.

CARTWRIGHT, Clarence; Private; C/9th Cav. At Ft D. A. Russell, WY, in 1910; resident of 65 Tatnall St., Atlanta. SOURCE: *Illustrated Review: Ninth Cavalry*, with picture.

CARTY, James; Private; 10th Cav. Arrived at Ft Leavenworth, KS, from Jefferson Barracks, MO. SOURCE: Adj, Ft Leavenworth, to HQ, Jefferson Barracks, 9 Oct 1866, LS, 10 Cav.

No clothing account issued for Private Carty. SOURCE: LS, 10 Cav.

CARVER, Charles; Sergeant; E/10th Cav. Private, E/10th Cavalry, served in 10th Cavalry in Cuba, 1898. SOURCE: Cashin, *Under Fire with the Tenth Cavalry*, 342.

Promoted from corporal. SOURCE: *ANJ* 37 (7 Oct 1899): 122.

CARVER, George; Sergeant; E/24th Inf. Ranked number 52 among expert riflemen with 74 percent, 1904. SOURCE: GO 79, AGO, 1 Jun 1905.

CARVIN, John; C/10th Cav. Original member of 10th Cavalry; in troop when organized, Ft Leavenworth, KS, 14 May 1867. SOURCE: McMiller, "Buffalo Soldiers," 70.

CARY, Wilson; Sergeant; I/9th Cav. Veteran of Philippine Insurrection; at Ft D. A. Russell, WY, in 1910; marksman; resident of Orange, VA. SOURCE: *Illustrated Review: Ninth Cavalry,* with picture.

CASEY, John F.; 1st Sgt; H/10th Cav. Honorable mention for services rendered as corporal in capture of Mangas and his Apache band, Rio Bonito, AZ, 18 Oct 1886. SOURCE: Baker, Roster.

Corporal, Ft Apache, AZ, sharpshooter. SOURCE: *ANJ* 24 (27 Nov 1886): 350.

First sergeant, Ft Apache, AZ, sharpshooter. SOURCE: *ANJ* 25 (13 Aug 1887): 42.

CASH, Richard; Private; C/24th Inf. Granted furlough from Ft D. A. Russell, WY, Apr 1899.

CASHIN, Daniel; Private; G/9th Cav. Recruit, Colored Detachment/Mounted Service, acquitted by general court martial of theft of overcoat owned by Recruit Perry Million, Colored Detachment, Jefferson Barracks, MO, 7 Oct 1885. SOURCE: GCMO 105, AGO, 28 Oct 1885.

In hands of civil authorities, Lincoln, NE, 29 Apr–Jun 1887. SOURCE: Regt Returns, 9 Cav.

CASHY, George S.; Private; D/24th Inf. At Cabanatuan, Philippines, 1901. *See* **MEAD**, James P., Private, K/24th Infantry

CASSAWAY, Charles; Private; G/9th Cav. Promoted to corporal, F/10th Cavalry; from private, Ft Washakie, WY. SOURCE: *Fremont Clipper,* 14 Dec 1906.

Veteran of Philippine Insurrection; private, G/9th Cavalry, at Ft. D. A. Russell, WY, in 1910; resident of San Antonio, TX. SOURCE: *Illustrated Review: Ninth Cavalry,* with picture.

CASSELLE, Nelson A.; Private; L/24th Inf. Letter from Skagway, AK, promotes his volume of poetry, *Consular of Light, or Casselle's Poetical Works*; Memphis, TN, resident and basso in L Company's "Magnolia Four"; sings with Benjamin Green, first tenor, George H. Williams, baritone, Edward J. Collins, second tenor; quartet has "won much popularity and praise from the Alaska press." SOURCE: Indianapolis *Freeman,* 11 Jan 1902.

Deserted from Ft Missoula, MT, 21 Jun 1902. SOURCE: Regt Returns, 24 Inf, Jul 1902.

CASTER, John W.; Private; L/9th Cav. Deserted from Ft Apache, AZ, 9 Sep 1900. SOURCE: Regt Returns, 9 Cav, Sep 1900.

CASTILLO, Pedro; Sergeant; C/10th Cav. Original member of 10th Cavalry; in troop when organized, Ft Leavenworth, KS, 14 May 1867. SOURCE: McMiller, "Buffalo Soldiers," 70.

Adjutant, 10th Cavalry, admonishes Capt. Edward Byrne, C/10th Cavalry, 8 Jul 1867: "When it is necessary to reduce a noncommissioned officer, commander will not issue order but will place the noncommissioned officer in arrest, appoint a temporary replacement, send full details and recommendations to regimental commander, and await reply; Castillo remains sergeant of company as proper reports have not been received by regiment; full report should have been promptly forwarded in case as serious as his; after reduction, charges cannot be brought for offenses that caused reduction; if you intend to prefer charges, it must be as sergeant, late first sergeant, with his vacancy as sergeant unfilled until reduction is decided." SOURCE: LS, 10 Cav, 1866–67.

Absent from duty in arrest. SOURCE: Adj, 10 Cav, to CO, C/10, 19 Jul 1867, LS, 10 Cav, 1866–67.

CATHEY, Joseph; Sergeant; G/9th Cav. Veteran of Philippine Insurrection; at Ft D. A. Russell, WY, in 1910; sharpshooter. SOURCE: *Illustrated Review: Ninth Cavalry,* with picture.

CATLETT, James H.; Private; F/10th Cav. Served in 10th Cavalry in Cuba, 1898. SOURCE: Cashin, *Under Fire with the Tenth Cavalry*, 344.

CAULDER, Nathan; Cook; K/9th Cav. Veteran of Philippine Insurrection; at Ft D. A. Russell, WY, in 1910; sharpshooter; resident of Lexington, KY. SOURCE: *Illustrated Review: Ninth Cavalry,* with picture.

CAUMP; Private; B/9th Cav. Wounded in action on Animas River, along with Private Freeland, B/9th Cavalry, 18 Sep 1879; later died of wounds. SOURCE: Hamilton, "History of the Ninth Cavalry," 42; *Illustrated Review: Ninth Cavalry.*

CAUSBY, John; Principal Musician; Band/24th Inf. Promoted from sergeant. SOURCE: *ANR* 38 (21 Oct 1905): 22.

CAUTHEN, Eddie; Private; A/9th Cav. At Ft D. A. Russell, WY, in 1910. SOURCE: *Illustrated Review: Ninth Cavalry,* with picture.

CAVILLE, Charles W.; I/48th Inf. Convicted of felonious assault with sharp instrument, Philippines, Nov 1900; sentenced to three months and $30 fine.

CAYSON, Frank; Private; C/9th Cav. Discharged from Ft Robinson, NE, 27 Jan 1887. SOURCE: GCMO 105, DP, 21 Dec 1886.

Military prisoner transferred to Ft Omaha, NE, Jan 1887. SOURCE: Post Returns, Ft Robinson.

CECIL, John; Private; G/24th Inf. Wounded in thigh at Deposito, Philippines. SOURCE: Richmond *Planet*, 19 Aug 1899; *ANJ* 36 (19 Aug 1899): 1223.

CEE, William; Private; Band/9th Cav. Private, with Band/9th Cavalry on detached service at headquarters, District of New Mexico, Santa Fe, 1880; played E-flat cornet. SOURCE: Billington, *New Mexico's Buffalo Soldiers*, 226.

At Ft Apache, AZ, 1890, subscribed $.50 to testimonial to General Grierson. SOURCE: List of subscriptions, 23 Apr 1890, 10th Cavalry papers, MHI.

CEIGHTON, Franklin; L/10th Cav. Original member of 10th Cavalry; in troop when organized, Ft Riley, KS, 21 Sep 1867. SOURCE: McMiller, "Buffalo Soldiers," 78.

CHAMBERS, Clifford; Corporal; A/49th Inf. Private, G/10th Cavalry, served in 10th Cavalry, 1898; remained in U.S. during war with Spain. SOURCE: Cashin, *Under Fire with the Tenth Cavalry*, 345.

Died of dysentery, Aparri, Luzon, Philippines, 4 Jun 1901. SOURCE: *ANJ* 38 (27 Jun 1901): 1169.

CHAMBERS, Henry; Private; K/10th Cav. Apprehended from desertion, Dec 1873. SOURCE: LS, 10 Cav, 1873–77.

Colonel Grierson says Chambers was apprehended in Philadelphia, 26 Nov 1873, and confined at St. Louis, MO. SOURCE: ES, 10 Cav, 1873–81.

CHAMBERS, Henry; F/24th Inf. *See* **PROCTOR**, John C., Color Sergeant, 9th Cavalry; **SMITH**, Jacob Clay, Sergeant, 10th Cavalry

CHAMBERS, John; Private; I/10th Cav. Released to duty from treatment for acute gonorrhea, Ft Robinson, NE, 18 Jan 1903. SOURCE: Post Surgeon to CO, I/10, 18 Jan 1903, LS, Post Surgeon, Ft Robinson.

Recommend discharge of this four-year veteran with venereal disease as unfit for service. SOURCE: Post Surgeon to Post Adj, 10 Feb 1904, LS, Post Surgeon, Ft Robinson.

Discharged on certificate of disability with chronic venereal disease, Ft Robinson, 13 Feb 1904. SOURCE: Certificates of Disability, Ft Robinson.

CHAMBERS, Robert; Private; C/9th Cav. Enlisted Baltimore, MD; discharged, end of term, Ft Robinson, NE, 20 Oct 1885. SOURCE: CO, C/9, to Chief Paymaster, DP, 23 Sep 1885, LS, C/9 Cav.

CHAMBERS, William; Private; C/24th Inf. Deserted, Honolulu, HI, 2 Jul 1899. SOURCE: Regt Returns, 24 Inf, Jul 1899.

CHAMBERS, William; Sergeant; M/25th Inf. Cited among men who distinguished themselves in 1893: as sergeant, D/25th Infantry, arrested Indian deserter, resisted and defeated nighttime attempt to rescue prisoner; displayed great coolness and bravery, Tongue River Agency, MT, 18 Jun 1893. SOURCE: GO 59, AGO, 10 Nov 1894.

As sergeant, H/25th Infantry, accompanied Chaplain Steward on visit to three saloon-keepers near Ft Missoula, MT, to ask them to close on Sunday during services, Jan 1894; all promised to do so. SOURCE: Chaplain T. G. Steward, Monthly Report, 31 Jan 1894, AGO File 4634ACP91.

At Bamban, Philippines, 1899. SOURCE: Nankivell, *History of the Twenty-fifth Infantry*, 93, with picture.

CHAMBLISS, Arthur; Warrant Officer; U.S. Army. At Ft D. A. Russell, WY, in 1910; resident of Dadeville, AL. SOURCE: *Illustrated Review: Ninth Cavalry*.

Sergeant, E/10th Cavalry, commissioned second lieutenant, 27 Sep 1918. SOURCE: Glass, *History of the Tenth Cavalry*, appendix M.

Warrant officer, stationed at Camp Stephen D. Little, Nogales, AZ. SOURCE: Work, *The Negro Yearbook, 1931–1932*, 334.

CHAMP, Abraham; Private; K/10th Cav. Private, G/9th Cavalry, threatened in saloon, Suggs, WY, 16 Jun 1892, triggering so-called Suggs Affray. SOURCE: Schubert, "The Suggs Affray," 63.

Served in 10th Cavalry in Cuba, 1898. SOURCE: Cashin, *Under Fire with the Tenth Cavalry*, 350.

CHANDLER, Alphonzo; C/10th Cav. Original member of 10th Cavalry; in troop when organized, Ft Leavenworth, KS, 14 May 1867. SOURCE: McMiller, "Buffalo Soldiers," 70.

CHANDLER, Ed D.; Private; E/9th Cav. At Ft D. A. Russell, WY, in 1910; sharpshooter; resident of St. Louis. SOURCE: *Illustrated Review: Ninth Cavalry*, with picture.

CHANDLER, Noah; Recruit; Colored Inf. Convicted of desertion, 5 Mar–28 Aug 1879, by general court martial, David's Island, NY; sentenced to dishonorable discharge and four years. SOURCE: GCMO 52, AGO, 3 Oct 1879.

CHANDLER, Richard; Private; I/9th Cav. Ordered to report to unit at Ft Wingate, NM. SOURCE: RO 2, 9 Cav, 22 Jan 1879, Name File, 9 Cav.

CHANDLER, W. H.; A/10th Cav. Served 1884–89; died Sumter, SC. SOURCE: *Winners of the West* 12 (May 1935): 3.

CHANLEY, Robert; Private; L/10th Cav. Served in 10th Cavalry, 1898; remained in U.S. during war with Spain. SOURCE: Cashin, *Under Fire with the Tenth Cavalry*, 350.

CHAPMAN, Charles; Private; C/9th Cav. Enlisted Ft McKinney, WY, 19 May 1893.

CHAPMAN, Henry; L/10th Cav. Original member of 10th Cavalry; in troop when organized, Ft Riley, KS, 21 Sep 1867. SOURCE: McMiller, "Buffalo Soldiers," 78.

CHAPMAN, James; Private; F/9th Cav. Recruit from depot arrived at Ft Robinson, NE, 1 Mar 1887.

CHAPMAN, James; Private; M/10th Cav. Served in 10th Cavalry, 1898; remained in U.S. during war with Spain. SOURCE: Cashin, *Under Fire with the Tenth Cavalry*, 351.

CHAPMAN, Joseph; 1st Sgt; G/25th Inf. Authorized four-month furlough from Ft Missoula, MT. SOURCE: *ANJ* 27 (2 Nov 1889): 185.

His retirement party at Ft Missoula described. SOURCE: *ANJ* 30 (19 Aug 1893): 860.

CHAPMAN, S.; Sergeant; E/9th Cav. Killed in action against Victorio at Camp Ojo Caliente, NM, Sep 1879. SOURCE: Billington, "Black Cavalrymen," 67; Billington, *New Mexico's Buffalo Soldiers*, 89.

Was in charge of herd guard, Ojo Caliente, 4 Sep 1879, when Indians jumped herd; he and Privates Graddon, Hoke, Murphy, and Percival were killed. SOURCE: Hamilton, "History of the Ninth Cavalry," 44; *Illustrated Review: Ninth Cavalry*.

CHAPMAN, Silas; Private; K/9th Cav. Veteran of Philippine Insurrection; at Ft D. A. Russell, WY, in 1910; resident of Philadelphia. SOURCE: *Illustrated Review: Ninth Cavalry*, with picture.

CHAPMAN, West P.; Private; I/25th Inf. Sentenced by summary court to two days for failure to learn sentry instructions, San Isidro, Philippines, second conviction. SOURCE: Register of Summary Court, San Isidro.

CHAPMAN, Wilson; G/10th Cav. Original member of 10th Cavalry; in troop when organized, Ft Leavenworth, KS, 5 Jul 1867. SOURCE: McMiller, "Buffalo Soldiers," 74.

CHAPPELL, Andrew; I/10th Cav. Admitted to Soldiers Home with disability, with eleven months' service, age 22. SOURCE: SecWar, *AR 1885*, 830.

CHAPPELL, Custer; Corporal; Band/25th Inf. Promoted from private. SOURCE: *ANR* 38 (14 Oct 1905): 21.

CHARLESTON, Oscar; 24th Inf. Served in Manila, Philippines, at age 15, from 1911–15; by 1923 an established Negro League baseball star and later manager; best outfielder in Negro baseball between about 1915 and 1930. SOURCE: Peterson, *Only the Ball Was White*, 241–42, with picture.

CHASE, Henry; K/9th Cav. Subscriber, age 73, served 1878–83. SOURCE: *Winners of the West* 10 (Aug 1933): 3.

CHASE, Henry; Private; K/9th Cav. Arrived Ft Robinson, NE, 28 Jul 1885; unable to march with troop.

Sentenced to dishonorable discharge and prison, Ft Robinson. SOURCE: GCMO 21, DP, 29 Mar 1887.

Commander, Ft Robinson, recommends remission of dishonorable discharge; Chase should be allowed to reenlist; "always a clean soldier," adequately punished for riding horse into Crawford, NE, saloon; original sentence dishonorable discharge and one year. SOURCE: CO, Ft Robinson, to AG, USA, 20 Apr 1888, LS, Ft Robinson.

Request for discharge disapproved. SOURCE: Letter, AGO, 3 Oct 1892.

CHASE, John; Sergeant; B/24th Inf. Retired May 1901. SOURCE: *ANJ* 37 (12 May 1900): 869.

CHASE, Levi; Private; C/9th Cav. As recruit, Colored Detachment, Mounted Service, tried by general court martial, Jefferson Barracks, MO, for engaging in disturbance and altercation with Recruit Francis J. Stokes, and trying to take carbine from rack to shoot Stokes, 5 Jul 1889; also tried for profane and abusive language toward Cpl. John M. Edwards, Company B of Instruction, who was conducting him to guardhouse; convicted of second charge only; fined $10 and jailed for one month. SOURCE: GCMO 48, AGO, 6 Aug 1889.

While private, C/9th Cavalry, convicted by garrison court martial, Ft Robinson, NE, of insubordination to first sergeant; sentenced to one month's imprisonment and fined one month's pay. SOURCE: SO 73, 10 Jul 1897, Post Orders, Ft Robinson.

Findings of board of officers in his case approved. SOURCE: Letter, DP, 19 Aug 1897, Post Returns, Ft Robinson.

CHATMAN, Calvin; Trumpeter; L/10th Cav. At Ft Bayard, NM, 1889; won Department of Arizona rifle competition. SOURCE: Billington, *New Mexico's Buffalo Soldiers*, 154.

Ranked number three, carbine competition, Departments of California and Arizona, at Ft Wingate, NM, 1889. SOURCE: GO 78, AGO, 12 Oct 1889; Baker, Roster.

CHATMAN, John; Private; E/9th Cav. Died of variola in the Philippines, 30 Sep 1901. SOURCE: *ANJ* 39 (7 Dec 1901): 339.

CHATMAN, William; QM Sgt; 25th Inf. Born Galveston, TX; age 42 in 1897; Ht 5'9", yellow complexion; served in I/10th Cavalry, 29 Mar 1873–29 Mar 1878; served in H/25th Infantry, 10 Apr 1878–9 Apr 1893; fifth enlistment, Ft Missoula, MT, 10 Apr 1893; married, no children; character excellent; marksman, 1892, 1893, 1894, 1896; promoted to regimental quartermaster sergeant from corporal, H/25th Infantry, 22 Mar 1897; deposits: $300 in 1893, $175 in 1894, $33 in 1896, $72 in 1897. SOURCE: Descriptive List, W. Chatman, Misc. Records, 25th Infantry.

First sergeant, G/25th Infantry, authorized furlough from Ft Missoula, 18 May–9 Jul 1891. SOURCE: *ANJ* 28 (30 May 1891): 677.

Reduced from sergeant, H/25th Infantry, to private, and fined $30 for abuse of civilian and for impertinence to commander, Ft Missoula. SOURCE: *ANJ* 29 (10 Oct 1891): 112.

In the Philippines, 1900. SOURCE: Richmond *Planet*, 28 Jul 1900.

Retired as quartermaster sergeant, 25th Infantry, Nov 1901. SOURCE: *ANJ* 39 (9 Nov 1901): 235.

CHATMON, Anderson; Private; L/9th Cav. At Ft D. A. Russell, WY, in 1910; resident of Batson, AL. SOURCE: *Illustrated Review: Ninth Cavalry,* with picture.

CHATMOUN, Littleton; Trumpeter; E/9th Inf. Enlisted Mobile, AL, 29 Mar 1899. SOURCE: Muster Roll, I/24 Inf, Mar–Apr 1899.

Allotted $10 per month to Virginia Chatmoun for six months. SOURCE: Muster Roll, I/24 Inf, Sep–Oct 1899.

Sergeant, I/24th Infantry, on detached service at Tarlac, Philippines, since 29 Dec 1899. SOURCE: Muster Roll, I/24 Inf, Nov–Dec 1899.

Trumpeter, D/9th Cavalry, at Ft D. A. Russell, WY, in 1910; sharpshooter. SOURCE: *Illustrated Review: Ninth Cavalry.*

Former sergeant, now age 89 and confined with paralysis in Manila hospital with stroke suffered ten years ago; draws $247 per month pension; second wife Juanita, age 48, is daughter of another black soldier. SOURCE: Thompson, "Veterans Who Never Came Home," 105–6.

CHATMOUN, Webb; H/10th Cav. Born Spartanburg Co., SC, 1863; parents unknown; enlisted Cincinnati, OH, Ht 5'8", black, laborer; served 16 Oct 1884–15 Oct 1889, including Apache wars, 1885–86; coal miner after service; incapacitated by rheumatism. SOURCE: VA File C 2360629, Webb Chatmoun.

Sick in lungs at Ft Davis, TX, hospital, Dec 1884–Jan 1885; sick at Ft Apache, AZ, with weak lungs and rheumatism, 1887 or 1888; sick at San Carlos, AZ, with piles, 1888. SOURCE: Affidavit, Chatmoun, Bevier, MO, 2 Mar 1912, VA File C 2360629, Webb Chatmoun.

Died of bronchial pneumonia, age 77. SOURCE: VA File C 2360629, Webb Chatmoun; *Winners of the West* 15 (Nov 1938): 4.

Widow Minerva Chatmoun of Bevier, MO, formerly married to Thomas West, who died 1896; pensioned after his death at St. Joseph, MO, 6 Oct 1938; her original widow's claim rejected because she was not married as of 4 Mar 1917; first wife Priscilla Davis Chatmoun died 31 Dec 1925. Probate Judge John V. Goodson, Macon Co., MO, to Veterans Administration, Washington, DC, writes that he does not know law but asks help for Minerva at request of her neighbors; she is "in distress, improperly nourished and dependent on the neighbors for fuel at her residence." SOURCE: VA File C 2360629, Webb Chatmoun.

See **CLEMENS**, James, Private, H/10th Cavalry; **BERRY**, Butler, H/10th Cavalry

CHATTELL, F. D.; Sergeant; F/24th Inf. Reports from Manila, Philippines, the death by drowning of nine men of 24th Infantry in accident, 21 Aug 1899. SOURCE: Indianapolis *Freeman*, 14 Oct 1899.

CHAVIES, Lewis C.; Private; L/9th Cav. At Ft D. A. Russell, WY, in 1910; resident of Kernersville, NC. SOURCE: *Illustrated Review: Ninth Cavalry,* with picture.

CHEATHAM, Alexander; Sergeant; C/10th Cav. Original member of 10th Cavalry; in L Troop when organized, Ft Riley, KS, 21 Sep 1867. SOURCE: McMiller, "Buffalo Soldiers," 78.

In support of Lieutenants Clark and Watson who were chasing marauders, Cheatham rode ninety miles with six mules loaded with supplies from San Carlos, AZ, to Salt River, AZ, from eleven P.M., 6 Mar, to sunset, 7 Mar 1890. SOURCE: Baker, Roster.

Cheatham and detachment from San Carlos brought breakfast out on trail of murderers after night march of forty-five miles; "the old fellow looked very tired and worn as he rode up, but his indomitable nerve and pluck carried him on forty-five miles more this day." SOURCE: Watson, "Scouting in Arizona," 131.

Sergeant, I/10th Cavalry, at Ft Apache, AZ, 1890, subscribed $.50 to testimonial to General Grierson. SOURCE: List of subscriptions, 23 Apr 1890, 10th Cavalry papers, MHI.

Retires as sergeant, C/10th Cavalry, from Ft Assiniboine, MT, 18 Mar 1895. SOURCE: *ANJ* 32 (16 Mar 1895): 52.

CHEATHAM, Boyd; Private; H/24th Inf. On special duty as fireman, post ice factory; to report to post surgeon. SOURCE: Order 125, Ft Huachuca, AZ, 21 Aug 1893, Name File, 24 Inf.

Enlisted Ft Douglas, UT, 8 Jan 1898, with nine years' continuous service. SOURCE: Muster Roll, H/24 Inf, May–Jun 1898.

Present for duty. SOURCE: Muster Roll, H/24 Inf, Jul–Aug 1898.

Absent, sick, disease contracted in line of duty, since 14 Sep 1898; whereabouts unknown. SOURCE: Muster Roll, H/24 Inf, Sep–Oct 1898.

Absent, sick, Plattsburg Barracks, NY, since 14 Sep 1898. SOURCE: Muster Roll, H/24 Inf, Nov–Dec 1898.

Discharged on surgeon's certificate, character excellent, single, Plattsburg Barracks, 3 Jan 1899; deposits $131.57; clothing $25.31. SOURCE: Muster Roll, H/24 Inf, Jan–Feb 1899.

CHEATHAM, Eugene B.; Private; A/9th Cav. Qualified but not teaching school, Ft Robinson, NE, 1 Feb–30 Apr 1893. SOURCE: Reports of Schools, Ft Robinson.

Relieved from extra duty as schoolteacher, Ft Robinson. SOURCE: Order 8, 29 Jan 1894, Post Orders, Ft Robinson.

CHEATHAM, Joseph; Private; M/10th Cav. Served in 10th Cavalry, 1898; remained in U.S. during war with Spain. SOURCE: Cashin, *Under Fire with the Tenth Cavalry*, 351.

CHEEK, Frank W.; 1st Lt; A/48th Inf. To report for temporary duty at recruiting station, Detroit, MI. SOURCE: *ANJ* 37 (30 Sep 1899): 101.

One of nineteen officers of 48th Infantry recommended as regular Army second lieutenants. SOURCE: CG, DivPI, Manila, 8 Feb 1901, to AGO, AGO File 355163.

Mentioned. SOURCE: Beasley, *Negro Trailblazers*, 284.

CHELF, Edward C.; Private; C/10th Cav. Served in 10th Cavalry in Cuba, 1898. SOURCE: Cashin, *Under Fire with the Tenth Cavalry*, 340.

CHELF, John; Private; H/9th Cav. At Ft D. A. Russell, WY, in 1910; marksman; resident of Chicago. SOURCE: *Illustrated Review: Ninth Cavalry,* with picture.

CHENAULT, Henry L.; Private; 24th Inf. Implicated himself in Houston riot, 1917, to Cpl. Daniel Rumpf, government plant in stockade, Ft Bliss, TX. SOURCE: Haynes, *A Night of Violence*, 286.

CHENAULT, Robert; Private; L/10th Cav. Served in 10th Cavalry, 1898; remained in U.S. during war with Spain. SOURCE: Cashin, *Under Fire with the Tenth Cavalry*, 350.

In M/10th Cavalry; his uniform overcoat stolen from barrack, Ft Robinson, NE, by Stratton, and returned before civil trial took place, Feb 1907.

CHENAULT, Walter; Private; C/10th Cav. Born Lexington, KY, son of parents he never knew, 6 May 1863; attended Russell Grade School, Lexington; served in 10th Cavalry, 1898–1902, including Cuba; attended Butler University, Indianapolis, IN, 1905–07; earned bachelor of science degree, Normal College, 1911; clerk, Indianapolis post office, 1914–17; licensed to preach in Indiana, Jun 1919; deacon, 1919; elder, 1922; published articles in Indianapolis dailies, Indianapolis *Recorder, Christian Recorder, Southern Christian Recorder*; assistant secretary, Indiana Annual Conference, 1937–43, and chief secretary, 1943; married to Estella Harris of Marion, IN, 1911; children William, Wade, Charles, Melvin, Harriet, Juanita, Evelyn; member National Association for the Advancement of Colored People; pastor, Shaffer Chapel, Muncie, IN, from Oct 1943. SOURCE: *Encyclopedia of African Methodism*, 64–65.

Served in 10th Cavalry, 1898; remained in U.S. during war with Spain. SOURCE: Cashin, *Under Fire with the Tenth Cavalry*, 340.

CHERRY, Ernest; Private; H/10th Cav. Served in 10th Cavalry, 1898; remained in U.S. during war with Spain. SOURCE: Cashin, *Under Fire with the Tenth Cavalry*, 346.

CHERRY, Jasper A.; Private; B/10th Cav. Served in 10th Cavalry, 1898; remained in U.S. during war with Spain. SOURCE: Cashin, *Under Fire with the Tenth Cavalry*, 339.

CHESNEY, Thomas; Private; F/9th Cav. Deserted from Ft Cummings, NM, 12 Jan 1881. SOURCE: Regt Returns, 9 Cav, Jan 1881.

CHESTER; Private; B/10th Cav. At Ft Apache, AZ, 1890, subscribed $.50 to testimonial to General Grierson. SOURCE: List of subscriptions, 23 Apr 1890, 10th Cavalry papers, MHI.

CHESTER, Lige; Private; G/10th Cav. Served in 10th Cavalry, 1898; remained in U.S. during war with Spain. SOURCE: Cashin, *Under Fire with the Tenth Cavalry*, 345.

CHESTER, Stanley; Private; 10th Cav. Recruit, Colored Detachment/Mounted Service, convicted by general court martial, Jefferson Barracks, MO, of violating Article 62, provoking and engaging in fight with Recruit Daniel Crutchfield, Colored Detachment, Mounted Service; after being cut with knife by Crutchfield, going to his quarters, getting his carbine, loading it, and pursuing Crutchfield near mess hall, 11 Nov 1886; sentenced to four months and fined $10 per month for four months. SOURCE: GCMO 101, AGO, 8 Dec 1886.

Involved in barroom brawl, Central City, NM, Mar 1891, in which Pvt. James Smith, 10th Cavalry, struck him with chair, fracturing his skull. SOURCE: Billington, *New Mexico's Buffalo Soldiers*, 164.

CHESTER, William L.; Private; Band/10th Cav. Served in 10th Cavalry in Cuba, 1898. SOURCE: Cashin, *Under Fire with the Tenth Cavalry*, 352.

CHESTNUT, Philip; Corporal; D/24th Inf. At Cabanatuan, Philippines, 1901. *See* **BLACK**, Henry, Private, K/24th Infantry

CHEVIN, John F., Jr.; Private; I/10th Cav. Served in 10th Cavalry in Cuba, 1898. SOURCE: Cashin, *Under Fire with the Tenth Cavalry*, 348.

CHILDERS, Samuel; Private; D/10th Cav. Served in 10th Cavalry, 1898; remained in U.S. during war with Spain. SOURCE: Cashin, *Under Fire with the Tenth Cavalry*, 341.

CHILDRESS, William; Saddler; E/9th Cav. At Ft D. A. Russell, WY, in 1910; resident of St. Louis. SOURCE: *Illustrated Review: Ninth Cavalry,* with picture.

CHILDS, Jacob; Private; B/10th Cav. Dishonorable discharge and jail, Ft Robinson, NE. SOURCE: SO 240, DeptMo, 10 Dec 1903.

Released Mar 1904.

CHINN, Charles H.; Ord Sgt; U.S. Army. Sergeant major, 24th Infantry, and post sergeant major, Ft Sill, Indian Territory. SOURCE: *ANJ* 24 (18 Dec 1886): 410.

First sergeant, 24th Infantry, Ft Sill, to be examined for post quartermaster sergeant. SOURCE: *ANJ* 25 (29 Oct 1887): 262.

First sergeant, E/24th Infantry, Ft Sill, authorized four-month furlough. SOURCE: *ANJ* 25 (17 Dec 1887): 403.

Ordnance sergeant, U.S. Army, recently ordered from Ft Pulaski, KY, to Ft McPherson, GA, to retire; had to ride Jim Crow car because railroad refused to honor army transportation request for sleeper; is suing railroad and state of Georgia. SOURCE: *ANJ* 34 (17 Apr 1897): 602.

CHINN, John; Private; B/10th Cav. Wounded in action, Santiago, Cuba, 1 Jul 1898. SOURCE: SecWar, *AR 1898*, 324.

CHISHOLM, Frank R.; 2nd Lt; K/48th Inf. Born Charleston, SC, 4 Jan 1875; attended Avery Normal Institute, Charleston; studied pharmacy in Boston, MA; private, L/6th Massachusetts Infantry; served in Cuba and Puerto Rico. SOURCE: *ANJ* 37 (4 Nov 1899): 219.

One of nineteen officers of 48th Infantry recommended as regular Army second lieutenants. SOURCE: CG, DivPI, Manila, 8 Feb 1901, to AGO, AGO File 355163.

Mentioned. SOURCE: Beasley, *Negro Trailblazers*, 284.

CHISHOLM, Lee; Private; 24th Inf. Involved in fight with Pvt. Dick Richardson, 24th Infantry, Ft Bayard, NM, Christmas 1889. SOURCE: Billington, *New Mexico's Buffalo Soldiers*, 164.

CHRISTIAN, George; Corporal; L/10th Cav. Served in 10th Cavalry, 1898; remained in U.S. during war with Spain. SOURCE: Cashin, *Under Fire with the Tenth Cavalry*, 350.

CHRISTIAN, Virgil; Private; L/10th Cav. Convicted of mutiny by general court martial, Bayamo, Cuba, 12 Oct 1899; sentenced to ten years. SOURCE: *ANJ* 37 (24 Feb 1900): 602

CHRISTON; Private; K/24th Inf. At Cabanatuan, Philippines, 1901. *See* **BLACK**, Henry, Private, K/24th Infantry

CHRISTOPHER; F/10th Cav. Original member of 10th Cavalry; in troop when organized, Ft Leavenworth, KS, 21 Jun 1867. SOURCE: McMiller, "Buffalo Soldiers," 73.

CHRISTY, William; Sergeant; F/10th Cav. Was 10th Cavalry's first fatality, near Ft Hays, KS, summer 1867; Christy a farmer from Pennsylvania with two months in regiment. SOURCE: Leckie, *The Buffalo Soldiers*, 22.

Shot through head and killed during attack by seventy-five Indians, 2 Aug 1867. SOURCE: Armes, *Ups and Downs*, 237.

Killed in action, by Indians, Saline Reservation, n.d.; Christy Avenue, Ft Huachuca, AZ, named for him. SOURCE: Orville A. Cochran to H. B. Wharfield, 5 Apr 1965, 10th Cavalry papers, MHI.

CHUBBS, Henry L.; Private; L/24th Inf. Died in Cuba, 30 Aug 1898. SOURCE: *ANJ* 36 (11 Feb 1899): 567.

CHURCHILL, Oliver; Corporal; I/24th Inf. Promoted from lance corporal. SOURCE: Order 12, I/24, Warwick Barracks, Cebu, Philippines, 1 Nov 1906, Name File, 24 Inf.

CICEL, Richard; Trumpeter; F/10th Cav. Served in 10th Cavalry in Cuba, 1898. SOURCE: Cashin, *Under Fire with the Tenth Cavalry*, 343.

CIRCY, James; F/10th Cav. Original member of 10th Cavalry; in troop when organized, Ft Leavenworth, KS, 21 Jun 1867. SOURCE: McMiller, "Buffalo Soldiers," 73.

CIRINTEE, Charles; K/10th Cav. Original member of 10th Cavalry; in troop when organized, Ft Riley, KS, 1 Sep 1867. SOURCE: McMiller, "Buffalo Soldiers," 77.

CISCO, Perry; Private; 25th Inf. Dishonorable discharge, Brownsville. SOURCE: SO 266, AGO, 9 Nov 1906.

CISSELL, William; Private; D/10th Cav. Served in 10th Cavalry, 1898; remained in U.S. during war with Spain. SOURCE: Cashin, *Under Fire with the Tenth Cavalry*, 341.

CLAGGETT, John H.; Blacksmith; H/10th Cav. Original member of 10th Cavalry; in troop when organized, Ft Leavenworth, KS, 21 Jul 1867. SOURCE: McMiller, "Buffalo Soldiers," 75.

Charged with petty larceny, Jun 1873; to be tried before field officers' court. SOURCE: ES, 10 Cav, 1873–81.

$30 reward paid for apprehension of Claggett, who deserted. SOURCE: CO, 10 Cav, to CO, H/10, 16 Nov 1873, ES, 10 Cav, 1873–81.

CLAGGETT, Joseph; Saddler; H/10th Cav. Original member of 10th Cavalry; in troop when organized, Ft Leavenworth, KS, 21 Jul 1867. SOURCE: McMiller, "Buffalo Soldiers," 75.

As sergeant he led patrol after Comanches from Ft Davis, TX, into Guadalupe Mountains, early summer 1877. SOURCE: Leckie, *The Buffalo Soldiers*, 157.

At Ft Apache, AZ, 1890, subscribed $.50 to testimonial to General Grierson. SOURCE: List of subscriptions, 23 Apr 1890, 10th Cavalry papers, MHI.

Was private and original member of troop; will retire soon and return "to his old Maryland home to enjoy a well earned rest." SOURCE: Baker, Roster.

Retires as saddler from Ft Assiniboine, MT. SOURCE: *ANJ* 35 (18 Sep 1897): 40.

CLANTON, Elbert B.; Private; K/25th Inf. At Ft Niobrara, NE, 1904. SOURCE: Wilson, "History of Fort Niobrara."

CLAPTON, Alexander; D/10th Cav. Original member of 10th Cavalry; in troop when organized, Ft Leavenworth, KS, 1 Jun 1867. SOURCE: McMiller, "Buffalo Soldiers," 71.

CLARK; Sergeant; H/9th Cav. Fought insurgents near Buloscan, Philippines, with detachment of five. SOURCE: Hamilton, "History of the Ninth Cavalry," 107; *Illustrated Review: Ninth Cavalry.*

CLARK, Ambers; Private; B/9th Cav. Private, H/24th Infantry; at Ft D. A. Russell, WY, in 1910. SOURCE: *Illustrated Review: Ninth Cavalry,* with picture.

CLARK, Andrew; Private; F/9th Cav. Private, H/24th Infantry, enlisted Camp Tampa, FL, 27 May 1898. SOURCE: Muster Roll, H/24 Inf, May–Jun 1898.

Sick, Siboney, Cuba, 2–25 Aug, and sick, en route to U.S., 25–31 Aug 1898, disease contracted in line of duty. SOURCE: Muster Roll, H/24 Inf, Jul–Aug 1898.

Rejoined unit 10 Oct 1898; absent sick, since 12 Oct 1898. SOURCE: Muster Roll, H/24 Inf, Sep–Oct 1898.

Sick in quarters since 12 Oct 1898. SOURCE: Muster Roll, H/24 Inf, Nov–Dec 1898.

Discharged, character good, single, 27 Jan 1899; deposits $53; due U.S. for clothing $3.76; reenlisted, Ft Douglas, UT, 28 Jan 1899. SOURCE: Muster Roll, H/24 Inf, Jan–Feb 1898.

Fined $2 by summary court, for violating Article 33, absent from eleven P.M. check roll call, San Isidro, Philippines, 12 May 1902. SOURCE: Register of Summary Court, San Isidro.

Veteran of Spanish-American War and Philippine Insurrection; at Ft D. A. Russell, WY, in 1910; resident of Quitman, GA. SOURCE: *Illustrated Review: Ninth Cavalry,* with picture.

CLARK, Arthur; Private; C/9th Cav. At Ft D. A. Russell, WY, in 1910; resident of Pembroke, KY. SOURCE: *Illustrated Review: Ninth Cavalry,* with picture.

CLARK, Charles; Private; D/10th Cav. Original member of 10th Cavalry; in troop when organized, Ft Leavenworth, KS, 1 Jun 1867. SOURCE: McMiller, "Buffalo Soldiers," 71.

Commander, 10th Cavalry, forwards final statement of late Private Clark to Adjutant General, U.S. Army, 13 Oct 1870. SOURCE: ES, 10 Cav, 1866–71.

CLARK, Charles; Private; K/10th Cav. Mentioned Mar 1869. SOURCE: LR, Det 10 Cav, 1868–69.

CLARK, Ennis; Private; D/10th Cav. Served in 10th Cavalry, 1898; remained in U.S. during war with Spain. SOURCE: Cashin, *Under Fire with the Tenth Cavalry,* 341.

CLARK, Gordon; Private; I/24th Inf. Enlisted Albany, GA, 21 Mar 1899. SOURCE: Muster Roll, I/24 Inf, Mar–Apr 1899.

Absent sick at Presidio of San Francisco, CA. SOURCE: Muster Roll, I/24 Inf, May–Jun 1899.

Sick in hospital, Presidio of San Francisco, 29 Apr–24 Jul 1899, disease not contracted in line of duty; rejoined

company 25 Aug 1899. SOURCE: Muster Roll, I/24 Inf, Jul–Aug 1899.

Fined $3 by summary court, 25 Sep 1899. SOURCE: Muster Roll, I/24 Inf, Sep–Oct 1899.

CLARK, J. W.; 1st Lt; 23rd Kans Inf. Mentioned. SOURCE: Beasley, *Negro Trailblazers,* 284.

CLARK, James; C/10th Cav. Original member of 10th Cavalry; in troop when organized, Ft Leavenworth, KS, 14 May 1867. SOURCE: McMiller, "Buffalo Soldiers," 70.

CLARK, John; Corporal; H/10th Cav. Commander of troop asks that Clark be detailed on daily duty as blacksmith; no other good blacksmiths in company. SOURCE: CO, H/10, to Adj, Det 10 Cav, 5 Jun 1869, LR, Det 10 Cav, 1868–69.

On daily duty as blacksmith, H/10th Cavalry. SOURCE: SO 32, Det 10 Cav, Camp Supply, Indian Territory, 7 Jun 1869, Orders, Det 10 Cav, 1868–69.

On extra duty, Quartermaster Department, as blacksmith. SOURCE: SO 56, Det 10 Cav, Camp Supply, Indian Territory, 6 Aug 1869, Orders, Det 10 Cav, 1868–69.

CLARK, John; Private; E/9th Cav. Discharge to be authorized if service has been faithful. SOURCE: TWX, DP, 4 May 1896, Post Returns, Ft Robinson.

Discharged. SOURCE: Letter, DP, 5 May 1896, Post Returns, Ft Robinson.

CLARK, Lewis; Private; E/10th Cav. Served in 10th Cavalry, 1898; remained in U.S. during war with Spain. SOURCE: Cashin, *Under Fire with the Tenth Cavalry,* 343.

CLARK, Lig J.; Corporal; H/24th Inf. Enlisted Dallas, TX, 10 Jun 1898. SOURCE: Muster Roll, H/24 Inf, Sep–Oct 1898.

Present for duty. SOURCE: Muster Roll, H/24 Inf, Nov–Dec 1898.

Discharged 29 Jan 1899, character excellent, single, deposits $50, clothing $2.71; reenlisted Ft Douglas, UT, 30 Jan 1899. SOURCE: Muster Roll, H/24 Inf, Jan–Feb 1899.

Recommended for certificate of merit for gallantry at Naguilian, Luzon, Philippines, 7 Dec 1899. SOURCE: *ANJ* 39 (15 Feb 1902): 594–95.

Awarded certificate of merit for distinguished gallantry, Naguilan, Luzon, 7 Dec 1899; discharged 18 Jan 1902; awarded 10 Mar 1902. SOURCE: GO 86, AGO, 24 Jul 1902.

See **WILLIAMS**, Walter B., Sergeant Major, 24th Infantry

Born Brownwood, TX, 1878; resided Temple, TX; stationed at Tampa, FL, during Cuban campaign; mustered out, Ft Douglass [*sic*], UT, 29 Jan 1899; reenlisted 30 Jan 1899; sailed to Philippines, 13 Jul 1899; in "fierce battle at Arayat," 12 Oct 1899, and many others; promoted to corporal, 14 Jul 1900; bought house for his mother on return; died of typhoid, 21 Apr 1902. "All Temple was proud of Lig J. Clark, and now mourn his death with a sorrow second only to that of his loving mother and two sisters who survive him. His discharge spoke of him as 'an excellent noncommissioned officer'; we say 'an excellent son and citizen.' " SOURCE: Letter, R. E. L. Holland, M.D., Temple, TX, to Editor, Indianapolis *Freeman*, 20 Sep 1902.

CLARK, Matthew R. C.; Private; H/10th Cav. Served in 10th Cavalry, 1898; remained in U.S. during war with Spain. SOURCE: Cashin, *Under Fire with the Tenth Cavalry*, 346.

CLARK, Oscar; Private; G/9th Cav. Witness for defense, Barney McKay court martial, Ft Robinson, NE, 1893. SOURCE: Court Martial Records, McKay.

CLARK, Richard; E/10th Cav. Original member of 10th Cavalry; in troop when organized, Ft Leavenworth, KS, 15 Jun 1867. SOURCE: McMiller, "Buffalo Soldiers," 72.
   Enlisted spring 1867. SOURCE: LS, 10 Cav, 1866–67.

CLARK, Robert; K/9th Cav. Surviving Indian war veteran. SOURCE: *Winners of the West* 3 (Jan 1926): 7.

CLARK, Samuel; Private; L/9th Cav. At Ft D. A. Russell, WY, in 1910; resident of Frezevant, TN. SOURCE: *Illustrated Review: Ninth Cavalry.*

CLARK, Sherman H.; Private; H/24th Inf. Enlisted Cleveland, OH, 6 Jun 1898; sick in U.S.; date of departure unknown. SOURCE: Muster Roll, H/24 Inf, Jul–Aug 1898.
   On furlough, surgeon's certificate, 17 Sep–31 Oct 1898; joined company 31 Oct; $30 due government for cost of transportation, Omaha, NE, to Salt Lake City, UT, in accordance with letter, Chief Quartermaster, Department of the Missouri. SOURCE: Muster Roll, H/24 Inf, Sep–Oct 1898.
   On special duty as printer, Quartermaster Department, since 4 Nov 1898; fined $5 and jailed for ten days by summary court, Ft Douglas, UT, 19 Dec 1898. SOURCE: Muster Roll, H/24 Inf, Nov–Dec 1898.
   Discharged, character good, single, due U.S. for clothing $22.95, 29 Jan 1899; reenlisted Washington Barracks, Washington, DC, 15 Feb 1899. SOURCE: Muster Roll, H/24 Inf, Jan–Feb 1899.

CLARK, Spencer; Private; F/9th Cav. Private, K/25th Infantry, at Ft Niobrara, NE, 1904. SOURCE: Wilson, "History of Fort Niobrara."
   Private, F/9th Cavalry, at Ft D. A. Russell, WY, in 1910; resident of Chattanooga, TN. SOURCE: *Illustrated Review: Ninth Cavalry*, with picture.

CLARK, Stephen; Private; L/10th Cav. Served in 10th Cavalry, 1898; remained in U.S. during war with Spain. SOURCE: Cashin, *Under Fire with the Tenth Cavalry*, 350.

CLARK, Thomas; Lieutenant. Graduate of Washington Colored High School; one of finest lieutenants in Spanish-

American War. SOURCE: *The Voice of the Negro* 1 (Jun 1904): 222.

CLARK, W. F.; Saddler; 10th Cav. Deposition of 11 Jul 1906 supports Caleb Benson's effort to get pension; Clark was 55 years old in 1906. SOURCE: VA File XC 2499129, Caleb Benson.

CLARK, William; Private; E/24th Inf. Wounded in action, Cuba, 1898. SOURCE: Muller, *The Twenty Fourth Infantry*, 18; Clark, "A History of the Twenty-fourth," 100.

CLARKE, Edward; Private; G/48th Inf. Died of malaria in the Philippines, 13 Dec 1900. SOURCE: *ANJ* 38 (29 Dec 1900): 431.

CLARKE, James; Private; E/9th Cav. Charges filed against him. SOURCE: Letter, DP, 27 Apr 1893, Post Returns, Ft Robinson.

CLARKE, John; Corporal; Band/10th Cav. Commissioned second lieutenant of cavalry, 27 Sep 1918. SOURCE: Glass, *History of the Tenth Cavalry*, appendix M.

CLARKE, John W.; E/10th Cav. Original member of 10th Cavalry; in troop when organized, Ft Leavenworth, KS, 15 Jun 1867. SOURCE: McMiller, "Buffalo Soldiers," 72.

CLARY, Heiney; K/10th Cav. Original member of 10th Cavalry; in troop when organized, Ft Riley, KS, 1 Sep 1867. SOURCE: McMiller, "Buffalo Soldiers," 77.

CLARY, Henry; G/10th Cav. Original member of 10th Cavalry; in troop when organized, Ft Leavenworth, KS, 5 Jul 1867. SOURCE: McMiller, "Buffalo Soldiers," 74.

CLAUDERS, Standley; Private; D/10th Cav. Served in 10th Cavalry, 1898; remained in U.S. during war with Spain. SOURCE: Cashin, *Under Fire with the Tenth Cavalry*, 341.

CLAY; Private; C/9th Cav. At Ft Sill, Indian Territory, 1883–84. *See* **COLE**, Private, C/9th Cavalry

CLAY; Private; F/24th Inf. Seriously cut on arm and head in fight with two ex-solders of 25th Infantry, Bentley and Crouch, from Ft Logan, CO. SOURCE: Cheyenne *Daily Leader*, 15 Sep 1899.

CLAY, Abraham L. J.; Private; A/9th Cav. Convicted by general court martial, Jefferson Barracks, MO, of desertion, 9 Oct 1883–14 Aug 1884; sentenced to dishonorable discharge and three years. SOURCE: GCMO 44, AGO, 7 Oct 1884.

CLAY, Albert; Private; I/24th Inf. Fined one month's pay by summary court for lying out of quarters and absence from eleven P.M. roll call, San Isidro, Philippines, n.d., third conviction. SOURCE: Register of Summary Court, San Isidro.

CLAY, Arons; Private; D/10th Cav. Served in 10th Cavalry, 1898; remained in U.S. during war with Spain. SOURCE: Cashin, *Under Fire with the Tenth Cavalry*, 341.

CLAY, Boston; Private; M/10th Cav. Served in 10th Cavalry, 1898; remained in U.S. during war with Spain. SOURCE: Cashin, *Under Fire with the Tenth Cavalry*, 351.

CLAY, C. C.; Private; 10th Cav. Wounded in right wrist, Naco, AZ, 27 Nov 1914. SOURCE: Cleveland *Gazette*, 13 May 1916.

CLAY, Charles F.; Private; G/24th Inf. Wounded in action, Cuba, 1898. SOURCE: Muller, *The Twenty Fourth Infantry*, 198.

CLAY, Henry; Private; K/10th Cav. Mentioned 1873. SOURCE: ES, 10 Cav, 1873–81.

CLAY, Henry; M/10th Cav. Original member of 10th Cavalry; in troop when organized, Ft Riley, KS, 15 Oct 1867. SOURCE: McMiller, "Buffalo Soldiers," 79.

CLAY, Henry; Private; M/10th Cav. Mentioned as newly enlisted, Apr 1873. SOURCE: ES, 10 Cav, 1873–81.

Died 18 May 1874; regiment commander forwards final statement and inventory of effects. SOURCE: CO, 10 Cav, to AG, USA, 27 May 1874, ES, 10 Cav, 1873–81.

CLAY, Henry; Private; I/24th Inf. Enlisted Mobile, AL, 31 Mar 1899. SOURCE: Muster Roll, I/24 Inf, Mar–Apr 1899.

Fined $2 by summary court, 10 May 1899. SOURCE: Muster Roll, I/24 Inf, May–Jun 1899.

Alloted $5 per month to Camilia Ballinger. SOURCE: Muster Roll, I/24 Inf, Sep–Oct 1899.

On detached service at Tarlac, Philippines, since 29 Dec 1899. SOURCE: Muster Roll, I/24 Inf, Nov–Dec 1899.

Captured by insurgents in the Philippines, 10 Oct 1900. *See* **BURNS**, William J., Corporal, I/24th Infantry

CLAY, Henry; Private; K/24th Inf. At Ft Douglas, UT, 1899. *See* **DICKERSON**, James M., Battalion Sergeant Major, 24th Infantry

CLAY, Henry; Private; L/49th Inf. Rescued from drowning with Pvt. Shelly Wilken by Pvts. David Walsh and George Hamilton on march from San Vicente to Aparri in northern Luzon, Philippines, Mar 1900. SOURCE: Company Returns, L/49 Inf.

CLAY, James; Private; D/10th Cav. Served in 10th Cavalry in Cuba, 1898. SOURCE: Cashin, *Under Fire with the Tenth Cavalry*, 341.

Missing in action, San Juan, Cuba, Jul 1898. SOURCE: SecWar, *AR 1898*, 711; Bigelow, *Reminiscences of Santiago*, 133.

CLAY, Matthew G.; Private; M/9th Cav. Sentenced by general court martial. SOURCE: SO 171, DeptMo, 7 Sep 1903.

At Ft D. A. Russell, WY, in 1910; resident of Evansville, IN. SOURCE: *Illustrated Review: Ninth Cavalry,* with picture.

CLAY, Sidney; Private; C/10th Cav. Served in 10th Cavalry, 1898; remained in U.S. during war with Spain. SOURCE: Cashin, *Under Fire with the Tenth Cavalry*, 340.

CLAY, William; D/10th Cav. Original member of 10th Cavalry; in troop when organized, Ft Leavenworth, KS, 1 Jun 1867. SOURCE: McMiller, "Buffalo Soldiers," 71.

CLAY, William; Private; B/9th Cav. On detached service at Ft Bayard, NM, 14 Jan–19 Feb 1881. SOURCE: Regt Returns, 9 Cav, Feb 1881.

CLAY, William; Drum Major; 9th Cav. First sergeant, E/9th Cavalry, at Ft Robinson, NE, 1893.

Promoted to drum major, Ft Grant, AZ; "an artist with the baton." SOURCE: Letter, Dr. J. Tempany, Ft Grant, Crawford *Tribune*, 17 Feb 1900.

Retired as drum major, 9th Cavalry, Apr 1902. SOURCE: *ANJ* 39 (3 May 1902): 879.

CLAY, William; Private; C/9th Cav. Died in the Philippines, 8 Sep 1900. SOURCE: *ANJ* 38 (10 Nov 1900): 259.

Drowned while bathing, Nagasaki, 8 Sep 1900; buried there. SOURCE: Hamilton, "History of the Ninth Cavalry," 92; *Illustrated Review: Ninth Cavalry.*

CLAY, William; A/25th Inf. Convicted of assault and battery on Filipino woman, Jun 1901.

CLAYBORN, John; Sergeant; 9th Cav. First enlisted in 24th Infantry; retired 1927; "John Clayborn Day" declared by mayor of Leavenworth, KS, celebrated 30 Oct 1971. SOURCE: *9th and 10th Cavalry Association Bulletin*, Jan–Mar 1972.

Enlisted 1899, sent to 25th Infantry; served in Philippine Insurrection and World War I; one of first enlisted men to organize "Colored Detachment" at Ft Leavenworth, KS, 1909; retired Oct 1927; died recently. SOURCE: *9th and 10th Cavalry Association Bulletin*, Jul 1973.

CLAYBORNE, Peter; Sergeant; D/10th Cav. Born in South Carolina; private, B/10th Cavalry, 7 Mar 1867–7 Mar 1872; private, corporal, sergeant, 4 Apr 1872–4 Apr 1877; private, E/10th Cavalry, 14 Apr 1877–13 Apr 1887; in D/10th Cavalry, 13 May 1887–12 May 1892; corporal, 8 Dec 1894; sergeant, 5 Mar 1897. SOURCE: Baker, Roster.

An original 10th Cavalryman, he came into regiment at its origin, Ft Leavenworth, KS; first action against Indians on Republican River, KS, May 1867, and Salt Creek, KS, 1867; in repulse of Black Kettle, Ft Dodge, KS, 1868; Foster Springs, TX, fight; engagement at Saragossa, Mexico, against Lipans and Kickapoos, 1876. SOURCE: Baker, Roster.

At Ft Apache, AZ, 1890, subscribed $.50 to testimonial to General Grierson. SOURCE: List of subscriptions, 23 Apr 1890, 10th Cavalry papers, MHI.

Retires from Ft Assiniboine, MT. SOURCE: *ANJ* 34 (26 Jun 1897): 801.

CLAYTON, Andy; Private; H/9th Cav. Acquitted of entering quarters of laundress Lydia Brown and threatening her, Ft Concho, TX, 1874. SOURCE: Leckie, *The Buffalo Soldiers*, 98; Stallard, *Glittering Misery*, 110.

See **BAYER**, Jacob, Private, H/10th Cavalry

CLAYTON, James; H/10th Cav. Original member of 10th Cavalry; in troop when organized, Ft Leavenworth, KS, 21 Jul 1867. SOURCE: McMiller, "Buffalo Soldiers," 75.

CLEMENS, James; Private; H/10th Cav. Often bunked with Webb Chatmoun, 1888–89; Chatmoun "suffered with piles"; Clemens is age 47 in 1912. SOURCE: Affidavit, Clemens, Mt. Olivet, Robertson Co., KY, 23 Oct 1912, VA File C 2360629, Webb Chatmoun.

At Ft Apache, AZ, 1890, subscribed $.50 to testimonial to General Grierson. SOURCE: List of subscriptions, 23 Apr 1890, 10th Cavalry papers, MHI.

CLEMENT, Thomas; Sergeant; K/10th Cav. Born in Texas; parents Virginians, educated at Hampton Institute, minister and teacher; worked as coal miner, hotel and railroad man, soldier, musician; in ninth year as minister, largest black congregation in Texas, at Wesley Chapel, Houston, 1947. SOURCE: *Encyclopedia of African Methodism*, 67.

Private, Ft Robinson, NE, 1904–05; captain and right halfback, K/10th Cavalry football team; author of "Athletics in the American Army," *Colored American Magazine*. SOURCE: *Colored American Magazine* 8 (Jan 1905): 21–29.

No Veterans Administration pension file.

CLEMMAN, Edward; Private; I/24th Inf. Enlisted Mobile, AL, 28 Mar 1899. SOURCE: Muster Roll, I/24 Inf, Mar–Apr 1899.

Allotted $5 per month for six months to Camilla Hollinger. SOURCE: Muster Roll, I/24 Inf, Nov–Dec 1899.

CLEMMENS; Corporal; K/25th Inf. *See* **THOMPSON**, Sergeant, M/25th Infantry

CLEVELAND, Jim; Private; A/9th Cav. At Ft D. A. Russell, WY, in 1910. SOURCE: *Illustrated Review: Ninth Cavalry,* with picture.

CLEVELAND, William A.; Private; L/10th Cav. Served in 10th Cavalry, 1898; remained in U.S. during war with Spain. SOURCE: Cashin, *Under Fire with the Tenth Cavalry*, 350.

CLIFFORD, Charles; Sergeant; G/10th Cav. Sergeant, M/10th Cavalry, Ft McDowell, AZ, 1887. SOURCE: Court Martial Charges against Pvt. Spencer Bright, Misc Records, 10 Cav, 1869–1918.

Promoted from private to corporal, G/10th Cavalry, 11 Nov 1897. SOURCE: *ANJ* 35 (11 Nov 1897): 212.

Sergeant, served in 10th Cavalry in Cuba, 1898. SOURCE: Cashin, *Under Fire with the Tenth Cavalry*, 344.

CLINTON, F. R.; 9th Cav. Sentinel, Crispus Attucks Lodge, No. 3, Knights of Pythias, State of Nebraska, Ft Robinson. SOURCE: Richmond *Planet*, 18 Dec 1897.

CLINTON, Francis; E/10th Cav. Original member of 10th Cavalry; in troop when organized, Ft Leavenworth, KS, 15 Jun 1867. SOURCE: McMiller, "Buffalo Soldiers," 72.

Enlisted Ft Gibson, Indian Territory, 3 Feb 1873. SOURCE: ES, 10 Cav, 1873–81.

CLINTON, Frank; QM Sgt; A/9th Cav. Veteran of Philippine Insurrection; sharpshooter; at Ft D. A. Russell, WY, in 1910. SOURCE: *Illustrated Review: Ninth Cavalry,* with picture.

CLINTON, Grant; Cook; A/9th Cav. At Ft D. A. Russell, WY, in 1910. SOURCE: *Illustrated Review: Ninth Cavalry,* with picture.

CLINTON, Princeton A.; Private; E/24th Inf. Wounded in action, Cuba, 1898. SOURCE: Muller, *The Twenty Fourth Infantry*, 18.

CLOMPTON, Jethro; H/10th Cav. Original member of 10th Cavalry; in troop when organized, Ft Leavenworth, KS, 21 Jul 1867. SOURCE: McMiller, "Buffalo Soldiers," 75.

CLOTTER, Dennis; Corporal; I/10th Cav. Released to duty from treatment for acute gonorrhea, Ft Robinson, NE, 30 Dec 1903. SOURCE: Post Surgeon to CO, I/10, 30 Dec 1903, LS, Post Surgeon, Ft Robinson.

CLOWERS, Earl; Corporal; I/24th Inf. Involved in Houston riot, 1917. SOURCE: Haynes, *A Night of Violence*, 130.

Sentenced to ten years for part in Houston riot. SOURCE: Cleveland *Gazette*, 5 Jan 1918.

CLYBURN, Peter; B/10th Cav. Original member of 10th Cavalry; in troop when organized, Ft Leavenworth, KS, 1 Apr 1867. SOURCE: McMiller, "Buffalo Soldiers," 69.

COAKGEE, Willie; Private; K/10th Cav. Served in 10th Cavalry, 1898; remained in U.S. during war with Spain. SOURCE: Cashin, *Under Fire with the Tenth Cavalry*, 349.

COATES, Benjamin; Private; C/9th Cav. Acquitted of conduct prejudicial to good order and discipline by garrison court martial, Ft Robinson, NE. SOURCE: Order 5, 10 Jan 1886, Post Orders, Ft Robinson.

Replaced Pvt. Thomas Benjamin, C/8th Infantry, in charge of post chapel, Ft Robinson. SOURCE: Order 25, 5 Feb 1888, Post Orders, Ft Robinson.

Replaced by Pvt. John Turner, I/8th Infantry, in charge of post chapel, Ft Robinson. SOURCE: Order 32, 14 Feb 1888, Post Orders, Ft Robinson.

COATES, John T.; Private; C/9th Cav. On detached service at Ft McKinney, WY, and reassigned to H/9th Cavalry there. SOURCE: Order 14, 9 Cav, 23 May 1887, Name File, 9 Cav.

COATES, Robert F.; F/25th Inf. Stationed at Botolin, Zambales, Philippines, Dec 1900; Methodist. SOURCE: Steward, *Fifty Years in the Gospel Ministry*, 362.

COATS, William H.; Private; H/24th Inf. Enlisted Baltimore, MD, 2 Jun 1898; joined company, San Juan, Cuba, 12 Jul 1898; sick, disease contracted in line of duty, Siboney, Cuba, 22–25 Aug, and en route to U.S., 25–31 Aug 1898. SOURCE: Muster Roll, H/24 Inf, Jul–Aug 1898.

Transferred to K/24th Infantry, 16 Sep 1898. SOURCE: Muster Roll, H/24 Inf, Sep–Oct 1898.

COATS, Willis; Private; A/10th Cav. Served in 10th Cavalry, 1898; remained in U.S. during war with Spain. SOURCE: Cashin, *Under Fire with the Tenth Cavalry*, 337.

COBB, Edward F.; Corporal; A/10th Cav. Served in 10th Cavalry in Cuba, 1898; drowned 22 Jun 1898. SOURCE: Cashin, *Under Fire with the Tenth Cavalry*, 337, 338.

COBB, Rufus; Private; H/10th Cav. Served in 10th Cavalry, 1898; remained in U.S. during war with Spain. SOURCE: Cashin, *Under Fire with the Tenth Cavalry*, 346.

COBB, Seadrick; Private; K/25th Inf. At Ft Niobrara, NE, 1904. SOURCE: Wilson, "History of Fort Niobrara."

COBLE, Andrew J.; Cook; B/9th Ohio Inf. Born Waterville, SC; died Minneapolis, MN, 22 Jul 1947. SOURCE: Taylor, "Minnesota Black Spanish-American War Veterans."

COCHRAN, Marion; Private; M/10th Cav. Served in 10th Cavalry, 1898; remained in U.S. during war with Spain. SOURCE: Cashin, *Under Fire with the Tenth Cavalry*, 351.

CODY, Nick; F/10th Cav. Original member of 10th Cavalry; in troop when organized, Ft Leavenworth, KS, 21 Jun 1867. SOURCE: McMiller, "Buffalo Soldiers," 73.

COFFEE, Nathan; Private; A/24th Inf. Died of malaria in the Philippines, 28 Jan 1900. SOURCE: *ANJ* 37 (10 Feb 1900): 562.

COKER, Abram; 38th Inf. Subscriber since 1929; member, Camp 11, National Indian War Veterans, St. Joseph, MO; died Austin, TX. SOURCE: *Winners of the West* 16 (Nov 1939): 2

COKER, Henry; Corporal; 9th Cav. At Ft Niobrara, NE, 1889. *See* **CARTER**, William H., Trumpeter, A/9th Cavalry

COLBERT, Boyd; D/10th Cav. Original member of 10th Cavalry; in troop when organized, Ft Leavenworth, KS, 1 Jun 1867. SOURCE: McMiller, "Buffalo Soldiers," 71.

COLBERT, Frederick; 10th Cav. Born in Maryland; parents Frederick Colbert and Rachel Sico; prior to enlistment, lived in Prince Georges Co., MD, worked as laborer; enlisted Baltimore, MD, 29 Aug 1889; was accidently shot in face by condemned pistol that had been issued to him, Ft Bayard, NM, early Jul 1890; discharged 4 Sep 1892; pension $4 per month, 7 Oct 1892. SOURCE: VA File XC 2643082, Frederick Colbert.

Married Agnes Malinda Sheppard, at St. Cyprian's Church, Washington, DC, 5 Nov 1902; resided in Washington; left wife, moved to Chesapeake Beach, MD, 1909, then moved to Baltimore, where he lived with brother at 173 West Lexington, 1913–31; died of pulmonary tuberculosis, Baltimore City Hospital, age 66, 16 May 1931. SOURCE: VA File XC 2643082, Frederick Colbert.

Applies for membership, Camp 11, National Indian War Veterans, St. Joseph, MO. SOURCE: *Winners of the West* 5 (Jun 1928): 3.

Died in Baltimore. SOURCE: *Winners of the West* 8 (Jun 1931): 8.

Widow awarded pension of $30 per month, 1 Apr 1935; $40 per month, 1944; died 28 Jul 1949.

COLBERT, John A.; Private; H/24th Inf. Enlisted Baltimore, MD, 31 Aug 1898. SOURCE: Muster Roll, H/24 Inf, Sep–Oct 1898.

Discharged, character good, single, $5 deposits, due U.S. for clothing $18.98, 28 Jan 1899; reenlisted Ft Douglas, UT, 29 Jan 1899. SOURCE: Muster Roll, H/24 Inf, Jan–Feb 1899.

COLBURN, Jessie; Private; H/9th Cav. Relieved from duty at regimental headquarters, Santa Fe, NM, and ordered to his troop at Ft Bayard, NM. SOURCE: RO 55, 9 Cav, Santa Fe, 7 Nov 1879, Name File, 9 Cav.

COLE; Private; C/9th Cav. Capt. Charles D. Beyer, 9th Cavalry, convicted by general court martial, Ft Sill, Indian Territory, of conduct unbecoming an officer and gentleman, at Ft Sill, Oct 1883–Jan 1884; failure to account properly for money received from Privates Cole and Clay, C/9th Cavalry, in payment for broken watercooler purchased with unit fund; also employed Private Turner, C/9th Cavalry, as his personal servant and had him paid by Private Ross, C/9th Cavalry, with $5 that Ross had obtained illegally by selling troop rations. SOURCE: GCMO 50, AGO, 11 Nov 1884.

COLE, Bud; Private; F/9th Cav. At Ft D. A. Russell, WY, in 1910; sharpshooter; resident of Walker Co., GA. SOURCE: *Illustrated Review: Ninth Cavalry,* with picture.

COLE, Charles; Private; C/9th Cav. Fined and jailed for thirty days for theft, Ft Cummings, NM, Jan 1881. SOURCE: Billington, *New Mexico's Buffalo Soldiers*, 130.

Deserted from Ft Cummings, NM, 17 Feb 1881. SOURCE: Regt Returns, 9 Cav, Feb 1881.

COLE, F. W.; Private; B/9th Cav. On detached service at Ft Bayard, NM, 16 Jan–9 Feb 1881. SOURCE: Regt Returns, 9 Cav, Feb 1881.

COLE, Felix J.; Private; H/24th Inf. Served in E/10th Cavalry in Cuba, 1898. SOURCE: Cashin, *Under Fire with the Tenth Cavalry*, 354.

Fined $2 by summary court, for absence from check roll call, San Isidro, Philippines, 11 Mar 1902, fourth conviction; acquitted of fighting and disorderly conduct in quarters, 12 Mar 1902. SOURCE: Register of Summary Court, San Isidro.

COLE, Gonza; Private; A/9th Cav. Detailed to special duty as post librarian, Ft Robinson, NE. SOURCE: Order 184, 29 Oct 1892, Post Orders, Ft Robinson.

Relieved from special duty as librarian. SOURCE: Order 9, 2 Feb 1894, Post Orders, Ft Robinson.

COLE, James E.; Private; B/24th Inf. Fined $10 for violating Article 62, engaging in fight with Pvt. Eugene Taylor, B/24th Infantry, while on guard duty at post guardhouse, Cabanatuan, Philippines, 3 Jan 1900; witnesses: Cpl. Charles Riz, B/24th Infantry, and Pvt. William Lee, D/24th Infantry. SOURCE: Name File, 24 Inf.

See **TAYLOR**, Eugene, Private, B/24th Infantry

COLE, James F.; Sergeant; 10th Cav. A non-commissioned officer who should be commissioned, according to unsigned letter from Montauk Point, NY, 1898. SOURCE: Gatewood, *"Smoked Yankees"*, 77.

COLE, James T.; Sergeant; A/10th Cav. Born in Louisiana; private, A/25th Infantry, 16 May 1889–15 May 1894; private, A/10th Cavalry, 14 Jun 1894; corporal, 2 Oct 1896. SOURCE: Baker, Roster.

Promoted sergeant, 14 Dec 1897. SOURCE: *ANJ* 35 (25 Dec 1897): 310.

Served in 10th Cavalry in Cuba, 1898. SOURCE: Cashin, *Under Fire with the Tenth Cavalry*, 336.

COLE, John H.; Private; F/10th Cav. Served in 10th Cavalry in Cuba, 1898. SOURCE: Cashin, *Under Fire with the Tenth Cavalry*, 344.

COLE, Lewis; Private; B/9th Cav. Sentenced by general court martial to dishonorable discharge and imprisonment. SOURCE: SO 209, DeptMo, 26 Oct 1903.

COLE, Pollard; Sergeant; H/10th Cav. Original member of 10th Cavalry; in troop when organized, Ft Leavenworth, KS, 21 Jul 1867. SOURCE: McMiller, "Buffalo Soldiers," 75.

Farrier, 1874; cited for gallantry against Kiowas and Comanches, Wichita Agency, Indian Territory, 22–23 Aug 1874. SOURCE: Baker, Roster.

Honorable mention for services rendered in capture of Mangas and his Apache band, Rio Bonito, AZ, 18 Oct 1886. SOURCE: Baker, Roster.

Sergeant, authorized four-month furlough from Ft Apache, AZ. SOURCE: *ANJ* 24 (25 Jun 1887): 954.

At Ft Apache, 1890, subscribed $.50 to testimonial to General Grierson. SOURCE: List of subscriptions, 23 Apr 1890, 10th Cavalry papers, MHI.

Retires as sergeant from Ft Buford, ND, 13 Aug 1894. SOURCE: Baker, Roster; *ANJ* 31 (14 Jul 1894): 803.

COLE, Samuel; Private; C/9th Cav. Veteran of Philippine Insurrection; at Ft D. A. Russell, WY, in 1910; resident of Baxter Springs, KS. SOURCE: *Illustrated Review: Ninth Cavalry.*

COLE, W.; Sergeant; 24th Inf. At Ft Grant, AZ, 1890. SOURCE: Cleveland *Gazette*, 28 Jun 1890.

COLEMAN; Private; C/10th Cav. At Ft Apache, AZ, 1890, subscribed $.50 to testimonial to General Grierson. SOURCE: List of subscriptions, 23 Apr 1890, 10th Cavalry papers, MHI.

COLEMAN, Andrew; Private; F/9th Cav. At Ft D. A. Russell, WY, in 1910; resident of Jackson, KY. SOURCE: *Illustrated Review: Ninth Cavalry,* with picture.

COLEMAN, Fortino; G/10th Cav. Original member of 10th Cavalry; in troop when organized, Ft Leavenworth, KS, 5 Jul 1867. SOURCE: McMiller, "Buffalo Soldiers," 74.

COLEMAN, Frank; 1st Sgt; F/25th Inf. Wounded in action, El Caney, Cuba, 1 Jul 1898. SOURCE: Nankivell, *History of the Twenty-fifth Infantry*, 83.

Pallbearer at funeral of Col. Andrew S. Burt, who had requested that men of 25th Infantry carry his coffin. SOURCE: Curtis, *The Black Soldier*, 49.

COLEMAN, Gardner; Private; I/10th Cav. Served in 10th Cavalry, 1898; remained in U.S. during war with Spain. SOURCE: Cashin, *Under Fire with the Tenth Cavalry*, 348.

COLEMAN, J.; Private; L/9th Cav. On detached service in field, New Mexico, 21 Jan–24 Feb 1881. SOURCE: Regt Returns, 9 Cav, Feb 1881.

COLEMAN, James; L/10th Cav. Original member of 10th Cavalry; in troop when organized, Ft Riley, KS, 21 Sep 1867. SOURCE: McMiller, "Buffalo Soldiers," 78.

COLEMAN, James; 9th Cav. Enlisted during Mexican border disturbance and was sent to Philippines in 1916; died there forty-four years later; founded furniture factory that former employees operate. SOURCE: Thompson, "Veterans Who Never Came Home," 114.

COLEMAN, James B.; 1st Lt; E/48th Inf. Mentioned. SOURCE: Beasley, *Negro Trailblazers*, 284.

COLEMAN, Jesse; Cook; B/9th Cav. Private, H/9th Cavalry, authorized three-month furlough. SOURCE: Letter, DP, 24 Oct 1895.
    Private, H/9th Cavalry, Ft Robinson, NE, 1896–98, with $82 deposited with paymaster, 1896.
    Retires as cook, B/9th Cavalry. SOURCE: *ANJ* 38 (9 Sep 1905): 19.

COLEMAN, John; Private; 48th Inf. Sick in the Philippines, Feb 1900. SOURCE: Richmond *Planet*, 14 Apr 1900.

COLEMAN, John; Sqdn Sgt Maj; 10th Cav. Commissioned second lieutenant, training camp at Leon Springs, TX, World War I. SOURCE: Glass, *History of the Tenth Cavalry*, appendix M.

COLEMAN, Leonard; Private; F/9th Cav. At Ft D. A. Russell, WY, in 1910; sharpshooter; resident of Nashville. SOURCE: *Illustrated Review: Ninth Cavalry*, with picture.

COLEMAN, Louis D.; Private; C/24th Inf. 1st Lt. Robert G. Rutherford acquitted by general court martial of agreeing to draw Coleman's pay for period starting 1 Jan 1909 and paying Coleman's debts through 31 Oct 1910 (total pay of $510.09), without making proper accounting to Coleman, although so requested, Madison Barracks, NY, Sep-Dec 1910; also acquitted of embezzling $100 that belonged to Coleman; convicted of other frauds. SOURCE: GCMO 123, AGO, 6 Sep 1911.

COLEMAN, Moses; Private; D/9th Cav. Resided at Junction City, Geary Co., KS, 1895. *See* **DENT**, Henry, Private, D/9th Cavalry

COLEMAN, Richard M.; Private; G/24th Inf. Wounded in action, Cuba, 1898. SOURCE: Muller, *The Twenty Fourth Infantry*, 198.

COLEMAN, Theodore; Recruit; Colored Detachment/Mounted Service. At Jefferson Barracks, MO, 1887. *See* **LEE**, Charles, Recruit, Colored Detachment/Mounted Service

COLEMAN, William M.; I/9th Cav. Clothing destroyed when fighting fire, Ft Wingate, NM, 15 Dec 1876. SOURCE: Billington, *New Mexico's Buffalo Soldiers*, 110.

COLEMAN, William N.; Private; Band/9th Cav. With band on detached service at headquarters, District of New Mexico, Santa Fe, 1880; played second B-flat cornet. SOURCE: Billington, *New Mexico's Buffalo Soldiers*, 226.

COLES; Bn Sgt Maj; 24th Inf. *See* **FARRIS**, Eugene, Sergeant, 24th Infantry

COLES, H.; Corporal; A/24th Inf. Third best infantry marksman, Department of Dakota, 1903. SOURCE: SecWar, *AR 1903*, I, 426.

COLES, W. H.; I/9th Cav. Enlistment for I/9th Cavalry authorized. SOURCE: TWX, AGO, 15 Oct 1896.

COLLANO, John; G/10th Cav. Original member of 10th Cavalry; in troop when organized, Ft Leavenworth, KS, 5 Jul 1867. SOURCE: McMiller, "Buffalo Soldiers," 74.

COLLEY, William E.; Private; C/9th Cav. At Ft D. A. Russell, WY, in 1910; resident of Lexington, MO. SOURCE: *Illustrated Review: Ninth Cavalry*, with picture.

COLLIER, Albert; Private; H/10th Cav. Served in 10th Cavalry, 1898; remained in U.S. during war with Spain. SOURCE: Cashin, *Under Fire with the Tenth Cavalry*, 346.

COLLIER, Babe; Private; I/24th Inf. Involved in Houston riot, 1917; sentenced to death. SOURCE: Haynes, *A Night of Violence*, 130, 277–78.
    To hang for part in Houston riot. SOURCE: Cleveland *Gazette*, 5 Jan 1918.

COLLIER, Robert L.; Private; C/25th Inf. Dishonorable discharge, Brownsville. SOURCE: SO 266, AGO, 9 Nov 1906.

COLLIER, Robert W.; Private; F/9th Cav. At Ft D. A. Russell, WY, in 1910; resident of Nashville. SOURCE: *Illustrated Review: Ninth Cavalry*, with picture.

COLLIER, Stephen J.; Private; M/10th Cav. Private, I/10th Cavalry, part of guard around Crawford, NE, while Sgt. John Reid, B/10th Cavalry was confined there; shot and killed Phil Murphy in line of duty. SOURCE: Crawford *Tribune*, 18 May 1906.
    Private, M/10th Cavalry, sick in Ft Robinson, NE hospital, 31 May 1907.

COLLIER, William; Sergeant; 10th Cav. Commissioned, Camp Des Moines, IA, 15 Oct 1917. SOURCE: Glass, *History of the Tenth Cavalry*, appendix M.

COLLINS, Daniel S.; Corporal; L/10th Cav. Ranked number 403 among rifle experts with 69 percent. SOURCE: GO 101, AGO, 31 May 1906.

COLLINS, Edward; Private; A/25th Inf. Dishonorably discharged, now confined at Ft Stockton, TX, in accordance with General Court Martial Order 19, Department of Texas, 8 Jun 1876; to be transferred to Kansas penitentiary. SOURCE: GCMO 107, AGO, 20 Jul 1876.

COLLINS, Edward J.; L/24th Inf. At Skagway, AK, 1902. *See* **CASSELLE**, Nelson A., Private, L/24th Infantry

COLLINS, Francis; Private; H/9th Cav. On detached service at Jefferson Barracks, MO, 4 Aug 1880–10 Feb 1881. SOURCE: Regt Returns, 9 Cav, Feb 1881.

COLLINS, George; Private; L/10th Cav. Excused from duty with illness by Assistant Surgeon M. F. Price but kept at work by Capt. George A. Armes, 10th Cavalry, Camp Santa Rosa, TX, May 1879; confined to quarters with pleurisy but arrested and placed under guard by Armes, 31 May 1879; prohibited by Armes from going in ambulance to hospital, Ft Stockton, TX, 4 Jun 1879, as were Cpl. Allen K. Sigalls and Trumpeter William Simmons, both also sick. SOURCE: GCMO 36, AGO, 27 May 1880.

COLLINS, Griffin; E/25th Inf. S. T. Collins seeks his brother Griffin, who served with E/25th Infantry, 1866–75. SOURCE: *Winners of the West* 7 (Oct 1930): 7.

COLLINS, James; Private; K/10th Cav. Served in 10th Cavalry, 1898; remained in U.S. during war with Spain. SOURCE: Cashin, *Under Fire with the Tenth Cavalry*, 349.

COLLINS, John; D/24th Inf. Served in E/9th Cavalry, 1875–85, and D/24th Infantry, 1885–90. SOURCE: *Winners of the West* 1 (Jan 1924): 8.

COLLINS, Joseph; Sergeant; H/25th Inf. Born Suffolk, VA; reenlisted, private, age 31, Ht 5'6", brown complexion, Baltimore, MD, 2 Aug 1881. SOURCE: Descriptive & Assignment Roll, 25 Inf.

Sergeant, acquitted of "threatening a member of the Hospital Corps at Ft Missoula with lynching." SOURCE: *ANJ* 31 (28 Jun 1894): 843.

Sergeant, ordered to Ft Huachuca, AZ. SOURCE: *ANJ* 36 (29 Oct 1898): 214.

COLLINS, McHenry; Private; I/9th Cav. Discharged on certificate of disability, Ojo Caliente, NM, Jan 1881. SOURCE: Regt Returns, 9 Cav, Jan 1881.

COLLINS, Robert; Blacksmith; C/9th Cav. Shot by Letcher, E/9th Cavalry, in Crawford, NE. SOURCE: Crawford *Tribune*, 1 Jan 1897.

Discharged. SOURCE: SO 14, AGO, 18 Jan 1897.

COLLINS, Stephen W.; Private; K/10th Cav. Served in 10th Cavalry, 1898; remained in U.S. during war with Spain. SOURCE: Cashin, *Under Fire with the Tenth Cavalry*, 349.

COLLINS, Thomas; Private; B/9th Cav. In hands of civil authorities, Salt Lake City, UT, 12 Nov 1887–May 1888. SOURCE: Regt Returns, 9 Cav, May 1888.

COLLINS, Thomas; Trumpeter; E/10th Cav. At Ft Apache, AZ, 1890, subscribed $.50 to testimonial to General Grierson. SOURCE: List of subscriptions, 23 Apr 1890, 10th Cavalry papers, MHI.

COLLINS, Walter; Private; A/10th Cav. Served in 10th Cavalry, 1898; remained in U.S. during war with Spain. SOURCE: Cashin, *Under Fire with the Tenth Cavalry*, 337.

COLLINS, William; Sergeant; E/10th Cav. Served in 10th Cavalry in Cuba, 1898. SOURCE: Cashin, *Under Fire with the Tenth Cavalry*, 342.

"An all-around soldier, a good rider, horse trainer, an excellent shot, and good drill instructor"; instructs at Wind River Indian School in company drills and formations. SOURCE: *Fremont Clipper*, 21 Sep 1906.

COLLINS, William; Private; D/24th Inf. At Cabanatuan, Philippines, 1900. *See* **TATES**, Rollins, Private, D/24th Infantry

COLLINS, William H.; Private; C/10th Cav. Served in 10th Cavalry in Cuba, 1898. SOURCE: Cashin, *Under Fire with the Tenth Cavalry*, 340.

COLLYER, S.; Private; F/9th Cav. Wounded in action, while with 1st Lt. P. Cusack's expedition east of Ft Davis, TX, against Mescalero Apaches, in which twenty-five Indians were killed, 198 animals captured, Sep 1868; Pvts. Lewis White, C/9th Cavalry, and John Foster, K/9th Cavalry, also were wounded. SOURCE: SecWar, *AR 1868*, 716.

COLMON, Charlie; Private; I/9th Cav. At Ft D. A. Russell, WY, in 1910; sharpshooter; resident of Houston. SOURCE: *Illustrated Review: Ninth Cavalry,* with picture.

COLSTON, Daniel; C/10th Cav. Paid $8.80 and served one day in Crawford, NE, jail in lieu of $5 fine and $4.80 costs, for being "beastly drunk and lying on the sidewalk," 19 Sep 1902.

COLTON, Willie; Private; K/9th Cav. At Ft D. A. Russell, WY, in 1910; resident of Howard Hill, AL. SOURCE: *Illustrated Review: Ninth Cavalry,* with picture.

COLTRANE, James A.; Corporal; B/25th Inf. Dishonorable discharge, Brownsville. SOURCE: SO 266, AGO, 9 Nov 1906.

One of fourteen cleared of involvement in Brownsville raid and allowed to reenlist. SOURCE: Weaver, *The Brownsville Raid*, 248.

COLWELL, Aaron; Private; 10th Cav. Arrived at Ft Leavenworth, KS, from Jefferson Barracks, MO. SOURCE: Adj, Ft Leavenworth, to HQ, Jefferson Bks, 9 Oct 1866, LS, 10 Cav.

Recruit not issued clothing account statement, Ft Leavenworth, Oct 1866. SOURCE: CO, Det 10 Cav, to AAG, DeptMo, 31 Oct 1886, LS, 10 Cav.

COLWELL, Lawrence; Private; G/9th Cav. At Ft D. A. Russell, WY, in 1910; resident of Chicago. SOURCE: *Illustrated Review: Ninth Cavalry,* with picture.

COMAGOR, Charles W.; Sergeant; I/9th Cav. Promoted from corporal, Ft Robinson, NE, May 1895. SOURCE: *ANJ* 32 (18 May 1895): 626.

COMBS, John; Sergeant; L/10th Cav. Commissioned first lieutenant, Camp Des Moines, IA, 15 Oct 1917. SOURCE: Glass, *History of the Tenth Cavalry*, appendix M.

COMBS, Richard; Cook; B/10th Cav. Private, at Ft Apache, AZ, 1890, subscribed $.50 to testimonial to General Grierson. SOURCE: List of subscriptions, 23 Apr 1890, 10th Cavalry papers, MHI.

Private, served in 10th Cavalry in Cuba, 1898. SOURCE: Cashin, *Under Fire with the Tenth Cavalry*, 338.

Retires. SOURCE: SO 117, AGO, 18 May 1904.

COMER, Levi; Private; K/9th Cav. Served 1872–73. *See* SLAUGHTER, Rufus, Private, K/9th Cavalry

COMMONS, John; Private; E/48th Inf. Died of variola in the Philippines, 17 Nov 1900. SOURCE: *ANJ* 38 (1 Dec 1900): 331.

COMPTON, Elisha; 24th Inf. Born in Virginia; died 28 Jul 1897; buried at Ft Douglas, UT. SOURCE: Clark, "A History of the Twenty-fourth," appendix A.

CONAC, Washington C.; Sergeant; A/9th Cav. Private, assigned to A/9th Cavalry, 17 Feb 1891.

Veteran of Spanish-American War and Philippine Insurrection; wagoner, at Ft D. A. Russell, WY, in 1910; marksman; resident of St. Louis. SOURCE: *Illustrated Review: Ninth Cavalry,* with picture.

To retire as sergeant, with twenty-six years' service, Jan 1912. SOURCE: Cheyenne *State Leader*, 16 Dec 1911.

CONE, William; D/10th Cav. Original member of 10th Cavalry; in troop when organized, Ft Leavenworth, KS, 1 Jun 1867. SOURCE: McMiller, "Buffalo Soldiers," 71.

CONLEY, Paschall; QM Sgt; 10th Cav. Born Huntsville, AL; enlisted H/24th Infantry, age 20, occupation clerk, Ht 5'5", mulatto, Memphis, TN, 26 Mar 1879; discharged, character excellent, 25 Mar 1884; reenlisted, D/24th Infantry, 1 Jul 1884; corporal, 16 Jul 1884; sergeant, 1 Jul 1886; marksman, 1883, 1884, 1887, 1888, and member, Department of the Missouri rifle team, 1886; fined $10 by garrison court martial, Ft Supply, Indian Territory, 1887; reduced to private and fined $10 per month for six months by garrison court martial, Ft Supply, 1888; sergeant major, 5 Oct 1888; reduced at own request and transferred to D/24th Infantry, 1 Feb 1889; character good, married, one child. SOURCE: Descriptive Book, 24 Inf NCS & Band.

Sharpshooter as corporal, D/24th Infantry, Ft Supply. SOURCE: *ANJ* 24 (21 Aug 1886): 70.

Private, L/10th Cavalry, 1 Jul 1889; corporal, 1 Mar 1890; transferred to H/10th Cavalry, 25 Aug 1890; quartermaster sergeant, 10th Cavalry, 14 May 1893; at Ft Assiniboine, MT, 1897. SOURCE: Baker, Roster.

An excellent noncommissioned officer who should be commissioned, according to John E. Lewis, H/10th Cavalry, in letter from Lakeland, FL, 5 Jun 1898. SOURCE: Gatewood, *"Smoked Yankees"*, 37.

Sergeant, M/10th Cavalry, 1898; remained in U.S. during war with Spain; narrates Spanish-American War experience. SOURCE: Cashin, *Under Fire with the Tenth Cavalry*, 351, 262–63.

Appointed squadron sergeant major, 10th Cavalry, 13 Jun 1899; served at Holguin, Cuba, 17 May 1899–12 May 1902; allotted $25 per month to Mrs. Mary J. Conley, 1 Jan–20 Jun 1900, 1 Oct 1900–31 Mar 1901, and $20 per month, 1 Jul–31 Dec 1901; discharged, character excellent, married, four minor children, 30 Jun 1902; reenlisted as squadron sergeant major, Ft Robinson, NE, 1 Jul 1902, wife and children residing in Havre, MT; reenlisted as regimental quartermaster sergeant, Ft Robinson, 1 Jul 1905; retired, character excellent, with $350 deposits and $250 due him for clothing, 19 Nov 1906. SOURCE: Descriptive Book, 10 Cav Officers & NCOs.

Guest with his wife at K/10th Cavalry Thanksgiving dinner, Ft Robinson, 1904. SOURCE: Simmons, "Thanksgiving Day," 664.

Sister Sallie married Beverly Thornton, Cook, K/10th Cavalry, at Ft Robinson.

Celebrated twentieth wedding anniversary, with large number of invited guests from Ft Robinson and Crawford, NE, 25 Apr 1905; to retire in about one year. SOURCE: Crawford *Tribune*, 5 May 1905.

Retired after thirty years with pension of $30 per month. SOURCE: Cleveland *Gazette*, 29 Dec 1906.

CONLIN, Edward; G/9th Cav. Admitted to Soldiers Home with disability after serving eighteen years and nine months, age 45, 24 Apr 1884. SOURCE: SecWar, *AR 1884*, 862.

CONN, George; Private; B/25th Inf. Dishonorable discharge, Brownsville. SOURCE: SO 266, AGO, 9 Nov 1906.

CONN, John; Corporal; D/24th Inf. Enlisted Philadelphia, PA, 23 Jan 1898; promoted to corporal, Tampa, FL, 10 May 1898; on detached service as recruiter, 20 Jun 1898; fourteen years' continuous service. SOURCE: Muster Roll, H/24 Inf, May–Jun 1898.

On special duty as clerk since 30 Aug 1898. SOURCE: Muster Roll, H/24 Inf, Jul–Aug 1898.

Letter from Siboney, Cuba, 24 Aug 1898. SOURCE: Gatewood, *"Smoked Yankees"*, 65–71.

Transferred to D/24th Infantry, 24 Oct 1898; due $5 for deposits and $15.66 for clothing. SOURCE: Muster Roll, H/24 Inf, Sep–Oct 1898.

Died Helena, MT, 20 Aug 1900; parents, brothers, and sisters have not answered letters; commander seeks permission to establish Court of Administration to sell his effects. SOURCE: Name File, 24 Inf.

CONNLEY, F.; Private; L/9th Cav. On detached service in field, New Mexico, 21 Jan–24 Feb 1881. SOURCE: Regt Returns, 9 Cav, Feb 1881.

CONNOR, Charles; Sergeant; F/24th Inf. At Ft Elliott, TX, 1886. *See* **SMITH**, Jacob Clay, Sergeant, 10th Cavalry

Sentenced by general court martial to reimburse government $26 for two pistols, reduced to private, dishonorably discharged, and imprisoned for two years, Ft Elliott; Brig. Gen. Orlando B. Willcox, approving authority, approved all but $26 reimbursement because it was not possible to fine man who drew no pay; Connor awaiting trial for murder. SOURCE: *ANJ* 24 (26 Mar 1887): 695.

CONNOR, F.; Private; G/9th Cav. On detached service, South Fork, NM, 17 Nov 1880–12 Jan 1881. SOURCE: Regt Returns, 9 Cav, Jan 1881.

CONONDY, Noah; L/10th Cav. Original member of 10th Cavalry; in troop when organized, Ft Riley, KS, 21 Sep 1867. SOURCE: McMiller, "Buffalo Soldiers," 78.

CONRAD, Barton; Corporal; A/10th Cav. Recommended for extra duty as schoolteacher, Ft Robinson, NE, 23 Nov 1902. SOURCE: CO, Ft Robinson, to AG, DeptMo, 23 Nov 1902, LS, Ft Robinson.

Transferred to Hospital Corps. SOURCE: SO 179, Dept Mo, 13 Sep 1903.

CONRAD, L.; Farrier; G/9th Cav. In hands of civil authorities, Valentine and Lincoln, NE, 29 Apr–30 Jun 1887. SOURCE: Regt Returns, 9 Cav, Jun 1887.

CONTEE, James S.; 1st Sgt; H/9th Cav. Sergeant, with detachment engaged against enemy, Lumagua, Philippines, 9 May 1901. SOURCE: Hamilton, "History of the Ninth Cavalry," 107; *Illustrated Review: Ninth Cavalry.*

Veteran of Spanish-American War and Philippine Insurrection; at Ft D. A. Russell, WY, in 1910; sharpshooter; resident of Washington, DC. SOURCE: *Illustrated Review: Ninth Cavalry,* with picture.

CONTEE, Clarence; Private; D/10th Cav. Ordered from Ft Robinson, NE, to General Hospital, Washington, DC. SOURCE: SO 44, DeptMo, 2 Mar 1903; Post Surgeon, Ft Robinson, to CO, D/10, 7 Mar 1903, LS, Post Surgeon, Ft Robinson.

CONWAY; Sergeant; D/9th Cav. Released from arrest. SOURCE: TWX, DP, 4 Oct 1980.

CONWAY, Henry; Private; M/9th Cav. Private, H/24th Infantry, enlisted St. Paul, MN, 30 Nov 1895; eight years' continuous service in 1898; due U.S. for set of shelter tent poles $.20. SOURCE: Muster Roll, H/24 Inf, May–Jun 1898.

Wounded in action, San Juan, Cuba, 1 Jul 1898; returned to U.S. for treatment. SOURCE: Muster Roll, H/24 Inf, Jul–Aug 1898.

Wounded in Cuba. SOURCE: Muller, *The Twenty Fourth Infantry,* 198.

Transferred to M/24th Infantry, 7 Oct 1898; $5 deposits and $3.45 retained; due U.S. for clothing $7.96. SOURCE: Muster Roll, H/24 Inf, Sep–Oct 1898.

Private, M/9th Cavalry, at Ft D. A. Russell, WY, in 1910; sharpshooter; resident of Columbia, SC. SOURCE: *Illustrated Review: Ninth Cavalry,* with picture.

CONWAY, James S.; Private; B/10th Cav. Served in 10th Cavalry, 1898; remained in U.S. during war with Spain. SOURCE: Cashin, *Under Fire with the Tenth Cavalry,* 339.

CONWAY, Louis; Private; 24th Inf. Involved in fight with ex-soldier Jeff Smith. SOURCE: Manila *Times,* 19 Mar 1902.

CONYERS, Alexander; K/10th Cav. Original member of 10th Cavalry; in troop when organized, Ft Riley, KS, 1 Sep 1867. SOURCE: McMiller, "Buffalo Soldiers," 77.

CONYERS, Boyd; Private; B/25th Inf. Dishonorable discharge, Brownsville. SOURCE: SO 266, AGO, 9 Nov 1906.

Mrs. Boyd Conyers, age 85, of Monroe, GA, regarding Brownsville: "He never talked about it. The only thing he would say was he didn't do it." SOURCE: *Newsweek,* 16 Oct 1972.

COOK; Private; A/10th Cav. At Ft Apache, AZ, 1890, subscribed $.50 to testimonial to General Grierson. SOURCE: List of subscriptions, 23 Apr 1890, 10th Cavalry papers, MHI.

COOK, A.; K/24th Inf. At Ft Reno, Indian Territory, 1887. *See* **GILES**, Henry, Sergeant, C/24th Infantry

COOK, Charlie; Private; B/9th Cav. At Ft D. A. Russell, WY, in 1910; sharpshooter. SOURCE: *Illustrated Review: Ninth Cavalry,* with picture.

COOK, Cycire; I/10th Cav. Original member of 10th Cavalry; in troop when organized, Ft Riley, KS, 15 Aug 1867. SOURCE: McMiller, "Buffalo Soldiers," 76.

COOK, Eddie; Private; B/10th Cav. Served in 10th Cavalry, 1898; remained in U.S. during war with Spain. SOURCE: Cashin, *Under Fire with the Tenth Cavalry,* 339.

COOK, Ermine; Private; E/24th Inf. Died of typhoid in the Philippines. SOURCE: *ANJ* 38 (9 Oct 1900): 187.

COOK, Isaiah; Private; K/24th Inf. Fined $8 for drunkenness in and around company quarters, Cabanatuan, Philippines, 20 Feb 1901. SOURCE: Name File, 24 Inf.

Fined $5 and jailed for fifteen days for being too drunk to perform duties, Cabanatuan, 19 May 1901; witness: 1st Sgt. J. Stevens, K/24th Infantry. SOURCE: Name File, 24 Inf.

COOK, James H.; Private; B/9th Cav. At Ft Robinson, NE, 1888. *See* **HERBERT**, Thomas H., Private, K/9th Cavalry

COOK, Jesse A.; Private; B/24th Inf. Transferred from Reserve Divisional Hospital, Siboney, Cuba, to U.S. on U.S. Army Transport *Santiago*, with yellow fever, 25 Jul 1898. SOURCE: Hospital Papers, Spanish-American War.

COOK, John; Private; B/25th Inf. Dishonorable discharge, Brownsville. SOURCE: SO 266, AGO, 9 Nov 1906.

COOK, Joshua; Blacksmith; C/10th Cav. Served in 10th Cavalry in Cuba, 1898. SOURCE: Cashin, *Under Fire with the Tenth Cavalry*, 340.

COOK, Julius; Private; B/24th Inf. Present enlistment began 29 Jan 1900; sentenced to ten days and $5 fine for sleeping on post as sentinel, Cabanatuan, Philippines, around one P.M., 5 Jan 1901; witnesses: Sgt. John W. Hall, B/24th Infantry, and Cpl. James W. Simes, D/24th Infantry. SOURCE: Name File, 24 Inf.

COOK, Lewis J.; H/9th Cav. Admitted to Soldiers Home with disability after seven months' service, age 27, 4 Sep 1884. SOURCE: SecWar, *AR 1885*, 830.

COOK, Samuel; Sergeant; K/24th Inf. At Camp Pilot Butte, WY, 1898–99; in hands of civil authorities, Rock Springs, WY, Jan 1899.

Fined $5 for violating Article 62, left guard duty without leave and found after taps in house of native woman, Cabanatuan, Philippines, 1901. SOURCE: Name File, 24 Inf.

See **TAYLOR**, George N., Private, K/24th Infantry

COOK, William; K/10th Cav. Served seven years; lives in Detroit, MI. SOURCE: *Winners of the West* 4 (Mar 1927): 8.

Pension up to $50 per month. SOURCE: *Winners of the West* 6 (Jul 1929): 5.

COOK, William H.; Private; I/10th Cav. Served in 10th Cavalry in Cuba, 1898. SOURCE: Cashin, *Under Fire with the Tenth Cavalry*, 348.

COOK, William L.; Artificer; H/24th Inf. Enlisted Tampa, FL, 29 May 1898. SOURCE: Muster Roll, H/24 Inf, May–Jun 1898.

Transferred from Reserve Divisional Hospital, Siboney, Cuba, to U.S. on U.S. Army Transport *Santiago* with yellow fever, 25 Jul 1898. SOURCE: Hospital Papers, Spanish-American War.

Sick in U.S., date of departure unknown; disease contracted in line of duty. SOURCE: Muster Roll, H/24 Inf, Jul–Aug 1898.

On furlough, authorized by surgeon's certificate, 20 Sep–19 Oct 1898; rejoined company 19 Oct 1898. SOURCE: Muster Roll, H/24 Inf, Sep–Oct 1898.

Discharged, as private, single, character good, $30 deposits, due U.S. $17.33 for clothing, 29 Jan 1899; reenlisted Ft Douglas, UT, 30 Jan 1899; on special duty, Quartermaster Department, since 23 Feb 1899; fined $1 by summary court, 15 Feb 1899. SOURCE: Muster Roll, H/24 Inf, Jan–Feb 1899.

Artificer, H/24th Infantry, fined $2 by summary court, for absence from check roll call, 9 Nov 1901, San Isidro, Philippines, 9 Nov 1901, fourth conviction; fined $10 and placed in solitary confinement for five days by summary court, for failure to attend eleven P.M. inspection and lying out of quarters, San Isidro, 21 May 1902. SOURCE: Register of Summary Court, San Isidro.

COOKSEY, Kirk; Private; I/10th Cav. Convicted by general court martial, Jefferson Barracks, MO, of desertion, 3 Jun–22 Jul 1882; sentenced to dishonorable discharge and five years, reduced to two years by General Sherman. SOURCE: GCMO 60, AGO, 11 Sep 1882.

COOLEY, Thomas; Private; D/9th Cav. At Ft D. A. Russell, WY, in 1910; resident of Winchester, TN. SOURCE: *Illustrated Review: Ninth Cavalry,* with picture.

COOMBS, S. J.; Private; A/9th Cav. Discharged on certificate of disability, Ft Stanton, NM, 11 Jan 1881. SOURCE: Regt Returns, 9 Cav, Jan 1881.

COOMBS, T.; Private; A/9th Cav. At Ft Stanton, NM, 1881. SOURCE: Regt Returns, 9 Cav, Jan 1881.

COOPER; Private; K/9th Cav. Transferred to Hospital Corps. SOURCE: SO 77, AGO, 3 Apr 1897.

COOPER; Sergeant; M/10th Cav. Discharged. SOURCE: SO 187, AGO, 9 Jul 1902.

COOPER, Allen; Private; B/10th Cav. Served in 10th Cavalry, 1898; remained in U.S. during war with Spain. SOURCE: Cashin, *Under Fire with the Tenth Cavalry*, 339.

COOPER, Andrew; Private; D/10th Cav. Corporal, served in 10th Cavalry in Cuba, 1898. SOURCE: Cashin, *Under Fire with the Tenth Cavalry*, 341.

In hands of civil authorities, Crawford, NE, 30 Jun–17 Jul 1903. SOURCE: Regt Returns, 10 Cav.

COOPER, Archie; Corporal; G/9th Cav. Veteran of Philippine Insurrection; at Ft D. A. Russell, WY, in 1910; sharpshooter; resident of Cuero, TX. SOURCE: *Illustrated Review: Ninth Cavalry,* with picture.

COOPER, Charles E.; Private; B/25th Inf. Dishonorable discharge, Brownsville. SOURCE: SO 266, AGO, 9 Nov 1906.

COOPER, Frank; Private; G/10th Cav. Honorable mention for bravery against Indians, Lake Quemado, TX, 3 Aug 1880. SOURCE: Baker, Roster.

COOPER, George B.; Private; G/25th Inf. Wounded in action, El Caney, Cuba, 1 Jul 1898. SOURCE: Nankivell, *History of the Twenty-fifth Infantry*, 83.

COOPER, George P.; Sergeant; M/9th Cav. Veteran of Spanish-American War and Philippine Insurrection; at Ft D. A. Russell, WY, in 1910. SOURCE: *Illustrated Review: Ninth Cavalry,* with picture.

COOPER, Horace; Color Sgt; 9th Cav. Private, restored to duty without trial. SOURCE: SO 278, AGO, 23 Nov 1891.

Corporal, C/9th Cavalry, since 6 Sep 1892. SOURCE: Roster, 9 Cav.

Promoted to sergeant, C/9th Cavalry, Ft Robinson, NE, Apr 1895. SOURCE: *ANJ* 32 (11 May 1895): 608.

Sergeant, authorized to reenlist as married. SOURCE: Letter, AGO, 2 Jun 1896, Post Returns, Ft Robinson.

Sergeant, on recruiting duty, early 1898. SOURCE: Cashin, *Under Fire with the Tenth Cavalry*, 112.

Appointed regimental color sergeant, May 1901. SOURCE: *ANJ* 38 (1 Jun 1901): 966.

COOPER, James H.; Trumpeter; G/10th Cav. Served in 10th Cavalry in Cuba, 1898. SOURCE: Cashin, *Under Fire with the Tenth Cavalry*, 345.

In Cuba with regiment, 1898. See **DAVIS**, William J., Sergeant Major, Second Squadron/10th Cavalry

COOPER, John; B/10th Cav. Original member of 10th Cavalry; in troop when organized, Ft Leavenworth, KS, 1 Apr 1867. SOURCE: McMiller, "Buffalo Soldiers," 69.

COOPER, John; Private; F/9th Cav. Awaiting trial for offenses committed on Crawford, NE, streets. SOURCE: CO, Ft Robinson, to Mr. A. Morrison, Marshal, Crawford, 8 Jun 1893, LS, Ft Robinson.

COOPER, John; 1st Sgt; D/9th Cav. Sergeant, on special duty in charge of recruits, Nueva Caceres, Philippines, 23–24 May 1902. SOURCE: SD List, D/9 Cav.

Veteran of Indian wars and Philippine Insurrection; first sergeant, at Ft D. A. Russell, WY, in 1910. SOURCE: *Illustrated Review: Ninth Cavalry,* with picture.

COOPER, Pleas; Private; D/10th Cav. Served in 10th Cavalry, 1898; remained in U.S. during war with Spain. SOURCE: Cashin, *Under Fire with the Tenth Cavalry*, 341.

COOPER, William; Private; M/49th Inf. Engaged against enemy, Tuao, Cagayan, Philippines, 18 Oct 1900. SOURCE: *ANJ* 38 (11 May 1901): 901.

COOPER, William A.; Private; A/10th Cav. Served in 10th Cavalry in Cuba, 1898. SOURCE: Cashin, *Under Fire with the Tenth Cavalry*, 336.

Wounded in action, Santiago, Cuba, 1 Jul 1898. SOURCE: SecWar, *AR 1898*, 324.

COOTS, Robert; I/10th Cav. Original member of 10th Cavalry; in troop when organized, Ft Riley, KS, 15 Aug 1867. SOURCE: McMiller, "Buffalo Soldiers," 76.

COPELAND, Charles L.; Private; G/9th Cav. Veteran of Philippine Insurrection; at Ft D. A. Russell, WY, in 1910; marksman. SOURCE: *Illustrated Review: Ninth Cavalry,* with picture.

COPELLE, Charles; Saddler; G/10th Cav. Served in 10th Cavalry in Cuba, 1898. SOURCE: Cashin, *Under Fire with the Tenth Cavalry*, 345.

COPES, Samuel; Private; C/24th Inf. Died of chronic diarrhea in the Philippines, 26 Sep 1899. SOURCE: *ANJ* 37 (7 Oct 1899): 119.

See **MURPHY**, George, Private, C/24th Infantry

CORBITT, George; Corporal; F/9th Cav. Veteran of Philippine Insurrection; at Ft D. A. Russell, WY, in 1910; resident of Orangeburg, SC. SOURCE: *Illustrated Review: Ninth Cavalry,* with picture.

CORDES, William; Sergeant; M/49th Inf. Performed bravely leading detachment against enemy, Tuao, Cagayan, Philippines, 18 Oct 1900; detachment consisted of Cpl. Archie Jestings and Pvts. Willie Allen, Wash C. Campbell, Hayes Carr, Henry Crofford, James Crofford, William Cooper, Madison W. Forman, Hezekiel Jones, Frank McCray, Samuel H. McNeil, James Oins, Homer M. Townes, Randall Wade, Jake Williams, and Charles Woods. SOURCE: *ANJ* 38 (11 May 1901): 901.

CORDIN, C. W.; Private; B/25th Inf. In clothing business, Troy, OH. SOURCE: Cleveland *Gazette*, 3 Aug 1889.

Seven letters, Camp Haskell, GA, n.d. [1898]. SOURCE: Gatewood, *"Smoked Yankees"*, 157–73.

Long-term resident of Cleveland, Lorain, Oberlin, Toledo, Norwalk, in northern Ohio. SOURCE: Cleveland *Gazette*, 17 Dec 1898.

Transferred from 7th Infantry, U.S. Volunteers, to 25th Infantry, and assigned to Ft Apache, AZ: "He is bright intellectually, looks very much like a dark-complexioned Spaniard, but is a loyal Afro-American, a close observer and a good writer." SOURCE: Cleveland *Gazette*, 15 Apr 1899.

Letter, from B/25th Infantry, Ft Apache, 20 Mar 1899, describes recreational facilities available to enlisted men on post. SOURCE: Cleveland *Gazette*, 6 May 1899.

Letters from Ft Apache and aboard U.S. Army Transport *Pennsylvania*. SOURCE: Cleveland *Gazette*, 1 and 15 Jul, 5 Aug 1899.

Letters from the Philippines. SOURCE: Cleveland *Gazette*, 16 and 30 Sep, 14 Oct, 2 Dec 1899; 3 and 10 Feb, 17 Mar, 21 and 28 Apr 1900.

Letter from Manila, 15 Oct 1899. SOURCE: Gatewood, *"Smoked Yankees"*, 249.

Letter to Professor W. A. Scarborough, Wilberforce University, from Palauig, Zambales, Philippines, 21 May 1901, advises of good opportunities for teachers in the Philippines. SOURCE: Indianapolis *Freeman*, 16 Nov 1901.

Letters from General Hospital, Presidio of San Francisco, CA. SOURCE: Cleveland *Gazette*, 26 Oct, 30 Nov 1901, 11 Jan 1902.

Still sick but home in Elyria, OH. SOURCE: Cleveland *Gazette*, 8 Feb 1902.

Resided in "the Sandusky home" from May 1902; still wears soldier's uniform; was in ten general engagements and many skirmishes while in the Philippines. SOURCE: Cleveland *Gazette*, 21 Feb 1903.

Resides at Soldiers and Sailors Home, VA; writes from Philadelphia that he expects to visit Cleveland. SOURCE: Cleveland *Gazette*, 5 Oct 1912.

Resides in National Military Home, CA, 1927. *See* SNOTEN, Peter, Sergeant, G/9th Cavalry

CORDLE, Wiley; Private; I/10th Cav. Served in 10th Cavalry, 1898; remained in U.S. during war with Spain. SOURCE: Cashin, *Under Fire with the Tenth Cavalry*, 348.

CORINGTON, Wiley; C/10th Cav. Original member of 10th Cavalry; in troop when organized, Ft Leavenworth, KS, 14 May 1867. SOURCE: McMiller, "Buffalo Soldiers," 70.

CORK, Adam; Private; E/10th Cav. Original member of 10th Cavalry; in troop when organized, Ft Leavenworth, KS, 15 Jun 1867. SOURCE: McMiller, "Buffalo Soldiers," 72.

Honorable mention for gallantry against Kiowas and Comanches, Wichita Agency, Indian Territory, 22–23 Aug 1874. SOURCE: Baker, Roster.

Wounded in action against Kiowas, Ft Sill, Indian Territory, Aug 1874. SOURCE: Leckie, *The Buffalo Soldiers*, 122.

CORNELIUS, George W.; K/25th Inf. Admitted to Soldiers Home with disability, with three years and nine months' service, age 32, 20 Dec 1890. SOURCE: SecWar, *AR 1891*, 751.

CORNELL, Hill; QM Sgt; A/25th Inf. Ranked number 147 among rifle experts with 69.33 percent in 1904. SOURCE: GO 79, AGO, 1 Jun 1905.

CORNISH, Harry; Private; I/24th Inf. Enlisted Baltimore, MD, 7 Feb 1899. SOURCE: Muster Roll, I/24 Inf, Jan–Feb 1899.

Fined $2 by summary court, 11 May 1899; Fined $1.50 by summary court, 15 May 1899; fined $10 and confined thirty days by summary court, 8 Jun 1899. SOURCE: Muster Roll, I/24 Inf, May–Jun 1899.

Fined $10 by summary court, 21 Oct 1899. SOURCE: Muster Roll, I/24 Inf, Sep–Oct 1899.

CORNISH, Isaac S.; M/10th Cav. Original member of 10th Cavalry; in troop when organized, Ft Riley, KS, 15 Oct 1867. SOURCE: McMiller, "Buffalo Soldiers," 79.

CORNISH, Samuel; Private; D/9th Cav. Resided at 122 Sharp St., Baltimore, MD, 1895. *See* DENT, Henry, Private, D/9th Cavalry

CORTER; Private; K/24th Inf. At Cabanatuan, Philippines, 1901. *See* NICKLE, Elijah, Private, K/24th Infantry

COSBY; Private; F/10th Cav. Wounded in battle against Indians, Kansas, 21 Aug 1867. SOURCE: Armes, *Ups and Downs*, 247.

COSBY, George S.; Private; D/24th Inf. At Cabanatuan, Philippines, 1901. *See* NEWELL, Frank, Private, D/24th Infantry

COSNAHAN, Charles; Private; 25th Inf. Born Aiken, SC; enlisted Charleston, SC, age 25, Ht 5'10", fair complexion, brown hair and eyes, occupation laborer, 18 Jul 1881. SOURCE: Descriptive & Assignment Roll, 25 Inf.

COSTLY, John; Staff Sgt; 10th Cav. Retires with thirty years' service from Ft Leavenworth, KS. SOURCE: *Cavalry Journal* 41 (Jul 1932): 61.

COSTON, W. Hilary; Chaplain; 9th Inf USV. Attended Yale Preparatory School, 1875–80; then sent by New England Conference, African Methodist Episcopal Church, for four years at Wilberforce University; Yale Seminary, 1884–1887; missionary in Ontario, Canada, Iowa, Pittsburgh, Northern Ohio, and Baltimore conferences; rebuilt church at Catonsville, MD; served ten years as pastor, Bethel African Methodist Episcopal Church, Hagerstown, MD, during which time forty-year-old mortgage was paid off; chaplain of 9th Infantry and Ohio Division, U.S. Reserve National Guard, 1899–1904; author of *A Freeman Yet a Slave*, *The African Abroad*, and *The Spanish-American War Volunteer*; editor of *Ringwood's Home Magazine*, first for colored women and children, for five years. SOURCE: Talbert, *The Sons of Allen*, 232–33.

Biographical sketch of wife Julia Ringwood Coston. SOURCE: Hine et al., eds., *Black Women in America*, 284–85.

COSY, John; Private; E/10th Cav. Served in 10th Cavalry, 1898; remained in U.S. during war with Spain. SOURCE: Cashin, *Under Fire with the Tenth Cavalry*, 343.

COTHRAN, Nesbert; Sergeant; F/25th Inf. Corporal, authorized four-month furlough from Ft Shaw, MT. SOURCE: *ANJ* 26 (3 Aug 1889): 1003.

Reduced to ranks from sergeant for attempting to leave post, Ft Missoula, MT, without proper authority.

COTTMAN, Charles W.; Private; I/24th Inf. Enlisted Baltimore, MD, 9 Feb 1899. SOURCE: Muster Roll, I/24 Inf, Jan–Feb 1899.

COTTON, J. H.; Sergeant; 24th Inf. Promoted from private to sergeant, E/24th Infantry, Ft Bayard, NM, 1890. SOURCE: Cleveland *Gazette*, 9 May 1891.

Sergeant and Mrs. Cotton of Nicholasville, KY, were guests of Mr. and Mrs. T. J. Weaver, East 30th St., Cleveland, for dinner. SOURCE: Cleveland *Gazette*, 8 Sep 1917.

COTTON, James T.; Private; 9th Cav. At Ft Niobrara, NE, 1889. *See* **CARTER**, William H., Trumpeter, A/9th Cavalry

COTTON, Stephen W.; L/10th Cav. Original member of 10th Cavalry; in troop when organized, Ft Riley, KS, 21 Sep 1867. SOURCE: McMiller, "Buffalo Soldiers," 78.

COUNCE, Joseph F. M.; Private; K/24th Inf. Born a slave, 21 May 1858; Col. Peter Counce owned him and his parents; mother and father, Angie and London Counce; lived on farm three miles east of Lawrenceburg, TN, until 1870; enlisted 30 Oct 1879, occupation schoolteacher, Ht 5'11", brown complexion; served until 12 Jul 1883; after service lived at Sedalia, MO, then eleven years in Soldiers Home, Washington, DC, and six years at Columbia, TN; worked at Camp Humphrey during World War I; original pension $4 per month, 13 Nov 1883; died of heart disease, 21 Feb 1931; widow Jennie Wigfall Counce, 451 High Street, Columbia, had pension discontinued because she married after 4 Mar 1917. SOURCE: VA File XC 921596, Joseph F. M. Counce.

Injured by explosion of rock in ash pit he was cleaning; employed as schoolteacher, Waynesboro, TN, 1883. SOURCE: Affidavit, Counce, 7 Nov 1883, VA File XC 921596, Joseph F. M. Counce.

Mentioned in acknowledgments. SOURCE: Mary Curtis, *The Black Soldier*.

Served 1879–83; wants to hear from old boys; pension just up from $17 to $40 per month. SOURCE: *Winners of the West* 6 (Nov 1929): 3.

Died Columbia. SOURCE: *Winners of the West* 8 (May 1931): 10.

Letter, Jennie Counce, to E. L. Bailey, Director, Dependent's Claims Service, 8 May 1942: "Please do something for me if you possibly can it won't be long you would have to help me for my time is nearly up but I do want comforts while living." Married Counce in Washington, DC, while he was in Soldiers Home. SOURCE: VA File XC 921596, Joseph F. M. Counce.

COUNTEE, Charles; Private; K/10th Cav. Deserted; was serving under name of Mark Manville, General Mounted Service, when recognized; now in confinement at cavalry depot. SOURCE: Superintendent, Mounted Recruiting Service, to CO, 10 Cav, Jul 1873, ES, 10 Cav, 1873–81.

COUNTEE, Thomas W.; Sergeant; 24th Inf. Drowned while crossing San Mateo River, Philippines, 21 Aug 1899. SOURCE: Richmond *Planet*, 2 Sep 1899.

COURTNEY, H. G.; B/24th Inf. Telegraph operator. SOURCE: Cleveland *Gazette*, 28 Oct 1899.

COUSINS, Benjamin; Corporal; H/25th Inf. Killed in action at El Caney, Cuba, 1 Jul 1898; buried one mile south of El Caney; wood headboard, surrounded by stones, has name cut into it; name enclosed in tightly corked bottle buried at head of grave. SOURCE: Scrapbook, 25 Inf, II.

Died in Cuba, 1 Jul 1898. SOURCE: *ANJ* 36 (11 Feb 1899): 567.

Killed in action, Cuba, 1898. SOURCE: Scipio, *Last of the Black Regulars*, 29.

COUTTS, Frank; D/10th Cav. Original member of 10th Cavalry; in troop when organized, Ft Leavenworth, KS, 1 Jun 1867. SOURCE: McMiller, "Buffalo Soldiers," 71.

COVINGTON, Charles; Private; Band/10th Cav. Formerly in Band/25th Infantry; enlisted in Band/10th Cavalry. SOURCE: Adj, 10 Cav, to AG, USA, 29 Jun 1875, LS, 10 Cav, 1873–83.

COVINGTON, James C.; Private; E/24th Inf. In K/24th Infantry at San Carlos, AZ, 1890. *See* **HARDEE**, James A., Private, K/24th Infantry

Resident of Chicago, IL; to be discharged from E/24th Infantry at end of term, Ft Bayard, NM, 15 Dec 1891. SOURCE: Cleveland *Gazette*, 12 Dec 1891.

COVINGTON, John; Wagoner; K/9th Cav. Promoted to corporal, L/9th Cavalry, from lance corporal, Apr 1902. SOURCE: *ANJ* 39 (10 May 1902): 904.

Veteran of Philippine Insurrection; wagoner, K/9th Cavalry, at Ft D. A. Russell, WY, in 1910; resident of Bowling Green, KY. SOURCE: *Illustrated Review: Ninth Cavalry*, with picture.

COVINGTON, Samuel; Corporal; C/10th Cav. Corporal, G/9th Cavalry, since 28 Jul 1893. SOURCE: Roster, 9 Cav.

Alternate for 9th Cavalry regimental color guard, Ft Robinson, NE, Mar 1896. SOURCE: *ANJ* 33 (28 Mar 1896): 540.

Corporal, C/10th Cavalry; served in 10th Cavalry in Cuba, 1898. SOURCE: Cashin, *Under Fire with the Tenth Cavalry*, 339.

COWINGS, Albert T.; Private; M/10th Cav. Served in 10th Cavalry, 1898; remained in U.S. during war with Spain. SOURCE: Cashin, *Under Fire with the Tenth Cavalry*, 351.

COX, Charles; Private; H/24th Inf. Discharged, end of term, single, character excellent, with $152.75 deposits, $9.25 clothing, Camp Tampa, FL, 17 May 1898; enlisted Lynchburg, VA, 20 May 1898. SOURCE: Muster Roll, H/24 Inf, May–Jun 1898.

COX, George; Private; I/9th Cav. At Ft D. A. Russell, WY, in 1910; resident of La Grange, GA. SOURCE: *Illustrated Review: Ninth Cavalry*.

COX, Henry; Private; A/9th Cav. At Ft D. A. Russell, WY, in 1910. SOURCE: *Illustrated Review: Ninth Cavalry*, with picture.

COX, James; I/10th Cav. Original member of 10th Cavalry; in troop when organized, Ft Riley, KS, 15 Aug 1867. SOURCE: McMiller, "Buffalo Soldiers," 76.

COX, Jonas W.; 1st Sgt; G/25th Inf. Son Walter D. Cox baptized by Chaplain Steward, Ft Missoula, MT, 10 Apr 1892. SOURCE: Monthly Report, Chaplain Steward, 1 May 1892, AGO File 4634 ACP 91.

COX, Richard; Private; D/24th Inf. Attacked Pvt. H. Lambert, D/24th Infantry, with hatchet, Ft Bayard, NM, Christmas 1888; disarmed by Sgt. E. Ramber and attacked Ramber with knife. SOURCE: Billington, *New Mexico's Buffalo Soldiers*, 164; Fowler, *The Black Infantry*, 83.

COX, Thomas; Sergeant; H/24th Inf. Enlisted Ft Huachuca, AZ, 17 Dec 1893; twenty-five years' continuous service. SOURCE: Muster Roll, H/24 Inf, May–Jun 1898.

Sick, Siboney, Cuba, disease contracted in line of duty, 24 Jul–25 Aug 1898; sick en route to U.S. since 25 Aug 1898. SOURCE: Muster Roll, H/24 Inf, Jul–Aug 1898.

On furlough, authorized by surgeon's certificate, 31 Sep– 22 Oct 1898; on special duty as overseer of laborers since 22 Oct 1898. SOURCE: Muster Roll, H/24 Inf, Sep–Oct 1898.

On special duty as overseer of laborers since 22 Oct 1898; discharged, character excellent, single, with $225 deposits, $116.14 clothing, $26.93 retained, 16 Dec 1898; reenlisted in company with warrant as sergeant continued from original date of 14 Sep 1897. SOURCE: Muster Roll, H/24 Inf, Nov–Dec 1898.

On special duty as overseer of laborers. SOURCE: Muster Roll, H/24 Inf, Jan–Feb 1899.

COX, William H., Jr.; Sergeant; I/48th Inf. Letters from Philippines, Manila, 14 Feb 1900, and La Trinidad, 3 Sep 1900. SOURCE: Gatewood, *"Smoked Yankees"*, 272, 282.

Letter. SOURCE: Richmond *Planet*, 3 Nov 1900.

COXE, James; Corporal; L/10th Cav. Served in 1879. *See* **THOMAS**, Benedict, Sergeant, L/10th Cavalry

COXMIRE, Amos; H/10th Cav. Original member of 10th Cavalry; in troop when organized, Ft Leavenworth, KS, 21 Jul 1867. SOURCE: McMiller, "Buffalo Soldiers," 75.

CRABB; Private; C/24th Inf. Confined four months for drunk and disorderly conduct, Ft Supply, OK. SOURCE: *ANJ* 25 (22 Oct 1887): 242.

CRADDOCK, Calvin; E/10th Cav. Original member of 10th Cavalry; in troop when organized, Ft Leavenworth, KS, 15 Jun 1867. SOURCE: McMiller, "Buffalo Soldiers," 72.

CRAGG, Allen; Sergeant; E/9th Cav. Sergeant, E/9th Cavalry, since 17 Jul 1885. SOURCE: Roster, 9 Cav.

Wife is one of three laundresses authorized E/9th Cavalry, Ft Robinson, NE, and authorized quartermaster stove and utensils, Jun 1891. SOURCE: Post Adj to Post QM, Ft Robinson, 22 Jul 91, LS, Ft Robinson.

Resides on Laundress Row with wife, Aug 1893. SOURCE: Medical History, Ft Robinson.

At Ft Robinson since 1885. SOURCE: *ANJ* 32 (4 May 1895): 591.

Retires from Ft Robinson, May 1885. SOURCE: *ANJ* 32 (11 May 1895): 609.

Retires to Sacramento, CA. SOURCE: Order 29, 11 May 1895, Post Orders, Ft Robinson.

Veterans Administration pension application 881404, by widow Violet Cragg, 16 Dec 1907, not found in search at National Archives.

CRAICE, George; L/10th Cav. Original member of 10th Cavalry; in troop when organized, Ft Riley, KS, 21 Sep 1867. SOURCE: McMiller, "Buffalo Soldiers," 78.

CRAIG, Benjamin F.; F/9th Cav. Served 1872–82; died at Delta, PA. SOURCE: *Winners of the West* 8 (Feb 1931): 10.

Mary Craig, his widow, died at Delta. SOURCE: *Winners of the West* 11 (Feb 1934): 3.

CRAIG, Daniel; Recruit; Colored Detachment/ Mounted Service. Convicted by general court martial, Jefferson Barracks, MO, of desertion 3–11 Dec 1885; sentenced to dishonorable discharge and three years. SOURCE: GCMO 122, AGO, 28 Dec 1885.

CRAIG, James; Private; H/9th Cav. Born Elizabethton, TN; enlisted Jonesboro, TN, age 23, occupation farmer, Ht 5'5", single, 6 Dec 1894; two summary court martial convictions, Ft Robinson, NE, 1895–96; six general court martial convictions, Ft Robinson, 1896–97; sentenced to dishonorable discharge and one year's confinement at Ft Logan, CO, 4 Nov 1897. SOURCE: Descriptive Book, H/9 Cav.

Returned to duty. SOURCE: Letter, DP, 13 Oct 1896, Post Returns, Ft Robinson.

Dishonorably discharged at Ft Robinson. SOURCE: SO 101, DP, 1897, Post Returns, Ft Robinson.

CRAIG, Peyton; Private; B/10th Cav. Served in 10th Cavalry, 1898; remained in U.S. during war with Spain. SOURCE: Cashin, *Under Fire with the Tenth Cavalry*, 339.

CRAIG, Richard; Color Sgt; 25th Inf. At Ft Niobrara, NE, 1903. SOURCE: Nankivell, *History of the Twenty-fifth Infantry*, 114, with picture.

CRAIG, Thomas; Private; F/24th Inf. Sentenced to dishonorable discharge and one year for shooting at Pvt. W. Warren, F/24th Infantry, with intent to kill, Ft Bayard, NM, 1 Jan 1894. SOURCE: *ANJ* 31 (3 Mar 1894): 459.

CRAIG, Thomas B.; Sergeant; E/9th Cav. Veteran of Spanish-American War and Philippine Insurrection; sergeant, D/9th Cavalry, wounded in action, San Juan, Cuba, 1 Jul 1898; sharpshooter; sergeant, E/9th Cavalry, at Ft D. A. Russell, WY, in 1910; resident of Washington, DC. SOURCE: *Illustrated Review: Ninth Cavalry,* with picture.

CRAIGMILES, John; Private; E/9th Cav. At Ft D. A. Russell, WY, in 1910; resident of Cleveland, TN. SOURCE: *Illustrated Review: Ninth Cavalry,* with picture.

CRAIGWELL, Ernest; Private; D/24th Inf. Transferred from Reserve Divisional Hospital, Siboney, Cuba, to U.S. Army Transport *Vigilancia* with remittent malarial fever. SOURCE: Hospital Papers, Spanish-American War.

CRANE, John T.; Corporal; M/10th Cav. Served in 10th Cavalry, 1898; remained in U.S. during war with Spain. SOURCE: Cashin, *Under Fire with the Tenth Cavalry,* 351.

CRANSHAW, Tennie; Sergeant; K/24th Inf. With seventy-five men of K Company, engaged 150 insurgents at Santa Ana, Philippines, 6 Oct 1899; repulsed enemy. SOURCE: Muller, *The Twenty Fourth Infantry,* 30.

Awarded certificate of merit for coolness and judgment in attack by insurgents, Santa Ana, 6 Oct 1899; discharged, 9 Sep 1901. SOURCE: GO 32, AGO, 6 Feb 1904.

CRANSON, James; 1st Sgt; E/10th Cav. Commissioned captain, Camp Des Moines, IA, 15 Oct 1917. SOURCE: Glass, *History of the Tenth Cavalry,* appendix M.

CRAPPER, John; F/10th Cav. Original member of 10th Cavalry; in troop when organized, Ft Leavenworth, KS, 21 Jun 1867. SOURCE: McMiller, "Buffalo Soldiers," 73.

CRAWFORD, E. L.; 24th Inf. At Ft Reno, Indian Territory, 1887. *See* **HAMILTON**, J. H., 24th Infantry

CRAWFORD, Eugene; Corporal; K/9th Cav. At Ft D. A. Russell, WY, in 1910; resident of Houston. SOURCE: *Illustrated Review: Ninth Cavalry,* with picture.

CRAWFORD, Guss; Private; D/9th Cav. At Ft D. A. Russell, WY, in 1910; resident of Press City, AL. SOURCE: *Illustrated Review: Ninth Cavalry,* with picture.

CRAWFORD, Henry; K/10th Cav. Original member of 10th Cavalry; in troop when organized, Ft Riley, KS, 1 Sep 1867. SOURCE: McMiller, "Buffalo Soldiers," 77.

CRAWFORD, Henry; Corporal; A/9th Cav. Promoted from lance corporal to corporal, C/9th Cavalry, Ft Robinson, NE. SOURCE: *ANJ* 32 (22 Dec 1894): 278.

Authorized to reenlist in A/9th Cavalry as married. SOURCE: Letter, AGO, 22 Jan 1897.

CRAWFORD, John H.; Private; M/9th Cav. Died of typhoid at Camp Wikoff, NY, 31 Aug 1898. SOURCE: Hospital Papers, Spanish-American War.

CRAWFORD, Lexis; Private; H/24th Inf. Reenlisted Ft Douglas, UT, 15 Dec 1897. SOURCE: Muster Roll, H/24 Inf, May–Jun 1898.

Sick in hospital, disease contracted in line of duty, Siboney, Cuba, 5–25 Aug 1898; sick en route to U.S. since 25 Aug 1898. SOURCE: Muster Roll, H/24 Inf, Jul–Aug 1898.

Rejoined company, 3 Oct 1898; sick, disease contracted in line of duty, since 6 Oct 1898. SOURCE: Muster Roll, H/24 Inf, Sep–Oct 1898.

On special duty as assistant plumber, Quartermaster Department, since 5 Oct 1898; sick in quarters to 14 Dec 1898. SOURCE: Muster Roll, H/24 Inf, Nov–Dec 1898.

On special duty as assistant plumber, Quartermaster Department. SOURCE: Muster Roll, H/24 Inf, Jan–Feb 1899.

CRAWFORD, Preston; Private; D/10th Cav. Mentioned, Feb 1873. SOURCE: LS, 10 Cav, 1873–77.

Died in hospital, Ft Dodge, KS. SOURCE: Letter, CO, 10 Cav, Ft Gibson, Indian Territory, to AG, USA, 20 Feb 1873, ES, 10 Cav, 1873–81.

CRAWFORD, W. A.; Private; F/9th Cav. On detached service in field, 30 Dec 1880–2 Jan 1881; at Ft Cummings, NM, 1881. SOURCE: Regt Returns, 9 Cav.

CRAWFORD, William; Corporal; K/25th Inf. Member, K/25th Infantry "Imperial Quartet" singers, Philippines. SOURCE: Richmond *Planet,* 16 Dec 1899.

Died at Angeles, Philippines, 29 Jan 1900; slipped running bases in baseball game and fell on dagger in his belt. SOURCE: *ANJ* 37 (24 Feb 1900): 611; *ANJ* 37 (14 Apr 1900): 780.

Prominent baseball player and leader of "Imperial Quartet"; died Jan 1900, Angeles field hospital, from injury by bolo he wore during baseball game. SOURCE: Richmond *Planet,* 7 April 1900.

CRAWFORD, William B.; 1st Lt; 8th Ill Inf. Sergeant, 24th Infantry, 1916; first lieutenant, 8th Illinois Infantry, 1917.

CRAYCROFT, Richard; Private; Band/24th Inf. Born Meade Co., KY; enlisted in E/24th Infantry, age 23, occupation laborer, Ht 5'9", hair, eyes, and complexion black, Louisville, KY, 28 May 1883; transferred to Band/24th Infantry to learn music, 14 Feb 1884, and for duty, 5 Sep 1884; discharged, end of term, single, character excellent, $60 deposits, $69.18 clothing, $72 retained, Ft Supply, Indian Territory, 27 May 1888. SOURCE: Descriptive Book, 24 Inf NCS & Band.

CREEK, Charles; Private; 9th Cav. Enlisted Annapolis, MD, 1880s: "tired of looking mules in the face from sunrise to sunset"; on Sioux campaign, 1890–91: "You ate out in the cold like a dog, [often] not in a tent, because the Indians gonna sneak up on you. It was so cold the spit froze when it left your mouth." SOURCE: Rickey, *Forty Miles a Day on Beans and Hay,* 4, 10.

CREGG, John L.; Private; G/9th Cav. While private, I/9th Cavalry, saw Cpl. Barney McKay, C/9th Cavalry, on crutches, lame in left leg, Ft Robinson, NE, around Nov 1887; served together in G/9th Cavalry, 1890–93; in June or Jul 1892, McKay was treated in field hospital, Suggs, WY, then had operation by post surgeon, Ft Robinson; Cregg resides at Soldiers Home, Washington, DC, 1916. SOURCE: Affidavit, Cregg, 4 Feb 1916, VA File XC 2659455, Barney McKay.

CREIGHTON, John R.; Private; F/10th Cav. Served in 10th Cavalry in Cuba, 1898. SOURCE: Cashin, *Under Fire with the Tenth Cavalry*, 344.

CRIFF, Samuel; F/10th Cav. Original member of 10th Cavalry; in troop when organized, Ft Leavenworth, KS, 21 Jun 1867. SOURCE: McMiller, "Buffalo Soldiers," 73.

CRINER, Walter; C/3rd Ala Inf. Died in Minnesota. SOURCE: Taylor, "Minnesota Black Spanish-American War Veterans."

CRIPPEN, Elijah A.; Sergeant; C/9th Cav. Private, wounded in action, San Juan, Cuba, 1 Jul 1898; private, at Ft D. A. Russell, WY, in 1910; resident of 809 Jackson St., Nashville, TN. SOURCE: *Illustrated Review: Ninth Cavalry*, with picture.

Sergeant; served in the Philippine Insurrection, led detachment from Sabang to Legaspi, Apr 1902. SOURCE: Hamilton, "History of the Ninth Cavalry," 109; *Illustrated Review: Ninth Cavalry*.

CRISTY, William; F/10th Cav. Original member of 10th Cavalry; in troop when organized, Ft Leavenworth, KS, 21 Jun 1867. SOURCE: McMiller, "Buffalo Soldiers," 73.

CRITTENDEN, Paul; Private; F/10th Cav. Served in 10th Cavalry in Cuba, 1898. SOURCE: Cashin, *Under Fire with the Tenth Cavalry*, 344.

CRITH, Frank; 38th Inf. Served 1867–70; resides in Topeka, KS; member, Camp 11, National Indian War Veterans, and attended recent convention. SOURCE: *Winners of the West* 4 (Sep 1927): 4.

Died. SOURCE: *Winners of the West* 7 (Sep 1930): 9.

CROCKET, Harry; Private; L/10th Cav. Served in 10th Cavalry, 1898; remained in U.S. during war with Spain. SOURCE: Cashin, *Under Fire with the Tenth Cavalry*, 350.

CROCKETT, George D.; Private; D/25th Inf. Born Lee Co., VA, father unknown, mother Susan Crockett, 1854; enlisted Cincinnati, OH, yellow complexion, occupation laborer, 8 Oct 1875; served until 7 Oct 1885; marksman, 1883; resided at Knoxville, TN, working as teamster, 1885–92; resided at 416 Prospect St., Cleveland, OH, 1897; resided at 6104 Euclid Ave., Cleveland, 1909; pension $17 per month, 28 Jul 1927, $50 per month, 29 Mar 1920; died of hypertrophy of prostate gland, U.S. Marine Hospital, Cleveland, 29 Oct 1929. SOURCE: VA File XC 2624113, George D. Crockett.

At Ft Stockton, TX, 1878; best marksman in company and in regiment. SOURCE: Scrapbook, 25 Inf, I.

Married to Josephine Nevares, Ft Stockton, Pecos Co., TX, by Chaplain B. L. Baldridge, U.S. Army, 22 Jan 1880; son John Henry Crockett born Ft Meade, SD, 3 Oct 1880; after Crockett died, his widow remained in Cleveland at 8809 Blaine Ave., with pension of $30 per month. SOURCE: VA File XC 2624113, George D. Crockett.

Letter from Cleveland reports that his pension increased from $17 to $40 per month. SOURCE: *Winners of the West* 5 (Mar 1928): 3.

See **BAILEY**, John H., Corporal, D/25th Infantry; **CRUISE**, John H., Sergeant, 25th Infantry; **DAVIS**, William H., First Sergeant, D/25th Infantry; **SHARP**, James, F/25th Infantry

CROCKETT, W. W.; Sergeant; K/8th Ill Inf. Letter from San Luis de Cuba expresses pride in ability of black soldiers to work under black officers; believes that experience of 8th Illinois proves this. SOURCE: Indianapolis *Freeman*, 25 Feb 1899.

CROFFORD, Henry; Private; M/49th Inf. Engaged against enemy, Tuao, Cagayan, Philippines, 18 Oct 1900. SOURCE: *ANJ* 38 (11 May 1901): 901.

CROFFORD, James; Private; M/49th Inf. Engaged against enemy, Tuao, Cagayan, Philippines, 18 Oct 1900. SOURCE: *ANJ* 38 (11 May 1901): 901.

CROLLY, James; Private; M/10th Cav. Served in 10th Cavalry in Cuba, 1898. SOURCE: Cashin, *Under Fire with the Tenth Cavalry*, 352.

CROOK, Anthony; L/10th Cav. Original member of 10th Cavalry; in troop when organized, Ft Riley, KS, 21 Sep 1867. SOURCE: McMiller, "Buffalo Soldiers," 78.

CROOK, James; Private; K/10th Cav. Served in 10th Cavalry, 1898; remained in U.S. during war with Spain. SOURCE: Cashin, *Under Fire with the Tenth Cavalry*, 349.

CROOKS, Richard; Private; D/25th Inf. Dishonorable discharge, Brownsville. SOURCE: SO 266, AGO, 9 Nov 1906.

CROPPER, Sam; Private; K/10th Cav. Assisted Lt. John Bigelow in planning Christmas program, at Mowry Mine, AZ, along with Private Hazzard, K/10th Cavalry, 1885. SOURCE: Bigelow, *On the Bloody Trail of Geronimo*, 103.

See **BRANSFORD**, Wesley, Private, K/10th Cavalry

CROSBY; Private; F/9th Cav. Application for transfer disapproved. SOURCE: Letter, AGO, 14 Apr 1894.

CROSBY, J.; Private; K/9th Cav. In hands of civil authorities, Crawford, NE, 21–22 Nov 1889. SOURCE: Regt Returns, 9 Cav, Nov 1889.

CROSBY, Scott; Corporal; A/24th Inf. While sergeant, D/24th Infantry, Ft Bayard, NM, reduced to ranks, confined for four months, and fined $10 per month for four months for being drunk on guard and allowing others on guard to get drunk. SOURCE: *ANJ* 28 (11 Oct 1890): 105.

Awarded certificate of merit for distinguished service while private, A/24th Infantry, battle of Santiago, Cuba, 1 Jul 1898. SOURCE: GO 15, AGO, 13 Feb 1900.

Certificate of merit mentioned. SOURCE: Steward, *The Colored Regulars*, 280; *ANJ* 37 (24 Feb 1900): 611; Scipio, *Last of the Black Regulars*, 130.

CROSBY, William H.; Private; K/10th Cav. Served in 10th Cavalry, 1898; remained in U.S. during war with Spain. SOURCE: Cashin, *Under Fire with the Tenth Cavalry*, 349.

CROSS, George W.; Private; I/24th Inf. Reenlisted Ft D. A. Russell, WY, 11 Feb 1899; appointed corporal same day. SOURCE: Muster Roll, I/24 Inf, Jan–Feb 1899.

Shot by Private Mahan in dive at west end of Cheyenne, WY; recovered and sentenced to one month's confinement and loss of one month's pay. SOURCE: Cheyenne *Daily Leader*, 13 Apr 1899.

CROSS, Harvey; G/10th Cav. Original member of 10th Cavalry; in troop when organized, Ft Leavenworth, KS, 5 Jul 1867. SOURCE: McMiller, "Buffalo Soldiers," 74.

CROSS, William; D/10th Cav. Original member of 10th Cavalry; in troop when organized, Ft Leavenworth, KS, 1 Jun 1867. SOURCE: McMiller, "Buffalo Soldiers," 71.

CROSS, William; Sergeant; E/10th Cav. Led detachment of eight on scout from station at San Felipe, TX, to Rio Grande, seeking murderers of Colson family, 13–20 Jun 1879; marched 150 miles. SOURCE: SecWar, *AR 1879*, 112.

CROSSWAY, Turner; Private; F/25th Inf. Retires from Ft Missoula, MT, Feb 1893. SOURCE: *ANJ* 30 (18 Feb 1893): 427.

CROTON, Henry; L/25th Inf. Wants his parents to answer his letters, according to Rienzi B. Lemus, staff correspondent. SOURCE: Richmond *Planet*, 8 Dec 1900.

CROUCH; Private; D/10th Cav. At Ft Apache, AZ, 1890, subscribed $.50 to testimonial to General Grierson. SOURCE: List of subscriptions, 23 Apr 1890, 10th Cavalry papers, MHI.

CROUCH, Albert S.; Private; 10th Cav. Former soldier, confined in guardhouse, Ft Bayard, NM, Jan 1889; planned and carried out escape with Pvt. Peter McCown, 10th Cavalry, who was confined for previously allowing prisoner to escape while serving as guard; guard Cpl. Lawrence J. Julius bribed into cooperation; both captured at Deming, NM. SOURCE: Billington, *New Mexico's Buffalo Soldiers*, 168–69.

CROWDER, John A.; Private; I/25th Inf. Fined $6 by summary court for lying out of quarters, San Isidro, Philippines, 29 Mar 1902, sixth conviction; fined $.50 for missing reveille, 29 Mar 1902. SOURCE: Register of Summary Court, San Isidro.

CROWDER, William; Private; 10th Cav. Recruit forwarded to Ft Leavenworth, KS, without statement of clothing account, Oct 1866. SOURCE: LS, 10 Cav, 1866–67.

CROWDY, George W.; Private; K/10th Cav. Original member of 10th Cavalry; in troop when organized, Ft Riley, KS, 1 Sep 1867. SOURCE: McMiller, "Buffalo Soldiers," 77.

His commander considers him an encumbrance and requests his transfer to guardhouse, Ft Dodge, KS, Oct 1868. SOURCE: CO, Det 10 Cav, to AAAG, District of the Upper Arkansas, 3 Oct 1868, LR, Det 10 Cav, 1868–69.

CROWELL, Julius; Corporal; I/24th Inf. With wife rented rooms in house on Washington Street, Houston 1917. SOURCE: Haynes, *A Night of Violence*, 44.

CROWER, Eugene; Private; G/24th Inf. Wounded in action, Cuba, 1898. SOURCE: Muller, *The Twenty Fourth Infantry*, 19.

CROWN, George; M/10th Cav. Original member of 10th Cavalry; in troop when organized, Ft Riley, KS, 15 Oct 1867. SOURCE: McMiller, "Buffalo Soldiers," 79.

CROXTON, Henry; Private; L/25th Inf. Sentenced to three months' confinement for indecent proposals to woman, San Marcelino, Philippines, 16 Nov 1901.

CRUDER, William; Private; 10th Cav. Recruit, arrived at Ft Leavenworth, KS, from Jefferson Barracks, MO, Oct 1866.

CRUISE, John H.; Sergeant; 25th Inf. Served as private, D/25th Infantry, with George D. Crockett; remembers Crockett's eye was badly injured when struck accidentally by comrade with fork, Ft Stockton, TX, Jul 1878; Cruise, as sergeant, age 43, Ft Custer, MT, 1891. SOURCE: Affidavit, Cruise, 20 Apr 1891, VA File XC 2624113, George D. Crockett.

CRUMBLE, C. A.; Sergeant; F/10th Cav. Commended for heroism in battle, Kansas, 21 Aug 1867. SOURCE: Armes, *Ups and Downs*, 247.

CRUMBLE, Richard; Private; G/9th Cav. Convicted by general court martial of conduct prejudicial to good order and discipline, attempted murder of Lieutenants Dimmick and

French, 9th Cavalry, theft of rifle, pistol, and ammunition, and desertion, 1 Aug 1875; sentenced to death by shooting; sentence commuted by Secretary of War to dishonorable discharge and five years in Kansas Penitentiary. SOURCE: GCMO 94, AGO, 15 Nov 1875.

CRUMBLES, Clayburn; Private; C/9th Cav. Deserter; $30 reward paid for his capture. SOURCE: CO, C/9, to Chief QM, DP, 12 Oct 1886, LS, C/9 Cav.

CRUMBLY, Floyd H.; Captain; 49th Inf. Born Rome, GA, 10 May 1859; father Robert a slave and mother Mariah free half-Indian; primary education from Rev. George Standing, early Methodist missionary at church in La Grange, GA; remaining education in Army and school of experience; enlisted 1876 and discharged, character excellent, 1881; returned to Atlanta as merchant and one-third owner of first drugstore owned and operated by blacks in Georgia, Butler-Slater Drug Co., Auburn Ave., Atlanta; sold out to Gate City Drug Co., also black; secretary of trustees of orphan home organized by Mrs. Carrie Steele; Mason; lieutenant, 10th U.S. Volunteer Infantry, 5 Jul 1898–Mar 1899. SOURCE: Beasley, *Negro Trailblazers*, 288.

Born of illiterate slave parents, 10 May 1855; mother free but virtually a slave because of her marriage to slave; mother died soon after Civil War, Nashville, TN, where she had gone with son to get within Union lines; returned to Georgia to live with grandparents, Hessie and Harriett Connally; mother had two other sons in second marriage, Hessie and Randolph Logan. SOURCE: Affidavit, Crumbly, 6 Oct 1919, VA File XC 2624105, Floyd H. Crumbly.

Joined 10th Cavalry from depot, 9 Mar 1877; with regiment until 16 Nov 1881. Locations: Ft Richardson, TX, 9 Mar–4 Jun 1877; in field scouting, 4–29 Jun 1877; Ft Richardson, 29 Jun 1877–Jan 1878; Ft Sill, Indian Territory, May 1878–Feb 1879; on detached service 26 Aug–Nov 1878; Ft Reno, Indian Territory, Mar–Jul 1879; Ft Sill, Jul 1879–Aug 1880; Eagle Springs, TX, Jul–Aug 1880; Ft Stockton, TX, 8 Sep–16 Nov 1881. SOURCE: VA File XC 2624105, Floyd H. Crumbly.

Enlisted 16 Nov 1876; corporal, Jan 1877; sergeant, Jan 1878; Victorio campaign, 1880; learned writing, arithmetic, spelling from his commander, Capt. T. A. Baldwin, and his wife; post sergeant major, Ft Stockton, Dec 1880–Nov 1881; discharged from I/10th Cavalry, 1881; first lieutenant and adjutant, Second Battalion, Georgia Volunteers (Colored), 1890; lieutenant colonel, Oct 1891–21 Jul 1898; first lieutenant, A/10th U.S. Volunteer Infantry, 21 Jul 1898; secretary, Negro Department, Georgia State Fair, Apr 1899; ten years as secretary, Georgia Real Estate Investment Company; ten years as secretary, Carrie Steele Orphanage; fifteen years with First Congregational Church, Atlanta. SOURCE: *ANJ* 37 (4 Nov 1899): 219.

Troop clerk for one year and acting post sergeant major for one year, 10th Cavalry; first lieutenant, 10th Volunteer Infantry, 21 Jul 1898–8 Mar 1899; captain, 49th Infantry, 9 Sep 1899; on recruiting duty, Atlanta, Sep 1899, and

Brunswick, GA, Oct 1899; provost judge, Paranaque, Philippines, 21 Aug–10 Oct 1900; commander, San Pablo Laguna, Philippines, 30 Nov–28 Dec 1900; in battle against General Juan Infania, Santa Catalina Laguna, Philippines, 20 Nov 1900. SOURCE: Descriptive Book, D/49 Inf.

Honorable discharge from A/10th U.S. Volunteer Infantry, age 38, Ht 5'7", dark brown complexion, occupation merchant, Camp Haskell, GA, Mar 1899. SOURCE: VA File XC 2624105, Floyd H. Crumbly.

Letters from the Philippines, Zapota Bridge, Luzon, 7 Feb 1900, and Tiason, 7 Mar 1901. SOURCE: Gatewood, *"Smoked Yankees"*, 269–71, 296.

Honorable discharge from 49th Infantry, Presidio of San Francisco, 30 Jul 1901; participated in battles at Paranaque, 25 Sep 1900, and Santa Catalina Laguna, 22 Nov 1900; no wounds, service honest and faithful, character excellent. SOURCE: Lt. Col. A. C. Ducat, CO, 49 Inf, VA File XC 2624105, Floyd H. Crumbly.

Claims that Philippine experience proves that blacks can follow other blacks. SOURCE: Beasley, *Negro Trailblazers*, 281.

Returned to Atlanta, 1901–02; resided in Los Angeles, CA, 1902–21; worked as grocer and real estate agent; fourth wife, born McMinnville, TN, worked as caterer and maid, 1931, received mail at 1649 W. 37th St., residence of Rev. N. P. Greggs, but had many addresses. SOURCE: Affidavit, Crumbly, 10 Jun 1931, VA File XC 2624105, Floyd H. Crumbly.

Moved to Los Angeles, 1903; assisted in organization of Columbia Department, United States Spanish War Veterans, which includes all states west of Mississippi River, and was first commander; led local movement to establish sanitarium for tuberculosis patients; worked in real estate and as notary public, Los Angeles Co.; prime mover in civic affairs, "thoroughly a race man" and a founder of Los Angeles Young Men's Christian Association and "Forum" club, which discusses "questions of importance to the race" each Sunday. SOURCE: Beasley, *Negro Trailblazers*, 288–89.

Daughter Flora Crumbly Jones born Atlanta, 25 Dec 1890; now housewife, married to Willis N. Jones, 9404 Pace Avenue, Los Angeles; her mother Lula, formerly of 204 Auburn Avenue, Atlanta, now deceased. SOURCE: Affidavit, F. C. Jones, 11 Jun 1931, VA File XC 2624105, Floyd H. Crumbly.

Married first wife Lula Goldsmith of Atlanta, 16 Apr 1881 (died 10 Oct 1892); married second wife Mary S. Goosby of Atlanta, 30 Aug 1893 (died 21 Nov 1902); married third wife Myrtle B. Carter of Los Angeles, 7 Sep 1904 (divorced 13 Jan 1922); married fourth wife Rebecca Bernice Tate, teacher, daughter of Alfred Vaughn and America Rhoades, and widow of John Marion Tate, 5 Apr 1922. SOURCE: VA File XC 2624105, Floyd H. Crumbly.

Received first pension for service as sergeant, I/10th Cavalry, against Northern Cheyennes, 1878–79, $20 per month, 10 May 1921; from 1923 until his death resided in Ward 9, Soldiers Home, Los Angeles; suffered from cerebral syphilis with psychosis; died of starvation, 14 Nov 1929. SOURCE: VA File XC 2624105, Floyd H. Crumbly.

Assistance acknowledged in preface of Beasley's book: *Negro Trailblazers*. Crumbly provided books, furnished names of black officers, offered helpful suggestions, critiqued chapter on black soldiers. SOURCE: Beasley, *Negro Trailblazers*.

See **CARROLL**, Joseph H., First Lieutenant, 49th Infantry; **GRANT**, Thomas, Captain, L/48th Infantry; **HEAGAN**, Joel, First Sergeant, D/49th Infantry; **LOVELACE**, Scott, Corporal, I/10th Cavalry; **THOMAS**, James H., First Lieutenant, D/49th Infantry; **WILLIAMS**, George A., Second Lieutenant, 49th Infantry

CRUMIEL, Christopher P.; Sergeant; F/10th Cav. Acquitted by general court martial, Ft Lyon, CO, of charges that he disobeyed order of Bvt. Maj. George Armes to cease playing with privates of company and that he neglected duty by marching troops to meals in unsoldierly manner. SOURCE: GCMO 25, DeptMo, 16 Apr 1869.

CRUMP, Edward W.; Private; C/9th Cav. Born St. Francisville, LA, to Lewis and Maria Crump, 1867; enlisted Washington, DC, Ht 5'9", occupation porter, 16 Apr 1885; discharged, Ft Meade, SD, as sergeant, H/25th Infantry; enlisted Baltimore, MD, 10 Jun 1889; discharged Ft Leavenworth, KS, 9 Sep 1892; retired from Washington public schools as steam engineer, with $100 per month pension, 1932; military pension $45 per month, 1932; wife earned $3100 per year from Washington public schools, 1932; died 21 Nov 1947; buried Arlington National Cemetery. SOURCE: VA File C 2359804, Edward W. Crump.

Served with Sgt. Barney McKay, C/9th Cavalry, Ft Duchesne, UT, 1889–90; was with detachment commanded by McKay, which went to crossing of Uintah River, around thirteen miles from post, as escort for Chaplain Scott, Mar 1889; with river over banks, waded through cold water from around nine A.M. to sundown; many contracted colds and rheumatism, including McKay, who was hospitalized. SOURCE: Affidavit, Crump, 1917, VA File XC 2659455, Barney McKay.

Lived with wife Sadie in Washington at 406 Franklin Street, NW, in 1894; at 1903 9 1/2 Street, NW, in 1895; at 117 U Street, NW, from 1933; pension of $55 per month as of 12 Aug 1942, increased to $60 as of 5 Jun 1944. SOURCE: VA File C 2359804, Edward W. Crump.

Renews subscription; is in good health; never drank, smoked, or gambled. SOURCE: *Winners of the West* 15 (Jul 1938): 8.

CRUMP, Horace; K/10th Cav. Original member of 10th Cavalry; in troop when organized, Ft Riley, KS, 1 Sep 1867. SOURCE: McMiller, "Buffalo Soldiers," 77.

CRUSE, Peter; Private; A/9th Cav. Born Rockcastle Co., KY; enlisted Landin, KY, occupation laborer, 22 Feb 1893; joined H Troop at Ft Robinson, NE, age 29, 28 May 1895; fined five times by summary court martials, 1893–96; discharged, character good, single, 21 May 1896; reenlisted. SOURCE: Descriptive Book, H/9 Cav.

Private, H/9th Cavalry, deposited $15 with paymaster, Ft Robinson, 1897–98.

Veteran of Spanish-American War and Philippine Insurrection; at Ft D. A. Russell, WY, in 1910. SOURCE: *Illustrated Review: Ninth Cavalry.*

CRUTCHEN, James; Private; L/10th Cav. Served in 10th Cavalry, 1898; remained in U.S. during war with Spain. SOURCE: Cashin, *Under Fire with the Tenth Cavalry*, 350.

CRUTCHER, Chesterfield; Private; 24th Inf. Harassed and arrested by police, Manila, Philippines, 19 Jun 1902. SOURCE: CO, 24 Inf, to Chief of Police, Manila, 21 Jun 1902.

CRUTCHER, James; Corporal; L/10th Cav. Promoted from private, Sep 1899. SOURCE: *ANJ* 37 (7 Oct 1899): 122.

CRUTCHFIELD, Daniel; Recruit; Colored Detachment/Mounted Service. Convicted by general court martial, Jefferson Barracks, MO, of fighting with Recruit Stanley Chester, Colored Detachment, without good and sufficient provocation, and cutting Chester on body with pocket knife, near mess hall of Company A of Instruction, Jefferson Barracks, 11 Nov 1886; sentenced to one month's confinement and $10 fine. SOURCE: GCMO 101, AGO, 8 Dec 1886.

CUGG, John; Corporal; G/9th Cav. Authorized to reenlist as married soldier. SOURCE: Letter, GO, 13 Aug 1897.

CUMBY, George; Trumpeter; H/9th Cav. Died of variola in the Philippines, 31 Dec 1901. SOURCE: *ANJ* 39 (1 Mar 1902): 645.

CUMMERS, William; A/10th Cav. Original member of 10th Cavalry; in troop when organized, Ft Leavenworth, KS, 18 Feb 1867. SOURCE: McMiller, "Buffalo Soldiers," 68.

CUMMINGS, Arthur. Twice married; Spanish war veteran died in the Philippines, 1941; granddaughter Sadie Burdett, formerly bar girl, now cooks in local barrooms, provides for four children with earnings and $50 per month from brother in U.S. SOURCE: Thompson, "Veterans Who Never Came Home," 112.

CUMMINGS, William; Private; F/24th Inf. Ranked number 190 among rifle experts with 68.33 percent. SOURCE: GO 79, AGO, 1 Jun 1905.

CUNNINGHAM, Eugene; Private; H/9th Cav. At Ft D. A. Russell, WY, in 1910; resident of Tuscaloosa, AL. SOURCE: *Illustrated Review: Ninth Cavalry,* with picture.

CUNNINGHAM, George; Private; H/10th Cav. Sick in Ft Robinson, NE, hospital, 19 Sep–20 Oct 1904.

CUNNINGHAM, Levi; Private; M/10th Cav. Served in 10th Cavalry, 1898; remained in U.S. during war with Spain. SOURCE: Cashin, *Under Fire with the Tenth Cavalry*, 351.

CUNNINGHAM, Samuel; Private; K/10th Cav. Original member of 10th Cavalry; in troop when organized, Ft Riley, KS, 1 Sep 1867. SOURCE: McMiller, "Buffalo Soldiers," 77.

Commander recommends remission of dishonorable discharge and disapproval of conviction for desertion. SOURCE: CO, Det 10 Cav, Ft Dodge, KS, to AAG, DeptMo, 17 May 1869, LR, Det 10 Cav, 1868–69.

CUNNINGHAM, Willie; Trumpeter; B/9th Cav. At Ft D. A. Russell, WY, in 1910; marksman. SOURCE: *Illustrated Review: Ninth Cavalry*, with picture.

CURD, R.; Private; B/24th Inf. Sentenced to dishonorable discharge and one year for trying to kill Pvt. Fred Hamilton by shooting him in head, Ft Huachuca, AZ, 16 Nov 1893. SOURCE: *ANJ* 30 (3 Mar 1894): 459.

CURING, George; Private; 24th Inf. Transferred from I/9th Cavalry. SOURCE: SO 154, AGO, 7 Jul 1891.

CURL, Henry W.; Private; H/10th Cav. Sentenced. SOURCE: SO 195, DeptMo, 24 Oct 1902.

CURRANT, Albert; Private; B/10th Cav. Served in 10th Cavalry, 1898; remained in U.S. during war with Spain. SOURCE: Cashin, *Under Fire with the Tenth Cavalry*, 339.

CURRY, Eugene; Private; E/10th Cav. Served in 10th Cavalry, 1898; remained in U.S. during war with Spain. SOURCE: Cashin, *Under Fire with the Tenth Cavalry*, 343.

CURRY, George; Private; C/9th Cav. While in F Troop, convicted by garrison court martial of conduct to prejudice of good order and discipline, Ft Robinson, NE; sentenced to thirty days, first seven of them in solitary on bread and water, and loss of one month's pay. SOURCE: Order 48, 10 Mar 1886, Post Orders, Ft Robinson.

Discharged, end of term, Ft Robinson, 15 Feb 1887.

CURRY, John; Corporal; H/25th Inf. Promoted from private. SOURCE: *ANR* 38 (23 Sep 1905): 21.

CURRY, Perry; H/10th Cav. Original member of 10th Cavalry; in troop when organized, Ft Leavenworth, KS, 21 Jul 1867. SOURCE: McMiller, "Buffalo Soldiers," 75.

See **JACKSON**, Orange, 10th Cavalry

CURTIS, Alexander; Corporal; C/25th Inf. Retired from San Carlos, AZ, Aug 1899. SOURCE: *ANJ* 36 (19 Aug 1899): 1215.

CURTIS, Edward O.; Private; F/24th Inf. Born in New York; third enlistment, Band/24th Infantry, Ft Supply,

Indian Territory, Ht 5'9", brown complexion, black eyes and hair, age 35, 27 Jan 1886; previously served until 20 Oct 1884; discharged, married with four children, character very good, $81 deposits, $101 clothing, $72 retained, Ft Bayard, NM, 26 Jan 1891; reenlisted, 27 Jan 1891; transferred to F/24th Infantry, 29 Jun 1893, married with three minor children, character very good, $155 deposits, $86 clothing, $29 retained. SOURCE: Descriptive Book, 24 Inf NCS & Band.

CURTIS, Felix; K/10th Cav. Original member of 10th Cavalry; in troop when organized, Ft Riley, KS, 1 Sep 1867. SOURCE: McMiller, "Buffalo Soldiers," 77.

CURTIS, Grant; Private; F/10th Cav. Served in 10th Cavalry in Cuba, 1898. SOURCE: Cashin, *Under Fire with the Tenth Cavalry*, 344.

CURTIS, J. Webb; Contract Surgeon; 48th Inf. Mentioned. SOURCE: San Francisco *Chronicle*, 15 Nov 1899.

CURTIS, John; Private; H/9th Cav. Told sergeant to go to hell when ordered to help feed horses; confined for two months, Ft Concho, TX, 1874. SOURCE: Leckie, *The Buffalo Soldiers*, 98.

CURTIS, Richard; Sergeant; G/24th Inf. Quartermaster sergeant, G/24th Infantry, commended for volunteering for duty at yellow fever hospital, Cuba, 17 Jul 1898. SOURCE: GO 15, AGO, 13 Feb 1900.

Distinguished service noted. SOURCE: *ANJ* 37 (24 Feb 1900): 611.

Retires as sergeant, G/24th Infantry. SOURCE: *ANJ* 38 (27 Apr 1901): 843.

CUSHINGBERRY, Porter; Private; I/24th Inf. Enlisted Louisville, KY, 29 Mar 1899. SOURCE: Muster Roll, I/24 Inf, Mar–Apr 1899.

On detached service, Arayat, Philippines, since 31 Oct 1899. SOURCE: Muster Roll, I/24 Inf, Sep–Oct 1899.

Sentenced by summary court to forfeit $10 and spend ten days under guard at hard labor. SOURCE: Muster Roll, I/24 Inf, Nov–Dec 1899.

CUSTARD, Elijah; Corporal; M/25th Inf. Promoted from private, Aug 1905; died Sep 1905.

CUSTER, Levi; Private; H/9th Cav. Wounded in side, Pagbilao, Luzon, Philippines, 26 May 1901. SOURCE: *ANJ* 38 (27 Jul 1901): 1169.

Wounded while with detachment commanded by Lieutenant Stodter at Mataray, Philippines, May 1901. SOURCE: Hamilton, "History of the Ninth Cavalry," 107; *Illustrated Review: Ninth Cavalry*.

CYRUS; Artificer; A/24th Inf. At Ft Huachuca, AZ, 1893. *See* **HAM**, James, Sergeant, B/24th Infantry

D

DABBS, Erasmus T.; Private; C/25th Inf. Dishonorable discharge, Brownsville. SOURCE: SO 266, AGO, 9 Nov 1906.

DABNEY, G.; Corporal; E/24th Inf. Promoted from private, Ft Bayard, NM, May 1891. SOURCE: Cleveland *Gazette*, 9 May 1891.

DABNEY, George; Private; I/10th Cav. Served in 10th Cavalry, 1898; remained in U.S. during war with Spain. SOURCE: Cashin, *Under Fire with the Tenth Cavalry*, 348.

DADE, Albert; Private; D/10th Cav. Served in 10th Cavalry, 1898; remained in U.S. during war with Spain. SOURCE: Cashin, *Under Fire with the Tenth Cavalry*, 341.

DADE, Allan; Private; B/9th Cav. On detached service, Ft Bayard, NM, 16 Jan-9 Feb 1881. SOURCE: Regt Returns, 9 Cav, Feb 1881.

DADE, Charles; Corporal; I/10th Cav. Served in 10th Cavalry in Cuba, 1898. SOURCE: Cashin, *Under Fire with the Tenth Cavalry*, 347.

DADE, Charles; Cook; D/25th Inf. Dishonorable discharge, Brownsville. SOURCE: SO 266, AGO, 9 Nov 1906.

The scene, while surrendering his rifle at Ft Reno, OK, after his discharge: " 'All right sir, all right, sir, Lieut. Higgins, here it is.' Dade handled the rifle caressingly as he passed it over to the officer. He turned his face to hide the tears which were falling from his eyes upon the shining barrel of the gun. 'I just can't help it,' he muttered apologetically to a comrade as he turned away. 'I've been in the service 22 years and it's hard to give up a gun that is about like my own kinfolks.' " SOURCE: Cleveland *Gazette*, 24 Nov 1906.

DAGGETT, Samuel; Private; D/9th Cav. Deserted San Francisco, CA, 9 Nov 1902. SOURCE: Regt Returns, 9 Cav, Nov 1902.

DAGGS, William H.; L/10th Cav. Original member of 10th Cavalry; in troop when organized, Ft Riley, KS, 21 Sep 1867. SOURCE: McMiller, "Buffalo Soldiers," 78.

DAILY; Private; E/24th Inf. Wife killed by Private Levi Johnson, Ft Sill, Indian Territory, 9 Aug 1887. SOURCE: *ANJ* 25 (3 Sep 1887): 103.
See JOHNSON, Levi, Private, C/24th Infantry

DAILY, Daniel T.; Private; I/10th Cav. Sergeant, released to duty from treatment for secondary syphilis, Ft Robinson, NE, 24 Aug 1903. SOURCE: Post Surgeon to CO, I/10, 24 Aug 1903, LS, Post Surgeon, Ft Robinson.

Transferred to Ft Leavenworth, KS. SOURCE: SO 207, AGO, 22 Oct 1903.

Private, five-year veteran, Ft Robinson; surgeon recommends his discharge; has venereal disease and is unfit for service. SOURCE: Post Surgeon to Post Adj, 10 Feb 1904, LS, Post Surgeon, Ft Robinson.

DAIS, William; Private; K/25th Inf. At Ft Niobrara, NE, 1904. SOURCE: Wilson, "History of Fort Niobrara."

DAKEY, Wesley; Private; D/24th Inf. Deserted on Balia Balia Road, Philippines, 15 Aug 1899, as reported in letter, Adjutant General's Office, 19 Sep 1899. SOURCE: Regt Returns, 24 Inf, Sep 1899.

DALE, Thomas; Corporal; H/9th Cav. Served in Lincoln County, NM, war, 1878. SOURCE: Leckie, *The Buffalo Soldiers*, 198.

DALE, Thomas; Corporal; H/9th Cav. Assigned with three privates to aid sheriff in maintaining order, Lincoln, NM, Apr 1878. SOURCE: Billington, *New Mexico's Buffalo Soldiers*, 75.

DALES, John; QM Sgt; E/25th Inf. Sergeant, at Ft Sisseton, SD, authorized three-month furlough. SOURCE: *ANJ* 25 (5 May 1888): 815.

First sergeant, at Ft Buford, ND, 1893. SOURCE: Nankivell, *History of the Twenty-fifth Infantry*, 50.

Quartermaster sergeant, retired, Jul 1901. SOURCE: *ANJ* 38 (20 Jul 1901): 1139.

Pallbearer for Col. Andrew Burt, who had requested that men of 25th Infantry carry his coffin. SOURCE: Curtis, *The Black Soldier*, 49.

DALLANGER, George; Corporal; E/9th Cav. At Ft D. A. Russell, WY, in 1910; resident of 3449 State St., Chicago. SOURCE: *Illustrated Review: Ninth Cavalry*, with picture.

DALRYMPLE, John; Private; E/9th Cav. Departed Ft Apache, AZ, with troop for California and transport to the Philippines; sailed aboard U.S. Army Transport *Warren*, Aug 1900; stationed at Albay with company, commanded by Capt. Frank West, Sep 1900; unit moved to Camalig, Albay, began scouting, convoying, patrolling duty, which they continued through tour of duty in islands. SOURCE: Regt Returns, 9 Cav, Jul–Oct 1900.

Deserted along with Pvts. Edmond DuBose and Lewis Russell, both of E/9th Cavalry, Camalig, 1 Mar 1901. SOURCE: Regt Returns, 9 Cav, Mar 1901.

"Comandante Toledo with five soldiers and five serviceable rifles and one Krag carbine . . . surrendered at Nueva Caceres, July 21st. He reported the death of the negro deserter Dalrymple from calentura (fever)." SOURCE: Manila *Times*, 26 Jul 1901.

See **DuBOSE**, Edmond, Private, E/9th Cavalry

DAMUS, Manie; Private; C/24th Inf. On special duty as assistant, post exchange, Ft Huachuca, AZ. SOURCE: Order 169, Ft Huachuca, 17 Nov 1893, Letters and Orders Received, 24 Inf, 1893.

DANCE, William; Private; K/24th Inf. Died of malaria in the Philippines, 25 Nov 1899. SOURCE: *ANJ* 37 (13 Jan 1900): 463.

Native of Richmond, died of fever in the Philippines "through bad treatment." SOURCE: Richmond *Planet*, 14 Apr 1900.

DANDRIDGE, George; Private; K/24th Inf. Fined $15 for quarrel with native woman, Anastacia Canido, in which he struck her several times, causing her to flee to camp in nightclothes, Cabanatuan, Philippines, 14 Apr 1904; also left quarters without permission while sick, 15 Apr 1901; witness: Private J. H. Faggins, K/24th Infantry. SOURCE: Name File, 24 Inf.

DANDRIDGE, Luther; Private; G/10th Cav. Commander, 10th Cavalry, refers the charges of petty larceny against him to field offficers' court for trial, 19 Jun 1873. SOURCE: ES, 10 Cav, 1873–83.

DANDRIDGE, Richard; F/10th Cav. Original member of 10th Cavalry; in troop when organized, Ft Leavenworth, KS, 21 Jun 1867. SOURCE: McMiller, "Buffalo Soldiers," 73.

DANDRIDGE, Turner; Private; I/24th Inf. Enlisted Richmond, VA, 10 Aug 1898. SOURCE: Muster Roll, I/24 Inf, Jan–Feb 1899.

Discharged, character good, $40 deposits, $4.98 clothing, 31 Dec 1899. SOURCE: Muster Roll, I/24 Inf, Nov–Dec 1899.

Chaplain, Col. Charles Young Camp No. 24, National Indian War Veterans, Washington, DC. SOURCE: *Winners of the West* 6 (Jun 1929): 4.

DANIEL, Boyd; Sergeant; L/10th Cav. Drowned late 1870. SOURCE: Leckie, *The Buffalo Soldiers*, 56.

DANIEL, J. R.; Corporal; H/25th Inf. Made oration, "Some Men Who Were in the Right Place," Ft Missoula, MT,

4 Jul 1892. SOURCE: Monthly Report, Chaplain Steward, Sep 1892, AGO File 4634 ACP 91.

DANIEL, Lawrence; Private; B/25th Inf. Dishonorable discharge, Brownsville. SOURCE: SO 266, AGO, 9 Nov 1906.

DANIEL, Thomas; D/10th Cav. Original member of 10th Cavalry; in troop when organized, Ft Leavenworth, KS, 1 Jun 1867. SOURCE: McMiller, "Buffalo Soldiers," 71.

DANIELL, Robert; Sergeant; A/9th Cav. Sergeant, A/9th Cavalry, at Ft Stanton, NM, 1881. SOURCE: Regt Returns, 9 Cav, Jan 1881.

Served in H/10th Cavalry with Benjamin Bard; resided at 914 North 8th Street, Richmond, VA, in 1912. SOURCE: VA File XC 2625176, Benjamin Bard.

DANIELS, Alvin; Private; G/25th Inf. Wounded in action, El Caney, Cuba, 1 Jul 1898. SOURCE: Nankivell, *History of the Twenty-fifth Infantry*, 83.

DANIELS, Blane J.; Private; H/9th Cav. At Ft D. A. Russell, WY, in 1910; resident of Evansville, IN. SOURCE: *Illustrated Review: Ninth Cavalry,* with picture.

DANIELS, Charles; Private; B/9th Cav. At Ft Robinson, NE, 1888. See **HERBERT**, Thomas H., Private, K/9th Cavalry

DANIELS, E. C.; Sergeant; K/25th Inf. In the Philippines, 1899. SOURCE: Richmond *Planet*, 16 Dec 1899.

DANIELS, Edward L.; Corporal; B/25th Inf. Veteran of Cuban campaign, skilled at topographical sketches. SOURCE: Weaver, *The Brownsville Raid*, 32.

Dishonorable discharge, Brownsville. SOURCE: SO 266, AGO, 9 Nov 1906.

One of fourteen cleared of involvement in Brownsville raid by court in 1910 and authorized to reenlist. SOURCE: Weaver, *The Brownsville Raid*, 298.

DANIELS, Hayes; Private; L/10th Cav. Served in 10th Cavalry, 1898; remained in U.S. during war with Spain. SOURCE: Cashin, *Under Fire with the Tenth Cavalry*, 350.

DANIELS, Henry; Private; 24th Inf. At Ft Bayard, NM, Jul 1888; selected for Department of Arizona rifle competition, Ft Wingate, NM. SOURCE: Billington, *New Mexico's Buffalo Soldiers*, 154.

DANIELS, John; I/10th Cav. Original member of 10th Cavalry; in troop when organized, Ft Riley, KS, 15 Aug 1867. SOURCE: McMiller, "Buffalo Soldiers," 76.

Wounded in action in Beecher's Island, KS, fight, 1868. SOURCE: Leckie, *The Buffalo Soldiers*, 38.

DANIELS, Jordan; Private; B/9th Cav. At Ft D. A. Russell, WY, in 1910; sharpshooter. SOURCE: *Illustrated Review: Ninth Cavalry,* with picture.

DANIELS, Moses; G/10th Cav. Original member of 10th Cavalry; in troop when organized, Ft Leavenworth, KS, 5 Jul 1867. SOURCE: McMiller, "Buffalo Soldiers," 74.

DANIELS, Thomas; H/10th Cav. Original member of 10th Cavalry; in troop when organized, Ft Leavenworth, KS, 21 Jul 1867. SOURCE: McMiller, "Buffalo Soldiers," 75.

DANIELS, William; Private; B/9th Cav. At Ft D. A. Russell, WY, in 1910; marksman. SOURCE: *Illustrated Review: Ninth Cavalry,*

DANIELS, William H.; Saddler; F/10th Cav. Served in 10th Cavalry in Cuba, 1898. SOURCE: Cashin, *Under Fire with the Tenth Cavalry,* 343.
Commended for conspicuous bravery with Hotchkiss Guns, Battle of Santiago, Cuba, 1 Jul 1898. SOURCE: GO 15, AGO, 13 Feb 1900; SecWar, *AR 1898,* 335.

DANSBURY, James W.; D/10th Cav. Admitted to Soldiers Home with disability, age 28, after three years and four months' service, 23 May 1889. SOURCE: SecWar, *AR 1889,* 1013.

DAPSON, Augustus; M/10th Cav. Original member of 10th Cavalry; in troop when organized, Ft Riley, KS, 15 Oct 1867. SOURCE: McMiller, "Buffalo Soldiers," 79.

DARCOTT, Thomas; F/10th Cav. Original member of 10th Cavalry; in troop when organized, Ft Leavenworth, KS, 21 Jun 1867. SOURCE: McMiller, "Buffalo Soldiers," 73.

DARCY; Private; K/10th Cav. His fine paid by Maj. J. E. Yard. SOURCE: Adj, Ft Hays, KS, to Adj, Det 10 Cav, camp near Ft Hays, 8 Jun 1868, LR, Det 10 Cav, 1868-69.

DARE, Lewis; D/10th Cav. Served 1867–72; present at 50th anniversary commemoration of Custer's defeat at Little Big Horn; now age 83, resides in Latiens, OK. SOURCE: *Winners of the West* 3 (Aug 1926): 5.

DARLING, A. W.; G/9th Cav. Discharged. SOURCE: SO 226, AGO, 25 Sep 1896.

DARLING, James A.; A/24th Inf. Convicted of felonious assault with intent to rape, Philippines, Jul 1901; sentenced to seven years.

DARNELL, Strowder; Private; D/25th Inf. Dishonorable discharge, Brownsville. SOURCE: SO 266, AGO, 9 Nov 1906.

DARRACE, John; M/10th Cav. Original member of 10th Cavalry; in troop when organized, Ft Riley, KS, 15 Oct 1867. SOURCE: McMiller, "Buffalo Soldiers," 79.

DARROW, Washington; Chief Musician; Band/ 10th Cav. Served in 10th Cavalry in Cuba, 1898; died of fever. SOURCE: Cashin, *Under Fire with the Tenth Cavalry,* 352.

DARTON, Stephen; Corporal; B/9th Cav. At Ft D. A. Russell, WY, in 1910; sharpshooter. SOURCE: *Illustrated Review: Ninth Cavalry,* with picture.

DAUGHERTY, Harvey; Private; K/25th Inf. At Ft Niobrara, NE, 1904. SOURCE: Wilson, "History of Fort Niobrara."

DAUGLASH, J. W. B., Jr.; Private; G/10th Cav. Served in 10th Cavalry in Cuba, 1898. SOURCE: Cashin, *Under Fire with the Tenth Cavalry,* 345.

DAULUPHUS, Jean; Private; F/9th Cav. Expert rifleman at Ft D. A. Russell, WY, in 1910; resident of Charlotte, NC. SOURCE: *Illustrated Review: Ninth Cavalry.*

DAVENGER, Jacob B.; Private; I/24th Inf. Enlisted Philadelphia, PA, 8 Jul 1899. SOURCE: Muster Roll, I/24 Inf, Jul–Aug 1899.
Fined $3 by summary court, 23 Sep 1899; joined company, 29 Sep 1899. SOURCE: Muster Roll, I/24 Inf, Sep–Oct 1899.

DAVENPORT, Leonard; A/49th Inf. Convicted of robbery in the Philippines, Apr 1900; sentenced to two years.

DAVES, John E.; Private; L/24th Inf. Came in first place in obstacle race, military tourney, Albany, NY, autumn 1909. SOURCE: Muller, *The Twenty Fourth Infantry,* 60.

DAVID, James; D/10th Cav. Original member of 10th Cavalry; in troop when organized, Ft Leavenworth, KS, 1 Jun 1867. SOURCE: McMiller, "Buffalo Soldiers," 71.

DAVIDSON, John A.; Private; A/10th Cav. Served in 10th Cavalry, 1898; remained in U.S. during war with Spain. SOURCE: Cashin, *Under Fire with the Tenth Cavalry,* 337.

DAVIDSON, Walter C.; Private; K/10th Cav. Served in 10th Cavalry, 1898; remained in U.S. during war with Spain. SOURCE: Cashin, *Under Fire with the Tenth Cavalry,* 349.

DAVIS; Corporal; L/10th Cav. Eighth best pistol shot, Departments of the Missouri and Texas, 1903. SOURCE: Glass, *History of the Tenth Cavalry,* 43.

DAVIS, Abraham; Sergeant; F/10th Cav. Served in 10th Cavalry in Cuba, 1898. SOURCE: Cashin, *Under Fire with the Tenth Cavalry,* 344.

DAVIS, Albert; Corporal; G/10th Cav. Served in 10th Cavalry in Cuba, 1898. SOURCE: Cashin, *Under Fire with the Tenth Cavalry,* 345.

DAVIS, Amos; Recruit; Colored Inf. Convicted of desertion by general court martial, Newport Barracks, KY; sentenced to dishonorable discharge and three years. SOURCE: GCMO 102, AGO, 8 Dec 1875.

DAVIS, Arthur; Private; H/10th Cav. Jailed for forgery. SOURCE: Cheyenne *Daily Leader*, 22 Feb 1907.

DAVIS, Ben; Private; L/9th Cav. Sick, Ft Bayard, NM, 25 Sep 1880–13 Jan 1881. SOURCE: Regt Returns, 9 Cav, Jan 1881.

DAVIS, Benjamin; Corporal; E/9th Cav. Private, I/9th Cavalry, sentenced to ten days and $3 fine for fighting with Pvt. Moses Harris, I/9th Cavalry, in barracks, Ft Robinson, NE, 6 Dec 1888. SOURCE: Order 239, 12 Dec 1888, Post Orders, Ft Robinson.

Private, I/9th Cavalry, convicted of conduct to prejudice of good order and discipline, throwing bowl at Pvt. William Victor, I/9th Cavalry, in troop dining room, Ft Robinson, 13 Mar 1889; sentenced to thirty days and $10 fine. SOURCE: Order 68, 22 Mar 1889, Post Orders, Ft Robinson.

Corporal, E/9th Cavalry, reprimanded by garrison court martial for being late for stable duty with troop. SOURCE: Order 15, 17 Feb 1893, Post Orders, Ft Robinson.

DAVIS, Benjamin; G/25th Inf. Admitted to Soldiers Home, age 42, after twenty-one years and four months' service, 2 Oct 1885. SOURCE: SecWar, *AR 1886*, 737.

DAVIS, Benjamin F.; QM Sgt; U.S. Army. Original member of M/10th Cavalry; in troop when organized, Ft Riley, KS, 15 Oct 1867. SOURCE: McMiller, "Buffalo Soldiers," 79.

Joined regiment in 1867; retired as post quartermaster sergeant. SOURCE: Baker, Roster.

Appointed post quartermaster sergeant, from regimental sergeant major, 9th Cavalry, 20 Jan 1885. SOURCE: Roster, 9 Cav.

Retired Ft Robinson, NE, after reception and banquet, 23 Apr 1895, with nineteen years as regimental sergeant major and post quartermaster sergeant. SOURCE: Cleveland *Gazette*, 4 May 1895.

Born Chester Co., PA, 1849; Civil War veteran; served over thirty-one years; appointed quartermaster sergeant, 1885; died 9 Nov 1921; buried with military honors, Soldiers Home Cemetery, Washington, DC; survived by widow, three daughters, three grandchildren; was member of National Association for the Advancement of Colored People. SOURCE: *Crisis* 24 (May 1922): 27.

Knew Robert Benjamin from Jun 1874 until his death; soldiered together in Texas, corresponded and kept track of each other; best man at Benjamin's wedding to Mary Young, Junction City, KS; now age 69 and residing at 1615 17th St., NW, Washington, DC. SOURCE: Affidavit, Davis, 9 Dec 1918, VA File WC 927337, Robert A. Benjamin.

DAVIS, Benjamin O.; G/10th Cav. Original member of 10th Cavalry; in troop when organized, Ft Leavenworth, KS, 5 Jul 1867. SOURCE: McMiller, "Buffalo Soldiers," 74.

DAVIS, Benjamin O.; Lt Col.; U.S. Army. First colored man to pass examination for regular Army commission, Ft Leavenworth, KS, and scored third of eighteen who took test; son of Messenger Davis of office of Secretary of the Interior; was major, Washington Colored High School cadet corps; former lieutenant, 8th U.S. Volunteer Infantry; then enlisted in 9th Cavalry and served one year as squadron sergeant major. SOURCE: Richmond *Planet*, 30 Mar 1901.

Appointment as second lieutenant, 10th Cavalry, dates from 2 Feb 1901. SOURCE: *ANJ* 38 (1 Jun 1901): 966.

First black officer commissioned from ranks into regular Army. SOURCE: Indianapolis *Freeman*, 15 Jun 1901.

Graduate of Washington Colored High School. SOURCE: *The Voice of the Negro* 1 (Jun 1904): 222.

Arrived Ft Washakie, WY, from Rawlins, WY. SOURCE: *Fremont Clipper*, 22 Aug 1902.

Was in Lander, WY, shopping with his wife last Saturday. SOURCE: *Fremont Clipper*, 19 Dec 1902.

One of three hundred enlisted men commissioned from the ranks into regular Army, 1898–1902, but one of two, with John E. Green, who were black. SOURCE: Fletcher, *The Black Soldier*, 165.

Returned to Ft Washakie from thirty-day leave in Washington, DC, where his wife will spend winter. SOURCE: *Fremont Clipper*, 30 Dec 1904.

Promoted to first lieutenant, Apr 1905.

Arrived Ft Robinson, NE, 21 Apr 1905; commander, M/10th Cavalry, 24–29 May and 23–28 Jun 1905; absent with leave, 4–15 Jun 1905; on detached service at Wilberforce University, OH, 27 Aug 1905, in accordance with Special Order 166, Adjutant General's Office, 1905. SOURCE: Post Returns, Ft Robinson.

Detailed to Wilberforce as military instructor. SOURCE: Indianapolis *Freeman*, 21 Oct 1905.

Dropped from post returns, Ft Robinson, May 1907; still at Wilberforce.

Named military attache to Liberia, a new position established to develop closer relations. SOURCE: Cleveland *Gazette*, 4 Dec 1909.

Will return from Liberia to duty with 9th Cavalry, Ft D. A. Russell, WY. SOURCE: Cleveland *Gazette*, 13 Jan 1912.

Joined regiment from duty as military attache in Africa. SOURCE: Cheyenne *State Leader*, 19 Jan 1912.

Mentioned. SOURCE: Work, *The Negro Yearbook, 1912*, 77.

Assigned as military instructor at Wilberforce. SOURCE: Cleveland *Gazette*, 5 Sep 1914.

As military instructor and commander at Wilberforce. SOURCE: Joiner, *A Half Century of Freedom*, 108.

Recently promoted to lieutenant colonel from major. SOURCE: Cleveland *Gazette*, 14 Sep 1918.

Mentioned. SOURCE: Work, *The Negro Yearbook, 1918–1919*, 228.

DAVIS, Charles; D/10th Cav. Original member of 10th Cavalry; in troop when organized, Ft Leavenworth, KS, 1 Jun 1867. SOURCE: McMiller, "Buffalo Soldiers," 71.

DAVIS, Charles; Sergeant; M/9th Cav. Corporal, ranked number 18, Northern Division rifle competition, Ft Sheridan, IL, 1906. SOURCE: GO 198, AGO, 6 Dec 1906.

Veteran of Philippine Insurrection; sergeant, at Ft D. A. Russell, WY, in 1910; sharpshooter. SOURCE: *Illustrated Review: Ninth Cavalry,* with picture.

DAVIS, Charles; Private; I/9th Cav. At Ft D. A. Russell, WY, in 1910; resident of Lexington, KY; sharpshooter. SOURCE: *Illustrated Review: Ninth Cavalry,* with picture.

DAVIS, Charles H.; Sergeant; G/10th Cav. Original member of 10th Cavalry; in troop when organized, Ft Leavenworth, KS, 5 Jul 1867. SOURCE: McMiller, "Buffalo Soldiers," 74.

Honorable mention for gallantry in attacking with small detachment of G Troop and repulsing large band of Cheyennes, Saline River, KS, 19 Sep 1867. SOURCE: Baker, Roster; Cashin, *Under Fire with the Tenth Cavalry,* 28–30.

See **FORD**, George W., Quartermaster Sergeant, 10th Cavalry

DAVIS, Clifford H.; Private; K/10th Cav. Released to duty from treatment for acute gonorrhea, Ft Robinson, NE, 15 Oct 1903. SOURCE: Post Surgeon to CO, Det 10 Cav, 15 Oct 1903, LS, Post Surgeon, Ft Robinson.

General court martial sentence published. SOURCE: SO 42, DeptMo, 4 Mar 1904.

DAVIS, Cornelius; B/10th Cav. Enlisted Memphis, TN. SOURCE: LS, 10 Cav, 1866–67.

Original member of 10th Cavalry; in troop when organized, Ft Leavenworth, KS, 1 Apr 1867. SOURCE: McMiller, "Buffalo Soldiers," 69.

DAVIS, David L.; Sergeant; F/10th Cav. At Ft Apache, AZ, 1890, subscribed $.50 to testimonial to General Grierson. SOURCE: List of subscriptions, 23 Apr 1890, 10th Cavalry papers, MHI.

To enter Army and Navy Hospital, Hot Springs, AR, from Ft Grant, AZ. SOURCE: *ANJ* 27 (24 May 1890): 738.

DAVIS, Dudley; Private; G/10th Cav. Honorable mention for bravery against Comanches, Double Mountain Fork, Brazos River, TX, 5 Feb 1874, and for bravery against Indians, Lake Quemado, TX, 3 Aug 1880. SOURCE: Baker, Roster.

DAVIS, Ed; Sergeant; G/10th Cav. In Kansas, 1867. SOURCE: Leckie, *The Buffalo Soldiers,* 25.

DAVIS, Edward; Private; K/9th Cav. Private, D/9th Cavalry, in hands of civil authorities, Buffalo, WY, 1–18

May 1890, and Crawford, NE, 28–30 Mar 1893. SOURCE: Regt Returns, 9 Cav.

Discharge disapproved. SOURCE: Letter, AGO, 15 Apr 1895.

Charges withdrawn. SOURCE: Letter, DP, 11 Sep 1895.

Discharged, end of term, private, H/9th Cavalry, with $8 clothing and $47 retained pay, 22 Apr 1897. SOURCE: CO, H/9, to Chief PM, DP, 17 Apr 1897, LS, H/9 Cav.

Wounded in action at San Juan, Cuba, 2 Jul 1898; suffering from scalp wound, blood streaming down his face, he waited only long enough for bandage, then joined troops in advance. SOURCE: SecWar, *AR 1898,* 707, 709.

Awarded certificate of merit for distinguished service in Cuba, Jul 1898. SOURCE: Steward, *The Colored Regulars,* 280; *ANJ* 37 (24 Feb 1900): 611.

Commended for gallantry, 1 Jul 1898. SOURCE: GO 15, AGO, 13 Feb 1900.

Veteran of Indian wars, Spanish-American War, and Philippine Insurrection; private, K/9th Cavalry, at Ft D. A. Russell, WY, in 1910; resident of Galveston, TX. SOURCE: *Illustrated Review: Ninth Cavalry,* with picture.

DAVIS, Elijah; Private; A/9th Cav. At Ft Stanton, NM, 1881. SOURCE: Regt Returns, 9 Cav, Jan 1881.

DAVIS, Elijah; Private; E/9th Cav. At Ft D. A. Russell, WY, in 1910; resident of Peneville, KY. SOURCE: *Illustrated Review: Ninth Cavalry.*

DAVIS, Frank; Corporal; K/10th Cav. With two privates, ordered to carry dispatches to commander, Ft Hays, KS, with three days' rations and one-half day forage; to rest at Ft Hays one day and return. SOURCE: SO 24, Det 10 Cav, Ft Dodge, 17 May 1896, Orders, Det 10 Cav, 1868–69.

DAVIS, George; Private; I/10th Cav. Deserter apprehended, Ft Gibson, Indian Territory, 13 Mar 1873. SOURCE: Adj, 10 Cav, to CO, I/10 Cav, 14 Mar 1873, LS, 10 Cav, 1873–77.

Reward of $30 paid in Davis case. SOURCE: ES, 10 Cav, 1873–83.

DAVIS, Henry; Private; A/10th Cav. Arrived at Ft Leavenworth, KS, from Jefferson Barracks, MO. SOURCE: Adj, Ft Leavenworth, to HQ, Jefferson Bks, 9 Oct 1866, LS, 10 Cav, 1866–67.

Arrived at Ft Leavenworth without statement of clothing or enlistment papers. SOURCE: LS, 10 Cav, 1866–67.

Original member of 10th Cavalry; in troop when organized, Ft Leavenworth, 18 Feb 1867. SOURCE: McMiller, "Buffalo Soldiers," 68.

DAVIS, Henry; Private; L/10th Cav. Released to duty from treatment for gonorrhea, Ft Robinson, NE, 29 Jun 1903. SOURCE: Post Surgeon to CO, L/10, 29 Jun 1903, LS, Post Surgeon, Ft Robinson.

DAVIS, Henry R.; Private; M/10th Cav. Released to duty from treatment for gonorrhea, Ft Robinson, NE, Jun

1903. SOURCE: Post Surgeon to CO, M/10, Jun 1903, LS, Post Surgeon, Ft Robinson.

Released to duty from treatment for gonorrheal rheumatism, Ft Robinson. SOURCE: Post Surgeon to CO, M/10, 4 Aug 1903, LS, Post Surgeon, Ft Robinson.

DAVIS, Horace G.; Private; E/9th Cav. At Ft D. A. Russell, WY, in 1910; resident of Birmingham, AL. SOURCE: *Illustrated Review: Ninth Cavalry,* with picture.

DAVIS, Ira B.; Private; I/24th Inf. Sentenced to death for part in Houston riot, 1917. SOURCE: Haynes, *A Night of Violence,* 271.

Hanged, Ft Sam Houston, TX, 13 Dec 1917, for part in Houston riot. SOURCE: Cleveland *Gazette,* 15 Dec 1917.

DAVIS, J. D.; Private; D/24th Inf. At Cabanatuan, Philippines, 1901. *See* **BROWN**, Philip, Private, D/24th Infantry

DAVIS, Jake; Staff Sgt; 10th Cav. Retired at U.S. Military Academy, West Point, NY, from second squadron, 10th Cavalry. SOURCE: *Cavalry Journal* 41 (Jul 1932): 62.

DAVIS, James; I/10th Cav. Original member of 10th Cavalry; in troop when organized, Ft Riley, KS, 15 Aug 1867. SOURCE: McMiller, "Buffalo Soldiers," 76.

DAVIS, James; M/10th Cav. Original member of 10th Cavalry; in troop when organized, Ft Riley, KS, 15 Sep 1867. SOURCE: McMiller, "Buffalo Soldiers," 79.

DAVIS, James; Corporal; B/24th Inf. At Ft Huachuca, AZ, 1893. *See* **BROWN**, Alfred, First Sergeant, H/24th Infantry

DAVIS, James; Private; F/24th Inf. Wounded in action, Cuba, 1898. SOURCE: Muller, *The Twenty Fourth Infantry,* 18; Clark, "A History of the Twenty-fourth," 100.

DAVIS, James; Private; I/24th Inf. Awaiting transportation to station from Ft Robinson, NE, Oct–11 Nov 1904.

DAVIS, James A.; Corporal; H/24th Inf. Enlisted Chicago, IL, 25 May 1896; six years' continuous service. SOURCE: Muster Roll, H/24 Inf, May–Jun 1898.

Sick, disease contracted in line of duty, at Siboney, Cuba, 5–25 Aug 1898, and en route to U.S. since 25 Aug 1898. SOURCE: Muster Roll, H/24 Inf, Jul–Aug 1898.

On furlough authorized by surgeon's certificate, 10 Sep–8 Oct 1898; en route to join company, 9–12 Oct 1898. SOURCE: Muster Roll, H/24 Inf, Sep–Oct 1898.

DAVIS, Jerry A.; Private; G/9th Cav. Admonished by commander, Ft Robinson, NE, that he is obligated to send his school-age children to class; under no circumstances will they be allowed to loiter around barracks during school hours.

SOURCE: CO, Ft Robinson, to Private Davis, 22 Mar 1893, LS, Ft Robinson.

His wife's sister is visiting Ft Robinson, early Apr 1893. SOURCE: Ft Robinson *Weekly Bulletin,* 5 Apr 1893, filed with Court Martial Records, McKay.

His funeral at Ft Robinson, 7 Apr 1893. SOURCE: Order 26, 6 Apr 1893, Post Orders, Ft Robinson; List of Interments, Ft Robinson.

DAVIS, John; Private; H/9th Cav. On detached service, Ft Bayard, NM, 16 Jan–10 Feb 1881. SOURCE: Regt Returns, 9 Cav, Feb 1881.

DAVIS, John; Private; C/10th Cav. Served in 10th Cavalry in Cuba, 1898. SOURCE: Cashin, *Under Fire with the Tenth Cavalry,* 340.

DAVIS, John; Private; K/10th Cav. Served in 10th Cavalry, 1898; remained in U.S. during war with Spain. SOURCE: Cashin, *Under Fire with the Tenth Cavalry,* 349.

DAVIS, John B.; Private; D/24th Inf. Deserted, Ft Harrison, MT, 20 Aug 1902. SOURCE: Regt Returns, 24 Inf, Aug 1902.

DAVIS, Lewis; D/10th Cav. Mentioned as surviving Indian war veteran. SOURCE: *Winners of the West* 3 (Jun 1926): 7.

DAVIS, Martin; Private; C/10th Cav. Killed in action, against Victorio, Eagle Springs, TX, 30 Jul 1880; street in Wharry housing area, Ft Huachuca, AZ, formerly named for him. SOURCE: Orville A. Cochran to H. B. Wharfield, 5 Apr 1965, 10th Cavalry papers, MHI; Leckie, *The Buffalo Soldiers,* 225.

Stationed at Ft Davis, TX, at time of death. SOURCE: SecWar, *AR 1880,* 149.

DAVIS, Martin; Private; C/9th Cav. Deserted from Ft Robinson, NE, prior to 10 Sep 1885. SOURCE: CO, C/9, to AG, USA, 10 Sep 1885, LS, C/9 Cav.

DAVIS, Matt; Sergeant; A/10th Cav. Born in Kentucky; private, A/10th Cavalry, 10 Dec 1892; corporal, 18 Feb 1895; sergeant, 19 Jul 1896; stationed at Ft Custer, MT, 1897. SOURCE: Baker, Roster.

DAVIS, Otey; Private; K/9th Cav. Maj. Gen. Elwell S. Otis, commander, Department of the Lakes, disapproves Davis's conviction for desertion by general court martial, citing "disregard of the plainest rules of the law of evidence and the rights of the accused." SOURCE: *ANJ* 38 (1 Jun 1901): 967.

DAVIS, Robert; Corporal; A/38th Inf. At Ft Cummings, NM, autumn 1867; tried at Ft Selden, NM, Jan 1868, for role in soldier revolt; convicted of participation and sentenced to dishonorable discharge and ten years at penitentiary, Jefferson City, MO. SOURCE: Billington, *New Mexico's Buffalo Soldiers*, 39–41.

DAVIS, Rufus A.; Private; K/24th Inf. Sentenced to thirty days and loss of month's pay for failure to give surgeon the name of Filipino woman from whom he contracted venereal disease, Cabanatuan, Philippines, 5 Jul 1901. SOURCE: Name File, 24 Inf.

DAVIS, Sam; B/10th Cav. Original member of 10th Cavalry; in troop when organized, Ft Leavenworth, KS, 1 Apr 1867. SOURCE: McMiller, "Buffalo Soldiers," 69.

DAVIS, Silas; A/10th Cav. Original member of 10th Cavalry; in troop when organized, Ft Leavenworth, KS, 18 Feb 1867. SOURCE: McMiller, "Buffalo Soldiers," 68.

DAVIS, Thomas; Private; D/24th Inf. Wounded in action, Cuba, 1898. SOURCE: Muller, *The Twenty Fourth Infantry*, 18; Clark, "A History of the Twenty-fourth," 100.

DAVIS, Thomas J.; Private; D/9th Cav. Died of dysentery, at Pasacao, Philippines, 11 Oct 1900. SOURCE: Hamilton, "History of the Ninth Cavalry," 103; *Illustrated Review: Ninth Cavalry.*

DAVIS, Ulysses; Private; C/10th Cav. Died in Cuba, 8 Aug 1898. SOURCE: *ANJ* 36 (11 Feb 1899): 567.

DAVIS, W. J.; 1st Sgt; A/25th Inf. Distinguished marksman; ranked third in Department of Dakota, with silver medal, as private, 1893; ranked first in department, with gold medal, as corporal, 1894. SOURCE: GO 64, AGO, 18 Nov 1894.

Ranked sixth in department, with bronze medal, as first sergeant, 1897. SOURCE: *ANJ* 35 (25 Sep 1897): 55.

DAVIS, Walter R.; Corporal; D/9th Cav. Veteran of Philippine Insurrection; private, at Ft D. A. Russell, WY, in 1910. SOURCE: *Illustrated Review: Ninth Cavalry.*

Corporal, on special duty at 9th Cavalry exchange, Ft D. A. Russell. SOURCE: *Wyoming State Tribune*, 10 Feb 1911.

DAVIS, William (1); M/10th Cav. Original member of 10th Cavalry; in troop when organized, Ft Riley, KS, 15 Oct 1867. SOURCE: McMiller, "Buffalo Soldiers," 79.

DAVIS, William (2); M/10th Cav. Original member of 10th Cavalry; in troop when organized, Ft Riley, KS, 15 Oct 1867. SOURCE: McMiller, "Buffalo Soldiers," 79.

DAVIS, William; Private; B/9th Cav. At Ft Robinson, NE, 1888. *See* **HERBERT**, Thomas H., Private, K/9th Cavalry

DAVIS, William; Private; A/10th Cav. Served in 10th Cavalry, 1898; remained in U.S. during war with Spain. SOURCE: Cashin, *Under Fire with the Tenth Cavalry*, 337.

DAVIS, William; Private; M/10th Cav. Promoted to corporal, 30 May 1901. SOURCE: *ANJ* 38 (15 Jun 1901): 1018–19.

Private, released to duty from treatment for acute gonorrhea, Ft Robinson, NE, 7 Aug 1903. SOURCE: Post Surgeon to CO, M/10, 7 Aug 1903, LS, Post Surgeon, Ft Robinson.

DAVIS, William; Private; K/24th Inf. Sentenced to ten days and $5 fine for being drunk and disorderly in camp, using loud, profane, threatening language toward Filipino woman, Cabanatuan, Philippines, 9 Jun 1901. SOURCE: Name File, 24 Inf.

DAVIS, William; Private; H/24th Inf. Fined $2 by summary court for absence from bed check, San Isidro, Philippines, 1 Nov 1901, third conviction; fined $5 for unauthorized absence through night of 5–6 Nov 1901, fourth conviction. SOURCE: Register of Summary Court, San Isidro.

DAVIS, William; Private; K/9th Cav. Veteran of Philippine Insurrection; at Ft D. A. Russell, WY, in 1910; resident of Boage, KY. SOURCE: *Illustrated Review: Ninth Cavalry*, with picture.

DAVIS, William H.; 1st Sgt; D/25th Inf. Served as first sergeant of company when soldier stuck fork in Pvt. George D. Crockett's eye; now age 50 and residing at Beaufort, Carteret Co., NC. SOURCE: Affidavit, Davis, 16 Feb 1891, VA File XC 2624113, George D. Crockett.

DAVIS, William J.; Sgt Maj; 2nd Sqdn/10th Cav. Private, 9th Cavalry, on special duty at post canteen, Ft Robinson, NE. SOURCE: Order 171, 23 Aug 1891, Post Orders, Ft Robinson.

In G/9th Cavalry, witness for defense, Barney McKay court martial, Ft Robinson, 1893.

With Trumpeter James Cooper, both of G/10th Cavalry, assisted 2nd Lt. T. A. Roberts, 10th Cavalry, to safety after Roberts was wounded, Cuba, 1 Jul 1898. SOURCE: Cashin, *Under Fire with the Tenth Cavalry*, 118, 345.

Private, G/10th Cavalry, detailed acting sergeant major, Ft Ringgold, TX, 6 Feb 1900. SOURCE: *ANJ* 37 (24 Feb 1900): 602.

Born Memphis, TN; age 33 in 1902, Ht 5'6", mulatto; ten years in E and G/9th Cavalry; reenlisted as corporal, G/10th Cavalry, 25 Mar 1901; appointed squadron sergeant major, 14 Oct 1901; fifteenth year of continuous service began 25 Mar 1902; $3 per month additional pay for ten years' continuous service; discharged, Ft Mackenzie, WY, 9 Dec 1902, character excellent; $43.70 in clothing, owes $11 for Colt revolver; married, wife resides in San Antonio, TX. SOURCE: Descriptive Book, 10 Cav Officers & NCOs.

DAVIS, William J.; Private; I/25th Inf. Died Ft Niobrara, NE, 28 Mar 1906. SOURCE: Monthly Report, Chaplain Steward, 31 Mar 1906.

DAVIS, William N.; Private; F/10th Cav. At Ft Robinson, NE, as general court martial witness, 4 Jan–7 Feb 1906.

DAWSON; Sergeant; K/24th Inf. At Cabanatuan, Philippines, 1901. *See* **WHITE**, Leonard, Private, D/24th Infantry

DAWSON, Eb; Blacksmith; F/9th Cav. Veteran of Philippine Insurrection; at Ft D. A. Russell, WY, in 1910; sharpshooter; resident of Bowling Green, KY. SOURCE: *Illustrated Review: Ninth Cavalry,* with picture.

DAWSON, George W.; E/48th Inf. Sentenced to one year for robbery and assault in the Philippines, Aug 1900.

DAWSON, John W.; Private; I/24th Inf. Enlisted Raleigh, NC, 23 Mar 1899. SOURCE: Muster Roll, I/24 Inf, Mar–Apr 1899.

Absent sick in Manila, Philippines, since 9 Sep 1899. SOURCE: Muster Roll, I/24 Inf, Nov–Dec 1899.

DAWSON, William L.; Private; K/10th Cav. Served in 10th Cavalry, 1898; remained in U.S. during war with Spain. SOURCE: Cashin, *Under Fire with the Tenth Cavalry,* 349.

DAY, Charles N.; Private; B/24th Inf. Born Bayou Sara, LA; enlisted Cincinnati, OH, occupation musician, age 23, Ht 5'4", saddle complexion, black eyes and hair, 21 Apr 1886; joined Band/24th Infantry, Ft Supply, Indian Territory, 13 Nov 1886; transferred to B/24th Infantry, character worthless, 19 Mar 1887. SOURCE: Descriptive Book, 24 Inf NCS & Band.

At Ft Elliott, TX, 1887. SOURCE: Cleveland *Gazette,* 8 Oct 1887.

DAY, James E.; Private; K/10th Cav. Killed in action, Carrizal, Mexico, 21 Jun 1916; buried in Arlington National Cemetery. SOURCE: Wharfield, *10th Cavalry and Border Fights,* 30, 39.

DAY, Louis; Sergeant; E/10th Cav. At Ft Apache, AZ, 1890, subscribed $.50 to testimonial to General Grierson. SOURCE: List of subscriptions, 23 Apr 1890, 10th Cavalry papers, MHI.

DAY, Nathon; Private; E/9th Cav. At Ft D. A. Russell, WY, in 1910; sharpshooter; resident of Benfort, SC. SOURCE: *Illustrated Review: Ninth Cavalry,* with picture.

DEAGONS, Joseph E.; Private; D/9th Cav. Convicted by general court martial, Jefferson Barracks, MO, of desertion, 5 May 1885–20 Sep 1888; sentenced to dishonorable discharge and five years. SOURCE: GCMO 61, AGO, 22 Nov 1888.

DEAN, Charles H.; Private; C/9th Cav. At Ft D. A. Russell, WY, in 1910; resident of 418 Center St., Louisville. SOURCE: *Illustrated Review: Ninth Cavalry,* with picture.

DEAN, John; Private; 24th Inf. Drowned crossing San Mateo River, Philippines, 21 Aug 1899. SOURCE: Richmond *Planet,* 2 Sep 1899.

DEAN, Milton T.; Major; U.S. Army. Expert rifleman and sergeant, K/9th Cavalry, at Ft D. A. Russell, WY, in 1910; resident of Shreveport, LA. SOURCE: *Illustrated Review: Ninth Cavalry,* with picture.

Squadron sergeant major, 9th Cavalry, Ft D. A. Russell, 1912; advocate of racial solidarity in business matters. SOURCE: Cleveland *Gazette,* 29 Jun 1912.

Commissioned at Camp Des Moines, IA, 15 Oct 1917. SOURCE: Sweeney, *History of the American Negro,* 120.

Senior among ten black officers on staff of Lt. Col. William G. Deane, Camp Dodge, IA, May 1918; recalled to 92nd Division. SOURCE: Williams, *Sidelights on Negro Soldiers,* 55.

Major, former sergeant major, 9th Cavalry, served with William Washington, 9th Cavalry, from 1903 at Ft Walla Walla, WA, to Washington's retirement, May 1910. SOURCE: VA File WC 894780, William Washington.

DEAN, Robert; Private; L/10th Cav. Served in 10th Cavalry, 1898; remained in U.S. during war with Spain. SOURCE: Cashin, *Under Fire with the Tenth Cavalry,* 350.

DEAN, William; Private; F/24th Inf. Wounded in action, Cuba, 1898. SOURCE: Muller, *The Twenty Fourth Infantry,* 18.

DEARING, Edward; Private; 25th Inf. Born Annsville, VA; enlisted Pittsburgh, PA, laborer, Ht 5'9", black complexion, 8 Mar 1892; at Ft Missoula, MT, character good, age 24, 18 Feb 1895. SOURCE: Descriptive Cards, 25 Inf.

DEARING, Ruben; Saddler; L/10th Cav. Served in 10th Cavalry, 1898; remained in U.S. during war with Spain. SOURCE: Cashin, *Under Fire with the Tenth Cavalry,* 350.

DEAVER, Alphonse W.; Private; I/24th Inf. Joined company, 29 Sep 1899; on detached service, Arayat, Philippines, 31 Oct 1899. SOURCE: Muster Roll, I/24 Inf, Sep–Oct 1899.

Allotted $10 per month for six months to Mary R. Deaver; on detached service at Cabanatuan since 30 Dec 1899. SOURCE: Muster Roll, I/24 Inf, Nov–Dec 1899.

DECKER, Edward; Private; I/10th Cav. Served in 10th Cavalry, 1898; remained in U.S. during war with Spain. SOURCE: Cashin, *Under Fire with the Tenth Cavalry,* 348.

DEGROAT; Private; H/10th Cav. At Ft Apache, AZ, 1890, subscribed $.50 to testimonial to General Grierson. SOURCE: List of subscriptions, 23 Apr 1890, 10th Cavalry papers, MHI.

DEHAVEN, John W.; Color Sgt; 24th Inf. Commissioned at Camp Des Moines, IA. SOURCE: Beasley, *Negro Trailblazers,* 285.

DEHENDERSON, Charles A.; Private; M/10th Cav. Served in 10th Cavalry, 1898; remained in U.S. during war with Spain. SOURCE: Cashin, *Under Fire with the Tenth Cavalry*, 351.

DELAND, Johnson; Private; D/10th Cav. Drowned, Mayari, Cuba, 28 Nov 1899. SOURCE: *ANJ* 37 (9 Dec 1899): 353.

DELANEY, George; Private; A/10th Cav. Served in 10th Cavalry in Cuba, 1898. SOURCE: Cashin, *Under Fire with the Tenth Cavalry*, 336.

DELLUM, Wesley; Corporal; I/25th Inf. Fined $3 by summary court for failure to report to noncommissioned officers' school, San Isidro, Philippines, first conviction. SOURCE: Register of Summary Court, San Isidro.

DELONG, George; Recruit; Colored Inf/General Recruits. Convicted by general court martial, Newport Barracks, KY, of theft from depot kitchen of twenty-two pounds of fresh beef and sixteen pounds of pork, 23 Sep 1875; sentenced to dishonorable discharge and one year. SOURCE: GCMO 88, AGO, 8 Nov 1875.

DEMARK, George; Private; G/10th Cav. *See* DEMORE, George, Private, G/10th Cavalry

DEMORE, George; Private; G/10th Cav. Served in 10th Cavalry in Cuba, 1898. SOURCE: Cashin, *Under Fire with the Tenth Cavalry*, 345.

Transferred from Reserve Divisional Hospital, Siboney, Cuba, with yellow fever, to Fortress Monroe, VA, on U.S. Army Transport *Concho*, 23 Jul 1898. SOURCE: Hospital Papers, Spanish-American War.

DENE, William; Private; B/9th Cav. In hands of civil authorities, Chadron, NE, 25 Feb–21 Mar 1893. SOURCE: Regt Returns, 9 Cav.

DENISON, Leon W.; Captain; E/48th Inf. One of nineteen officers of 48th Infantry recommended as regular Army second lieutenants. SOURCE: CG, DivPI, Manila, 8 Feb 1901, to AGO, AGO File 355163.

Mentioned. SOURCE: Beasley, *Negro Trailblazers*, 284.

DENNEY, Labian; Private; M/10th Cav. Convicted by general court martial, Columbus Barracks, OH, of desertion, 5 Aug 1874–18 May 1885; sentenced to dishonorable discharge and five years. SOURCE: GCMO 69, AGO, 27 Jun 1885.

DENNIS, Abraham; 1st Sgt; D/25th Inf. Authorized six-month furlough from Ft Meade, SD. SOURCE: *ANJ* 24 (6 Nov 1886): 290.

DENNIS, Alfred; K/10th Cav. Original member of 10th Cavalry; in troop when organized, Ft Riley, KS, 1 Sep 1867. SOURCE: McMiller, "Buffalo Soldiers," 77.

DENNIS, Clark; D/10th Cav. Original member of 10th Cavalry; in troop when organized, Ft Leavenworth, KS, 1 Jun 1867. SOURCE: McMiller, "Buffalo Soldiers," 71.

DENNIS, Herman; Private; F/25th Inf. Transferred to Hospital Corps at Ft Snelling, MN. SOURCE: *ANJ* 25 (4 Feb 1888): 546.

DENNIS, Janius; M/10th Cav. Original member of 10th Cavalry; in troop when organized, Ft Riley, KS, 15 Oct 1867. SOURCE: McMiller, "Buffalo Soldiers," 79.

DENNY, Elbiron; Saddler; F/10th Cav. Sergeant, fined $10 for "sundry offenses," camp on Deaver Creek, MT. SOURCE: *ANJ* 30 (12 Nov 1892): 186.

Knew Thomas H. Allsup at Ft Assiniboine, MT, 1891, and until 1898; resides at 1567 E. Adams, Los Angeles, CA, for eight years, age 74, employed as janitor. SOURCE: VA File XC 2659797, Thomas H. Allsup.

Served in 10th Cavalry in Cuba, 1898. SOURCE: Cashin, *Under Fire with the Tenth Cavalry*, 344.

DENNY, John; Sergeant; 9th Cav. Born Big Flats, NY; Medal of Honor for service against Victorio in 1880 awarded to him later at Ft Robinson, NE. SOURCE: Carroll, *The Black Military Experience*, 413–14.

Awarded Medal of Honor for rescue of Private Freeland during battle of Las Animas, NM, Sep 1879. SOURCE: Billington, *New Mexico's Buffalo Soldiers*, 91.

Medal of Honor transmitted to him in letter, Adjutant General, U.S. Army, 10 Jan 1895.

Awarded Medal of Honor for distinguished service as private, C/9th Cavalry, against Apaches, removed wounded comrade to safety under fire, 18 Sep 1879; regimental commander, Col. James Biddle, says that "such acts of gallantry not only reflect credit upon the individual, but also on the organization to which he belongs, and the 9th Cavalry may well feel proud of having in its ranks a man so signally honored." SOURCE: *ANJ* 32 (26 Jan 1895): 358.

Promoted from lance corporal to corporal, C/9th Cavalry, Ft Robinson, 23 Mar 1895. SOURCE: *ANJ* 32 (6 Apr 1895): 523.

To retire, Ft Robinson, 11 Sep 1897. SOURCE: SO 205, AGO, 7 Sep 1897.

Employed at post exchange, Ft Robinson, Jan–Jun 1899; paid $10 per month. SOURCE: QM Consolidated File, Ft Robinson.

No Veterans Administration pension file.

DENT, Henry; Private; D/9th Cav. Born St. Mary's Co., MD, 29 Oct 1856; parents Henry L. Dent and Julia Dorsey of Maryland; Ht 5'6", enlisted, black complexion, occupation butler, 4 Jan 1878; served at Ft Riley, KS, Fts Selden and Craig, NM, Fts Garland and Lewis, CO, "which I helped to build"; discharged 3 Jan 1883; married Rosa B. Ross, age 25, Baltimore, MD, 27 Apr 1897; resided at 1434 Presstman, Baltimore; pensions: $30 per month, 5 Mar 1927; $40, 29 Oct 1928; $50, 1 Apr 1935; $55, 1 Sep 1937;

$72, 26 Nov 1937; died 12 Sep 1938. Widow's pension $30 per month, 16 Sep 1938, $40, 21 Mar 1944; moved to 822 Carrollton Avenue, Baltimore, in 1947; died 11 Jan 1949. SOURCE: VA File C 2363092, Henry Dent.

Former comrades in D/9th Cavalry, with locations, 6 Jul 1895: Edward Scott, private, Forest Glen, Montgomery Co., MD; Moses Coleman, private, Junction City, Geary Co., KS; Samuel Cornish, private, 122 Sharp Street, Baltimore; James Haskins, Private, Pueblo, CO. SOURCE: VA File C 2363092, Henry Dent.

Served 1878–83; member, Camp 11, National Indian War Veterans, St. Joseph, MO; died recently, Baltimore. SOURCE: *Winners of the West* 16 (Dec 1938): 2.

DENTY, John; Private; 24th Inf. Served in Houston, 1917; "a raw recruit" at time of riot. SOURCE: Haynes, *A Night of Violence*, 122, 264.

DERBIGNY, Benjamin; 25th Inf. Letter, Capt. Gamis Lawson, 25th Infantry, Columbus Barracks, OH, to Hon. Blanche K. Bruce, U.S. Senate, Washington, DC, 25 May 1879, transmits papers in case of Derbigny, alias Benjamin Olivia, late sergeant, I/84th U.S. Colored Troops, regarding his claim for bounty, at Derbigny's request; after Civil War, Olivia enlisted in C/39th Infantry as Derbigny; while stationed at Ft Pike, LA, someone drew his bounty from Freedmen's Bureau agent at New Orleans; "There is no doubt in my mind but what the man has been cheated out of money, and as he is a very deserving fellow (he having served in my command for ten years) I hope you will be able to recover him his money"; his address is Brackettvile, Kinney Co., TX. SOURCE: Bruce misc. manuscripts, RBHL.

DERRETT, George; QM Sgt; D/25th Inf. Ranked number 124 among rifle experts with 73.33 percent, 1905. SOURCE: GO 101, AGO, 31 May 1906.

DERRETT, Thurston G.; Private; H/10th Cav. Served in 10th Cavalry, 1898; remained in U.S. during war with Spain. SOURCE: Cashin, *Under Fire with the Tenth Cavalry*, 346.

DERRICK, David; Private; B/9th Cav. At Ft D. A. Russell, WY, in 1910. SOURCE: *Illustrated Review: Ninth Cavalry*, with picture.

DERRICK, Silas E.; Private; H/24th Inf. Enlisted Ft Douglas, UT, 25 May 1898; transferred from M/9th Cavalry, 28 Oct 1898. SOURCE: Muster Roll, H/24 Inf, Nov–Dec 1898.

Musician, 29 Jan 1899. SOURCE: Muster Roll, H/24 Inf, Jan–Feb 1899.

DERRY, Lewis; Farrier; A/9th Cav. Veteran of Philippine Insurrection; at Ft D. A. Russell, WY, in 1910; sharpshooter. SOURCE: *Illustrated Review: Ninth Cavalry*.

DERWIN, Isaac; Private; A/10th Cav. Died on Staked Plains expedition, Aug 1877. SOURCE: Leckie, *The Buffalo Soldiers*, 161.

Final statement of deceased Derwin transmitted by commander, 10th Cavalry, to Adjutant General's Office, 3 Sep 1877. SOURCE: ES, 10 Cav, 1873–81.

DESAUSSURE, Carolina; Private; B/25th Inf. Dishonorable discharge, Brownsville. SOURCE: SO 266, AGO, 9 Nov 1906.

DEWEY, Taliaferro Miles; 9th Ohio Inf. Letters. SOURCE: Gatewood, *"Smoked Yankees"*, 115–16, 119–20.

DEWHURST, Moses; Private; Hospital Corps. Fined $3 by summary court for absence from eleven P.M. inspection, San Isidro, Philippines, 28 Apr 1902, first conviction; fined $15 for carelessly discharging rifle while guarding prisoner, 24 Jun 1902. SOURCE: Register of Summary Court, San Isidro.

DEYO, Isaac A.; Private; I/24th Inf. Forced to accompany mutineers, Houston riot, 1917. SOURCE: Haynes, *A Night of Violence*, 126.

DIAL, Charles L.; Private; I/9th Cav. At Ft D. A. Russell, WY, in 1910; resident of Caseyville, KY. SOURCE: *Illustrated Review: Ninth Cavalry*.

DIAL, Samuel; Private; I/24th Inf. Enlisted Birmingham, AL, 3 Jul 1899. SOURCE: Muster Roll, I/24 Inf, Jul–Aug 1899.

DICEY, Dennis; H/10th Cav. Original member of 10th Cavalry; in troop when organized, Ft Leavenworth, KS, 21 Jul 1867. SOURCE: McMiller, "Buffalo Soldiers," 75.

DICKERSON; Sergeant; 9th Cav. At Ft Craig, NM, 1881. *See* **RICHARDSON**, William, Private, D/9th Cavalry

DICKERSON; Corporal; 24th Inf. Performed solo, "Asleep in the Deep," at Christian Endeavor Society, Ft Harrison, MT, Nov 1904; married. SOURCE: Indianapolis *Freeman*, 17 Dec 1904.

DICKERSON, Clarence; Private; B/9th Cav. At Ft D. A. Russell, WY, in 1910. SOURCE: *Illustrated Review: Ninth Cavalry*.

DICKERSON, Frank K.; Private; H/10th Cav. Served in 10th Cavalry, 1898; remained in U.S. during war with Spain. SOURCE: Cashin, *Under Fire with the Tenth Cavalry*, 346.

At Camp Forse, AL, Nov 1898. SOURCE: Richmond *Planet*, 3 Dec 1898.

DICKERSON, Hugh; Private; F/10th Cav. Served in 10th Cavalry in Cuba, 1898. SOURCE: Cashin, *Under Fire with the Tenth Cavalry*, 344.

DICKERSON, James; Private; F/24th Inf. At Ft Bayard, NM, 1895. SOURCE: Billington, *New Mexico's Buffalo Soldiers*, 158.

DICKERSON, James M.; Bn Sgt Maj; 24th Inf. Detailed to escort general prisoner Henry Clay, formerly of K/24th Infantry, to Ft Leavenworth, KS, military prison from Ft Douglas, UT. SOURCE: *ANJ* 36 (11 Feb 1899): 564.

Regimental postmaster, handled tickets on Salt Lake City, UT, streetcar line, Mar 1899; frequent speaker, 24th Infantry Christian Endeavor Society, Ft Douglas; appointed sergeant major, Mar 1899; in charge of Ft Douglas baseball park. SOURCE: Clark, "A History of the Twenty-fourth," 68.

DICKERSON, James M.; 2nd Lt; F/49th Inf. Born Jamestown, MD; age 33 on 23 Nov 1899; former service in 10th Cavalry. SOURCE: Descriptive Book, 49 Inf NCS.

Enlisted as sergeant major, 49th Infantry, 12 Oct 1899; promoted to second lieutenant vice Blaney, 13 Nov 1899; sick in hospital, disease contracted in line of duty, Manila, Philippines, 6–13 Jan 1900; on detached service, scouting, 18–19 Jan, 31 Jan–1 Feb, and 30–31 Jul 1900; on detached service, Tuguegarao, Luzon, 1–31 Oct and 9–17 Dec 1900. SOURCE: Descriptive Book, F/49 Inf.

Promoted to second lieutenant as of 10 Nov 1899. SOURCE: *ANJ* 37 (18 Nov 1899): 217; *ANJ* 37 (2 Dec 1899): 319.

Acquitted of charges of improper relations with Filipino women, 8 Feb 1901.

DICKERSON, Jefferson; Blacksmith; D/10th Cav. At Ft Apache, AZ, 1890, subscribed $.50 to testimonial to General Grierson. SOURCE: List of subscriptions, 23 Apr 1890, 10th Cavalry papers, MHI.

DICKERSON, John; Private; M/10th Cav. Served in 10th Cavalry, 1898; remained in U.S. during war with Spain. SOURCE: Cashin, *Under Fire with the Tenth Cavalry*, 351.

DICKERSON, Lamar M.; Private; F/9th Cav. Expert rifleman at Ft D. A. Russell, WY, in 1910; resident of Burke Co., NC. SOURCE: *Illustrated Review: Ninth Cavalry,* with picture.

DICKERSON, William; Private; I/9th Cav. At Ft D. A. Russell, WY, in 1910; resident of Staunton, VA. SOURCE: *Illustrated Review: Ninth Cavalry,* with picture.

DICKSON, Ben; F/10th Cav. Served 1886–91; died Phoenix, AZ. SOURCE: *Winners of the West* 11 (Jul 1934): 3.

DICKSON, Benjamin J.; Private; F/9th Cav. At Ft D. A. Russell, WY, in 1910; marksman; resident of Patrick Co., VA. SOURCE: *Illustrated Review: Ninth Cavalry,* with picture.

DICKSON, John; Band/9th Cav. Reenlistment authorized by letter, Adjutant General's Office, 28 Sep 1895.

DICKSON, Leonard E.; Private; H/9th Cav. Born Stanton, VA; prior service, H/9th Cavalry, 24 Aug 1892–23

Nov 1895; enlisted Ft Omaha, NE, age 26, occupation laborer, 5 Feb 1896; two summary court martial convictions and fines, 1896; garrison court martial conviction and fine, 1898; discharged, end of term, character good, Ft Wingate, NM, 4 Feb 1899. SOURCE: Descriptive Book, H/9 Cav.

Convicted by garrison court martial of conduct prejudcial to good order and discipline, Ft Robinson, NE; fined $5. SOURCE: SO 73, 18 Apr 1898, Post Orders, Ft Robinson.

DIEKSON, Solomon; C/10th Cav. Original member of 10th Cavalry; in troop when organized, Ft Leavenworth, KS, 14 May 1867. SOURCE: McMiller, "Buffalo Soldiers," 70.

DIGGS, Albert L.; Private; K/10th Cav. Served in 10th Cavalry, 1898; remained in U.S. during war with Spain. SOURCE: Cashin, *Under Fire with the Tenth Cavalry*, 349.

DIGGS, Charles H.; Private; D/24th Inf. Died of yellow fever at Siboney, Cuba, 7 Aug 1898. SOURCE: *ANJ* 36 (11 Feb 1899): 567; AG, *Correspondence Regarding the War with Spain*, I:213; Hospital Papers, Spanish-American War.

DIGGS, James; Private; C/9th Cav. Commander, C/9th Cavalry, asks remission of rest of confinement of enlisted men sentenced by General Court Martial Order 78, Department of the Platte, 10 Nov 1885; all have been confined since 16 Oct 1885, long enough to learn their lesson; in addition to Diggs, they are Pvt. Philip H. Dover, Wagoner Charles Perry, and Farrier William Smith, all of C/9th Cavalry. SOURCE: CO, C/9, to AAG, DP, 4 Jan 1886, LS, C/9 Cav.

In guardhouse, Ft Robinson, NE, Mar 1887, after dishonorable discharge. SOURCE: GCMO 16, DP, 16 Feb 1887.

DILLARD, C. D.; Private; K/9th Cav. Directed to proceed with Pvt. William S. Jones, K/9th Cavalry, and a private of F/9th Cavalry without delay to repair military telegraph line between Ft Robinson, NE, and Ft Laramie, WY. SOURCE: Order 207, 13 Dec 1886, Post Orders, Ft Robinson.

Telegraph operator, Ft Robinson, 1887; between Apr and Jun repaired Ft Robinson telegraph line five times: four times to Running Water and once to Crawford.

Relieved as post librarian, Ft Robinson. SOURCE: Order 98, 21 May 1887, Post Orders, Ft Robinson.

Replaced Pvt. John Vaughn, C/8th Infantry, as post librarian, Ft Robinson. SOURCE: Order 111, 4 Jun 1887, Post Orders, Ft Robinson.

Ordered to take four days' rations and one private, K/9th Cavalry, to repair telegraph line to Running Water without delay. SOURCE: Order 161, 9 Aug 1887, Post Orders, Ft Robinson.

Ordered to take three days' rations, one private from F/9th Cavalry, and one private from C/9th Cavalry, and proceed along military telegraph line to Running Water without delay. SOURCE: Order 197, 27 Nov 1887, Post Orders, Ft Robinson.

Relieved as post librarian, Ft Robinson, by Pvt. Barney Sullivan, I/8th Infantry. SOURCE: Order 14, 22 Jan 1888, Post Orders, Ft Robinson.

Ordered to take one private, F/9th Cavalry, to repair telegraph line to Running Water. SOURCE: Order 104, 31 May 1888, Post Orders, Ft Robinson.

Relieved as post librarian, Ft Robinson, by Pvt. Thomas McKenzie, C/8th Infantry, and detailed clerk to post adjutant. SOURCE: Order 8, 10 Jan 1889, Post Orders, Ft Robinson.

DILLARD, Charlie; Private; A/9th Cav. Veteran of Philippine Insurrection; at Ft D. A. Russell, WY, in 1910. SOURCE: *Illustrated Review: Ninth Cavalry,* with picture.

DILLARD, James; Private; H/10th Cav. Honorable mention for services rendered in capture of Mangas and his Apache band, Rio Bonito, AZ, 18 Oct 1886. SOURCE: Baker, Roster.

DILLON, David R.; Sergeant; Band/9th Cav. Enlisted 6 Jan 1877; discharged, character good, 5 Jan 1882; enlisted 6 Jun 1883; discharged, character good, "an excellent cornet player," 5 Jun 1888; current enlistment began 19 Dec 1893; reduced from sergeant to private, dishonorably discharged, for disobeying orders and conduct to prejudice of good order, Ft Robinson, NE, in accordance with Special Order 100, Department of the Platte, 27 Sep 1894. SOURCE: Court Martial Records, Dillon.

Col. James Biddle, commander, 9th Cavalry, requests that Dillon, formerly chief trumpeter, 10th Cavalry, be sent to 9th Cavalry; Dillon desires to enlist "and is an excellent musician, something difficult to get"; also will accept William Jenkins, Andrew Murry, and Samuel A. Warfield, all old soldiers deserving to enlist, to keep his regiment from becoming training center for others. SOURCE: CO, 9 Cav, to AG, USA, 24 Feb 1894, Appointment File 3406 PRD 1894, Dillon.

Biddle reiterates interest in Dillon and other veterans: "Would like to have these men if possible especially Recruit Dillon as he is an excellent musician." Source: TWX, CO, 9 Cav, to AG, USA, 14 Mar 1894, Appointment File 3406 PRD 1894, Dillon.

Arrived Ft Robinson, NE, 31 Mar 1894; widower, whose wife died in Santa Fe, NM, and with minor children who did not live with him; taught organ to daughter of Saddler Sgt. Robert Benjamin, 9th Cavalry. SOURCE: Court Martial Records, Plummer.

DILLON, Robert; Chief Musician; 49th Inf. Born St. Louis, MO; age 39, occupation musician, in 1899; ten years' service in 10th Cavalry; eight months in 7th U.S. Volunteer Infantry; married to Mary J. Dillon, 3113 Cass Avenue, St. Louis. SOURCE: Descriptive Book, 49 Inf NCS.

DILLON, Thomas; Private; L/10th Cav. Promoted to sergeant, 1 Jun 1894. SOURCE: *ANJ* 31 (16 Jun 1894): 735.

Private, released to duty from treatment for secondary syphilis, Ft Robinson, NE, 27 Dec 1903. SOURCE: Post

Surgeon to CO, L/10, 27 Dec 1903, LS, Post Surgeon, Ft Robinson.

DILWOOD, Thomas J.; B/10th Cav. Lives in San Antonio, TX; would like to hear from old comrades. SOURCE: *Winners of the West* 5 (May 1928): 5.

Commander of new all-black Abraham Lincoln Camp No. 30, National Indian War Veterans, San Antonio, organized 14 Oct 1929. SOURCE: *Winners of the West* 6 (Oct 1929): 7.

Picture, with three comrades of Camp 30, National Indian War Veterans. SOURCE: *Winners of the West* 9 (Mar 1932): 7.

Age 83; served ten years. SOURCE: *Winners of the West* 10 (Aug 1933): 3.

Congratulates editor on efforts for veterans; can hardly talk, is paralyzed, weak, and feeble; aged wife and son help him get around. SOURCE: *Winners of the West* 11 (Sep 1933): 3.

DIMPLE; Private; H/10th Cav. Hospitalized at Ft D. A. Russell, WY, as result of attempted assault on prostitute. SOURCE: Cheyenne *Daily Leader*, 22 Feb 1907.

DIRKS, Harrison; Private; H/48th Inf. Committed suicide in the Philippines. SOURCE: *ANJ* 37 (26 May 1900): 927.

DISBERRY; Private; B/10th Cav. At Ft Apache, AZ, 1890, subscribed $.50 to testimonial to General Grierson. SOURCE: List of subscriptions, 23 Apr 1890, 10th Cavalry papers, MHI.

DIVINS, James; Private; I/24th Inf. Involved in Houston riot, 1917; sentenced to death. SOURCE: Haynes, *A Night of Violence*, 167, 271.

Hanged, Ft Sam Houston, TX, 13 Dec 1917, for his part in Houston riot. SOURCE: Cleveland *Gazette*, 15 Dec 1917.

DIXON; Private; F/9th Cav. Absent from post school for two weeks, Ft Robinson, NE, Mar 1889. SOURCE: CO, Ft Robinson, to CO, F/9, 30 Mar 1889, LS, Ft Robinson.

DIXON, Alfred; H/10th Cav. Original member of 10th Cavalry; in troop when organized, Ft Leavenworth, KS, 21 Jul 1867. SOURCE: McMiller, "Buffalo Soldiers," 75.

DIXON, Charles; A/10th Cav. Original member of 10th Cavalry; in troop when organized, Ft Leavenworth, KS, 18 Feb 1867. SOURCE: McMiller, "Buffalo Soldiers," 68.

DIXON, Charley; Private; E/9th Cav. At Ft D. A. Russell, WY, in 1910; marksman; resident of St. Louis. SOURCE: *Illustrated Review: Ninth Cavalry,* with picture.

DIXON, David; E/10th Cav. Original member of 10th Cavalry; in troop when organized, Ft Leavenworth, KS, 15 Jun 1867. SOURCE: McMiller, "Buffalo Soldiers," 72.

Served 1867–72; died Muskogee, OK. SOURCE: *Winners of the West* 12 (Oct 1935): 3.

DIXON, Dennis; Private; E/9th Cav. Family resides at Ft Robinson, NE, and claims to be indigent, dependent on charity of garrison for subsistence. SOURCE: CO, Ft Robinson, to CO, 9 Cav, 25 Jul 1898, LS, Ft Robinson.

Died of malaria, Camp Wikoff, NY, 5 Sep 1898. SOURCE: Hospital Papers, Spanish-American War.

DIXON, Frank; K/10th Cav. Original member of 10th Cavalry; in troop when organized, Ft Riley, KS, 1 Sep 1867. SOURCE: McMiller, "Buffalo Soldiers," 77.

DIXON, Henry; M/10th Cav. Original member of 10th Cavalry; in troop when organized, Ft Riley, KS, 15 Oct 1867. SOURCE: McMiller, "Buffalo Soldiers," 79.

DIXON, James; Private; B/9th Cav. Knew Arthur Smith before they enlisted together and were assigned to B/9th Cavalry; now age 47, resides at 126 E. Vine Street, Knoxville, TN. SOURCE: VA File C 2410890, Arthur Smith.

DIXON, Jerry; Private; 10th Cav. Enlisted Little Rock, AR, 18 Feb 1867. SOURCE: LS 10 Cav, 1866–67.

DIXON, John; D/10th Cav. Enlisted Little Rock, AR, 18 Feb 1867. SOURCE: LS 10 Cav, 1866–67.

Original member of 10th Cavalry; in troop when organized, Ft Leavenworth, KS, 1 Jun 1867. SOURCE: McMiller, "Buffalo Soldiers," 71.

DIXON, Joseph; Corporal; I/10th Cav. Acquitted at Whipple Barracks, AZ, of calling troop commander "a damned old scoundrel" and "an old drunken sot." SOURCE: *ANJ* 25 (19 Nov 1887): 323.

DIXON, Will; Private; M/10th Cav. Served in 10th Cavalry, 1898; remained in U.S. during war with Spain. SOURCE: Cashin, *Under Fire with the Tenth Cavalry*, 351.

DIXON, William; Corporal; B/10th Cav. Served in 10th Cavalry in Cuba, 1898. SOURCE: Cashin, *Under Fire with the Tenth Cavalry*, 337.

DIXON, Willie; Private; L/10th Cav. Served in 10th Cavalry, 1898; remained in U.S. during war with Spain. SOURCE: Cashin, *Under Fire with the Tenth Cavalry*, 350.

DOBBS, George; B/10th Cav. Original member of 10th Cavalry; in troop when organized, Ft Leavenworth, KS, 1 Apr 1867. SOURCE: McMiller, "Buffalo Soldiers," 69.

DOBBS, Scipin; A/10th Cav. Original member of 10th Cavalry; in troop when organized, Ft Leavenworth, KS, 18 Feb 1867. SOURCE: McMiller, "Buffalo Soldiers," 68.

DOBSON, Theophilus; Private; E/9th Cav. Buried at Ft Robinson, NE, 11 Jun 1890. SOURCE: List of Interments, Ft Robinson.

DOBYNS, Samuel; Private; A/10th Cav. Served in 10th Cavalry, 1898; remained in U.S. during war with Spain. SOURCE: Cashin, *Under Fire with the Tenth Cavalry*, 337.

DOCKEY, Stanton; Private; I/24th Inf. Enlisted Anniston, AL, 25 Mar 1899. SOURCE: Muster Roll, I/24 Inf, Mar–Apr 1899.

Fined $10 and jailed for one month by summary court, 20 May 1899. SOURCE: Muster Roll, I/24 Inf, May–Jun 1899.

Fined $2 by summary court, 22 Jul 1899. SOURCE: Muster Roll, I/24 Inf, Jul–Aug 1899.

Allotted $10 per month for six months to Jinnie Dockey. SOURCE: Muster Roll, I/24 Inf, Sep–Oct 1899.

Absent sick, Cabanatuan, Philippines, since 25 Dec 1899. SOURCE: Muster Roll, I/24 Inf, Nov–Dec 1899.

DODD, Charles; Sergeant; C/10th Cav. Original member of 10th Cavalry; in troop when organized, Ft Leavenworth, KS, 14 May 1867. SOURCE: McMiller, "Buffalo Soldiers," 70.

Sergeant, vacancy unfilled. SOURCE: Adj, 10 Cav, to CO, C/10, 19 Jul 1867, LS, 10 Cav, 1866–67.

DODD, James H.; Private; K/10th Cav. Served in 10th Cavalry, 1898; remained in U.S. during war with Spain. SOURCE: Cashin, *Under Fire with the Tenth Cavalry*, 349.

DODGE, Cleveland; D/10th Cav. Original member of 10th Cavalry; in troop when organized, Ft Leavenworth, KS, 1 Jun 1867. SOURCE: McMiller, "Buffalo Soldiers," 71.

DODSON, John H.; Private; C/10th Cav. Killed in action, San Juan, Cuba, 1 Jul 1898; Dodson Street, Ft Huachuca, AZ, named for him. SOURCE: Orville A. Cochran to H. B. Wharfield, 5 Apr 1965, 10th Cavalry papers, MHI.

Killed at Santiago, Cuba, 1 Jul 1898. SOURCE: SecWar, *AR 1898*, 323; *ANJ* 36 (11 Feb 1898): 567.

Killed in action, Cuba, 1898. SOURCE: Scipio, *Last of the Black Regulars*, 29.

DODSON, Lucious; Private; K/10th Cav. Transferred to K/10th Cavalry. SOURCE: SO 45, AGO, 24 Feb 1903.

Released to duty from treatment for acute chancroids, Ft Robinson, NE, 17 May 1903. SOURCE: Post Surgeon to CO, K/10, 17 May 1903, LS, Post Surgeon, Ft Robinson.

Released to duty from treatment for acute chancroids, Ft Robinson, NE, 4 Jun 1903. SOURCE: Post Surgeon to CO, K/10, 4 Jun 1903, LS, Post Surgeon, Ft Robinson.

At Ft Robinson, 1904.

DOLBY; Private; M/10th Cav. At Ft Apache, AZ, 1890, subscribed $.50 to testimonial to General Grierson. SOURCE: List of subscriptions, 23 Apr 1890, 10th Cavalry papers, MHI.

DOLBY, Eli R.; Sergeant; Band/10th Cav. Private, at Ft Apache, AZ, 1890, subscribed $.50 to testimonial to General Grierson. SOURCE: List of subscriptions, 23 Apr 1890, 10th Cavalry papers, MHI.

Private, served in 10th Cavalry in Cuba, 1898. SOURCE: Cashin, *Under Fire with the Tenth Cavalry*, 359.

Sergeant; his quarters at Ft Robinson, NE, contain three wash tubs and sink without sewer connection, with water running over ground to adjoining yard. SOURCE: Post Surgeon to CO, Ft Robinson, 3 Sep 1903, LS, Post Surgeon, Ft Robinson,.

Musician from Ohio; plays bass drum and violin. SOURCE: Lowe, "Camp Life," 206.

Son Eli Ross, Jr., born to wife, maiden name Maria Angela Elias, Ft Robinson, 1 Sep 1905; third child. SOURCE: Medical History, Ft Robinson.

DOLMAN, Norman; L/10th Cav. Original member of 10th Cavalry; in troop when organized, Ft Riley, KS, 21 Sep 1867. SOURCE: McMiller, "Buffalo Soldiers," 78.

DONNELLY, Thomas; Private; E/10th Cav. Deserted at Seminole Agency, Indian Territory, 7 Nov 1869. SOURCE: CO, 10 Cav, to AG, USA, 12 Dec 1969, ES, 10 Cav, 1866–71.

DONSON, Robert; Private; K/10th Cav. Served in 10th Cavalry, 1898; remained in U.S. during war with Spain. SOURCE: Cashin, *Under Fire with the Tenth Cavalry*, 349.

DOOLEY, William; F/38th Inf. Enlisted Columbia, TN, 4 Mar 1867; assigned to F/38th Infantry, Ft Leavenworth, KS: "We fought many Indians in Kansas, Colorado, and New Mexico and for nearly two years kept on the trails of different tribes. Had quite a few skirmishes with the Indians along the western and northern part of Mexico, and saw many Indians while in service, and scalped quite a number"; will be age 89 next Feb; lives with nephew and niece, "and if it was not for them I do not know what would become of me." SOURCE: *Winners of the West* 6 (Feb 1929): 7.

DOOLEY, William J.; Private; E/9th Cav. Transferred from E/25th Infantry. SOURCE: SO 21, AGO, 26 Jan 1898.

Returned from furlough to duty at Ft Robinson, NE, 10 Sep 1898.

DOOMS, Thomas; Corporal; M/10th Cav. Born in Kentucky; private, corporal, sergeant, C/10th Cavalry, 4 Jan 1887-3 Jan 1892; private, 29 Sep 1892; corporal, 1 Feb 1897; stationed at Ft Assiniboine, MT, 1897. SOURCE: Baker, Roster.

Corporal, C/10th Cavalry, served in 10th Cavalry in Cuba, 1898. SOURCE: Cashin, *Under Fire with the Tenth Cavalry*, 339.

Born Bourbon Co., KY; corporal, M/10th Cavalry, age 42, fourteen years' service, died Ft Robinson, NE, 17 Mar 1904. SOURCE: Monthly Report, Chaplain Anderson, AGO File 53901.

Buried at Ft Robinson, 17 Mar 1904. SOURCE: List of Interments, Ft Robinson.

DORAM, Shaler; Private; B/9th Cav. At Ft D. A. Russell, WY, in 1910. SOURCE: *Illustrated Review: Ninth Cavalry.*

DORILY, John; K/10th Cav. Original member of 10th Cavalry; in troop when organized, Ft Riley, KS, 1 Sep 1867. SOURCE: McMiller, "Buffalo Soldiers," 77.

DORSET, Edward; G/10th Cav. Original member of 10th Cavalry; in troop when organized, Ft Leavenworth, KS, 5 Jul 1867. SOURCE: McMiller, "Buffalo Soldiers," 74.

DORSEY; 9th Cav. Served at Ft Duchesne, UT; son George married Viola Rucker, daughter of Sgt. Alfred Rucker, 24th Infantry, and resided in Salt Lake City, UT. SOURCE: Clark, "A History of the Twenty Fourth," 79.

DORSEY, Charles A.; Sergeant; G/10th Cav. Born in West Virginia; private and corporal, L/10th Cavalry, 6 Sep 1882–5 Sep 1887; private, 13 Sep 1887; transferred to F/10th Cavalry, 25 Aug 1890; transferred to G/10th Cavalry, 17 Oct 1890; farrier, 9 Aug 1892; corporal, 13 Dec 1895; sergeant, 17 Dec 1895; stationed at Ft Assiniboine, MT, 1897. SOURCE: Baker, Roster.

Served in 10th Cavalry in Cuba, 1898. SOURCE: Cashin, *Under Fire with the Tenth Cavalry*, 344.

DORSEY, Edward A.; Corporal; K/10th Cav. Served in 10th Cavalry, 1898; remained in U.S. during war with Spain. SOURCE: Cashin, *Under Fire with the Tenth Cavalry*, 348.

DORSEY, F. E.; Private; B/9th Cav. Enlisted at Ft D. A. Russell, WY, 14 Oct 1885.

DORSEY, Frank; Private; C/9th Cav. Killed in action against Victorio, Mimbres Mountains, NM, 28 May 1879; Pvt. George W. Moore wounded in same fight. SOURCE: Hamilton, "History of the Ninth Cavalry," 43; *Illustrated Review: Ninth Cavalry.*

Buried where he fell, in well-marked grave. SOURCE: Billington, "Black Cavalrymen," 64.

DORSEY, G.; Private; L/9th Cav. On detached service in field, New Mexico, 21 Jan–24 Feb 1881. SOURCE: Regt Returns, 9 Cav, Feb 1881.

DORSEY, G.; Trumpeter; H/9th Cav. On furlough in Buffalo, WY, 15 Jul–4 Aug 1890.

DORSEY, Harry; Private; K/10th Cav. Transferred to 24th Infantry. SOURCE: SO 303, AGO, 27 Dec 1902.

Released to duty from treatment for venereal warts and gonorrhea, Ft Robinson, NE, 11 Jan 1903. SOURCE: Post Surgeon to CO, K/10, 11 Jan 1903, LS, Post Surgeon, Ft Robinson.

DORSEY, Henry; Private; K/10th Cav. Original member of 10th Cavalry; in troop when organized, Ft Riley, KS, 1 Sep 1867. SOURCE: McMiller, "Buffalo Soldiers," 77.

Ordered to Wilmington, DE, as witness in William Bater murder trial. SOURCE: TWX, AAG, DeptMo, to CO, Det, 10 Cav, 15 May 1868, LR, Det 10 Cav, 1868–69.

DORSEY, James; M/10th Cav. Original member of 10th Cavalry; in troop when organized, Ft Riley, KS, 15 Oct 1867. SOURCE: McMiller, "Buffalo Soldiers," 79.

DORSEY, John; G/10th Cav. Original member of 10th Cavalry; in troop when organized, Ft Leavenworth, KS, 5 Jul 1867. SOURCE: McMiller, "Buffalo Soldiers," 74.

DORSEY, Osborne; Private; A/9th Cav. At Ft D. A. Russell, WY, in 1910. SOURCE: *Illustrated Review: Ninth Cavalry,* with picture.

DORSEY, Robert; Private; I/10th Cav. Served in 10th Cavalry, 1898; remained in U.S. during war with Spain. SOURCE: Cashin, *Under Fire with the Tenth Cavalry,* 348.

Fined $10 and $4.80 court costs for carrying concealed weapon, Crawford, NE, 12 Mar 1903.

Dishonorably discharged and confined at Ft Robinson, NE, Feb 1904, in accordance with Special Order 17, Department of the Missouri; released Apr 1904.

DORSEY, Solomon T.; Sgt; B/10th Cav. Born in Pennsylvania; private, B/10th Cavalry, 21 Mar 1890; corporal, 11 May 1894; sergeant, 24 Jul 1896; stationed at Ft Custer, MT, 1897. SOURCE: Baker, Roster.

DORSEY, Trace; M/10th Cav. Original member of 10th Cavalry; in troop when organized, Ft Riley, KS, 15 Oct 1867. SOURCE: McMiller, "Buffalo Soldiers," 79.

DORSEY, Wesley; Private; I/24th Inf. Enlisted Wilmington, DE, 4 Aug 1898. SOURCE: Muster Roll, I/24 Inf, Jan–Feb 1899.

Absent sick, whereabouts unknown; commander asks that his name be dropped. SOURCE: Muster Roll, I/24 Inf, Mar–Apr 1899.

Absent sick, whereabouts unknown. SOURCE: Muster Roll, I/24 Inf, May–Jun and Jul–Aug 1899.

Listed as having deserted, Montauk Point, NY, since 21 Sep 1899. SOURCE: Muster Roll, I/24 Inf, Sep–Oct 1899.

DORSEY, William H.; Private; A/24th Inf. On extra duty as blacksmith, Quartermaster Department. SOURCE: Order 52, Ft Huachuca, AZ, 7 Apr 1893, Name File, 24 Inf.

Died in the Philippines, 5 Apr 1901. SOURCE: *ANJ* 38 (13 Apr 1901): 803.

DOSIER, Edward; Private; H/10th Cav. Served in 10th Cavalry, 1898; remained in U.S. during war with Spain. SOURCE: Cashin, *Under Fire with the Tenth Cavalry,* 346.

DOUGHERTY, Charles; Private; 10th Cav. Arrived at Ft Leavenworth, KS, from Jefferson Barracks, MO. SOURCE: Adj, Ft Leavenworth, to HQ, Jefferson Bks, 9 Oct 1866.

DOUGLAS, Barney; Private; A/10th Cav. Released to duty from treatment for chancroids, Ft Robinson, NE, 8 Jul 1903. SOURCE: Post Surgeon to CO, A/10, 8 Jul 1903, LS, Post Surgeon, Ft Robinson.

Released to duty from treatment for gonorrhea, Ft Robinson, 13 Jul 1903. SOURCE: Post Surgeon to CO, A/10, 13 Jul 1903, LS, Post Surgeon, Ft Robinson.

DOUGLAS, Boney; Private; G/25th Inf. Wounded in action, El Caney, Cuba, 1 Jul 1898. SOURCE: Nankivell, *History of the Twenty-fifth Infantry,* 83.

DOUGLAS, Daniel; F/10th Cav. Original member of 10th Cav; in troop when organized, Ft Leavenworth, KS, 21 Jun 1867. SOURCE: McMiller, "Buffalo Soldiers," 73.

DOUGLAS, Joseph; 1st Sgt; E/9th Cav. Witness in court martial of 1st Lt. E. M. Heyle, 9th Cavalry, for brutality, camp near San Antonio, TX, Apr 1867; other witnesses: Sgt. Johnson Smith, Corporal Lock, Cpl. Henry Cants, all of E/9th Cavalry.

DOUGLAS, Turner; Staff Sgt; 10th Cav. Retired after thirty years' service, Ft Leavenworth, KS. SOURCE: *Cavalry Journal* 41 (Jul 1932): 61.

DOUGLAS, Vest; Sergeant; Machine Gun Troop/ 10th Cav. Veteran of Philippine Insurrection; private, G/9th Cavalry, at Ft D. A. Russell, WY, in 1910; sharpshooter; resident of Charlotte, NC. SOURCE: *Illustrated Review: Ninth Cavalry,* with picture.

Commissioned first lieutenant in regular Army, Camp Des Moines, IA, 15 Oct 1917. SOURCE: Glass, *History of the Tenth Cavalry,* appendix M.

DOUGLAS, William; K/10th Cav. Original member of 10th Cavalry; in troop when organized, Ft Riley, KS, 1 Sep 1867. SOURCE: McMiller, "Buffalo Soldiers," 77.

DOUGLASS, John; Private; K/10th Cav. At Ft Robinson, NE, 1904.

DOUGLASS, John H.; Private; K/10th Cav. Detailed as teamster, Camp Supply, Indian Territory. SOURCE: SO 54, HQ, Det 10 Cav, 31 Jul 1869, Orders, Det 10 Cav.

Inventory of his effects and final statement transmitted. SOURCE: CO, K/10, to CO, 10 Cav, Apr 1870, ES, 10 Cav, 1866–71.

DOUGLASS, Samuel W.; Sergeant; B/10th Cav. Born in Georgia; private, B/10th Cavalry, 1 Jan 1893; corporal, 15 Aug 1896; stationed at Ft Custer, MT, 1897. SOURCE: Baker, Roster.

Served in 10th Cavalry in Cuba, 1898; narrates experience as sergeant in Spanish-American War. SOURCE: Cashin, *Under Fire with the Tenth Cavalry,* 337, 257–62.

DOVER, Augustus; Private; M/10th Cav. Wounded in action, Jul 1882. SOURCE: Leckie, *The Buffalo Soldiers*, 238.

See **SCOTT**, Winfield, Sergeant, B/25th Infantry

DOVER, Philip H.; Private; C/9th Cav. Confined at Ft Robinson, NE, 1885. *See* **DIGGS**, James, Private, C/9th Cavalry

DOVLEY, William; Private; 9th Cav. Capt. Clarence A. Stedman, Dovley's troop commander, asks payment of full amount due Dovley, who transferred to his troop from 5th Cavalry. SOURCE: Stedman to Chief Paymaster, DP, 11 Aug 1897, Misc Records, DP.

DOWD; Corporal; A/9th Cav. Discharged by purchase. SOURCE: SO 97, AGO, 25 Apr 1894.

DOWD, Charles H.; Color Sgt; 9th Cav. At Ft Niobrara, NE, 1889. *See* **CARTER**, William H., Trumpeter, A/9th Cavalry

Corporal, A/9th Cavalry, since 6 Sep 1892. SOURCE: Roster, 9 Cav.

Promoted from corporal, A/9th Cavalry, to saddler sergeant, 9th Cavalry, vice Benjamin, promoted. SOURCE: *ANJ* 32 (3 Nov 1894): 154.

Discharged as color sergeant, 9th Cavalry, Ft Robinson, NE, Apr 1896. SOURCE: *ANJ* 33 (9 May 1896): 652.

Dowd was married and had no children; his widow married Sgt. Elisha Jackson, H/9th Cavalry, Ft Robinson, 15 Jun 1897. SOURCE: CO, Ft Robinson, to AG, USA, 17 Jun 1897, LS, Ft Robinson.

DOWLING, Jefferson; Sergeant; L/10th Cav. Born in Tennessee; private, D/10th Cavalry, 2 Apr 1894; corporal, 20 May 1895; stationed at Ft Assiniboine, MT, 1897. SOURCE: Baker, Roster.

Sergeant, L/10th Cavalry, served in 10th Cavalry, 1898; remained in U.S. during war with Spain. SOURCE: Cashin, *Under Fire with the Tenth Cavalry*, 350.

DOWNEY, John; Corporal; B/9th Cav. *See* **POTTER**, Cain, Private, B/9th Cavalry; **WATERS**, George, Private, B/9th Cavalry

DOWNING, D.; Sergeant; E/9th Cav. On detached service in field, New Mexico, 27 Jan–1 Feb 1881. SOURCE: Regt Returns, 9 Cav, Feb 1881.

DOWNS; Private; H/10th Cav. *See* **BATTLES**, Private, H/10th Cavalry

DOWNS, William; Private; D/10th Cav. Served in 10th Cavalry, 1898; remained in U.S. during war with Spain. SOURCE: Cashin, *Under Fire with the Tenth Cavalry*, 341.

DOYLE, Richard F.; Private; B/10th Cav. Served in 10th Cavalry in Cuba, 1898. SOURCE: Cashin, *Under Fire with the Tenth Cavalry*, 338.

DOZIER, Edward; Private; M/10th Cav. Transferred from M/10th Cavalry. SOURCE: SO 243, AGO, 16 Oct 1902.

DRAIN, S.; Private; K/9th Cav. On detached service in field, New Mexico, 21 Jan–8 Feb 1881. SOURCE: Regt Returns, 9 Cav, Feb 1881.

DRAIN, Simeon; B/10th Cav. Original member of 10th Cavalry; in troop when organized, Ft Leavenworth, KS, 1 Apr 1867. SOURCE: McMiller, "Buffalo Soldiers," 69.

DRAKE, Alonzo; Private; G/9th Cav. Carried request for help from Sgt. James Robinson's detachment when attacked by Apaches, Agua Chiquita Canyon, NM, Sep 1880. SOURCE: Billington, *New Mexico's Buffalo Soldiers*, 98.

DRAKE, Ellie; Horseshoer; K/9th Cav. At Ft D. A. Russell, WY, in 1910; resident of Madison Co., AL. SOURCE: *Illustrated Review: Ninth Cavalry,* with picture.

DRAKE, Grover C.; Corporal; K/9th Cav. At Ft D. A. Russell, WY, in 1910; resident of Columbus, OH. SOURCE: *Illustrated Review: Ninth Cavalry,* with picture.

DRAKE, Luther; Private; I/10th Cav. Served in 10th Cavalry, 1898; remained in U.S. during war with Spain. SOURCE: Cashin, *Under Fire with the Tenth Cavalry,* 348.

DRAKE, Robert I.; Private; G/10th Cav. Intelligent and highly educated; athlete and orator; enlisted in G/10th Cavalry, 1898. SOURCE: Lynk, *The Black Troopers,* 5.

Served in 10th Cavalry in Cuba, 1898. SOURCE: Cashin, *Under Fire with the Tenth Cavalry,* 345.

Born Woodford Co., KY; resident of Lexington, KY; noted athlete, actor, and "orator of rare power and ability"; enlisted for Cuban war and served with Band/10th Cavalry; now in G/10th Cavalry. SOURCE: Indianapolis *Freeman*, 4 Mar 1899.

DRANE, Lucilius; Sergeant; H/10th Cav. Born in Tennessee; private, H/10th Cavalry, 13 Apr 1894; corporal, 14 Oct 1896; stationed at Ft Assiniboine, MT, 1897. SOURCE: Baker, Roster.

Promoted to sergeant. SOURCE: *ANJ* 35 (22 Jan 1898): 382.

Served in 10th Cavalry, 1898; remained in U.S. during war with Spain. SOURCE: Cashin, *Under Fire with the Tenth Cavalry,* 346.

Visited by wife from Kansas City, MO, at Camp Forse, AL, for Thanksgiving 1898. SOURCE: Richmond *Planet*, 3 Dec 1898.

At Ft Sam Houston, TX, 1899. *See* **JENNINGS**, Andrew J., Sergeant, H/10th Cavalry

DRAPER, Frank; Private; M/24th Inf. Served in Houston, 1917; refused to turn in his rifle when ordered before mutiny for fear of reprisals; Eugenia Bennett, his sweetheart in Houston, later married him; veteran of 4.5 years. SOURCE: Haynes, *A Night of Violence*, 112, 121, 264.

DRAPER, Thomas M.; Private; I/24th Inf. Enlisted Mobile, AL, 31 Mar 1899. SOURCE: Muster Roll, I/24 Inf, Mar–Apr 1899.

Fined $2 by summary court. SOURCE: Muster Roll, I/24 Inf, May–Jun 1899.

Appointed cook, 1 Jul 1898. SOURCE: Muster Roll, I/24 Inf, Jul–Aug 1899.

Allotted $10 per month for six months to Margie A. Gibbs. SOURCE: Muster Roll, I/24 Inf, Sep–Oct 1899.

DRAYTON, Abram; Private; 25th Inf. Born Charleston, SC; enlisted, Charleston, occupation farmer, Ht 5'9", dark complexion, black hair and eyes, age 22, 14 Jun 1881. SOURCE: Descriptive & Assignment Roll, 25 Inf.

DREW, Albert; Sergeant; H/9th Cav. Private, fined $5 and costs for fast riding in town, Buffalo, WY, Sep 1886. SOURCE: *Big Horn Sentinel*, 2 Oct 1886.

Ranked number 47 among carbine sharpshooters with 72 percent, 1890. SOURCE: GO 1, AGO, 2 Jan 1891.

Sergeant, H/9th Cavalry, since 5 Nov 1885. SOURCE: Roster, 9 Cav.

Sergeant, H/9th Cavalry, Ft Robinson, NE, deposited $30 with paymaster, 1897.

DREW, James L.; Sergeant; 9th Cav. Letter, Ft Duchesne, UT, to editor asks about truth of Washington *Post* report that Mason Mitchell, former Rough Rider, was hooted off a Richmond stage for praising 10th Cavalry; editor verifies report. SOURCE: Richmond *Planet*, 21 Jan 1899.

DREW, John B.; Private; Band/10th Cav. Served in 10th Cavalry in Cuba, 1898. SOURCE: Cashin, *Under Fire with the Tenth Cavalry*, 352.

DRISCOLL, George; Sergeant; D/24th Inf. At Cabanatuan, Philippines, 1901. *See* **HALE**, Moses, Private, K/24th Infantry; **JOHNSON**, Otto, Private, D/24th Infantry; **STONE**, John H., Private, D/24th Infantry; **TATES**, Rollins, Private, D/24th Infantry

DRIVERS, Edward; Private; D/10th Cav. Served in 10th Cavalry, 1898; remained in U.S. during war with Spain. SOURCE: Cashin, *Under Fire with the Tenth Cavalry*, 341.

DRUMMAN, Hamilton; C/10th Cav. Original member of 10th Cavalry; in troop when organized, Ft Leavenworth, KS, 14 May 1867. SOURCE: McMiller, "Buffalo Soldiers," 70.

DRY, Clarence; Private; M/10th Cav. Served in 10th Cavalry, 1898; remained in U.S. during war with Spain. SOURCE: Cashin, *Under Fire with the Tenth Cavalry*, 351.

DRY, Will; Private; H/24th Inf. Enlisted Louisville, KY, 6 Jun 1893; discharged, Camp Tampa, FL, end of term, character excellent, single, 5 Jun 1898; $25 deposits and $57.33 retained pay; due U.S. for clothing $8.54. SOURCE: Muster Roll, H/24 Inf, May–Jun 1898.

Reenlisted for H/24th Infantry, Ft Douglas, UT, 28 Jun 1898; joined 3 Oct 1898; six years' continuous service; on special duty, laborer, Quartermaster Department, since 5 Oct 1898. SOURCE: Muster Roll, H/24 Inf, Sep–Oct 1898.

On special duty, laborer, Quartermaster Department, since 5 Oct 1898. SOURCE: Muster Roll, H/24 Inf, Nov–Dec 1898.

Discharged, character good, single, 29 Jan 1899; $17.85 clothing; reenlisted, Ft Douglas, 30 Jan 1899; on special duty as laborer, Quartermaster Department, since 5 Oct 1898. SOURCE: Muster Roll, H/24 Inf, Jan–Feb 1899.

DRYE, Frank L.; Private; Band/9th Cav. At Ft D. A. Russell, WY, in 1910; resident of Little Rock, AR. SOURCE: *Illustrated Review: Ninth Cavalry*, with picture.

DUBOISE, Stephen H.; Private; I/10th Cav. Served in 10th Cavalry in Cuba, 1898. SOURCE: Cashin, *Under Fire with the Tenth Cavalry*, 348.

DuBOSE, Edmond; Private; E/9th Cav. Participated in twelve-man scouting expedition commanded by Sgt. D. Williamson, E/9th Cavalry, 30 Jan–2 Feb 1902; detachment fought no engagements. SOURCE: Regt Returns, 9 Cav, Feb 1901.

"On 24th [June] left Legaspi, and shortly after arriving at Camalig two deserters from Ninth Cav (Russell and Dubose) surrendered to Lieutenant Pritchard, commanding officer at Camalig. I learned from them where Toledo was, and asked Pritchard to take DuBose as a guide and go after Toledo that night. I took Russell with me and went to Guinobatan and then to Jovellar, where I arrived at 10 o'clock. All reports indicated that the insurgents were rapidly disintegrating. Our country was kept well patrolled." SOURCE: Report of Capt. E. Wittenmyer, 15th Infantry, Sorsogon, Philippines, 10 Jul 1901, SecWar, *AR 1902*, 360.

Capture of Dubose and Russell at Camalig, 24 Jun 1901, reported. SOURCE: Col. Theodore J. Wint, 6th Cav, Commanding Subdistrict of Albay, 13 Aug 1901, SecWar, *AR 1902*, 346; Manila *Times*, 28 Jun 1901.

Press releases report surrender by deserters Dubose and Russell and that Bellarmino gave up two others, Hunter and Victor. SOURCE: *ANJ* 38 (20 Jul 1901): 1147.

Dubose and Russell moved to Guinobatan in confinement, 20 Dec 1901. SOURCE: Regt Returns, 9 Cav, Dec 1901.

Dubose and Russell, E/9th Cavalry, were hanged yesterday; they belonged to "a negro regiment. While their troop was operating against the insurgents in the province of Albay last August these men deserted and were afterward discovered serving in the ranks of the enemy." SOURCE: San Francisco *Chronicle*, dateline Washington, DC, 7, 8 Feb 1902.

Dubose and Russell were hanged, Guinobatan, Albay, 7 Feb 1902; orderly execution before about 3,000 spectators; several native petitions for clemency were received and rejected. SOURCE: San Francisco *Chronicle*, dateline Manila, 11, 12 Feb 1902.

Notice of hanging of Dubose and Russell, 7 Feb 1902. SOURCE: *ANJ* 39 (14 Jun 1902): 1046.

According to record of court martial, Dubose and Russell deserted at Camalig, about March 1, 1901, with six stolen carbines, three revolvers, three belts filled with ammunition and other government property, and then presented themselves to enemy, whom they joined and cooperated with, each as lieutenant of insurgent forces, in expeditions and engagements against U.S. troops for nearly four months. Gen. Adna Chaffee, in approving death sentence, said: "The evidence against these accused is strong and convincing, and their attempt to show their irresponsibility at the time of their desertion on account of drunkenness is negated by their systematic and felonious taking of arms and ammunition to be delivered to the enemy. No extenuating circumstances appear of record. The laws of war provide but one adequate penalty for the soldier who deserts his flag to fight in the ranks of the enemy against his own people." SOURCE: Washington *Evening Star*, 13 Feb 1902.

DUDLEY; Private; K/24th Inf. *See* **NICKLE**, Elijah, Private, K/24th Infantry

DUDLEY, G. W.; Private; H/9th Cav. On detached service, Ft Bayard, NM, 16 Jan–10 Feb 1881. SOURCE: Regt Returns, 9 Cav, Feb 1881.

DUDLEY, John H.; Corporal; H/24th Inf. Born Wilmington, DE; occupation musician; first enlistment, H/25th Infantry, Aug 1870; second discharge, Band/10th Cavalry, 17 Mar 1878; third discharge, Band/10th Cavalry, 17 Mar 1883; fourth discharge, married, character excellent, Ft Reno, Indian Territory, 12 Apr 1888; deposits, $500, 1885–87, clothing $127.05, retained $60; additional pay $3 per month; fifth enlistment, Ft Supply, Indian Territory, 13 Apr 1888; discharged, married, no children, character excellent, Ft Bayard, NM, 12 Apr 1893; deposits, $225, 1888–92, clothing $155.69, retained $60; additional pay $4 per month; enlisted Ft Bayard, 13 Apr 1893; transferred from band to E/24th Infantry, character very good, married, no children, 15 Jul 1893; deposits $250, retained $3.07; additional pay $5 per month. SOURCE: Descriptive Book, 24 Inf NCS & Band.

Mentioned as not absent without leave, Jan 1874. SOURCE: LS, 10 Cav, 1873–77.

Deposited $60 with paymaster. SOURCE: CO, 10 Cav, to Paymaster General, 26 Dec 1876, 12 Mar, 7 May 1877, LS, 10 Cav, 1873–77.

Enlisted 13 Apr 1898, Ft Douglas, UT; promoted from private to corporal, Tampa, FL, 10 May 1898; twenty-nine years' continuous service. SOURCE: Muster Roll, H/24 Inf, May–Jun 1898.

Wounded in action, San Juan, Cuba, 2 Jul 1898; returned to U.S. for treatment. SOURCE: Muster Roll, H/24 Inf, Jul–Aug 1898.

On furlough, authorized by surgeon's certificate, 15 Aug–13 Oct 1899; on special duty as clerk, Subsistence Department, since 15 Oct 1898.

On special duty as clerk, Subsistence Department, since 15 Oct 1898. SOURCE: Muster Roll, H/24 Inf, Nov–Dec 1898 and Jan–Feb 1899.

Corporal, H/24th Infantry, wounded in action, Cuba, 1898. SOURCE: Muller, *The Twenty Fourth Infantry*, 96.

Picture. SOURCE: Indianapolis *Freeman*, 18 Mar 1899.

Corporal, H/24th Infantry, retired May 1901. SOURCE: *ANJ* 37 (19 May 1900): 895.

DUESCAIR, Ortise; I/10th Cav. Original member of 10th Cavalry; in troop when organized, Ft Riley, KS, 15 Aug 1867. SOURCE: McMiller, "Buffalo Soldiers," 76.

DUEWSON, Harry; Private; C/9th Cav. At Ft D. A. Russell, WY, in 1910; resident of 216 Sixth St., Connersville, IN. SOURCE: *Illustrated Review: Ninth Cavalry*, with picture.

DUFF, Hall; Sergeant; L/10th Cav. Private, served in 10th Cavalry, 1898; remained in U.S. during war with Spain. SOURCE: Cashin, *Under Fire with the Tenth Cavalry*, 350.

Promoted from corporal, Sep 1899. SOURCE: *ANJ* 37 (7 Oct 1899): 122.

DUFF, John; Blacksmith; G/10th Cav. Served in 10th Cavalry in Cuba, 1898. SOURCE: Cashin, *Under Fire with the Tenth Cavalry*, 344.

DUFFRE, Charles; Recruit; Colored Detachment/ Mounted Service. Convicted by general court martial, Jefferson Barracks, MO, of drunkenness near water closet behind quarters of Company D of Instruction, Mounted Service, night of 9 Nov 1886; refusal to obey order of Lance Corporal Nadall, Colored Detachment, to go to quarters, flourishing revolver, threatening Nadall's life, discharging revolver repeatedly in quarters and on landing between there and river; sentenced to four months and loss of $10 per month for four months. SOURCE: GCMO 101, AGO, 8 Dec 86.

DUKE, James; Private; 24th Inf. Under arrest for embezzlement, Manila, Philippines. SOURCE: Manila *Times*, 29 Jan 1902.

DUKE, Thomas; Private; B/9th Cav. Killed in action against Indians, Boca Grande Mountains, 30 Apr 1881. SOURCE: Hamilton, "History of the Ninth Cavalry," 57; *Illustrated Review: Ninth Cavalry.*

DULTON, John; I/10th Cav. Original member of 10th Cavalry; in troop when organized, Ft Riley, KS, 15 Aug 1867. SOURCE: McMiller, "Buffalo Soldiers," 76.

DUMAS, Clark; Sergeant; M/10th Cav. Mentioned as deceased, Sep 1877. SOURCE: ES, 10 Cav, 1873–81.

DUMAS, Washington W.; E/10th Cav. Original member of 10th Cavalry; in troop when organized, Ft Leavenworth, KS, 15 Jun 1867. SOURCE: McMiller, "Buffalo Soldiers," 72.

DUNCAN, Austin; C/10th Cav. Original member of 10th Cavalry; in troop when organized, Ft Leavenworth, KS, 14 May 1867. SOURCE: McMiller, "Buffalo Soldiers," 70.

Papers in case of State of Kentucky v. Austin Duncan forwarded to Adjutant General, U.S. Army, 8 Jun 1867; Duncan removed by civil authorities from rendezvous where enlisted and held without cause. SOURCE: ES, 10 Cav, 1866–71.

DUNCAN, D.; Private; A/9th Cav. At Ft Stanton, NM, 1881. SOURCE: Regt Returns, 9 Cav, Jan 1881.

DUNCAN, James; Private; G/25th Inf. Dishonorable discharge, Brownsville. SOURCE: SO 266, AGO, 9 Nov 1906.

DUNCAN, Lee; Private; C/9th Cav. At Ft D. A. Russell, WY, in 1910; marksman; resident of 111 W. Indiana St., Evansville, IN. SOURCE: *Illustrated Review: Ninth Cavalry,* with picture.

DUNCAN, R.; Private; B/9th Cav. On detached service, Ft Bayard, NM, 16 Jan–9 Feb 1881. SOURCE: Regt Returns, 9 Cav, Feb 1881.

DUNCAN, Samuel; Private; G/48th Inf. Died in the Philippines, 10 Dec 1900. SOURCE: *ANJ* 38 (29 Dec 1900): 431.

DUNCAN, William; E/9th Cav. Born Saginaw, MI; enlisted, age 22, occupation grocer, yellow complexion, New York City, 11 Nov 1880; sustained compound fracture of right thigh as military prisoner, Ft Cummings, NM, 8 Mar 1882; received at Ft Leavenworth, KS, military prison as hospital case with recovery "remote and uncertain"; discharged on surgeon's certificate, U.S. Military Prison, Leavenworth, 5 May 1882. SOURCE: Certificates of Disability, DivMo, 1875–1887.

DUNDEE, James P.; Sgt Maj; 25th Inf. Deserted San Francisco, CA, 11 Jul 1899. SOURCE: Regt Returns, 25 Inf, Aug 1899.

DUNGEY, William L.; Private; D/9th Cav. At Ft D. A. Russell, WY, in 1910; resident of Nashville. SOURCE: *Illustrated Review: Ninth Cavalry,* with picture.

DUNIVANT, Boston; Private; B/9th Cav. At Ft D. A. Russell, WY, in 1910. SOURCE: *Illustrated Review: Ninth Cavalry,* with picture.

DUNKERSON, Pomp; Private; F/24th Inf. Died in the Philippines, 15 Dec 1900. SOURCE: *ANJ* 38 (29 Dec 1900): 431.

DUNLAP; Corporal; B/9th Cav. Led detachment in pursuit of Camp Bowie, AZ, Indians; followed them to Ft Stanton, NM, reservation and recovered five horses, 11–27 May 1876. SOURCE: Hamilton, "History of the Ninth Cavalry," 26; *Illustrated Review: Ninth Cavalry.*

DUNLAP, Cruise; Private; C/9th Cav. At Ft D. A. Russell, WY, in 1910; resident of Ross View, TN. SOURCE: *Illustrated Review: Ninth Cavalry,* with picture.

DUNLAP, Nicholas; Private; Band/9th Cav. With band on detached service at headquarters, District of New Mexico, Santa Fe, 1880; played B-flat tuba. SOURCE: Billington. *New Mexico's Buffalo Soldiers,* 226.

DUNLAP, Shurley; Private; H/9th Cav. At Ft D. A. Russell, WY, in 1910; resident of Paducah, KY. SOURCE: *Illustrated Review: Ninth Cavalry,* with picture.

DUNLAP, William; Private; M/10th Cav. Served in 10th Cavalry, 1898; remained in U.S. during war with Spain. SOURCE: Cashin, *Under Fire with the Tenth Cavalry,* 351.

DUNN, David; C/10th Cav. Original member of 10th Cavalry; in troop when organized, Ft Leavenworth, KS, 14 May 1867. SOURCE: McMiller, "Buffalo Soldiers," 70.

DUNN, Henry; Private; A/9th Cav. At Ft D. A. Russell, WY, in 1910. SOURCE: *Illustrated Review: Ninth Cavalry,* with picture.

DUNN, Howard P.; Private; K/10th Cav. Served in 10th Cavalry, 1898; remained in U.S. during war with Spain. SOURCE: Cashin, *Under Fire with the Tenth Cavalry,* 349.

DUNN, James; Private; I/25th Inf. Wounded in the head, Botelan, Philippines, 9 Dec 1899. SOURCE: *ANJ* 37 (3 Feb 1900): 526.

DUNTON, John; Sergeant; I/10th Cav. Born in Virginia; private, I/10th Cavalry, 10 Jul 1889; corporal, 5 Oct 1894; sergeant, 9 Apr 1896; stationed at Ft Assiniboine, MT, 1897. SOURCE: Baker, Roster.

His heroism in Cuban campaign, 1898, mentioned. SOURCE: Cashin, *Under Fire with the Tenth Cavalry,* 185, 347.

DUPEE, Louis; Private; F/10th Cav. Died 30 Dec 1876. SOURCE: ES, 10 Cav, 1873–81.

DURANT, Empire Adam; Corporal; I/7th Vol Inf. Born Wilmington, NC; died in Minnesota. SOURCE: Taylor, "Minnesota Black Spanish-American War Veterans."

DURANT, Will; 25th Inf. Body transferred from Montauk Point, NY, to National Cemetery, Cypress Hills, NY. SOURCE: *ANJ* 36 (21 Jan 1899): 480.

DURDEN, Theodore; Private; I/10th Cav. Served in 10th Cavalry, 1898; remained in U.S. during war with Spain. SOURCE: Cashin, *Under Fire with the Tenth Cavalry*, 348.

DURLESS, Alonzo J.; Private; 24th Inf. Transferred to B/10th Cavalry. SOURCE: SO 33, AGO, 9 Feb 1903.

Transferred to 24th Infantry. SOURCE: SO 56, AGO, 9 Mar 1903.

DUTTON, W. V.; Private; K/9th Cav. On detached service in field, New Mexico, 21 Jan–8 Feb 1881. SOURCE: Regt Returns, 9 Cav, Feb 1881.

DUVALL, Robert L.; QM Sgt; D/24th Inf. At Cabanatuan, Philippines, 1900–1901. *See* **BUFORD**, James J., Private, D/24th Infantry; **JOHNSON**, James, Private, D/24th Infantry; **LEE**, George, Private, D/24th Infantry; **ROBINSON**, Mason, Private, D/24th Infantry; **TATES**, Rollins, Private, D/24th Infantry

DUVALL, William H.; Private; D/10th Cav. Honorable mention for bravery against Comanches, Double Mountain Fork, Brazos River, TX, 5 Feb 1874. SOURCE: Baker, Roster.

DYALS, George; Sergeant; D/10th Cav. Born in North Carolina; private, M and H/9th Cavalry, 4 May 1887–3 May 1892; private, D/10th Cavalry, 4 Feb 1895; corporal, 22 Aug 1896; stationed at Ft Assiniboine, MT, 1897. SOURCE: Baker, Roster.

Promoted from corporal to sergeant, 13 Feb 1898. SOURCE: *ANJ* 35 (26 Feb 1898): 478.

Wounded in action, with loss of sight in one eye, 30 Jun 1898, and later discharged for disability. SOURCE: SecWar, *AR 1898*, 709; Bigelow, *Reminiscences of Santiago*, 113–14.

DYER; Private; I/9th Cav. *See* **MOORE**, Private, K/9th Cavalry

DYER, John; Private; Band/9th Cav. At Ft D. A. Russell, WY, in 1910; resident of New York City. SOURCE: *Illustrated Review: Ninth Cavalry,* with picture.

DYSON, James A.; Private; E/10th Cav. Served in 10th Cavalry in Cuba, 1898. SOURCE: Cashin, *Under Fire with the Tenth Cavalry*, 342.

E

EAGLIN, Thomas; Private; H/24th Inf. Enlisted Baltimore, MD, 21 Apr 1896; three years' continuous service. SOURCE: Muster Roll, H/24 Inf, May–Jun 1898.

Sick, disease contracted in line of duty, in hospital, Siboney, Cuba, 2–25 Aug 1898; sick en route to U.S. since 25 Aug 1898. SOURCE: Muster Roll, H/24 Inf, Jul–Aug 1898.

On furlough, authorized by surgeon's certificate, 9 Sep–8 Oct 1898; sick in hospital since 14 Oct 1898, disease contracted in line of duty. SOURCE: Muster Roll, H/24 Inf, Sep–Oct 1898.

Sick in hospital with chronic rheumatism, contracted in line of duty, until 30 Nov 1898; discharged on surgeon's certificate, character excellent, single, with $20.54 for clothing; degree of disability 50 percent. SOURCE: Muster Roll, H/24 Inf, Nov–Dec 1898.

EALY, John; Private; B/10th Cav. Relieved of duty with Commissary Department. SOURCE: SO 20, Det 10 Cav, Ft Dodge, KS, 16 Apr 1869, Orders, Det 10 Cav, 1868–69.

EARLES, Armstead; 1st Sgt; G/10th Cav. Sergeant, C/10th Cavalry, at San Carlos, AZ, authorized two-month furlough. SOURCE: ANJ 25 (28 Apr 1888): 794.

First sergeant, G/10th Cavalry, retired 1 Aug 1892. SOURCE: Baker, Roster.

Retired, convicted by general court martial, Ft Grant, AZ, of embezzlement and sentenced to dishonorable discharge and forfeiture of pay and allowances; Brig. Gen. Elwell S. Otis approved but mitigated sentence on recommendation of court to reimbursement of $89.40, which was cost of his subsistence and transportation for trial from Ft Clark, TX; clemency was due to his long and honorable service and restitution of funds. SOURCE: ANJ 34 (3 Jul 1897): 821.

EARLY, Anthony; Corporal; D/9th Cav. Enlistment in I/9th Cavalry authorized. SOURCE: Letter, AGO, 27 Sep 1893, Post Returns, Ft Robinson.

Promoted from lance corporal, D/9th Cavalry, to corporal, Jul 1895. SOURCE: ANJ 32 (13 Jul 1895): 758.

Mentioned as surviving Indian war veteran. SOURCE: Winners of the West 3 (Jul 1926): 7.

EARLY, Herbert; Private; G/10th Cav. Served in 10th Cavalry in Cuba, 1898. SOURCE: Cashin, Under Fire with the Tenth Cavalry, 345.

EASLEY, James; Private; A/24th Inf. Sharpshooter, at Ft Bayard, NM. SOURCE: ANJ 26 (8 Sep 1888): 27.

EASLY, Reuben; Private; A/10th Cav. Served in 10th Cavalry in Cuba, 1898. SOURCE: Cashin, Under Fire with the Tenth Cavalry, 336.

EASTMAN, Frank; Private; D/9th Cav. Died of tuberculosis in the Philippines, 3 Jan 1902. SOURCE: ANJ 39 (1 Mar 1902): 645.

EATON; Private; B/10th Cav. At Ft Apache, AZ, 1890, subscribed $.50 to testimonial to General Grierson. SOURCE: List of subscriptions, 23 Apr 1890, 10th Cavalry papers, MHI.

EATON; Private; H/10th Cav. Transferred from A/10th Cavalry. SOURCE: SO 89, AGO, Apr 1903.

EATON, James; Corporal; H/10th Cav. Served in 10th Cavalry, 1898; remained in U.S. during war with Spain. SOURCE: Cashin, Under Fire with the Tenth Cavalry, 346.

Toastmaster at H/10th Cavalry's Thanksgiving dinner, Camp Forse, AL, 1898. SOURCE: Richmond Planet, 3 Dec 1898.

EAVES, Pike; Private; M/10th Cav. Served in 10th Cavalry, 1898; remained in U.S. during war with Spain. SOURCE: Cashin, Under Fire with the Tenth Cavalry, 341.

ECTON, Charles; Sup Sgt; 24th Inf. Commissioned at Camp Des Moines, IA. SOURCE: Beasley, Negro Trailblazers, 285.

EDDINGS, James; D/48th Inf. Died in Minnesota. SOURCE: Taylor, "Minnesota Black Spanish-American War Veterans."

EDDINGS, W.; Private; A/9th Cav. At Ft Stanton, NM, 1881. SOURCE: Regt Returns, 9 Cav, Jan 1881.

On detached service in field, New Mexico, 29 Jan–15 Feb 1881. SOURCE: Regt Returns, 9 Cav, Feb 1881.

EDDY, William; M/10th Cav. Original member of 10th Cavalry; in troop when organized, Ft Riley, KS, 15 Oct 1867. SOURCE: McMiller, "Buffalo Soldiers," 79.

EDMONDS, John; Private; G/9th Cav. Born Charlotte Co., VA; father Henry Edmonds from Campbell Co., VA; mother unknown; enlisted Washington, DC, occupation laborer, Ht 5'5", 18 Aug 1887; discharged, Camp Bettens, WY, 17 Aug 1892; married Mary Hancock, daughter of

Benjamin and Sarah Hancock, of Campbell Co., age 23, 28 Sep 1892, while residing in Lynchburg, VA; resided in Rochester, Beaver Co., PA, 1899; pension $20 per month, 3 May 1930, while residing at 438 Holly, Philadelphia, PA; died of benign prostatic hypertrophy, U.S. Navy Hospital, Philadelphia, 19 Jan 1936; widow's pension $30 per month 4 Feb 1936, $40 per month 22 Mar 1944; died 5 Dec 1944. SOURCE: VA File C 2359453, John Edmonds.

Served 1887–92; age 71. SOURCE: *Winners of the West* 13 (Dec 1935): 2.

EDMONDS, Ralph; L/10th Cav. Original member of 10th Cavalry; in troop when organized, Ft Riley, KS, 21 Sep 1867. SOURCE: McMiller, "Buffalo Soldiers," 78.

EDMONDS, Robert; H/10th Cav. Original member of 10th Cavalry; in troop when organized, Ft Leavenworth, KS, 21 Jul 1867. SOURCE: McMiller, "Buffalo Soldiers," 75.

EDMONDS, Thomas; H/10th Cav. Original member of 10th Cavalry; in troop when organized, Ft Leavenworth, KS, 21 Jul 1867. SOURCE: McMiller, "Buffalo Soldiers," 75.

EDMONDSON, John; 1st Sgt; F/10th Cav. Lt. Col. A. D. Nelson, commander, Camp Supply, Indian Territory, transmits copy of Special Order 207, Camp Supply, promoting Edmondson to sergeant, F/10th Cavalry, 30 Oct 1870; commander, 10th Cavalry, replies that regimental records show Edmondson as first sergeant and contain no evidence of legal reduction, so promotion from private to sergeant is disapproved, 31 Oct 1870. SOURCE: ES, 10 Cav, 1866–71.

See **TAYLOR**, John, Private, F/10th Cavalry

EDMONDSON, Sam L.; Sergeant; I/9th Cav. Sergeant in troop since 6 May 1893. SOURCE: Roster, 9 Cav.

EDMUNDS; Private; B/10th Cav. At Ft Apache, AZ, 1890, subscribed $.50 to testimonial to General Grierson. SOURCE: List of subscriptions, 23 Apr 1890, 10th Cavalry papers, MHI.

EDMUNDSON, William; Private; B/49th Inf. Wounded in leg above knee, San Pablo, Luzon, Philippines. SOURCE: *ANJ* 38 (9 Feb 1901): 579.

EDWARDS; Private; E/10th Cav. Was frostbitten on way from Ft Washakie, WY, to Thermopolis, WY, in deep snow, Jan 1906.

EDWARDS, Alonzo; Private; L/24th Inf. On pass, involved in incident that triggered Houston riot, 1917; badly beaten in jail. SOURCE: Haynes, *A Night of Violence*, 95–96, 101.

EDWARDS, Amos K.; Saddler; I/10th Cav. Served in 10th Cavalry in Cuba, 1898. SOURCE: Cashin, *Under Fire with the Tenth Cavalry*, 347.

EDWARDS, Benjamin; Private; K/25th Inf. Captured by insurgents at Subig Pass, Philippines, 10 Nov 1900. SOURCE: Richmond *Planet*, 12 Jan 1901.

Returned by insurgent General Arsi, who surrendered to K/25th Infantry at Castillejos, 10 Apr 1901. SOURCE: Richmond *Planet*, 8 Jun 1901.

EDWARDS, E. W.; Sergeant. Leaving Army after five years with $1,400 in savings, to open business, in Atlanta, GA. SOURCE: Cleveland *Gazette*, 26 May 1888.

EDWARDS, George F.; Sergeant; H/10th Cav. Commissioned first lieutenant, Camp Des Moines, IA, 15 Oct 1917. SOURCE: Glass, *History of the Tenth Cavalry*, appendix M.

EDWARDS, Granville; Private; K/9th Cav. Discharged, end of term, Ft Robinson, NE, 13 Feb 1887.

EDWARDS, Guy; Private; Band/9th Cav. At Ft D. A. Russell, WY, in 1910; resident of Shelbyville, IN. SOURCE: *Illustrated Review: Ninth Cavalry*, with picture.

EDWARDS, Guy; Trumpeter; C/9th Cav. Expert rifleman at Ft D. A. Russell, WY, in 1910. SOURCE: *Illustrated Review: Ninth Cavalry*, with picture.

EDWARDS, James; Private; K/24th Inf. At San Carlos, AZ, 1890. *See* **HARDEE**, James A., Private, K/24th Infantry

EDWARDS, Joe; Private; C/9th Cav. Discharged on certificate of disability, with gonorrhea, Ft Robinson, NE, 2 Mar 1898. SOURCE: Certificates of Disability, Ft Robinson.

EDWARDS, John; Private; C/9th Cav. Discharged without honor. SOURCE: SO 68, AGO, 22 Mar 1898.

EDWARDS, John; Private; K/24th Cav. Left Mexico, Philippines, without authorization, accompanied by Pvt. David Scott, K/24th Infantry, 27 Sep 1899; died while prisoner of insurgents at Tarlac. SOURCE: Muller, *The Twenty Fourth Infantry*, 28.

EDWARDS, Joseph S.; Private; C/10th Cav. Served in 10th Cavalry in Cuba, 1898. SOURCE: Cashin, *Under Fire with the Tenth Cavalry*, 340.

EDWARDS, Julius; F/10th Cav. Original member of 10th Cavalry; in troop when organized, Ft Leavenworth, KS, 21 Jun 1867. SOURCE: McMiller, "Buffalo Soldiers," 73.

EDWARDS, L.; Private; E/9th Cav. On detached service in field, New Mexico, 27 Jan–1 Feb 1881. SOURCE: Regt Returns, 9 Cav, Feb 1881.

EDWARDS, L. J.; Private; A/9th Cav. At Ft Stanton, NM, 1881. SOURCE: Regt Returns, 9 Cav, Jan 1881.

EDWARDS, Lewis; Private; 25th Inf. Born Charleston, SC; enlisted, age 23, Ht 5'9", dark complexion, black hair and eyes, occupation driver, Charleston, 15 Jul 1881. SOURCE: Descriptive & Assignment Cards, 25 Inf.

EDWARDS, Randolph; Private; L/9th Cav. At Ft D. A. Russell, WY, in 1910; resident of Kansas City, MO. SOURCE: *Illustrated Review: Ninth Cavalry.*

EDWARDS, Richard C.; Private; K/9th Cav. At Ft D. A. Russell, WY, in 1910; sharpshooter; resident of Cumberland, MD. SOURCE: *Illustrated Review: Ninth Cavalry*, with picture.

EDWARDS, Robert; Private; G/9th Cav. Served as private, H/10th Cavalry, 1898; remained in U.S. during war with Spain. SOURCE: Cashin, *Under Fire with the Tenth Cavalry*, 346.

Veteran of Spanish-American War and Philippine Insurrection; at Ft D. A. Russell, WY, in 1910; resident of St. Louis. SOURCE: *Illustrated Review: Ninth Cavalry*, with picture.

EDWARDS, William; Private; F/25th Inf. Born Leavenworth, KS; Ht 5'11", age 30, in seventh year of service, 1902, character very good; tattoos: heart with female head and dagger on right forearm, and cross and heart on left forearm. SOURCE: Descriptive & Assignment Cards, 25 Inf.

EDWARDS, William D.; Corporal; A/10th Cav. At Bellevue, NE, rifle range, 1886. See **SHEPERD**, Frank, Private, M/9th Cavalry

Was clerk, G/9th Cavalry, when Barney McKay joined unit at Rosebud Agency, SD, Dec 1890; served continuously with McKay until close of campaign, spring 1891. SOURCE: VA File XC 2659455, Barney McKay.

Lance corporal, G/9th Cavalry, Ft Robinson, NE, promoted to corporal. SOURCE: *ANJ* 32 (8 Jun 1895): 674.

Corporal, A/10th Cavalry, served in 10th Cavalry, 1898; remained in U.S. during war with Spain. SOURCE: Cashin, *Under Fire with the Tenth Cavalry*, 337.

Captain, 49th Infantry, formerly with 10th Cavalry, ordered to New York City. SOURCE: *ANJ* 37 (7 Oct 1899): 122.

Captain, H/49th Infantry, commanded troops in attack at Alminos, Philippines, 2 Jan 1901. SOURCE: Manila *Times*, 6 Jan 1901.

One of twenty-three officers of 49th Infantry recommended as regular Army second lieutenants. SOURCE: CG, DivPI, Manila, 8 Feb 1901, to AGO, AGO File 355163.

Corporal, A/10th Cavalry, ordered to hospital, Hot Springs, AR. SOURCE: SO 161, DeptMo, 27 Aug 1902.

EGLIN, Ellis Moss; G/10th Cav. Original member of 10th Cavalry; in troop when organized, Ft Leavenworth, KS, 5 Jul 1867. SOURCE: McMiller, "Buffalo Soldiers," 74.

EIGHMIE, Isaac G.; Private; E/10th Cav. Served in 10th Cavalry in Cuba, 1898. SOURCE: Cashin, *Under Fire with the Tenth Cavalry*, 342.

ELIXANDER, Charles; C/10th Cav. Fined $1 and $4.80 costs for disturbing the peace by breaking a window of Annie Mathews, Crawford, NE, 7 Mar 1903.

ELLETT, Luther M.; A/24th Inf. Died of atrophy of liver, Philippines, 25 Sep 1899. SOURCE: *ANJ* 37 (7 Oct 1899): 119.

ELLINGTON, Jack; Private; G/10th Cav. Mentioned 1873. SOURCE: ES, 10 Cav, 1873–81.

Honorable mention for bravery against Comanches, Double Mountain Fork, Brazos River, TX, 5 Feb 1874. SOURCE: Baker, Roster.

ELLINGTON, Jacob; F/10th Cav. Original member of 10th Cavalry; in troop when organized, Ft Leavenworth, KS, 21 Jun 1867. SOURCE: McMiller, "Buffalo Soldiers," 73.

ELLIOT, George J.; Private; K/24th Inf. Fined $5 for absence from quarters after taps without proper authority, Cabanatuan, Philippines, 2 Apr 1901. SOURCE: Name File, 24 Inf.

ELLIOTT, James; Sergeant; D/10th Cav. Born in Georgia; private, farrier, corporal, in M, C, D/10th Cavalry, 16 May 1887–15 May 1892; private, 15 Jun 1892; sergeant, 18 Jun 1893; stationed at Ft Assiniboine, MT, 1897. SOURCE: Baker, Roster.

Former deserter, "now a very active and consistent Christian," assisting Chaplain Steward with series of gospel meetings, Ft Missoula, MT, Feb 1893. SOURCE: Monthly report, Chaplain Steward, 1 Mar 1893.

Served in 10th Cavalry in Cuba, 1898. SOURCE: Cashin, *Under Fire with the Tenth Cavalry*, 340–41.

Commended for distinguished service, battle of Santiago, Cuba, 1 Jul 1898. SOURCE: GO 15, AGO, 13 Feb 1900; SecWar, *AR 1898*, 709–10.

Activities in Cuba mentioned. SOURCE: Bigelow, *Reminiscences of Santiago*, 105, 114–15, 120–21, 130, 163.

Heroism mentioned in unsigned letter, Montauk, NY, 8 Oct 1898. SOURCE: Gatewood, *"Smoked Yankees"*, 80.

Awarded certificate of merit for distinguished service in Cuba, 1 Jul 1898. SOURCE: *ANJ* 37 (24 Feb 1900): 611; Steward, *The Colored Regulars*, 280.

ELLIOTT, Rufus; 24th Inf. Wounded in action, Cuba, 1898. SOURCE: Clark, "A History of the Twenty-fourth," 100; Muller, *The Twenty Fourth Infantry*, 18.

ELLIS; Corporal; K/25th Inf. With four privates was surprised by 100 Filipino insurgents and forced to retreat; Private McPheeters got lost but made it back; L/25th Infantry from Mabalacat four miles away came to rescue, early Jan 1900. SOURCE: Richmond *Planet*, 17 Feb 1900.

ELLIS, Arthur; Private; Band/9th Cav. Born St. Louis, MO; private, 8th Illinois Infantry, Jun 1898–Apr

1899; enlisted in regular Army, age 30, occupation laborer, Jefferson Barracks, MO; private, A/9th Cavalry, March 1908–March 1911, character on discharge excellent; grandson of pioneer Oakland, CA, barber, George Ellis. SOURCE: Beasley, *Negro Trailblazers*, 299–300.

Fought with Private Johnson, A/9th Cavalry, over ownership of dog; Ellis was knifed and Johnson was jailed, Ft. D. A. Russell, WY. SOURCE: *Wyoming State Tribune*, 18 Nov 1910.

Private, Band/9th Cavalry, at Ft. D. A. Russell, 1910. SOURCE: *Illustrated Review: Ninth Cavalry*, with picture.

ELLIS, Charles E.; Private; C/10th Cav. Served in 10th Cavalry, 1898; remained in U.S. during war with Spain. SOURCE: Cashin, *Under Fire with the Tenth Cavalry*, 340.

ELLIS, Edward; Private; H/24th Inf. Fined $2 by summary court, San Isidro, Philippines, for allowing his commander to approach within three yards while sentinel without saluting, 14 Jan 1902, fourth conviction; fined $2 for absence from bed check roll call, 10 Mar 1902; sentenced to fifteen days and $10 fine for entering native shack contrary to orders, Apr 1902. SOURCE: Register of Summary Court, San Isidro.

ELLIS, James; Sergeant; G/9th Cav. Veteran of Philippine Insurrection; at Ft D. A. Russell, WY, in 1910; marksman; resident of Chattanooga, TN. SOURCE: *Illustrated Review: Ninth Cavalry*, with picture.

ELLIS, James; Sergeant; L/10th Cav. Authorized four-month furlough from Ft Grant, AZ. SOURCE: *ANJ* 35 (28 Jan 1898): 526.

ELLIS, James; QM Sgt; L/9th Cav. Retired May 1902. SOURCE: *ANJ* 39 (24 May 1902): 955.

ELLIS, Merriman H.; 1st Sgt; D/24th Inf. In D/24th Infantry; authorized four-month furlough from Ft Supply, Indian Territory. SOURCE: *ANJ* 24 (5 Feb 1887): 550.

In E/24th Infantry; examined for ordnance sergeant, Ft Bayard, NM, 1893. SOURCE: *ANJ* 30 (8 Jul 1893): 763.

In D/24th Infantry; wounded in foot, Santiago, Cuba, 1 Jul 1898. SOURCE: SecWar, *AR 1898*, 437; Muller, *The Twenty Fourth Infantry*, 18.

In D/24th Infantry, at Cabanatuan, Philippines, 1900–01. *See* **BERRY**, William H., Private, D/24th Infantry; **BROWN**, Philip, Private, D/24th Infantry; **BUFORD**, James J., Private, D/24th Infantry; **JOHNSON**, George, Private, D/24th Infantry; **JOHNSON**, James, Private, D/24th Infantry; **JOHNSON**, Jason, Corporal, D/24th Infantry; **JOHNSON**, Otto, Private, D/24th Infantry; **LEAVELL**, William, Private, D/24th Infantry; **MOORE**, Cato, Private, D/24th Infantry; **MOORE**, Simon, Private, D/24th Infantry; **MORANDERS**, Joseph, Private, D/24th Infantry; **NEWELL**, Frank, Private, D/24th Infantry; **PREAR**, Wilson, Sergeant, D/24th Infantry; **RANSOM**, Henry, Private, D/24th Infantry; **ROBINSON**, Mason,

Private, D/24th Infantry; **SIMPSON**, James A., Private, D/24th Infantry; **TAGGART**, Henry, Private, D/24th Infantry; **TATES**, Rollins, Private, D/24th Infantry

Retired, Aug 1901. SOURCE: *ANJ* 38 (17 Aug 1901): 1235.

ELLIS, Robert; Private; H/24th Inf. At Ft McIntosh, TX, 1877. *See* **GRAYSON**, Charles H., Private, G/24th Infantry

ELLIS, Roscoe; Color Sgt; 24th Inf. Commissioned at Camp Des Moines, IA. SOURCE: Beasley, *Negro Trailblazers*, 285.

ELLIS, Thomas; I/25th Inf. Performed vocal solo at YMCA meeting, Marcelinas, Philippines, 24 Aug 1900. SOURCE: Richmond *Planet*, 20 Oct 1900.

ELLISON, James; K/10th Cav. Original member of 10th Cavalry; in troop when organized, Ft Riley, KS, 1 Sep 1867. SOURCE: McMiller, "Buffalo Soldiers," 77.

ELLISON, Lewis A.; F/25th Inf. At Botolen, Zambales, Philippines, Dec 1900; Methodist. SOURCE: Steward, *Fifty Years in the Gospel Ministry*, 326.

ELLISON, Sam; Private; D/9th Cav. At Ft D. A. Russell, WY, in 1910; resident of Chicago. SOURCE: *Illustrated Review: Ninth Cavalry*, with picture.

ELLISTON, Amos; Sergeant; F/10th Cav. Born in Tennessee; private, Band/25th Infantry, 12 Nov 1875–11 Nov 1880; private and sergeant, Band and G/10th Cavalry, 15 Feb 1881–14 Feb 1886; private, F/10th Cavalry, 15 Feb 1886; corporal, 22 Oct 1896; stationed at Ft Assiniboine, MT, 1897. SOURCE: Baker, Roster.

At Ft Apache, AZ, 1890, subscribed $.50 to testimonial to General Grierson. SOURCE: List of subscriptions, 23 Apr 1890, 10th Cavalry papers, MHI.

First sergeant, F/10th Cavalry, served in 10th Cavalry in Cuba, 1898. SOURCE: Cashin, *Under Fire with the Tenth Cavalry*, 343.

Sergeant, F/10th Cavalry, wounded in action, Santiago, Cuba, 1 Jul 1898. SOURCE: SecWar, *AR 1898*, 324.

ELMORE, Thomas; B/10th Cav. Original member of 10th Cavalry; in troop when organized, Ft Leavenworth, KS, 1 Apr 1867. SOURCE: McMiller, "Buffalo Soldiers," 69.

ELSBERRY, Isaiah C.; L/10th Cav. Original member of 10th Cavalry; in troop when organized, Ft Riley, KS, 21 Sep 1867. SOURCE: McMiller, "Buffalo Soldiers," 78.

ELZY, Robert; 1st Sgt; C/10th Cav. Recruit awaiting assignment to regiment, at St. Louis, MO, depot, May 1875. SOURCE: LS, 10 Cav, 1873–77.

Ranked number 91 among sharpshooters with over 90 percent, 1886. SOURCE: GO 97, AGO, 31 Dec 1886.

EMBRA, Isaac; Private; B/10th Cav. Served in 10th Cavalry, 1898; remained in U.S. during war with Spain. SOURCE: Cashin, *Under Fire with the Tenth Cavalry*, 339.

EMBREE, Benjamin; E/7th Inf USV. Died in Minnesota. SOURCE: Taylor, "Minnesota Black Spanish-American War Veterans."

EMERSON, William; Private; D/24th Inf. Won first place in bayonet fencing, military tournament, Albany, NY, autumn 1909. SOURCE: Muller, *The Twenty Fourth Infantry*, 60.

EMPOIRE, Theodore; K/10th Cav. Original member of 10th Cavalry; in troop when organized, Ft Riley, KS, 1 Sep 1867. SOURCE: McMiller, "Buffalo Soldiers," 77.

EMPSON, Theodore; Private; K/10th Cav. Ordered to Wilmington, DE, as witness in William Bater murder trial. SOURCE: TWX, AAG, DeptMo, to CO, Det 10 Cav, 15 May 1868, LR, Det 10 Cav, 1868–69.

ENGLISH, Charles; Private; G/10th Cav. Served in 10th Cavalry, 1898; remained in U.S. during war with Spain. SOURCE: Cashin, *Under Fire with the Tenth Cavalry*, 345.

ENGLISH, Ernest; Private; B/25th Inf. Dishonorable discharge, Brownsville. SOURCE: SO 266, AGO, 9 Nov 1906.

ENGLISH, George; Private; B/10th Cav. Served in 10th Cavalry in Cuba, 1898; drowned there, 22 Jun 1898. SOURCE: Cashin, *Under Fire with the Tenth Cavalry*, 338.

Died in Cuba, 22 Jun 1898. SOURCE: *ANJ* 36 (11 Feb 1899): 567.

ENNIS; Private; E/10th Cav. At Ft Apache, AZ, 1890, subscribed $.50 to testimonial to General Grierson. SOURCE: List of subscriptions, 23 Apr 1890, 10th Cavalry papers, MHI.

ENNIS, Evan; Private; C/9th Cav. Sentenced to dishonorable discharge and two years at Leavenworth military prison. SOURCE: GCMO 88, DP, 15 Dec 1885.

Escaped from guardhouse, Ft Robinson, NE, 18 Mar 1886.

ENOICE, William; D/10th Cav. Original member of 10th Cavalry; in troop when organized, Ft Leavenworth, KS, 1 Jun 1867. SOURCE: McMiller, "Buffalo Soldiers," 71.

EPHRAIM, Randall; Corporal; M/9th Cav. Veteran of Philippine Insurrection; at Ft D. A. Russell, WY, in 1910. SOURCE: *Illustrated Review: Ninth Cavalry*, with picture.

EPPERSON, Perry; Private; 10th Cav. Mentioned Mar 1874. SOURCE: ES, 10 Cav, 1873–81.

EPPERSON, Stephen O.; Private; C/9th Cav. At Ft D. A. Russell, WY, in 1910; resident of Columbia, MO. SOURCE: *Illustrated Review: Ninth Cavalry*, with picture.

EPPS, J.; Private; B/9th Cav. In hands of civil authorities, Uintah, UT, 20 Oct–2 Nov 1886, 25 Dec 1886–25 Feb 1887, and Salt Lake City, UT, 25 Feb–Jul 1887. SOURCE: Regt Returns, 9 Cav.

EPPS, Richard; Private; 9th Cav. Commended for bravery, Florida Mountains, MN, 1877. SOURCE: Billington, "Black Cavalrymen," 62; Billington, *New Mexico's Buffalo Soldiers*, 91.

ERICKSON, William E.; Private; I/25th Inf. Enlisted 1901. *See* **MURRY**, Mat, Private, 24th Infantry

Fined $1.50 by summary court for carelessness in counting off on guard mount, San Isidro, Philippines, 23 May 1902, first conviction. SOURCE: Register of Summary Court, San Isidro.

ERNEST, Thomas A.; Private; E/24th Inf. Wrote letter to editor, Salt Lake City *Tribune*, from Ft Bayard, NM, 1896, in response to rumors that city had reservations about impending arrival of black troops; letter published. SOURCE: Billington, *New Mexico's Buffalo Soldiers*, 186.

ERVIN, William A.; Private; E/9th Cav. Has measles, Apr 1896; at Ft Robinson, NE, only eight days when it developed; he probably brought it onto post; no other cases. SOURCE: Medical History, Ft Robinson.

ERVINE, C. V.; Private; D/10th Cav. Served in 10th Cavalry, 1898; remained in U.S. during war with Spain. SOURCE: Cashin, *Under Fire with the Tenth Cavalry*, 341.

ERVINE, James W.; Corporal; C/9th Cav. Private, I/9th Cavalry, on extra duty as painter, Ft Robinson, NE. SOURCE: Order 252, 22 Nov 1890, Post Orders, Ft Robinson.

Private on extra duty as mechanic, Quartermaster Department, Ft Robinson. SOURCE: Order 25, 23 Apr 1895, Post Orders, Ft Robinson.

Corporal, C/9th Cavalry, wounded in action, San Juan, Cuba, 1 Jul 1898. SOURCE: *Illustrated Review: Ninth Cavalry*.

Corporal, C/9th Cavalry, transferred from Reserve Divisional Hospital, Siboney, Cuba, to U.S. on U.S. Army Transport *Santiago* with yellow fever, 25 Jul 1898. SOURCE: Hospital Papers, Spanish-American War.

ERWIN, George; Private; I/10th Cav. Sentenced to dishonorable discharge and confinement, Ft Robinson, NE, Jan 1903. SOURCE: SO 9, DeptMo, 13 Jan 1903.

Released 30 Mar 1903.

ESTES, William; I/9th Cav. Private pension law grants him $20 per month. SOURCE: *Winners of the West* 3 (Apr 1926): 2.

ESTILL, Allen P.; Sergeant; C/24th Inf. Private, schoolteacher at Ft Huachuca, AZ, since 16 Dec 1892; relieved from extra duty as schoolteacher at Ft Huachuca, 28 Apr 1893. SOURCE: Name File, 24 Inf.

On extra duty as schoolteacher, Ft Huachuca, 1 Nov 1893. SOURCE: Letters and Orders Received, 24 Inf.

Sergeant, C/24th Infantry, transferred from Reserve Divisional Hospital, Siboney, Cuba, to U.S. on U.S. Army Transport *Vigilancia* with yellow fever, 6 Sep 1898. SOURCE: Hospital Papers, Spanish-American War.

ESTILL, Robert L.; Private; I/9th Cav. Awaiting transportation from Ft Robinson, NE, to station at Ft Washakie, WY, May–Jun 1896.

EUBANKS, John; Saddler; B/10th Cav. Saddler, F/9th Cavalry, 1893.

Served in 10th Cavalry in Cuba, 1898. SOURCE: Cashin, *Under Fire with the Tenth Cavalry*, 338.

EUSTON, Henry; Private; M/9th Cav. Convicted by general court martial, Jefferson Barracks, MO, of desertion, 7 Sep 1881; sentenced to dishonorable discharge and four years; sentence reduced to two years by General Sherman. SOURCE: GCMO 74, AGO, 4 Dec 1881.

EVANS, Aaron; A/10th Cav. Original member of 10th Cavalry; in troop when organized, Ft Leavenworth, KS, 18 Feb 1867. SOURCE: McMiller, "Buffalo Soldiers," 68.

EVANS, Charles; H/10th Cav. Original member of 10th Cavalry; in troop when organized, Ft Leavenworth, KS, 21 Jul 1867. SOURCE: McMiller, "Buffalo Soldiers," 75.

EVANS, Elleck; Private; 10th Cav. Arrived from Jefferson Barracks, MO, at Ft Leavenworth, KS. SOURCE: Adj, Ft Leavenworth, to HQ, Jefferson Bks, 9 Oct 1866.

EVANS, F.; Private; A/9th Cav. At Ft Stanton, NM, 1881. SOURCE: Regt Returns, 9 Cav, Jan 1881.

EVANS, Frank; Private; G/24th Inf. Born Wilmington, NC; enlisted Baltimore, MD, Ht 5'6", age 29, 7 Jun 1890; transferred from Band/10th Cavalry to Band/24th Infantry, Ft Bayard, NM, May 1892; transferred to G/24th Infantry, 1 Sep 1892. SOURCE: Descriptive Book, 24 Inf NCS & Band.

EVANS, Frank, Sr.; Private; D/24th Inf. Served 1876–81; member, Camp 11, National Indian War Veterans, St. Joseph, MO; died in Wichita, KS. SOURCE: *Winners of the West* 15 (Apr 1938): 5.

Born a slave, six miles south of Griffin, Spalding Co., GA, parents unknown, 13 Jan 1855; enlisted Nashville, TN, Ht 5'3", yellow complexion, 4 Jan 1876; served in Indian war of 1876, TX and Indian Territory; wagoner, 21 Sep 1876; private, Apr 1878; discharged Ft Sill, Indian Territory, 3 Jan 1881; residences: Nashville, 1875–1901, Wellston, OK,

1901, Fallis, OK, 1904, Chandler, OK, 1908, Wichita, 1923; worked as barber until 1929; married Mollie Steward, 15 Nov 1883; five children include daughter Jessie L. Douglass, 1021 Cleveland, Wichita; three sons served in World War I: Willie in 803rd Pioneer Infantry, Frank in U.S. Navy, Lillard in 25th Infantry; pension $50 per month, 24 Mar 1927, $72 per month, 29 Nov 1937; died of chronic interstitial nephritis, 27 Feb 1938. SOURCE: VA File C 2577383, Frank Evans, Sr.

EVANS, Harry V.; Private; E/10th Cav. Served in 10th Cavalry in Cuba, 1898. SOURCE: Cashin, *Under Fire with the Tenth Cavalry*, 342.

EVANS, Henry; Private; A/10th Cav. Original member of 10th Cavalry; in troop when organized, Ft Leavenworth, KS, 18 Feb 1867. SOURCE: McMiller, "Buffalo Soldiers," 68.

Commander wants immediate report of this case; Evans enlisted by you and sent per descriptive roll of 5 Feb 1867 but identified at Jefferson Barracks, MO, as deserter from 38th Infantry, 6 Feb 1867; turned over to 38th Infantry at Jefferson Barracks. SOURCE: Adj, 10 Cav, to Capt. Henry Davis, Recruiting Officer, Memphis, TN, 20 Feb 1867, LS, 10 Cav, 1866–67.

EVANS, Henry; Private; H/10th Cav. Enlisted Sep 1867; discharged Jan 1873. SOURCE: LS, 10 Cav, 1873–83.

EVANS, Isaac; Private; I/10th Cav. Original member of 10th Cavalry; in troop when organized, Ft Riley, KS, 15 Aug 1867. SOURCE: McMiller, "Buffalo Soldiers," 76.

Detailed as teamster. SOURCE: SO 54, HQ, Det 10 Cav, Camp Supply, Indian Territory, 31 Jul 1869.

EVANS, James; Private; A/9th Cav. At Ft D. A. Russell, WY, in 1910; sharpshooter. SOURCE: *Illustrated Review: Ninth Cavalry*, with picture.

EVANS, John; Private; F/10th Cav. Original member of 10th Cavalry; in troop when organized, Ft Leavenworth, KS, 21 Jun 1867. SOURCE: McMiller, "Buffalo Soldiers," 73.

2nd Lt. M. M. Maxon, commander, F/10th Cavalry, Camp Supply, Indian Territory, asks that Evans be returned from regimental headquarters to his troop, 9 Nov 1869; headquarters agrees to do so at first opportunity, 2 Dec 1869. SOURCE: ES, 10 Cav, 1866–71.

EVANS, John; Private; C/49th Inf. Drowned in Cagayan River, Alcala, Philippines, 22 Jul 1900. SOURCE: *ANJ* 38 (20 Oct 1900): 186; *ANJ* 37 (11 Aug 1900): 1191.

Drowned because he got cramp while bathing and could not swim against swift current. SOURCE: Fletcher, *The Black Soldier*, 297.

EVANS, Joseph B.; Private; E/9th Cav. Died of cholera in the Philippines, 14 Jun 1902. SOURCE: *ANJ* 39 (9 Aug 1902): 1248.

EVANS, Owen; Private; B/10th Cav. Served in 10th Cavalry, 1898; remained in U.S. during war with Spain. SOURCE: Cashin, *Under Fire with the Tenth Cavalry*, 339.

EVANS, Robert; Private; D/9th Cav. At Ft D. A. Russell, WY, in 1910; resident of St. Louis. SOURCE: *Illustrated Review: Ninth Cavalry*, with picture.

EVANS, Robert; Sergeant; C/10th Cav. Killed in action, Gayleysville Canyon, AZ, 3 Jul 1886; Evans Road, Ft Huachuca, AZ, named for him. SOURCE: Orville A. Cochran to H. B. Wharfield, 5 Apr 1965, 10th Cavalry papers, MHI; Baker, Roster.

EVANS, Samuel T.; Corporal; H/24th Inf. Enlisted Indianapolis, IN, 9 Feb 1899. SOURCE: Muster Roll, H/24 Inf, Jan–Feb 1899.

Letter, San Nicolas, Philippines, 30 Mar 1900. SOURCE: Gatewood, *"Smoked Yankees"*, 273.

EVANS, Thomas; Private; I/10th Cav. Served in 10th Cavalry, 1898; remained in U.S. during war with Spain. SOURCE: Cashin, *Under Fire with the Tenth Cavalry*, 348.

EVANS, Tommie; Private; K/10th Cav. Sentenced to dishonorable discharge and jail, Ft Robinson, NE. SOURCE: SO 101, DeptMo, 1 Jul 1904.

EVERETT, James; Private; I/25th Inf. Fined $2.50 by summary court, San Isidro, Philippines, for disobeying adjutant's order to deliver communication to an officer. SOURCE: Register of Summary Court, San Isidro.

EVERETT, James; Corporal; E/10th Cav. Commissioned second lieutenant of cavalry, Camp Des Moines, IA, 27 Sep 1918. SOURCE: Glass, *History of the Tenth Cavalry*, appendix M.

EVERHART, Harry; Private; 9th Cav. Wounded in knee, Naco, AZ, 11 Oct 1914. SOURCE: Cleveland *Gazette*, 11 Oct 1914.

EWELL, William C.; Blacksmith; H/10th Cav. Born in Virginia; private and corporal, K/10th Cavalry, 17 Oct 1887–20 Apr 1892; private, H/10th Cavalry, 13 Nov 1895; corporal, 12 Feb 1896; stationed at Ft Assiniboine, MT, 1897. SOURCE: Baker, Roster.

Corporal, K/10th Cavalry, at Ft Apache, AZ, 1890, subscribed $.50 to testimonial to General Grierson. SOURCE: List of subscriptions, 23 Apr 1890, 10th Cavalry papers, MHI.

Blacksmith, served in 10th Cavalry, 1898; remained in U.S. during war with Spain. SOURCE: Cashin, *Under Fire with the Tenth Cavalry*, 346.

EWING, Calvin; C/24th Cav. Leader of C/24th Infantry's string band, San Carlos, AZ, 1890. SOURCE: Cleveland *Gazette*, 19 Jul 1890.

EWING, George W.; Corporal; H/24th Inf. On special duty at target range, Ft Huachuca, AZ, 30 Apr–30 Jun 1893. SOURCE: Name File, 24 Inf.

EWING, Jack; 24th Inf. Resided at 545 South 10th East, Salt Lake City, UT, in 1898. SOURCE: Clark, "A History of the Twenty-fourth," appendix E.

EWING, Jacob; H/10th Cav. Original member of 10th Cavalry; in troop when organized, Ft Leavenworth, KS, 21 Jul 1867. SOURCE: McMiller, "Buffalo Soldiers," 75.

𝟳

FACE, Bucker; M/10th Cav. Original member of 10th Cavalry; in troop when organized, Ft Riley, KS, 15 Oct 1867. SOURCE: McMiller, "Buffalo Soldiers," 79.

FACIT; Private; E/10th Cav. At Ft Apache, AZ, 1890, subscribed $.50 to testimonial to General Grierson. SOURCE: List of subscriptions, 23 Apr 1890, 10th Cavalry papers, MHI.

FACTOR, Pompey; Private; 24th Inf. Seminole-Negro scout; won Medal of Honor for heroism, with Lieutenant Bullis, Pecos River, TX, 26 Apr 1875. SOURCE: Carroll, *The Black Military Experience*, 390.

FAGEN, David; Private; I/24th Inf. Enlisted Tampa, FL, 4 Jun 1898; assigned to H/24th Infantry; sick in hospital, Siboney, Cuba, 21–25 Aug 1898, and en route to U.S., 25–31 Aug 1898, disease contracted in line of duty. SOURCE: Muster Roll, H/24 Inf, Jul–Aug 1898.

Rejoined company, 2 Sep 1898; due U.S. for ordnance (one oiler) $.25. SOURCE: Muster Roll, H/24 Inf, Sep–Oct 1898.

Fined $2 by summary court, 25 Nov 1898; due U.S. for ordnance (one knife and one fork) $.12. SOURCE: Muster Roll, I/24 Inf, Nov–Dec 1898.

Discharged, single, character good, Ft Douglas, UT, 28 Jan 1899; due U.S. for clothing $20.93; enlisted, Ft McPherson, GA, 9 Feb 1899; assigned to I/24th Infantry. SOURCE: Muster Roll, I/24 Inf, Jan–Feb 1899.

Fined $1 by garrison court martial, 25 Mar 1899. SOURCE: Muster Roll, I/24 Inf, Mar–Apr 1899.

On detached service at Three Rivers, CA, 3 May–21 Jun 1899; on detached service at Presidio of San Francisco, 22 Jun 1899. SOURCE: Muster Roll, I/24 Inf, May–Jun 1899.

Rejoined company, 26 Jul 1899; fined $5 by summary court, 7 Jun 1899; fined $2 by summary court, 14 Jul 1899. SOURCE: Muster Roll, I/24 Inf, Jul–Aug 1899.

Fined $10 by summary court, 11 Sep 1899; fined $5 by summary court, 22 Sep 1899; fined $6 by summary court, 26 Oct 1899. SOURCE: Muster Roll, I/24 Inf, Sep–Oct 1899.

Sentenced to thirty days and $15 fine by summary court, 2 Oct 1899; deserted at San Isidro, Philippines, 17 Nov 1899; due U.S. for clothing $.86. SOURCE: Muster Roll, I/24 Inf, Nov–Dec 1899.

Deserted, San Isidro, Nueva Ecija, 28 Nov 1899. SOURCE: Regt Returns, 24 Inf, Nov 1899.

Biographical sketch. SOURCE: Logan and Winston, *Dictionary of American Negro Biography*, 217–18.

See AGO Files 198322, 215561, 356799, 431081; Robinson and Schubert, "David Fagen."

FAGG, John; Private; K/10th Cav. Sentenced to dishonorable discharge and imprisonment, Ft Robinson, NE, Feb 1904. SOURCE: SO 25, DeptMo, 1904.

Released Apr 1904.

FAGGINS, John H.; Private; K/24th Inf. Fined $4, Cabanatuan, Philippines, 25 Jan 1901, for failure to come to attention on signal of attention and continuing to talk in ranks after being ordered to stop; witness: Sergeant Green, K/24th Infantry. Fined $5 for failure to repair for reveille, Cabanatuan, 22 Apr 1901; witness: 1st. Sgt. Jacob Stevens, K/24th Infantry. Fined one month's pay and jailed for thirty days for concealing bottle of spirits in clothes and trying to take it into guardhouse while on guard duty, Cabanatuan, 17 Jul 1901; witness: Sergeant Prear, D/24th Infantry; signed consent to be tried by summary court with "X." SOURCE: Name File, 24 Inf.

See **DANDRIDGE**, George, Private, K/24th Infantry

FAIN, Frank; 1st Sgt; F/9th Cav. First sergeant as of 16 Jul 1892. SOURCE: Roster, 9 Cav

FAIRFAX, Jesse J. A.; Private; F/9th Cav. Began eighteen-month sentence, Ft Robinson, NE, 8 Mar 1895. SOURCE: SO 30, DP, 1895.

Transferred to Ft Logan, CO. SOURCE: SO 80, DP, 5 Nov 1895.

FAIRHOLDS, Charles; M/10th Cav. Original member of 10th Cavalry; in troop when organized, Ft Riley, KS, 15 Oct 1867. SOURCE: McMiller, "Buffalo Soldiers," 79.

FALL, William H.; Private; E/10th Cav. Served in 10th Cavalry in Cuba, 1898. SOURCE: Cashin, *Under Fire with the Tenth Cavalry*, 342.

Confined for trial, Ft Robinson, NE, 26 Jan 1906; returned to station, Ft Washakie, WY, Mar 1906.

FANT, Daniel; Private; H/10th Cav. Served in 10th Cavalry, 1898; remained in U.S. during war with Spain. SOURCE: Cashin, *Under Fire with the Tenth Cavalry*, 348.

FARMAN, John; Private; C/48th Inf. Died of nephritis in the Philippines, 9 May 1900. SOURCE: *ANJ* 37 (19 May 1900): 903.

FARR, John H.; Private; K/10th Cav. At Ft Robinson, NE, 1904.

FARRALL, William H.; Cook; I/10th Cav. Died of self-inflicted gunshot wound, Holguin, Cuba, 2 Apr 1901. SOURCE: *ANJ* 38 (13 Apr 1901): 803.

FARRELL, Charles H.; Private; M/10th Cav. "Our mascot," enlisted Memphis, TN, 11 Sep 1867, and reported one week later, Ft Riley, KS; saw action against Indians at Quartermaster Creek, Indian Territory, autumn 1868, and against Cheyennes, Kiowas, Comanches, 1874; one of first signal men in regiment; lost left hand in shotgun blast, hunting quail in Texas, and since "a protege of the regiment"; "he wore himself out by hard and unsparing service, and deserves to be held in grateful memory by our regiment." SOURCE: Baker, Roster.

FARRELL, Charles J.; 9th Cav. *See* **McKAY**, Barney, Sergeant, G/9th Cavalry

FARRINGTON, George W.; Private; I/9th Cav. *See* **FEARINGTON**, George W., Private, I/9th Cavalry

FARRIS, Eugene; Sergeant; 24th Inf. Married Miss Nannie T. Coles, sister of his battalion sergeant major. SOURCE: Fletcher, *The Black Soldier*, 75–76.

FASIT, Benjamin; Sergeant; E/10th Cav. Served in 10th Cavalry in Cuba, 1898. SOURCE: Cashin, *Under Fire with the Tenth Cavalry*, 342.

Commended for distinguished service, battle of Santiago, Cuba, 1 Jul 1898. SOURCE: GO 15, AGO, 13 Feb 1900.

Awarded certificate of merit. SOURCE: Steward, *The Colored Regulars*, 280; *ANJ* 37 (24 Feb 1900): 611.

FAULKIN; Private; L/25th Inf. Wounded in ambush in the Philippines, 29 Jan 1900. SOURCE: Richmond *Planet*, 17 Mar 1900.

FAULKNER; Private; G/9th Cav. Wounded at Ft D. A. Russell, WY, 28 Oct 1910; died 31 Oct 1910. SOURCE: Cheyenne *State Leader*, 29 Oct and 1 Nov 1910.

FAULKNER, Charles S. C.; Sergeant; F/10th Cav. Born in Kentucky; private, H/10th Cavalry, 29 Jul 1879; corporal, 20 Mar 1881; sergeant, 11 Sep 1881; stationed at Ft Assiniboine, MT, 1897. SOURCE: Baker, Roster.

Sergeant, H/10th Cavalry, at Ft Apache, AZ, 1890, subscribed $.50 to testimonial to General Grierson. SOURCE: List of subscriptions, 23 Apr 1890, 10th Cavalry papers, MHI.

Sergeant, F/10th Cavalry, national standard bearer. SOURCE: *ANJ* 35 (19 Feb 1898): 458.

Served in 10th Cavalry in Cuba, 1898. SOURCE: Cashin, *Under Fire with the Tenth Cavalry*, 346.

FAULKNER, George; Private; K/24th Inf. At San Carlos, AZ, 1890. *See* **HARDEE**, James A., Private, K/24th Infantry

FEARINGTON, George W.; Private; I/9th Cav. Awarded certificate of merit, 24 Nov 1903, for excellent conduct and heroic service when troop barrack was destroyed by fire, Ft Duchesne, UT, 13 Dec 1899; took position on peak of building and stayed there applying water, although in serious danger, until fire was brought under control. SOURCE: GO 32, AGO, 6 Feb 1904.

At post hospital, Presidio of San Francisco, CA, with hole in chest; shot by Cpl. Walter Lockett, I/9th Cavalry, while in tent, early morning, 7 Nov 1902; Lockett was apparently drunk; both are ten-year men and veterans of Cuba and the Philippines; commander is Capt. Charles Young, whose troop "has always enjoyed a splendid reputation for discipline and good behavior." SOURCE: San Francisco *Chronicle*, 8 Nov 1902.

Veteran of Philippine Insurrection; at Ft D. A. Russell, WY, in 1910; sharpshooter; resident of Durham, NC. SOURCE: *Illustrated Review: Ninth Cavalry*, with picture.

FEARN, Henry; Private; D/10th Cav. Served in 10th Cavalry in Cuba, 1898. SOURCE: Cashin, *Under Fire with the Tenth Cavalry*, 341.

Wounded in action, Santiago, Cuba, 1898. SOURCE: SecWar, *AR 1898*, 711; Bigelow, *Reminiscences of Santiago*, 133.

FEASON, Henry; D/10th Cav. Resides in Cuba, 1933. *See* **WILSON**, George, Private, I/10th Cavalry

FEASTER, Thomas; Private; G/48th Inf. Convicted of rape and desertion by general court martial, San Fernando de la Union, Philippines; death sentence commuted to twenty years by President McKinley. SOURCE: *ANJ* 38 (22 Dec 1900): 407.

Released from confinement at Leavenworth military prison in accordance with Supreme Court's Deming decision, 19 May 1902. SOURCE: *ANJ* 39 (7 Jun 1902): 1005.

FEDER, Mathew; G/10th Cav. Original member of 10th Cavalry; in troop when organized, Ft Leavenworth, KS, 5 Jul 1867. SOURCE: McMiller, "Buffalo Soldiers," 74.

FELTON; Private; E/10th Cav. Frostbitten on way from Ft Washakie, WY, to Thermopolis, WY, in deep snow, Jan 1906.

FENNELL, Eugene S.; Trumpeter; B/10th Cav. Served in 10th Cavalry in Cuba, 1898. SOURCE: Cashin, *Under Fire with the Tenth Cavalry*, 338.

FENNELL, George M.; Private; A/9th Cav. At Ft D. A. Russell, WY, in 1910. SOURCE: *Illustrated Review: Ninth Cavalry*.

FENWICK, William J; Sergeant; C/9th Cav. Veteran of Philippine Insurrection; at Ft D. A. Russell, WY, in 1910; resident of 320 D. St., NE, Washington, DC. SOURCE: *Illustrated Review: Ninth Cavalry*, with picture.

FERGUSON; Sergeant; D/9th Cav. Led detachment scouting vicinity of Ft Lewis, CO, Jun 1883. SOURCE: Regt Returns, 9 Cav, Jun 1883.

FERGUSON, Albert; Private; M/10th Cav. Served in 10th Cavalry, 1898; remained in U.S. during war with Spain. SOURCE: Cashin, *Under Fire with the Tenth Cavalry*, 351.

FERGUSON, Arthur J.; Private; M/10th Cav. Confined awaiting trial, Ft Robinson, NE, 31 May–31 Aug 1907.

FERGUSON, James; G/10th Cav. Original member of 10th Cavalry; in troop when organized, Ft Leavenworth, KS, 5 Jul 1867. SOURCE: McMiller, "Buffalo Soldiers," 74.

FERGUSON, John H.; Sergeant; A/9th Cav. Discharged. SOURCE: SO 257, AGO, 4 Nov 1891.

FERRER, Jackson; Trumpeter; H/10th Cav. Honorable mention for gallantry against Kiowas and Comanches, Wichita Agency, Indian Territory, 22–23 Aug 1874. SOURCE: Baker, Roster.

FERRICK, Silas E.; H/24th Inf. Sentenced to eighteen months for larceny in the Philippines, 5 Oct 1900.

FERRIS; Private; E/25th Inf. Best in sixteen-pound shot put in Department of the Missouri, third in Army, with 37'6", 1903. SOURCE: SecWar, *AR 1903*, I, 430.

FICKLIN, Ezekiel; Private; D/10th Cav. Served in 10th Cavalry, 1898; remained in U.S. during war with Spain. SOURCE: Cashin, *Under Fire with the Tenth Cavalry*, 341.

FIELDING, F. P.; C/10th Cav. Served 1872–77; member, Camp 11, National Indian War Veterans, St. Joseph, MO; later minister. SOURCE: *Winners of the West* 9 (Mar 1932): 7, with picture.

FIELDS, A.; Farrier; B/9th Cav. On detached service, Ft Bayard, NM, 16 Jan–9 Feb 1881. SOURCE: Regt Returns, 9 Cav, Feb 1881.

FIELDS, Alfred H.; Private; K/9th Cav. At Ft D. A. Russell, WY, in 1910; marksman; resident of Indianapolis. SOURCE: *Illustrated Review: Ninth Cavalry*, with picture.

FIELDS, Alonzo; Private; E/10th Cav. Mentioned May 1874 as enlisting Aug 1872. SOURCE: LS, 10 Cav, 1873–77.

FIELDS, Eddie; Private; I/24th Inf. Enlisted Philadelphia, PA, 28 Mar 1899. SOURCE: Muster Roll, I/24 Inf, Mar–Apr 1899.

Fined $3 by summary court, 26 Oct 1899. SOURCE: Muster Roll, I/24 Inf, Sep–Oct 1899.

Fined $10 and confined for thirty days by summary court, 28 Dec 1899. SOURCE: Muster Roll, I/24 Inf, Nov–Dec 1899.

Killed in action in the Philippines, 31 Jul 1900. *See* SMITH, C. H., Sergeant, I/24th Infantry

FIELDS, Ernest E.; Private; 24th Inf. Served in Houston, 1917; telephone orderly, 3rd Battalion, Houston, 1917; considered Sgt. Vida Henry an obedient soldier and strict first sergeant. SOURCE: Haynes, *A Night of Violence*, 86, 110, 116.

FIELDS, Frank; H/10th Cav. Original member of 10th Cavalry; in troop when organized, Ft Leavenworth, KS, 21 Jul 1867. SOURCE: McMiller, "Buffalo Soldiers," 75.

FIELDS, George; D/10th Cav. Original member of 10th Cavalry; in troop when organized, Ft Leavenworth, KS, 1 Jun 1867. SOURCE: McMiller, "Buffalo Soldiers," 71.

FIELDS, Harvey; 1st Sgt; H/25th Inf. Sergeant, H/25th Infantry, led detachment of thirteen men of I/20th Infantry and C and H/10th Cavalry, 665 miles from camp at Seven Springs, TX, in pursuit of Indian raiders; discovered no recent signs or information on depredations, 30 Jul–1 Dec 1879. SOURCE: SecWar, *AR 1880*, 137.

Retires as first sergeant from Ft Missoula, MT, Sep 1894. SOURCE: *ANJ* 32 (6 Oct 1894): 86.

FIELDS, Harvey; Private; A/10th Cav. Served in 10th Cavalry, 1898; remained in U.S. during war with Spain. SOURCE: Cashin, *Under Fire with the Tenth Cavalry*, 337.

FIELDS, Henry; Sergeant; D/10th Cav. Commander, 10th Cavalry, forwards final statement of late Private Fields to Adjutant General, 10 Sep 1870. SOURCE: ES, 10 Cav, 1866–71.

FIELDS, Henry; Sergeant; G/9th Cav. Sergeant, G/9th Cavalry, since 11 Jun 1889. SOURCE: Roster, 9 Cav.

At Ft Robinson, NE, 1892.

With detachment fired on by insurgents, Donsoll, Philippines, 4 Jun 1901; also in small engagement at Bonga River, 27 Jun 1901. SOURCE: Hamilton, "History of the Ninth Cavalry," 107; *Illustrated Review: Ninth Cavalry*.

FIELDS, Howard W.; Sergeant; L/10th Cav. Commissioned second lieutenant of cavalry, Leon Springs, TX, 27 Sep 1918. SOURCE: Glass, *History of the Tenth Cavalry*, appendix M.

FIELDS, J. M.; Corporal; E/9th Cav. On detached service in field, New Mexico, 26 Jan–1 Feb 1881. SOURCE: Regt Returns, 9 Cav, Feb 1881.

FIELDS, John W.; Private; A/10th Cav. At Ft Apache, AZ, 1890, subscribed $.50 to testimonial to General Grierson. SOURCE: List of subscriptions, 23 Apr 1890, 10th Cavalry papers, MHI.

Farrier, served in 10th Cavalry in Cuba, 1898. SOURCE: Cashin, *Under Fire with the Tenth Cavalry*, 336.

Retired Aug 1901. SOURCE: *ANJ* 38 (17 Aug 1901): 1235.

FIELDS, William; Cook; F/9th Cav. Born Louisville, 1881; served in 9th Cavalry, 24th and 25th Infantry; worked twenty-three years for Southern Pacific Railroad; settled in Oakland, CA, area; died 17 Aug 1964.

Private, I/24th Infantry, relieved from duty as cook, Warwick Barracks, Cebu, Philippines. SOURCE: Order 10, I/24, 5 Jan 1906, Name File, 24 Inf.

Veteran of Philippine Insurrection; cook, F/9th Cavalry, at Ft D. A. Russell, WY, in 1910; sharpshooter; resident of Louisville. SOURCE: *Illustrated Review: Ninth Cavalry*, with picture.

FILL, Haron; G/10th Cav. Original member of 10th Cavalry; in troop when organized, Ft Leavenworth, KS, 5 Jul 1867. SOURCE: McMiller, "Buffalo Soldiers," 74.

FILLMORE, Lurid; Cook; B/9th Cav. At Ft D. A. Russell, WY, in 1910; sharpshooter. SOURCE: *Illustrated Review: Ninth Cavalry*.

FINLEY; Private; C/9th Cav. Discharge disapproved. SOURCE: Letter, AGO, 9 Apr 1895, Post Returns, Ft Robinson.

FINLEY, Augustus; Private; G/9th Cav. Enlisted in D/9th Cavalry, Ft McKinney, WY, 10 Feb 1888.

Commander, Captain Finley, G/9th Cavalry, calls him "a gambling, ill-natured, sulky man . . . captious, fault-finding soldier." SOURCE: Report of inspection, Ft Robinson, NE, 21 Aug 1893, Reports of Inspections, DP.

Turned over to civil authorities, 30 Aug 1893. SOURCE: CO, Ft Robinson, to CO, G/9, 1 Sep 1893, LS, Ft Robinson.

Alleged to have stolen some money; case not reported to post commander until U.S. Marshal Ledyard appeared with warrant. SOURCE: CO, Ft Robinson, to AAG, DP, 25 Nov 1893, LS, Ft Robinson.

In hands of civil authorities, Omaha, NE, 30 Aug–14 Dec 1893. SOURCE: Regt Returns, 9 Cav.

Funeral, Ft Robinson, 6 Dec 1897. SOURCE: SO 161, 5 Dec 1897, Post Orders, Ft Robinson.

Money due deceased Private Finley from sale of his personal effects $15.60, money he left $16.50, pay $21, sent to Department of the Platte. SOURCE: CO, G/9, to Chief Paymaster, DP, 21 Jan 1898, Miscellaneous Records, DP.

FINLEY, Ernest; Sergeant; K/10th Cav. Private, served in 10th Cavalry, 1898; remained in U.S. during war with Spain. SOURCE: Cashin, *Under Fire with the Tenth Cavalry*, 349.

Promoted from corporal, Aug 1902. SOURCE: *ANJ* 39 (30 Aug 1902): 1315.

FINLEY, Louis G.; Private; D/25th Inf. Died of acute diarrhea aboard U.S. Army Transport *Thomas*, bound for San Francisco, CA, 5 Jul 1901. SOURCE: *ANJ* 39 (9 Aug 1902): 1249.

FINLEY, Rae; Private; F/24th Inf. Retires from Ft Douglas, UT. SOURCE: *ANJ* 34 (7 Aug 1897): 909.

FINNEGAN, John; Private; M/25th Inf. Died of erysipelas in the Philippines, 18 Jul 1900. SOURCE: *ANJ* 37 (28 Jul 1900): 1142.

FINNEGAN, Michael; Sergeant; A/10th Cav. Corporal, H/10th Cavalry, sharpshooter, at Ft Apache, AZ. SOURCE: *ANJ* 25 (21 Jul 1888): 1034.

Acquitted of assault on civilian employee of Quartermaster Department, Ft Apache. SOURCE: *ANJ* 27 (28 Dec 1889): 352.

First sergeant, H/10th Cavalry, at Ft Apache, 1890, subscribed $.50 to testimonial to General Grierson. SOURCE: List of subscriptions, 23 Apr 1890, 10th Cavalry papers, MHI.

As corporal, A/10th Cavalry, ranked number nine with carbine, Departments of Arizona and Texas, bronze medal, Ft Wingate, NM, 17–22 Aug 1891. SOURCE: Baker, Roster; GO 81, AGO, 6 Oct 1891.

Ranked number 49 among carbine sharpshooters with over 72 percent, 1891. SOURCE: GO 1, AGO, 2 Jan 1892.

As sergeant, A/10th Cavalry, ranked number five with carbine, Departments of Columbia and Dakota, bronze medal, Ft Keogh, MT, 15–21 Aug 1892. SOURCE: Baker, Roster; GO 75, AGO, 3 Nov 1892.

FINNEY; Private; M/10th Cav. General court martial sentence. SOURCE: SO 120, DeptMo, 23 Jun 1903.

FINNEY; Sergeant; E/24th Inf. Promoted from corporal, Ft Bayard, NM, May 1890. SOURCE: Cleveland *Gazette*, 9 May 1891.

FINNEY, Corbin B.; Corporal; C/9th Cav. Commended for gallantry as private, C/9th Cavalry, in charge on San Juan Hill, battle of Santiago, Cuba, 1 Jul 1898. SOURCE: GO 15, AGO, 13 Feb 1900.

Cited for distinguished service, 1 Jul 1898. SOURCE: *ANJ* 37 (24 Feb 1900): 611.

FINNEY, Richard; Private; F/10th Cav. Served in 10th Cavalry in Cuba, 1898. SOURCE: Cashin, *Under Fire with the Tenth Cavalry*, 345.

FIRMES, Thomas A.; Bn Sgt Maj; 24th Inf. Private, K/25th Infantry, at Ft Niobrara, NE, 1904. SOURCE: Wilson, "History of Fort Niobrara."

Promoted to corporal. SOURCE: *ANR* 38 (26 Aug 1905): 21.

Battalion sergeant major, 24th Infantry, when commissioned captain at Camp Des Moines, IA, 15 Oct 1917. SOURCE: Glass, *History of the Tenth Cavalry*, appendix M; Beasley, *Negro Trailblazers*, 285.

Wife Mary I. Firmes was daughter of Elizabeth Wilson and late J. B. Wilson of Oakland, CA; graduated from Oakland High School, expert stenographer, employed as such in law firm for several years before marriage; was only black among three stenographers employed at Camp Des Moines and the most proficient; member, St. Augustine Episcopal Mission, Oakland. SOURCE: Beasley, *Negro Trailblazers*, 232.

Warrant officer, headquarters, Hawaiian Department, Ft Shafter, HI. SOURCE: Work, *The Negro Yearbook, 1931–1932*, 334.

FISH, Henry R.; F/9th Cav. Served 1869–74; resides in Washington, DC. SOURCE: *Winners of the West* 4 (May 1927): 2.

FISHBACK, Benjamin; Saddler; M/9th Cav. Veteran of Spanish-American War and Philippine Insurrection; at Ft D. A. Russell, WY, in 1910. SOURCE: *Illustrated Review: Ninth Cavalry*, with picture.

FISHBACK, Moses; Recruit; Colored Recruits. At Columbus Barracks, OH, 1885. *See* **PETERSON**, George, Recruit, Colored Recruits

FISHBURN, William G.; Private; C/9th Cav. Returned from Douglas, WY; sick in quarters, Ft Robinson, NE, Jun 1888.

FISHER; Private; B/10th Cav. At Ft Apache, AZ, 1890, subscribed $.50 to testimonial to General Grierson. SOURCE: List of subscriptions, 23 Apr 1890, 10th Cavalry papers, MHI.

FISHER, Adam; Private; D/9th Cav. At Ft D. A. Russell, WY, in 1910; resident of Los Angeles. SOURCE: *Illustrated Review: Ninth Cavalry*, with picture.

FISHER, Fred; Cook; F/10th Cav. Private, served in 10th Cavalry in Cuba, 1898. SOURCE: Cashin, *Under Fire with the Tenth Cavalry*, 344.

In hands of civil authorities, Lander, WY, 30 Jun 1904. SOURCE: Regt Returns, 10 Cav, Jul 1904.

FISHER, Henry; E/10th Cav. Original member of 10th Cavalry; in troop when organized, Ft Leavenworth, KS, 15 Jun 1867. SOURCE: McMiller, "Buffalo Soldiers," 72.

FISHER, Leonard; Corporal; A/9th Cav. Private, A/9th Cavalry, relieved from extra duty as packer, Quartermaster Department, Ft Robinson, NE. SOURCE: SO 90, 20 Aug 1896, Post Orders, Ft Robinson.

Promoted to corporal. SOURCE: *ANJ* 34 (17 Jul 1897): 854.

FISHER, Robert; F/10th Cav. Original member of 10th Cavalry; in troop when organized, Ft Leavenworth, KS, 21 Jun 1867. SOURCE: McMiller, "Buffalo Soldiers," 73.

FISHER, Ruben; I/10th Cav. Original member of 10th Cavalry; in troop when organized, Ft Riley, KS, 15 Aug 1867. SOURCE: McMiller, "Buffalo Soldiers," 76.

FISHER, Samuel; C/10th Cav. Original member of 10th Cavalry; in troop when organized, Ft Leavenworth, KS, 14 May 1867. SOURCE: McMiller, "Buffalo Soldiers," 70.

FISHER, Walter R.; Private; K/9th Cav. Recruit from depot, arrived at Ft Robinson, NE, 1 Mar 1887.

At Ft Robinson, 1888. *See* **IRVING**, Lee, Private, B/10th Cavalry

FITCH, Thomas N.; Private; Band/24th Inf. Born Lexington, KY; enlisted, age 21, occupation farmer, Ht 5'5", brown complexion, Ft Leavenworth, KS, 15 Jul 1886; marksman, 1887, 1888; transferred from D/24th Infantry to band, 27 Apr 1889; discharged, end of term, single, character excellent, Ft Bayard, NM, 14 Jun 1891; deposits $90, clothing $29, retained $72, owed $2.19 for subsistence stores; enlisted, Ft Bayard, 15 Jun 1891; absent in hands of civil authorities, charged with murder, Silver City, NM, 9 Aug–1 Sep 1891, single, character "up to date of confinement: Good, since that date bad"; transferred from D/24th Infantry to band, 2 Sep 1893; discharged, end of term, single, character very good, Ft Bayard, 14 Jun 1896; additional pay $2 per month, clothing $94.41, retained $57. SOURCE: Descriptive Book, 24 Inf NCS & Band.

FITCHUE, Roland; Private; M/9th Cav. At Ft D. A. Russell, WY, in 1910; resident of Chicago. SOURCE: *Illustrated Review: Ninth Cavalry*.

FITTISWATER, John; E/10th Cav. Original member of 10th Cavalry; in troop when organized, Ft Leavenworth, KS, 15 Jun 1867. SOURCE: McMiller, "Buffalo Soldiers," 72.

FITTS, Charles; Private; I/9th Cav. In hands of civil authorities, Hyannis, NE, 13 Jun–29 Nov 1893. SOURCE: Regt Returns, 9 Cav.

FITTS, Ned; Private; A/9th Cav. At Ft D. A. Russell, WY, in 1910; resident of Flat Lick, KY. SOURCE: *Illustrated Review: Ninth Cavalry*, with picture.

FITZGERALD; Private; K/10th Cav. Cook, served with Capt. John Bigelow, Clifton, AZ, Oct 1885. SOURCE: Bigelow, *On the Bloody Trail of Geronimo*, 86.

FITZGERALD; Private; G/10th Cav. At Ft Apache, AZ, 1890, subscribed $.25 to testimonial to General Grierson. SOURCE: List of subscriptions, 23 Apr 1890, 10th Cavalry papers, MHI.

FITZGERALD, John; Ord Sgt; U.S. Army. Born Philadelphia, PA; served first enlistment with I/24th Infantry, discharged as sergeant, 27 Mar 1870; appointed regimental quartermaster sergeant, 1 Mar 1877; fifth enlistment, Ft Supply, Indian Territory, single, character excellent, 26 Mar 1885; additional pay $4 per month; deposits $300 in 1881, $150 in 1882, retained $60, clothing $159; appointed ordnance sergeant, U.S. Army, 28 May 1885. SOURCE: Descriptive Book, 24 Inf NCS & Band.

FLADGER, John J.; Private; 25th Inf. Born Marion, SC; enlisted, Charleston, SC, age 27, occupation brakeman, Ht 5'9", dark complexion, black eyes and hair, 20 Jun 1881. SOURCE: Descriptive & Assignment Rolls, 25 Inf.

FLAKE, Stephen; I/9th Cav. Clothing destroyed when fighting fire, Ft Wingate, NM, 15 Dec 1876. SOURCE: Billington, *New Mexico's Buffalo Soldiers*, 110.

FLAMER, Burdell; Private; M/25th Inf. Ranked number 174 among rifle experts with 68.67 percent, 1904. SOURCE: GO 79, AGO, 1 Jun 1905.

FLEMING, Clarence T.; Private; F/49th Inf. Killed by comrade in the Philippines, 8 Oct 1900. SOURCE: *ANJ* 38 (27 Oct 1900): 211.

FLEMING, Faust; Private; C/9th Cav. At Ft D. A. Russell, WY, in 1910; resident of Morganton, NC. SOURCE: *Illustrated Review: Ninth Cavalry*, with picture.

FLEMING, Harry; Private; I/24th Inf. Enlisted Anniston, AL, 25 Mar 1899. SOURCE: Muster Roll, I/24 Inf, Mar–Apr 1899.

Discharged, character good, 16 May 1899; owes U.S. $25.04 for clothing. SOURCE: Muster Roll, I/24 Inf, May–Jun 1899.

FLEMING, James; B/49th Inf. Released from five-year sentence for desertion at Alcatraz, CA, based on Supreme Court's Deming decision. SOURCE: San Francisco *Chronicle*, 4 Jun 1902.

FLEMING, John; Private; L/25th Inf. Wounded in knee, Cabangan, Philippines, 15 Jul 1900. SOURCE: *ANJ* 37 (18 Aug 1900): 1214.

Permanently injured knee in Cabangan fight, 7 Jul 1900. SOURCE: Richmond *Planet*, 8 Sep 1900.

FLEMING, Richard; Private; H/24th Inf. Enlisted Ft Douglas, UT, 20 Feb 1898, with twenty-one years' continuous service; on extra duty as teamster, Quartermaster Department, 17 Mar–7 Apr 1898. SOURCE: Muster Roll, H/24 Inf, Mar–Apr 1898.

Sick in hospital, disease contracted in line of duty, Siboney, Cuba, 8–25 Aug 1898, and en route to U.S., 25–31 Aug 1898. SOURCE: Muster Roll, H/24 Inf, Jul–Aug 1898.

On furlough, authorized by surgeon's certificate, 12 Sep–11 Oct 1898; sick since 11 Oct 1898. SOURCE: Muster Roll, H/24 Inf, Nov–Dec 1898.

Sick in hospital until 11 Jan 1899; sick in quarters since 31 Jan 1899, disease contracted in line of duty. SOURCE: Muster Roll, H/24 Inf, Jan–Feb 1899.

FLEMING, William M.; Private; K/24th Inf. At San Carlos, AZ, 1890. *See* **HARDEE**, James A., Private, K/24th Infantry

FLEMMING, Jim H.; E/24th Inf. Died in Nashville, TN. SOURCE: *Winners of the West* 14 (Apr 1937): 4.

FLETCHER, Edward; 1st Sgt; F/9th Cav. Sergeant as of 1 Jan 1887. SOURCE: Roster, 9 Cav.

At Ft Robinson, NE, 1887–91. *See* **ROSS**, Edward, Private, G/9th Cavalry; **SMITH**, Walter, Private, F/9th Cavalry; **WILLIAMS**, Charles, Private, F/9th Cavalry

Fined $10 by garrison court martial for allowing and engaging in gambling in barracks after taps; leniency due to his good record. SOURCE: Order 132, Jul 1888, Post Orders, Ft Robinson.

First sergeant, F/9th Cavalry, 1891. *See* **BRADFORD**, Rudolph, Private, F/9th Cavalry

FLETCHER, Isaiah; Private; M/10th Cav. Original member of 10th Cavalry; in troop when organized, Ft Riley, KS, 15 Oct 1867. SOURCE: McMiller, "Buffalo Soldiers," 79.

Capt. Henry E. Alvord, former commander of troop, certifies to previous good character of late Private Fletcher and asks remission of unexpired part of sentence of dishonorable discharge and four years, in accordance with General Court Martial Order 156, Department of the Missouri, 1868; regimental commander agrees. SOURCE: ES, 10 Cav, 1866–71.

FLETCHER, J. R.; Trumpeter; K/10th Cav. At Ft Apache, AZ, 1890, subscribed $.25 to testimonial to General Grierson. SOURCE: List of subscriptions, 23 Apr 1890, 10th Cavalry papers, MHI.

FLETCHER, James. Color bearer, Col. Charles Young Camp No. 24, National Indian War Veterans, Washington, DC. SOURCE: *Winners of the West* 6 (Jun 1929): 4.

Commander of Camp No. 24. SOURCE: *Winners of the West* 7 (May 1930): 1.

FLETCHER, John; Private; H/9th Cav. Sentence for desertion, which began 5 Aug 1876, reduced to eighteen months. SOURCE: GCMO 22, AGO, 23 Feb 1877.

FLETCHER, Nathan; 1st Sgt; E/9th Cav. Fifteen years' continuous service in Army; now in F/9th Cavalry. SOURCE: Cleveland *Gazette*, 26 Jul 1886.

Sergeant, F/9th Cavalry, as of 3 Feb 1880. SOURCE: Roster, 9 Cav.

Authorized four-month furlough from Ft Robinson, NE. SOURCE: *ANJ* 24 (25 Jun 1887): 954.

Replaced recently killed first sergeant (*see* **STANCE**, Emanuel, First Sergeant, F/9th Cavalry) just before arrival of Simpson Mann in troop. SOURCE: Rickey, Mann interview.

Mrs. Fannie Fletcher, wife of 1st Sgt. Nathan Fletcher, to be directed to leave post with understanding that she is never to return. SOURCE: Post QM, Ft Robinson, to CO, Ft Robinson, 29 Mar 1888, Register of Correspondence, Ft Robinson.

Sergeant, F/9th Cavalry, on special duty as post provost sergeant, Ft Robinson, vice Sgt. Arthur Ransom, G/9th Cavalry. SOURCE: Order 5, 16 Jan 1893, Post Orders, Ft Robinson.

Reenlistment as first sergeant, E/9th Cavalry, married, authorized. SOURCE: Letter, AGO, 14 Jun 1897.

FLETCHER, Oliver; Private; M/24th Inf. Forced out of camp at gunpoint by mutineers, Houston riot, 1917; able to convince court martial of his alibi, escape to home of Carl W. Guy; found guilty of disobeying orders and sentenced to two and one-half years in prison. SOURCE: Haynes, *A Night of Violence*, 126, 267–68, 271.

FLETCHER, Samuel. Standard bearer, Col. Charles Young Camp No. 24, National Indian War Veterans, Washington, DC. SOURCE: *Winners of the West* 6 (Jun 1929): 4.

FLETCHER, Stephen; D/10th Cav. Original member of 10th Cavalry; in troop when organized, Ft Leavenworth, KS, 1 Jun 1867. SOURCE: McMiller, "Buffalo Soldiers," 71.

FLINT, Robert T.; 1st Sgt; E/25th Inf. At Ft Buford, ND, 1893. SOURCE: Nankivell, *History of the Twenty-fifth Infantry*, 50, with picture.

Applies for retirement; previously recommended for Medal of Honor for control of detachment of eleven facing threat of drowning in the Philippines with Moros nearby. SOURCE: CO, E/25, to AG, USA, 23 Oct 1913, in Scrapbook, 25 Inf, vol. III.

Retired Nov 1913, as first sergeant, E/25th Infantry, known as "Flint, the lion-hearted" and famed as Indian fighter. SOURCE: Curtis, *The Black Soldier*, 49.

FLIPPER, Henry O.; 2nd Lt; 10th Cav. Biographical sketch. SOURCE: Logan and Winston, *Dictionary of American Negro Biography*, 227–28.

Mentioned as 1877 graduate of U.S. Military Academy. SOURCE: Billington, *New Mexico's Buffalo Soldiers*, 190.

Offered services to government in war with Spain, 1898. SOURCE: Clark, "A History of the Twenty-fourth," 87.

FLIPPINS, Benjamin; Private; M/10th Cav. In hands of civil authorities, Crawford, NE, 31 Jan 1903. SOURCE: Regt Returns, 10 Cav, Jan 1903.

Miss Laura Lyons of Crawford asks that he be kept away from her premises; he threatens her life and she fears him; he also damages her property each time he comes around. SOURCE: Lyons to CO, Ft Robinson, 16 Feb 1903, Register, LR, Ft Robinson.

Sentenced by court martial. SOURCE: SO 54, DeptMo, 18 Mar 1903.

Spent two days in jail and paid fine of $5 plus $4.80 costs for carrying concealed weapon, Crawford, 14 Dec 1903.

Sentenced to dishonorable discharge and confinement, Ft Robinson, NE, Feb 1904. SOURCE: SO 17, DeptMo, 1904.

FLOODMAN; Private; H/24th Inf. Reduced to ranks from sergeant. SOURCE: *ANJ* 34 (17 Jul 1897): 855.

FLORENCE, Alexander; Private; M/10th Cav. Discharged on certificate of disability with chronic gonorrhea from Ft Robinson, NE, 15 Nov 1902. SOURCE: Certificates of Disability, Ft Robinson.

FLOWERS, Benjamin; F/10th Cav. Original member of 10th Cavalry; in troop when organized, Ft Leavenworth, KS, 21 Jun 1867. SOURCE: McMiller, "Buffalo Soldiers," 73.

FLOWERS, James; 24th Inf. Excellent baseball player; dishonorable discharge from Ft Douglas, UT. SOURCE: Clark, "A History of the Twenty-fourth," 70–71.

FLOWERS, Robert; I/10th Cav. Original member of 10th Cavalry; in troop when organized, Ft Riley, KS, 15 Aug 1867. SOURCE: McMiller, "Buffalo Soldiers," 76.

FLOYD, John; Sergeant; M/9th Cav. Lance corporal, I/9th Cavalry, promoted to corporal vice Bailey, promoted. SOURCE: *ANJ* 31 (19 May 1894): 663.

Promoted to sergeant, Ft Washakie, WY, Nov 1895. SOURCE: *ANJ* 33 (16 Nov 1895): 179.

Quartermaster sergeant, M/9th Cavalry, ranked number five, Army pistol competition, and number nine, Northern Division pistol competition, both at Ft Sheridan, IL, 1906. SOURCE: GO 198, AGO, 6 Dec 1906.

Veteran of Spanish-American War and Philippine Insurrection; sergeant, at Ft D. A. Russell, WY, in 1910; marksman. SOURCE: *Illustrated Review: Ninth Cavalry*, with picture.

FLOYD, William; Cook; K/10th Cav. At Ft Robinson, NE, 1904.

Ranked number 11 in competition of Northern Division pistol team, Ft Riley, KS, 1904. SOURCE: GO 167, AGO, 28 Oct 1904; Glass, *History of the Tenth Cavalry*, 44.

Ranked number 11 in Northern Division cavalry competition, bronze medal, Ft Riley, 1905. SOURCE: GO 173, AGO, 20 Oct 1905; Glass, *History of the Tenth Cavalry*, 45.

FLYNT, Robert; Private; G/9th Cav. Corporal, served in C/10th Cavalry in Cuba, 1898. SOURCE: Cashin, *Under Fire with the Tenth Cavalry*, 341.

Private, C/10th Cavalry, fined $1 and $4.80 costs for being drunk and disorderly, Crawford, NE, 28 Jun 1902.

Paid $13.80 of $10 fine and $4.80 costs for carrying concealed weapon, Crawford, 25 Jul 1902.

Veteran of Spanish-American War and Philippine Insurrection; at Ft. D. A. Russell, WY, in 1910; sharpshooter. SOURCE: *Illustrated Review: Ninth Cavalry*, with picture.

FOBUS, Perry J.; Recruit; 10th Cav. Mentioned Sep 1875 as having enlisted at New Orleans, LA. SOURCE: LS, 10 Cav, 1873–83.

FOLLIERAU, Frank; I/10th Cav. Original member of 10th Cavalry; in troop when organized, Ft Riley, KS, 15 Aug 1867. SOURCE: McMiller, "Buffalo Soldiers," 76.

FOLLIS; Private; K/10th Cav. Killed in action against Geronimo, Pineto Mountains, Mexico, 3 May 1886. SOURCE: Baker, Roster.

FOLSOM, William; Trumpeter; H/9th Cav. Veteran of Philippine Insurrection; at Ft D. A. Russell, WY, in 1910; sharpshooter; resident of Washington, DC. SOURCE: *Illustrated Review: Ninth Cavalry*, with picture.

FONTANO, Joseph; Private; E/9th Cav. At Ft D. A. Russell, WY, in 1910; sharpshooter; resident of 1513 34th St., Galveston, TX. SOURCE: *Illustrated Review: Ninth Cavalry*, with picture.

FORD; Private; D/10th Cav. At Ft Apache, AZ, 1890, subscribed $.50 to testimonial to General Grierson. SOURCE: List of subscriptions, 23 Apr 1890, 10th Cavalry papers, MHI.

FORD; Private; G/10th Cav. At Ft Apache, AZ, 1890, subscribed $.50 to testimonial to General Grierson. SOURCE: List of subscriptions, 23 Apr 1890, 10th Cavalry papers, MHI.

FORD, Abe; Private; H/9th Cav. At Ft D. A. Russell, WY, in 1910; resident of Concord, TN. SOURCE: *Illustrated Review: Ninth Cavalry*, with picture.

FORD, Charles; Private; K/10th Cav. Served in 10th Cavalry, 1898; remained in U.S. during war with Spain. SOURCE: Cashin, *Under Fire with the Tenth Cavalry*, 349.

FORD, F.; Private; A/9th Cav. At Ft Stanton, NM, 1881. SOURCE: Regt Returns, 9 Cav, Jan 1881.

FORD, George W.; QM Sgt; 10th Cav. Lived on Duke Street, Alexandria, VA, between St. Asaph and Columbia; moved with parents to farm at Gum Spring, adjoining Mt. Vernon estate, 1857; went to live with aunt Mary V. Bell, 543 Broome St., New York, NY, Mar 1860; returned late winter, 1861. SOURCE: Affidavit, Ford, 28 Nov 1921, VA File C 2580332, George W. Ford.

Father a free man, owned farm inherited from West Ford; baptized at age 5, St. Paul's Episcopal Church, where Washingtons worshipped; family respected and active communicants of Episcopal Church; as lad he sold pictures at entrance to Mt. Vernon; grandfather was wheelwright, carpenter, overseer of house servants at Mt. Vernon, slaves at Mt. Vernon frequently did chores on Ford farm; in New York City with parents during draft riots; delegate from Kansas to 1900 Republican convention in Philadelphia, voted for Theodore Roosevelt as vice president; wife a native of Charleston, SC, speaks with clear English accent acquired as girl living with English family in Brooklyn, NY, is daughter of well-known Baptist minister. SOURCE: Rev. Gay C. White, "From Mt. Vernon to Springfield," (Springfield) *Illinois State Register*, 17 Jan 1937.

Born Fairfax Co., VA; enlisted Washington, DC, age 21, farmer, Ht 5'7", yellow complexion, 10 Sep 1867; assigned to L/10th Cavalry; discharged, expiration of service, as first sergeant, Ft Sill, OK, 10 Sep 1872; enlisted Ft Sill, 11 Sep 1872; assigned to field and staff, 10th Cavalry; discharged Ft Concho, TX, expiration of service, quartermaster sergeant, "character most excellent," 11 Sep 1877. SOURCE: Register of Enlistments.

Original member of 10th Cavalry; in L Troop when organized, Ft Riley, KS, 21 Sep 1867. SOURCE: McMiller, "Buffalo Soldiers," 78.

Enlisted at age 19, 1867; served two enlistments; appointed superintendent of Negro section, Chattanooga National Cemetery, 1878; supervised several national cemeteries; granted leave of absence to serve as major, 23rd Kansas Infantry, 1898; retired 1930. SOURCE: Rickey, *Forty Miles a Day on Beans and Hay*, 344.

"Dear Sir: I feel that my first duty should be an apology for intruding on your valuable time on a subject for which you possibly have little or no interest. I have been wondering if I am the last man or are there any survivors of the 10th Cavalry who were in at its organization. I enlisted Sept. 10, 1867. Discharged Sept. 11, 1877. I entered the regiment at the age of 19 as trumpeter, served seven years as first sergeant of L Troop, and was discharged as Q.M. Sergt. in 1877 through the recommendation of Col. B. H. Grierson, our commander. I received an appointment as Supt. National Cemeteries and served in that position for fifty-three years, retiring in August, 1930. At the outbreak of the Spanish-American War, I was stationed at the National Cemetery at Fort Scott, Kansas. Through the recommendation of Colonel Grierson I was commissioned Major of the 23rd Kansas Volunteers, and served with my regiment in Cuba having obtained leave of absence from my cemeterial duties. I just imagined you might have knowledge of another survivor. I must in closing ask you to kindly overlook any defects in this letter. You know a man 89 years old is not expected to be a good penman. Sincerely yours, Geo. W. Ford." Letter, Ford to Sergeant Major, 10th Cavalry, West Point, NY, 17 Nov 1936. SOURCE: *Cavalry Journal* 46 (Jul–Aug 1937): 394.

Among Ford's most prized possessions is letter from Lt. Col. N. B. Briscoe, Commander, 10th Cavalry, Ft Leavenworth, KS, 27 Nov 1936: "I am most pleased to hear from one of the charter members of the tenth cavalry, and am taking the liberty of publishing your letter in the regiment, and of making inquiry through the service papers for other original members. The long and honorable record attained during the years since 1867 is a great pride to those of us now in the regiment and I am sure you will be gratified to learn that we hold annually an organization day celebration on July 28. Among the men in the regiment there are about fifteen whose fathers also served in the 10th Cavalry. . . . It is a great pleasure to hear from you and I assure you that anything you want from the 10th Cavalry is yours." SOURCE: Rev. Gay C. White, "From Mt. Vernon to Springfield," (Springfield) *Illinois State Register*, 17 Jan 1937.

Born in Virginia; 10th Cavalry, 1867–1877, discharged as quartermaster sergeant; superintendent, Military Cemetery, Springfield, 1916. SOURCE: *Crisis* 11 (Apr 1916): 290.

Honorable mention for gallantry against Kiowas and Comanches, Wichita Agency, Indian Territory, 22–23 Aug 1874. SOURCE: Baker, Roster.

Served as mail courier in L/10th Cavalry and D/10th Cavalry, between Ft Arbuckle, KS, and Ft Gibson, Indian Territory, winter 1868: "This was no pleasure ride when one considers that besides fording the icy waters of the Canadian, the Washita, and Wild Horse, there was also the danger of capture by Indians"; Filmore Roberts, "a boy of 19," drowned in Canadian River with his pouch; reported as absent without leave when he did not arrive at Ft Arbuckle; body found months later. From Ford letter, dated Rural Route 1, Springfield, IL. SOURCE: *Winners of the West* 1 (Apr 1924): 1.

Pvt. John Randall, G/10th Cavalry, was wounded eleven times with lances and shot in hip about forty-five miles west of Ft Hays, KS, while hiding in hole under railroad cut, Oct 1867; Sgt. Charles H. Davis performed gallantly in main battle. SOURCE: *Winners of the West* 2 (Nov 1925): 2.

First sergeant, L/10th Cavalry, accidentally shot in leg by loaded revolver he unpacked from arms chest, while issuing arms to guard, Ft Sill, Sep 1871. SOURCE: Affidavit, Thomas J. Spencer, former first lieutenant, 10th Cavalry, Washington, DC, 23 May 1890, VA File C 2580332, George W. Ford.

Former comrade Joseph A. Blackburn saw Ford accidentally wounded with Colt revolver in line of duty. SOURCE: Affidavit, Blackburn, former first sergeant, L/10th Cavalry, Henrietta, Clay Co., TX, 16 May 1890, VA File C 2580332, George W. Ford.

Ford writes from Ft Scott, KS, that he was commended in General Order 53, 1874, for gallantry in action; desires to know if conditions permit issue to him of Medal of Honor. SOURCE: J. D. Bowersock, Member of Congress, to Secretary of War, 23 Apr 1902, AGO File 431605.

War Department reports to Bowersock no indication of recommendation for Medal of Honor or certificate of merit for Ford. SOURCE: AAG to Bowersock, 3 May 1902, AGO File 431605.

First Sergeant Ford present Jul–Aug 1874; L/10th Cavalry in accordance with Special Order 155, Headquarters, Ft Richardson, TX, 12 Aug, left 14 Aug, arrived Ft Sill 18 Aug; left post 21 Aug, arrived Wichita Agency 22 Aug, engaged Nocomi and Kiowa Indians with one noncommissioned officer wounded in action; marched 160 miles. SOURCE: Report of Rolls Division, AGO, 26 Apr 1902, AGO File 431605.

Born 23 Nov 1847; lived with parents, Fairfax Co., VA, until he went to school in New York City; returned and lived one year with sister; enlisted Washington, DC, 10 Sep 1867; served ten years to discharge as quartermaster sergeant, noncommissioned staff, 10th Cavalry, Ft Concho, 11 Sep 1877; worked at Arlington National Cemetery, Mar–May 1878; transferred to Chattanooga Cemetery until Nov 1878; then Beaufort, SC, National Cemetery to Aug 1894; Ft Scott, until 1904; Port Hudson, LA, until Nov 1906; enlisted Topeka, KS, 15 Jul 1898; discharged Ft Leavenworth, 10 Apr 1899. SOURCE: Affidavit, Ford, 29 Dec 1931, VA File C 2580332, George W. Ford.

Children: George, Jr., born 1880, resided at 10750 Glenroy, Chicago, IL; Noel B., born 1881, deceased; Harriet C., born 1884, married Goin, resided at 920 Shipman, Peoria, IL; James I., born 1886, resided at 1605 East Capitol, Springfield; Donald G., born 1888, deceased; Cecil B., born 1891, resided at 303 Gale, Peoria; Elise, married Jenkins, 1414 Pine, Columbia, SC; Vera, married E. C. Powell, 916 First Avenue, Charleston, WV. SOURCE: VA File C 2580332, George W. Ford.

Major, 23rd Kansas, and commander, 2nd Battalion. SOURCE: Beasley, *Negro Trailblazers*, 284.

President has referred to War Department Ford letter of 21 Jun 1899, asking authority to recruit Negro regiment for service in the Philippines; Secretary of War says present plans do not include additional volunteer regiments for Philippine service; Ford letter to remain on file for future consideration. SOURCE: AAG to Ford, 27 Jun 1899, AGO File 246901.

Ford asks return of papers he filed when commissioned in volunteers. SOURCE: Ford to SecWar, 2 Nov 1899, AGO File 246901.

War Department complies with Ford request for return of papers. SOURCE: AAG to Ford, 17 Nov 1899, AGO File 246901.

Letter, Theodore Roosevelt to "My Dear Major Ford," dated Oyster Bay, NY, 9 Jul 1900, responds to Ford query regarding Roosevelt's attacks on black troops; Roosevelt explains his respect for black soldiers and his pointing out of shortcomings of others. SOURCE: Morison and Blum, *Letters of Theodore Roosevelt*, II.

Ford request for position in colored regiment has been placed on file and will receive due consideration at proper time. SOURCE: AG to J. D. Bowersock, 21 Jan 1901, AGO File 246901.

In response to inquiry, informed that vacancies in Philippine Scouts are filled at lieutenant level; Ford letter to president will be referred to General Chaffee. SOURCE: AG to Ford, 2 Dec 1901, AGO File 246901.

"Should the present crisis demand that men be enlisted and drilled for the defense of the country, I beg to offer my services and ask that when needed, I be authorized to enlist and prepare a regiment of Colored Men, more if necessary, to be used in any emergency that may arise. The Colored Men of Illinois are loyal and ready to defend their country whenever called upon. My military experience has been gained by ten years' service as a non. com. officer in the regular Army, and one year as Major, 23 Kans Vol., War with Spain." SOURCE: Ford to SecWar, 6 Feb 1917, AGO File 246901.

Born in Alexandria, 23 Nov 1850; educated in grade schools of New York City; "have been a student of drill regulations for the past 40 years, have drilled and instructed several cos. of the National Guard"; speak and read Spanish fairly well; physical condition "nearly perfect." SOURCE: Ford, questionnaire, AGO, 9 Feb 1917, AGO File 246901.

Son Cecil B. Ford served as dental assistant, 8th Illinois Infantry Hospital Corps, 370th Infantry (National Guard), 24 Jul 1917–24 Jan 1918. SOURCE: Affidavit, Ford, 1 Oct 1921, VA File, C 2580332, George W. Ford.

Pension: $20 per month, 4 Mar 1917; $24 per month, 16 Jun 1920; $30 per month, 23 Nov 1922; $72 per month, 4 May 1931; $60 per month, 29 Dec 1931; $72 per month, 13 Aug 1935; $100 per month, 9 Jun 1938. SOURCE: VA File C 2580332, George W. Ford.

Complains about veto of pension bill by President Coolidge. SOURCE: *Winners of the West* 1 (Jul 1924): 1.

Complains about unfair pension treatment. SOURCE: *Winners of the West* 1 (Oct 1924): 4.

Renews subscription; expresses gratitude for pension fight carried on by magazine. SOURCE: *Winners of the West* 4 (Aug 1927): 4.

Said goodbye to boyhood friend Joseph A. Blackburn, Ft Worth, TX, 12 Sep 1877; recently saw his name in your magazine and you have helped me locate him and have reunion. SOURCE: *Winners of the West* 5 (Sep 1928): 3.

Ford: "I sometimes wonder if some white persons hope to inherit a different and separate heaven and let us have such a one as is depicted in *Green Pastures*. I am fully aware of the shortcomings of many of my people, but the great majority are peaceful and law abiding. There are very many noble and high-minded white people, who do not subscribe to the treatment to which we are subjected, but they lack the courage and the interest to come out in the open and protest against it. Many persons think of us as the carefree, shiftless characters shown in the farcical skit of 'Amos 'n' Andy' "; calls attention to *Harper's* 1859 article ["Mount Vernon as it is," *Harper's Monthly* 18 (March 1859)] and his grandfather West Ford, whom he recalled as a "picturesque old fellow" and privileged character at Mt. Vernon and Alexandria. SOURCE: Rev. Gay C. White, "From Mt. Vernon to Springfield," (Springfield) *Illinois State Register*, 17 Jan 1937.

Ford and wife are sick but improving; he was 90 on 23 Nov 1937; "am the only living survivor of the original regiment, the 10th U.S. Cavalry, who marched away toward the Rio Grande, 1,225 strong in 1867"; renews subscription. SOURCE: *Winners of the West* 15 (Feb 1938): 3.

Picture, "Oldest Known Survivor"; with letter, Sgt. Maj. L. M. Carter, 10th Cavalry, Ft Leavenworth, KS, requesting photograph of Ford for regimental archives. SOURCE: *Winners of the West* 15 (Jun 1938): 7.

Superintendent, National Cemetery, Chattanooga, 1878; then cemeteries at Beaufort, Ft Scott, Port Hudson; superintendent at Camp Butler, IL, 1906–30; died at home, Springfield, 30 Jun 1939; survived by wife, to whom he was married 28 Aug 1879, three daughters, one sister, eight grandchildren; buried at Camp Butler. SOURCE: *Winners of the West* 16 (Aug 1939): 1.

Ford died of bronchial pneumonia; father William Ford of Alexandria; mother Henrietta Bruce Ford of Virginia; buried at Camp Butler National Cemetery; widow Harriett E. (Bythewood) Ford born 16 Sep 1861; married at Beaufort, 28 Aug 1879; resided at 1525 South 11th, Springfield; resided at 916 First Avenue, Charleston, 30 Aug 1939; pension $50 per month, 1 Apr 1944. SOURCE: VA File C 2580332, George W. Ford.

See **ANDERSON**, Henry, Private, L/10th Cavalry

FORD, Harry; Private; K/24th Inf. Stationed at Camp Pilot Butte, WY; in hands of civil authorities, Rock Springs, WY, 26–31 Dec 1898.

FORD, James A.; Sergeant; A/10th Cav. At Ft Apache, AZ, 1890, subscribed $.50 to testimonial to General Grierson. SOURCE: List of subscriptions, 23 Apr 1890, 10th Cavalry papers, MHI.

FORD, James W.; QM Sgt; B/10th Cav. Born in South Carolina; private and saddler, B/10th Cavalry, 21 Nov 1884–20 Nov 1889; private, corporal, sergeant, H/9th Cavalry, 5 Dec 1889–4 Dec 1894; private, B/10th Cavalry, 20 Feb 1895; corporal, 22 Jul 1895; sergeant, 24 Jul 1896; stationed at Ft Custer, MT, 1897. SOURCE: Baker, Roster.

Corporal, H/9th Cavalry, as of 10 Apr 1891. SOURCE: Roster, 9 Cav.

Promoted to sergeant, H/9th Cavalry, Ft Robinson, NE, 22 Aug 1894. SOURCE: *ANJ* 32 (1 Sep 1894): 6.

Quartermaster sergeant, B/10th Cavalry, served in 10th Cavalry in Cuba, 1898; recommended for Medal of Honor for gallantry, assault on San Juan, Cuba, 1 Jul 1898; sergeant, B/10th Cavalry, testified to heroism of Pvt. Arthur G. Wheeler, B/10th Cavalry, at Las Guasimas, Cuba, 24 Jun 1898, in deposition at Camp Forse, AL, 4 Dec 1898. SOURCE: Cashin, *Under Fire with the Tenth Cavalry*, 337, 186, 179.

FORD, Jefferson; E/10th Cav. Original member of 10th Cavalry; in troop when organized, Ft Leavenworth, KS, 15 Jun 1867. SOURCE: McMiller, "Buffalo Soldiers," 72.

FORD, John A.; Sergeant; Machine Gun Troop/ 10th Cav. Commissioned second lieutenant of cavalry, Leon Springs, TX, 27 Sep 1918. SOURCE: Glass, *History of the Tenth Cavalry*, appendix M.

FORD, John W.; Sergeant; C/10th Cav. At Ft Apache, AZ, 1890, subscribed $.50 to testimonial to General Grierson. SOURCE: List of subscriptions, 23 Apr 1890, 10th Cavalry papers, MHI.

FORD, Richard; Private; I/25th Inf. Fined $4 by summary court, San Isidro, Philippines, for lying out of quarters, 24 Mar 1902, first conviction. SOURCE: Register of Summary Court, San Isidro.

FORD, S. S.; Sergeant; H/10th Cav. Sergeant, B/10th Cavalry, at Ft Apache, AZ, 1890, subscribed $.50 to testimonial to General Grierson. SOURCE: List of subscriptions, 23 Apr 1890, 10th Cavalry papers, MHI.

Ranked ninth in revolver competition, Departments of Columbia, California, Arizona, bronze medal, at Ft Wingate, NM, 4–9 Aug 1890; distinguished marksman. SOURCE: GO 112, AGO, 2 Oct 1890; Baker, Roster.

Sergeant, B/10th Cavalry, sharpshooter, Ft Apache, 1891. SOURCE: *ANJ* 31 (4 Jul 1891): 765.

Second in carbine competition, silver medal, and fifth in revolver competition, bronze medal, Departments of Arizona and Texas, Ft Wingate, 17–22 Aug 1891; distinguished marksman. SOURCE: GO 81, AGO, 6 Oct 1891; Baker, Roster.

Sergeant, H/10th Cavalry; tenth in Army with carbine; distinguished marksman, 1893. SOURCE: GO 82, AGO, 24 Oct 1893.

FORD, Thomas; C/10th Cav. Original member of 10th Cavalry; in troop when organized, Ft Leavenworth, KS, 14 May 1867. SOURCE: McMiller, "Buffalo Soldiers," 70.

FORD, Thomas; Sergeant; A/9th Cav. Assisted Lt. Matthias W. Day in pursuing deserters in New Mexico, late 1880. SOURCE: Billington, *New Mexico's Buffalo Soldiers,* 132.

FORD, William; Private; G/9th Cav. On detached service, Ft Stanton, NM, 29 Jan–5 Feb 1881. SOURCE: Regt Returns, 9 Cav, Feb 1881.

Admitted to Soldiers Home with disability, age 41, after seventeen years and six months' service, 14 May 1886. SOURCE: SecWar, *AR 1887,* 747.

FORD, William H.; M/10th Cav. Original member of 10th Cavalry; in troop when organized, Ft Riley, KS, 15 Oct 1867. SOURCE: McMiller, "Buffalo Soldiers," 79.

FOREMAN, William A.; K/24th Inf. At Ft Reno, Indian Territory, 1887. *See* **GILES**, Henry, Sergeant, C/24th Infantry

Leads ten-string band, Ft Grant, AZ. SOURCE: Cleveland *Gazette,* 26 Jan 1889.

FORMAN, Andrew; Private; B/10th Cav. Served 1883. *See* **LOCKETT**, Howard, Corporal, B/10th Cavalry

FORMAN, Elwood A.; Corporal; H/25th Inf. Died in the Philippines, 22 Apr 1901. SOURCE: *ANJ* 38 (4 May 1901): 876.

FORMAN, Madison W.; Private; M/49th Inf. Engaged against enemy, Tuao, Cagayan, Philippines, 18 Oct 1900. SOURCE: *ANJ* 38 (11 May 1901): 901.

FORREST, Samuel H.; Saddler; M/10th Cav. At Ft Apache, AZ, 1890, subscribed $.50 to testimonial to General Grierson. SOURCE: List of subscriptions, 23 Apr 1890, 10th Cavalry papers, MHI.

FORT, Lewis; Trumpeter; H/9th Cav. Born Alexandria, VA; in D/9th Cavalry, Sep 1878–Jan 1896; transferred to H/9th Cavalry, age 37, Ht 5'8", seventeen years' continuous service, $4 per month additional pay, 25 Jan 1896; seven summary court martial convictions, Ft Robinson, NE, 1896–97. SOURCE: Descriptive Book, H/9 Cav.

Reenlistment in D/9th Cavalry, married, authorized. SOURCE: Letter, AGO, 28 Jul 1893.

Wife Bertie G. Fort writes Secretary of War from Crawford, NE, asking quarters at Ft Robinson, 28 Jul 1894; she left post in Apr 1894 of her own accord "to keep from having trouble with a man, I would not do as he wanted me to do"; commander said when she returned that he could not give her permission to reside on post; husband has fifteen years' service, married nine years; she worked for Capt. John Loud, 1886–93: "I always did my duty as a servant"; commander, Ft Robinson, defends his position as based on fact that there are too many enlisted men's wives on post, 8 Aug 1894; Adjutant General supports commander, 14 Aug 1894. SOURCE: QM Consolidated File, Ft Robinson.

Killed in action, San Juan, Cuba, 2 Jul 1898. SOURCE: SecWar, *AR 1898,* 707; *ANJ* 36 (11 Feb 1899): 567.

Killed in action, Cuba, 1898. SOURCE: Scipio, *Last of the Black Regulars,* 29.

FORTNER, Hugh; Corporal; K/24th Inf. At Cabanatuan, Philippines, 1901. *See* **SHAVER**, Lee, Private, K/24th Infantry

FORTUNE, John T.; Corporal; H/24th Inf. Convicted of neglect of duty; sentence remitted because of conflicting and inconclusive evidence, in accordance with Special Order 47, 1879. SOURCE: Report of Trials, Department of Texas, 1878–79.

FORTUNE, William H.; Corporal; H/9th Cav. Promoted from lance corporal, Ft Robinson, NE, 16 Jul 1894. SOURCE: *ANJ* 31 (4 Aug 1894): 858.

FOSTER; Private; G/10th Cav. At Ft Apache, AZ, 1890, subscribed $.50 to testimonial to General Grierson. SOURCE: List of subscriptions, 23 Apr 1890, 10th Cavalry papers, MHI.

FOSTER, Charles; Sergeant; B/10th Cav. Born in Wisconsin; private, B/9th Cavalry, 1 Feb 1888–31 Jan 1893; private, B/10th Cavalry, 2 Mar 1893; corporal, 16 Sep 1894; sergeant, 28 Dec 1896. SOURCE: Baker, Roster.

FOSTER, George; C/10th Cav. Original member of 10th Cavalry; in troop when organized, Ft Leavenworth, KS, 14 May 1867. SOURCE: McMiller, "Buffalo Soldiers," 70.

FOSTER, George; C/9th Cav. Served 1881–86; died at National Military Home, Dayton, OH. SOURCE: *Winners of the West* 9 (May 1932): 8.

FOSTER, George; Sergeant; H/10th Cav. Private, wounded in battle with Indians near Sulphur Springs, TX, while part of Capt. M. L. Courtney's command of H/10th Cavalry and H/25th Infantry, Jul 1879; two Indians also killed. SOURCE: SecWar, *AR 1879,* 107.

Honorable mention as private, H/10th Cavalry, for services rendered in capture of Mangas and his Apache band, Rio Bonito, AZ, 18 Oct 1886. SOURCE: Baker, Roster.

Sergeant, H/10th Cavalry, shot by interpreter John Glass, Ft Apache, AZ, 20 Feb 1891, and died two days later; Glass in guardhouse to await action of civil authorities; "Sergt. Foster was a good soldier of twenty-one years service in the 10th Cavalry, and bore on his body the marks of a wound received in an Indian fight. His death is much regretted by all who knew him." SOURCE: *ANJ* 28 (14 Mar 1891): 493.

FOSTER, George R.; Private; F/24th Inf. Fined $10 by summary court, San Isidro, Philippines, for disrespectful and obscene language, 3 Mar 1902, first conviction. SOURCE: Register of Summary Court, San Isidro.

FOSTER, John; Private; G/10th Cav. On daily duty with Quartermaster Department, camp near Ft Lyon, CO, 1868. SOURCE: Orders, Det 10 Cav, 1868–69.

FOSTER, John; Private; K/9th Cav. At Ft Davis, TX, 1868. *See* **COLLYER**, S., Private, F/9th Cavalry

FOSTER, Lankin; B/10th Cav. Original member of 10th Cavalry; in troop when organized, Ft Leavenworth, KS, 1 Apr 1867. SOURCE: McMiller, "Buffalo Soldiers," 69.

FOSTER, Leslie J.; Private; I/24th Inf. Enlisted Kansas City, MO, 9 Feb 1899. SOURCE: Muster Roll, I/24 Inf, Jan–Feb 1899.

On detached service at Three Rivers, CA, 3 May–21 Jun 1899. SOURCE: Muster Roll, I/24 Inf, May–Jun 1899.

Fined three times by summary court martials. SOURCE: Muster Roll, I/24 Inf, Jul–Aug 1899.

On detached service at Arayat, Philippines, beginning 31 Oct 1899; allotted $10 per month for three months to George Foster. SOURCE: Muster Roll, I/24 Inf, Sep–Oct 1899.

FOSTER, Lorenzo; C/10th Cav. Original member of 10th Cavalry; in troop when organized, Ft Leavenworth, KS, 14 May 1867. SOURCE: McMiller, "Buffalo Soldiers," 70.

FOSTER, Peter; D/10th Cav. Original member of 10th Cavalry; in troop when organized, Ft Leavenworth, KS, 1 Jun 1867. SOURCE: McMiller, "Buffalo Soldiers," 71.

FOSTER, Robert; Corporal; L/25th Inf. Drowned while on mounted expedition to mountains under Lt. J. DeCamp Hall, Aug 1900; Richmond-born resident of Malory Street; served in 6th Virginia Infantry; enlisted in G/25th Infantry and transferred to L/25th Infantry; "a good soldier and very popular"; had just made corporal. SOURCE: Richmond *Planet*, 20 Oct 1900.

FOSTER, Saint; 2nd Lt; 10th Inf, USV. Born in Texas; private, D/25th Infantry, 12 Nov 1875–11 Nov 1880; private, corporal, sergeant, first sergeant, M and C/10th Cavalry; private, corporal, sergeant, D/10th Cavalry, 12 Feb 1881–27 Apr 1893; private, G/10th Cavalry, 2 Mar 1896;

sergeant, 9 Mar 1896; first sergeant, 5 Sep 1896; stationed at Ft Assiniboine, MT, as first sergeant, G/10th Cavalry, 1897. SOURCE: Baker, Roster.

Sharpshooter, stationed at Ft McDowell, AZ. SOURCE: *ANJ* 24 (18 Jun 1887): 934.

Honorable mention for skill in trailing raiding parties in Arizona, 1888. SOURCE: Baker, Roster; Steward, *The Colored Regulars*, 244.

First sergeant, M/10th Cavalry, at Ft Apache, AZ, 1890, subscribed $.50 to testimonial to General Grierson. SOURCE: List of subscriptions, 23 Apr 1890, 10th Cavalry papers, MHI.

First sergeant, G/10th Cavalry, served in 10th Cavalry in Cuba, 1898. SOURCE: Cashin, *Under Fire with the Tenth Cavalry*, 344.

Commanded G/10th Cavalry, at Las Guasimas, Cuba, 1898, and won commission due to success with troops in battle. SOURCE: Steward, *The Colored Regulars*, 139.

Second lieutenant, 10th Infantry, U.S. Volunteers. SOURCE: Cashin, *Under Fire with the Tenth Cavalry*, 320, with picture.

FOSTER, Wiley; Private; F/10th Cav. Served in 10th Cavalry, 1898; remained in U.S. during war with Spain. SOURCE: Cashin, *Under Fire with the Tenth Cavalry*, 344.

FOWLER, Fred; Private; L/10th Cav. Served in 10th Cavalry, 1898; remained in U.S. during war with Spain. SOURCE: Cashin, *Under Fire with the Tenth Cavalry*, 350.

FOWLIS, Elmer; Private; G/49th Inf. Deserted while outpost guard, cause unknown, Zapote Bridge, Philippines, 9 Jul 1900; killed by insurgents. SOURCE: Descriptive Book, G/49 Inf.

FOWLISS, Kirk; Private; G/24th Inf. Wounded in action, Bongabon, Philippines, 29 Dec 1899. SOURCE: Muller, *The Twenty Fourth Infantry*, 36.

Wounded in the head, 28 Feb 1900. SOURCE: *ANJ* 37 (14 Apr 1900): 779.

FOX; Sergeant; K/9th Cav. Stationed at Ft Robinson, NE, 1887.

FOX, George; L/10th Cav. Original member of 10th Cavalry; in troop when organized, Ft Riley, KS, 21 Sep 1867. SOURCE: McMiller, "Buffalo Soldiers," 78.

FOX, Oscar; Sergeant; D/25th Inf. In D/25th Infantry, ranked fourth among infantry marksmen, Department of Dakota, and on department team. SOURCE: *ANJ* 35 (25 Sep 1897): 55.

Resident of Flushing, NY; thirteen years' service, including heroism at El Caney, Cuba, 1898; discharged, character excellent; expected to reenlist after home leave; presented medal for valor by fellow townsmen, 1899. SOURCE: *ANJ* 38 (3 Aug 1901): 1187.

Third best marksman, Department of the Missouri, 1903. SOURCE: SecWar, *AR 1903*, 1:427.

Ranked number 24 among expert riflemen with 72.6 percent, 1904. SOURCE: GO 52, AGO, 19 Mar 1904.

Ranked number 17 in Northern Division rifle team competition, Ft Sheridan, IL, awarded bronze medal, 1904. SOURCE: GO 167, AGO, 28 Oct 1904.

Ranked number 14 among expert riflemen with 79.67 percent, 1905. SOURCE: GO 79, AGO, 1 Jun 1905.

Distinguished marksman, 1905. SOURCE: GO 173, AGO, 20 Oct 1905.

Ranked number 160 among expert riflemen with 72.67 percent, 1906. SOURCE: GO 101, AGO, 31 May 1906.

Ranked number ten on U.S. infantry team that won first place, National Rifle Match, Sea Girt, NJ, 1906; each member of team won $300 and medal. SOURCE: GO 190, AGO, 15 Nov 1906.

Member of U.S. Army infantry team of seventeen riflemen, 1907. SOURCE: GO 162, AGO, 1 Aug 1907.

Ranked number six on ninth-place U.S. Army team, National Rifle Match, Camp Perry, OH, 28–31 Aug 1907. SOURCE: GO 4, AGO, 6 Jan 1908.

FOX, Robert J.; Private; K/10th Cav. Convicted by general court martial, Ft Robinson, NE, 11 Jan 1906; sentenced to two months' confinement; transferred from F/10th Cavalry, 24 Mar 1906.

FOX, William; Private; B/24th Inf. Reduced from sergeant, D/24th Infantry, to ranks and fined $30 for threatening his first sergeant and assaulting a corporal. SOURCE: *ANJ* 30 (4 Feb 1893): 395.

Unassigned recruit, 24th Infantry, forwarded to Ft Huachuca, AZ, under Order 246, Ft Bayard, NM, 19 Dec 1893, with Pvt. James Phillips, assigned to B/24th Infantry, Pvt. Loyd D. Allen, assigned to H/24th Infantry, and Pvt. Samuel Kennedy, assigned to H/24th Infantry. SOURCE: Order 188, Ft Huachuca, 22 Dec 1893, Letters & Orders Received, 24 Inf, 1893.

At Ft Niobrara, NE, 1904. SOURCE: Wilson, "History of Fort Niobrara."

An old buddy of Sgt. Vida Henry, at Houston, 1917; tried to warn Henry not to go through with attack on town. SOURCE: Haynes, *A Night of Violence*, 127.

FRANCIS, Dan; Private; H/24th Inf. Fined $5 by summary court, for being drunk and disorderly in streets, San Isidro, Philippines, 5 Dec 1901, second conviction; sentenced to three months for being drunk and disorderly, nuisance, disrespect to noncommissioned officer in quarters, 9 Dec 1901; fined $10 for carelessly discharging weapon while provost guard, 8 Mar 1902. SOURCE: Register of Summary Court, San Isidro.

FRANCIS, Dongel; 24th Inf. Died Ft Douglas, UT, 6 Apr 1899; buried at Ft Douglas. SOURCE: Clark, "A History of the Twenty-fourth," appendix A.

FRANCIS, Richard; Corporal; A/38th Inf. Arrested for part in soldier revolt at Ft Cummings, NM, autumn 1867; acquitted by court martial of involvement. SOURCE: Billington, *New Mexico's Buffalo Soldiers*, 40, 42.

FRANKLIN, Alfred J.; 24th Inf. Native of Gallatin, TN; married Miss Annie B. Walker of Mobeetie, TX, at Ft Elliott, TX, Dec 1885. SOURCE: Cleveland *Gazette*, 9 Jan 1886.

At Ft Elliott; his wife just returned from visit with friends. SOURCE: Cleveland *Gazette*, 15 Jan 1887.

Resided at 471 South 9th East, Salt Lake City, UT, in 1898. SOURCE: Clark, "A History of the Twenty-fourth," appendix B.

FRANKLIN, Anthony; Corporal; B/25th Inf. Dishonorable discharge, Brownsville. SOURCE: SO 266, AGO, 9 Nov 1906.

FRANKLIN, Benjamin; Private; A/10th Cav. Served in 10th Cavalry in Cuba, 1898. SOURCE: Cashin, *Under Fire with the Tenth Cavalry*, 336.

Wounded in action, Santiago, Cuba, 1 Jul 1898. SOURCE: SecWar, *AR 1898*, 324.

FRANKLIN, George; Corporal; F/9th Cav. Private, I/24th Infantry, enlisted Mobile, AL, 28 Mar 1899. SOURCE: Muster Roll, I/24 Inf, Mar–Apr 1899.

Allotted $5 per month for twelve months to Mary Stafford. SOURCE: Muster Roll, I/24 Inf, Sep–Oct 1899.

Veteran of Philippine Insurrection; corporal, F/9th Cavalry, at Ft D. A. Russell, WY, in 1910; resident of Mobile. SOURCE: *Illustrated Review: Ninth Cavalry*, with picture.

FRANKLIN, Henry O.; 2nd Lt; 9th Inf USV. Born Thibodaux, Lafourche Parish, LA, 25 Mar 1874; attended Thibodaux public schools, Straight University at New Orleans, and Meilley's Commercial Night School, New Orleans; worked six years for Citizens' Bank of New Orleans prior to appointment to 9th Infantry, U.S. Volunteers, 25 Jun 1898; intends to quit South and seek home in some new possession of U.S.; three years on board of trustees of Central Church and for some time superintendent of Sunday School; secretary of New Orleans Christian Endeavor Union and delegate to Christian Endeavor convention, Boston, MA, 1895; until 1898, his father one of wealthiest and most prosperous colored men in Louisiana; then forced to leave Thibodaux for New Orleans by "regulators." SOURCE: Coston, *The Spanish-American War Volunteer*, 27.

FRANKLIN, James A.; Private; H/9th Cav. Veteran of Spanish-American War and Philippine Insurrection; at Ft D. A. Russell, WY, in 1910; resident of Shirley, IN. SOURCE: *Illustrated Review: Ninth Cavalry*, with picture.

FRANKLIN, James Edward; D/10th Cav. Seven-year veteran; native of Richmond, VA; is home with bullet wound through neck, suffered at Santiago, Cuba, 4 Jul 1898, while seeking to rescue white Pvt. William Murphy, 71st New York Infantry; now invalid awaiting pension. SOURCE: Richmond *Planet*, 24 Jun 1899.

FRANKLIN, John; 1st Sgt; D/25th Inf. At Ft Custer, MT. SOURCE: *ANJ* 26 (16 Feb 1889): 491.

FRANKLIN, John; Private; H/9th Cav. Private, H/24th Infantry, enlisted Ft Douglas, UT, 11 Jan 1897; seven years' continuous service. SOURCE: Muster Roll, H/24 Inf, May–Jun 1898.

Transferred to L/24th Infantry, 7 Oct 1898; deposits $60, clothing $4.10. SOURCE: Muster Roll, H/24 Inf, Sep–Oct 1898.

Private, H/9th Cavalry, at Ft D. A. Russell, WY, in 1910; resident of Gallatin, TN. SOURCE: *Illustrated Review: Ninth Cavalry*, with picture.

FRANKLIN, Simon P.; Sergeant; Band/9th Cav. Born Sumner Co., TN, 1850; Ht 6'0", black complexion; enlisted A/24th Infantry, 7 Mar 1870; sergeant, 1 May 1870; reduced to ranks by garrison court martial, 19 Apr 1872; discharged 7 Mar 1875; reenlisted, Band/24th Infantry, 9 Mar 1875; principal musician, 24th Infantry, 16 Jul 1875; reduced to ranks, 1 Jul 1880; principal musician, 5 Sep 1884; discharged, Ft Supply, Indian Territory, character excellent, single, additional pay $3 per month, clothing $51.81, retained $60, 8 Mar 1885. SOURCE: Descriptive Book, 24 Inf NCS & Band.

Sergeant, Band/9th Cavalry, retires from Camp Bettens, WY, Aug 1892, in accordance with Special Order 182, Adjutant General's Office, 4 Aug 1892. SOURCE: *ANJ* 29 (13 Aug 1892): 880.

Retired from Band/9th Cavalry, 11 Aug 1892. SOURCE: Roster, 9 Cav.

Retired and employed as post exchange steward, Ft Robinson, NE, for $25 per month. SOURCE: Report of Inspection, Ft Robinson, 12 Aug 1893, Reports of Inspection, DP.

Retired, post exchange steward, Ft Robinson, 1894. SOURCE: Investigation of Charges against Chaplain Plummer.

Retired, resides at Ft Robinson, one of six soldiers, four of them black, on retired list paid in Department of the Platte by mail. SOURCE: Misc Records, DP, 1894–98.

In business near Ft Grant, AZ, 1900. SOURCE: Crawford *Bulletin*, 17 Feb 1900.

No Veterans Administration pension file.

FRANKLIN, W. W.; Private; E/25th Inf. Died of chronic dysentery on U.S. Army Transport *Warren* bound for San Francisco, CA, Jan 1901. SOURCE: *ANJ* 38 (9 Feb 1901): 579.

FRANKLIN, Walter; Private; E/10th Cav. Honorable mention for gallantry against Kiowas and Comanches, Wichita Agency, Indian Territory, 22–23 Aug 1874. SOURCE: Baker, Roster.

FRANKLIN, Walter; Private; A/9th Cav. Born Jackson Co., MO; enlisted, Cincinnati, OH, 18 Jul 1878; received at U.S. Military Prison, Leavenworth, age 31, occupation cook, brown complexion, 16 Jun 1882; discharged on certificate of disability with goiter. SOURCE: Certificates of Disability, DivMo, 1875–87.

FRANKLIN, William H.; 1st Lt; 9th Inf USV. Born Gallatin, Sumner Co., TN, 25 Mar 1857; enlisted 16 Apr 1876; private, corporal, sergeant, first sergeant, I and E/24th Infantry, to 17 Aug 1898; participated in battle of Santiago, Cuba, 1898; commissioned at Siboney, Cuba, first lieutenant, 9th Infantry, U.S. Volunteers, 16 Aug 1898. SOURCE: Coston, *The Spanish-American War Volunteer*, 24.

Sergeant, 24th Infantry, officiated at evening church services, Ft Apache, AZ, 1888. SOURCE: *ANJ* 25 (7 Jul 1888): 995.

Granted six-month furlough from San Carlos, AZ. SOURCE: *ANJ* 28 (30 May 1891): 667.

First sergeant, E/24th Infantry, distinguished marksman, rifle, 1892, 1893, 1894. SOURCE: GO 15, AGO, 15 Nov 1894.

First sergeant, E/24th Infantry, when commissioned. SOURCE: Cashin, *Under Fire with the Tenth Cavalry*, 360.

FRANKS, Benjamin; Private; E/25th Inf. Died of dysentery in the Philippines, 26 Aug 1900. SOURCE: *ANJ* 38 (8 Sep 1900): 43.

Died in the Philippines, 25 Aug 1900. SOURCE: Richmond *Planet*, 8 Sep 1900.

FRASER, Carlos; Corporal; F/10th Cav. Born Waterboro, SC; enlisted in 25th Infantry, Charleston, SC, age 22, laborer, Ht 5'6", black complexion, eyes, hair, 18 Jun 1881. SOURCE: Descriptive & Assignment Cards, 25 Inf.

Corporal, F/10th Cavalry; ranked number ten in revolver competition, Departments of Arizona and California, bronze medal, Ft Wingate, NM, 1889. SOURCE: GO 78, AGO, 12 Oct 1889; Baker, Roster.

FRAZER, Solomon; Private; Band/24th Inf. Enlisted Charleston, SC, drayman and stonemason, Ht 5'5", dark complexion, black hair and eyes, 18 May 1881; transferred from G/24th Infantry to Band/24th Infantry, 1 Apr 1886; discharged, end of term, Ft Supply, Indian Territory, single, character excellent, 17 May 1886; deposits $422.50, 1881–86, retained $72, clothing $67.01. SOURCE: Descriptive Book, 24 Inf NCS & Band.

FRAZIER, Benjamin T.; Private; B/24th Inf. Wounded in Cuba, 1898. SOURCE: Muller, *The Twenty Fourth Infantry*, 18.

Wounded in hand, San Juan, Cuba; discharged Jan 1899; former president, post literary society, Ft Douglas, UT. SOURCE: Clark, "A History of the Twenty-fourth," 100–101.

FRAZIER, Jacob; 1st Sgt; D/25th Inf. Dishonorable discharge, Brownsville. SOURCE: SO 266, AGO, 9 Nov 1906.

When discharged, fourteen-year veteran; wife's name Hattie. SOURCE: Weaver, *The Brownsville Raid*, 38.

FRAZIER, John W.; Private; I/10th Cav. Served in 10th Cavalry, 1898; remained in U.S. during war with Spain. SOURCE: Cashin, *Under Fire with the Tenth Cavalry*, 348.

FRAZIER, Petrum R.; Private; A/9th Cav. On special duty as cook, Nueva Caceres, Philippines, as of 19 Apr 1902. SOURCE: Special Duty List, A/9 Cav.

FREAR, Wilson; Private; D/24th Inf. Died of sclerosis in the Philippines, 9 Oct 1901. SOURCE: *ANJ* 39 (7 Dec 1901): 339.

FREDERICK, John; G/10th Cav. Original member of 10th Cavalry; in troop when organized, Ft Leavenworth, KS, 5 Jul 1867. SOURCE: McMiller, "Buffalo Soldiers," 74.

FREDERICKS, George; Private; K/9th Cav. Refused quarters, Ft Robinson, NE, Mar 1887, because commander was unsure his wife had divorced her first husband. SOURCE: Register of Correspondence, Ft Robinson.

FREDERICKS, Harry; Trumpeter; H/9th Cav. Veteran of Philippine Insurrection; at Ft D. A. Russell, WY, in 1910; sharpshooter; resident of Cincinnati. SOURCE: *Illustrated Review: Ninth Cavalry.*

FREDERICKS, John; Private; G/9th Cav. Served 1875–76. *See* **BLACKSTONE**, Charley, Private, G/9th Cavalry; **TROUTMAN**, Edward, Sergeant, G/9th Cavalry

FREDERICKS, Thomas; Sergeant; H/9th Cav. Praised for bravery against Victorio by Maj. Albert P. Morrow, Nov 1879. SOURCE: Billington, "Black Cavalrymen," 68; Billington, *New Mexico's Buffalo Soldiers*, 93.

FREELAND; Private; B/9th Cav. Wounded in action against Indians, 18 Sep 1879. *See* **CAUMP**, Private, B/9th Cavalry; **DENNY**, John, Sergeant, 9th Cavalry

FREEMAN; Sergeant; L/10th Cav. A noncommissioned officer who should be commissioned, according to unsigned letter, probably written by John E. Lewis, H/10th Cavalry, from Lakeland, FL, 12 Aug 1898. SOURCE: Gatewood, *"Smoked Yankees"*, 63.

FREEMAN, Albert; Private; A/9th Cav. At Ft D. A. Russell, WY, in 1910; marksman. SOURCE: *Illustrated Review: Ninth Cavalry*, with picture.

FREEMAN, Augustus C.; H/10th Cav. Original member of 10th Cavalry; in troop when organized, Ft Leavenworth, KS, 21 Jul 1867. SOURCE: McMiller, "Buffalo Soldiers," 75.

FREEMAN, Charles L.; Private; H/24th Inf. Enlisted Ft Huachuca, AZ, 27 Nov 1895; eight years' continuous service; due U.S. for ordnance lost, one fork, $.05. SOURCE: Muster Roll, H/24 Inf, May–Jun 1898.

Transferred to M/24th Infantry, 7 Oct 1898; retained $3.60; clothing $18.35. SOURCE: Muster Roll, H/24 Inf, Sep–Oct 1898.

FREEMAN, F. P.; Private; A/9th Cav. At Ft Stanton, NM, 1881. SOURCE: Regt Returns, 9 Cav, Jan 1881.

FREEMAN, George M.; L/10th Cav. Original member of 10th Cavalry; in troop when organized, Ft Riley, KS, 21 Sep 1867. SOURCE: McMiller, "Buffalo Soldiers," 78.

FREEMAN, Henry; Private; E/10th Cav. Served in 10th Cavalry, 1898; remained in U.S. during war with Spain. SOURCE: Cashin, *Under Fire with the Tenth Cavalry*, 343.

FREEMAN, Jerry B.; F/10th Cav. Original member of 10th Cavalry; in troop when organized, Ft Leavenworth, KS, 21 Jun 1867. SOURCE: McMiller, "Buffalo Soldiers," 73.

FREEMAN, Jerry R.; Private; A/10th Cav. Mentioned 1873. SOURCE: ES, 10 Cav, 1873–81.

FREEMAN, Pete; Corporal; L/10th Cav. Mentioned Oct 1870. SOURCE: ES, 10 Cav, 1873–81.

FREEMAN, Samuel; Private; H/25th Inf. At Ft Missoula, MT, 1894, according to Sgt. Dalbert P. Green, he was "one of the classiest [baseball] players that I've met in the Army." SOURCE: Nankivell, *History of the Twenty-fifth Infantry*, 164.

Served 1890–95; now age 65. SOURCE: *Winners of the West* 12 (Mar 1935): 2.

Writes and renews subscription; enjoys paper "these cold days in Wyoming." SOURCE: *Winners of the West* 14 (Mar 1937): 9.

Writes and renews subscription; pension up $5 per month. SOURCE: *Winners of the West* 15 (Mar 1938): 8.

Writes; pension up from $55 to $72 per month, for which he is grateful; bad eyesight keeps him from writing more. SOURCE: *Winners of the West* 15 (Jun 1938): 6.

Subscriber since 1929; died at his Wyoming home Aug 1939. SOURCE: *Winners of the West* 16 (Aug 1939): 2.

FREEMAN, William H.; Private; Band/10th Cav. Deposited $10 with paymaster, Ft Concho, TX, 29 Jan 1877. SOURCE: Adj, 10 Cav, to PMG, 30 Jan 1877, LS, 10 Cav, 1873–83.

Deposited $10 with paymaster, Ft Concho, 12 Mar 1877. SOURCE: Adj, 10 Cav, to PMG, 12 Mar 1877, LS, 10 Cav, 1873–83.

FRELAND, G.; Corporal; A/9th Cav. At Ft Stanton, NM, 1881. SOURCE: Regt Returns, 9 Cav, Jan 1881.

FREMONT, George W.; L Corp; A/10th Cav. Enlisted as private, A/10th Cavalry, Apr 1876. SOURCE: ES, 10 Cav, 1873–81.

Former post librarian, Ft Concho, TX; deserted Staked Plains expedition, Aug 1877, and sentenced to dishonorable discharge and one year's confinement. SOURCE: Leckie, *The Buffalo Soldiers*, 160, 162.

Deserter from Staked Plains expedition. SOURCE: Sullivan, "Fort McKavett," 147.

Convicted by general court martial, Ft Clark, TX, 10 Dec 1877. SOURCE: Miles, "Fort Concho in 1877," 49.

FRENCH, Robert; Private; C/10th Cav. Served in 10th Cavalry, 1898; remained in U.S. during war with Spain. SOURCE: Cashin, *Under Fire with the Tenth Cavalry*, 340.

FRIEDMAN, Arthur; Private; A/10th Cav. Sergeant, D/10th Cavalry; released to duty from treatment for gonorrhea, Ft Robinson, NE, 11 Aug 1903. SOURCE: Post Surgeon to CO, D/10, 11 Aug 1903, LS, Post Surgeon, Ft Robinson.

Private, A/10th Cavalry; released to duty from treatment for multiple chancroids, Ft Robinson, 17 Dec 1903. SOURCE: Post Surgeon to CO, A/10, 17 Dec 1903, LS, Post Surgeon, Ft Robinson.

FRIERSON, Eugene; Sgt Maj; 10th Cav. Born in Tennessee; private, K/10th Cavalry, 19 Oct 1892; corporal, 13 Jun 1895; stationed at Ft Custer, MT, 1897. SOURCE: Baker, Roster.

Born Columbia, TN, around 1873; Ht 5'6", brown complexion; marksman, 1893, 1894, 1900; sharpshooter, 1896, 1897, 1901, 1902; lance corporal, corporal, sergeant, 17 Oct 1894-1 Dec 1902; squadron sergeant major, 1 Dec 1902; served in Cuba, 22 May 1899–30 Oct 1900, 13 Dec 1900–5 May 1902; reenlisted, character excellent, $3 per month additional pay for ten years' continuous service, 19 Oct 1902; married to Julia E. Frierson, one child; deposits $250, 13 Nov 1900, $15, 11 Mar 1903, $30, 9 Apr 1903; proficient at noncommissioned officers' school, Ft Robinson, NE, in Army regulations, minor tactics, hippology, drill regulations, and as expert rifleman, 13 Jul 1905. SOURCE: Descriptive Book, 10 Cav Officers & NCOs.

At Ft Robinson as corporal, K/10th Cavalry, for cavalry competition, Sep 1897.

Served in 10th Cavalry, 1898; remained in U.S. during war with Spain. SOURCE: Cashin, *Under Fire with the Tenth Cavalry*, 349.

Guest of former troop, K/10th Cavalry, at Christmas dinner, 1904, with wife. SOURCE: Barrow, "Christmas in the United States Army," 96–97.

Ranked number 16 among marksmen, Northern Division cavalry, 1905. SOURCE: Glass, *History of the Tenth Cavalry*, 45.

Author of "An Adventure in the Big Horn Mountains, or, the Trials and Tribulations of a Recruit," in *Colored American Magazine*. SOURCE: *Colored American Magazine* 8 (Apr 1905): 196–99; (May 1905): 277–79; (Jun 1905): 338–40.

Ranked number 16, Northern Division cavalry competition, bronze medal, Ft Riley, KS, 1905. SOURCE: GO 173, AGO, 20 Oct 1905.

Ranked number 133 among expert riflemen with 73.33 percent, 1905. SOURCE: GO 101, AGO, 31 May 1906.

Regimental sergeant major, 1914, first lieutenant, 8th Illinois Infantry, 1916; first lieutenant, 9th Cavalry, 1916; passed examination for commission, Ft Huachuca, AZ, May 1914; commissioned at El Paso. TX, 1916; retired with thirty years, 1919. SOURCE: *Crisis* 9 (Nov 1914): 13; 12 (Sep 1916): 247; 17 (Sep 1919): 259.

Author of preface to *The Black Soldier*. SOURCE: Curtis, *The Black Soldier*.

As sergeant major, 10th Cavalry, Ft Huachuca, 28 Aug 1914, he wrote: "If there is any doubt on the part of any citizen as to our valor, courage, and obedience in the Army, I simply refer him to the records of the War Department, in Washington, DC. . . . Men are not superior by reason of the accident of race or color. They are superior who have the best heart and the best brain. Superiority is born of honesty, of virtue, of charity, and above all of the love of liberty." SOURCE: Curtis, *The Black Soldier*, 56, with pictures.

Regimental sergeant major, 10th Cavalry, commissioned second lieutenant from training camp at Leon Springs, TX. SOURCE: Glass, *History of the Tenth Cavalry*, appendix M.

FRIERSON, Watts; Farrier; E/9th Cav. Corporal, K/10th Cavalry, served in 10th Cavalry, 1898; remained in U.S. during war with Spain. SOURCE: Cashin, *Under Fire with the Tenth Cavalry*, 349.

Private, G/24th Infantry, ranked number 207 among rifle experts with 68 percent, 1904. SOURCE: GO 79, AGO, 1 Jul 1905.

Farrier, E/9th Cavalry, at Ft D. A. Russell, WY, in 1910; sharpshooter. SOURCE: *Illustrated Review: Ninth Cavalry*, with picture.

FRISBY, Isaac; Private; G/10th Cav. Original member of 10th Cavalry; in troop when organized, Ft Leavenworth, KS, 5 Jul 1867. SOURCE: McMiller, "Buffalo Soldiers," 74.

Charges and specifications against him transmitted. SOURCE: 2nd Lt. S. R. Colladay, CO, G/10, to Adj, Det 10 Cav, Ft Lyon, CO, 23 Feb 1869, LR, Det 10 Cav, 1868–69.

Prisoner Frisby to report tomorrow to court martial room. SOURCE: 1st Lt. C. Parker, CO, 5 Inf, Judge Advocate, Ft Lyon, CO, to CO, Det 10 Cav, 14 Mar 1869, LR, Det 10 Cav, 1868–69.

Convicted by general court martial, Ft Lyon, CO, of deserting sentry post at camp on Hackberry Creek, Indian Territory, 3 Dec 1868, until caught 15 Dec 1868, and of theft of weapons and ammunition at the same time; sentenced "to forfeit to the United States all pay now due or that may become due, excepting the just dues of his laundress; to be indelibly marked on the left hip with the letter D, two inches long and one inch broad, in vermillion," dishonorably discharged, and confined for five years; all but the confinement approved by commander, Department of the Missouri. SOURCE: GCMO 25, DeptMo, 16 Apr 1869.

FRISLEY, John L.; Private; K/24th Inf. Stationed at Camp Pilot Butte, WY; in hands of civil authorities, Rock Springs, WY, 2–13 Feb 1899.

FRONTMAN, William; Private; A/10th Cav. Served in 10th Cavalry in Cuba, 1898. SOURCE: Cashin, *Under Fire with the Tenth Cavalry*, 336.

FROST, John; M/10th Cav. Original member of 10th Cavalry; in troop when organized, Ft Riley, KS, 15 Oct 1867. SOURCE: McMiller, "Buffalo Soldiers," 79.

FRY, Edward; B/10th Cav. Original member of 10th Cavalry; in troop when organized, Ft Leavenworth, KS, 1 Apr 1867. SOURCE: McMiller, "Buffalo Soldiers," 69.

FRY, Edward; 1st Sgt; A/24th Inf. Retired Jun 1901.

FRY, Frank; Farrier; E/10th Cav. At Ft Apache, AZ, 1890, subscribed $.50 to testimonial to General Grierson. SOURCE: List of subscriptions, 23 Apr 1890, 10th Cavalry papers, MHI.

Served in 10th Cavalry, 1898; remained in U.S. during war with Spain. SOURCE: Cashin, *Under Fire with the Tenth Cavalry*, 343.

Farrier, drowned in Rio Grandera, Samar, Philippines, 28 Jun 1901; body recovered. SOURCE: *ANJ* 39 (28 Sep 1901): 81.

FRY, John; A/10th Cav. As surviving Indian war veteran. SOURCE: *Winners of the West* 3 (Jun 1926): 7.

FRYE, William G.; Private; A/9th Cav. Buried at Ft Robinson, NE, 14 Jul 1896. SOURCE: List of Interments, Ft Robinson.

FULBRIGHT, William R.; Private; H/25th Inf. Corporal, M/25th Infantry; two letters to editor, in Manila *Times*, 1899, one a tribute to Robert Ingersoll. SOURCE: Manila *Times*, 7 Aug and 18 Sep 1899.

Corporal, Band/25th Infantry; letter describes his colleagues as veterans of Cuba, "brave and daring" and eager for combat. SOURCE: Indianapolis *Freeman*, 4 Feb 1899.

An infielder on regimental baseball team that beat 12th Infantry 15 to 3 at Christmas 1899. SOURCE: Richmond *Planet*, 10 Feb 1900.

Fined $5 by summary court for failure to repair for reveille, San Marcelino, Philippines, 1 Nov 1900; acquitted of disrespectful language toward and challenge to fight Sgt. John H. Jackson, Band/25th Infantry, 31 Oct 1900; witnesses: Sgts. George Hampton, Robert Warick, and James Nolan, all of Band/25th Infantry. SOURCE: Misc Records, 25 Inf.

Principal speaker at entertainment of Reading Club, 25th Infantry, Castillejos, Philippines, Nov 1900. SOURCE: Richmond *Planet*, 23 Feb 1901.

Private, H/25th Infantry; letter from Manila, 10 Jun 1901. SOURCE: Gatewood, *"Smoked Yankees"*, 304.

FULLER, Cornelius; QM Sgt; 24th Inf. Born Cartersville, GA; first enlisted in G/24th Infantry; discharged as corporal, 16 Nov 1884; reenlisted, Ft Leavenworth, KS, age 26, Ht 5'5", black complexion, 21 Nov 1884; transferred to Band/24th Infantry, Ft Supply, Indian Territory, 10 Apr 1885; fined $5 by garrison court martial, Ft Bayard, NM, 1889; discharged, end of term, Ft Bayard, character very good, single, with $2 per month additional pay, deposits $15, retained $60, clothing $41.59, 20 Nov 1889; reenlisted, Ft Bayard, 21 Nov 1889; discharged, end of term, Ft Bayard, character excellent, married, no children, with $3 per month additional pay, retained $60, clothing $48.83, owes government $7.06 for subsistence stores, 20 Nov 1894. SOURCE: Descriptive Book, 24 Inf NCS & Band.

Retires as quartermaster sergeant, 24th Infantry, with thirty years' service and $30 per month pension. SOURCE: Cleveland *Gazette*, 29 Dec 1906.

FULLER, James D.; Private; B/10th Cav. Served in 10th Cavalry, 1898; remained in U.S. during war with Spain. SOURCE: Cashin, *Under Fire with the Tenth Cavalry*, 339.

FULLER, Jefferson; Sergeant; A/10th Cav. At Ft Apache, AZ, 1890, subscribed $.50 to testimonial to General Grierson. SOURCE: List of subscriptions, 23 Apr 1890, 10th Cavalry papers, MHI.

Admitted to Soldiers Home with disability, age 37, after thirteen years and six months' service, 26 Sep 1890. SOURCE: SecWar, *AR 1890*, 1044.

FULLER, John; Private; A/48th Inf. Drowned in the Philippines, 18 Aug 1900. SOURCE: *ANJ* 38 (8 Sep 1900): 43.

Died in the Philippines, 18 Aug 1900. SOURCE: Richmond *Planet*, 8 Sep 1900.

FULLER, John R.; Private; E/24th Inf. Transferred from Reserve Divisional Hospital, Siboney, Cuba, to Fortress Monroe, VA, with remittent malarial fever, on U.S. Army Transport *Concho*, 23 Jul 1898. SOURCE: Hospital Papers, Spanish-American War.

FULLER, Lewis E.; Chief Musician; Band/9th Cav. Led regimental band in concert at Hot Springs, SD, Oct 1895. SOURCE: *ANJ* 33 (12 Oct 1895): 92.

FULLER, Peter; L/10th Cav. Original member of 10th Cavalry; in troop when organized, Ft Riley, KS, 21 Sep 1867. SOURCE: McMiller, "Buffalo Soldiers," 78.

FULLER, Richard; Private; L/10th Cav. Mentioned May 1877 as having transferred from A/10th Cavalry. SOURCE: ES, 10 Cav, 1873–81.

FULSOME, A.; QM Sgt; 25th Inf. Served as pallbearer for Col. Andrew S. Burt, who had requested that men of 25th

Infantry carry his coffin. SOURCE: Curtis, *The Black Soldier*, 49.

FULTZ, George; Private; K/10th Cav. Served in 10th Cavalry in Cuba, 1898. SOURCE: Cashin, *Under Fire with the Tenth Cavalry*, 359.

FUQUA, William R.; Private; A/10th Cav. Jailed and put to work on city streets, Crawford, NE, in lieu of $5 fine and $4.80 costs for fast riding, 30 Jun 1902.

Deserter from Ft Robinson, NE, Oct 1902. SOURCE: Certificate, Capt. W. H. Hay, 10th Cav, 15 Jan 1903, 10th Cavalry papers, MHI.

FUREMAN, A.; Sergeant; A/9th Cav. Ranked number eight in competition of Army carbine team, 1892. SOURCE: GO 75, AGO, 3 Nov 1892.

FURGESON, DeWitt; Private; B/9th Cav. On detached service at Ft Bayard, NM, 16 Jan–9 Feb 1881. SOURCE: Regt Returns, 9 Cav, Feb 1881.

G

GABBOND, Moses; B/10th Cav. Original member of 10th Cavalry; in troop when organized, Ft Leavenworth, KS, 1 Apr 1867. SOURCE: McMiller, "Buffalo Soldiers," 69.

GADDEN, Parris; M/10th Cav. Original member of 10th Cavalry; in troop when organized, Ft Riley, KS, 15 Oct 1867. SOURCE: McMiller, "Buffalo Soldiers," 79.

GADDIS, John; Private; Band/10th Cav. Deposited $100 with paymaster. SOURCE: CO, 10 Cav, to PMG, 13 Jan 1874, LS, 10 Cav, 1873–77.

Deposited $100 with paymaster. SOURCE: CO, 10 Cav, to PMG, 4 May 1874, LS, 10 Cav, 1873–77.

Former private, Band/10th Cavalry, plays very important instrument; regimental commander recommends approval of his enlistment. SOURCE: CO, 10 Cav, to AG, USA, 31 Dec 1874, LS, 10 Cav, 1873–77.

GADMIN, Willis; A/10th Cav. Original member of 10th Cavalry; in troop when organized, Ft Leavenworth, KS, 18 Feb 1867. SOURCE: McMiller, "Buffalo Soldiers," 68.

GADSDEN, Peter; Sergeant; A/9th Cav. Retires Apr 1901. SOURCE: *ANJ* 38 (27 Apr 1901): 843.

GAGE; Private; Band/10th Cav. At Ft Apache, AZ, 1890, subscribed $.50 to testimonial to General Grierson. SOURCE: List of subscriptions, 23 Apr 1890, 10th Cavalry papers, MHI.

GAGE, Henry; Private; H/25th Inf. Died of heart disease in the Philippines, 30 Nov 1900. SOURCE: *ANJ* 38 (8 Dec 1900): 355.

GAGE, James H.; Private; D/9th Cav. His sentence for desertion, which began 4 Feb 1876, reduced to eighteen months. SOURCE: GCMO 22, AGO, 23 Feb 1877.

GAINES, George W.; 1st Sgt; A/10th Cav. At Wounded Knee Creek, SD, at time of massacre as private, E/9th Cavalry; sergeant, A/10th Cavalry, Ft Robinson, NE, 1906. SOURCE: Ricker Tablet no. 35, NSHS.

Promoted to corporal, E/9th Cavalry, in accordance with regimental order 27, Ft Robinson, 23 Apr 1891. SOURCE: Cleveland *Gazette*, 16 May 1891.

Sergeant, E/9th Cavalry, since 15 Mar 1893. SOURCE: Roster, 9 Cav.

As sergeant, E/9th Cavalry, led detachment of one private from each troop, which proceeded to Ft Robinson's wood reservation to cut for new corral fence, 25 Mar 1895; carried three days' rations; accompanied by four mules and one civilian packer. SOURCE: Post Order 18, 23 Mar 1895, Post Orders, Ft Robinson.

Reenlistment for A/10th Cavalry authorized. SOURCE: TWX, AGO, USA, 6 Nov 1897.

Served in A/10th Cavalry, 1898; remained in U.S. during war with Spain. SOURCE: Cashin, *Under Fire with the Tenth Cavalry*, 337

Promoted to corporal, Sep 1899. SOURCE: *ANJ* 37 (23 Sep 1899): 80.

First sergeant, A/10th Cavalry; was in charge of detachment of regiment camped on timber reserve, Ft Robinson, when sudden storm caused stove explosion that partially blinded Caleb Benson. SOURCE: Deposition, Gaines, 25 Aug 1905, VA File XC 2499129, Caleb Benson.

First sergeant, A/10th Cavalry, age 51; supports Benson's claim for pension. SOURCE: Deposition, Gaines, 11 Jul 1906, VA File XC 2499129, Caleb Benson.

GAINES, Henry P.; Private; H/10th Cav. Served in 10th Cavalry, 1898; remained in U.S. during war with Spain. SOURCE: Cashin, *Under Fire with the Tenth Cavalry*, 346.

At Camp Forse, AL, Nov 1898. SOURCE: Richmond *Planet*, 3 Dec 1898.

GAINES, Joseph; L/10th Cav. Original member of 10th Cavalry; in troop when organized, Ft Riley, KS, 21 Sep 1867. SOURCE: McMiller, "Buffalo Soldiers," 78.

GAINES, Mosely; Private; B/10th Cav. Enlisted Pittsburgh, PA; wounded in action, Santiago, Cuba, 1898. SOURCE: Cleveland *Gazette*, 2 Jul 1898.

Served in 10th Cavalry in Cuba, 1898. SOURCE: Cashin, *Under Fire with the Tenth Cavalry*, 338.

Wounded in finger of left hand, Santiago, 24 Jun 1898. SOURCE: SecWar, *AR 1898*, 339.

Died of typhoid followed by yellow fever, in Cuba, 19 Aug 1898. SOURCE: *ANJ* 36 (11 Feb 1899): 567; *ANJ* 36 (3 Sep 1898): 19; AG, *Correspondence Regarding the War with Spain*, I:246.

GAINES, Underwood; Sergeant; A/9th Cav. Veteran of Philippine Insurrection; expert rifleman at Ft D. A. Russell, WY, in 1910. SOURCE: *Illustrated Review: Ninth Cavalry,* with picture.

GAINS, Henry; C/10th Cav. Original member of 10th Cavalry; in troop when organized, Ft Leavenworth, KS, 14 May 1867. SOURCE: McMiller, "Buffalo Soldiers," 70.

GAITHER, Ozrow; Sergeant; E/10th Cav. Served in 10th Cavalry in Cuba, 1989. SOURCE: Cashin, *Under Fire with the Tenth Cavalry*, 342.

Commended for distinguished service, battle of Santiago, Cuba, 1 Jul 1898; now out of service. SOURCE: GO 15, AGO, 13 Feb 1900.

Born and enlisted Nashville, TN; awarded certificate of merit for distinguished service in Cuba. SOURCE: *ANJ* 36 (10 Jun 1899): 967.

Certificate of merit mentioned. SOURCE: Steward, *The Colored Regulars*, 280; *ANJ* 37 (24 Feb 1900): 611.

GALAGER, Samuel; L/10th Cav. Original member of 10th Cavalry; in troop when organized, Ft Riley, KS, 21 Sep 1867. SOURCE: McMiller, "Buffalo Soldiers," 78.

GALBREATH, J. F.; Private; K/9th Cav. On detached service in field, New Mexico, 21 Jan–8 Feb 1881. SOURCE: Regt Returns, 9 Cav, Feb 1881.

GALE, William; Private; G/10th Cav. Served in 10th Cavalry, 1898; remained in U.S. during war with Spain. SOURCE: Cashin, *Under Fire with the Tenth Cavalry*, 345.

GALLOWAY, Alonzo; Private; I/24th Inf. Enlisted Philadelphia, PA, 30 Mar 1899. SOURCE: Muster Roll, I/24 Inf, Mar–Apr 1899.

On detached service, Three Rivers, CA, 3 May–21 Jun 1899, and at Presidio of San Francisco, CA, 22 Jun 1899. SOURCE: Muster Roll, I/24 Inf, May–Jun 1899.

Allotted $10 per month for six months to James Galloway. SOURCE: Muster Roll, I/24 Inf, Sep–Oct 1899.

GALLOWAY, Henry T.; Private; H/10th Cav. Served in 10th Cavalry, 1898; remained in U.S. during war with Spain. SOURCE: Cashin, *Under Fire with the Tenth Cavalry*, 347.

GALLOWAY, Lawrence; Blacksmith; H/9th Inf. Born Augusta, GA; age 46 in Apr 1895; Ht 5'6", complexion yellow; $5 per month additional pay for twenty years continuous service, all in H Troop. SOURCE: Descriptive Book, H/9 Cav.

GALLOWAY, William; A/10th Cav. Original member of 10th Cavalry; in troop when organized, Ft Leavenworth, KS, 18 Feb 1867. SOURCE: McMiller, "Buffalo Soldiers," 68.

GALVIN, Orpheus; L/9th Cav. Born Buckingham, VA; enlisted Baltimore, MD, occupation laborer, complexion black, 24 Jan 1879; received at U.S. Military Prison, Ft Leavenworth, KS, age 33, 14 Feb 1883; discharged on certificate of disability with pulmonary consumption, 8 Mar 1883. SOURCE: Certificates of Disability, DivMo.

GAMBLE, John; Sergeant; K/25th Inf. At Ft Niobrara, NE, 1904. SOURCE: Wilson, "History of Fort Niobrara."

GANAWAY; Private; F/10th Cav. At Ft Apache, AZ, 1890, subscribed $.50 to testimonial to General Grierson. SOURCE: List of subscriptions, 23 Apr 1890, 10th Cavalry papers, MHI.

GANSON, Charles; Private; K/10th Cav. Served in 10th Cavalry, 1898; remained in U.S. during war with Spain. SOURCE: Cashin, *Under Fire with the Tenth Cavalry*, 346.

GANSON, Stertes; Private; M/10th Cav. Served in 10th Cavalry, 1898; remained in U.S. during war with Spain. SOURCE: Cashin, *Under Fire with the Tenth Cavalry*, 351.

GANT, Elias; Private; D/25th Inf. In K/25th Infantry at Ft Niobrara, NE, 1904. SOURCE: Wilson, "History of Fort Niobrara."

In D/25th Infantry; dishonorable discharge, Brownsville. SOURCE: SO 266, AGO, 9 Nov 1906.

One of fourteen cleared of involvement in Brownsville raid and allowed to reenlist. SOURCE: Weaver, *The Brownsville Raid*, 248.

GANT, John; Private; H/24th Inf. Enlisted Ft Douglas, UT, twenty-ninth year of continuous service, 14 Feb 1899. SOURCE: Muster Roll, H/24 Inf, Jan–Feb 1899.

GANT, Stephen; Private; G/10th Cav. Honorable mention for bravery against Indians, Lake Quemado, TX, 3 Aug 1880. SOURCE: Baker, Roster.

GANT, Thomas; F/9th Cav. Surviving Indian war veteran. SOURCE: *Winners of the West* 3 (Jun 1926): 7.

GANTZ, Frank; 24th Inf. Drunk at Halfway House between Havre and Ft Assiniboine, MT; took three shots at John Dolan, proprietor, then shot at bartender L. Groves; Groves shot Gantz; Gantz shot Private Robinson, M/24th Infantry; constable A. C. White arrested Groves, who claimed self-defense; both wounded soldiers are in post hospital. SOURCE: San Francisco *Chronicle*, 26 Dec 1902.

GARDNER, Charles; 25th Inf. Willing to submit to any test for reenlistment. SOURCE: Washington *Post*, 13 Dec 1906.

GARDNER, Jacob N.; Private; 10th Cav. Mentioned Jun 1875. SOURCE: ES, 10 Cav, 1873–83.

Commander, 10th Cavalry, transmits charges and specifications against Gardner to St. Louis Barracks, MO; Gardner remains in hospital, Ft Sill, Indian Territory. SOURCE: CO, 10 Cav, to CO, Ft Sill, 7 Jan 1877, LS, 10 Cav, 1873–81.

GARDNER, Sandy; Sergeant; 25th Inf. Born Russell Co., VA; enlisted in Band/25th Infantry, San Diego Barracks, CA, occupation carpenter, Ht 5'11", dark brown complexion, single, age 28, 13 Jul 1896. SOURCE: Descriptive & Assignment Cards, 25 Inf.

Age 70, retires as sergeant with forty-two years' service, Ft Huachuca, AZ. SOURCE: *Winners of the West* 16 (Dec 1938): 2.

GARDNER, Seymour; Private; B/10th Cav. Served in 10th Cavalry in Cuba, 1898. SOURCE: Cashin, *Under Fire with the Tenth Cavalry*, 338.

GARDNER, William; Private; Band/25th Inf. Born Russell Co., VA; enlisted in Band/25th Infantry, San Diego Barracks, CA, Ht 5'9", dark brown complexion, age 25, 6 Jun 1896; three years and three months' previous service in unit. SOURCE: Descriptive & Assignment Cards, 25 Inf.

GARDNER, William A.; A/10th Cav. Original member of 10th Cavalry; in troop when organized, Ft Leavenworth, KS, 18 Feb 1867. SOURCE: McMiller, "Buffalo Soldiers," 68.

GARDNER, William George; Private; M/9th Cav. Born in Virginia; enlisted Baltimore, MD, age 25, 24 May 1898; served in Tampa, FL, Camp Wikoff, NY, Ft Grant, AZ, and Cuban campaign; discharged 13 Dec 1898. Married Suzie Gambel, age 40, widow of Fields Wilder, 26 Apr 1898; pensioned with one-third disability for rheumatism, died an invalid, of pulmonary tuberculosis and alcoholism, 8 Apr 1908; buried in National Cemetery, Baltimore; widow had no property or insurance; her pension claim rejected because his death was unrelated to service. SOURCE: VA File C 2497800, William G. Gardner.

When he came home from Army, he was "all broken down" from rheumatism and heart trouble and could not work although willing to do so; short winded, pains in chest. SOURCE: Affidavit, Emma Gardner, sister, Baltimore, 6 Apr 1905, VA File C 2497800, William G. Gardner.

GARDNER, William H.; Corporal; E/9th Cav. Trumpeter, E/9th Cavalry, at Ft Robinson, NE. SOURCE: Court Martial Records, Hector.

Will marry Miss Mattie Hughes at Ft Robinson chapel, 25 Nov 1897. SOURCE: Crawford *Tribune*, 19 Nov 1897.

Corporal, E/9th Cavalry, stationed at Ft Leavenworth, KS; hero of San Juan Hill, Cuba, and veteran of the Philippines, recently tendered reception by "admiring citizens" at Easton, MD. SOURCE: Indianapolis *Freeman*, 14 Apr 1906.

GAREY, Charles; B/10th Cav. Original member of 10th Cavalry; in troop when organized, Ft Leavenworth, KS, 1 Apr 1867. SOURCE: McMiller, "Buffalo Soldiers," 69.

Mentioned Apr 1877 as formerly in B/10th Cavalry. SOURCE: ES, 10 Cav, 1873–81.

GARFIELD, George A.; Private; H/10th Cav. Served in 10th Cavalry, 1898; remained in U.S. during war with Spain. SOURCE: Cashin, *Under Fire with the Tenth Cavalry*, 347.

GARLAND, G.; Private; A/9th Cav. At Ft Stanton, NM, 1881. SOURCE: Regt Returns, 9 Cav, Jan 1881.

GARMON, Mark; Private; C/25th Cav. Dishonorable discharge, Brownsville. SOURCE: SO 266, AGO, 9 Nov 1906.

GARNER, Clarence; Private; H/24th Inf. Acquitted by summary court, San Isidro, Philippines, of absence from check roll call, 21 Apr 1902, and reveille, 22 Apr 1902. SOURCE: Register of Summary Court, San Isidro.

GARNETT; Private; B/9th Cav. Wounded in action, Mimbres Mountains, NM, 3 Feb 1880. SOURCE: Hamilton, "History of the Ninth Cavalry," 50; *Illustrated Review: Ninth Cavalry*.

GARNETT, George R.; Sgt Maj; 10th Cav. Original member of E/10th Cavalry; in troop when organized, Ft Leavenworth, KS, 15 Jun 1867. SOURCE: McMiller, "Buffalo Soldiers," 72.

As first sergeant, H/10th Cavalry, cited for gallantry against Kiowas and Comanches, Wichita Agency, Indian Territory, 22–23 Aug 1874. SOURCE: Baker, Roster.

Authorized four-month furlough from Ft Apache, AZ. SOURCE: *ANJ* 26 (20 Apr 1889): 678.

At Ft Apache, 1890, subscribed $.50 to testimonial to General Grierson. SOURCE: List of subscriptions, 23 Apr 1890, 10th Cavalry papers, MHI.

On furlough, to be discharged. SOURCE: *ANJ* 28 (3 Jan 1891): 312.

GARNETT, Robert; K/10th Cav. Original member of 10th Cavalry; in troop when organized, Ft Riley, KS, 1 Sep 1867. SOURCE: McMiller, "Buffalo Soldiers," 77.

GARNEY, John D.; Private; Band/25th Inf. Born Savannah, GA; enlisted New Orleans, LA, Ht 5'9", complexion brown, occupation paperhanger, age 21, 1 May 1895; stationed at Ft Missoula, MT. SOURCE: Descriptive & Assignment Cards, 25 Inf.

GARR, Henry B.; Private; K/25th Inf. Died of beriberi in the Philippines. SOURCE: *ANJ* 39 (8 Feb 1902): 577.

GARRARD, Chester; Private; G/25th Inf. Served 1910. *See* **JAMES**, John, Sergeant, G/25th Infantry

GARRET, John; Private; D/24th Inf. Died of dysentery, Camp Wikoff, NY, 18 Sep 1898. SOURCE: Hospital Papers, Spanish-American War.

GARRETT; Private; D/10th Cav. At Ft Apache, AZ, 1890, subscribed $.50 to testimonial to General Grierson. SOURCE: List of subscriptions, 23 Apr 1890, 10th Cavalry papers, MHI.

GARRETT, Clarence; Private; G/9th Cav. At Ft D. A. Russell, WY, in 1910; resident of Chicago. SOURCE: *Illustrated Review: Ninth Cavalry*.

GARRETT, Daniel; Corporal; H/10th Cav. Served in 10th Cavalry, 1898; remained in U.S. during war with Spain. SOURCE: Cashin, *Under Fire with the Tenth Cavalry*, 346.

Killed, Camp Forse, AL, 11 Nov 1898. *See* **BROOKS**, John R., Private, H/10th Cavalry

GARRETT, James; L/10th Cav. Original member of 10th Cavalry; in troop when organized, Ft Riley, KS, 21 Sep 1867. SOURCE: McMiller, "Buffalo Soldiers," 78.

GARRETT, John H.; Private; E/10th Cav. Served in 10th Cavalry, 1898; remained in U.S. during war with Spain. SOURCE: Cashin, *Under Fire with the Tenth Cavalry*, 343.

GARRETT, Stephen; Private; K/24th Cav. At Camp Pilot Butte, WY, 1898–99; in hands of civil authorities, Rock Springs, WY, 31 Jan–4 Feb 1899.

GARRETT, William; B/49th Inf. Released from five-year sentence at Alcatraz, CA, for disobedience of orders, based on Supreme Court's Deming decision. SOURCE: San Francisco *Chronicle*, 4 Jun 1902; *ANJ* 39 (7 Jun 1902): 1005.

GARRISON, Richard; H/10th Cav. Original member of 10th Cavalry; in troop when organized, Ft Leavenworth, KS, 21 Jul 1867. SOURCE: McMiller, "Buffalo Soldiers," 75.

GARROTT, Clarence; Private; K/25th Inf. At Ft Niobrara, NE, 1904. SOURCE: Wilson, "History of Fort Niobrara."

GARROTT, Langston E.; Private; L/10th Cav. Released to duty from treatment for acute gonorrhea, Ft Robinson, NE, 17 May 1903. SOURCE: Post Surgeon to CO, L/10, 17 May 1903, LS, Post Surgeon, Ft Robinson.

GARTRILL, Christopher; F/10th Cav. Original member of 10th Cavalry; in troop when organized, Ft Leavenworth, KS, 21 Jun 1867. SOURCE: McMiller, "Buffalo Soldiers," 73.

Commander, detachment, 10th Cavalry, Ft Dodge, KS, recommends to assistant adjutant general, Department of the Missouri, remission of his sentence except discharge, 17 May 1869; judge advocate, Department of the Missouri, recommends disapproval, 24 May 1869; conviction of Gartrill was for desertion. SOURCE: LR, Det 10 Cav, 1868–69.

GARY, Bartly R.; E/10th Cav. Died of consumption, age 23, U.S. Soldiers Home, 21 Apr 1898. SOURCE: SecWar, *AR 1898*, 1015.

GASKINS, Albert; Private; Band/10th Cav. Served in F/10th Cavalry in Cuba, 1898. SOURCE: Cashin, *Under Fire with the Tenth Cavalry*, 344.

Transferred from F Troop, Ft Assiniboine, MT. SOURCE: SO 15, 10 Cav, 25 Mar 1898.

GASKINS, Alfred; Private; H/9th Cav. Deposited $10 with paymaster, Ft Robinson, NE, 1897.

GASKINS, Benjamin F.; Corporal; C/10th Cav. Served in 10th Cavalry in Cuba, 1898. SOURCE: Cashin, *Under Fire with the Tenth Cavalry*, 339.

Wounded in action, Santiago, Cuba, 1 Jul 1898. SOURCE: SecWar, *AR 1898*, 324.

GASKINS, Forest; Private; Band/9th Cav. At Ft D. A. Russell, WY, in 1910; resident of Waterford, VA. SOURCE: *Illustrated Review: Ninth Cavalry*, with picture.

GASKINS, John; Private; L/49th Inf. Drowned in the Philippines, 5 May 1900. SOURCE: *ANJ* 37 (30 Jun 1900): 1046.

GASKINS, William E.; L Corp; D/9th Cav. On special duty, troop clerk, Nueva Caceres, Philippines, since 10 Mar 1902. SOURCE: Special Duty List, D/9 Cav, 24 May 1902.

GASTON, Albert; Private; Band/10th Cav. Served in 10th Cavalry in Cuba, 1898. SOURCE: Cashin, *Under Fire with the Tenth Cavalry*, 353.

GASTON, Herbert J.; Private; M/10th Cav. Served in 10th Cavalry, 1898; remained in U.S. during war with Spain. SOURCE: Cashin, *Under Fire with the Tenth Cavalry*, 351.

GASTON, William H.; Private; H/10th Cav. Served in 10th Cavalry, 1898; remained in U.S. during war with Spain. SOURCE: Cashin, *Under Fire with the Tenth Cavalry*, 346.

Died in Minnesota, 16 Nov 1942. SOURCE: Taylor, "Minnesota Black Spanish-American War Veterans."

GATCHELL, Walter G.; 1st Lt; 48th Inf. One of nineteen officers of 48th Infantry recommended as regular Army second lieutenants. SOURCE: CG, DivPI, Manila, 8 Feb 1901, to AGO, AGO File 355163.

GATES, George; Private; F/9th Cav. At Ft Robinson, NE, 1887. *See* **BOWSER**, Frank T., Private, F/9th Cavalry

GATES, Joseph; Private; G/10th Cav. Served in 10th Cavalry in Cuba, 1898. SOURCE: Cashin, *Under Fire with the Tenth Cavalry*, 345.

GATEWOOD, Aquilla; Private; H/24th Inf. Fined $5 by summary court, San Isidro, Philippines, for lying out of quarters, 22 Mar 1902, third conviction. SOURCE: Register of Summary Court, San Isidro.

GATEWOOD, George; Private; K/25th Inf. Died of ruptured aortic aneurism in the Philippines, 15 Jan 1900. SOURCE: *ANJ* 37 (27 Jan 1900): 515.

GAY, Jesse; Private; B/10th Cav. Served in 10th Cavalry, 1898; remained in U.S. during war with Spain. SOURCE: Cashin, *Under Fire with the Tenth Cavalry*, 339.

GAYHART, Scott L.; Private; A/9th Cav. At Ft D. A. Russell, WY, in 1910. SOURCE: *Illustrated Review: Ninth Cavalry*, with picture.

GAYTION, William; Private; H/24th Inf. Enlisted Pittsburgh, PA, 13 Nov 1895; on special duty as assistant cook, 19 Dec 1897–24 May 1898. SOURCE: Muster Roll, H/24 Inf, May–Jun 1898.

Absent sick, disease contracted in line of duty, 15 Sep– 2 Oct 1898; on special duty as cook since 2 Oct 1898; due U.S. for ordnance, one oiler, $.25. SOURCE: Muster Roll, H/24 Inf, Sep–Oct 1898.

Discharged, Ft Douglas, UT, end of term, character excellent, single, deposits $96, clothing $10.39, 12 Nov 1898. SOURCE: Muster Roll, H/24 Inf, Nov–Dec 1898.

GEASON, James; Private; F/9th Cav. Discharged on surgeon's certificate, due to old wounds in left leg, Ft Robinson, NE, Mar 1888.

GEE, Herbert; 2nd Lt; L/48th Inf. Promoted from sergeant major, 24 Dec 1899. SOURCE: *ANJ* 37 (6 Jan 1900): 437; Richmond *Planet*, 14 Apr 1900.

Sick in hospital, San Fernando de la Union, Philippines, Jun 1900. SOURCE: Richmond *Planet*, 29 Jul 1900.

GEE, William; Private; Band/10th Cav. Retires from Ft Assiniboine, MT. SOURCE: *ANJ* 34 (29 May 1897): 725.

GEORGE, Lorenzo; Private; G/10th Cav. Convicted of desertion, 13 Apr 1876 until he surrendered himself 22 Dec 1883, by general court martial, Jefferson Barracks, MO; sentenced to dishonorable discharge and three years. SOURCE: GCMO 7, AGO, 8 Feb 1884.

GETER, John; Corporal; I/24th Inf. Accused of role in Houston riot, 1917; sentenced to death; commuted to life in prison; reduced to twenty years in 1922. SOURCE: Haynes, *A Night of Violence*, 287, 294, 302, 312–13.

GIBBONS, William; 1st Sgt; K/10th Cav. Served 1885–86. *See* **KELLY**, William H., K/10th Cavalry

GIBBS; Private; B/10th Cav. At Ft Apache, AZ, 1890, subscribed $.50 to testimonial to General Grierson. SOURCE: List of subscriptions, 23 Apr 1890, 10th Cavalry papers, MHI.

GIBBS, Franklin; E/10th Cav. Original member of 10th Cavalry; in troop when organized, Ft Leavenworth, KS, 15 Jun 1867. SOURCE: McMiller, "Buffalo Soldiers," 72.

Mentioned Apr 1873 as having joined from desertion. SOURCE: ES, 10 Cav, 1873–81.

GIBBS, James; M/10th Cav. Original member of 10th Cavalry; in troop when organized, Ft Riley, KS, 15 Oct 1867. SOURCE: McMiller, "Buffalo Soldiers," 79.

GIBBS, John; E/10th Cav. Original member of 10th Cavalry; in troop when organized, Ft Leavenworth, KS, 15 Jun 1867. SOURCE: McMiller, "Buffalo Soldiers," 72.

GIBBS, Senior; A/10th Cav. Original member of 10th Cavalry; in troop when organized, Ft Leavenworth, KS, 18 Feb 1867. SOURCE: McMiller, "Buffalo Soldiers," 68.

GIBBS, William; Private; A/9th Cav. Died of pneumonia, Ft Robinson, NE, Apr 1888. SOURCE: Medical History, Ft Robinson.

Funeral, Ft Robinson, 18 Apr 1888. SOURCE: Post Order 74, Ft Robinson, 17 Apr 1888; List of Interments, Ft Robinson.

GIBINS, William; L/10th Cav. Original member of 10th Cavalry; in troop when organized, Ft Riley, KS, 21 Sep 1867. SOURCE: McMiller, "Buffalo Soldiers," 78.

GIBSON; Private; K/24th Inf. At Cabanatuan, Philippines, 1901. *See* **TAYLOR**, George N., Private, K/24th Infantry

GIBSON, E. D.; Sergeant; G/24th Inf. Born Wythe Co., VA, 4 Dec 1852; enlisted in 10th Cavalry, Nov 1869; saw "many hard fights with the Indians"; transferred to 24th Infantry, 1880; wrote narrative of 24th Infantry in Cuba. SOURCE: Johnson, *History of Negro Soldiers*, 145–47.

Private, K/24th Infantry, at San Carlos, AZ, 1890. *See* **HARDEE**, James A., Private, K/24th Infantry

GIBSON, George; Private; F/10th Cav. Original member of 10th Cavalry; in troop when organized, Ft Leavenworth, KS, 21 Jun 1867. SOURCE: McMiller, "Buffalo Soldiers," 73.

Resided at 1409 Currant Street, Harrisburg, PA, in 1922. SOURCE: VA File SC 11405, John Taylor.

GIBSON, James; Private; A/38th Inf. At Ft Selden, NM, Oct 1869; arrested with Pvt. George Hammond, A/38th Infantry, for murder of teamster Leandro Benardo. SOURCE: Billington, *New Mexico's Buffalo Soldiers*, 35.

GIBSON, James; Private; H/10th Cav. Honorable mention for services rendered in capture of Mangas and his Apache band, Rio Bonito, AZ, 18 Oct 1886. SOURCE: Baker, Roster.

GIBSON, James W.; I/10th Cav. Original member of 10th Cavalry; in troop when organized, Ft Riley, KS, 15 Aug 1867. SOURCE: McMiller, "Buffalo Soldiers," 76.

GIBSON, Murry; Private; E/10th Cav. At Ft Apache, AZ, 1890, subscribed $.50 to testimonial to General

Grierson. SOURCE: List of subscriptions, 23 Apr 1890, 10th Cavalry papers, MHI.

Served in 10th Cavalry in Cuba, 1898. SOURCE: Cashin, *Under Fire with the Tenth Cavalry*, 342.

GIBSON, Peter G.; 1st Sgt; A/49th Inf. In the Philippines, 1900. *See* **SHEPARDSON**, George, Private, A/49th Infantry

GIBSON, Philip; Corporal; A/9th Cav. Corporal, A/9th Cavalry, since 30 Apr 1892. SOURCE: Roster, 9 Cav.

On special duty as chief gardener, Ft Robinson, NE. SOURCE: Post Order 13, Ft Robinson, 23 Feb 1894.

On special duty as chief gardener, Ft Robinson, NE. SOURCE: Post Order 11, Ft Robinson, 20 Feb 1895.

Relieved from special duty as chief gardener, Ft Robinson, NE. SOURCE: Post Order 31, Ft Robinson, 21 May 1895.

GIBSON, Robert; B/10th Cav. Original member of 10th Cavalry; in troop when organized, Ft Leavenworth, KS, 1 Apr 1867. SOURCE: McMiller, "Buffalo Soldiers," 69.

Enlisted Memphis, TN. SOURCE: LS, 10 Cav, 1866–68.

GIBSON, Rubie; Private; K/10th Cav. Served in 10th Cavalry, 1898; remained in U.S. during war with Spain. SOURCE: Cashin, *Under Fire with the Tenth Cavalry*, 349.

GIBSON, Thomas; F/10th Cav. Original member of 10th Cavalry; in troop when organized, Ft Leavenworth, KS, 21 Jun 1867. SOURCE: McMiller, "Buffalo Soldiers," 73.

GIBSON, William; C/10th Cav. Original member of 10th Cavalry; in troop when organized, Ft Leavenworth, KS, 14 May 1867. SOURCE: McMiller, "Buffalo Soldiers," 70.

GIBSON, William H.; L/10th Cav. Served 1882–87; resides in San Diego, CA; subscriber. SOURCE: *Winners of the West* 4 (May 1927): 2.

GILBERT, Albert; Private; K/10th Cav. Served in 10th Cavalry, 1898; remained in U.S. during war with Spain. SOURCE: Cashin, *Under Fire with the Tenth Cavalry*, 346.

GILBERT, C.; Private; A/9th Cav. Released and restored to duty. SOURCE: TWX, DP, 14 May 1894.

GILBERT, Henry; Private; H/25th Inf. Wounded in action, El Caney, Cuba, 1 Jul 1898. SOURCE: Nankivell, *History of the Twenty-fifth Infantry*, 83.

GILBERT, I. W.; Private; K/24th Inf. At San Carlos, AZ, 1890. *See* **HARDEE**, James A., Private, K/24th Infantry

GILBERT, Saint; Sergeant; F/9th Cav. Promoted from corporal, Apr 1902. SOURCE: *ANJ* 39 (10 May 1902): 904.

Veteran of Philippine Insurrection; at Ft D. A. Russell, WY, in 1910; sharpshooter; resident of Manchester, KY. SOURCE: *Illustrated Review: Ninth Cavalry*, with picture.

GILBERT, Samuel; Private; F/9th Cav. Transferred to Hospital Corps, Ft Duchesne, UT, May 1896. SOURCE: *ANJ* 33 (23 May 1896): 692.

GILBERT, William M.; Private; L/9th Cav. At Ft D. A. Russell, WY, in 1910; sharpshooter; resident of Mt. Airy, NC. SOURCE: *Illustrated Review: Ninth Cavalry*, with picture.

GILBERT, Wilson S.; F/10th Cav. Original member of 10th Cavalry; in troop when organized, Ft Leavenworth, KS, 21 Jun 1867. SOURCE: McMiller, "Buffalo Soldiers," 73.

GILES; Sergeant; H/24th Inf. With two privates of each company, 24th Infantry, fully armed, to escort paymaster tomorrow from Huachuca siding to post. SOURCE: Order 140, Ft Huachuca, AZ, 21 Sep 1893, Name File, 24 Inf.

GILES, Henry; Sergeant; C/24th Inf. Corporal, K/24th Infantry, married Miss Maria Smith of Washington, DC, at Ft Reno, Indian Territory, Apr 1887; best men: A. Cook of Nashville, TN, and William A. Foreman of Louisville, KY, both in K/24th Infantry. SOURCE: Cleveland *Gazette*, 23 Apr 1887.

Corporal, K/24th Infantry, San Carlos, AZ, 1890. *See* **HARDEE**, James A., Private, K/24th Infantry

Resided at 1130 East Third South, Salt Lake City, UT, in 1898. SOURCE: Clark, "A History of the Twenty-fourth," appendix E.

Sergeant, C/24th Infantry; drowned in the Philippines, 23 Aug 1900. SOURCE: *ANJ* 38 (1 Sep 1900): 19.

GILES, Hollie; Private; M/9th Cav. At Ft D. A. Russell, WY, in 1910; resident of Boston. SOURCE: *Illustrated Review: Ninth Cavalry*, with picture.

GILES, Isaiah P. H.; Blacksmith; K/10th Cav. Mentioned as private, K/10th Cavalry, Oct 1876. SOURCE: LS, 10 Cav, 1873–83.

Blacksmith, K/10th Cavalry, complained of stomach pains, Mowry Mines, AZ, 21 Dec 1885; treated by Dr. Terrell. SOURCE: Bigelow, *On the Bloody Trail of Geronimo*, 101.

GILES, W.; Private; E/9th Cav. On detached service in field, New Mexico, 27 Jan–1 Feb 1881. SOURCE: Regt Returns, 9 Cav, Feb 1881.

GILFRED, Alfred; Private; C/10th Cav. Released to duty from treatment for chronic gonorrhea, Ft Robinson, NE, 17 May 1903. SOURCE: Post Surgeon to CO, C/10, 17 May 1903, LS, Post Surgeon, Ft Robinson.

GILL, James C.; Private; D/25th Inf. Dishonorable discharge, Brownsville. SOURCE: SO 266, AGO, 9 Nov 1906.

GILL, Robert; Private; B/9th Cav. Detailed to regimental headquarters near Ft Selden, NM, for duty. SOURCE: RO 57, 9 Cav, 4 Dec 1875.

GILL, Wesley; Private; M/10th Cav. Court martial in his case convened. SOURCE: SO 46, DeptMo, 10 Mar 1904.

Sentenced to dishonorable discharge and jail, Ft Robinson, NE, Jun 1904. SOURCE: SO 118, DeptMo, 27 Jun 1904.

GILLAM, David C.; Private; E/25th Inf. Wounded in action, El Caney, Cuba, 1 Jul 1898. SOURCE: Nankivell, *History of the Twenty-fifth Infantry*, 83.

GILLEM, T.; Private; E/9th Cav. On detached service in field, New Mexico, 26 Jan–1 Feb 1881. SOURCE: Regt Returns, 9 Cav, Feb 1881.

GILLENWATER, Walter; Corporal; Band/25th Inf. Private, G/9th Cavalry, witness for defense in Barney McKay court martial, Ft Robinson, NE, 1893; heard Private Wyatt threaten to get McKay, as did Isaac Anderson; other witnesses: Pvts. Samuel Rivers and William Thompkins. SOURCE: Court Martial Records, McKay.

Promoted from private, Iba, Zambales, Philippines. SOURCE: SO 135, 25 Inf, 24 Dec 1900, Misc Records, 25 Inf.

GILLESPIE, Archie H.; Private; A/9th Cav. At Ft D. A. Russell, WY, in 1910; sharpshooter. SOURCE: *Illustrated Review: Ninth Cavalry*, with picture.

GILLESPIE, Vivian; Private; B/9th Cav. At Ft D. A. Russell, WY, in 1910. SOURCE: *Illustrated Review: Ninth Cavalry*.

GILLIAM, Chauncey; Private; 25th Inf. Born Charleston, SC; enlisted Charleston, occupation miner, age 22, Ht 5'6", dark complexion, black eyes and hair, 16 Jun 1881. SOURCE: Descriptive & Assignment Rolls, 25 Inf.

GILLIARD, William; Private; I/24th Inf. Enlisted Mobile, AL, 29 Mar 1899. SOURCE: Muster Roll, I/24 Inf, Mar–Apr 1899.

Rejoined company from Three Rivers, CA, 26 Jul 1899. SOURCE: Muster Roll, I/24 Inf, Jul–Aug 1899.

Confined at hard labor for three months by summary court martial, 15 Dec 1899. SOURCE: Muster Roll, I/24 Inf, Nov–Dec 1899.

GILLISPIE, James R.; QM Sgt; U.S. Army. Corporal, A/10th Cavalry, at Ft Apache, AZ, 1890, subscribed $.50 to testimonial to General Grierson. SOURCE: List of subscriptions, 23 Apr 1890, 10th Cavalry papers, MHI.

Sergeant, A/10th Cavalry, stationed at Ft Grant, AZ; to report to Lt. Col. Edward P. Pearson, 24th Infantry, president, board of officers, Ft Grant, for examination for position of post quartermaster sergeant. SOURCE: *ANJ* 28 (21 Mar 1891): 510.

Appointed post quartermaster sergeant from sergeant, A/10th Cavalry, 5 May 1891. SOURCE: Baker, Roster.

Ordered from Ft Grant to Ft Missoula, MT; comrades "regret his and his amiable wife's departure." SOURCE: Cleveland *Gazette*, 19 Mar 1892.

His child baptized by Chaplain Steward, Ft Missoula, 25 Dec 1892. SOURCE: Monthly Report, Chaplain Steward, Dec 1892.

Sends $1.50 from Ft Duchesne, UT, for one-year subscription to Richmond *Planet*; writes that every colored man who can afford a paper should have *Planet*; praises paper's "bold and manly stand," prays for journalistic unity, wishes *Planet* "a greater success and a long and useful life." SOURCE: Richmond *Planet*, 2 Feb 1895.

An excellent noncommissioned officer who should be commissioned, according to John E. Lewis, H/10th Cavalry, in letter from Lakeland, FL, 5 Jun 1898. SOURCE: Gatewood, *"Smoked Yankees"*, 36.

First lieutenant of volunteers, 1898. SOURCE: Steward, *The Colored Regulars*, 291.

Retired Army officer and veteran of Spanish-American War and Philippines; now captain of Liberian Frontier Police with $1,600 per year pay and $250 per year quarters allowance. SOURCE: Cleveland *Gazette*, 18 Dec 1915.

No Veterans Administration pension file.

GILLUM, William; 10th Cav. Commissioned captain from Camp Des Moines, IA, 15 Oct 1917. SOURCE: Glass, *History of the Tenth Cavalry*, appendix M.

Retired as warrant officer; resides at 3408 S. Raymond Ave., Los Angeles, CA. SOURCE: Work, *The Negro Yearbook, 1931–1932*, 334.

GILMER, David J.; 1st Lt; Philippine Scouts. Born Greensboro, NC, 8 Apr 1872; educated in Greensboro schools, first lieutenant and captain, 3rd North Carolina Infantry. SOURCE: *ANJ* 37 (9 Dec 1899): 353.

Lieutenant, 49th Infantry; with thirty men killed two insurgents, captured arms and ammunition, Philippines, 20 Mar 1900. SOURCE: *ANJ* 37 (12 May 1900): 879.

With sixteen men reconnoitered Linao-Sanchez Mira, Philippines, surprised insurgents, killed two, 21 Mar 1900. SOURCE: *ANJ* 37 (26 May 1900): 926.

Recently successful in reconnaissance and hot fight. SOURCE: *ANJ* 37 (9 Jun 1900): 975.

Promoted to captain, Oct 1900. SOURCE: *ANJ* 38 (3 Nov 1900): 235.

Captain, A/49th Infantry, vice Charles W. Jefferson, resigned, 6 Oct 1900. SOURCE: Descriptive Book, A/49 Inf.

Quoted as working for his race in the Philippines. SOURCE: *ANJ* 38 (1 Dec 1900): 331; *ANJ* 38 (6 Apr 1901): 777.

Letter from Linao, Philippines, 19 Jan 1901. SOURCE: Gatewood, *"Smoked Yankees"*, 292.

Resident of Greensboro has passed tests and been commissioned in regular Army, according to Charlotte, NC, *Africo-American Presbyterian*. SOURCE: Cleveland *Gazette*, 2 Nov 1901.

Interviewed by editor; on Filipino view of black soldier, Gilmer said that "they seem to love him as a brother and the Negro soldier, fighting them as he did, taught the natives that all American white men were not unfair to colored people and that their great hope rested in the American government";

never met a white officer "who did not accord to me every right that I would seek as an officer." SOURCE: Washington *Colored American*, 23 Nov 1901.

Greensboro native, who distinguished himself in the Philippines, has passed examination and is now lieutenant in regular Army; "this is highly creditable to Lieutenant Gilmer and reflects credit on the race." SOURCE: Indianapolis *Freeman*, 30 Nov 1901.

Appointed lieutenant in Philippine Scouts; will be "regularly appointed by the war department at the first opportunity." SOURCE: Cleveland *Gazette*, 21 Feb 1903.

Stationed at Aparri, Cagayan, Philippines. SOURCE: Division of the Philippines, *Alphabetical List of Officers Serving in the Division*, 9.

In Philippines, 1906. *See* **WOODS**, Robert Gordon, Captain, I/49th Infantry

To be tried by court martial for false statement on official document; other black officer, Thompson, also to be tried for misconduct; "Taft's 'new southern policy' has reached Manila." SOURCE: Cleveland *Gazette*, 20 Nov 1909.

Tried by general court martial, Camp Daraga, Albay, Philippines, for conduct unbecoming officer and gentleman, three specifications of false and malicious statements to and regarding 2nd Lt. Frank C. O'Loughlin, Philippine Scouts; convicted and sentenced to dismissal; sentence reduced by president to reduction in rank of first lieutenant by fifteen files of seniority. SOURCE: GO 93, AGO, 19 May 1910.

Booker T. Washington used his influence to help have Gilmer's dismissal commuted and was profusely thanked by Gilmer. SOURCE: Fletcher, *The Black Soldier*, 172.

Convicted by court martial; retains rank but is reduced in seniority. SOURCE: Cleveland *Gazette*, 4 Jun 1910.

GILMER, Floyd; Sergeant; A/10th Cav. Commissioned first lieutenant at Camp Des Moines, IA, 15 Oct 1917. SOURCE: Glass, *History of the Tenth Cavalry*, appendix M.

GILMORE; Sergeant; F/9th Cav. Assaulted Private Jones, F/9th Cavalry, for foul and insulting language in barracks, Ft Robinson, NE. SOURCE: CO, Ft Robinson, to CO, F/9, 25 Jun and 2 Jul 1889, LS, Ft Robinson.

GILMORE, Charles H.; Corporal; A/10th Cav. Deserted Staked Plains expedition, Aug 1877; sentenced to dishonorable discharge and one year. SOURCE: Leckie, *The Buffalo Soldiers*, 160, 162.

Convicted by general court martial of desertion, Ft Clark, TX, 10 Dec 1877. SOURCE: Miles, "Ft Concho in 1877," 49.

GILMORE, Frank; D/10th Cav. Original member of 10th Cavalry; in troop when organized, Ft Leavenworth, KS, 1 Jun 1867. SOURCE: McMiller, "Buffalo Soldiers," 71.

GILMORE, Robert C.; Corporal; H/24th Inf. Enlisted Ft Douglas, UT, 9 Dec 1898; private with four years' continuous service; promoted to lance corporal, 20 Dec 1898. SOURCE: Muster Roll, H/24 Inf, Nov–Dec 1898.

Promoted to corporal, 27 Jan 1899. SOURCE: Muster Roll, H/24 Inf, Jan–Feb 1899.

GILYARD, William; Private; L/10th Cav. Served in 10th Cavalry, 1898; remained in U.S. during war with Spain. SOURCE: Cashin, *Under Fire with the Tenth Cavalry*, 350.

GISH, Thomas; Corporal; F/10th Cav. Died 14 Jul 1918. SOURCE: VA File SC 11405, John Taylor.

GIST, John S.; Private; I/10th Cav. Wants to hear from old veterans; served in E/9th Cavalry, 1886–91, and I/10th Cavalry, 1891–94; pension is $20 per month. SOURCE: *Winners of the West* 6 (Oct 1929): 3.

GIVENS, Edward; Private; D/10th Cav. Original member of 10th Cavalry; in troop when organized, Ft Leavenworth, KS, 1 Jun 1867. SOURCE: McMiller, "Buffalo Soldiers," 71.

Wounded in action against Kiowas, Ft Sill, Indian Territory, May 1871. SOURCE: Leckie, *The Buffalo Soldiers*, 61–62.

GIVENS, George; Sergeant; M/49th Inf. Died of variola in the Philippines, 30 Nov 1900. SOURCE: *ANJ* 38 (15 Dec 1900): 373.

GIVENS, Gilmore; Private; E/10th Cav. Served in 10th Cavalry in Cuba, 1898. SOURCE: Cashin, *Under Fire with the Tenth Cavalry*, 342.

Wounded in action, Santiago, Cuba, 1 Jul 1898. SOURCE: SecWar, *AR 1898*, 324.

GIVENS, William H.; 1st Sgt; D/10th Cav. Born in Kentucky; private, sergeant, quartermaster sergeant, B/10th Cavalry, 20 Aug 1869–20 Aug 1874; private, corporal, sergeant, first sergeant, B/10th Cavalry, 1 Aug 1876–4 Aug 1881; private, first sergeant, quartermaster sergeant, sergeant, first sergeant, K/10th Cavalry, 8 Nov 1881–21 Nov 1891; private, F/9th Cavalry, 14 Nov 1893–10 Apr 1894; private, H/10th Cavalry, 10 Apr 1894; corporal, 9 May 1894; sergeant, 12 Mar 1895; stationed at Ft Assiniboine, MT, 1897. SOURCE: Baker, Roster.

Enlisted 1869; served on Mexican border, 1876–78, and in Victorio campaign; commended by Lt. Col. Theodore J. Wint for service in Cuba, 1898. SOURCE: Steward, *The Colored Regulars*, 245.

At Ft Grant, AZ; to be examined for ordnance sergeant. SOURCE: *ANJ* 24 (14 May 1887): 834.

At Ft Grant; to be examined for post quartermaster sergeant. SOURCE: *ANJ* 25 (7 Jan 1888): 462.

First sergeant, K/10th Cavalry; at Ft Apache, AZ, 1890, subscribed $.50 to testimonial to General Grierson. SOURCE: List of subscriptions, 23 Apr 1890, 10th Cavalry papers, MHI.

At Ft Thomas, AZ; to enter Army and Navy Hospital, Hot Springs, AR. SOURCE: *ANJ* 27 (21 Jun 1890): 808.

At San Carlos, AZ; to be examined for commissary sergeant. SOURCE: *ANJ* 28 (25 Apr 1891): 595.

Authorized six-month furlough from Ft Grant. SOURCE: *ANJ* 29 (14 Nov 1891): 198.

Transferred to H/10th Cavalry. SOURCE: SO 83, AGO, 9 Apr 1894.

At Ft Assiniboine, 1895; examined for ordnance sergeant. SOURCE: *ANJ* 33 (16 Nov 1895): 179.

Served in 10th Cavalry in Cuba, 1898. SOURCE: Cashin, *Under Fire with the Tenth Cavalry*, 340.

Commanded company at Las Guasimas, Cuba, and won commission due to success with troops in battle. SOURCE: Steward, *The Colored Regulars*, 139.

At San Juan, Cuba, exercised "a steadying and encouraging influence upon the men" and conducted himself like "the thorough soldier which I have long known him to be," according to Capt. John Bigelow. SOURCE: SecWar, *AR 1898*, 711.

Cited for distinguished service in Cuba. SOURCE: *ANJ* 37 (24 Feb 1900): 611.

As first sergeant, D/10th Cavalry, commended "for exercising a steady and encouraging influence upon the men of his troop and conducting himself in a thoroughly efficient manner," at battle of Santiago, Cuba, 1 Jul 1898. SOURCE: GO 15, AGO, 13 Feb 1900.

Should be commissioned, according to John E. Lewis, H/10th Cavalry, in letter from Lakeland, FL, c. 1 Aug 1898. SOURCE: Gatewood, *"Smoked Yankees"*, 580.

Commissioned second lieutenant, 10th U.S. Volunteer Infantry. SOURCE: Cashin, *Under Fire with the Tenth Cavalry*, 361.

Capt. John Bigelow's recollections of his service with Givens on the frontier and in Cuba. SOURCE: Bigelow, *Reminiscences of Santiago*, 9, 96-97, 133, 135, 163, 166-67.

Retired Jun 1901. SOURCE: *ANJ* 38 (29 Jun 1901): 1067

GLADDEN, Washington W. E.; Chaplain; 25th Inf. Born in South Carolina, 1866; moved to Great Bend, KS, age 14; worked twelve years for Hulme and Kelly flour mills as roustabout to chief engineer and as champion sack-sewer (sewed and packed 616 in ten hours): while there mastered electrical engineering; at 14 organized Sunday School; held religious meetings in rural Kansas, 1889; went to Africa in interest of missions and to evaluate emigration schemes; reported mission work in Africa a failure, people in field lacked medical and sanitary information to protect against epidemics of southcentral Africa; entered ministry at Great Bend, 1890; organized St. John's Baptist Church, Colorado Springs, CO, 1895; appointed chaplain, 21 May 1906; in the Philippines during Pulahan insurrection, 1906–7; at Madison Barracks, NY, 1908–10; only black member of board of chaplains appointed to recommend more chaplains, 1909, and recorder of board; performed first baptism by immersion in the Philippines, 1911; qualified as expert rifleman; installed modern picture show theater, Camp Stotsenburg, Pampanga, Philippines; went with regiment from Ft D. A. Russell, WY, to Mexican border with Pershing expedition, 26 Mar 1915; injured there by large sack of mail; retired 23 May 1917; resides "in a modern beautiful home" on Dona Street, Colorado Springs, with his family; praises men of 24th Infantry and lauds opportunities provided by Army. SOURCE: Beasley, *Negro Trailblazers*, 294–95.

Born in South Carolina; appointed first lieutenant, 21 May 1906; now with regiment, Madison Barracks; Baptist, previously built up congregation at Colorado Springs. SOURCE: *Colored American Magazine* 16 (Apr 1909): 224.

Baptist minister of Denver, replacing Chaplain Allensworth, who is retiring. SOURCE: Cleveland *Gazette*, 12 May 1906.

"A new chaplain is to 'Gladden' the hearts of the men of the 25th [*sic*] Infantry." SOURCE: Indianapolis *Freeman*, 2 Jun 1906.

Appointed captain and assigned to regiment in the Philippines. SOURCE: Indianapolis *Freeman*, 16 Jun 1906.

On furlough at home in Colorado Springs to bury his wife. SOURCE: Indianapolis *Freeman*, 29 Dec 1906.

At Ft Leavenworth, KS, as member of board of inquiry. SOURCE: Cleveland *Gazette*, 12 Jun 1909.

Visited enlisted men in barracks daily for conversations on religious subjects; oriented new Chaplain Louis A. Carter, summer of 1910, Madison Barracks and Pine Camp, NY. SOURCE: Stover, *Up from Handymen*, 152.

Stationed at Manila, Philippines; promoted to captain; only black captain in Army. SOURCE: Cleveland *Gazette*, 11 Oct 1913.

Served as regimental postmaster on Mexican border, 1915. SOURCE: Stover, *Up from Handymen*, 173.

Retires as major, chaplain of 25th Infantry. SOURCE: Cleveland *Gazette*, 23 Jun 1917.

Mentioned. SOURCE: Work, *The Negro Year Book, 1912*, 77; Work, *The Negro Yearbook, 1918–1919*, 228; Work, *The Negro Yearbook, 1925–1926*, 253.

GLADNEY, Culp D.; Corporal; 24th Inf. Served in Houston, 1917. SOURCE: Haynes, *A Night of Violence*, 122.

GLASGOW, Aaron; Recruit; K/10th Cav. Mentioned Oct 1875. SOURCE: ES, 10 Cav, 1873–81.

GLASS; Private; A/10th Cav. At Ft Apache, AZ, 1890, subscribed $.50 to testimonial to General Grierson. SOURCE: List of subscriptions, 23 Apr 1890, 10th Cavalry papers, MHI.

GLAZIER, F. H.; Corporal; F/48th Inf. Letter, Manila, 26 Feb 1900: "The natives of Manila and all over Luzon are very friendly and kind towards American soldiers, and especially toward the colored soldiers." SOURCE: Cleveland *Gazette*, 26 May 1900.

GLEASON, J.; Private; H/9th Cav. Served in 1891.

GLEAVES, Will; Private; K/10th Cav. Served in 10th Cavalry, 1898; remained in U.S. during war with Spain. SOURCE: Cashin, *Under Fire with the Tenth Cavalry*, 349.

GLEEDON, James; Private; M/10th Cav. Served in 10th Cavalry, 1898; remained in U.S. during war with Spain. SOURCE: Cashin, *Under Fire with the Tenth Cavalry*, 351.

GLENN, John T.; Sergeant; D/9th Cav. At Ft D. A. Russell, WY, in 1910; sharpshooter; resident of Chicago. SOURCE: *Illustrated Review: Ninth Cavalry*, with picture.

GLENN, Judge; Sergeant; D/9th Cav. At Ft D. A. Russell, WY, in 1910; marksman. SOURCE: *Illustrated Review: Ninth Cavalry*.

GLENN, Louis; Private; F/9th Cav. Sentenced to ten days and $5 fine by garrison court martial, Ft Robinson, NE, for insubordination to 1st Sgt. Emanuel Stance, F/9th Cavalry. SOURCE: Post Order 188, 23 Sep 1887, Post Orders, Ft Robinson.

Sentenced to thirty days and $12 fine by garrison court martial, Ft Robinson, for failure to report serious disease to surgeon and deception regarding it. SOURCE: Post Order 241, 6 Dec 1887, Post Orders, Ft Robinson.

See **HARRIS**, Robert, Sergeant, F/9th Cavalry

GLENN, Shepherd; Private; B/25th Inf. Dishonorable discharge, Brownsville. SOURCE: SO 266, AGO, 9 Nov 1906.

GLOVER, Benjamin; Corporal; Band/25th Inf. Promoted from private. SOURCE: *ANR* 39 (22 Jul 1905): 21.

GLOVER, Charles; Private; I/24th Inf. Enlisted Huntington, WV, 24 Mar 1899. SOURCE: Muster Roll, I/24 Inf, Mar–Apr 1899.

Allotted $10 per month for six months to Clara Glover. SOURCE: Muster Roll, I/24 Inf, Sep–Oct 1899.

GLOVER, John; Private; M/10th Cav. Served in 10th Cavalry, 1898; remained in U.S. during war with Spain. SOURCE: Cashin, *Under Fire with the Tenth Cavalry*, 351.

GLOVER, Robert; Sergeant; L/10th Cav. Served in 10th Cavalry in Cuba, 1898. SOURCE: Cashin, *Under Fire with the Tenth Cavalry*, 348.

Ranked number 14 among marksmen in Northern Division cavalry team competition, Ft Riley, KS, 1904. SOURCE: GO 167, AGO, 28 Oct 1904; Glass, *History of the Tenth Cavalry*, 44.

Ranked number 547 among rifle experts with 68 percent, 1905. SOURCE: GO 101, AGO, 31 May 1906.

GLOVER, William; Private; F/10th Cav. Served in 10th Cavalry, 1898; remained in U.S. during war with Spain. SOURCE: Cashin, *Under Fire with the Tenth Cavalry*, 344.

GODFIELD, G.; Private; F/10th Cav. Wounded in action against Indians, Kansas, 21 Aug 1867. SOURCE: Armes, *Ups and Downs*, 247.

GOENS, Henry; Sergeant; L/10th Cav. Authorized six-month furlough from Ft Grant, AZ. SOURCE: *ANJ* 25 (4 Feb 1888): 545.

Retires from Ft Custer, MT, May 1894. SOURCE: *ANJ* 31 (2 Jun 1894): 699; Baker, Roster.

GOENS, Robert; E/24th Inf. At Ft Bayard, NM, 1891. SOURCE: *ANJ* 29 (17 Oct 1891): 133.

GOFF, George W.; Sergeant; K/9th Cav. Recording secretary, Diamond Club, K/9th Cavalry, Ft Robinson, NE. SOURCE: *ANJ* 28 (2 May 1891): 620.

Promoted from lance corporal to corporal, Ft Robinson, 2 Sep 1895. SOURCE: *ANJ* 33 (14 Sep 1895): 23.

Corporal, K/9th Cavalry, alternate for regimental color guard, Ft Robinson. SOURCE: *ANJ* 33 (28 Mar 1896): 540.

Sir Knight Captain, Crispus Attucks Lodge No. 3, Knights of Pythias, State of Nebraska. SOURCE: Richmond *Planet*, 18 Dec 1897.

Enlisted Memphis, TN; sergeant, won certificate of merit for service in Cuba, 1898; now out of service. SOURCE: *ANJ* 36 (10 Jun 1899): 967.

Commended for gallantry in Cuba, 1 Jul 1898; awarded certificate of merit; now out of service. SOURCE: GO 15, AGO, 13 Feb 1900.

Sergeant, awarded certificate of merit for service in Cuba, 1898; now out of service. SOURCE: Steward, *The Colored Regulars*, 280; *ANJ* 37 (24 Feb 1900): 611.

GOFF, Henry A.; 10th Cav. Served in F/24th Infantry and 10th Cavalry; died at Newville, PA. SOURCE: *Winners of the West* 6 (Nov 1929): 3.

GOFF, Robert L.; 2nd Lt; B/49th Inf. Mentioned. SOURCE: Beasley, *Negro Trailblazers*, 284.

GOING, James; Private; E/10th Cav. Mentioned Jun 1867. SOURCE: LS, 10 Cav, 1866–67.

GOINS, Charles M.; Private; F/9th Cav. Fractured skull while absent without leave from Ft Robinson, NE; discharged on certificate of disability, 7 Jan 1887. SOURCE: Certificates of Disability, Ft Robinson.

GOINS, Joshua Van Buren. Born Xenia, OH, 2 Feb 1848; enlisted Jul 1863; during enlistment led many soldier comrades to Jesus; discharged, end of term, Ft McKavett, TX, Jul 1870; licensed to preach, San Antonio, TX, 1870; made career as itinerant preacher, Texas, Louisiana, Indian Territory; established Delhi Institute, Delhi, LA, and was president for four years; twenty years as trustee, Paul Quinn College; three-time delegate to general conference, African Methodist Episcopal Church; oldest active itinerant minister in Texas. SOURCE: Talbert, *The Sons of Allen*, 218–19.

GOLDEN, John; Sergeant; H/9th Cav. Ranked number four, Pacific Division pistol team competition, Ord Barracks, CA, 1904. SOURCE: GO 167, AGO, 28 Oct 1904.

GOLDEN, Thomas; Saddler; B/9th Cav. On detached service at Ft Craig, NM, 20 Dec 1880–20 Feb 1881. SOURCE: Regt Returns, 9 Cav, Feb 1881.

Killed in action at Gavillon Pass in Mimbres Mountains, NM, 19 Aug 1881; Pvts. James Brown and Monroe Overstreet of B/9th Cavalry also killed; Pvt. William A. Hollins wounded. SOURCE: Hamilton, "History of the Ninth Cavalry," 57; Billington, *New Mexico's Buffalo Soldiers*, 105; *Illustrated Review: Ninth Cavalry*.

GOLDING, Thomas; Saddler; B/9th Cav. *See* **GOLDEN**, Thomas, Saddler, B/9th Cavalry

GOLDSBURY; Chief Musician; 10th Cav. At Ft Apache, AZ, 1890, subscribed $.50 to testimonial to General Grierson. SOURCE: List of subscriptions, 23 Apr 1890, 10th Cavalry papers, MHI.

GOLDSBY, George; 1st Sgt; G/10th Cav. Born Selma, AL; enlisted 1867; became sergeant major; reenlisted, 1872, as first sergeant, D/10th Cavalry; led soldiers on raid to avenge insults, from Ft Concho, TX, into San Angelo, TX, 1877, then deserted. SOURCE: Leckie, *The Buffalo Soldiers*, 164.

First sergeant, G/10th Cavalry, Ft Lyon, CO, Mar 1869. SOURCE: LR, Det 10 Cav, 1868–69.

Ex-sergeant, first sergeant, sergeant major, 10th Cavalry; according to W. A. Haynes and Fred Scott of San Francisco, he is really Pancho Villa. SOURCE: Cleveland *Gazette*, 7 Mar 1914.

GOLDSMITH, Jefferson; L/10th Cav. Original member of 10th Cavalry; in troop when organized, Ft Riley, KS, 21 Sep 1867. SOURCE: McMiller, "Buffalo Soldiers," 78.

At Ft Sill, Indian Territory, 1870. *See* **ANDERSON**, Henry, Private, L/10th Cavalry

GOLDWAITE, Silas; Cook; G/10th Cav. Served in 10th Cavalry in Cuba, 1898. SOURCE: Cashin, *Under Fire with the Tenth Cavalry*, 345.

GONZALES, Ralph W.; Private; K/9th Cav. At Ft D. A. Russell, WY, in 1910; resident of Colebrook, CT. SOURCE: *Illustrated Review: Ninth Cavalry*, with picture.

GOOCH, John H.; Private; I/24th Inf. Enlisted Nashville, TN, 27 Jul 1898. SOURCE: Muster Roll, I/24 Inf, Jan–Feb 1899.

Allotted $12 per month for eighteen months to First National Bank, San Francisco, CA. SOURCE: Muster Roll, I/24 Inf, Sep–Oct 1899.

Discharged 31 Dec 1899; deposits $25, clothing $9.96; owes U.S. $.20 for ordnance. SOURCE: Muster Roll, I/24 Inf, Nov–Dec 1899.

GOOCH, Philip; Private; F/25th Inf. Died of malaria at Camp Wikoff, NY, 31 Aug 1898. SOURCE: Hospital Papers, Spanish-American War.

Body transferred from Montauk, NY, to National Cemetery, Cypress Hills, NY. SOURCE: *ANJ* 36 (21 Jan 1899): 480.

GOODALL, Bert; Corporal; I/24th Inf. With wife Maggie rented rooms in house on Washington Street, Houston, 1917. SOURCE: Haynes, *A Night of Violence*, 44.

GOODE, Benjamin H.; Private; H/24th Inf. Enlisted Ft McPherson, GA, 20 Jan 1899. SOURCE: Muster Roll, H/24 Inf, Jan–Feb 1899.

Awarded certificate of merit for distinguished gallantry, Naguilian, Luzon, Philippines, 7 Dec 1899; award made 10 Mar 1902; discharged 18 Jan 1902. SOURCE: *ANJ* 39 (15 Feb 1902): 594–95; GO 86, AGO, 24 Jul 1902.

GOODE, Clyde F.; Private; L/24th Inf. Stationed at Houston, 1917; did not participate in mutiny. SOURCE: Haynes, *A Night of Violence*, 260.

GOODLOE, Thomas; 1st Sgt; G/9th Cav. In I/9th Cavalry, married, desires to reenlist with six-month furlough, Mar 1890.

Sergeant, G/9th Cavalry, since 11 Dec 1891; first sergeant as of 15 Dec 1891. SOURCE: Roster, 9 Cav.

At Ft Robinson, NE, 1893; heard by Sgt. A. E. Ransom to say regarding Barney McKay affair: "The niggers won't hang together; they are always ready to hang one another." SOURCE: Court Martial Records, McKay.

See **JEFFERSON**, Charles W., Sergeant, B/9th Cavalry

Resided with wife and mother-in-law at quarters of Captain Day, 9th Cavalry, Ft Robinson, Aug 1893. SOURCE: Medical History, Ft Robinson.

Reenlistment, married, authorized. SOURCE: TWX, AGO, 17 Feb 1896.

Convicted of conduct to prejudice of good order and discipline by garrison court martial, Ft Robinson; sentenced to $10 fine and public reprimand, in consideration of his previous good character. SOURCE: *ANJ* 33 (11 Jul 1896): 816.

Born Nashville, TN; knew Archy Wall, born Franklin, Maury Co., TN, since boyhood; enlisted around same time in 1876; served together in 24th Infantry for number of years; saw each other and kept in touch for nearly fifty years, including when in different regiments; resides at 1319 66th Street, Berkeley, CA, age 72. SOURCE: Affidavit, Goodloe, 18 May 1931, VA File C 2643745, Archy Wall.

GOODLOW, George; Private; E/10th Cav. Mentioned 1873 as having enlisted Jun 1872. SOURCE: ES, 10 Cav, 1873–81.

GOODMAN, Alfred; K/10th Cav. Original member of 10th Cavalry; in troop when organized, Ft Riley, KS, 1 Sep 1867. SOURCE: McMiller, "Buffalo Soldiers," 77.

GOODMAN, Alphonse; Private; E/9th Cav. 1st Lt. Edward Heyle charged with ordering Goodman tied up by the hands for one hour as punishment for disobedience, Apr 1867.

GOODMAN, John; Private; M/25th Inf. Wounded in leg, Botelan, Philippines, 9 Dec 1899. SOURCE: *ANJ* 37 (3 Feb 1900): 526.

GOODMAN, Paul; Cook; I/24th Inf. Enlisted Mobile, AL, 21 Jan 1899. SOURCE: Muster Roll, I/24 Inf, Jan–Feb 1899.

Appointed cook 20 Mar 1899. SOURCE: Muster Roll, I/24 Inf, Mar–Apr 1899.

Transferred to Hospital Corps per instructions from War Department, 19 Jun 1899. SOURCE: Muster Roll, I/24 Inf, May–Jun 1899.

GOODMAN, Robert; Private; D/9th Cav. At Ft D. A. Russell, WY, in 1910; resident of Jasper, TN. SOURCE: *Illustrated Review: Ninth Cavalry*, with picture.

GOODNER, Frank M.; Sergeant; M/10th Cav. Commissioned first lieutenant at Camp Des Moines, IA, 15 Oct 1917. SOURCE: Glass, *History of the Tenth Cavalry*, appendix M.

GOODSON, Isaac; Private; L/9th Cav. At Ft D. A. Russell, WY, in 1910; resident of Lafayette, GA. SOURCE: *Illustrated Review: Ninth Cavalry*, with picture.

GOODWIN, Albert; Private; 24th Inf. Killed by sergeant for refusing to obey orders and pulling gun on him, while on Pershing expedition in Mexico. SOURCE: *ANJ* 53 (13 May 1916): 1197.

GOODWIN, Robert; Private; D/25th Inf. Wounded in action, El Caney, Cuba, 1 Jul 1898. SOURCE: Nankivell, *History of the Twenty-fifth Infantry*, 83.

GOODWIN, Theophilus; Private; B/24th Inf. Relieved from duty as assistant, post exchange. SOURCE: Order 63, Ft Huachuca, AZ, 4 May 1893, Name File, 24 Inf.

On extra duty as schoolteacher. SOURCE: Order 162, Ft Huachuca, 1 Nov 1893, Letters & Orders Received, 24 Inf.

Relieved from extra duty as schoolteacher. SOURCE: Order 177, Ft Huachuca, 30 Nov 1893, Letters & Orders Received, 24 Inf.

GOODWIN, Willie; Private; A/9th Cav. At Ft D. A. Russell, WY, in 1910. SOURCE: *Illustrated Review: Ninth Cavalry*, with picture.

GOOLSBY, Isaac; Private; B/25th Inf. Dishonorable discharge, Brownsville. SOURCE: SO 266, AGO, 9 Nov 1906.

GOOSLEY, Samuel; Private; A/25th Inf. At Camp Cary Sanger, KS, 1903. *See* **WILLIAMS**, John S., Private, H/25th Infantry

GORDON, Bryant; Sergeant; M/10th Cav. At Ft Apache, AZ, 1890, subscribed $.50 to testimonial to General Grierson. SOURCE: List of subscriptions, 23 Apr 1890, 10th Cavalry papers, MHI.

GORDON, J.; Private; B/25th Inf. Best infantry marksman in Department of Dakota competition, Ft Shaw, MT; first colored soldier to head department rifle team. SOURCE: *ANJ* 27 (23 Aug 1890): 963.

Distinguished marksman with rifle, 1890, 1892, 1893. SOURCE: GO 82, AGO, 24 Oct 1893.

Ranked number five, competition of Army rifle team of distinguished marksmen, 1894. SOURCE: GO 62, AGO, 15 Nov 1894.

GORDON, John; Private; C/9th Cav. At Ft D. A. Russell, WY, in 1910; sharpshooter; resident of Clarksdale, MS. SOURCE: *Illustrated Review: Ninth Cavalry*, with picture.

GORDON, John T.; Private; A/10th Cav. Died on Staked Plains expedition, Aug 1877. SOURCE: Leckie, *The Buffalo Soldiers*, 161–62.

Commander, 10th Cavalry, transmits final statement of deceased Gordon to Adjutant General, 3 Sep 1877. SOURCE: ES, 10 Cav, 1873–81.

GORDON, William; Private; H/24th Inf. Enlisted Nashville, TN, 8 Oct 1898; on special duty as assistant company cook since 16 Oct 1898. SOURCE: Muster Roll, H/24 Inf, Sep–Oct 1898.

Discharged, Ft Douglas, UT, character good, single, due U.S. for clothing $14.31, 27 Jan 1899. SOURCE: Muster Roll, H/24 Inf, Jan–Feb 1899.

GORMER, Richard; K/10th Cav. Original member of 10th Cavalry; in troop when organized, Ft Riley, KS, 1 Sep 1867. SOURCE: McMiller, "Buffalo Soldiers," 77.

GOUGH, Robert; 2nd Lt; B/49th Inf. Private, corporal, E/10th Cavalry, 20 Mar 1890–19 Mar 1895; private, corporal, D/24th Infantry, 20 Mar 1895–9 Apr 1901; in battles at San Juan and Santiago, Cuba, 1–5 Jul 1898; at Siboney yellow fever hospital, 16 Jul–26 Aug 1898; battalion adjutant, 1 Sep 1900–Jun 1901. SOURCE: Descriptive Book, B/49 Inf.

Mentioned as second lieutenant, 49th Infantry, and former corporal, D/24th Infantry. SOURCE: *ANJ* 37 (9 Dec 1899): 345.

One of twenty-three officers of 49th Infantry recommended as regular Army second lieutenants. SOURCE: CG, DivPI, Manila, 8 Feb 1901, to AGO, AGO File 355163.

GOULD, Charley; Private; M/10th Cav. Transferred from K/25th Infantry. SOURCE: SO 16, AGO, 20 Jan 1904.

Deserter from Ft Robinson, NE; caught by Marshal Messenger of Crawford, NE, 10 Sep 1904; escaped on 12 Sep, caught, and taken to post. SOURCE: Crawford *Tribune*, 16 Sep 1904.

GOULD, Luther D.; Private; A/10th Cav. Served in 10th Cavalry in Cuba, 1898. SOURCE: Cashin, *Under Fire with the Tenth Cavalry*, 336.

Wounded in action, Santiago, Cuba, 2 Jul 1898. SOURCE: SecWar, *AR 1898*, 324.

Former corporal, married to Fanny Cuff; served against Indians and in Cuba; father was Lorenzo F. Gould, Civil War veteran. SOURCE: Steward and Steward, *Gouldtown*, 98, 219.

GOULD, Samuel; Private; C/10th Cav. Released to duty from treatment for gonorrhea, Ft Robinson, NE, 19 Aug 1903. SOURCE: Post Surgeon to CO, C/10, 19 Aug 1903, LS, Post Surgeon, Ft Robinson.

GOULDEN, Ruck; Private; E/25th Inf. Died of tuberculosis in the Philippines. SOURCE: *ANJ* 39 (8 Feb 1902): 577.

GRACE, James; Private; K/10th Cav. Served in 10th Cavalry, 1898; remained in U.S. during war with Spain. SOURCE: Cashin, *Under Fire with the Tenth Cavalry*, 349.

GRADDON; Private; E/9th Cav. Killed in action, 4 Sep 1879. *See* **CHAPMAN**, S., Sergeant, E/9th Cavalry

GRAHAM; Private; G/10th Cav. At Ft Apache, AZ, 1890, subscribed $.50 to testimonial to General Grierson. SOURCE: List of subscriptions, 23 Apr 1890, 10th Cavalry papers, MHI.

GRAHAM; Private; B/25th Inf. Sick in hospital, Castillejos, Philippines, May 1900. SOURCE: Richmond *Planet*, 30 Jun 1900.

GRAHAM, Henry; Private; C/10th Cav. Served in 10th Cavalry, 1898; remained in U.S. during war with Spain. SOURCE: Cashin, *Under Fire with the Tenth Cavalry*, 340.

GRAHAM, John; Sergeant; D/25th Inf. Born in Virginia; private, D/10th Cavalry, 14 Feb 1877–13 Feb 1882; transferred to K/10th Cavalry, 13 Mar 1882–12 Mar 1887; transferred to E/10th Cavalry, 21 Mar 1887; corporal, 21 Mar 1887; sergeant, 1 Feb 1892; stationed at Ft Custer, MT, 1897. SOURCE: Baker, Roster.

Corporal, E/10th Cavalry, subscribed $.50 to testimonial to General Grierson. SOURCE: List of subscriptions, 23 Apr 1890, 10th Cavalry papers, MHI.

Sergeant, E/10th Cavalry, served in 10th Cavalry in Cuba, 1898. SOURCE: Cashin, *Under Fire with the Tenth Cavalry*, 342.

Awarded certificate of merit for distinguished service, Cuba, 1 Jul 1898. SOURCE: Steward, *The Colored Regulars*, 280; *ANJ* 37 (24 Feb 1900): 611.

Sergeant, D/25th Infantry, 1900. SOURCE: GO 15, AGO, 13 Feb 1900.

Retired, Aug 1902. SOURCE: *ANJ* 39 (30 Aug 1902): 1315.

No Veterans Administration pension file.

GRAHAM, John; Private; I/10th Cav. Served in 10th Cavalry, 1898; remained in U.S. during war with Spain. SOURCE: Cashin, *Under Fire with the Tenth Cavalry*, 348.

GRAHAM, Joseph; Private; 25th Inf. Born Waterboro, SC; enlisted, age 33, occupation rock miner, dark complexion, black hair and eyes, Charleston, SC, 21 Jun 1881. SOURCE: Descriptive & Assignment Rolls, 25 Inf.

GRAHAM, William; Corporal; I/24th Inf. Enlisted Louisville, KY, 7 Feb 1899. SOURCE: Muster Roll, I/24 Inf, Jan–Feb 1899.

Promoted from private, 10 Jul 1899. SOURCE: Muster Roll, I/24 Inf, Jul–Aug 1899.

Allotted $5 per month to Hettie Graham. SOURCE: Muster Roll, I/24 Inf, Sep–Oct 1899.

GRAHAM, William H.; Sergeant; D/9th Cav. Veteran of Philippine Insurrection; at Ft D. A. Russell, WY, in 1910. SOURCE: *Illustrated Review: Ninth Cavalry*, with picture.

GRAMMAR, Nelson; Private; G/25th Inf. Born Brunswick Co., NY; occupation sailor; admitted to Soldiers Home at age of 24 [*sic*] with ten years and six months' service and pension of $17 per month; discharged from home at own request, 1 Jul 1893. SOURCE: SecWar, *AR 1893*, 4:845.

GRAMMER, Edward L.; Private; H/9th Cav. Born Cassville, MO; enlisted, age 24, Ht 5'6", Cincinnati, OH, 27 May 1897; joined unit at Ft Robinson, NE, 1 Jun 1897. SOURCE: Descriptive Book, H/9 Cav.

Deserted from Ft Robinson, 22 Sep 1897.

GRANDON, John; A/24th Inf. Remained in Huiningan, Philippines, after service; occupation farmer. SOURCE: Funston papers, KSHS.

GRANT; Corporal; A/38th Inf. At Ft Cummings, NM, autumn 1867. SOURCE: Billington, *New Mexico's Buffalo Soldiers*, 39.

GRANT; Private; B/10th Cav. At Ft Apache, AZ, 1890, subscribed $.50 to testimonial to General Grierson. SOURCE: List of subscriptions, 23 Apr 1890, 10th Cavalry papers, MHI.

GRANT, Frank; G/10th Cav. Original member of 10th Cavalry; in troop when organized, Ft Leavenworth, KS, 5 Jul 1867. SOURCE: McMiller, "Buffalo Soldiers," 74.

GRANT, Frank; Private; L/24th Inf. Best all-around athlete, Division of the Atlantic, 1908. SOURCE: Muller, *The Twenty Fourth Infantry*, 56.

GRANT, General Lee; Corporal; H/10th Cav. Commissioned second lieutenant of cavalry, 27 Sep 1918. SOURCE: Glass, *History of the Tenth Cavalry*, appendix M.

GRANT, John; A/9th Cav. Served in 1896.
    Died of stomach cancer at U.S. Soldiers Home, 30 Mar 1904. SOURCE: SecWar, *AR 1904*, 4:289.

GRANT, John; Sergeant; I/24th Inf. Enlisted Ft Huachuca, AZ, 28 May 1894; discharged, end of term, with fifteen years' continuous service, character good, 27 May 1899. SOURCE: Muster Roll, I/24 Inf, May–Jun 1899.
    Enlisted Presidio of San Francisco, CA, 28 May 1899; promoted from corporal, 17 Aug 1899. SOURCE: Muster Roll, I/24 Inf, Jul–Aug 1899.
    Allotted $20 per month for six months to Emma Grant. SOURCE: Muster Roll, I/24 Inf, Sep–Oct 1899.

GRANT, John; 24th Inf. Died 1 Apr 1899; buried at Ft Douglas, UT. SOURCE: Clark, "A History of the Twenty-fourth," appendix A.

GRANT, Thomas; Musician; B/24th Inf. Served in Second Brigade, Second Division, V Corps, during Civil War. SOURCE: CO, B/24, to Adj, Ft Huachuca, 13 Jul 1893, Name File, 24 Inf.
    Seeks permission to take B/24th Infantry band and buckboard to Tombstone, AZ, 5–6 Nov 1893, to play for ball. SOURCE: Grant to Adj, Ft Huachuca, 2 Nov 1893, Letters & Orders Received, 24 Inf.
    Retires from Ft Huachuca, AZ, Jan 1896. SOURCE: *ANJ* 33 (11 Jan 1896): 329.

GRANT, Thomas; Captain; L/48th Inf. Son of Col. John T. Grant, "wealthy citizen" of Atlanta, GA, born 4 Jun 1862; educated at Atlanta University; second lieutenant, 10th U.S. Volunteer Infantry, 21 Jul 1898; first lieutenant, 26 Jul 1898; mustered out with regiment, Macon, GA, 8 Mar 1899; in Georgia State Militia (Colored), private, sergeant major, lieutenant colonel, Second Battalion. SOURCE: *ANJ* 37 (14 Oct 1899): 145.
    One of nineteen officers of 48th Infantry recommended as regular Army second lieutenants. SOURCE: CG, DivPI, Manila, 8 Feb 1901, to AGO, AGO File 355163.
    Mentioned. SOURCE: Beasley, *Negro Trailblazers*, 284.
    Attests to illness of Floyd Crumbly, even when he left Atlanta in spring of 1903; resides at 136 Houston Street, Atlanta, in 1905. SOURCE: Affidavit, Grant, 16 Sep 1905, VA File XC 2624105, Floyd H. Crumbly.

GRANT, Tony; Private; 25th Inf. Wounded in thigh, Botolan, Philippines, 28 Feb 1900. SOURCE: *ANJ* 37 (14 Apr 1900): 779.

GRANT, William; Recruit; 10th Cav. Mentioned Jun 1867 as scheduled for assignment to F/10th Cavalry. SOURCE: LS, 10 Cav, 1866–67.

GRANT, William; Private; 10th Cav. Killed by fellow prisoner during fight in guardhouse, Ft Davis, TX, Jun 1878. SOURCE: Carroll, *The Black Military Experience*, 276.

GRANT, William B.; QM Sgt; H/9th Cav. Veteran of Spanish-American War and Philippine Insurrection; at Ft D. A. Russell, WY, in 1910; resident of Onancock, VA. SOURCE: *Illustrated Review: Ninth Cavalry*, with picture.

GRANVILLE, John A.; A/10th Cav. Original member of 10th Cavalry; in troop when organized, Ft Leavenworth, KS, 18 Feb 1867. SOURCE: McMiller, "Buffalo Soldiers," 68.

GRASS, Harry; Private; F/9th Cav. Recruit from depot, arrived Ft Robinson, NE, 1 Mar 1887.

GRATES, Lawson; Private; K/10th Cav. Original member of 10th Cavalry; in troop when organized, Ft Riley, KS, 1 Sep 1867. SOURCE: McMiller, "Buffalo Soldiers," 77.
    Mentioned Mar 1869. SOURCE: LR, Det 10 Cav, 1868–69.

GRAVELY, G. S.; Private; F/9th Cav. Stationed at Ft Robinson, NE; in hands of civil authorities, Chadron, NE, 5 Jun 1889–3 Jan 1890. SOURCE: Regt Returns, 9 Cav.

GRAVES, Johnson; Sergeant; A/10th Cav. Private, A/10th Cavalry, at Ft Apache, AZ, 1890, subscribed $.50 to testimonial to General Grierson. SOURCE: List of subscriptions, 23 Apr 1890, 10th Cavalry papers, MHI.
    Served in A and D/10th Cavalry; knew Thomas Allsup, his first sergeant, 1875–98; age 65, watchman, Salvation Army Building, 7th and P Streets, NW, Washington, DC, with residence at same address. SOURCE: Affidavit, Graves, VA File XC 2659797, Thomas H. Allsup.

GRAVES, Thomas R.; Private; I/10th Cav. Original member of 10th Cavalry; in troop when organized, Ft Riley, KS, 15 Aug 1867. SOURCE: McMiller, "Buffalo Soldiers," 76.
    Arrested today for desertion; will be sent to Ft Sill, Indian Territory. SOURCE: Adj, 10 Cav, to CO, I/10 Cav, 9 Jan 1873, LS, 10 Cav, 1873–81.
    Reward of $30 paid for apprehension of Graves. SOURCE: CO, 10 Cav, to CO, I/10, 19 Mar 1873, ES, 10 Cav, 1873–81.

GRAVES, William; Private; H/10th Cav. Served in 10th Cavalry, 1898; remained in U.S. during war with Spain. SOURCE: Cashin, *Under Fire with the Tenth Cavalry*, 346.

GRAW, George R.; 1st Lt; 49th Inf. One of twenty-three officers of 49th Infantry recommended as regular Army second lieutenants. SOURCE: CG, DivPI, Manila, 8 Feb 1901, to AGO, AGO File 355163.

GRAY, Charles; Sergeant; A/9th Cav. Trumpeter, H/10th Cavalry, at Ft Apache, AZ, 1890, subscribed $.50 to testimonial to General Grierson. SOURCE: List of subscriptions, 23 Apr 1890, 10th Cavalry papers, MHI.
    Promoted to corporal, B/9th Cavalry, from private, Ft Duchesne, UT, Apr 1895. SOURCE: *ANJ* 32 (4 May 1895): 590.

Promoted to sergeant, G/10th Cavalry, from corporal, Jun 1902. SOURCE: *ANJ* 39 (7 Jun 1902): 1004.

Veteran of Indian wars and Philippine Insurrection; sergeant, A/9th Cavalry, at Ft D. A. Russell, WY, in 1910. SOURCE: *Illustrated Review: Ninth Cavalry*, with picture.

GRAY, Conny; Private; H/25th Inf. Awarded certificate of merit for special gallantry, while private, D/25th Infantry, El Caney, Cuba, 1 Jul 1898; fearlessly exposed self to hostile fire, applied first-aid bandage, and carried his wounded captain to shelter, then rejoined company and participated in action; now private, I/25th Infantry. SOURCE: GO 32, AGO, 6 Feb 1904.

Reason for certificate of merit described; now private, H/25th Infantry. SOURCE: Cleveland *Gazette*, 24 Nov 1906.

GRAY, Edward; Private; F/10th Cav. Served in 10th Cavalry in Cuba, 1898. SOURCE: Cashin, *Under Fire with the Tenth Cavalry*, 344.

GRAY, Fred W.; Private; B/9th Cav. At Ft D. A. Russell, WY, in 1910. SOURCE: *Illustrated Review: Ninth Cavalry*, with picture.

GRAY, George W.; Private; C/25th Inf. Dishonorable discharge, Brownsville. SOURCE: SO 266, AGO, 9 Nov 1906.

GRAY, Joseph H.; Private; C/25th Inf. Dishonorable discharge, Brownsville. SOURCE: SO 266, AGO, 9 Nov 1906.

GRAY, Lewis; D/10th Cav. Original member of 10th Cavalry; in troop when organized, Ft Leavenworth, KS, 1 Jun 1867. SOURCE: McMiller, "Buffalo Soldiers," 71.

GRAY, Robert; Private; Band/25th Inf. Fined $1 by summary court for absence from drill, Ft Missoula, MT, 3 Aug 1896. SOURCE: Descriptive & Assignment Cards, 25 Inf.

Fined $1 by summary court for absence from retreat, Iba, Zambales, Philippines, 25 Oct 1900. SOURCE: Misc Records, 25 Inf.

GRAY, William H.; Private; B/10th Cav. Served in 10th Cavalry, 1898; remained in U.S. during war with Spain. SOURCE: Cashin, *Under Fire with the Tenth Cavalry*, 339.

GRAYSON; Corporal; E/9th Cav. Wife is one of three laundresses authorized for E/9th Cavalry; authorized use of cooking stove and utensils, Ft Robinson, NE. SOURCE: Post Adj to Post QM, 22 Jun 1891, LS, Ft Robinson.

GRAYSON, A. L.; Private; H/25th Inf. Transferred from C/9th Cavalry. SOURCE: SO 70, AGO, 24 Mar 1892.

Read Declaration of Independence at celebration, Ft Missoula, MT, 4 Jul 1892. SOURCE: Monthly Report, Chaplain Steward, Sep 1892.

GRAYSON, Charles H.; Private; G/24th Inf. Born Zanesville, OH; complexion yellow; enlisted in B/24th Infantry, 10 Apr 1876; reenlisted 28 Apr 1881 and 28 Apr 1886; transferred to Band/24th Infantry, age 33, 6 Jun 1887; transferred as sergeant to I/24th Infantry, character good, single, Ft Bayard, NM, 1 Aug 1888. SOURCE: Descriptive Book, 24 Inf NCS & Band.

Capt. John B. Nixon, 24th Infantry, convicted by general court martial of defrauding Grayson of $7.20 due him for extra duty pay, Ft McIntosh, TX, Feb 1877; also defrauded others in B/24th Infantry: Cpl. Thomas E. Hurst ($7.20), Pvts. Robert Ellis ($13.40), William Brown ($8.40), John Lane ($8.40), James Sanders ($8.40), Loss Seaton ($8.40), Thomas Winsted ($8.40), and Daniel Johnson ($13.80). SOURCE: GCMO 4, AGO, 2 Feb 1878.

Ranked number 15 among sharpshooters over 90 percent, 1885. SOURCE: GO 25, AGO, 12 Mar 1885.

Returned from four-month furlough to Ft Elliott, TX. SOURCE: *ANJ* 24 (9 Oct 1886): 210.

In G/24th Infantry; reduced to ranks, confined for six months, fined $60 for "sundry offences, including 'drunk and disorderly,'" Ft Bayard, NM. SOURCE: *ANJ* 31 (25 Nov 1893): 222.

Distinguished marksman with rifle, as sergeant, B/24th Infantry, 1882 and 1884, and as private, G/24th Infantry, 1894. SOURCE: GO 62, AGO, 15 Nov 1894.

GRAYSON, Perry; Private; K/10th Cav. Served in 10th Cavalry, 1898; remained in U.S. during war with Spain. SOURCE: Cashin, *Under Fire with the Tenth Cavalry*, 346.

GREAVES, Clinton; Corporal; C/9th Cav. Born Madison Co., VA; resided Prince Georges Co., MD; Ht 5'7"; won Medal of Honor for heroism against Apaches, Florida Mountains, NM, 24 Jan 1877; stationed at Ft Cummings, NM, at time. SOURCE: Leckie, *The Buffalo Soldiers*, 178–79; Carroll, *The Black Military Experience*, 407; Lee, *Negro Medal of Honor Men*, 61–63; Koger, *The Maryland Negro in Our Wars*, 23; Billingon, "Black Cavalrymen," 62; Billington, *New Mexico's Buffalo Soldiers*, 51.

Joined Army, age 22, in 1872; served over twenty years; retired to Columbus, OH, where he died, 1906. SOURCE: Amos, *Above and Beyond in the West*, 8.

GREEN; Private; G/9th Cav. To go to Ft Crook, NE, for medical treatment. SOURCE: SO 62, AGO, 17 Mar 1897.

GREEN; Sergeant; K/24th Inf. At Cabanatuan, Philippines, 1901. *See* **FAGGINS**, John H., Private, K/24th Infantry

GREEN, Alfred; Private; 25th Inf. Born Santee, SC; enlisted Charleston, SC, age 23, occupation brakeman, Ht 5'7", dark complexion, black eyes and hair. SOURCE: Descriptive & Assignment Rolls, 25 Inf.

GREEN, Archer; I/10th Cav. Original member of 10th Cavalry; in troop when organized, Ft Riley, KS, 15 Aug 1867. SOURCE: McMiller, "Buffalo Soldiers," 76.

GREEN, Bailey; 1st Sgt; C/9th Cav. Authorized four-month furlough from Ft Leavenworth, KS. SOURCE: *ANJ* 25 (19 Nov 1887): 322.

At Ft Leavenworth; warrant as noncommissioned officer dates from 1 Dec 1873. SOURCE: *ANJ* 25 (18 Feb 1888): 586.

Transferred from Ft Leavenworth to Army and Navy Hospital, Hot Springs, AR. SOURCE: *ANJ* 27 (14 Sep 1889): 42.

Recovered; returned from hospital to his company at Ft Leavenworth. SOURCE: *ANJ* 27 (4 Jan 1890): 368.

Retired as first sergeant, C/9th Cavalry, 2 Sep 1892. SOURCE: Roster, 9 Cav.

GREEN, Benjamin; L/24th Inf. At Skagway, AL, 1902. *See* **CASSELLE**, Nelson A., Private, L/24th Infantry

GREEN, Callie; Private; 24th Inf. Participated in Houston riot, 1917; slightly wounded. SOURCE: Haynes, *A Night of Violence*, 163.

GREEN, Charles; F/48th Inf. Convicted of robbery in the Philippines, May 1900; sentenced to three years.

GREEN, Charles; Private; L/9th Cav. At Ft D. A. Russell, WY, in 1910; resident of Cincinnati. SOURCE: *Illustrated Review: Ninth Cavalry*.

GREEN, Charles A.; Private; H/10th Cav. Honorable mention for services rendered in capture of Mangas and his Apache band, Rio Bonito, AZ, 18 Oct 1886. SOURCE: Baker, Roster.

GREEN, Dalbert P.; Master Sgt; 25th Inf. Born 25 Mar 1873; enlisted Washington, DC; served in B and E/25th Infantry, 27 Aug 1891–26 Aug 1896; B/25th Infantry and Noncommissioned Staff/25th Infantry, 27 Aug 1896–26 Aug 1899; on Noncommissioned Staff/25th Infantry, 27 Aug 1899-retirement, Schofield Barracks, HI, 30 Aug 1916; corporal, 12 Jun 1893; sergeant, 19 Jan 1895; commissary sergeant, 23 Mar 1895; regimental supply sergeant, 7 Aug 1916; served in Cuba, 22 Jun–13 Aug 1898, and in the Philippines, 31 Jun 1899–17 Jul 1902 and 13 Sep 1907–11 Sep 1909; character on all discharges excellent; retired in accordance with Special Order 189, War Department, 14 Aug 1916; resided at 31 Pierce Street, NW, Washington, DC.

At Bamban, Philippines, 1899. SOURCE: Nankivell, *History of the Twenty-fifth Infantry*, 93, with picture.

In charge of commissary while commissary officer, Lt. R. J. Burt, was absent with 1st Battalion. SOURCE: Richmond *Planet*, 27 Jan 1900.

Heroism in the Philippines, 2 Dec 1899, discussed. SOURCE: *Leslie's Weekly* 90 (10 Feb 1900): 107.

Leslie's story reprinted. SOURCE: Richmond *Planet*, 17 Feb 1900; Cleveland *Gazette*, 10 Mar 1900.

Mentioned. SOURCE: Richmond *Planet*, 28 Jul 1900.

"Indignant Sergeant D. P. Green, 25th Inf., sent a protest recently to the Manila *Times* for referring to the ballplayers of that command as 'darkies.'. . . The *Times* made a manly apology." SOURCE: *ANJ* 35 (22 Jul 1901): 1049.

Along with regimental noncommissioned staff, initiated move to buy Brig. Gen. Andrew Burt a retirement gift. SOURCE: Richmond *Planet*, 7 Dec 1901.

Letter to editor. SOURCE: Manila *Times*, 8 May 1901.

"Mickey" Green "a man of great gallantry," who saved life of Sgt. George Thompson, Band/25th Infantry, according to Colonel Burt in Chicago speech, 11 Sep 1902. SOURCE: Cleveland *Gazette*, 11 Oct 1902.

Retired 1916 with over twenty-five years' service. SOURCE: *Crisis* 13 (Dec 1916): 93.

When retired, Honolulu *Star-Gazette* wrote that he "has been the best known and most liked man in the 25th for years. He has well earned his retirement and can proceed to his home feeling that he has given the active years of his life to his country and has a splendid record behind him of duty well performed." SOURCE: Cleveland *Gazette*, 25 Nov 1917.

Former captain, manager, coach regimental baseball team, 1894–1908, "the happiest days of my life"; now master sergeant, retired; thanked for assistance in preparation of chapter on regimental baseball team. SOURCE: Nankivell, *History of the Twenty-fifth Infantry*, introduction, 163.

GREEN, Edward; G/10th Cav. Original member of 10th Cavalry; in troop when organized, Ft Leavenworth, KS, 5 Jul 1867. SOURCE: McMiller, "Buffalo Soldiers," 74.

GREEN, Edward; Trumpeter; L/10th Cav. Served in 10th Cavalry, 1898; remained in U.S. during war with Spain. SOURCE: Cashin, *Under Fire with the Tenth Cavalry*, 350.

GREEN, Elder; Private; K/10th Cav. At Ft Robinson, NE, 1904; member of troop orchestra. SOURCE: Barrow, "Christmas in the United States Army," 96.

GREEN, Ernest; Corporal; C/10th Cav. Private, A/10th Cavalry; released to duty from treatment for acute gonorrhea, Ft Robinson, NE, 7 Aug 1903. SOURCE: Post Surgeon to CO, A/10, 7 Aug 1903, LS, Post Surgeon, Ft Robinson.

Corporal, C/10th Cavalry; released to duty from treatment for gonorrhea, Ft Robinson, 21 Aug 1903. SOURCE: Post Surgeon to CO, A/10, 21 Aug 1903, LS, Post Surgeon, Ft Robinson.

GREEN, Ezekiel; 1st Sgt; L/10th Cav. Served in 10th Cavalry, 1898; remained in U.S. during war with Spain. SOURCE: Cashin, *Under Fire with the Tenth Cavalry*, 349.

Ranked number 360 among rifle experts with 69.67 percent, 1905. SOURCE: GO 101, AGO, 31 May 1906.

GREEN, F. E.; Sergeant; F/25th Inf. Discharged and remained in Manila, Philippines. SOURCE: Manila *Times*, 11 May 1901.

GREEN, Frank E.; Private; A/10th Cav. Arrived at Ft Leavenworth, KS, from Jefferson Barracks, MO. SOURCE: Adj, Ft Leavenworth, to HQ, Jefferson Barracks, 9 Oct 1866.

Original member of 10th Cavalry; in troop when organized, Ft Leavenworth, KS, 18 Feb 1867. SOURCE: McMiller, "Buffalo Soldiers," 68.

GREEN, Garfield; Private; D/10th Cav. Served in 10th Cavalry, 1898; remained in U.S. during war with Spain. SOURCE: Cashin, *Under Fire with the Tenth Cavalry*, 341.

GREEN, George; E/10th Cav. Original member of 10th Cavalry; in troop when organized, Ft Leavenworth, KS, 15 Jun 1867. SOURCE: McMiller, "Buffalo Soldiers," 72.

GREEN, George; F/10th Cav. Original member of 10th Cavalry; in troop when organized, Ft Leavenworth, KS, 21 Jun 1867. SOURCE: McMiller, "Buffalo Soldiers," 73.

GREEN, Hamilton; Private; A/10th Cav. Served in 10th Cavalry in Cuba, 1898. SOURCE: Cashin, *Under Fire with the Tenth Cavalry*, 336.

GREEN, Henry; 1st Sgt; M/9th Cav. At Ft McKavett, TX, 1872–73. *See* **STANCE**, Emanuel, First Sergeant, F/9th Cavalry

GREEN, Henry; Private; K/25th Inf. At Ft Niobrara, NE, 1904. SOURCE: Wilson, "History of Fort Niobrara."

GREEN, Isaac; Private; A/10th Cav. Served in 10th Cavalry, 1898; remained in U.S. during war with Spain. SOURCE: Cashin, *Under Fire with the Tenth Cavalry*, 337.

GREEN, James; Private; I/10th Cav. Served in 10th Cavalry, 1898; remained in U.S. during war with Spain. SOURCE: Cashin, *Under Fire with the Tenth Cavalry*, 348.

GREEN, James; Musician; I/25th Inf. Sentenced to one month by summary court, San Isidro, Philippines, for going beyond prescribed limits of post, Apr 1902, first conviction; fined $1.50 for permitting sounding of retreat at time not appointed, 13 Jun 1902; fined $4 for street fight, 20 Jun 1902. SOURCE: Register of Summary Court, San Isidro.

GREEN, James; Private; I/9th Cav. Served with Henry McClain, in 10th Cavalry and later in I/9th Cavalry. SOURCE: Affidavit, Green, Ft Robinson, NE, 27 Feb 1904, VA File XC 2705872, Henry McClain.

GREEN, James; Trumpeter; L/9th Cav. Transferred from A/10th Cavalry to 9th Cavalry. SOURCE: SO 115, AGO, 16 May 1904.

Veteran of Philippine Insurrection; trumpeter, L/9th Cavalry, at Ft D. A. Russell, WY, in 1910; sharpshooter; resident of St. Louis. SOURCE: *Illustrated Review: Ninth Cavalry*, with picture.

GREEN, James H.; Private; L/49th Inf. Died in the Philippines, 16 Aug 1900. SOURCE: Richmond *Planet*, 8 Sep 1900.

Killed by comrade in the Philippines, 16 Aug 1900. SOURCE: *ANJ* 38 (8 Sep 1900): 43.

GREEN, James H.; 1st Sgt; K/24th Inf. Commissioned first lieutenant, 8th Illinois Infantry.

GREEN, John; I/10th Cav. Original member of 10th Cavalry; in troop when organized, Ft Riley, KS, 15 Aug 1867. SOURCE: McMiller, "Buffalo Soldiers," 76.

GREEN, John; M/10th Cav. Original member of 10th Cavalry; in troop when organized, Ft Riley, KS, 15 Oct 1867. SOURCE: McMiller, "Buffalo Soldiers," 79.

GREEN, John; Private; D/25th Inf. Dishonorable discharge, Brownsville. SOURCE: SO 266, AGO, 9 Nov 1906.

GREEN, John; Private; D/10th Cav. Casualty in fight at Cheyenne Agency, Indian Territory, 6 Apr 1875. SOURCE: Leckie, *The Buffalo Soldiers*, 139.

GREEN, John C.; Private; K/10th Cav. At Ft Robinson, NE, 1904.

GREEN, John E.; 24th Inf. At Ft Bayard, NM, 1890. *See* **HENDRICKS**, Lewis, 24th Infantry

GREEN, John E.; Lt Col; U.S. Army. Enlisted by Chaplain Allensworth, 24th Infantry, Louisville, KY, 1898, while student in Walden University, Nashville, TN; served as Allensworth's clerk while in H/24th Infantry, 1899; later commissioned in 25th Infantry. SOURCE: Alexander, *Battles and Victories*, 364, 392.

Green and Benjamin O. Davis were the only two blacks among 300 enlisted men commissioned from ranks, 1898–1902. SOURCE: Fletcher, *The Black Soldier*, 165.

Corporal, H/24th Infantry, when appointed second lieutenant, 25th Infantry. SOURCE: Cleveland *Gazette*, 13 Jul 1901.

Appointed second lieutenant, 25th Infantry. SOURCE: Indianapolis *Freeman*, 20 Jul 1901.

Second lieutenant, 1901; first lieutenant, 1916, Mexican border; military attache to Liberia; lieutenant colonel and chief, Military Department, Wilberforce University, 1920; retired, Camp Henry J. Jones, AZ, 1929. SOURCE: *Crisis* 12 (Jun 1916): 62; *Crisis* 20 (May 1920): 270; *Crisis* 38 (Jul 1929): 218.

Second lieutenant, 25th Infantry, led detachment against bandits, Indang, Batangas, Philippines, 29 Nov 1901. SOURCE: *ANJ* 39 (18 Jan 1902): 487.

In the Philippines, 1906. *See* **WOODS**, Robert Gordon, Captain, I/49th Infantry

Mentioned as first lieutenant. SOURCE: Work, *The Negro Year Book, 1912*, 77.

First lieutenant, stationed at Wilberforce; appointed chairman of board of judges to pass on annual competitive drill of separate battalion, high-school cadets, Washington, DC. SOURCE: Cleveland *Gazette*, 17 May 1913.

Promoted to captain, stationed in Liberia. SOURCE: Cleveland *Gazette*, 18 Nov 1916.

Lieutenant colonel, military attache, in Liberia. SOURCE: Work, *The Negro Yearbook, 1918–1919*, 228.

Lieutenant colonel at Camp Henry J. Jones. SOURCE: Work, *The Negro Yearbook, 1925–1926*, 253.

GREEN, John R.; Sergeant; A/24th Inf. Private, recruited from Ft Apache, AZ, to teach in Chaplain Allensworth's post school, Ft Bayard, NM, 1889. SOURCE: Billington, *New Mexico's Buffalo Soldiers*, 162.

Post schoolteacher, Ft Huachuca, AZ, since 6 Dec 1892. SOURCE: Report of Schools, Ft Huachuca, 1 Dec 1892–1 Feb 1893, Name File, 24 Inf.

Relieved from extra duty as schoolteacher. SOURCE: Order 66, Ft Huachuca, 7 May 1893, Name File, 24 Inf.

With his wife contributed $2 of $4.50 sent from Ft Huachuca for defense fund of three black women charged with murder, Lunenburg Co., VA, Jan 1896. SOURCE: Richmond *Planet*, 11 Jan 1896.

GREEN, Joseph; Private; H/24th Inf. Enlisted Philadelphia, PA, 18 Feb 1899. SOURCE: Muster Roll, H/24 Inf, Jan–Feb 1899.

Convicted of larceny in the Philippines and sentenced to eighteen months, 5 Oct 1900.

GREEN, Joseph H.; Recruit; Colored Detachment/Mounted Service. Convicted by general court martial of absence without leave from morning of 12 Nov 1888 until arrested by sergeant of the guard, morning of 13 Nov 1888, and of loss of military clothing worth $25.25; sentenced to dishonorable discharge and two years. SOURCE: GCMO 2, AGO, 18 Jan 1889.

Confinement later reduced to six months by Adjutant General.

GREEN, Lewis T.; Sergeant; H/9th Cav. Sergeant since 12 Feb 1885. SOURCE: Roster, 9 Cav.

At Ft Robinson, NE, 1895; sergeant since 12 Feb 1885. SOURCE: *ANJ* 32 (13 Jun 1895): 758.

Deposits with paymaster, 1897–98: $35.

GREEN, McCallin; Trumpeter; M/10th Cav. Served in 10th Cavalry in Cuba, 1898. SOURCE: Cashin, *Under Fire with the Tenth Cavalry*, 352.

GREEN, Miles M.; Sergeant; Machine Gun Troop/10th Cav. Commissioned captain, Camp Des Moines, IA, 15 Oct 1917. SOURCE: Glass, *History of the Tenth Cavalry*, appendix M.

GREEN, Morris; Private; I/10th Cav. Served in 10th Cavalry in Cuba, 1898. SOURCE: Cashin, *Under Fire with the Tenth Cavalry*, 348.

GREEN, Moses; F/9th Cav. Intends to marry, Ft Robinson, NE, Christmas 1886. SOURCE: Cleveland *Gazette*, 27 Nov 1886.

GREEN, Nathan; Private; M/10th Cav. Honorable mention for skill in successful pursuit of raiding parties, Arizona, 1888. SOURCE: Baker, Roster.

GREEN, Richard; Private; F/10th Cav. Apprehended as deserter; now in confinement at St. Louis, MO, cavalry depot. SOURCE: CO, 10 Cav, to CO, F/10, 28 Jan 1877, ES, 10 Cav, 1873–81.

Escaped confinement 7 Feb 1877. SOURCE: CO, F/10, to CO, 10 Cav, [?] Feb 1877, ES, 10 Cav, 1873–81.

GREEN, Robert T.; Private; B/10th Cav. Served in 10th Cavalry, 1898; remained in U.S. during war with Spain. SOURCE: Cashin, *Under Fire with the Tenth Cavalry*, 339.

GREEN, Roy; Private; G/25th Inf. Served in 1910. *See* **JAMES**, John, Sergeant, G/25th Infantry

GREEN, T. W.; Private; A/9th Cav. At Ft Stanton, NM, 1881; on detached service at Ft Craig, NM, 26 Dec 1880–14 Jan 1881. SOURCE: Regt Returns, 9 Cav, Jan 1881.

GREEN, Thomas E.; Chief Musician; 24th Inf. Commissioned at Camp Des Moines, IA, during World War I. SOURCE: Beasley, *Negro Trailblazers*, 285.

GREEN, Thomas J.; QM Sgt; D/25th Inf. Dishonorable discharge, Brownsville. SOURCE: SO 266, AGO, 9 Nov 1906.

GREEN, Wallace W.; Private; L/9th Cav. At Ft D. A. Russell, WY, in 1910; resident of Columbia, MO. SOURCE: *Illustrated Review: Ninth Cavalry*, with picture.

GREEN, Walter; 2nd Lt; H/48th Inf. Born in North Carolina; private, K/25th Infantry, 2 Aug 1879–1 Aug 1884; private, corporal, sergeant, first sergeant, I/9th Cavalry, 9 Aug 1884–8 Aug 1889; private, K/10th Cavalry, 13 Aug 1889; corporal, 15 Jan 1890; sergeant, 10 May 1890; first sergeant, 16 Feb 1894; stationed at Ft Custer, MT, 1897. SOURCE: Baker, Roster.

First sergeant, I/9th Cavalry, Ft Robinson, NE, 1889. *See* **WHITEN**, Walter J., Private, 24th Infantry

Served in 10th Cavalry, 1898; remained in U.S. during war with Spain. SOURCE: Cashin, *Under Fire with the Tenth Cavalry*, 349.

First sergeant, K/10th Cavalry, discharged to take commission in 48th Infantry. SOURCE: *ANJ* 37 (25 Nov 1899): 294.

Mentioned as second lieutenant, H/48th Infantry. SOURCE: Beasley, *Negro Trailblazers*, 284.

Commissioned captain, Camp Des Moines, IA, Oct 1917. SOURCE: Glass, *History of the Tenth Cavalry*, appendix M.

GREEN, Walter; Corporal; H/10th Cav. Promoted from private, 16 Mar 1902. SOURCE: *ANJ* 39 (10 May 1902): 904.

GREEN, Warren; Private; H/24th Inf. Enlisted Jefferson Barracks, MO, with eleven years' continuous service, 4 Jun 1898; died in field hospital, Siboney, Cuba, of disease contracted in line of duty; clothing $18.32. SOURCE: Muster Roll, H/24 Inf, Jul–Aug 1898.

Died in Cuba, 5 Aug 1898. SOURCE: *ANJ* 36 (11 Feb 1899): 567.

Death caused by yellow fever. SOURCE: AG, *Correspondence Regarding the War with Spain* I:209.

GREEN, Wesley; Private; G/10th Cav. To be assigned to F/10th Cavalry, Jun 1867. SOURCE: LS, 10 Cav, 1866–67.

Original member of 10th Cavalry; in troop when organized, Ft Leavenworth, KS, 5 Jul 1867. SOURCE: McMiller, "Buffalo Soldiers," 74.

GREEN, William; Recruit; Colored Detachment/ Mounted Service. Convicted by general court martial, Jefferson Barracks, MO, of overstaying pass, from midnight to seven A.M., 5 Dec 1886; sentenced to three months.

GREEN, William; 2nd Lt; 23rd Kans Inf. Mentioned. SOURCE: Beasley, *Negro Trailblazers*, 285.

GREEN, William E.; Private; K/10th Cav. In hands of civil authorities, Crawford, NE, 24–26 Aug 1902. SOURCE: Regt Returns, 10 Cav, Aug 1902.

Sentenced to dishonorable discharge and nine months, 13 Oct 1902; escaped from Ft Robinson, NE, guardhouse, 20 Oct 1902.

GREEN, William H.; Private; D/9th Cav. Died in the Philippines, 27 Mar 1901. SOURCE: *ANJ* 38 (13 Apr 1901): 803.

GREEN, William W.; Private; I/24th Inf. Enlisted Ft D. A. Russell, WY, 16 Feb 1899; on special duty at post exchange, 22 Feb 1899. SOURCE: Muster Roll, I/24 Inf, Jan–Feb 1899.

Fined $.50 by summary court, Presidio of San Francisco, CA, 13 Jun 1899. SOURCE: Muster Roll, I/24 Inf, May–Jun 1899.

Allotted $10 per month for twelve months to Margaret Green. SOURCE: Muster Roll, I/24 Inf, Sep–Oct 1899.

GREENBERRY, Grant; Private; G/25th Inf. Died of dysentery at Bani, Luzon, Philippines, 3 Aug 1901. SOURCE: *ANJ* 39 (28 Sep 1901): 81.

GREENE, Hallett; Signal Corps. Graduate of City College of New York; enlisted at insistence of Secretary of War Robert T. Lincoln, over protest of Brig. Gen. William B. Hazen, and broke color line in Signal Corps, 1884. SOURCE: *Leslie's Weekly* 59 (11 Oct 1884): 114.

GREENE, William; E/10th Cav. Original member of 10th Cavalry; in troop when organized, Ft Leavenworth, KS, 15 Jun 1867. SOURCE: McMiller, "Buffalo Soldiers," 72.

GREENHOW, George; Corporal; I/24th Inf. Enlisted Washington, DC, 7 Apr 1897; fined $6 by garrison court martial, Ft D. A. Russell, WY, 9 Feb 1899. SOURCE: Muster Roll, I/24 Inf, Jan–Feb 1899.

Fined one month's pay by garrison court martial, 23 Mar 1899. SOURCE: Muster Roll, I/24 Inf, Mar–Apr 1899.

Fined $8 by garrison court martial, 18 May 1899; fined $5 by garrison court martial, 27 May 1899. SOURCE: Muster Roll, I/24 Inf, May–Jun 1899.

GREENLEAF, Edward; Private; G/48th Inf. Died of variola in the Philippines, 3 May 1900. SOURCE: *ANJ* 37 (19 May 1900): 903.

GREENWOOD, Ceabron; Sergeant; I/9th Cav. Expert rifleman at Ft D. A. Russell, WY, in 1910; resident of Cleveland, AR. SOURCE: *Illustrated Review: Ninth Cavalry*, with picture.

GREENWOOD, George; Corporal; K/25th Inf. As first sergeant, K/25th Infantry, encouraged company YMCA, Castillejos, Philippines, 1900. SOURCE: Richmond *Planet*, 20 Oct 1900.

Corporal, K/25th Infantry, at Ft Niobrara, NE, 1904. SOURCE: Wilson, "History of Fort Niobrara."

GREER, Willis; Private; C/9th Cav. At Ft D. A. Russell, WY, in 1910; resident of Lyles, Gibson Co., IN. SOURCE: *Illustrated Review: Ninth Cavalry*, with picture.

GREGG; Private; K/9th Cav. At Ft Robinson, NE, 1887.

GREGG; Sergeant; C/9th Cav. Reenlistment, married, authorized by letter, Adjutant General's Office, 4 Apr 1895.

GREGG, John A.; QM Sgt; 23rd Kans Inf. Born Eureka, KS, 18 Feb 1877; graduated from high school in Eureka, 1897; graduated from Southern Kansas Academy science department, 1897, and entered Kansas State University, Lawrence; enlisted in 23rd Kansas, Jun 1898; after war, returned to Kansas State; graduated with bachelor of arts degree in 1902, only Negro graduate in class of 215; licensed to preach, 1899; pastorate in Emporia, KS, then South Africa, Leavenworth, KS, St. Joseph, MO, and president, Edward Waters College, Jacksonville, FL; deacon, 1903, and elder, 1906; doctor of divinity, Wilberforce University, 1915; married Miss Celia Ann Nelson of Lawrence, 21 Aug 1900. SOURCE: Wright, *Centennial Encyclopedia of the AME Church*, 99–100, with picture.

GREGGS, Austin; Private; C/24th Inf. Died of variola in the Philippines, 25 Dec 1899. SOURCE: *ANJ* 37 (20 Jan 1900): 488.

GREGGS, James; Private; L/10th Cav. Served in 10th Cavalry, 1898; remained in U.S. during war with Spain. SOURCE: Cashin, *Under Fire with the Tenth Cavalry*, 350.

GREGOR, William; Private; A/9th Cav. His sentence for desertion, which began 13 Sep 1875, reduced to eighteen months. SOURCE: GCMO 22, AGO, 23 Feb 1877.

GREGORY, John G.; Private; B/10th Cav. Served in 10th Cavalry, 1898; remained in U.S. during war with Spain. SOURCE: Cashin, *Under Fire with the Tenth Cavalry*, 339.

GREGORY, John T.; Sergeant; M/10th Cav. Enlisted, with brother Will, in B/10th Cavalry, Jul 1897; transferred to M/10th Cavalry as sergeant when war with Spain broke out; wounded in action at Santiago, Cuba, 2 Jul 1898, and carried to hospital by two privates of 1st Cavalry; at Ft McPherson, GA, hospital for one month before coming home to Indianapolis, IN; brother still in B/10th Cavalry. SOURCE: Indianapolis *Freeman*, 20 Aug 1898.

GREGORY, Nathanial; Private; E/24th Inf. Transferred from Reserve Divisional Hospital, Siboney, Cuba, to Fortress Monroe, VA, with yellow fever, via U.S. Army Transport *Concho*, 24 Jul 1898. SOURCE: Hospital Papers, Spanish-American War.

GREGORY, William; Private; B/10th Cav. Served in 10th Cavalry in Cuba, 1898. SOURCE: Cashin, *Under Fire with the Tenth Cavalry*, 338.

Wounded in action at Santiago, Cuba, 1 Jul 1898. SOURCE: SecWar, *AR 1898*, 324.

See **GREGORY**, John T., Sergeant, M/10th Cavalry

GRESON, William; B/10th Cav. Original member of 10th Cavalry; in troop when organized, Ft Leavenworth, KS, 1 Apr 1867. SOURCE: McMiller, "Buffalo Soldiers," 69.

GREY, Charles H.; Private; K/9th Cav. Funeral at Ft Robinson, NE, 17 Mar 1890. SOURCE: Order 54, 16 Mar 1890, Post Orders, Ft Robinson.

Died Ft Robinson, 16 Mar 1890. SOURCE: List of Interments, Ft Robinson.

GREY, John R.; Blacksmith; G/9th Cav. Denied privileges of Ft Robinson, NE, post exchange for non-payment of indebtedness; in effect until he pays in full. SOURCE: SO 42, 17 Apr 1897, Post Orders, Ft Robinson.

GREY, Lawrence T.; Private; D/25th Inf. Died of malaria in the Philippines, 26 Dec 1900. SOURCE: *ANJ* 38 (12 Jan 1901): 479.

GRICE, Theodore; Private; B/10th Cav. Served in 10th Cavalry in Cuba, 1898; wounded in action. SOURCE: Cashin, *Under Fire with the Tenth Cavalry*, 338–39.

GRIDER, Henry; B/10th Cav. Original member of 10th Cavalry; in troop when organized, Ft Leavenworth, KS, 1 Apr 1867. SOURCE: McMiller, "Buffalo Soldiers," 69.

GRIER, George; Cook; C/25th Inf. Dishonorable discharge, Brownsville. SOURCE: SO 266, AGO, 9 Nov 1906.

GRIFFIE, William; Private; D/24th Inf. At Cabanatuan, Philippines, 1901. *See* **MOORE**, Cato, Private, D/24th Infantry

GRIFFIN, Alfred E.; Private; C/10th Cav. Served in 10th Cavalry in Cuba, 1898. SOURCE: Cashin, *Under Fire with the Tenth Cavalry*, 340.

GRIFFIN, George; Musician; G/25th Inf. Retires. SOURCE: *ANJ* 28 (17 Jan 1891): 349.

GRIFFIN, George; Private; 10th Cav. Recruit, arrived Ft Robinson, NE, 7 May 1902.

GRIFFIN, Henry; B/10th Cav. Original member of 10th Cavalry; in troop when organized, Ft Leavenworth, KS, 1 Apr 1867. SOURCE: McMiller, "Buffalo Soldiers," 69.

GRIFFIN, Isaac; Private; D/24th Inf. His sentence in accordance with General Court Martial Order 3, Department of Texas, 4 Feb 1876, to be carried out at Kansas Penitentiary, Leavenworth. SOURCE: GCMO 42, AGO, 4 Apr 1876.

GRIFFIN, Jeremiah; Private; 10th Cav. Killed in action, Ojo Caliente, TX, 28 Oct 1880. SOURCE: Leckie, *The Buffalo Soldiers*, 230.

Killed in action, Ojo Caliente, 29 Oct 1880. SOURCE: Baker, Roster.

GRIFFIN, John; Sergeant; I/9th Cav. Shot and killed Cpl. William Taylor, I/9th Cavalry, in dining room just before Christmas feast, Ft Sheridan, IL, 1906. SOURCE: Washington *Post*, 26 Dec 1906.

GRIFFIN, Samuel; M/10th Cav. Original member of 10th Cavalry; in troop when organized, Ft Riley, KS, 15 Oct 1867. SOURCE: McMiller, "Buffalo Soldiers," 79.

GRIFFIN, Stephen; QM Sgt; K/9th Cav. Veteran of Philippine Insurrection; at Ft D. A. Russell, WY, in 1910; resident of Manchester, KY. SOURCE: *Illustrated Review: Ninth Cavalry*, with picture.

GRIFFIN, Thomas; Sergeant; C/10th Cav. Born in Kentucky; private, C/10th Cavalry, 23 Apr 1879; corporal, 1 Jul 1890; sergeant, 1 Jul 1891; at Ft Assiniboine, MT, 1897. SOURCE: Baker, Roster.

Trumpeter, C/10th Cavalry; at Ft Apache, AZ, 1890, subscribed $.50 to testimonial to General Grierson. SOURCE: List of subscriptions, 23 Apr 1890, 10th Cavalry papers, MHI.

Served in 10th Cavalry in Cuba, 1898. SOURCE: Cashin, *Under Fire with the Tenth Cavalry*, 339.

Cut barbed wire at base of San Juan, Cuba, 1 Jul 1898, according to letter, Sgt. William Ancrum, C/10th Cavalry. SOURCE: Cashin, *Under Fire with the Tenth Cavalry*, 190.

His heroism in Cuba slighted, according to unsigned letter [John E. Lewis, H/10th Cavalry], Montauk, NY. SOURCE: Gatewood, *"Smoked Yankees"*, 78.

GRIFFITH, William B.; Private; B/9th Cav. Relieved from daily duty at post canteen, Ft Robinson, NE, by Pvt. E. W. Maden, F/9th Cavalry. SOURCE: Order 131, [?] Jun 1890, Post Orders, Ft Robinson.

GRIFFITH, William B.; Sergeant; I/24th Inf. Transferred from 25th Infantry to M/10th Cavalry. SOURCE: SO 2, AGO, 4 Jan 1904.

Promoted from corporal to sergeant, I/24th Infantry, Warwick Barracks, Cebu, Philippines. SOURCE: Order 12, I/24, 1 Nov 1906, Name File, 24 Inf.

GRIGGS, Marcellus; Private; D/9th Cav. At Ft D. A. Russell, WY, in 1910; resident of Cuero, TX. SOURCE: *Illustrated Review: Ninth Cavalry*, with picture.

GRIGGS, Richard; Private; L/24th Inf. Served in Houston, 1917; involved in racial incident on trolley, 19 Aug 1917; in jail at time of mutiny for violating local Jim Crow laws. SOURCE: Haynes, *A Night of Violence*, 87, 91, 192.

GRIGGS, William H.; Private; H/24th Inf. Enlisted Richmond, VA, 10 Nov 1897; four years' continuous service. SOURCE: Muster Roll, H/24 Inf, Mar–Apr 1898.

Sick in hospital, Siboney, Cuba, 8–25 Aug 1898 and en route to U.S., 25–31 Aug 1898, disease contracted in line of duty. SOURCE: Muster Roll, H/24 Inf, Jul–Aug 1898.

Died at Camp Wikoff, NY, 9 Sep 1898; deposits $15; due U.S. for clothing $1.91. SOURCE: Muster Roll, H/24 Inf, Sep–Oct 1898.

GRIGSBY, Jeff; Private; H/9th Cav. Born Baton Rouge, LA; enlisted, age 19, laborer, Ht 5'5", dark complexion, single, Ft Leavenworth, KS, 14 Jun 1898; joined unit at Camp Wikoff, NY, 27 Aug 1898; discharged at Ft Wingate, NM, 26 Jan 1899, in accordance with telegram, Adjutant General's Office, 24 Jan 1899; reenlisted, Ft Wingate, 12 Mar 1899; fined $5 by summary court, Guinobatan, Philippines, 10 Dec 1900; sentenced to dishonorable discharge and four months, at Guinobatan, 20 Mar 1901, in accordance with Special Order 66, Department of Southern Luzon, 7 Mar 1901.

GRILLS, Eugene H.; Sergeant; I/24th Inf. Private, enlisted Huntington, WV, 14 Mar 1899. SOURCE: Muster Roll, I/24 Inf, Mar–Apr 1899.

Fined $5 by summary court, 25 Sep 1899. SOURCE: Muster Roll, I/24 Inf, Sep–Oct 1899.

Sergeant, West Virginian, and Spanish-American War veteran who stayed in the Philippines; died at age 56 after seventeen years as superintendent of transportation, Manila Electrical Company; widow Antonia Penaflor is 87. SOURCE: Thompson, "Veterans Who Never Came Home," 106.

GRIMES, James; Sergeant; B/24th Inf. Corporal, B/24th Infantry, wounded in Cuba, 1898. SOURCE: Muller, *The Twenty Fourth Infantry*, 18.

Retired sergeant, owns three lots and ten acres at Allensworth, CA. SOURCE: Beasley, *Negro Trailblazers*, 156.

GRIMES, Willie; Private; B/9th Cav. At Ft D. A. Russell, WY, in 1910. SOURCE: *Illustrated Review: Ninth Cavalry*, with picture.

GRIMES, Woody W.; Private; F/9th Cav. At Ft D. A. Russell, WY, in 1910; resident of Parsons, KS. SOURCE: *Illustrated Review: Ninth Cavalry*.

GRIMKE, Washington; Private; A/9th Cav. *See* **GRUNKE**, Washington, Private, A/9th Cavalry

GRISHON, David; Trumpeter; I/9th Cav. At Ft D. A. Russell, WY, in 1910; sharpshooter; resident of Canton, GA. SOURCE: *Illustrated Review: Ninth Cavalry*, with picture.

GRISSEN, Daniel; H/10th Cav. Original member of 10th Cavalry; in troop when organized, Ft Leavenworth, KS, 21 Jul 1867. SOURCE: McMiller, "Buffalo Soldiers," 75.

GRISWOLD, Sam; 25th Inf. Arrested and fined $40 for drunken shooting, Missoula, MT, Nov 1889. SOURCE: Fowler, *The Black Infantry*, 67.

GROCE, John; Private; E/10th Cav. Transferred to Hospital Corps. SOURCE: *ANJ* 25 (10 Dec 1887): 382.

GROOMS, George A.; Private; I/24th Inf. Enlisted Baltimore, MD, 8 Feb 1899. SOURCE: Muster Roll, I/24 Inf, Jan–Feb 1899.

Fined $3 by garrison court martial, 4 May 1899. SOURCE: Muster Roll, I/24 Inf, May–Jun 1899.

Fined $5 by summary court, 2 Nov 1899; fined $5 by summary court, 14 Dec 1899. SOURCE: Muster Roll, I/24 Inf, Nov–Dec 1899.

GROSE, Henry; Private; H/10th Cav. Set at liberty from Kansas Penitentiary, where he was serving in accordance with General Court Martial Order 29, Adjutant General's Office, 18 Jun 1868; unexpired portion of sentence remitted. SOURCE: GCMO 73, AGO, 2 Jun 1876.

GROSS, D. J.; Sergeant; F/9th Cav. Killed in action on headwaters of Rio Perches, 12 Jan 1880, along with Pvt. I. H. James, F/9th Cavalry. SOURCE: Hamilton, "History of the Ninth Cavalry," 52; *Illustrated Review: Ninth Cavalry*.

GROSS, Harry; Private; C/9th Cav. Transferred from F/9th Cavalry to C/9th Cavalry and attached to Band/9th Cavalry for instruction in music, Ft Robinson, NE. SOURCE: Order 16, 9 Cav, 26 May 1887.

See **WHITING**, John, Private, F/9th Cavalry

GROSS, Robert G. Sergeant-at-arms, Col. Charles Young Camp No. 24, National Indian War Veterans, Washington, DC. SOURCE: *Winners of the West* 6 (Jun 1929): 4.

GROSS, Thomas; Private; C/9th Cav. Recruit, Colored Detachment, Mounted Service, Jefferson Barracks, MO, 1888. *See* **GUNTER**, William H., Recruit, Colored Detachment/Mounted Service

Enlisted Ft McKinney, WY, 12 Mar 1894.

Charges against him contained in letter, Department of the Platte, 7 Sep 1895, are withdrawn by letter, Department of the Platte, 16 Sep 1895.

Reenlistment, married, authorized by letter, Adjutant General's Office, 14 Oct 1896.

GROSS, W.; Private; E/9th Cav. On detached service in field, New Mexico, 27 Jan–1 Feb 1881. SOURCE: Regt Returns, 9 Cav, Feb 1881.

GROVER, John; Private; F/10th Cav. Served in 10th Cavalry in Cuba, 1898. SOURCE: Cashin, *Under Fire with the Tenth Cavalry*, 344.

GROVES, Wills; Private; I/10th Cav. Served in 10th Cavalry in Cuba, 1898. SOURCE: Cashin, *Under Fire with the Tenth Cavalry*, 348.

GRUBE, Howard A.; Captain; 48th Inf. One of nineteen officers of 48th Infantry recommended as regular Army second lieutenants. SOURCE: CG, DivPI, Manila, 8 Feb 1901, to AGO, AGO File 355163.

GRUNKE, Washington; Private; 9th Cav. He and Sgt. Bush Johnson killed by "a desperate horse thief," while taking him from Henrietta, TX, to Ft Sill, Indian Territory, Aug 1882. SOURCE: Hamilton, "History of the Ninth Cavalry," 64; *Illustrated Review: Ninth Cavalry.*

GUDDY, P.; Trumpeter; D/9th Cav. Wounded in action against Victorio, 6–7 Apr 1880, along with Private Morgan, D/9th Cavalry. SOURCE: Hamilton, "History of the Ninth Cavalry," 51; *Illustrated Review: Ninth Cavalry.*

With troop when it left Ft Riley, KS, for three-month march into Indian Territory, Feb 1885. SOURCE: Regt Returns, 9 Cav, Feb 1885.

GUILFORD, Alfred; Private; C/10th Cav. Discharged on certificate of disability with chronic gonorrhea, Ft Robinson, NE, 15 Nov 1902. SOURCE: Certificates of Disability, Ft Robinson.

GUILLORY, Jerome; Private; D/9th Cav. At Ft D. A. Russell, WY, in 1910; resident of Louisville. SOURCE: *Illustrated Review: Ninth Cavalry*, with picture.

GULLION, George W.; Private; B/10th Cav. Served in 10th Cavalry in Cuba, 1898. SOURCE: Cashin, *Under Fire with the Tenth Cavalry*, 338.

GULLION, John; Private; B/10th Cav. Served in 10th Cavalry in Cuba, 1898. SOURCE: Cashin, *Under Fire with the Tenth Cavalry*, 338.

GULLIVER, Cassius M.; Private; I/10th Cav. Sentenced to dishonorable discharge and three years for desertion by general court martial, Columbia Barracks, WA. SOURCE: GCMO 6, AGO, 29 Jan 1879.

GUNN, J.; Private; A/9th Cav. At Ft Stanton, NM, 1881. SOURCE: Regt Returns, 9 Cav, Jan 1881.

GUNN, W. P.; 24th Inf. At Ft Douglas, UT; fined for drunkenness and carrying machete, Salt Lake City, UT, police court, 1896. SOURCE: Clark, "A History of the Twenty-fourth," 84–85.

GUNN, William; Private; A/24th Inf. On extra duty as teamster, Quartermaster Department. SOURCE: Order 163, Ft Huachuca, 2 Nov 1893, Name File, 24 Inf.

GUNTER, James; Private; G/9th Cav. Served as private, C/10th Cavalry, 1898; remained in U.S. during war with Spain. SOURCE: Cashin, *Under Fire with the Tenth Cavalry*, 340.

Veteran of Spanish-American War and Philippine Insurrection; private, G/9th Cavalry, at Ft D. A. Russell, WY, in 1910; resident of Atlanta. SOURCE: *Illustrated Review: Ninth Cavalry.*

GUNTER, Ulysses G.; Sergeant; I/10th Cav. Born in Virginia; private, I/10th Cavalry, 16 Jul 1892; corporal, 1 Mar 1896; stationed at Ft Assiniboine, MT, 1897. SOURCE: Baker, Roster.

Served in 10th Cavalry in Cuba, 1898. SOURCE: Cashin, *Under Fire with the Tenth Cavalry*, 347.

Wounded in action at Santiago, Cuba, 1 Jul 1898. SOURCE: SecWar, *AR 1898*, 324.

GUNTER, Wash; Private; H/24th Inf. Sentenced by summary court to fifteen days and $10 fine for insubordinate language to noncommissioned officer, San Isidro, Philippines, 5 Nov 1901, first conviction. SOURCE: Register of Summary Court, San Isidro.

GUNTER, William H.; Recruit; Colored Detachment/Mounted Service. Convicted by general court martial of striking without provocation and seriously injuring Recruit Thomas Gross, Colored Detachment, Mounted Service, Jefferson Barracks, MO, 21 Dec 1888; also broke carbine stock, same date; sentenced to dishonorable discharge and two years. SOURCE: GCMO 2, AGO, 18 Jan 1889.

GURNELL, Oscar; Private; E/10th Cav. Served in 10th Cavalry in Cuba, 1898. SOURCE: Cashin, *Under Fire with the Tenth Cavalry*, 342.

Departed Ft Robinson, NE, to join his troop at Ft D. A. Russell, WY, 4 Jan 1903.

GUTRIDGE; Private; I/10th Cav. His general court martial discussed. SOURCE: SO 142, DeptMo, 30 Jul 1902.

GUY, Frank; Recruit; Colored Detachment/ Mounted Service. Convicted by general court martial, Jefferson Barracks, MO, for enlisting fraudulently, representing that he had never been discharged before by court sentence; had been dishonorably discharged in accordance with Special Order 209, Adjutant General's Office, 1892, for fraudulent enlistment and served term in U.S. Military Prison pursuant to general court martial sentence; sentenced to dishonorable discharge and one year at Military Prison, Leavenworth, KS. SOURCE: GCMO 87, AGO, 12 Aug 1893.

GUY, John R.; Blacksmith; G/9th Cav. Died aboard U.S. Army Transport *Yucatan* bound for Camp Wikoff, NY. SOURCE: *ANJ* 36 (3 Sep 1898): 19.

Died at sea en route from Cuba to Camp Wikoff. SOURCE: Cleveland *Gazette*, 3 Sep 1898.

GUYWN, Edward; Farrier; E/10th Cav. At Ft Apache, AZ, 1890, subscribed $.50 to testimonial to General Grierson. SOURCE: List of subscriptions, 23 Apr 1890, 10th Cavalry papers, MHI.

GYNN, Edward; Private; H/10th Cav. Served in 10th Cavalry, 1898; remained in U.S. during war with Spain. SOURCE: Cashin, *Under Fire with the Tenth Cavalry*, 346.

H

HACKET, Robert; E/10th Cav. Original member of 10th Cavalry; in troop when organized, Ft Leavenworth, KS, 15 Jun 1867. SOURCE: McMiller, "Buffalo Soldiers," 72.

HADDOX, Press; Sergeant; M/10th Cav. After discharge at end of term as sergeant, K/10th Cavalry, Dec 1885, established store in old adobe building rented for $1 per month with Pvt. John Hall of K/10th Cavalry at Mowry Mine, AZ; stocked liquor, cigars, some clothing; renovated building with aid of men in 10th Cavalry and named store Hall & Haddox. SOURCE: Bigelow, *On the Bloody Trail of Geronimo*, 99.

At Ft Apache, AZ, 1890, subscribed $.50 to testimonial to General Grierson. SOURCE: List of subscriptions, 23 Apr 1890, 10th Cavalry papers, MHI.

Mentioned as survivor of Indian wars. SOURCE: *Winners of the West* 3 (Jun 1926): 7.

Wants to hear from old boys; served five years in E/25th Infantry, five years in K/10th Cavalry, five years in M/10th Cavalry, two years in general mounted service, three years in F/24th Infantry. SOURCE: *Winners of the West* 6 (Dec 1929): 5.

Died. SOURCE: *Winners of the West* 8 (Jul 1932): 5.

HAGEN, Abram; Sergeant; G/24th Inf. Commended for distinguished service, battle of Santiago, Cuba, 1 Jul 1898, as corporal, G/24th Infantry; awarded certificate of merit. SOURCE: GO 15, AGO, 13 Feb 1900.

Certificate of merit mentioned. SOURCE: Steward, *The Colored Regulars*, 280; *ANJ* 37 (24 Feb 1900): 611; Scipio, *Last of the Black Regulars*, 130.

Wounded in action in Cuba, 1898. SOURCE: Muller, *The Twenty Fourth Infantry*, 98.

HAGER; Private; B/10th Cav. At Ft Apache, AZ, 1890, subscribed $.50 to testimonial to General Grierson. SOURCE: List of subscriptions, 23 Apr 1890, 10th Cavalry papers, MHI.

HAGUE, Lucious J.; Corporal; E/9th Cav. Promoted from lance corporal, E/9th Cavalry, Ft Robinson, NE, 10 May 1895. SOURCE: *ANJ* 32 (25 May 1895): 642.

Corporal, K/9th Cavalry, ranked number 75 among rifle experts with 75 percent, 1905. SOURCE: GO 101, AGO, 31 May 1906.

Veteran of Spanish-American War and Philippine Insurrection; corporal, E/9th Cavalry, at Ft D. A. Russell, WY, in 1910; sharpshooter. SOURCE: *Illustrated Review: Ninth Cavalry*, with picture.

HAILEY, Benjamin; Private; K/49th Inf. In the Philippines, 1900. See **BLUNT**, Hamilton H., Captain, K/49th Infantry

HAILSTALK, James; C/10th Cav. Original member of 10th Cavalry; in troop when organized, Ft Leavenworth, KS, 14 May 1867. SOURCE: McMiller, "Buffalo Soldiers," 70.

HAINER, Levi; M/10th Cav. Original member of 10th Cavalry; in troop when organized, Ft Riley, KS, 15 Oct 1867. SOURCE: McMiller, "Buffalo Soldiers," 79.

HAINES, Jack; E/24th Inf. At Ft Bayard, NM, 1893–96. *See* **BROWN**, Thomas Hatcher, E/24th Infantry

HAINES, Peter; Private; G/9th Cav. Killed in action against Victorio, Las Animas River, NM, 18 Sep 1879. SOURCE: Hamilton, "History of the Ninth Cavalry," 46; *Illustrated Review: Ninth Cavalry*.

HAINES, Reuben F.; Artificer; A/24th Inf. Retires from Ft Douglas, UT. SOURCE: *ANJ* 34 (26 Jun 1897): 801

HAINES, William; Sergeant; G/24th Inf. At Ft Brown, TX, 1872. *See* **SMITH**, John, Private, H/24th Infantry

HAIRSTON, Charley; Private; B/25th Inf. Dishonorable discharge, Brownsville. SOURCE: SO 266, AGO, 9 Nov 1906.

HAIRSTON, William; Private; C/10th Cav. Born in North Carolina; age 26; accidentally killed, Ft Robinson, NE, 25 May 1903; body shipped to Pittsburgh. SOURCE: Monthly Report, Chaplain Anderson, Ft Robinson, 1 Jun 1903.

Accidentally shot at target practice on morning of 25 May 1903; died around eleven A.M. SOURCE: Post Surgeon to CO, C/10, 25 May 1903, LS, Post Surgeon, Ft Robinson.

HAITMAN, James S.; 1st Sgt; B/9th Cav. At Ft D. A. Russell, WY, in 1910; sharpshooter. SOURCE: *Illustrated Review: Ninth Cavalry*.

HALE; Private; B/10th Cav. At Ft Apache, AZ, 1890, subscribed $.50 to testimonial to General Grierson. SOURCE: List of subscriptions, 23 Apr 1890, 10th Cavalry papers, MHI.

HALE, Andrew J.; Sergeant; G/10th Cav. Ranked number 375 among rifle experts with 69.33 percent, 1905. SOURCE: GO 101, AGO, 31 May 1906.

HALE, Harvey; M/10th Cav. Original member of 10th Cavalry; in troop when organized, Ft Riley, KS, 15 Oct 1867. SOURCE: McMiller, "Buffalo Soldiers," 79.

HALE, James D.; Private; M/10th Cav. Served in 10th Cavalry, 1898; remained in U.S. during war with Spain. SOURCE: Cashin, *Under Fire with the Tenth Cavalry*, 351.

HALE, Joseph; Recruit; Colored Detachment/ General Service. Convicted by general court martial, Columbus Barracks, OH, of allowing prisoner Pvt. Daniel Huffman, Battery D, 5th Artillery, to escape, 20 Jan 1887; sentenced to two months and $10 fine for two months; conviction disapproved as not sustained by evidence, by Lt. Gen. William T. Sherman; Hale released to duty. SOURCE: GCMO 15, AGO, 15 Feb 1887.

HALE, Lewis; F/10th Cav. Original member of 10th Cavalry; in troop when organized, Ft Leavenworth, KS, 21 Jun 1867. SOURCE: McMiller, "Buffalo Soldiers," 73.

HALE, Moses; Private; K/24th Inf. Fined $15 for being unable to perform mounted guard, Cabanatuan, Philippines, as too drunk to ride and needing to be carried in wagon, 11 Feb 1901; witnesses: Sgt. George Driscoll, D/24th Infantry, and Pvt. Charles Allen, D/24th Infantry. SOURCE: Name File, 24 Inf.

HALE, U.; Private; 10th Cav. Recruit, arrived Ft Robinson, NE, 7 May 1902.

HALE, Wesley; F/9th Cav. Served 1875–80; eighty years old; resides in Topeka, KS, with pension of $50 per month; subscribes. SOURCE: *Winners of the West* 5 (Apr 1928): 6.

HALE, William; E/10th Cav. Original member of 10th Cavalry; in troop when organized, Ft Leavenworth, KS, 15 Jun 1867. SOURCE: McMiller, "Buffalo Soldiers," 72.

HALEY, Alonzo; Private; D/24th Inf. Dishonorable discharge, Brownsville. SOURCE: SO 266, AGO, 9 Nov 1906.

HALEY, Frank; Private; H/48th Inf. Died of variola in the Philippines, 3 Jun 1900. SOURCE: *ANJ* 37 (16 Jun 1900): 999.

HALEY, James; Wagoner; D/9th Cav. Veteran of Philippine Insurrection; at Ft D. A. Russell, WY, in 1910; resident of Frankfort. KY. SOURCE: *Illustrated Review: Ninth Cavalry,* with picture.

HALL; Private; A/10th Cav. At Ft Apache, AZ, 1890, subscribed $.50 to testimonial to General Grierson. SOURCE: List of subscriptions, 23 Apr 1890, 10th Cavalry papers, MHI.

HALL, Arthur; Private; I/9th Cav. At Ft D. A. Russell, WY, in 1910; resident of Birmingham. AL. SOURCE: *Illustrated Review: Ninth Cavalry.*

HALL, Brice; Private; F/10th Cav. Resided at 333 Winnie Street, Paris, KY, in 1922. SOURCE: VA File SC 11405, John Taylor.

HALL, Christian; E/9th Cav. Mentioned as surviving Indian War veteran. SOURCE: *Winners of the West* 3 (Jun 1926): 7.

HALL, Clarence; Private; D/10th Cav. Served in 10th Cavalry in Cuba, 1898. SOURCE: Cashin, *Under Fire with the Tenth Cavalry*, 341.

HALL, Clarence; Private; I/10th Cav. Served in 10th Cavalry in Cuba, 1898. SOURCE: Cashin, *Under Fire with the Tenth Cavalry*, 348.

HALL, David; H/10th Cav. Transferred from A/10th Cavalry. SOURCE: SO 307, AGO, 19 Dec 1903.

HALL, Fayette; Private; E/9th Cav. 1st Lt. Edward Heyle charged with tying Hall up by the thumbs and striking him with sabre, camp near San Antonio, TX, 9 Apr 1867.

HALL, George C.; Sergeant; L/10th Cav. Commissioned captain, Camp Des Moines, IA, 15 Oct 1917. SOURCE: Glass, *History of the Tenth Cavalry*, appendix M.

An able noncommissioned officer who was commissioned a captain of infantry during World War I and was returned at his own request at Ft Apache, AZ, to sergeant. SOURCE: Wharfield, *10th Cavalry and Border Fights*, 97.

HALL, George W.; Private; D/25th Inf. Dishonorable discharge, Brownsville. SOURCE: SO 266, AGO, 9 Nov 1906.

HALL, Harry; Private; G/25th Inf. Served in 1898. SOURCE: Nankivell, *History of the Twenty-fifth Infantry*, 67.

HALL, Henry; Private; A/10th Cav. Admitted to Soldiers Home with disability at age 39 with fourteen years and eleven months' service, 24 Mar 1885. SOURCE: SecWar, *AR 1885*, 829.

HALL, James; Private; I/24th Inf. Enlisted Baltimore, MD, 29 Jul 1898. SOURCE: Muster Roll, I/24 Inf, Jan–Feb 1899.

On detached service, Three Rivers, CA, 3 May–21 Jun 1899, and on detached service, Presidio of San Francisco, CA, 22 Jun–26 Jul 1899. SOURCE: Muster Roll, I/24 Inf, May–Jun and Jul–Aug 1899.

Discharged, character good, with $25 deposits and $6.59 clothing, 31 Dec 1899. SOURCE: Muster Roll, I/24 Inf, Nov–Dec 1899.

HALL, James B.; Private; A/10th Cav. Served in 10th Cavalry, 1898; remained in U.S. during war with Spain. SOURCE: Cashin, *Under Fire with the Tenth Cavalry*, 337.

HALL, John; Private; K/10th Cav. Discharged, end of term, Dec 1885. *See* **BRANSFORD**, Wesley, Private, K/10th Cavalry; **HADDOX**, Press, Sergeant, M/10th Cavalry

HALL, John W.; Sergeant; B/24th Inf. Corporal, B/24th Infantry, wounded in action in Cuba, 1898. SOURCE: Muller, *The Twenty Fourth Infantry*, 18.

Sergeant at Cabanatuan, Philippines, 1901. *See* **COOK**, Julius, Private, B/24th Infantry

HALL, Lafayette; Blacksmith; A/10th Cav. Served in 10th Cavalry in Cuba, 1898. SOURCE: Cashin, *Under Fire with the Tenth Cavalry*, 336.

HALL, Raymond; Private; F/9th Cav. At Ft D. A. Russell, WY, in 1910; resident of Chicago. SOURCE: *Illustrated Review: Ninth Cavalry,* with picture.

HALL, Thomas; Private; H/9th Cav. Killed Pvt. Amos Palmer with pistol in fight, Ft McKinney, WY, 2 Nov 1887.

In hands of civil authorities, Buffalo, WY, until 29 Jan 1888. SOURCE: Regt Returns, 9 Cav, Jan 1888.

HALL, Thomas E.; Private; E/9th Cav. At Ft D. A. Russell, WY, in 1910. SOURCE: *Illustrated Review: Ninth Cavalry,* with picture.

HALL, William; Private; M/10th Cav. Convicted by general court martial, Jefferson Barracks, MO, of desertion, 25 Jun 1884–7 Jun 1887; sentenced to dishonorable discharge and four years. SOURCE: GCMO 65, AGO, 25 Aug 1887.

HAM, James; Sergeant; B/24th Inf. To report to Assistant Surgeon Ebert for special duty in post garden, Ft Huachuca, AZ, along with Private Brent, A/24th Infantry; Artificer Cyrus, A/24th Infantry; Private Robertson, B/24th Infantry; Private Smith, H/24th Infantry; Private Varnes, H/24th Infantry. SOURCE: Order 74, Ft Huachuca, 28 May 1893, Letters & Orders Received, 24 Inf, 1893.

HAMBRIGHT; Private; B/24th Inf. On detached service, to report to acting post engineer, Ft Huachuca, AZ, 1st Lt. Joseph B. Batchelor, Jr. SOURCE: Order 115, Ft Huachuca, 5 Aug 1893, Name File, 24 Inf.

HAMBRIGHT, Peter; Private; Band/10th Cav. Served in 10th Cavalry in Cuba, 1898. SOURCE: Cashin, *Under Fire with the Tenth Cavalry*, 359.

HAMES, Thomas; Private; H/10th Cav. Served in 10th Cavalry, 1898; remained in U.S. during war with Spain. SOURCE: Cashin, *Under Fire with the Tenth Cavalry*, 346.

HAMILTON, Albert; Corporal; F/9th Cav. Private, A/9th Cavalry; teacher, Ft Robinson, NE, school, 27 Feb–30 Apr 1893. SOURCE: Report of Schools, Ft Robinson, 1892–96.

Witness for prosecution in general court martial of Sgt. Barney McKay, G/9th Cavalry, Ft Robinson, 1893.

Promoted from private, F/9th Cavalry, Ft Duchesne, UT, 22 Jun 1894. SOURCE: *ANJ* 31 (4 Aug 1894): 858.

HAMILTON, Arthur; Private; B/10th Cav. Served in 10th Cavalry in Cuba, 1898. SOURCE: Cashin, *Under Fire with the Tenth Cavalry*, 338.

HAMILTON, Charles; Private; G/10th Cav. Deserter received at Ft Leavenworth, KS. SOURCE: CO, 7 Cav, to CO, 10 Cav, 12 Oct 1870, ES, 10 Cav, 1866–71.

HAMILTON, Denmark; Recruit; 10th Cav. Mentioned Apr 1867. SOURCE: LS, 10 Cav, 1866–67.

HAMILTON, Edward; Private; Band/10th Cav. Mentioned Apr 1873 as having been discharged, Ft Gibson, Indian Territory. SOURCE: ES, 10 Cav, 1873–81.

HAMILTON, Edward; Private; C/9th Cav. Deserted from Ft Robinson, NE, 17 Jul 1886.

HAMILTON, George; Private; L/49th Inf. In the Philippines, 1900. *See* **CLAY**, Henry, Private, L/49th Infantry

HAMILTON, J. H.; 24th Inf. President, Western Star Literary Club, Ft Reno, Indian Territory, which gave grand ball, 18 Jun 1887; other officers: J. Campbell, secretary; E. L. Crawford, treasurer; also J. S. Miner and C. C. Mathews; total membership, twenty-five. SOURCE: Cleveland *Gazette*, 2 Jul 1887.

HAMILTON, Paul; Private; F/9th Cav. Relieved from duty at regimental headquarters, Santa Fe, NM; to join his unit at Ft Stanton, NM. SOURCE: Order 31, 27 Jun 1879, Regimental Orders, 9 Cav.

Fined and jailed for thirty days for theft, Ft Cummings, NM, Dec 1880. SOURCE: Billington, *New Mexico's Buffalo Soldiers*, 130.

HAMILTON, Thomas; E/10th Cav. Original member of 10th Cavalry; in troop when organized, Ft Leavenworth, KS, 15 Jun 1867. SOURCE: McMiller, "Buffalo Soldiers," 72.

Enlisted St. Louis, MO, spring 1867. SOURCE: LS, 10 Cav, 1866–67.

HAMILTON, William; Private; F/24th Inf. Died in Cuba, 29 Aug 1898. SOURCE: *ANJ* 36 (11 Feb 1899): 567.

HAMILTON, William H.; Sergeant; D/10th Cav. Born in Tennessee; private, D/10th Cavalry, 20 Feb 1895;

corporal, 20 Jan 1896; at Ft Assiniboine, MT, 1897. SOURCE: Baker, *Roster.*

Promoted to sergeant, 5 Nov 1897. SOURCE: *ANJ* 35 (20 Nov 1897): 212.

Served in 10th Cavalry in Cuba, 1898. SOURCE: Cashin, *Under Fire with the Tenth Cavalry,* 341.

Heroism in Cuba mentioned in unsigned letter [John E. Lewis, H/10th Cavalry], Montauk, NY, 8 Oct 1898. SOURCE: Gatewood, *"Smoked Yankees",* 80.

Commissioned captain, 49th Infantry, as of 9 Sep 1899; ordered to report at Jefferson Barracks, MO. SOURCE: *ANJ* 37 (7 Oct 1899): 123.

Ranked number ten on Northern Division Pistol Team, Ft Riley, KS, 1904; also number ten, Army Pistol Team competition, Ft Riley, 18–19 Aug 1904; twelfth best in Army. SOURCE: GO 167, AGO, 28 Oct 1904; Glass, *History of the Tenth Cavalry,* 44–45.

Ranked number one, gold medal, in Northern Division pistol competition, Ft Riley, 1905; Distinguished Pistol Shot. SOURCE: GO 173, AGO, 20 Oct 1905; Glass, *History of the Tenth Cavalry,* 44–45.

Ranked number six, silver medal and $15, National Pistol Match, Sea Girt, NJ, 1906. SOURCE: GO 190, AGO, 15 Nov 1906.

Ranked number six, Army Pistol Team competition, Ft Sheridan, IL, 1906; Distinguished Pistol Shot. SOURCE: GO 198, AGO, 6 Dec 1906.

Sergeant, D/10th Cavalry; son Woodrow Henry Hamilton, second child, born to wife Rosa Arnold Hamilton, Ft Robinson, NE, 20 Jul 1906. SOURCE: Medical History, Ft Robinson.

HAMILTON, William M.; Private; A/9th Cav. Relieved from extra duty as laborer, Quartermaster Department, Ft Robinson, NE. SOURCE: Special Order 90, 20 Aug 1896, Post Orders, Ft Robinson.

HAMLIN, James E.; Captain; A/48th Inf. Born Raleigh, NC; worked as tailor, then worked at Raleigh post office before opening fish market, which he quit to enter dining car service, then returned to Raleigh and opened restaurant; captain, B/32nd North Carolina Volunteers, during Spanish-American War; captain, 48th Infantry; returned to Raleigh, opened drugstore, 1904; owned two drugstores, lunchroom, and large farm, 1919; member, African Methodist Episcopal Church; secretary, Negro State Fair, North Carolina, twelve years; only Negro notary, Raleigh; connected with North Carolina Mutual Industrial Association; owns home, store, fourteen rental houses, and farm valued at $6,800; total wealth estimated at $65,000 to $78,000; married Annie W. Foushee of Raleigh, 1885; two children Annie Ethel, now Mrs. Rogers, and Dr. V. C. Hamlin of Raleigh. SOURCE: Richardson, *National Cyclopedia,* 290.

One of nineteen officers of 48th Infantry recommended as regular Army second lieutenants. SOURCE: CG, DivPI, Manila, 8 Feb 1901, to AGO, AGO File 355163.

Mentioned. SOURCE: Beasley, *Negro Trailblazers,* 284.

HAMLIN, Thomas; Corporal; K/25th Inf. At Ft Niobrara, NE, 1904. SOURCE: Wilson, "History of Fort Niobrara."

HAMMIN, Wyle; A/10th Cav. Original member of 10th Cavalry; in troop when organized, Ft Leavenworth, KS, 18 Feb 1867. SOURCE: McMiller, "Buffalo Soldiers," 68.

HAMMOCK, Charles E.; Sergeant; Band/9th Cav. Veteran of Philippine Insurrection; at Ft D. A. Russell, WY, in 1910; resident of Boston. SOURCE: *Illustrated Review: Ninth Cavalry,* with picture.

HAMMOND, George; Private; A/38th Inf. At Ft Selden, NM, Oct 1869; arrested with Pvt. James Gibson, A/38th Infantry, for murder of teamster Leandro Benardo. SOURCE: Billington, *New Mexico's Buffalo Soldiers,* 35.

HAMMOND, Noah; Private; I/24th Inf. Enlisted Pittsburgh, 26 Jun 1898; on special duty as teamster, 4 Feb 1899. SOURCE: Muster Roll, I/24 Inf, Jan–Feb 1899.

Appointed corporal, 3 May 1899. SOURCE: Muster Roll, I/24 Inf, May–Jun 1899.

Reduced to private, 21 Oct 1899; fined one month's pay by summary court, 27 Oct 1899. SOURCE: Muster Roll, I/24 Inf, Sep–Oct 1899.

Discharged, character good, owes government $7.33 for clothing, 31 Dec 1899. SOURCE: Muster Roll, I/24 Inf, Nov–Dec 1899.

HAMMOND, Pleasant H.; Sergeant; G/24th Inf. Private, G/24th Infantry; wounded in action, Cuba, 1898. SOURCE: Muller, *The Twenty Fourth Infantry,* 19.

Sergeant, G/24th Infantry, died of dysentery in the Philippines, 11 Dec 1900. SOURCE: *ANJ* 38 (29 Dec 1900): 431.

HAMMOND, Thomas C.; Principal Musician; Band/10th Cav. Private, Band/10th Cavalry; served in 10th Cavalry in Cuba, 1898. SOURCE: Cashin, *Under Fire with the Tenth Cavalry,* 359.

From Pittsburgh; plays violin and cornet; at Ft Robinson, NE. SOURCE: Lowe, "Camp Life," 206.

Played Rossini solo in concert, Crawford, NE, Saturday, 11 Jun 1905. SOURCE: Crawford *Tribune,* 16 Jun 1905.

Ira T. Bryant of Washington, DC, protests reenlistment of George F. Tyrell as chief musician, 10th Cavalry, on basis of "no competent colored man"; suggests Hammond, solo B-flat cornet and first violin, who is competent instructor and leader; decision to keep Tyrell "is discouraging to all colored army musicians." SOURCE: Bryant to SecWar, 12 Aug 1907, AGO File 1285422.

HAMMOND, Wade H.; Chief Musician; Band/9th Cav. Appointed from Western University, Quindaro, KS, where he had been bandmaster for two years. SOURCE: Cleveland *Gazette,* 25 Sep 1909.

His band gave successful concert for African Methodist Episcopal Church in Kiefe Hall, Cheyenne, WY; "perhaps the most accomplished negro musician in the service and deserves all the laurels that have come to him since his venture in the service." SOURCE: Cheyenne *Daily Leader*, 23 Mar 1910.

At Ft D. A. Russell, WY, in 1910; resident of Durham, NC. SOURCE: *Illustrated Review: Ninth Cavalry*, with picture.

On soldiers' trolley boycott committee, Ft D. A. Russell. SOURCE: Cheyenne *Daily Leader*, 15 Jan 1911.

Received permission to attend course at Royal Music School for Bandmasters, London. SOURCE: Fletcher, *The Black Soldier*, 86.

Back at Ft D. A. Russell after two-month trip to Europe, studying music, financed by regiment fund. SOURCE: Cheyenne *State Leader*, 24 Aug 1912.

At Ft Huachuca, AZ. SOURCE: Work, *The Negro Yearbook, 1925–1926*, 254.

Warrant officer, Ft Huachuca, 1930. SOURCE: Work, *The Negro Yearbook, 1931–1932*, 334.

10th Cavalry band under Hammond completed "remarkable tour" through Arizona, New Mexico, Texas; covered 2,261 miles and gave twenty concerts, including at Waco, Dallas, San Antonio, Austin, and El Paso. SOURCE: *Cavalry Journal*, 40 (Sep–Oct 1931): 58.

HAMMONDS, Virgil; Private; K/10th Cav. Served in 10th Cavalry, 1898; remained in U.S. during war with Spain. SOURCE: Cashin, *Under Fire with the Tenth Cavalry*, 349.

HAMMONS, Isaiah; Private; 10th Cav. Enlisted by recruiting officer, Santa Fe, NM, 17 Dec 1866. SOURCE: CO, 10 Cav, to Lt George McDermott, 10 May 1867, ES, 10 Cav, 1866–71.

Regimental headquarters has final statement but no inventory of effects for late Private Hammons. SOURCE: CO, 10 Cav, to Lt T. A. Jennings, K/25, 22 Apr 1867, LS, 10 Cav, 1866–67.

HAMON, Charles; G/10th Cav. Original member of 10th Cavalry; in troop when organized, Ft Leavenworth, KS, 5 Jul 1867. SOURCE: McMiller, "Buffalo Soldiers," 74.

HAMPTON, Forrest; Private; I/10th Cav. Served in 10th Cavalry, 1898; remained in U.S. during war with Spain. SOURCE: Cashin, *Under Fire with the Tenth Cavalry*, 348.

HAMPTON, George W.; Sergeant; Band/10th Cav. At San Marcelino, Philippines, 1900. *See* **FULBRIGHT, William R., Private, H/25th Infantry**

Acquitted of absence from concert by summary court, Iba, Zambales, Philippines, 25 Oct 1900. SOURCE: Misc Records, 25 Inf.

At Ft Niobrara, NE, Mar 1903; his "disease appears fatal and [he] has reached a remarkably clear faith and awaits his earthly end with perfect composure. His bible has become to him his trusted guide." SOURCE: Monthly Report, Chaplain Steward, Mar 1903.

HAMPTON, Jesse; Private; H/24th Inf. Enlisted Indianapolis, 6 Oct 1898. SOURCE: Muster Roll, H/24 Inf, Nov–Dec 1898.

Discharged, Ft Douglas, UT, character good, single, due U.S. for clothing $47.55, 27 Jan 1899; reenlisted, Indianapolis, 16 Feb 1899; joined company, 25 Feb 1899. SOURCE: Muster Roll, H/24 Inf, Jan–Feb 1899.

Fined $5 by summary court, San Isidro, Philippines, for leaning on sentry box with arms folded and rifle not in hand while on duty as sentry. 15 Jan 1902. SOURCE: Register of Summary Court, San Isidro.

HAMPTON, Moat; K/10th Cav. Original member of 10th Cavalry; in troop when organized, Ft Riley, KS, 1 Sep 1867. SOURCE: McMiller, "Buffalo Soldiers," 77.

HAMPTON, Nathan; Private; H/9th Cav. Born Knoxville, TN; enlisted, age 18, occupation farmer, Ht 5'5", 28 Nov 1894; sentenced to two months' confinement by garrison court martial, Ft Robinson, NE, for conduct prejudicial to good order and discipline, 26 May 1896; discharged, end of term, single, character very good, 1897; deposits $54, retained $10, clothing $13. SOURCE: Descriptive Book, H/9 Cav.

HAMPTON, Thornton; B/10th Cav. Original member of 10th Cavalry; in troop when organized, Ft Leavenworth, KS, 1 Apr 1867. SOURCE: McMiller, "Buffalo Soldiers," 69.

HAMPTON, Wade; D/10th Cav. Served five years; recent subscriber. SOURCE: *Winners of the West* 4 (Mar 1927): 8.

Subscriber and member, Camp 11, National Indian War Veterans, St. Joseph, MO; served 1867–72; died Okmulgee, OK, 14 Dec 1932. SOURCE: *Winners of the West* 10 (Jan 1933): 3.

HAMPTON, Wade; Private; B/24th Inf. Fined $8 by summary court, Cabanatuan, Philippines, for four counts of conduct prejudicial to good order and discipline, 30 Jan 1901, drunk and disorderly on streets of Cabanatuan; "generally obnoxious" in "canteens" of Auria Reenda; refused order of Cpl. Samuel T. Henry, M/24th Infantry, to accompany him to the guardhouse; disrespectful to Corporal Henry; witnesses: Corporal Henry and Pvt. George Lacy, B/24th Infantry. SOURCE: Name File, 24 Inf.

HAMRICK, Clarence C.; 10th Cav. Deserter; physically fit for duty. SOURCE: Post Surgeon to Post Adjutant, 14 Feb 1903, LS, Post Surgeon, Ft Robinson.

HAMS, Thornton; Private; C/10th Cav. Mentioned among men who distinguished themselves in 1889; awarded certificate of merit for gallant and meritorious service while escort for Maj. Joseph W. Wham, paymaster, when attacked by robbers between Fts Grant and Thomas, AZ. SOURCE: GO 18, AGO, 1891.

At Ft Grant, 1890; certificate of merit mentioned. SOURCE: SecWar, *AR 1890*, 289; Baker, Roster.

Letter, Adjutant General's Office, 1 May 1896, concerns his enlistment for A/9th Cavalry.

HANCE, George W.; B/25th Inf. Died of valvular heart disease on arrival at U.S. Soldiers Home, age 57, 15 Mar 1904. SOURCE: SecWar, *AR 1904*, 4:289.

HANCOCK, George W.; 25th Inf. At Ft Niobrara, NE, 1902; wife arrived from Oakland, CA, 1 Nov 1902. SOURCE: Indianapolis *Freeman*, 15 Nov 1902.

HAND, William; Private; A/9th Cav. In hands of civil authorities, Omaha, NE, 20 Jul–22 Nov 1889. SOURCE: Regt Returns, 9 Cav.

HANES, George; C/10th Cav. Original member of 10th Cavalry; in troop when organized, Ft Leavenworth, KS, 14 May 1867. SOURCE: McMiller, "Buffalo Soldiers," 70.

HANKINS, Andrew; Private; G/10th Cav. Served in 10th Cavalry, 1898; remained in U.S. during war with Spain. SOURCE: Cashin, *Under Fire with the Tenth Cavalry*, 346.

HANKINS, W. A.; Captain; F/48th Inf. Impresses all "by his gentlemanly conduct and military conception." SOURCE: Richmond *Planet*, 14 Apr 1900.

Born Halifax Co., VA; was member of Mt. Vernon Baptist Church, Halifax Co., and vice president, Mechanics Savings Bank, Richmond; died, age 41, 11 May 1902; funeral from Third Street African Methodist Episcopal Church, Richmond; left widow of thirteen years and two children. SOURCE: Richmond *Planet*, 17 May 1902.

HANKS, Frank; Private; F/10th Cav. Served in 10th Cavalry in Cuba, 1898. SOURCE: Cashin, *Under Fire with the Tenth Cavalry*, 344.

HANLEY, Edward; Private; F/10th Cav. Deceased; final statement sent to Adjutant General, 27 Jul 1873. SOURCE: LS, 10 Cav, 1873–83.

HANNOVER, John; H/10th Cav. Original member of 10th Cavalry; in troop when organized, Ft Leavenworth, KS, 21 Jul 1867. SOURCE: McMiller, "Buffalo Soldiers," 75.

HANSON, Edward; Sergeant; B/9th Cav. Appointed sergeant, 8 Apr 1877. SOURCE: Roster, 9 Cav.

Stationed at Ft Duchesne, UT; to report for examination for appointment as ordnance sergeant. SOURCE: *ANJ* 28 (1 Aug 1891): 539.

Retires from Ft Duchesne, Apr 1895. SOURCE: *ANJ* 32 (13 Apr 1895): 539.

HANSON, George W.; M/10th Cav. Original member of 10th Cavalry; in troop when organized, Ft Riley, KS, 15 Oct 1867. SOURCE: McMiller, "Buffalo Soldiers," 79.

HANSON, John; Private; L/9th Cav. Killed 24 Jan 1876. *See* **HARVEY**, Anthony, Private, L/9th Cavalry

Killed in saloon shootout with Pvts. Anthony Harvey and George Small, L/9th Cavalry, Cimarron, NM, Apr 1876; buried at Ft Union, NM. SOURCE: Billington, *New Mexico's Buffalo Soldiers*, 67.

HANSON, William; Private; E/10th Cav. Mentioned 1873 as having enlisted Aug 1872. SOURCE: ES, 10 Cav, 1873–81.

HANSTON, Charles H.; Private; I/24th Inf. Enlisted Dayton, OH, 27 Mar 1899. SOURCE: Muster Roll, I/24 Inf. Mar–Apr 1899.

Absent without leave since 22 Jun 1899. SOURCE: Muster Roll, I/24 Inf, May–June 1899.

Absent without leave, 22 Jun–3 Jul 1899; confined at Presidio of San Francisco, CA, 3–23 Jul 1899; en route to the Philippines, 24 Jul 1899; joined company, 25 Aug 1899; in confinement since 29 Aug 1899. SOURCE: Muster Roll, I/24 Inf, Jul–Aug 1899.

Fined one month's pay by summary court, 29 Aug 1899. SOURCE: Muster Roll, I/24 Inf, Sep–Oct 1899.

HARDAWAY, Benjamin; Corporal; K/25th Inf. In the Philippines, 1900. SOURCE: Richmond *Planet*, 16 Jun 1900.

HARDAWAY, Henry; Private; I/10th Cav. Served in 10th Cavalry in Cuba, 1898. SOURCE: Cashin, *Under Fire with the Tenth Cavalry*, 348.

HARDAY, Wesley; 10th Cav. *See* **LOVELACE**, Scott, Corporal, I/10th Cavalry

HARDEE, James A.; Private; K/24th Inf. Corporal; writes from San Carlos, AZ, 25 Mar 1890, to Henry Thompson and wife Ruth, daughter of John Brown; men of 24th Infantry want to respond to solicitation on behalf of destitute Thompsons. SOURCE: Cleveland *Gazette*, 19 Apr 1890.

Private, K/24th Infantry, reports in letter, 30 May 1890, collection of $23 for destitute daughter and son-in-law of John Brown; following men contributed: Sgt. George D. Powell, C/24th Infantry, $1; Sgt. E. D. Bordinghammer, K/24th Infantry, $.50; Sgt. James Larkins, K/24th Infantry, $.50; Sgt. R. A. Porter, K/24th Infantry, $.50; Sgt. W. H. Barkley, K/24th Infantry, $.25; Cpl. Henry Giles, K/24th Infantry, $.50; Pvt. Charley Henry, I/24th Infantry, $1; Pvt. John Burton, I/24th Infantry, $.50; Pvts. W. M. Thompson, $.25, James A. Hardee, $1, Henry Batie, $1, W. S. Bouncler, $.50, A. F. Butcher, $1, J. C. Covington, $1, James Edwards, $.50, George Faulkner, $.50, W. M. Fleming, $1, E. D. Gibson, $.50, I. W. Gilbert, $.50, D. A. Kyle, $1, W. H. Myers,

$.50, R. M. Odom, $.25, T. H. Patterson, $1, Henry Richardson, $.50, Richard Scott, $1.50, Albert H. Squires, $1, George Steward, $.50, George Sulliven, $.75, James Taylor, $1.50, P. J. Jones, $.50, all K/24th Infantry; Musician P. A. Moulton, K/24th Infantry; Pvt. H. H. Rhodes, K/24th Infantry, $.50. SOURCE: Cleveland *Gazette*, 7 Jun 1890.

On special duty at post exchange, Ft Huachuca, AZ. SOURCE: Order 140, Ft Huachuca, 21 Sep 1893, Name File, 24 Inf.

Relieved from special duty at post exchange, Ft Huachuca. SOURCE: Order 148, Ft Huachuca, 6 Oct 1893, Name File, 24 Inf.

HARDEN, Henry; Private; K/9th Cav. Veteran of Philippine Insurrection; at Ft D. A. Russell, WY, in 1910; resident of Johnson Co., TN. SOURCE: *Illustrated Review: Ninth Cavalry*, with picture.

HARDEN, James T.; Private; C/25th Inf. Dishonorable discharge, Brownsville. SOURCE: SO 266, AGO, 9 Nov 1906.

Willing to submit to any test to prove innocence and reenlist. SOURCE: Washington *Post*, 13 Dec 1906.

HARDEN, William; Private; B/25th Inf. Dishonorable discharge, Brownsville. SOURCE: SO 266, AGO, 9 Nov 1906.

HARDEN, William K.; Private; G/48th Inf. Died of variola in the Philippines, 4 Dec 1900. SOURCE: *ANJ* 38 (15 Dec 1900): 373.

HARDIMAN, Henry; Private; D/9th Cav. At Ft D. A. Russell, WY, in 1910; resident of Lyles, Gibson Co., IN. SOURCE: *Illustrated Review: Ninth Cavalry*, with picture.

HARDIN, Richard; Private; I/10th Cav. Served in 10th Cavalry, 1898; remained in U.S. during war with Spain. SOURCE: Cashin, *Under Fire with the Tenth Cavalry*, 348.

HARDMAN, Benjamin H.; Private; E/24th Inf. Wounded in action, Cuba, 1898. SOURCE: Muller, *The Twenty Fourth Infantry*, 18.

HARDWICKS, William; Private; E/9th Cav. *See* **JOHNSON**, Starks H., Private, E/9th Cavalry

HARDY; Private; H/10th Cav. Missing in action, Rattlesnake Springs, TX, 6 Aug 1880. SOURCE: Baker, Roster.

HARDY, Thomas S.; Private; I/10th Cav. Wounded in action, Santiago, Cuba, 1 Jul 1898. SOURCE: SecWar, *AR 1898*, 324.

Served with distinction in Cuba, 1898. SOURCE: Cashin, *Under Fire with the Tenth Cavalry*, 185, 348.

HARDY, William; Private; K/9th Cav. Veteran of Philippine Insurrection; at Ft D. A. Russell, WY, in 1910;

sharpshooter; resident of Graham, NC. SOURCE: *Illustrated Review: Ninth Cavalry*, with picture.

HARE, Solomon; Private; F/25th Inf. Sergeant, I/25th Infantry, authorized two-month furlough from Ft Missoula, MT. SOURCE: *ANJ* 27 (22 Feb 1890): 491.

Reduced from sergeant, F/25th Infantry, to private, Ft Missoula; while sergeant of guard, gambled with prisoner under sentence; portion of sentence calling for three months' confinement remitted by Brig. Gen. Thomas H. Ruger. SOURCE: *ANJ* 28 (18 Oct 1890): 121.

Private, F/25th Infantry, retires from Ft Missoula, Dec 1892. SOURCE: *ANJ* 30 (17 Dec 1892): 271.

HARGIS, William; Private; E/9th Cav. At Ft D. A. Russell, WY, in 1910; sharpshooter; resident of Blue Level, KY. SOURCE: *Illustrated Review: Ninth Cavalry*, with picture.

HARGRAVES, John C.; Private; K/24th Inf. Sentenced to $10 fine and twenty days, Cabanatuan, Philippines, 24 Apr 1901, for being drunk and disorderly in camp, saying to 1st Sgt. Jacob W. Stevens that he would be damned if he would go on detached service and would go back to saloon and drink more. SOURCE: Name File, 24 Inf.

HARGROVE, Augustus; Private; H/10th Cav. Served in 10th Cavalry, 1898; remained in U.S. during war with Spain. SOURCE: Cashin, *Under Fire with the Tenth Cavalry*, 346.

HARKINS, Charles; K/10th Cav. Original member of 10th Cavalry; in troop when organized, Ft Riley, KS, 1 Sep 1867. SOURCE: McMiller, "Buffalo Soldiers," 77.

HARKINS, John; K/10th Cav. Original member of 10th Cavalry; in troop when organized, Ft Riley, KS, 1 Sep 1867. SOURCE: McMiller, "Buffalo Soldiers," 77.

HARKLESS, J. D.; 2nd Lt; 23rd Kans Inf. Mentioned. SOURCE: Beasley, *Negro Trailblazers*, 285.

HARLAN, William; Private; E/24th Inf. Private, K/24th Infantry; convicted of stealing forage cap and other articles; sentence disapproved because of incomplete findings, in accordance with Special Order 51, 1879. SOURCE: Report of Trials, Department of Texas, 1878–79.

At Ft Bayard, NM, 1891. SOURCE: *ANJ* 29 (17 Oct 1891): 133.

Retires as private, E/24th Infantry, from Ft Bayard, 2 Mar 1895. SOURCE: *ANJ* 32 (9 Mar 1895): 455.

Resided at 323 South 11th East, Salt Lake City, UT, in 1898. SOURCE: Clark, "A History of the Twenty-fourth," appendix E.

Buried at Ft Douglas, UT, 7 Sep 1905. SOURCE: Clark, "A History of the Twenty-fourth," appendix A.

HARLEY, Samuel W.; Sergeant; C/25th Inf. Served in 9th Cavalry, 1891–94; in 25th Infantry, 1894–1906;

wounded in action at El Caney, Cuba, 1898. SOURCE: Weaver, *The Brownsville Raid*, 124.

Private, C/25th Infantry, wounded at El Caney, 1 Jul 1898. SOURCE: Nankivell, *History of the Twenty-fifth Infantry*, 83.

Acting first sergeant, C/25th Infantry, 37 years old, sixteen years' service, in 1906. SOURCE: Weaver, *The Brownsville Raid*, 40.

Sergeant, C/25th Infantry; dishonorable discharge, Brownsville. SOURCE: SO 266, AGO, 9 Nov 1906.

HARMAN, James R.; Private; H/24th Inf. Enlisted Columbus Barracks, OH, 19 Jan 1899. SOURCE: Muster Roll, H/24 Inf, Jan–Feb 1899.

HARMON, Charles; G/10th Cav. Original member of 10th Cavalry; in troop when organized, Ft Leavenworth, KS, 5 Jul 1867. SOURCE: McMiller, "Buffalo Soldiers," 74.

HARPER, Charles; Private; G/9th Cav. Private, C/9th Cavalry, promoted to corporal. SOURCE: Order 46, 20 Sep 1888, Regimental Orders, 9 Cav.

Reduced from sergeant, G/9th Cavalry, to private and fined $40 for insubordination, Ft Robinson, NE, Oct 1891. SOURCE: *ANJ* 29 (7 Nov 1891): 176.

HARPER, Clay; QM Sgt; E/9th Cav. Veteran of Philippine Insurrection; at Ft D. A. Russell, WY, in 1910. SOURCE: *Illustrated Review: Ninth Cavalry*, with picture.

HARPER, Henry; Private; H/10th Cav. Original member of 10th Cavalry; in troop when organized, Ft Leavenworth, KS, 21 Jul 1867. SOURCE: McMiller, "Buffalo Soldiers," 75.

At Ft Apache, AZ, 1890, subscribed $.50 to testimonial to General Grierson. SOURCE: List of subscriptions, 23 Apr 1890, 10th Cavalry papers, MHI.

HARPER, James; Private; F/9th Cav. At Ft D. A. Russell, WY, in 1910; resident of Selma, AL. SOURCE: *Illustrated Review: Ninth Cavalry*, with picture.

HARPER, John W.; 1st Sgt; H/25th Inf. At Ft Davis, TX, 1878; best marksman in company, tied for fourth in regiment. SOURCE: Scrapbook, 25 Inf, I.

Son born to wife Fanny, Ft Davis, 30 Aug 1879. SOURCE: Thompson, "The Negro Regiments."

HARPER, John W.; Private; I/25th Inf. Deserted at Mexico, Luzon, Philippines, 14 Nov 1899. SOURCE: Regt Returns, 25 Inf, Nov 1899.

HARPER, Jordan; M/10th Cav. Original member of 10th Cavalry; in troop when organized, Ft Riley, KS, 15 Oct 1867. SOURCE: McMiller, "Buffalo Soldiers," 79.

HARPER, Michael; Private; M/25th Inf. Ranked number 160 among rifle experts with 69 percent, 1904. SOURCE: GO 79, AGO, 1 Jun 1905.

HARPER, W. R.; Sergeant; F/9th Cav. Discharged, end of term, Ft Robinson, NE, Aug 1885. SOURCE: Post Returns, Ft Robinson, Aug 1885.

HARPER, William; Private; L/10th Cav. Served in 10th Cavalry, 1898; remained in U.S. during war with Spain. SOURCE: Cashin, *Under Fire with the Tenth Cavalry*, 350.

HARPER, William H.; Corporal; E/9th Cav. At Ft Robinson, NE, 1894. *See* **TURNER**, Peter H., Blacksmith, E/9th Cavalry

On permanent color guard, Ft Robinson, 1895. *See* **LYMAN**, George, Color Sergeant, 9th Cavalry. SOURCE: *ANJ* 32 (3 Aug 1895): 807.

Appointed to regimental color guard, Ft Robinson, Mar 1896. SOURCE: *ANJ* 33 (28 Mar 1896): 540.

HARRIEL, Philip; Private; K/9th Cav. At Ft D. A. Russell, WY, in 1910; resident of Montgomery, AL. SOURCE: *Illustrated Review: Ninth Cavalry*, with picture.

HARRILL, Doc L.; Sergeant; K/25th Inf. Corporal, K/25th Infantry; at Ft Niobrara, NE, 1904. SOURCE: Wilson, "History of Fort Niobrara."

Promoted to sergeant. SOURCE: *ANR* 38 (26 Aug 1905): 21.

HARRILLA, Lews; B/10th Cav. Original member of 10th Cavalry; in troop when organized, Ft Leavenworth, KS, 1 Apr 1867. SOURCE: McMiller, "Buffalo Soldiers," 69.

HARRINGTON, William; Private; I/10th Cav. Served in 10th Cavalry in Cuba, 1898. SOURCE: Cashin, *Under Fire with the Tenth Cavalry*, 348.

HARRIS; Private; A/10th Cav. At Ft Apache, AZ, 1890, subscribed $.50 to testimonial to General Grierson. SOURCE: List of subscriptions, 23 Apr 1890, 10th Cavalry papers, MHI.

HARRIS; Private; C/10th Cav. At Ft Apache, AZ, 1890, subscribed $.25 to testimonial to General Grierson. SOURCE: List of subscriptions, 23 Apr 1890, 10th Cavalry papers, MHI.

HARRIS; Private; F/10th Cav. At Ft Apache, AZ, 1890, subscribed $.50 to testimonial to General Grierson. SOURCE: List of subscriptions, 23 Apr 1890, 10th Cavalry papers, MHI.

HARRIS; Private; C/9th Cav. Excused from daily school attendance; is post printer, reads and writes with ease. SOURCE: CO, Ft Robinson, NE, to 1st Lt James A. Swift, Superintendent, Post School, 21 Nov 1894, LS, Ft Robinson.

HARRIS, A.; Private; H/9th Cav. On detached service, Ft Bayard, NM, 16 Jan–10 Feb 1881. SOURCE: Regt Returns, 9 Cav, Feb 1881.

HARRIS, A.; Private; L/9th Cav. On detached service in field, New Mexico, 21 Jan–24 Feb 1881. SOURCE: Regt Returns, 9 Cav, Feb 1881.

HARRIS, Aleck; C/10th Cav. Original member of 10th Cavalry; in troop when organized, Ft Leavenworth, KS, 14 May 1867. SOURCE: McMiller, "Buffalo Soldiers," 70.

HARRIS, Barney; Private; D/25th Inf. Dishonorable discharge, Brownsville. SOURCE: SO 266, AGO, 9 Nov 1906.

HARRIS, Ben; Private; I/9th Cav. At Ft D. A. Russell, WY, in 1910; resident of Muskogee, OK. SOURCE: *Illustrated Review: Ninth Cavalry*, with picture.

HARRIS, Charles; Private; G/24th Inf. Wounded in action in Cuba, 1898. SOURCE: Muller, *The Twenty Fourth Infantry*, 19.

HARRIS, Charles, Jr.; Private; G/9th Cav. At Ft D. A. Russell, WY, in 1910; resident of Evansville, IN. SOURCE: *Illustrated Review: Ninth Cavalry*,

HARRIS, Charles G.; Sergeant; H/10th Cav. At Ft Apache, AZ, 1890, subscribed $.50 to testimonial to General Grierson. SOURCE: List of subscriptions, 23 Apr 1890, 10th Cavalry papers, MHI.

HARRIS, D.; Farrier; E/9th Cav. On detached service in field, New Mexico, 27 Jan–1 Feb 1881. SOURCE: Regt Returns, 9 Cav, Feb 1881.

HARRIS, David H.; Musician; I/24th Inf. Enlisted 16 Jan 1899. SOURCE: Muster Roll, I/24 Inf, Jan–Feb 1899.

Fined $.50 by garrison court martial, 19 Apr 1899. SOURCE: Muster Roll, I/24 Inf, Mar–Apr 1899.

Appointed artificer, 21 May 1899; fined $1 by garrison court martial, 24 May 1899; fined $3 by garrison court martial, 13 June 1899. SOURCE: Muster Roll, I/24 Inf, May–Jun 1899.

HARRIS, Douglas; Private; E/10th Cav. Served in 10th Cavalry in Cuba, 1898. SOURCE: Cashin, *Under Fire with the Tenth Cavalry*, 342.

HARRIS, Edward H.; Private; Band/10th Cav. Deposited $20 with paymaster. SOURCE: CO, 10 Cav, to PMG, 4 May 1874, LS, 10 Cav, 1873–83.

HARRIS, Ellis; Cook; G/9th Cav. Veteran of Philippine Insurrection; at Ft D. A. Russell, WY, in 1910; marksman; resident of Chattanooga, TN. SOURCE: *Illustrated Review: Ninth Cavalry*, with picture.

HARRIS, Eugene; 1st Sgt; 24th Inf. Picture. SOURCE: Curtis, *The Black Soldier*, opposite 39.

HARRIS, Fenton H.; Sqdn Sgt Maj; 10th Cav. Born Bristow, VA; Ht 5'7", light brown complexion; enlisted, I/10th Cavalry, May 1899; marksman, 1903; sharpshooter, 1904; sergeant major, second squadron, 10th Cavalry, as of 5 Sep 1904; discharged, end of term, character excellent, single, Ft Washakie, WY, 4 Aug 1905; deposits $671; clothing $102; reenlisted Ft Washakie, continued as sergeant major, 15 Sep 1905; marksman, 1905; discharged in accordance with General Order 48, War Department, 1904, character good, "an inefficient Squadron Sergeant Major," single, 29 Nov 1905; deposits $80, clothing $53. SOURCE: Descriptive Book, 10 Cav Officers & NCOs.

Private, I/10th Cavalry; released to duty from treatment for gonorrhea, Ft Robinson, NE, 29 May 1903. SOURCE: Post Surgeon to CO, A/10, 29 May 1903, LS, Post Surgeon, Ft Robinson.

Shot by Henderson, D/10th Cavalry, in Crawford, NE, 14 Sep 1903. SOURCE: Crawford *Tribune*, 18 Sep 1903.

Not expected to recover from shooting. SOURCE: Crawford *Bulletin*, 18 Sep 1903.

Appointed squadron sergeant major from sergeant, I/10th Cavalry, Ft Mackenzie, WY, 5 Sep 1904; post sergeant major, Ft Washakie, 22 Apr 1905. SOURCE: Muster Roll, Det Field & Staff, 10 Cav.

At Ft Robinson, NE, guarding prisoners, as of 29 Nov 1904.

HARRIS, Gene; H/10th Cav. Original member of 10th Cavalry; in troop when organized, Ft Leavenworth, KS, 21 Jul 1867. SOURCE: McMiller, "Buffalo Soldiers," 75.

HARRIS, George; Recruit; C/10th Cav. Mentioned Apr 1867. SOURCE: LS, 10 Cav, 1866–67.

On extra duty, Ft Leavenworth, KS. SOURCE: CO, 10 Cav, to Adj, Ft Leavenworth, 15 May 1867, LS, 10 Cav, 1866–67.

HARRIS, George; Private; C/9th Cav. Deserted from Ft Robinson, NE, 17 Jul 1886.

Sentenced to dishonorable discharge by general court martial, Ft Robinson, 2 Nov 1886.

HARRIS, George H.; Corporal; K/25th Inf. In the Philippines, 1900; guest at wedding of Pvt. Willie Redding, K/25th Infantry, 15 Apr 1900. SOURCE: Richmond *Planet*, 16 Jun 1900.

HARRIS, George W.; M/10th Cav. Original member of 10th Cavalry; in troop when organized, Ft Riley, KS, 15 Oct 1867. SOURCE: McMiller, "Buffalo Soldiers," 79.

HARRIS, George W.; Private; C/25th Inf. Dishonorable discharge, Brownsville. SOURCE: SO 266, AGO, 9 Nov 1906.

HARRIS, Henry (1); E/10th Cav. Original member of 10th Cavalry; in troop when organized, Ft Leavenworth, KS, 15 Jun 1867. SOURCE: McMiller, "Buffalo Soldiers," 72.

HARRIS, Henry (2); E/10th Cav. Original member of 10th Cavalry; in troop when organized, Ft Leavenworth, KS, 15 Jun 1867. SOURCE: McMiller, "Buffalo Soldiers," 72.

HARRIS, Henry; Private; M/10th Cav. Died in Columbia, TN. SOURCE: *Winners of the West* 12 (Mar 1935): 3.

HARRIS, Isaiah F.; Private; L/10th Cav. Served in 10th Cavalry, 1898; remained in U.S. during war with Spain. SOURCE: Cashin, *Under Fire with the Tenth Cavalry*, 350.

HARRIS, Israel; 1st Sgt; D/25th Inf. Dishonorable discharge, Brownsville. SOURCE: SO 266, AGO, 9 Nov 1906.

Now special officer and porter, Eliot National Bank, Boston, MA. SOURCE: Cleveland *Gazette*, 29 Dec 1906.

HARRIS, James; B/10th Cav. Original member of 10th Cavalry; in troop when organized, Ft Leavenworth, KS, 1 Apr 1867. SOURCE: McMiller, "Buffalo Soldiers," 69.

HARRIS, James H.; Private; C/10th Cav. Served 1887–91; subscriber. SOURCE: *Winners of the West* 10 (Aug 1933): 3.

Born Richmond, VA, 1854, parents unknown; anchor tattoo on left forearm; enlisted St. Louis, MO, occupation hostler, Ht 5'4", complexion black, 11 Oct 1887; troop and post clerk, Ft Grant, AZ; discharged, 10 Jan 1891; janitor after service; resided 1118 Argyle Avenue, Baltimore, MD; pension $20 per month, 8 Feb 1932, increased to $50 per month, 16 Sep 1932; died of bronchial pneumonia, age 81, Baltimore, 26 Oct 1935. SOURCE: VA File C 2583656, James H. Harris.

HARRIS, Jeff; 1st Sgt; B/25th Inf. Twenty-five-year veteran, at Ft Apache, AZ. SOURCE: Cleveland *Gazette*, 20 May 1899.

HARRIS, Jeremiah; Private; A/10th Cav. Dishonorably discharged, then enlisted Ft Sill, Indian Territory, 12 Feb 1870, under assumption he was discharged by mistake for another man in company of same name. SOURCE: CO, 10 Cav, to CO, A/10, 28 Feb 1870, ES, 10 Cav, 1866–71.

Dishonorably discharged in accordance with Special Order 106, War Department, 16 May 1869; dropped from rolls, 20 Apr 1870. SOURCE: CO, A/10 Cav, to CO, 10 Cav, 20 Apr 1870, ES, 10 Cav, 1866–71.

HARRIS, Jerry; Private; A/10th Cav. Arrived Ft Leavenworth, KS, from Jefferson Barracks, MO, Oct 1866. SOURCE: Adj, Ft Leavenworth, to Headquarters, Jefferson Barracks, 9 Oct 1866, LS, 10 Cav, 1866–67.

Original member of 10th Cavalry; in troop when organized, Ft Leavenworth, KS, 18 Feb 1867. SOURCE: McMiller, "Buffalo Soldiers," 68.

HARRIS, Jesse; D/10th Cav. Original member of 10th Cavalry; in troop when organized, Ft Leavenworth, KS, 1 Jun 1867. SOURCE: McMiller, "Buffalo Soldiers," 71.

HARRIS, Joe; Private; H/9th Cav. At Ft D. A. Russell, WY, in 1910; marksman; resident of Daytona, FL. SOURCE: *Illustrated Review: Ninth Cavalry*, with picture.

HARRIS, John; Blacksmith; G/10th Cav. At Ft Apache, AZ, 1890, subscribed $.50 to testimonial to General Grierson. SOURCE: List of subscriptions, 23 Apr 1890, 10th Cavalry papers, MHI.

HARRIS, John; Sergeant; Band/9th Cav. Corporal, served in 10th Cavalry in Cuba, 1898. SOURCE: Cashin, *Under Fire with the Tenth Cavalry*, 352.

Native of Kentucky; played tuba and bass viol; on 10th Cavalry regimental baseball team, Ft Robinson, NE, 1904. SOURCE: Lowe, "Camp Life," 206.

Veteran of Indian wars and Spanish-American War; sergeant, Band/9th Cavalry, at Ft D. A. Russell, WY, 1910; resident of Lawrenceburg, KY. SOURCE: *Illustrated Review: Ninth Cavalry*, with picture.

HARRIS, John W.; Private; K/10th Cav. Born Winchester, VA; died, age 49, with twenty-seven years' service, Ft Robinson, NE, 27 Jun 1904. SOURCE: Monthly Report, Chaplain Anderson, 1 Jul 1904.

Buried, Ft Robinson, 27 Jun 1904. SOURCE: List of Interments, Ft Robinson.

HARRIS, Joseph; Sergeant; A/10th Cav. Died of pistol shot wound, 6 Apr 1870. SOURCE: CO, A/10, to CO, 10 Cav, 12 Apr 1870, ES, 10 Cav, 1866–71.

HARRIS, Lee; Private; K/25th Inf. At Ft Niobrara, NE, 1904. SOURCE: Wilson, "History of Fort Niobrara."

HARRIS, Lewis; Cook; M/24th Inf. Retires Oct 1901. SOURCE: *ANJ* 39 (26 Oct 1901): 183.

HARRIS, Louis; Private; H/24th Inf. On extra duty as teamster, Quartermaster Department, Ft Huachuca, AZ, and to accompany detachment to Nogales, AZ. SOURCE: Order 89, Ft Huachuca, 17 Jun 1893, Name File, 24 Inf.

HARRIS, Louis; Private; F/25th Inf. Killed Capt. Nicholas Beck of scow schooner *James Burns*, Angel Island, CA, 25 Jun 1902, when Beck failed to respond to challenge by Harris while on sentry duty. SOURCE: San Francisco *Chronicle*, 28 Jun 1902.

HARRIS, Louis; Private; H/10th Cav. Died of wounds, Ft Mackenzie, WY, 14 Sep 1902.

HARRIS, Mack; Private; H/10th Cav. Corporal, A/10th Cavalry; at Ft Apache, AZ, 1890, subscribed $.50 to testimonial to General Grierson. SOURCE: List of subscriptions, 23 Apr 1890, 10th Cavalry papers, MHI.

Cook, served in 10th Cavalry, 1898; remained in U.S. during war with Spain. SOURCE: Cashin, *Under Fire with the Tenth Cavalry*, 346.

Cook, H/10th Cavalry, prepared Thanksgiving dinner, Camp Forse, AL, 1898. SOURCE: Richmond *Planet*, 3 Dec 1898.

Private, H/10th Cavalry, retires, Aug 1901. SOURCE: *ANJ* 38 (31 Aug 1901): 1283.

HARRIS, Maston; H/9th Cav. Served 1879–84; member, Camp 11, National Indian War Veterans. SOURCE: *Winners of the West* 6 (May 1929): 5.

Mentioned. SOURCE: *Winners of the West* 6 (Oct 1929): 3; *Winners of the West* 12 (Dec 1935): 2.

On detached service, Ft Bayard, NM, 16 Jan–10 Feb 1881. SOURCE: Regt Returns, 9 Cav, Feb 1881.

HARRIS, Milton; Private; A/38th Inf. On extra duty with Quartermaster Department, Ft Cummings, NM, 1868, and considered "trustworthy, reliable, and faithful." SOURCE: Billington, *New Mexico's Buffalo Soldiers*, 192.

HARRIS, Moses; Private; I/9th Cav. At Ft Robinson, NE, 1888. *See* **DAVIS**, Benjamin, Corporal, E/9th Cavalry

HARRIS, Nathaniel; Private; K/10th Cav. Served in 10th Cavalry, 1898; remained in U.S. during war with Spain. SOURCE: Cashin, *Under Fire with the Tenth Cavalry*, 349.

HARRIS, Nelson; Private; G/10th Cav. Served in 10th Cavalry, 1898; remained in U.S. during war with Spain. SOURCE: Cashin, *Under Fire with the Tenth Cavalry*, 346.

HARRIS, Norbin; Private; F/9th Cav. Sentenced to thirty days by garrison court martial for insubordination to Corporal McKeen, F/9th Cavalry, saying "I am tired of you goddamn niggers bulldozing me and I will not stand it." SOURCE: Order 126, 25 Jun 1887, Post Orders, Ft Robinson.

HARRIS, Perry; Private; H/9th Cav. Died of tuberculosis at 2nd Reserve Hospital, Manila, Philippines, 22 Jun 1901. SOURCE: *ANJ* 38 (17 Aug 1901): 1241.

HARRIS, Rand; Wagoner; B/10th Cav. Served in 10th Cavalry in Cuba, 1898. SOURCE: Cashin, *Under Fire with the Tenth Cavalry*, 338.

HARRIS, Robert; Sergeant; F/9th Cav. Fined one month's pay by garrison court martial, Ft Robinson, NE, for fight with Sgt. Ebbert Maden, F/9th Cavalry, and for threatening sentinel, Pvt. Louis Glenn, F/9th Cavalry, 14 Nov 1887. SOURCE: Order 225, 17 Nov 1887, Post Orders, Ft Robinson.

See **BOWSER**, Frank T., Private, F/9th Cavalry

HARRIS, Robert; Private; D/24th Inf. Transferred from Reserve Divisional Hospital, Siboney, Cuba, to U.S. on U.S. Army Transport *Berkshire*, 23 Aug 1898, with remittent malarial fever. SOURCE: Hospital Papers, Spanish-American War.

HARRIS, S.; Private; B/9th Cav. On detached service, Santa Fe, NM, 28 Jan 1878–20 Feb 1881. SOURCE: Regt Returns, 9 Cav, Feb 1881.

HARRIS, Samuel; Sergeant; 25th Inf. Left Army to work on Dakota ranch, 1890. SOURCE: Rickey, *Forty Miles a Day on Beans and Hay*, 346.

HARRIS, Sherman; Farrier; I/10th Cav. Served in 10th Cavalry in Cuba, 1898. SOURCE: Cashin, *Under Fire with the Tenth Cavalry*, 347.

Cited for conspicuous coolness and gallantry under fire, Las Guasimas, Cuba, 24 Jun 1898. SOURCE: SecWar, *AR 1898*, 349; GO 15, AGO, 13 Feb 1900; *ANJ* 37 (24 Feb 1900): 611; Cashin, *Under Fire with the Tenth Cavalry*, 185; Steward, *The Colored Regulars*, 137.

Resides in Cuba, 1933. *See* **WILSON**, George, Private, I/10th Cavalry

HARRIS, Silas; Private; D/9th Cav. Veteran of Philippine Insurrection; at Ft D. A. Russell, WY, in 1910; resident of Macon, GA. SOURCE: *Illustrated Review: Ninth Cavalry*, with picture.

HARRIS, Simon P.; QM Sgt; 9th Cav. Sergeant, D/9th Cavalry, promoted to saddler sergeant, 9th Cavalry, Ft Robinson, NE, 23 Apr 1891. SOURCE: Cleveland *Gazette*, 16 May 1891.

Appointed regimental quartermaster sergeant, 12 Oct 1892. SOURCE: Roster, 9 Cav.

Shares duplex on post with Sergeant Major Jones, Ft Robinson, 1894. SOURCE: Investigation of Charges against Chaplain Plummer.

HARRIS, Sylvestor; M/10th Cav. Original member of 10th Cavalry; in troop when organized, Ft Riley, KS, 15 Oct 1867. SOURCE: McMiller, "Buffalo Soldiers," 79.

HARRIS, Theodore; 9th Cav. Married Miss Frances Jones in Crawford, NM, 18 Nov 1896, at home of Mrs. L. Jackson. SOURCE: Crawford *Tribune*, 20 Nov 1896.

No Veterans Administration pension file.

HARRIS, Thomas M.; Private; K/24th Inf. Native of Pittsburgh; wounded in head near Payug, Philippines. SOURCE: Richmond *Planet*, 14 Apr 1900.

Fined $5 for failure to repair for reveille, Cabanatuan, Philippines, 2 Jun 1902; witness 1st Sgt. Jacob W. Stevens, K/24th Infantry. SOURCE: Name File, 24 Inf.

HARRIS, Wade; Corporal; B/25th Inf. Promoted from private. SOURCE: *ANR* 38 (23 Sep 1905): 21.

HARRIS, Wesley; Private; H/9th Cav. Seriously wounded in action against Nana, 19 Aug 1881. SOURCE: *Illustrated Review: Ninth Cavalry.*

    See **WILLIAMS**, John, Private, H/9th Cavalry

HARRIS, William; Private; K/9th Cav. Arrested and fined for being drunk and disorderly and carrying concealed weapon after shooting chase. SOURCE: Cheyenne *Daily Leader*, 9 and 10 Jul 1887.

HARRIS, William; Private; H/10th Cav. Served in 10th Cavalry in Cuba, 1898. SOURCE: Cashin, *Under Fire with the Tenth Cavalry*, 347.

HARRIS, William; Private; H/24th Inf. Fined $3 by summary court, San Isidro, Philippines, for absence from ten P.M. inspection, 14 Feb 1902, first conviction; sentenced to one month and $10 fine for sitting down on sentry duty, failing to halt corporal of guard, San Isidro, 10 May 1902. SOURCE: Register of Summary Court, San Isidro.

HARRIS, William; Private; K/10th Cav. At Ft Robinson, NE, 1904.

HARRIS, William; Corporal; B/9th Cav. Veteran of Philippine Insurrection; at Ft D. A. Russell, WY, in 1910; sharpshooter. SOURCE: *Illustrated Review: Ninth Cavalry*, with picture.

HARRIS, William C.; Sergeant; E/24th Inf. Cited for bravery under fire against Pulahanes, Tabon Tabon, Philippines, 24 Jun 1906, along with Sgt. John Ash, Cpl. Preston Askew, Pvt. Albert W. Piner, and Pvt. Andrew M. Blackman. SOURCE: Muller, *The Twenty Fourth Infantry*, 45.

HARRIS, Willie; L/10th Cav. Original member of 10th Cavalry; in troop when organized, Ft Riley, KS, 21 Sep 1867. SOURCE: McMiller, "Buffalo Soldiers," 78.

HARRISON, Charlie; Trumpeter; G/9th Cav. At Ft D. A. Russell, WY, in 1910; sharpshooter; resident of Los Angeles. SOURCE: *Illustrated Review: Ninth Cavalry*, with picture.

HARRISON, Garfield; Private; A/49th Inf. Deserted at Tuguegarao, Philippines, 15 Apr 1899; was in confinement for murder when he escaped guard. SOURCE: Descriptive Book, A/49 Inf.

HARRISON, George; B/10th Cav. Original member of 10th Cavalry; in troop when organized, Ft Leavenworth, KS, 1 Apr 1867. SOURCE: McMiller, "Buffalo Soldiers," 69.

HARRISON, Henry; D/10th Cav. Original member of 10th Cavalry; in troop when organized, Ft Leavenworth, KS, 1 Jun 1867. SOURCE: McMiller, "Buffalo Soldiers," 71.

HARRISON, Isaac; Private; A/9th Cav. Served 1872. *See* **NELSON**, William, Trumpeter, A/9th Cavalry

HARRISON, Julius; Private; B/24th Inf. Mentioned among men who distinguished themselves in 1889; awarded certificate of merit for gallant and meritorious service while escort for Maj. Joseph W. Wham, paymaster, when attacked by robbers between Fts Grant and Thomas, AZ. SOURCE: GO 18, AGO, 1891.

    At Ft Grant, AZ, 1890; certificate of merit mentioned. SOURCE: SecWar, *AR 1890*, 289.

HARRISON, Lee; Private; E/9th Cav. Sentenced to two months for robbery near Camalig, Philippines, 9 Dec 1901.

HARRISON, Richard; Private; C/10th Cav. Corporal, at Ft Bayard, NM, Jul 1888; selected for Department of Arizona rifle competition, Ft Wingate, NM. SOURCE: Billington, *New Mexico's Buffalo Soldiers*, 154.

    Sergeant; at Ft Apache, AZ, 1890; subscribed $.50 to testimonial to General Grierson. SOURCE: List of subscriptions, 23 Apr 1890, 10th Cavalry papers, MHI.

    First sergeant, reduced to private for adversely criticizing troop commander in presence of enlisted men and inciting men to desertion. SOURCE: *ANJ* 27 (23 Aug 1890): 964.

HARRISON, Samuel A.; Musician; K/25th Inf. At Ft Niobrara, NE, 1904. SOURCE: Wilson, "History of Fort Niobrara."

HARRISON, William; Private; F/10th Cav. Prisoner Harrison to report to court martial room tomorrow. SOURCE: 1st Lt C. Parker to CO, Det 10 Cav, Ft Lyon, CO, 14 Mar 1869, LR, Det 10 Cav, 1868–69.

    Convicted by general court martial, Ft Lyon, for sleeping while sentinel, camp in field near Ft Wallace, KS, 29 Jul 1868; sentenced to six months, then having head shaved and being bugled out of service. SOURCE: GCMO 25, DeptMo, 16 Apr 1869.

    Capt. George Armes asks Harrison's return to duty from guardhouse; his court martial was two months ago and no sentence set yet; Harrison a good soldier who, it appears, was not asleep on post as charged. SOURCE: Armes to AAG, DeptMo, 15 May 1869, LR, Det 10 Cav, 1868–69.

HARRISON, William H.; Private; E/9th Cav. Sentenced to dishonorable discharge and two years for desertion, St. Louis Barracks, MO. SOURCE: GCMO 18, AGO, 20 Feb 1875.

HARRISTON; C/10th Cav. Killed at target practice, Ft Robinson, NE, 25 May 1903. SOURCE: Crawford *Tribune*, 29 May 1903.

HART, Charles; Corporal; L/9th Cav. Retired Jun 1901. SOURCE: *ANJ* 38 (29 Jun 1901): 1067.

HARTNETT, Allen J.; Private; F/24th Inf. Transferred from Reserve Divisional Hospital, Siboney, Cuba, to U.S. on U.S. Army Transport *Vigilancia*, 6 Sep 1898, with remittent malarial fever. SOURCE: Hospital Papers, Spanish-American War.

HARTSELL, Clarence L.; Corporal; H/9th Cav. At Ft D. A. Russell, WY, in 1910; sharpshooter; resident of Bedford, IN. SOURCE: *Illustrated Review: Ninth Cavalry*, with picture.

HARTSFIELD, Edward; Corporal; H/10th Cav. Served in 10th Cavalry, 1898; remained in U.S. during war with Spain. SOURCE: Cashin, *Under Fire with the Tenth Cavalry*, 346.

HARTWELL, O. B.; Private; K/10th Cav. At Ft Robinson, NE, 1904; member of troop orchestra. SOURCE: Barrow, "Christmas in the United States Army," 96.

HARTWOOD, Andrew; Private; G/24th Inf. Born Evansville, IN; served ten years in Band/10th Cavalry; enlisted and joined Band/24th Infantry, age 28, Ht 5'7", yellow complexion, black hair and grey eyes, Ft Bayard, NM, 14 Dec 1891; transferred to G/24th Infantry, married, 25 Dec 1893; additional pay $3 per month; retained $24.40, clothing $50.15. SOURCE: Descriptive Book, 24 Inf NCS & Band.

Private, Band/10th Cavalry; at Ft Apache, AZ, 1890, subscribed $.50 to testimonial to General Grierson. SOURCE: List of subscriptions, 23 Apr 1890, 10th Cavalry papers, MHI.

HARVEY, Anthony; Private; L/9th Cav. Killed by cattle herders at Cimarron, NM, 24 Jan 1876, along with Pvts. John Hanson and George Smallow, L/9th Cavalry. SOURCE: Hamilton, "History of the Ninth Cavalry," 28; *Illustrated Review: Ninth Cavalry*.

HARVEY, B.; Private; K/9th Cav. Reenlistment, married, authorized. SOURCE: Letter, AGO, 17 Jun 1896.

HARVEY, George; Private; K/10th Cav. Mentioned as reenlisting Feb 1873. SOURCE: ES, 10 Cav, 1873–81.

HARVEY, Isaiah; Private; L/25th Inf. Sentenced to one month and $10 fine for sitting down on guard post, San Isidro, Philippines, third conviction; fined $5 for going off limits, Jun 1902. SOURCE: Register of Summary Court, San Isidro.

HARVEY, J. W.; Private; K/9th Cav. On detached service in field, New Mexico, 30 Jan–2 Feb 1881. SOURCE: Regt Returns, 9 Cav, Feb 1881.

HARVEY, John; Private; L/9th Cav. At Ft D. A. Russell, WY, in 1910; resident of Huntington, WV. SOURCE: *Illustrated Review: Ninth Cavalry*, with picture.

HARVEY, John W.; Private; K/25th Inf. Wounded in action, Comanzi, Philippines, 5 Jan 1900. SOURCE: *ANJ* 37 (20 Jan 1900): 488.

Wounded in head during ambush near Arayat, early Jan 1900; native of Missouri. SOURCE: Richmond *Planet*, 17 Feb 1900.

HARVEY, Robert F.; Private; A/10th Cav. Served in 10th Cavalry in Cuba, 1898. SOURCE: Cashin, *Under Fire with the Tenth Cavalry*, 336.

HARVEY, William; Private; C/9th Cav. Recruit, enlisted for C/9th Cavalry at Omaha, NE; arrived at Ft Robinson, NE, Mar 1887.

HARWARD, Lewis; B/10th Cav. Original member of 10th Cavalry; in troop when organized, Ft Leavenworth, KS, 1 Apr 1867. SOURCE: McMiller, "Buffalo Soldiers," 69.

HARWOOD, Thomas; Drum Major; Band/25th Inf. Warrant as sergeant continued as of 1 Dec 1889. SOURCE: SO 13, 25 Inf, Ft Missoula, MT, 4 Mar 1898, Descriptive Cards, 25 Inf.

Sergeant, authorized two-month furlough from Ft Missoula. SOURCE: *ANJ* 27 (22 Feb 1890): 491.

Retired as drum major, Jun 1900. SOURCE: *ANJ* 37 (23 Jun 1900): 1015.

HASKINS, David; 1st Sgt; F/10th Cav. Born in Virginia; private, sergeant, quartermaster sergeant, first sergeant, L/10th Cavalry, and sergeant major, F/10th Cavalry, 6 Sep 1867–5 Sep 1882; private, F/10th Cavalry, 17 Feb 1883; sergeant, 22 Feb 1883; first sergeant, 1 Mar 1883. SOURCE: Baker, Roster.

Original member of 10th Cavalry; in L Troop when organized, Ft Riley, KS, 21 Sep 1867. SOURCE: McMiller, "Buffalo Soldiers," 78.

His request for reduction to the ranks approved by commander, L/10th Cavalry, but not by regimental commander, Feb 1873; proper application for resignation of warrant will be considered; order reducing him to ranks would imply misconduct on his part. SOURCE: ES, 10 Cav, 1873–81.

Resignation as first sergeant accepted. SOURCE: CO, 10 Cav, to CO, L/10 Cav, 20 Mar 1873, ES, 10 Cav, 1873–81.

First sergeant, F/10th Cavalry, at Ft Grant, AZ, to be examined for post quartermaster sergeant. SOURCE: *ANJ* 24 (26 Feb 1887): 610.

First sergeant, F/10th Cavalry, at Ft Apache, AZ, 1890, subscribed $.50 to testimonial to General Grierson. SOURCE: List of subscriptions, 23 Apr 1890, 10th Cavalry papers, MHI.

Retires from Ft Assiniboine, MT, as first sergeant, F/10th Cavalry. SOURCE: *ANJ* 35 (12 Mar 1898): 519.

HASKINS, James; Private; D/9th Cav. Resided in Pueblo, CO, 1895. *See* **DENT**, Henry, Private, D/9th Cavalry

HATCHER; Private; E/10th Cav. At Ft Apache, AZ, 1890, subscribed $.50 to testimonial to General Grierson. SOURCE: List of subscriptions, 23 Apr 1890, 10th Cavalry papers, MHI.

HATCHER, Alex; Musician; H/25th Inf. Born Nashville, TN, 6 Jun 1869; parents Samuel Hatcher and Millie Pitway; occupation railroad porter; Ht 5'4", dark brown complexion; enlisted Evansville, IN; served 7 Mar 1892–6 Mar 1897; disability based on burned feet, incurred crossing desert between Ft Huachuca, AZ, and Mexico, first treated at Ft Huachuca; discharged Ft Douglas, UT; pension $20 per month, 23 Sep 1928, $25 per month, Apr 1932, $60 per month, 6 May 1944, $101.59 when he died; worked for Santa Fe Railroad, 1932; resided at 1043 Walker Avenue, Kansas City, KS; survived by widow Sally E. Hatcher; died of pulmonary edema, Veterans Administration Hospital, Kansas City, MO, 29 Jul 1961; buried National Cemetery, Nashville. SOURCE: VA File C 2349975, Alex Hatcher.

HATCHER, James C.; Private; C/25th Inf. Drowned in the Philippines, 7 Apr 1902. SOURCE: *ANJ* 39 (14 Jun 1902): 1046.

HATCHER, Richard; A/25th Inf. Admitted to Soldiers Home with disability at age 38 with fifteen years' service, 15 Nov 1890. SOURCE: SecWar, *AR 1890*, 751.

HATCHER, Willie; Private; I/24th Inf. Enlisted New Orleans, LA, 26 Jun 1899; assigned to company 10 Jul 1899; never joined; absent sick in Honolulu, HI. SOURCE: Muster Roll, I/24 Inf, Jul–Aug and Nov–Dec 1899.

Joined company, 4 Sep 1899; absent sick in Manila, Philippines, since 11 Oct 1899. SOURCE: Muster Roll, I/24 Inf, Sep–Oct 1899.

HATCHER, Willis; Sergeant; D/10th Cav. Served in 10th Cavalry in Cuba, 1898. SOURCE: Cashin, *Under Fire with the Tenth Cavalry*, 341.

Wounded in action, Santiago, Cuba. SOURCE: SecWar, *AR 1898*, 711; Bigelow, *Reminiscences of Santiago*, 133.

HAUGER, William; Private; K/25th Inf. At Ft Niobrara, NE, 1904. SOURCE: Wilson, "History of Fort Niobrara."

HAUGHTON, Will; Private; I/10th Cav. Served in 10th Cavalry, 1898; remained in U.S. during war with Spain. SOURCE: Cashin, *Under Fire with the Tenth Cavalry*, 348.

HAWK, Luther M.; Private; L/9th Cav. At Ft D. A. Russell, WY, in 1910; resident of Atlanta. SOURCE: *Illustrated Review: Ninth Cavalry*, with picture.

HAWKER, Thomas; Trumpeter; A/9th Cav. At Ft D. A. Russell, WY, in 1910; marksman. SOURCE: *Illustrated Review: Ninth Cavalry*, with picture.

HAWKINS; Corporal; G/9th Cav. At Ft Robinson, NE, 1893; Pvt. Mathew Wyatt heard him say that G Troop was hanging together pretty well behind Barney McKay at time of McKay's court martial. SOURCE: Court Martial Records, McKay.

HAWKINS, Alfred; Corporal; G/10th Cav. Promoted from lance corporal, Jun 1902. SOURCE: *ANJ* 39 (7 Jun 1902): 1004.

HAWKINS, Benjamin; Private; C/10th Cav. Served in 10th Cavalry, 1898; remained in U.S. during war with Spain. SOURCE: Cashin, *Under Fire with the Tenth Cavalry*, 340.

HAWKINS, Charles; Bn Sgt Maj; 10th Cav. Private, on daily duty at headquarters. SOURCE: SO 5, Ft Lyon, CO, 16 Mar 1869, Orders, Det 10 Cav, 1868–69.

Promoted to corporal but to remain on daily duty as clerk in detachment headquarters, because no private of command capable of doing job. SOURCE: SO 8, "in the Field, Kansas," 30 Mar 1869, Orders, Det 10 Cav, 1868–69.

Relieved of duty as clerk. SOURCE: SO 20, Ft Dodge, KS, 16 Apr 1869, Orders, Det 10 Cav, 1868–69.

Sergeant, appointed battalion sergeant major. SOURCE: GO 44, Ft Dodge, KS, 15 May 1869, Orders, Det 10 Cav, 1868–69.

HAWKINS, Charles; Private; D/25th Inf. Dishonorable discharge, Brownsville. SOURCE: SO 266, AGO, 9 Nov 1906.

HAWKINS, D. C.; Private; G/9th Cav. Discharged on surgeon's certificate of disability, Ft Stanton, NM, 11 Jan 1881. SOURCE: Regt Returns, 9 Cav, Jan 1881.

HAWKINS, Emmett; QM Sgt; K/24th Inf. Enlisted Ft Douglas, UT, 22 Feb 1897, with thirteen years' continuous service; sergeant, F/24th Infantry, until 3 Apr 1899; transferred to I Company, 10 Apr 1899, as corporal. SOURCE: Muster Roll, I/24 Inf, Mar–Apr 1899.

Promoted to sergeant, 1 May 1899; on detached service, Three Rivers, CA, 3 May–21 Jun 1899; on detached service, Presidio of San Francisco, CA, 22 Jun 1899. SOURCE: Muster Roll, I/24 Inf, May–Jun 1899.

Fined $1 by summary court, 22 Jul 1899; rejoined company, 26 Jul 1899; reduced to private by summary court, 20 Aug 1899. SOURCE: Muster Roll, I/24 Inf, Jul–Aug 1899.

Promoted to corporal, 21 Oct 1899; allotted $21.60 per month to Mary Hawkins. SOURCE: Muster Roll, I/24 Inf, Sep–Oct 1899.

Corporal; harassed and arrested by Manila, Philippines, police, 19 Jun 1902. SOURCE: CO, 24 Inf to Chief, Manila Police, 21 Jun 1902.

Best infantry marksman, Department of Dakota, 1903. SOURCE: SecWar, *AR 1903*, 1:426.

Stationed at Ft Missoula, MT; won first prize at recent tournament at Sea Girt, NJ; now "ranked among the most remarkable rifle shots in the world"; received "with scant courtesy by his brother officers upon his return to his post at Fort Missoula, Mont. The jealousy engendered may result in his asking for a transfer to Fort Assiniboine." SOURCE: Indianapolis *Freeman*, 28 Nov 1903.

Eighteen-year veteran of Cuba and the Philippines; won Department of Dakota gold medal at Sea Girt, NJ. SOURCE: Cleveland *Gazette*, 26 Sep 1903.

His officers refused his fellows' plans for reception in his honor on return; men are furious; Hawkins has asked for transfer to Second Battalion, Ft Assiniboine, MT. SOURCE: Cleveland *Gazette*, 14 Nov 1903.

Ranked number 18 among expert riflemen, with 74.67 percent, 1903; distinguished marksman, 1897, as private, F/24th Infantry, and 1903. SOURCE: GO 52, AGO, 19 Mar 1904.

Ranked number 175 among expert riflemen, with 68.67 percent, 1904. SOURCE: GO 79, AGO, 1 Jun 1905.

Distinguished marksman, 1905. SOURCE: GO 173, AGO, 20 Oct 1905.

Ranked number five among expert riflemen, with 81.33 percent, 1905. SOURCE: GO 101, AGO, 31 May 1906.

Distinguished marksman, 1906. SOURCE: GO 198, AGO, 6 Dec 1906.

Quartermaster sergeant, K/24th Infantry; ranked number eight, Army Rifle Competition, Ft Sheridan, IL, 1909; distinguished marksman. SOURCE: GO 228, AGO, 12 Nov 1909.

First in recent Ft Niagara, NY, rifle competition for Departments of the East and Gulf; five-time member of Army rifle team of fourteen; eighty-seven officers and enlisted men at competition. SOURCE: Cleveland *Gazette*, 14 Aug 1909.

HAWKINS, G. S.; Corporal; A/9th Cav. Wounded in action against Victorio, Membrillo Canyon, NM, 5 Mar 1880. SOURCE: *Illustrated Review: Ninth Cavalry*.

At Ft Stanton, NM, 1881; on detached service, Ft Craig, NM, 29 Dec 1880–2 Jan 1881. SOURCE: Regt Returns, 9 Cav, Jan 1881.

HAWKINS, George; Recruit; Colored Detachment/ Mounted Service. Convicted by general court martial, Jefferson Barracks, MO, of desertion, 10–13 Oct 1888; sentenced to dishonorable discharge and five years; sentence reduced to six months, without discharge. SOURCE: GCMO 59, AGO, 15 Nov 1888.

HAWKINS, Ham; Recruit; 10th Cav. Mentioned May 1877 as private, 9th Cavalry, 8 Dec 1866–8 Dec 1871 and 14 Jan 1872–1 Jan 1877; now unassigned, 10th Cavalry. SOURCE: LS, 10 Cav, 1873–83.

HAWKINS, Henry; Private; E/10th Cav. Original member of 10th Cavalry; in troop when organized, Ft Leavenworth, KS, 15 Jun 1867. SOURCE: McMiller, "Buffalo Soldiers," 72.

Assigned to E Troop, Jun 1867. SOURCE: LS, 10 Cav, 1866–67.

HAWKINS, Henry; Private; B/10th Cav. Served in 10th Cavalry, 1898; remained in U.S. during war with Spain. SOURCE: Cashin, *Under Fire with the Tenth Cavalry*, 339.

HAWKINS, John T.; Private; C/25th Inf. Dishonorable discharge, Brownsville. SOURCE: SO 266, AGO, 9 Nov 1906.

HAWKINS, Monroe; Blacksmith; B/9th Cav. Veteran of Spanish-American War and Philippine Insurrection; at Ft D. A. Russell, WY, in 1910; sharpshooter. SOURCE: *Illustrated Review: Ninth Cavalry*, with picture.

HAWKINS, Thomas C.; Private; 24th Inf. Sentenced to death for role in Houston riot, 1917. SOURCE: Haynes, *A Night of Violence*, 271.

Hanged, Ft Sam Houston, TX, 13 Dec 1917, for part in Houston riot. SOURCE: Cleveland *Gazette*, 15 Dec 1917.

HAWKINS, William; Corporal; H/10th Cav. Honorable mention for services rendered in capture of Mangas and his Apache band, Rio Bonito, AZ, 18 Oct 1886. SOURCE: Baker, Roster.

HAWKINS, William; Private; A/10th Cav. Served in 10th Cavalry in Cuba, 1898. SOURCE: Cashin, *Under Fire with the Tenth Cavalry*, 336.

HAWKINS, William F.; Captain; M/49th Inf. Appointed as of 9 Sep 1899. SOURCE: Descriptive Book, M/49 Inf.

HAWLEY; Private; K/9th Cav. Discharged in accordance with Special Order 62, Adjutant General's Office, 16 Mar 1898.

HAY, P.; Private; H/9th Cav. Enlisted Ft McKinney, WY, 10 Aug 1888.

HAYDEN, David F.; Private; M/24th Inf. Fatally shot by civilian, Coeur d'Alene, ID. SOURCE: *ANJ* 37 (24 Mar 1900): 698; Richmond *Planet*, 24 Mar 1900.

HAYDEN, James; Private; K/9th Cav. Recruit from depot, arrived Ft Robinson, NE, 1 Mar 1887.

Discharged with staph infection, right eye, Ft Robinson, Jun 1888.

HAYDEN, Thomas; H/10th Cav. Original member of 10th Cavalry; in troop when organized, Ft Leavenworth, KS, 21 Jul 1867. SOURCE: McMiller, "Buffalo Soldiers," 75.

HAYDEN, William; Private; A/10th Cav. Served in 10th Cavalry, 1898; remained in U.S. during war with Spain. SOURCE: Cashin, *Under Fire with the Tenth Cavalry*, 337.

HAYDEN, William; Private; K/24th Inf. Fined $5, Cabanatuan, Philippines, 25 Apr 1901, for being drunk and disorderly in quarters and refusing to stop loud talking, making it necessary to take him to guardhouse; witness 1st Sgt. Jacob Stevens, K/24th Infantry. SOURCE: Name File, 24 Inf.

HAYE, Henry; B/10th Cav. Original member of 10th Cavalry; in troop when organized, Ft Leavenworth, KS, 1 Apr 1867. SOURCE: McMiller, "Buffalo Soldiers," 69.

HAYES, Allen; 24th Inf. Resided at 1276 East 5th South, Salt Lake City, UT, in 1898. SOURCE: Clark, "A History of the Twenty-fourth," appendix E.

HAYES, Burton; Private; F/9th Cav. At Ft D. A. Russell, WY, in 1910; sharpshooter. SOURCE: *Illustrated Review: Ninth Cavalry.*

HAYES, Frank, Jr.; Private; I/10th Cav. Served in 10th Cavalry, 1898; remained in U.S. during war with Spain. SOURCE: Cashin, *Under Fire with the Tenth Cavalry*, 348.

HAYES, Hugh; Private; I/10th Cav. Served in 10th Cavalry, 1898; remained in U.S. during war with Spain. SOURCE: Cashin, *Under Fire with the Tenth Cavalry*, 348.

HAYES, James C.; Corporal; A/10th Cav. At Ft Keogh, MT; promoted from private, 3 Mar 1898. SOURCE: *ANJ* 35 (12 Mar 1898): 518.

Served in 10th Cavalry, 1898; remained in U.S. during war with Spain. SOURCE: Cashin, *Under Fire with the Tenth Cavalry*, 337.

HAYES, Leander W.; 2nd Lt; E/49th Inf. In North Carolina volunteer infantry, 2 Jun 1898–2 Jan 1899; appointed second lieutenant, 49th Infantry, 9 Sep 1899; participated in engagement between Las Pinas and Paranaque, Philippines, 25 Sep 1900; commanded detachment against insurgents at Bibin, Laguna, Philippines, 10 Feb 1900. SOURCE: Descriptive Book, E/49 Inf.

HAYES, Preston; Private; K/10th Cav. Served in 10th Cavalry, 1898; remained in U.S. during war with Spain. SOURCE: Cashin, *Under Fire with the Tenth Cavalry*, 349.

HAYES, West; Private; M/24th Inf. Fatally shot by civilian, Coeur d'Alene, ID. SOURCE: *ANJ* 37 (24 Mar 1900): 698; Richmond *Planet*, 24 Mar 1900.

HAYES, William; Private; K/10th Cav. Served in 10th Cavalry, 1898; remained in U.S. during war with Spain. SOURCE: Cashin, *Under Fire with the Tenth Cavalry*, 349.

HAYGOOD, Claude; Private; K/10th Cav. Discharged on surgeon's certificate, with gonorrhea, Ft Robinson, NE, 26 Sep 1904. SOURCE: Certificates of Disability, Ft Robinson.

HAYMAN, Perry A.; B/25th Inf. Born Sharon Hill, PA; enlisted, age 20, Philadelphia, PA; served ten years;

Charles Holder, M/10th Cavalry, shot peddler to steal whisky, was turned over to civil authorities, Ft Smith, AR, Apr 1874; Cpl. George Berry was wounded in fight at Cheyenne Agency, Apr 1875; participated in battle at Cheyenne Agency and served at Ft Reno, Indian Territory; then served in 25th Infantry; now age 71. SOURCE: *Winners of the West* 2 (Mar 1925): 2–3.

Corporal, M/10th Cavalry, wounded in Cheyenne Agency fight, 6 Apr 1875. SOURCE: Leckie, *The Buffalo Soldiers*, 139.

HAYNE; Trumpeter; K/10th Cav. Shaved Lt. John Bigelow at Mowry Mine, AZ, 31 Dec 1885. SOURCE: Bigelow, *On the Bloody Trail of Geronimo*, 109.

HAYNES, Oscar; Private; C/23rd Kans Inf. Born Hemenla, AL; died in Minnesota, 1 Sep 1941. SOURCE: Taylor, "Minnesota Black Spanish-American War Veterans."

HAYNES, William J.; 1st Sgt; F/25th Inf. Took pledge renouncing participation in games of chance or skill for wagers, Ft Missoula, MT, 21 Apr 1892. SOURCE: Monthly Report, Chaplain Steward, 1 May 1892.

Ranked number 485 among rifle experts with 68.33 percent in 1905. SOURCE: GO 101, AGO, 31 May 1906.

An extremely capable noncommissioned officer. SOURCE: Steward, *Fifty Years in the Gospel Ministry*, 352.

HAYS; Corporal; L/24th Inf. Retires with thirty years' service from Madison Barracks, NY. SOURCE: Cleveland *Gazette*, 18 Apr 1908.

HAYS, J. E.; Private; E/9th Cav. Restored to duty in accordance with letter, Department of the Platte, 21 Jul 1891.

Letter, Department of the Platte, 9 Aug 1891, concerns his unjust confinement.

HAYS, J. H.; Corporal; E/24th Inf. Promoted from private, Ft Bayard, NM, May 1891. SOURCE: Cleveland *Gazette*, 9 May 1891.

HAYS, Jackson; Recruit; C/10th Cav. Enlisted Memphis, TN, spring 1867. SOURCE: LS, 10 Cav, 1866–67.

Original member of 10th Cavalry; in troop when organized, Ft Leavenworth, KS, 14 May 1867. SOURCE: McMiller, "Buffalo Soldiers," 70.

HAYS, James; C/10th Cav. Arrived at Ft Leavenworth, KS, from Jefferson Barracks, MO. SOURCE: Adj, Ft Leavenworth, to headquarters, Jefferson Barracks, 9 Oct 1866, LS, 10 Cav, 1866–67.

Original member of 10th Cavalry; in troop when organized, Ft Leavenworth, KS, 14 May 1867. SOURCE: McMiller, "Buffalo Soldiers," 70.

HAYS, John; A/10th Cav. Original member of 10th Cavalry; in troop when organized, Ft Leavenworth, KS, 18 Feb 1867. SOURCE: McMiller, "Buffalo Soldiers," 70.

HAYS, John R.; Sergeant; H/24th Inf. Enlisted Ft Bayard, NM, 17 Nov 1895; on detached service at Ft Douglas, UT, since 20 Apr 1898, in charge of company property. SOURCE: Muster Roll, H/24 Inf, May–Jun 1899.

Promoted sergeant from artificer, 14 Sep 1898; on special duty as acting quartermaster sergeant since 29 Oct 1898; on special duty at Ft Douglas, 20 Apr–1 Oct 1898. SOURCE: Muster Roll, H/24 Inf, Sep–Oct 1898.

Acting quartermaster sergeant until 4 Nov 1898; discharged, end of term, character excellent, single, retained $3.97, clothing, $32.30, Ft Douglas, 16 Nov 1898; reenlisted, 17 Nov 1898; warrant continued; fourteenth year of continuous service; on special duty, overseer of laborers, since 17 Nov 1898. SOURCE: Muster Roll, H/24 Inf, Nov–Dec 1898.

On special duty as overseer of laborers through Feb 1899. SOURCE: Muster Roll, H/24 Inf, Jan–Feb 1899.

HAYS, Lewis; Recruit; 10th Cav. Application made for his discharge as he is underage. SOURCE: AG, USA, to CO, 10 Cav, Jan 1870, ES, 10 Cav, 1866–71.

HAYWOOD, Charles; Private; D/9th Cav. Killed in action, Pine Ridge, SD, 30 Dec 1890, while part of wagon guard. SOURCE: Hamilton, "History of the Ninth Cavalry," 74; *Illustrated Review: Ninth Cavalry*.

Killed along with horse when troop, commanded by Capt. John Loud, repulsed Sioux attack on regiment's wagon train. SOURCE: Kelley, *Pine Ridge, 1890*, 192.

Killed by Indian in cavalry uniform in "exchange of a few shots." SOURCE: Perry, "The Ninth U.S. Cavalry in the Sioux Campaign of 1890," 39.

Buried at Ft Robinson, NE. SOURCE: List of Interments, Ft Robinson.

HAYWOOD, Larry; Private; F/9th Cav. Prisoner awaiting trial for absence without leave, Dec 1887, complains of abuse and unfairness in his troop and being cursed by his captain, Ft Robinson, NE. SOURCE: Reports of Inspection, DeptPlatte, I.

HAZZARD; Private; K/10th Cav. With Lt. John Bigelow, Dec 1885. *See* **CROPPER**, Sam, Private, K/10th Cavalry

HAZZARD, Frank; Recruit; Colored Detachment/ Mounted Service. Convicted by general court martial, Jefferson Barracks, MO, of loss of clothing worth $24.90 and desertion, 8–9 Feb 1887; sentenced to dishonorable discharge and four years. SOURCE: GCMO 24, AGO, 14 Mar 1887.

HAZZARD, George H.; Private; H/24th Inf. Born West Chester, PA. SOURCE: Clark, "A History of the Twenty-fourth," 101.

Enlisted Philadelphia, PA, 19 Jun 1897, with two years' continuous service. SOURCE: Muster Roll, H/24 Inf, May–Jun 1898.

Wounded in action at San Juan, Cuba, 1 Jul 1898; returned to U.S. for treatment. SOURCE: Muster Roll, H/24 Inf, Jul–Aug 1898.

Wounded in Cuba. SOURCE: Muller, *The Twenty Fourth Infantry*, 19.

Rejoined company from absence, sick, 24 Sep 1898; on special duty in charge of post bathhouse, Ft Douglas, UT, since 2 Oct 1898. SOURCE: Muster Roll, H/24 Inf, Sep–Oct 1898.

On special duty in charge of post bathhouse 2 Oct–13 Nov 1898; on special duty, laborer, Quartermaster Department, since 13 Nov 1898. SOURCE: Muster Roll, H/24 Inf, Nov–Dec 1898.

On special duty as laborer since 4 Dec 1898; fined $8 by summary court, 1 Jan 1899. SOURCE: Muster Roll, H/24 Inf, Jan–Feb 1899.

HAZZARD, Miller; Trumpeter; M/10th Cav. Original member of 10th Cavalry; in troop when organized, Ft Riley, KS, 15 Oct 1867. SOURCE: McMiller, "Buffalo Soldiers," 79.

Mentioned Jan 1873 as having served Sep 1867–Oct 1872. SOURCE: LS, 10 Cav, 1873–83.

Commander, 10th Cavalry, approves request of Captain Norvell to reenlist Trumpeter Hazzard, discharged 1 Jun 1877, but Adjutant General does not approve. SOURCE: ES, 10 Cav, 1873–81.

HEAD, Monroe; Private; L/10th Cav. Served in 10th Cavalry, 1898; remained in U.S. during war with Spain. SOURCE: Cashin, *Under Fire with the Tenth Cavalry*, 351.

HEAGAN, Joel; 1st Sgt; D/49th Inf. Resides at 871 West 11th Street, Indianapolis; served in the Philippines; verifies Floyd Crumbly's illness in the Philippines. SOURCE: Affidavit, Heagan, 1 May 1905, VA File XC 2624105, Floyd H. Crumbly.

HEAGOOD, George; Private; I/9th Cav. At Ft D. A. Russell, WY, in 1910; resident of Mt. Fension, AL. SOURCE: *Illustrated Review: Ninth Cavalry*, with picture.

HEARD, Alonzo; Private; K/25th Inf. Fined $5 by summary court, San Isidro, Philippines, for being drunk and disorderly in quarters after taps and failing to obey order to stop, 4 Jun 1902. SOURCE: Register of Summary Court, San Isidro.

HEARD, Mack; Private; I/25th Inf. Fined one month's pay by summary court, San Isidro, Philippines, for breach of arrest, Mar 1902, sixth conviction; fined $3 for failure to attend formation for company vaccinations, 3 Apr 1902. SOURCE: Register of Summary Court, San Isidro.

HEATDER, Randolph; Private; K/9th Cav. At Ft D. A. Russell, WY, in 1910; resident of Austin, TX. SOURCE: *Illustrated Review: Ninth Cavalry*.

HEATH, Ulysses G.; Private; K/48th Inf. Wounded in thigh in the Philippines, 6 May 1900. SOURCE: *ANJ* 37 (9 Jun 1900): 975.

HECTOR, Herman, Jr.; Private; E/9th Cav. Enlisted Ft Washakie, WY, 25 Dec 1889. SOURCE: Regt Returns, 9 Cav, Dec 1889.

Relieved of special duty as clerk, Adjutant's Office, Ft Robinson, NE. SOURCE: Order 71, 30 Apr 1892, Post Orders, Ft Robinson.

Wife is pyromaniac although "a very good quiet woman of excellent character." SOURCE: CO, Ft Robinson, to AAG, DP, 8 and 9 Aug 1893, LS, Ft Robinson.

Teacher, Ft Robinson schools, 4 Nov 1893–30 Apr 1894. SOURCE: Reports of Schools, Ft Robinson.

Relieved of extra duty as schoolteacher, Ft Robinson. SOURCE: Order 27, 29 Apr 1894, Post Orders, Ft Robinson.

Child buried at Ft Robinson, 1894. SOURCE: List of Interments, Ft Robinson.

Enlisted 22 Oct 1886; sentenced to dishonorable discharge and one year, Ft Washakie, 2 Dec 1888, in accordance with General Court Martial Order 103, Department of the Platte, Nov 1888; reenlisted, 23 Dec 1889, in accordance with message, Adjutant General's Office, 23 Dec 1889; convicted of theft of gold watch and chain worth $59 from Blacksmith Peter H. Turner, E/9th Cavalry, in accordance with Special Order 100, Department of the Platte, 27 Sep 1894; sentenced to dishonorable discharge and eighteen months; was his own counsel at court martial. SOURCE: Court Martial Records, Hector.

Military Convict Hector conducted to Ft Omaha, NE, with Military Convict George Washington, 9th Cavalry, by 1st Sgt. George Tracy and Pvt. Harry Rice, D/9th Cavalry. SOURCE: Order 77, 3 Oct 1894, Post Orders, Ft Robinson.

HEGWOOD, Samuel; A/10th Cav. Original member of 10th Cavalry; in troop when organized, Ft Leavenworth, KS, 18 Feb 1867. SOURCE: McMiller, "Buffalo Soldiers," 68.

HELLEMS, Frank; Private; H/24th Inf. Enlisted Providence, RI, 9 Oct 1896, with eight years' continuous service; transferred from C/24th Infantry, 21 Sep 1898. SOURCE: Muster Roll, H/24 Inf, Sep–Oct 1898.

Musician, C/24th Infantry, wounded in Cuba, 1898. SOURCE: Muller, *The Twenty Fourth Infantry*, 18.

Present for duty. SOURCE: Muster Roll, H/24 Inf, Nov–Dec 1898 and Jan–Feb 1899.

HELM, Joshua; Corporal; C/25th Inf. Late private, F/114th U.S. Colored Troops; late corporal, C/25th Infantry; reenlisted in C/25th Infantry and now at Newport Barracks, KY; adjutant, 10th Cavalry, forwards check for $90 to Adjutant General to pay Helm's claim. SOURCE: Adj, 10 Cav, to AG, USA, 27 Feb 1875, LS, 10 Cav, 1873–83.

HELM, Sherred; Private; G/10th Cav. Honorable mention for bravery against Comanches, Double Mountains Fork, Brazos River, TX, 5 Feb 1874. SOURCE: Baker, Roster.

HEMPHILL, Lank; Private; H/24th Inf. On request of company commander, board of officers convened to examine his mental condition. SOURCE: Order 172, Ft Huachuca, AZ, 25 Nov 1893, Orders Received, 24 Inf.

HENDERSON; Sergeant; 10th Cav. Wife Agnes died suddenly of acute bronchitis and laryngitis, morning of 27 Jun 1902; remains shipped to Kansas City, MO, for burial. SOURCE: Medical History, Ft Robinson.

HENDERSON; D/10th Cav. Shot Fenton Harris, I/10th Cavalry, on Main Street, Crawford, NE, 14 Sep 1903. SOURCE: Crawford *Tribune*, 18 Sep 1903.

HENDERSON, Albert J.; Private; L/10th Cav. Released to duty from treatment for gonorrhea, Ft Robinson, NE, 27 Sep 1903. SOURCE: Post Surgeon to CO, L/10, 27 Sep 1903, LS, Post Surgeon, Ft Robinson.

HENDERSON, Albert W.; Private; L/9th Cav. At Ft D. A. Russell, WY, in 1910; resident of Cleveland, TN. SOURCE: *Illustrated Review: Ninth Cavalry*, with picture.

HENDERSON, Almando; Sergeant; K/10th Cav. Commissioned first lieutenant, Camp Des Moines, IA, 15 Oct 1917. SOURCE: Glass, *History of the Tenth Cavalry*, appendix M.

HENDERSON, Charles; Private; A/10th Cav. Arrived Ft Leavenworth, KS, from Jefferson Barracks, MO. SOURCE: Adj, Ft Leavenworth, to Headquarters, Jefferson Barracks, 9 Oct 1866.

Original member of 10th Cavalry; in troop when organized, Ft Leavenworth, KS, 18 Feb 1867. SOURCE: McMiller, "Buffalo Soldiers," 68.

HENDERSON, Charles H.; Private; L/10th Cav. Served in 10th Cavalry, 1898; remained in U.S. during war with Spain. SOURCE: Cashin, *Under Fire with the Tenth Cavalry*, 351.

Sentenced to ten years for mutiny by general court martial, Bayamo, Cuba, 12 Oct 1899. SOURCE: *ANJ* 37 (24 Oct 1900): 602.

HENDERSON, Edward; A/10th Cav. Original member of 10th Cavalry; in troop when organized, Ft Leavenworth, KS, 18 Feb 1867. SOURCE: McMiller, "Buffalo Soldiers," 68.

Born Morgan Co., MO; enlisted, occupation laborer, age 23, Ht 5'9", black complexion, St. Louis, MO, 26 Jan 1867; feet frozen while on stable guard, Ft Leavenworth, c. 25 Feb 1867; discharged on surgeon's certificate with permanent disability, 16 Jan 1868.

HENDERSON, Elmer; Private; D/10th Cav. Married Mary Suaya, with consent of commander, Ft Robinson, NE, 17 Feb 1906 [two months earlier civilian Walter P. Tate married Carlota Suaya]. SOURCE: Monthly Report, Chaplain Anderson, 1 Mar 1906.

Age 29 when he married Mary Theodosia Ardella Suaya, age 39, born Kingston, Jamaica. SOURCE: Medical History, Ft Robinson.

HENDERSON, Harrison; Private; Band/9th Cav. At Ft Robinson, NE, 1894. SOURCE: Court Martial Records, Plummer.

HENDERSON, J. W.; Sergeant; C/9th Cav. Appointed corporal, F/9th Cavalry, 14 Apr 1893. SOURCE: Roster, 9 Cav.

Ranked number two in cavalry carbine competition, Departments of the Platte, Dakota, and Columbia, 27–30 Sep 1894. SOURCE: GO 64, AGO, 18 Nov 1897.

Trumpeter, C/9th Cavalry, transferred from C/10th Cavalry. SOURCE: SO 64, AGO, 17 Mar 1896.

Commended for gallantry in charge on San Juan Hill, battle of Santiago, Cuba, 1 Jul 1898, as corporal, C/9th Cavalry; now sergeant, C/9th Cavalry. SOURCE: GO 15, AGO, 13 Feb 1900.

Awarded certificate of merit for distinguished service, 1 Jul 1898. SOURCE: *ANJ* 37 (24 Feb 1900): 611.

HENDERSON, John; Private; A/10th Cav. Fined $12.80 and worked on streets 1 1/2 days for fast riding, being drunk and disorderly, and running horse into Fremont House, Crawford, NE, 30 Jun 1902.

In hands of civil authorities, Crawford, 1–4 Jul 1902. SOURCE: Regt Returns, 9 Cav, Jul 1902.

Transferred to E/10th Cavalry in accordance with Special Order 235, Adjutant General's Office, 6 Oct 1902.

HENDERSON, John; Sergeant; G/10th Cav. Served in 10th Cavalry in Cuba, 1898. SOURCE: Cashin, *Under Fire with the Tenth Cavalry*, 345.

HENDERSON, John; Private; G/10th Cav. Served in 10th Cavalry in Cuba, 1898. SOURCE: Cashin, *Under Fire with the Tenth Cavalry*, 345.

HENDERSON, John, Jr.; Private; 9th Cav. At Ft Niobrara, NE, 1889. *See* **CARTER**, William H., Trumpeter, A/9th Cavalry

HENDERSON, John H.; Corporal; I/9th Cav. Served as corporal, E/10th Cavalry, in Cuba, 1898. SOURCE: Cashin, *Under Fire with the Tenth Cavalry*, 342.

Veteran of Spanish-American War and Philippine Insurrection; corporal, I/9th Cavalry, at Ft D. A. Russell, WY, in 1910; sharpshooter; resident of Manchester, NH. SOURCE: *Illustrated Review: Ninth Cavalry*, with picture.

HENDERSON, Lewis; Private; I/10th Cav. Served in 10th Cavalry in Cuba, 1898. SOURCE: Cashin, *Under Fire with the Tenth Cavalry*, 348.

HENDERSON, Monola; Corporal; K/10th Cav. With Captain Morey and three others who were found twenty miles west of Carrizal, Mexico, three days after 1916 battle. SOURCE: Wharfield, *10th Cavalry and Border Fights*, 43.

HENDERSON, Norman; K/25th Inf. At San Marcelino, Philippines, 1900. *See* **WISEMAN**, Turner H., Corporal, K/25th Infantry

HENDERSON, Reuben W.; G/25th Inf. Born Caroline Co., VA; enlisted, age 45, Ht 5'7", dark complexion, brown eyes, grey hair, Ft Grant, AZ, 1 Mar 1899; twenty-four years' continuous service; character excellent. SOURCE: Descriptive & Assignment Cards, 25 Inf.

HENDERSON, Richard; Private; E/24th Inf. Wounded in action in Cuba, 1898. SOURCE: Muller, *The Twenty Fourth Infantry*, 18.

HENDERSON, William; F/10th Cav. Born and reared Richmond, VA; enlisted, age 19, Washington, DC, 13 Aug 1867; discharged, end of term, Ft Sill, Indian Territory, 13 Aug 1873; age 78, laborer, resided at 1373 West Pleasant Street, Springfield, OH, for thirty-six years, 1922. SOURCE: Affidavit, Henderson, 1922, VA File SC 11405, John Taylor.

HENDERSON, William; Private; E/24th Inf. Born Wheeling, WV; died in Minnesota, 26 Sep 1938. SOURCE: Taylor, "Minnesota Black Spanish-American War Veterans."

HENDERSON, William A.; C/9th Cav. Served 1873–78; member, Camp 11, National Indian War Veterans, St. Joseph, MO; died El Paso, TX, age 85. SOURCE: *Winners of the West* 12 (Jun 1935): 2.

HENDERSON, William N.; Private; E/10th Cav. Served in 10th Cavalry in Cuba, 1898. SOURCE: Cashin, *Under Fire with the Tenth Cavalry*, 342.

HENDRICKS, Caesar; Private; M/10th Cav. Served in 10th Cavalry, 1898; remained in U.S. during war with Spain. SOURCE: Cashin, *Under Fire with the Tenth Cavalry*, 351.

HENDRICKS, J. F.; Musician; Band/10th Cav. Served in 10th Cavalry in Cuba, 1898. SOURCE: Cashin, *Under Fire with the Tenth Cavalry*, 352.

From Pulaski City, VA; played clarinet, saxophone, organ, cello. SOURCE: Lowe, "Camp Life," 206.

HENDRICKS, Lewis; 24th Inf. Died Ft Bayard, NM, Aug 1890; resolution of respect signed by James W. Abbott, Goodson M. Newlands, and John E. Green, of Noah's Ark Lodge, No. 3207, Grand Union of Odd Fellows, Ft Bayard. SOURCE: Cleveland *Gazette*, 30 Aug 1890.

HENDRICKS, William; Private; E/9th Cav. Application for Hospital Corps rejected by letter, Adjutant General's Office, 20 Dec 1897.

HENRY; Private; C/9th Cav. Wounded in action at San Juan, Cuba, 1 Jul 1898. SOURCE: *Illustrated Review: Ninth Cavalry.*

HENRY, Boston; Private; 9th Cav. Killed by white civilian, San Angelo, TX, Jun 1869. SOURCE: Carroll, *The Black Military Experience*, 454.

HENRY, Cash; Corporal; I/24th Inf. Captured by insurgents, 10 Oct 1900; died same day of sunstroke after his hat was taken from him. *See* **BURNS**, William J., Corporal, I/24th Infantry

HENRY, Charles; Private; I/24th Inf. Enlisted Pittsburgh, 26 Jul 1898. SOURCE: Muster Roll, I/24 Inf, Jan–Feb 1899.

Sentenced to one month's confinement by garrison court martial, Ft D. A. Russell, WY, 16 Mar 1899. SOURCE: Muster Roll, I/24 Inf, Mar–Apr 1899.

Discharged, character very good, 31 Dec 1899; deposits $40, clothing $12.25. SOURCE: Muster Roll, I/24 Inf, Nov–Dec 1899.

HENRY, Charley; Private; I/24th Inf. At San Carlos, AZ, 1890. *See* **HARDEE**, James A., Private, K/24th Infantry

HENRY, Edward; Private; B/10th Cav. At Camp Forse, AL, Nov 1898. SOURCE: Richmond *Planet*, 3 Dec 1898.

Sentenced to dishonorable discharge and confinement at Ft Robinson, NE, in accordance with Special Order 120, Department of the Missouri, 30 Jun 1904.

HENRY, Frank C.; Private; H/10th Cav. At Camp Forse, AL, Nov 1898. SOURCE: Richmond *Planet*, 3 Dec 1898. Served in 10th Cavalry in Cuba, 1898. SOURCE: Cashin, *Under Fire with the Tenth Cavalry*, 345.

HENRY, H.; Private; B/9th Cav. On detached service at Ft Bayard, NM, 16 Jan–9 Feb 1881. SOURCE: Regt Returns, 9 Cav, Feb 1881.

HENRY, Hiram A.; Private; K/9th Cav. To be discharged from Ft Myers, VA, in accordance with Special Order 124, Division of the Atlantic, 13 Jun 1891. SOURCE: *ANJ* 28 (20 Jun 1891): 732.

HENRY, Horace T.; QM Sgt; K/25th Inf. Sergeant, in charge of Gatling gun, and provost sergeant, San Fernando, Luzon, Philippines, autumn 1899. SOURCE: Richmond *Planet*, 20 Jan 1900.

"The pride of the 25th" is again first sergeant and "we will again enjoy peace and discipline combined as a result." SOURCE: Richmond *Planet*, 30 Jun 1900.

Accidentally shot and killed Pvt. Jesse B. Smith, K/25th Infantry, at Castillejos, Philippines, 31 Dec 1901. SOURCE: *ANJ* 38 (30 Mar 1901): 753; Richmond *Planet*, 9 Mar 1901.

Quartermaster sergeant, K/25th Infantry, at Ft Niobrara, NE, 1904. SOURCE: Wilson, "History of Fort Niobrara."

HENRY, J. E.; Corporal; I/25th Inf. In charge of commissary, battalion headquarters, San Felipe, Philippines, Jun 1900. SOURCE: Richmond *Planet*, 18 Aug 1900.

HENRY, James; A/10th Cav. Original member of 10th Cavalry; in troop when organized, Ft Leavenworth, KS, 18 Feb 1867. SOURCE: McMiller, "Buffalo Soldiers," 68.

HENRY, James L.; Private; D/25th Inf. Sentenced to ten years in prison after brief court martial for using "a profane word in retort to a command of an officer," Dec 1906. SOURCE: Cleveland *Gazette*, 12 Jan 1907; Washington *Bee*, 5 Jan 1907.

HENRY, John; K/10th Cav. Original member of 10th Cavalry; in troop when organized, Ft Riley, KS, 1 Sep 1867. SOURCE: McMiller, "Buffalo Soldiers," 77.

HENRY, John; L/10th Cav. Original member of 10th Cavalry; in troop when organized, Ft Riley, KS, 21 Sep 1867. SOURCE: McMiller, "Buffalo Soldiers," 78.

HENRY, John; Private; M/10th Cav. Served in 10th Cavalry in Cuba, 1898. SOURCE: Cashin, *Under Fire with the Tenth Cavalry*, 352.

HENRY, John; Private; F/25th Inf. Former soldier, owned laundry in Botolen, Zambales, Philippines, Dec 1900. SOURCE: Steward, *Fifty Years in the Gospel Ministry*, 326–27.

HENRY, John; Private; L/9th Cav. At Ft D. A. Russell, WY, in 1910; resident of Charlottesville, VA. SOURCE: *Illustrated Review: Ninth Cavalry*, with picture.

HENRY, Philip; Private; F/9th Cav. Shot it out with Pvt. William H. Holloway, F/9th Cavalry, at Ft Cummings, NM, Nov 1880; died while Holloway escaped with leg wounds. SOURCE: Billington, *New Mexico's Buffalo Soldiers*, 129.

HENRY, Robert A.; Private; H/24th Inf. Enlisted Philadelphia, PA, 4 Feb 1899. SOURCE: Muster Roll, H/24 Inf, Jan–Feb 1899.

HENRY, Samuel T.; Corporal; M/24th Inf. At Cabanatuan, Philippines, 1901. *See* **HAMPTON**, Wade, Private, B/24th Infantry

HENRY, Thomas; A/10th Cav. Original member of 10th Cavalry; in troop when organized, Ft Leavenworth, KS, 18 Feb 1867. SOURCE: McMiller, "Buffalo Soldiers," 68.

HENRY, Thomas; F/10th Cav. Original member of 10th Cavalry; in troop when organized, Ft Leavenworth, KS, 21 Jun 1867. SOURCE: McMiller, "Buffalo Soldiers," 73.

HENRY, Thomas; Private; G/10th Cav. At Ft Lyon, CO, Mar 1869. SOURCE: LR, Det 10 Cav, 1868–69.

HENRY, Vida; Private; I/24th Inf. Ranked number 216 among rifle experts with 71.33 percent in 1905. SOURCE: GO 101, AGO, 31 May 1906.

Accused of leading Houston riot, 1917. SOURCE: Haynes, *A Night of Violence*, 46.

Acting first sergeant, 35 years old, veteran of thirteen years, light complexion, deep scar on outer edge of right eye, "muscular and well-proportioned," on eve of mutiny; warned officers of possible trouble; unable to write; stern disciplinarian. SOURCE: Haynes, *A Night of Violence*, 115–16.

Plainly in charge of mutineers, Houston; actual role in riot murky because he committed suicide immediately afterward. SOURCE: Haynes, *A Night of Violence*, 127, 136–37.

HENRY, Vodrey; Sergeant; H/10th Cav. Born in North Carolina; private, C/10th Cavalry, 27 May 1892; corporal, 2 Oct 1896; at Ft Assiniboine, MT, 1897. SOURCE: Baker, Roster.

At Ft Robinson, NE, for cavalry competition, Sep 1897.

Promoted to sergeant, 6 Dec 1897. SOURCE: *ANJ* 35 (18 Dec 1897): 292.

Sergeant, C/10th Cavalry; served in 10th Cavalry in Cuba, 1898. SOURCE: Cashin, *Under Fire with the Tenth Cavalry*, 339.

Ranked number ten, Division of the Philippines pistol competition, Ft William McKinley, Rizal, Philippines, 1907. SOURCE: GO 213, AGO, 19 Oct 1907.

Sergeant, H/10th Cavalry, commissioned first lieutenant, Camp Des Moines, IA, Oct 1917. SOURCE: Glass, *History of the Tenth Cavalry*, appendix M.

HENSHAW, Thomas H.; Private; I/9th Cav. Veteran of Spanish-American War and Philippine Insurrection; at Ft D. A. Russell, WY, in 1910; resident of Washington, DC. SOURCE: *Illustrated Review: Ninth Cavalry*, with picture.

HENSLEY, Charles; Sergeant; K/9th Cav. Retires in accordance with Special Order 22, Adjutant General's Office, 27 Jan 1898.

No Veterans Administration pension file.

HENSLEY, John; H/10th Cav. Original member of 10th Cavalry; in troop when organized, Ft Leavenworth, KS, 21 Jul 1867. SOURCE: McMiller, "Buffalo Soldiers," 75.

HENSON; Private; C/9th Cav. At Ft Robinson, NE, 1886.

HENSON, Barry; Sergeant; I/10th Cav. Born in Maryland; private, I/10th Cavalry, 14 Nov 1892; corporal, 14 Apr 1896; at Ft Assiniboine, MT, 1897. SOURCE: Baker, Roster.

Served in 10th Cavalry in Cuba, 1898. SOURCE: Cashin, *Under Fire with the Tenth Cavalry*, 347.

HENSON, Clem; Recruit; Colored Detachment/ Mounted Service. At Jefferson Barracks, MO, 1889. *See* **SHERWOOD**, James H., Recruit, Colored Detachment/ Mounted Service

HENSON, George J.; Cook; I/10th Cav. Served in 10th Cavalry in Cuba, 1898. SOURCE: Cashin, *Under Fire with the Tenth Cavalry*, 348.

Fined $5 and $4.80 costs for carrying and drawing concealed weapon, Crawford, NE, 16 Mar 1903; served four days in jail to cover costs and released.

Wounded in action, Naco, AZ, 18 Oct 1914. SOURCE: Cleveland *Gazette*, 13 May 1916.

HENSON, John; Private; C/9th Cav. Born Anne Arundel Co., MD; enlisted, occupation farmer, Ht 5'7", black complexion, single, 14 May 1889; injured left arm and leg when thrown by horse, Ft Leavenworth, KS; discharged, end of term, 13 May 1894; resided at 1466 Hildreth Avenue, Columbus, OH, in 1930; pension $40 per month, 15 Jan 1930, $72, 24 Jun 1938, $86.40, 1 Mar 1948, $120, 22 Apr 1948; resided at 15 North Indiana Avenue, Apartment B-37, Atlantic City, NJ, 1952; died of coronary thrombosis, 2 May 1952; survived by widow, age 71; son Jonah Edward served with Motor Truck Company 22, 15 Nov 1917–13 Dec 1919. SOURCE: VA File C 2598484, John Henson.

Served 1889–94; now age 67. SOURCE: *Winners of the West* 10 (Aug 1933): 3.

HENSON, William; Sergeant; H/24th Inf. Authorized six-month furlough from San Carlos, AZ. SOURCE: *ANJ* 26 (22 Jun 1889): 882.

HENSON, William H.; Wagoner; L/9th Cav. Veteran of Philippine Insurrection; at Ft D. A. Russell, WY, in 1910; sharpshooter; resident of Baltimore. SOURCE: *Illustrated Review: Ninth Cavalry*, with picture.

HERBERT, Thomas H.; Private; K/9th Cav. Private, B/9th Cavalry; sentenced to thirty days by garrison court martial, Ft Robinson, NE, for vile and obscene language toward Pvts. Charles Daniels and William Davis; threw rock at Davis and hit Pvt. James H. Cook; resisted arrest by Cpl. Gus Bailey, 26 Dec 1888. SOURCE: Order 255, 30 Dec 1888, Post Orders, Ft Robinson.

Served in 10th Cavalry in Cuba, 1898 SOURCE: Cashin, *Under Fire with the Tenth Cavalry*, 342.

Commended for distinguished service, battle of Santiago, Cuba, 1 Jul 1898, as corporal, E/10th Cavalry. SOURCE: GO 15, AGO, 13 Feb 1900.

Awarded certificate of merit for distinguished service in Cuba, 1 Jul 1898. SOURCE: *ANJ* 37 (24 Feb 1900): 611; Steward, *The Colored Regulars*, 280.

Born Montgomery Co., MD; received Distinguished Service Medal for distinguished service, battle of Santiago,

1 Jul 1898. SOURCE: Koger, *The Maryland Negro in Our Wars*, 23.

Veteran of Spanish-American War and Philippine Insurrection; private, K/9th Cavalry, at Ft D. A. Russell, WY, in 1910; resident of Montgomery, AL. SOURCE: *Illustrated Review: Ninth Cavalry*, with picture.

HERRING, Hardy; Private; B/9th Cav. At Ft D. A. Russell, WY, in 1910. SOURCE: *Illustrated Review: Ninth Cavalry*, with picture.

HERRON, William; Private; F/38th Inf. At Ft Cummings, NM, 1868. *See* **TOWNSEND**, Allen, Private, F/38th Infantry

HEYMAN, George L.; Private; C/10th Cav. Served in 10th Cavalry, 1898; remained in U.S. during war with Spain. SOURCE: Cashin, *Under Fire with the Tenth Cavalry*, 340.

HIBBARD, George; M/10th Cav. Original member of 10th Cavalry; in troop when organized, Ft Riley, KS, 15 Oct 1867. SOURCE: McMiller, "Buffalo Soldiers," 79.

HICKMAN, Charles; Horseshoer; C/9th Cav. Private, D/10th Cavalry, released to duty from treatment for acute chancroids, Ft Robinson, NE, 29 May 1903. SOURCE: Post Surgeon to CO, D/10, 29 May 1903, LS, Post Surgeon, Ft Robinson.

Horseshoer, C/9th Cavalry, at Ft D. A. Russell, WY, in 1910; resident of Carlyle, IL. SOURCE: *Illustrated Review: Ninth Cavalry*, with picture.

HICKS, Absom; Corporal; F/10th Cav. Served in 10th Cavalry in Cuba, 1898. SOURCE: Cashin, *Under Fire with the Tenth Cavalry*, 343.

HICKS, Charles; Private; F/24th Inf. Died of yellow fever in Cuba, 12 Aug 1898. SOURCE: *ANJ* 36 (11 Feb 1899): 567; AG, *Correspondence Regarding the War with Spain*, I:223.

HICKS, Charles H.; Private; F/10th Cav. Original member of 10th Cavalry; in troop when organized, Ft Leavenworth, KS, 21 Jun 1867. SOURCE: McMiller, "Buffalo Soldiers," 73.

Mentioned, Ft Lyon, CO, Mar 1869. SOURCE: LR, Det 10 Cav, 1868–69.

HICKS, Early; F/24th Inf. Letter from Ft Assiniboine, MT. SOURCE: Indianapolis *Freeman*, 27 Dec 1902.

HICKS, Edmond; 24th Inf. Died Ft Douglas, UT, 17 Jun 1899; buried there. SOURCE: Clark, "A History of the Twenty-fourth," appendix A.

HICKS, George; Sergeant; 24th Inf. Retired; owns three lots and ten acres of alfalfa, Allensworth, CA. SOURCE: Beasley, *Negro Trailblazers*, 156.

HICKS, Howard F.; Corporal; K/9th Cav. Veteran of Philippine Insurrection; at Ft D. A. Russell, WY, in 1910; resident of Baltimore. SOURCE: *Illustrated Review: Ninth Cavalry*, with picture.

HICKS, Peter; Private; 10th Cav. Former musician, Band/25th Infantry, application for enlistment in 10th Cavalry approved by Lieutenant Stiles, Austin, TX. SOURCE: CO, 10 Cav, to AG, USA, 1 Nov 1875, ES, 10 Cav, 1872–81.

HICKS, Stephen; A/10th Cav. Deserted from Ft Leavenworth, KS, 1 Mar 1867. SOURCE: McMiller, "Buffalo Soldiers," 53.

HICKS, William B.; Private; G/9th Cav. Funeral, Ft Robinson, NE, 8 Oct 1896, handled by regular Army and Navy Union of Ft Robinson. SOURCE: SO 114, 7 Oct 1896, Post Orders, Ft Robinson.

Buried Ft Robinson. SOURCE: List of Interments, Ft Robinson.

His effects sold for $27, which sum was forwarded to department headquarters. SOURCE: 2nd Lt M. Batson, CO, G/9 Cav, to Chief PM, DP, 2 Feb 1897, Miscellaneous Records, DeptPlatte.

HIGGINS, Ansas; G/10th Cav. Original member of 10th Cavalry; in troop when organized, Ft Leavenworth, KS, 5 Jul 1867. SOURCE: McMiller, "Buffalo Soldiers," 74.

HIGH, John H.; Private; L/10th Cav. Original member of 10th Cavalry; in troop when organized, Ft Riley, KS, 21 Sep 1867. SOURCE: McMiller, "Buffalo Soldiers," 78.

William C. Drew, Chief, Claims Division, asked commander, 10th Cavalry, whether High had ever served with K/9th U.S. Colored Troops, Feb 1870.

HILDRETH, Sandy; Private; B/10th Cav. Original member of 10th Cavalry; in troop when organized, Ft Leavenworth, KS, 1 Apr 1867. SOURCE: McMiller, "Buffalo Soldiers," 69.

Mentioned Jun 1867. SOURCE: ES, 10 Cav, 1866–71.

HILL, Abraham; M/10th Cav. Original member of 10th Cavalry; in troop when organized, Ft Riley, KS, 15 Oct 1867. SOURCE: McMiller, "Buffalo Soldiers," 79.

HILL, Abraham; Color Sgt; 24th Inf. Helped Chaplain Allensworth lay foundation for chapel furnace, Ft Douglas, UT. SOURCE: Alexander, *Battles and Victories*, 269.

"One of the Army's great rifle shots," with picture. SOURCE: Muller, *The Twenty Fourth Infantry*, 29.

Ranked number ten, Northern Division infantry team competition, Ft Sheridan, IL, 1904. SOURCE: GO 167, AGO, 28 Oct 1904.

Sergeant, B/24th Infantry; ranked number 197 among expert riflemen, 1904; Northern Division bronze medal.

SOURCE: GO 79, AGO, 1 Jun 1905; GO 198, AGO, 6 Dec 1906.

Sergeant, B/24th Infantry; ranked number one among expert riflemen, with 86.33 percent, 1905; Northern Division rifle team; silver medal. SOURCE: GO 101, AGO, 31 May 1906; GO 198, AGO, 6 Dec 1906; Muller, *The Twenty Fourth Infantry*, 42.

Color sergeant, 24th Infantry, ranked number nine in Philippine Division competition, Malabang, Mindanao, silver medal. SOURCE: GO 198, AGO, 6 Dec 1906.

HILL, Alonzo D.; Sergeant; L/9th Cav. Veteran of Philippine Insurrection; expert rifleman at Ft D. A. Russell, WY, in 1910; sharpshooter; resident of Nashville. SOURCE: *Illustrated Review: Ninth Cavalry*, with picture.

HILL, Charles; Principal Musician; 9th Cav. Killed by civilian, Ft Davis, TX, Jul 1876. SOURCE: Carroll, *The Black Military Experience*, 279.

HILL, Coleman; Private; M/10th Cav. Discharged without honor. SOURCE: SO 146, AGO, 22 Jun 1904.

HILL, E. H.; 24th Inf. Married "Spanish lady, name unknown," Ft Elliott, TX, Dec 1885. SOURCE: Cleveland *Gazette*, 9 Jan 1886.

HILL, Ezekiel; Corporal; B/24th Inf. On detached service as scorer, department rifle meet, Ft Bayard, NM. SOURCE: Order 118, Ft Huachuca, 9 Aug 1893, Name File, 24 Inf.

HILL, Frank; Private; A/24th Inf. Wounded in action, Santiago, Cuba, 1898. SOURCE: SecWar, *AR 1898*, 437; Muller, *The Twenty Fourth Infantry*, 16.

HILL, H. W.; C/9th Cav. Native of Monroe, LA; enlisted, Ft Leavenworth, KS, 10 May 1895; served at Ft Robinson, NE, and in Cuba; one thousand residents of Monroe turned out for reception in his honor, Apr 1899. SOURCE: Indianapolis *Freeman*, 8 Apr 1899.

HILL, Herbert; Private; K/10th Cav. Died of yellow fever at Siboney, Cuba, 13 Aug 1898. SOURCE: *ANJ* 36 (11 Feb 1899): 567; AG, *Correspondence Regarding the War with Spain*, I:228; Hospital Papers, Spanish-American War.

HILL, J. H.; QM Sgt; 10th Cav. At Ft Grant, AZ; to be examined for position of post quartermaster sergeant. SOURCE: *ANJ* 24 (26 Feb 1887): 610.

Ordered to duty at Santa Fe, NM. SOURCE: *ANJ* 25 (20 Aug 1887): 62.

HILL, J. H.; Sergeant; 24th Inf. Commissioned lieutenant of volunteers, 1898, for bravery in action at Santiago, Cuba. SOURCE: Cashin, *Under Fire with the Tenth Cavalry*, 354.

HILL, Jacob; Corporal; D/9th Cav. Veteran of Spanish-American War and Philippine Insurrection; at Ft D. A. Russell, WY, in 1910; resident of Baltimore. SOURCE: *Illustrated Review: Ninth Cavalry*, with picture.

HILL, James; Wagoner; H/10th Cav. Appointed from private, Jun 1868. SOURCE: LR, Det 10 Cav, 1868–69.

HILL, John; Private; E/10th Cav. At camp near San Antonio, TX, Apr 1867.

HILL, John; Private; A/9th Cav. Discharged on surgeon's certificate, Ft Robinson, NE, 24 Apr 1888.

HILL, John H.; Corporal; C/25th Inf. Dishonorable discharge, Brownsville. SOURCE: SO 266, AGO, 9 Nov 1906.

HILL, Rubin; D/10th Cav. Original member of 10th Cavalry; in troop when organized, Ft Leavenworth, KS, 1 Jun 1867. SOURCE: McMiller, "Buffalo Soldiers," 71.

HILL, Thomas; Private; F/9th Cav. At Ft D. A. Russell, WY, in 1910; sharpshooter; resident of Shawnee, KS. SOURCE: *Illustrated Review: Ninth Cavalry*, with picture.

HILL, Walter; Sergeant; K/9th Cav. At Ft D. A. Russell, WY, in 1910; sharpshooter; resident of Nashville. SOURCE: *Illustrated Review: Ninth Cavalry*, with picture.

HILL, William; Private; D/10th Cav. Served in 10th Cavalry, 1898; remained in U.S. during war with Spain. SOURCE: Cashin, *Under Fire with the Tenth Cavalry*, 341.

HILL, William B.; Corporal; E/10th Cav. Served in 10th Cavalry, 1898; remained in U.S. during war with Spain. SOURCE: Cashin, *Under Fire with the Tenth Cavalry*, 343.

HILL, William C.; Private; H/24th Inf. Fined $10 by summary court for standing sentry duty with weapon leaning against sentry box and with hands in pockets, San Isidro, Philippines, ca. 1902, first conviction. SOURCE: Register of Summary Court, San Isidro.

HILL, William H.; Comsy Sgt; 10th Cav. Born St. Francis Co., MO; served in A/9th Cavalry, 20 May 1890–1 Aug 1893; in K/10th Cavalry, 4 Oct 1893–24 Oct 1899; drum major, Band/10th Cavalry, 25 Oct–8 Dec 1899; commissary sergeant, 10 Dec 1901; stationed in Cuba, 21 May 1899–20 May 1902; character excellent; married to Mrs. Missouri Hill, no children; deposits $105, 1900, $70, 1901; clothing $49; enlisted Ft Robinson, NE, 9 Dec 1902, character excellent; discharge, 8 Dec 1905, character excellent, clothing $97. SOURCE: Descriptive Book, 10 Cav Officers & NCOs.

Private, A/9th Cavalry, teacher, Ft Robinson school, 1 Nov 1892–30 Apr 1893. SOURCE: Report of Schools, Ft

Robinson, 1892–96; Order 33, 29 Apr 1893, Post Orders, Ft Robinson.

Sergeant, served in K/10th Cavalry, 1898; remained in U.S. during war with Spain. SOURCE: Cashin, *Under Fire with the Tenth Cavalry*, 349.

Commissary sergeant, guest with wife at K/10th Cavalry Thanksgiving dinner. SOURCE: Simmons, "Thanksgiving Day," 663.

HILL, Winmon; Private; A/9th Cav. At Ft D. A. Russell, WY, in 1910; sharpshooter. SOURCE: *Illustrated Review: Ninth Cavalry*, with picture.

HILLIARD, Henry; Private; H/9th Cav. Relieved from extra duty as laborer, Quartermaster Department, Ft Robinson, NE. SOURCE SO 90, 20 Aug 1896, Post Orders, Ft Robinson.

Deposited with paymaster $25, 1897, and $5, 1898.

HILLIARD, Mack; Private; F/9th Cav. At Ft D. A. Russell, WY, in 1910; marksman; resident of Macon, GA. SOURCE: *Illustrated Review: Ninth Cavalry*, with picture.

HILLIARD, Peter; 38th Inf. Letter from Xenia, OH, age 81, congratulates editor on work. SOURCE: *Winners of the West* 2 (Mar 1925): 6.

Will be 82 in Feb 1926; encourages editor to keep up good work. SOURCE: *Winners of the West* 3 (Jan 1926): 5.

Over 83; gets $30 per month pension; no increase because he did not participate in Indian campaign; served 1867–70; got rheumatism on recruiting duty, Jefferson Barracks, MO. SOURCE: *Winners of the West* 4 (Feb 1928): 8.

Died Xenia, OH; member, Camp 11, National Indian War Veterans. SOURCE: *Winners of the West* 8 (Mar 1931): 10.

HILTON, George T.; Private; G/24th Inf. Wounded in action, Cuba, 1898. SOURCE: Muller, *The Twenty Fourth Infantry*, 19.

HINES, Joseph J.; Private; E/9th Cav. Died in Cuba, 4 Aug 1898. SOURCE: *ANJ* 36 (11 Feb 1899): 567.

Died, no cause of death reported. SOURCE: AG, *Correspondence Regarding the War with Spain*, 1:206.

HINES, Peter; L/10th Cav. Original member of 10th Cavalry; in troop when organized, Ft Riley, KS, 21 Sep 1867. SOURCE: McMiller, "Buffalo Soldiers," 78.

HINES, Sylvester; C/10th Cav. Original member of 10th Cavalry; in troop when organized, Ft Leavenworth, KS, 14 May 1867. SOURCE: McMiller, "Buffalo Soldiers," 70.

HINES, Will; Sergeant; C/10th Cav. Killed in action, near Carrizal, Mexico, 21 Jun 1916; Hines Road at Ft Huachuca, AZ, named for him. SOURCE: Orville A. Cochran to H. B. Wharfield, 5 Apr 1965, 10th Cavalry papers, MHI.

"With great courage crawled up to a Mexican machine gun post, put it out of action, and then was killed"; buried at Arlington Cemetery. SOURCE: Wharfield, *10th Cavalry and Border Fights*, 36, 39.

HINKLE, Jonee; Private; K/10th Cav. Sentenced to dishonorable discharge and one year's confinement, Ft Robinson, NE, Jul 1902; released Nov 1902.

HINSLEY, Joseph; Private; B/49th Inf. Deserted, Jefferson Barracks, MO, 24 Sep 1899. SOURCE: Descriptive Book, B/49 Inf.

HINSON, Walter; Private; H/24th Inf. Enlisted Louisville, 12 Sep 1898. SOURCE: Muster Roll, H/24 Inf, Sep–Oct 1898.

Discharged Ft Douglas, UT, character good, single, 28 Jan 1899; deposits $10; due U.S. for clothing $40.98. SOURCE: Muster Roll, H/24 Inf, Jan–Feb 1899.

HIPPLE, James E.; A/9th Cav. Admitted to Soldiers Home with disability, age 47, after twenty-six years and one month's service, 19 Jun 1891. SOURCE: SecWar, *AR 1891*, 829.

HIPSHER, Wiley; Private; E/9th Cav. Private, E/9th Cavalry, relieved from extra duty as teamster with Quartermaster Department, Ft Robinson, NE. SOURCE: SO 86, 8 Aug 1896, Post Orders, Ft Robinson.

Served as private, A/10th Cavalry, in Cuba, 1898; wounded in action, 1 Jul 1898. SOURCE: Cashin, *Under Fire with the Tenth Cavalry*, 336–37.

Wounded at Santiago, Cuba, 1 Jul 1898. SOURCE: SecWar, *AR 1898*, 324.

Veteran of Spanish-American War and Philippine Insurrection; sergeant, E/9th Cavalry, at Ft D. A. Russell, WY, in 1910; sharpshooter. SOURCE: *Illustrated Review: Ninth Cavalry*, with picture.

HIPSHER, William; Corporal; C/9th Cav. Veteran of Spanish-American War; at Ft D. A. Russell, WY, in 1910. SOURCE: *Illustrated Review: Ninth Cavalry*, with picture.

HIPSHIRE, Riley; Private; D/24th Inf. Transferred from Reserve Divisional Hospital, Siboney, Cuba, to U.S. on Hospital Ship *Missouri* with typhoid, 3 Sep 1898. SOURCE: Hospital Papers, Spanish-American War.

Private, Hospital Corps, Cabanatuan, Philippines, 1901. *See* **MOORE**, Cato, Private, D/24th Infantry

HIRBERT, John; I/10th Cav. Original member of 10th Cavalry; in troop when organized, Ft Riley, KS, 15 Aug 1867. SOURCE: McMiller, "Buffalo Soldiers," 76.

HISLE, Charles; Private; K/9th Cav. At Ft D. A. Russell, WY, in 1910; resident of Covington, KY. SOURCE: *Illustrated Review: Ninth Cavalry*, with picture.

HITE, Samuel; Private; M/10th Cav. Served in 10th Cavalry, 1898; remained in U.S. during war with Spain. SOURCE: Cashin, *Under Fire with the Tenth Cavalry*, 351.

HOBBS, Louis; Private; I/24th Inf. Enlisted Mobile, AL, 28 Mar 1899. SOURCE: Muster Roll, I/24 Inf, Mar–Apr 1899.

Fined $3 by summary court, 25 Sep 1899; on detached service, Mexico, Philippines, since 16 Oct 1899. SOURCE: Muster Roll, I/24 Inf, Sep–Oct 1899.

HOBSON, Winslow; 9th Ohio Inf. Letter, Camp Meade, PA, 15 Oct 1898. SOURCE: Gatewood, *"Smoked Yankees"*, 117–18.

HOCKER, Jesse C.; Private; B/9th Cav. At Ft D. A. Russell, WY, in 1910. SOURCE: *Illustrated Review: Ninth Cavalry*, with picture.

HOCKINS, Benjamin; Corporal; G/9th Cav. 1st Lt. F. Bears Taylor said to Hockins, "Don't look at me, God damn you," "I could kill you," and "Go on, you God damn black son of a bitch," also struck him several blows on head, face, shoulders with carbine, after Hockins was on the ground, helpless, handcuffed, shackled, while in E/9th Cavalry, at Ft Cummings, NM, 21 Oct 1880. SOURCE: GCMO 61, AGO, 4 Nov 1881.

Transferred to B/9th Cavalry, Ft Duchesne, UT. SOURCE: Order 22, 9 Cav, 1 May 1888.

Corporal, B/9th Cavalry, fined $5 by garrison court martial, Ft Robinson, NE, for insubordination to 1st Sgt. David Badie, B/9th Cavalry. SOURCE: Order 162, 22 Aug 1888, Post Orders, Ft Robinson.

Appointed corporal, G/9th Cavalry, 17 Jul 1892. SOURCE: Roster, 9 Cav.

HOCKINS, Major; Private; B/10th Cav. Served in 10th Cavalry in Cuba, 1898. SOURCE: Cashin, *Under Fire with the Tenth Cavalry*, 338.

Sentence published in Special Order 198, Department of the Missouri, 28 Oct 1902.

HODGE, Arthur; Corporal; L/9th Cav. Veteran of Philippine Insurrection; at Ft D. A. Russell, WY, in 1910; sharpshooter; resident of Ahrdeen, OH. SOURCE: *Illustrated Review: Ninth Cavalry*, with picture.

HODGE, William J.; Private; C/24th Inf. On special duty in charge of post library, Ft Huachuca, AZ. SOURCE: Order 157, Ft Huachuca, 23 Oct 1893, Name File, 24 Inf.

HODGES, George; Private; L/25th Inf. Fined $2 by summary court, San Isidro, Philippines, for unmilitary behavior at retreat formation, 16 May 1902, third conviction. SOURCE: Register of Summary Court, San Isidro.

HODGES, Lonnie; Private; D/9th Cav. At Ft D. A. Russell, WY, in 1910; resident of Houston. SOURCE: *Illustrated Review: Ninth Cavalry*.

Deserter from Ft D. A. Russell, captured in Chicago, IL. SOURCE: Wyoming *Tribune*, 11 Dec 1911.

HOFFMAN, Oscar; Private; H/10th Cav. Served in 10th Cavalry, 1898; remained in U.S. during war with Spain. SOURCE: Cashin, *Under Fire with the Tenth Cavalry*, 346.

HOGEKINS, John; A/10th Cav. Original member of 10th Cavalry; in troop when organized, Ft Leavenworth, KS, 18 Feb 1867. SOURCE: McMiller, "Buffalo Soldiers," 68.

HOGINS, Jerry; H/10th Cav. Original member of 10th Cavalry; in troop when organized, Ft Leavenworth, KS, 21 Jul 1867. SOURCE: McMiller, "Buffalo Soldiers," 75.

HOGUE, William; Private; G/25th Inf. Served 1910. *See* **JAMES**, John, Sergeant, G/25th Infantry

HOKE; Private; E/9th Cav. Killed in action against Victorio, Camp Ojo Caliente, NM, 4 Sep 1879. SOURCE: Billington, "Black Cavalrymen," 67; Billington, *New Mexico's Buffalo Soldiers*, 89.

See **CHAPMAN**, S., Sergeant, E/9th Cavalry

HOLBROOK, Isaac; Private; H/9th Cav. Cited for gallantry against Victorio, Nov 1879, by Maj. Albert P. Morrow. SOURCE: Billington, "Black Cavalrymen," 68; Billington, *New Mexico's Buffalo Soldiers*, 93.

HOLDEN, David; Sergeant; F/24th Inf. Private, recruited from Ft Huachuca, AZ, to teach in Chaplain Allensworth's post school, Ft Bayard, NM, 1889. SOURCE: Billington, *New Mexico's Buffalo Soldiers*, 162.

Corporal, A/24th Infantry; military telegraph operator at Silver City, NM, late 1889. SOURCE: Billington, *New Mexico's Buffalo Soldiers*, 146.

Corporal, A/24th Infantry, authorized six-month furlough from Ft Bayard, NM. SOURCE: *ANJ* 28 (11 Feb 1891): 439.

Sergeant, F/24th Infantry, wounded in action, Cuba, 1898. SOURCE: Muller, *The Twenty Fourth Infantry*, 18.

Wounded in action, Santa Ana, Philippines, 7 Oct 1899. SOURCE: *ANJ* 37 (21 Oct 1899): 178; Muller, *The Twenty Fourth Infantry*, 30; Manila *Times*, 12 Oct 1899.

HOLDEN, James; 1st Sgt; H/24th Inf. Authorized four-month furlough from Ft Supply, Indian Territory. SOURCE: *ANJ* 24 (19 Feb 1887): 590.

HOLDEN, James; Sergeant; K/9th Cav. Appointed corporal, 10 Jul 1892. SOURCE: 9 Cav, Roster.

Promoted to sergeant, Ft Robinson, NE, 26 Aug 1895. SOURCE: *ANJ* 33 (7 Sep 1895): 7.

HOLDEN, Samuel; Farrier; C/10th Cav. Served in 10th Cavalry in Cuba, 1898. SOURCE: Cashin, *Under Fire with the Tenth Cavalry*, 340.

HOLDER, Charles; Private; M/10th Cav. Served 1874. *See* **HAYMAN**, Perry A., B/25th Infantry

Discharge of Holder, convicted of murder by civil court, approved by regimental commander, 4 Jun 1875. SOURCE: ES, 10 Cav, 1872–81.

Discharged as of 18 May 1874, date turned over to civil authorities. SOURCE: LS, 10 Cav, 1873–83.

HOLDMAN, Lyman; Private; H/10th Cav. Served in 10th Cavalry, 1898; remained in U.S. during war with Spain. SOURCE: Cashin, *Under Fire with the Tenth Cavalry*, 346.

HOLEMAN, Edmond; L/10th Cav. Original member of 10th Cavalry; in troop when organized, Ft Riley, KS, 21 Sep 1867. SOURCE: McMiller, "Buffalo Soldiers," 78.

HOLLADAY, Thomas; Private; A/24th Inf. Died of appendicitis, Manila, Philippines, 18 Sep 1899. SOURCE: Richmond *Planet*, 30 Sep 1899.

Died of ascending paralysis, Philippines, 18 Sep 1899. SOURCE: *ANJ* 37 (30 Sep 1899): 99.

HOLLAND, Alphonso; Private; C/25th Inf. Dishonorable discharge, Brownsville. SOURCE: SO 266, AGO, 9 Nov 1906.

HOLLAND, Charles; Private; H/10th Cav. Served in 10th Cavalry, 1898; remained in U.S. during war with Spain. SOURCE: Cashin, *Under Fire with the Tenth Cavalry*, 346.

HOLLAND, Elijah; Private; H/48th Inf. Died of variola in the Philippines, 25 Jun 1900. SOURCE: *ANJ* 37 (7 Jul 1900): 1071.

HOLLAND, George A.; Sergeant; 24th Inf. Corporal, D/24th Infantry, at Cabanatuan, Philippines, 1901. *See* **JOHNSON**, Jason, Corporal, D/24th Infantry

Commissioned at Camp Des Moines, IA, 1917. SOURCE: Beasley, *Negro Trailblazers*, 285.

HOLLAND, Irvin W.; Private; C/9th Cav. At Ft D. A. Russell, WY, in 1910; sharpshooter; resident of 3626 Vernon Ave., Chicago. SOURCE: *Illustrated Review: Ninth Cavalry*, with picture.

HOLLAND, James T.; K/10th Cav. Original member of 10th Cavalry; in troop when organized, Ft Riley, KS, 1 Sep 1867. SOURCE: McMiller, "Buffalo Soldiers," 77.

HOLLAND, Richard; Private; D/9th Cav. At Ft D. A. Russell, WY, in 1910; resident of Martinsville, VA. SOURCE: *Illustrated Review: Ninth Cavalry*, with picture.

HOLLAND, Robert; Private; E/10th Cav. Awaiting trial for desertion, Apr 1895.

Sentenced to dishonorable discharge and twelve months' confinement, 11 Apr 1895, in accordance with Special Order 69, Department of the Platte.

Transferred to Ft Logan, CO, Nov 1895.

HOLLAND, Robert C.; Private; H/9th Cav. Died of cholera in the Philippines, 15 Jun 1902. SOURCE: *ANJ* 39 (9 Aug 1902): 1248.

HOLLAND, William H.; Private; G/10th Cav. Served in 10th Cavalry, 1898; remained in U.S. during war with Spain. SOURCE: Cashin, *Under Fire with the Tenth Cavalry*, 346.

HOLLEY, Sylvester S.; Private; M/24th Inf. Died of malaria at Second Reserve Hospital, Manila, Philippines, 21 Jun 1901. SOURCE: *ANJ* 38 (17 Aug 1901): 1241.

HOLLIDAY, Henry; Private; F/49th Inf. Released from confinement at Ft Leavenworth, KS, in accordance with Supreme Court's Deming decision, 19 May 1902. SOURCE: *ANJ* 39 (7 Jun 1902): 1005

HOLLIDAY, John; Recruit; 10th Cav. Acquitted by general court martial and restored to duty, Feb 1877.

HOLLIDAY, Presley; Sgt Maj; 10th Cav. Born Orange Court House, VA; Ht 5'8"; served in B/10th Cavalry, 19 Jun 1893–6 Mar 1899; in Cuba, at Las Guasimas, San Juan, and Santiago, 22 Jun–14 Aug 1898, 21 May 1899–10 Jul 1900, 9 Oct 1900–24 Apr 1902; sergeant major, 10th Cavalry, 1 Oct 1899; en route to New York, NY, for treatment of eye disease, 2 Oct 1899; nearest living relative Mrs. Elizabeth Brown, sister, Steelton, PA; reenlisted Manzanillo, Cuba, character excellent, single, deposits $500, 1899–1900, clothing $90, 7 Mar 1902; reenlisted, continued as sergeant major, character excellent, married, deposits $35, clothing $114, Ft Robinson, NE, 7 Mar 1905; honorable discharge in accordance with General Order 207, War Department, 1906, character excellent, 23 Jan 1907. SOURCE: Descriptive Book, 10 Cav Officers & NCOs.

Private, B/10th Cavalry; corporal, 15 Oct 1894; stationed at Ft Custer, MT, 1897. SOURCE: Baker, Roster.

Sergeant, B/10th Cavalry, in Cuba, 1898; recommended for Medal of Honor for bravery, assault on San Juan Hill, 1 Jul 1898; narrates experience in Spanish-American War. SOURCE: Cashin, *Under Fire with the Tenth Cavalry*, 337, 186, 231–42.

Letter, Ft Ringgold, TX, 22 Apr 1899. SOURCE: Gatewood, *"Smoked Yankees"*, 92.

Letter to editor, as sergeant, B/10th Cavalry, Gibara, Cuba, 10 Jul 1899, defends 24th Infantry against slurs in San Francisco *Chronicle*. SOURCE: Richmond *Planet*, 29 Jul 1899.

"That brave Afro-American soldier, Sergeant Major Presley Holliday, of the Tenth Cavalry, stationed at Manzanillo, Cuba, gave Gov. Roosevelt a mighty 'punch in the face,' in a recent and second communication which completely wipes out the latter's *Scribner's Magazine* charge of cowardice directed against the colored troops that fought in Cuba during the Spanish-American war. It is about time the colonel was retracting and apologizing." SOURCE: Cleveland *Gazette*, 26 May 1900.

Letter to New York *Age*, including his version of battle at San Juan Hill, responding to *Age's* publication of Theodore Roosevelt's account. SOURCE: Johnson, *History of Negro Soldiers*, 41–46.

Married Estelle M. Hill of Farmington, MO, at Congregational Church, Crawford, NE, 16 Sep 1903. SOURCE: Crawford *Tribune*, 18 Sep 1903.

Letter, Ft Robinson, 16 Dec 1904, complains about apathy and ignorance of blacks regarding Army; reads Washington *Post* and New York *Age*. SOURCE: Cleveland *Gazette*, 11 Feb 1905 (reprinted from New York *Age*).

Daughter Hope Louise born to wife, Estelle M. (Hill) Holliday, Ft Robinson, 18 Dec 1904, first child. SOURCE: Monthly Report, Chaplain Anderson, Dec 1904; Medical History, Ft Robinson.

Son Presley Jr. born Ft Robinson, 16 Aug 1906, second child. SOURCE: Monthly Report, Chaplain Anderson, Aug 1906; Medical History, Ft Robinson.

Wrote to Booker T. Washington's secretary, E. J. Scott, 24 Feb 1907, suggesting possiblity of securing some Negro artillery units with help of president. SOURCE: Fletcher, *The Black Soldier*, 69.

HOLLIER, William; E/10th Cav. Original member of 10th Cavalry; in troop when organized, Ft Leavenworth, KS, 15 Jun 1867. SOURCE: McMiller, "Buffalo Soldiers," 72.

HOLLINGSWORTH, Isaac M.; F/24th Inf. Paid $1.50 for his third annual subscription to *Gazette*. SOURCE: Cleveland *Gazette*, 18 Oct 1887.

Won two races, Ft Bayard, NM, 4 Jul 1888. SOURCE: Cleveland *Gazette*, 14 Jul 1888.

HOLLINS, William A.; Private; B/9th Cav. Severely wounded in action against Apaches, Gabaldon Canyon, NM, 19 Aug 1881. SOURCE: Billington, *New Mexico's Buffalo Soldiers*, 105.

See **GOLDEN**, Thomas, Saddler, B/9th Cavalry

HOLLMAN, Clifton; Private; 10th Cav. Transferred from 25th Infantry. SOURCE: SO 155, AGO, 3 Jul 1903.

HOLLOMAN, Solomon; 1st Sgt; A/9th Cav. At Ft Niobrara, NE, 1889. *See* **CARTER**, William H., Trumpeter, A/9th Cavalry

Sergeant as of 1 Mar 1889; first sergeant as of 10 Mar 1889. SOURCE: Roster, 9 Cav.

Author of resolution of tribute to deceased Sgt. Israel Valentine, Ft Robinson, NE, 1892. SOURCE: *ANJ* 28 (2 Jun 1892): 782.

Resides with wife, mother-in-law, and brother-in-law on laundress row, Ft Robinson, 1893. SOURCE: Medical History, Ft Robinson.

Reenlistment, married, authorized, by letter, Adjutant General's Office, 11 Jan 1894.

Daughter Ida Rebecca, age sixteen months, died of capillary bronchitis, complication of pneumonia, Ft Robinson, 20 Feb 1897. SOURCE: Post Surgeon to Surgeon General, USA, 6 Apr 1897, LS, Post Surgeon, Ft Robinson.

Transferred from Reserve Divisional Hospital, Siboney, Cuba, with yellow fever, on U.S. Army Transport *Concho* to Fortress Monroe, VA, 24 Jun 1898. SOURCE: Hospital Papers, Spanish-American War.

HOLLOWAY; Private; H/10th Cav. At Ft Apache, AZ, 1890, subscribed $.50 to testimonial to General Grierson. SOURCE: List of subscriptions, 23 Apr 1890, 10th Cavalry papers, MHI.

HOLLOWAY, James; Private; L/10th Cav. Sentenced to seven years' confinement for mutiny by general court martial, Bayamo, Cuba, 12 Oct 1899. SOURCE: *ANJ* 37 (24 Oct 1899): 602.

HOLLOWAY, Lewis W.; Private; B/10th Cav. Served in 10th Cavalry in Cuba, 1898. SOURCE: Cashin, *Under Fire with the Tenth Cavalry*, 338.

HOLLOWAY, William H.; Private; F/9th Cav. At Ft Cummings, NM, 1880. *See* HENRY, Philip, Private, F/9th Cavalry

HOLLSMEER, George; H/10th Cav. Original member of 10th Cavalry; in troop when organized, Ft Leavenworth, KS, 21 Jul 1867. SOURCE: McMiller, "Buffalo Soldiers," 75.

HOLLY, A.; Private; L/25th Inf. Fined $3 by summary court, San Isidro, Philippines, for going off limits, 25 May 1902, first conviction; sentenced to three days' solitary confinement and fined three months' pay for loafing around native canteen, resisting arrest, insulting sergeant of the guard, 30 Jun 1902. SOURCE: Register of Summary Court, San Isidro.

HOLLY, Henry J.; Private; M/48th Inf. Died of dysentery in the Philippines, 13 Mar 1901. SOURCE: *ANJ* 38 (30 Mar 1901): 755.

HOLLY, Thomas; E/10th Cav. Chaplain, Camp 30, National Indian War Veterans, San Antonio, TX. SOURCE: *Winners of the West* 6 (Oct 1929): 7.

Served 1867–77; died. SOURCE: *Winners of the West* 7 (Jan 1930): 1.

HOLLY, W. C.; Corporal; F/25th Inf. Authorized two-month furlough from Ft Snelling, MN, to visit relatives in Baltimore, MD. SOURCE: Cleveland *Gazette*, 30 Oct 1886.

HOLMAN, James W.; F/10th Cav. Admitted to Soldiers Home with disability at age 31 with two years and two months' service, 14 Mar 1891. SOURCE: SecWar, *AR 1891*, 753.

HOLME, C. E.; Private; A/9th Cav. At Ft Stanton, NM, 1881. SOURCE: Regt Returns, 9 Cav, Jan 1881.

HOLMES; Private; B/10th Cav. At Ft Apache, AZ, 1890, subscribed $.50 to testimonial to General Grierson. SOURCE: List of subscriptions, 23 Apr 1890, 10th Cavalry papers, MHI.

HOLMES, Alexander H.; Corporal; F/9th Cav. Died of cholera in the Philippines, 15 Jun 1902. SOURCE: *ANJ* 39 (9 Aug 1902): 1248.

HOLMES, Conley; Private; A/10th Cav. Served in 10th Cavalry in Cuba, 1898. SOURCE: Cashin, *Under Fire with the Tenth Cavalry*, 336.

Sentenced to dishonorable discharge and three months' confinement, Ft Robinson, NE, 18 Jul 1902, in accordance with Special Order 133, Department of the Missouri, 1902; released 2 Oct 1902.

HOLMES, John; Private; G/10th Cav. Served in 10th Cavalry, 1898; remained in U.S. during war with Spain. SOURCE: Cashin, *Under Fire with the Tenth Cavalry*, 346.

HOLMES, John; Private; L/10th Cav. Served in 10th Cavalry, 1898; remained in U.S. during war with Spain. SOURCE: Cashin, *Under Fire with the Tenth Cavalry*, 351.

HOLMES, King; Private; K/9th Cav. Veteran of Philippine Insurrection; at Ft D. A. Russell, WY, in 1910; resident of Galveston, TX. SOURCE: *Illustrated Review: Ninth Cavalry*, with picture.

HOLMES, Robert; Corporal; I/9th Cav. At Ft D. A. Russell, WY, in 1910; sharpshooter; resident of Du Quoin, IL. SOURCE: *Illustrated Review: Ninth Cavalry*, with picture.

HOLMES, Robert H.; Private; C/9th Cav. Arrived at Ft Robinson, NE, from depot, 1 Mar 1887.

HOLMES, Sims; Private; C/10th Cav. Served in 10th Cavalry, 1898; remained in U.S. during war with Spain. SOURCE: Cashin, *Under Fire with the Tenth Cavalry*, 340.

HOLMES, Thomas; Sergeant; H/9th Cav. Veteran of Philippine Insurrection; expert rifleman at Ft D. A. Russell, WY, in 1910; resident of Macon, GA. SOURCE: *Illustrated Review: Ninth Cavalry*, with picture.

HOLOMAN, John; Private; B/25th Inf. Dishonorable discharge, Brownsville. SOURCE: SO 266, AGO, 9 Nov 1906.

HOLOWELL, Lowery; Corporal; K/10th Cav. Served in 10th Cavalry, 1898; remained in U.S. during war with Spain. SOURCE: Cashin, *Under Fire with the Tenth Cavalry*, 349.

HOLSEN, Bailey; Private; L/10th Cav. Released to duty from treatment for acute gonorrhea, Ft Robinson, NE, 18 Jan 1903. SOURCE: Post Surgeon to CO, L/10 Cav, 18 Jan 1903, LS, Post Surgeon, Ft Robinson.

HOLT, James; Artificer; C/24th Inf. Private; relieved from special duty as janitor, post hall, Ft Huachuca, AZ. SOURCE: Order 115, Ft Huachuca, 4 Aug 1893, Name File, 24 Inf.

Retires from Ft Douglas, UT. SOURCE: *ANJ* 35 (5 Feb 1898): 422.

HOLT, John; Private; A/38th Inf. At Ft Cummings, NM, autumn 1867; acquitted of involvement in soldiers' revolt. Billington, *New Mexico's Buffalo Soldiers*, 41–42.

HOLT, John W.; Private; H/24th Inf. Enlisted Ft Douglas, UT, with sixteen years' continuous service, 4 Aug 1898; transferred from F/24th Infantry. SOURCE: Muster Roll, H/24 Inf, Sep–Oct 1898.

Present for duty. SOURCE: Muster Roll, H/24 Inf, Nov–Dec 1898 and Jan–Feb 1899.

HOLT, Levi; 1st Lt; 23rd Kans Inf. Mentioned. SOURCE: Beasley, *Negro Trailblazers*, 285.

HOLT, Lindsey P.; Private; F/10th Cav. Served in 10th Cavalry in Cuba, 1898; killed Pvt. James P. Twisby, F/10th Cavalry, at Montauk Point, NY. SOURCE: Cashin, *Under Fire With the Tenth Cavalry*, 344.

Convicted by general court martial, Huntsville, AL, of premeditated murder of Pvt. James P. Twisby, F/10th Cavalry, Camp Wikoff, NY, 25 Sep 1898; death sentence commuted by President McKinley to life in military prison, Ft Leavenworth, KS. SOURCE: GO 187, AGO, 22 Dec 1898.

Sentenced to death by general court martial for murder of comrade, Montauk, NY. SOURCE: *ANJ* 36 (3 Dec 1898): 332.

Death sentence commuted to life in military prison, Ft Leavenworth, KS. SOURCE: *ANJ* 36 (17 Dec 1898): 375.

HOLTZINGER, George; H/10th Cav. Admitted to Soldiers Home with disability at age 42 with three years and five months' service, 11 Jan 1888. SOURCE: SecWar, *AR 1888*, 902.

HOOD, Perry; Private; D/9th Cav. Born 14 Feb 1866; parents Roxie Fletcher Hood and Jordan Hood; Ht 5'5"; occupation farmer, served 10 Jun 1893–9 Jun 1898; thrown from horse and injured in abdomen while in service; discharged Ft Washakie, WY; first wife Millie Wilson died 1910; married Fannie Rice, Winchester, KY, 25 Nov 1911; worked on farms and other labor until he took up lathing trade, 1921; pension $30 per month, 13 Apr 1927; died 26 Apr 1937; widow's pension $30 per month, 28 May 1937, $40 per month, 11 Aug 1947, $65 per month when she died 30 Mar 1960; one daughter Lorraine Hood, resided with widow, 337 E. Hickman, Winchester, KY, in 1937. SOURCE: VA File C 2326719, Perry Hood.

In Lander, WY, publicizing appearance of Ft Washakie minstrels. SOURCE: Fremont *Clipper*, 9 Aug 1897.

Served 1893–98; died Winchester, KY. SOURCE: *Winners of the West* 14 (May 1937): 5.

HOOKER, Robert; Private; 24th Inf. Died late Aug 1898. SOURCE: *ANJ* 36 (3 Sep 1898): 19.

HOOVER, Alfred C.; Private; G/9th Cav. Served Sep 1883–Sep 1884; was in room with Pvt. James F. Jackson, G/9th Cavalry, Ft Niobrara, NE, when Jackson was shot; now age 47, resides at 1215 Harvey, Omaha, NE, in 1889. SOURCE: Affidavit, Hoover, VA File C 2555351, James F. Jackson.

HOPE, Henry; I/10th Cav. Original member of 10th Cavalry; in troop when organized, Ft Riley, KS, 15 Aug 1867. SOURCE: McMiller, "Buffalo Soldiers," 76.

HOPE, Jasper Pickens; F/9th Cav. Served 1875–85; now age 81. SOURCE: *Winners of the West* 12 (Nov 1935): 3.

HOPINGS, John T.; Private; K/10th Cav. Served in 10th Cavalry, 1898; remained in U.S. during war with Spain. SOURCE: Cashin, *Under Fire with the Tenth Cavalry*, 349.

HOPKINS, Charles; Private; G/10th Cav. Wounded in action, Santiago, Cuba, 1 Jul 1898. SOURCE: SecWar, *AR 1898*, 324.

HOPKINS, Clarence; Private; E/9th Cav. Veteran of Philippine Insurrection; at Ft D. A. Russell, WY, in 1910; resident of Brunswick, MO. SOURCE: *Illustrated Review: Ninth Cavalry*, with picture.

HOPKINS, James; M/10th Cav. Original member of 10th Cavalry; in troop when organized, Ft Riley, KS, 15 Oct 1867. SOURCE: McMiller, "Buffalo Soldiers," 79.

HOPKINS, John; Private; Band/10th Cav. Served in 10th Cavalry in Cuba, 1898. SOURCE: Cashin, *Under Fire with the Tenth Cavalry*, 359.

HOPKINS, Peter; Private; D/9th Cav. At Ft Robinson, NE, 1892. SOURCE: Order 181, 25 Oct 1892, Post Orders, Ft Robinson.

HOPKINS, Richard; Sergeant; G/10th Cav. Served in 10th Cavalry in Cuba, 1898; wounded in action. SOURCE: Cashin, *Under Fire with the Tenth Cavalry*, 345.

HOPKINS, Richard; Private; K/25th Inf. At Ft Niobrara, NE, 1904. SOURCE: Wilson, "History of Fort Niobrara."

HOPKINS, Robert; I/10th Cav. Original member of 10th Cavalry; in troop when organized, Ft Riley, KS, 15 Aug 1867. SOURCE: McMiller, "Buffalo Soldiers," 76.

HOPKINS, Voll; Corporal; E/10th Cav. Corporal, 24th Infantry, at Ft Elliott, TX, 1885. SOURCE: Cleveland *Gazette*, 9 Jan 1886.

Corporal, E/10th Cavalry, at Ft Apache, AZ, 1890, subscribed $.50 to testimonial to General Grierson. SOURCE: List of subscriptions, 23 Apr 1890, 10th Cavalry papers, MHI.

Sharpshooter, Ft Apache, 1891. SOURCE: *ANJ* 31 (4 Jul 1891): 765.

HOPKINS, William; Private; I/10th Cav. Mentioned 1872. SOURCE: ES, 10 Cav, 1872–81.

HOPKINS, William H.; Sergeant; A/9th Cav. On special duty in charge of laundry since 9 Apr 1902, Nueva Caceres, Philippines. SOURCE: SD List, A/9 Cav, 24 May 1902.

HOPPER, James; Sergeant; H/10th Cav. Private, at Ft Apache, AZ, 1890, subscribed $.50 to testimonial to General Grierson. SOURCE: List of subscriptions, 23 Apr 1890, 10th Cavalry papers, MHI.

Served in 10th Cavalry, 1898; remained in U.S. during war with Spain. SOURCE: Cashin, *Under Fire with the Tenth Cavalry*, 346.

HOPSON, Henry; Corporal; A/9th Cav. On special duty in charge of laundry since 28 Apr 1902, Nueva Caceres, Philippines. SOURCE: SD List, A/9 Cav, 10 May 1902.

HORN, George W.; Private; K/10th Cav. At Ft Robinson, NE, 1904.

HORN, Leroy; Cook; B/25th Inf. Dishonorable discharge, Brownsville. SOURCE: SO 266, AGO, 9 Nov 1906.

HORNER, Joseph; Private; I/24th Inf. Appointed cook, Warwick Barracks, Cebu, Philippines. SOURCE: Order 10, I/24 Inf, 6 Jan 1906, Name File, 24 Inf.

HORNER, Reuben; Sergeant; HQ Troop/10th Cav. Commissioned captain from Camp Des Moines, IA, 15 Oct 1917. SOURCE: Glass, *History of the Tenth Cavalry*, appendix M.

Warrant officer, stationed at Camp Stephen B. Little, Nogales, AZ, 1930. SOURCE: Work, *The Negro Yearbook, 1931–1932*, 334.

HORNOLD, Aleck; A/10th Cav. Original member of 10th Cavalry; in troop when organized, Ft Leavenworth, KS, 18 Feb 1867. SOURCE: McMiller, "Buffalo Soldiers," 68.

HORTON, George; Saddler; H/10th Cav. Sentenced to six months and $60 fine for false allegations of assault and abuse against Capt. C. D. Viele, 10th Cavalry, Ft Apache, AZ. SOURCE: *ANJ* 25 (28 Jan 1887): 527.

HORTON, George; Sergeant; C/25th Inf. Authorized three-month furlough from Ft Shaw, MT. SOURCE: *ANJ* 28 (7 Mar 1891): 474.

HOSE, William; Private; H/10th Cav. Served in 10th Cavalry, 1898; remained in U.S. during war with Spain. SOURCE: Cashin, *Under Fire with the Tenth Cavalry*, 346.

HOSTON, John; Private; I/24th Inf. Enlisted Richmond, VA, 4 Aug 1898. SOURCE: Muster Roll, I/24 Inf, Jan–Feb 1899.

Discharged, character good, 31 Dec 1899; deposits $55, clothing $2.21, due U.S. for ordnance $.05. SOURCE: Muster Roll, I/24 Inf, Nov–Dec 1899.

HOUGH, William; Private; 24th Inf. Convinced court martial that he hid in camp during Houston riot, 1917. SOURCE: Haynes, *A Night of Violence*, 268.

HOUSTON, Adam; QM Sgt; 10th Cav. Born Pulaski Co., VA, 1858; Ht 5'10", brown complexion; served in Cuba 23 Jun–3 Jul 1898, 8 May 1899–24 Apr 1902; twenty-two years' continuous service as of 21 Jan 1901; $2 per month additional pay for certificate of merit; $5 per month additional pay for twenty years' continuous service; married, no children; sergeant, B/10th Cavalry, promoted to color sergeant, 10th Cavalry, 10 Mar 1901; reenlisted 21 Jan 1904; promoted to regimental quartermaster sergeant, 27 Dec 1906; widowed by 20 Jan 1907. SOURCE: Descriptive Book, 10 Cav Officers & NCOs.

Private, corporal, sergeant, K/24th Infantry, 1 Dec 1879–30 Nov 1884; private, corporal, sergeant, B/10th Cavalry, 29 Dec 1884–28 Dec 1889; private, C/10th Cavalry, 20 Jan 1890; corporal, 1 Jul 1890; sergeant, 15 Mar 1891; first sergeant, 20 Jul 1891; stationed at Ft Assiniboine, MT, 1897. SOURCE: Baker, Roster.

Served with Thomas Allsup in K/24th Infantry, Ft Concho, TX, Jul 1880; after divorce, Allsup's first wife married Sgt. Lewis M. Smith, E/10th Cavalry, Ft Apache, AZ; now age 66, resides at Soldiers Home, CA. SOURCE: Affidavit, Houston, 14 Apr 1926, VA File XC 2659797, Thomas H. Allsup.

Served in C/10th Cavalry in Cuba, 1898. SOURCE: Cashin, *Under Fire with the Tenth Cavalry*, 190, 360.

Wounded in action, Santiago, Cuba, 1 Jul 1898. SOURCE: SecWar, *AR 1898*, 324.

His heroism in Cuba slighted according to unsigned letter [Cpl. John E. Lewis], Montauk, NY, n.d. SOURCE: Gatewood, *"Smoked Yankees"*, 78.

Awarded certificate of merit for distinguished service in Cuba, 1 Jul 1898. SOURCE: *ANJ* 37 (24 Feb 1900): 611; Steward, *The Colored Regulars*, 280.

Commended for distinguished service, battle of Santiago, 1 Jul 1898. SOURCE: GO 15, AGO, 13 Feb 1900.

HOUSTON, Earl E.; Private; C/9th Cav. At Ft D. A. Russell, WY, in 1910; resident of 1045 Forest Ave., Moberly, MO. SOURCE: *Illustrated Review: Ninth Cavalry*, with picture.

HOUSTON, Henry C.; Corporal; K/10th Cav. Corporal, K/10th Cavalry, on march to Carrizal, Mexico:

"The water was the worst I ever drank"; walked away from fight with Cpl. H. D. Queen, stole U.S. cavalry horses from Mexicans, and found own lines. SOURCE: Clendenen, *Blood on the Border*, 305, 310.

At Carrizal. SOURCE: Carroll, *The Black Military Experience*, 502.

Wrote letter to sister of his commander, 1st Lt. Jerome H. Howe, 11 Sep 1916, describing fight at Carrizal; during World War I, served in France as captain. SOURCE: Wharfield, *10th Cavalry and Border Fights*, 31.

Commissioned captain from Camp Des Moines, IA, 15 Oct 1917. SOURCE: Glass, *History of the Tenth Cavalry*, appendix M.

HOUSTON, Henry P.; Private; G/10th Cav. Served in 10th Cavalry, 1898; remained in U.S. during war with Spain. SOURCE: Cashin, *Under Fire with the Tenth Cavalry*, 346.

HOUSTON, John; Farrier; K/9th Cav. Born Lee Co., VA; enlisted Cincinnati, OH, Ht 5'9", laborer, 14 Sep 1881; does not write; discharged, end of term, character excellent, age 29, Ft Robinson, NE, 13 Sep 1886. SOURCE: CO to AAG, DP, 17 Sep 1886, LS, Ft Robinson.

HOUSTON, Lewis; Private; I/9th Cav. At Ft D. A. Russell, WY, in 1910; resident of Savannah, GA. SOURCE: *Illustrated Review: Ninth Cavalry*, with picture.

HOUSTON, William; Private; C/9th Cav. At Ft D. A. Russell, WY, in 1910; resident of 718 S. 4th St., Moberly, MO. SOURCE: *Illustrated Review: Ninth Cavalry*, with picture.

HOUSTON, William A.; Private; C/24th Inf. Wounded in action, Cuba, 1898. SOURCE: Muller, *The Twenty Fourth Infantry*, 18.

HOWARD; Corporal; F/10th Cav. At Ft Harker, KS, Jul 1867. SOURCE: LS, 10 Cav, 1866–67.

HOWARD, Andrew; H/10th Cav. Resided in Purcell, McClain Co., OK, in 1912. *See* **BARD**, Benjamin, Private, H/10th Cavalry

HOWARD, B. F.; Private; B/9th Cav. Ranked number seven in revolver competition, Departments of the East, Platte, and California, Bellevue, NE, 14–19 Aug 1893. SOURCE: GO 82, AGO, 24 Oct 1893.

HOWARD, Barney; Private; A/10th Cav. On Staked Plains expedition, Aug 1877. SOURCE: Leckie, *The Buffalo Soldiers*, 160–61.

HOWARD, Charles; Private; I/10th Cav. Served in 10th Cavalry in Cuba, 1898. SOURCE: Cashin, *Under Fire with the Tenth Cavalry*, 348.

HOWARD, Charley; Private; K/10th Cav. *See* BRANSFORD, Wesley, Private, K/10th Cavalry

HOWARD, Fountain; Private; E/10th Cav. Served in 10th Cavalry, 1898; remained in U.S. during war with Spain. SOURCE: Cashin, *Under Fire with the Tenth Cavalry*, 343.

Acquitted of conduct to prejudice of good order and discipline, Iloilo, Panay, Philippines. SOURCE: Manila *Times*, 20 Mar 1902.

HOWARD, Frank; Private; F/10th Cav. Served in 10th Cavalry, 1898; remained in U.S. during war with Spain. SOURCE: Cashin, *Under Fire with the Tenth Cavalry*, 344.

HOWARD, Henry L.; Private; H/9th Cav. Veteran of Philippine Insurrection; at Ft D. A. Russell, WY, in 1910; resident of Mecklinburg Co., VA. SOURCE: *Illustrated Review: Ninth Cavalry*, with picture.

HOWARD, James; Private; F/10th Cav. Original member of 10th Cavalry; in troop when organized, Ft Leavenworth, KS, 21 Jun 1867. SOURCE: McMiller, "Buffalo Soldiers," 73.

Commander of detachment at Ft Dodge, KS, recommends remission of Howard's sentence so he can be discharged, 17 May 1869; judge advocate, Department of the Missouri, recommends disapproval because Howard is convicted deserter, 24 May 1869. SOURCE: LR, Det 10 Cav, 1868–69.

HOWARD, James; Private; E/25th Inf. Wounded in action, El Caney, Cuba, 1 Jul 1898. SOURCE: Nankivell, *History of the Twenty-fifth Infantry*, 83.

HOWARD, John A.; K/10th Cav. Original member of 10th Cavalry; in troop when organized, Ft Riley, KS, 1 Sep 1867. SOURCE: McMiller, "Buffalo Soldiers," 77.

HOWARD, John D.; Principal Musician; 25th Inf. Retires from Ft Missoula, MT, May 1894. SOURCE: *ANJ* 31 (26 May 1894): 679.

HOWARD, Joseph H.; Private; D/25th Inf. Dishonorable discharge, Brownsville. SOURCE: SO 266, AGO, 9 Nov 1906.

HOWARD, Lewis; Recruit; 10th Cav. Enlisted Memphis, TN, spring 1867. SOURCE: LS, 10 Cav, 1866–67.

HOWARD, Robert; Private; D/9th Cav. Veteran of Philippine Insurrection; at Ft D. A. Russell, WY, in 1910; marksman; resident of Charleston, SC. SOURCE: *Illustrated Review: Ninth Cavalry*, with picture.

HOWARD, Rodney; QM Sgt; C/24th Inf. Coerced by 1st Lt. Robert G. Rutherford, 24th Infantry, into preparing false vouchers, Madison Barracks, NY, Aug–Sep 1910; Rutherford convicted of this and other frauds by general court martial. SOURCE: GCMO 123, AGO, 6 Sep 1911.

HOWARD, Washington; Private; F/10th Cav. Mentioned Apr 1873 as having deserted Nov 1872. SOURCE: ES, 10 Cav, 1872–81.

HOWARD, William; Sergeant; E/9th Cav. Wife is one of three authorized laundresses, E/9th Cavalry, and so entitled to Quartermaster stove and utensils if available, Ft Robinson, NE, Jun 1891. SOURCE: Post Adj to Post QM, 22 Jun 1891, LS, Ft Robinson.

Retires from Ft Robinson as sergeant, E/9th Cavalry, 14 Feb 1893. SOURCE: *ANJ* 30 (11 Mar 1893): 479; Roster, 9 Cav.

Retired; lives with wife in old barrack, Ft Robinson. SOURCE: Medical History, Ft Robinson.

Retired; employed as laborer, Ft Robinson post exchange, at $5 per month. SOURCE: Report of Inspection, Ft Robinson, 3 Sep 1894, Reports of Inspections, DeptPlatte, 2.

Emma Howard, washerwoman, resided at Ft Robinson, 1894. SOURCE: Court Martial Records, Plummer.

One of six retirees, four of whom are black, at Ft Robinson. SOURCE: Misc Records, DeptPlatte, 1894–98.

Wife Emma buried at Ft Robinson, 20 Aug 1908. SOURCE: List of Interments, Ft Robinson.

Resided in Crawford, NE, 1912, with personal property assessed at $21 and paid $2 tax; personal property assessed at $10 and paid $1 tax, 1916.

Resided in Crawford, 1921, age 75, with no income except retired pay; knew Louisa McClain from time of her marriage to Henry McClain; identified as "respected by everyone and . . . credited with being truthful and honest in each and every respect" by Veterans Administration Special Examiner C. R. Franks. SOURCE: VA File XC 2705872, Henry McClain.

HOWARD, William; Private; I/9th Cav. Promoted from lance corporal to corporal, Ft Duchesne, UT, Nov 1895. SOURCE: *ANJ* 33 (16 Nov 1895): 179.

Reduced to ranks, Ft Duchesne, Feb 1896. SOURCE: *ANJ* 33 (7 Mar 1896): 480.

HOWARD, William; 24th Inf. Wounded in action, Cuba, 1898; returned to Salt Lake City, UT, with regiment; promoted. SOURCE: Clark, "A History of the Twenty-fourth," 100–101.

HOWE, Tom; Private; D/25th Inf. Killed in action, Cuba, 1898. SOURCE: Scipio, *Last of the Black Regulars*, 29.

Died in Cuba, 1 Jul 1898. SOURCE: *ANJ* 36 (11 Feb 1899): 567.

Killed in action at El Caney, 1 Jul 1898; buried one mile south of El Caney; wooden headboard with name cut in, stones around board, name in tightly corked bottle buried at head of grave. SOURCE: Capt. M. L. Loughborough to Adj,

25th Inf, Santiago, Cuba, 11 Aug 1898, Scrapbook, 25 Inf, II.

HOWE, Willis; Corporal; G/24th Inf. Wounded in thigh, Deposito, Philippines, summer 1899. SOURCE: *ANJ* 36 (19 Aug 1899): 1223; Richmond *Planet*, 19 Aug 1899.

HOWELL, Joseph; Sergeant; B/9th Cav. At Ft D. A. Russell, WY, in 1910; sharpshooter. SOURCE: *Illustrated Review: Ninth Cavalry*, with picture.

HOWERTON, John C.; Private; A/10th Cav. Born 16 Apr 1854; enlisted Indianapolis, IN, Ht 5'5", mulatto, served 26 Sep 1882–25 Sep 1887, including Geronimo campaign; married Mary Eliza Pollard, Braidwood, IL, 1888; laborer for city of Chicago, IL; pensioned at $4 per month, 21 Feb 1890, with injury to right shoulder and rheumatism; resided at 2971 Dearborn, Chicago; sons Robert and Dewey, daughter Ursula; wife died 1931; he died 11 May 1934. SOURCE: VA File XC 896871, John C. Howerton.

Horse fell on Howerton, Ft Stockton, TX, Apr 1884. SOURCE: Affidavit, Green Trice (age 28, Hiram, OH, former private, L/10 Cav), 19 Feb 1894, VA File XC 896871, John C. Howerton.

Howerton was thrown from horse while herd guide. SOURCE: Affidavit, Robert Anderson (sergeant, B/10th Cavalry, Ft Custer, MT), 14 Sep 1893, VA File XC 896871, John C. Howerton.

Died in Chicago; late member, Camp 11, National Indian War Veterans. SOURCE: *Winners of the West* 11 (May 1934): 3.

Born 16 Apr 1854, slave of William B. Bruce, on farm five miles north of Brunswick, MO; mother also belonged to Bruce; father Henry Howerton, slave of Joseph Howerton, was sold South in 1860 or 1861; year later learned of father's death; in 1860–63 was at home "with my old master William B. Bruce"; mother loaded all four children in wagon she had hired to escape to LaClede, MO, 1864; there hidden by white man, fed for two to three days in his cellar, put on Hannibal & St. Joseph Railroad to St. Joseph, where he was told to cross to Kansas when he could; crossed Missouri River on ferry of Captain Blackston, taken to Mr. Bryant's farm, Doniphan Co.; stayed until he returned to St. Joseph, summer 1869; then got work on farm of John Britton, nineteen miles west of Omaha and three miles south of Elkhorn Station, on Union Pacific Railroad; stayed there until 1871. SOURCE: Affidavit, Howerton, 10 Sep 1927, VA File XC 896871, John C. Howerton.

HOWSAM, Barry; Sergeant; I/10th Cav. General court martial sentence. SOURCE: SO 233, DeptMo, 30 Nov 1903.

HOYLE; Private; E/9th Cav. Wounded in action at San Juan, Cuba, 1 Jul 1898. SOURCE: *Illustrated Review: Ninth Cavalry.*

HUBBARD, David W.; G/10th Cav. Original member of 10th Cavalry; in troop when organized, Ft Leavenworth, KS, 5 Jul 1867. SOURCE: McMiller, "Buffalo Soldiers," 74.

HUBBARD, George; 1st Sgt; I/24th Inf. Corporal, enlisted Ft Douglas, UT, 22 Oct 1897; fourteen years' continuous service. SOURCE: Muster Roll, I/24 Inf, Nov–Dec 1898.

Rejoined company from detached service, Three Rivers, CA, 26 Jul 1899; reduced to private, 20 Aug 1899. SOURCE: Muster Roll, I/24 Inf, Jul–Aug 1899.

Appointed corporal, 9 Sep 1899; allotted $10 per month to cashier, First National Bank, San Francisco, CA. SOURCE: Muster Roll, I/24 Inf, Sep–Oct 1899.

Promoted from sergeant to first sergeant, Warwick Barracks, Cebu, Philippines. SOURCE: Order 12, I/24 Inf, 1 Nov 1906, Name File, 24 Inf.

HUBBARD, John; Sergeant; I/10th Cav. Mentioned 1872. SOURCE: ES, 10 Cav, 1866–71.

HUBBARD, Walter; Private; L/9th Cav. At Ft D. A. Russell, WY, in 1910; resident of Newport, AR. SOURCE: *Illustrated Review: Ninth Cavalry*, with picture.

HUBBERT, Lewellen; I/10th Cav. Original member of 10th Cavalry; in troop when organized, Ft Riley, KS, 15 Aug 1867. SOURCE: McMiller, "Buffalo Soldiers," 76.

HUBBRET, Edward; Saddler; K/10th Cav. At Ft Robinson, NE, 1904; member of troop orchestra. SOURCE: Barrow, "Christmas in the United States Army," 96.

HUCKSTEP, Henderson; Corporal; G/9th Cav. Private, L/10th Cavalry, assaulted female servant of post trader, Ft Bayard, NM, Aug 1890. SOURCE: Billington, *New Mexico's Buffalo Soldiers*, 166.

Promoted from private, Ft Robinson, NE, Oct 1895. SOURCE: *ANJ* 33 (12 Oct 1895): 87.

HUDNELL, George; Private; B/10th Cav. Served in 10th Cavalry; as private, K/10th Cavalry, 1898; remained in U.S. during war with Spain. SOURCE: Cashin, *Under Fire with the Tenth Cavalry*, 349.

First American killed in action on Pershing punitive expedition into Mexico. SOURCE: *ANJ* 53 (1 Apr 1916): 996; Cleveland *Gazette*, 15 Apr 1916.

HUDSON, Charles; Private; M/9th Cav. At Ft D. A. Russell, WY, in 1910; resident of New Albany, IN. SOURCE: *Illustrated Review: Ninth Cavalry*, with picture.

HUDSON, Gus; Private; H/24th Inf. Enlisted Ft Huachuca, AZ, 28 Nov 1896. SOURCE: Muster Roll, H/24 Inf, May–Jun 1898.

Killed at San Juan, Cuba, 1 Jul 1898; due U.S. for clothing overdrawn $7.64; deposits $25. SOURCE: Muster Roll, H/24 Inf, Jul–Aug 1898.

Killed in action, Cuba, 1898. SOURCE: Scipio, *Last of the Black Regulars*, 29.

Death mentioned. SOURCE: *ANJ* 36 (11 Feb 1899): 567.

HUDSON, John H.; Private 1st Cl; 24th Inf. Tried to convince court martial that he remained in camp on night of Houston riot, 1917; sentenced to life in prison, with clemency recommended by court. SOURCE: Haynes, *A Night of Violence*, 269, 271.

HUDSON, Joseph; Private; I/25th Inf. Fined $10 by summary court, San Isidro, Philippines, for failure to cease talking in ranks when so ordered and using vile and abusive language in ranks, 16 Apr 1902, sixth conviction. SOURCE: Register of Summary Court, San Isidro.

HUDSON, McHenry; Private; C/10th Cav. Served in 10th Cavalry, 1898; remained in U.S. during war with Spain. SOURCE: Cashin, *Under Fire with the Tenth Cavalry*, 340.

HUDSON, Squire; Private; L/10th Cav. Served in 10th Cavalry, 1898; remained in U.S. during war with Spain. SOURCE: Cashin, *Under Fire with the Tenth Cavalry*, 351.

HUFF, Albert; Recruit; G/9th Cav. Convicted by general court martial, Jefferson Barracks, MO, of desertion, 25 Jun 1883; sentenced to dishonorable discharge and three years' confinement. SOURCE: GCMO 39, AGO, 27 Aug 1883.

HUFF, Walter; Private; L/10th Cav. Served in 10th Cavalry, 1898; remained in U.S. during war with Spain. SOURCE: Cashin, *Under Fire with the Tenth Cavalry*, 351.

HUFF, Willis; Private; C/9th Cav. Convicted by garrison court martial, Ft Robinson, NE, of assault on Pvt. Charles H. Young with knife, 11 Sep 1887; sentenced to thirty days' confinement. SOURCE: Post Order 188, 23 Sep 1887, Post Orders, Ft Robinson.

See **TAYLOR**, George, Private, C/9th Cavalry

HUFFMAN, Wyatt; 1st Lt; C/49th Inf. Served in G/25th Infantry, 10 Jan 1872–10 Jan 1897; corporal, 25 May 1875; sergeant, 1 Aug 1876; first sergeant, 1 Jan–1 Sep 1891; sergeant, 1 Sep 1891–29 Jul 1898; second lieutenant, 8th Infantry, U.S. Volunteers, 29 Jul 1898–6 Mar 1899; in M/25th Infantry, 14 Mar–9 Sep 1899; second lieutenant, 49th Infantry, 9 Sep 1899; first lieutenant, 2 Jan 1901; served at El Caney and Santiago, Cuba, 1898; marksman and sharpshooter. SOURCE: Descriptive Book, C/49 Inf.

With G/25th Infantry, in Cuba, 1898; "one of the finest soldiers in the regiment and carried so many service stripes on his arm that little of his sleeve showed," according to Col. Reynolds J. Burt. SOURCE: Nankivell, *History of the Twenty-fifth Infantry*, 67.

Commissioned second lieutenant, 8th Volunteer Infantry. SOURCE: Cashin, *Under Fire with the Tenth Cavalry*, 360.

Resident of Tennessee; commissioned for bravery at El Caney. SOURCE: Johnson, *History of Negro Soldiers*, 32.

Commissioned for gallantry and meritorious service around Santiago. SOURCE: New York *Journal*, quoted in Thweatt, *What the Newspapers Say*, 10; Richmond *Planet*, 13 Aug 1898.

Philippine service mentioned. SOURCE: Villard, "The Negro in the Regular Army," 724.

Second lieutenant, K/49th Infantry, on detached service with 25th Infantry, 22 Sep 1899–30 May 1900; commander, K/49th Infantry, 23 Jul–1 Aug and 14 Sep–5 Oct 1900.

Promoted to first lieutenant, 49th Infantry, 2 Jan 1901. SOURCE: *ANJ* 38 (19 Jan 1901): 503.

HUGGINS, Cumsey; Private; 25th Inf. Born Christ Church, SC; enlisted Charleston, SC, age 22, Ht 5'6", dark complexion, black hair and eyes, occupation farmer, 28 Jun 1881. SOURCE: Descriptive & Assignment Rolls, 25 Inf.

HUGHES, David; Private; M/10th Cav. Served in 10th Cavalry, 1898; remained in U.S. during war with Spain. SOURCE: Cashin, *Under Fire with the Tenth Cavalry*, 351.

HUGHES, Grant; Private; A/10th Cav. Served in 10th Cavalry in Cuba, 1898. SOURCE: Cashin, *Under Fire with the Tenth Cavalry*, 336.

HUGHES, Isack; C/10th Cav. Original member of 10th Cavalry; in troop when organized, Ft Leavenworth, KS, 14 May 1867. SOURCE: McMiller, "Buffalo Soldiers," 70.

HUGHES, James N. C.; Private; M/10th Cav. Served in 10th Cavalry, 1898; remained in U.S. during war with Spain. SOURCE: Cashin, *Under Fire with the Tenth Cavalry*, 351.

HUGHES, John; Private; A/38th Inf. At Ft Cummings, NM, autumn 1867. SOURCE: Billington, *New Mexico's Buffalo Soldiers*, 41.

HUGHES, John; Corporal; E/10th Cav. Served in 10th Cavalry in Cuba, 1898. SOURCE: Cashin, *Under Fire with the Tenth Cavalry*, 342.

HUGHES, Sam; Corporal; C/24th Inf. Private, C/24th Infantry, on special duty as fireman, ice factory, Ft Huachuca, AZ; relieved of special duty as fireman. SOURCE: Order 50, Ft Huachuca, 5 Apr 1893, Orders Received, 24 Inf.

Corporal, C/24th Infantry, died in Cuba, 29 Aug 1898. SOURCE: *ANJ* 36 (3 Sep 1898): 19; *ANJ* 36 (11 Feb 1899): 567.

HUGHES, Samuel; Private; B/10th Cav. Served in 10th Cavalry, 1898; remained in U.S. during war with Spain. SOURCE: Cashin, *Under Fire with the Tenth Cavalry*, 339.

HUKA, Stephen; A/10th Cav. Original member of 10th Cavalry; in troop when organized, Ft Leavenworth, KS, 18 Feb 1867. SOURCE: McMiller, "Buffalo Soldiers," 68.

HULEY, James; E/10th Cav. Original member of 10th Cavalry; in troop when organized, Ft Leavenworth, KS, 15 Jun 1867. SOURCE: McMiller, "Buffalo Soldiers," 72.

HULL, James; Corporal; 25th Inf. Shot and killed in El Paso, TX; buried with full military honors, post cemetery, Ft Bliss, TX, 18 Feb 1900. SOURCE: *ANJ* 37 (3 Mar 1900): 632.

HULL, Moses W.; Private; H/10th Cav. Served in 10th Cavalry, 1898; remained in U.S. during war with Spain. SOURCE: Cashin, *Under Fire with the Tenth Cavalry*, 346.

HULL, Thornton; Private; C/10th Cav. Original member of 10th Cavalry; in troop when organized, Ft Leavenworth, KS, 14 May 1867. SOURCE: McMiller, "Buffalo Soldiers," 70.

On extra duty, Ft Leavenworth, KS. SOURCE: CO, 10 Cav, to Adj, Ft Leavenworth, 15 May 1867, LS, 10 Cav, 1866–67.

HUMBLES, John C.; Sergeant; C/24th Inf. Authorized six-month furlough from Ft Grant, AZ, 1891. SOURCE: *ANJ* 28 (11 Jul 1891): 786.

HUMKINS, Andrew; A/10th Cav. Original member of 10th Cavalry; in troop when organized, Ft Leavenworth, KS, 18 Feb 1867. SOURCE: McMiller, "Buffalo Soldiers," 68.

HUMPHERY, John H.; F/10th Cav. Original member of 10th Cavalry; in troop when organized, Ft Leavenworth, KS, 21 Jun 1867. SOURCE: McMiller, "Buffalo Soldiers," 73.

HUMPHREY, Cornelius; Corporal; B/10th Cav. Born in Kentucky; private, Band/10th Cavalry, 23 Jul 1892; trumpeter, B/10th Cavalry, 26 Oct 1893; corporal, 28 Dec 1896; stationed at Ft Custer, MT, 1897. SOURCE: Baker, Roster.

HUMPHREY, John A.; Artificer; 24th Inf. Private, H/24th Infantry, relieved from extra duty as laborer, and detailed on extra duty as plasterer, Quartermaster Department, Ft Huachuca, AZ. SOURCE: Order 16, Ft Huachuca, 1 Feb 1893, Name File, 24 Inf.

Served as private, I/10th Cavalry in Cuba, 1898. SOURCE: Cashin, *Under Fire with the Tenth Cavalry*, 348.

Certificate of merit awarded for gallant conduct in voluntarily clearing path up side of hill through heavy and impassible weeds and brush while under heavy fire, Las Guasimas, Cuba, 24 Jun 1898, when private, I/10th Cavalry; discharged, as artificer, 24th Infantry, 7 Jun 1903.

Heroism mentioned. SOURCE: Cashin, *Under Fire with the Tenth Cavalry*, 185.

Private, H/24th Infantry, fined $3 by summary court, San Isidro, Philippines, for being drunk in quarters, 31 Mar 1902, first conviction. SOURCE: Register of Summary Court, San Isidro.

HUNT; Trumpeter; C/9th Cav. Wife Celeste F. buried, Ft Robinson, NE, 28 Mar 1895. SOURCE: List of Interments, Ft Robinson.

HUNT; Private; F/25th Inf. Son Clayton buried, Ft Robinson, NE, 2 Sep 1895. SOURCE: List of Interments, Ft Robinson.

HUNT; Private; K/9th Cav. Day engineer at pumphouse, so excused from Saturday inspections until further notice, Ft Robinson, NE. SOURCE: CO, Ft Robinson, to CO, K/9 Cav, 4 Mar 1898, LS, Ft Robinson.

HUNT, Arthur; Private; A/48th Inf. Died of malaria in the Philippines, 5 Oct 1900. SOURCE: *ANJ* 38 (20 Oct 1900): 187.

HUNT, George W.; Private; K/25th Inf. At Ft Niobrara, NE, 1904. SOURCE: Wilson, "History of Fort Niobrara."

HUNT, John; Sergeant; C/25th Inf. Authorized three-month furlough from Ft Shaw, MT. SOURCE: *ANJ* 28 (7 Mar 1891): 474.

HUNT, Simon; D/10th Cav. Enlisted Nashville. SOURCE: LS, 10 Cav, 1866–67.

Original member of 10th Cavalry; in troop when organized, Ft Leavenworth, KS, 1 Jun 1867. SOURCE: McMiller, "Buffalo Soldiers," 71.

HUNT, William; Private; H/24th Inf. Fined $1.50 by summary court, San Isidro, Philippines, for reporting to guard mount with dirty, rusty rifle, 7 Nov 1901, second conviction; fined $4 by summary court, San Isidro, for lying out of quarters, 22 Mar 1902; fined $2 by summary court for absence from eleven P.M. check roll call, Apr 1902; sentenced to six days for unauthorized communication with general prisoner, U.S. Military Prison, 20 Apr 1902. SOURCE: Register of Summary Court, San Isidro.

HUNT, William S.; Private; G/9th Cav. Relieved from extra duty as laborer, Quartermaster Department, Ft Robinson, NE. SOURCE: Special Order 86, 8 Aug 1896, Post Orders, Ft Robinson.

HUNTER, Bedford B.; Sgt Maj; 49th Inf. Born Junction City, KS; age 27 in 1900; occupation stenographer; yellow complexion; two years' prior service in F/24th Infantry; nine months in 23rd Kansas Infantry as acting sergeant major; married; character excellent. SOURCE: Descriptive Book, 49 Inf NCS & Band.

HUNTER, Charles; Sergeant; K/9th Cav. Private, on detached service in field, New Mexico, 30 Jan–2 Feb 1881. SOURCE: Regt Returns, 9 Cav, Feb 1881.

Private, reenlistment, married, authorized by letter, Adjutant General's Office, 27 Dec 1897.

Retires from Ft Robinson, NE. SOURCE: *ANJ* 35 (5 Feb 1898): 422.

HUNTER, Edward; Private; D/9th Cav. At Ft D. A. Russell, WY, in 1910; marksman; resident of Greenville, GA. SOURCE: *Illustrated Review: Ninth Cavalry*, with picture.

HUNTER, Ellis; Recruit; Colored Detachment/ Mounted Service. Convicted by general court martial, Jefferson Barracks, MO, of stealing suspenders worth $1 from Recruit Walter Grubb, Company A of Instruction, Mounted Service, and selling same to Recruit Jesse Boggs, Colored Detachment, Mounted Service, for $.30, rather than to Recruit James Jones, Colored Detachment, for $.50, as originally charged; sentenced to dishonorable discharge and one year. SOURCE: GCMO 11, AGO, 19 Feb 1889.

HUNTER, F. C.; Private; A/9th Cav. At Ft Stanton, NM, 1881. SOURCE: Regt Returns, 9 Cav, Jan 1881.

HUNTER, Fred; Private; G/9th Cav. Born Aiken, GA; enlisted Ft McPherson, GA, occupation soldier, age 26, Ht 5'4", dark complexion, brown hair and eyes, single, 18 Feb 1899; two summary court convictions, Ft Wingate, NM: sentenced to seven days' confinement, 12 Jan 1900, and to thirty days' confinement, 18 May 1900; "deserted to the insurrectos, at Guinobatan, P.I., Feb 13, 1901. Taking clothing, 2 carbines, 1 pistol, 3 belts full ammunition"; surrendered with insurgent forces, Legaspi, Philippines, 5 Jul 1901, with Pvts. Garth Shores and William Victor; killed in attempt to escape confinement, Albay, Philippines, 26 Aug 1901. SOURCE: Descriptive Book, H/9 Cav.

See D**U**BOSE, Edmond, Private, E/9th Cavalry; VICTOR, William, Private, H/9th Cavalry

HUNTER, George; Private; K/9th Cav. *See* PUMPHREY, George W., Sergeant, H/9th Cavalry

HUNTER, Isaac; Horseshoer; I/9th Cav. Served as private, L/10th Cavalry, 1898; remained in U.S. during war with Spain. SOURCE: Cashin, *Under Fire with the Tenth Cavalry*, 351.

Expert rifleman and horseshoer, I/9th Cavalry, at Ft D. A. Russell, WY, in 1910; resident of Enfield, NC. SOURCE: *Illustrated Review: Ninth Cavalry*, with picture.

HUNTER, James; Private; 10th Cav. Transferred to 10th Cavalry in accordance with Special Order 200, Adjutant General's Office, 25 Jul 1902.

HUNTER, James O.; Bn Sgt Maj; 49th Inf. Born Sumner, TN; age 47 in 1899; formerly corporal and sergeant, G/25th Infantry, and first sergeant, L/49th Infantry, before becoming battalion sergeant major; character excellent, single; mother Mrs. Edith Hunter, Brightwood, IN; deposits $300, Jan–Nov 1900. SOURCE: Descriptive Book, 49 Inf NCS.

Wounded in action as corporal, G/25th Infantry, El Caney, Cuba, 1 Jul 1898. SOURCE: Nankivell, *History of the Twenty-fifth Infantry*, 83.

In command of L/49th Infantry, as first sergeant, much of Jul–Aug 1900 during absence of Capt. Edward L. Baker. SOURCE: Monthly Returns, L/49 Inf.

HUNTER, Jerry; 24th Inf. Died 4 Dec 1898; buried at Ft Douglas, UT. SOURCE: Clark, "A History of the Twenty-fourth," appendix A.

HUNTER, John M.; Private; K/9th Cav. Expert rifleman at Ft D. A. Russell, WY, in 1910; resident of Union, SC. SOURCE: *Illustrated Review: Ninth Cavalry*.

HUNTER, Jordan; Saddler; D/9th Cav. Retires from Ft Washakie, WY. SOURCE: *ANJ* 34 (8 May 1897): 663.

HUNTER, Samuel; A/10th Cav. Original member of 10th Cavalry; in troop when organized, Ft Leavenworth, KS, 18 Feb 1867. SOURCE: McMiller, "Buffalo Soldiers," 68.

HURBURT, J. D. C.; E/9th Cav. Served 1886–91; resides at St. Joseph, MO; member, Camp 11, National Indian War Veterans, and attended recent convention. SOURCE: *Winners of the West* 4 (Sep 1927): 4.

HURD, John; K/25th Inf. Admitted to Soldiers Home at age 44 with twenty-one years and six months' service, 16 Jun 1888. SOURCE: SecWar, *AR 1888*, 904.

HURD, William; Corporal; M/9th Cav. At Ft D. A. Russell, WY, in 1910; marksman; resident of Chicago. SOURCE: *Illustrated Review: Ninth Cavalry*, with picture.

HURLEY, Otto; Private; K/10th Cav. At Ft Robinson, NE, 1904.

HURNS, Thomas H.; K/10th Cav. Original member of 10th Cavalry; in troop when organized, Ft Riley, KS, 1 Sep 1867. SOURCE: McMiller, "Buffalo Soldiers," 77.

HURST, Thomas E.; Corporal; B/24th Inf. At Ft McIntosh, TX, 1877. *See* GRAYSON, Charles H., Private, G/24th Infantry

HURT, Burnett J.; Private; I/9th Cav. At Ft D. A. Russell, WY, in 1910; resident of Selma, AL. SOURCE: *Illustrated Review: Ninth Cavalry*, with picture.

HURT, John; Sergeant; H/9th Cav. Private, served in H/10th Cavalry, 1898; remained in U.S. during war with Spain. SOURCE: Cashin, *Under Fire with the Tenth Cavalry*, 346.

Expert rifleman and sergeant, H/9th Cavalry, at Ft D. A. Russell, WY, in 1910; resident of Bluefield, WV. SOURCE: *Illustrated Review: Ninth Cavalry*, with picture.

HURT, John L.; Corporal; K/10th Cav. At Ft Robinson, NE, 1904.

HUTCHINSON, Charles; 24th Inf. Died 28 Jan 1899; buried at Ft Douglas, UT. SOURCE: Clark, "A History of the Twenty-fourth," appendix A.

HUTSON, Charles G.; Private; I/24th Inf. Enlisted Louisville, KY, 7 Jul 1899; joined company 29 Sep 1899. SOURCE: Muster Roll, I/24 Inf, Sep–Oct 1899.

Absent sick, Tarlac, Philippines, since 12 Dec 1899. SOURCE: Muster Roll, I/24 Inf, Nov–Dec 1899.

HUTSON, Julius; Private; I/9th Cav. At Ft D. A. Russell, WY, in 1910; resident of Gallatin, TN. SOURCE: *Illustrated Review: Ninth Cavalry.*

HUTTON, George R.; Private; H/24th Inf. Enlisted Springfield, MA, 8 Jun 1895; discharged, end of term, Camp Tampa, FL, character excellent, single, with $55 deposits, $9.23 retained, $7.79 clothing, 7 Jun 1898; discharged with nine years' continuous service; enlisted, Tampa, 8 Jun 1898. SOURCE: Muster Roll, H/24 Inf, May–Jun 1898.

Recommended for commission as second lieutenant for bravery at San Juan Hill, Cuba. SOURCE: Lynk, *The Black Troopers*, 61, with drawing.

Appointed corporal, 15 Sep 1898; authorized furlough by surgeon's certificate, 19 Sep–18 Oct 1898; present sick, disease contracted in line of duty, since 29 Oct 1898. SOURCE: Muster Roll, H/24 Inf, Sep–Oct 1898.

Sick in quarters until 23 Nov 1898. SOURCE: Muster Roll, H/24 Inf, Nov–Dec 1898.

Discharged as private, Ft Douglas, UT, character good, single, 26 Jan 1899; deposits $47.75; clothing $29.20. SOURCE: Muster Roll, H/24 Inf, Jan–Feb 1899.

Picture. SOURCE: Indianapolis *Freeman*, 28 Jan 1899.

HUTTON, James T.; Private; H/24th Inf. Enlisted Springfield, MA, 8 Jun 1895; discharged, end of term, Camp Tampa, FL, character excellent, single, with $93.14 deposits, $1.14 clothing, 7 Jun 1898; discharged with three years' continuous service; enlisted Tampa, 8 Jun 1898. SOURCE: Muster Roll, H/24 Inf, May–Jun 1898.

Enlisted Boston, MA, 19 Jul 1898; joined company 16 Sep 1898. SOURCE: Muster Roll, H/24 Inf, Sep–Oct 1898.

Discharged Ft Douglas, UT, character good, single, 26 Jan 1899; deposits $33; clothing $10.27. SOURCE: Muster Roll, H/24 Inf, Jan–Feb 1899.

HUTTON, William A.; Farrier; H/9th Cav. Veteran of Philippine Insurrection; at Ft D. A. Russell, WY, in 1910; resident of Washington, DC. SOURCE: *Illustrated Review: Ninth Cavalry*, with picture.

HUTTON, William H.; Private; A/10th Cav. Wounded in action, Lancaster River, TX, Apr 1874.

HYDE, Alexander; QM Sgt; I/24th Inf. Enlisted Nashville, TN, 1 May 1896; thirteen years' continuous service in 1898. SOURCE: Muster Roll, I/24 Inf, Jan–Feb 1899.

Discharged, character excellent, deposits $149.25 and clothing $53.64, 30 Apr 1899. SOURCE: Muster Roll, I/24 Inf, May–Jun 1899.

HYMES, Pompy; Private; G/49th Inf. Died of variola in the Philippines, 9 Mar 1900. SOURCE: *ANJ* 37 (14 Apr 1900): 779.

ILL, James B.; Private; A/24th Inf. Died in Cuba, 19 Aug 1898. SOURCE: *ANJ* 36 (11 Feb 1899): 567.

Died of yellow fever. SOURCE: AG, *Correspondence Regarding the War with Spain*, I:244.

IMES, James; Private; K/9th Cav. Served 1872–73. *See* **SLAUGHTER**, Rufus, Private, K/9th Cavalry; **WILLIAMS**, Jerry, Private, K/9th Cavalry

INGMAN, James; Sergeant; K/24th Inf. Fined $10 for failure to repair for retreat, Cabanatuan, Philippines, 31 May 1901; witness: 1st Sgt. Stevens, K/24th Infantry. SOURCE: Name File, 24 Inf.

Fined one month's pay, confined for thirty days, and reduced to private for allowing native *vino* in guardhouse while in command of guard and drinking *vino* in guardhouse; witness: Musician Thurman, K/24th Infantry. SOURCE: Name File, 24 Inf.

See **THURMAN**, Harry, Musician, K/24th Infantry

INGOMAN, Madison; QM Sgt; D/9th Cav. Served in G/10th Cavalry, 1873. SOURCE: ES, 10 Cav, 1872–81.

Sergeant, D/9th Cavalry, from 1 May 1880. SOURCE: Roster, 9 Cav.

Ambushed while commanding wagon train escort of six privates between Ft Craig and Camp Ojo Caliente, NM, Jan 1881; Pvt. William Jones severely wounded and died next day. SOURCE: Billington, *New Mexico's Buffalo Soldiers*, 101.

Sergeant, D/9th Cavalry, at Ft Robinson, NE, as witness in Brown and Wormsley court martial, 26 Oct–27 Dec 1889; then returned to station at Ft McKinney, WY.

Admonished by commander, Ft Robinson, that while his family resides on post, his children of proper school age must attend post school or some other school; under no circumstances will they loiter around barracks during school hours. SOURCE: CO to Sgt. Ingoman, 22 Mar 1893, LS, Ft Robinson.

Resides at Ft Robinson on laundresses' row with wife, three children, and sister-in-law with one child. SOURCE: Medical History, Ft Robinson, Entry for Aug 1893.

Quartermaster sergeant, D/9th Cavalry, died in Cuba, 8 Aug 1898. SOURCE: *ANJ* 36 (11 Feb 1899): 567.

Died of fever in Cuba and buried with honors, Ft Leavenworth, KS, 3 Mar 1900; two citations for actions against Apaches en route to Ojo Caliente, NM, 21 Jan 1881, and at Canada Alamosa, NM, 25 Jan 1881. SOURCE: *ANJ* 37 (10 Mar 1900): 651.

INMAN, William F.; Private; K/10th Cav. At Ft Robinson, NE, 1904.

IRVIN; Private; I/9th Cav. Resides at Ft Robinson, NE, with his wife, 1893. SOURCE: Medical History, Ft Robinson.

IRVIN, William N.; Private; H/9th Cav. At Ft D. A. Russell, WY, in 1910; resident of Knoxville, TN. SOURCE: *Illustrated Review: Ninth Cavalry*, with picture.

IRVING, Lee; Private; B/10th Cav. Private, K/9th Cavalry, directed to leave Ft Robinson, NE, with Pvt. Walter R. Fisher, K/9th Cavalry, and three days' rations to repair telegraph line to Running Water, 18 Jul 1888. SOURCE: Order 135, 17 Jul 1888, Post Orders, Ft Robinson.

Private, K/9th Cavalry, wounded in action at Pine Ridge, SD, 1890; returned to Ft Robinson, 4 Jan 1891. SOURCE: Kelley, *Pine Ridge, 1890*, 219.

Retires from Ft Custer, MT, as private, B/10th Cavalry, 28 Apr 1896. SOURCE: *ANJ* 33 (25 Apr 1896): 616; Baker, Roster.

IRWIN, J. W.; Sergeant; A/9th Cav. Authorized furlough from Ft Stanton, NM, beginning 27 Jan 1881. SOURCE: Regt Returns, 9 Cav, Jan 1881.

ISAACS, John; Private; A/10th Cav. Died on Staked Plains expedition, Aug 1877. SOURCE: Leckie, *The Buffalo Soldiers*, 162.

ISAACS, Thomas; Private; H/24th Inf. Enlisted Louisville, KY, 5 May 1893; discharged, end of term, character excellent, single, Ft Douglas, UT, 4 May 1898; deposits $95, retained $58.33, owes U.S. $5.12 for clothing. SOURCE: Muster Roll, H/24 Inf, May–Jun 1898.

Enlisted Louisville, 1 Aug 1898; assigned to H/24th Infantry, 9 Sep 1898; musician, 16 Sep 1898. SOURCE: Muster Roll, H/24 Inf, Sep–Oct 1898.

Discharged, character good, single, Ft Douglas, 26 Jan 1899; deposits $40, clothing $1.85. SOURCE: Muster Roll, H/24 Inf, Jan–Feb 1899.

ISAACS, Will; QM Sgt; D/24th Inf. Private, B/24th Infantry, transferred from Reserve Divisional Hospital, Siboney, Cuba, to U.S. with remittent malarial fever, on U.S. Army Transport *Santiago*, 25 Jul 1898. SOURCE: Hospital Papers, Spanish-American War.

Ranked number 113 among rifle experts with 73.67 percent, 1905. SOURCE: GO 101, AGO, 31 May 1906.

ISAIAH, Basil; B/10th Cav. Original member of 10th Cavalry; in troop when organized, Ft Leavenworth, KS, 1 Apr 1867. SOURCE: McMiller, "Buffalo Soldiers," 69.

ISAM, Frank J.; Saddler; I/10th Cav. At Ft Apache, AZ, 1890, subscribed $.50 to testimonial to General Grierson. SOURCE: List of subscriptions, 23 Apr 1890, 10th Cavalry papers, MHI.

ITSON, Albert; Private; I/24th Inf. Enlisted Louisville, KY, 7 Feb 1899. SOURCE: Muster Roll, I/24 Inf, Jan–Feb 1899.

Fined $1.50 by summary court, 23 May 1899. SOURCE: Muster Roll, I/24 Inf, May–Jun 1899.

Fined $1 by summary court, 22 Jul 1899. SOURCE: Muster Roll, I/24 Inf, Jul–Aug 1899.

Fined $3 by summary court, 25 Sep 1899. SOURCE: Muster Roll, I/24 Inf, Sep–Oct 1899.

On detached service at Cabanatuan, Philippines, since 30 Dec 1899. SOURCE: Muster Roll, I/24 Inf, Nov–Dec 1899.

JACKSON; Private; A/10th Cav. At Ft Apache, AZ, 1890, subscribed $.50 to testimonial to General Grierson. SOURCE: List of subscriptions, 23 Apr 1890, 10th Cavalry papers, MHI.

JACKSON; Private; B/10th Cav. At Ft Apache, AZ, 1890, subscribed $.50 to testimonial to General Grierson. SOURCE: List of subscriptions, 23 Apr 1890, 10th Cavalry papers, MHI.

JACKSON; Private; D/10th Cav. At Ft Apache, AZ, 1890, subscribed $.50 to testimonial to General Grierson. SOURCE: List of subscriptions, 23 Apr 1890, 10th Cavalry papers, MHI.

JACKSON; Private; I/9th Cav. Wounded in action, Pine Ridge, SD; returned to Ft Robinson, NE, 4 Jan 1891. SOURCE: Kelley, *Pine Ridge, 1890*, 219.

JACKSON; Corporal; K/24th Inf. At Cabanatuan, Philippines, 1901. *See* **TAYLOR**, George N., Private, K/24th Infantry

JACKSON, Abraham; Private; H/10th Cav. Served in 10th Cavalry, 1898; remained in U.S. during war with Spain. SOURCE: Cashin, *Under Fire with the Tenth Cavalry*, 346–47.

JACKSON, Albert; Private; E/24th Inf. Transferred from Reserve Divisional Hospital, Siboney, Cuba, to U.S. on U.S. Army Transport *Santiago*, with remittent malarial fever. SOURCE: Hospital Papers, Spanish-American War.

JACKSON, Alexander; C/10th Cav. Original member of 10th Cavalry; in troop when organized, Ft Leavenworth, KS, 14 May 1867. SOURCE: McMiller, "Buffalo Soldiers," 70.

JACKSON, Andrew; D/10th Cav. Original member of 10th Cavalry; in troop when organized, Ft Leavenworth, KS, 1 Jun 1867. SOURCE: McMiller, "Buffalo Soldiers," 71.

JACKSON, Andrew; Private; K/24th Inf. Arrested for drunkenness and making threats with weapon at Presidio of San Francisco entrance after being missing for four days; reduced from sergeant. SOURCE: San Francisco *Chronicle*, 2 Dec 1899.
  With B/24th Infantry at San Juan, Cuba, 1898; sharpshooter. SOURCE: San Francisco *Chronicle*, 6 Dec 1899.

JACKSON, Benjamin; Private; B/10th Cav. Mentioned Mar 1874. SOURCE: LS, 10 Cav, 1873–83.

JACKSON, Bernard A.; Private; K/10th Cav. Served in 10th Cavalry in Cuba, 1898. SOURCE: Cashin, *Under Fire with the Tenth Cavalry*, 348.

JACKSON, Brown; Private; 10th Cav. Arrived at Ft Leavenworth, KS, from Jefferson Barracks, MO, Oct 1866.

JACKSON, Claude; Private; C/10th Cav. Served in 10th Cavalry, 1898; remained in U.S. during war with Spain. SOURCE: Cashin, *Under Fire with the Tenth Cavalry*, 333.

JACKSON, Daniel; 49th Inf. Identified Pvt. Andrew Jackson, K/24th Infantry, for San Francisco police. SOURCE: San Francisco *Chronicle*, 6 Dec 1899.

JACKSON, Edgar; Private; B/9th Cav. At Ft D. A. Russell, WY, in 1910. SOURCE: *Illustrated Review: Ninth Cavalry*, with picture.

JACKSON, Edward; Sergeant; H/10th Cav. Letter to editor from Covington, KY; grateful for increased pension. SOURCE: *Winners of the West* 4 (Jun 1927): 5.
  Calls *Winners of the West* "a dandy little paper." SOURCE: *Winners of the West* 8 (Mar 1931): 9.

JACKSON, Edward; Corporal; 48th Inf. Sick in the Philippines, Feb 1900. SOURCE: Richmond *Planet*, 14 Apr 1900.

JACKSON, Elisha; 2nd Lt; 10th Inf USV. Appointed corporal, H/9th Cavalry, 19 Apr 1893. SOURCE: Roster, 9 Cav.
  Promoted to sergeant from corporal, Ft Robinson, NE, Dec 1894. SOURCE: *ANJ* 32 (22 Dec 1894): 278.
  To be discharged from H/9th Cavalry, 24 May 1897, with $175 deposits, $92 clothing, $48 retained. SOURCE: CO, H/9, to Chief QM, DeptPlatte, May 1897, LS, H/9 Cav.
  Born Richmond Co., VA; enlisted, age 31, Ft Robinson, 20 May 1897, with ten years' continuous service in M and H/9th Cavalry; married without children; commissioned second lieutenant, 10th Infantry, U.S. Volunteers. SOURCE: Descriptive Book, H/9 Cav.
  Married widow of Saddler Sgt. Charles H. Dowd, 9th Cavalry, Ft Robinson, 15 Jun 1897. SOURCE: CO, 9 Cav, to AG, USA, 17 Jun 1897, LS, Ft Robinson.

On point, Cuba, 1 Jul 1898, and "ever in front and by his example encouraged all about him." SOURCE: SecWar, *AR 1898*, 708.

Sergeant, H/9th Cavalry, commissioned second lieutenant, 10th Volunteer Infantry, after Spanish-American War. SOURCE: Cashin, *Under Fire with the Tenth Cavalry*, 360.

Awarded certificate of merit for meritorious service, Cuba, 1898; out of service by 1900. SOURCE: *ANJ* 37 (24 Feb 1900): 611; Steward, *The Colored Regulars*, 280.

Commended for gallantry, 1 Jul 1898; now out of service. SOURCE: GO 15, AGO, 13 Feb 1900.

JACKSON, Emmett J.; Corporal; 24th Inf. Corporal, D/24th Infantry, at Cabanatuan, Philippines, 1901. *See* **MOORE**, Cato, Private, D/24th Infantry

Corporal, C/25th Infantry, married Agnes Marshall of Valentine, NE, at Ft Niobrara, NE, 9 Nov 1904, at age 27, by Chaplain Steward. SOURCE: Monthly Report, Chaplain Steward, Nov 1904.

In 24th Infantry, Ft Madison, NY; visited parents at their home, 1407 East Capitol Street, Washington, DC, after ten-year absence; brother H. Oliver Jackson of Philadelphia, PA, also visited. SOURCE: Washington *Bee*, 2 May 1908.

JACKSON, Ernest; Private; G/9th Cav. Veteran of Philippine Insurrection; at Ft D. A. Russell, WY, in 1910; marksman; resident of Indianapolis. SOURCE: *Illustrated Review: Ninth Cavalry*, with picture.

JACKSON, F.; Corporal; G/25th Inf. Baseball player at Ft Missoula, MT, 1894. SOURCE: Nankivell, *History of the Twenty-fifth Infantry*, 164, with picture on 165.

JACKSON, Frank; Private; B/10th Cav. Served in 10th Cavalry, 1898; remained in U.S. during war with Spain. SOURCE: Cashin, *Under Fire with the Tenth Cavalry*, 339.

JACKSON, Frank; Private; E/9th Cav. Returned from furlough to duty at Ft Robinson, NE, 14 Sep 1898.

JACKSON, Frank; Private; B/24th Inf. Fined one month's pay for drunkenness in streets of Cabanatuan, Philippines, and assault on Regina Carlos Satornina by striking her on cheek with his hand, 4 Jan 1901; witness: Pvt. Wheeler Pride, D/24th Infantry. SOURCE: Name File, 24 Inf.

JACKSON, G. A.; Private; E/9th Cav. On detached service in field, New Mexico, 26 Jan–1 Feb 1881. SOURCE: Regt Returns, 9 Cav, Feb 1881.

JACKSON, Garfield; Private; D/10th Cav. Released to duty from treatment for acute gonorrhea, Ft Robinson, NE, 18 Jan 1903. SOURCE: Post Surgeon to CO, D/10 Cav, 18 Jan 1903, LS, Post Surgeon, Ft Robinson.

JACKSON, George; Private; F/10th Cav. Served in 10th Cavalry in Cuba, 1898. SOURCE: Cashin, *Under Fire with the Tenth Cavalry*, 344.

JACKSON, George; Private; B/25th Inf. Enlisted 1898. SOURCE: Weaver, *The Brownsville Raid*, 71.

Ranked number 16, Northern Division Infantry Team competition, Ft Sheridan, IL, 1904. SOURCE: GO 167, AGO, 28 Oct 1904.

Dishonorable discharge, Brownsville. SOURCE: SO 266, AGO, 9 Nov 1906.

JACKSON, George H.; 1st Sgt; H/9th Cav. Deposited $440 with paymaster, Ft Robinson, NE, 1898.

JACKSON, George W.; Private; A/10th Cav. Enlisted Philadelphia, PA, 5 Jul 1898. SOURCE: Muster Roll, I/24 Inf, Nov–Dec 1899.

Captured in Philippines, 31 Jul 1900. *See* **SMITH**, C. H., Sergeant, I/24th Infantry

Wounded in action, Munoz, Luzon, and captured, 10 Oct 1900. SOURCE: *ANJ* 38 (3 Nov 1900): 235. *See* **BURNS**, William J., Corporal, I/24th Infantry

Letter to editor. SOURCE: Manila *Times*, 14 May 1901.

JACKSON, H.; Private; L/9th Cav. On detached service in field, New Mexico, 21 Jan–24 Feb 1881. SOURCE: Regt Returns, 9 Cav, Feb 1881.

JACKSON, Harvey; G/10th Cav. Original member of 10th Cavalry; in troop when organized, Ft Leavenworth, KS, 5 Jul 1867. SOURCE: McMiller, "Buffalo Soldiers," 74.

JACKSON, Henry; L/10th Cav. Original member of 10th Cavalry; in troop when organized, Ft Riley, KS, 21 Sep 1867. SOURCE: McMiller, "Buffalo Soldiers," 78.

JACKSON, Henry; Private; F/10th Cav. Served in 10th Cavalry in Cuba, 1898; wounded in action. SOURCE: Cashin, *Under Fire with the Tenth Cavalry*, 344.

JACKSON, Henry; Private; I/24th Inf. Enlisted Kansas City, MO, 9 Feb 1899. SOURCE: Muster Roll, I/24 Inf, Jan–Feb 1899.

Sick, disease contracted in line of duty, since 29 Apr 1899. SOURCE: Muster Roll, I/24 Inf, Mar–Apr 1899.

Allotted $6 per month for twelve months to Robert Jackson. SOURCE: Muster Roll, I/24 Inf, Sep–Oct 1899.

Captured by insurgents in the Philippines, 10 Oct 1900. *See* **BURNS**, William J., Corporal, I/24th Infantry

JACKSON, Isaac; Sergeant; H/10th Cav. Honorable mention for services rendered in capture of Mangas and his Apache band, Rio Bonito, AZ, 18 Oct 1886. SOURCE: Baker, Roster.

JACKSON, Isaac L.; Private; H/24th Inf. Enlisted Columbus Barracks, OH, 23 Dec 1898; assigned and joined company 14 Jan 1899; on special duty as painter, Quartermaster Department, since 23 Feb 1899. SOURCE: Muster Roll, H/24 Inf, Jan–Feb 1899.

JACKSON, J.; Private; 24th Inf. Sentenced to life in prison for part in Houston riot, 1917; released from prison with terminal tuberculosis, 1921. SOURCE: Haynes, *A Night of Violence*, 308–09.

JACKSON, J. H.; Private; H/10th Cav. Jailed for disturbance, Cheyenne, WY. SOURCE: Wyoming *Tribune*, 26 Dec 1906.

JACKSON, J. T.; Private; G/9th Cav. On detached service, Ft Stanton, NM, 29 Jan–5 Feb 1881. SOURCE: Regt Returns, 9 Cav, Feb 1881.

JACKSON, James; G/10th Cav. Original member of 10th Cavalry; in troop when organized, Ft Leavenworth, KS, 5 Jul 1867. SOURCE: McMiller, "Buffalo Soldiers," 74.

JACKSON, James; Private; D/10th Cav. Mentioned Feb 1877 as having reenlisted and transferred from C/10th Cavalry. SOURCE: LS, 10 Cav, 1873–83.

JACKSON, James; Private; A/9th Cav. Resides on laundress row, Ft Robinson, NE, with wife and child, Aug 1893. SOURCE: Medical History, Ft Robinson.

Post commander recently "bothered a great deal" listening to "innumerable complaints" of conduct of Private Jackson's wife, who appears "a quarrelsome and vindictive woman" and is suspected of carrying on illicit whisky and beer trade; orders already given regarding her leaving post will be obeyed. SOURCE: CO, Ft Robinson, to CO, A/9 Cav, 19 Nov 1894, LS, Ft Robinson.

Reenlistment, married, authorized by letter, Adjutant General's Office, 11 Jun 1897.

Retires from Ft Robinson, in accordance with Special Order 179, Adjutant General's Office, 5 Aug 1897. SOURCE: *ANJ* 34 (7 Aug 1897): 909.

JACKSON, James; Sergeant; C/10th Cav. Served as private, C/10th Cavalry, 1898; remained in U.S. during war with Spain. SOURCE: Cashin, *Under Fire with the Tenth Cavalry*, 333.

Retires, Mar 1901. SOURCE: *ANJ* 38 (23 Mar 1901): 721.

JACKSON, James; Private; L/10th Cav. Served in 10th Cavalry, 1898; remained in U.S. during war with Spain. SOURCE: Cashin, *Under Fire with the Tenth Cavalry*, 351.

JACKSON, James F.; Private; G/9th Cav. Born Waynesboro, MS, 1 May 1863; enlisted Louisville, KY, occupation laborer, dark complexion, 10 Nov 1880; corporal, 1 Aug 1882; sergeant, 1 Mar 1883; private, 27 Sep 1884; corporal, 16 Jan 1886; sergeant, 10 Apr 1888; first sergeant, 15 Sep 1889; private, 27 Oct 1896; dishonorable

discharge, Ft Robinson, NE, in accordance with Special Order 120, Department of the Platte, 1896, for embezzlement; pension of $6 per month as of 6 Jan 1898 for rheumatism in right arm and shoulder, caused by gunshot wound inflicted by Private Moseby, G/9th Cavalry at Ft Niobrara, NE, 12 May 1888; when shot, Jackson was in charge of quarters on duty in squad room, ordered Moseby to report to sergeant of the guard, Moseby left, returned, ordered Jackson to raise his hands, said he had come to kill him, shot him in right shoulder; married Annie B. Thompson, 3 Oct 1891, Louisville; no children. SOURCE: VA File C 2555351, James F. Jackson.

Appointed sergeant, 10 Apr 1888. SOURCE: Roster, 9 Cav.

Ranked number six, carbine competition, Departments of the Platte and Columbia, at Bellevue, NE, 1889. SOURCE: GO 78, AGO, 12 Oct 1889.

Distinguished marksman, 1889. SOURCE: GO 112, AGO, 2 Oct 1890.

Ranked number three in rifle competition, Departments of the Platte and Dakota, and number seven, revolver competition, Bellevue, NE, 4–9 Aug 1890; distinguished marksman, 1890. SOURCE: *ANJ* 27 (16 Aug 1890): 943; GO 112, AGO, 2 Oct 1890.

At Ft Sheridan, IL, for rifle competition, Sep 1891. SOURCE: *ANJ* 29 (5 Sep 1891): 25.

Ranked number three, competition of Army carbine team, 1891. SOURCE: GO 81, AGO, 6 Oct 1891.

Distinguished marksman, 1892. SOURCE: *ANJ* 30 (27 Aug 1892): 5.

Witness for defense, Barney McKay court martial, Ft Robinson, 1893.

Ranked number ten, Army carbine team of distinguished marksmen, 1893. SOURCE: GO 82, AGO, 24 Oct 1893.

Ranked number five, Army carbine team of distinguished marksmen, 1894. SOURCE: GO 15, AGO, 15 Nov 1894.

See **BELL**, Wade, G/9th Cavalry; **BLEW**, Joseph, Sergeant, G/9th Cavalry; **HOOVER**, Alfred C., Private, G/9th Cavalry; **TAYLOR**, Alexander, Private, I/9th Cavalry; **WATTS**, Willis, Private, G/24th Infantry

JACKSON, James H.; Private; L/9th Cav. At Ft D. A. Russell, WY, in 1910; resident of Columbia, SC. SOURCE: *Illustrated Review: Ninth Cavalry*, with picture.

JACKSON, Jason J.; Sergeant; 9th Cav. Stationed at Ord Barracks, Monterey, CA, 1903; vice president of literary and social club organized with civilians of Pacific Grove, CA. SOURCE: Indianapolis *Freeman*, 5 Dec 1903.

JACKSON, Jerry; A/10th Cav. Original member of 10th Cavalry; in troop when organized, Ft Leavenworth, KS, 18 Feb 1867. SOURCE: McMiller, "Buffalo Soldiers," 68.

JACKSON, Jesse; A/10th Cav. Deserted from Ft Leavenworth, KS, 19 Mar 1867. SOURCE: McMiller, "Buffalo Soldiers," 53.

JACKSON, John; Sergeant; C/9th Cav. Private, C/9th Cavalry; child buried at Ft Robinson, NE, 28 Aug 1886. SOURCE: List of Interments, Ft Robinson.

Appointed sergeant, 22 Aug 1887. SOURCE: Roster, 9 Cav.

Killed Artificer Cornelius Donovan, C/8th Infantry, in line of duty as sergeant of guard, Ft Robinson, "greatly outraged by the most insulting language"; Donovan threatened him and he had to take threat literally; nine years of service in D/9th Cavalry and his officers consider him "thoroughly good and reliable." SOURCE: CO, Ft Robinson, to AAG, DP, 16 and 19 Oct 1891, LS, Ft Robinson.

In hands of civil authorities, Omaha, NE, 25 Oct–21 Dec 1891. SOURCE: Regt Returns, 9 Cav.

Resided in quarters adjacent to Saddler Sergeant Benjamin, Ft Robinson, 1894. SOURCE: Court Martial Records, Dillon.

Ordered from Ft Robinson to Douglas, WY, to receive deserter Myles Smith, D/9th Cavalry, from city marshal. SOURCE: Order 89, 30 Nov 1894, Post Orders, Ft Robinson.

At Ft Washakie, WY, 1896.

JACKSON, John; Private; C/10th Cav. Served in 10th Cavalry, 1898; remained in U.S. during war with Spain. SOURCE: Cashin, *Under Fire with the Tenth Cavalry*, 340.

JACKSON, John; Private; M/10th Cav. Transferred from 25th Infantry in accordance with Special Order 295, Adjutant General's Office, 3 Dec 1903.

JACKSON, John; Corporal; H/24th Inf. Ranked number two, with gold medal, Northern Division infantry team competition, Ft Sheridan, IL, 1904. SOURCE: GO 167, AGO, 28 Oct 1904.

Ranked number 530 among rifle experts with 68 percent, 1905. SOURCE: GO 101, AGO, 31 May 1906.

JACKSON, John A.; Private; D/25th Inf. Dishonorable discharge, Brownsville. SOURCE: SO 266, AGO, 9 Nov 1906.

One of fourteen cleared of involvement in Brownsville raid by court, 1910; authorized to reenlist. SOURCE: Weaver, *The Brownsville Raid*, 248.

JACKSON, John H.; Private; A/10th Cav. Joined regiment 1867, as private A/10th Cavalry. SOURCE: Baker, Roster.

Sergeant, authorized three-month furlough from San Carlos, AZ. SOURCE: *ANJ* 25 (24 Dec 1887): 423.

At Ft Apache, AZ, 1890, subscribed $.50 to testimonial to General Grierson. SOURCE: List of subscriptions, 23 Apr 1890, 10th Cavalry papers, MHI.

Retires as private, from Ft Keogh, MT. SOURCE: *ANJ* 35 (18 Dec 1897): 293.

JACKSON, John H.; Corporal; Band/25th Inf. Born Smithton, MO; second enlistment, age 26, Ht 5'8", yellow complexion, Ft Omaha, NE, 24 Jun 1893; previously discharged from D/9th Cavalry, 21 Jan 1893; assigned to Band/25th Infantry, 8 Mar 1895. SOURCE: Descriptive & Assignment Cards, 25 Inf.

Sergeant, Band/25th Infantry, at San Marcelino, Philippines, 1901. *See* **FULBRIGHT**, William R., Private, H/25th Infantry

Promoted from private to corporal. SOURCE: *ANR* 38 (5 Aug 1905): 21.

JACKSON, John H.; Private; Band/10th Cav. Recruit, arrived at Ft Robinson, NE, 7 May 1902.

JACKSON, John I.; Saddler; K/9th Cav. At Ft D. A. Russell, WY, in 1910; resident of St. Clairsville, OH. SOURCE: *Illustrated Review: Ninth Cavalry.*

JACKSON, John J.; 1st Sgt; C/9th Cav. Captain of Ft Robinson, NE, baseball team. SOURCE: Cleveland *Gazette*, 24 Jul 1886.

Sergeant, to open dancing school for enlisted men, Ft Robinson, 1 Dec 1886. SOURCE: Cleveland *Gazette*, 27 Nov 1886.

Appointed sergeant, 6 Sep 1892. SOURCE: Roster, 9 Cav.

Promoted to first sergeant, Ft Robinson, vice Mason, retired. SOURCE: *ANJ* 32 (11 May 1895): 608.

Awarded certificate of merit for gallantry, Cuba, 1 Jul 1898. SOURCE: GO 15, AGO, 13 Feb 1900; Steward, *The Colored Regulars*, 245; *ANJ* 37 (24 Feb 1900): 611.

Shot and killed, Ft Douglas, UT, 8 Aug 1899, by Pvt. W. H. Carter, C/9th Cavalry, who was then chased into Salt Lake City and shot fatally by pursuers. SOURCE: *ANJ* 36 (19 Aug 1899): 1214.

Buried at Ft Douglas. SOURCE: Clark, "A History of the Twenty-fourth," appendix A.

JACKSON, Joseph; Private; L/25th Inf. Fined $8 by summary court, San Isidro, Philippines, for failure to obey promptly sergeant of guard, 18 Jun 1902, first conviction; fined $2 for absence from 11 P.M. roll call, 29 Jun 1902. SOURCE: Register of Summary Court, San Isidro.

JACKSON, Julius; Private; E/25th Inf. Awarded certificate of merit, 12 Sep 1908, for saving comrade from drowning at risk of own life, Malabang, Mindanao, Philippines, 16 Dec 1907. SOURCE: GO 134, AGO, 1 Jul 1909.

JACKSON, Levorsiear; Private; H/24th Inf. Enlisted Tampa, FL, 1 Jun 1898. SOURCE: Muster Roll, H/24 Inf, May–Jun 1898.

Sick in hospital, Siboney, Cuba, until 25 Aug 1898, and en route to U.S., 25–31 Aug 1898. SOURCE: Muster Roll, H/24 Inf, Jul–Aug 1898.

Sick in quarters since 29 Oct 1898, disease contracted in line of duty; furlough on surgeon's certificate, 6 Sep–5 Oct 1898. SOURCE: Muster Roll, H/24 Inf, Sep–Oct 1898.

Sick in quarters until 28 Nov 1898. SOURCE: Muster Roll, H/24 Inf, Nov–Dec 1898.

Discharged, character good, single, Ft Douglas, UT, 28 Jan 1899; due U.S. for clothing $21.58. SOURCE: Muster Roll, H/24 Inf, Jan–Feb 1899.

JACKSON, London; Private; K/25th Inf. At Ft Niobrara, NE, 1904. SOURCE: Wilson, "History of Fort Niobrara."

Commissioned first lieutenant, Camp Des Moines, IA, Oct 1917. SOURCE: Sweeney, *History of the American Negro*, 124 [first name given as "Landen"]

JACKSON, Mack; Private; Band/10th Cav. Deposited $20 with paymaster, Dec 1876. SOURCE: LS, 10 Cav, 1873–83.

JACKSON, Mark; Private; L/10th Cav. Served in 10th Cavalry, 1898; remained in U.S. during war with Spain. SOURCE: Cashin, *Under Fire with the Tenth Cavalry*, 351.

JACKSON, Matthew; Corporal; I/24th Inf. Enlisted Montgomery, AL, 7 Jul 1899. SOURCE: Muster Roll, I/24 Inf, Nov–Dec 1899.

Private, joined company 29 Sep 1899. SOURCE: Muster Roll, I/24 Inf, May–Jun 1899.

Corporal, requests transfer to 25th Infantry, 19 Jun 1902, with view toward discharge in Philippines at end of term of enlistment. SOURCE: Press Copies of Letters Sent, 24 Inf.

JACKSON, Orange; 10th Cav. Original member of 10th Cavalry; in troop when organized, Ft Riley, KS, 15 Aug 1867. SOURCE: McMiller, "Buffalo Soldiers," 76.

Adjutant, 10th Cavalry, complains to Capt. Henry Davis, Recruiting Officer, 10th Cavalry, Memphis, TN, 16 Jul 1867, that on reexamination of last detachment of recruits from Davis, Orange Jackson was found to have bad chronic ulcers of his legs, which totally unfit him for duty; Jackson in hospital and "will probably never come out except to be discharged"; ulcers must have been apparent at time of enlistment; Recruit Perry Curry "almost as bad," and only duty he can perform is cooking; "both are very ignorant specimens of humanity." SOURCE: LS, 10 Cav, 1866–67.

JACKSON, Perry; Private; E/10th Cav. Recruit Henry Long with detachment sent by you recognized here as Perry Jackson, recently discharged dishonorably from your company and escaped confinement; is being sent so you can take proper action. SOURCE: Adj, 10 Cav, to CO, E/10, 13 Apr 1876, LS, 10 Cav, 1873–83.

JACKSON, Peter; Sergeant; G/24th Inf. Awarded certificate of merit for service in Cuban campaign, 1898. SOURCE: Scipio, *Last of the Black Regulars*, 130.

Commended for distinguished service, battle of Santiago, Cuba, 1 Jul 1898, as corporal; now sergeant; awarded certificate of merit. SOURCE: GO 15, AGO, 13 Feb 1900; Steward, *The Colored Regulars*, 280; *ANJ* 37 (24 Feb 1900): 611.

Ranked number 67 among expert riflemen with 73 percent, 1904. SOURCE: GO 79, AGO, 1 Jun 1905.

JACKSON, Preston; I/10th Cav. Original member of 10th Cavalry; in troop when organized, Ft Riley, KS, 15 Aug 1867. SOURCE: McMiller, "Buffalo Soldiers," 76.

JACKSON, R.; Corporal; K/10th Cav. Ranked sixth best marksman in Army with carbine, 1894. SOURCE: *ANJ* 32 (20 Oct 1894): 119.

JACKSON, Robert; Private; 10th Cav. Mentioned Mar 1874. SOURCE: ES, 10 Cav, 1872–81.

JACKSON, Robert; Private; C/9th Cav. On extra duty as teamster, Ft Robinson, NE, 1886.

JACKSON, Robert; B/9th Cav. Age 62; gets $6 per month disability pension and has filed for increase based on information in this paper; encloses subscription. SOURCE: *Winners of the West* 6 (Jan 1929): 5.

Enjoys paper very much; pension up to $10 per month. SOURCE: *Winners of the West* 6 (Jul 1929): 5.

Died in Baltimore, MD. SOURCE: *Winners of the West* 7 (Feb 1930): 3.

JACKSON, Robert R.; Major; 8th Ill Inf. Born Malta, IL, 1 Sep 1870; educated through high school in Chicago public schools and worked as newsboy; clerk, Chicago post office, 21 years; assistant superintendent, Armour Street post office, 12 years; veteran of 25 years' service, including Spanish-American War and on Mexican border; honorable discharge, 1917; charter member of 8th Illinois Infantry; member 48th through 50th general assemblies; alderman, second ward; author of "the famous Jackson law," which put *Birth of a Nation* out of business; owns Fraternal Printing & Publishing Company, worth $55,000; married Miss Annie Green of Chicago, May 1888; son George is clerk, City of Chicago; daughter Naomi married. SOURCE: Richardson, *National Cyclopedia*, 426.

JACKSON, Romeo; Private; K/24th Inf. Died of variola in the Philippines. SOURCE: *ANJ* 37 (24 Mar 1900): 707.

JACKSON, S.; B/9th Cav. Telegraph operator. SOURCE: Cleveland *Gazette*, 28 Oct 1899.

JACKSON, Samuel; B/10th Cav. Original member of 10th Cavalry; in troop when organized, Ft Leavenworth, KS, 1 Apr 1867. SOURCE: McMiller, "Buffalo Soldiers," 69.

JACKSON, Samuel; H/10th Cav. Original member of 10th Cavalry; in troop when organized, Ft Leavenworth, KS, 21 Jul 1867. SOURCE: McMiller, "Buffalo Soldiers," 75.

Enlisted Memphis, TN. SOURCE: LS, 10 Cav, 1866–67.

JACKSON, Samuel; Private; G/24th Inf. Born Hookstown, PA; enlisted, age 22, occupation laborer, Ht 5'8", yellow complexion, brown eyes, black hair, Youngstown, OH, 5 Mar 1891; joined Band/24th Infantry, Ft Bayard, NM, 26 Aug 1891; transferred to G/24th Infantry, 11 Mar 1892; $4 per month retained since enlistment under act of 16 Jun 1890. SOURCE: Descriptive Book, 24 Inf NCS & Band.

JACKSON, Samuel; Private; C/9th Cav. Veteran of Philippine Insurrection; at Ft D. A. Russell, WY, in 1910; sharpshooter; resident of Paris, KY. SOURCE: *Illustrated Review: Ninth Cavalry*, with picture.

JACKSON, Stephen. Quartermaster, Camp 30, National Indian War Veterans, San Antonio, TX. SOURCE: *Winners of the West* 6 (Oct 1929): 7.

JACKSON, Thomas; Private; A/10th Cav. Convicted by general court martial of desertion; deserted 14 Feb 1889; apprehended same day; and loss of government clothing worth $13.41, Jefferson Barracks, MO, 14 Feb 1889; sentenced to dishonorable discharge and five years. SOURCE: GCMO 17, AGO, 6 Apr 1889

JACKSON, Thomas; Private; K/49th Inf. In the Philippines, 1900. *See* **BLUNT**, Hamilton H., Captain, K/49th Infantry

JACKSON, Thomas; Sergeant; F/10th Cav. Promoted from corporal, Ft Washakie, WY. SOURCE: Fremont *Clipper*, 14 Dec 1906.

JACKSON, Thornton; Corporal; C/24th Inf. At Ft Huachuca, AZ, 1893. *See* **BROWN**, Benjamin, Drum Major, 24th Infantry

Served with Sgt. Alfred Rucker at Ft Huachuca; arrived at Salt Lake City, UT, together; also served with Buford Parker, and settled in Salt Lake City; daughter Viola Dorsey born at Ft Douglas, UT, 24 Jan 1897. SOURCE: Clark, "A History of the Twenty-fourth," 77–78.

JACKSON, Turner; Corporal; A/10th Cav. Served in 10th Cavalry in Cuba, 1898. SOURCE: Cashin, *Under Fire with the Tenth Cavalry*, 336.

Participated in Houston riot, 1917; slightly wounded. SOURCE: Haynes, *A Night of Violence*, 163.

JACKSON, W. A.; Trumpeter; G/9th Cav. On detached service at Ft Stanton, NM, 29 Jan–5 Feb 1881. SOURCE: Regt Returns, 9 Cav, Feb 1881.

JACKSON, Walter B.; Corporal; D/24th Inf. At Cabanatuan, Philippines, 1901. *See* **PRIDE**, Wheeler, Private, D/24th Infantry; **STONE**, John H., Private, D/24th Infantry

JACKSON, William; E/10th Cav. Original member of 10th Cavalry; in troop when organized, Ft Leavenworth, KS, 15 Jun 1867. SOURCE: McMiller, "Buffalo Soldiers," 72.

JACKSON, William; Private; Band/10th Cav. Commander, 10th Cavalry, forwards effects of late Private Jackson to Adjutant General, 30 Jan 1877. SOURCE: ES, 10 Cav, 1872–81.

JACKSON, William; Private; G/9th Cav. In Army four months; can read but "not very well"; witness for defense, Barney McKay court martial, Ft Robinson, NE, 1893.

JACKSON, William; Private; H/9th Cav. Commander requests his discharge with gonorrhea; has been in hospital at Ft Robinson, NE, two weeks and will remain at least six more; "too dull and stupid to learn the duties of a cavalry soldier." SOURCE: CO, H/9 Cav, to AG, USA, 25 Nov 1897.

Discharged by letter, Adjutant General's Office, 10 Dec 1897.

JACKSON, William; Private; B/10th Cav. Served in 10th Cavalry in Cuba, 1898; wounded in action. SOURCE: Cashin, *Under Fire with the Tenth Cavalry*, 338–39.

JACKSON, William; Private; H/10th Cav. Served in 10th Cavalry, 1898; remained in U.S. during war with Spain. SOURCE: Cashin, *Under Fire with the Tenth Cavalry*, 347.

JACKSON, William; Private; A/9th Cav. At Ft D. A. Russell, WY, in 1910; sharpshooter. SOURCE: *Illustrated Review: Ninth Cavalry*, with picture.

JACKSON, William H.; Private; G/10th Cav. Served in 10th Cavalry in Cuba, 1898. SOURCE: Cashin, *Under Fire with the Tenth Cavalry*, 345.

JACKSON, William H.; Private; I/10th Cav. Served in 10th Cavalry, 1898; remained in U.S. during war with Spain. SOURCE: Cashin, *Under Fire with the Tenth Cavalry*, 348.

JACKSON, William H.; Private; I/25th Inf. Fined $5 by summary court, San Isidro, Philippines, for lying out of quarters, 24 Mar 1902, fourth conviction; fined one month's pay for disobeying orders of sergeant of guard while on guard, 20 Apr 1902. SOURCE: Register of Summary Court, San Isidro.

JACKSON, William H.; Private; D/9th Cav. At Ft D. A. Russell, WY, in 1910; resident of Culloden, GA. SOURCE: *Illustrated Review: Ninth Cavalry*, with picture.

JACKSON, William Hubert; Captain; H/48th Inf. Graduate of Boston University; served with 6th Massachusetts Infantry, as captain, 48th Infantry, as major, 15th New York Infantry (National Guard); still in 15th New York Infantry in 1922; died 1930, resident of New York City, former appointments clerk to president, Borough of

Manhattan, age 56. SOURCE: *Crisis* 23 (Feb 1922): 173; *Crisis* 40 (Aug 1930): 276.

Mentioned as captain, H/48th Infantry. SOURCE: Beasley, *Negro Trailblazers*, 284.

One of nineteen officers of 48th Infantry recommended as regular Army second lieutenants. SOURCE: CG, DivPI, Manila, 8 Feb 1901, to AGO, AGO File 355163.

Former correspondent, *Afro-American Press*, Worcester, MA. SOURCE: Richmond *Planet*, 3 Feb 1901.

JACKSON, William M.; Sergeant; G/9th Cav. In F/9th Cavalry; enlisted as laborer; request for relief from extra duty as schoolteacher and return to duty with troop approved. SOURCE: CO, F/9 Cav, to CO, Ft Robinson, 13 Mar 1887, LS, Ft Robinson.

Promoted from lance corporal, G/9th Cavalry, to corporal, Ft Robinson, Oct 1895.

Sergeant, reenlistment, married, authorized by letter, Department of the Platte, 24 Oct 1895.

JACKSON, William M.; Sergeant; A/10th Cav. Served in 10th Cavalry in Cuba, 1898. SOURCE: Cashin, *Under Fire with the Tenth Cavalry*, 336.

JACKSON, Willie H.; L/10th Cav. Original member of 10th Cavalry; in troop when organized, Ft Riley, KS, 21 Sep 1867. SOURCE: McMiller, "Buffalo Soldiers," 78.

JACOBS, Camp; Corporal; H/9th Cav. Born Chattanooga, TN; enlisted with three years' prior service in H/9th Cavalry, age 24, occupation laborer, Ht 5'5", Cincinnati, OH, 4 Nov 1895; fined $3 by summary court, Ft Robinson, NE, 8 Jul 1896; fined $7 and confined for twenty days by summary court, Ft Robinson, 12 Jul 1896; promoted to corporal, 13 Sep 1898; discharged, end of term, Ft Sill, Indian Territory, 3 Nov 1898. SOURCE: Descriptive Book, H/9 Cav.

Guard, Crispus Attucks Lodge No. 3, Knights of Pythias, State of Nebraska, Ft Robinson. SOURCE: Richmond *Planet*, 18 Dec 1897.

Deposited $14 with paymaster, Ft Robinson, 1898.

JACOBS, Henry; A/10th Cav. Original member of 10th Cavalry; in troop when organized, Ft Leavenworth, KS, 18 Feb 1867. SOURCE: McMiller, "Buffalo Soldiers," 68.

JAM, James; 24th Inf. Died 21 Jun 1897; buried at Ft Douglas, UT. SOURCE: Clark, "A History of the Twenty-fourth," appendix A.

JAMAR, Hessiekiah; Private; K/9th Cav. Veteran of Philippine Insurrection; at Ft D. A. Russell, WY, in 1910; sharpshooter; resident of Madison Co., AL. SOURCE: *Illustrated Review: Ninth Cavalry*, with picture.

JAMES; Private; D/9th Cav. Resides with wife at Ft Robinson, NE, 1891, in improvised dwelling across Soldiers Creek, which he shares with Private Walker, Walker's wife, sister-in-law, and five children. SOURCE: Medical History, Ft Robinson.

JAMES; Private; E/10th Cav. At Ft Apache, AZ, 1890, subscribed $.50 to testimonial to General Grierson. SOURCE: List of subscriptions, 23 Apr 1890, 10th Cavalry papers, MHI.

JAMES, Augustus; I/10th Cav. Original member of 10th Cavalry; in troop when organized, Ft Riley, KS, 15 Aug 1867. SOURCE: McMiller, "Buffalo Soldiers," 76.

Deceased; commander, I/10th Cavalry, forwards copies of final statement and inventory of his personal effects, Mar 1870. SOURCE: ES, 10 Cav, 1866–71.

JAMES, Edward; Private; H/9th Cav. At Ft D. A. Russell, WY, in 1910; resident of Davidson Co., KY. SOURCE: *Illustrated Review: Ninth Cavalry*, with picture.

JAMES, Frank; Private; K/24th Inf. Sentenced to thirty days, ten on bread and water, and fined one month's pay for enticing thirteen-year-old girl to live with him for immoral purposes, Cabanatuan, Philippines, Apr or May 1901. SOURCE: Name File, 24 Inf.

JAMES, Frank; Private; B/10th Cav. Sentenced to dishonorable discharge and confinement, Ft Robinson, NE, Feb 1903, in accordance with Special Order 26, Department of the Missouri, 1903; escaped 26 Mar 1903.

JAMES, Henry; Recruit; 10th Cav. Arrived at Ft Leavenworth, KS, from Jefferson Barracks, MO, Oct 1866. SOURCE: LS, 10 Cav, 1866–67.

JAMES, Henry; Corporal; D/24th Inf. Entered backyard of officer's quarters, later found drunk in room of woman servant, Ft Bayard, NM, Jan 1889. SOURCE: Billington, *New Mexico's Buffalo Soldiers*, 165.

JAMES, I. H.; Private; F/9th Cav. Killed in action, 12 Jan 1880, on headwaters of Rio Perches. SOURCE: Hamilton, "History of the Ninth Cavalry," 52.

JAMES, Isaac; Private; D/10th Cav. Served in 10th Cavalry in Cuba, 1898. SOURCE: Cashin, *Under Fire with the Tenth Cavalry*, 341.

JAMES, Jesse; Private; F/10th Cav. Served in 10th Cavalry in Cuba, 1898. SOURCE: Cashin, *Under Fire with the Tenth Cavalry*, 344.

JAMES, John; Private; I/9th Cav. At Ft Robinson, NE, 1891. *See* **JEMSON**, Joe, Private, I/9th Cavalry

JAMES, John; Sergeant; G/25th Inf. Commended by forest ranger for leading special railroad train with women and children away from forest fire, Avery, ID, Aug 1910; assisted by Pvts. Chester Garrard, Roy Green, William

Hogue, and Grandvill W. Bright, all from Ft George Wright, WA; all maintained order and protected passengers. SOURCE: Nankivell, *History of the Twenty-fifth Infantry*, 134.

JAMES, Louis M.; D/23rd Kans Inf. Died in Minnesota. SOURCE: Taylor, "Minnesota Black Spanish-American War Veterans."

JAMES, Morris; Sergeant; D/3rd Ala Inf. Born in Alabama; died in Minnesota, 26 Jun 1936. SOURCE: Taylor, "Minnesota Black Spanish-American War Veterans."

JAMES, Oscar; A/24th Inf. Admitted to Soldiers Home with disability at age 37 with eleven years and six months' service, 15 Aug 1891. SOURCE: SecWar, *AR 1891*, 754.

JAMES, Richard; Private; A/10th Cav. Served in 10th Cavalry in Cuba, 1898; wounded in action. SOURCE: Cashin, *Under Fire with the Tenth Cavalry*, 336–37; SecWar, *AR 1898*, 324.

JAMES, Robert; Private; C/49th Inf. Died of dysentery in the Philippines, 3 Jan 1901. SOURCE: *ANJ* 38 (19 Jan 1901): 503.

JAMES, Robert; Private; 9th Cav. Stationed at Ft Riley, KS; with 25th Infantry at Ft Brown, TX, during raid; received dishonorable discharge. SOURCE: Cleveland *Gazette*, 1 Dec 1906.

JAMES, William; F/10th Cav. Original member of 10th Cavalry; in troop when organized, Ft Leavenworth, KS, 21 Jun 1867. SOURCE: McMiller, "Buffalo Soldiers," 73.

JAMES, William F.; Private; G/10th Cav. Served in 10th Cavalry, 1898; remained in U.S. during war with Spain. SOURCE: Cashin, *Under Fire with the Tenth Cavalry*, 346.

JAMES, William H.; Private; I/24th Inf. Enlisted Ft D. A. Russell, WY, 13 Feb 1899. SOURCE: Muster Roll, I/24 Inf, Jan–Feb 1899.

Fined $.50 by summary court, San Francisco, CA, 22 Apr 1899. SOURCE: Muster Roll, I/24 Inf, Mar–Apr 1899.

Fined $2 by summary court, 10 May 1899; fined $3 by summary court, 23 May 1899. SOURCE: Muster Roll, I/24 Inf, May–Jun 1899.

Fined one month's pay by summary court, 8 Aug 1899. SOURCE: Muster Roll, I/24 Inf, Jul–Aug 1899.

Absent sick in Manila, Philippines, since 11 Oct 1899. SOURCE: Muster Roll, I/24 Inf, Sep–Oct 1899.

Captured by insurgents, 10 Oct 1900; killed same day while attempting to escape. *See* **BURNS**, William J., Corporal, I/24th Infantry

JAMESON, Henry W.; 1st Lt; 8th Ill Inf. Born Mexico, MO, 15 Jun 1865, to William and Elizabeth (Miller) Jameson; educated in public schools, Macon, MO, 1871–78,

and Galesburg, IL, 1878–80; graduate of Knox College, Galesburg, 1888, Wesleyan Law School, Bloomington, IL, 1897; doctorate, Central Law School, Louisville, KY, 1906; doctor of divinity, Morris Brown College, 1907; married Nannie L. Crabb of Galena, IL, 18 Jun 1887, and Lilliam E. Jenkins, Evansville, IN, 19 Nov 1903; one son, Henry W., Jr.; admitted to Illinois bar, 1896; editor and publisher, Bloomington *American Pilot*; licensed to preach, 1896; now pastor, Bethel Church, Champaign, IL; trustee, Wilberforce University; served as judge advocate and court martial, Military District of Mayari, Province of Santiago, Cuba; first colored chaplain of Wisconsin legislature; now chaplain, Spanish-American War Veterans, Department of Illinois; major, U.S. Boy Scouts; Republican. SOURCE: Wright, *Centennial Encyclopedia of the AME Church*, 276–77, with picture.

JANES, Edward; Private; A/10th Cav. Served in 10th Cavalry in Cuba, 1898. SOURCE: Cashin, *Under Fire with the Tenth Cavalry*, 336.

JANEY, George A.; Drum Major; Band/24th Inf. Enlisted Ft Douglas, UT, 14 Jan 1897; promoted to quartermaster sergeant, H/24th Infantry, from sergeant, 10 May 1898; seventeen years' continuous service. SOURCE: Muster Roll, H/24 Inf, May–Jun 1898.

Acting first sergeant, 1 Jul–4 Nov 1898. SOURCE: Muster Roll, H/24 Inf, Jul–Aug through Nov–Dec 1898.

Transferred to Band as drum major, 13 Jan 1899; due soldier $35.56 for clothing. SOURCE: Muster Roll, H/24 Inf, Jan–Feb 1899.

JARRELL, Thomas W.; Corporal; A/25th Inf. Ranked number 49 among expert riflemen with 69.0 percent, 1903. SOURCE: GO 52, AGO, 19 Mar 1904.

Ranked number 549 among expert riflemen with 68.0 percent, 1905. SOURCE: GO 101, AGO, 31 May 1906.

JARRETT, William; Private; A/10th Cav. Served in 10th Cavalry, 1898; remained in U.S. during war with Spain. SOURCE: Cashin, *Under Fire with the Tenth Cavalry*, 337.

JASPER, Cornelius; Private; A/10th Cav. Served in 10th Cavalry, 1898; remained in U.S. during war with Spain. SOURCE: Cashin, *Under Fire with the Tenth Cavalry*, 337.

JASPER, James; E/24th Inf. At Ft Bayard, NM, 1891. SOURCE: *ANJ* 31 (17 Oct 1891): 133.

JEFFERDS, Wesley; Sergeant; A/9th Cav. In L/9th Cavalry, on detached service in field, New Mexico, 21 Jan–24 Feb 1881. SOURCE: Regt Returns, 9 Cav, Feb 1881.

In A/9th Cavalry, at Ft Niobrara, NE; to be examined for appointment as ordnance sergeant. SOURCE: *ANJ* 26 (3 Aug 1889): 1002.

At Ft Niobrara; to be examined for appointment as ordnance sergeant. SOURCE: *ANJ* 27 (23 Aug 1890): 902.

Retires from Ft Robinson, NE, Apr 1892. SOURCE: *ANJ* 29 (30 Apr 1892): 625.

Retired as sergeant, A/9th Cavalry, 29 Apr 1892. SOURCE: Roster, 9 Cav.

Resided at 306 Third Street, SE, Washington, DC, in 1906; served over ten years with Sgt. Maj. Jeremiah Jones, 9th Cavalry. SOURCE: Affidavit, Jefferds, 19 May 1906, VA File WC 611769, Jeremiah Jones.

Age 69; resided at 306 Third Street, SE, Washington, DC, in 1918; knew Sgt. Robert Benjamin personally from 1872 until Benjamin's death. SOURCE: Affidavit, Jefferds, 2 Dec 1918, VA File WC 927337, Robert A. Benjamin.

JEFFERS, David B.; 1st Lt; E/48th Inf. Appointed commissary sergeant, U.S. Army, 5 Jun 1879. SOURCE: Roster, 9 Cav.

One of only two blacks in noncommissioned general staff positions, along with Commissary Sergeant Sullivant, 1879.

At Ft McKinney, WY, friend to Chaplain Plummer and Sergeant Benjamin, as quartermaster sergeant, 9th Cavalry; from Angel Island, CA, 1894, wrote threatening letter to Mrs. Robert Benjamin, warning against testimony about Plummer; former quartermaster sergeant, 9th Cavalry, Ft McKinney. SOURCE: Court Martial Records, Plummer.

Retires from Ft Custer, MT. SOURCE: *ANJ* 34 (22 May 1897): 705.

To report as second lieutenant, 48th Infantry, to Ft Thomas, KY. SOURCE: *ANJ* 37 (30 Sep 1899): 101.

First lieutenant, E/48th Infantry, and veteran of thirty years. SOURCE: San Francisco *Chronicle*, 15 Nov 1899.

JEFFERSON, Charles W.; Sergeant; B/9th Cav. Enlisted in 9th Cavalry, 23 May 1890; corporal, G/9th Cavalry, 1 Jan 1895; discharged 23 May 1895; reenlisted in B/9th Cavalry, 28 May 1895, promoted to corporal, sergeant, first sergeant; discharged 27 May 1898; reenlisted 28 May 1898; discharged 3 Feb 1899; reenlisted 4 Feb 1899; appointed captain, 49th Infantry, 9 Sep 1899; resigned in accordance with Special Order 226, Adjutant General's Office, Oct 1900. SOURCE: Descriptive Book, A/49 Inf.

At Ft Robinson, NE, 1893, refused to serve meal to prisoner Diggs in guardhouse; told by First Sergeant Goodloe, "Any of you men that don't want to carry this man's meals don't have to, but hereafter you had better walk the chalk." Testimony of Sgt. Arthur E. Ransom. SOURCE: Court Martial Records, McKay.

Lance corporal, B/9th Cavalry, conducted deserter Hiram Tolmatier, H/8th Infantry, from Ft Robinson to Ft D. A. Russell, WY. SOURCE: Order 9, 10 Feb 1895, Post Orders, Ft Robinson.

Lance corporal, promoted to corporal, Ft Robinson, 11 Feb 1895. SOURCE: *ANJ* 32 (9 Mar 1895): 434.

Corporal, G/9th Cavalry, discharged May 1895. SOURCE: *ANJ* 32 (8 Jun 1895): 674.

Promoted from private to corporal, B/9th Cavalry, Ft Duchesne, UT, Nov 1895. SOURCE: *ANJ* 33 (7 Dec 1895): 236.

Wounded in action, El Caney, Cuba, 1898; recommended for certificate of merit by troop and squadron commanders. SOURCE: Cashin, *Under Fire with the Tenth Cavalry*, 116–17; *Illustrated Review: Ninth Cavalry*.

Commended and awarded certificate of merit for distinguished service, battle of Santiago, Cuba, as first sergeant, B/9th Cavalry. SOURCE: GO 15, AGO, 13 Feb 1900; Steward, *The Colored Regulars*, 280; *ANJ* 37 (9 Dec 1899): 345.

Promoted to captain, 49th Infantry. SOURCE: *ANJ* 37 (9 Dec 1899): 345.

Mentioned as captain, A/49th Infantry. SOURCE: Beasley, *Negro Trailblazers*, 284.

Veteran of Indian wars, Spanish-American War, and Philippine Insurrection; expert rifleman; sergeant, B/9th Cavalry, at Ft D. A. Russell, WY, in 1910. *Illustrated Review: Ninth Cavalry*, with picture.

JEFFERSON, George B.; Private; G/9th Cav. To be tried by general court martial. SOURCE: *ANJ* 34 (3 Apr 1897): 564.

JEFFERSON, Horace; Private; B/9th Cav. Corporal, ranked number two, Army pistol competition, Ft Sheridan, IL, 1906; ranked number seven, Northern Division pistol competition, Ft Sheridan, 1906. SOURCE: GO 198, AGO, 6 Dec 1906.

Distinguished marksman, 1906; distinguished marksman, ranked number three, Division of the Philippines, 1907. SOURCE: GO 207, AGO, 19 Dec 1908.

Second best pistol shot among Army privates, B/9th Cavalry. SOURCE: Indianapolis *Freeman*, 26 Jan 1907.

Veteran of Philippine Insurrection; private, B/9th Cavalry, at Ft D. A. Russell, WY, in 1910; sharpshooter. SOURCE: *Illustrated Review: Ninth Cavalry*, with picture.

JEFFERSON, John; Private; K/25th Inf. Deserted, San Francisco, CA, 1 Aug 1902. SOURCE: Regt Returns, 25 Inf, Aug 1902.

JEFFERSON, John; Trumpeter; D/10th Cav. Released to duty from treatment for gonorrhea, Ft Robinson, NE, 21 Aug 1903. SOURCE: Post Surgeon to CO, D/10 Cav, 21 Aug 1903, LS, Post Surgeon, Ft Robinson.

JEFFERSON, Mathes; Private; G/9th Cav. At Ft D. A. Russell, WY, in 1910; resident of Guthrie, OK. SOURCE: *Illustrated Review: Ninth Cavalry*.

JEFFERSON, Thomas; Private; C/25th Inf. Dishonorable discharge, Brownsville. SOURCE: SO 266, AGO, 9 Nov 1906.

JEFFERSON, Thomas E.; QM Sgt; I/49th Inf. Letter to editor from Camp Pierson, Philippines, 12 Feb 1900. SOURCE: Indianapolis *Freeman*, 21 Apr 1900.

JEFFERSON, William; Sergeant; M/10th Cav. Original member of 10th Cavalry; in troop when organized,

Ft Riley, KS, 15 Oct 1867. SOURCE: McMiller, "Buffalo Soldiers," 79.

Commander of M/10th Cavalry reports incomplete company records so cannot furnish final statement regarding Jefferson, casualty. SOURCE: ES, 10 Cav, 1866–71.

JELKES, James B.; QM Sergeant; M/10th Cav. Served as sergeant, M/10th Cavalry, Cuba, 1898; relates experience. SOURCE: Cashin, *Under Fire with the Tenth Cavalry*, 175–76, 352.

Veteran of Spanish-American War and Philippine Insurrection; quartermaster sergeant, D/9th Cavalry, at Ft D. A. Russell, WY, in 1910; resident of Jacksonville, FL. SOURCE: *Illustrated Review: Ninth Cavalry*, with picture.

JEMSON, Joe; Private; I/9th Cav. Fined $2 by summary court, Ft Robinson, NE, 6 May 1891, for conduct prejudicial to good order and discipline; complained, "Sergeant, by God, I don't know how it is, I was on fatigue every day last week, and here it is, the same this week," 5 May 1891; complained to 1st Sgt. George Tracy, on order to fall out for water call, "I can't see how it is that every time I am detached for Guard, I have something to do," 30 Apr 1891; witnesses: 1st Sgt. George Tracy, Sgt. Houston Lust, Pvt. John James. SOURCE: Summary Court Record, Ft Robinson, I.

JENIFER, Theopolous E.; Sergeant; Band/10th Cav. Private, at Ft Apache, AZ, 1890, subscribed $.50 to testimonial to General Grierson. SOURCE: List of subscriptions, 23 Apr 1890, 10th Cavalry papers, MHI.

Promoted from private to sergeant, 17 Nov 1897. SOURCE: *ANJ* 35 (4 Dec 1897): 252.

Served in 10th Cavalry in Cuba, 1898; performed heroically caring for wounded at San Juan. SOURCE: Cashin, *Under Fire with the Tenth Cavalry*, 271, 352.

JENIFER, William; A/9th Cav. Admitted to Soldiers Home with disability at age 39 with sixteen years and five months' service, 16 Jun 1886. SOURCE: SecWar, *AR 1886*, 738.

JENKINS; Private; A/10th Cav. At Ft Apache, AZ, 1890, subscribed $.50 to testimonial to General Grierson. SOURCE: List of subscriptions, 23 Apr 1890, 10th Cavalry papers, MHI.

JENKINS, Albert; M/10th Cav. Original member of 10th Cavalry; in troop when organized, Ft Riley, KS, 15 Oct 1867. SOURCE: McMiller, "Buffalo Soldiers," 79.

JENKINS, Andrew; F/10th Cav. Original member of 10th Cavalry; in troop when organized, Ft Leavenworth, KS, 21 Jun 1867. SOURCE: McMiller, "Buffalo Soldiers," 73.

JENKINS, Blunt; Corporal; G/10th Cav. At Ft Apache, AZ, 1890, subscribed $.50 to testimonial to General Grierson. SOURCE: List of subscriptions, 23 Apr 1890, 10th Cavalry papers, MHI.

JENKINS, Frank; Corporal; C/9th Cav. Promoted from lance corporal, vice Corporal Staff, deceased. SOURCE: *ANJ* 31 (18 Nov 1893): 206.

At Ft McKinney, WY, 1893; hunting in Big Horn Mountains with five privates of C/9th Cavalry, 26 Jul–4 Aug 1893; on hunting pass in Big Horns, 24 Oct–7 Nov 1893.

Resigns warrant, Ft Robinson, NE. SOURCE: *ANJ* 32 (30 Mar 1895): 506.

JENKINS, John; Private; K/9th Cav. Died at Santiago, Cuba, 3 Sep 1898. SOURCE: *ANJ* 36 (10 Sep 1898): 43; *ANJ* 36 (11 Feb 1899): 567.

JENKINS, Joseph; Sergeant; A/10th Cav. Original member of 10th Cavalry; in L Troop when organized, Ft Riley, KS, 21 Sep 1867. SOURCE: McMiller, "Buffalo Soldiers," 78.

Sergeant, A/10th Cavalry, at Ft Apache, AZ, 1890, subscribed $.50 to testimonial to General Grierson. SOURCE: List of subscriptions, 23 Apr 1890, 10th Cavalry papers, MHI.

Retires from Ft Grant, AZ, 5 Apr 1892. SOURCE: *ANJ* 29 (2 Apr 1892): 553; Baker, Roster.

JENKINS, L. H.; Private; G/9th Cav. On detached service at South Fork, NM, 17 Nov 1880–12 Jan 1881. SOURCE: Regt Returns, 9 Cav, Jan 1881.

JENKINS, Randolph; Musician; I/24th Inf. Enlisted Tampa, FL, 30 May 1898, with five years' continuous service; joined company 21 Jan 1899; sentenced to ten days and $5 fine by garrison court martial, 24 Jan 1899; appointed musician, Ft D. A. Russell, WY, 13 Feb 1899. SOURCE: Muster Roll, I/24 Inf, Jan–Feb 1899.

Fined $1.50 by garrison court martial, 25 Mar 1899. SOURCE: Muster Roll, I/24 Inf, Mar–Apr 1899.

Discharged 31 Dec 1899, with $17.18 due him for clothing, character good. SOURCE: Muster Roll, I/24 Inf, Nov–Dec 1899.

JENKINS, Thomas H.; K/24th Inf. Also served in G/10th Cavalry; resides in Washington, DC. SOURCE: *Winners of the West* 13 (Oct 1936): 3.

JENKINS, Tillmon; A/10th Cav. Recruit from Jefferson Barracks, MO, died in Ft Leavenworth, KS, hospital shortly after arrival on post, early 1867. SOURCE: McMiller, "Buffalo Soldiers," 52.

JENKINS, William; Private; H/9th Cav. On detached service at Ft Bayard, NM, 16 Jan–10 Feb 1881. SOURCE: Regt Returns, 9 Cav, Feb 1881.

JENKINS, William; Corporal; F/9th Cav. Wagoner, Ft Robinson, NE, 1891.

Served 1894. *See* **DILLON**, David R., Sergeant, Band/9th Cavalry

Promoted from lance corporal to corporal. SOURCE: *ANJ* 34 (21 Nov 1896): 196.

JENNINGS, Andrew J.; Sergeant; H/10th Cav. Corporal, served in 10th Cavalry, 1898; remained in U.S. during war with Spain. SOURCE: Cashin, *Under Fire with the Tenth Cavalry*, 346.

Promoted to sergeant vice Drane, discharged. SOURCE: SO 35, 10 Cav, Ft Sam Houston, TX, 1 Apr 1899, SO, 10 Cav.

JENNINGS, Irving; Private; D/24th Inf. Transferred from Ft Grant, AZ, to Hospital Corps at Ft Thomas, AZ. SOURCE: *ANJ* 28 (16 Mar 1889): 576.

JENNINGS, Julius; Corporal; A/24th Inf. Private, ranked number ten in rifle competition, Division of the Philippines, Ft William McKinley, Rizal, Philippines, 1907; silver medal. SOURCE: Muller, *The Twenty Fourth Infantry*, 48; GO 213, AGO, 19 Oct 1907.

Corporal, A/24th Infantry, Madison Barracks, NY, 1908. *See* **WHITE**, George W., Cook, C/24th Infantry

JENNINGS, Oliver; Private; K/10th Cav. Original member of 10th Cavalry; in troop when organized, Ft Riley, KS, 1 Sep 1867. SOURCE: McMiller, "Buffalo Soldiers," 77.

Died 24 Jan 1869 on San Francisco Creek, Indian Territory, of wounds inflicted 23 Jan 1869. SOURCE: Baker, Roster.

JENNISON, Perry; L/10th Cav. Original member of 10th Cav; in troop when organized, Ft Riley, KS, 21 Sep 1867. SOURCE: McMiller, "Buffalo Soldiers," 78.

JENSON, Joseph; Private; D/9th Cav. On special duty as attendant, post canteen, Ft Robinson, NE, 19–23 Sep 1891. SOURCE: Order 183, 19 Sep 1891, Post Orders, Ft Robinson; Order 186, 23 Sep 1891, Post Orders, Ft Robinson.

JERKINS, Moses A.; Corporal; D/9th Cav. Promoted from lance corporal, 9 May 1901. SOURCE: *ANJ* 38 (29 Jun 1901): 1065.

On special duty as assistant to ordnance officer since 6 Jul 1901, Nueva Caceres, Philippines. SOURCE: Special Duty List, D/9 Cav, 24 May 1901.

JERMINNIE, Henry; Private; L/25th Inf. Sentenced to thirty days and fined one month's pay by summary court, San Isidro, Philippines, for going off limits and resisting arrest, 10 May 1902. SOURCE: Register of Summary Court, San Isidro.

JERMON, W. S.; Private; H/25th Inf. On special duty at headquarters, Second Brigade, Camp Sanger, KY. SOURCE: SO 2, 2d Bde, 18 Oct 1903, Misc Records, 25 Inf.

JERNIGAN. Isaac; Private; H/10th Cav. Served in 10th Cavalry, 1898; remained in U.S. during war with Spain. SOURCE: Cashin, *Under Fire with the Tenth Cavalry*, 347.

JESTINGS, Archie; Corporal; M/49th Inf. Cited for heroism against insurgents, Tuao, Cagayan, Philippines, 18 Oct 1900. SOURCE: *ANJ* 38 (11 May 1901): 901.

JETER, John; Corporal; C/10th Cav. With Pershing expedition to Mexico; in Carrizal helped wounded comrade to safety; removed papers from body of Captain Boyd to avoid their capture; had three bullet holes in his clothes; later minister, Vallejo, CA. SOURCE: Clendenen, *Blood on the Border*, 228, 247, 305, 307, 309–10.

JEWELL, Bradey; Private; B/10th Cav. Served in 10th Cavalry in Cuba, 1898. SOURCE: Cashin, *Under Fire with the Tenth Cavalry*, 338.

JIMISON, Charles D.; I/10th Cav. Original member of 10th Cav; in troop when organized, Ft Riley, KS, 15 Aug 1867. SOURCE: McMiller, "Buffalo Soldiers," 76.

JINKINS, Joseph; Private; H/9th Cav. Died of cholera in the Philippines, 8 Jun 1902. SOURCE: *ANJ* 39 (9 Aug 1902): 1248.

JOHNS, Edward C.; Private; L/9th Cav. At Ft D. A. Russell, WY, in 1910; resident of Topeka, KS. SOURCE: *Illustrated Review: Ninth Cavalry*, with picture.

JOHNSON; Private; L/9th Cav. Killed in action, Mimbres Mountains, along with Private Woodward, 30 Sep 1879. SOURCE: Hamilton, "History of the Ninth Cavalry," 47; *Illustrated Review: Ninth Cavalry*.

JOHNSON; Private; M/10th Cav. At Ft Apache, AZ, 1890, subscribed $.50 to testimonial to General Grierson. SOURCE: List of subscriptions, 23 Apr 1890, 10th Cav papers, MHI.

JOHNSON; Private; A/9th Cav. Authorized to be sent to insane asylum according to telegram, Department of the Platte, 21 Jan 1897.

JOHNSON; Private; A/9th Cav. Served 1910. *See* **ELLIS**, Arthur, Private, Band/9th Cavalry

JOHNSON, A.; Private; K/9th Cav. On detached service in field, New Mexico, 21 Jan–8 Feb 1881. SOURCE: Regt Returns, 9 Cav, Feb 1881.

JOHNSON, Albert; K/10th Cav. Original member of 10th Cavalry; in troop when organized, Ft Riley, KS, 1 Sep 1867. SOURCE: McMiller, "Buffalo Soldiers," 77.

JOHNSON, Albert; Corporal; D/9th Cav. Veteran of Philippine Insurrection; at Ft D. A. Russell, WY, in 1910; sharpshooter; resident of Nashville. SOURCE: *Illustrated Review: Ninth Cavalry*, with picture.

JOHNSON, Alexander; Private; G/9th Cav. In hands of civil authorities, Omaha, NE, 14 Feb–31 May 1893. SOURCE: Regt Returns, 9 Cav.

On special duty as lamplighter, Ft Robinson, NE, vice Pvt. Joseph Price, G/9th Cavalry. SOURCE: SO 86, 8 Aug 1896, Post Orders, Ft Robinson.

Letter, Adjutant General's Office, 5 Jun 1897, concerns errors in his enlistment papers.

Returns to duty, Ft Robinson, from furlough, 6 Oct 1898.

On special duty as clerk, Adjutant's Office, Nueva Caceres, Philippines, since 17 May 1902. SOURCE: Special Duty List, A/9 Cav, 24 May 1902.

JOHNSON, Alfred; Private; G/10th Cav. Died of disease, Ft Griffin, TX, 2 Dec 1874. SOURCE: CO, 10 Cav, to AG, USA, 19 Dec 1874, LS, 10 Cav, 1873–83.

JOHNSON, Andrew; Private; K/9th Cav. Recruit from depot arrived at Ft Robinson, NE, 1 Mar 1887.

JOHNSON, B. F.; Farrier; E/10th Cav. Served in 10th Cavalry in Cuba, 1898. SOURCE: Cashin, *Under Fire with the Tenth Cavalry*, 342.

JOHNSON, B. J.; Corporal; G/9th Cav. On detached service at South Fork, NM, with three privates of G/9th Cavalry, 17 Nov 1880–12 Jan 1881. SOURCE: Regt Returns, 9 Cav, Jan 1881.

JOHNSON, Benjamin; Private; C/9th Cav. Enlisted Louisville, KY; discharged, Ft Robinson, NE, end of term, 2 Nov 1886; unable to write. SOURCE: CO, C/9, to Chief Paymaster, DP, 5 Oct 1886, LS, C/9 Cav.

No Veterans Administration pension file.

JOHNSON, Benjamin; Private; H/24th Inf. Fined $2 by summary court, San Isidro, Philippines, for being on street with his blouse unbuttoned. SOURCE: Register of Summary Court, San Isidro.

JOHNSON, Benjamin F.; Private; D/25th Inf. Dishonorable discharge, Brownsville. SOURCE: SO 266, AGO, 9 Nov 1906.

JOHNSON, Bush; Sergeant; G/9th Cav. Left in charge of unit garden and property by Lt. Patrick Cusack when unit departed for field duty, Sep 1881. SOURCE: Billington, *New Mexico's Buffalo Soldiers*, 114–15.

Killed by horse thief, Aug 1882. *See* **GRUNKE**, Washington, Private, 9th Cavalry

JOHNSON, C. J.; Private; L/10th Cav. Transferred from 25th Infantry to 10th Cavalry; at Ft Robinson, NE, 1903. SOURCE: SO 104, AGO, 4 May 1903.

JOHNSON, C. W.; 25th Inf. Pallbearer at Col. A. W. Burt's funeral. SOURCE: Curtis, *The Black Soldier*, 49.

JOHNSON, Charles; Private; C/9th Cav. Buried at Ft Robinson, NE, 13 Apr 1886. SOURCE: List of Interments, Ft Robinson.

JOHNSON, Charles; Trumpeter; G/9th Cav. One of six enlisted men of G/9th Cavalry to testify against Lt. John Conline at his 1877 court martial for misconduct, including drunkenness, sexual misconduct, and misappropriation of funds belonging to men of his troop, Ft Garland, CO. SOURCE: Billington, *New Mexico's Buffalo Soldiers*, 121–23.

JOHNSON, Charles; Private; B/24th Inf. Relieved from extra duty as plasterer, Quartermaster Department, and will report to company for duty. SOURCE: Order 16, Ft Huachuca, AZ, 1 Feb 1893; Name File, 24 Inf.

Relieved of extra duty as laborer, Quartermaster Department. SOURCE: Order 96, Ft Huachuca, 30 Jun 1893.

On extra duty as carpenter, Quartermaster Department. SOURCE: Order 116, Ft Huachuca, 7 Aug 1893.

Relieved of extra duty as carpenter, Quartermaster Department, and detailed extra duty, plasterer, Quartermaster Department. SOURCE: Order 139, Ft Huachuca, 20 Sep 1893.

To lead detachment of six privates, 24th Infantry, with rations to 31 Dec 1893, to Tanner's Canyon, to burn lime. SOURCE: Order 185, Ft Huachuca, 18 Dec 1893.

JOHNSON, Charles; Private; C/10th Cav. Served in 10th Cavalry, 1898; remained in U.S. during war with Spain. SOURCE: Cashin, *Under Fire with the Tenth Cavalry*, 333.

JOHNSON, Charles; Private; D/9th Cav. At Ft D. A. Russell, WY, in 1910; resident of Indianapolis. SOURCE: *Illustrated Review: Ninth Cavalry*, with picture.

JOHNSON, Charles; Private; H/9th Cav. At Ft D. A. Russell, WY, in 1910; resident of Cincinnati. SOURCE: *Illustrated Review: Ninth Cavalry*, with picture.

JOHNSON, Charles J.; Private; I/48th Inf. Died in the Philippines, 28 Apr 1901. SOURCE: *ANJ* 38 (18 May 1901): 925.

JOHNSON, Charles W.; Private; F/9th Cav. With Pvt. C. W. Prann of F/9th Cavalry, complained of being cursed and abused by first sergeant, who denies charges; commander is investigating. SOURCE: Report, 2 Dec 1889, Reports of Investigations, DP, I.

JOHNSON, Charlie; Private; A/9th Cav. At Ft D. A. Russell, WY, in 1910. SOURCE: *Illustrated Review: Ninth Cavalry*, with picture.

JOHNSON, Clarence; Private; A/9th Cav. At Ft D. A. Russell, WY, 1910. SOURCE: *Illustrated Review: Ninth Cavalry*, with picture.

JOHNSON, Clarence; Private; G/9th Cav. At Ft D. A. Russell, WY, in 1910; marksman. SOURCE: *Illustrated Review: Ninth Cavalry*, with picture.

JOHNSON, Clarence W.; Private; I/9th Cav. At Ft D. A. Russell, WY, in 1910; resident of Mount Pleasant, PA. SOURCE: *Illustrated Review: Ninth Cavalry*, with picture.

JOHNSON, Clifford; Private; I/10th Cav. Discharged without honor. SOURCE: SO 148, AGO, 24 Jun 1904.

JOHNSON, Daniel; Sergeant; K/10th Cav. Born Washington, DC; enlisted in K/10th Cavalry, 1 Oct 1867; trumpeter, 28 Dec 1869; corporal, 1 Nov 1873; sergeant, 1 Mar 1874; stationed at Ft Custer, MT, 1897. SOURCE: Baker, Roster.

JOHNSON, Daniel; Private; B/24th Inf. Stationed at Ft McIntosh, TX, early 1877. *See* **GRAYSON**, Charles H., Private, G/24th Infantry

Servant of 1st Lt. M. W. Saxton, 24th Infantry, Ft Duncan, TX. SOURCE: GCMO 4, AGO, 2 Feb 1878.

JOHNSON, David; Recruit; K/10th Cav. Mentioned Nov 1873. SOURCE: LS, 10 Cav, 1873–83.

JOHNSON, David Albert; Private; K/10th Cav. Application for discharge of Johnson, who was under eighteen when he enlisted at Syracuse, NY, 2 Oct 1869, has been referred to commander, K/10th Cavalry. SOURCE: AG, USA, to CO, 10 Cav, 19 Oct 1869, ES, 10 Cav, 1866–71.

JOHNSON, Edward; F/10th Cav. Original member of 10th Cavalry; in troop when organized, Ft Leavenworth, KS, 21 Jun 1867. SOURCE: McMiller, "Buffalo Soldiers," 73.

JOHNSON, Edward; Private; D/10th Cav. Served in 10th Cavalry, 1898; remained in U.S. during war with Spain. SOURCE: Cashin, *Under Fire with the Tenth Cavalry*, 341.

JOHNSON, Edward; Private; L/10th Cav. Served in 10th Cavalry, 1898; remained in U.S. during war with Spain. SOURCE: Cashin, *Under Fire with the Tenth Cavalry*, 351.

JOHNSON, Edward; Private; G/24th Inf. Deserted, Presidio of San Francisco, CA, 19 May 1899. SOURCE: Regt Returns, 24 Inf, Jul 1899.

JOHNSON, Edward; Private; C/24th Inf. Killed in action, Gapan, Philippines, 13 Sep 1900. SOURCE: Muller, *The Twenty Fourth Infantry*, 38.

JOHNSON, Edward; Private; C/25th Inf. Dishonorable discharge, Brownsville. SOURCE: SO 266, AGO, 9 Nov 1906.

JOHNSON, Edward B.; 2nd Lt; I/49th Inf. Served in B and E/25th Infantry, 2 Jun 1889–1 Jun 1895; in 10th Cavalry, 10 Jun 1895–9 Jun 1896; in 25th Infantry, 10 Jun 1896–17 Jun 1899; in emergency notify Mrs. Cornelia Robinson, 9 Pinckney Street, Boston, MA; arrested awaiting charge, trial, sentence, Feb–Mar 1900; dismissed from service 31 Mar 1900 in accordance with General Order 21, Department of the Pacific. SOURCE: Descriptive Book, I/49 Inf.

Formerly sergeant, 10th Cavalry. SOURCE: *ANJ* 37 (9 Dec 1899): 345b.

Commissioned in 49th Infantry from E/25th Infantry. SOURCE: Richmond *Planet*, 20 Jan 1900.

JOHNSON, Enoch; Private; D/10th Cav. Served in 10th Cavalry, 1898; remained in U.S. during war with Spain. SOURCE: Cashin, *Under Fire with the Tenth Cavalry*, 341.

JOHNSON, Ernest; Private; F/10th Cav. Served in 10th Cavalry in Cuba, 1898; died of fever. SOURCE: Cashin, *Under Fire With the Tenth Cavalry*, 344.

Died of yellow fever in Cuba, 13 Aug 1898. SOURCE: *ANJ* 36 (11 Feb 1899): 567; AG, *Correspondence Regarding the War with Spain*, I:228.

Died of yellow fever, Siboney, Cuba, 14 Aug 1898. SOURCE: Hospital Papers, Spanish-American War.

JOHNSON, Ernie; H/10th Cav. Original member of 10th Cavalry; in troop when organized, Ft Leavenworth, KS, 21 Jul 1867. SOURCE: McMiller, "Buffalo Soldiers," 75.

JOHNSON, Eugene; Private; L/25th Inf. Fined $3 by summary court, San Isidro, Philippines, for going off limits, 25 May 1902, first conviction. SOURCE: Register of Summary Court, San Isidro.

JOHNSON, Frank; Recruit; E/10th Cav. Original member of 10th Cavalry; in troop when organized, Ft Leavenworth, KS, 15 Jun 1867. SOURCE: McMiller, "Buffalo Soldiers," 72.

Assigned to E/10th Cavalry, Jun 1867. SOURCE: LS, 10 Cav, 1866–67.

JOHNSON, Frank; Private; E/9th Cav. At Ft D. A. Russell, WY, in 1910; resident of Chellath, OH. SOURCE: *Illustrated Review: Ninth Cavalry*, with picture.

In Laramie County, WY, jail for three burglaries. SOURCE: Cheyenne *Daily Leader*, 11 Jan 1910.

JOHNSON, Frank; Private; I/24th Inf. Nickname "Big Frank"; before execution for part in Houston riot, 1917, declared he was dying "not for Uncle Sam but for God." SOURCE: Haynes, *A Night of Violence*, 5, 123, 271.

Hanged, Ft Sam Houston, TX, 13 Dec 1917, for part in Houston riot. SOURCE: Cleveland *Gazette*, 15 Dec 1917.

JOHNSON, G.; Private; A/9th Cav. On detached service at Ft Cummings, NM, 24 Dec 1880–16 Jan 1881, from station at Ft Stanton, NM. SOURCE: Regt Returns, 9 Cav, Jan 1881.

JOHNSON, George; Private; M/10th Cav. Original member of 10th Cavalry; in troop when organized, Ft Riley, KS, 15 Oct 1867. SOURCE: McMiller, "Buffalo Soldiers," 79.

Deserter, apprehended at Ft Gibson, Indian Territory, 12 Mar 1873. SOURCE: Adj, 10 Cav, to CO, M/10 Cav, 14 Mar 1873, LS, 10 Cav, 1873–83.

Reward of $30 paid for apprehension of deserter Johnson. SOURCE: CO, 10 Cav, to CO, M/10 Cav, 19 Mar 1873, ES, 10 Cav, 1872–81.

Sentence for desertion, which began 2 Mar 1876, reduced to eighteen months. SOURCE: GCMO 22, AGO, 23 Feb 1877.

JOHNSON, George; Corporal; Band/10th Cav. Private, served in 10th Cavalry, 1898; remained in U.S. during war with Spain. SOURCE: Cashin, *Under Fire with the Tenth Cavalry*, 359.

Died at Ft Robinson, NE, Jun 1902; buried, Ft Robinson, 26 Jun 1902. SOURCE: Medical History, Ft Robinson; List of Interments, Ft Robinson.

JOHNSON, George; Private; D/24th Inf. Fined $5 at Cabanatuan, Philippines, 17 May 1901, for looking at 1st Sgt. M. H. Ellis in insubordinate and threatening manner and saying, "I wasn't talking"; witness: First Sergeant Ellis, D/24th Infantry. SOURCE: Name File, 24 Inf.

Jailed for thirty days and fined one month's pay for being absent without leave overnight 4–5 Jul 1901 and taking horse from Quartermaster corral and riding it into San Isidro, Philippines, and back without authorization; witness: Private Neil, D/24th Infantry. SOURCE: Name File, 24 Inf.

JOHNSON, George; Private; C/25th Inf. Dishonorable discharge, Brownsville. SOURCE: SO 266, AGO, 9 Nov 1906.

JOHNSON, George; Corporal; E/9th Cav. Expert rifleman at Ft D. A. Russell, WY, in 1910; resident of 3151 Forest Ave., Chicago. SOURCE: *Illustrated Review: Ninth Cavalry*, with picture.

JOHNSON, George H.; 1st Sgt; H/9th Cav. Sergeant since 1 Jul 1880; first sergeant since 17 Jul 1881. SOURCE: Roster, 9 Cav.

Authorized five-month furlough. SOURCE: *ANJ* 25 (14 Jul 1888): 1014.

JOHNSON, Gilbert; Private; A/9th Cav. At Ft D. A. Russell, WY, in 1910. SOURCE: *Illustrated Review: Ninth Cavalry*, with picture.

JOHNSON, Green; C/10th Cav. Original member of 10th Cavalry; in troop when organized, Ft Leavenworth, KS, 14 May 1867. SOURCE: McMiller, "Buffalo Soldiers," 70.

JOHNSON, H.; Sergeant; A/9th Cav. Stationed at Ft Stanton, NM, 1881. SOURCE: Regt Returns, 9 Cav, Jan 1881.

JOHNSON, Hansom; Warrant Officer; U.S. Army. Sergeant, Supply Troop/10th Cavalry, commissioned captain from Camp Des Moines, IA, 15 Oct 1917. SOURCE: Glass, *History of the Tenth Cavalry*, appendix M.

Retired, resides at 2444 7th Ave, New York City, 1930. SOURCE: Work, *The Negro Yearbook, 1931–1932*, 334.

JOHNSON, Harry; Private; A/10th Cav. Mentioned Jan 1877 as discharged, character good. SOURCE: ES, 10 Cav, 1872–81.

JOHNSON, Henry; F/10th Cav. Original member of 10th Cavalry; in troop when organized, Ft Leavenworth, KS, 21 Jun 1867. SOURCE: McMiller, "Buffalo Soldiers," 73.

JOHNSON, Henry; A/10th Cav. Original member of 10th Cavalry; in troop when organized, Ft Leavenworth, KS, 18 Feb 1867. SOURCE: McMiller, "Buffalo Soldiers," 68.

JOHNSON, Henry; G/10th Cav. Original member of 10th Cavalry; in troop when organized, Ft Leavenworth, KS, 5 Jul 1867. SOURCE: McMiller, "Buffalo Soldiers," 74.

JOHNSON, Henry; L/10th Cav. Original member of 10th Cavalry; in troop when organized, Ft Riley, KS, 21 Sep 1867. SOURCE: McMiller, "Buffalo Soldiers," 78.

JOHNSON, Henry; Private; B/10th Cav. Ordered to Wilmington, DE, as witness in William Bater murder trial. SOURCE: TWX, AAG, DeptMo, to CO, Det 10 Cav, 15 May 1868, LR, Det 10 Cav, 1868–69.

JOHNSON, Henry; Corporal; H/10th Cav. Prisoner sentenced in accordance with General Court Martial orders 143 and 145, Department of the Missouri, to be sent to headquarters under guard for imprisonment at penitentiary, Jefferson City, MO. SOURCE: AAAG, District of the Upper Arkansas, to CO, Det 10 Cav, 8 Sep 1868, LR, Det 10 Cav, 1868–69.

JOHNSON, Henry; Private; F/10th Cav. Recruit from depot, 1873; mentioned Mar 1874. SOURCE: ES, 10 Cav, 1872–81.

JOHNSON, Henry; Private; I/9th Cav. Convicted by general court martial, Jefferson Barracks, MO, of desertion, from 11 Jun 1881 until surrender, 3 Dec 1881; sentenced to dishonorable discharge and five years, reduced to two years by General Sheridan. SOURCE: GCMO 9, AGO, 26 Jan 1882.

JOHNSON, Henry; Trumpeter; I/10th Cav. Request for transfer to D/10th Cavalry disapproved. SOURCE: CO, 10 Cav, to Johnson, 16 Aug 1873, ES, 10 Cav, 1872–81.

JOHNSON, Henry; Private; K/9th Cav. Born Boynton, VA; awarded Medal of Honor for distinguished service, Milk River, CO, Sep 1879. SOURCE: Carroll, *The Black Military Experience*, 386.

Sergeant, D/9th Cavalry, when awarded Medal of Honor. SOURCE: Leckie, *The Buffalo Soldiers*, 208.

Enlisted Baltimore, MD, Jun 1877; Medal of Honor awarded at Ft Robinson, NE, 1890. SOURCE: Lee, *Negro Medal of Honor Men*, 68–71.

Reduced from sergeant, K/9th Cavalry, to private for abusive language to bartender, post canteen, Ft Robinson, when told he could have no more beer. SOURCE: *ANJ* 27 (28 Dec 1889): 352.

Private, K/9th Cavalry, authorized to wear knot in lieu of Medal of Honor, by letter, Adjutant General's Office, 7 Sep 1897.

Reported to Ft Robinson from furlough, Jul 1898; retired and went home to Washington, DC, 29 Aug 1898, in accordance with telegram, Adjutant General's Office, 29 Jul 1898.

Retires to his home, Washington, DC, from Ft Robinson, as private, K/9th Cavalry. SOURCE: *ANJ* 35 (6 Aug 1898): 1007; SO 112, 29 Aug 1898, Post Orders, Ft Robinson.

JOHNSON, Henry; Private; Band/24th Inf. Born Edenton, NC; Ht 5'8", brown complexion; enlisted 25 Jul 1870, G/24th Infantry, transferred to I/24th Infantry, 1 Nov 1874; reenlisted Band/24th Infantry, 26 Jul 1875; transferred to G/24th Infantry, 16 Aug 1875; transferred to K/24th Infantry, 1 Mar 1876; transferred to Band/24th Infantry, 30 Sep 1876; transferred to F/24th Infantry, 11 Jul 1877; transferred to Band/24th Infantry, 8 Dec 1877; married, no children, character excellent, on reenlistments, Ft Supply, Indian Territory, Jul 1885 and Ft Bayard, NM, Jul 1890; married, no children, character very good, on reenlistment, Ft Bayard, Jun 1895; deposits: $100 in 1880, $250 in 1883, $15 in 1884, $280 in 1885, $10 in 1886, $55 in 1890, $20 in 1891, $10 in 1892. SOURCE: Descriptive Book, 24 Inf NCS & Band.

Retired from Presidio of San Francisco, CA, Aug 1900. SOURCE: *ANJ* 37 (11 Aug 1900): 1183.

JOHNSON, Henry; I/10th Cav. Mentioned as Indian War survivor. SOURCE: *Winners of the West* 3 (Jun 1926): 7.

Recent subscriber; served 1881–88; resides in Baltimore, MD. SOURCE: *Winners of the West* 4 (May 1927): 2.

JOHNSON, Henry; Hospital Corps. Remained in San Quentin, Philippines, after service. SOURCE: Funston papers, KSHS.

JOHNSON, Henry E.; K/25th Inf. At San Marcelino, Philippines, 1900. *See* **WISEMAN**, Turner H., Corporal, K/25th Infantry

President, K/25th Infantry YMCA, Castillejos, Philippines, 1900. SOURCE: Richmond *Planet*, 20 Oct 1900.

JOHNSON, Henry W.; E/10th Cav. Original member of 10th Cavalry; in troop when organized, Ft Leavenworth, KS, 15 Jun 1867. SOURCE: McMiller, "Buffalo Soldiers," 72.

JOHNSON, Horace; Sergeant; M/9th Cav. Stationed at Ft McKavett, TX, 1872–73. *See* **STANCE**, Emanuel, First Sergeant, F/9th Cavalry

JOHNSON, Isaac; Private; G/9th Cav. On detached service, Ft Stanton, NM, 29 Jan–5 Feb 1881. SOURCE: Regt Returns, 9 Cav, Feb 1881.

JOHNSON, Isaac M.; Private; 10th Cav. Born Huntland, TN; father was Ben Johnson of Huntland; recruit, enlisted for colored cavalry, Harriman, TN, age 25, Ht 5'6", dark brown complexion, occupation miner, 20 Dec 1907. SOURCE: Terrell, Recruiting Officer, Descriptive Book of Recruits, 1907–1908.

JOHNSON, Isaiah; Private; I/9th Cav. Private, C/9th Cavalry, Ft Robinson, NE, 1886.

Transferred to Hospital Corps, Ft Robinson, Oct 1887.

Private, L/9th Cavalry, Ft Leavenworth, KS, transferred to Hospital Corps and assigned to Ft Missoula, MT. SOURCE: *ANJ* 26 (17 Nov 1888): 226.

Private, F/9th Cavalry, being tried by general court martial, Ft Duchesne, UT, with Lt. H. A. Barker, 9th Cavalry, as his counsel. SOURCE: *ANJ* 35 (22 Jan 1898): 382.

Private, I/9th Cavalry, in hands of civil authorities, Cheyenne, WY, 30 Aug 1897–23 Feb 1898; sentenced to ten years in Wyoming State Penitentiary, Laramie. SOURCE: Regt Returns, 9 Cav.

JOHNSON, Isher; Corporal; I/9th Cav. At Ft Washakie, WY, 1897. *See* **PAULEY**, Charles J., Private, D/9th Cavalry

JOHNSON, Isiak E.; G/10th Cav. Original member of 10th Cavalry; in troop when organized, Ft Leavenworth, KS, 5 Jul 1867. SOURCE: McMiller, "Buffalo Soldiers," 74.

JOHNSON, Israel; Private; A/10th Cav. At Ft Apache, AZ, 1890, subscribed $.50 to testimonial to General Grierson. SOURCE: List of subscriptions, 23 Apr 1890, 10th Cav papers, MHI.

JOHNSON, J.; Private; A/9th Cav. Stationed at Ft Stanton, NM, 1881. SOURCE: Regt Returns, 9 Cav, Jan 1881.

JOHNSON, J.; Private; E/9th Cav. On detached service in field, New Mexico, 27 Jan–1 Feb 1881. SOURCE: Regt Returns, 9 Cav, Feb 1881.

JOHNSON, J.; 9th Cav. Treasurer, Chrispus Attucks Lodge No. 3, Knights of Pythias, State of Nebraska, Ft Robinson, NE. SOURCE: Richmond *Planet*, 18 Dec 1897.

JOHNSON, J. E.; Private; 24th Inf. Drowned crossing San Mateo River, Philippines, 21 Aug 1899. SOURCE: Richmond *Planet*, 2 Sep 1899.

JOHNSON, J. J.; Private; G/25th Inf. Discharged, Ft Missoula, MT, May 1892; "he was a most faithful Sunday School teacher and Temperance man." SOURCE: Monthly Report, Chaplain Steward, Jun 1892.

JOHNSON, Jacob; Private; F/9th Cav. Discharged on surgeon's certificate with epilepsy, Ft Robinson, NE, 21 Jun 1887.

JOHNSON, Jacob B.; Private; I/24th Inf. Enlisted Philadelphia, PA, 1 Jul 1899; joined company 29 Sep 1899. SOURCE: Muster Roll, I/24 Inf, Sep–Oct and Nov–Dec 1899.

JOHNSON, James; Sergeant; A/10th Cav. Original member of 10th Cavalry; in troop when organized, Ft Leavenworth, KS, 18 Feb 1867. SOURCE: McMiller, "Buffalo Soldiers," 68.

Discharged Jan 1877, character fair. SOURCE: ES, 10 Cav, 1872–81.

JOHNSON, James; M/10th Cav. Original member of 10th Cav; in troop when organized, Ft Riley, KS, 15 Oct 1867. SOURCE: McMiller, "Buffalo Soldiers," 79.

JOHNSON, James; Sgt Maj; 25th Inf. Private, I/25th Infantry, at Ft Snelling, MN, to be examined for post quartermaster sergeant. SOURCE: *ANJ* 25 (26 Nov 1887): 342.

Sergeant major, 25th Infantry, Ft Missoula, MT, 1892. SOURCE: *ANJ* 29 (4 Jul 1892): 711.

At Ft Missoula, 1893, examined for ordnance sergeant. SOURCE: *ANJ* 30 (1 Jul 1893): 745.

Retires Jun 1894; Col. A. W. Burt regrets "losing such an efficient and faithful soldier . . . eminently worthy of emulation by the men of this regiment." SOURCE: *ANJ* 31 (23 Jun 1894): 755.

JOHNSON, James; Recruit; Colored Detachment/Mounted Service. Tried and acquitted by general court martial, Jefferson Barracks, MO, 18 Feb 1893, of stealing rations, released from confinement, restored to duty. SOURCE: GCMO 33, AGO, 20 Mar 1893.

JOHNSON, James; Private; H/9th Cav. Killed in action, Cuba, 1898. SOURCE: Scipio, *Last of the Black Regulars*, 29.

Died in Cuba, 1 Jul 1898. SOURCE: *ANJ* 36 (11 Feb 1899): 567.

Killed in action, San Juan, Cuba, 2 Jul 1898. SOURCE: SecWar, *AR 1898*, 707.

JOHNSON, James; Private; A/10th Cav. Served in 10th Cavalry in Cuba, 1898. SOURCE: Cashin, *Under Fire with the Tenth Cavalry*, 336.

JOHNSON, James; Private; I/10th Cav. Served in 10th Cavalry, 1898; remained in U.S. during war with Spain. SOURCE: Cashin, *Under Fire with the Tenth Cavalry*, 348.

JOHNSON, James; Private; D/24th Inf. Fined $10, Cabanatuan, Philippines, 2 Jan 1901, for swearing in loud and boisterous manner in company quarters and continuing after being ordered to stop by 1st Sgt. M. H. Ellis; witnesses: First Sergeant Ellis, QM Sgt. Robert L. Duvall, D/24th Infantry. SOURCE: Name File, 24 Inf.

JOHNSON, James; Private; B/25th Inf. Dishonorable discharge, Brownsville. SOURCE: SO 266, AGO, 9 Nov 1906.

JOHNSON, James E.; E/10th Cav. Original member of 10th Cavalry; in troop when organized, Ft Leavenworth, KS, 15 Jun 1867. SOURCE: McMiller, "Buffalo Soldiers," 72.

JOHNSON, James F.; Saddler; L/9th Cav. At Ft D. A. Russell, WY, in 1910; resident of Columbia, SC. SOURCE: *Illustrated Review: Ninth Cavalry*, with picture.

JOHNSON, James M.; Private; A/24th Inf. At Ft Bayard, NM, 1894. *See* **WATERS**, Charles, Private, L/10th Cavalry

JOHNSON, James M.; Private; K/10th Cav. Mentioned as Indian War survivor. SOURCE: *Winners of the West* 3 (Jun 1926): 7.

JOHNSON, Jason; Corporal; D/24th Inf. Fined $5, Cabanatuan, Philippines, 25 Mar 1901, for being absent without leave; witnesses: 1st Sgt. M. H. Ellis, Sgt. Pat Keys, Cpl. George A. Holland, Musician Moses Reynolds, all of D/24th Infantry. SOURCE: Name File, 24 Inf.

JOHNSON, Jim; Private; 10th Cav. Arrived at Ft Leavenworth, KS, from Jefferson Barracks, MO. SOURCE: Adj, Ft Leavenworth, to HQ, Jefferson Barracks, 9 Oct 1866.

JOHNSON, John; L/10th Cav. Original member of 10th Cavalry; in troop when organized, Ft Riley, KS, 21 Sep 1867. SOURCE: McMiller, "Buffalo Soldiers," 78.

JOHNSON, John; Sergeant; K/9th Cav. Restored to duty at Ft Robinson, NE, in accordance with telegram, Department of the Platte, 14 Dec 1889.

Retired, Nov 1901. SOURCE: *ANJ* 39 (16 Nov 1901): 259.

JOHNSON, John; Private; L/25th Inf. Apprehended from desertion at Ft Robinson, NE, 16 Sep 1905; dishonorable discharge, 10 Oct 1905, in accordance with Special Order 230, Adjutant General's Office, 1905.

JOHNSON, John; Private; A/9th Cav. At Ft D. A. Russell, WY, in 1910; marksman. SOURCE: *Illustrated Review: Ninth Cavalry.*

JOHNSON, John A.; F/10th Cav. Served five years; resides in Santa Ana, CA; recent subscriber. SOURCE: *Winners of the West* 4 (May 1927): 2.

JOHNSON, John A.; A/24th Inf. Stationed at Ft Bayard, NM, 1889. *See* **WOOLEY**, William, Band/24th Infantry

JOHNSON, John A.; Private; K/10th Cav. Served in 10th Cavalry, 1898; remained in U.S. during war with

Spain. SOURCE: Cashin, *Under Fire with the Tenth Cavalry*, 349.

Stationed at Ft Robinson, NE, 1904.

JOHNSON, John A.; G/25th Inf. Convicted of assault with loaded revolver, Philippines, Jan 1901; sentenced to six months and $60 fine.

JOHNSON, John C.; K/10th Cav. Original member of 10th Cavalry; in troop when organized, Ft Riley, KS, 1 Sep 1867. SOURCE: McMiller, "Buffalo Soldiers," 77.

JOHNSON, John H.; Sergeant; I/10th Cav. Original member of 10th Cavalry; in troop when organized, Ft Riley, KS, 15 Aug 1867. SOURCE: McMiller, "Buffalo Soldiers," 76.

Assisted in capture of Pvts. James Reed, B/10th Cavalry, and Frank Wilson, H/10th Cavalry, at Hays City, KS, when they tried to board eastbound train, 25 May 1868. SOURCE: CO, Ft Hays, KS, to Adj, Det 10 Cav, Camp near Ft Wallace, KS, 28 May 1868, LR, Det 10 Cav, 1868–69.

With fifteen dismounted men will escort train to Ft Dodge, KS, with five days' rations and forty rounds of ammunition per man, and return without delay. SOURCE: SO 35, Det 10 Cav, Camp Supply, Indian Territory, Orders, Det 10 Cav, 1868–69.

JOHNSON, John H.; Private; A/10th Cav. Retires from Ft Logan, CO, Jan 1899. SOURCE: *ANJ* 36 (14 Jan 1899): 471.

JOHNSON, John H.; Corporal; H/24th Inf. At Ft Grant, AZ, 1890, he and comrades Cpl. O. R. Lawrence, Sgt. J. Holden, Pvts. William Richardson, Charles H. Thompson, Albert Steed, John C. Perkins, and others, bought casket for burial of Sgt. Edward Berry, H/24th Infantry, because they were dissatisfied with casket provided by government. SOURCE: Cleveland *Gazette*, 26 Apr 1890.

Gave speech at picnic of E/24th Infantry band, Ft Grant, Jun 1890. SOURCE: Cleveland *Gazette*, 28 Jun 1890.

Acquitted of neglect of duty, Ft Bayard, NM. SOURCE: *ANJ* 28 (3 Jan 1891): 313.

Enlisted Ft Bayard, 10 Jul 1896, with ten years' continuous service; promoted from private to corporal, Tampa, FL, 10 May 1898. SOURCE: Muster Roll, H/24 Inf, May–Jun 1898.

Is presently sick, disease contracted in line of duty, since 1 Oct 1898. SOURCE: Muster Roll, H/24 Inf, Nov–Dec 1898.

Sick until 27 Jan 1899; on special duty as painter, Quartermaster Department, since 1 Feb 1899. SOURCE: Muster Roll, H/24 Inf, Jan–Feb 1899.

Recommended for certificate of merit for gallantry, Naguilian, Luzon, Philippines, 7 Dec 1899. SOURCE: *ANJ* 39 (15 Feb 1902): 595.

Certificate of merit for distinguished gallantry, Naguilian, Luzon, 7 Dec 1899, awarded 10 Mar 1902. SOURCE: GO 86, AGO, 24 Jul 1902.

Corporal, drowned in the Philippines. SOURCE: Muller, *The Twenty Fourth Infantry*, 34.

JOHNSON, John J.; Private; L/24th Inf. Enlisted Ft Douglas, UT, 17 Dec 1896. SOURCE: Muster Roll, H/24 Inf, May–Jun 1898.

Private, H/24th Infantry, wounded in action, San Juan, Cuba, 1 Jul 1898, and returned to U.S. for treatment. SOURCE: Muster Roll, H/24 Inf, Jul–Aug 1898; Muller, *The Twenty Fourth Infantry*, 19.

Transferred to L/24th Infantry, 7 Oct 1898; due U.S. for clothing $3.58. SOURCE: Muster Roll, H/24 Inf, Sep–Oct 1898.

JOHNSON, John S.; Private; K/10th Cav. Detailed as teamster. SOURCE: SO 54, HQ, Det 10 Cav, Camp Supply, Indian Territory, 31 Jul 1869.

JOHNSON, John W.; Private; A/10th Cav. At Ft Apache, AZ, 1890, subscribed $.50 to testimonial to General Grierson. SOURCE: List of subscriptions, 23 Apr 1890, 10th Cav papers, MHI.

JOHNSON, John W. L.; Private; Band/9th Cav. Died at Ft Robinson, NE, hospital, 14 Dec 1897. SOURCE: Crawford *Tribune*, 17 Dec 1897.

Funeral, Ft Robinson, 15 Dec 1897. SOURCE: SO 168, 15 Dec 1897, Post Orders, Ft Robinson; List of Interments, Ft Robinson.

JOHNSON, Joseph; Private; G/10th Cav. Original member of 10th Cavalry; in troop when organized, Ft Leavenworth, KS, 5 Jul 1867. SOURCE: McMiller, "Buffalo Soldiers," 74.

Prisoner and encumbrance to command; commander would like him transferred to Ft Dodge, KS, guardhouse. SOURCE: CO, Det 10 Cav, to AAAG, District of the Upper Arkansas, 3 Oct 1868, LR, Det 10 Cav, 1868–69.

JOHNSON, Joseph; Private; H/9th Cav. Killed in action at San Juan, Cuba, 1 Jul 1898. SOURCE: *Illustrated Review: Ninth Cavalry*, with picture.

Also known as James Johnson. *See* **JOHNSON**, James, Private, H/9th Cavalry

JOHNSON, Joseph L.; Private; L/9th Cav. Private, C/25th Infantry, wounded in action, El Caney, Cuba, 1 Jul 1898. SOURCE: Nankivell, *History of the Twenty-fifth Infantry*, 83.

Quartermaster Sergeant, L/9th Cavalry, ranked number 374 among rifle experts with 69.33 percent, 1905. SOURCE: GO 101, AGO, 31 May 1906.

Veteran of Spanish-American War and Philippine Insurrection; private, L/9th Cavalry, at Ft D. A. Russell, WY, in 1910; marksman; resident of Baltimore. SOURCE: *Illustrated Review: Ninth Cavalry*, with picture.

JOHNSON, Joseph S.; 25th Inf. One of original members of 25th Infantry, joining from 40th Infantry; served previously on three different ships during Civil War; commander of Charles Sumner Post 9, Grand Army of the Republic, Washington, DC, on way home from annual encampment; guest in New York City of son-in-law and daughter, Mr. and Mrs. John T. Addison. SOURCE: New York *Age*, 21 Sep 1929.

JOHNSON, Joseph T.; Private; K/10th Cav. Transferred from F/9th Cavalry, Sep 1876. SOURCE: LS, 10 Cav, 1873–83.

JOHNSON, K. A.; Private; F/9th Cav. Discharged, end of term, Ft Robinson, NE, Aug 1885. SOURCE: Post Returns, Ft Robinson, Aug 1885.

JOHNSON, L.; Private; G/9th Cav. On detached service at Ft Stanton, NM, 29 Jan–5 Feb 1881. SOURCE: Regt Returns, 9 Cav, Feb 1881.

JOHNSON, Lawrence; Corporal; M/9th Cav. At Ft McKavett, TX, 1872–73. *See* **STANCE**, Emanuel, First Sergeant, F/9th Cavalry

JOHNSON, Leoid; Recruit; Colored Detachment/ Mounted Service. Tried by general court martial, Jefferson Barracks, MO, for desertion 18 Aug 1887, until apprehended at St. Louis, MO, 24 Aug 1887; convicted of absence without leave; sentenced to dishonorable discharge and four years' confinement. SOURCE: GCMO 76, AGO, 29 Oct 1887.

JOHNSON, Levi; Private; C/24th Inf. At Ft Sill, Indian Territory, killed wife of Private Dailey, E/24th Infantry, 9 Aug 1887, because she rejected his attentions, then shot himself in left breast; not expected to recover. SOURCE: *ANJ* 25 (3 Sep 1887): 102.

JOHNSON, Lewis; Private; H/10th Cav. Served in 10th Cavalry, 1898; remained in U.S. during war with Spain. SOURCE: Cashin, *Under Fire with the Tenth Cavalry*, 347.

JOHNSON, Louis; Corporal; H/24th Inf. Enlisted New York City, 15 Sep 1893, with five years' continuous service; promoted from private, Tampa, FL, 10 May 1898. SOURCE: Muster Roll, H/24 Inf, May–Jun 1898.

Resided at 331 South 11th East, Salt Lake City, UT, in 1898. SOURCE: Clark, "A History of the Twenty-fourth," appendix E.

On detached service on board U.S. Army Transport *City of Washington*, 21 Jun–7 Aug 1898. SOURCE: Muster Roll, H/24 Inf, Jul–Aug 1898.

Died at Camp Wikoff, NY, 14 Sep 1898, of disease contracted at yellow fever hospital, Siboney, Cuba; due soldier $5 deposits, $30 retained, $8.63 clothing. SOURCE: Muster Roll, H/24 Inf, Sep–Oct 1898.

JOHNSON, Luther; Private; Band/24th Inf. Born Williamson Co., KY; Ht 5'3", yellow complexion; enlisted in A/24th Infantry, 23 Feb 1876; transferred to Band/24th Infantry, 18 Oct 1876; transferred to G/24th Infantry, 11 Jul 1877; transferred to Band/24th Infantry, 8 Dec 1877; fined $5 by garrison court martial, Ft Duncan, TX, 1878; fined $10 by garrison court martial, Ft Supply, Indian Territory, 1882; fined one month's pay by garrison court martial, Ft Supply, 1884; promoted to principal musician, character excellent, single, 2 Nov 1885; enlisted Ft Bayard, NM, 23 Feb 1886; private, 27 Oct 1888; discharged Ft Bayard, character very good, "a good B-flat cornet player," married, no children, 22 Feb 1891; retained $60, clothing $18; enlisted, Ft Bayard, 23 Feb 1891; discharged, character very good, married, no children, 22 Feb 1896; additional pay $4 per month. SOURCE: Descriptive Book, 24 Inf NCS & Band.

JOHNSON, Mack; F/10th Cav. Original member of 10th Cavalry; in troop when organized, Ft Leavenworth, KS, 21 Jun 1867. SOURCE: McMiller, "Buffalo Soldiers," 73.

JOHNSON, Marshall H.; M/10th Cav. Original member of 10th Cavalry; in troop when organized, Ft Riley, KS, 15 Oct 1867. SOURCE: McMiller, "Buffalo Soldiers," 79.

JOHNSON, Monroe; Sergeant; M/9th Cav. At Ft McKavett, TX, 1872–73. *See* **STANCE**, Emanuel, First Sergeant, F/9th Cavalry

JOHNSON, Mose; Private; G/9th Cav. At Ft D. A. Russell, WY, in 1910; sharpshooter; resident of Buffalo, NY. SOURCE: *Illustrated Review: Ninth Cavalry*, with picture.

JOHNSON, Moses; Private; C/10th Cav. Mentioned Jan 1873 as having enlisted Sep 1867 and transferred to G/10th Cavalry. SOURCE: LS, 10 Cav, 1873–83.

Mentioned 1873 as private, G/10th Cavalry. SOURCE: ES, 10 Cav, 1872–81.

Applies for membership in Camp No. 11, National Indian War Veterans, St. Joseph, MO. SOURCE: *Winners of the West* 5 (Jun 1928): 3.

Served in C/10th Cavalry, 1872–73; died at Hutchinson, KS. SOURCE: *Winners of the West* 8 (Jul 1931): 8.

JOHNSON, Napoleon; Private; A/10th Cav. Served in 10th Cavalry, 1898; remained in U.S. during war with Spain. SOURCE: *Cashin, Under Fire with the Tenth Cavalry*, 337.

JOHNSON, Natter; Private; K/24th Inf. Sentenced to ten days and fined $5 for striking Filipino woman in face and tearing her dress. SOURCE: Name File, 24 Inf.

JOHNSON, Otto; Private; D/24th Inf. Fined $4 for being drunk and disorderly in quarters, Cabanatuan, Philippines, 12 Feb 1901; witnesses: Sgt. Wilson Prear and Pvt. John Smith, both D/24th Infantry. SOURCE: Name File, 24 Inf.

Acquitted of failure to keep quiet in pay line, Cabanatuan, 17 May 1901; witness: 1st Sgt. M. H. Ellis. SOURCE: Name File, 24 Inf.

Fined $5 for failure to repair for stable duty, Cabanatuan, 8 Jul 1901; witness: Sgt. George Driscoll, D/24th Infantry.

JOHNSON, Peter; I/10th Cav. Original member of 10th Cavalry; in troop when organized, Ft Riley, KS, 15 Aug 1867. SOURCE: McMiller, "Buffalo Soldiers," 76.

JOHNSON, Peter; Corporal; C/9th Cav. At Ft D. A. Russell, WY, in 1910; sharpshooter. SOURCE: *Illustrated Review: Ninth Cavalry*, with picture.

JOHNSON, Reuben; Private; F/24th Inf. Convicted by general court martial, Ft Columbus, NY, for desertion; sentenced to dishonorable discharge and two years. SOURCE: GCMO 48, AGO, 8 Jun 1875.

Prisoner released from military prison, Ft Leavenworth, KS. SOURCE: GCMO 22, AGO, 23 Feb 1877.

JOHNSON, Richard; A/10th Cav. Mentioned as recruit, Oct 1866. SOURCE: LS, 10 Cav, 1866–67.

Original member of 10th Cavalry; in troop when organized, Ft Leavenworth, KS, 18 Feb 1867. SOURCE: McMiller, "Buffalo Soldiers," 68.

JOHNSON, Richard; C/10th Cav. Original member of 10th Cavalry; in troop when organized, Ft Leavenworth, KS, 14 May 1867. SOURCE: McMiller, "Buffalo Soldiers," 70.

JOHNSON, Richard; Private; H/10th Cav. Served in 10th Cavalry, 1898; remained in U.S. during war with Spain. SOURCE: Cashin, *Under Fire with the Tenth Cavalry*, 347.

JOHNSON, Richard; Musician; I/25th Inf. Fined $1 by summary court, San Isidro, Philippines, for absence from reveille, 26 May 1902, second conviction; fined $5 for absence from duty at adjutant's office, 25 Jun 1902. SOURCE: Register of Summary Court, San Isidro.

JOHNSON, Robert; A/10th Cav. Mentioned Oct 1866. SOURCE: LS, 10 Cav, 1866–67.

Mentioned as enlisted at St. Louis, MO, Nov 1866. SOURCE: ES, 10 Cav, 1866–71.

Original member of 10th Cavalry; in troop when organized, Ft Leavenworth, KS, 18 Feb 1867. SOURCE: McMiller, "Buffalo Soldiers," 68.

JOHNSON, Robert; Sergeant; G/9th Cav. One of six enlisted men of G/9th Cavalry to testify against Lt. John Conline at his 1877 court martial for misconduct, including drunkenness, sexual misconduct, and misappropriation of funds belonging to men of his troop, Ft Garland, CO. SOURCE: Billington, *New Mexico's Buffalo Soldiers*, 121–23.

JOHNSON, Robert; Farrier; I/9th Cav. At Ft D. A. Russell, WY, in 1910; sharpshooter; resident of Lonoke, AR. SOURCE: *Illustrated Review: Ninth Cavalry*, with picture.

JOHNSON, Robert; Private; K/9th Cav. At Ft D. A. Russell, WY, in 1910; marksman; resident of Iron City, AL. SOURCE: *Illustrated Review: Ninth Cavalry*.

JOHNSON, Robert J.; Private; G/9th Cav. Witness for defense, Barney McKay general court martial, Ft Robinson, NE, 1893.

JOHNSON, Robert J.; Private; M/10th Cav. Served in 10th Cavalry in Cuba, 1898. SOURCE: Cashin, *Under Fire with the Tenth Cavalry*, 352.

JOHNSON, Robert J.; Corporal; K/9th Cav. Veteran of Indian wars, Spanish-American War, and Philippine Insurrection; at Ft D. A. Russell, WY, in 1910; sharpshooter; resident of Moffat's Creek, VA. SOURCE: *Illustrated Review: Ninth Cavalry*, with picture.

JOHNSON, Robert M.; 1st Sgt; K/10th Cav. Born in Kentucky; enlisted in K/10th Cavalry, 22 Nov 1887; corporal, 11 Nov 1892; sergeant, 7 Apr 1895; stationed at Ft Custer, MT, 1897. SOURCE: Baker, Roster.

Ranked number nine, carbine competition, and number four, revolver competition, Departments of Dakota and Columbia, at Ft Keogh, MT, 15–23 Aug 1892. SOURCE: GO 75, AGO, 3 Nov 1892.

Veteran of Geronimo campaign; won medals with carbine and revolver at marksmanship contests, Ft Keogh. SOURCE: Cleveland *Gazette*, 5 Nov 1892.

Ranked number seven on carbine team and tenth on revolver team, Departments of Columbia and Dakota competition, Ft Keogh, 14–22 Aug 1893; distinguished marksman with carbine and pistol, 1892 and 1893. SOURCE: GO 82, AGO, 24 Oct 1893.

Corporal, ranked number six, competition of Army carbine team, 1894. SOURCE: GO 15, AGO, 15 Nov 1894.

Ranked number three among carbine sharpshooters with 82.67 percent, 1894. SOURCE: GO 1, AGO, 2 Jan 1895.

Sergeant, served in 10th Cavalry, 1898; remained in U.S. during war with Spain. SOURCE: Cashin, *Under Fire with the Tenth Cavalry*, 349.

First sergeant, K/10th Cavalry, stationed at Ft Robinson, NE, seventh best marksman, U.S. Army team, 1904. SOURCE: Glass, *History of the Tenth Cavalry*, 44.

Ranked number seven in competition of Army cavalry carbine team, Ft Riley, KS, 11–17 Aug 1904. SOURCE: GO 167, AGO, 28 Oct 1904.

Paid postage on subscriptions to black newspapers of men of his company "to advance a good cause." SOURCE: Schubert, "The Fort Robinson Y.M.C.A.," 178.

Ranked number 79 among expert riflemen with 72.33 percent, 1904. SOURCE: GO 79, AGO, 1 Jun 1905.

Ranked number 32, national individual marksmanship competition, Sea Girt, NJ, 1905; distinguished marksman. SOURCE: SecWar, *AR 1905*, 1:160; GO 195, AGO, 18 Nov 1905.

Ranked number ten on second place U.S. Cavalry team at national rifle match, Sea Girt, 1906; team awarded $200 and medals for each member. SOURCE: GO 190, AGO, 15 Nov 1906.

Married to Fannie Trueheart by Chaplain Anderson at Ft Robinson, 27 Nov 1905, with commander's permission; 136 attended. SOURCE: Monthly Report, Chaplain Anderson, Nov 1905.

First sergeant, K/10th Cavalry, Ft Ethan Allen, VT, 1909; states he knew Henry McClain until 1894 and after 1902; McClain complained of stomach pains from time horse fell over backward on him in 1893. SOURCE: VA File XC 2705872, Henry McClain.

JOHNSON, Robert T.; G/9th Cav. Was recruit at St. Louis with Joseph Blew, Oct 1873; then served together in G/9th Cavalry until discharged in 1883; met again in Omaha, NE, 1904, when Johnson was working on the Overland Limited Train. SOURCE: Affidavit, Johnson, age 70, 916 Cypress, Oakland, CA, 31 May 1924, VA File XC 970422, Joseph Blew.

JOHNSON, Rubin; I/10th Cav. Original member of 10th Cavalry; in troop when organized, Ft Riley, KS, 15 Aug 1867. SOURCE: McMiller, "Buffalo Soldiers," 76.

JOHNSON, Samuel; A/10th Cav. Original member of 10th Cavalry; in troop when organized, Ft Leavenworth, KS, 18 Feb 1867. SOURCE: McMiller, "Buffalo Soldiers," 68.

JOHNSON, Samuel; Private; Band/24th Inf. Born Ft Leavenworth, KS; enlisted in Band/24th Infantry, age 21, Ht 5'9", brown complexion; black hair and eyes, Nov 1879; corporal, A/24th Infantry, 6 Mar–31 Jul 1882; reduced to private by garrison court martial, 31 Jul 1882; reenlisted Ft Leavenworth, 1884; fined $1 by garrison court martial, Ft Bayard, NM, 13 Nov 1889; discharged, end of term, character very good, married, no children, Ft Bayard, 13 Nov 1889; deposits $300 in 1885, $450 in 1888, $385 in 1889, retained $60, clothing $58.66. SOURCE: Descriptive Book, 24 Inf NCS & Band.

JOHNSON, Scott; Private; L/10th Cav. Served in 10th Cavalry, 1898; remained in U.S. during war with Spain. SOURCE: Cashin, *Under Fire with the Tenth Cavalry*, 351.

JOHNSON, Scott; Private; L/9th Cav. At Ft D. A. Russell, WY, in 1910; resident of Savannah, GA. SOURCE: *Illustrated Review: Ninth Cavalry*, with picture.

JOHNSON, Sidney; Private; D/10th Cav. Mentioned 1873. SOURCE: ES, 10 Cav, 1872–81.

JOHNSON, Silas; Sergeant; D/10th Cav. Farrier, served in 10th Cavalry in Cuba, 1898. SOURCE: Cashin, *Under Fire with the Tenth Cavalry*, 341.

President McKinley congratulated him and shook his hand on trip from New York City to Long Island City, NY. SOURCE: Cleveland *Gazette*, 17 Sep 1898.

Son born to wife at Ft Robinson, NE, 10 Feb 1906. SOURCE: Monthly Report, Chaplain Anderson, Mar 1906.

JOHNSON, Silvester; Private; C/10th Cav. Honorably discharged from C/10th Cavalry, 11 Oct 1874; reenlistment application approved. SOURCE: CO, 10 Cav, to AG, USA, 5 Apr 1876, ES, 10 Cav, 1872–81.

JOHNSON, Smith; QM Sgt; A/10th Cav. Born in Kentucky; private, corporal, sergeant, A and G/10th Cavalry, 11 Sep 1872–31 Oct 1892; private, A/10th Cavalry, 16 Nov 1892; corporal, 10 Jan 1893; sergeant, 28 Jan 1896; stationed at Ft Custer, MT, 1897. SOURCE: Baker, Roster.

Private, A/10th Cavalry, at Ft Apache, AZ, 1890, subscribed $.50 to testimonial to General Grierson. SOURCE: List of subscriptions, 23 Apr 1890, 10th Cav papers, MHI.

Served in 10th Cavalry in Cuba, 1898; wounded in action. SOURCE: Cashin, *Under Fire with the Tenth Cavalry*, 336–37.

Heroism in Cuba slighted according to unsigned letter [John E. Lewis, H/10th Cavalry], Montauk, NY, n.d. SOURCE: Steward, *The Colored Regulars*, 77.

Sergeant, A/10th Cavalry, wounded in action at Santiago, Cuba, 1 Jul 1898. SOURCE: SecWar, *AR 1898*, 323.

Retires as quartermaster sergeant, A/10th Cavalry, Jan 1901. SOURCE: *ANJ* 38 (26 Jan 1901): 519.

JOHNSON, Solomon; Cook; B/25th Inf. Private, E/9th Cavalry, letter. SOURCE: *ANJ* 39 (12 Oct 1901): 141.

Dishonorable discharge, Brownsville. SOURCE: SO 266, AGO, 9 Nov 1906.

JOHNSON, Starks H.; Private; E/9th Cav. Changed name from William Hardwicks. SOURCE: SO 37, AGO, 14 Feb 1898.

JOHNSON, T. A.; Private; A/9th Cav. Discharged from Ft Stanton, NM, 26 Feb 1881, in accordance with Special Order 36, Adjutant General's Office, 1881. SOURCE: Regt Returns, 9 Cav, Feb 1881.

JOHNSON, Thomas; L/10th Cav. Original member of 10th Cavalry; in troop when organized, Ft Riley, KS, 21 Sep 1867. SOURCE: McMiller, "Buffalo Soldiers," 78.

JOHNSON, Thomas; A/9th Cav. Surviving Indian War veteran. SOURCE: *Winners of the West* 3 (Jan 1926): 7.

Mentioned. SOURCE: *Winners of the West* 13 (Dec 1935): 2.

JOHNSON, Thomas; Corporal; D/24th Inf. At Cabanatuan, Philippines, 1900–1901. *See* **BROWN**, Philip, Private, D/24th Infantry; **MOORE**, Cato, Private, D/24th Infantry; **PRIDE**, Wheeler, Private, D/24th Infantry

JOHNSON, Thomas; 1st Sgt; I/24th Inf. Commended in general orders by Maj. Gen. J. Franklin Bell, Commanding General, Department of the Philippines, for distinguished service, Camp McGrath, Batangas, Philippines. SOURCE: Curtis, *The Black Soldier*, 42.

Awarded certificate of merit for distinguished service at risk of his own life in pursuit and disarming of enlisted man bent on murdering his first sergeant, Camp McGrath, Batangas, Philippines, 22 Aug 1912. SOURCE: AGO, Bulletin 29, 13 Jul 1914.

JOHNSON, W. A.; Private; M/9th Cav. Enlisted Ft Washakie, WY, 29 Nov 1887.

JOHNSON, W. S.; I/10th Cav. Sheriff George A. Olney, Graham Co., AZ, asks information regarding his whereabouts from commander, Ft Huachuca, AZ, 31 Mar 1893. SOURCE: Letters & Orders Received, 24 Inf.

JOHNSON, Walker; Sergeant; C/10th Cav. Private, at Ft Apache, AZ, 1890, subscribed $.25 to testimonial to General Grierson. SOURCE: List of subscriptions, 23 Apr 1890, 10th Cav papers, MHI.

Corporal, acquitted by general court martial, Ft Custer, MT, of conduct to prejudice of good order and discipline. SOURCE: *ANJ* 33 (28 Mar 1896): 540.

Served in 10th Cavalry in Cuba, 1898. SOURCE: Cashin, *Under Fire with the Tenth Cavalry*, 339.

Wounded in action, Santiago, Cuba, 1 Jul 1898. SOURCE: SecWar, *AR 1898*, 324.

JOHNSON, Walter; Private; M/10th Cav. Served in 10th Cavalry, 1898; remained in U.S. during war with Spain. SOURCE: Cashin, *Under Fire with the Tenth Cavalry*, 351.

JOHNSON, Walter; Private; D/25th Inf. Dishonorable discharge, Brownsville. SOURCE: SO 266, AGO, 9 Nov 1906.

JOHNSON, Will; Private; I/9th Cav. Discharge disapproved by Adjutant General. SOURCE: Letter, DP, 10 Jun 1895.

JOHNSON, William; Private; F/10th Cav. Original member of 10th Cavalry; in troop when organized, Ft Leavenworth, KS, 21 Jun 1867. SOURCE: McMiller, "Buffalo Soldiers," 73.

Sergeant, convicted by garrison court martial, Ft Lyon, CO, of neglect of duty, failure to obey standing troop order to lead, not ride, horses to water on march near Saline River, 20 Aug 1868; reduced to private. SOURCE: GCMO 25, DeptMo, 16 Apr 1869.

Private, mentioned Mar 1873. SOURCE: LS, 10 Cav, 1873–83.

"One of the few colored telegraph operators," died Ft Grant, AZ, 15 Jul 1887. SOURCE: Cleveland *Gazette*, 30 Jul 1887.

JOHNSON, William; H/10th Cav. Original member of 10th Cavalry; in troop when organized, Ft Leavenworth, KS, 21 Jul 1867. SOURCE: McMiller, "Buffalo Soldiers," 75.

JOHNSON, William; Private; B/25th Inf. Serving sentence at Kansas Penitentiary in accordance with General Court Martial Order 21, Department of Texas, 28 Feb 1876, which is reduced to five years. SOURCE: GCMO 40, AGO, 26 Mar 1876.

JOHNSON, William; Private; Band/10th Cav. Killed in personal altercation with Private Sneed, F/10th Cavalry, night of 28 Nov 1876, when both were absent without leave; Sneed arrested by civil authorities, escaped, now at large; balance owed Jackson of around $140 can be obtained by kin through Adjutant General. SOURCE: 1st Lt. J. T. Morrison, 10 Cav, to CO, 10 Cav, 15 Apr 1877, ES, 10 Cav, 1872–81.

JOHNSON, William; Private; E/24th Inf. Resident of New York City; discharged, end of term, from Ft Bayard, NM, 7 Dec 1891. SOURCE: Cleveland *Gazette*, 12 Dec 1891.

JOHNSON, William; Cook; C/10th Cav. Corporal, accompanied 1st Lt. L. Hardeman on march from Havre, MT, 15 Jun 1896, along with Trumpeter Sulder and five privates, to intercept Crees moving to Dakota; on 15–16 Jun covered 110 miles in 25 hours. SOURCE: Baker, Roster.

Retires as cook, C/10th Cavalry. SOURCE: SO 6, AGO, 8 Jan 1904.

Buried at Ft Robinson, NE, 20 Jan 1914. SOURCE: List of Interments, Ft Robinson.

JOHNSON, William; Private; 9th Cav. Enlisted in H/24th Infantry, Ft Douglas, UT, 8 Dec 1897; entitled to reenlistment pay. SOURCE: Muster Roll, H/24 Inf, May–Jun 1898.

Sick in hospital, Siboney, Cuba, 25–31 Aug 1898, and en route to U.S., 25–31 Aug 1898, disease contracted in line of duty. SOURCE: Muster Roll, H/24 Inf, Jul–Aug 1898.

On furlough, authorized by surgeon's certificate, 11 Sep–10 Oct 1898; appointed lance corporal, 8 Oct 1898. SOURCE: Muster Roll, H/24 Inf, Sep–Oct 1898.

Transferred to 9th Cavalry, 6 Dec 1898, with $10 deposits, $11.42 clothing. SOURCE: Muster Roll, H/24 Inf, Nov–Dec 1898.

Born Philadelphia, PA, 27 May 1849; member, St. Paul, MN, Camp 21, National Indian War Veterans; died. SOURCE: *Winners of the West* 8 (Sep 1931): 8.

JOHNSON, William; Private; A/10th Cav. Served in 10th Cavalry, 1898; remained in U.S. during war with Spain. SOURCE: Cashin, *Under Fire with the Tenth Cavalry*, 337.

JOHNSON, William; Private; D/10th Cav. Served in 10th Cavalry in Cuba, 1898. SOURCE: Cashin, *Under Fire with the Tenth Cavalry*, 341.

JOHNSON, William; Private; E/10th Cav. Served in 10th Cavalry, 1898; remained in U.S. during war with Spain. SOURCE: Cashin, *Under Fire with the Tenth Cavalry*, 343.

JOHNSON, William; Private; G/10th Cav. Served in 10th Cavalry, 1898; remained in U.S. during war with Spain. SOURCE: Cashin, *Under Fire with the Tenth Cavalry*, 346.

JOHNSON, William; Sergeant; L/10th Cav. Served in 10th Cavalry, 1898; remained in U.S. during war with Spain. SOURCE: Cashin, *Under Fire with the Tenth Cavalry*, 350.

JOHNSON, William (1); Private; L/10th Cav. Served in 10th Cavalry, 1898; remained in U.S. during war with Spain. SOURCE: Cashin, *Under Fire with the Tenth Cavalry*, 351.

JOHNSON, William (2); Private; L/10th Cav. Served in 10th Cavalry, 1898; remained in U.S. during war with Spain. SOURCE: Cashin, *Under Fire with the Tenth Cavalry*, 351.

JOHNSON, William; Private; D/24th Inf. Wounded in the arm, Santiago, Cuba, 1 Jul 1898. SOURCE: Clark, "A History of the Twenty-fourth," 100; SecWar, *AR 1898*, 436; Muller, *The Twenty Fourth Infantry*, 18.

JOHNSON, William; Corporal; B/24th Inf. At Cabanatuan, Philippines, 1900. *See* **LEAVELL**, William, Private, D/24th Infantry

JOHNSON, William; Private; F/25th Inf. Drowned, body recovered, in the Philippines, 27 Feb 1901. SOURCE: *ANJ* 38 (16 Mar 1901): 703.

JOHNSON, William; Private; 10th Cav. Sentence in Special Order 186, Department of the Missouri, 10 Oct 1902.

JOHNSON, William D.; Master Sgt; 25th Inf. Private, K/25th Infantry, at Ft Niobrara, NE, 1904. SOURCE: Wilson, "History of Fort Niobrara."

Master sergeant at Camp Stephen D. Little, Nogales, AZ, 1925. SOURCE: Nankivell, *History of the Twenty-fifth Infantry*, 159.

JOHNSON, William F.; Sergeant; F/9th Cav. Appointed sergeant 11 Dec 1891. SOURCE: Roster, 9 Cav.

JOHNSON, William F.; Corporal; B/10th Cav. Served in 10th Cavalry in Cuba, 1898; killed in action, Jul 1898. SOURCE: Cashin, *Under Fire With the Tenth Cavalry*, 337–38.

Commended for "efficiency and perfect coolness under fire," as noncommissioned officer in charge, Hotchkiss battery, Santiago, Cuba, 24 Jun 1898. SOURCE: SecWar, *AR 1898*, 323; GO 15, AGO, 13 Feb 1900; Steward, *The Colored Regulars*, 146.

Killed in action, San Juan, Cuba, 1 Jul 1898; Johnson Road, Ft Huachuca, AZ, named for him. SOURCE: Orville A. Cochran to H. B. Wharfield, 5 Apr 1965, 10th Cavalry papers, MHI.

Killed in action, Cuba, 1 Jul 1898. SOURCE: Scipio, *Last of the Black Regulars*, 29; *ANJ* 36 (11 Feb 1899): 567.

JOHNSON, William H.; I/10th Cav. Original member of 10th Cavalry; in troop when organized, Ft Riley, KS, 15 Aug 1867. SOURCE: McMiller, "Buffalo Soldiers," 76.

JOHNSON, William H.; 1st Sgt; E/10th Cav. Corporal, at Ft Apache, AZ, 1890, subscribed $.50 to testimonial to General Grierson. SOURCE: List of subscriptions, 23 Apr 1890, 10th Cavalry papers, MHI.

Trumpeter, served in 10th Cavalry in Cuba, 1898. SOURCE: Cashin, *Under Fire with the Tenth Cavalry*, 342.

Wounded in action at Santiago, Cuba, 24 Jun 1898. SOURCE: SecWar, *AR 1898*, 355.

Retired "with fine record" as first sergeant. SOURCE: Fremont *Clipper*, 30 Nov 1906.

JOHNSON, William H.; Private; B/10th Cav. Transferred to Hospital Corps, Feb 1895. SOURCE: *ANJ* 32 (16 Feb 1895): 406.

JOHNSON, William H. (1); Private; C/10th Cav. Served in 10th Cavalry in Cuba, 1898. SOURCE: Cashin, *Under Fire with the Tenth Cavalry*, 340.

JOHNSON, William H. (2); Private; C/10th Cav. Served in 10th Cavalry, 1898; remained in U.S. during war with Spain. SOURCE: Cashin, *Under Fire with the Tenth Cavalry*, 340.

JOHNSON, William H.; Private; I/24th Inf. Enlisted Baltimore, MD, 26 Jul 1898. SOURCE: Muster Roll, I/24 Inf, Jan–Feb 1899.

On detached service at Three Rivers, CA, 3 May–21 Jun 1899; on detached service at Presidio of San Francisco, CA, 22 Jun–26 Jul 1899. SOURCE: Muster Roll, I/24 Inf, May–Jun and Jul–Aug 1899.

Discharged, character good, 31 Dec 1899, with $95 deposits and $7.25 clothing. SOURCE: Muster Roll, I/24 Inf, Nov–Dec 1899.

JOHNSON, William H.; Private; I/9th Cav. At Ft D. A. Russell, WY, in 1910; resident of Carbondale, KS. SOURCE: *Illustrated Review: Ninth Cavalry*, with picture.

JOHNSON, William L.; L/25th Inf. Letter from San Marcelino, Philippines, 19 Dec 1900, praises *Planet*: "Your paper is all O.K." SOURCE: Richmond *Planet*, 16 Feb 1901.

JOHNSON, William L.; Corporal; M/9th Cav. At Ft D. A. Russell, WY, in 1910; resident of Lexington, MO. SOURCE: *Illustrated Review: Ninth Cavalry*, with picture.

JOHNSON, William M.; Private; F/9th Cav. Recruit from depot arrived at Ft Robinson, NE, 1 Mar 1887.

Deserted from Ft Robinson, 23 Apr 1887.

Buried at Ft Robinson, 24 Oct 1890. SOURCE: List of Interments, Ft Robinson.

JOHNSON, William T.; Sergeant; A/10th Cav. Commissioned first lieutenant at Camp Des Moines, IA, 15 Oct 1917. SOURCE: Glass, *History of the Tenth Cavalry*, appendix M.

JOHNSON, Willie; Private; G/10th Cav. Served in 10th Cavalry in Cuba, 1898. SOURCE: Cashin, *Under Fire with the Tenth Cavalry*, 345.

JOHNSON, Willie; Private; M/10th Cav. Served in 10th Cavalry, 1898; remained in U.S. during war with Spain. SOURCE: Cashin, *Under Fire with the Tenth Cavalry*, 351.

JOHNSON, Willie; Private; G/49th Inf. Died in the Philippines, 18 Oct 1900. SOURCE: *ANJ* 38 (10 Nov 1900): 259.

JOHNSON, Wyatt; B/10th Cav. Original member of 10th Cavalry; in troop when organized, Ft Leavenworth, KS, 1 Apr 1867. SOURCE: McMiller, "Buffalo Soldiers," 69.

JOHNSON, Y.; C/9th Cav. Jailed, Crawford, NE, 6 Dec 1896, in lieu of $5 fine and $6.40 court costs for being drunk and disorderly and fast riding, to which he had pled not guilty.

JOHNSON, York; Private; C/10th Cav. Original member of 10th Cavalry; in troop when organized, Ft Leavenworth, KS, 14 May 1867. SOURCE: McMiller, "Buffalo Soldiers," 70.

Recruit on extra duty, Ft Leavenworth, assigned to C/10th Cavalry. SOURCE: CO, 10 Cav, to Adjutant, Ft Leavenworth, 15 May 1867, LS, 10 Cav, 1866–67.

Shot to death along with Pvt. Charles Smith by Lt. Robert Price in fit of rage after quarrel en route to Santa Fe, NM, Aug 1871. SOURCE: Leckie, *The Buffalo Soldiers*, 60.

JOHNSTON; Sergeant; F/10th Cav. Wounded in action, Kansas, 21 Aug 1867. SOURCE: Armes, *Ups and Downs*, 247.

JOHNSTON, Brooks; 9th Cav. One of twenty-nine former Tuskegee Institute students who enlisted for Spanish-American War; letter to *The Tuskegee Student*, 9 Jun 1898, from Tampa. SOURCE: Thweatt, *What the Newspapers Say*, 8–9.

JOHNSTON, Charles; Private; D/9th Cav. On extra duty as carpenter, Ft Robinson, NE. SOURCE: Order 56, 9 Aug 1894, Post Orders, Ft Robinson.

JOHNSTON, William; Corporal; I/10th Cav. Born in North Carolina; private, I/10th Cavalry, 6 May 1894; corporal, 9 Feb 1897; stationed at Ft Assiniboine, MT, 1897. SOURCE: Baker, Roster.

JOHNSTON, Willis J.; Private; 25th Inf. Wounded in thigh, Botolon, Philippines, 28 Feb 1900. SOURCE: *ANJ* 37 (14 Apr 1900): 779.

JOHNSTONE, John H.; Corporal; H/25th Inf. Drowned at Tayug, Philippines, 2 Dec 1899. SOURCE: *ANJ* 37 (23 Dec 1899): 389.

JONES; Private; B/10th Cav. General court martial sentence. SOURCE: SO 171, DeptMo, 7 Sep 1903.

JONES, A.; Private; B/10th Cav. At Ft Apache, AZ, 1890, subscribed $.50 to testimonial to General Grierson. SOURCE: List of subscriptions, 23 Apr 1890, 10th Cavalry papers, MHI.

JONES, A. H.; Private; L/10th Cav. Served in 10th Cavalry, 1898; remained in U.S. during war with Spain. SOURCE: Cashin, *Under Fire with the Tenth Cavalry*, 351.

JONES, A. J.; Sergeant; M/10th Cav. Private, M/10th Cavalry, and sharpshooter, at Ft McDowell, AZ. SOURCE: *ANJ* 24 (18 Jan 1887): 934.

Ranked number three in revolver competition, Departments of California and Arizona, Ft Wingate, NM, 1889; silver medal. SOURCE: Baker, Roster; GO 78, AGO, 12 Oct 1889.

Corporal, at Ft Apache, AZ, 1890, subscribed $.25 to testimonial to General Grierson. SOURCE: List of subscriptions, 23 Apr 1890, 10th Cavalry papers, MHI.

Ranked number two in revolver competition, Departments of California, Columbia, and Arizona, Ft Wingate, 4–9 Aug 1890. SOURCE: GO 112, AGO, 2 Oct 1890.

Sergeant, ranked number 35 among carbine sharpshooters with 72.71 percent, 1890. SOURCE: GO 1, AGO, 2 Jan 1891.

JONES, Adrian; Private; 10th Cav. At Ft Bayard, NM, Jul 1888; selected for Department of Arizona rifle competition, Ft Wingate, NM; also selected 1889 and 1890, and ranked second with silver medal, 1890. SOURCE: Billington, *New Mexico's Buffalo Soldiers*, 154.

JONES, Alex; Private; F/9th Cav. At Ft D. A. Russell, WY, in 1910; resident of Huntsville, AL. SOURCE: *Illustrated Review: Ninth Cavalry*, with picture.

JONES, Alexander; 1st Sgt; C/9th Cav. Mentioned Mar 1877 as discharged 4 Oct 1876 and reenlisted as private, D/10th Cavalry, 26 Oct 1876. SOURCE: ES, 10 Cav, 1872–81.

Discharged, end of term, as first sergeant, D/24th Infantry, 4 Oct 1873; entitled to reenlistment pay. SOURCE: AG, USA, to CG, Division of the Missouri, 4 Apr 1877, ES, 10 Cav, 1872–81.

First sergeant, C/9th Cavalry; inspector general says he has justifiable complaint regarding excessive guard and fatigue details, Ft Robinson, NE, Nov 1886. SOURCE:

Report of Inspection, Ft Robinson, 15 Nov 1886, Reports of Inspections, DeptPlatte.

JONES, Alexander; K/25th Inf. In the Philippines, 1900. *See* **WISEMAN**, Turner H., Corporal, K/25th Infantry

JONES, Alfred; E/10th Cav. Original member of 10th Cavalry; in troop when organized, Ft Leavenworth, KS, 15 Jun 1867. SOURCE: McMiller, "Buffalo Soldiers," 72.

JONES, Allen; Corporal; F/10th Cav. Served in 10th Cavalry in Cuba, 1898; died of fever. SOURCE: Cashin, *Under Fire with the Tenth Cavalry*, 343–44.
    Wounded in action, Santiago, Cuba, 1 Jul 1898, SOURCE: SecWar, *AR 1898*, 324.
    Buried Washington Barracks, Washington, DC, 20 Aug 1898. SOURCE: *ANJ* 36 (3 Sep 1898): 10.

JONES, Andrew; Sergeant; H/9th Cav. Born King Co., VA; age 49 in 1895; Ht 5'8"; three years in 38th Infantry; five years in E/24th Infantry; twenty years in H/9th Cavalry; $6 per month additional pay for 25 years' continuous service; character excellent, single. SOURCE: Descriptive Book, H/9 Cav.
    Sergeant since 1 Jan 1881. SOURCE: *ANJ* 32 (8 Jun 1895): 674.
    Sergeant since 17 Jan 1881. SOURCE: Roster, 9 Cav.
    Retires from Ft Robinson, NE, as sergeant, H/9th Cavalry. SOURCE: *ANJ* 34 (22 May 1897): 705.

JONES, Archie; Private; K/9th Cav. At Ft D. A. Russell, WY, in 1910; resident of Huntsville, AL. SOURCE: *Illustrated Review: Ninth Cavalry*, with picture.

JONES, Archie; Master Sgt; K/10th Cav. Began career at Ft Ethan Allen, VT, 1913; wounded in action twice and captured at Carrizal, Mexico, 21 Jun 1916; on release from hospital at Ft Bliss, TX, rejoined troop at Ojo Federico; served at border camps, Naco, Ft Huachuca, AZ, and Philippines; retired 1944 as master sergeant to Tucson, AZ; commander, Veterans of Foreign Wars Post 1717, Tucson, 1946; biographical article in (Tucson) *Arizona Daily Star*, 11 Dec 1965. SOURCE: Wharfield, *10th Cavalry and Border Fights*, 36–37.

JONES, B.; Private; C/9th Cav. At Ft Cummings, NM, 1881; on detached service in field, New Mexico, 30 Jan–3 Feb 1881. SOURCE: Regt Returns, 9 Cav, Feb 1881.

JONES, Benjamin; H/10th Cav. Original member of 10th Cavalry; in troop when organized, Ft Leavenworth, KS, 21 Jul 1867. SOURCE: McMiller, "Buffalo Soldiers," 75.

JONES, Beverly; M/9th Cav. Admitted to Soldiers Home with disability at age 40 with nineteen years and eight months' service, 23 Jan 1888. SOURCE: SecWar, *AR 1888*, 902.

JONES, Buber; Private; H/24th Inf. Fined $5 by summary court, San Isidro, Philippines, for absence from eleven P.M. inspection, 30 Jan 1902, second conviction; fined $1.75 for absence from eleven P.M. bed check, 31 Mar 1902. SOURCE: Register of Summary Court, San Isidro.

JONES, Charles; Private; C/10th Cav. Served in 10th Cavalry, 1898; remained in U.S. during war with Spain. SOURCE: Cashin, *Under Fire with the Tenth Cavalry*, 340.

JONES, Charles; Private; D/25th Inf. Dishonorable discharge, Brownsville. SOURCE: SO 266, AGO, 9 Nov 1906.

JONES, Charles S.; G/10th Cav. Original member of 10th Cavalry; in troop when organized, Ft Leavenworth, KS, 5 Jul 1867. SOURCE: McMiller, "Buffalo Soldiers," 74.

JONES, Crawford; L/9th Cav. $50 per month pension as of 7 Jan 1929; died "with the consoling thought that his widow would now be allowed a pension." SOURCE: *Winners of the West* 6 (Feb 1929): 7.

JONES, Daniel; Private; L/9th Cav. Veteran of Philippine Insurrection; at Ft D. A. Russell, WY, in 1910; marksman; resident of Orange, VA. SOURCE: *Illustrated Review: Ninth Cavalry*, with picture.

JONES, David; Private; E/10th Cav. In hands of civil authorities, Cheyenne, WY, 22 Dec 1902. SOURCE: Regt Returns, 10 Cav, 1902.

JONES, Douglas; M/10th Cav. Original member of 10th Cavalry; in troop when organized, Ft Riley, KS, 15 Oct 1867. SOURCE: McMiller, "Buffalo Soldiers," 79.

JONES, Ed; Private; C/9th Cav. In hands of civil authorities, Salt Lake City, UT, 28 Sep 1888–May 1889. SOURCE: Regt Returns, 9 Cav.

JONES, Edward; Private; 10th Cav. Not yet arrived at Ft Leavenworth, KS, from Jefferson Barracks, MO. SOURCE: Adj, Ft Leavenworth, to HQ, Jefferson Barracks, 9 Oct 1866.

JONES, Edward; Corporal; C/10th Cav. Promoted from private, 6 Dec 1897. SOURCE: *ANJ* 35 (18 Dec 1897): 292.

JONES, Edward; Private; H/10th Cav. Served in 10th Cavalry, 1898; remained in U.S. during war with Spain. SOURCE: Cashin, *Under Fire with the Tenth Cavalry*, 347.

JONES, Edward; Private; 24th Inf. Drowned crossing San Mateo River, Philippines, 21 Aug 1899. SOURCE: Richmond *Planet*, 2 Sep 1899.

JONES, Edward; Private; B/49th Inf. Died in the Philippines, 12 Dec 1900. SOURCE: *ANJ* 38 (29 Dec 1900): 431.

JONES, Edward; Sergeant; A/10th Cav. Son William, fifth child, born to wife Josie (Lee) Jones at Ft Robinson, NE, 20 May 1905. SOURCE: Medical History, Ft Robinson; Monthly Report, Chaplain Anderson, 1 Jun 1905.

JONES, Eldridge T.; Private; D/9th Cav. Killed in action near Ft Lancaster, by Kickapoos, 11 Oct 1867, while escorting Camp Hudson-Ft Stockton, TX, mail along with Corporal Samuel Wright, D/9th Cavalry. SOURCE: Leckie, *The Buffalo Soldiers*, 84–85; Hamilton, "History of the Ninth Cavalry," 7.

See **WRIGHT**, Samuel, Corporal, D/9th Cavalry

JONES, Elsie; Corporal; I/10th Cav. Private, served in 10th Cavalry in Cuba, 1898. SOURCE: Cashin, *Under Fire with the Tenth Cavalry*, 348.

Distinguished himself twice in Cuba; showed "unusual coolness and gallantry," Las Guasimas, 24 Jun 1898; despite only two months in service "behaved like a veteran." SOURCE: SecWar, *AR 1898*, 349; Steward, *The Colored Regulars*, 137.

Mentioned for conspicuous coolness and gallantry under fire, Las Guasimas, 24 Jun 1898; corporal in 1900. SOURCE: GO 15, AGO, 13 Feb 1900.

JONES, Emanuel; F/10th Cav. Original member of 10th Cavalry; in troop when organized, Ft Leavenworth, KS, 21 Jun 1867. SOURCE: McMiller, "Buffalo Soldiers," 73.

Born Frederick, MD; enlisted Harrisburg, PA, 1 May 1867; assigned to F/10th Cavalry, Ft Leavenworth; discharged Ft Sill, Indian Territory, Sep 1870; went to Springfield, OH, in 1872; resided at 618 Wiley Avenue, Springfield, in 1915; thereafter for seven years at National Military Home, Ohio; age 75 in 1922. SOURCE: Affidavit, 1922, VA File SC 11405, John Taylor.

JONES, Ernest; Private; F/25th Inf. Died in the Philippines, 5 Feb 1902; "concussion of Brain from stone held in hands of comrade." SOURCE: *ANJ* 39 (5 Apr 1902): 786.

JONES, Ernest; Private; D/9th Cav. At Ft D. A. Russell, WY, in 1910; resident of Murfreesboro, TN. SOURCE: *Illustrated Review: Ninth Cavalry*.

JONES, Eugene; Private; G/25th Inf. In H/25th Infantry; member of bicycle corps that rode from Ft Missoula, MT, to St. Joseph, MO, and sent back ill; only one of twenty who became sick and was faking, according to 2nd Lt. James A. Moss. SOURCE: *ANJ* 35 (2 Oct 1897): 71.

Wounded in action, El Caney, Cuba, 1 Jul 1898. SOURCE: Nankivell, *History of the Twenty-fifth Infantry*, 83.

JONES, Fielding; Private; Band/9th Cav. With band on detached service at headquarters, District of New Mexico, Santa Fe, 1880; played second alto. SOURCE: Billington, *New Mexico's Buffalo Soldiers*, 226.

JONES, Frank; Private; K/10th Cav. At Ft Robinson, NE, 1904.

JONES, Frank; Private; B/25th Inf. Dishonorable discharge, Brownsville. SOURCE: SO 266, AGO, 9 Nov 1906.

JONES, Frank H.; Private; E/24th Inf. Transferred from Reserve Divisional Hospital, Siboney, Cuba, to U.S. on U.S. Army Transport *Santiago* with acute dysentery, 25 Jul 1898. SOURCE: Hospital Papers, Spanish-American War.

JONES, G.; Private; B/10th Cav. At Ft Apache, AZ, 1890, subscribed $.50 to testimonial to General Grierson. SOURCE: List of subscriptions, 23 Apr 1890, 10th Cavalry papers, MHI.

JONES, G. M.; Private; Band/10th Cav. Served in 10th Cavalry in Cuba, 1898. SOURCE: Cashin, *Under Fire with the Tenth Cavalry*, 359.

JONES, George; M/10th Cav. Original member of 10th Cavalry; in troop when organized, Ft Riley, KS, 15 Oct 1867. SOURCE: McMiller, "Buffalo Soldiers," 79.

JONES, George; Sergeant; Band/24th Inf. Born Carroll Co., MD; Ht 5'11", yellow complexion, black hair and eyes; enlisted, age 20, Baltimore, MD, Jul 1888; served in E/25th Infantry and A and F/24th Infantry, before joining band; corporal 11 Jul 1892; sergeant 26 Feb 1893; fined $2 by garrison court martial, 1893; single; discharged, end of term, character excellent, Ft Bayard, NM, 4 Jul 1893, with $72 retained and $8.43 clothing. SOURCE: Descriptive Book, 24 Inf NCS & Band.

JONES, George; Private; I/24th Inf. Enlisted Baltimore, MD, 26 Jul 1898; on special duty as teamster, 24 Feb 1899. SOURCE: Muster Roll, I/24 Inf, Jan–Feb 1899.

Fined one month's pay by summary court, 8 Aug 1899; in confinement since 14 Aug 1899. SOURCE: Muster Roll, I/24 Inf, Jul–Aug 1899.

Discharged, character good, with $10 deposits and $9.71 clothing, 31 Dec 1899. SOURCE: Muster Roll, I/24 Inf, Nov–Dec 1899.

JONES, George; Private; E/10th Cav. Convicted of conduct prejudicial to good order and discipline, Iloilo, Panay, Philippines; sentenced to dishonorable discharge and five years. SOURCE: Manila *Times*, 20 Mar 1902.

JONES, George; Private; M/9th Cav. At Ft D. A. Russell, WY, in 1910; sharpshooter; resident of Madison, IN. SOURCE: *Illustrated Review: Ninth Cavalry*, with picture.

JONES, George F.; Private; F/9th Cav. Fined $3 by garrison court martial for disobeying Cook William H. Perrin, K/9th Cavalry, while on kitchen police, Ft Robinson, NE, 20 Nov 1887. SOURCE: Order 241, 6 Dec 1887, Post Orders, Ft Robinson.

In hands of civil authorities, Crawford, NE, 5–9 Jun 1889. SOURCE: Regt Returns, 9 Cav, Jun1889.

JONES, George W.; Private; L/10th Cav. Served in 10th Cavalry, 1898; remained in U.S. during war with Spain. SOURCE: Cashin, *Under Fire with the Tenth Cavalry*, 351.

JONES, George W.; Private; C/10th Cav. Died of pyemia, Bayamo, Cuba, 13 Jun 1901. SOURCE: *ANJ* 38 (29 Jun 1901): 1073.

JONES, H. M.; Private; L/10th Cav. Served in 10th Cavalry, 1898; remained in U.S. during war with Spain. SOURCE: Cashin, *Under Fire with the Tenth Cavalry*, 351.

JONES, Harry R.; Private; K/10th Cav. Served in 10th Cavalry, 1898; remained in U.S. during war with Spain. SOURCE: Cashin, *Under Fire with the Tenth Cavalry*, 349.

JONES, Henry; E/10th Cav. Original member of 10th Cavalry; in troop when organized, Ft Leavenworth, KS, 15 Jun 1867. SOURCE: McMiller, "Buffalo Soldiers," 72.

JONES, Henry; I/10th Cav. Original member of 10th Cavalry; in troop when organized, Ft Riley, KS, 15 Aug 1867. SOURCE: McMiller, "Buffalo Soldiers," 76.

JONES, Henry; Private; B/10th Cav. Mentioned May 1875 as having deserted 11 Sep 1874. SOURCE: ES, 10 Cav, 1872–81.

JONES, Henry; Recruit; 10th Cav. Late unassigned recruit, 10th Cavalry, died at Ft Concho, TX, 14 Apr 1876. SOURCE: CO, 10 Cav, to AG, USA, 21 Apr 1876, ES, 10 Cav, 1872–81.

JONES, Henry; Recruit; Colored Detachment/ Mounted Service. Convicted by general court martial, Jefferson Barracks, MO, of disposing of greatcoat valued at $12.36 issued to him, 8 Dec 1882; sentenced to one month's confinement and fined $6.18 per month for two months. SOURCE: GCMO 7, AGO, 16 Jan 1883.

JONES, Henry; Private; B/25th Inf. Dishonorable discharge, Brownsville. SOURCE: SO 266, AGO, 9 Nov 1906.

JONES, Henry C.; Private; Band/10th Cav. Born Montgomery Co., TX; Ht 5'9", brown eyes and black hair, dark brown complexion; discharged from Band/10th Cavalry, 2 Apr 1895; fourth enlistment in B/25th Infantry, Ft Missoula, MT, 2 Jun 1895. SOURCE: Misc Records, 25 Inf.

Transferred from E/10th Cavalry, to Hospital Corps, Ft Grant, AZ. SOURCE: *ANJ* 25 (10 Dec 1887): 382.

In E/10th Cavalry, at Ft Apache, AZ, 1890, subscribed $.50 to testimonial to General Grierson. SOURCE: List of subscriptions, 23 Apr 1890, 10th Cavalry papers, MHI.

Served in Band/10th Cavalry in Cuba, 1898. SOURCE: Cashin, *Under Fire with the Tenth Cavalry*, 359.

JONES, Hezekiah; Private; M/49th Inf. Engaged against enemy, Tuao, Cagayan, Philippines, 18 Oct 1900. SOURCE: *ANJ* 38 (11 May 1901): 901.

JONES, Horatio F. M.; I/10th Cav. Mentioned as Indian War survivor. SOURCE: *Winners of the West* 3 (Jun 1926): 7.

JONES, Ira; Private; E/24th Inf. Drowned near Mount Arayat, Philippines, 15 Oct 1899, while trying to swim with comrade after a carabao. SOURCE: Manila *Times*, 19 Oct 1899.

JONES, Isaac L.; Private; K/9th Cav. At Ft D. A. Russell, WY, in 1910; sharpshooter; resident of Beaver Falls, PA. SOURCE: *Illustrated Review: Ninth Cavalry*, with picture.

JONES, J. H.; Private; L/9th Cav. On detached service in the field, New Mexico, 21 Jan–24 Feb 1881. SOURCE: Regt Returns, 9 Cav, Feb 1881.

JONES, J. H.; Private; D/25th Inf. Among first in El Caney blockhouse, Cuba, 1898. SOURCE: SecWar, *AR 1898*, 387.

Mentioned for bravery at El Caney in general orders, 11 Aug 1898. SOURCE: Cashin, *Under Fire with the Tenth Cavalry*, 144.

JONES, Jack; Sergeant; Band/24th Inf. Sergeant, C/25th Infantry, Ft Sill, Indian Territory, reduced to private, fined $10, confined for one month for refusal to obey legal order of first sergeant. SOURCE: *ANJ* 25 (21 Jan 1888): 506.

Enlisted San Carlos, AZ, 5 Aug 1890; Ht 6'0", yellow complexion; joined Band/24th Infantry, Jul 1893, Ft Bayard, NM; has had smallpox; discharged, end of term, character very good, single, Ft Bayard, 4 Aug 1895; additional pay $4 per month, retained $60, clothing $6. SOURCE: Descriptive Book, 24 Inf NCS & Band.

Sergeant, C/24th Infantry, to proceed to Ft Bayard, 1 Jul 1893, to report to commander, 24th Infantry. SOURCE: Order 97, Ft Huachuca, AZ, 1 Jul 1893, Name File, 24 Inf.

Sergeant, Band/24th Infantry, transferred from Reserve Divisional Hospital, Siboney, Cuba, to U.S. on U.S. Army Transport *Vigilancia*, 6 Sep 1898, with remittent malarial fever. SOURCE: Hospital Papers, Spanish-American War.

Retires from Ft Douglas, UT, Jun 1899. SOURCE: *ANJ* 36 (14 Jan 1899): 471.

JONES, Jacob; 25th Inf. Fined $25 at Missoula, MT, Dec 1889, for assault on Lizzie Maroney of "notorious 'four-mile' house." SOURCE: Fowler, *The Black Infantry*, 68.

JONES, James; Private; C/10th Cav. Also served in I/24th Infantry; died in Philadelphia, PA. SOURCE: *Winners of the West* 8 (Feb 1931): 10.

JONES, James; Private; E/25th Inf. Acquitted of stealing money from comrade, 1879. SOURCE: Report of Trials, Department of Texas, 1878–79.

JONES, James; Private; G/9th Cav. On detached service at Ft Stanton, NM, 29 Jan–5 Feb 1881. SOURCE: Regt Returns, 9 Cav, Feb 1881.

JONES, James; C/25th Inf. Died of consumption, U.S. Soldiers Home, 24 Sep 1894. SOURCE: SecWar, *AR 1894*, 526.

JONES, James; Private; L/10th Cav. Recruit, Colored Detachment, Mounted Service, at Jefferson Barracks, MO, 1889. *See* **HUNTER**, Ellis, Recruit, Colored Detachment/Mounted Service

Born in Virginia; private, H/10th Cavalry, 10 Jul 1889–9 Oct 1892; private, I/10th Cavalry, 7 Nov 1894; wagoner, 16 Jan 1895; corporal, 21 Feb 1897; at Ft Assiniboine, MT, 1897. SOURCE: Baker, Roster.

Served in 10th Cavalry, 1898; remained in U.S. during war with Spain. SOURCE: Cashin, *Under Fire with the Tenth Cavalry*, 351.

JONES, James W.; G/24th Inf. Admitted to Soldiers Home with disability at age 54 with five years and one month's service, 14 Feb 1891. SOURCE: SecWar, *AR 1891*, 752.

JONES, Jasper; Private; F/9th Cav. Discharged on surgeon's certificate with syphilis from Ft Robinson, NE, 4 May 1887. SOURCE: Certificates of Disability, Ft Robinson.

JONES, Jefferson; Private; D/10th Cav. Served in 10th Cavalry in Cuba, 1898. SOURCE: Cashin, *Under Fire with the Tenth Cavalry*, 341.

JONES, Jefferson; Horseshoer; M/9th Cav. Veteran of Spanish-American War; at Ft D. A. Russell, WY, in 1910; resident of St. Louis. SOURCE: *Illustrated Review: Ninth Cavalry.*

JONES, Jeremiah; Ord Sgt; U.S. Army. Born Charles Co., MD, 18 Oct 1861; Ht 5'7", black complexion; private, corporal, sergeant, sergeant major, 9th Cavalry, 22 Jan 1881–21 Jan 1896; had syphilis, 1881; served as ordnance sergeant at Ft Huachuca, AZ, Jefferson Barracks, MO, Ft Logan, CO; died of pneumonia, while on active duty as ordnance sergeant, Ft Logan, 20 Mar 1906; married Annie L. Brown at 431 8th Street, SW, Washington, DC; widow resided at 1812 11th St., NW, Washington, until 1906, then moved to 431 8th Street, SW. SOURCE: VA File WC 611769, Jeremiah Jones.

See **JEFFERDS**, Wesley, Sergeant, A/9th Cavalry

Date of rank as regimental sergeant major, 9th Cavalry, 12 Feb 1885. SOURCE: *ANJ* 25 (18 Feb 1888): 586; Roster, 9 Cav.

Deposited $450 with paymaster, Ft McKinney, WY, 21 Jan 1886. SOURCE: CO, 9 Cav, to Paymaster General, USA, 15 Feb 1886, LS, 9 Cav.

Senior man on Ft Robinson, NE, canteen committee of nine noncommissioned officers, five of whom are in 9th Cavalry, others 8th Infantry, appointed to make recommendations to canteen council. SOURCE: Order 136, 1 Jul 1890, Post Orders, Ft Robinson.

With regiment on practice march from Ft Robinson, Aug 1890.

Authorized six-month furlough by Special Order 108, Division of the Missouri, 26 Dec 1890. SOURCE: *ANJ* 28 (3 Jan 1891): 312.

Furlough revoked by telegram, Adjutant General's Office, 8 Apr 1891.

Acts as chief clerk and is so busy attending to proper classification and administrative details that he has little time for clerical work; forced with adjutant to work far into night, far more than regular hours. SOURCE: CO, Ft Robinson, to AAG, DP, 5 May 1892, LS, Ft Robinson.

On expedition from Ft Robinson to Butte, MT, and back, under Lt. Col. Reuben Bernard, 18–31 Jul 1894.

Managed church benefit concerts for Chaplain Plummer, also sang; shared duplex on old post with QM Sgt. Simon Harris, 9th Cavalry. SOURCE: Investigation of Charges against Chaplain Plummer.

Examined for ordnance sergeant, Ft Robinson, Nov 1895. SOURCE: *ANJ* 33 (16 Nov 1895): 179.

Reenlisted at Ft Robinson, 22 Jan 1896. SOURCE: *ANJ* 33 (1 Feb 1896): 388.

Appointed ordnance sergeant as of 22 Jun 1897; departed Ft Robinson 24 Jun 1897, for duty at Whipple Barracks, AZ. SOURCE: SO 80, 23 Jul 1897, Post Orders, Ft Robinson.

JONES, Jesse; Private; G/24th Inf. Killed in action, Tulavero, Philippines, 28 Dec 1899. SOURCE: Muller, *The Twenty Fourth Infantry*, 36.

JONES, John; E/10th Cav. Original member of 10th Cavalry; in troop when organized, Ft Leavenworth, KS, 15 Jun 1867. SOURCE: McMiller, "Buffalo Soldiers," 72.

JONES, John; I/10th Cav. Original member of 10th Cavalry; in troop when organized, Ft Riley, KS, 15 Aug 1867. SOURCE: McMiller, "Buffalo Soldiers," 76.

JONES, John; Private; 38th Inf. Tried by court martial, Ft Cummings, NM, 1869. SOURCE: Billington, *New Mexico's Buffalo Soldiers*, 37.

JONES, John; Private; K/10th Cav. Died spring 1870. SOURCE: ES, 10 Cav, 1866–71.

JONES, John; Private; K/38th Inf. Renews subscription; wants to hear from old boys. SOURCE: *Winners of the West* 7 (Feb 1930): 3.

Died El Paso, TX. SOURCE: *Winners of the West* 8 (Feb 1931): 10.

JONES, John A.; Private; H/9th Cav. Wife buried at Ft Robinson, NE, 25 Nov 1897. SOURCE: List of Interments, Ft Robinson.

JONES, John A.; Wagoner; E/9th Cav. Veteran of Spanish-American War and Philippine Insurrection; at Ft D. A. Russell, WY, in 1910; resident of Baltimore. SOURCE: *Illustrated Review: Ninth Cavalry*, with picture.

JONES, John M.; Private; E/25th Inf. Died of nephritis in the Philippines, 19 Nov 1900. SOURCE: *ANJ* 38 (1 Dec 1900): 331.

JONES, John P.; Private; K/9th Cav. At Ft D. A. Russell, WY, in 1910; resident of Macon, GA. SOURCE: *Illustrated Review: Ninth Cavalry*, with picture.

JONES, John R.; Private; D/25th Inf. Dishonorable discharge, Brownsville. SOURCE: SO 266, AGO, 9 Nov 1906.

JONES, John S.; L/10th Cav. Original member of 10th Cavalry; in troop when organized, Ft Riley, KS, 21 Sep 1867. SOURCE: McMiller, "Buffalo Soldiers," 78.

JONES, Joseph; Private; D/25th Inf. Dishonorable discharge, Brownsville. SOURCE: SO 266, AGO, 9 Nov 1906.

JONES, Joseph L.; QM Sgt; 24th Inf. Commissioned second lieutenant, 9th Volunteer Infantry, after Spanish-American War. SOURCE: Cashin, *Under Fire with the Tenth Cavalry*, 360.

JONES, Lee A.; Private; A/10th Cav. Served in 10th Cavalry, 1898; remained in U.S. during war with Spain. SOURCE: Cashin, *Under Fire with the Tenth Cavalry*, 337.

JONES, Leon; 1st Sgt; D/25th Inf. Retired from Ft Sam Houston, TX, Jul 1900. SOURCE: *ANJ* 37 (21 Jul 1900): 1119.

JONES, Leroy C.; Private; H/48th Inf. Died of variola in the Philippines, 21 Jun 1900. SOURCE: *ANJ* 37 (7 Jul 1900): 1071.

JONES, Lewis; Cook; M/9th Cav. Private, D/9th Cavalry, charges against him forwarded to Ft Robinson, NE, from Ft Washakie, WY, in accordance with letter, Department of the Platte, 23 Oct 1895.

Confined for trial at Ft Robinson, 4 Nov 1895; released to station at Ft Washakie, 7 Dec 1895.

Member of committee which presented departure gift to Maj. John Loud, former commander, on his promotion; others on committee 1st Sgt. George Tracy and Post Sgt. Maj. William Williams. SOURCE: *ANJ* 35 (4 Sep 1897): 5.

Veteran of Indian wars, Spanish-American War, and Philippine Insurrection; cook, M/9th Cavalry, at Ft D. A. Russell, WY, in 1910. SOURCE: *Illustrated Review: Ninth Cavalry*, with picture.

JONES, Lewis; Private; L/10th Cav. General court martial trial in accordance with Special Order 101, Department of the Missouri, 1 Jun 1904.

Sentence mitigated by Special Order 128, Department of the Missouri, 12 Jul 1904.

Discharged by Special Order 160, Department of the Missouri, 24 Aug 1904.

JONES, Manuel; H/10th Cav. Original member of 10th Cavalry; in troop when organized, Ft Leavenworth, KS, 21 Jul 1867. SOURCE: McMiller, "Buffalo Soldiers," 75.

JONES, Maurice; Private; H/24th Inf. On special duty at post exchange, Ft Huachuca, AZ, 24 Jul–16 Aug and 21 Sep–6 Oct 1893. SOURCE: Name File, 24 Inf.

JONES, Mitchell; H/10th Cav. Original member of 10th Cavalry; in troop when organized, Ft Leavenworth, KS, 21 Jul 1867. SOURCE: McMiller, "Buffalo Soldiers," 75.

JONES, Moses H. Graduate of Howard University; worked in Charleston, WV, law office before Spanish-American War; then in law office in Dayton, OH; died in Dayton, 1924. SOURCE: *Crisis* 27 (Apr 1924): 267.

JONES, Nathan; Private; F/9th Cav. Killed in action by Indians, Eagle Springs, TX, 100 miles from Ft Davis, TX, while escorting mail, 5 Dec 1867. SOURCE: Hamilton, "History of the Ninth Cavalry," 7; *Illustrated Review: Ninth Cavalry*; Ninth Cavalry, *Historical and Pictorial Review*, 45.

JONES, Nathan; 1st Sgt; L/9th Cav. Distinguished marksman, as private, L/9th Cavalry; Department of Colorado gold medal and Army silver medal, 1903. SOURCE: GO 11, AGO, 27 Jan 1905.

Stationed near Yosemite Park, CA; won gold medal in pistol competition, Prescott, AZ, for Departments of Colorado, Utah, Columbia; scored 287 of 300 and beat 56 competitors. SOURCE: Cleveland *Gazette*, 12 Sep 1903; SecWar, *AR 1903*, 1:427.

Ranked number three, Pacific Division pistol team, Ord Barracks, CA, 1904. SOURCE: GO 167, AGO, 28 Oct 1904.

Division of the Pacific bronze medal as corporal, L/9th Cavalry, 1904. SOURCE: GO 11, AGO, 27 Jan 1905.

Distinguished pistol shot, 1905. SOURCE: GO 173, AGO, 20 Oct 1905.

Distinguished marksman and veteran of Philippine Insurrection; first sergeant, L/9th Cavalry, at Ft D. A. Russell, WY, in 1910; sharpshooter; resident of Macon, GA. SOURCE: *Illustrated Review: Ninth Cavalry*, with picture.

JONES, Nelson; Saddler; E/10th Cav. Recently died, Oct 1870. SOURCE: ES, 10 Cav, 1866–71.

JONES, Palmer; B/25th Inf. Out of Army; running canteens at Subig and Castillejos, Philippines, Dec 1900. SOURCE: Richmond *Planet*, 16 Feb 1901.

JONES, Patrick J.; Private; K/24th Inf. At San Carlos, AZ, 1890. *See* **HARDEE**, James A., Private, K/24th Infantry

Admitted to Soldiers Home with disability at age 39 with fourteen years and seven months' service, 19 Sep 1891. SOURCE: SecWar, *AR 1891*, 754.

JONES, Paul; Musician; F/24th Inf. Wounded in action in Cuba, 1898. SOURCE: Muller, *The Twenty Fourth Infantry*, 18.

JONES, Philip; Corporal; H/10th Cav. Born in Virginia; private, M/10th Cavalry, 27 Sep 1867–27 Sep 1872; private, corporal, sergeant, 5 Oct 1874–4 Oct 1882; private, corporal, sergeant, D/10th Cavalry, 5 Oct 1882–4 Oct 1892; private, 11 Oct 1892; sergeant, 12 Oct 1892; private, H/10th Cavalry, 1 Sep 1896; corporal, 3 Sep 1896; at Ft Assiniboine, MT, 1897. SOURCE: Baker, Roster.

Original member of 10th Cavalry; in troop when organized, Ft Riley, KS, 15 Oct 1867. SOURCE: McMiller, "Buffalo Soldiers," 79.

An original member of M Troop; involved in his first Indian fight around Ft Sill, Indian Territory, under 2nd Lt. William R. Harman, defending beef, wood, and hay contractors with employees; participated in arrest of Satanta and Satank, Ft Sill, Apr 1871; performed much duty as courier between Indian Territory and Texas post in early days. SOURCE: Baker, Roster.

Sergeant, D/10th Cavalry, at Ft Apache, AZ, 1890, subscribed $.50 to testimonial to General Grierson. SOURCE: List of subscriptions, 23 Apr 1890, 10th Cavalry papers, MHI.

Retired from Ft Assiniboine and moved to Havre, MT, 28 Nov 1897. SOURCE: *ANJ* 36 (13 Nov 1897): 192; Indianapolis *Freeman*, 11 Dec 1897.

JONES, Richard; Private; I/9th Cav. On extra duty with Quartermaster Department, 1881. SOURCE: Billington, *New Mexico's Buffalo Soldiers*, 200.

JONES, Richard; Corporal; K/10th Cav. At Ft Robinson, NE, 1904.

JONES, Robert; F/10th Cav. Original member of 10th Cavalry; in troop when organized, Ft Leavenworth, KS, 21 Jun 1867. SOURCE: McMiller, "Buffalo Soldiers," 73.

JONES, Robert; D/24th Inf. Served 1884–89; subscriber, age 75. SOURCE: *Winners of the West* 10 (Jan 1933): 3.

Broke into room of Lizzy McCarthy, domestic servant of post surgeon, Ft Bayard, NM, Dec 1888. SOURCE: Billington, *New Mexico's Buffalo Soldiers*, 165.

JONES, Robert; Private; C/24th Inf. Recommended by commander for duty in ice factory, Ft Huachuca, AZ, Apr 1893. SOURCE: Name File, 24 Inf.

JONES, Robert H.; Private; L/10th Cav. Original member of 10th Cavalry; in troop when organized, Ft Riley, KS, 21 Sep 1867. SOURCE: McMiller, "Buffalo Soldiers," 78.

Mentioned Apr 1873 as apprehended from desertion. SOURCE: ES, 10 Cav, 1872–81.

JONES, Robert R.; Corporal; 24th Inf. Sentenced to ten years for part in Houston riot. SOURCE: Cleveland *Gazette*, 5 Jan 1918.

JONES, Samuel; Private; K/10th Cav. Original member of 10th Cavalry; in troop when organized, Ft Riley, KS, 1 Sep 1867. SOURCE: McMiller, "Buffalo Soldiers," 77.

Prisoner sentenced in accordance with General Court Martial Orders 143 and 145, Department of the Missouri, to be sent to headquarters under guard for imprisonment at penitentiary, Jefferson City, MO, Sep 1868. SOURCE: LR, Det 10 Cav, 1868–69.

JONES, Samuel E.; Corporal; C/9th Cav. Appointed corporal as of 8 Sep 1892. SOURCE: Roster, 9 Cav.

Resigned as corporal, Ft Robinson, NE, 1 Jun 1894. SOURCE: *ANJ* 31 (16 Jun 1894): 735.

JONES, Samuel M.; Private; C/10th Cav. Served in 10th Cavalry in Cuba, 1898. SOURCE: Cashin, *Under Fire with the Tenth Cavalry*, 340.

JONES, Seth; A/9th Cav. In I/9th Cavalry; clothing destroyed when fighting fire, Ft Wingate, NM, 15 Dec 1876. SOURCE: Billington, *New Mexico's Buffalo Soldiers*, 110.

Married Fannie Butler, 1912; divorced her, 1919; she then married Alex Stepney, also late of 9th Cavalry. SOURCE: VA File SC 874522, Alex Stepney.

JONES, Sherman; Private; I/9th Cav. At Ft D. A. Russell, WY, in 1910; resident of Madison Co., KY. SOURCE: *Illustrated Review: Ninth Cavalry*, with picture.

JONES, Silas; Trumpeter; H/10th Cav. Original member of 10th Cavalry; in troop when organized, Ft Leavenworth, KS, 21 Jul 1867. SOURCE: McMiller, "Buffalo Soldiers," 75.

In H/10th Cavalry since it was organized; honorable mention for service rendered in capture of Mangas and his Apache band, Rio Bonito, AZ, 18 Oct 1886. SOURCE: Baker, Roster.

Retires from Ft Assiniboine, MT. SOURCE: *ANJ* 34 (7 Aug 1897): 909.

JONES, Stephen; Recruit; 25th Inf. Convicted by general court martial, Jefferson Barracks, MO, of conduct prejudicial to good order and discipline; while en route to regiment by train, he tried to engage Recruit Frank Banks, 25th Infantry, in fight; when sent to other part of car, he made unprovoked attack on Recruits George H. Malborne,

Lewis Penny, Henry Maitland, 25th Infantry; after separated from them, he took out razor, and when ordered by Sgt. James Condon, Company B of Instruction, General Service Recruits, to give it up, said, "I will kill some of them damn yellow niggers before I get to Chicago; yes, if I swing for it, I have it in for them"; made second attack on Maitland, Penny, Malborne and had to be restrained by conductor, brakeman, passengers; when train reached Philadelphia, PA, he made third attack on Penny and Maitland with jackknife; cut conductor when being turned over to police in Philadelphia; all on Pennsylvania Railroad, 27 May 1884; sentenced to dishonorable discharge. SOURCE: GCMO 32, AGO, 2 Aug 1884.

JONES, Thomas; Private; M and G/10th Cav. Served 1887–92; wants to hear from former comrades. SOURCE: *Winners of the West* 8 (Feb 1931): 10.

JONES, Thomas; Corporal; K/25th Inf. At Castillejos, Philippines, 1900. *See* **WISEMAN**, Turner H., Corporal, K/25th Infantry

JONES, Thomas H.; Private; C/9th Cav. Enlisted Ft McKinney, WY, 18 Apr 1894.

Application for transfer disapproved by letter, Department of the Platte, 24 Aug 1895.

JONES, Thomas P.; Corporal; K/25th Inf. Born Memphis, TN; died in Minnesota, 23 Feb 1948. SOURCE: Taylor, "Minnesota Black Spanish-American War Veterans."

JONES, Wallace; A/10th Cav. Original member of 10th Cavalry; in troop when organized, Ft Leavenworth, KS, 18 Feb 1867. SOURCE: McMiller, "Buffalo Soldiers," 68.

JONES, Walter S.; Corporal; H/10th Cav. Private, served in 10th Cavalry, 1898; remained in U.S. during war with Spain. SOURCE: Cashin, *Under Fire with the Tenth Cavalry*, 347.

Promoted to corporal. SOURCE: Special Order 35, 10 Cav, Ft Sam Houston, TX, 1 Apr 1899, Special Orders, 10 Cav.

JONES, Wesley; Sergeant; I/10th Cav. Private, served in 10th Cavalry in Cuba, 1898. SOURCE: Cashin, *Under Fire with the Tenth Cavalry*, 348.

Wounded in hand, Las Guasimas, Cuba, 24 Jun 1898, but remained in fight. SOURCE: SecWar, *AR 1898*, 324, 349.

Corporal, released to duty from treatment for secondary syphilis, Ft Robinson, NE, 16 Sep 1903. SOURCE: Post Surgeon to CO, I/10 Cav, 16 Sep 1903, LS, Post Surgeon, Ft Robinson.

Spent five months and three days in Ft Robinson hospital with syphilis; sergeant, released to duty from treatment for secondary syphilis, Ft Robinson, 31 Dec 1903. SOURCE: Post Surgeon to CO, I/10, 31 Dec 1903, LS, Post Surgeon, Ft Robinson.

Paid $5 fine and $4.80 costs for assault on complaint of Maggie Patrick, Crawford, NE, 28 May 1904. SOURCE: Police Court Docket, Crawford.

Sergeant, in hands of civil authorities, Crawford, 29–31 May 1904. SOURCE: Regt Returns, 9 Cav, May 1904.

JONES, William; A/10th Cav. Deserted from Ft Leavenworth, KS, 24 Mar 1867. SOURCE: McMiller, "Buffalo Soldiers," 53.

JONES, William; C/10th Cav. Original member of 10th Cavalry; in troop when organized, Ft Leavenworth, KS, 14 May 1867. SOURCE: McMiller, "Buffalo Soldiers," 70.

JONES, William; Private; D/9th Cav. In I/9th Cavalry; cited for gallantry against Victorio, Nov 1879, by Maj. Albert P. Morrow. SOURCE: Billington, "Black Cavalrymen," 68; Billington, *New Mexico's Buffalo Soldiers*, 93.

Killed in action by Indians, Canada, NM, while on escort duty, 27 Jan 1881. SOURCE: Regt Return, 9 Cav, Jan 1881; Hamilton, "History of the Ninth Cavalry," 58; *Illustrated Review: Ninth Cavalry.*

JONES, William; Private; A/9th Cav. Unassigned, arrived at Ft Robinson, NE, 26 May 1891; assigned to A/9th Cavalry, 3 Jan 1891.

JONES, William; Corporal; B/9th Cav. Promoted from private, Ft Duchesne, UT, Jun 1895. SOURCE: *ANJ* 32 (22 Jun 1895): 706.

JONES, William; Private; 9th Cav. To be tried by general court martial, Ft Duchesne, UT. SOURCE: *ANJ* 35 (25 Dec 1897): 310.

JONES, William; Private; M/10th Cav. Served in 10th Cavalry, 1898; remained in U.S. during war with Spain. SOURCE: Cashin, *Under Fire with the Tenth Cavalry*, 351.

JONES, William; Private; C/24th Inf. Died of malaria in the Philippines, 29 Dec 1901. SOURCE: *ANJ* 39 (5 Apr 1902): 786.

JONES, William; Private; F/9th Cav. At Ft D. A. Russell, WY, in 1910; resident of Mt. Sterling, KY. SOURCE: *Illustrated Review: Ninth Cavalry*, with picture.

JONES, William E.; Private; D/25th Inf. Dishonorable discharge, Brownsville. SOURCE: SO 266, AGO, 9 Nov 1906.

JONES, William H.; E/10th Cav. Original member of 10th Cavalry; in troop when organized, Ft Leavenworth, KS, 15 Jun 1867. SOURCE: McMiller, "Buffalo Soldiers," 72.

JONES, William M.; Private; B/10th Cav. Served in 10th Cavalry, 1898; remained in U.S. during war with

Spain. SOURCE: Cashin, *Under Fire with the Tenth Cavalry*, 339.

JONES, William R.; Private; D/25th Inf. Dishonorable discharge, Brownsville. SOURCE: SO 266, AGO, 9 Nov 1906.

JONES, William S.; 1st Sgt; I/9th Cav. Private, K/9th Cavalry, at Ft Robinson, NE, 1886.

Veteran of Philippine Insurrection; first sergeant, I/9th Cavalry, at Ft D. A. Russell, WY, in 1910; sharpshooter; resident of St. Louis. SOURCE: *Illustrated Review: Ninth Cavalry*, with picture.

See **DILLARD**, C. D., Private, K/9th Cavalry

JORDAN, Acey; Private; A/25th Inf. Ranked number 162 among rifle experts with 69 percent, 1904. SOURCE: GO 79, AGO, 1 Jul 1905.

JORDAN, Andrew; Recruit; Colored Detachment/Mounted Service. Convicted by general court martial, Columbus Barracks, OH, of desertion, 24 Feb–22 Aug 1882; sentenced to six months' confinement and fined $10 per month for six months; leniency due to "evident ignorance of the accused." SOURCE: GCMO 61, AGO, 12 Sep 1882.

JORDAN, Charles; Private; A/10th Cav. Deserted from Ft Robinson, NE, Oct 1902. SOURCE: Certificate, Capt. W. H. Hay, 10th Cav, 15 Jan 1903, 10th Cavalry papers, MHI.

JORDAN, David; Sergeant; A/25th Inf. Retired from Ft Bliss, TX, Jun 1900. SOURCE: *ANJ* 37 (14 Jul 1900): 1087.

JORDAN, Edward; Private; D/25th Inf. Dishonorable discharge, Brownsville. SOURCE: SO 266, AGO, 9 Nov 1906.

JORDAN, George; 1st Sgt; K/9th Cav. Born Williamson Co., KY; enlisted, age 19, Nashville, TN, 25 Dec 1866; occupation farmer, Ht 5'4", black complexion. SOURCE: Register of Enlistments, 1866.

Second enlistment, Ft Davis, TX, 3 Jan 1870, as corporal. SOURCE: Register of Enlistments, 1870.

Third enlistment, Ft Griffin, TX, 3 Jan 1875, as corporal. SOURCE: Register of Enlistments, 1875.

Fourth enlistment, Farmington, NM, 3 Jan 1880, as sergeant; discharged, Ft Supply, Indian Territory, 2 Jan 1880, character good. SOURCE: Register of Enlistments, 1880.

Won Medal of Honor for organizing and directing defense of civilian settlement at old Ft Tularosa, NM, against Victorio. SOURCE: Leckie, *The Buffalo Soldiers*, 221.

Rifleman with "sure finger and keen eyesight," commanded detachment of 25 that repulsed 100 Apaches, 14 May 1880, old Ft Tularosa; with 19 men forced Apaches back

in Carrizo Canyon, 12 Aug 1881; [erroneously states] Jordan retired to U.S. Soldiers Home, Washington, DC. SOURCE: Lee, *Negro Medal of Honor Men*, 70–71; Billington, *New Mexico's Buffalo Soldiers*, 95–96, 105.

Heroism Aug 1881 mentioned. SOURCE: Carroll, *The Black Military Experience*, 378.

Commended by post commander, Ft Robinson, NE, for role in capture of escapee, 24 Jan 1887. SOURCE: CO, Ft Robinson, to CO, K/9 Cav, 24 Jan 1887, LS, Ft Robinson.

Fifth enlistment, Ft Supply, 3 Jan 1885, as first sergeant; discharged, Ft Robinson, 2 Jan 1890, character very good. SOURCE: Register of Enlistments, 1885.

Sixth enlistment, Ft Robinson, 3 Jan 1890; discharged 2 Jan 1895, character excellent. SOURCE: Register of Enlistments, 1890.

Award of Medal of Honor published in Order 23, 9th Cavalry, 4 Jan 1890.

President, Diamond Club, K/9th Cavalry, Ft Robinson. SOURCE: *ANJ* 28 (2 May 1891): 620.

First sergeant, K/9th Cavalry, since 20 Jul 1896. SOURCE: Roster, 9 Cav.

Retires from Ft Robinson in accordance with Special Order 73, Adjutant General's Office, 30 Mar 1897.

Affidavit, from Crawford, NE, 13 Dec 1898. SOURCE: VA File XC 2648848, Rufus Slaughter.

Assessed value of personal property, 1902, was $11.

Died in Crawford 24 Oct 1904; thirty-year veteran, at Ft Robinson 1885–98; retired and lived in Crawford; buried with military honors, Ft Robinson. SOURCE: Crawford *Tribune*, 28 Oct 1904.

Funeral, Ft Robinson, 26 Oct 1904, attended by entire command; died preceding day; according to Dr. J. H. Hartwell of Crawford, "First Sergt. George Jordan, retired, died for the want of proper attention. He lived alone and had no one to attend to his wants. The Doctor made two applications for his admittance into Fort Robinson Hospital and was refused." SOURCE: Monthly Report, Chaplain Anderson, 1 Nov 1904.

Jordan applied for admission to hospital when Col. Jacob Augur was absent; hospital did not have facilities and Jordan was not destitute; he was advised to go to Soldiers Home but said he could not due to business at Crawford. SOURCE: Endorsement, Colonel Augur, to Monthly Report, Chaplain Anderson, 1 Nov 1904.

Surgeon General states that retiree has no right to treatment in military hospitals; privilege may be granted on decision of commander with advice of surgeon based on situation; "at the same time, surgeons should be careful to show all practicable consideration towards retired soldiers, especially when their records and services are as excellent as were those of 1st Sergeant Geroge Jordan, Retired." SOURCE: Endorsement, Surgeon General, to Monthly Report, Chaplain Anderson, 1 Nov 1904.

Biography erroneously follows Lee regarding Jordan's retirement. SOURCE: Reasons and Patrick, *They Had a Dream*.

Biographical sketch. SOURCE: Logan and Winston, eds., *Dictionary of American Negro Biography*, 371–72.

No Veterans Administration pension file.

JORDAN, Henry; Private; M/10th Cav. Served in 10th Cavalry, 1898; remained in U.S. during war with Spain. SOURCE: Cashin, *Under Fire with the Tenth Cavalry*, 351.

JORDAN, Henry; Private; B/10th Cav. Discharged on surgeon's certificate with gonorrhea from Ft Robinson, NE, 24 Dec 1904. SOURCE: Certificates of Disability, Ft Robinson.

JORDAN, James H.; K/10th Cav. Original member of 10th Cavalry; in troop when organized, Ft Riley, KS, 1 Sep 1867. SOURCE: McMiller, "Buffalo Soldiers," 77.

JORDAN, Leon H.; 1st Lt; B/49th Inf. Born Leavenworth, KS, 19 Sep 1868; educated at Lincoln State Normal, Jefferson City, MO, and Oberlin College; deputy U.S. marshal, Western District of Missouri; assistant recorder of deeds, Washington, DC; first lieutenant, 7th U.S. Volunteer Infantry, 26 Aug 1898. SOURCE: *ANJ* 37 (14 Oct 1899): 145.

First lieutenant, 7th Volunteer Infantry, 26 Jul 1898–28 Feb 1899; first lieutenant, A/49th Infantry, 9 Sep 1899. SOURCE: Descriptive Book, A/49 Inf.

Transferred to B/49th Infantry, 29 Oct 1899. SOURCE: Descriptive Book, B/49 Inf.

Mentioned. SOURCE: *ANJ* 38 (6 Oct 1900): 131; Beasley, *Negro Trailblazers*, 284.

JORDAN, Moses; Sergeant; K/9th Cav. Corporal as of 16 Apr 1892. SOURCE: Roster, 9 Cav.

Stationed at Ft Myers, VA, 1894. SOURCE: *ANJ* 31 (7 Jul 1894): 786.

Promoted to sergeant, Ft Robinson, NE, Mar 1895. SOURCE: *ANJ* 32 (30 Mar 1895): 506.

JORDAN, Thomas; 1st Sgt; F/10th Cav. Private, served in 10th Cavalry in Cuba, 1898. SOURCE: Cashin, *Under Fire with the Tenth Cavalry*, 344.

Served in Philippines as troop quartermaster sergeant, 1907–09; during fight at Nogales, AZ, 27 Aug 1918, pulled wounded Capt. Henry Caron out of harm's way and took over troop until Caron received first aid. SOURCE: Wharfield, *10th Cavalry and Border Fights*, 76, 20, with picture.

First sergeant, Nogales, 1918; wise and keen observer of human nature. SOURCE: Wharfield, *With Scouts and Cavalry at Fort Apache*, 81.

JORDAN, Thomas W.; QM Sgt; 9th Cav. Ordered from Washington Barracks, Washington, DC, to Montauk, NY. SOURCE: *ANJ* 36 (17 Sep 1898): 61.

Ordered to Philippines. SOURCE: *ANJ* 39 (26 Apr 1902): 852.

JOSEPH, Leon E.; Private; K/10th Cav. At Ft Robinson, NE, 1904; left end, troop football team, and hero of 1904 Thanksgiving game's 10–10 tie with B/10th Cavalry. SOURCE: Simmons, "Thanksgiving Day," 663.

JOURDAN, John; Private; 25th Inf. Blinded in one eye when artillery piece he was loading prematurely discharged, Ft Davis, TX, 4 Jul 1874. SOURCE: Carroll, *The Black Military Experience*, 272; Thompson, "The Negro Regiments."

JUDSON, John; Sergeant; C/9th Cav. At Ft McKinney, WY, 1893; in Big Horn Mountains hunting, 24 Oct–7 Nov 1893.

JULIUS, Lawrence J.; Corporal; F/24th Inf. Sent to quell disturbance in quarters of post laundress, Ft Bayard, NM, Oct 1888; became drunk and added to disturbance. SOURCE: Billington, *New Mexico's Buffalo Soldiers*, 164.

Dishonorably discharged from Ft Bayard, NM, 1889, and confined at Alcatraz, CA, for four years. SOURCE: Billington, *New Mexico's Buffalo Soldiers*, 169.

See **CROUCH**, Albert S., Private, 10th Cavalry

JUNIFER, Samuel; I/10th Cav. Original member of 10th Cavalry; in troop when organized, Ft Riley, KS, 15 Aug 1867. SOURCE: McMiller, "Buffalo Soldiers," 76.

K

KAHOLOKULA, John; Private; I/10th Cav. Served in 10th Cavalry, 1898; remained in U.S. during war with Spain. SOURCE: Cashin, *Under Fire with the Tenth Cavalry*, 348.

Stationed at Ft Robinson, NE, 1903.

KANE; Private; M/10th Cav. At Ft Apache, AZ, 1890, subscribed $.50 to testimonial to General Grierson. SOURCE: List of subscriptions, 23 Apr 1890, 10th Cavalry papers, MHI.

KANE, George; Private; F/9th Cav. Arrived at Ft Leavenworth, KS, from Jefferson Barracks, MO, Oct 1866.

Original member of A/10th Cavalry; in troop when organized, Ft Leavenworth, KS, 18 Feb 1867. SOURCE: McMiller, "Buffalo Soldiers," 68.

In F/9th Cavalry, attached to Band/9th Cavalry, for instruction in music. SOURCE: Order 15, 9 Cav, 25 May 1887, Regimental Orders, 9 Cav.

Prisoner in Ft Robinson, NE, guardhouse; greatly in need of shoes and stockings and change of underwear. SOURCE: Report of Inspection, 2 Aug 1888, Reports of Inspections, DP, I.

KANE, William; Private; 24th Inf. Sentenced to life in prison for role in Houston riot, 1917; agreed to cooperate with military investigators; pardoned for testimony. SOURCE: Haynes, *A Night of Violence*, 285–86, 308.

KAPPS. Isaac; I/10th Cav. Original member of 10th Cavalry; in troop when organized, Ft Riley, KS, 15 Aug 1867. SOURCE: McMiller, "Buffalo Soldiers," 76.

KATO, Kersye; Private; I/9th Cav. At Ft D. A. Russell, WY, in 1910; resident of Philadelphia. SOURCE: *Illustrated Review: Ninth Cavalry*.

KEARNEY, Robert; Sergeant; D/10th Cav. At Ft Apache, AZ, 1890, subscribed $.50 to testimonial to General Grierson. SOURCE: List of subscriptions, 23 Apr 1890, 10th Cavalry papers, MHI.

KEATES, Charles; G/10th Cav. Original member of 10th Cavalry; in troop when organized, Ft Leavenworth, KS, 5 Jul 1867. SOURCE: McMiller, "Buffalo Soldiers," 74.

KEATON, Shannon; Sergeant; B/9th Cav. Retired Aug 1901. SOURCE: *ANJ* 38 (10 Aug 1901): 1211.

KEEL, Arthur; Private; 9th Cav. Arrested in Buffalo, WY, Mar 1886, and fined $50 for "displaying a six-shooter too freely." SOURCE: *Big Horn Sentinel*, 27 Mar 1886.

KEITH, Howard; Corporal; C/10th Cav. Born in Virginia; private C/10th Cavalry, 26 Nov 1894; corporal, 1 Apr 1897; at Ft Assiniboine, MT, 1897. SOURCE: Baker, Roster.

KEITH, Porter; Private; I/24th Inf. Born and resided in Athens, TN; father Charles Keith of same location; also served in I/38th Infantry; single; died as prisoner number 187, U.S. Military Prison, Ft Leavenworth, KS, of inflammation of lungs, 4 Jun 1876. SOURCE: Certificates of Disability, Military Divison of the Missouri.

KELHANY; Private; M/10th Cav. Mentioned as recently died, Mar 1874. SOURCE: ES, 10 Cav, 1872–81.

KELL, John; Private; G/10th Cav. On extra duty in hospital, Ft Lyon, CO, 16 Mar–18 Apr 1869. SOURCE: Orders, Det 10 Cav, 1868–69.

KELLAM, Alfred; Sergeant; H/9th Cav. Promoted to corporal, H/9th Cavalry, from lance corporal, Ft Duchesne, UT, Dec 1894. SOURCE: *ANJ* 32 (22 Dec 1894): 278.

Veteran of Philippine Insurrection; sergeant, H/9th Cavalry, at Ft D. A. Russell, WY, in 1910; sharpshooter; resident of Fairmount Heights, MD. SOURCE: *Illustrated Review: Ninth Cavalry*, with picture.

KELLAR, George H.; Private; I/10th Cav. Served in 10th Cavalry, 1898; remained in U.S. during war with Spain. SOURCE: Cashin, *Under Fire with the Tenth Cavalry*, 348.

KELLEY, George B.; 1st Sgt; C/9th Cav. Born Galipolis, OH; served in G/24th Infantry, 27 Aug 1897–18 Jun 1899; age 23 in 1900; served in D/49th Infantry, before becoming battalion sergeant major, 7 Oct 1900; served at Tuguegarao, Cagayan, Philippines, Nov 1900; regimental sergeant major, 23 Dec 1900; reduced to private and confined 14 Feb–14 Jul 1900; discharged, character excellent; wife is Mrs. Rena B. Kelley, 267 Everett Street, Portland, OR. SOURCE: Descriptive Book, 49 Inf NCS.

Served in Cuba at San Juan and Santiago; spent 40 days at Siboney, Cuba, hospital; private and corporal, G/24th Infantry; enlisted in 49th Infantry, San Francisco; second lieutenant, K/49th Infantry, 6 Feb 1901; discharged Aparri,

Philippines, 20 May 1901, character excellent. SOURCE: Descriptive Book, K/49 Inf.

Stationed at Ord Barracks, Monterey, CA, 1903; president of Literary and Social Club organized with civilians of Pacific Grove, CA; manager of squadron baseball team that lost to 15th Infantry. SOURCE: Indianapolis *Freeman*, 5 Dec 1903.

Letter to editor, n.d., on opportunities in the Philippines, observes that there are no windfalls available and opportunities for small capital investment have leveled off; success "depends on the man himself for a successful grasping of them as elsewhere." SOURCE: Indianapolis *Freeman*, 20 Feb 1904.

Former private, G/24th Infantry; died in Minnesota, 9 Oct 1938. SOURCE: Taylor, "Minnesota Black Spanish-American War Veterans."

KELLEY, George S.; Private; H/9th Cav. Veteran of Spanish-American War, and Philippine Insurrection; at Ft D. A. Russell, WY, in 1910; marksman; resident of Harrisburg, PA. SOURCE: *Illustrated Review: Ninth Cavalry*, with picture.

KELLEY, George W.; G/10th Cav. Original member of 10th Cavalry; in troop when organized, Ft Leavenworth, KS, 5 Jul 1867. SOURCE: McMiller, "Buffalo Soldiers," 74.

KELLEY, James; Trumpeter; L/9th Cav. Discharged on certificate of disability, Ft Bliss, TX, 2 Jan 1881. SOURCE: Regt Returns, 9 Cav, Jan 1881.

KELLEY, John; Private; E/10th Cav. Honorable mention for gallantry against Kiowas and Comanches, Wichita Agency, Indian Territory, 22–23 Aug 1874. SOURCE: Baker, Roster.

KELLEY, William; Blacksmith; M/10th Cav. Served in 10th Cavalry in Cuba, 1898. SOURCE: Cashin, *Under Fire with the Tenth Cavalry*, 352.

KELLIS, John; Private; E/10th Cav. At Ft Apache, AZ, 1890, subscribed $.50 to testimonial to General Grierson. SOURCE: List of subscriptions, 23 Apr 1890, 10th Cavalry papers, MHI.

Served in 10th Cavalry, 1898; remained in U.S. during war with Spain. SOURCE: Cashin, *Under Fire with the Tenth Cavalry*, 343.

KELLUM, D. F.; Private; B/9th Cav. On detached service at Ft Bliss, TX, 8 Jan–9 Feb 1881. SOURCE: Regt Returns, 9 Cav, Jan 1881.

KELLUM, George; Private; D/10th Cav. Served in 10th Cavalry in Cuba, 1898. SOURCE: Cashin, *Under Fire with the Tenth Cavalry*, 341.

KELLY, Alonzo B.; Musician; F/24th Inf. Wounded in thigh, Naguilan, Philippines, 7 Dec 1899.

SOURCE: *ANJ* 37 (10 Mar 1900): 659; Muller, *The Twenty Fourth Infantry*, 35.

KELLY, George H.; Chief Musician; Band/10th Cav. Resides in Boston; cornet soloist and band master, Ft Robinson, NE. SOURCE: Lowe, "Camp Life," 206.

KELLY, James; M/10th Cav. Original member of 10th Cavalry; in troop when organized, Ft Riley, KS, 15 Oct 1867. SOURCE: McMiller, "Buffalo Soldiers," 79.

KELLY, Vernon; Private; H/24th Inf. Fined $10 by summary court, San Isidro, Philippines, for being drunk and disorderly in street, 30 Jan 1902, fourth conviction; sentenced to two days in solitary confinement on bread and water and fined one month's pay for disobeying legal order to remain in quarters, 13 Feb 1902; fined $5 for being drunk in streets, 6 Apr 1902. SOURCE: Register of Summary Court, San Isidro.

KELLY, William; Private; CA/10th Cav. Sentenced to dishonorable discharge and confinement, Ft Robinson, NE, Jan 1903, in accordance with Special Order 16, Department of the Missouri, 1903; released 7 Apr 1903.

KELLY, William H.; K/10th Cav. Sergeant-at-arms, Camp 30, National Indian War Veterans, San Antonio, TX. SOURCE: *Winners of the West* 6 (Oct 1929): 7.

Commander, Camp 30; World War I veteran. SOURCE: *Winners of the West* 7 (Oct 1930): 7.

Fought in Apache campaign, 1885–86, while at Ft Grant, AZ; recalls that Pvt. Frank Scott was killed in action; Bill Gibbons was first sergeant. SOURCE: *Winners of the West* 15 (Jan 1938): 7.

KELSEY, Edward; Private; 9th Cav. At Ft Craig, NM, 1881. *See* **RICHARDSON**, William, Private, D/9th Cavalry

KEMP, Joseph; Private; H/10th Cav. Served in 10th Cavalry, 1898; remained in U.S. during war with Spain. SOURCE: Cashin, *Under Fire with the Tenth Cavalry*, 347.

KENDAL, Hampton; Private; 24th Inf. Drowned crossing San Mateo River, Philippines, 21 Aug 1899. SOURCE: Richmond *Planet*, 2 Sep 1899.

KENDALL, Jackson; Private; K/10th Cav. Served in 10th Cavalry, 1898; remained in U.S. during war with Spain. SOURCE: Cashin, *Under Fire with the Tenth Cavalry*, 349.

KENDELL, David; Private; E/9th Cav. At Ft D. A. Russell, WY, in 1910; resident of Pequa, OH. SOURCE: *Illustrated Review: Ninth Cavalry*, with picture.

KENDRICK, Allen; Sergeant; A/24th Inf. Acquitted of neglect of duty as sergeant of the guard. SOURCE: Report of Trials, Department of Texas, 1878–79.

KENDRICK, David; Private; F/9th Cav. Recruit from depot, arrived Ft Robinson, NE, 1 Mar 1887.

Released by garrison court martial, Ft Robinson, which determined he did strike Pvt. W. Smith, F/9th Cavalry, on head with bowl in troop dining room, but not to prejudice of good order and discipline. SOURCE: Order 140, 13 Jul 1887, Post Orders, Ft Robinson.

Prisoner in guardhouse, Ft Robinson, Dec 1889; complained to inspector general that before he was tried, letter from his mother, asking his discharge as her only support, was returned by his commander to Washington with claim that Kendrick had written it himself; Military Convict Jones, F/9th Cavalry, acknowledges writing letter. SOURCE: Report of Inspection, 2 Dec 1889, Reports of Inspections, DP, I.

KENDRICK, Lindsay; Sergeant; I/10th Cav. Served 1876. *See* **BRITTON**, William H., Recruit, Mounted Service

Deposited $20 with paymaster, Ft Concho, TX, Jan 1877. SOURCE: LS, 10 Cav, 1873–83.

At Ft Apache, AZ, 1890, subscribed $.50 to testimonial to General Grierson. SOURCE: List of subscriptions, 23 Apr 1890, 10th Cavalry papers, MHI.

KENEDY, Lee; Private; D/9th Cav. At Ft D. A. Russell, WY, in 1910; resident of Cleveland Co., AL. SOURCE: *Illustrated Review: Ninth Cavalry.*

KENEDY, Washington; B/10th Cav. Original member of 10th Cavalry; in troop when organized, Ft Leavenworth, KS, 1 Apr 1867. SOURCE: McMiller, "Buffalo Soldiers," 69.

KENNEDY, Henry; L/10th Cav. Original member of 10th Cavalry; in troop when organized, Ft Riley, KS, 21 Sep 1867. SOURCE: McMiller, "Buffalo Soldiers," 78.

KENNEDY, John; K/10th Cav. Original member of 10th Cavalry; in troop when organized, Ft Riley, KS, 1 Sep 1867. SOURCE: McMiller, "Buffalo Soldiers," 77.

KENNEDY, Richard; Private; A/9th Cav. At Ft Stanton, NM, 1881. SOURCE: Regt Returns, 9 Cav, Jan 1881.

KENNEDY, Samuel; Private; H/24th Inf. At Ft Huachuca, AZ, 1893. *See* **FOX**, William, Private, B/24th Infantry

KENNEDY, William B.; Private; E/10th Cav. Served in 10th Cavalry, 1898; remained in U.S. during war with Spain. SOURCE: Cashin, *Under Fire with the Tenth Cavalry*, 343.

KENNELY, John; Private; I/25th Inf. Drowned, body recovered, in the Philippines, 14 Oct 1901. SOURCE: *ANJ* 39 (18 Jan 1902): 502.

KERNAN, William J.; Private; B/25th Inf. Dishonorable discharge, Brownsville. SOURCE: SO 266, AGO, 9 Nov 1906.

KERR, Moses; Trumpeter; E/10th Cav. At Ft Apache, AZ, 1890, subscribed $.50 to testimonial to General Grierson. SOURCE: List of subscriptions, 23 Apr 1890, 10th Cavalry papers, MHI.

KERRY, Issac; I/10th Cav. Original member of 10th Cavalry; in troop when organized, Ft Riley, KS, 15 Aug 1867. SOURCE: McMiller, "Buffalo Soldiers," 76.

KEWCONDA, Benjamin; Private; E/10th Cav. Original member of 10th Cavalry; in troop when organized, Ft Leavenworth, KS, 15 Jun 1867. SOURCE: McMiller, "Buffalo Soldiers," 72.

Drunk at Ft Sill, Indian Territory, Aug 1869. SOURCE: Leckie, *The Buffalo Soldiers*, 49.

KEY, Charles; Ord Sgt; U.S. Army. Original member of E/10th Cavalry; in troop when organized, Ft Leavenworth, KS, 15 Jun 1867. SOURCE: McMiller, "Buffalo Soldiers," 72.

Mentioned as private, formerly sergeant, E/10th Cavalry, Mar 1874. SOURCE: ES, 10 Cav, 1872–81.

Private, E/10th Cavalry; honorable mention for gallantry against Kiowas and Comanches, Wichita Agency, Indian Territory, 22–23 Aug 1874. SOURCE: Baker, Roster.

Appointed ordnance sergeant from sergeant, E/10th Cavalry, 8 Feb 1889. SOURCE: Baker, Roster.

Ordnance sergeant at Ft Trumbull, CT, with twenty-seven years of service. SOURCE: Cleveland *Gazette*, 12 Mar 1892.

KEYS, Pat; Sergeant; D/24th Inf. Corporal, wounded in both legs, Santiago, Cuba, 1 Jul 1898. SOURCE: SecWar, *AR 1898*, 436; Muller, *The Twenty Fourth Infantry*, 18.

Sergeant, at Cabanatuan, Philippines, 1901. *See* **JOHNSON**, Jason, Corporal, D/24th Infantry; **LEAVELL**, William, Private, D/24th Infantry; **MOORE**, Cato, Private, D/24th Infantry; **PRIDE**, Wheeler, Private, D/24th Infantry

KIBBY; Private; D/24th Inf. At Cabanatuan, Philippines, 1901. *See* **TAYLOR**, George N., Private, K/24th Infantry

KIDD, Henry; C/10th Cav. Original member of 10th Cavalry; in troop when organized, Ft Leavenworth, KS, 14 May 1867. SOURCE: McMiller, "Buffalo Soldiers," 70.

KIDD, Robert; Private; K/49th Inf. In the Philippines, 1900. *See* **BLUNT**, Hamilton H., Captain, K/49th Infantry

KILLEAN, Thomas P.; Private; F/9th Cav. Buried at Ft Robinson, NE [1893?]. SOURCE: List of Interments, Ft Robinson.

KIMBLE, Richmond; D/10th Cav. Original member of 10th Cavalry; in troop when organized, Ft Leavenworth, KS, 1 Jun 1867. SOURCE: McMiller, "Buffalo Soldiers," 71.

KIMBLERN, Calvin; Private; D/25th Inf. Cited among men who distinguished themselves in 1893, for promptness, perseverance, rapidity in pursuit and capture, after severe struggle, of deserter at Sheridan, WY, 12–13 Oct; and endurance in long ride from Ft Custer, MT, to Sheridan. SOURCE: GO 56, AGO, 10 Nov 1894.

KINARD, Thomas; Private; D/9th Cav. On special duty as assistant baker, Nueva Caceres, Philippines, since 5 Apr 1901. SOURCE: SD List, D/9 Cav, 17 May 1902.

KINCAID, M. L.; Saddler; A/9th Cav. Ranked number eight in revolver competition, Departments of the Platte, East, and California, Bellevue, NE, 18–25 Sep 1894. SOURCE: GO 62, AGO, 15 Nov 1894.

KINEAD, Caspar; Private; D/24th Inf. Transferred from Reserve Divisional Hospital, Siboney, Cuba, to U.S. on U.S. Army Transport *Berkshire* with yellow fever, 23 Aug 1898. SOURCE: Hospital Papers, Spanish-American War.

KING, Charles; Private; C/9th Cav. At Ft D. A. Russell, WY, in 1910; resident of Columbus, GA. SOURCE: *Illustrated Review: Ninth Cavalry*, with picture.

KING, H. B.; Private; Band/9th Cav. At Ft McKinney, WY, 1886. *See* **THOMPSON**, Harvey A., 9th Cavalry

KING, James; Farrier; K/9th Cav. Discharged, end of term, from Ft Cummings, NM, 4 Jan 1881. SOURCE: Regt Returns, 9 Cav, Jan 1881.

KING, John; Farrier; M/9th Cav. At Ft D. A. Russell, WY, in 1910; marksman; resident of Chattanooga, TN. SOURCE: *Illustrated Review: Ninth Cavalry*, with picture.

KING, L. S.; Sergeant; F/25th Inf. At Ft Reno, OK, 1903. SOURCE: Indianapolis *Freeman*, 21 Feb 1903.

KING, Leslie; Corporal; Band/25th Inf. In D/25th Infantry; convicted of assault in the Philippines, Aug 1901; sentenced to eight months and $80 fine.
Promoted to corporal, Band/25th Infantry. SOURCE: *ANJ* 38 (22 Jul 1905): 21.
Warrant officer stationed at Nogales, AZ, 1930. SOURCE: Work, *The Negro Yearbook, 1931–1932*, 334.

KING, Randall; E/10th Cav. Original member of 10th Cavalry; in troop when organized, Ft Leavenworth, KS, 15 Jun 1867. SOURCE: McMiller, "Buffalo Soldiers," 72.

KING, Taylor; K/10th Cav. Original member of 10th Cavalry; in troop when organized, Ft Riley, KS, 1 Sep 1867. SOURCE: McMiller, "Buffalo Soldiers," 77.

KING, William; B/10th Cav. Original member of 10th Cavalry; in troop when organized, Ft Leavenworth, KS, 1 Apr 1867. SOURCE: McMiller, "Buffalo Soldiers," 69.

KING, Willie; Private; A/9th Cav. Veteran of Philippine Insurrection; at Ft D. A. Russell, WY, in 1910. SOURCE: *Illustrated Review: Ninth Cavalry*.

KINNEY, Jerry; Private; M/10th Cav. Acquitted of selling clothing of comrade, 1879. SOURCE: Report of Trials, Department of Texas, 1878–79.

KINSLOW, Thomas; Private; F/10th Cav. Private, G/9th Cavalry, to be tried by general court martial. SOURCE: *ANJ* 34 (3 Apr 1897): 564.
Authorized to enlist in 10th Cavalry, Ft Assiniboine, MT, by telegram, Adjutant General's Office, 4 Mar 1898.
Served in F/10th Cavalry in Cuba, 1898. SOURCE: Cashin, *Under Fire with the Tenth Cavalry*, 344.

KIPPER, John; Sergeant; A/25th Inf. Sentenced to life in prison for leading mob of Negro soldiers against El Paso, TX, police station, 17 Feb 1900, and for murder of policeman Newton Stewart. SOURCE: *ANJ* 37 (12 May 1900): 869.

KIRBY, Wesley; Private; H/24th Inf. Shot and seriously wounded by comrade, Presidio of San Francisco, CA, 26 Jun 1899. SOURCE: *ANJ* 36 (1 Jul 1899): 1047.

KIRK, James; M/10th Cav. Original member of 10th Cavalry; in troop when organized, Ft Riley, KS, 15 Oct 1867. SOURCE: McMiller, "Buffalo Soldiers," 79.

KIRK, William; Corporal; D/24th Inf. At Cabanatuan, Philippines, 1901. *See* **MOORE**, Cato, Private, D/24th Infantry

KIRKLEY, Samuel; Corporal; G/9th Cav. One of six enlisted men of G/9th Cavalry to testify against Lt. John Conline at his 1877 court martial for misconduct, including drunkenness, sexual misconduct, and misappropriation of funds belonging to men of his troop, Ft Garland, CO. SOURCE: Billington, *New Mexico's Buffalo Soldiers*, 121–23.

KIRKPATRICK, John; Private; C/25th Inf. Dishonorable discharge, Brownsville. SOURCE: SO 266, AGO, 9 Nov 1906.

KIRTLEY, Preston; M/10th Cav. Mentioned as Indian war survivor. SOURCE: *Winners of the West* 3 (Jun 1926): 7.

KIRTLEY, Sidney; Private; M/10th Cav. Served in C/10th Cavalry in Cuba, 1898. SOURCE: Cashin, *Under Fire with the Tenth Cavalry*, 340.
Sick in Ft Robinson, NE, hospital, Jun–Sep 1907.

Requested transfer to post hospital, Ft Riley, KS, for continued treatment of fracture of right leg: "I am a colored man and belong to troop M, 10th Cavalry, and as my troop is at Ft Riley, feel that I would be much better satisfied there"; request approved by post surgeon, Ft Robinson, same day. SOURCE: Kirtley to Post Surgeon, Ft Robinson, 14 Oct 1907, and endorsement, Register of Correspondence, Post Surgeon, Ft Robinson.

KITCHEN, George; Private; K/24th Inf. Died of cerebral hemorrhage in the Philippines, 24 Dec 1899. SOURCE: *ANJ* 37 (20 Jan 1900): 488.

KLINE, Frank; Private; E/9th Cav. At Ft D. A. Russell, WY, in 1910. SOURCE: *Illustrated Review: Ninth Cavalry*, with picture.

KNIFFLEY, Charles H.; Private; M/10th Cav. Served in 10th Cavalry, 1898; remained in U.S. during war with Spain. SOURCE: Cashin, *Under Fire with the Tenth Cavalry*, 351.

KNIGHT, A.; Private; H/10th Cav. Best standing broad jump, Department of Colorado, 1903, and third best in Army, at 10'1"; stationed at Ft Washakie, WY. SOURCE: SecWar, *AR 1903*, 1:430.

KNIGHT, David; Private; K/49th Inf. In the Philippines, 1900. *See* **BLUNT**, Hamilton H., Captain, K/49th Infantry

Died of typhoid in the Philippines, 21 Mar 1900. SOURCE: *ANJ* 37 (31 Mar 1900): 731.

KNOX, Durward B.; Private; Band/25th Inf. Born Natchez, MS; Ht 5'7", yellow complexion, occupation laborer; enlisted, age 21, St. Paul, MN, 1 May 1893; previous service in F/25th Infantry, 8 Oct 1889–22 Mar 1891, discharged as minor, character very good; $4 per month retained for total of $48 through Apr 1894; second class marksman 1893; first class marksman 1894; transferred to Band/25th Infantry, character excellent, single, 16 Mar 1895. SOURCE: Descriptive Book, 24 Inf NCS & Band.

KNOX, George; Private; G/9th Cav. At Ft D. A. Russell, WY, in 1910; resident of Denver. SOURCE: *Illustrated Review: Ninth Cavalry*, with picture.

KROH, Warren B.; Corporal; L/25th Inf. Died of malaria, Iriga, Luzon, Philippines, 4 Aug 1901. SOURCE: *ANJ* 39 (12 Oct 1901): 140.

KURNEY, Robert; Sergeant; H/10th Cav. Born in Virginia; private, D/10th Cavalry, 21 Apr 1867–21 Apr 1872; private, corporal, sergeant, 19 Apr 1873–18 Apr 1893; private, E/25th Infantry, 19 Apr 1893–23 Nov 1895; private, H/10th Cavalry, 23 Nov 1895; corporal, 5 Dec 1895; sergeant, 14 Oct 1896; at Ft Assiniboine, MT, 1897. SOURCE: Baker, Roster.

Original member of D/10th Cavalry; in troop when organized, Ft Leavenworth, KS, 1 Jun 1867. SOURCE: McMiller, "Buffalo Soldiers," 71.

First Indian action at Ft Sill, Indian Territory, May 1871; in action against band of twenty cattle thieves, Elm Creek, TX, 5 Dec 1873; with D Troop assisted sheriff in bringing desperadoes to justice, killing four and capturing rest of thieves, recovering one thousand head of cattle. SOURCE: Baker, Roster.

Sergeant, H/10th Cavalry, in campaign against Indians around Ft Sill, 1871. SOURCE: Cashin, *Under Fire with the Tenth Cavalry*, 36.

KYLE, D. A.; Private; K/24th Inf. At San Carlos, AZ, 1890. *See* **HARDEE**, James A., Private, K/24th Infantry

L

LACUE, Samuel; Private; A/9th Cav. At Ft D. A. Russell, WY, in 1910; sharpshooter. SOURCE: *Illustrated Review: Ninth Cavalry*, with picture.

LACY, George; Private; B/24th Inf. At Cabanatuan, Philippines, 1901. *See* **HAMPTON**, Wade, Private, B/24th Infantry

LACY, William; Sergeant; L/10th Cav. Served in 10th Cavalry, 1898; remained in U.S. during war with Spain. SOURCE: Cashin, *Under Fire with the Tenth Cavalry*, 350.

LAFFERTY, Benjamin; Sqdn Sgt Maj; 9th Cav. Promoted from lance corporal to corporal, I/9th Cavalry, Ft Duchesne, UT, Feb 1896. SOURCE: *ANJ* 33 (7 Mar 1896): 480.

Promoted from first sergeant, C/9th Cavalry, to sergeant major, first squadron/9th Cavalry, Apr 1902. SOURCE: *ANJ* 39 (7 Jun 1902): 1004.

LAIRE, James; I/10th Cav. Original member of 10th Cavalry; in troop when organized, Ft Riley, KS, 15 Aug 1867. SOURCE: McMiller, "Buffalo Soldiers," 76.

LAMBERT, H.; Private; D/24th Inf. At Ft Bayard, NM, 1888. *See* **COX**, Richard, Private, D/24th Infantry

LAMPKIN, William M.; Private; G/10th Cav. Corporal, at Ft Apache, AZ, 1890, subscribed $.50 to testimonial to General Grierson. SOURCE: List of subscriptions, 23 Apr 1890, 10th Cavalry papers, MHI.

Ranked number 51 among carbine sharpshooters over 72 percent, 1891. SOURCE: GO 1, AGO, 2 Jan 1892.

LAMPKINS, Amanias; Sergeant; I/10th Cav. Born in Virginia; private, I/10th Cavalry, 5 Jan 1884; corporal, 14 Oct 1892; sergeant, 5 Oct 1894; at Ft Assiniboine, MT, 1897. SOURCE: Baker, Roster.

LAMPKINS, William; Private; 24th Inf. Served in Houston, 1917; convinced court martial he remained in camp during riot. SOURCE: Haynes, *A Night of Violence*, 290.

LAMPLEY, Wellington H.; Private; MG Co/25th Inf. Letter, from Schofield Barracks, HI, dated 9 Jul 1917. SOURCE: Cleveland *Gazette*, 1 Sep 1917.

LANAM, George; Private; K/9th Cav. Sentenced to twenty days and $5 fine by garrison court martial, Ft Robinson, NE; when ordered by Corporal McTrammick, K/9th Cavalry, to sort cabbages in troop garden, he refused, and said, "I don't give a damn, put me in the Guard House." SOURCE: Order 236, 11 Nov 1889, Post Orders, Ft Robinson.

LANCASTER, Thomas D.; Private; M/10th Cav. Served in 10th Cavalry, 1898; remained in U.S. during war with Spain. SOURCE: Cashin, *Under Fire with the Tenth Cavalry*, 351.

LAND, Robert; D/10th Cav. Original member of 10th Cavalry; in troop when organized, Ft Leavenworth, KS, 1 Jun 1867. SOURCE: McMiller, "Buffalo Soldiers," 71.

LANDER, William H.; Private; L/10th Cav. Served in 10th Cavalry, 1898; remained in U.S. during war with Spain. SOURCE: Cashin, *Under Fire with the Tenth Cavalry*, 351.

LANDERS, M.; 1st Sgt; B/25th Inf. Mentioned. SOURCE: Cleveland *Gazette*, 21 Apr 1900.

LANDIES, George; C/10th Cav. Original member of 10th Cavalry; in troop when organized, Ft Leavenworth, KS, 14 May 1867. SOURCE: McMiller, "Buffalo Soldiers," 70.

LANE, Edward; 1st Sgt; C/10th Cav. Born in Virginia; private, corporal, sergeant, A/9th Cavalry, 13 Sep 1886–12 Sep 1891; private, C/10th Cavalry, 24 Sep 1891; corporal, 1 Sep 1894; sergeant, 21 Mar 1895; at Ft Assiniboine, MT, 1897. SOURCE: Baker, Roster.

Served in 10th Cavalry in Cuba, 1898. SOURCE: Cashin, *Under Fire with the Tenth Cavalry*, 339.

Wounded in action, Santiago, Cuba, 1 Jul 1898. SOURCE: SecWar, *AR 1898*, 324.

First sergeant, C/10th Cavalry, posted $300 bond for prostitute Lizzie Carr, Crawford, NE, arrested for assault, 1 Apr 1904. SOURCE: Police Court Docket, Crawford, NE.

LANE, Eugene F.; Private; I/9th Cav. Deserted, San Francisco, 15 Nov 1902. SOURCE: Regt Returns, 9 Cav, Nov 1902.

LANE, John; Private; B/24th Inf. At Ft McIntosh, TX, 1877. *See* **GRAYSON**, Charles H., Private, G/24th Infantry

Capt. John B. Nixon, 24th Infantry, convicted of attempting to withhold $10 of Lane's pay, Ft Duncan, TX,

Feb–Sep 1877, but not guilty of defrauding him of $12 extra duty pay in exchange for paying Lane's post trader debts.

LANE, John M.; Corporal; B/10th Cav. Served in 10th Cavalry in Cuba, 1898. SOURCE: Cashin, *Under Fire with the Tenth Cavalry*, 338.

LANE, Thomas; Private; M/10th Cav. Honorable mention for skill in successful pursuit of raiding parties, Arizona, 1888. SOURCE: Baker, Roster.

At Ft Apache, AZ, 1890, subscribed $.50 to testimonial to General Grierson. SOURCE: List of subscriptions, 23 Apr 1890, 10th Cavalry papers, MHI.

LANE, William; Private; K/10th Cav. Recruit at St Louis depot, awaiting assignment to regiment, May 1875. SOURCE: LS, 10 Cav, 1873–83.

In A/10th Cavalry; promised promotion to first sergeant but told needed more as regimental quartermaster sergeant. SOURCE: CO, 10 Cav, to CO, A/10, 6 Nov 1875, ES, 10 Cav, 1872–81.

Private, K/10th Cavalry, mentioned Apr 1877. SOURCE: LS, 10 Cav, 1873–83.

LANE, William; F/10th Cav. Admitted to Soldiers Home with disability at age 38 with eighteen years' service, 21 Feb 1885. SOURCE: SecWar, *AR 1885*, 829.

LANG, Robert; Sergeant; H/10th Cav. Served in 10th Cavalry, 1898; remained in U.S. during war with Spain. SOURCE: Cashin, *Under Fire with the Tenth Cavalry*, 346.

LANG, William; Private; M/9th Cav. Enlisted Ft Washakie, WY, 26 Oct 1885.

LANGFORD, Edward; Corporal; D/25th Inf. Retired from Ft Grant, AZ, Nov 1898. SOURCE: *ANJ* 36 (12 Nov 1898): 262.

LANGFORD, Hayes; Private; I/9th Cav. At Ft D. A. Russell, WY, in 1910; resident of Huntsville, AL. SOURCE: *Illustrated Review: Ninth Cavalry.*

LANGFORD, William; Private; 24th Inf. Served in Houston, 1917; convinced court martial he remained in camp during riot. SOURCE: Haynes, *A Night of Violence*, 269.

LANN, Charles; Private; H/10th Cav. Served in 10th Cavalry, 1898; remained in U.S. during war with Spain. SOURCE: Cashin, *Under Fire with the Tenth Cavalry*, 347.

LAOOS, Lewis; E/10th Cav. Original member of 10th Cavalry; in troop when organized, Ft Leavenworth, KS, 15 Jun 1867. SOURCE: McMiller, "Buffalo Soldiers," 72.

LAPSLEY, George; Private; K/10th Cav. Served in 10th Cavalry, 1898; remained in U.S. during war with Spain. SOURCE: Cashin, *Under Fire with the Tenth Cavalry*, 349.

LARKINS, James; Sergeant; K/24th Inf. At San Carlos, AZ, 1890. *See* **HARDEE**, James A., Private, K/24th Infantry

Authorized three-month furlough from San Carlos. SOURCE: *ANJ* 28 (25 Oct 1890): 137.

LARRIMORE, Herman F.; Private; D/24th Inf. At Cabanatuan, Philippines, 1901. *See* **NEWELL**, Frank, Private, D/24th Infantry

LARTER; Private; B/10th Cav. At Ft Apache, AZ, 1890, subscribed $.50 to testimonial to General Grierson. SOURCE: List of subscriptions, 23 Apr 1890, 10th Cavalry papers, MHI.

LARUE, Bernhard; K/10th Cav. Original member of 10th Cavalry; in troop when organized, Ft Riley, KS, 1 Sep 1867. SOURCE: McMiller, "Buffalo Soldiers," 77.

LAST, H.; Regt QM Sgt; 9th Cav. With regiment on practice march from Ft Robinson, NE, Aug 1890.

LATIMER, Grant; Private; E/48th Inf. Died of variola in the Philippines, 8 Dec 1900. SOURCE: *ANJ* 38 (15 Dec 1900): 373.

LATIMER, James C.; Private; A/24th Inf. Private, K/25th Infantry, at Ft Niobrara, NE, 1904. SOURCE: Wilson, "History of Fort Niobrara."

Ranked number 125 among rifle experts with 72.67 percent, 1905. SOURCE: GO 101, AGO, 31 May 1906.

LATONE, Foichoill; G/10th Cav. Original member of 10th Cavalry; in troop when organized, Ft Leavenworth, KS, 5 Jul 1867. SOURCE: McMiller, "Buffalo Soldiers," 74.

LATTIMORE, Allen; 1st Lt; 23rd Kans Inf. Mentioned. SOURCE: Beasley, *Negro Trailblazers*, 285.

LATTY, John; A/10th Cav. Original member of 10th Cavalry; in troop when organized, Ft Leavenworth, KS, 18 Feb 1867. SOURCE: McMiller, "Buffalo Soldiers," 68.

LAWERANCE, Frank E.; G/10th Cav. Original member of 10th Cavalry; in troop when organized, Ft Leavenworth, KS, 5 Jul 1867. SOURCE: McMiller, "Buffalo Soldiers," 74.

LAWRENCE, Earnest; Private; I/9th Cav. Veteran of Philippine Insurrection; trumpeter, I/9th Cavalry, at Ft D. A. Russell, WY, in 1910; sharpshooter; resident of Chattanooga, TN. SOURCE: *Illustrated Review: Ninth Cavalry*, with picture.

Private, I/9th Cavalry, killed by Raymond Hall, late of F/9th Cavalry, at Autumn Leaf Club dance last night at Keefe Hall, Cheyenne, WY; Hall escaped. SOURCE: Cheyenne *State Leader*, 13 Oct 1911.

LAWRENCE, Frank; Private; E/25th Inf. Convicted by general court martial, Columbus Barracks, OH, of desertion, from 1 Aug 1884 until surrendered 27 Aug 1884; sentenced to dishonorable discharge and 2 1/2 years. SOURCE: GCMO 47, AGO, 20 Oct 1884.

LAWS, A.; Private; I/10th Cav. Sentenced to dishonorable discharge and confinement, Ft Robinson, NE, Apr 1904, in accordance with Special Order 56, Department of the Missouri; released Jun 1904.

LAWS, Clinton; Private; 10th Cav. Recently deceased, Aug 1874.

LAWS, John H.; Private; F/10th Cav. Served in 10th Cavalry in Cuba, 1898. SOURCE: Cashin, *Under Fire with the Tenth Cavalry*, 344.

LAWSON; Private; C/10th Cav. Killed in action, Gayleyville Canyon, AZ, 3 Jan 1886. SOURCE: Baker, Roster.

LAWSON, George; Private; B/25th Inf. Dishonorable discharge, Brownsville. SOURCE: SO 266, AGO, 9 Nov 1906.

LAWSON, Gillespie; Private; B/9th Cav. Veteran of Philippine Insurrection; at Ft D. A. Russell, WY, in 1910; marksman. SOURCE: *Illustrated Review: Ninth Cavalry*, with picture.

LAWSON, Isa; I/10th Cav. Original member of 10th Cavalry; in troop when organized, Ft Riley, KS, 15 Aug 1867. SOURCE: McMiller, "Buffalo Soldiers," 76.

LAWSON, James; Private; C/24th Inf. Transferred from Reserve Divisional Hospital, Siboney, Cuba, to U.S. on U.S. Army Transport *Santiago* with remittent malarial fever, 25 Jul 1898. SOURCE: Hospital Papers, Spanish-American War.

LAWSON, James H.; Private; M/10th Cav. Served in 10th Cavalry in Cuba, 1898. SOURCE: Cashin, *Under Fire with the Tenth Cavalry*, 352.

LAWSON, John E.; Private; K/10th Cav. On extra duty with Medical Department as hospital nurse as of 21 Jul 1883. SOURCE: Order 5, Sub-Post Camp Rice, TX, 31 Jul 1883, Misc Records, 10 Cav.

LAWSON, L. W.; Private; 9th Cav. In confinement at Ft Bayard, NM, 16 Jan–9 Feb 1881. SOURCE: Regt Returns, 9 Cav, Feb 1881.

LAWSON, Samuel; Private; A/24th Inf. Second place, obstacle race, military tournament, Albany, NY, autumn, 1909; also second place in equipment race. SOURCE: Muller, *The Twenty Fourth Infantry*, 60.

LAWSON, T. J.; Private; E/9th Cav. On detached service in field, New Mexico, 26 Jan–1 Feb 1881. SOURCE: Regt Returns, 9 Cav, Feb 1881.

LAWSON, Walter; E/25th Inf. Alias Walker Lawson; widow Millie gets private bill passed for $20 per month pension. SOURCE: *Winners of the West* 3 (Apr 1926): 2.

LAWSON, William; Private; A/10th Cav. Served in 10th Cavalry in Cuba, 1898. SOURCE: Cashin, *Under Fire with the Tenth Cavalry*, 336.

LAWSON, William A.; Recruit; Colored Detachment/Mounted Service. At Jefferson Barracks, MO, 1885. *See* **MORE**, Charles, Recruit, Colored Detachment/Mounted Service

LAY, Rufus; Private; K/9th Cav. At Ft D. A. Russell, WY, in 1910; resident of Atlanta. SOURCE: *Illustrated Review: Ninth Cavalry*.

LAYNE, George; Private; L/10th Cav. Served in 10th Cavalry, 1898; remained in U.S. during war with Spain. SOURCE: Cashin, *Under Fire with the Tenth Cavalry*, 351.

LEACH, Samuel; Private; G/9th Cav. Served 1892–96 and discharged with character excellent; reenlisted in F/25th Infantry and deserted 15 Apr 1897 due to dissatisfaction with commander's denial of privileges to all when a few misbehaved; went home and mother persuaded him to return; served in B and I/9th Cavalry; recommended for restoration to duty in 9th Cavalry without trial. SOURCE: CO, 9 Cav, to AG, DP, 5 Dec 1897, LS, Ft Robinson.

Dropped from G/9th Cavalry as deserter from F/25th Infantry; confined since 3 Dec 1897 at Ft Robinson, NE, awaiting trial; sentenced to dishonorable discharge, 28 Jan 1898, in accordance with Special Order 5, Department of the Platte, 31 Jan 1898; sent under guard to Ft Logan, CO.

Forwarded to department headquarters the amount of $5.20 belonging to Private Leach, deserter from 25th Infantry who fraudulently enlisted in 9th Cavalry and assigned to G/9th Cavalry on 19 Nov 1897. SOURCE: CO, G/9, to Chief Paymaster, DP, 19 Feb 1898, Misc Records, DP.

LEAVELL, Saint; Private; I/10th Cav. Served in 10th Cavalry, 1898; remained in U.S. during war with Spain. SOURCE: Cashin, *Under Fire with the Tenth Cavalry*, 348.

LEAVELL, William; Private; D/24th Inf. Fined for disobeying order of Cpl. William Johnson to stop talking and remarking that no one could stop him from talking if he wanted to do so, Cabanatuan, Philippines, 8 Jan 1900; witnesses: Cpl. William Johnson, B/24th Infantry; Cpl. Charles Riz, B/24th Infantry; Pvt. David Short, D/24th Infantry; Pvt. Edward Ridgely, D/24th Infantry; Pvt. Wallace Streeter, D/24th Infantry; Pvt. Willie Berts, D/24th Infantry. SOURCE: Name File, 24 Inf.

Fined $7 for appearing at reveille without his hat and being insubordinate to 1st Sgt. M. H. Ellis's order to get it; witnesses: First Sergeant Ellis, D/24th Infantry; Sgt. William H. Brice, D/24th Infantry; Sgt. Pat Keys, D/24th Infantry.

LEE; Private; E/10th Cav. At Ft Apache, AZ, 1890, subscribed $.50 to testimonial to General Grierson. SOURCE: List of subscriptions, 23 Apr 1890, 10th Cavalry papers, MHI.

LEE; Trumpeter; 10th Cav. Fined $2 and $4.80 costs, Crawford, NE, for carrying concealed weapon (razor) and disturbing peace, 15 Jan 1906.

LEE, Alexander; Private; K/9th Cav. On detached service in field, New Mexico, 21 Jan–8 Feb 1881. SOURCE: Regt Returns, 9 Cav, Feb 1881.

Served 1878–83; new member, Camp No. 11, National Indian War Veterans. SOURCE: *Winners of the West* 5 (Mar 1928): 3.

LEE, Allen H.; 10th Cav. Died in Minnesota. SOURCE: Taylor, "Minnesota Black Spanish-American War Veterans."

LEE, Arthur; Private; G/10th Cav. At Ft Grant, AZ, transferred to Hospital Corps. SOURCE: *ANJ* 28 (25 Jul 1891): 817.

LEE, Asberry; Recruit; Colored Detachment/ Mounted Service. Convicted by general court martial, Jefferson Barracks, MO, of desertion, 6–23 Sep 1887; sentenced to dishonorable discharge and four years. SOURCE: GCMO 79, AGO, 7 Nov 1887.

LEE, Charles; Recruit; Colored Detachment/ Mounted Service. Convicted by general court martial, Jefferson Barracks, MO, of theft of $8.42 in government clothing from Recruit Theo Coleman, Colored Detachment, Mounted Service, 11 Jul 1887; acquitted of desertion, 12–13 Jul 1887; sentenced to dishonorable discharge and one year.

LEE, Charles A.; Private; B/10th Cav. Served in 10th Cavalry, 1898; remained in U.S. during war with Spain. SOURCE: Cashin, *Under Fire with the Tenth Cavalry*, 339.

LEE, Claude; Private; 9th Cav. Stopped runaway team of two mules pulling empty carriage in Cheyenne, WY. SOURCE: Cheyenne *State Leader*, 13 Jul 1910.

LEE, Daniel; Corporal; I/48th Inf. In the Philippines, 1900. *See* **SMITH**, Lewis M., First Sergeant, M/10th Cavalry

LEE, David; I/10th Cav. Original member of 10th Cavalry; in troop when organized, Ft Riley, KS, 15 Aug 1867. SOURCE: McMiller, "Buffalo Soldiers," 76.

LEE, Dillard; Private; E/10th Cav. Served in 10th Cavalry, 1898; remained in U.S. during war with Spain. SOURCE: Cashin, *Under Fire with the Tenth Cavalry*, 343.

LEE, Edward; Color Sgt.; 24th Inf. Corporal, Band/9th Cavalry; on detached service with band at headquarters, District of New Mexico, Santa Fe, 1880; played solo alto. SOURCE: Billington, *New Mexico's Buffalo Soldiers*, 226.

Sergeant, Band/9th Cavalry, returned to duty in accordance with letter, Department of the Platte, 24 Feb 1890.

Reduced to private and fined $20, Ft Robinson, NE, for involvement in drunken and disgraceful altercation with a private named Scruggs. SOURCE: *ANJ* 28 (11 Apr 1891): 561.

Sergeant, Band/9th Cavalry; secretary of Oak & Ivy Dancing Club of Ft Robinson, which gives dancing lessons on post. SOURCE: Ft Robinson *Weekly Bulletin*, 5 Apr 1893, in Court Martial Records, McKay.

Retired as color sergeant, 24th Infantry, Mar 1902. SOURCE: *ANJ* 39 (5 Apr 1902): 776.

Born in Ohio; died 7 Feb 1922; buried Ft Douglas, UT. SOURCE: Clark, "A History of the Twenty-fourth," appendix A.

LEE, Edward; Private; C/25th Inf. Dishonorable discharge, Brownsville. SOURCE: SO 266, AGO, 9 Nov 1906.

Willing to submit to any test so he could reenlist. SOURCE: Washington *Post*, 13 Dec 1906.

LEE, Ernest; Musician; H/24th Inf. Fined by summary court, San Isidro, Philippines, for drunkenness in street, 18 Nov 1901, third conviction; fined $6 for absence from company evening inspection, 22 Feb 1902; fined $2.50 for absence from check roll call, 10 Mar 1902; fined $5 for lying out of quarters, 8 Apr 1902. SOURCE: Register of Summary Court, San Isidro.

LEE, Fitz; Private; M/10th Cav. Served in 10th Cavalry, 1898. SOURCE: Cashin, *Under Fire with the Tenth Cavalry*, 351–52.

Awarded Medal of Honor for service in Cuba, 1898. *See* **THOMPKINS**, William H., Sergeant, H/25th Infantry

Medal of Honor mentioned; Lee out of service in 1900. SOURCE: *ANJ* 37 (24 Feb 1900): 611; Steward, *The Colored Regulars*, 205.

Born Dinwiddie Co., VA; received medal 3 Jun 1899 while in hospital, Ft Bliss, TX. SOURCE: Lee, *Negro Medal of Honor Men*, 92, 98.

LEE, Fred; Private; E/9th Cav. At Ft D. A. Russell, WY, in 1910. SOURCE: *Illustrated Review: Ninth Cavalry*, with picture.

LEE, George; C/9th Cav. Family resides at Ft Robinson, NE, and claims to be indigent, dependent on charity of garrison for subsistence. SOURCE: CO, Ft Robinson, to CO, 9 Cav, 25 Jul 1898, LS, Ft Robinson.

LEE, George; Private; D/24th Inf. Fined $5 at Cabanatuan, Philippines, for appearing at guard mount with dirty rifle, 10 Jul 1901; witness: QM Sgt. Robert Duvall, D/24th Infantry. SOURCE: Name File, 24 Inf.

LEE, George; Private; M/10th Cav. Transferred in accordance with Special Order 242, Adjutant General's Office, 15 Oct 1902.

LEE, Harvey M.; Private; K/10th Cav. Captured at Carrizal, Mexico, 21 Jun 1916; resides in Tucson, AZ, 1965. SOURCE: Wharfield, *10th Cavalry and Border Fights*, 37.

LEE, Henry; A/10th Cav. Original member of 10th Cavalry; in troop when organized, Ft Leavenworth, KS, 18 Feb 1867. SOURCE: McMiller, "Buffalo Soldiers," 68.

LEE, Henry; B/10th Cav. Original member of 10th Cavalry; in troop when organized, Ft Leavenworth, KS, 1 Apr 1867. SOURCE: McMiller, "Buffalo Soldiers," 69.

LEE, Henry; Private; K/9th Cav. Reduced to the ranks from sergeant and fined $50 for absence without leave from Ft Robinson, NE, and other offenses. SOURCE: *ANJ* 26 (8 Jun 1889): 842.

LEE, Herman; A/10th Cav. Original member of 10th Cavalry; in troop when organized, Ft Leavenworth, KS, 18 Feb 1867. SOURCE: McMiller, "Buffalo Soldiers," 68.

LEE, James; Sergeant; D/9th Cav. Promoted from lance corporal to corporal, vice Jones; resigned, Ft Robinson, NE, 11 Jun 1894.

Corporal and post gardener, Ft Robinson, 21 May– 16 Aug 1895. SOURCE: Order 31, 21 May 1895, and Order 54, 16 Aug 1895, Post Orders, Ft Robinson.

Corporal, I/9th Cavalry, on special duty as chief gardener, Ft Robinson. SOURCE: Special Order 29, Ft Robinson, 22 Mar 1897.

Authorized to reenlist as married soldier by letter, Adjutant General's Office, 19 Nov 1897.

Commended for gallantry in charge on San Juan Hill, battle of Santiago, Cuba, 1 Jul 1898. SOURCE: GO 15, AGO, 13 Feb 1900; *ANJ* 37 (24 Feb 1900): 611.

Sergeant, D/9th Cavalry, on special duty in charge of recruits, Nueva Caceres, Philippines, since 24 Mar 1902. SOURCE: Special Duty List, D/9, 31 May 1902.

LEE, James K.; Private; F/10th Cav. Served in 10th Cavalry in Cuba, 1898. SOURCE: Cashin, *Under Fire with the Tenth Cavalry*, 343.

LEE, Joel; Sergeant; M/10th Cav. Sharpshooter at Ft McDowell, AZ. SOURCE: *ANJ* 24 (18 Jun 1887): 934.

LEE, John H.; Private; G/10th Cav. Served in 10th Cavalry, 1898; remained in U.S. during war with Spain. SOURCE: Cashin, *Under Fire with the Tenth Cavalry*, 346.

LEE, Jordan; D/10th Cav. Original member of 10th Cavalry; in troop when organized, Ft Leavenworth, KS, 1 Jun 1867. SOURCE: McMiller, "Buffalo Soldiers," 71.

LEE, Joseph; Private; H/9th Cav. Convicted by general court martial, Jefferson Barracks, MO, of desertion, 20 May 1883–12 Aug 1884; sentenced to dishonorable discharge and three years. SOURCE: GCMO 39, AGO, 22 Sep 1884.

Convicted by general court martial, Jefferson Barracks, of desertion, 11 May 1883–12 Aug 1884 and 19 Sep 1884– 30 Aug 1886, when apprehended in St. Louis; sentenced to dishonorable discharge and four years. SOURCE: GCMO 91, AGO, 29 Oct 1886.

LEE, Joseph H.; Sergeant. Retired; served as usher, first anniversary celebration, Col. Charles Young Camp No. 24, National Indian War Veterans, Washington, DC. SOURCE: *Winners of the West* 7 (May 1930): 1.

LEE, Nathaniel; Private; A/10th Cav. At Ft Apache, AZ, 1890, subscribed $.50 to testimonial to General Grierson. SOURCE: List of subscriptions, 23 Apr 1890, 10th Cavalry papers, MHI.

LEE, Richard; Private; A/10th Cav. At Ft Apache, AZ, 1890, subscribed $.50 to testimonial to General Grierson. SOURCE: List of subscriptions, 23 Apr 1890, 10th Cavalry papers, MHI.

LEE, Robert E.; Wagoner; F/24th Inf. Born Mercer Co., KY; Ht 5'10", occupation laborer, black complexion; enlisted, age 23, Ft Leavenworth, KS, 15 Nov 1883; transferred from H/24th Infantry to Band/24th Infantry, 1 Oct 1888; discharged, end of term, Ft Bayard, NM, single, character excellent, 14 Nov 1888; retained $72, clothing overdrawn $9; reenlisted, Ft Bayard, 15 Nov 1888; transferred to F/24th Infantry, single, character very good, retained $60, clothing overdrawn $23, 12 Nov 1893; reenlisted 21 Nov 1893. SOURCE: Descriptive Book, 24 Inf NCS & Band.

Married Miss R. Rainey, Ft Bayard, Sep 1891. SOURCE: *ANJ* 29 (17 Oct 1891): 133.

LEE, Robert E.; Private; A/10th Cav. Served in 10th Cavalry in Cuba, 1898; wounded in action. SOURCE: Cashin, *Under Fire with the Tenth Cavalry*, 336-37; SOURCE: SecWar, *AR 1898*, 324.

LEE, Samuel; F/10th Cav. Original member of 10th Cavalry; in troop when organized, Ft Leavenworth, KS, 21 Jun 1867. SOURCE: McMiller, "Buffalo Soldiers," 73.

LEE, Ulysses; Private; F/9th Cav. At Ft D. A. Russell, WY, in 1910; sharpshooter; resident of Washington, DC. SOURCE: *Illustrated Review: Ninth Cavalry*, with picture.

LEE, W.; Private; B/9th Cav. In confinement, Ft Bayard, NM, 16 Jan–9 Feb 1881. SOURCE: Regt Returns, 9 Cav, Feb 1881.

LEE, Wane; Recruit; 10th Cav. Enlisted Memphis, spring 1867. SOURCE: LS, 10 Cav, 1866–67.

LEE, Warren; C/10th Cav. Original member of 10th Cavalry; in troop when organized, Ft Leavenworth, KS, 14 May 1867. SOURCE: McMiller, "Buffalo Soldiers," 70.

LEE, William; Recruit; General Service. Convicted by general court martial, Columbus Barracks, OH, of desertion, 9 Jul 1881 until apprehended 18 Nov 1881; sentenced to dishonorable discharge and one year. SOURCE: GCMO 4, AGO, 7 Jan 1882.

LEE, William; Musician; I/24th Inf. Convicted by general court martial, Columbus Barracks, OH, of desertion, Ft Sill, Indian Territory, 11 Aug 1884 until apprehended in Chicago, 17 Sep 1884; sentenced to dishonorable discharge and three years. SOURCE: GCMO 47, AGO, 20 Oct 1884.

LEE, William; Private; D/10th Cav. Served in 10th Cavalry, 1898; remained in U.S. during war with Spain. SOURCE: Cashin, *Under Fire with the Tenth Cavalry*, 341.

LEE, William; Private; F/10th Cav. Served in 10th Cavalry in Cuba, 1898. SOURCE: Cashin, *Under Fire with the Tenth Cavalry*, 344.

LEE, William; Private; K/24th Inf. In D/24th Infantry, at Cabanatuan, Philippines, 1900. *See* **COLE**, James E., Private, B/24th Infantry

Fined $7 at Cabanatuan for being disorderly in camp, loud and disrespectful, and handling weapon in threatening manner and refusing order to give it to first sergeant; witnesses: First Sergeant Stevens and Private Washington, K/24th Infantry. SOURCE: Name File, 24 Inf.

LEE, William T.; Private; Band/9th Cav. With band on detached service at headquarters, District of New Mexico, Santa Fe, 1880; played bells. SOURCE: Billington, *New Mexico's Buffalo Soldiers*, 226.

LEE, Willie; Private; 25th Inf. Sends love from the Philippines to parents and friends. SOURCE: Richmond *Planet*, 20 Jan 1900.

LEELY, Robert; D/10th Cav. Original member of 10th Cavalry; in troop when organized, Ft Leavenworth, KS, 1 Jun 1867. SOURCE: McMiller, "Buffalo Soldiers," 71.

LEFTWICH, Aaron; Private; G/25th Inf. Killed in action, Cuba, 1898. SOURCE: Scipio, *Last of the Black Regulars*, 29.

Died in Cuba, 1 Jul 1898. SOURCE: *ANJ* 36 (11 Feb 1899): 567.

Killed in action at El Caney, Cuba, 1 Jul 1898; buried one mile south of El Caney, with wooden headboard with his name cut into it, stones around headboard; name in tightly corked bottle, buried at head of grave. SOURCE: Scrapbook, 25 Inf, II.

LEGRAND, John; I/10th Cav. Original member of 10th Cavalry; in troop when organized, Ft Riley, KS, 15 Aug 1867. SOURCE: McMiller, "Buffalo Soldiers," 76.

LEIGH, Wade H.; Private; K/10th Cav. Served in 10th Cavalry, 1898; remained in U.S. during war with Spain. SOURCE: Cashin, *Under Fire with the Tenth Cavalry*, 349.

LELOT, John; Private; K/25th Inf. Behaved heroically, 23 Jul 1901; on guard while his patrol slept, he chased off three native attackers while under fire for first time. SOURCE: Lemus, "The Enlisted Man in Action," 52.

LEMONS, Willie; Private; B/25th Inf. Dishonorable discharge, Brownsville. SOURCE: SO 266, AGO, 9 Nov 1906.

LEMUS, Rienzi Brock; Private; K/25th Inf. Born Richmond, VA, to Charles H. and Mamie L. (Brock) Lemus, 8 Jan 1881; educated in Richmond public schools; soldier, 1 Aug 1899–18 Mar 1902; Pullman porter, 2 1/2 years; dining car waiter, twenty years; led organized movement of dining car cooks and waiters, 1918; organized Brotherhood of Dining Car Employees, 1919; Grand President of Brotherhood, 1919–present; columnist, Boston *Chronicle*; special correspondent, New York *Age*; member, Masons and Elks; Baptist; address 204 W. 136th Street, New York City; coleader in movement effecting amalgamation of Brotherhood of Dining Car Employees (New England railroads and New York Central) and Dining Car Cooks and Waiters Association (Pennsylvania and lines west of Hudson River centering on New York), 1920; instrumental in securing from U.S. Railroad Administration, for first time, extension of eight-hour day and overtime for dining car cooks and waiters, 1919; made three successful presentations to late U.S. Railroad Labor Board against efforts of railroad management to restore pre-World War I rates of pay and rules, 1921 and 1924; won first formal agreement on rules governing employment of dining car men of any class with New York, New Haven, and Hartford Railroad's general manager, 1921; conducted negotiations in conference resulting in contracts on pay and rules with Boston and Albany, Boston and Maine, New York Central, Pennsylvania Railroads, 1921, Atlantic Coast line, 1924, Southern Railroad, 1925, and New Haven line, 1926. SOURCE: Yenser, *Who's Who in Colored America 1933–37*, 327 (same article in 1938–40 edition, 328).

Letter from LaLoma, Philippines, 4 Nov 1899. SOURCE: Gatewood, *"Smoked Yankees"*, 246.

Secretary, Y.M.C.A., Marcelina, Philippines, which was organized 21 Aug 1900; explained organization and accomplishments. SOURCE: Richmond *Planet*, 20 Oct 1900.

Letters to editor, Richmond *Planet*, in following issues: 30 Sep, 4, 11, 18 Nov, and 16 and 30 Dec 1899; 20 and 27 Jan, 10 and 17 Feb, 10 and 17 Mar, 7 and 14 Apr, 12 May, 16 and 30 Jun, 28 Jul, 18 Aug, 8 Sep, 20 and 27 Oct, 8 and 29 Dec, 1900; 12 Jan, 16 and 23 Feb, 9, 16, and 23 Mar, 27 Apr, 1, 8, and 22 Jun, and 7 Dec 1901; 12 and 26 Apr and 3 May 1902.

Letter regarding Y.M.C.A., Castillegos, Zambales, Philippines. SOURCE: *ANJ* 38 (10 Aug 1901): 1219.

Author of three articles in *The Colored American Magazine*: "The Philippine Islands; or, Opportunities for Colored Americans in the Far East," 4 (March 1902), 259–68; "The Enlisted Man in Action, or, the Colored American Soldier in the Philippines," 5 (May 1902), 46–54; "The Negro and the Philippines," 6 (March 1903), 314–18.

Leader in amalgamation of two dining car unions, 1920. SOURCE: Spero and Harris, *The Black Worker*, 125.

Author of "A Successful Negro Labor Union," *Opportunity* 1 (May 1923): 21.

Grand President, Brotherhood of Dining Car Employees, address 147 Massachusetts Avenue, NW, Washington, DC. SOURCE: Work, *The Negro Yearbook, 1925–1926*, 459.

Letter criticizing John P. Davis for attacks on Lawrence Oxley, Chief, Negro Division, U.S. Department of Labor. SOURCE: New York *Age*, 25 Aug 1934.

Revolt in Brotherhood deposed Lemus, president since inception, and amalgamated Brotherhood with United Transport Services Employees. SOURCE: Northrup, *Organized Labor and the Negro*, 99.

LENARD, Clarence M.; Private; L/10th Cav. Served in 10th Cavalry, 1898; remained in U.S. during war with Spain. SOURCE: Cashin, *Under Fire with the Tenth Cavalry*, 351.

LENIOUS, Alfred; D/10th Cav. Original member of 10th Cavalry; in troop when organized, Ft Leavenworth, KS, 1 Jun 1867. SOURCE: McMiller, "Buffalo Soldiers," 71.

LENOIR, Noha; Private; D/48th Inf. Died of variola in the Philippines, 2 Jul 1900. SOURCE: *ANJ* 37 (14 Jul 1900): 1083.

LENTZ, Lorantus U.; Private; K/25th Inf. Died of variola in the Philippines, 22 Jul 1901. SOURCE: *ANJ* 39 (21 Sep 1901): 59.

LEONARD, John E.; Sergeant; H/9th Cav. Veteran of Philippine Insurrection; at Ft D. A. Russell, WY, in 1910; marksman; resident of Boston. SOURCE: *Illustrated Review: Ninth Cavalry*, with picture.

LEONARD, John H.; Private; C/9th Cav. Deserted from Ft Robinson, NE, 11 May 1886.

LEONARD, Samuel J.; Private; G/10th Cav. In Band/10th Cavalry, deposited $15 with paymaster, Ft Concho, TX, Sep 1881. SOURCE: LS, 10 Cav, 1873–83.

Served in G/10th Cavalry, 1898; remained in U.S. during war with Spain. SOURCE: Cashin, *Under Fire with the Tenth Cavalry*, 346.

LESLIE, Robert; Private; C/9th Cav. At Ft D. A. Russell, WY, in 1910; marksman; resident of La Grange, GA. SOURCE: *Illustrated Review: Ninth Cavalry*, with picture.

LESTER, Isaac A.; Private; E/24th Inf. Died of yellow fever in Cuba, 1 Aug 1898. SOURCE: *ANJ* 36 (11 Feb 1899): 567; AG, *Correspondence Regarding the War with Spain*, I:197.

LETCHER, Philip E.; Sergeant; K/10th Cav. Born in Kentucky; private, corporal, sergeant, F/10th Cavalry, 17 Oct 1879–16 Oct 1884; private, corporal, sergeant, K/10th Cavalry, 28 Oct 1884–27 Oct 1889; private, K/10th Cavalry, 21 Nov 1889; sergeant, 13 Jan 1890; at Ft Custer, MT, 1897. SOURCE: Baker, Roster.

Served as quartermaster sergeant, K/10th Cavalry, 1898; remained in U.S. during war with Spain. SOURCE: Cashin, *Under Fire with the Tenth Cavalry*, 349.

Quartermaster sergeant, A/10th Cavalry, Ft Robinson, NE, 1902, detailed to color guard. SOURCE: SO 62, 10 Cav, 9 Jul 1902.

Sergeant, K/10th Cavalry, Ft Robinson, 1904.

Age 48 in 1906 when wrote deposition in support of pension claim of Caleb Benson. SOURCE: VA File XC 2499129, Caleb Benson.

Enlisted Ft Leavenworth, KS, 1879; retired at Ft Robinson, 1906; after retirement worked nearly twenty years in postal service; resides at 3415 N. 28th Street, Omaha, NE; recently visited regiment. SOURCE: *Cavalry Journal* 46 (Nov 1937): 578.

LETCHERE; C/9th Cav. Shot Collins of C/9th Cavalry and arrested, turned over to military authorities in Crawford, NE, Jan 1897. SOURCE: Crawford *Tribune*, 1 Jan 1897.

LEVENBERRY, Arthur; Private; H/24th Inf. Enlisted Philadelphia, 10 Feb 1899; assigned and joined 22 Feb 1899. SOURCE: Muster Roll, I/24 Inf, Jan–Feb 1899.

LEVINS, John; A/10th Cav. Original member of 10th Cavalry; in troop when organized, Ft Leavenworth, KS, 18 Feb 1867. SOURCE: McMiller, "Buffalo Soldiers," 68.

LEWELLYN, John; Private; C/10th Cav. Arrested while sleeping behind forage barn near post several hours after command had departed. SOURCE: CO, Monument Station, KS, to CO, 10 Cav, 1 Jul 1868, LR, Det 10 Cav, 1868–69.

LEWERS, Carey; Trumpeter; F/10th Cav. Served in 10th Cavalry in Cuba, 1898. SOURCE: Cashin, *Under Fire with the Tenth Cavalry*, 343.

LEWIS; Private; B/10th Cav. At Ft Apache, AZ, 1890, subscribed $.50 to testimonial to General Grierson. SOURCE: List of subscriptions, 23 Apr 1890, 10th Cavalry papers, MHI.

LEWIS; Private; 10th Cav. Transferred from Hospital Corps in accordance with Special Order 226, Adjutant General's Office, 25 Sep 1902.

LEWIS, Asa L.; Private; F/24th Inf. At Ft Elliott, TX, 1886. *See* **SMITH**, Jacob Clay, Sergeant, 10th Cavalry

LEWIS, Bert; Private; I/48th Inf. Died of malaria in San Fernando, Luzon, Philippines, 26 May 1901. SOURCE: *ANJ* 38 (13 Jul 1901): 1110.

LEWIS, C.; Private; E/9th Cav. On detached service in field, New Mexico, 27 Jan–1 Feb 1881. SOURCE: Regt Returns, 9 Cav, Feb 1881.

LEWIS, C. J.; M/10th Cav. "Thinks the army is a good place for the colored man to learn discipline, regular habits, and save money, and affords an opportunity to study on the side. He speaks well of Santiago as an outlet for American negro talent. He joins his troop at Fort Robinson, Neb." SOURCE: Indianapolis *Freeman*, 27 Sep 1902.

LEWIS, Cary H.; QM Sgt; I/9th Cav. Veteran of Philippine Insurrection; at Ft D. A. Russell, WY, in 1910; sharpshooter; resident of Red Oak, OH. SOURCE: *Illustrated Review: Ninth Cavalry*, with picture.

LEWIS, Charles; H/10th Cav. Original member of 10th Cavalry; in troop when organized, Ft Leavenworth, KS, 21 Jul 1867. SOURCE: McMiller, "Buffalo Soldiers," 75.

LEWIS, Charles; Private; A/9th Cav. Returned to duty in accordance with telegram, Department of the Platte, 7 Sep 1891.

LEWIS, Charles; Private; A/10th Cav. Served in 10th Cavalry, 1898; remained in U.S. during war with Spain. SOURCE: Cashin, *Under Fire with the Tenth Cavalry*, 337.

LEWIS, Charles; Private; M/9th Cav. Veteran of Philippine Insurrection; at Ft D. A. Russell, WY, in 1910. SOURCE: *Illustrated Review: Ninth Cavalry*, with picture.

LEWIS, Clarence; Private; B/10th Cav. Released to duty from treatment for acute chancroids, Ft Robinson, NE, 4 Aug 1903. SOURCE: Post Surgeon to CO, B/10, 4 Aug 1903, LS, Post Surgeon, Ft Robinson.

General court martial mentioned in Special Order 118, Adjutant General's Office, 27 Jun 1904.

LEWIS, Coleman; K/10th Cav. Died of consumption at age 24 in U.S. Soldiers Home, 12 Oct 1897. SOURCE: SecWar, *AR 1898*, 1015.

LEWIS, Edward; M/10th Cav. Original member of 10th Cavalry; in troop when organized, Ft Riley, KS, 15 Oct 1867. SOURCE: McMiller, "Buffalo Soldiers," 79.

Certificate of disability regarding Lewis not received. SOURCE: AG, USA, to CO, 10 Cav, Jan 1870, ES, 10 Cav, 1866–71.

Senior vice commander, Col. Charles Young Camp 25, National Indian War Veterans, Washington, DC. SOURCE: *Winners of the West* 6 (Jun 1929): 4.

LEWIS, Edward; Private; I/10th Cav. Served in 10th Cavalry, 1898; remained in U.S. during war with Spain. SOURCE: Cashin, *Under Fire with the Tenth Cavalry*, 348.

LEWIS, Edward F.; Private; M/9th Cav. At Ft D. A. Russell, WY, in 1910; resident of Connersville, IN. SOURCE: *Illustrated Review: Ninth Cavalry*, with picture.

LEWIS, Ezekiel; Private; C/9th Cav. In D/9th Cavalry; teacher, Ft Robinson, NE, schools, Oct 1893–30 Apr 1894. SOURCE: Report of Schools, Ft Robinson, 1892–96.

Relieved of extra duty as schoolteacher, Ft Robinson. SOURCE: Order 39, 20 Jun 1894, Post Orders, Ft Robinson.

Qualified but not teaching, Ft Robinson, 1 Nov 1894–30 Apr 1895. SOURCE: Report of Schools, Ft Robinson, 1892-96.

Teacher, Ft Washakie, WY, 1 Nov 1895–27 Feb 1896. SOURCE: Report of Schools, Ft Washakie.

In C/9th Cavalry; fined $5 and $4.45 costs for being drunk and disorderly and fast riding, Crawford, NE, 6 Dec 1896. SOURCE: Police Court Docket, Crawford.

On extra duty as schoolteacher, Ft Robinson. SOURCE: SO 57, 1 Jun 1897, Post Orders, Ft Robinson.

Relieved of extra duty as schoolteacher and detailed on special duty as clerk, Adjutant's Office. SOURCE: SO 165, 10 Dec 1897, Post Orders, Ft Robinson.

LEWIS, Frank; Trumpeter; K/9th Cav. Company commander asks that enforcement of order banning wife of Trumpeter Lewis, K/9th Cavalry, be stayed until after payday so he can find place for his wife and family to live; commander, Ft Robinson, NE, says he is inclined to agree but a woman of her character should not be allowed on post. SOURCE: CO, K/9, to CO, Ft Robinson, 10 Feb 1887, and endorsement, CO, Ft Robinson, to CO, K/9, 10 Feb 1887, Register of Correspondence, Ft Robinson.

Discharged, end of term, Ft Robinson, character very good, 27 Apr 1887.

Promoted from private to corporal, G/9th Cavalry, 28 Jun 1892. SOURCE: Roster, 9 Cav.

Witness for defense, Barney McKay general court martial, Ft Robinson, NE, 1893. SOURCE: Court Martial Records, McKay.

Resides with wife, two grown daughters, and three children, at quarters of Lieutenant Alexander, Ft Robinson, 1893.

Authorized to reenlist in K/9th Cavalry as married soldier by letter, Adjutant General's Office, 18 Jan 1898.

LEWIS, Fred; Private; I/9th Cav. At Ft D. A. Russell, WY, in 1910; sharpshooter; resident of St. Louis. SOURCE: *Illustrated Review: Ninth Cavalry*, with picture.

LEWIS, George; H/10th Cav. Original member of 10th Cavalry; in troop when organized, Ft Leavenworth, KS, 21 Jul 1867. SOURCE: McMiller, "Buffalo Soldiers," 75.

On extra duty as teamster, Camp Supply, Indian Territory, Jul 1869. SOURCE: SO 54, HQ, Det 10 Cav, Camp Supply, 31 Jul 1869.

LEWIS, George; Corporal; I/9th Cav. Born Caroline Co., VA; brown complexion, Ht 6'0"; enlisted in H/24th Infantry, 10 Jan 1880; sergeant, 1 Aug 1884; reenlisted Ft Supply, Indian Territory, 12 Jan 1885; sergeant major, 29 Jun 1885; resigned 19 Dec 1887; transferred to G/24th Infantry; sharpshooter 1884 and 1885; transferred to 9th Cavalry, Feb 1888, single, character excellent. SOURCE: Descriptive Book, 24 Inf NCS & Band.

Corporal, I/9th Cavalry, deserter brought to Ft Robinson, NE, from Alliance, NE, by 2nd Lt. Guy H. Preston, 9th Cavalry, and two enlisted men of 8th Infantry. SOURCE: Order 61, 12 Mar 1889, Post Orders, Ft Robinson.

Former sergeant major, 24th Infantry, in Ft Robinson guardhouse charged with desertion and forgery; offered $150 check signed by Col. James Brisbin for goods bought in Alliance; "has the reputation of being a smart individual and writes a splendid hand." SOURCE: *ANJ* 26 (30 Mar 1889): 620.

Former member of 9th Cavalry and War Department messenger ingeniously forged General Grant's signature to pardon while serving sentence for forgery and nearly escaped, 11 Feb 1893. SOURCE: *ANJ* 30 (18 Mar 1893): 429.

LEWIS, George; Sergeant; D/10th Cav. Served in 10th Cavalry in Cuba, 1898. SOURCE: Cashin, *Under Fire with the Tenth Cavalry*, 341.

LEWIS, George P.; Private; L/10th Cav. Released to duty from treatment for gonorrhea, Ft Robinson, NE, 5 Jun 1903. SOURCE: Post Surgeon to CO, L/10, 5 Jun 1903, LS, Post Surgeon, Ft Robinson.

LEWIS, George W.; M/10th Cav. Original member of 10th Cavalry; in troop when organized, Ft Riley, KS, 15 Oct 1867. SOURCE: McMiller, "Buffalo Soldiers," 79.

LEWIS, Glendee; Private; I/9th Cav. At Ft D. A. Russell, WY, in 1910; resident of Madisonville, KY. SOURCE: *Illustrated Review: Ninth Cavalry*, with picture.

LEWIS, Hamilton; Private; B/24th Inf. Among men who distinguished themselves in 1889; awarded certificate of merit for gallant and meritorious conduct while escorting paymaster, Maj. Joseph W. Wham, when attacked by robbers between Fts Grant and Thomas, AZ; now out of service. SOURCE: GO 18, AGO, 1891.

At Ft Grant, 1890; certificate of merit mentioned. SOURCE: SecWar, *AR 1890*, 289.

LEWIS, Henry C.; Private; C/10th Cav. Assigned to machine gun platoon, Ft Ethan Allen, VT. SOURCE: SO 89, 10 Cav, 26 Nov 1909.

LEWIS, Isaac; Private; K/10th Cav. Served in 10th Cavalry in Cuba, 1898. SOURCE: Cashin, *Under Fire with the Tenth Cavalry*, 350.

LEWIS, Jackson; Private; G/9th Cav. To serve as guard for General Prisoner Frank H. Bosley from Ft Robinson, NE, to Ft Logan, CO, 6 Apr 1898. SOURCE: SO 58, 5 Apr 1898, Post Orders, Ft Robinson.

Check for $400 sent to Department of the Missouri headquarters for credit to Private Lewis, who did not endorse check. SOURCE: Letter, HQ, DeptMo, to CO, Det 9 Cav, Ft Robinson, 3 Aug 1898, Misc Records, DP.

LEWIS, James; D/10th Cav. Original member of 10th Cavalry; in troop when organized, Ft Leavenworth, KS, 1 Jun 1867. SOURCE: McMiller, "Buffalo Soldiers," 71.

LEWIS, James C.; Private; C/10th Cav. Served in 10th Cavalry, 1898; remained in U.S. during war with Spain. SOURCE: Cashin, *Under Fire with the Tenth Cavalry*, 340.

LEWIS, James P.; Private; A/9th Cav. At Ft D. A. Russell, WY, in 1910. SOURCE: *Illustrated Review: Ninth Cavalry*.

LEWIS, John; Sergeant; A/9th Cav. Retired from Ft Grant, AZ, Mar 1900. SOURCE: *ANJ* 37 (10 Mar 1900): 650.

LEWIS, John; Private; E/9th Cav. At Ft D. A. Russell, WY, in 1910; resident of Muskogee, OK. SOURCE: *Illustrated Review: Ninth Cavalry*, with picture.

LEWIS, John A.; Private; A/25th Inf. Died of chronic diarrhea in Cuba, 5 Aug 1898. SOURCE: *ANJ* 36 (11 Feb 1899): 567; AG, *Correspondence Regarding the War with Spain*, I:211.

Died at Siboney, Cuba, 6 Aug 1898. SOURCE: Hospital Papers, Spanish-American War.

LEWIS, John E.; Corporal; H/10th Cav. Letters from Lakeland, FL, 5 Jun and 1 Aug 1898, and from Manzanillo, Cuba, 30 Dec 1898. SOURCE: Gatewood, *"Smoked Yankees"*, 30–37, 58–59, 233–34.

Served in 10th Cavalry, 1898; remained in U.S. during war with Spain. SOURCE: Cashin, *Under Fire with the Tenth Cavalry*, 346.

At Camp Forse, AL, Nov 1898. SOURCE: Richmond *Planet*, 3 Dec 1898.

LEWIS, Joseph; Private; C/9th Cav. At Ft D. A. Russell, WY, in 1910; resident of Worow, GA. SOURCE: *Illustrated Review: Ninth Cavalry*, with picture.

LEWIS, Matthew; Private; M/9th Cav. Deserted at San Francisco, 11 Nov 1902. SOURCE: Regt Returns, 9 Cav, Nov 1902.

LEWIS, Morgan; C/10th Cav. Served 1873–78; new member, Camp No. 11, National Indian War Veterans. SOURCE: *Winners of the West* 5 (Mar 1928): 3.

Died at San Antonio, TX. SOURCE: *Winners of the West* 7 (Aug 1930): 9.

LEWIS, Peter; L/10th Cav. Original member of 10th Cavalry; in troop when organized, Ft Riley, KS, 21 Sep 1867. SOURCE: McMiller, "Buffalo Soldiers," 78.

LEWIS, Reuben; Private; C/25th Inf. To be tried for murder, San Antonio, TX. SOURCE: *ANJ* 38 (13 Apr 1901): 800.

Lawyer succeeded in getting indictment quashed because there were no blacks on either grand or petit jury. SOURCE: Fletcher, "The Negro Soldier," 139.

Still awaiting trial for killing another cook in mess kitchen of post. SOURCE: *ANJ* 39 (2 Nov 1901): 216.

Convicted of manslaughter for shooting Cook Brown, after waiting more than one year for trial. SOURCE: *ANJ* 39 (16 Nov 1901): 266.

LEWIS, Richard; Sergeant; D/10th Cav. Wounded in action during fight at Cheyenne Agency, Indian Territory, 6 Apr 1875. SOURCE: Leckie, *The Buffalo Soldiers*, 139.

Former deserter and dishonorably discharged from A/10th Cavalry; has served well and was badly wounded last year; should be allowed to serve out enlistment and get honorable discharge; request approved by Adjutant General, 1 Feb 1876. SOURCE: CO, 10 Cav, to AG, USA, 1 Feb 1876, ES, 10 Cav, 1873–81.

LEWIS, Richard D.; Private; H/25th Inf. Died in the Philippines, 2 Apr 1901. SOURCE: *ANJ* 38 (13 Apr 1901): 803.

LEWIS, Richmond D.; Corporal; M/9th Cav. Veteran of Philippine Insurrection; at Ft D. A. Russell, WY, in 1910. SOURCE: *Illustrated Review: Ninth Cavalry*, with picture.

LEWIS, Sprague; Trumpeter; D/10th Cav. Wounded in action at Santiago, Cuba, 2 Jul 1898. SOURCE: SecWar, *AR 1898*, 324.

LEWIS, Stephen; Sergeant; K/25th Inf. At Ft Niobrara, NE, 1904. SOURCE: Wilson, "History of Fort Niobrara."

LEWIS, T.; Musician; K/9th Cav. On detached service in field, New Mexico, 30 Jan–2 Feb 1881. SOURCE: Regt Returns, 9 Cav, Feb 1881.

LEWIS, Thomas; Private; C/10th Cav. His general court martial mentioned in Special Order 118, Department of the Missouri, 27 Jun 1904.

LEWIS, Thomas E.; A/49th Inf. Convicted of assault in the Philippines, Apr 1900; sentenced to one month.

LEWIS, William; Private; L/10th Cav. Sentenced to ten years for mutiny by general court martial, Bayamo, Cuba, 12 Oct 1899. SOURCE: *ANJ* 37 (24 Feb 1900): 602.

LEWIS, William H.; Corporal; Band/10th Cav. Stationed at Ft Robinson, NE; played "Les Bluets" euphonium solo, Crawford, NE, 13 May 1905. SOURCE: Crawford *Tribune*, 12 May 1905.

Commissioned second lieutenant at Camp Des Moines, IA, 27 Sep 1918. SOURCE: Glass, *History of the Tenth Cavalry*, appendix M.

LIDELL, Thomas; Private; F/24th Inf. Killed in action, Cuba, 1898. SOURCE: Scipio, *Last of the Black Regulars*, 29.

Died in Cuba, 2 Jul 1898. SOURCE: *ANJ* 36 (11 Feb 1899): 567.

LIEUSS, George; Recruit; Colored Detachment/ General Service. Convicted by general court martial, Columbus Barracks, OH, of being drunk while general prisoner, trying to strike Sgt. Robert van der Goltz with whiskey flask, putting his fist through prison window, trying to strike 1st Lt. John McMartin, 25th Infantry, Officer of the Day, and grabbing him by the coat until compelled to desist by members of guard, all on 21 Oct 1885; sentenced to dishonorable discharge and one year. SOURCE: GCMO 112, AGO, 19 Nov 1885.

LIGGINS, Robert; D/10th Cav. Original member of 10th Cavalry; in troop when organized, Ft Leavenworth, KS, 1 Jun 1867. SOURCE: McMiller, "Buffalo Soldiers," 71.

LIGGINS, William; G/10th Cav. Original member of 10th Cavalry; in troop when organized, Ft Leavenworth, KS, 5 Jul 1867. SOURCE: McMiller, "Buffalo Soldiers," 74.

LIGHER, James; E/10th Cav. Original member of 10th Cavalry; in troop when organized, Ft Leavenworth, KS, 15 Jun 1867. SOURCE: McMiller, "Buffalo Soldiers," 72.

LIGHT, General; Private; K/49th Inf. In the Philippines, 1900. *See* **BLUNT**, Hamilton H., Captain, K/49th Infantry

LIGHTFOOT, James R.; Sergeant; K/25th Inf. Born Culpepper Co., VA; moved to Washington, DC, as child; enlisted in C/25th Infantry, 1895; served in Montana; discharged mid-1898 and reenlisted for duty in Cuba; never fully rcovered from yellow fever contracted in Cuba; transferred to K/25th Infantry as corporal, then promoted to sergeant; killed eight miles north of San Felipe in enemy attack. SOURCE: Richmond *Planet*, 8 Sep 1900.

Awarded certificate of merit for distinguished gallantry in advance on concealed enemy at capture of insurgent stronghold, Camansi, Luzon, Philippines, 5 Jan 1900; killed in action, 14 Jul 1900. SOURCE: GO 32, AGO, 6 Feb 1904.

Virginian who showed "vim and coolheadedness"; wounded in arm and chest in ambush, 29 Jan 1900. SOURCE: Richmond *Planet*, 17 Mar 1900.

Killed in action, Cabangan, Luzon, 15 Jul 1900. SOURCE: *ANJ* 37 (28 Jul 1900): 1142; Cleveland *Gazette*, 15 Sep 1900.

LILLY; Private; E/10th Cav. At Ft Apache, AZ, 1890, subscribed $.50 to testimonial to General Grierson. SOURCE: List of subscriptions, 23 Apr 1890, 10th Cavalry papers, MHI.

LIMISON, Frank; A/10th Cav. Original member of 10th Cavalry; in troop when organized, Ft Leavenworth, KS, 18 Feb 1867. SOURCE: McMiller, "Buffalo Soldiers," 68.

LIMONS, Benjamin; Private; L/10th Cav. Mentioned Jan 1873 as having enlisted Sep 1867. SOURCE: LS, 10 Cav, 1873–83.

LINAIRE; Private; I/25th Inf. Shot and killed Sgt. Robert Yours, I/25th Infantry, at Ft Niobrara, NE, 25 Apr 1903, "during a fit of passion"; sergeant had called him vile names after he had refused to obey order to get up from bunk; Linaire shot Yours and was surrounded and disarmed; Yours "is said to have been rather overbearing"; Linaire in guardhouse. SOURCE: Crawford *Bulletin*, 1 May 1903.

LINCOLN, Robert; Private; 25th Cav. Born Beaufort, SC; occupation laborer, fair complexion, Ht 5'4 1/2"; enlisted, age 22, Charleston, SC, 2 Jul 1881. SOURCE: Descriptive & Assignment Rolls, 25 Inf.

LINDSAY, Gus; Sergeant; K/10th Cav. At Ft Robinson, NE, 1904.

LINDSEY, Henry; L/10th Cav. Served 1872–82; died in Chicago. SOURCE: *Winners of the West* 11 (Jul 1934): 3.

LINDSEY, John Q.; Sergeant; HQ Troop/10th Cav. Commissioned first lieutenant, Camp Des Moines, IA, 15 Oct 1917. SOURCE: Glass, *History of the Tenth Cavalry*, appendix M.

LINDSEY, William; Private; K/10th Cav. Served in 10th Cavalry, 1898; remained in U.S. during war with Spain. SOURCE: Cashin, *Under Fire with the Tenth Cavalry*, 349.

LIPPS, O. H.; Private; 25th Inf. Schoolteacher, Ft Missoula, MT, 1891. SOURCE: *ANJ* 29 (9 Jan 1892): 347.

LIPSCOMB, Frank J.; Private; C/25th Inf. Dishonorable discharge, Brownsville. SOURCE: SO 266, AGO, 9 Nov 1906.

LISK, Obey D.; Sergeant; E/25th Inf. Recommended for certificate of merit for support of Sgt. Robert Flint in saving lives and weapons of men of E/25th Infantry in perilous situation, Misamis Bay, Mindanao, Philippines; Flint also recommended for certificate. SOURCE: CO, E/25, to AG, USA, 23 Oct 1913, Scrapbook, 25 Inf, III.

LISLE, Frank; Corporal; C/10th Cav. Promoted from private, Aug 1902. SOURCE: *ANJ* 39 (30 Aug 1902): 1315.

LITTLE, Frank; Private; K/25th Inf. At Ft Niobrara, NE, 1904. SOURCE: Wilson, "History of Fort Niobrara."

LITTLE, William; B/10th Cav. Original member of 10th Cavalry; in troop when organized, Ft Leavenworth, KS, 1 Apr 1867. SOURCE: McMiller, "Buffalo Soldiers," 69.

LITTLEJOHN, James C.; Sergeant; D/9th Cav. Promoted from corporal, 9 May 1901. SOURCE: *ANJ* 38 (29 Jun 1901): 1065.

At Ord Barracks, CA, 1903; captain and shortstop of first squadron baseball team that lost to 15th Infantry on Sunday, 1 Nov 1903. SOURCE: Indianapolis *Freeman*, 5 Dec 1903.

LITTLEPAGE, Junius; Private; H/9th Cav. At Ft D. A. Russell, WY, in 1910; resident of Madisonville, KY. SOURCE: *Illustrated Review: Ninth Cavalry*, with picture.

LITTLES, Dillard; Private; B/25th Inf. Deserted from Santa Mora Hospital, Manila, Philippines, 25 Nov 1899. SOURCE: Regt Returns, 25 Inf, Dec 1899.

LIVAS, Harry; Private; F/9th Cav. At Ft D. A. Russell, WY, in 1910; resident of Jefferson Co., IN. SOURCE: *Illustrated Review: Ninth Cavalry*, with picture.

LIVINGSTON, James; Farrier; D/10th Cav. Without permission took pony belonging to Capt. A. S. B. Keyes, 10th Cavalry, from post at Ft Bayard, NM, to Central City, NM, Nov 1888. SOURCE: Billington, *New Mexico's Buffalo Soldiers*, 168.

Affidavit from PO Box 831, Mesa, AZ, 30 Nov 1925, verifies that Thomas Allsup was his first sergeant. SOURCE: VA File XC 2659797, Thomas H. Allsup.

LIVINGSTONE, Charles; E/10th Cav. Original member of 10th Cavalry; in troop when organized, Ft Leavenworth, KS, 15 Jun 1867. SOURCE: McMiller, "Buffalo Soldiers," 72.

LLOYD, Isaac H.; F/9th Cav. Telegraph operator. SOURCE: Cleveland *Gazette*, 28 Oct 1899.

Born in North Carolina; became farmer and logger after Spanish-American War; Army contractor and postmaster, Mariveles, Philippines; married Ynez Rocha, Filipino of Spanish descent; father of singing broadcaster Cecilio Lloyd. SOURCE: Thompson, "Veterans Who Never Came Home," 108, 112.

LLOYD, Lewis; Private; K/10th Cav. Served in 10th Cavalry, 1898; remained in U.S. during war with Spain. SOURCE: Cashin, *Under Fire with the Tenth Cavalry*, 349.

LOCK; Corporal; E/9th Cav. Served in 1867. *See* **DOUGLAS**, Joseph, First Sergeant, E/9th Cavalry

LOCKADOO, Matthew; Sergeant; B/25th Inf. Sick in Manila, Philippines, May 1900. SOURCE: Richmond *Planet*, 30 Jun 1900.

LOCKERY, Luther; Private; I/10th Cav. Served in 10th Cavalry, 1898; remained in U.S. during war with Spain. SOURCE: Cashin, *Under Fire with the Tenth Cavalry*, 348.

LOCKETT, George; Private; M/9th Cav. At Ft D. A. Russell, WY, in 1910; resident of Augusta, GA. SOURCE: *Illustrated Review: Ninth Cavalry*, with picture.

LOCKETT, Howard; Corporal; B/10th Cav. With Pvt. Andrew Forman escorted transport for quartermaster supplies en route to Ft Davis, TX, from camp near Pasadena, TX, May 1883.

LOCKETT, Walter; Corporal; I/9th Cav. At Presidio of San Francisco, CA, 1902. *See* **FARRINGTON**, George W., Private, I/9th Cavalry

LOCKHART, Fred; Private; E/9th Cav. At Ft D. A. Russell, WY, in 1910; resident of Atlanta. SOURCE: *Illustrated Review: Ninth Cavalry*, with picture.

LOCKMAN, George H.; Saddler; H/9th Cav. At Ft Robinson, NE, 1897.

Deposited $10 with paymaster, Ft Robinson, 1898.

In charge of unit bedrolls as H/9th Cavalry moved to ford Aguadores River, morning of 1 Jul 1898, prior to assault on San Juan, Cuba. SOURCE: SecWar, *AR 1898*, 706.

LOCKS, Walter F.; Private; B/10th Cav. Served in 10th Cavalry, 1898; remained in U.S. during war with Spain. SOURCE: Cashin, *Under Fire with the Tenth Cavalry*, 339.

LOCKSLEY, Thomas I.; Private; E/9th Cav. 2nd Lt. Guy H. Preston assigned as his defense counsel for general court martial, Ft Robinson, NE. SOURCE: CO, to Second Lieutenant Preston, 9 Cav, 4 Feb 1895, LS, Ft Robinson.

LOGAN, Addie L.; Private; C/9th Cav. At Ft D. A. Russell, WY, in 1910; sharpshooter; resident of Springfield, IL. SOURCE: *Illustrated Review: Ninth Cavalry*.

LOGAN, Frank; Private; M/10th Cav. Served in 10th Cavalry, 1898; remained in U.S. during war with Spain. SOURCE: Cashin, *Under Fire with the Tenth Cavalry*, 352.

LOGAN, Fred; Private; L/10th Cav. At Ft Robinson, NE, 1903; commander recommends general court martial. SOURCE: Register of LR, Ft Robinson.

Sentence in Special Order 233, Department of the Missouri, 30 Nov 1903.

Post surgeon recommends his discharge from Ft Robinson, Feb 1904; chronic venereal disease makes him unfit for duty. SOURCE: Post Surgeon to Post Adjutant, 10 Feb 1904, LS, Post Surgeon, Ft Robinson.

Discharged on certificate of disability with chronic venereal disease, 12 Feb 1904. SOURCE: Certificates of Disability, Ft Robinson.

LOGAN, Henry; Private; H/24th Inf. Fined $10 and jailed for one month by summary court, San Isidro, Philippines, for being drunk in quarters, 11 Nov 1901.

Sentenced to three months for failure to do certain extra fatigue and for being drunk and a nuisance in quarters, Dec 1901. SOURCE: Register of Summary Court, San Isidro.

LOGAN, Isam; Private; K/38th Inf. At Ft Cummings, NM, 1869; on escort duty between Fts Cummings and Selden, NM, traded his issue trousers for one dozen eggs; fined one month's pay. SOURCE: Billington, *New Mexico's Buffalo Soldiers*, 36.

LOGAN, J.; Sergeant; G/24th Inf. Qualified as sharpshooter with rifle, with 80.86 percent. SOURCE: GO 1, AGO, 3 Jan 1893.

LOGAN, Jacob; B/10th Cav. Original member of 10th Cavalry; in troop when organized, Ft Leavenworth, KS, 1 Apr 1867. SOURCE: McMiller, "Buffalo Soldiers," 69.

LOGAN, James; Saddler Sgt; 10th Cav. Honorable mention for gallantry against Kiowas and Comanches, Wichita Agency, Indian Territory, 22-23 Aug 1874. SOURCE: Baker, Roster.

Led detachment of eight from San Felipe, TX, on 150-mile scout of Rio Grande, seeking murderers of Colson family, 6–14 Jun 1879. SOURCE: SecWar, *AR 1879*, 112.

At Ft Grant, AZ, 1888. *See* **WELLINGTON**, William, Corporal, G/10th Cavalry

LOGAN, James E.; Sergeant; I/9th Cav. Served in K/10th Cavalry, as private, 1898; remained in U.S. during war with Spain. SOURCE: Cashin, *Under Fire with the Tenth Cavalry*, 349.

Corporal, second best marksman, Departments of the Missouri and Texas, 1903; third best in U.S. cavalry. SOURCE: Glass, *History of the Tenth Cavalry*, 43; SecWar, *AR 1903*, 1:427.

Ranked number 11, competition of Army cavalry team, and number seven, with silver medal and $19 cash prize, individual pistol match, Ft Riley, KS, 11–17 Aug 1904; ranked number one, competition of Pacific Division cavalry team, and number two, competition of Pacific Division pistol team, Ord Barracks, CA, 1904. SOURCE: GO 167, AGO, 28 Oct 1904.

Member of fourth place team, U.S. Army cavalry, national matches, Ft Riley, 1904, which split $150 and received medals. SOURCE: GO 172, AGO, 10 Nov 1904.

Distinguished marksman, 1903, as corporal, K/10th Cavalry; Department of the Missouri silver medal and Army gold medal; Division of the Pacific gold medal and Army silver medal, as private, I/9th Cavalry, 1904. SOURCE: GO 11, AGO, 27 Jan 1905.

Ranked number 12, Army pistol competition, and number nine, Northern Division pistol competition, Ft Riley, 1905; distinguished pistol shot, 1904, as private, I/9th Cavalry; Division of the Pacific silver medal, 1904; Northern Division bronze medal and Army silver medal, as corporal, I/9th Cavalry, 1905. SOURCE: GO 173, AGO, 20 Oct 1905.

Ranked number 109 among expert riflemen with 73.67 percent in 1905. SOURCE: GO 191, AGO, 31 May 1906.

Sergeant, I/9th Cavalry, best Northern Division marksman after 10–13 Aug 1906 meet at Ft Sheridan, IL; scored 779 out of 1,000. SOURCE: Indianapolis *Freeman*, 25 Aug 1906.

Ranked number nine, national pistol match, Sea Girt, NJ, bronze medal and $10, 1906. SOURCE: GO 190, AGO, 15 Nov 1906.

Ranked number 10, Army pistol competition, Ft Sheridan, 1906; distinguished marksman and pistol shot as sergeant, I/9th Cavalry. SOURCE: GO 198, AGO, 6 Dec 1906.

Expert rifleman and sergeant, I/9th Cavalry, at Ft D. A. Russell, WY, in 1910; resident of Washington, DC. SOURCE: *Illustrated Review: Ninth Cavalry*, with picture.

LOGAN, John; F/10th Cav. Original member of 10th Cavalry; in troop when organized, Ft Leavenworth, KS, 21 Jun 1867. SOURCE: McMiller, "Buffalo Soldiers," 73.

LOGAN, John; Sergeant; C/25th Inf. Retires Mar 1901. SOURCE: *ANJ* 38 (23 Mar 1901): 721.

LOGAN, John A.; Sgt Maj; 9th Cav. Promoted from lance corporal, C/9th Cavalry, Ft Robinson, NE, Apr 1895. SOURCE: *ANJ* 32 (11 May 1895): 608.

Reduced to ranks, C/9th Cavalry, Ft Robinson, Oct 1895. SOURCE: *ANJ* 33 (12 Oct 1895): 87.

Enlisted Chattanooga, TN, 23 Aug 1892, and assigned to C/9th Cavalry; served five years in C/9th Cavalry, six years in L/9th Cavalry, and six years on regimental noncommissioned staff; veteran of Spanish-American War and Philippine Insurrection; sergeant major since 29 Aug 1904; marksman, 1907. SOURCE: *Illustrated Review: Ninth Cavalry*, with picture.

Sergeant major, on soldiers boycott committee, Cheyenne, WY. SOURCE: Cheyenne *State Leader*, 15 Jan 1911.

LOGAN, Robert; Private; D/10th Cav. Casualty, fight at Cheyenne Agency, Indian Territory, 6 Apr 1875. SOURCE: Leckie, *The Buffalo Soldiers*, 139.

LOGAN, West; Private; C/25th Inf. Dishonorable discharge, Brownsville. SOURCE: SO 266, AGO, 9 Nov 1906.

LOGAN, William H.; A/9th Cav. Letter from Nueva Caceres, Philippines, 25 Dec 1900. SOURCE: Gatewood, *"Smoked Yankees"*, 290.

LOGERN, Thomas; A/10th Cav. Original member of 10th Cavalry; in troop when organized, Ft Leavenworth, KS, 18 Feb 1867. SOURCE: McMiller, "Buffalo Soldiers," 68.

LOKEMAN, Alferdo; G/10th Cav. Original member of 10th Cavalry; in troop when organized, Ft Leavenworth, KS, 5 Jul 1867. SOURCE: McMiller, "Buffalo Soldiers," 74.

LOMAX, John; Corporal; H/24th Inf. Enlisted Washington Barracks, Washington, DC, 22 May 1896, with five years' service. SOURCE: Muster Roll, H/24 Inf, May–Jun 1898.

Wounded in action, San Juan, Cuba, 1 Jul 1898; returned to U.S. for treatment. SOURCE: Muster Roll, H/24 Inf, Jul–Aug 1898.

Rejoined company from absence due to sickness, 9 Sep 1898; promoted to corporal, 14 Sep 1898. SOURCE: Muster Roll, H/24 Inf, Sep–Oct 1898.

On special duty as company clerk since 6 Nov 1898. SOURCE: Muster Roll, H/24 Inf, Nov–Dec 1898 and Jan–Feb 1899.

Wounded in Cuba, 1898. SOURCE: Muller, *The Twenty Fourth Infantry*, 19.

LONE, Milton; C/10th Cav. Original member of 10th Cavalry; in troop when organized, Ft Leavenworth, KS, 14 May 1867. SOURCE: McMiller, "Buffalo Soldiers," 70.

LONDON; Private; G/10th Cav. Wounded in action, Alamo, TX, 3 Aug 1880. SOURCE: Baker, Roster.

LONG, Charles; C/10th Cav. Original member of 10th Cavalry; in troop when organized, Ft Leavenworth, KS, 14 May 1867. SOURCE: McMiller, "Buffalo Soldiers," 70.

LONG, Edward; Private; E/10th Cav. Served in 10th Cavalry, 1898; remained in U.S. during war with Spain. SOURCE: Cashin, *Under Fire with the Tenth Cavalry*, 343.

LONG, Frank; Private; K/25th Inf. At Ft Niobrara, NE, 1904. SOURCE: Wilson, "History of Fort Niobrara."

LONG, Gid; Private; L/10th Cav. Served in 10th Cavalry, 1898; remained in U.S. during war with Spain. SOURCE: Cashin, *Under Fire with the Tenth Cavalry*, 351.

LONG, Henry; Recruit; 10th Cav. Served 1876. *See* **JACKSON**, Perry, Private, E/10th Cavalry

LONG, Isaiah; Private; C/10th Cav. Released to duty from treatment for acute gonorrhea, Ft Robinson, NE, 14 Nov 1903. SOURCE: Post Surgeon to CO, C/10, 14 Nov 1903, LS, Post Surgeon, Ft Robinson.

LONG, James; Private; H/49th Inf. Died of acute exacerbation of chronic dysentery aboard U.S. Army Transport *Grant*, bound for San Francisco, 10 Jun 1901. SOURCE: *ANJ* 38 (29 Jun 1901): 1073.

LONG, Louis; Private; L/25th Inf. Fined $10 per month for three months and confined to quarters for ten days by summary court, San Isidro, Philippines, for loafing around native canteen, resisting arrest, and insulting sergeant of the guard, 30 Jun 1902, first conviction. SOURCE: Register of Summary Court, San Isidro.

LONG, Robert; 10th Cav. Born Cardiff, TN; occupation miner, Ht 5'9", dark complexion; enlisted for colored infantry, age 22, Harriman, TN; grandfather Frank Butler resides at 155 Willis Street, Knoxville, TN. SOURCE: Recruiting Officer's Descriptive Book of Recruits, 1907–1908.

LONG, Roy; Private; F/10th Cav. Served in 10th Cavalry, 1898; remained in U.S. during war with Spain. SOURCE: Cashin, *Under Fire with the Tenth Cavalry*, 344.

LOOMIS, Amos; B/10th Cav. Original member of 10th Cavalry; in troop when organized, Ft Leavenworth, KS, 1 Apr 1867. SOURCE: McMiller, "Buffalo Soldiers," 69.

Mentioned as enlisting spring 1867, Memphis. SOURCE: LS, 10 Cav, 1866–67.

LOTT, Mert; Private; A/9th Cav. At Ft D. A. Russell, WY, in 1910. SOURCE: *Illustrated Review: Ninth Cavalry*, with picture.

LOTTERBERRY, John; Private; L/10th Cav. Served in 10th Cavalry, 1898; remained in U.S. during war with Spain. SOURCE: Cashin, *Under Fire with the Tenth Cavalry*, 351.

LOUIS, Marshell; Private; G/10th Cav. Served in 10th Cavalry, 1898; remained in U.S. during war with Spain. SOURCE: Cashin, *Under Fire with the Tenth Cavalry*, 346.

LOVE; Corporal; B/10th Cav. Wounded in action at Santiago, Cuba, 24 Jun 1898; left arm grazed by bullet. SOURCE: SecWar, *AR 1898*, 339.

LOVE, Charles H.; Sergeant; E/10th Cav. Private, E/10th Cavalry, at Ft Apache, AZ, 1890, subscribed $.50 to testimonial to General Grierson. SOURCE: List of subscriptions, 23 Apr 1890, 10th Cavalry papers, MHI.

Retired as sergeant, E/10th Cavalry, 13 Jun 1894. SOURCE: Baker, Roster.

LOVE, Cleda; Private; I/24th Inf. Mutineer, Houston, 1917, who had second thoughts; six-month veteran, age 20, testified under grant of immunity at court martial. SOURCE: Haynes, *A Night of Violence*, 147, 266.

LOVE, Frank W.; Sqdn Sgt Maj; 9th Cav. Born Kansas City, MO, 20 Nov 1877; enlisted Kansas City, 18 Aug 1900; served in D/25th Infantry, 18 Aug 1900–17 Aug 1903; E/9th Cavalry, 18 Aug 1903–17 Aug 1906; E/9th Cavalry and on noncommissioned staff, 9th Cavalry, Aug 1906–17 Aug 1909; appointed sergeant major, first squadron, 9th Cavalry, from sergeant, E/9th Cavalry, 16 Aug 1909; marksman, 1906; sharpshooter, 1908; expert rifleman, 1909; at Ft D. A. Russell, WY, in 1910. SOURCE: *Illustrated Review: Ninth Cavalry*, with picture.

LOVE, John; Private; K/24th Inf. Sentenced to eight years in military prison for assaulting his wife with intent to kill; escaped from guardhouse at Ft Brown, TX, 31 Dec 1878. SOURCE: Report of Trials, Department of Texas, 1878–79.

LOVE, Thomas; Private; E/48th Inf. Died of variola in the Philippines, 14 Dec 1900. SOURCE: *ANJ* 38 (29 Dec 1900): 431.

LOVELACE, Scott; Corporal; I/10th Cav. Age 65; resides at 547 West Orange, Jacksonville, FL; was at Ft Richardson, TX, Ft Sill, Indian Territory, and Ft Stockton, TX, with Floyd Crumbly; participated together in Indian campaigns under Capt. T. A. Baldwin. SOURCE: VA File XC 2624105, Floyd H. Crumbly.

Mentioned as Indian war survivor. SOURCE: *Winners of the West* 3 (Jun 1926): 7.

Enlisted Atlanta, 6 Nov 1876, and served five years; came out an invalid with rheumatism and catarrh; "I have slept many a night on the cold frozen ground covered with five foot of snow, without an overcoat, blanket, or shelter tent, with half rations, chasing the redskins to help blaze a right of way for the settlers of the wild west"; gets pension of $20 per month and is subscriber; resides in Jacksonville, FL. SOURCE: *Winners of the West* 4 (Dec 1926): 2.

Mentioned as subscriber. SOURCE: *Winners of the West* 9 (Oct 1932): 4.

Wants to hear from all who served in I/10th Cavalry, 1885–86; knew 1st Sgt. James Brown. SOURCE: *Winners of the West* 10 (Jan 1933): 1.

Renews subscription; now almost blind; has Spanish-American War veteran friend who reads *Winners of the West* to him; age 80; next door are illiterate Indians; came to California from home in Florida for cure for blindness; doctors have done nothing but take his money; pension reduced from $50 to $45 per month; guarded Indian prisoners at Ft Sill in 1876; campaigned three years against Apaches while Geronimo raided Texas; Indians captured Wesley Harday, comrade from Georgia, and burned him alive; saddler by trade. SOURCE: *Winners of the West* 11 (Apr 1934): 3.

Mentioned. SOURCE: *Winners of the West* 15 (Dec 1935): 1.

LOVELL; Private; F/10th Cav. Best running high jump in Department of Colorado, 1903, at 5'4", performed at Ft Washakie, WY. SOURCE: SecWar, *AR 1903*, 430.

LOVERY, Crawford; L/10th Cav. Original member of 10th Cavalry; in troop when organized, Ft Riley, KS, 21 Sep 1867. SOURCE: McMiller, "Buffalo Soldiers," 78.

LOVING, Charles K.; Private; C/9th Cav. Absent without leave from Ft Robinson, NE, 29 Mar 1887.

LOVING, John; Private; D/9th Cav. Joined as recruit from Jefferson Barracks, MO, 24 Dec 1880. SOURCE: Regt Returns, 9 Cav, Feb 1881.

LOVING, Lelwood; Private; H/10th Cav. Served in 10th Cavalry in Cuba, 1898. SOURCE: Cashin, *Under Fire with the Tenth Cavalry*, 345.

LOVING, Walter H.; Major; Philippine Constabulary. Born Livingston, VA; occupation musician, Ht 5'9", brown complexion; enlisted, age 21, St. Paul, MN, 22 Jun 1893; joined Band/24th Infantry, Ft Bayard, NM, 1 Jul 1893; transferred to D/24th Infantry, character very good, single, retained $14, 2 Sep 1893. SOURCE: Descriptive Book, 24 Inf NCS & Band.

Gave free vocal lessons and directed community band called High School Minstrels in Salt Lake City. SOURCE: Clark, "A History of the Twenty-fourth Infantry," 72.

Wrote E. J. Scott, secretary to Booker T. Washington, that he should look for Negroes outside Army for positions as chief musician in Negro regiments because only most competent could overcome opposition of regimental commanders. SOURCE: Fletcher, "The Negro Soldier," 147.

Captain, Philippine Constabulary; principal musician, 24th Infantry, and chief musician, 8th Illinois Infantry, before taking over constabulary band; in U.S. for President Taft's inauguration; will give concert at Keith's Hippodrome, Sunday afternoon and evening. SOURCE: Cleveland *Gazette*, 27 Feb 1909.

Captain, Philippine Constabulary Band, with pay of $2,525 per year. SOURCE: Cleveland *Gazette*, 26 Oct 1912.

Retires as major; will return to U.S. SOURCE: Cleveland *Gazette*, 4 Mar 1916.

Leaves Los Angeles to spend two months at Ft Bayard. SOURCE: Cleveland *Gazette*, 1 Apr 1916.

Director of famous Philippine Constabulary Band for twenty years as commissioned officer. SOURCE: *Crisis* 29 (Jan 1925): 125.

LOWE, Albert S.; Private; Band/10th Cav. Served in 10th Cavalry in Cuba, 1898. SOURCE: Cashin, *Under Fire with the Tenth Cavalry*, 359.

Picture. SOURCE: *Colored American Magazine* 6 (Aug 1903): 609.

Resides in Atlanta; plays violin, trombone soloist, trap drum; author of "Camp Life of the Tenth U.S. Cavalry," *Colored American Magazine* 7 (Mar 1904).

Was guest with wife at K/10th Cavalry's Thanksgiving dinner, Ft Robinson, NE, 1904. SOURCE: Simmons, "Thanksgiving Day in the Tenth Cavalry," 664.

LOWE, Charles H.; Private; G/10th Cav. Mentioned Apr 1877 as honorably discharged from Ft Sill, Indian Territory, Sep 1872, and as reenlisting, Kansas City, MO, 14 Dec 1872. SOURCE: ES, 10 Cav, 1872-81.

LOWE, Clifford; Private; Band/10th Cav. Served in 10th Cavalry in Cuba, 1898. SOURCE: Cashin, *Under Fire with the Tenth Cavalry*, 359.

LOWE, Hampton; Private; F/10th Cav. Original member of 10th Cavalry; in troop when organized, Ft Leavenworth, KS, 21 Jun 1867. SOURCE: McMiller, "Buffalo Soldiers," 73.

At Ft Lyon, CO, Mar 1869. SOURCE: LR, Det 10 Cav, 1868–69.

Relieved of duty in hospital. SOURCE: Special Order 21, Det 10 Cav, 18 Apr 1869, Orders, Det 10 Cav, 1868–69.

LOWE, James; K/10th Cav. Original member of 10th Cavalry; in troop when organized, Ft Riley, KS, 1 Sep 1867. SOURCE: McMiller, "Buffalo Soldiers," 77.

LOWRY, Richard T.; Trumpeter; D/9th Cav. At Ft D. A. Russell, WY, in 1910; marksman; resident of Huntsville, AL. SOURCE: *Illustrated Review: Ninth Cavalry*, with picture.

LOYD, Edgar; Private; G/10th Cav. Served in 10th Cavalry, 1898; remained in U.S. during war with Spain. SOURCE: Cashin, *Under Fire with the Tenth Cavalry*, 346.

LUCAS; Corporal; C/24th Inf. Absent without leave from Ft Huachuca, AZ, 1 Oct 1893. SOURCE: Name File, 24 Inf.

LUCAS, Aron; E/10th Cav. Original member of 10th Cavalry; in troop when organized, Ft Leavenworth, KS, 15 Jun 1867. SOURCE: McMiller, "Buffalo Soldiers," 72.

LUCAS, Gurnzie M.; Private; Band/9th Cav. At Ft D. A. Russell, WY, in 1910; resident of Washington, DC. SOURCE: *Illustrated Review: Ninth Cavalry*, with picture.

LUCAS, Jefferson; Private; B/10th Cav. Served in 10th Cavalry, 1898; remained in U.S. during war with Spain. SOURCE: Cashin, *Under Fire with the Tenth Cavalry*, 338.

LUCAS, John R.; Private; L/10th Cav. Served in 10th Cavalry, 1898; remained in U.S. during war with Spain. SOURCE: Cashin, *Under Fire with the Tenth Cavalry*, 351.

LUCAS, M.; Corporal; C/9th Cav. At Ft Cummings, NM, 1881; on detached service at Ft Bayard, NM, 2 Aug 1880–15 Jan 1881. SOURCE: Regt Returns, 9 Cav, Jan 1881.

LUCAS, William; Private; 38th Inf. Tried by court martial, Ft Cummings, NM, 1869. SOURCE: Billington, *New Mexico's Buffalo Soldiers*, 37.

LUCAS, Willie; Private; H/9th Cav. Veteran of Philippine Insurrection; at Ft D. A. Russell, WY, in 1910; resident of Savannah, GA. SOURCE: *Illustrated Review: Ninth Cavalry.*

LUCKETT, Thomas; Private; H/24th Inf. Fined $1 by summary court, San Isidro, Philippines, for absence from check roll call, 27 Mar 1902, first conviction. SOURCE: Register of Summary Court, San Isidro.

LUCKY, Joseph D.; Corporal; I/24th Inf. Enlisted Mobile, AL, 25 Jan 1899. SOURCE: Muster Roll, I/24 Inf, Jan–Feb 1899.

Promoted to corporal, 17 Aug 1899. SOURCE: Muster Roll, I/24 Inf, Jul–Aug 1899.

Allotted $15 per month to William H. Larkins. SOURCE: Muster Roll, I/24 Inf, Sep–Oct 1899.

LUMKINS, Ananias; Sergeant; I/10th Cav. Served in 10th Cavalry in Cuba, 1898. SOURCE: Cashin, *Under Fire with the Tenth Cavalry*, 347.

LUMPKIN, J. H.; Private; 9th Cav. Wounded in action, left arm, Naco, AZ, 21 Nov 1914. SOURCE: Cleveland *Gazette*, 13 May 1916.

LUMPKINS, Douglas; Private; 24th Inf. Served in Houston, 1917; convinced court martial he remained in camp during riot. SOURCE: Haynes, *A Night of Violence*, 86, 268.

LUMPKINS, John; Sergeant; M/9th Cav. Veteran of Philippine Insurrection; at Ft D. A. Russell, WY, in 1910; marksman. SOURCE: *Illustrated Review: Ninth Cavalry*, with picture.

LUNNEY, Mack; Private; 25th Inf. Born Darlington, SC; enlisted age 22, occupation miner, Ht 5'8", dark complexion, black eyes and hair, Charleston, SC, 25 May 1881. SOURCE: Descriptive & Assignment Rolls, 25 Inf.

LURSERRS, Henry; Private; D/9th Cav. On special duty at post headquarters, Nueva Caceres, Philippines, since 9 Oct 1901. SOURCE: SD List, D/9, 24 May 1902.

LUSK, John H.; G/10th Cav. Original member of 10th Cavalry; in troop when organized, Ft Leavenworth, KS, 5 Jul 1867. SOURCE: McMiller, "Buffalo Soldiers," 74.

LUST, Houston; Sergeant; D/9th Cav. Private, H/9th Cavalry, on detached service, Ft Bayard, NM, 29 Jan–16 Feb 1881. SOURCE: Regt Returns, 9 Cav, Feb 1881.

Sergeant, I/9th Cavalry, Ft Robinson, NE, 1881. *See* **JEMSON**, Joe, Private, I/9th Cavalry

Sergeant, D/9th Cavalry, appointed 1 Mar 1884. SOURCE: Roster, 9 Cav.

Resides at Ft Robinson with wife and one child, Aug 1893. SOURCE: Medical History, Ft Robinson.

Sergeant of guard, 11 Sep 1894, who arrested Sgts. David Dillon and Robert Benjamin; lived in quarters on post with wife. SOURCE: Court Martial Records, Dillon.

Sergeant, D/9th Cavalry, at Ft Robinson, 1895; sergeant since 1884. SOURCE: *ANJ* 32 (23 Mar 1895): 490.

Retires as sergeant, D/9th Cavalry, from Ft Washakie, WY. SOURCE: *ANJ* 34 (20 Mar 1897): 525.

LYLE, George; Private; F/9th Cav. Discharged on certificate of disability from Ft Stanton, NM, 11 Jan 1881. SOURCE: Regt Returns, 9 Cav, Jan 1881.

LYLE, Julius R.; Private; D/9th Cav. At Ft D. A. Russell, WY, in 1910; resident of Columbus, OH. SOURCE: *Illustrated Review: Ninth Cavalry*, with picture.

LYLES; Private; K/10th Cav. At Ft Apache, AZ, 1890, subscribed $.50 to testimonial to General Grierson. SOURCE: List of subscriptions, 23 Apr 1890, 10th Cavalry papers, MHI.

LYMAN, George; Color Sgt; 9th Cav. Singled out by Capt. Charles D. Beyer for bravery and gallantry against Victorio, Jun 1879. SOURCE: Billington, "Black Cavalrymen," 64; Billington, *New Mexico's Buffalo Soldiers*, 88–89.

Sergeant, C/9th Cavalry, at Ft Cummings, NM, 1881; on detached service in field in charge of five privates, C/9th Cavalry, scouting, 30 Jan–3 Feb 1881. SOURCE: Regt Returns, 9 Cav, Feb 1881.

Served with Henry Briscoe, Nov 1879–Jul 1882; in campaign against Victorio, including fight at Santa Rita Mountains, and remembers that someone was wounded. SOURCE: Affidavit, Leavenworth, KS, 29 Apr 1922, VA File C 2349975, Henry Briscoe.

Appointed corporal A/9th Cavalry, 26 Jun 1892. SOURCE: Roster, 9 Cav.

Corporal, A/9th Cavalry, Ft Robinson, NE, 1894.

Corporal, E/9th Cavalry, detailed as permanent color guard, 9th Cavalry, Ft Robinson, Jul 1895, with Cpl. W. H. Harper, E/9th Cavalry, and Cpl. E. N. Reynolds, H/9th Cavalry. SOURCE: *ANJ* 32 (3 Aug 1895): 807.

Corporal, A/9th Cavalry, appointed to regimental color guard, Ft Robinson, Mar 1896. SOURCE: *ANJ* 33 (28 Mar 1896): 540.

Sergeant, A/9th Cavalry, authorized to reenlist as married soldier by letter, Adjutant General's Office, 29 Dec 1896.

Ranked number three, carbine competition, Departments of Dakota, Columbia, and the Platte, at Ft Robinson, 27–30 Sep 1897. SOURCE: GO 64, AGO, 18 Nov 1897.

Color sergeant, 9th Cavalry, second best marksman in Department of the Platte, 1898. SOURCE: Cleveland *Gazette*, 21 May 1898.

Sergeant, 9th Cavalry, color-bearer in Cuba, 1898. SOURCE: Cashin, *Under Fire with the Tenth Cavalry*, 117.

LYNCH, George W.; Recruit; Colored Detachment/Mounted Service. Convicted by general court martial, Columbus Barracks, OH, of permitting prisoner he was guarding to get whiskey, Columbus Barracks, 9 Sep 1895; fined $5 with clemency based on recommendation of investigating officer, Captain Fletcher. SOURCE: GCMO 101, AGO, 12 Oct 1885.

LYNCH, Luther; Private; E/9th Cav. At Ft D. A. Russell, WY, in 1910; resident of Dallas, GA. SOURCE: *Illustrated Review: Ninth Cavalry*, with picture.

LYNCH, Washington; C/10th Cav. Original member of 10th Cavalry; in troop when organized, Ft Leavenworth, KS, 14 May 1867. SOURCE: McMiller, "Buffalo Soldiers," 70.

LYNN, Albert; Sergeant; 10th Cav. Died Mar 1973, "almost 90 years old"; served in Punitive Expedition, and in the Philippines, with 10th Cavalry; "He related how he cooked beans that were so sandy they were barely able to eat," during Pershing expedition; was cook and once cooked steer to serve his unit; in the Philippines troops on guard always went in pairs "to the little house," one guarding until the other returned. SOURCE: 9th & 10th Cavalry Association, *Bulletin*, Jul 1973.

LYONS; Sergeant; C/10th Cav. Wounded in action, Carrizal, Mexico, 1916; helped to safety by Cpl. John Jeter, C/10th Cavalry. SOURCE: Clendenen, *Blood on the Border*, 309–10.

LYONS, Daniel; Private; H/24th Inf. Enlisted Dallas, 7 Jun 1898; joined company 6 Sep 1898; owes U.S. $1 for ordnance (canteen, canteen straps, tin cup). SOURCE: Muster Roll, H/24 Inf, Sep–Oct 1898.
    Discharged Ft Douglas, UT, character excellent, single, 29 Jan 1899; due soldier $2.77 for clothing; reenlisted Ft Douglas, 30 Jan 1899; formerly served under name Daniel Lyon, Sep 1898–Jan 1899.
    Died of variola in the Philippines, 14 Mar 1900. SOURCE: *ANJ* 37 (24 Mar 1900): 707.

LYONS, Edward; Sergeant; G/9th Cav. Private, Band/9th Cavalry, with Band on detached service at headquarters, District of New Mexico, Santa Fe, 1880; played E-flat cornet. SOURCE: Billington, *New Mexico's Buffalo Soldiers*, 226.
    At Ft Cummings, NM, 1881. SOURCE: Billington, *New Mexico's Buffalo Soldiers*, 130.
    Wife returns to Ft Robinson, NE, from visit to Leavenworth, KS. SOURCE: Cleveland *Gazette*, 12 Jan 1888.
    Private, G/9th Cavalry, authorized to reenlist as married soldier by letter, Adjutant General's Office, 12 Jan 1898.
    Retires as sergeant, G/9th Cavalry, Apr 1900. SOURCE: *ANJ* 37 (5 May 1900): 851.

LYONS, Henry; Private; C/9th Cav. At Ft D. A. Russell, WY, in 1910; sharpshooter; resident of East Chattanooga, TN. SOURCE: *Illustrated Review: Ninth Cavalry*, with picture.

LYONS, J.; Sergeant; E/9th Cav. On detached service in field, New Mexico, 27 Jan–1 Feb 1881. SOURCE: Regt Returns, 9 Cav, Feb 1881.

LYONS, James; F/10th Cav. Served 1882–87; resides in Elkhart, IN; recent subscriber. SOURCE: *Winners of the West* 4 (May 1927): 2.
    Now gets $30 per month pension; credits *Winners of the West* with providing information needed to get increase. SOURCE: *Winners of the West* 7 (Feb 1930): 3.
    Expresses thanks for help with pension. SOURCE: *Winners of the West* 11 (Oct 1934): 4.
    Renews subscription; pension up to $50 per month; "thank God and also thank Comrade Webb." SOURCE: *Winners of the West* 14 (Feb 1937): 6.

LYONS, John; E/10th Cav. Original member of 10th Cavalry; in troop when organized, Ft Leavenworth, KS, 15 Jun 1867. SOURCE: McMiller, "Buffalo Soldiers," 72.

LYONS, John R.; Private; D/10th Cav. Risked life to save drowning comrade, at Mallets Bay near Ft Ethan Allen, VT, 6 Jul 1911; certificate of merit awarded 21 Aug 1911. SOURCE: AGO, Bulletin 9, 1912.

LYONS, Lewis; E/10th Cav. Original member of 10th Cavalry; in troop when organized, Ft Leavenworth, KS, 15 Jun 1867. SOURCE: McMiller, "Buffalo Soldiers," 72.

LYONS, Walter; Sergeant; L/10th Cav. Commissioned first lieutenant at Camp Des Moines, IA, 15 Oct 1917. SOURCE: Glass, *History of the Tenth Cavalry*, appendix M.

LYONS, Wilson; D/10th Cav. Original member of 10th Cavalry; in troop when organized, Ft Leavenworth, KS, 1 Jun 1867. SOURCE: McMiller, "Buffalo Soldiers," 71.

LYTLE, Claude; Private; A/3rd NC Inf. Died in Minnesota. SOURCE: Taylor, "Minnesota Black Spanish-American War Veterans."

LYTLE, John; F/10th Cav. Original member of 10th Cavalry; in troop when organized, Ft Leavenworth, KS, 21 Jun 1867. SOURCE: McMiller, "Buffalo Soldiers," 73.

LYTLE, William F.; Private; G/10th Cav. Served in 10th Cavalry, 1898; remained in U.S. during war with Spain. SOURCE: Cashin, *Under Fire with the Tenth Cavalry*, 346.

LYTTLE, Peter; Private; I/9th Cav. Arrived at Ft Robinson, NE, from Ft Washakie, WY, 24 Jan 1896, and sentenced by general court martial to six months; released 15 Jul 1896 and sent back to station.

LYTTLE, Samuel L.; Private; F/10th Cav. Judge advocate of Department of the Missouri disapproves recommendation of Lyttle's commander, Mar 1869, that his sentence be remitted so he can be discharged; Lyttle had been convicted of desertion. SOURCE: LR, Det 10 Cav, 1868–69.

M

MABERRY, Kelley; Private; I/10th Cav. Served in 10th Cavalry in Cuba, 1898. SOURCE: Cashin, *Under Fire with the Tenth Cavalry*, 348.

Enlisted in Nashville; wounded in action at Santiago, Cuba, 1898. SOURCE: Cleveland *Gazette*, 2 Jul 1898.

MABREY, Alfred; Private; B/24th Inf. Recruit from Tennessee; had his foot crushed trying to board train after it had started at Kearney, NE; had to have the foot amputated. SOURCE: Salt Lake City *Tribune*, 1 Oct 1898.

MABREY, York; L/10th Cav. Original member of 10th Cavalry; in troop when organized, Ft Riley, KS, 21 Sep 1867. SOURCE: McMiller, "Buffalo Soldiers," 78.

Admitted to Soldiers Home at age 43 with twenty-one years and nine months' service, 22 Jul 1889. SOURCE: SecWar, *AR 1889*, 1013.

Died of valvular disease of heart at age 51, U.S. Soldiers Home. SOURCE: SecWar, *AR 1903*, 4:257.

MABRY, Isam; Private; 9th Cav. Cited for gallantry against Victorio, Jun 1879, by Capt. Charles D. Beyer. SOURCE: Billington, "Black Cavalrymen," 64; Billington, *New Mexico's Buffalo Soldiers*, 88–89.

McADAMS, Clifford; Private; Band/9th Cav. At Ft D. A. Russell, WY, in 1910; resident of Colorado Springs, CO. SOURCE: *Illustrated Review: Ninth Cavalry*, with picture.

McADOO, Robert; Private; K/10th Cav. Served in 10th Cavalry, 1898; remained in U.S. during war with Spain. SOURCE: Cashin, *Under Fire with the Tenth Cavalry*, 349.

McADOO, Thomas; 1st Lt; 23rd Kans Inf. Resident of San Diego. SOURCE: Beasley, *Negro Trailblazers*, 284.

McALISTER; E/24th Inf. Remained in Tayug, Philippines, after service. SOURCE: Funston papers, KSHS.

McALLISTER, James. Junior vice commander, Col. Charles Young Camp No. 24, Washington, DC, National Indian War Veterans. SOURCE: *Winners of the West* 6 (Jun 1929): 4.

McALLISTER, Noah; Corporal; 9th Cav. Wounded in hand, Naco, AZ, 11 Oct 1914, and in left leg, Naco, 30 Nov 1914. SOURCE: Cleveland *Gazette*, 13 May 1916.

McBAIN, E.; Private; G/9th Cav. On detached service at Ft Stanton, NM, 29 Jan–5 Feb 1881. SOURCE: Regt Returns, 9 Cav, Feb 1881.

McBRIDE, George; Recruit; Colored Detachment/Mounted Service. Convicted by general court martial, Jefferson Barracks, MO, of loss of clothing and desertion, 8–9 Feb 1887; sentenced to dishonorable discharge and five years. SOURCE: GCMO 24, AGO, 14 Mar 1887.

McBRIDE, Martin C.; Private; H/10th Cav. Served in 10th Cavalry, 1898; remained in U.S. during war with Spain. SOURCE: Cashin, *Under Fire with the Tenth Cavalry*, 347.

McBRIDE, William; Private; A/10th Cav. Served in 10th Cavalry, 1898; remained in U.S. during war with Spain. SOURCE: Cashin, *Under Fire with the Tenth Cavalry*, 337.

McBROOM, James; Private; A/9th Cav. At Ft D. A. Russell, WY, in 1910; resident of Springfield, MO. SOURCE: *Illustrated Review: Ninth Cavalry*, with picture.

McBRYAR, William; Sergeant; H/25th Inf. Born Elizabethtown, NC; Ht 5'5 1/2", brown complexion. SOURCE: Descriptive & Assignment Cards of Recruits, 25 Inf.

First enlisted New York City, 3 Jan 1887. SOURCE: Lee, *Negro Medal of Honor Men*, 80–81.

Served as private, corporal, sergeant, first sergeant, K/10th Cavalry, and private, corporal, sergeant, and quartermaster sergeant, H/25th Infantry, 3 Jan 1887–8 Sep 1898; second lieutenant, 8th Volunteer Infantry, 29 Jul 1898; first lieutenant, 7 Sep 1898; discharged 6 Mar 1899; private and battalion sergeant major, 25th Infantry, 9 Mar–9 Sep 1899; second lieutenant, 49th Infantry, 30 Sep 1899; on detached service with 25th Infantry, 30 Sep 1899–30 Jul 1900; commander, K/49th Infantry, 5 Jan–27 Mar 1901. SOURCE: Descriptive Book, K/49 Inf.

Stationed at Ft Thomas, AZ, when he won Medal of Honor in engagement against Apaches, Salt River, AZ, 7 Mar 1890. SOURCE: SecWar, *AR 1890*, 290; Baker, Roster; Carroll, *The Black Military Experience*, 421.

Cited among men who distinguished themselves in 1890, for coolness, bravery, and good marksmanship against Apaches, Salt River. SOURCE: GO 100, AGO, 17 Dec 1891.

Sergeant, K/10th Cavalry at Ft Apache, AZ, 1890, subscribed $.50 to testimonial to General Grierson. SOURCE: List of subscriptions, 23 Apr 1890, 10th Cavalry papers, MHI.

Commissioned first lieutenant, 8th Volunteer Infantry, after Spanish-American War. SOURCE: Cashin, *Under Fire with the Tenth Cavalry*, 360.

Picture. SOURCE: Cashin, *Under Fire with the Tenth Cavalry*, 134.

Won commission for gallantry and meritorious service around Santiago, Cuba, 1898. SOURCE: Thweatt, *What the Newspapers Say*, 9–10.

Commissioned for bravery at El Caney, Cuba. SOURCE: Johnson, *History of Negro Soldiers*, 32.

Sergeant, H/25th Infantry, commissioned for gallantry at Santiago, Cuba, 1–2 Jul 1898. SOURCE: Richmond *Planet*, 13 Aug 1898.

Enlisted in 25th Infantry, Chattanooga, TN, 9 Mar 1899; most recent service in M/8th Volunteer Infantry; thirteen years' continuous service; arrived from furlough at Ft Logan, CO, 30 May 1899. SOURCE: Descriptive & Assignment Cards of Recruits, 25 Inf.

Appointed second lieutenant, 49th Infantry, from sergeant major, 25th Infantry. SOURCE: *ANJ* 37 (9 Dec 1899): 345b.

Second lieutenant, M/49th Infantry, as of 9 Sep 1899. SOURCE: Descriptive Book, M/49 Inf.

First lieutenant, 49th Infantry, as of 6 Oct 1900. SOURCE: *ANJ* 38 (24 Nov 1900): 307.

Philippine service mentioned. SOURCE: Villard, "The Negro in the Regular Army," 724.

M c CABE, Lorenzo; K/25th Inf. At Castillejos, Philippines, 1900. *See* **WISEMAN**, Turner H., Corporal, K/25th Infantry

M c CABE, William; Sergeant; E/9th Cav. Appointed sergeant Jul 1889. SOURCE: Roster, 9 Cav.

M c CALL, Henry; L/10th Cav. Original member of 10th Cavalry; in troop when organized, Ft Riley, KS, 21 Sep 1867. SOURCE: McMiller, "Buffalo Soldiers," 78.

M c CAMPBELL, George; Sergeant; M/9th Cav. On pass in Lander, WY, 31 Dec 1887–7 Jan 1888; died of spinal meningitis at Ft Washakie, WY, 3 Feb 1888.

M c CANTS, William; Private; 25th Inf. Born Mount Pleasant, SC; occupation farmer, Ht 5'4 1/2", fair complexion, black hair and eyes; enlisted Charleston, SC, age 21, 14 Jun 1881. SOURCE: Descriptive and Assignment Rolls, 25 Inf.

M c CANTS, William S.; QM Sgt; G/24th Inf. Ranked number 185 among rifle experts with 68.33 percent, 1904. SOURCE: GO 79, AGO, 1 Jun 1905.

M c CARTHY; Private; I/9th Cav. Probable author of petition to replace Capt. John Guilfoyle as commander of I/9th Cavalry, Ft Robinson, NE. SOURCE: CO to AAG, DP, 26 Jun 1891, LS, Ft Robinson.

M c CARTHY, Archie; Private; D/23rd Kans Inf. Born Riceville, TN; died in Minnesota, 25 Jan 1929. SOURCE: Taylor, "Minnesota Black Spanish-American War Veterans."

M c CARTHY, Elijah; Sergeant; K/9th Cav. Veteran of Philippine Insurrection; at Ft D. A. Russell, WY, in 1910; resident of Macon, GA. SOURCE: *Illustrated Review: Ninth Cavalry*, with picture.

M c CARVER, P. N.; Private; 9th Cav. Wounded in left leg, Naco, AZ, 17 Oct 1914. SOURCE: Cleveland *Gazette*, 13 May 1916.

M c CASKELL, Grant; K/49th Inf. Convicted of larceny in the Philippines, Sep 1900; sentenced to six months.

M c CAULEY, William; 1st Sgt; 24th Inf. Served as wagoner, F/10th Cavalry in Cuba, 1898. SOURCE: Cashin, *Under Fire with the Tenth Cavalry*, 343.

Last man left in regiment of those who stormed San Juan Hill; just retired with over thirty years' service; comes from "fighting stock," of parents who were former slaves of Confederate Gen. Fitzhugh Lee; born near Spottsylvania, VA, battlefield in town of same name; joined Army 1896; saw active service against renegade Indians, in Montana, who were fleeing Canadian authorities after Red River rebellion in Manitoba; on Samar, Philippines, with Pershing while in F/10th Cavalry; retired from 24th Infantry at Ft Benning, GA, Infantry School; almost 60, still hale and hearty, and to quote him "just lazy enough to make a good shot, 'cause I liked to lie down." SOURCE: *Infantry Journal* 41 (May–Jun 1934): 224.

M c CAW, Melvin; Sergeant; F/9th Cav. Promoted from lance corporal to corporal, Ft Duchesne, UT, 1 Jul 1895. SOURCE: *ANJ* 32 (13 Jul 1895): 758.

Promoted to sergeant. SOURCE: *ANJ* 34 (21 Nov 1896): 196.

M c CLAIN, Allen; Private; I/10th Cav. Released to duty from treatment for acute gonorrhea, Ft Robinson, NE, 13 Dec 1903. SOURCE: Post Surgeon to CO, I/10, 13 Dec 1903, LS, Post Surgeon, Ft Robinson.

M c CLAIN, Henry; Private; I/9th Cav. Born Bardstown, Nelson Co., KY; occupation carpenter, black complexion; enlisted Louisville, Dec 1888; discharged 9 Dec 1893; enlisted in I/9th Cavalry, Evansville, IN, 15 Mar 1894; farrier, 1 Sep 1894; corporal, 1 Jan 1895; private, 30 Dec 1895; blacksmith, 15 Jun 1896; private, 1 Aug 1896; discharged, Ft Washakie, WY, 14 Jun 1897; enlisted in I/9th Cavalry, Ft Robinson, NE, 27 Mar 1899; blacksmith, 1 Apr 1899; corporal, 1 Feb 1900; sergeant, 6 Aug 1900; private,

20 Feb 1902; discharged 23 Apr 1902; stations: Jefferson Barracks, MO, Dec 1888–Nov 1889; Ft Thomas, AZ, Nov 1889–Feb 1891; San Carlos, AZ, Feb 1891–Aug 1891; Ft Grant, AZ, Aug 1891–Apr 1892; Ft Custer, MT, Apr 1892–Dec 1893; Jefferson Barracks, Mar–Jul 1894; Ft Robinson, Jul 1894–Dec 1895; Ft Washakie, Dec 1895–Jun 1897; Ft Duchesne, UT, Mar 1897–Apr 1901; in the Philippines, May 1901–Apr 1902. SOURCE: VA File XC 2705872, Henry McClain.

Blacksmith, K/10th Cavalry, at Ft Apache, AZ, 1890, subscribed $.50 to testimonial to General Grierson. SOURCE: List of subscriptions, 23 Apr 1890, 10th Cavalry papers, MHI.

Corporal, I/9th Cavalry, at Ft Robinson, 4 Nov–7 Dec 1895, from Ft Washakie as witness in court martial of Pvt. Lewis Jones. SOURCE: Post Returns, Ft Robinson.

Reduced to ranks, Ft Duchesne, Jan 1896. SOURCE: *ANJ* 33 (18 Jan 1896): 348.

Married Louisa M. Massey in Chadron, NE, 21 Mar 1899; previously knew each other and lived together 1890–1894 while at Jefferson Barracks; she followed him to Crawford, NE, and they lived together until married. SOURCE: VA File XC 2705872, Henry McClain.

Died at residence three miles east of Crawford, age 43; leaves widow; came to Crawford about thirteen years ago, veteran of 10th Cavalry, enlisted in 9th Cavalry for war with Spain, and returned; born Nelson Co., KY, 1865. SOURCE: Crawford *Tribune*, 22 Nov 1907.

Widow Louisa M. McClain resided on "a dry ranch," to which she hauled water to do wash, against bluffs, about seven miles from Crawford; "well and favorably known in and around Crawford"; very poor, lived in one-room shack with fourteen-year-old boy, who picked up and delivered laundry she did; owned eighty acres worth about $1,000, a few chickens and pigs, one horse, one cow, a buggy; parents were Benjamin and Mary E. Nelson; her mother later married Daniel Joiner, farmer, of Madison Co., near Troy, IL; Louisa went to Crawford in 1896, same year her first husband, George Massey, died in St. Louis; husband Henry died 17 Nov 1907; pension: $30 per month in 1928; $15 per month in 1933; $50 per month as of 1 Apr 1944; died 1945. SOURCE: VA File XC 2705872, Henry McClain.

See **BECKETT**, William C., Sergeant, E/10th Cavalry; **GREEN**, James, Private, I/9th Cavalry; **HOWARD**, William, Sergeant, E/9th Cavalry; **JOHNSON**, Robert M., First Sergeant, K/10th Cavalry; **MITCHELL**, Woody, Private, B/10th Cavalry; **PRICE**, Charles E., 9th Cavalry

McCLAIN, John H.; Private; D/9th Cav. Convicted by general court martial, Jefferson Barracks, MO, of desertion, 7 May–17 Jun 1885; sentenced to dishonorable discharge and three years. SOURCE: GCMO 99, AGO, 29 Sep 1885.

McCLARE, Allen; Cook; L/9th Cav. At Ft D. A. Russell, WY, in 1910; marksman; resident of Greenwood, SC. SOURCE: *Illustrated Review: Ninth Cavalry*, with picture.

McCLELLAND, B.; Private; F/24th Inf. Died of disease at Ft D. A. Russell, WY, 18 Jan 1899.

Died at Ft D. A. Russell, 17 Jan 1899; buried on post with full military honors, 20 Jan 1899. SOURCE: Wyoming *Tribune*, 21 Jan 1899.

McCLOUD, Washington; I/10th Cav. Original member of 10th Cavalry; in troop when organized, Ft Riley, KS, 15 Aug 1867. SOURCE: McMiller, "Buffalo Soldiers," 76.

Mentioned Mar 1873; also known as Frank Richardson. SOURCE: ES, 10 Cav, 1872–81.

McCLUNG, Samuel; Private; L/10th Cav. Served in 10th Cavalry, 1898; remained in U.S. during war with Spain. SOURCE: Cashin, *Under Fire with the Tenth Cavalry*, 351.

McCOMBS, Henry; E/10th Cav. Resides in Greenwood, SC; expresses thanks for help in increasing pensions; "we made the West; defeated the hostile tribes of Indians; and made the country safe to live in." SOURCE: *Winners of the West* 4 (Dec 1927): 3.

Served in E/10th Cavalry, 1867–71; wants to hear from old buddies; age 84 and unable to work; he and his "good wife" appreciate their $50 per month pension. SOURCE: *Winners of the West* 8 (Feb 1931): 8.

Age 85; wants to hear from old comrades; "Let's keep up the good fight, and all stick together, and try to obtain justice for the ex-service men of Indian Wars." SOURCE: *Winners of the West* 8 (Aug 1931): 7.

Age 86; resides in Georgia; member Camp 11, St. Joseph, MO, National Indian War Veterans. SOURCE: *Winners of the West* 9 (Jun 1932): 3, with picture.

Mentioned as subscriber. SOURCE: *Winners of the West* 10 (Jan 1933): 3.

Died, age 90, at Dalton, GA. SOURCE: *Winners of the West* 11 (Jun 1934): 3.

McCONKEY, Nathan; Private; I/24th Inf. Enlisted Baltimore, 9 Feb 1899. SOURCE: Muster Roll, I/24 Inf, Jan–Feb 1899.

Fined $1 by summary court. SOURCE: Muster Roll, I/24 Inf, Jul–Aug 1899.

Allotted $5 per month for six months to Mary McConkey; on detached service at Ararat, Philippines, since 31 Oct 1899. SOURCE: Muster Roll, I/24 Inf, Sep–Oct 1899.

McCORMACK, Henry; Corporal; E/10th Cav. Born in Missouri; private, E/10th Cavalry, 27 Mar 1888–26 Mar 1893; private, 9 Sep 1893; corporal, 1 Feb 1897; at Ft Custer, MT, 1897. SOURCE: Baker, Roster.

Private, E/10th Cavalry, at Ft Apache, AZ, 1890, subscribed $.50 to testimonial to General Grierson. SOURCE: List of subscriptions, 23 Apr 1890, 10th Cavalry papers, MHI.

Served as private, E/10th Cavalry in Cuba, 1898. SOURCE: Cashin, *Under Fire with the Tenth Cavalry*, 342.

Wounded in action, Santiago, Cuba, 1 Jul 1898. SOURCE: SecWar, *AR 1898*, 324.

Corporal, E/10th Cavalry, frostbitten en route from Ft Washakie, WY, to Thermopolis, WY, in deep snow, Jan 1906. Name also spelled McCormick.

McCORMICK; Private; L/25th Inf. Killed in action, Subig Pass, Philippines, 10 Nov 1900. SOURCE: Richmond *Planet*, 12 Jan 1901.

McCOWAN, James G.; Recruit; G/Colored Inf General Service Recruits. Convicted by general court martial, Newport Barracks, KY, of refusing order of sergeant of guard to leave vicinity of guardhouse and when taken in charge by corporal of guard of striking him, 18 Sep 1875; sentenced to one month's confinement and $10 fine. SOURCE: GCMO 88, AGO, 8 Nov 1875.

McCOWN, Peter; 1st Lt; L/48th Inf. Born in Detroit; resided in Cincinnati, on enlistment; awarded distinguished service medal for gallantry at Santiago, Cuba, 1 Jul 1898, in lieu of certificate of merit. SOURCE: *Decorations, U.S. Army. Supplement I*, 36.

Private, D/10th Cavalry, 4 Dec 1885–3 Dec 1890, and 12 Dec 1890–31 May 1891; transferred to E/10th Cavalry, 1 Jun 1891; corporal, 1 Feb 1892; sergeant, 16 Jun 1893; at Ft Custer, MT, 1897. SOURCE: Baker, Roster.

Private, D/10th Cavalry, twice found in room of female servant of officer at reveille, Ft Bayard, NM. SOURCE: Billington, *New Mexico's Buffalo Soldiers*, 166.

Served as first sergeant, E/10th Cavalry in Cuba, 1898. SOURCE: Cashin, *Under Fire With the Tenth Cavalry*, 342.

Enlisted Philadelphia, 1885; won certificate of merit for distinguished service in battle of Santiago, 1898. SOURCE: *ANJ* 37 (24 Feb 1900): 610; Steward, *The Colored Regulars*, 280; GO 15, AGO, 13 Feb 1900.

Narrates Spanish-American War experience. SOURCE: Cashin, *Under Fire with the Tenth Cavalry*, 217–20.

Commissioned second lieutenant, 7th Volunteer Infantry, after Spanish-American War. SOURCE: Cashin, *Under Fire with the Tenth Cavalry*, 359.

Mentioned as first lieutenant, 48th Infantry. SOURCE: *ANJ* 37 (7 Oct 1899): 123; Beasley, *Negro Trailblazers*, 285.

Mentioned. SOURCE: San Francisco *Chronicle*, 15 Nov 1899.

Picture as first lieutenant, 48th Infantry. SOURCE: Indianapolis *Freeman*, 18 Nov 1899.

One of nineteen officers of 48th Infantry recommended as regular Army second lieutenants. SOURCE: CG, DivPI, Manila, 8 Feb 1901, to AGO, AGO File 355163.

See **SMITH**, Jacob Clay, Sergeant, 10th Cavalry; **CROUCH**, Albert S., Private, 10th Cavalry

McCOY, Burt; Corporal; H/25th Inf. Wounded in thigh, Tarlac, Philippines, 10 Dec 1899. SOURCE: *ANJ* 37 (30 Dec 1899): 412.

McCOY, Charles; Recruit; Colored Detachment/ General Mounted Service. Convicted by general court martial, Jefferson Barracks, MO, of desertion, from 5 Nov 1882 until his surrender, 28 Nov 1882; sentenced to dishonorable discharge and four years. SOURCE: GCMO 2, AGO, 3 Jan 1883.

McCOY, Emmett; Private; H/9th Cav. Single, discharged from H/9th Cavalry, Ft Robinson, NE, character very good; wants to reenlist for Ft Washakie, WY; vacancy exists there in I/9th Cavalry; requests authorization to enlist and to be forwarded there. SOURCE: Recruiting Officer to AG, DP, 11 Aug 1897, LS, Ft Robinson.

To be discharged 14 Aug 1897, with $75 retained and $1 clothing. SOURCE: CO, H/9, to Chief Paymaster, DP, 13 Aug 1897, LS, H/9.

Reenlistment authorized by telegram, Department of the Platte, Aug 1897.

MacCRARY, Andrew; G/10th Cav. Original member of 10th Cavalry; in troop when organized, Ft Leavenworth, KS, 5 Jul 1867. SOURCE: McMiller, "Buffalo Soldiers," 74.

McCRAY, Frank; Private; M/49th Inf. Engaged against insurgents, Tuao, Cagayan, Philippines, 18 Oct 1900. SOURCE: *ANJ* 38 (11 May 1901): 901.

McCRAY, Joseph; Private; K/10th Cav. Transferred from H/10th Cavalry in accordance with Special Order 64, Department of the Missouri, 1 Apr 1904.

McCREMENS, David; 49th Inf. Operated gas station, Quezon City, Philippines, until his death in 1924; left Filipino widow and four children; son Thomas is captain and operations officer, traffic bureau, Quezon City police department. SOURCE: Thompson, "Veterans Who Never Came Home," 108.

McCULLEN, George; Corporal; F/10th Cav. Promoted from private at Ft Washakie, WY. SOURCE: *Fremont Clipper*, 14 Dec 1906.

McCURDY, Walter; Sergeant; B/25th Inf. In the Philippines, 1899. SOURCE: Richmond *Planet*, 27 Jan 1900.

Developed bad leg cramp on march from Magalong to Mt Arayat, Philippines, 20 Dec 1899. SOURCE: Richmond *Planet*, 10 Feb 1900.

Before Brownsville, never charged with violation of discipline. SOURCE: Cleveland *Gazette*, 23 Feb 1907.

Dishonorable discharge, Brownsville. SOURCE: SO 266, AGO, 9 Nov 1906.

Acting quartermaster sergeant, B/25th Infantry, and sixteen-year veteran with Cuban and Philippine service when discharged. SOURCE: Weaver, *The Brownsville Raid*, 179.

McCUTCHIN, Ephriam; Private; H/10th Cav. On extra duty as teamster, Camp Supply, Indian Territory, 31 Jul–13 Aug 1869. SOURCE: SO 54, Det 10 Cav, 31 Jul 1869; SO 58, Det 10 Cav, 13 Aug 1869.

McDANIEL, Jackson; Private; F/9th Cav. At Ft D. A. Russell, WY, in 1910; resident of Birmingham, AL. SOURCE: *Illustrated Review: Ninth Cavalry*, with picture.

McDANIEL, Nathaniel; Private; C/10th Cav. Taken to asylum in Washington, DC, as insane, Sep 1892, by Sgt. B. Perea, Band/24th Infantry. SOURCE: Descriptive Book, 24 Inf NCS & Band.

McDONALD; Private; 10th Cav. Acquitted of murder in Yuma, AZ; last Dec threatened by white man Bert McBee in saloon and beat McBee to the draw. SOURCE: Cleveland *Gazette*, 18 Jul 1914.

McDONALD, E.; Private; D/25th Inf. Transferred from E/9th Cavalry in accordance with Special Order 179, AGO, 7 Aug 1893.

McDONALD, James M.; Private; H/9th Cav. At Ft D. A. Russell, WY, in 1910; resident of Dolgeville, CA. SOURCE: *Illustrated Review: Ninth Cavalry*, with picture.

McDONALD, John; Sergeant; F/9th Cav. Appointed 1 Jan 1889. SOURCE: Roster, 9 Cav.

Resides with wife and child under photo gallery, Ft Robinson, NE, Aug 1893. SOURCE: Medical History, Ft Robinson.

Sentenced to dishonorable discharge and two years for assault and shooting at a lance corporal, Ft Robinson. SOURCE: *ANJ* 31 (14 Apr 1894): 566.

McDONALD, Robert; Farrier; B/10th Cav. Reduced from sergeant to private, fined $30, and jailed for three months for allowing prisoner to escape through carelessness, Ft Thomas, AZ. SOURCE: *ANJ* 25 (24 Mar 1888): 694.

At Ft Apache, AZ, 1890, subscribed $.50 to testimonial to General Grierson. SOURCE: List of subscriptions, 23 Apr 1890, 10th Cavalry papers, MHI.

Served in 10th Cavalry in Cuba, 1898. SOURCE: Cashin, *Under Fire with the Tenth Cavalry*, 338.

Stabbed to death in Havana, Cuba, 12 Feb 1899. SOURCE: *ANJ* 36 (18 Feb 1899): 582.

McDONALD, Thomas; Private; I/24th Inf. Involved in Houston riot, 1917; sentenced to death. SOURCE: Haynes, *A Night of Violence*, 130, 277–78; Cleveland *Gazette*, 5 Jan 1918.

McDONALD, Timothy; Corporal; L/9th Cav. Veteran of Philippine Insurrection; at Ft D. A. Russell, WY, in 1910; resident of Austin, TX. SOURCE: *Illustrated Review: Ninth Cavalry*, with picture.

McDOUGAL, Barney; 24th Inf. Also called McKay. *See* **McKAY**, Barney, Sergeant, G/9th Cavalry

McDOUGAL, John; Private; 25th Inf. Enlisted Wichita, KS, and left for California en route to the Philippines, 13 Nov 1900. SOURCE: Wichita *Searchlight*, 17 Nov 1900.

McDOWELL, Edward C.; Private; L/10th Cav. Served in 10th Cavalry, 1898; remained in U.S. during war with Spain. SOURCE: Cashin, *Under Fire with the Tenth Cavalry*, 351.

McDOWELL, John; Private; B/24th Inf. On extra duty as teamster with Quartermaster Department, Ft Huachuca, AZ, 1–30 Nov 1893. SOURCE: Order 162, Ft Huachuca, 1 Nov 1893, and Order 177, Ft Huachuca, 30 Nov 1893, Letters and Orders Received, 24 Inf, 1893.

McDOWELL, John H.; A/24th Inf. Served 1879–84; subscriber, gets $40 per month pension. SOURCE: *Winners of the West* 9 (Jun 1932): 7.

Died Des Moines, IA; member Camp 11, St. Joseph, MO, National Indian War Veterans. SOURCE: *Winners of the West* 14 (Aug 1937): 5.

McDOWELL, Lewis Sanford; E/10th Cav. Served 1876–81; now age 81. SOURCE: *Winners of the West* 12 (Dec 1935): 2.

McDOWELL, Martin; Master Sgt; HQ Troop/10th Cav. Wagoner, G/9th Cavalry, at Ft D. A. Russell, WY, in 1910; sharpshooter; resident of Louisville. SOURCE: *Illustrated Review: Ninth Cavalry*, with picture.

Retires with thirty years' service. SOURCE: *Cavalry Journal*, 43 (Sep–Oct 1934): 77.

McDOWELL, William A.; Private; K/10th Cav. At Ft Robinson, NE, 1904.

Ranked number 534 among rifle experts with 68 percent, 1905. SOURCE: GO 101, AGO, 31 May 1906.

McDUFFIN, Ennis; Recruit; 9th Cav. To be sent from Louisville, via New Orleans, to 9th Cavalry in Texas. SOURCE: SO 147, Department of the Cumberland, 13 Aug 1868.

MACE, Alfred; Private; C/9th Cav. Murdered Pvt. Henry Roberts, F/9th Cavalry, at Ft Robinson, NE, 7 Dec 1886. SOURCE: Cleveland *Gazette*, 1 Jan 1887.

In hands of civil authorities, Chadron, NE, 11 Dec 1886–6 Jun 1887. SOURCE: Regt Returns, 9 Cav.

MACE, William; Private; D/10th Cav. Convicted of murder and won appeal, 1877. SOURCE: Leckie, *The Buffalo Soldiers*, 164.

McELROY, Archie; Private; F/10th Cav. Served in 10th Cavalry, 1898; remained in U.S. during war with Spain. SOURCE: Cashin, *Under Fire with the Tenth Cavalry*, 344.

McELROY, Marshall; Private; I/24th Inf. Enlisted Louisville, 20 Feb 1899. SOURCE: Muster Roll, I/24 Inf, Jan–Feb 1899.

Dishonorably discharged, Bali, Philippines, 18 Sep 1899, in accordance with sentence of general court martial. SOURCE: Muster Roll, I/24 Inf, Sep–Oct 1899.

McELROY, William W.; Private; A/9th Cav. At Ft D. A. Russell, WY, in 1910; sharpshooter. SOURCE: *Illustrated Review: Ninth Cavalry.*

McEWING, Duke; Private; Band/24th Inf. Born Nashville, TN; Ht 5'5", black complexion; first enlisted in Band/25th Infantry, and discharged 11 Nov 1880; enlisted Indianapolis, 18 Feb 1882; fined $10 and $5 by garrison court martials, 1884; discharged, end of term, character good, married, retained pay $72, deposits $50, clothing $92, 9 Feb 1887; enlisted Ft Leavenworth, KS, 14 Feb 1887; fined $5 by garrison court martial, 1889; discharged Ft Bayard, NM, married, in accordance with Special Order 30, Adjutant General's Office, 6 Feb 1891, retained pay $48, deposits $30, clothing $31; "He sometimes drinks too much, otherwise a good soldier." SOURCE: Descriptive Book, 24 Inf NCS & Band.

Chaplain Allensworth's striker at Ft Supply, Indian Territory, 1886. SOURCE: Alexander, *Battles and Victories*, 259.

McFADDEN, Charles; Private; E/9th Cav. At Ft D. A. Russell, WY, in 1910. SOURCE: *Illustrated Review: Ninth Cavalry*, with picture.

McFADDEN, Eddie M.; G/25th Inf. Convicted of entry, assault, and larceny in the Philippines Aug 1901; sentenced to two years.

McFADDEN, William C.; 3rd NC Inf. Died in Minnesota. SOURCE: Taylor, "Minnesota Black Spanish-American War Veterans."

McFARLAND; Private; K/10th Cav. At Ft Apache, AZ, 1890, subscribed $.50 to testimonial to General Grierson. SOURCE: List of subscriptions, 23 Apr 1890, 10th Cavalry papers, MHI.

McFARLAND, Lewis; Private; I/9th Cav. At Ft D. A. Russell, WY, in 1910; resident of Xenia, OH. SOURCE: *Illustrated Review: Ninth Cavalry*, with picture.

McGAUGHEY, George; 24th Inf. Enlisted Knoxville, TN, in 38th or 41st Infantry; in 24th Infantry for seven years after consolidation; in Mar 1928 will be 78 years old; resides in Chattanooga, TN, and gets pension of $50 per month. SOURCE: *Winners of the West* 5 (Feb 1928): 8.

McGEE, Allen; Private; C/24th Inf. Transferred from Reserve Divisional Hospital, Siboney, Cuba, to U.S. with yellow fever on U.S. Army Transport *Vigilancia*, 6 Sep 1898. SOURCE: Hospital Papers, Spanish-American War.

McGEE, Charles; Private; H/10th Cav. Served in 10th Cavalry, 1898; remained in U.S. during war with Spain. SOURCE: Cashin, *Under Fire with the Tenth Cavalry*, 347.

McGEE, Henry; D/25th Inf. Died of gunshot wound inflicted by comrade, Ft Niobrara, NE, 17 Sep 1902; buried on post with military honors, 18 Sep 1902. SOURCE: Monthly Report, Chaplain Steward, 30 Sep 1902.

Funeral of "our deceased brother, Henry McGee," Ft Niobrara, NE, 31 Oct 1902. SOURCE: Indianapolis *Freeman*, 15 Nov 1902.

Name also spelled McGhee.

McGEE, William; Private; B/48th Inf. Died of variola in the Philippines, Apr 1901. SOURCE: *ANJ* 38 (13 Apr 1901): 803.

McGHEE, Oscar; Sergeant; D/9th Cav. Private, D/9th Cavalry, at Ft Washakie, WY, 1897. *See* **STEED**, Luke, Private, D/9th Cavalry

Veteran of Philippine Insurrection; sergeant, D/9th Cavalry, at Ft D. A. Russell, WY, in 1910. SOURCE: *Illustrated Review: Ninth Cavalry*, with picture.

McGHEE, Samuel; Private; B/25th Inf. Dishonorable discharge, Brownsville. SOURCE: SO 266, AGO, 9 Nov 1906.

McGINNIS, Samuel R.; Sergeant; C/9th Cav. Veteran of Philippine Insurrection; at Ft D. A. Russell, WY, in 1910; sharpshooter. SOURCE: *Illustrated Review: Ninth Cavalry*, with picture.

McGOINS, Charles; Private; F/9th Cav. Discharged on surgeon's certificate, "character indifferent," 7 Jan 1887.

McGRAW; Private; G/10th Cav. At Ft Apache, AZ, 1890, subscribed $.50 to testimonial to General Grierson. SOURCE: List of subscriptions, 23 Apr 1890, 10th Cavalry papers, MHI.

McGUIRE, William Jr.; Private; C/25th Inf. Dishonorable discharge, Brownsville. SOURCE: SO 266, AGO, 9 Nov 1906.

McHENRY, Joseph; Private; K/24th Inf. Fined $5 for failure to repair for retreat, Cabanatuan, Philippines, 31 May 1901; witness: 1st Sgt. J. W. Stevens, K/24th Infantry. SOURCE: Name File, 24 Inf.

McHUE, Martin; L/10th Cav. Original member of 10th Cavalry; in troop when organized, Ft Riley, KS, 21 Sep 1867. SOURCE: McMiller, "Buffalo Soldiers," 78.

McINTOSH, Henry; Private; 25th Inf. Born Sumter, SC; Ht 5'5 1/2", black hair and eyes, dark complexion, occupation laborer; enlisted, age 28, Charleston, SC, 2 Jul 1881. SOURCE: Descriptive & Assignment Rolls, 25 Inf.

McINTOSH, Julius C.; Private; E/10th Cav. Served in 10th Cavalry, 1898; remained in U.S. during war with Spain. SOURCE: Cashin, *Under Fire with the Tenth Cavalry*, 343.

McINTOSH, Robert; Private; I/24th Inf. Enlisted Baltimore, 28 Mar 1899. SOURCE: Muster Roll, I/24 Inf, Mar–Apr 1899.

On detached service, Arayat, Philippines, since 3 Oct 1899. SOURCE: Muster Roll, I/24 Inf, Sep–Oct 1899.

McINTYRE, Burnett A.; Private; I/24th Inf. Enlisted Lexington, KY, 24 Jun 1899. SOURCE: Muster Roll, I/24 Inf, May–Jun 1899.

Allotted $10 month for twelve months to McIntyre. SOURCE: Muster Roll, I/24 Inf, Sep–Oct 1899.

Absent sick at Cabanatuan, Philippines, since 23 Dec 1899. SOURCE: Muster Roll, I/24 Inf, Nov–Dec 1899.

Died of pneumonia at Rosales, Luzon, Philippines, 28 Jul 1901. SOURCE: *ANJ* 39 (28 Sep 1901): 81.

McINTYRE, Calvin; Recruit; Colored Inf/ General Service. Acquitted by general court martial, Columbus Barracks, OH, of fraudulently enlisting at Cincinnati, by misrepresenting himself as unmarried. SOURCE: GCMO 36, AGO, 27 Mar 1893.

MACK; Private; A/10th Cav. Second best 100-yard dash in Department of the Missouri, at 10.4 seconds, in 1903. SOURCE: SecWar, *AR 1903*, 1:429.

Trumpeter and broadjumper. SOURCE: Clement, "Athletics in the American Army," 22, with picture.

Boxed Schiston, I/10th Cavalry, at Ft Robinson, NE, 15 Jan 1905. SOURCE: Crawford *Tribune*, 13 Jan 1905.

MACK, Clayborn; Private; B/10th Cav. 1st Lt. W. H. Beck, 10th Cavalry, was convicted of forcing Mack without cause to walk three days to camp at Pena Blanco, TX, 16–18 Oct 1878; Mack claimed that Beck called him "You Goddamn black ignorant son of a bitch," and that Mack respectfully informed Beck that his mother was a lady, although a colored woman, but that this was deleted from finding of guilty. SOURCE: GCMO 34, AGO, 30 May 1879.

MACK, Dolpheus; Private; D/10th Cav. Jailed to work on streets in lieu of $15 fine and $8.75 costs for carrying concealed weapon, Crawford, NE, 29 Jul 1902.

In hands of civil authorities, Crawford, 30 Jul–17 Aug 1902. SOURCE: Regt Returns, 10 Cav.

MACK, James L.; Private; H/25th Inf. Convicted by general court martial, Jefferson Barracks, MO, of desertion, 30 Jul–2 Aug 1880; sentenced to dishonorable discharge and five years. SOURCE: GCMO 58, AGO, 9 Nov 1880.

MACK, Louis; Sergeant; H/10th Cav. Honorable mention for gallantry against Kiowas and Comanches,

Wichita Agency, Indian Territory, 22–23 Aug 1874. SOURCE: Baker, Roster.

Wounded in action by Kiowas, Ft Sill, Indian Territory, Aug 1874. SOURCE: Leckie, *The Buffalo Soldiers*, 122.

MACKADOO, Richard; Private; C/9th Cav. Commended for bravery in fight against Apaches, Florida Mountains, NM, 24 Jan 1877. SOURCE: Leckie, *The Buffalo Soldiers*, 179; Billington, "Black Cavalrymen," 62; Billington, *New Mexico's Buffalo Soldiers*, 51.

Private bill passed for $20 per month pension. SOURCE: *Winners of the West* 3 (Apr 1926): 2.

Mentioned as surviving Indian war veteran. SOURCE: *Winners of the West* 3 (Jun 1926): 7.

Name also spelled Mackadew.

McKAY, Albert; Private; G/10th Cav. Served in 10th Cavalry, 1898; remained in U.S. during war with Spain. SOURCE: Cashin, *Under Fire with the Tenth Cavalry*, 346.

McKAY, Barney; Sergeant; G/9th Cav. Also known as McDougal.

Born in Kentucky, son of Barney McKay and Mary McDougal; one sister Hannah Taylor; occupation laborer, complexion brown; enlisted Indianapolis, IN, 16 Aug 1881, as private, general dismounted service; honorably discharged, 12 Jan 1892. SOURCE: VA File XC 2659455, Barney McKay.

Injured left leg on march from Ft Sill to Boulder Creek, Indian Territory, when thrown from baggage wagon which overturned, May 1882; reinjured when thrown by mule, 4 Aug 1884; had surgery on knee for floating cartilage, by Dr. Adair, Ft Robinson, NE, spring 1892. SOURCE: Affidavit, McKay, 1417 17th Street, Washington, 24 Jan 1916, VA File XC 2659455, Barney McKay.

Private, C/9th Cavalry, arrived Ft Robinson, NE, from depot, 1 Mar 1887.

Corporal, C/9th Cavalry, promoted to sergeant. SOURCE: Order 46, 9 Cav, 20 Sep 1888.

Sergeant, G/9th Cavalry, sentenced to dishonorable discharge and two years for "circulating an incendiary circular" among Ft Robinson troops, inciting them to lawless acts against civilians of Crawford, NE. SOURCE: *ANJ* 30 (22 Jul 1893): 795.

George W. Jackson met McKay right after he was released from military prison; friend Drayton Moffett in same regiment and company had written that McKay was in prison; Moffett was trying to enlist support to get him out. SOURCE: Affidavit, George W. Jackson, 1211 Linden Street, NE, Washington, DC, occupation bookkeeper, age 71, 5 Nov 1925, VA File XC 2659455, Barney McKay.

Worked in 1896 and subsequent political campaigns. SOURCE: Affidavit, Thomas H. R. Clarke, 6 Nov 1925, VA File XC 2659455, Barney McKay.

Ella Farrell first knew McKay around Jan 1897, when he resided at house of Mrs. Lacey's family, on K Street, between 17th and 18th Streets, NW; husband Charles J. Farrell, chauffeur, served with McKay in 9th Cavalry. SOURCE: Affidavit, Ella Farrell, 1416 P Street, NW, Washington, age 48, 30 Oct 1925, VA File XC 2659455, Barney McKay.

Coauthor with T. H. R. Clarke of *A Republican Text-Book for Colored Voters*, 1900, 48 pages.

Julia McKay, born and raised Hillsdale, Bergen Co., NJ, daughter of Samuel and Mary Moore, met McKay in Washington, 1900, while he worked for law firm of Lambert and Baker; married in Washington, 5 Jun 1902; no children; he had come to Washington after military service, was Pullman porter for some time, then ran newspaper in Camden, NJ, for a few months; notice of wedding published in Denver *Statesman* because he had number of friends in West whom he wanted to inform of marriage. SOURCE: Affidavit, Julia McKay, age 60, occupation dressmaker, 28 Oct 1925, VA File XC 2659455, Barney McKay.

Before enlistment worked as railroad porter and iron puddler and incapable of doing either; worked on New York Central Railroad, Oct 1896–May 1897, until knee and back gave way on New York-Chicago run; was carried off train at Buffalo, NY. SOURCE: McKay to Commissioner of Pensions Vespasian Warner, 13 Oct 1905, VA File XC 2659455, Barney McKay.

Letter, from 1620 L Street, NW, Washington, protests support by department commander Mitchell, of Spanish-American War Veterans, of dismissal of 25th Infantry battalion after Brownsville affray. SOURCE: Washington *Post*, 25 Jan 1907.

Mentioned. SOURCE: Acknowledgements to Curtis, *The Black Soldier*.

Editor, *Jersey Tribune* and *New England Torch-Light*; author of *Republican Text Book for Colored Voters* (1896), *Republican Party and the Negro* (1904), and *Hughes' Attitude Towards the Negro* (1916). SOURCE: Business card, "SERGT. B. M. MCKAY," VA File XC 2659455, Barney McKay.

Had $6 per month pension for injury to left knee; increased to $20 per month on 26 Oct 1922 based on syrionitis and floating cartilage in left knee; died 30 Apr 1925; widow, 1340 Corcoran Street, NW, Washington, died 2 Apr 1941. SOURCE: VA File XC 2659455, Barney McKay.

Born 27 Oct 1862; occupation watchman and government service; died at 1340 Corcoran Street from arteriosclerotic nephritis, myocarditis, and oremic toxemia; buried Harmony Cemetery, E. R. Jones, undertaker, 3 May 1925. SOURCE: Certificate of Death #2915000, District of Columbia, VA File XC 2659455, Barney McKay.

See CREGG, John L., Private, G/9th Cavalry; CRUMP, Edward W., Private, C/9th Cavalry; EDWARDS, William D., Corporal, A/10th Cavalry; PAYNE, Hayes B., Sergeant, K/24th Infantry; POWELL, George D., Sergeant Major, 24th Infantry

McKAY, George; Private; K/24th Inf. Soldiered in K/24th Infantry with William Branch at Ft Sill, Indian Territory, and Ft Duncan, TX; saw Branch in hospital, 1874. SOURCE: Affidavit, McKay, San Antonio, TX, age 30 [*sic*], VA File C 2581520, William Branch.

McKEE, Henry; Private; D/25th Inf. At Ft Niobrara, NE, 1902. *See* MORRIS, Edward, Private, D/25th Infantry

McKEEN, Robert; Corporal; F/9th Cav. Served in D/25th Infantry, and A and F/9th Cavalry, 1880–90; wishes to hear from old buddies. SOURCE: *Winners of the West* 5 (Aug 1928): 7.

Corporal, F/9th Cavalry, at Ft Robinson, NE. *See* HARRIS, Norbin, Private, F/9th Cavalry

Adjutant of newly organized Abraham Lincoln Camp 30, National Indian War Veterans, San Antonio, TX; resides at 501 Nevada Street, San Antonio. SOURCE: *Winners of the West* 6 (Oct 1929): 7.

Camp 30 busy lobbying for House of Representatives Bill No. 8976; meets in Odd Fellows Hall, under picture of Lincoln; "we are sure making the colored Spanish-American camp here awfully small." SOURCE: *Winners of the West* 7 (Mar 1930): 7.

Picture with three Camp 30 colleagues. SOURCE: *Winners of the West* 9 (Mar 1932): 7.

McKENNEY, Ed; Private; 24th Inf. Sentenced to seven years for part in Houston riot of 1917. SOURCE: Cleveland *Gazette*, 5 Jan 1918.

McKENNEY, Robert; Private; G/9th Cav. At Ft D. A. Russell, WY, in 1910; marksman; resident of Washington, DC. SOURCE: *Illustrated Review: Ninth Cavalry*, with picture.

MACKENS, Wallace; L/10th Cav. Original member of 10th Cavalry; in troop when organized, Ft Riley, KS, 21 Sep 1867. SOURCE: McMiller, "Buffalo Soldiers," 78.

McKENZIE, Edward; Sergeant; B/9th Cav. Sergeant, I/9th Cavalry, since 1 Aug 1880. SOURCE: Roster, 9 Cav.

On extra duty as wagonmaster, Ft Robinson, NE. SOURCE: Order 92, 4 Mar 1891, Post Orders, Ft Robinson.

Denies signing petition for removal of Capt. John Guilfoyle as commander of I Troop. SOURCE: CO, Ft Robinson, to AAG, Department of the Platte, 1 May 1891, LS, Ft Robinson.

Resides with wife and five children in old barrack, Ft Robinson, Aug 1893. SOURCE: Medical History, Ft Robinson.

In I/9th Cavalry; wife Annie died of paralysis, Ft Robinson, Feb 1895; she was sister of wife of 1st Sgt. George Mason, C/9th Cavalry; buried at post cemetery, 16 Feb 1895. SOURCE: ANJ 32 (2 Mar 1895): 439; List of Interments, Ft Robinson.

Retires from B/9th Cavalry, Ft Duchesne, UT. SOURCE: ANJ 35 (25 Dec 1897): 311.

McKENZIE, Frank; Private; G/9th Cav. Came out second best in fray with woman in Crawford, NE, Jun 1894; badly slashed with razor. SOURCE: Crawford *Gazette*, 22 Jun 1894.

McKIBBIN, Care; Private; H/10th Cav. Honorable mention for services rendered in capture of Mangas and his Apache band, Rio Bonito, AZ, 18 Oct 1886. SOURCE: Baker, Roster.

McKINNEY, James; Private; H/10th Vol Inf. Died in Minnesota. SOURCE: Taylor, "Black Spanish-American War Veterans."

McKINSEY, Meack; D/10th Cav. Original member of 10th Cavalry; in troop when organized, Ft Leavenworth, KS, 1 Jun 1867. SOURCE: McMiller, "Buffalo Soldiers," 71.

McKINZIE, Job; Private; G/9th Cav. Wounded in action at Tagitay, Philippines, 26 Oct 1900; died of wounds at Camalig, Philippines, 27 Oct 1900. SOURCE: Hamilton, "History of the Ninth Cavalry," 103.

McKNIGHT, A. H.; Corporal; 24th Inf. Served in Houston, 1917; did not participate in riot; on pass for date with daughter of David G. Burney, Houston's only black detective; spent the night at Burney's house rather than risk trying to get back to camp. SOURCE: Haynes, *A Night of Violence*, 185–86.

McKNIGHT, Clarence; Private; A/25th Inf. Ranked number 175 among rifle experts with 72.33 percent, 1905. SOURCE: GO 101, AGO, 31 May 1906.

Ranked number four at Southwestern Division rifle competition, Leon Springs, TX, 1907. SOURCE: GO 213, AGO, 19 Oct 1907.

McKNIGHT, Robert; Sergeant; G/9th Cav. Expert rifleman and veteran of Philippine Insurrection; at Ft D. A. Russell, WY, in 1910. SOURCE: *Illustrated Review: Ninth Cavalry*, with picture.

McKNIGHT, Roberts; Private; E/24th Inf. Died of typhoid, 31 Oct 1899. SOURCE: *ANJ* 37 (20 Jan 1900): 488.

McKOY, William; Trumpeter; C/9th Cav. At Ft D. A. Russell, WY, in 1910; sharpshooter. SOURCE: *Illustrated Review: Ninth Cavalry*, with picture.

McLAUGHLIN, Ephraim; H/10th Cav. Original member of 10th Cavalry; in troop when organized, Ft Leavenworth, KS, 21 Jul 1867. SOURCE: McMiller, "Buffalo Soldiers," 75.

McLANE, Carey P.; Sergeant; L/10th Cav. Private, L/10th Cavalry, first child, son Lorenzo A., born to wife, maiden name Cornelia E. Lindsay, Ft Robinson, NE, 10 Nov 1904. SOURCE: Medical History, Ft Robinson; Monthly Report, Chaplain Anderson, 1 Dec 1904.

Sergeant, L/10th Cavalry, commissioned first lieutenant at Camp Des Moines, IA, 15 Oct 1917. SOURCE: Glass, *History of the Tenth Cavalry*, appendix M; Sweeney, *History of the American Negro*, 126.

McLEARY, James; G/10th Cav. Original member of 10th Cavalry; in troop when organized, Ft Leavenworth, KS, 5 Jul 1867. SOURCE: McMiller, "Buffalo Soldiers," 74.

McLEOD, Gabrial; Private; A/24th Inf. Murdered by natives in the Philippines, 1899.

McMICHAEL, William; Private; L/10th Cav. Served in 10th Cavalry, 1898; remained in U.S. during war with Spain. SOURCE: Cashin, *Under Fire with the Tenth Cavalry*, 351.

McMICKEN, William; Private; E/9th Cav. Veteran of Philippine Insurrection; at Ft D. A. Russell, WY, in 1910. SOURCE: *Illustrated Review: Ninth Cavalry*, with picture.

McMILLAN, Emmett; Private; 24th Inf. Drowned crossing San Mateo River, Philippines, 21 Aug 1899. SOURCE: Richmond *Planet*, 2 Sep 1899.

McMURRAY, George W.; QM Sgt; C/25th Inf. Dishonorable discharge, Brownsville. SOURCE: SO 266, AGO, 9 Nov 1906.

McNABB, Lewis W.; Captain; K/49th Inf. Private, corporal, sergeant, first sergeant, D/24th Infantry, 19 Jul 1881–12 Oct 1899; captain, 49th Infantry, 13 Oct 1899; sick in quarters, disease contracted in line of duty, 1–7 Nov 1899; "died from gunshot wounds inflicted by his own hands Nov. 7, 1899." SOURCE: Descriptive Book, K/49 Inf.

Distinguished marksman as corporal, 1885 and 1886, and as sergeant, 1888. SOURCE: GO 73, AGO, 3 Oct 1888.

Sharpshooter, at Ft Meade, SD. SOURCE: *ANJ* 24 (21 Aug 1886): 70.

Sharpshooter, at Ft Bayard, NM. SOURCE: *ANJ* 26 (8 Aug 1888): 27.

At Ft Bayard, NM, Jul 1888; selected for Department of Arizona rifle competition, Ft Wingate, NM. SOURCE: Billington, *New Mexico's Buffalo Soldiers*, 154.

Sharpshooter, at Ft Bayard. SOURCE: *ANJ* 26 (20 Jul 1889): 962.

Sharpshooter, at Ft Bayard. SOURCE: *ANJ* 28 (27 Sep 1890): 70.

Sergeant, D/24th Infantry, ranked number 18 among rifle sharpshooters with 81.86 percent, 1890. SOURCE: GO 1, AGO, 2 Jan 1891.

Sergeant, D/24th Infantry, ranked number eight in competition of Army rifle team of distinguished marksmen, 1891. SOURCE: GO 81, AGO, 6 Oct 1891.

Led his company up San Juan Hill, Santiago, Cuba, 1898, after his officers were killed in action. SOURCE: Curtis, *The Black Soldier*, 41.

Suicide at Jefferson Barracks, MO, 7 Nov 1899; shot self through head with rifle; former first sergeant, D/24th Infantry. SOURCE: *ANJ* 37 (9 Nov 1899): 254, 345b.

McNEAL, S. H.; Private; M/49th Inf. Letter, Piat, Philippines, 3 Aug 1900, claims "our war is about over here";

resident of Galveston, TX; mentions L. M. Van Buren of Indianapolis, also in M/49th Infantry. SOURCE: Indianapolis *Freeman*, 6 Oct 1900.

Engaged against insurgents at Tuao, Cagayan, Philippines, 18 Oct 1900. SOURCE: *ANJ* 38 (11 May 1901): 901.

MᴄNEAR, Elijah; G/10th Cav. Original member of 10th Cavalry; in troop when organized, Ft Leavenworth, KS, 5 Jul 1867. SOURCE: McMiller, "Buffalo Soldiers," 74.

MᴄNEIL, Levy V.; Private; 24th Inf. Served in Houston, 1917; acquitted of participation in riot. SOURCE: Haynes, *A Night of Violence*, 290.

MᴄNEIL, Lewis O.; Private; 24th Inf. Sentenced to seven years for part in Houston riot, 1917. SOURCE: Cleveland *Gazette*, 5 Jan 1918.

MᴄNORTON, Burman; Private; H/9th Cav. At Ft D. A. Russell, WY, in 1910; marksman; resident of Christianville, VA. SOURCE: *Illustrated Review: Ninth Cavalry*, with picture.

MACON, Joseph; A/10th Cav. Original member of 10th Cavalry; in troop when organized, Ft Leavenworth, KS, 18 Feb 1867. SOURCE: McMiller, "Buffalo Soldiers," 68.

MᴄPHEETERS; Private; K/25th Inf. In the Philippines, 1900. *See* **ELLIS**, Corporal, K/25th Infantry

MᴄPHERSON, Alfred; H/10th Cav. Original member of 10th Cavalry; in troop when organized, Ft Leavenworth, KS, 21 Jul 1867. SOURCE: McMiller, "Buffalo Soldiers," 75.

MᴄREYNOLDS, George; Private; I/10th Cav. Served in 10th Cavalry, 1898; remained in U.S. during war with Spain. SOURCE: Cashin, *Under Fire with the Tenth Cavalry*, 348.

MᴄTRAMMICK, Charles; Private; L/9th Cav. Private, K/9th Cavalry, on detached service in field, New Mexico, 21 Jan–8 Feb 1881. SOURCE: Regt Returns, 9 Cav, Feb 1881.

Corporal, K/9th Cavalry, 1889. *See* **LANAM**, George, Private, K/9th Cavalry

Private, L/9th Cavalry, died in Sta. Mesa Hospital, Philippines, 16 Jul 1901. SOURCE: *ANJ* 39 (7 Sep 1901): 17.

MᴄWHORTER, Pat; Private; M/24th Inf. Served in Houston, 1917; sentenced to three months for threatening white contractor. SOURCE: Haynes, *A Night of Violence*, 79.

Urged comrades not to turn in weapons prior to mutiny. SOURCE: Haynes, *A Night of Violence*, 120.

"The company troublemaker"; sentenced to death for part in Houston riot. SOURCE: Haynes, *A Night of Violence*, 127, 271.

Hanged, Ft Sam Houston, TX, 13 Dec 1917, for part in Houston riot. SOURCE: Cleveland *Gazette*, 15 Dec 1917.

MADDEN, David; Private; F/25th Inf. Shot, apparently accidentally, by white man who was in midst of argument with white cavalryman, Rome, GA. SOURCE: Cleveland *Gazette*, 7 May 1898.

MADDEN, James; Corporal; F/9th Cav. Private, F/9th Cavalry; letter, Adjutant General's Office, 20 Sep 1892, concerns his transfer to 24th Infantry.

Private, F/9th Cavalry; letter, Department of the Platte, 23 Sep 1893, concerns his discharge in accordance with General Order 80, Adjutant General's Office, 1893.

Corporal, reenlistment as married soldier authorized by letter, Adjutant General's Office, 18 Jan 1895.

MADDERSON, Charles J.; K/10th Cav. Original member of 10th Cavalry; in troop when organized, Ft Riley, KS, 1 Sep 1867. SOURCE: McMiller, "Buffalo Soldiers," 77.

MADDISON, Charles; Private; K/10th Cav. At Ft Lyon, CO, Mar 1869. SOURCE: LR, Det 10 Cav, 1868–69.

MADEN, Ebbert W.; Captain; M/49th Inf. Enlisted in F/9th Cavalry, 1880; saddler, K/9th Cavalry, 1888; corporal, F and E/9th Cavalry, 1890; participated in Sioux campaign, 1890–91; served in Cuban campaign, 1898. SOURCE: *ANJ* 37 (18 Nov 1899): 278.

First sergeant, F/9th Cavalry; married Miss Annie Ewing, "one of Omaha's belles," at Chadron, NE. SOURCE: Cleveland *Gazette*, 24 Jul 1886.

Assigned south-end quarters, Laundress Row, Ft Robinson. SOURCE: CO to QM, Ft Robinson, 30 Oct 1886, LS, Ft Robinson.

Son buried at Ft Robinson [1886?]. SOURCE: List of Interments, Ft Robinson.

Sergeant, F/9th Cavalry, at Ft Robinson, 1887. *See* **HARRIS**, Robert, Sergeant, F/9th Cavalry

Reduced to ranks by garrison court martial, Ft Robinson, for quarrel with Sgt. Robert Harris, F/9th Cavalry, 13 Nov 1887; also careless with candle in stable, 12 Nov 1887. SOURCE: Order 226, 18 Nov 1887, Post Orders, Ft Robinson.

Private, F/9th Cavalry, transferred to K/9th Cavalry. SOURCE: Order 12, 9 Cav, 13 Mar 1888.

Private, F/9th Cavalry, assigned daily duty at post canteen, Ft Robinson. SOURCE: Order 36, 24 Feb 1890, Post Orders, Ft Robinson.

Private, F/9th Cavalry, assigned daily duty at post canteen, Ft Robinson, vice Pvt. William B. Griffith, B/9th Cavalry. SOURCE: Order 131, Jun 1890, Post Orders, Ft Robinson.

Private, F/9th Cavalry, assigned daily duty at post canteen, Ft Robinson. SOURCE: Order 183, 31 Aug 1890, Post Orders, Ft Robinson.

Relieved from duty at canteen. SOURCE: Order 248, 18 Nov 1890, Post Orders, Ft Robinson.

On special duty as assistant, post canteen, Ft Robinson. SOURCE: Order 61, 31 Mar 1891, Post Orders, Ft Robinson.

Appointed corporal, F/9th Cavalry, 3 Nov 1891. SOURCE: Roster, 9 Cav.

Commander recognizes his prompt notification of guard of escape of prisoner and his energy and good judgment in capture and return of prisoner: "Such devotion to the interest of the service when off as well as on duty is a worthy example to all"; corporal, F/9th Cavalry. SOURCE: Order 77, 7 May 1892, Post Orders, Ft Robinson.

Ranked number eight in carbine competition, Departments of the East, California, and the Platte, Bellevue, NE, 18–25 Sep 1894. SOURCE: GO 62, AGO, 15 Nov 1894.

At Ft Robinson, NE, 1895; corporal since 3 Nov 1892. SOURCE: *ANJ* 32 (23 Feb 1895): 422.

Promoted to sergeant, Ft Robinson, 10 May 1895. SOURCE: *ANJ* 32 (25 May 1895): 642.

Reenlistment as married soldier authorized by letter, Adjutant General's Office, 14 Jan 1898.

Family resides at Ft Robinson and claims to be indigent, dependent on charity of garrison for subsistence. SOURCE: CO, Ft Robinson, to CO, 9 Cav, 25 Jul 1898, LS, Ft Robinson.

First lieutenant, B/49th Infantry, as of 9 Sep 1899; transferred to M/49th Infantry, 28 Oct 1899; promoted to captain, 14 Nov 1899. SOURCE: Descriptive Book, B/49 Inf.

MADISON, Charles H.; Corporal; C/25th Inf. Dishonorable discharge, Brownsville. SOURCE: SO 266, AGO, 9 Nov 1906.

MAGRUDER, John; Private; K/10th Cav. *See* **BRANSFORD**, Wesley, Private, K/10th Cavalry

MAHAN, Foster; Private; E/24th Inf. At Ft D. A. Russell, WY, 1899; in hands of civil authorities, Cheyenne, WY, 10 Mar–Apr and 22 Jun–31 Jul 1899.

Shot Private Cross in west-end dive, Cheyenne. SOURCE: Cheyenne *Daily Sun-Leader*, 13 Apr 1899.

MAHI, Joe; Private; C/49th Inf. Deserted, Honolulu, HI, 12 Dec 1899. SOURCE: Descriptive Book, M/49 Inf.

MAHIN, Edward; Private; I/9th Cav. At Ft D. A. Russell, WY, in 1910; resident of Nashville, TN. SOURCE: *Illustrated Review: Ninth Cavalry*, with picture.

MAILEY, Thomas; I/10th Cav. Original member of 10th Cavalry; in troop when organized, Ft Riley, KS, 15 Aug 1867. SOURCE: McMiller, "Buffalo Soldiers," 76.

MAIN, Mark; D/10th Cav. Original member of 10th Cavalry; in troop when organized, Ft Leavenworth, KS, 1 Jun 1867. SOURCE: McMiller, "Buffalo Soldiers," 71.

MAITLAND, Henry; Recruit; 25th Inf. Served in 1884. *See* **JONES**, Stephen, Recruit, 25th Infantry

MAJOR, Melvin; Private; H/24th Inf. Fined $4 by summary court, San Isidro, Philippines, for absence from eleven P.M. inspection, 30 Jan 1902, second conviction. SOURCE: Register of Summary Court, San Isidro.

MAJOR, Oliver; I/10th Cav. Admitted to Soldiers Home with disability at age 24 with one year and five months' service, 24 Apr 1885. SOURCE: SecWar, *AR 1885*, 829.

MAJORS, William; Private; D/10th Cav. Served in 10th Cavalry, 1898; remained in U.S. during war with Spain. SOURCE: Cashin, *Under Fire with the Tenth Cavalry*, 341.

MALBORNE, George H.; Recruit; 25th Inf. Served in 1884. *See* **JONES**, Stephen, Recruit, 25th Infantry

MALLORY, Joseph; Private; A/9th Cav. Veteran of Philippine Insurrection; at Ft D. A. Russell, WY, in 1910. SOURCE: *Illustrated Review: Ninth Cavalry*.

MALONE, Edgar; Sergeant; F/10th Cav. Private, F/10th Cavalry, promoted to corporal. SOURCE: SO 93, 10 Cav, Ft Ethan Allen, VT, 11 Dec 1909.

Sergeant, F/10th Cavalry, commissioned captain at Camp Des Moines, IA, 15 Oct 1917. SOURCE: Glass, *History of the Tenth Cavalry*, appendix M.

MALONE, Henry; I/10th Cav. Original member of 10th Cavalry; in troop when organized, Ft Riley, KS, 15 Aug 1867. SOURCE: McMiller, "Buffalo Soldiers," 76.

MALONE, James E.; G/10th Cav. Original member of 10th Cavalry; in troop when organized, Ft Leavenworth, KS, 5 Jul 1867. SOURCE: McMiller, "Buffalo Soldiers," 74.

MALONE, John; Private; D/24th Inf. Born Courtland, AL; occupation laborer, dark complexion; enlisted, age 22 1/2, Tuscumbia, AL, for three years; deserted Ft Harrison, MT, 12 Jun 1904; apprehended at Sweet Grass, MT, 14 Jul 1904; dishonorably discharged from Ft Harrison, 23 Jul 1904. SOURCE: Misc Records, DeptMo, 1904–1912.

MANAGAULT, William; Private; K/10th Cav. Released to duty from treatment for acute gonorrhea, Ft Robinson, NE, 8 Dec 1903. SOURCE: Post Surgeon to CO, K/10, 8 Dec 1903, LS, Post Surgeon, Ft Robinson.

At Ft Robinson, 1904.

MANLEY, Edward W.; Private; F/10th Cav. Served in 10th Cavalry in Cuba, 1898. SOURCE: Cashin, *Under Fire with the Tenth Cavalry*, 344.

MANN, Frank T.; Private; I/24th Inf. Enlisted Cleveland, OH, 8 Feb 1899. SOURCE: Muster Roll, I/24 Inf, Jan–Feb 1899.

On detached service at Three Rivers, CA, 3 May–21 Jun 1899; on detached service at Presidio of San Francisco, CA, 22 Jun–26 Jul 1899. SOURCE: Muster Roll, I/24 Inf, May–Jun and Jul–Aug 1899.

Allotted $10 per month for twelve months to Wella Mann. SOURCE: Muster Roll, I/24 Inf, Sep–Oct 1899.

MANN, Louis; Private; F/9th Cav. Discharged on surgeon's certificate with syphilis at Ft Robinson, NE, Feb 1888.

MANN, Simpson; Private; F/9th Cav. Resided Mickles Mill, Monroe Co., WV; enlisted, age 27, Cincinnati, 1888; served one three-year enlistment at Ft Robinson, NE. SOURCE: Rickey, Mann interview.

Convicted by garrison court martial of absence without permission over night of 2–3 Nov 1889; $5 retained from pay until discharge. SOURCE: Order 233, 8 Nov 1899, Post Orders, Ft Robinson.

One hundred-three-year-old veteran awarded Indian wars campaign medal at Wadsworth Hospital, 13 May 1965. SOURCE: Rickey, "The Negro Regulars," 1.

MANNING, Charles; Private; G/10th Cav. Served in 10th Cavalry, 1898; remained in U.S. during war with Spain. SOURCE: Cashin, *Under Fire with the Tenth Cavalry,* 346.

MANNING, James E.; Private; C/9th Cav. In hands of civil authorities, Crawford, NE, 22 Jun–14 Jul 1887, and Salt Lake City, 28 Sep 1888–May 1889. SOURCE: Regt Returns, 9 Cav.

MANNY, George; K/10th Cav. Original member of 10th Cavalry; in troop when organized, Ft Riley, KS, 1 Sep 1867. SOURCE: McMiller, "Buffalo Soldiers," 77.

MANSON, William; D/24th Inf. Letter from Ft Supply, Indian Territory, described Christmas, 1885. SOURCE: Cleveland *Gazette,* 9 Jan 1886.

MANVILLE, Mark (pseud.); Recruit; General Mounted Service. *See* **COUNTEE**, Charles, Private, K/10th Cavalry

MAPP, Wesley; Private; D/25th Inf. Dishonorable discharge, Brownsville. SOURCE: SO 266, AGO, 9 Nov 1906.

MAPP, William; Private; C/25th Inf. Dishonorable discharge, Brownsville. SOURCE: SO 266, AGO, 9 Nov 1906.

MARATTA, William H.; Private; Band/9th Cav. At Ft D. A. Russell, WY, in 1910; resident of Louisville. SOURCE: *Illustrated Review: Ninth Cavalry,* with picture.

MARCHBANKS, Vance H.; Sergeant; C/10th Cav. Private, A/9th Cavalry, detailed on special duty as assistant librarian, Ft Robinson, NE. SOURCE: SO 103, 16 Sep 1896, Post Orders, Ft Robinson.

Transferred to Hospital Corps in accordance with Special Order 274, Adjutant General's Office, 22 Nov 1897.

Squadron sergeant major, 10th Cavalry, at Ft Washakie, WY; letter. SOURCE: *The Voice of the Negro* (Dec 1906).

Sergeant, C/10th Cavalry, commissioned captain at Camp Des Moines, IA, 15 Oct 1917. SOURCE: Glass, *History of the Tenth Cavalry,* appendix M; Sweeney, *History of the American Negro in the Great War,* 126.

Warrant officer, at Ft Huachuca, AZ. SOURCE: Work, *The Negro Yearbook, 1925–1926,* 254; Work, *The Negro Yearbook, 1931–1932,* 334.

MAREE, James B.; Private; 25th Inf. Born Charleston, SC; occupation laborer, Ht 5'8", fair complexion, black hair and eyes; enlisted, age 21, Charleston, 21 Jan 1881. SOURCE: Descriptive & Assignment Rolls, 25 Inf.

MARIN, Benjamin; A/10th Cav. Original member of 10th Cavalry; in troop when organized, Ft Leavenworth, KS, 18 Feb 1867. SOURCE: McMiller, "Buffalo Soldiers," 68.

MARION, G. F.; 2nd Lt; B/48th Inf. Mentioned. SOURCE: Beasley, *Negro Trailblazers,* 284.

MARLAND, John; Private; A/10th Cav. Served in 10th Cavalry, 1898; remained in U.S. during war with Spain. SOURCE: Cashin, *Under Fire with the Tenth Cavalry,* 337.

MARLEY, Will; Private; E/9th Cav. At Ft D. A. Russell, WY, in 1910; resident of Columbus, OH. SOURCE: *Illustrated Review: Ninth Cavalry,* with picture.

MARRIS, Eugene; Private; A/24th Inf. Transferred from Reserve Divisional Hospital, Siboney, Cuba, to U.S. on U.S. Army Transport *Vigilancia* with remittent malarial fever, 6 Sep 1898. SOURCE: Hospital Papers, Spanish-American War.

MARROW, Anthony A.; Sgt Maj; 25th Inf. Born Bullock, NC; father Anthony Marrow of Bullock; occupation farmer; first enlisted age 23, Newark, NJ; served in H/24th Infantry, 12 Jun 1895–11 Jun 1898; A/25th Infantry, 5 Jul 1898–27 Mar 1899; noncommissioned staff, 25th Infantry, 28 Mar 1899–5 Feb 1910; enlisted, occupation schoolteacher, complexion light brown, married, Ft Lawton, WA, 6 Feb 1910. SOURCE: Descriptive & Assignment Cards, 25 Inf.

Enlisted in H/24th Infantry, Newark, 12 Jun 1895; discharged on board steamship *City of Washington,* end of term, character excellent, single, in Tampa Bay, FL, 11 Jun 1898; $18 deposits, $3.42 clothing. SOURCE: Muster Roll, H/24 Inf, May–Jun 1898.

At Bamban, Philippines, 1899. SOURCE: Nankivell, *History of the Twenty-fifth Infantry,* 93, with picture.

In the Philippines, 1900. SOURCE: Richmond *Planet,* 28 Jun 1900.

Rumored to have commission in native regiments, in the Philippines. SOURCE: Richmond *Planet,* 22 Jun 1901.

Sends copy of Col. Andrew S. Burt's farewell to regiment, which is printed in full. SOURCE: Cleveland *Gazette,* 9 Aug 1902.

Mentioned as extremely efficient noncommissioned officer. SOURCE: Steward, *Fifty Years in the Gospel Ministry*, 352.

MARRS, Charles; Cook; H/9th Cav. At Ft D. A. Russell, WY, in 1910; marksman; resident of Patrick Co., VA. SOURCE: *Illustrated Review: Ninth Cavalry.*

MARSENGALE, Walter; Private; A/10th Cav. Served in 10th Cavalry, 1898; remained in U.S. during war with Spain. SOURCE: Cashin, *Under Fire with the Tenth Cavalry*, 337.

MARSHALL; Saddler; K/9th Cav. Commended for role in capture of escapee from Ft Robinson, NE, guardhouse, 24 Jan 1887. SOURCE: CO, Ft Robinson, to CO, K/9, 25 Jan 1887, LS, Ft Robinson.

MARSHALL; Private; A/10th Cav. At Ft Apache, AZ, 1890, subscribed $.50 to testimonial to General Grierson. SOURCE: List of subscriptions, 23 Apr 1890, 10th Cavalry papers, MHI.

MARSHALL, Albert; Corporal; F/9th Cav. Killed by white civilian John Jackson at Ft McKavett, TX, 1870. SOURCE: Leckie, *The Buffalo Soldiers*, 99.

Killed near Manadrill, TX, 2 Feb 1870. SOURCE: *Historical and Pictorial Review, Second Cavalry Division*, 45.

Killed in vicinity of San Angelo, TX, 1871. SOURCE: Carroll, *The Black Military Experience*, 456.

Killed along with Pvt. Charles Murray, 9th Cavalry, by friends of Jackson while standing guard at Jackson home. SOURCE: Sullivan, "Fort McKavett," 144.

MARSHALL, E.; 9th Cav. At Ft Robinson, NE, 1886. *See* **MOORE**, Joseph, Quartermaster Sergeant, 9th Cavalry

MARSHALL, Frank W.; Private; I/9th Cav. At Ft D. A. Russell, WY, in 1910; sharpshooter; resident of St. Louis. SOURCE: *Illustrated Review: Ninth Cavalry*, with picture.

MARSHALL, Henry; Corporal; F/9th Cav. Killed by horse thieves near Manadrill, TX, 2 Feb 1870. SOURCE: *Illustrated Review: Ninth Cavalry. See* **MARSHALL**, Albert, Corporal, F/9th Cavalry

MARSHALL, Hoyle; Sergeant; A/10th Cav. Born in South Carolina; private, A/10th Cavalry, 12 Jul 1882; corporal, 1 Sep 1889; sergeant, 1 Feb 1892; at Ft Custer, MT, 1897. SOURCE: Baker, Roster.

MARSHALL, Issac; F/10th Cav. Original member of 10th Cavalry; in troop when organized, Ft Leavenworth, KS, 21 Jun 1867. SOURCE: McMiller, "Buffalo Soldiers," 73.

MARSHALL, J.; Private; F/10th Cav. Wounded in action, Kansas, 21 Aug 1867. SOURCE: Armes, *Ups and Downs*, 247.

MARSHALL, James H.; Private; I/9th Cav. At Ft D. A. Russell, WY, in 1910; resident of Rockland, SC. SOURCE: *Illustrated Review: Ninth Cavalry.*

MARSHALL, John; Sergeant; A/10th Cav. Original member of 10th Cavalry; in troop when organized, Ft Leavenworth, KS, 18 Feb 1867. SOURCE: McMiller, "Buffalo Soldiers," 68.

Led patrol which intercepted eight Indians and killed one, near Catfish Creek, TX, 6 May 1875. SOURCE: Leckie, *The Buffalo Soldiers*, 142.

MARSHALL, John R.; Colonel; 8th Ill Inf. Letter from Santiago, Cuba, 3 Sep 1898. SOURCE: Gatewood, *"Smoked Yankees"*, 186.

Alternate at-large delegate to Republican Convention, Chicago, 1908. SOURCE: *Colored American Magazine* 14 (Apr 1908): 176.

MARSHALL, Joseph; Sergeant; Band/9th Cav. With band on detached service at headquarters, District of New Mexico, Santa Fe, 1880; played baritone. SOURCE: Billington, *New Mexico's Buffalo Soldiers*, 226.

MARSHALL, Louis; Private; C/10th Cav. Served in 10th Cavalry in Cuba, 1898. SOURCE: Cashin, *Under Fire with the Tenth Cavalry*, 340.

Wounded in action at Santiago, Cuba, 1 Jul 1898. SOURCE: SecWar, *AR 1898*, 324.

MARSHALL, Moses; Private; H/25th Inf. Sergeant at Ft Davis, TX, 1878. *See* **ROBINSON**, Richard, Corporal, H/25th Infantry

Convicted of murder, District Court, Presidio Co., TX, and sentenced to nine years in Texas State Penitentiary, Huntsville, TX, 9 Apr 1879. SOURCE: Report of Trials, Department of Texas, 1878–79.

MARSHALL, Robert; Private; G/10th Cav. Honorable mention for bravery against Comanches, Double Mountains Fork, Brazos River, TX, 5 Feb 1874. SOURCE: Baker, Roster.

MARSHALL, William H.; Private; D/10th Cav. Commissioned second lieutenant of cavalry, 27 Sep 1918. SOURCE: Glass, *History of the Tenth Cavalry*, appendix M.

MARSHELL, James E.; Private; I/10th Cav. Served in 10th Cavalry, 1898; remained in U.S. during war with Spain. SOURCE: Cashin, *Under Fire with the Tenth Cavalry*, 348.

MARSHELL, Victor L.; Private; I/10th Cav. Served in 10th Cavalry in Cuba, 1898. SOURCE: Cashin, *Under Fire with the Tenth Cavalry*, 348.

MARTIN, Albert; Farrier; F/9th Cav. At Ft D. A. Russell, WY, in 1910; sharpshooter; resident of Henderson, KY. SOURCE: *Illustrated Review: Ninth Cavalry*, with picture.

MARTIN, Charles; Private; B/10th Cav. Served in 10th Cavalry, 1898; remained in U.S. during war with Spain. SOURCE: Cashin, *Under Fire with the Tenth Cavalry*, 339.

MARTIN, Cornelius; Private; F/10th Cav. Served in 10th Cavalry in Cuba, 1898. SOURCE: Cashin, *Under Fire with the Tenth Cavalry*, 344.

MARTIN, Cuby; Private; B/24th Inf. Second place in bayonet fencing, military tournament, Albany, NY, autumn 1909. SOURCE: Muller, *The Twenty Fourth Infantry*, 60.

Commissioned first lieutenant at Camp Des Moines, IA, Oct 1917. SOURCE: Sweeney, *History of the American Negro*, 126.

MARTIN, Eugene; Private; I/9th Cav. At Ft D. A. Russell, WY, in 1910; resident of Bedford Co., TN. SOURCE: *Illustrated Review: Ninth Cavalry*.

MARTIN, George; H/10th Cav. Original member of 10th Cavalry; in troop when organized, Ft Leavenworth, KS, 21 Jul 1867. SOURCE: McMiller, "Buffalo Soldiers," 75.

MARTIN, George; Private; L/10th Cav. Served in 10th Cavalry, 1898; remained in U.S. during war with Spain. SOURCE: Cashin, *Under Fire with the Tenth Cavalry*, 351.

MARTIN, Henry L.; Private; L/25th Inf. Deserted from confinement at Ft Santiago, Philippines, 9 Sep 1899; apprehended 17 Oct 1899. SOURCE: Regt Returns, 25 Inf, Sep–Oct 1899.

MARTIN, James W.; Private; A/24th Inf. Transferred from Reserve Divisional Hospital, Santiago, Cuba, to U.S. with yellow fever on U.S. Army Transport *Santiago*, 25 Jul 1898. SOURCE: Hospital Papers, Spanish-American War.

MARTIN, Jerry; Private; D/9th Cav. Convicted by garrison court martial, Ft Robinson, NE, of scuffling and wrestling in troop quarters and refusing order of Cpl. Thomas C. Butler to stop; fined $4.50 and confined for ten days. SOURCE: Order 34, 3 May 1893, Post Orders, Ft Robinson.

MARTIN, Landon; Private; 24th Inf. Sentenced to seven years for part in Houston riot, 1917. SOURCE: Cleveland *Gazette*, 5 Jan 1918.

MARTIN, Richard; Farrier; G/9th Cav. At Ft Robinson, NE; deposited $125 with paymaster. SOURCE: Misc Records, DP, 1894–98.

MARTIN, Samuel; Recruit; E/10th Cav. Enlisted St. Louis, spring 1867. SOURCE: LS, 10 Cav, 1866–67.

Original member of 10th Cavalry; in troop when organized, Ft Leavenworth, KS, 15 Jun 1867. SOURCE: McMiller, "Buffalo Soldiers," 72.

MARTIN, Thomas P. Senior vice commander, Camp No. 30, National Indian War Veterans, San Antonio, TX. SOURCE: *Winners of the West* 6 (Oct 1929): 7.

MARTIN, Walker; Private; H/25th Inf. Transferred from Reserve Divisional Hospital, Siboney, Cuba, to Fortress Monroe, VA, with yellow fever on U.S. Army Transport *Concho*, 24 Jul 1898. SOURCE: Hospital Papers, Spanish-American War.

MARTIN, William; Corporal; E/25th Inf. Picture, Ft Buford, ND, 1893. SOURCE: Nankivell, *History of the Twenty-fifth Infantry*, 50.

MARTIN, William C.; Hospital Corps. Resided in Cuba, 1933; still alive in 1951. *See* **WILSON**, George, Private, I/10th Cavalry

MARTIN, William J.; Private; G/24th Inf. Died of septicemia and shock following operation in the Philippines, 17 Jun 1902. SOURCE: *ANJ* 39 (9 Aug 1902): 1248.

MARTIN, Willie; Corporal; E/10th Cav. Promoted from private, Sep 1899. SOURCE: *ANJ* 37 (7 Oct 1899): 122.

MASON, Calvin; K/25th Inf. Treasurer, K/25th Infantry Y.M.C.A., Castillejos, Philippines, 1900. SOURCE: Richmond *Planet*, 20 Oct 1900.

MASON, Elijah; Corporal; Band/9th Cav. With band on detached service at headquarters, District of New Mexico, Santa Fe, 1880; played bass drum. SOURCE: Billington, *New Mexico's Buffalo Soldiers*, 226.

MASON, George; 1st Sgt; C/9th Cav. First sergeant, L/9th Cavalry, Ft Leavenworth, KS, with warrant dating from 3 Jan 1872. SOURCE: *ANJ* 25 (18 Feb 1888): 586.

First sergeant, C/9th Cavalry, since 1 Oct 1892; sergeant since 1 Aug 1889. SOURCE: Roster, 9 Cav.

First sergeant, C/9th Cavalry; letter, Adjutant General's Office, 14 Apr 1895, concerns his retirement.

Married, stationed at Ft Robinson, NE, 1895; wife is sister of wife of Sgt. Edward McKenzie, I/9th Cavalry. SOURCE: *ANJ* 32 (2 Mar 1895): 439.

Retires from Ft Robinson, Apr 1895. SOURCE: *ANJ* 32 (20 Apr 1895): 555.

Praised by commander, Capt. Charles W. Taylor, upon retirement. SOURCE: *ANJ* 32 (11 May 1895): 608.

Retired and residing in Crawford, NE, one of six retirees there, four of whom are black. SOURCE: Soldiers on the Retired List Paid in the Department of the Platte by Mail, Misc Records, DP, 1894–98.

Died at home in Crawford with asthma, 15 Apr 1916; 9th Cavalry retiree and twenty-year resident; "was very agreeable and pleasant in all his dealings with his fellow men." SOURCE: Crawford *Tribune*, 17 Apr 1916.

Buried at Ft Robinson, 15 Apr 1916. SOURCE: List of Interments, Ft Robinson.

MASON, George F.; Private; M/10th Cav. Born Houston; enlisted, age 23 1/2, occupation laborer, brown complexion; served in Spanish-American War as private, I/9th Volunteer Infantry, in M/10th Cavalry, 25 Jun 1898–14 Sep 1903, in B/9th Cavalry, 11 Apr 1904–10 Apr 1907, including Cuban occupation; married Ada White of Smith Grove, Warren Co., KY, at Junction City, KS, 11 Apr 1907; sister Rose Gardner of Houston, age 63 in 1931. SOURCE: VA File XC 2628090, George F. Mason.

Resided in Colorado Springs, CO, 1907–1929; pensioned as of 9 Aug 1929, for disability; mentally deranged and occasionally violent before death, 21 Dec 1929; left $280 in bank and half-interest in property, 514 North Pine, worth $600; Knights of Pythias death benefits $375; after 1930, widow resided at 1427 West 35th Street, Los Angeles; pension: $30 per month, 13 Aug 1935; $40 per month, 22 Nov 1944; died 17 Mar 1953. SOURCE: VA File XC 2628090, George F. Mason.

MASON, George H.; Private; K/9th Cav. Discharged from Ft Robinson, NE, on certificate of disability with syphilis, 16 Oct 1894. SOURCE: Certificates of Disability, Ft Robinson.

MASON, Iscar; Private; E/10th Cav. Served in 10th Cavalry, 1898; remained in U.S. during war with Spain. SOURCE: Cashin, *Under Fire with the Tenth Cavalry*, 343.

MASON, John; Sergeant; H/9th Cav. Born Wytheville, TN; Ht 5'4 1/2", occupation waiter; enlisted, age 21, Bristol, TN, 6 Dec 1894; discharged, end of term, character excellent, Ft Robinson, NE, 5 Dec 1897; fined $.50 by summary court, 7 Nov 1895, and $2.50, 18 Sep 1896; deposits $5; retained $8.80; clothing $12.71. SOURCE: Descriptive Book, H/9 Cav.

Corporal, H/9th Cavalry, wounded in action, San Juan, Cuba, 2 Jul 1898; despite bad wound charged up hill near head of troops. SOURCE: SecWar, *AR 1898*, 707–08; *Illustrated Review: Ninth Cavalry*.

Corporal, H/9th Cavalry, returned from furlough to duty, Ft Robinson, NE, 7 Oct 1898.

Commended for gallantry in charging at head of troops up San Juan Hill in battle of Santiago, Cuba, in which he was seriously wounded; now sergeant, H/9th Cavalry. SOURCE GO 15, AGO, 13 Feb 1900.

MASON, John H.; D/10th Cav. Admitted to Soldiers Home with disability at age 40 with ten years and ten months' service, 18 May 1886; died later in year. SOURCE: SecWar, *AR 1886*, 738.

MASON, Patrick; Sergeant; I/24th Inf. Enlisted with twenty-eight years' continuous service, Ft D. A. Russell, WY, 9 Dec 1898; appointed corporal, at Ft Douglas, UT, 23 Jan 1899; promoted to sergeant, 3 Feb 1899. SOURCE: Muster Roll, I/24 Inf, Jan–Feb 1899.

Reduced to private, 3 May 1899. SOURCE: Muster Roll, I/24 Inf, May–Jun 1899.

Sick in First Reserve Hospital, Manila, Philippines, since 24 Aug 1899; disease contracted in line of duty. SOURCE: Muster Roll, I/24 Inf, Jul–Aug 1899.

Absent sick at Convalescent Hospital, Corregidor, Philippines, since 24 Aug 1899. SOURCE: Muster Roll, I/24 Inf, Sep–Oct 1899.

Absent at Cabanatuan, Philippines, since 23 Dec 1899. SOURCE: Muster Roll, I/24 Inf, Nov–Dec 1899.

Letter from Corregidor, 19 Nov 1899. SOURCE: Gatewood, *"Smoked Yankees"*, 257.

MASON, Samuel; B/10th Cav. Original member of 10th Cavalry; in troop when organized, Ft Leavenworth, KS, 1 Apr 1867. SOURCE: McMiller, "Buffalo Soldiers," 69.

MASON, Thomas; Private; A/10th Cav. Arrived at Ft Leavenworth, KS, from Jefferson Barracks, MO, Oct 1866.

Died at Ft Concho, TX, 5 Jul 1875. SOURCE: ES, 10 Cav, 1872–81.

MASON, Thomas; Private; B/10th Cav. Served in 10th Cavalry in Cuba, 1898. SOURCE: Cashin, *Under Fire with the Tenth Cavalry*, 338.

MASON, Thomas; Private; D/10th Cav. Served in 10th Cavalry in Cuba, 1898. SOURCE: Cashin, *Under Fire with the Tenth Cavalry*, 341.

MASON, William; Saddler; C/10th Cav. Private, B/9th Cavalry, ranked number eight with carbine, Department of the Platte competition, Bellevue, NE, 17–22 Aug 1891, bronze medal. SOURCE: Baker, Roster.

Private, B/9th Cavalry, qualified for first time as carbine sharpshooter with 74.86 percent. SOURCE: GO 1, AGO, 3 Jan 1893.

Saddler, C/10th Cavalry, and distinguished marksman, ranked number eight with revolver and number nine with carbine, Departments of Dakota and the Columbia, two bronze medals, 1893. SOURCE: Baker, Roster.

Distinguished marksman, carbine, 1891, and carbine and revolver, 1893. SOURCE: GO 82, AGO, 24 Oct 1893.

Ranked number 50 among carbine sharpshooters with 74.14 percent, 1893. SOURCE: GO 1, AGO, 2 Jan 1894.

MASON, William; Trumpeter; D/9th Cav. At Ft D. A. Russell, WY, in 1910; sharpshooter; resident of Acworth, GA. SOURCE: *Illustrated Review: Ninth Cavalry*, with picture.

MASON, Willie; Private; C/10th Cav. Right foot lacerated by rabid wolf, Ft Larned, KS, late 1860s. SOURCE: Leckie, *The Buffalo Soldiers*, 22.

MASSEY, James H.; Sergeant; F/10th Cav.
Resided at 1324 Avenue B, Galveston, TX, in 1922.
SOURCE: VA File SC 11405, John Taylor.

MASSEY, John; Sergeant; D/9th Cav. Appointed
sergeant 29 Dec 1885. SOURCE: Roster, 9 Cav.

MATCHETT, John R.; Private; C/9th Cav. Died in
post hospital, Ft Craig, NM, of gunshot wound inflicted
during fight, Mar 1881. SOURCE: Billington, *New Mexico's
Buffalo Soldiers*, 128.

MATES, Barlett; H/10th Cav. Original member of
10th Cavalry; in troop when organized, Ft Leavenworth, KS,
21 Jul 1867. SOURCE: McMiller, "Buffalo Soldiers," 75.

MATHES, George M.; H/49th Inf. Convicted of
throwing fish in face of native woman in the Philippines,
Mar 1900; sentenced to four months and $40 fine.

MATHEWS, Abraham. "Old Indian fighter and pioneer";
member of Camp 30, National Indian War Veterans, San
Antonio, TX; married fifty-five years. SOURCE: *Winners of
the West* 9 (Mar 1932): 7, with picture of him and his wife.

MATHEWS, C. C.; 24th Inf. At Ft Reno, Indian
Territory, 1887. *See* **HAMILTON**, J. H., 24th Infantry

MATHEWS, Charles; 1st Sgt; A/24th Inf. Ranked
number 12, Northern Division Infantry Team competition, Ft
Sheridan, IL, 1904. SOURCE: GO 167, AGO, 28 Oct 1904.

MATHEWS, Charles E.; G/10th Cav. Original
member of 10th Cavalry; in troop when organized, Ft
Leavenworth, KS, 5 Jul 1867. SOURCE: McMiller, "Buffalo
Soldiers," 74.

MATHEWS, Charlie; Private; K/10th Cav. Killed
in action at Carrizal, Mexico, 21 Jun 1916; buried at
Arlington National Cemetery. SOURCE: Wharfield, *10th
Cavalry and Border Fights*, 30, 39.

MATHEWS, Edward; H/10th Cav. Served with Webb
Chatmoun, 1880s; resided in Colorado Springs, CO, 1913.
SOURCE: VA File C 2360629, Webb Chatmoun.

MATHEWS, Gene H.; M/10th Cav. Original member
of 10th Cavalry; in troop when organized, Ft Riley, KS,
15 Oct 1867. SOURCE: McMiller, "Buffalo Soldiers," 79.

MATHEWS, Gletcheri; I/10th Cav. Original member
of 10th Cavalry; in troop when organized, Ft Riley, KS,
15 Aug 1867. SOURCE: McMiller, "Buffalo Soldiers," 76.

MATHEWS, J.; Private; C/9th Cav. Died of
pulmonary disease at Ft Robinson, NE, 16 Feb 1888.
SOURCE: Medical History, Ft Robinson.

Funeral at Ft Robinson, 18 Feb 1888. SOURCE: Order
35, 17 Feb 1888, Post Orders, and List of Interments, Ft
Robinson.

MATHEWS, Pleas; K/10th Cav. Original member of
10th Cavalry; in troop when organized, Ft Riley, KS, 1 Sep
1867. SOURCE: McMiller, "Buffalo Soldiers," 77.

MATHEWS, William; E/10th Cav. Original member
of 10th Cavalry; in troop when organized, Ft Leavenworth,
KS, 15 Jun 1867. SOURCE: McMiller, "Buffalo Soldiers,"
72.

MATJOY, James; H/9th Cav. Private pension bill
granting him $30 per month passed by Congress. SOURCE:
Winners of the West 3 (Apr 1926): 2.
    Recent subscriber; resides in El Paso, TX; served 1875–
80. SOURCE: *Winners of the West* 4 (May 1927): 2.

MATLOCK, William T.; Private; H/24th Inf.
Drowned in the Philippines, 8 Oct 1901; body not recovered.
SOURCE: *ANJ* 39 (7 Dec 1901): 339.

MATTHEWS, Courtney; Private; B/10th Cav.
Original member of L/10th Cavalry; in troop when
organized, Ft Riley, KS, 21 Sep 1867. SOURCE: McMiller,
"Buffalo Soldiers," 78.
    In B/10th Cavalry; at Ft Apache, AZ, 1890, subscribed
$.50 to testimonial to General Grierson. SOURCE: List of
subscriptions, 23 Apr 1890, 10th Cavalry papers, MHI.
    Served in 10th Cavalry, 1898; remained in U.S. during
war with Spain. SOURCE: Cashin, *Under Fire with the Tenth
Cavalry*, 338.
    Retires as private, B/10th Cavalry, from Ft Keogh, MT,
Nov 1898. SOURCE: *ANJ* 36 (12 Nov 1898): 262.

MATTHEWS, Edward L.; Private; A/24th Inf.
Murdered by natives in the Philippines, 1899.

MATTHEWS, H.; Private; C/10th Cav. Released to
duty from treatment for acute gonorrhea, Ft Robinson, NE,
4 Aug 1903. SOURCE: Post Surgeon to CO, C/10, 4 Aug
1903, LS, Post Surgeon, Ft Robinson.

MATTHEWS, Robert; F/24th Inf. Writes from
Manila, Philippines: "I am all right and all I want now is my
gun, belt, and plenty of cartridges." SOURCE: Cleveland
Gazette, 28 Oct 1899.

MATTHEWS, William; Private; C/10th Cav.
Served in 10th Cavalry in Cuba, 1898. SOURCE: Cashin,
Under Fire with the Tenth Cavalry, 340.
    Wounded in action at Santiago, Cuba, 1 Jul 1898.
SOURCE: SecWar, *AR 1898*, 324.

MATTHEWS, William A.; Private; D/25th Inf.
Dishonorable discharge, Brownsville. SOURCE: SO 266,
AGO, 9 Nov 1906.

MAXWELL, George; E/10th Cav. Original member of 10th Cavalry; in troop when organized, Ft Leavenworth, KS, 15 Jun 1867. SOURCE: McMiller, "Buffalo Soldiers," 72.

MAXWELL, William; C/24th Inf. At San Carlos, AZ, 1890. SOURCE: Cleveland *Gazette*, 19 Jun 1890.

MAY, Anderson N.; 1st Sgt; G/9th Cav. Veteran of Spanish-American War and Philippine Insurrection; at Ft D. A. Russell, WY, in 1910; sharpshooter; resident of Portland, OR. SOURCE: *Illustrated Review: Ninth Cavalry*, with picture.

MAYBERRY, Kelly; Private; I/10th Cav. Wounded in action in Cuba, 24 Jun 1898, and sent to hospital ship. SOURCE: SecWar, *AR 1898*, 349.

MAYES, Hilliard; Private; H/24th Inf. Funeral at Ft Huachuca, AZ, 14 May 1893. SOURCE: Name File, 24 Inf.

MAYFIELD, John; Private; K/25th Inf. At Ft Niobrara, NE, 1904. SOURCE: Wilson, "History of Fort Niobrara."

MAYO, Benjamin; Corporal; I/10th Cav. Served in 10th Cavalry, 1898; remained in U.S. during war with Spain. SOURCE: Cashin, *Under Fire with the Tenth Cavalry*, 348.

MAYO, George; Private; F/10th Cav. Served in 10th Cavalry in Cuba, 1898; died of fever. SOURCE: Cashin, *Under Fire with the Tenth Cavalry*, 344.

MAYO, William; Sergeant; A/9th Cav. Promoted from corporal. SOURCE: Order 46, 9 Cav, 20 Sep 1888.

MAYOR, J. H.; Private; C/9th Cav. At Ft Cummings, NM; on detached service in field, 30 Jan–3 Feb 1881.

MAYS, Henry; Private; H/24th Inf. Fined $2 by summary court, San Isidro, Philippines, for smoking on sentinel duty and saluting officer of day with cigarette in mouth, 6 Dec 1901. SOURCE: Register of Summary Court, San Isidro.

MAYS, Isaiah; Corporal; B/24th Inf. Among men who distinguished themselves in 1889; awarded Medal of Honor for gallant and meritorious service while escort for Maj. Joseph W. Wham, paymaster, when attacked by robbers between Fts Grant and Thomas, AZ, 11 May 1889. SOURCE: GO 18, AGO, 1891.

Born Carter's Ridge, VA. SOURCE: Carroll, *The Black Military Experience*, 278, 417.

MAYS, James E.; Corporal; A/9th Cav. Veteran of Philippine Insurrection; at Ft D. A. Russell, WY, in 1910. SOURCE: *Illustrated Review: Ninth Cavalry*, with picture.

MAYS, Peter; Private; I/24th Inf. Enlisted Macon, GA, 26 Jun 1899. SOURCE: Muster Roll, I/24 Inf, Jul–Aug 1899.

MEAD, David H.; H/10th Cav. Original member of 10th Cavalry; in troop when organized, Ft Leavenworth, KS, 21 Jul 1867. SOURCE: McMiller, "Buffalo Soldiers," 75.

MEAD, James P.; Private; K/24th Inf. Sentenced to fifteen days and $8 fine for being drunk and disorderly near officers' quarters, Cabanatuan, Philippines, 6 Jul 1901; witness: Pvt. George S. Cashy, D/24th Infantry. SOURCE: Name File, 24 Inf.

MEADE; Private; A/10th Cav. At Ft Apache, AZ, 1890, subscribed $.50 to testimonial to General Grierson. SOURCE: List of subscriptions, 23 Apr 1890, 10th Cavalry papers, MHI.

MEADE, Robert; Musician; L/24th Inf. Died in Minnesota. SOURCE: Taylor, "Minnesota Black Spanish-American War Veterans."

MEADOWS, Benjamin; Private; A/38th Inf. On extra duty in subsistence department, Ft Cummings, NM, 1868; reliable and trustworthy. SOURCE: Billington, *New Mexico's Buffalo Soldiers*, 200.

MEADOWS, Edward; Private; 25th Inf. Parents Mr. and Mrs. Hiram Meadows at Denver depot, bid goodbye to sons Edward and John, bound for the Philippines with regiment, Jun 1899. SOURCE: Nankivell, *History of the Twenty-fifth Infantry*, 200.

MEADOWS, John; Private; 25th Inf. Parents Mr. and Mrs. Hiram Meadows at Denver depot, bid goodbye to sons Edward and John, bound for the Philippines with regiment, Jun 1899. SOURCE: Nankivell, *History of the Twenty-fifth Infantry*, 200.

MEANS, George; Private; L/25th Inf. Fined $8 by summary court, San Isidro, Philippines, for insubordination to sergeant of guard, 18 Jun 1902, first conviction. SOURCE: Register of Summary Court, San Isidro.

MEARS, George W.; Sergeant; G/9th Cav. Sergeant, M/10th Cavalry, at Ft Apache, AZ, 1890, subscribed $.50 to testimonial to General Grierson. SOURCE: List of subscriptions, 23 Apr 1890, 10th Cavalry papers, MHI.

Appointed sergeant, G/9th Cavalry, 28 Jul 1892. SOURCE: Roster, 9 Cav.

At Ft Robinson, NE, 1893, Pvt. Mathew Wyatt, G/9th Cavalry, testified that Mears sent home a copy of incendiary circular that Sgt. Barney McKay allegedly brought into barracks. SOURCE: Court Martial Records, McKay.

Discharged Ft Robinson, Oct 1895. SOURCE: *ANJ* 33 (12 Oct 1895): 87.

MEDLER, Felix; A/9th Cav. Convicted of theft from and threat to native policeman in the Philippines, Nov 1900; sentenced to six months.

MEEKS, Stephen; Private; L/10th Cav. Served in 10th Cavalry, 1898; remained in U.S. during war with Spain. SOURCE: Cashin, *Under Fire with the Tenth Cavalry*, 351.

MEIKS, William; Trumpeter; C/10th Cav. Honorable mention for gallantry against Kiowas and Comanches, Wichita Agency, Indian Territory, 22–23 Aug 1874. SOURCE: Baker, Roster.

MEINE, James; G/10th Cav. Original member of 10th Cavalry; in troop when organized, Ft Leavenworth, KS, 5 Jul 1867. SOURCE: McMiller, "Buffalo Soldiers," 74.

MELROSE, Charles H.; Private; E/9th Cav. At Ft D. A. Russell, WY, in 1910. SOURCE: *Illustrated Review: Ninth Cavalry*, with picture.

MELTON, William; Private; K/9th Cav. Sentenced to 30 days' confinement by garrison court martial, Ft Robinson, NE. SOURCE: Order 4, 9 Jan 1886, Post Orders, Ft Robinson.

MEMS, Grant; Private; 24th Inf. Served in Houston, 1917. SOURCE: Haynes, *A Night of Violence*, 87.

MENDENHAL, William; Sergeant; 24th Inf. Former soldier; tried to shoot bartender John Castro. SOURCE: San Francisco *Chronicle*, 16 Oct 1899, with picture.

MENLOW, Thomas; Private; C/9th Cav. Murdered in tent, Ft Robinson, NE, 15 Sep 1886. SOURCE: CO, C/9, to AG, USA, 1 Nov 1886, LS, C/9.

MERCHANT, Walter E.; Corporal; 48th Inf. Letter from San Fernando de la Union, Philippines, 12 Jun 1900. SOURCE: Gatewood, *"Smoked Yankees"*, 281.

MERRIMAN, David; Private; F/10th Cav. Served in 10th Cavalry, 1898; remained in U.S. during war with Spain. SOURCE: Cashin, *Under Fire with the Tenth Cavalry*, 344.

MERRITT, Julius; 49th Inf. Cincinnati native; married sister of Filipino congressman; licensed to practice medicine in the Philippines after left Army in 1905; died 1920 at age 43; son Jesus served four years on Quezon City six-man administrative council, now public relations man of budget commission; another son works for government and another is retired colonel, Philippine army. SOURCE: Thompson, "Veterans Who Never Came Home," 106.

MERRITT, Wesley; Private; K/48th Inf. Drowned in the Philippines, 23 Mar 1900. SOURCE: *ANJ* 37 (5 May 1900): 851.

MERRIWEATHER, Henry C.; Private; I/9th Cav. Discharged from Ft Robinson, NE, on surgeon's certificate with hernia, Jul 1888.

MERRIWEATHER, Luke; Private; M/10th Cav. Served in 10th Cavalry, 1898; remained in U.S. during war with Spain. SOURCE: Cashin, *Under Fire with the Tenth Cavalry*, 352.

MERRYFIELD, William; Private; L/9th Cav. Convicted by general court martial, Jefferson Barracks, MO, of desertion, 13 Nov 1882–28 Oct 1884; sentenced to dishonorable discharge and two years. SOURCE: GCMO 63, AGO, 31 Dec 1884.

METCALF, George; Private; I/10th Cav. Served in 10th Cavalry, 1898; remained in U.S. during war with Spain. SOURCE: Cashin, *Under Fire with the Tenth Cavalry*, 348.

MEYART, Isaac; Private; A/10th Cav. Mentioned Jan 1873 as having enlisted 30 Sep 1867. SOURCE: LS, 10 Cav, 1873–83.

MEYER, Robert S.; Cook; I/9th Cav. At Ft D. A. Russell, WY, in 1910; resident of Winston, NC. SOURCE: *Illustrated Review: Ninth Cavalry*, with picture.

MICHAEL; Private; K/10th Cav. Accidentally shot and killed himself at Henshaw Station, 2 Jun 1868; body buried by side of road in woolen blanket. SOURCE: Armes, *Ups and Downs*, 267.

MIDDLETON, Charles N.; Private; F/9th Cav. Turned over to deputy U.S. Marshal for assaulting woman on military reservation, Ft Robinson, NE. SOURCE: CO, Ft Robinson, to CO, F/9, 28 May 1892, LS, Ft Robinson.

Sentenced to dishonorable discharge and six months for malingering, Ft Robinson, Feb 1893. SOURCE: *ANJ* 30 (18 Feb 1893): 426.

MIDDLETON, Robert; Private; 25th Inf. Born Barnwell Court House, SC; Ht 5'4 1/2", occupation farmer, black hair and eyes, dark complexion; enlisted, age 22, Charleston, SC, 13 Jun 1881. SOURCE: Descriptive & Assignment Rolls, 25 Inf.

MIKELL, Henry; Private; F/9th Cav. At Ft D. A. Russell, WY, in 1910; resident of Pulaski, TN. SOURCE: *Illustrated Review: Ninth Cavalry*, with picture.

MILBURN, Alex; Private; A/25th Inf. Convicted of being drunk on guard and asleep at post; sentence remitted on unanimous recommendation of court. SOURCE: Report of Trials, Department of Texas, 1878–79.

MILDS, Miller; Private; F/9th Cav. At Ft Robinson, NE, 1887; suspect in murder of 1st Sgt. Emanuel Stance, F/9th Cavalry. SOURCE: Schubert, "The Violent World of Emanuel Stance," 213–14.

In hands of civil authorities, Chadron, NE, 13 Jan–2 Mar 1888, and Omaha, NE, 16 Mar–10 May 1888, after which confined at Ft Omaha, NE. SOURCE: Regt Returns, 9 Cav.

See Schubert, "The Violent World of Emanuel Stance," 213–14.

MILERTON, Filevions; F/10th Cav. Original member of 10th Cavalry; in troop when organized, Ft Leavenworth, KS, 21 Jun 1867. SOURCE: McMiller, "Buffalo Soldiers," 73.

MILES, Candy; K/10th Cav. Original member of 10th Cavalry; in troop when organized, Ft Riley, KS, 1 Sep 1867. SOURCE: McMiller, "Buffalo Soldiers," 77.

MILES, Charles; Private; A/10th Cav. Released to duty from treatment for gonorrhea, Ft Robinson, NE, 5 Jun 1903. SOURCE: Post Surgeon to CO, A/10, 5 Jun 1903, LS, Post Surgeon, Ft Robinson.

MILES, Chester; Private; K/10th Cav. At Ft Robinson, NE, 1904.

MILES, Grabt A.; Private; E/9th Cav. At Ft D. A. Russell, WY, in 1910; resident of Louisville. SOURCE: *Illustrated Review: Ninth Cavalry*, with picture.

MILES, Henry; Private; B/25th Inf. Dishonorably discharged; to serve sentence promulgated in General Court Martial Order 2, Department of Texas, 25 Jan 1876, at Kansas Penitentiary, Leavenworth, KS. SOURCE: GCMO 21, AGO, 28 Feb 1876.

MILES, James; E/10th Cav. Original member of 10th Cavalry; in troop when organized, Ft Leavenworth, KS, 15 Jun 1867. SOURCE: McMiller, "Buffalo Soldiers," 72.

MILES, James; Private; H/24th Inf. Enlisted St. Louis, 28 Apr 1898. SOURCE: Muster Roll, H/24 Inf, May–Jun 1898.

Discharged 29 Jan 1899; reenlisted Ft Douglas, UT, character excellent, single, 30 Jan 1899; deposits $58; clothing $1.54; on special duty with Subsistence Department since 14 Jan 1899. SOURCE: Muster Roll, H/24 Inf, Jan–Feb 1899.

MILES, John B.; Sergeant; F/10th Cav. At Ft Supply, Indian Territory, 1870. *See* **TAYLOR**, John, Private, F/10th Cavalry

MILES, Joseph; F/10th Cav. To be assigned to F/10th Cavalry, Jun 1867. SOURCE: LS, 10 Cav, 1866–67.

Original member of 10th Cavalry; in troop when organized, Ft Leavenworth, KS, 21 Jun 1867. SOURCE: McMiller, "Buffalo Soldiers," 73.

MILES, Julius; L/10th Cav. Original member of 10th Cavalry; in troop when organized, Ft Riley, KS, 21 Sep 1867. SOURCE: McMiller, "Buffalo Soldiers," 78.

MILES, M.; Private; H/9th Cav. On detached service at Ft Bayard, NM, 16 Jan–10 Feb 1881. SOURCE: Regt Returns, 9 Cav, Feb 1881.

MILES, Sandy; Private; K/10th Cav. Deserter Miles arrested this morning by Mr. O. L. Warren, who was paid a $30 reward. SOURCE: CO, Ft Hays, KS, to Adj, Det 10 Cav, camp near Ft Wallace, KS, 28 May 1868, LR, Det 10 Cav, 1868–69.

MILES, Silas; A/10th Cav. Recruit from Jefferson Barracks, MO, died in Ft Leavenworth, KS, hospital shortly after arrival on post, early 1867. SOURCE: McMiller, "Buffalo Soldiers," 52.

MILES, Thomas; Private; 10th Cav. In Captain Armes's company at Ft Lyon, CO, Oct 1868. SOURCE: ES, 10 Cav, 1866–71.

MILES, Williams; E/10th Cav. Original member of 10th Cavalry; in troop when organized, Ft Leavenworth, KS, 15 Jun 1867. SOURCE: McMiller, "Buffalo Soldiers," 72.

MILLBROWN, Robert; 1st Sgt; I/10th Cav. Born in Maryland; private, I/10th Cavalry, 17 Nov 1873; corporal, 5 Feb 1877; sergeant, 1 Jul 1877; first sergeant, 11 Feb 1895; at Ft Assiniboine, MT, 1897. SOURCE: Baker, Roster.

Sergeant, at Ft Apache, AZ, 1890, subscribed $.50 to testimonial to General Grierson. SOURCE: List of subscriptions, 23 Apr 1890, 10th Cavalry papers, MHI.

Served in 10th Cavalry in Cuba, 1898. SOURCE: Cashin, *Under Fire with the Tenth Cavalry*, 347.

Wounded in action at Santiago, Cuba, 1 Jul 1898. SOURCE: SecWar, *AR 1898*, 324.

Wound and heroism in Cuba, 1898, mentioned. SOURCE: Cashin, *Under Fire with the Tenth Cavalry*, 185.

MILLER; Private; B/10th Cav. At Ft Apache, AZ, 1890, subscribed $.50 to testimonial to General Grierson. SOURCE: List of subscriptions, 23 Apr 1890, 10th Cavalry papers, MHI.

MILLER; Private; D/10th Cav. At Ft Apache, AZ, 1890, subscribed $.50 to testimonial to General Grierson. SOURCE: List of subscriptions, 23 Apr 1890, 10th Cavalry papers, MHI.

MILLER, Abner; Corporal; G/10th Cav. On daily duty with Commissary Department, 9–16 Apr 1869. SOURCE: SO 16, Det 10 Cav, in field, 9 Apr 1869, and SO 20, Det 10 Cav, Ft Dodge, KS, 16 Apr 1869, Orders, Det 10 Cav, 1868–69.

MILLER, Alexander; F/10th Cav. Original member of 10th Cavalry; in troop when organized, Ft Leavenworth, KS, 21 Jun 1867. SOURCE: McMiller, "Buffalo Soldiers," 73.

MILLER, Bernard; Corporal; F/9th Cav. Appointed corporal, 16 Jul 1893. SOURCE: Roster, 9 Cav.

MILLER, Charles; Recruit; Colored Detachment/ Mounted Service. Convicted by general court martial, Jefferson Barracks, MO, of desertion, 14 Sep 1886, until apprehended by Police Officer John W. Murphy of Carondolet, MO, 18 Sep 1886, of theft of trousers and suspenders from Recruit Isaac W. Romons, Colored Detachment/Mounted Service, Jefferson Barracks, 14 Sep 1884, and of selling or losing military shoes, week of 11 Sep 1886; sentenced to dishonorable discharge and four years. SOURCE: GCMO 94, AGO, 10 Nov 1886.

MILLER, Charles; Private; I/24th Inf. Enlisted Savannah, GA, 3 Apr 1898. SOURCE: Muster Roll, I/24, May–Jun 1899.

On detached service at Cabanatuan, Philippines, since 30 Dec 1899. SOURCE: Muster Roll, I/24 Inf, Nov–Dec 1899.

MILLER, Chris; Sergeant; E/10th Cav. Mentioned Aug 1875 as just enlisted in E/10th Cavalry. SOURCE: ES, 10 Cav, 1872–81.

Led detachment of eight on scout from station at San Felipe, TX, in vicinity of Rio Grande, seeking murderers of Colson family, 21–27 Jun 1879; marched one hundred miles. SOURCE: SecWar, *AR 1879*, 112.

MILLER, Colonel E.; Sergeant; H/10th Cav. Served with Webb Chatmoun in 1880s; resided at 300 Walnut Street, Kansas City, MO, in 1913. SOURCE: VA File C 2360629, Webb Chatmoun.

Honorable mention for services rendered as private in capture of Mangas and his Apache band, Rio Bonito, AZ, 18 Oct 1886. SOURCE: Baker, Roster.

Sergeant, authorized four-month furlough from Ft Apache, AZ. SOURCE: *ANJ* 29 (14 Nov 1891): 198.

MILLER, Cooper; Artificer; E/25th Inf. Suzie Hart, who was unmarried when she knew Sadie Allsup at Ft Keogh, MT, in 1892, later married Cooper Miller, then in D/10th Cavalry, now deceased. SOURCE: Affidavit, Suzie G. Hart, age 49, residing at 1047 W. 49th, Los Angeles, widow of John Hart, 13 Apr 1926; VA File XC 2659797, Thomas H. Allsup.

Retired as artificer, E/25th Infantry, Jun 1902. SOURCE: *ANJ* 39 (21 Jun 1902): 1067.

MILLER, Edward; L/10th Cav. Original member of 10th Cavalry; in troop when organized, Ft Riley, KS, 21 Sep 1867. SOURCE: McMiller, "Buffalo Soldiers," 78.

MILLER, Edward; 9th Cav. Served 1886–91; "We gladly did all we could to smooth the way for our great west"; *Winners of the West* "reminds me of the strenuous and also the happy life we led in our younger days in the army." SOURCE: *Winners of the West* 7 (Feb 1930): 3.

MILLER, Edwin; B/10th Cav. Enlisted Memphis. SOURCE: LS, 10 Cav, 1866–67.

Original member of 10th Cavalry; in troop when organized, Ft Leavenworth, KS, 1 Apr 1867. SOURCE: McMiller, "Buffalo Soldiers," 69.

MILLER, Emanueal; Private; E/9th Cav. Veteran of Philippine Insurrection; at Ft D. A. Russell, WY, in 1910. SOURCE: *Illustrated Review: Ninth Cavalry*, with picture.

MILLER, Frank A.; Private; B/10th Cav. Served in 10th Cavalry in Cuba, 1898; wounded in action. SOURCE: Cashin, *Under Fire With the Tenth Cavalry*, 338-39.

Enlisted Indianapolis; wounded at Santiago, Cuba. SOURCE: Cleveland *Gazette*, 2 Jul 1898.

Wounded in right arm; Indianapolis address is 517 Railroad Street. SOURCE: Indianapolis *Freeman*, 20 Aug 1898.

MILLER, G.; Private; H/10th Cav. Ranked number 18 among sharpshooters over 90 percent in 1885. SOURCE: GO 25, AGO, 12 Mar 1885.

MILLER, George A.; Private; G/10th Cav. Original member of 10th Cavalry; in troop when organized, Ft Leavenworth, KS, 5 Jul 1867. SOURCE: McMiller, "Buffalo Soldiers," 74.

Prisoner to be transferred to Ft Dodge, KS, guardhouse as encumbrance to command. SOURCE: CO, Det 10 Cav, to AAAG, District of the Upper Arkansas, 3 Oct 1868, LR, Det 10 Cav, 1868-69.

Commander of detachment, Ft Dodge, recommends remission of his sentence so he can be discharged, 17 May 1869; judge advocate, Department of the Missouri, recommends disapproval because he is convicted deserter, 24 May 1869. SOURCE: LR, Det 10 Cav, 1868–69.

MILLER, George D.; Private; H/24th Inf. Fined $1 by summary court, San Isidro, Philippines, for being dirty at company inspection, 8 Feb 1902, second conviction; fined $5 for lying out of quarters, 25 Mar 1902; fined $3 for carelessly discharging rifle while prison guard, 4 Apr 1902; fined $5 for absence from quarters without authority while being treated for venereal disease, 24 Apr 1902. SOURCE: Register of Summary Court, San Isidro.

MILLER, Harry; Private; H/24th Inf. Transferred from Reserve General Hospital, Siboney, Cuba, to Fortress Monroe, VA, on U.S. Army Transport *Concho* with remittent malarial fever, 24 Jul 1898. SOURCE: Hospital Papers, Spanish-American War.

MILLER, Henry; Corporal; E/9th Cav. Appointed corporal, 7 Jul 1893. SOURCE: Roster, 9 Cav.

MILLER, Henry; Private; M/10th Cav. Served in 10th Cavalry, 1898; remained in U.S. during war with Spain. SOURCE: Cashin, *Under Fire with the Tenth Cavalry*, 352.

MILLER, Henry; Private; A/24th Inf. Wounded in action, Santiago, Cuba, 1898. SOURCE: SecWar, *AR 1898*, 437.

MILLER, Henry; QM Sgt; L/9th Cav. Veteran of Philippine Insurrection; at Ft D. A. Russell, WY, in 1910; resident of Easton, MD. SOURCE: *Illustrated Review: Ninth Cavalry*, with picture.

MILLER, Henry C.; Sergeant; 10th Cav. Mentioned 1873 as deceased. SOURCE: ES, 10 Cav, 1872–81.

MILLER, Homer; G/10th Cav. Original member of 10th Cavalry; in troop when organized, Ft Leavenworth, KS, 5 Jul 1867. SOURCE: McMiller, "Buffalo Soldiers," 74.

MILLER, Isaiah; Private; H/9th Cav. Died of dysentery in the Philippines, 22 Sep 1901. SOURCE: *ANJ* 39 (7 Dec 1901): 339.

MILLER, J. W.; Private; 10th Cav. Wounded in left thigh, Naco, AZ, 4 Dec 1914. SOURCE: Cleveland *Gazette*, 13 May 1916.

MILLER, James E.; Private; B/10th Cav. Served in 10th Cavalry, 1898; remained in U.S. during war with Spain. SOURCE: Cashin, *Under Fire with the Tenth Cavalry*, 339.

MILLER, James H.; Private; B/10th Cav. Enlisted Richmond, VA; wounded in action at Santiago, Cuba, 1898. SOURCE: Cleveland *Gazette*, 2 Jul 1898.

Served in 10th Cavalry in Cuba, 1898. SOURCE: Cashin, *Under Fire with the Tenth Cavalry*, 338.

MILLER, Jesse C.; Sergeant; M/24th Inf. Private, C/24th Infantry, transferred from Reserve Divisional Hospital, Siboney, Cuba, to U.S. on U.S. Army Transport *Santiago* with remittent malarial fever, 25 Jul 1898. SOURCE: Hospital Papers, Spanish-American War.

Sergeant, M/24th Infantry, married to Nola Montgomery at Ft Douglas, UT, by Chaplain Allensworth. SOURCE: *ANJ* 36 (18 Mar 1899): 686.

MILLER, John; M/10th Cav. Original member of 10th Cavalry; in troop when organized, Ft Riley, KS, 15 Oct 1867. SOURCE: McMiller, "Buffalo Soldiers," 79.

MILLER, John D.; Sergeant; D/9th Cav. Private, D/9th Cavalry, at Ft Robinson, NE, 1894, resided with wife Elizabell in room at Chaplain Plummer's quarters. SOURCE: Investigation of Charges against Chaplain Plummer.

Private, D/9th Cavalry, on recruiting duty early 1898. SOURCE: Cashin, *Under Fire with the Tenth Cavalry*, 112.

Sergeant, D/9th Cavalry, at Ft D. A. Russell, WY, in 1910. SOURCE: *Illustrated Review: Ninth Cavalry*, with picture.

MILLER, John E.; Sergeant; K/9th Cav. Private, teacher, Ft Robinson, NE, school, 15 Nov 1894–31 Jan 1895 and 1 Feb–30 Apr 1895. SOURCE: Reports of Schools, Ft Robinson, 1892–96.

Lance corporal, relieved from extra duty as schoolteacher, Ft Robinson. SOURCE: Order 26, 29 Apr 1895, Post Orders, Ft Robinson.

Promoted to corporal, Ft Robinson, 9 May 1895. SOURCE: *ANJ* 32 (18 May 1895): 626.

Promoted to sergeant, Ft Robinson, 1 Oct 1895. SOURCE: *ANJ* 33 (12 Oct 1895): 87.

Sergeant, G/9th Cavalry, authorized to reenlist as married, K/9th Cavalry, by letter, Adjutant General's Office, 28 Dec 1897.

MILLER, John G.; Sgt Maj; 24th Inf. Sergeant major, Second Battalion/25th Infantry, in the Philippines, 1900. SOURCE: Richmond *Planet*, 28 Jul 1900.

Retires with thirty years' service as sergeant major, 24th Infantry, from Madison Barracks, NY. SOURCE: Cleveland *Gazette*, 18 Apr 1908.

MILLER, John R.; Corporal; G/24th Inf. Killed in action, Cuba, 1898. SOURCE: Scipio, *Last of the Black Regulars*, 29.

Died in Cuba, 1 Jul 1898. SOURCE: *ANJ* 36 (18 Feb 1899): 590.

MILLER, Lewis; E/10th Cav. Original member of 10th Cavalry; in troop when organized, Ft Leavenworth, KS, 15 Jun 1867. SOURCE: McMiller, "Buffalo Soldiers," 72.

MILLER, Nathan B.; Private; F/9th Cav. At Ft D. A. Russell, WY, in 1910; resident of Anderson, SC. SOURCE: *Illustrated Review: Ninth Cavalry*, with picture.

MILLER, Richard; Color Sgt; 9th Cav. Corporal, B/10th Cavalry, honorable mention for daring effort to capture Indian outlaw, San Carlos, AZ, 28 Aug 1886. SOURCE: Baker, Roster.

Trumpeter, B/10th Cavalry; at Ft Apache, AZ, 1890, subscribed $.50 to testimonial to General Grierson. SOURCE: List of subscriptions, 23 Apr 1890, 10th Cavalry papers, MHI.

Sergeant, F/9th Cavalry, and drum major, troop band, Ft Duchesne, UT. SOURCE: *ANJ* 34 (29 May 1897): 733.

Seriously wounded in thigh, Guinobatan, Albay, Philippines, 17 Dec 1900. SOURCE: *ANJ* 38 (2 Feb 1901): 555; Hamilton, "History of the Ninth Cavalry," 103; *Illustrated Review: Ninth Cavalry*.

Appointed regimental color sergeant, May 1901. SOURCE: *ANJ* 38 (1 Jun 1901): 966.

Awarded certificate of merit, 17 Dec 1903, for distinguished conduct in engagement with insurgents, Taybac, Albay, Philippines, 17 Dec 1900, where attacked and wounded by several bolomen, while sergeant, F/9th Cavalry. SOURCE: GO 32, AGO, 6 Feb 1904.

MILLER, Robert; H/10th Cav. Resided at 1430 South 13th, Terre Haute, IN, in 1912. *See* **BARD**, Benjamin, Private, H/10th Cavalry

MILLER, Samuel; Blacksmith; H/9th Cav. Veteran of Philippine Insurrection; at Ft D. A. Russell, WY, in 1910; sharpshooter; resident of Atlanta. SOURCE: *Illustrated Review: Ninth Cavalry*, with picture.

MILLER, Thomas; K/10th Cav. Original member of 10th Cavalry; in troop when organized, Ft Riley, KS, 1 Sep 1867. SOURCE: McMiller, "Buffalo Soldiers," 77.

MILLER, Thomas; Private; L/49th Inf. Died in Minnesota. SOURCE: Taylor, "Minnesota Spanish-American War Veterans."

MILLER, Walter; Private; H/9th Cav. Transferred from furlough to sick leave, illness not contracted in line of duty, Ft Robinson, NE, 29 Sep 1898.

MILLER, William; 9th Cav. Served in G and K/9th Cavalry, 1890–93; had $6 per month pension in 1900, discontinued 1903; then $6 per month, 1929, increased to $25 per month later in same year. SOURCE: *Winners of the West* 7 (Sep 1930): 7.

"I am a half-breed"; would like to hear from comrades with pack train at Rosebud, SD, 1890; asks help to get increased pension; can't get work because everyone says he is too old. SOURCE: *Winners of the West* 8 (Dec 1930): 12.

MILLER, William; Private; D/10th Cav. Served in 10th Cavalry, 1898; remained in U.S. during war with Spain. SOURCE: Cashin, *Under Fire with the Tenth Cavalry*, 341.

MILLER, William; Private; G/24th Inf. Died of dysentery in the Philippines, 19 Jul 1901. SOURCE: *ANJ* 39 (21 Sep 1901): 51.

MILLER, William; Private; D/9th Cav. At Ft D. A. Russell, WY, in 1910; sharpshooter; resident of Louisville. SOURCE: *Illustrated Review: Ninth Cavalry*.

MILLER, William F.; Private; K/10th Cav. Original member of 10th Cavalry; in troop when organized, Ft Riley, KS, 1 Sep 1867. SOURCE: McMiller, "Buffalo Soldiers," 77.

Mrs. Henrietta Miller's request for information about her son referred from War Department, 29 Feb 1869, and forwarded to commander, K/10th Cavalry. SOURCE: ES, 10 Cav, 1866–71.

MILLER, William H.; Corporal; C/25th Inf. Promoted from private, M/25th Infantry. SOURCE: *ANR* 38 (30 Sep 1905): 21.

Dishonorable discharge, Brownsville. SOURCE: SO 266, AGO, 9 Nov 1906.

MILLER, William W.; L/10th Cav. Original member of 10th Cavalry; in troop when organized, Ft Riley, KS, 21 Sep 1867. SOURCE: McMiller, "Buffalo Soldiers," 78.

MILLINGTON, Samuel; Private; 24th Inf. Transferred from Reserve Divisional Hospital, Siboney, Cuba, to U.S. on U.S. Army Transport *Santiago* with remittent yellow fever, 25 Jul 1898. SOURCE: Hospital Papers, Spanish-American War.

MILLION, Perry; Recruit; Colored Detachment/ Mounted Service. At Jefferson Barracks, MO, 1885. *See* **CASHIN**, Daniel, Private, G/9th Cavalry

MILLS, Archie; Sergeant; K/10th Cav. Saddler, served in 10th Cavalry, 1898; remained in U.S. during war with Spain. SOURCE: Cashin, *Under Fire with the Tenth Cavalry*, 349.

Private, transferred from B/25th Infantry, to K/10th Cavalry, in accordance with Special Order 19, Adjutant General's Office, 23 Jan 1903.

Sergeant, K/10th Cavalry, at Ft Robinson, NE, 1904.

MILLS, D. M.; 10th Cav. Regimental printer, Cuba; resident of San Antonio, TX. SOURCE: Indianapolis *Freeman*, 30 Nov 1901.

MILLS, George; Private; B/10th Cav. Killed in action at Ojo Caliente, TX, 29 Oct 1880. SOURCE: Baker, Roster; Leckie, *The Buffalo Soldiers*, 230.

MILLS, Robert; 1st Sgt; M/25th Inf. Promoted from sergeant, vice Wyatt Huffman, commissioned second lieutenant. SOURCE: Richmond *Planet*, 20 Jan 1900.

MIMS, Charles; C/10th Cav. Original member of 10th Cavalry; in troop when organized, Ft Leavenworth, KS, 14 May 1867. SOURCE: McMiller, "Buffalo Soldiers," 70.

MIMS, Lewis; Private; E/9th Cav. At Ft D. A. Russell, WY, in 1910; resident of 254 Chestnut St., Macon, GA. SOURCE: *Illustrated Review: Ninth Cavalry*, with picture.

MINAR, James L.; Sergeant; M/10th Cav. Born in Virginia; private, F/10th Cavalry, 1 Dec 1876–30 Nov 1881; private, 7 Dec 1881; corporal, 31 Oct 1883; sergeant, 11 Sep 1884; at Ft Assiniboine, MT, 1897. SOURCE: Baker, Roster.

Sergeant, F/10th Cavalry, at Ft Apache, AZ, 1890, subscribed $.50 to testimonial to General Grierson. SOURCE: List of subscriptions, 23 Apr 1890, 10th Cavalry papers, MHI.

Sergeant, F/10th Cavalry, reduced to ranks. SOURCE: *ANJ* 35 (12 Mar 1898): 518.

Served as sergeant, M/10th Cavalry in Cuba, 1898. SOURCE: Cashin, *Under Fire with the Tenth Cavalry*, 352.

Retires as sergeant, M/10th Cavalry, in accordance with Special Order 300, Adjutant General's Office, 11 Dec 1903.

MIND, George; Private; H/24th Inf. Fined $1 by summary court, San Isidro, Philippines, for appearing in street with blouse unbuttoned in violation of standing orders, 3 Nov 1901, third conviction; fined $5 and jailed for five days, first three in solitary on bread and water, for leaving rifle outside company quarters, 28 Feb 1902. SOURCE: Register of Summary Court, San Isidro.

MINER, James S.; 24th Inf. At Ft Reno, Indian Territory, 1887. *See* **HAMILTON**, J. H., 24th Infantry

MINER, William; A/10th Cav. Original member of 10th Cavalry; in troop when organized, Ft Leavenworth, KS, 18 Feb 1867. SOURCE: McMiller, "Buffalo Soldiers," 68.

MINGO, Arthur; Private; C/9th Cav. Veteran of Philippine Insurrection; at Ft D. A. Russell, WY, in 1910; resident of 21 Douglas St., Chattanooga, TN. SOURCE: *Illustrated Review: Ninth Cavalry*, with picture.

MINGUS, Charles; Corporal; G/10th Cav. Born in North Carolina; private, G/10th Cavalry, 5 Nov 1892; corporal, 14 Mar 1897; at Ft Assiniboine, MT, 1897. SOURCE: Baker, Roster.

Discharged. SOURCE: *ANJ* 35 (5 Mar 1898): 498.

MINOR, Abraham L.; Private; I/24th Inf. Enlisted Baltimore, 1 Feb 1899; sick since 14 Feb 1899, disease contracted in line of duty. SOURCE: Muster Roll, I/24 Inf, Jan–Feb 1899.

Fined $.50 by summary court, 13 May 1899. SOURCE: Muster Roll, I/24 Inf, May–Jun 1899.

Fined $2 by summary court, 25 Sep 1899; absent sick in Manila, Philippines, since 18 Oct 1899. SOURCE: Muster Roll, I/24 Inf, Sep–Oct 1899.

Absent sick in First Reserve Hospital, Manila, since 18 Oct 1899. SOURCE: Muster Roll, I/24 Inf, Nov–Dec 1899.

MINOR, Dennis; Private; H/24th Inf. Enlisted Mobile, AL, 7 Jan 1899; on special duty as post baker since 2 Feb 1899. SOURCE: Muster Roll, H/24 Inf, Jan–Feb 1899.

MINOR, Francis; Private; E/10th Cav. Original member of 10th Cavalry; in troop when organized, Ft Leavenworth, KS, 15 Jun 1867. SOURCE: McMiller, "Buffalo Soldiers," 72.

Mentioned Apr 1873 as joined from desertion. SOURCE: ES, 10 Cav, 1872–81.

MINOR, Samuel T.; Private; G/10th Cav. Served in 10th Cavalry in Cuba, 1898; wounded in action. SOURCE: Cashin, *Under Fire with the Tenth Cavalry*, 345.

Wounded in action at Santiago, Cuba, 1 Jul 1898. SOURCE: SecWar, *AR 1898*, 324.

VA File C 2462167 missing, Federal Records Center, Suitland, MD.

MINOR, William; Private; E/9th Cav. On detached service in field, New Mexico, 27 Jan–1 Feb 1881. SOURCE: Regt Returns, 9 Cav, Feb 1881.

MINOTT, Joseph; Corporal; F/9th Cav. Sergeant, B/9th Cavalry, in field with troops, San Francisco Mountains, NM, on detached service from Ft Craig, NM, 4–15 Jan 1881. SOURCE: Regt Returns, 9 Cav, Jan 1881.

Appointed corporal, F/9th Cavalry, 25 Apr 1891. SOURCE: Roster, 9 Cav.

Retires from Ft Duchesne, UT, Apr 1896. SOURCE: *ANJ* 33 (25 Apr 1896): 616.

Died, U.S. Soldiers Home, age 52, 1 Jul 1897, with lockjaw. SOURCE: SecWar, *AR 1897*, 792.

MINTUS, Aurelius; Private; G/9th Cav. At Ft D. A. Russell, WY, in 1910; resident of Boston. SOURCE: *Illustrated Review: Ninth Cavalry*, with picture.

MISTY, John; I/10th Cav. Original member of 10th Cavalry; in troop when organized, Ft Riley, KS, 15 Aug 1867. SOURCE: McMiller, "Buffalo Soldiers," 76.

MITCHELL; Private; L/10th Cav. Discharged in accordance with Special Order 170, Adjutant General's Office, 21 Jul 1904.

MITCHELL, Albert M; Trumpeter; M/9th Cav. At Ft D. A. Russell, WY, in 1910. SOURCE: *Illustrated Review: Ninth Cavalry*, with picture.

MITCHELL, Andrew; Private; C/25th Inf. Dishonorable discharge, Brownsville. SOURCE: SO 266, AGO, 9 Nov 1906.

MITCHELL, Basil; Sergeant; L/10th Cav. Original member of 10th Cavalry; in troop when organized, Ft Riley, KS, 21 Sep 1867. SOURCE: McMiller, "Buffalo Soldiers," 78.

Commander, 10th Cavalry, disapproves L/10th Cavalry order reducing Sergeant Mitchell to ranks and says trial by court martial would be proper action. SOURCE: ES, 10 Cav, 1872–81.

MITCHELL, Charles F.; Private; D/24th Inf. At Cabanatuan, Philippines, 1901. *See* **BROWN**, Philip, Private, D/24th Infantry; **SIMPSON**, James A., Private, D/24th Infantry; **TATES**, Rollins, Private, D/24th Infantry

MITCHELL, Cornelius; Private; B/10th Cav. Served in 10th Cavalry, 1898; remained in U.S. during war with Spain. SOURCE: Cashin, *Under Fire with the Tenth Cavalry*, 339.

MITCHELL, Edward; Private; B/10th Cav. Served in 10th Cavalry in Cuba, 1898. SOURCE: Cashin, *Under Fire with the Tenth Cavalry*, 338.

MITCHELL, George; C/10th Cav. Original member of 10th Cavalry; in troop when organized, Ft Leavenworth, KS, 14 May 1867. SOURCE: McMiller, "Buffalo Soldiers," 70.

MITCHELL, George W.; Private; D/9th Cav. On special duty as messenger for signal officer, since 3 Feb 1902. SOURCE: SD List, D/9, Nueva Caceres, Philippines, 24 May 1902.

MITCHELL, George W.; Private; B/25th Inf. Dishonorable discharge, Brownsville. SOURCE: SO 266, AGO, 9 Nov 1906.

MITCHELL, Harry; Private; B/24th Inf. Transferred from Reserve Divisional Hospital, Siboney, Cuba, to U.S. on U.S. Army Transport *Santiago* with remittent yellow fever, 1898. SOURCE: Hospital Papers, Spanish-American War.

MITCHELL, Henry H.; Private; L/25th Inf. Fined $8 by summary court, San Isidro, Philippines, for being drunk on kitchen police duty, 23 May 1902, first conviction; fined three months' pay for being drunk on guard duty, Jul 1902. SOURCE: Register of Summary Court, San Isidro.

MITCHELL, James; Recruit; Mounted Service. Convicted by general court martial, St. Louis Barracks, MO, of desertion; sentenced to dishonorable discharge and three years. SOURCE: GCMO 23, AGO, 20 Apr 1878.

MITCHELL, James; Private; B/25th Inf. Died of dysentery at Palanig, Luzon, Philippines, 2 Jul 1901. SOURCE: *ANJ* 38 (24 Aug 1901): 1256.

MITCHELL, James A.; H/10th Cav. Died in Minnesota. SOURCE: Taylor, "Minnesota Black Spanish-American War Veterans."

MITCHELL, James H.; Corporal; I/24th Inf. Served in Houston, 1917; expressed desire to be transferred from Texas; accused of role in riot; sentenced to death; sentence commuted to life in prison and reduced to twenty years in 1922. SOURCE: Haynes, *A Night of Violence*, 119–20, 287, 294, 302, 312–13.

MITCHELL, Joseph; Private; H/24th Inf. Enlisted Ft McPherson, GA, 30 Jan 1899. SOURCE: Muster Roll, H/24 Inf, Jan–Feb 1899.

MITCHELL, Joseph G.; Corporal; A/10th Cav. Private, A/10th Cavalry, contributed $1.50 of $3.25 sent by men of A/10th Cavalry, Ft Keogh, MT, to Richmond *Planet* for defense fund of three black women accused of murder, Lunenburg Co., VA. SOURCE: Richmond *Planet*, 21 Sep 1895.
  Corporal, served in A/10th Cavalry in Cuba, 1898; wounded in action. SOURCE: Cashin, *Under Fire with the Tenth Cavalry*, 336–37; SecWar, *AR 1898*, 323.

Heroism in Cuba slighted according to unsigned letter (Cpl. John E. Lewis, H/10th Cavalry) from Montauk, NY. SOURCE: Gatewood, *"Smoked Yankees"*, 77.

MITCHELL, Loyd; Corporal; H/24th Inf. Enlisted Ft McPherson, GA, 3 Nov 1897; six years' continuous service; promoted from lance corporal, 10 May 1898, Tampa, FL. SOURCE: Muster Roll, H/24 Inf, May–Jun 1898.
  On special duty in charge of rations since 28 Aug 1898. SOURCE: Muster Roll, H/24 Inf, Jul–Aug 1898.
  On special duty as clerk, adjutant's office, since 2 Oct 1898. SOURCE: Muster Roll, H/24 Inf, Sep–Oct 1898.
  On special duty as clerk, adjutant's office; seventh year of continuous service starts 3 Nov 1898. SOURCE: Muster Roll, H/24 Inf, Nov–Dec 1898.
  On special duty as clerk, adjutant's office. SOURCE: Muster Roll, H/24 Inf, Jan–Feb 1899.

MITCHELL, Luke; Saddler; I/9th Cav. Veteran of Philippine Insurrection; at Ft D. A. Russell, WY, in 1910; resident of Glenwood, LA. SOURCE: *Illustrated Review: Ninth Cavalry*, with picture.

MITCHELL, Poindexter; Private; C/9th Cav. At Ft D. A. Russell, WY, in 1910; resident of 1436 Pierce Pl., NW, Washington, DC. SOURCE: *Illustrated Review: Ninth Cavalry*, with picture.

MITCHELL, William; K/10th Cav. Original member of 10th Cavalry; in troop when organized, Ft Riley, KS, 1 Sep 1867. SOURCE: McMiller, "Buffalo Soldiers," 77.

MITCHELL, William H.; Private; E/10th Cav. Served in 10th Cavalry in Cuba, 1898. SOURCE: Cashin, *Under Fire with the Tenth Cavalry*, 342.

MITCHELL, Woody; Private; B/10th Cav. Enlisted I/9th Cavalry, May 1899; served at Ft Duchesne, UT, 1900; private, B/10th Cavalry, Ft Robinson, NE, 1904. SOURCE: Affidavit, Mitchell, age 25, Ft Robinson, 10 Jun 1904, VA File XC 2705872, Henry McClain.

MITCHEM, Thomas; Private; H/10th Cav. Served in 10th Cavalry in Cuba, 1898. SOURCE: Cashin, *Under Fire with the Tenth Cavalry*, 345.

MITCHEM, William H.; Corporal; F/10th Cav. Served in 10th Cavalry in Cuba, 1898. SOURCE: Cashin, *Under Fire with the Tenth Cavalry*, 343.

MODELIN, Alexander; B/10th Cav. Original member of 10th Cavalry; in troop when organized, Ft Leavenworth, KS, 1 Apr 1867. SOURCE: McMiller, "Buffalo Soldiers," 69.

MOFFETT, Drayton H.; Private; A/10th Cav. On extra duty as schoolteacher, Ft Robinson, NE. SOURCE: Order 211, 31 Oct 1891, Post Orders, Ft Robinson.

Teacher, Ft Robinson school, 1 Nov 1891–30 Apr 1892 and 1 Feb–30 Apr 1893. SOURCE: Reports of Schools, Ft Robinson, 1879–92.

On special duty as clerk, office of post adjutant, Ft Robinson. SOURCE: Order 71, 30 Oct 1892, Post Orders, Ft Robinson.

Relieved from extra duty as schoolteacher. SOURCE: Order 57, 11 Jul 1893, Post Orders, Ft Robinson.

"As far as known, there is no authority for Private Moffett to have a wife," so he cannot expect any privileges because of marriage. SOURCE: CO, Ft Robinson, to CO, G/9, 19 Jul 1893, LS, Ft Robinson.

Called Pvt. Mathew Wyatt, G/9th Cavalry, "a cock-sucking son-of-a-bitch" and said Wyatt "was pimping around the troop and among the white folks." SOURCE: Court Martial Records, McKay.

MOLOCK, Andrew M.; K/9th Cav. Served 1879–90; he and wife Carey are new members of Camp No. 11, National Indian War Veterans. SOURCE: *Winners of the West* 5 (Mar 1928): 3.

Died Baltimore, 15 Nov 1929; buried London Park National Cemetery, Baltimore; loyal supporter and member, Camp 11, National Indian War Veterans. SOURCE: *Winners of the West* 6 (Nov 1929): 3.

MOLONY, Isaac W.; 1st Lt; 49th Inf. One of twenty-three officers of 49th Infantry recommended as regular Army second lieutenants. SOURCE: CG, DivPI, Manila, 8 Feb 1901, to AGO, AGO File 355163.

MONROE, Edward M.; Sergeant. Awarded distinguished service cross for heroism in the Philippines, 7 Dec 1899. SOURCE: *Crisis* 30 (June 1925): 78.

MONROE, F. J.; Corporal; K/24th Inf. At Cabanatuan, Philippines, 1901. *See* **WILLIAMS**, Anderson, Private, K/24th Infantry

MONROE, George; Sergeant; A/9th Cav. Appointed sergeant, 30 Apr 1892. SOURCE: Roster, 9 Cav.

Wife Sallie buried at Ft Robinson, NE, 1894. SOURCE: List of Interments, Ft Robinson.

At Ft Robinson, 1895. SOURCE: *ANJ* 32 (23 Feb 1895): 422.

MONTGOMERY, Gilbert; Private; H/9th Cav. At Ft D. A. Russell, WY, in 1910; resident of Cleveland, TN. SOURCE: *Illustrated Review: Ninth Cavalry.*

MONTGOMERY, Henry; Private; F/9th Cav. At Ft D. A. Russell, WY, in 1910; resident of Pineville, AL. SOURCE: *Illustrated Review: Ninth Cavalry.*

MONTGOMERY, Humphrey; Private; A/24th Inf. Died of yellow fever in Cuba, 17 Aug 1898. SOURCE: *ANJ* 36 (18 Feb 1898): 590; AG, *Correspondence Regarding the War with Spain*, I:241.

MONTGOMERY, James B.; Private; M/10th Cav. Served in 10th Cavalry, 1898; remained in U.S. during war with Spain. SOURCE: Cashin, *Under Fire with the Tenth Cavalry*, 352.

MONTGOMERY, Jesse; Private; M/10th Cav. Original member of 10th Cavalry; in troop when organized, Ft Riley, KS, 15 Oct 1867. SOURCE: McMiller, "Buffalo Soldiers," 79.

Mentioned Oct 1870. SOURCE: ES, 10 Cav, 1866–71.

MONTGOMERY, Morgan; Private; E/25th Inf. Quartermaster Department to furnish him transportation from furlough at Louisville to Ft Thomas, AZ. SOURCE: *ANJ* 28 (28 Mar 1891): 529.

MONTGOMERY, S.; A/10th Cav. Original member of 10th Cavalry; in troop when organized, Ft Leavenworth, KS, 18 Feb 1867. SOURCE: McMiller, "Buffalo Soldiers," 68.

MOODY, George; Private; 24th Inf. Drowned while crossing San Mateo River, Philippines, 21 Aug 1899. SOURCE: Richmond *Planet*, 2 Sep 1899.

MOODY, Henry; Private; E/24th Inf. Dishonorably discharged; now confined at Ft Brown, TX, in accordance with General Court Martial Order 5, Department of Texas, 28 Feb 1876; to serve sentence at Kansas Penitentiary, Leavenworth, KS. SOURCE: GCMO 38, AGO, 24 Mar 1876.

MOODY, Thomas E.; 1st Lt; 23rd Kans Inf. Served in 1898.

MOORE; Private; E/10th Cav. At Ft Apache, AZ, 1890, subscribed $.50 to testimonial to General Grierson. SOURCE: List of subscriptions, 23 Apr 1890, 10th Cavalry papers, MHI.

MOORE; Private; K/9th Cav. Wounded by Private Dyer, I/9th Cavalry, in I Troop's railroad car bound for Mexican border. SOURCE: Cheyenne *State Leader*, 12 Mar 1911.

MOORE, Abraham; Corporal; I/24th Inf. Enlisted Indianapolis, 29 Jul 1898. SOURCE: Muster Roll, I/24 Inf, Jan–Feb 1899.

On detached service, Three Rivers, CA, 3 May–21 Jun 1899; on detached service at Presidio of San Francisco, CA, 22 Jun 1899. SOURCE: Muster Roll, I/24 Inf, May–Jun 1899.

Rejoined company from detached service, 26 Jul 1899. SOURCE: Muster Roll, I/24 Inf, Jul–Aug 1899.

Discharged, character very good, 31 Dec 1899; $156 deposits, $26.81 clothing. SOURCE: Muster Roll, I/24 Inf, Nov–Dec 1899.

MOORE, Adam; Sergeant; C/9th Cav. Appointed corporal, C/9th Cavalry, 23 Mar 1889. SOURCE: Roster, 9 Cav.

Promoted to sergeant, vice Rock, retired, Ft Robinson, NE, Dec 1894. SOURCE: *ANJ* 32 (22 Dec 1894): 278.

Commended for gallantry in charge on San Juan Hill, battle of Santiago, Cuba, 1 Jul 1898; now out of service. SOURCE: GO 15, AGO, 13 Feb 1900; *ANJ* 37 (24 Feb 1900): 611.

Wounded in action at San Juan, Cuba, 1 Jul 1898. SOURCE: *Illustrated Review: Ninth Cavalry*, with picture.

MOORE, Bazil B.; Sergeant; L/10th Cav. Original member of 10th Cavalry; in troop when organized, Ft Riley, KS, 21 Sep 1867. SOURCE: McMiller, "Buffalo Soldiers," 78.

Citizens of Lewiston, PA, petition for pardon of Moore, late sergeant, L/10th Cavalry; Capt. Robert Gray, troop commander, applied for reprieve six months ago, considered Moore honest, sober, reliable before offense, and best noncommissioned officer in troop, potential first sergeant, agrees that he fully merits pardon, 25 Jul 1870; regiment commander concurs, 26 Jul 1870. SOURCE: ES, 10 Cav, 1866–71.

MOORE, Cato; Private; D/24th Inf. Acquitted of wasting two rounds of ammunition, Cabanatuan, Philippines, 24 Nov 1900; witness: 1st Sgt. M. H. Ellis, D/24th Infantry. SOURCE: Name File, 24 Inf.

Fined $2 for absence without leave from guard mount, Cabanatuan, 12 Dec 1900; witnesses: 1st Sgt. M. H. Ellis, D/24th Infantry; Cpl. William Kirk, D/24th Infantry; Cpl. Thomas Johnson, D/24th Infantry. SOURCE: Name File, 24 Inf.

Fined one month's pay and confined for thirty days for theft of dark blue shirt, property of Pvt. George Brownie, D/24th Infantry, Cabanatuan, 15 May 1901; witnesses: 1st Sgt. M. H. Ellis, D/24th Infantry; Pvt. Simon Moore, D/24th Infantry; Pvts. Edward A. Ridgely, D/24th Infantry, George Brownie, D/24th Infantry, William Griffie, D/24th Infantry; Cpl. Emmett Jackson, D/24th Infantry. SOURCE: Name File, 24 Inf.

Fined one month's pay and confined for thirty days for felonious theft of one noncommissioned officer's waist belt and belt plate, U.S. property, Cabanatuan, 28 Jun 1901; witnesses: Sgt. Pat Keys, D/24th Infantry; Pvts. Frank Young, K/24th Infantry, Lemuel Rogers, Hospital Corps, Riley Hipshire, Hospital Corps. SOURCE: Name File, 24 Inf.

MOORE, Columbus; D/10th Cav. Original member of 10th Cavalry; in troop when organized, Ft Leavenworth, KS, 1 Jun 1867. SOURCE: McMiller, "Buffalo Soldiers," 71.

MOORE, Daniel; M/10th Cav. Original member of 10th Cavalry; in troop when organized, Ft Riley, KS, 15 Oct 1867. SOURCE: McMiller, "Buffalo Soldiers," 79.

MOORE, David; Corporal; A/9th Cav. Promoted from private. SOURCE: Order 46, 9 Cav, 20 Sep 1888.

MOORE, Edward; Private; D/9th Cav. In hands of civil authorities, Buffalo, WY, 24 Mar–6 Apr 1889. SOURCE: Regt Returns, 9 Cav.

MOORE, Edward W.; Private; L/10th Cav. Served in 10th Cavalry, 1898; remained in U.S. during war with Spain. SOURCE: Cashin, *Under Fire with the Tenth Cavalry*, 351.

MOORE, Elbridge; Private; I/10th Cav. Served in 10th Cavalry, 1898; remained in U.S. during war with Spain. SOURCE: Cashin, *Under Fire with the Tenth Cavalry*, 348.

MOORE, Ellis E.; H/10th Cav. Original member of 10th Cavalry; in troop when organized, Ft Leavenworth, KS, 21 Jul 1867. SOURCE: McMiller, "Buffalo Soldiers," 75.

MOORE, George W.; Private; C/9th Cav. Wounded in action against Victorio in Mimbres Mountains, NM, 28 May 1879. SOURCE: Billington, "Black Cavalrymen," 64; *Illustrated Review: Ninth Cavalry*. See **DORSEY**, Frank, Private, C/9th Cavalry

MOORE, Harry; Private; A/24th Inf. Wounded in action at Santiago, Cuba, 1898. SOURCE: SecWar, *AR 1898*, 437.

MOORE, Henry; E/10th Cav. On temporary duty for training, Ft Bascom, NM. SOURCE: SO 3, District of New Mexico, 23 Jan 1867.

Original member of 10th Cavalry; in troop when organized, Ft Leavenworth, KS, 15 Jun 1867. SOURCE: McMiller, "Buffalo Soldiers," 72.

MOORE, Henry; Sergeant; K/9th Cav. Sergeant, E/9th Cavalry, authorized four-month furlough from Ft Duchesne, UT. SOURCE: *ANJ* 24 (7 May 1887): 814.

Appointed corporal, K/9th Cavalry, 20 Feb 1889. SOURCE: Roster, 9 Cav.

Corporal and assistant treasurer, Diamond Club of K/9th Cavalry, Ft Robinson, NE, 1891. SOURCE: *ANJ* 28 (2 May 1891): 620.

Promoted to sergeant, Ft Robinson, Feb 1895. SOURCE: *ANJ* 32 (9 Mar 1895): 454.

Sergeant, retires from Ft Robinson, Mar 1895. SOURCE: *ANJ* 32 (16 Mar 1895): 474.

VA File C 2459666 missing from Federal Records Center, Suitland, MD.

MOORE, Henry; Private; L/10th Cav. Served in 10th Cavalry, 1898; remained in U.S. during war with Spain. SOURCE: Cashin, *Under Fire with the Tenth Cavalry*, 350.

MOORE, Henry; Private; F/48th Inf. Committed suicide, 20 Jan 1901. SOURCE: *ANJ* 38 (2 Feb 1901): 555.

MOORE, Henry; Cook; K/9th Cav. Veteran of Philippine Insurrection; at Ft D. A. Russell, WY, in 1910; marksman; resident of Lee Co., AL. SOURCE: *Illustrated Review: Ninth Cavalry*, with picture.

MOORE, Herman; Private; G/9th Cav. At Ft D. A. Russell, WY, in 1910; resident of Houston. SOURCE: *Illustrated Review: Ninth Cavalry*, with picture.

MOORE, J.; Private; D/9th Cav. In hands of civil authorities, Buffalo, WY, 1–18 May 1890. SOURCE: Regt Returns, 9 Cav, May 1890.

MOORE, Jack; Private; L/10th Cav. Mentioned Jan 1873 as recruit en route to Ft Gibson, Indian Territory. SOURCE: LS, 10 Cav, 1873–83.

MOORE, Jesse; Corporal; I/24th Inf. One of Sergeant Henry's "most dedicated disciples," Houston riot, 1917; sentenced to death. SOURCE: Haynes, *A Night of Violence*, 128, 271.

Hanged, Ft Sam Houston, TX, for part in Houston riot. SOURCE: Cleveland *Gazette*, 15 Dec 1917.

MOORE, John; F/10th Cav. Original member of 10th Cavalry; in troop when organized, Ft Leavenworth, KS, 21 Jun 1867. SOURCE: McMiller, "Buffalo Soldiers," 73.

MOORE, John; H/10th Cav. Original member of 10th Cavalry; in troop when organized, Ft Leavenworth, KS, 21 Jul 1867. SOURCE: McMiller, "Buffalo Soldiers," 75.

MOORE, John; Sergeant; K/24th Inf. Requests transfer to H/10th Cavalry so he can serve with his brother; commander approves transfer of Moore, one of his best men: "I am willing to gratify a good soldier," 10th Cavalry will gain a good soldier; commanders of H/10th Cavalry and 10th Cavalry willing to accept him, Jun 1873. SOURCE: ES, 10 Cav, 1872–81.

MOORE, John T.; Private; C/25th Inf. Reduced from sergeant for absence without leave from guard duty, Ft Buford, ND. SOURCE: *ANJ* 30 (12 Nov 1892): 187.

MOORE, Joseph; QM Sgt; 9th Cav. Private, arrived at Ft Robinson, NE, from Jefferson Barracks, MO, 14 Aug 1885. SOURCE: Monthly Return, Ft Robinson, Aug 1885.

Along with E. Marshall, 9th Cavalry, responsible for establishment of Sunday School at Ft Robinson. SOURCE: Cleveland *Gazette*, 11 Aug 1886.

Private, F/9th Cavalry, relieved from extra duty as schoolteacher, Ft Robinson. SOURCE: Order 111, 4 Jun 1887, Post Orders, Ft Robinson.

Corporal, F/9th Cavalry, relieved from extra duty as schoolteacher, Ft Robinson. SOURCE: Order 217, 7 Nov 1887, Post Orders, Ft Robinson.

Sergeant, F/9th Cavalry, on extra duty as schoolteacher, Ft Robinson. SOURCE: Order 226, 31 Oct 1889, Post Orders, Ft Robinson.

Relieved from extra duty as schoolteacher, Ft Robinson. SOURCE: Order 61, 25 Mar 1890, Post Orders, Ft Robinson.

Proposes to raise sufficient money among four colored regiments to buy site of John Brown fort, Harper's Ferry,

WV, for monument. SOURCE: Cleveland *Gazette*, 9 Aug 1890.

Private, A/9th Cavalry, relieves Sgt. Harry S. Ogilvie, C/8th Infantry, as schoolteacher, Ft Robinson. SOURCE: Order 88, 29 Apr 1891, Post Orders, Ft Robinson.

Commander, Ft Robinson, asks for report from superintendent of post schools on qualifications of Private Moore as schoolteacher. SOURCE: CO, Ft Robinson, to Chaplain Plummer, 28 Apr 1891, LS, Ft Robinson.

On extra duty as schoolteacher, Ft Robinson. SOURCE: Order 183, 19 Sep 1891, Post Orders, Ft Robinson.

Corporal, retained on extra duty as schoolteacher in accordance with telegram, Adjutant General's Office, 4 Dec 1891.

Teacher, Ft Robinson, 1 Nov 1891–30 Apr 1892. SOURCE: Reports of Schools, Ft Robinson, 1892–96.

Commander, Ft Robinson, asks authority to keep Corporal Moore on as schoolteacher because of his experience; Moore has organized post schools for enlisted men and children under direction of chaplain; his relief would seriously hinder progress. SOURCE: CO, Ft Robinson, to AG, USA, 15 Nov 1891, LS, Ft Robinson.

Appointed sergeant, A/9th Cavalry, 26 Jun 1892. SOURCE: Roster, 9 Cav.

Letter, Ft Robinson, to editor. SOURCE: Cleveland *Gazette*, 4 Mar 1895.

Sergeant, on special regimental recruiting duty with 1st Lt. Montgomery D. Parker, 9th Cavalry, at Cincinnati. SOURCE: *ANJ* 32 (24 Aug 1895): 855.

Examined for ordnance sergeant at Ft Robinson, Nov 1895, while sergeant, A/9th Cavalry. SOURCE: *ANJ* 33 (16 Nov 1895): 179.

Reenlistment authorized by letter, Adjutant General's Office, 19 Jan 1898.

Sergeant, A/9th Cavalry; commissioned first lieutenant, 8th Volunteer Infantry, after Spanish-American War. SOURCE: Cashin, *Under Fire with the Tenth Cavalry*, 355, 359, with picture in uniform of 8th Volunteer Infantry.

Mentioned. SOURCE: San Francisco *Chronicle*, 15 Nov 1899.

Mentioned as second lieutenant, F/48th Infantry. SOURCE: Beasley, *Negro Trailblazers*, 284.

Formerly with 8th and 48th Volunteer Infantry regiments; now quartermaster sergeant, 9th Cavalry, Ord Barracks, CA, with first squadron. SOURCE: Indianapolis *Freeman*, 5 Dec 1903.

MOORE, Loney; Corporal; L/24th Inf. Awarded certificate of merit for service in Cuban campaign, 1898. SOURCE: Scipio, *Last of the Black Regulars*, 130.

Wounded in Cuba, 1898. SOURCE: Muller, *The Twenty Fourth Infantry*, 16.

Commended for distinguished service as private, A/24th Infantry, battle of Santiago, Cuba, 1 Jul 1898; awarded certificate of merit. SOURCE: GO 15, AGO, 13 Feb 1900.

Certificate of merit mentioned. SOURCE: Steward, *The Colored Regulars*, 280; *ANJ* 37 (24 Feb 1900): 611.

MOORE, Preston; Sergeant; C/24th Inf. Letter from Manicling, Philippines, 22 Oct 1900. SOURCE: Gatewood, *"Smoked Yankees"*, 288.

MOORE, Richard; Private; L/10th Cav. Served in 10th Cavalry, 1898; remained in U.S. during war with Spain. SOURCE: Cashin, *Under Fire with the Tenth Cavalry*, 350.

MOORE, Richard; Sergeant; 10th Cav. Enlisted 14 Nov 1911; served in Mexican punitive expedition and saw action at Aguas Calientes, 1 Apr 1916; accomplished athlete who was on U.S. Olympic team, 1920; retired 12 Dec 1943; buried, Ft Leavenworth, KS, 27 Dec 1971. SOURCE: *9th and 10th Cavalry Association Bulletin*, Jun 1973.

MOORE, Robert B.; Private; K/10th Cav. Served in 10th Cavalry, 1898; remained in U.S. during war with Spain. SOURCE: Cashin, *Under Fire with the Tenth Cavalry*, 349.

MOORE, Rufus; Private; K/10th Cav. Served in 10th Cavalry, 1898; remained in U.S. during war with Spain. SOURCE: Cashin, *Under Fire with the Tenth Cavalry*, 349.

MOORE, Samuel; Private; F/9th Cav. Detailed gardener, post hospital, Ft Robinson, NE. SOURCE: Order 141, 14 Aug 1886, Post Orders, Ft Robinson.

Discharged, end of term, from Ft Robinson, 28 Feb 1887.

MOORE, Simon; Private; D/24th Inf. Fined $5 at Cabanatuan, Philippines, for assault on Volentina De Los Ris, native woman of Cabanatuan, striking her with piece of bamboo, 25 Apr 1901; witness: Sgt. W. Prear, D/24th Infantry. SOURCE: Name File, 24 Inf.

Jailed for fifteen days, Cabanatuan, May 1901, for failure to obey commander's order to pay native woman Catalina Peneda for his wash; witness: 1st Sgt. M. H. Ellis, D/24th Infantry. SOURCE: Name File, 24 Inf.

See **MOORE**, Cato, Private, D/24th Infantry

MOORE, William; Private; K/9th Cav. At Ft D. A. Russell, WY, in 1910; resident of Covington, KY. SOURCE: *Illustrated Review: Ninth Cavalry*, with picture.

MOORE, William T.; Private; F/9th Cav. Died of variola in the Philippines, 19 Jul 1901. SOURCE: *ANJ* 39 (21 Sep 1901): 59.

MORAN, Shelley; Private; F/10th Cav. Drowned in the Philippines, 13 May 1901; body not recovered. SOURCE: *ANJ* 38 (25 May 1901): 948.

Body reported recovered in telegram, Maj. Gen. Arthur MacArthur to Adjutant General, 3 Jun 1901.

MORANDERS, Joseph; Private; D/24th Inf. Fined $1 for wasting seven rounds of ammunition, Cabanatuan, Philippines, 24 Nov 1900; witness: 1st Sgt. M. H. Ellis, D/24th Infantry. SOURCE: Name File, 24 Inf.

See **SMITH**, Horace J., Private, D/24th Infantry

MORATIER, Charles; F/10th Cav. Original member of 10th Cavalry; in troop when organized, Ft Leavenworth, KS, 21 Jun 1867. SOURCE: McMiller, "Buffalo Soldiers," 73.

MORE, Charles; Recruit; Colored Detachment/ Mounted Service. Acquitted by general court martial, Jefferson Barracks, MO, of theft of woolen blankets from Recruit William A. Lawson, Colored Detachment, 3 Feb 1885, and from Recruit Anthony Jenson, 12 Feb 1885. SOURCE: GCMO 24, AGO, 6 Mar 1885.

MORGAN; Private; D/9th Cav. Wounded in action against Victorio, 6–7 Apr 1880, along with Trumpeter Guddy, D/9th Cavalry. SOURCE: Hamilton, "History of the Ninth Cavalry," 31.

MORGAN, Arthur W.; Corporal; H/24th Inf. Promoted from lance corporal. SOURCE: *ANJ* 34 (17 Jul 1897): 855.

MORGAN, Charles P.; Private; K/10th Cav. At Ft Robinson, NE, 1904.

Ranked number 143 among rifle experts with 69.33 percent, 1904. SOURCE: GO 79, AGO, 1 Jun 1905.

Member of troop orchestra. SOURCE: Barrow, "Christmas in the United States Army," 96.

MORGAN, David; Private; D/24th Inf. Fined $5 for failure to clean rifle properly for guard mount, Cabanatuan, Philippines, 30 Mar 1901. SOURCE: Name File, 24 Inf.

MORGAN, John; B/10th Cav. Original member of 10th Cavalry; in troop when organized, Ft Leavenworth, KS, 1 Apr 1867. SOURCE: McMiller, "Buffalo Soldiers," 69.

MORGAN, Lindsey; Private; K/10th Cav. Served in 10th Cavalry, 1898; remained in U.S. during war with Spain. SOURCE: Cashin, *Under Fire with the Tenth Cavalry*, 349.

MORGAN, Richard; Cook; D/9th Cav. At Ft D. A. Russell, WY, in 1910; resident of Winchester, KY. SOURCE: *Illustrated Review: Ninth Cavalry*, with picture.

MORI, Philip; Corporal; F/10th Cav. Born Washington, DC; private, F/10th Cavalry, 2 Jun 1892; corporal, 22 Jan 1896; at Ft Assiniboine, MT, 1897. SOURCE: Baker, Roster.

MORRELL, Benjamin; Ord Sgt; U.S. Army. First sergeant, A/25th Infantry, at Ft Concho, TX, 1878; best marksman in company and eighth in regiment. SOURCE: 25 Inf, Scrapbook, I:145.

Wrote two letters to Richmond *Planet* from Dutch Island, Jamestown, RI, contributing money to defense of three black women accused of murder in Lunenburg Co., VA; letter of 26 Aug 1895 contained $2.50; letter of 17 Jul 1896 contained $2.25, including $1 from his wife and $.25 from his young son Freddie. SOURCE: Richmond *Planet*, 21 Sep 1895 and 25 Jul 1896.

MORRIS; Private; E/10th Cav. At Ft Apache, AZ, 1890, subscribed $.50 to testimonial to General Grierson. SOURCE: List of subscriptions, 23 Apr 1890, 10th Cavalry papers, MHI.

MORRIS, Burrell; Corporal; C/9th Cav. Veteran of Philippine Insurrection; at Ft D. A. Russell, WY, in 1910. SOURCE: *Illustrated Review: Ninth Cavalry*, with picture.

MORRIS, Edward; Private; D/25th Inf. Charged with murder of Pvt. Henry McKee, D/25th Infantry, at Ft Niobrara, NE, 17 Sep 1902, during evening crap game in rear of D Company barracks; Morris claims gun went off accidentally; Walter Johnson ran game. SOURCE: Crawford *Bulletin*, 17 Oct 1902.

On trial for murder of Private McKee at Omaha, NE. SOURCE: Crawford *Bulletin*, 26 Jun 1903.

MORRIS, James; Private; A/24th Inf. Murdered by natives in the Philippines, 1899.

MORRIS, John; D/24th Inf. Admitted to Soldiers Home with disability at age 30 with two years and four months' service, 21 May 1891. SOURCE: SecWar, *AR 1891*, 753.

MORRIS, John; Private; B/10th Cav. Served in 10th Cavalry in Cuba, 1898; wounded in action. SOURCE: Cashin, *Under Fire with the Tenth Cavalry*, 338–39.

MORRIS, Reuben B.; Private; D/9th Cav. Letter, Department of the Platte, 20 Jun 1894, concerns his application for transfer.

In hands of civil authorities, Crawford, NE, 11–23 Jan 1895. SOURCE: Regt Returns, 9 Cav, Jan 1895.

MORRIS, Richard M.; Sergeant; A/10th Cav. Commissioned first lieutenant at Camp Des Moines, IA, 15 Oct 1917. SOURCE: Glass, *History of the Tenth Cavalry*, appendix M.

MORRIS, T.; Private; H/9th Cav. On detached service at Ft Bayard, NM, 16 Jan–10 Feb 1881. SOURCE: Regt Returns, 9 Cav, Feb 1881.

MORRIS, Thomas; Private; K/24th Inf. Jailed for thirty days and fined one month's pay for taking weapon from quarters, although ordered by noncommissioned officer not to, firing it, and causing alarm in camp, Cabanatuan, Philippines, 12 Apr 1901; witnesses: Cpl. James Roston, K/24th Infantry, and Sgt. Jacob Stevens, K/24th Infantry. SOURCE: Name File, 24 Inf.

MORRIS, Thomas H.; Private; I/24th Inf. Captured in the Philippines, 10 Oct 1900. *See* **BURNS**, William J., Corporal, I/24th Infantry

MORRIS, William S.; Sergeant; E/9th Cav. Private, E/9th Cavalry, on special duty as assistant librarian, Ft Robinson, NE. SOURCE: Order 48, 18 Jul 1894, Post Orders, Ft Robinson.

Veteran of Indian wars, Spanish-American War, and Philippine Insurrection; sergeant, E/9th Cavalry, at Ft D. A. Russell, WY, in 1910. SOURCE: *Illustrated Review: Ninth Cavalry*, with picture.

MORRISON, Henry J.; K/10th Cav. Original member of 10th Cavalry; in troop when organized, Ft Riley, KS, 1 Sep 1867. SOURCE: McMiller, "Buffalo Soldiers," 77.

MORRISON, James; K/10th Cav. Original member of 10th Cavalry; in troop when organized, Ft Riley, KS, 1 Sep 1867. SOURCE: McMiller, "Buffalo Soldiers," 77.

MORRISON, James N.; Private; H/24th Inf. Enlisted Pittsburgh, PA, 12 Jan 1899; on special duty as carpenter, Quartermaster Department, since 23 Feb 1899. SOURCE: Muster Roll, H/24 Inf, Jan–Feb 1899.

MORROW, Alexander; Private; H/24th Inf. Saddler, C/10th Cavalry, at Ft Apache, AZ, 1890, subscribed $.50 to testimonial to General Grierson. SOURCE: List of subscriptions, 23 Apr 1890, 10th Cavalry papers, MHI.

Enlisted Ft Douglas, UT, 29 Dec 1897; eleven years' continuous service; transferred from C/24th Infantry, 8 Oct 1898; on special duty as shoemaker since 18 Oct 1898. SOURCE: Muster Roll, H/24 Inf, Sep–Oct 1898.

Private, C/24th Infantry; wounded in action in Cuba, 1898. SOURCE: Clark, "A History of the Twenty-fourth," 100; Muller, *The Twenty Fourth Infantry*, 18.

On special duty as post saddler since 18 Oct 1898; twelfth year began 23 Oct 1898. SOURCE: Muster Roll, H/24 Inf, Nov–Dec 1899.

Post saddler. SOURCE: Muster Roll, H/24 Inf, Jan–Feb 1899.

MORROW, Alston; Private; D/24th Inf. At Cabanatuan, Philippines, 1901. *See* **BLACK**, Henry, Private, K/24th Infantry

MORROW, Cleveland; Sergeant; B/10th Cav. Corporal, D/24th Infantry, won first place in equipment race, military tournament, Albany, NY, autumn 1909. SOURCE: Muller, *The Twenty Fourth Infantry*, 60.

Sergeant, B/10th Cavalry, commissioned first lieutenant at Camp Des Moines, IA, 15 Oct 1917. SOURCE: Glass, *History of the Tenth Cavalry*, appendix M; Sweeney, *History of the American Negro*, 126.

MORROW, Henry; Sergeant; I/9th Cav. Expert rifleman and veteran of Philippine Insurrection; at Ft D. A. Russell, WY, in 1910; resident of Americus, GA. SOURCE: *Illustrated Review: Ninth Cavalry*, with picture.

MORROW, Nelson; 24th Inf. Served in G and K companies; wants to hear from comrades; receives $50 per month pension. SOURCE: *Winners of the West* 7 (Jan 1930): 6.

MORROW, William; B/10th Cav. Original member of 10th Cavalry; in troop when organized, Ft Leavenworth, KS, 1 Apr 1867. SOURCE: McMiller, "Buffalo Soldiers," 69.

MORSE, Abraham; F/24th Inf. Remained in Bautista, Philippines, after service; occupation saloonkeeper. SOURCE: Funston papers, KSHS.

MORSE, Albert; Private; E/9th Cav. At Ft D. A. Russell, WY, in 1910. SOURCE: *Illustrated Review: Ninth Cavalry*, with picture.

MORSE, G.; Private; F/9th Cav. Authorized to reenlist as married soldier by letter, Adjutant General's Office, 6 Jan 1890.

MORSE, H. C.; Color Sgt; 25th Inf. Picture, at Ft Niobrara, NE, 1903. SOURCE: Nankivell, *History of the Twenty-fifth Infantry*, 114.

MORTON, George; Sergeant; A/9th Cav. Private, attendant at Ft Robinson, NE, post exchange store at $15 per month. SOURCE: Reports of Inspections, Department of the Platte, II.

Promoted to corporal at Ft Robinson, 21 Jan 1895. SOURCE: *ANJ* 32 (2 Feb 1895): 374.

Sergeant, on special duty as provost sergeant since 27 Jan 1901. SOURCE: SD List, A/9, Nueva Caceres, Philippines, 24 May 1902.

Veteran of Indian wars, Spanish-American War, and Philippine Insurrection; at Ft D. A. Russell, WY, in 1910. SOURCE: *Illustrated Review: Ninth Cavalry*, with picture.

MORTON, John; Principal Musician; 25th Inf. In the Philippines, 1900. SOURCE: Richmond *Planet*, 28 Jul 1900.

MORTON, Thomas; Private; G/10th Cav. On extra duty at Ft Dodge, KS, hospital, May 1869. SOURCE: Orders, Det 10 Cav, 1868-69.

MORTON, Thomas; Private; C/9th Cav. Fined $5 by garrison court martial for conduct prejudicial to good order and discipline, Ft Robinson, NE. SOURCE: Order 5, 10 Jan 1886, Post Orders, Ft Robinson.

Buried at Ft Robinson, 14 Sep 1886. SOURCE: List of Interments, Ft Robinson.

MOSBY, Thomas; Private; 25th Inf. Born Whiteville, NC; occupation laborer, Ht 5'4 1/2", brown complexion, black eyes and hair; enlisted, age 21, Charleston, SC, 18 Jul 1881. SOURCE: Descriptive & Assignment Rolls, 25 Inf.

MOSEBY; Private; G/9th Cav. At Ft Niobrara, NE, 1886. *See* **BLEW**, Joseph, Sergeant, G/9th Cavalry

MOSELEY, William; Private; H/24th Inf. Enlisted Ft Huachuca, AZ, 16 Jun 1898; assigned to H/24th Infantry, San Juan, Cuba, 12 Jul 1898; died in field hospital, Siboney, Cuba, 11 Aug 1898, of disease contracted in line of duty; clothing $16.44. SOURCE: Muster Roll, H/24 Inf, Jul–Aug 1898.

Died in Cuba, 10 Aug 1898. SOURCE: *ANJ* 36 (18 Feb 1898): 590.

Died of yellow fever. SOURCE: AG, *Correspondence Regarding the War with Spain*, I:218.

Died at Siboney of yellow fever, 9 Aug 1898. SOURCE: Hospital Papers, Spanish-American War.

MOSES, Joe; Private; 24th Inf. Served in Houston, 1917. SOURCE: Haynes, *A Night of Violence*, 117.

MOSES, Thomas; Private; C/10th Cav. Killed in action at Carrizal, Mexico, 21 Jun 1916; burial place unknown. SOURCE: Wharfield, *Tenth Cavalry and Border Fights*, 30, 40.

MOSLEY, Benedict; Private; I/9th Cav. At Ft D. A. Russell, WY, in 1910; resident of Bluffton, IN. SOURCE: *Illustrated Review: Ninth Cavalry*, with picture.

MOSLEY, Prince; Private; C/10th Cav. Served in 10th Cavalry, 1898; remained in U.S. during war with Spain. SOURCE: Cashin, *Under Fire with the Tenth Cavalry*, 340.

MOSLEY, Robert; Corporal; H/24th Inf. Fined $5 by summary court, San Isidro, Philippines, for absence from evening inspection, 7 Feb 1902, first conviction; fined $5 for absence from eleven P.M. inspection, 26 May 1902. SOURCE: Register of Summary Court, San Isidro.

MOSLEY, Thomas L.; Private; G/10th Cav. Served in 10th Cavalry, 1898; remained in U.S. during war with Spain. SOURCE: Cashin, *Under Fire with the Tenth Cavalry*, 346.

In C/25th Infantry; dishonorable discharge, Brownsville. SOURCE: SO 266, AGO, 9 Nov 1906.

MOSLEY, Zechoriah; Trumpeter; M/10th Cav. Original member of 10th Cavalry; in troop when organized, Ft Riley, KS, 15 Oct 1867. SOURCE: McMiller, "Buffalo Soldiers," 79.

Sharpshooter at Ft McDowell, AZ. SOURCE: *ANJ* 24 (18 Jun 1887): 934.

MOSS, Don; Private; Band/9th Cav. Discharged, end of term, 2 Apr 1893; will visit friends and relatives back East. SOURCE: Ft Robinson *Weekly Bulletin*, 5 Apr 1893, in Court Martial Records, McKay.

MOSS, James; Private; D/10th Cav. Served in 10th Cavalry in Cuba, 1898. SOURCE: Cashin, *Under Fire with the Tenth Cavalry*, 341.

Married to Miss Laures Juana, "a belle of Cuba," by Judge Charles F. Babcock, at Ft Robinson, NE, 17 Sep 1902. SOURCE: Crawford *Bulletin*, 19 Sep 1902.

MOSS, Jesse S.; Corporal; B/24th Inf. Killed in action, Cuba, 1898. SOURCE: Scipio, *Last of the Black Regulars*, 29.

Died in Cuba, 1 Jul 1898. SOURCE: *ANJ* 36 (18 Feb 1899): 590.

MOSS, Joel M.; Chief Trumpeter; 10th Cav. Private, Band/10th Cavalry, request for furlough disapproved because regiment about to take field for active operations; request submitted after campaign will be granted. SOURCE: CO, 10 Cav, to Pvt. Joel M. Moss, 12 Aug 1874, ES, 10 Cav, 1872–81.

Mentioned, Dec 1876. SOURCE: LS, 10 Cav, 1873–83.

To be discharged with certificate of disability. SOURCE: Adj, 10 Cav, to AG, USA, 18 Feb 1877, LS, 10 Cav, 1873–83.

Discharged 18 Dec 1877. SOURCE: LS, 10 Cav, 1873–83.

MOSS, John; Sergeant; L/9th Cav. Private, I/9th Cavalry, furlough extended ten days by letter, Department of the Platte, 9 Oct 1894.

Veteran of Indian wars and Philippine Insurrection; at Ft D. A. Russell, WY, in 1910; resident of Vance Co., NC. SOURCE: *Illustrated Review: Ninth Cavalry*, with picture.

MOSS, Parker; Private; K/25th Inf. At Ft Niobrara, NE, 1904. SOURCE: Wilson, "History of Fort Niobrara."

MOTHOW, Simon; Private; H/10th Cav. Served in 10th Cavalry, 1898; remained in U.S. during war with Spain. SOURCE: Cashin, *Under Fire with the Tenth Cavalry*, 347.

MOTLEY, George; Private; H/24th Inf. Died of general debility in the Philippines, 11 Dec 1899. SOURCE: *ANJ* 37 (30 Dec 1899): 412.

MOTLEY, Solomon; Private; A/10th Cav. At Ft Apache, AZ, 1890, subscribed $.50 to testimonial to General Grierson. SOURCE: List of subscriptions, 23 Apr 1890, 10th Cavalry papers, MHI.

At Ft Robinson, NE, for cavalry competition, Sep 1897.

Served in 10th Cavalry in Cuba, 1898. SOURCE: Cashin, *Under Fire with the Tenth Cavalry*, 336.

Discharged in accordance with Special Order 20, Adjutant General's Office, 24 Jan 1903.

MOULTON, Edward; Recruit; Colored Detachment/Mounted Service. Convicted by general court martial, Jefferson Barracks, MO, of striking without cause Recruit Albert Blouski, Company A of Instruction, Mounted Service, and threatening to kill Lance Cpl. Frank G. French, Company C of Instruction, Mounted Service; sentenced to four months' confinement and loss of pay. SOURCE: GCMO 44, AGO, 1 May 1885.

MOULTON, P. A.; Musician; K/24th Inf. Letter from Ft Reno, Indian Territory, 14 Apr 1887; plays bass drum in Ft Reno band. SOURCE: Cleveland *Gazette*, 23 Apr 1887.

At San Carlos, AZ, 1890. *See* **HARDEE**, James A., Private, K/24th Infantry

MOULTRIE; Private; I/10th Cav. At Ft Apache, AZ, 1890, subscribed $.25 to testimonial to General Grierson. SOURCE: List of subscriptions, 23 Apr 1890, 10th Cavalry papers, MHI.

MUCKER, William; Corporal; A/9th Cav. Veteran of Spanish-American War and Philippine Insurrection; at Ft D. A. Russell, WY, in 1910. SOURCE: *Illustrated Review: Ninth Cavalry*, with picture.

MUDD, Martin; Private; C/24th Inf. At Ft D. A. Russell, WY; in hands of civil authorities, Cheyenne, WY, 16–17 Nov 1898.

MUDD, Robert; Private; H/24th Inf. Fined $10 by summary court, San Isidro, Philippines, for failure to salute commander while sentry, 21 Feb 1902, second conviction. SOURCE: Register of Summary Court, San Isidro.

MUKES, Matthew; Private; F/9th Cav. Recruit from depot, arrived Ft Robinson, NE, 1 Mar 1887.

Discharged from Ft Robinson, 23 Jul 1887, after reporting sick with old injury, in accordance with Special Order 169, Adjutant General's Office, 23 Jul 1887.

MULFORD, Charles; QM Sgt; C/9th Cav. Veteran of Philippine Insurrection; at Ft D. A. Russell, WY, in 1910; resident of 62 Plane St., Newark, NJ. SOURCE: *Illustrated Review: Ninth Cavalry*, with picture.

MULLEN, Harry F.; Private; M/9th Cav. Convicted of entry, assault, and rape, Legaspi, Philippines, 15 Nov 1901; sentenced to five years.

MULLIN, George C.; Private; L/10th Cav. Served in 10th Cavalry, 1898; remained in U.S. during war with Spain. SOURCE: Cashin, *Under Fire with the Tenth Cavalry*, 350.

MULLINS, William; Private; K/10th Cav. Born Nashville; occupation laborer, Ht 5'8", dark brown complexion; enlisted, age 22, 12 Feb 1882; dishonorably discharged by General Court Martial Order 40, Department of Texas, 6 Nov 1882; escaped confinement at Ft Davis, TX, 20 Jul 1883.

MUNDIN, George A.; D/9th Bn, Ohio Inf. Died in Minnesota. SOURCE: Taylor, "Minnesota Black Spanish-American War Veterans."

MUNDY, LaFayette; Recruit; 10th Cav. Sergeant, L/10th Cavalry, Feb 1873; commander disapproves troop order reducing him to ranks and says trial by court martial would be appropriate. SOURCE: ES, 10 Cav, 1872–81.

Resignation of his warrant as sergeant approved. SOURCE: CO, 10 Cav, to CO, L/10, 17 Mar 1873, ES, 10 Cav, 1872–81.

Mentioned May 1875 as recruit at St. Louis depot awaiting assignment to regiment. SOURCE: LS, 10 Cav, 1873–83.

MUNROE, William; Recruit; 10th Cav. Enlisted Memphis, spring 1867. SOURCE: LS, 10 Cav, 1866–67.

MUNSEY, Lawrence W.; I/48th Inf. Convicted of larceny in the Philippines, Jul 1900; sentenced to one year.

MURDOCK, Thomas W.; Corporal; K/10th Cav. Served in 10th Cavalry, 1898; remained in U.S. during war with Spain. SOURCE: Cashin, *Under Fire with the Tenth Cavalry*, 349.

MURPHEY, Moses L.; Private; I/10th Cav. Served in 10th Cavalry, 1898; remained in U.S. during war with Spain. SOURCE: Cashin, *Under Fire with the Tenth Cavalry*, 348.

MURPHY; Private; E/9th Cav. Killed in action at Camp Ojo Caliente, NM, 4 Sep 1879. SOURCE: Billington, "Black Cavalrymen," 67; Billington, *New Mexico's Buffalo Soldiers*, 89. *See* **CHAPMAN**, S., Sergeant, E/9th Cavalry

MURPHY, George; Private; C/24th Inf. Shot Samuel Cops [*sic*] of same unit in Manila, Philippines, as result of grudge, 26 Sep 1899; both Louisianans, enlisted at New Orleans. SOURCE: Manila *Times*, 26 Sep 1899.

Convicted by general court martial of murder of Pvt. Samuel Copes, C/24th Infantry, with .38 caliber Colt pistol, El Deposito, Philippines, 25–26 Sep 1899; sentence of death by hanging reduced to life in prison by President McKinley. SOURCE: GO 29, AGO, 9 Mar 1900; *ANJ* 37 (17 Mar 1900): 674.

MURPHY, George; Warrant Officer; U.S. Army. Retired; resides at 5352 Prairie Avenue, Chicago, 1930. SOURCE: Work, *The Negro Yearbook, 1931–1932*, 334.

MURPHY, Harry; Private; F/9th Cav. At Ft D. A. Russell, WY, in 1910; resident of Kalamazoo, MI. SOURCE: *Illustrated Review: Ninth Cavalry*, with picture.

MURPHY, Israel B.; 1st Sgt; B/9th Cav. Sergeant since 8 Apr 1877; first sergeant since 1 Jan 1886. SOURCE: Roster, 9 Cav.

Ranked number six in revolver competition, Departments of Dakota and the Platte, at Bellevue, NE, 4–9 Aug 1890. SOURCE: GO 112, AGO, 2 Oct 1890.

First Sergeant, B/9th Cavalry, to be examined for ordnance sergeant, Ft Duchesne, UT. SOURCE: *ANJ* 29 (31 Oct 1891): 159.

Retires from Ft Duchesne, May 1895. SOURCE: *ANJ* 32 (18 May 1895): 627.

Retired soldier, resident of 1666 West 35th, Los Angeles for thirty years; served as sergeant, F/9th Cavalry, at Ft Concho, TX, 1873. SOURCE: Affidavit, Murphy, age 81, 13 Apr 1926, VA File XC 2659797, Thomas H. Allsup.

MURPHY, Joseph; H/10th Cav. Original member of 10th Cavalry; in troop when organized, Ft Leavenworth, KS, 21 Jul 1867. SOURCE: McMiller, "Buffalo Soldiers," 75.

MURPHY, Marion W.; Private; B/10th Cav. Served in 10th Cavalry in Cuba, 1898; then at Camp Forse, AL. SOURCE: Cashin, *Under Fire with the Tenth Cavalry*, 181, 338.

MURPHY, Samuel; 1st Sgt; M/24th Inf. Sergeant, B/24th Infantry, Ft Huachuca, AZ, 1893; served in 1st Brigade, 1st Division, 25th Corps, during Civil War. SOURCE: Name File, 24 Inf.

Retires from Ft Douglas, UT, Feb 1899. SOURCE: *ANJ* 36 (18 Feb 1899): 583.

MURRAY; Private; E/10th Cav. At Ft Apache, AZ, 1890, subscribed $.50 to testimonial to General Grierson. SOURCE: List of subscriptions, 23 Apr 1890, 10th Cavalry papers, MHI.

MURRAY, A.; Corporal; F/9th Cav. Promoted from lance corporal, Ft Duchesne, UT. SOURCE: *ANJ* 33 (26 Oct 1895): 119.

MURRAY, C.; Private; F/10th Cav. Wounded in action in Kansas, 21 Aug 1867. SOURCE: Armes, *Ups and Downs*, 247.

MURRAY, Charles; Private; F/9th Cav. *See* **MARSHALL**, Albert, Corporal, F/9th Cavalry

MURRAY, Charles E.; Trumpeter; D/10th Cav. At Ft Apache, AZ, 1890, subscribed $.50 to testimonial to General Grierson. SOURCE: List of subscriptions, 23 Apr 1890, 10th Cavalry papers, MHI.

MURRAY, Freeman; Private; D/9th Cav. Enlistment authorized by letter, Adjutant General's Office, 9 May 1900.

At Ft D. A. Russell, WY, in 1910; resident of Bismarck, ND. SOURCE: *Illustrated Review: Ninth Cavalry*, with picture.

MURRAY, George; Private; I/24th Inf. Enlisted Birmingham, AL, 3 Jul 1899. SOURCE: Muster Roll, I/24 Inf, Jul–Aug 1899.

MURRAY, Henry; Corporal; F/9th Cav. Promoted from private, Apr 1902. SOURCE: *ANJ* 39 (10 May 1902): 904.

MURRAY, John; Private; I/10th Cav. Died 24 Apr 1870. SOURCE: ES, 10 Cav, 1866–71.

MURRAY, Jordan; Corporal; I/9th Cav. At Ft D. A. Russell, WY, in 1910; resident of Morgan, LA. SOURCE: *Illustrated Review: Ninth Cavalry*, with picture.

MURRAY, Othniel III; 25th Inf. At Ft Reno, OK, 1913; parents are Othniel Murray II and Angeline Pierce, granddaughter of Revolutionary War soldier Aram Pierce. SOURCE: Steward and Steward, *Gouldtown*, 125.

MURRAY, Renzy; A/24th Inf. Admitted to Soldiers Home with disability at age 30 with three years and seven months' service, 27 Jun 1888. SOURCE: SecWar, *AR 1888*, 904.

MURRAY, William; Private; F/24th Inf. Private, F/24th Infantry, qualified as sharpshooter, Ft Bayard, NM, 1890. SOURCE: *ANJ* 28 (27 Sep 1890): 70.

Resided at 327 South 13th East, Salt Lake City, 1898. SOURCE: Clark, "A History of the Twenty-fourth," 100.

Wife left residence, 327 South 13th, on Saturday to go to Ft Douglas, UT, to greet her husband and learned that he had died in hospital at Montauk Point, NY, just before regiment came west. SOURCE: Salt Lake City *Tribune*, 4 Oct 1898.

MURRELL; Private; F/10th Cav. At Ft Apache, AZ, 1890, subscribed $.50 to testimonial to General Grierson. SOURCE: List of subscriptions, 23 Apr 1890, 10th Cavalry papers, MHI.

MURRELL, James; Sergeant; H/10th Cav. Private, served in A/10th Cavalry in Cuba, 1898. SOURCE: Cashin, *Under Fire with the Tenth Cavalry*, 336.

Sergeant, A/10th Cavalry, narrates Spanish-American War experience. SOURCE: Cashin, *Under Fire with the Tenth Cavalry*, 263-64.

Sergeant, H/10th Cavalry, and post quartermaster sergeant, Ft Mackenzie, WY. SOURCE: Sheridan *Post*, 8 Jul 1904.

MURRY, Andrew; 9th Cav. Served at Ft Robinson, NE, 1894. *See* **DILLON**, David R., Sergeant, Band/9th Cavalry

MURRY, Charles; F/10th Cav. Original member of 10th Cavalry; in troop when organized, Ft Leavenworth, KS, 21 Jun 1867. SOURCE: McMiller, "Buffalo Soldiers," 73.

MURRY, Frank; Private; I/10th Cav. Served in 10th Cavalry in Cuba, 1898. SOURCE: Cashin, *Under Fire with the Tenth Cavalry*, 348.

MURRY, Mat; Private; 24th Inf. Murry and William Erickson, "two young colored boys," left Wichita, KS, to join 24th Infantry in the Philippines, 4 Feb 1901. SOURCE: Wichita *Searchlight*, 9 Feb 1901.

MURRY, Mose; Private; M/10th Cav. Served in 10th Cavalry, 1898; remained in U.S. during war with Spain. SOURCE: Cashin, *Under Fire with the Tenth Cavalry*, 352.

MUSON, Thomas; A/10th Cav. Original member of 10th Cavalry; in troop when organized, Ft Leavenworth, KS, 18 Feb 1867. SOURCE: McMiller, "Buffalo Soldiers," 68.

MYERS, Alfred; L/10th Cav. Original member of 10th Cavalry; in troop when organized, Ft Riley, KS, 21 Sep 1867. SOURCE: McMiller, "Buffalo Soldiers," 78.

MYERS, Frank; Private; K/24th Inf. Fined $3 for failure and neglect to turn out guard at approach to his post of officer of the day, Cabanatuan, Philippines, 3 Apr 1901. SOURCE: Name File, 24 Inf.

Fined $5 for being too drunk to fall in with company, Cabanatuan, Philippines, 7 May 1901; witness: 1st Sgt. Jacob Stevens, K/24th Infantry. SOURCE: Name File, 24 Inf.

MYERS, James C.; Sergeant; E/10th Cav. Private, served in L/10th Cavalry, 1898; remained in U.S. during war with Spain. SOURCE: Cashin, *Under Fire with the Tenth Cavalry*, 350.

Sergeant, E/10th Cavalry, and witness at a general court martial, Ft Robinson, NE, 26 Jan–21 Feb 1906.

MYERS, Rath; Sergeant; I/24th Inf. Corporal, A/9th Cavalry, at Ft Stanton, NM, 1881. SOURCE: Regt Returns, 9 Cav, Jan 1881.

On furlough 27 Jan–3 Feb 1881.

Enlisted Ft Douglas, UT, 14 Apr 1898, twenty-three years' continuous service; fined $2 by garrison court martial, Ft D. A. Russell, WY, 13 Feb 1899. SOURCE: Muster Roll, I/24 Inf, Jan–Feb 1899.

On detached service at Three Rivers, CA, 3 May–21 Jun 1899; on detached service at Presidio of San Francisco, CA, since 22 Jun 1899. SOURCE: Muster Roll, I/24 Inf, May–Jun 1899.

Rejoined company from detached service, 26 Jul 1899; allotted $20 per month for twelve months to Mallisee Myers. SOURCE: Muster Roll, I/24 Inf, Jul–Aug 1899.

Retired Aug 1902. SOURCE: *ANJ* 39 (30 Aug 1902): 1315.

MYERS, Thomas C.; Sergeant; D/25th Inf. Escorting deserter Jones Barber, 9th Cavalry, from Vicksburg, MS, to New Orleans via steamer *Bart Able*. SOURCE: SO 166, Sub-District of Missouri, 26 Dec 1867.

MYERS, William H.; Sergeant; K/24th Inf. Born Georgetown, SC; occupation waiter, Ht 5'8", dark complexion, black hair and eyes; enlisted in 25th Infantry, age 20, Charleston, SC, 15 Jul 1881. SOURCE: Descriptive & Assignment Rolls, 25 Inf.

Private, K/24th Infantry, at San Carlos, AZ, 1890.

Private, I/24th Infantry; enlisted Ft Grant, AZ, 3 Sep 1896; eighteen years' continuous service in 1899; absent on furlough since 20 Feb 1899. SOURCE: Muster Roll, I/24 Inf, May–Jun 1899.

Transferred to K/24th Infantry. SOURCE: Muster Roll, I/24 Inf, Mar–Apr 1899.

Retires as sergeant, K/24th Infantry, Feb 1901. SOURCE: *ANJ* 38 (23 Feb 1901): 623. *See* **HARDEE**, James A., Private, K/24th Infantry

MYLA, William; Private; B/10th Cav. Served in 10th Cavalry, 1898; remained in U.S. during war with Spain. SOURCE: Cashin, *Under Fire with the Tenth Cavalry*, 339.

MYRICK, Sam; Private; C/9th Cav. At Ft D. A. Russell, WY, in 1910; resident of 541 S. 8th St., Griffin, GA. SOURCE: *Illustrated Review: Ninth Cavalry*

MYRICKS, John; Private; L/9th Cav. At Ft D. A. Russell, WY, in 1910; resident of Gaston, AL. SOURCE: *Illustrated Review: Ninth Cavalry*, with picture.

N

NADELL, Alexander; Sergeant; L/10th Cav. Promoted from corporal to sergeant, G/10th Cavalry, 11 Nov 1897. SOURCE: *ANJ* 35 (20 Nov 1897): 212.

Reduced to ranks. SOURCE: *ANJ* 35 (9 Apr 1898): 602.

Served in 10th Cavalry, 1898; remained in U.S. as sergeant, L/10th Cavalry, during war with Spain. SOURCE: Cashin, *Under Fire with the Tenth Cavalry*, 350.

NANCE, Fred; QM Sgt; A/24th Inf. Ranked number seven, Army rifle competition, Ft Sheridan, IL, 1909. SOURCE: GO 228, AGO, 12 Nov 1909.

Distinguished marksman, 1909, as sergeant, A/24th Infantry, ranked number three in Division of the Atlantic, and number seven in Army; distinguished marksman, 1913, as quartermaster sergeant, A/24th Infantry, ranked number three in Division of the Philippines. SOURCE: AGO, Bulletin 6, 6 Mar 1914.

NANCE, Mack T. C.; Private; F/24th Inf. Wounded in pelvis at San Luis Isabela, Philippines, 3 Dec 1899. SOURCE: *ANJ* 37 (10 Mar 1900): 659; Muller, *The Twenty Fourth Infantry*, 32.

NAPIER, Henry F.; Private; L/9th Cav. At Ft D. A. Russell, WY, in 1910; resident of DeSoto, MO. SOURCE: *Illustrated Review: Ninth Cavalry*, with picture.

NASH, Robert N.; Private; 10th Cav. Acquitted in accordance with Special Order 164, Department of the Missouri, 24 Aug 1903.

Boxer, fought at Ft Robinson, NE, 1906. SOURCE: Crawford *Tribune*, 2 Mar 1906.

NAYES, John; Private; K/25th Inf. At Ft Niobrara, NE, 1904. SOURCE: Wilson, "History of Fort Niobrara."

NEAL, Burr; Private; E/10th Cav. Private, contributed $1 of $3.25 sent by men of A/10th Cavalry to Richmond *Planet* for defense fund of three black women accused of murder, Lunenburg Co., VA, Sep 1895. SOURCE: Richmond *Planet*, 21 Sep 1895.

Served in 10th Cavalry in Cuba, 1898. SOURCE: Cashin, *Under Fire with the Tenth Cavalry*, 342.

Showed "great gallantry" before Santiago, Cuba, 24 Jun 1898; helped Captain Ayres and Pvts. W. R. Nelson, A. Wally, and A. C. White drag Major Bell, First Cavalry, who had been wounded in action, to safety. SOURCE: SecWar, *AR 1898*, 355.

Murdered at Ft Washakie, WY, 31 May 1905.

NEAL, David; Private; L/25th Inf. Fined $7 by summary court, San Isidro, Philippines, for going off limits, 13 Jan 1902, first conviction. SOURCE: Register of Summary Court, San Isidro.

NEAL, Thomas; Private; A/25th Inf. Died in Minnesota. SOURCE: Taylor, "Minnesota Black Spanish-American War Veterans."

NEAL, William; Private; H/10th Cav. Served in 10th Cavalry, 1898; remained in U.S. during war with Spain. SOURCE: Cashin, *Under Fire with the Tenth Cavalry*, 347.

NEALY, James; Private; 24th Inf. Shot and killed in Hampton, GA, because he asked for a glass of soda water: "This business is getting serious, and the end is not far off. No use to look to the government. It has been slumbering for some time. Colored men must protect themselves, if they hang for it. Lynch-law must go!" SOURCE: Richmond *Planet*, 27 Aug 1898.

NEELY; Private; M/10th Cav. At Ft Apache, AZ, 1890, subscribed $.50 to testimonial to General Grierson. SOURCE: List of subscriptions, 23 Apr 1890, 10th Cavalry papers, MHI.

NEELY, Walter; Recruit; Colored Detachment/ General Service. Convicted by general court martial, Columbus Barracks, OH, of assaulting, with intent to kill, Recruit Charley Osborne, Colored Detachment, Company B of Instruction, by repeatedly cutting him with knife, 3 Jul 1889; pled guilty to assault but without intent to kill; found guilty; sentenced to six months' confinement and fined six months' pay. SOURCE: GCMO 49, AGO, 8 Aug 1889.

Convicted by general court martial of desertion, 30 Jul 1889, apprehended same day; sentenced to dishonorable discharge and five years. SOURCE: GCMO 51, AGO, 27 Aug 1889.

NEEN, Frank B.; Private; A/25th Inf. Drowned in the Philippines, 3 Mar 1900. SOURCE: *ANJ* 37 (24 Mar 1900): 707.

NEESE, Kern; Private; F/49th Inf. Deserted, Springfield, MO, 6 Oct 1899; "no trace of this man has been known." SOURCE: Descriptive Book, F/49 Inf.

NEIL; Private; D/24th Inf. At Cabanatuan, Philippines, 1901. *See* **JOHNSON**, George, Private, D/24th Infantry

NELIS; QM Sgt; E/10th Cav. At Ft Harker, KS, Jul 1867. SOURCE: LS, 10 Cav, 1866–67.

NELLIS, J. B.; Private; A/9th Cav. Native of Providence, RI; died near Ft Robinson, NE, while training troop's horses to swim, 17 Jun 1896. SOURCE: *ANJ* 33 (27 Jun 1896): 782.

Buried at Ft Robinson. SOURCE: List of Interments, Ft Robinson.

NELSON; Private; H/10th Cav. At Ft Apache, AZ, 1890, subscribed $.50 to testimonial to General Grierson. SOURCE: List of subscriptions, 23 Apr 1890, 10th Cavalry papers, MHI.

NELSON, Calab; L/10th Cav. Original member of 10th Cavalry; in troop when organized, Ft Riley, KS, 21 Sep 1867. SOURCE: McMiller, "Buffalo Soldiers," 78.

NELSON, Edward; Private; K/10th Cav. Served in 10th Cavalry, 1898; remained in U.S. during war with Spain. SOURCE: Cashin, *Under Fire with the Tenth Cavalry*, 349.

NELSON, Edward D.; Corporal; 10th Cav. Wounded in action, San Juan, Cuba, 2 Jul 1898; despite bad wound, charged up hill near head of troop, while private, H/9th Cavalry. SOURCE: SecWar, *AR 1898*, 707–08; *Illustrated Review: Ninth Cavalry.*

Awarded certificate of merit for distinguished service, 1 Jul 1898. SOURCE: *ANJ* 37 (24 Feb 1900): 611.

Commended for gallantry in charging at head of troop up San Juan Hill in battle of Santiago, Cuba, in which act seriously wounded. SOURCE: GO 15, AGO, 13 Feb 1900.

Corporal, 10th Cavalry, married to Miss Annie Ray by Chaplain Anderson, Crawford, NE, 24 Nov 1904, with understanding that he could not have quarters on post at Ft Robinson, NE; resides in Crawford. SOURCE: Monthly Report, Chaplain Anderson, 1 Dec 1904.

NELSON, Foster L.; Private; H/9th Cav. At Ft D. A. Russell, WY, in 1910; resident of Chicago. SOURCE: *Illustrated Review: Ninth Cavalry*, with picture.

NELSON, Henry; L/10th Cav. Original member of 10th Cavalry; in troop when organized, Ft Riley, KS, 21 Sep 1867. SOURCE: McMiller, "Buffalo Soldiers," 78.

NELSON, James; Private; 9th Cav. Deserted 1880. *See* **BURKS**, Henry, Private, 9th Cavalry

NELSON, James H.; Corporal; E/9th Cav. Veteran of Spanish-American War, and Philippine Insurrection; at Ft D. A. Russell, WY, in 1910. SOURCE: *Illustrated Review: Ninth Cavalry*, with picture.

NELSON, Louis; Private; H/9th Cav. Sentenced to death by hanging by general court martial, Guinobatan, Luzon, Philippines; sentence commuted to ten years by President Roosevelt. SOURCE: *ANJ* 39 (1 May 1902): 646.

NELSON, Moses; Private; M/10th Cav. Original member of 10th Cavalry; in troop when organized, Ft Riley, KS, 15 Oct 1867. SOURCE: McMiller, "Buffalo Soldiers," 79.

Mentioned Jan 1873 as deserted 8 Aug 1868 and apprehended 19 Aug 1868. SOURCE: LS, 10 Cav, 1873–83.

NELSON, Robert; Private; A/9th Cav. Seriously wounded in action while on courier duty between South Fork and Ft Stanton, NM, 1 Dec 1880. SOURCE: Hamilton, "History of the Ninth Cavalry," 50; *Illustrated Review: Ninth Cavalry.*

NELSON, Samuel A.; Corporal; F/25th Inf. Convicted of murder by general court martial, Iba, Philippines; death sentence commuted to life in prison at Leavenworth, KS, by President McKinley. SOURCE: *ANJ* 38 (22 Dec 1900): 399.

Died of dysentery in the Philippines, 25 Dec 1900. SOURCE: *ANJ* 38 (12 Jan 1901): 479.

NELSON, William; Trumpeter; A/9th Cav. With Pvt. Isaac Harrison, rescued his commander, Capt. Michael Cooney, near Howard's Well on the El Paso-San Antonio, TX, road, Apr 1872. SOURCE: Leckie, *The Buffalo Soldiers,* 101.

NELSON, William R.; Private; E/10th Cav. Served in 10th Cavalry in Cuba, 1898. SOURCE: Cashin, *Under Fire with the Tenth Cavalry,* 342.

Showed "great gallantry" before Santiago, Cuba, 24 Jun 1898; helped Captain Ayres and Pvts. Burr Neal, A. Wally, and A. C. White drag Major Bell, First Cavalry, who had been wounded in action, to safety. SOURCE: SecWar, *AR 1898,* 355.

NERO, Ambrose; 9th Cav. Body transferred from Montauk, NY, to national cemetery, Cypress Hills, NY. SOURCE: *ANJ* 36 (21 Jan 1899): 480.

NESBITT, Charles; Private; E/49th Inf. Wounded in knee in the Philippines, Feb 1901. SOURCE: *ANJ* 38 (23 Feb 1901): 631.

NESBITT, William C.; Sergeant; I/24th Inf. *See* proceedings of court martial in case of Houston riot: *United States v. Sergeant William C. Nesbitt et al.*

Long-time buddy of Sgt. Vida Henry; led those who favored abandoning raid by midnight. SOURCE: Haynes, *A Night of Violence,* 165.

Tried, San Antonio, TX, Nov 1917, with sixty-two other defendants; his name on case because he was the senior noncommissioned officer accused; sentenced to death. SOURCE: Haynes, *A Night of Violence,* 254, 271.

Hanged, Ft Sam Houston, TX, 13 Dec 1917, for part in Houston riot. SOURCE: Cleveland *Gazette,* 15 Dec 1917.

NETHERLAND, Robert K.; Private; I/24th Inf. Enlisted Louisville, 2 Aug 1898. SOURCE: Muster Roll, I/24 Inf, Jan–Feb 1899.

Fined $6 by summary court, 11 May 1899. SOURCE: Muster Roll, I/24 Inf, May–Jun 1899.

Fined $5 by summary court, 2 Sep 1898. SOURCE: Muster Roll, I/24 Inf, Sep–Oct 1899.

Discharged, character very good, 31 Dec 1899, with $35 deposits and $11 clothing. SOURCE: Muster Roll, I/24 Inf, Nov–Dec 1899.

NETHERLAND, Walter; Private; H/24th Inf. Convicted of insult and violence to native woman in the Philippines, May 1900; sentenced to four months.

Fined $3 by summary court, San Isidro, Philippines, for allowing prisoner under his guard to obtain and hide bottle of "vino," 26 Feb 1902, second conviction; fined $4 for carelessly discharging rifle while guarding prisoners, 11 Mar 1902. SOURCE: Register of Summary Court, San Isidro.

NEVITT, John W.; E/10th Cav. Original member of 10th Cavalry; in troop when organized, Ft Leavenworth, KS, 15 Jun 1867. SOURCE: McMiller, "Buffalo Soldiers," 72.

NEWELL, Frank; Private; D/24th Inf. Fined $7 for being drunk and disorderly around quarters, Cabanatuan, Philippines, 2 Jun 1901; witnesses: 1st Sgt. M. H. Ellis, and Pvts. George S. Cosby and Herman F. Larrimore, D/24th Infantry. SOURCE: Name File, 24 Inf.

NEWHOUSE, Robert; Private; K/24th Inf. Born Chicago; resided in Chicago on enlistment; awarded distinguished service medal in lieu of certificate of merit for rescue of comrade from drowning near Camp McGrath, Philippines, 12 Nov 1914. SOURCE: *Decorations. US Army, Supplement I*, 36

NEWKIRK; Private; A/10th Cav. At Ft Apache, AZ, 1890, subscribed $.50 to testimonial to General Grierson. SOURCE: List of subscriptions, 23 Apr 1890, 10th Cavalry papers, MHI.

NEWLANDS, Goodson M.; Private; 24th Inf. Born Asheville, NC; resided in Summerville, SC; occupation foreman, Ht 5'11". brown complexion; enlisted, age 22, Charleston, SC, 20 Feb 1888; assigned to F/24th Infantry, 27 Jul 1888; regimental clerk, 17 Jun 1889; fined three times by court martials; sentenced to seven days' confinement when not on duty in adjutant's office, Ft Bayard, NM, 6 Jul 1891; discharged, end of term, single, character excellent, 19 Feb 1893, with $5 deposits, $72 retained, $8 clothing. SOURCE: Descriptive Book, 24 Inf NCS & Band.

At Ft Bayard, 1890. *See* **HENDRICKS**, Lewis, 24th Infantry

Enlisted San Francisco, 24 Feb 1893; joined Band/24th Infantry, 27 Feb 1893; on special duty as regimental clerk, 1 Mar 1893; also clerk in Subsistence Department, 3 Mar 1893; single; at Ft Douglas, UT, $45 clothing and $37

retained, 1 Nov 1896. SOURCE: Descriptive Book, 24 Inf NCS & Band.

NEWMAN, George W.; Corporal; M/10th Cav. Honorable mention for services rendered in capture of Mangas and his Apache band, Rio Bonito, AZ, 18 Oct 1886. SOURCE: Baker, Roster.

Served as corporal H/10th Cavalry, 1898; remained in U.S. during war with Spain. SOURCE: Cashin, *Under Fire with the Tenth Cavalry*, 351.

NEWMAN, George W.; Saddler; B/9th Cav. Veteran of Philippine Insurrection; at Ft D. A. Russell, WY, in 1910. SOURCE: *Illustrated Review: Ninth Cavalry*, with picture.

NEWMAN, John D.; Private; G/24th Inf. On special duty as schoolteacher, Ft Douglas, UT. SOURCE: Clark, "A History of the Twenty-fourth," 82.

Wounded in action, Cuba, 1898. SOURCE: Muller, *The Twenty Fourth Infantry*, 19.

NEWMAN, William; Private; C/9th Cav. At Ft Cummings, NM, 1881; on detached service in field, 30 Jan–3 Feb 1881. SOURCE: Regt Returns, 9 Cav, Feb 1881.

Discharged, end of term, Ft Robinson, NE, Aug 1885. SOURCE: Monthly Return, Ft Robinson, Aug 1885.

NEWTON, Bertie T.; Private; E/9th Cav. At Ft D. A. Russell, WY, in 1910. SOURCE: *Illustrated Review: Ninth Cavalry*, with picture.

NEWTON, Ferdinand C.; Private; M/10th Cav. Served in 10th Cavalry, 1898; remained in U.S. during war with Spain. SOURCE: Cashin, *Under Fire with the Tenth Cavalry*, 352.

NEWTON, George; Private; A/38th Inf. Arrested for part in soldiers' revolt at Ft Cummings, NM, autumn 1867. SOURCE: Billington, *New Mexico's Buffalo Soldiers*, 40.

NEWTON, George; Private; 48th Inf. Died in Minnesota. SOURCE: Taylor, "Minnesota Black Spanish-American War Veterans."

NEWTON, George W.; Artificer; D/25th Inf. Dishonorable discharge, Brownsville. SOURCE: SO 266, AGO, 9 Nov 1906.

NEWTON, James; Private; D/25th Inf. Insulted and struck on head by U.S. customs officer, Brownsville, TX, 5 Aug 1906. SOURCE: Haynes, *A Night of Violence*, 55.

Dishonorable discharge, Brownsville. SOURCE: SO 266, AGO, 9 Nov 1906.

NEWTON, James W.; Private; C/25th Inf. Dishonorable discharge, Brownsville. SOURCE: SO 266, AGO, 9 Nov 1906.

NEWTON, John R.; Private; D/9th Cav. Deserted from Ft Craig, NM, 20 Jan 1881. SOURCE: Regt Returns, 9 Cav, Jan 1881.

NEWTON, Richard H.; 1st Sgt; C/9th Cav. Veteran of Philippine Insurrection; first sergeant, C/9th Cavalry, at Ft D. A. Russell, WY, in 1910; sharpshooter; resident of 1132 Druid Hill Ave., Baltimore. SOURCE: *Illustrated Review: Ninth Cavalry*, with picture.

Served in L and C/9th Cavalry; then second lieutenant and first lieutenant, Philippine Scouts, before going to Liberian Frontier Police, with total thirteen years and four months' service. SOURCE: Cleveland *Gazette*, 25 Dec 1915.

VA File XC 2653514 on file in Veterans Benefit Office, rather than in National Archives.

NICHOLAS, Wesley; Private; 25th Inf. Enlisted as private, I/24th Infantry, Richmond, VA, 26 Jun 1899. SOURCE: Muster Roll, I/24 Inf, Jul–Aug 1898.

Private, 25th Infantry; sends love to parents and friends from the Philippines. SOURCE: Richmond *Planet*, 20 Jan 1900.

NICHOLSON, Edward; Private; L/9th Cav. Served as private, C/10th Cavalry in Cuba, 1898. SOURCE: Cashin, *Under Fire with the Tenth Cavalry*, 340.

Died of cerebral hemorrhage aboard U.S. Army Transport *Logan*, bound from San Francisco to Manila, Philippines, 24 May 1907. SOURCE: Hamilton, "History of the Ninth Cavalry," 116.

NICHOLSON, George H.; Private; Band/24th Inf. Born Accomack, VA; enlisted Baltimore, 26 Jun 1880; served in E/9th Cavalry until deserted, 27 Apr 1881; enlisted in D/24th Infantry, Ft Leavenworth, KS, 17 Sep 1881, as George Williams; surrendered, Ft Sill, Indian Territory, 2 Jan 1882; restored to duty without trial; enlisted Ft Leavenworth, 29 Oct 1885; transferred to Band/24th Infantry, Ft Bayard, NM, 5 Nov 1889; marksman, 1883–88; discharged, end of term, single, character good, Ft Bayard, 28 Oct 1890, with $72 retained, and owing government $3 for clothing. SOURCE: Descriptive Book, 24 Inf NCS & Band.

On detached service in field, New Mexico, 27 Jan–1 Feb 1881. SOURCE: Regt Returns, 9 Cav, Feb 1881.

NICHOLSON, Thomas; Private; M/9th Cav. Drowned at Santa Rosa, Samar, Philippines, 28 Jul 1901; body recovered. SOURCE: *ANJ* 39 (28 Sep 1901): 81.

NICOLS, Richard; G/10th Cav. Original member of 10th Cavalry; in troop when organized, Ft Leavenworth, KS, 5 Jul 1867. SOURCE: McMiller, "Buffalo Soldiers," 74.

NICKLE, Elijah; Private; K/24th Inf. Fined $5 and jailed for ten days for fight with "a Chinaman" in public place, Cabanatuan, Philippines, 19 May 1901. SOURCE: Name File, 24 Inf.

Confined for thirty days for refusal to work while guardhouse prisoner and refusal to stop talking and empty cans; sentry had to hit him with weapon to prevent further disorder; witnesses: Privates Banks, Corter, and Dudley of K/24th Infantry. SOURCE: Name File, 24 Inf.

NIEL; Private; H/10th Cav. Jailed for attempted assault on prostitute, Cheyenne, WY. SOURCE: Cheyenne *Daily Leader*, 22 Feb 1907.

NIELSON, George A.; Private; G/10th Cav. Served in 10th Cavalry, 1898; remained in U.S. during war with Spain. SOURCE: Cashin, *Under Fire with the Tenth Cavalry*, 346.

NILES, John R.; F/10th Cav. Original member of 10th Cavalry; in troop when organized, Ft Leavenworth, KS, 21 Jun 1867. SOURCE: McMiller, "Buffalo Soldiers," 73.

NILSON, Arbet; Private; G/10th Cav. Served in 10th Cavalry, 1898; remained in U.S. during war with Spain. SOURCE: Cashin, *Under Fire with the Tenth Cavalry*, 346.

NIMMS, Edward W.; Sergeant; M/10th Cav. Served in 10th Cavalry, 1898; remained in U.S. during war with Spain. SOURCE: Cashin, *Under Fire with the Tenth Cavalry*, 351.

NOAL, Robert J.; Sergeant; M/10th Cav. Born in Maryland; private and corporal, G/10th Cavalry, 2 Mar 1883–1 Mar 1888; private, 28 Mar 1888; corporal, 25 Jan 1889; sergeant, 14 Mar 1897. SOURCE: Baker, Roster.

Corporal, G/10th Cavalry, at Ft Apache, AZ, 1890, subscribed $.50 to testimonial to General Grierson. SOURCE: List of subscriptions, 23 Apr 1890, 10th Cavalry papers, MHI.

Served as sergeant, M/10th Cavalry, in Cuba, 1898. SOURCE: Cashin, *Under Fire with the Tenth Cavalry*, 352.

NOEL; Private; B/10th Cav. At Ft Apache, AZ, 1890, subscribed $.50 to testimonial to General Grierson. SOURCE: List of subscriptions, 23 Apr 1890, 10th Cavalry papers, MHI.

NOID, James; Private; E/24th Inf. Killed in action, San Luis, Philippines, summer 1899. SOURCE: *ANJ* 36 (19 Aug 1899): 1223; Richmond *Planet*, 19 Aug 1899.

NOLAN, Alexander; Private; A/10th Cav. Convicted by general court martial, Ft Clark, TX, 10 Dec 1887. SOURCE: Miles, "Fort Concho in 1877," 49.

Sentenced to dishonorable discharge and one year for desertion from Staked Plains expedition, Aug 1877. SOURCE: Leckie, *The Buffalo Soldiers*, 49; Sullivan, "Fort McKavett," 147.

NOLAN, James L.; Private; Band/25th Inf. Transferred from M/25th Infantry, 1 Nov 1900. SOURCE: Misc Records, 25 Inf.

At San Marcelino, Philippines, 1900. *See* FULBRIGHT, William R., Private, H/25th Infantry

NOLAN, Martin; Private; G/10th Cav. Served in 10th Cavalry, 1898; remained in U.S. during war with Spain. SOURCE: Cashin, *Under Fire with the Tenth Cavalry*, 346.

NOLAND, Henry C.; Private; L/10th Cav. Served in 10th Cavalry, 1898; remained in U.S. during war with Spain. SOURCE: Cashin, *Under Fire with the Tenth Cavalry*, 350.

NOLAND, William; Private; L/10th Cav. Served in 10th Cavalry, 1898; remained in U.S. during war with Spain. SOURCE: Cashin, *Under Fire with the Tenth Cavalry*, 350.

NOOMAN, Joseph D.; Private; D/10th Cav. Mentioned Jul 1877 as having enlisted Oct 1873. SOURCE: ES, 10 Cav, 1872–81.

NORMAN, Almer; Private; D/9th Cav. At Ft D. A. Russell, WY, in 1910; sharpshooter; resident of Bessemer, AL. SOURCE: *Illustrated Review: Ninth Cavalry*, with picture.

NORMAN, John; Private; I/10th Cav. Served in 10th Cavalry, 1898; remained in U.S. during war with Spain. SOURCE: Cashin, *Under Fire with the Tenth Cavalry*, 348.

NORMAN, John D.; Private; A/10th Cav. Mentioned Jan 1873. SOURCE: LS, 10 Cav, 1873–83.

NORMAN, Willie; Private; F/10th Cav. Wounded in action on observation duty, Douglas, AZ, Nov 1915. SOURCE: Wharfield, *10th Cavalry and Border Fights*, 84.

NORRIS, Benjamin; Private; G/10th Cav. Original member of 10th Cavalry; in troop when organized, Ft Leavenworth, KS, 5 Jul 1867. SOURCE: McMiller, "Buffalo Soldiers," 74.

At Ft Lyon, CO, Mar 1869. SOURCE: LR, Det 10 Cav, 1868–69.

NORRIS, Charles E.; Private; E/9th Cav. At Ft D. A. Russell, WY, in 1910; resident of Washington, DC. SOURCE: *Illustrated Review: Ninth Cavalry*, with picture.

NORRIS, J. B.; Corporal; 48th Inf. Sick in the Philippines, Feb 1900. SOURCE: Richmond *Planet*, 14 Apr 1900.

NORRIS, James; Private; H/10th Cav. Served in 10th Cavalry, 1898; remained in U.S. during war with Spain. SOURCE: Cashin, *Under Fire with the Tenth Cavalry*, 347.

At Camp Forse, AL, Nov 1898. SOURCE: Richmond *Planet*, 3 Dec 1898.

NORRIS, Jerry; Private; F/10th Cav. Served in 10th Cavalry in Cuba, 1898. SOURCE: Cashin, *Under Fire with the Tenth Cavalry*, 344.

NORRIS, Thomas H.; Private; I/24th Inf. Enlisted Baltimore, 20 Feb 1899. SOURCE: Muster Roll, I/24 Inf, Jan–Feb 1899.

Fined $.50 by garrison court martial, Presidio of San Francisco, CA, 24 Apr 1899. SOURCE: Muster Roll, I/24 Inf, Mar–Apr 1899.

NORTHROP, Clark H.; Corporal; G/10th Cav. Original member of 10th Cavalry; in troop when organized, Ft Leavenworth, KS, 5 Jul 1867. SOURCE: McMiller, "Buffalo Soldiers," 74.

At Ft Lyon, CO, Mar 1869. SOURCE: LR, Det 10 Cav, 1868–69.

NORTON, George; I/9th Cav. Served in 1891.

NORTON, Thomas; K/10th Cav. Original member of 10th Cavalry; in troop when organized, Ft Riley, KS, 1 Sep 1867. SOURCE: McMiller, "Buffalo Soldiers," 77.

NORWOOD, West; Private; H/9th Cav. Veteran of Philippine Insurrection; at Ft D. A. Russell, WY, in 1910; resident of Atlanta. SOURCE: *Illustrated Review: Ninth Cavalry*, with picture.

NOTHINGTON, Emery; Private; M/10th Cav. Served in 10th Cavalry, 1898; remained in U.S. during war with Spain. SOURCE: Cashin, *Under Fire with the Tenth Cavalry*, 352.

NUBLE, John; Trumpeter; I/10th Cav. Served in 10th Cavalry in Cuba, 1898. SOURCE: Cashin, *Under Fire with the Tenth Cavalry*, 347.

NUNN, Duffy; Corporal; H/24th Inf. Enlisted Washington Barracks, Washington, DC, with four years' continuous service, 16 Apr 1898. SOURCE: Muster Roll, H/24 Inf, May–Jun 1898.

Sick, returned to U.S. SOURCE: Muster Roll, I/24 Inf, Jul–Aug 1898.

Transferred from Reserve Divisional Hospital, Siboney, Cuba, to U.S. on U.S. Army Transport *Santiago* with remittent yellow fever, 25 Jul 1898. SOURCE: Hospital Papers, Spanish-American War. 1898.

Rejoined company, 14 Oct 1898. SOURCE: Muster Roll, H/24 Inf, Sep–Oct 1898.

Corporal. SOURCE: Indianapolis *Freeman*, 4 Feb 1899, with picture.

NYPHON, Andrew; Private; K/10th Cav. Discharged in accordance with Special Order 124, Adjutant General's Office, 26 May 1904.

O

OAKELY, Bud; Private; A/9th Cav. At Ft D. A. Russell, WY, in 1910. SOURCE: *Illustrated Review: Ninth Cavalry*, with picture.

OATFIELD, Francis L.; Private; K/10th Cav. Mentioned 1873. SOURCE: ES, 10 Cav, 1872–81.

OATMAN, Walter; Private; Band/24th Inf. Born Murray Co., TN; mulatto, black hair, brown eyes, Ht 5'6", enlisted, age 21, F/24th Infantry, 6 Jan 1876; transferred to Band/24th Infantry, 1 Nov 1876; transferred to H/24th Infantry, 11 Jul 1877; transferred to Band/24th Infantry, 8 Dec 1877; discharged 5 Jan 1881; enlisted in Band/24th Infantry, Ft Supply, Indian Territory, 6 Jan 1881; discharged, end of term, single, character excellent, "a good solo alto player," 5 Jan 1886; deposits $20, retained $60, clothing $22.27. SOURCE: Descriptive Book, 24 Inf NCS & Band.

OBANION, Otis; Private; K/10th Cav. Served in 10th Cavalry in Cuba, 1898. SOURCE: Cashin, *Under Fire with the Tenth Cavalry*, 350.
    Died of malaria at Holguin, Cuba, 30 Oct 1900. SOURCE: *ANJ* 38 (3 Nov 1900): 235.
    Name also spelled O'Bannon.

OBEY, Thomas; Private; K/10th Cav. Original member of 10th Cavalry; in troop when organized, Ft Riley, KS, 1 Sep 1867. SOURCE: McMiller, "Buffalo Soldiers," 77.
    Discharged on certificate of disability before end of Feb 1868. SOURCE: LR, Det 10 Cav, 1868-69.

O'CONNOR; Sergeant; L/24th Inf. At Skagway, AK, 1901. *See* WILLIAMS, Edward, First Sergeant, L/24th Infantry

ODEN, James; Corporal; L/10th Cav. Served in 10th Cavalry, 1898; remained in U.S. during war with Spain. SOURCE: Cashin, *Under Fire with the Tenth Cavalry*, 350.

ODEN, Oscar N.; Private; I/10th Cav. Served in 10th Cavalry in Cuba, 1898. SOURCE: Cashin, *Under Fire with the Tenth Cavalry*, 185, 347.
    Awarded certificate of merit for distinguished service in Cuba, 1898. SOURCE: *ANJ* 37 (24 Feb 1900): 611; Steward, *The Colored Regulars*, 280.
    Commended for distinguished service, Battle of Santiago, Cuba, 1 Jul 1898. SOURCE: GO 15, AGO, 13 Feb 1900.
    Convicted by general court martial, Holguin, Cuba, of carelessly wounding soldier with revolver; sentenced to five months' confinement and loss of pay. SOURCE: *ANJ* 38 (8 Jun 1901): 993.

ODOM, Henry; Musician; B/25th Inf. Dishonorable discharge, Brownsville. SOURCE: SO 266, AGO, 9 Nov 1906.

ODOM, R. M.; Private; K/24th Inf. At San Carlos, AZ, 1890. *See* HARDEE, James A., Private, K/24th Infantry

ODOM, Zack; Private; K/49th Inf. In the Philippines, 1900. *See* BLUNT, Hamilton H., Captain, K/49th Infantry

OFFUTT, Benjamin F.; Private; M/10th Cav. Served in 10th Cavalry in Cuba, 1898. SOURCE: Cashin, *Under Fire with the Tenth Cavalry*, 352.

OGDEN, Henry; Band/10th Cav. Died at Santa Fe, NM. SOURCE: *ANJ* 25 (7 Jun 1888): 994.

OGGS, Samuel B.; Private; G/9th Cav. Died in the Philippines, 19 Apr 1901. SOURCE: *ANJ* 38 (4 May 1901): 876.

OGLESBY, Charles, Sr.; C/25th Inf. Died at Shelbyville, KY; over 90 years old. SOURCE: *Winners of the West* 11 (Jun 1934): 3.

OGLESBY, John E.; Private; G/9th Cav. Qualified but not teaching school, Ft Robinson, NE, 1 Nov 1895–29 Feb 1896. SOURCE: Reports of Schools, Ft Robinson, 1892–96.
    On extra duty as schoolteacher, Ft Robinson. SOURCE: Special Order 111, 1 Oct 1896, Post Orders, Ft Robinson.
    Relieved of extra duty as schoolteacher, Ft Robinson. SOURCE: Special Order 117, 16 Oct 1896, Post Orders, Ft Robinson.
    On extra duty as schoolteacher, Ft Robinson. SOURCE: Special Order 2, 4 Jan 1897, Post Orders, Ft Robinson.
    Relieved of extra duty as schoolteacher, Ft Robinson. SOURCE: Special Order 34, 30 Mar 1897, Post Orders, Ft Robinson.
    Relieved of special duty as assistant librarian and detailed on extra duty as schoolteacher, Ft Robinson. SOURCE: Special Order 45, 21 Apr 1897, Post Orders, Ft Robinson.
    Relieved of extra duty as schoolteacher, Ft Robinson. SOURCE: Special Order 57, 17 May 1897, Post Orders, Ft Robinson.

Lance corporal, relieved of extra duty as schoolteacher, Ft Robinson. SOURCE: Special Order 58, 30 May 1898, Post Orders, Ft Robinson.

OINS, James; Private; M/49th Inf. Engaged against enemy, Tuao, Cagayan, Philippines, 18 Oct 1900. SOURCE: *ANJ* 38 (11 May 1901): 901.

O'KELLY, John A.; Private; H/9th Cav. At Ft D. A. Russell, WY, in 1910; sharpshooter; resident of Raleigh, NC. SOURCE: *Illustrated Review: Ninth Cavalry*, with picture.

OLE, Henry R.; QM Sgt; U.S. Army. Born Thomasville, MO; Ht 5'6 1/2", light medium complexion, black hair and brown eyes; served in G/10th Cavalry, 21 Feb 1882–21 Feb 1887, character excellent; in D/10th Cavalry, 15 Mar 1887–14 Mar 1892, character excellent; in I/10th Cavalry, 22 Mar 1892–13 Oct 1895, character excellent; in A/24th Infantry, 28 Apr 1896–27 Apr 1899, character excellent; in A/24th Infantry, 28 Apr 1899, corporal, 15 Sep 1896, sergeant, 10 May 1898; participated in Geronimo campaign, 1885–86, Spanish-American War battles at San Juan and Santiago, Cuba, 1898, and Philippine Insurrection, 1899–1901; second class marksman, 1894, 1897; first class marksman, 1896; appointed post quartermaster sergeant, U.S. Army, 18 Feb 1901; single, age 40, father of Leonard A. Ole. SOURCE: Name File, 24 Inf.

Corporal, D/10th Cavalry; at Ft Apache, AZ, 1890, subscribed $.50 to testimonial to General Grierson. SOURCE: List of subscriptions, 23 Apr 1890, 10th Cavalry papers, MHI.

OLIVER, John J.; Captain; K/49th Inf. Former second lieutenant, 10th Volunteer Infantry. SOURCE: *ANJ* 37 (9 Dec 1899): 345b.

Mentioned. SOURCE: Beasley, *Negro Trailblazers*, 284.

OLIVER, Philip; Sergeant; H/9th Cav. Corporal, wounded in action near Bololo, Philippines, 31 Jan 1901. SOURCE: Hamilton, "History of the Ninth Cavalry," 107; *Illustrated Review: Ninth Cavalry*.

Sergeant, died of variola, Guinobatan, Luzon, Philippines, 29 Jul 1901. SOURCE: *ANJ* 39 (28 Sep 1901): 81.

OLIVER, William; Private; K/10th Cav. Original member of 10th Cavalry; in H/10th Cavalry when organized, Ft Leavenworth, KS, 21 Jul 1867. SOURCE: McMiller, "Buffalo Soldiers," 75.

Commander asks transfer of Oliver, who is prisoner, to Ft Dodge, KS, guardhouse as he is an encumbrance to command, 3 Oct 1868. SOURCE: LR, Det 10 Cav, 1868–69.

OLIVER, William; Private; B/10th Cav. Released to duty from treatment for acute gonorrhea, Ft Robinson, NE, 18 Jan 1903. SOURCE: Post Surgeon to CO, B/10, 18 Jan 1903, LS, Post Surgeon, Ft Robinson.

OLIVER, William H.; Chief Trumpeter; Band/9th Cav. At Ft Walla Walla, WA, 1904. *See* **BROWN**, William W., 24th and 25th Infantry

Veteran of Philippine Insurrection; at Ft D. A. Russell, WY, in 1910; resident of Richmond, TX. SOURCE: *Illustrated Review: Ninth Cavalry*, with picture.

OLIVIA, Benjamin (pseud.); 25th Infantry. *See* DERBIGNY, Benjamin, 25th Infantry

O'NEAL, Arthur; Private; H/9th Cav. At Ft D. A. Russell, WY, in 1910; resident of Columbus, GA. SOURCE: *Illustrated Review: Ninth Cavalry*, with picture.

O'NEAL, Clarence E.; Private; G/10th Cav. Served in 10th Cavalry, 1898; remained in U.S. during war with Spain. SOURCE: Cashin, *Under Fire with the Tenth Cavalry*, 346.

O'NEAL, Lucius H.; Private; L/10th Cav. Served in 10th Cavalry, 1898; remained in U.S. during war with Spain. SOURCE: Cashin, *Under Fire with the Tenth Cavalry*, 350.

O'NEAL, Thomas; Private; M/10th Cav. Served in 10th Cavalry, 1898; remained in U.S. during war with Spain. SOURCE: Cashin, *Under Fire with the Tenth Cavalry*, 352.

O'NEAL, Ned; Private; A/10th Cav. Served in 10th Cavalry, 1898; remained in U.S. during war with Spain. SOURCE: Cashin, *Under Fire with the Tenth Cavalry*, 337.

O'NEIL, Solomon P.; Corporal; C/25th Inf. Dishonorable discharge, Brownsville. SOURCE: SO 266, AGO, 9 Nov 1906.

ONLY, John; Private; C/9th Cav. In L/9th Cavalry, on detached service in field, New Mexico, 21 Jan–24 Feb 1881. SOURCE: Regt Returns, 9 Cav, Feb 1881.

In C/9th Cavalry, authorized to reenlist as married soldier by letter, Adjutant General's Office, 21 May 1895.

Retires from Ft Robinson, NE, in accordance with Special Order 94, Adjutant General's Office, 23 Apr 1897. SOURCE: *ANJ* 34 (1 May 1897): 645.

Served during Civil War in H/43rd U.S. Colored Troops; pension application made by widow Sarah J. Only from Chicago, 1920; married in Wisconsin, 1903. SOURCE: VA File C 2493371, John Only.

ORR, Charles F.; Private; A/9th Cav. At Ft D. A. Russell, WY, in 1910. SOURCE: *Illustrated Review: Ninth Cavalry*, with picture.

ORSBY, Bose; Private; H/24th Inf. Fined $5 by summary court, San Isidro, Philippines, for failure to arrange cot and bedding for inspection, 21 Dec 1901. SOURCE: Register of Summary Court, San Isidro.

OSBORN, Stanley; Private; F/9th Cav. Wounded in action against Apaches in Mimbres Mountains, NM, 3 Feb 1880. SOURCE: *Illustrated Review: Ninth Cavalry.*

Died of pulmonary tuberculosis at age 45, Soldiers Home, 1 Mar 1905. SOURCE: SecWar, *AR 1905*, 4:168.

OSBORNE, Anthony; 2nd Lt; 49th Inf. Promoted from sergeant, L/25th Infantry. SOURCE: Richmond *Planet*, 16 Jun 1900.

OSBORNE, Charley; Recruit; Colored Detachment/General Service. At Columbus Barracks, OH, 1889. *See* **NEELY**, Walter, Recruit, Colored Detachment/General Service

OULDO, James; Private; K/25th Inf. At Ft Niobrara, NE, 1904. SOURCE: Wilson, "History of Fort Niobrara."

OUSLEY, Horace; A/24th Inf. Admitted to Soldiers Home with disability at age 30 with eight years and four months' service, 21 Apr 1888; died since admission. SOURCE: SecWar, *AR 1888*, 903.

OVERALL, Nathaniel; I/10th Cav. Original member of 10th Cavalry; in troop when organized, Ft Riley, KS, 15 Aug 1867. SOURCE: McMiller, "Buffalo Soldiers," 76.

OVERR, Oscar; 2nd Lt; 23rd Kans Inf. Resident of Allensworth, CA; first black justice of the peace in California; owns twenty-four acres and has claim on six hundred forty acres of nearby government land; has contract for irrigation water, four wells, and pumping station; irrigates thirteen hundred acres; raises chickens, turkeys, ducks, cattle; failed in "untiring efforts" to locate polytechnic school in Allensworth. SOURCE: Beasley, *Negro Trailblazers*, 157, 285.

Overr became first black justice of the peace in California, 1914, when Allensworth became judicial district. SOURCE: New York *Times*, 22 Oct 1972.

OVERSTREET, Monroe; Private; B/9th Cav. Killed in action against Apaches, Gabaldon Canyon, NM, 19 Aug 1881. SOURCE: Billington, *New Mexico's Buffalo Soldiers*, 105. *See* **GOLDEN**, Thomas, Saddler, B/9th Cavalry

OVERTON, George; K/10th Cav. Original member of 10th Cavalry; in troop when organized, Ft Riley, KS, 1 Sep 1867. SOURCE: McMiller, "Buffalo Soldiers," 77.

OWENS, Charles H.; QM Sgt; U.S. Army. Born Philadelphia; dark complexion, Ht 5'4"; enlisted, Philadelphia, age 22, 13 Nov 1886; formerly served in E/10th Cavalry; in D/24th Infantry, 11 Jan 1887; corporal, 1 Oct 1888; sergeant, 1 Jan 1890, regimental quartermaster sergeant, 25 Feb 1890; discharged, end of term, character excellent, single, Ft Bayard, NM, 12 Nov 1891, with $60 retained and $10.65 clothing, owing government $4.70 for subsistence stores; enlisted Ft Bayard, 13 Nov 1891; became post quartermaster sergeant, U.S. Army, 1 Feb 1895, and transferred to Ft Custer, MT, with $50.67 retained, owing government $7.36 for subsistence stores. SOURCE: Descriptive Book, 24 Inf NCS & Band.

OWENS, Clarence H.; Private; M/10th Cav. Served in 10th Cavalry, 1898; remained in U.S. during war with Spain. SOURCE: Cashin, *Under Fire with the Tenth Cavalry*, 352.

OWENS, Fred; Private; D/10th Cav. Served in 10th Cavalry in Cuba, 1898. SOURCE: Cashin, *Under Fire with the Tenth Cavalry*, 341.

OWENS, Frederick; M/10th Cav. Original member of 10th Cavalry; in troop when organized, Ft Riley, KS, 15 Oct 1867. SOURCE: McMiller, "Buffalo Soldiers," 79.

OWENS, George; G/10th Cav. Served 1876–81; Reverend Owens would like to hear from old buddies. SOURCE: *Winners of the West* 9 (Apr 1932): 2.

Wants to hear from former comrades. SOURCE: *Winners of the West* 11 (Nov 1934): 3.

OWENS, Horace; E/24th Inf. Served 1887–90; renews subscription. SOURCE: *Winners of the West* 8 (Apr 1931): 7.

OWENS, Richard; Private; C/25th Inf. Died of peritonitis in the Philippines, 21 Oct 1901. SOURCE: *ANJ* 39 (18 Jan 1902): 502.

OWENS, Stephan; D/10th Cav. Original member of 10th Cavalry; in troop when organized, Ft Leavenworth, KS, 1 Jun 1867. SOURCE: McMiller, "Buffalo Soldiers," 71.

OWENS, William; Sergeant; H/9th Cav. Committed suicide at Guinobatan, Luzon, Philippines, 9 Aug 1901. SOURCE: *ANJ* 39 (12 Oct 1901): 140.

OWSLEY, Jeremiah; Private; G/9th Cav. Stationed at Ft Ringgold, TX; killed in action in attack by large party of Mexican desperadoes and cattle thieves, along with Pvt. Moses Turner, G/9th Cavalry, 26 Jan 1875. SOURCE: Hamilton, "History of the Ninth Cavalry," 23; *Illustrated Review: Ninth Cavalry.*

Murdered 1875. SOURCE: Leckie, *The Buffalo Soldiers*, 108. *See* **TROUTMAN**, Edward, Sergeant, G/9th Cavalry

P

PADGETT, Andrew; Corporal; B/24th Inf. Wounded in action, Cuba, 1898. SOURCE: Muller, *The Twenty Fourth Infantry*, 18.

PAGE, Bassett; Private; E/24th Inf. Retires from Ft Bayard, NM, Feb 1892. SOURCE: *ANJ* 29 (6 Feb 1892): 411.

PAGE, Clarence; Private; A/9th Cav. Served as corporal in M/10th Cavalry, 1898; remained in U.S. during war with Spain. SOURCE: Cashin, *Under Fire with the Tenth Cavalry*, 351.

On special duty at brigade headquarters, in the Philippines, since 9 May 1902. SOURCE: SD List, A/9 Cav, 24 May 1902, Nueva Caceres.

PAGE, Edward W.; QM Sgt; B/10th Cav. Served as private in 10th Cavalry in Cuba, 1898. SOURCE: Cashin, *Under Fire with the Tenth Cavalry*, 338.

Seriously cut black civilian in saloon, Crawford, NE, 5 Feb 1905. SOURCE: Crawford *Tribune*, 10 Feb 1905.

Won second place in one-hundred-yard dash and won hurdle race, Wyoming State Fair, 1905. SOURCE: Cheyenne *Daily Leader*, 7 Oct 1905.

PAGE, Felix; 1st Sgt; K/10th Cav. Served with regiment at Carrizal, Mexico, 1916. SOURCE: Wharfield, *10th Cavalry and Border Fights*, 38.

PAGE, William; Private; F/24th Inf. Born Union, SC; mulatto complexion, black hair and eyes, Ht 5'9"; enlisted in Band/24th Infantry, age 29, Ft Bayard, NM, 10 Mar 1892; ten years' prior service, five with Band/9th Cavalry, and five with Band/10th Cavalry; transferred to F/24th Infantry, character excellent, married with one child, 1 Jul 1895, with $39.73 retained. SOURCE: Descriptive Book, 24 Inf NCS & Band.

PAINE, James; Trumpeter; 24th Inf. Picture. SOURCE: Indianapolis *Freeman*, 28 Jan 1899.

Drawing. SOURCE: Lynk, *The Black Troopers*, 57.

PAINE, Samson; Private; E/9th Cav. Sentence for desertion, which began 24 Dec 1875, reduced to eighteen months. SOURCE: GCMO 22, AGO, 23 Feb 1877.

PALMER, Alexander; Recruit; Colored Detachment/General Service. Convicted by general court martial, Columbus Barracks, OH, of neglecting duty while on guard, 19 Jan 1887, by annoying female servants at quarters of two officers; acquitted of trying to open window to servant's room at quarters of another officer; sentenced to dishonorable discharge and two months. SOURCE: GCMO 19, AGO, 26 Feb 1887.

PALMER, Amos; Private; D/9th Cav. Died in hospital, Ft McKinney, WY, 2 Nov 1887, after being shot in fight by Pvt. Thomas Hall, H/9th Cavalry.

PALMER, Joseph; Private; H/9th Cav. Veteran of Philippine Insurrection; at Ft D. A. Russell, WY, in 1910; resident of Jamaica. SOURCE: *Illustrated Review: Ninth Cavalry*, with picture.

PALMER, Will; Private; B/10th Cav. Served in 10th Cavalry, 1898; remained in U.S. during war with Spain. SOURCE: Cashin, *Under Fire with the Tenth Cavalry*, 33.

PALMER, William; Private; C/10th Cav. Served in 10th Cavalry, 1898; remained in U.S. during war with Spain. SOURCE: Cashin, *Under Fire with the Tenth Cavalry*, 340.

PANNELL, John; Corporal; I/25th Inf. Fined $3 by summary court, San Isidro, Philippines, for failure to report to noncommissioned officers' school, 4 Apr 1902, first conviction. SOURCE: Register of Summary Court, San Isidro.

PAPPY, John H.; Private; K/10th Cav. At Ft Robinson, NE, 1904.

PARHAM, Julius; Private; I/10th Cav. Sentenced to dishonorable discharge and confinement, Ft Robinson, NE, by Special Order 248, Department of the Missouri, 19 Dec 1903; released Mar 1904.

PARHAM, Richard C.; Private; L/10th Cav. Served in 10th Cavalry, 1898; remained in U.S. during war with Spain. SOURCE: Cashin, *Under Fire with the Tenth Cavalry*, 350.

PARILLA, Juan G.; Private; A/24th Inf. Second place in hasty entrenchment contest, military tournament, Albany, NY, autumn 1909. SOURCE: Muller, *The Twenty Fourth Infantry*, 60.

PARIS, Joseph A.; Sergeant; K/10th Cav. Corporal, released to duty from treatment for gonorrhea, Ft Robinson, NE, 9 Sep 1903. SOURCE: Post Surgeon to CO, K/10, 9 Sep 1903, LS, Post Surgeon, Ft Robinson.

Sergeant, at Ft Robinson, 1904.

PARISH, Willie; Private; G/9th Cav. At Ft D. A. Russell, WY, in 1910; resident of Chicago. SOURCE: *Illustrated Review: Ninth Cavalry*, with picture.

PARKER, Amos A.; Private; E/10th Cav. Mentioned 1873 as having enlisted Jun 1872. SOURCE: ES, 10 Cav, 1873–83.

At Ft Apache, AZ, 1890, subscribed $.50 to testimonial to General Grierson. SOURCE: List of subscriptions, 23 Apr 1890, 10th Cavalry papers, MHI.

PARKER, Andrew; Recruit; Colored Detachment/ Mounted Service. Convicted by general court martial, Jefferson Barracks, MO, of falling asleep on guard, 14 Sep 1889; sentenced to six months' confinement and loss of pay. SOURCE: GCMO 63, AGO, 31 Oct 1889.

PARKER, Archie; Private; D/49th Inf. Joined company 8 Oct 1899; deserted from Jefferson Barracks, MO, 9 Oct 1899. SOURCE: Descriptive Book, D/49 Inf.

PARKER, Calvin; Private; E/25th Inf. Died in Minnesota. SOURCE: Taylor, "Minnesota Black Spanish-American War Veterans."

PARKER, Charles E.; Corporal; G/10th Cav. Private, L/10th Cavalry, at Camp Santa Rosa, TX, May 1879; excused from duty by Surgeon M. F. Price because of fever and debility, but kept at work by Capt. George A. Armes, causing suffering and impeding recovery. SOURCE: GCMO 36, AGO, 27 May 1880.

Farrier, at Ft Apache, AZ, 1890, subscribed $.50 to testimonial to General Grierson. SOURCE: List of subscriptions, 23 Apr 1890, 10th Cavalry papers, MHI.

Served in 10th Cavalry in Cuba, 1898. SOURCE: Cashin, *Under Fire with the Tenth Cavalry*, 345.

PARKER, Charles L.; Private; G/9th Cav. Corporal, praised for bravery against Victorio, Nov 1879, by Maj. Albert P. Morrow. SOURCE: Billington, "Black Cavalrymen," 68; Billington, *New Mexico's Buffalo Soldiers*, 93.

Private, on detached service at Ft Stanton, NM, 29 Jan– 5 Feb 1881. SOURCE: Regt Returns, 9 Cav, Feb 1881.

PARKER, Edward; Private; Band/24th Inf. Born King William Co., VA; occupation barber, Ht 5'6", black complexion, dark eyes, black hair; enlisted, age 31, Philadelphia, 13 Nov 1889; transferred from C/24th Infantry to Band/24th Infantry, 11 Jul 1890; previous service in H/9th Cavalry, discharged 18 Oct 1885; discharged from 24th Infantry, single, character very good, Ft Bayard, NM, 12 Feb 1893, with $18 retained and $41.95 clothing. SOURCE: Descriptive Book, 24 Inf NCS & Band.

PARKER, Eugene; Private; A/9th Cav. At Ft D. A. Russell, WY, in 1910; marksman. SOURCE: *Illustrated Review: Ninth Cavalry*, with picture.

PARKER, George; Corporal; E/24th Inf. Wounded in action in Cuba, 1898. SOURCE: Muller, *The Twenty Fourth Infantry*, 18.

PARKER, H. J.; 1st Lt; H/48th Inf. Private, 10th Volunteer Infantry, 7 Jul 1899; first sergeant, A/10th Infantry, 22 Jul 1899; first lieutenant, 48th Infantry, 9 Sep 1899. SOURCE: *ANJ* 37 (4 Nov 1899): 219.

Mentioned. SOURCE: Beasley, *Negro Trailblazers*, 284.

PARKER, Harry; 1st Sgt; M/24th Inf. Served in Houston, 1917; veteran of five years. SOURCE: Haynes, *A Night of Violence*, 105, 120.

PARKER, Hiram C.; Sergeant; D/10th Cav. Corporal, recommended for extra duty as schoolteacher, Ft Robinson, NE, 23 Nov 1902. SOURCE: CO, Ft Robinson, to AG, DeptMo, 23 Nov 1902, LS, Ft Robinson.

Sergeant, directed from Ft Robinson to Ft Leavenworth, KS, for instruction prior to competition and examination. SOURCE: AG, DeptMo, to CO, Ft Robinson, 22 Jun 1904, Register of LR, Ft Robinson.

Ordered to Ft Leavenworth by Special Order 145, Adjutant General's Office, 21 Jun 1904.

Took preliminary examination for commission and passed; examination board recommended waiver of weight and chest standards, which he missed slightly; commander, Department of the Missouri, and surgeon general disapproved; blacks became upset; Parker failed to pass final examinations. SOURCE: Fletcher, *The Black Soldier and Officer*, 75.

PARKER, James E.; Private; M/10th Cav. Original member of M/10th Cavalry; in troop when organized, Ft Riley, KS, 15 Oct 1867. SOURCE: McMiller, "Buffalo Soldiers," 79.

Mentioned as sergeant, D/10th Cavalry, Dec 1875. SOURCE: ES, 10 Cav, 1873–83.

Mentioned as private, M/10th Cavalry, transferred from A/10th Cavalry, May 1877. SOURCE: ES, 10 Cav, 1873-83.

PARKER, Jefferson; Private; M/10th Cav. Served in 10th Cavalry, 1898; remained in U.S. during war with Spain. SOURCE: Cashin, *Under Fire with the Tenth Cavalry*, 352.

PARKER, Jesse C.; Pvt 1st Cl; Hospital Corps. While artificer, D/24th Infantry, commended for assisting wounded officer to safety, Santiago, Cuba, 1 Jul 1898. SOURCE: Cleveland *Gazette*, 24 Nov 1906.

PARKER, John; E/10th Cav. Original member of 10th Cavalry; in troop when organized, Ft Leavenworth, KS, 15 Jun 1867. SOURCE: McMiller, "Buffalo Soldiers," 72.

PARKER, John H.; Private; G/9th Cav. At Ft D. A. Russell, WY, in 1910; resident of Louisville. SOURCE: *Illustrated Review: Ninth Cavalry*, with picture.

PARKER, Joseph; Sgt Maj; 10th Cav. Private, K/10th Cavalry, detailed for duty at detachment headquarters, Ft Lyon, CO. SOURCE: SO 1, Det 10 Cav, 22 Feb 1869, Orders, Det 10 Cav, 1868–69.

Reported absent without leave, Jan 1873, but on recruiting duty. SOURCE: ES, 10 Cav, 1873–83.

Sergeant, K/10th Cavalry; commander, 10th Cavalry, asks orders transferring Parker to Ft Gibson, Indian Territory, as saddler sergeant, 10th Cavalry. SOURCE: CO, 10 Cav, to AAG, Department of Texas, 21 Feb 1873, LS, 10 Cav, 1873–83.

Sergeant major, 10th Cavalry, deposited $25 with paymaster, Ft Concho, TX, Sep 1881. SOURCE: TS, 10 Cav.

PARKER, Nathan; Private; F/9th Cav. At Ft D. A. Russell, WY, in 1910; resident of Cairo, IL. SOURCE: *Illustrated Review: Ninth Cavalry*, with picture.

PARKER, Richard; Private; H/9th Cav. Fingers frozen while on scout in Florida Mountains, NM, Nov 1880. SOURCE: Billington, *New Mexico's Buffalo Soldiers*, 126–27.

Buried at Ft Robinson, NE, 2 Mar 1890. SOURCE: List of Interments, Ft Robinson.

PARKER, Richard C.; Private; A/10th Cav. Died 2 Oct 1898. SOURCE: Cashin, *Under Fire with the Tenth Cavalry*, 354.

PARKER, Theodore; Private; A/9th Cav. At Ft D. A. Russell, WY, in 1910. SOURCE: *Illustrated Review: Ninth Cavalry*, with picture.

PARKER, Walter; Private; A/10th Cav. Sentenced to one month's confinement and fined two months' pay by summary court, San Isidro, Philippines, for sitting on guard duty and failing to walk post, 4 Dec 1901, third conviction. SOURCE: Register of Summary Court, San Isidro.

PARKER, William; Private; L/10th Cav. Beat and kicked Fannie Potter when she did not yield to his advances, Ft Bayard, NM, Jan 1889. SOURCE: Billington, *New Mexico's Buffalo Soldiers*, 166.

PARKER, William; Musician; E/25th Inf. Ranked number 106 among expert riflemen with 70.67 percent, 1904. SOURCE: GO 79, AGO, 1 Jul 1905.

PARKS, Frank H.; Musician; K/25th Inf. At Ft Niobrara, NE, 1904. SOURCE: Wilson, "History of Fort Niobrara."

PARKS, John; Corporal; C/9th Cav. At Ft Robinson, NE, 1887. *See* **WINFIELD**, Arthur, Trumpeter, C/9th Cavalry

Fined $3 by garrison court martial, Ft Robinson, for neglect of duty in failure to give intelligent answers to any questions in tactics at noncommissioned officers' school despite repeated warnings regarding his carelessness and inattention. SOURCE: Order 62, 31 Mar 1888, Post Orders, Ft Robinson.

PARKS, Thomas; Wagoner; M/9th Cav. Veteran of Philippine Insurrection; at Ft D. A. Russell, WY, in 1910. SOURCE: *Illustrated Review: Ninth Cavalry*, with picture.

PARKS, Tolbert; Private; A/25th Inf. Ranked number 191 among expert riflemen with 68.33 percent, 1904. SOURCE: GO 79, AGO, 1 Jul 1905.

PARKS, Virgil H.; Private; A/10th Cav. Served in 10th Cavalry, 1898; remained in U.S. during war with Spain. SOURCE: Cashin, *Under Fire with the Tenth Cavalry*, 337.

PARNELL, Edward; Trumpeter; E/25th Inf. Trumpeter, 10th Cavalry; at Ft Bayard, NM, 1890; competed in Department of Arizona marksmanship contest. SOURCE: Billington, *New Mexico's Buffalo Soldiers*, 154.

Trumpeter, D/10th Cavalry, at Ft Apache, AZ, 1890, subscribed $.50 to testimonial to General Grierson. SOURCE: List of subscriptions, 23 Apr 1890, 10th Cavalry papers, MHI.

Trumpeter, E/25th Infantry, died of enteritis in the Philippines. SOURCE: *ANJ* 37 (21 Oct 1899): 178.

Died of heart failure in attack on LaLoma Church, Philippines; veteran of twenty-nine years. SOURCE: Cleveland *Gazette*, 18 Nov 1899.

PARNELL, William; Private; D/49th Inf. Died of dysentery in the Philippines, 23 Jan 1901. SOURCE: *ANJ* 38 (23 Feb 1901): 631.

PARNETT, John H.; I/10th Cav. Original member of 10th Cavalry; in troop when organized, Ft Riley, KS, 15 Aug 1867. SOURCE: McMiller, "Buffalo Soldiers," 76.

PASCHALL, Lincoln; Private; D/9th Cav. Funeral at post hall, Ft Robinson, NE, 5:15 P.M., 21 Aug 1894. SOURCE: Order 60, 20 Aug 1894, Post Orders, Ft Robinson.

Buried, Ft Robinson. SOURCE: List of Interments, Ft Robinson.

PASH, George B.; Corporal; D/9th Cav. Appointed 4 Aug 1889. SOURCE: Roster, 9 Cav.

PATE, Frank; Corporal; I/10th Cav. Promoted from private. SOURCE: SO 92, 10 Cav, Ft Ethan Allen, VT, 10 Dec 1909.

PATON, Jerome; Sergeant; E/9th Cav. In hands of civil authorities, Omaha, NE, 29 Jan–23 May 1893. SOURCE: Regt Returns, 9 Cav.

Appointed sergeant, 7 Jul 1893. SOURCE: Roster, 9 Cav.

Convicted by garrison court martial, Ft Robinson, NE, of failure to repair at correct time for stable duty; fined $5. SOURCE: Order 50, 21 Jul 1894, Post Orders, Ft Robinson.

At Ft Robinson; date of rank 7 Jul 1893. SOURCE: *ANJ* 32 (9 Feb 1895): 390.

PATTERSON, Albert; F/10th Cav. Original member of 10th Cavalry; in troop when organized, Ft Leavenworth, KS, 21 Jun 1867. SOURCE: McMiller, "Buffalo Soldiers," 73.

PATTERSON, Andrew; C/10th Cav. Mentioned as surviving Indian war veteran. SOURCE: *Winners of the West* 3 (Jan 1926): 7.

PATTERSON, George; Private; L/10th Cav. Served in 10th Cavalry, 1898; remained in U.S. during war with Spain. SOURCE: Cashin, *Under Fire with the Tenth Cavalry*, 350.

Mrs. George Patterson wants to hear from comrades of her husband; she only knows he served in 9th or 10th Cavalry, 24th or 25th Infantry. SOURCE: *Winners of the West* 7 (Dec 1929): 5.

PATTERSON, James E.; Private; G/9th Cav. At Ft D. A. Russell, WY, in 1910; resident of Baltimore. SOURCE: *Illustrated Review: Ninth Cavalry*, with picture.

PATTERSON, John; Private; K/10th Cav. *See* **BRANSFORD**, Wesley, Private, K/10th Cavalry

PATTERSON, Stephen; Corporal; H/24th Inf. Enlisted Ft Snelling, MN, 30 Oct 1897; on special duty as cook, 18 Dec 1897–28 Jan 1898; four years' continuous service. SOURCE: Muster Roll, H/24 Inf, Jan–Feb 1898.

Corporal and company cook. SOURCE: Muster Roll, H/24 Inf, Jan–Feb 1899.

Witness in trial of assailant of Pvt. George Washington, San Francisco; told court: "We did our duty in Cuba, and we don't think we should be insulted because we are black." SOURCE: San Francisco *Chronicle*, 30 Jun 1899.

Promoted to corporal, 14 Sep 1898. SOURCE: Muster Roll, H/24 Inf, Sep–Oct 1898.

Corporal and cook since 14 Sep 1898; fifth year continuous service started 30 Oct 1898. SOURCE: Muster Roll, H/24 Inf, Nov–Dec 1899.

PATTERSON, T. H.; Private; K/24th Inf. At San Carlos, AZ, 1890. *See* **HARDEE**, James A., Private, K/24th Infantry

PATTERSON, Walter; Private; 10th Cav. Wounded in left leg, Naco, AZ, 7 Dec 1914. SOURCE: Cleveland *Gazette*, 13 May 1916.

PATTERSON, William; C/10th Cav. Original member of 10th Cavalry; in troop when organized, Ft Leavenworth, KS, 14 May 1867. SOURCE: McMiller, "Buffalo Soldiers," 70.

PATTERSON, William; Private; H/10th Cav. Served in 10th Cavalry, 1898; remained in U.S. during war

with Spain. SOURCE: Cashin, *Under Fire with the Tenth Cavalry*, 347.

PATTON, George; L/48th Inf. Convicted of larceny in the Philippines, Mar 1901; sentenced to four months.

PATTON, Homer; Private; G/24th Inf. Died of tuberculosis in the Philippines, 11 Feb 1901. SOURCE: *ANJ* 38 (23 Feb 1901): 631.

PATTON, Jesse; Private; I/10th Cav. Served in 10th Cavalry, 1898; remained in U.S. during war with Spain. SOURCE: Cashin, *Under Fire with the Tenth Cavalry*, 348.

PATTON, John; B/10th Cav. Original member of 10th Cavalry; in troop when organized, Ft Leavenworth, KS, 1 Apr 1867. SOURCE: McMiller, "Buffalo Soldiers," 69.

PAULEY, Charles J.; Private; D/9th Cav. Shot dead in barracks by Cpl. Isher Johnson, I/9th Cavalry, in dispute over monte game, Ft Washakie, WY, 14 Aug 1897; buried on post with full military honors. SOURCE: *Fremont Clipper*, 20 Aug 1897.

Deposit of $48.90 made to account of deceased Private Pauley. SOURCE: CO, D/9, to Chief Paymaster, DP, 16 Sep 1897, Misc Records, DP.

PAYNE, Charles; Private; A/9th Cav. Born Cincinnati; enlisted Xenia, OH, 6 Sep 1895; occupation janitor; Ht 5'5 1/2", brown complexion, brown eyes and hair; discharged Ft Grant, AZ, character excellent, 6 Oct 1898; remained in service. SOURCE: Register of Enlistments.

Released from extra duty as schoolteacher, Ft Robinson, NE. SOURCE: SO 45, 21 Apr 1897, Post Orders, Ft Robinson.

Deserted "while sick in hospital," Buceria Barracks, Philippines, 10 Jan 1902. SOURCE: Regt Returns, 9 Cav, Apr 1902.

PAYNE, French; Private; B/25th Inf. Chaplain Steward's janitor at Ft Missoula, MT; also cared for singing books and was chief schoolteacher; killed in action at El Caney, Cuba. SOURCE: Steward, *The Colored Regulars*, 93–94.

Killed in action, Cuba, 1898. SOURCE: Scipio, *Last of the Black Regulars*, 29.

Killed in action at El Caney, 1 Jul 1898; buried one mile south of El Caney, with wooden headboard with his name cut into it, stones around headboard; name in tightly corked bottle buried at head of grave. SOURCE: Scrapbook, 25 Inf, II.

PAYNE, George E.; 2nd Lt; D/49th Inf. Served in D/9th Cavalry, 4 Aug 1884–3 Aug 1889; in 23rd Kansas Infantry, 16 Jun 1898; commissioned second lieutenant, 15 Jun 1899; second lieutenant, 49th Infantry, 9 Sep 1899. SOURCE: Descriptive Book, D/49 Inf.

Corporal, D/9th Cavalry, at Ft McKinney, WY, best rifle shot among cavalrymen in Department of the Platte. SOURCE: *ANJ* 25 (14 Jul 1888): 1014.

Reduced to ranks at own request. SOURCE: Order 46, 9 Cav, 20 Sep 1888.

Mentioned as second lieutenant, 23rd Kansas Infantry. SOURCE: Beasley, *Negro Trailblazers*, 285.

Ordered to report to 49th Infantry, Jefferson Barracks, MO, 9 Sep 1899. SOURCE: *ANJ* 37 (7 Oct 1899): 123.

Mentioned (incorrectly) as second lieutenant, E/48th Infantry. SOURCE: Beasley, *Negro Trailblazers*, 284.

Mentioned. SOURCE: Manila *Times*, 6 Jan 1901.

One of twenty-three officers of 49th Infantry recommended as regular Army second lieutenants. SOURCE: CG, DivPI, Manila, 8 Feb 1901, to AGO, AGO File 355163.

PAYNE, Godfrey J.; Private; H/24th Inf. On extra duty as painter, Quartermaster Department, Ft Huachuca, AZ, 16–30 Jun 1893. SOURCE: Name File, 24 Inf.

PAYNE, Hayes B.; Sergeant; K/24th Inf. Served in K/24th Infantry 1880–90; knew Barney McKay as McDougal; did not see him again until he came to Washington, DC. SOURCE: Affidavit, Payne, 1924 New Hampshire Avenue, NW, Washington, DC, age 68, occupation laborer, 31 Oct 1925, VA File XC 2659455, Barney McKay.

Authorized six-month furlough from Ft Grant, AZ. SOURCE: *ANJ* 27 (15 Feb 1890): 473.

PAYNE, Isaac; Trumpeter; 10th Cav. Seminole-Negro scout; awarded Medal of Honor for heroism with Lieutenant Bullis, Pecos River, TX, 26 Apr 1875. SOURCE: Carroll, *The Black Military Experience*, 390.

PAYNE, James; Corporal; H/24th Inf. Enlisted Ft Douglas, UT, 23 Oct 1898; four years of continuous service. SOURCE: Muster Roll, H/24 Inf, Nov–Dec 1898.

Appointed lance corporal 30 Jan 1899. SOURCE: Muster Roll, H/24 Inf, Jan–Feb 1899.

Corporal, deserted from Presidio of San Francisco, CA, 23 Jun 1899. SOURCE: Regt Returns, 24 Inf, Jul 1899.

PAYNE, James H.; Corporal; G/10th Cav. Born in Virginia; private, L and A/10th Cavalry, 27 Apr 1889–26 Aug 1894; enlisted in G/10th Cavalry, 13 Oct 1894; wagoner, 10 Sep 1895; corporal, 16 Mar 1897; at Ft Assiniboine, MT, 1897. SOURCE: Baker, Roster.

PAYNE, John H.; Private; C/10th Cav. Served in 10th Cavalry in Cuba, 1898. SOURCE: Cashin, *Under Fire with the Tenth Cavalry*, 340.

PAYNE, Matthew; Private; M/9th Cav. At Ft D. A. Russell, WY, in 1910; resident of Chicago. SOURCE: *Illustrated Review: Ninth Cavalry*, with picture.

PAYNE, Robert A.; Private; I/10th Cav. Served in 10th Cavalry in Cuba, 1898. SOURCE: Cashin, *Under Fire with the Tenth Cavalry*, 348.

PAYNE, Thomas; Corporal; 9th Cav. Mentioned for bravery and gallantry against Victorio, 1879, by Capt. Charles D. Beyer. SOURCE: Billington, "Black Cavalrymen," 64.

PAYNE, William; QM Sgt; E/10th Cav. Enlisted, age 16, 4 Feb 1892; at Ft Keogh, MT, when Spanish-American War broke out; narrates war experience. SOURCE: Cashin, *Under Fire with the Tenth Cavalry*, 220–24.

Served in 10th Cavalry in Cuba, 1898; wounded in action. SOURCE: Cashin, *Under Fire with the Tenth Cavalry*, 342; SecWar, *AR 1898*, 324.

Awarded certificate of merit for distinguished service in Cuba, 1 Jul 1898. SOURCE: *ANJ* 37 (24 Feb 1900): 611; Steward, *The Colored Regulars*, 280.

Commended for distinguished service as sergeant, E/10th Cavalry, battle of Santiago, Cuba, 1 Jul 1898. SOURCE: GO 15, AGO, 13 Feb 1898.

At Ft Huachuca, AZ, 1914; passed examination for commission as captain of volunteers, May 1914. SOURCE: *Crisis* 9 (Nov 1914): 14.

PAYNTER; Private; B/10th Cav. At Ft Apache, AZ, 1890, subscribed $.50 to testimonial to General Grierson. SOURCE: List of subscriptions, 23 Apr 1890, 10th Cavalry papers, MHI.

PEACE, Bradford; Private; F/25th Inf. Deserted, Subig, Philippines, "cause unknown," 23 Nov 1900. SOURCE: Regt Returns, 25 Inf, Nov 1900.

PEACOCK, Henry; Lance Cpl; 24th Inf. Involved in Houston riot, 1917: "Well, if we die, we will die like men"; with Pvt. Hezekiah Turner of I/24th Infantry, dressed wounds of Sergeant Henry and Private McWhorter. SOURCE: Haynes, *A Night of Violence*, 157–58, 163.

Twenty-nine-year veteran, with nine years in regiment; testified in exchange for immunity. SOURCE: Haynes, *A Night of Violence*, 216.

PEAL, Allen S.; Lieutenant; 7th Inf USV. Lieutenant, 7th Volunteer Infantry; letter from Columbus, OH, 15 Mar 1899. SOURCE: Gatewood, *"Smoked Yankees"*, 174–77.

Born Cleveland, OH; attended Miss Purdy's kindergarten on Cedar Avenue; moved to central Ohio in 1879; bachelor of arts, Ohio State University, 1895; taught, Red River Normal School, Clarksville, TX, where he conducted summer Teachers' Normal School; recommended for commission by Colonel Heistand, his military instructor at Ohio State; commanded cadets in President McKinley's inauguration parade; deputy county auditor, Columbus, OH; principal, Tulsa, OK, separate schools; wife teacher; now custodian, disciplinarian, teacher of pedagogy, Latin, and military, Western University, Kansas. SOURCE: Cleveland *Gazette*, 28 Sep 1912.

Maj. Allen S. Peal of Chicago, formerly of Western University, has accepted teaching position at Bluefield, WV, Institute. SOURCE: Cleveland *Gazette*, 18 Sep 1915.

Principal of our Bluefield, WV, schools; at Des Moines, IA, officer training camp. SOURCE: Cleveland *Gazette*, 23 Jun 1917.

PEARCALL, W.; Sergeant; E/24th Inf. At Ft Grant, AZ, 1890. *See* **BERRY**, Edward, Sergeant, H/24th Infantry

PEARCE, Thomas; Private; L/10th Cav. Forged name of Pvt. William Wilson on $3 check, post trader's store, Ft Bayard, NM, Aug 1888; escaped from guardhouse. SOURCE: Billington, *New Mexico's Buffalo Soldiers*, 169.

PEARM, John; Sergeant; C/9th Cav. Accidentally killed Cpl. James Billions, C/9th Cavalry, while they were together on detached service from Ft Bayard, NM, Oct 1877. SOURCE: Billington, *New Mexico's Buffalo Soldiers*, 128.

PEARSON, Edmond; Private; E/9th Cav. Transferred to Hospital Corps in accordance with Special Order 269, Adjutant General's Office, 14 Nov 1896.

PEARSON, Frank; Private; K/24th Inf. Died of disease of liver in the Philippines, 18 Jan 1902. SOURCE: *ANJ* 39 (15 Mar 1902): 706.

PEARSON, John F.; Cook; E/9th Cav. At Ft D. A. Russell, WY, in 1910. SOURCE: *Illustrated Review: Ninth Cavalry*, with picture.

PEARSON, London; F/9th Cav. Served 1875–80. SOURCE: *Winners of the West* 13 (Nov 1936): 12.

PECK, George W.; Private; E/10th Cav. Served in 10th Cavalry, 1898; remained in U.S. during war with Spain. SOURCE: Cashin, *Under Fire with the Tenth Cavalry*, 343.

PECK, Henry; Private; 10th Cav. Ordered to Ft Leavenworth, KS, by Special Order 165, Adjutant General's Office, 15 Jul 1904.

Died Ft Robinson, NE, 15 Jun 1904; five-year veteran; buried at Ft Robinson. SOURCE: Monthly Report, Chaplain Anderson, 1 Aug 1904; List of Interments, Ft Robinson.

PEDEE, Martin; Musician; 25th Inf. Convicted of attempted rape of white wife of corporal in same company, 25th Infantry, Ft Davis, TX, Nov 1872. SOURCE: Carroll, *The Black Military Experience*, 274–75.

PEEKS, William D.; 1st Sgt; D/10th Cav. Commissioned captain at Camp Des Moines, IA, 15 Oct 1917. SOURCE: Glass, *History of the Tenth Cavalry*, appendix M.

PEMBERTON, Harce; Private; Band/10th Cav. Resides in Philadelphia; at Ft Robinson, NE, 1904; played clarinet and violin. SOURCE: Lowe, "Camp Life of the Tenth U.S. Cavalry," 206.

PENDER, Freeman E.; Private; I/25th Inf. Served as private, E/10th Cavalry in Cuba, 1898. SOURCE: Cashin, *Under Fire with the Tenth Cavalry*, 342.

Fined $10 by summary court, San Isidro, Philippines, for going off limits, 20 May 1902, third conviction; fined $20 for allowing prisoner to obtain liquor while on provost guard. SOURCE: Register of Summary Court, San Isidro.

PENDERGRASS, John C.; Color Sgt; 10th Cav. Born Jamestown, IL; Ht 5'9", mulatto; served in A/10th Cavalry, 5 Dec 1881–4 Dec 1886, 1 Jun 1887–31 May 1892, 1 Jun 1892–31 May 1897, 1 Jun 1897–18 Aug 1898, character excellent on all discharges; served in Cuba 14 Jun–14 Aug 1898 and 12 Dec 1900–25 Apr 1902; sergeant, A/10th Cavalry, 10 Mar 1900; first sergeant, A/10th Cavalry, 11 Mar 1900; sharpshooter 1885, 1888, 1889, 1891, 1893, 1894, 1896, 1901; wounded in right arm and bone broken, 1 1/2" above elbow, with carbine, during sham battle, Manzanillo, Cuba, 8 May 1901; in hospital in Cuba, 8–26 May 1901; promoted to regimental color sergeant, 5 Jun 1901; married to Mrs. Amanda Pendergrass, 118 11th Street, Springfield, IL, no children; deposits Jul–Sep 1902 $123, clothing $83; reenlisted Ft Robinson, NE, 13 Nov 1903; expert rifleman 1904 and 1905; wife at Ft Robinson; deposits, $700 in 1903, $100 in 1904, $100 in 1905, $300 in 1906; clothing $106; sharpshooter 1906. SOURCE: Descriptive Book, 10 Cav Officers and NCOs.

Born in Illinois; private, corporal, sergeant, A/10th Cavalry, 5 Dec 1881–4 Dec 1886; private, 1 Jun 1887; sergeant, 10 Oct 1887; first sergeant, 1 Feb 1888. SOURCE: Baker, Roster.

Distinguished marksman, 1884 and 1885. SOURCE: GO 78, AGO, 20 Oct 1886.

Distinguished marksman, 1886; fifth in Division of the Pacific with rifle, silver medal. SOURCE: Baker, Roster.

First sergeant, A/10th Cavalry, sharpshooter, at Ft Apache, AZ, 1888. SOURCE: *ANJ* 25 (21 Jul 1888): 1034.

Ranked number ten in competition of Army carbine team of distinguished marksmen as first sergeant, A/10th Cavalry, 1889. SOURCE: GO 78, AGO, 12 Oct 1889.

First sergeant, A/10th Cavalry, at Ft Apache, AZ, 1890, subscribed $.50 to testimonial to General Grierson. SOURCE: List of subscriptions, 23 Apr 1890, 10th Cavalry papers, MHI.

Served as first sergeant, A/10th Cavalry in Cuba, 1898. SOURCE: Cashin, *Under Fire with the Tenth Cavalry*, 336.

Picture. SOURCE: Cashin, *Under Fire with the Tenth Cavalry*, 250.

Letter from Santiago, Cuba, no date. SOURCE: Gatewood, *"Smoked Yankees"*, 50–52.

Commissioned second lieutenant, 10th Volunteer Infantry, after Spanish-American War. SOURCE: Cashin, *Under Fire with the Tenth Cavalry*, 360–61; Johnson, *History of Negro Soldiers*, 50.

Color sergeant, 10th Cavalry; commander asks authority to detail him as schoolteacher in emergency; no other competent man available. SOURCE: CO, Ft Robinson, to AGO, 24 Oct 1902, LS, Ft Robinson.

Ranked number 123 among expert riflemen with 70.33 percent in 1904. SOURCE: GO 79, AGO, 1 Jun 1905.

Ranked number 589 among expert riflemen with 67 percent in 1905. SOURCE: GO 101, AGO, 31 May 1906.

PENDLETON, Joseph; Sergeant; I/25th Inf. Authorized two-month furlough from Ft Snelling, MN. SOURCE: *ANJ* 24 (25 Dec 1886): 430.

Transferred from Ft Missoula, MT, to take charge of Ft Snelling mess. SOURCE: *ANJ* 25 (14 Jul 1888): 1015.

PENDLETON, Ross; Private; I/10th Cav. Served in 10th Cavalry in Cuba, 1898. SOURCE: Cashin, *Under Fire with the Tenth Cavalry*, 348.

PENN, Delaware; Sergeant; I/9th Cav. Cited for gallantry against Victorio, Jun 1879, by Capt. Charles D. Beyer. SOURCE: Billington, "Black Cavalrymen," 64; Billington, *New Mexico's Buffalo Soldiers*, 88–89.

PENN, Edward; Private; B/24th Inf. Died in Cuba, 5 Aug 1898. SOURCE: *ANJ* 36 (18 Feb 1899): 590.

Died of pernicious malaria. SOURCE: AG, *Correspondence Regarding the War with Spain*, I:209.

Died of yellow fever at Siboney, Cuba, 5 Aug 1898. SOURCE: Hospital Papers, Spanish-American War.

PENN, Irvin; Private; L/25th Inf. Died of dysentery at Cabagan, Luzon, Philippines, 16 Aug 1901. SOURCE: *ANJ* 39 (12 Oct 1901): 140.

PENN, William H.; 1st Sgt; K/9th Cav. Born Baltimore, 1863; enlisted 1880 and served against Indians, and in Cuba, the Philippines, and Samoa; many years as ranking sergeant in 3rd Squadron, 9th Cavalry; retired 4 Feb 1908. SOURCE: *Crisis* 27 (Jan 1924): 126.

On furlough from Ft Robinson, NE, at Crawford, NE, Mar 1887.

Appointed sergeant, 30 Dec 1889. SOURCE: Roster, 9 Cav.

Detached as provost sergeant, Ft Myer, VA. SOURCE: *ANJ* 31 (14 Apr 1894): 570.

Relieved from extra duty with Quartermaster Department, Ft Myer. SOURCE: *ANJ* 32 (5 Jan 1895): 310.

Sergeant, K/9th Cavalry, sent to Hot Springs, SD, to pick up deserter, Pvt. William Smith, E/9th Cavalry. SOURCE: SO 129, 21 Nov 1896, Post Orders, Ft Robinson.

Reenlistment as married soldier at Ft Robinson authorized by letter, Adjutant General's Office, 3 Dec 1897.

As first sergeant, K/9th Cavalry, 1901, met William Washington and his first wife; Washington remained unmarried 1903–1910; Penn retired and resided 1012 6 1/2 Street, SE, Washington, DC, in 1920. SOURCE: VA File WC 894780, William Washington.

PENNEAN, William H.; Sergeant; L/10th Cav. Served in 10th Cavalry, 1898; remained in U.S. during war with Spain. SOURCE: Cashin, *Under Fire with the Tenth Cavalry*, 350.

PENNICK, Lloyd; Private; C/9th Cav. At Ft D. A. Russell, WY, in 1910; resident of Lebanon, KY. SOURCE: *Illustrated Review: Ninth Cavalry.*

PENNISTON, James W.; Sqdn Sgt Maj; 10th Cav. Born Petersburg, VA; enlisted 23 Dec 1897; Ht 5'5", brown complexion; served three years and three months in E/10th Cavalry, 8 May 1894–7 Aug 1897; five months in B/25th Infantry; in K/10th Cavalry, 23 Dec 1897–24 Mar 1899; joined noncommissioned staff 25 Mar 1899; marksman 1894; served in Cuban campaign; regimental clerk 26 Aug 1898–24 Mar 1899; squadron sergeant major 25 Mar 1899; discharged, end of term, Manzanillo, Cuba, 22 Dec 1900, with $53 clothing; reenlisted, married 23 Dec 1900; examined for ordnance sergeant, rated "fair," Feb 1901; discharged, "service no longer required," in accordance with Special Order 217, Adjutant General's Office, 29 Nov 1902, with $15 deposits and $66 clothing; sharpshooter, 1900, 1901, 1902, service honest and faithful, character excellent. SOURCE: Descriptive Book, 10 Cav Officers and NCOs.

Served as private K/10th Cavalry in Cuba, 1898. SOURCE: Cashin, *Under Fire with the Tenth Cavalry*, 350.

Private, promoted to squadron sergeant major for bravery at Las Guasimas, Cuba, 1898. SOURCE: Steward, *The Colored Regulars*, 281.

Sergeant major, relieved as schoolteacher, Ft Robinson, NE, 26 Oct 1902, SOURCE: CO, Ft Robinson, to AG, DeptMo, 22 Nov 1902, LS, Ft Robinson,

PENNY, James T.; 1st Sgt; C/10th Cav. Corporal, C/10th Cavalry, promoted to sergeant, Aug 1902. SOURCE: *ANJ* 39 (30 Aug 1902): 1315.

As first sergeant, took over troop in fight against Mexicans at Nogales, 27 Aug 1918, after Capt. Joseph D. Hungerford was killed. SOURCE: Wharfield, *10th Cavalry and Border Fights*, 21.

PENNY, Lewis; Recruit; 25th Inf. Served in 1884. *See* **JONES**, Stephen, Recruit, 25th Infantry

PEON, Robinson; Private; B/9th Cav. At Ft D. A. Russell, WY, in 1910. SOURCE: *Illustrated Review: Ninth Cavalry*, with picture.

PEOPLES, R.; Corporal; B/25th Inf. Married Miss A. Charis of Gallatin, TN, at Ft Elliott, TX, Sep 1887. SOURCE: Cleveland *Gazette*, 8 Oct 1887.

PERCIVAL; Private; E/9th Cav. Killed in action at Camp Ojo Caliente, NM, 4 Sep 1879. SOURCE: Billington, "Black Cavalrymen," 67; Billington, *New Mexico's Buffalo Soldiers*, 89; *Illustrated Review: Ninth Cavalry. See* **CHAPMAN**, S., Sergeant, E/9th Cavalry

PEREA, Beverly; 1st Sgt; 24th Inf. Born Mecklenburg Co., VA; Ht 5'8", black complexion; served in A/24th Infantry, 25 Jul 1871–25 Jul 1876, character excellent; in I/24th Infantry, 31 Jul 1876–30 Jul 1881 and 31 Jul 1881–

30 Jul 1886, character excellent; enlisted Ft Sill, Indian Territory, 31 Jul 1886, transferred to Band/24th Infantry, 1 Aug 1886; discharged, Ft Bayard, NM, character excellent, married, no children; deposits $80 in 1889, $100 in 1890, $30 in 1891, retained $60, clothing $84; reenlisted Ft Bayard, 31 Jul 1891; on detached service at Washington, DC, conducting insane Pvt. Nathaniel McDaniel, C/10th Cavalry, to asylum, 4 Sep–2 Oct 1891; sergeant, E/24th Infantry, 1 Sep 1892; character "excellent, a fine noncommissioned officer," married, no children, deposits $200 in 1892, retained $13, clothing $56. SOURCE: Descriptive Book, 24 Inf NCS & Band.

Sergeant, E/24th Infantry, examined for ordnance sergeant while stationed at Ft Bayard, NM, Sep 1893. SOURCE: *ANJ* 30 (8 Sep 1893): 763.

Stationed at Vancouver Barracks, WA. SOURCE: San Francisco *Chronicle*, 15 Sep 1899.

Former second lieutenant, 7th Infantry, U.S. Volunteers, commissioned second lieutenant, 49th Infantry. SOURCE: *ANJ* 37 (9 Dec 1899): 345b.

Private, corporal, sergeant, first sergeant, regimental quartermaster sergeant, 24th Infantry, 25 Jul 1871–8 Sep 1899; second and first lieutenant, 7th Infantry, U.S. Volunteers, 16 Sep 1898–28 Feb 1899; second lieutenant, 49th Infantry, 9 Sep 1899; in battle of San Juan, Cuba, 1–3 Jul 1898. SOURCE: Descriptive Book, C/49 Inf.

Mentioned as second lieutenant, C/49th Infantry. SOURCE: Beasley, *Negro Trailblazers*, 284.

Retired as first sergeant; married for second time, age 52, to Missouri Johns, age 41, in Boston, 19 Apr 1905, by Reverend J. Horatio Carter; daughter Margaret M. Perea born Cambridge, MA, 1 Mar 1906; died of arteriosclerosis due to rheumatism, Cambridge, 15 Oct 1915; widow resided at his home, 15 Van Norden Street, Cambridge; pension of $27 per month as of 14 Mar 1919 authorized by private law. SOURCE: VA File XC 866859, Beverly Perea.

PERKINS, Frank; E/10th Cav. Original member of 10th Cavalry; in troop when organized, Ft Leavenworth, KS, 15 Jun 1867. SOURCE: McMiller, "Buffalo Soldiers," 72.

PERKINS, George W.; Private; C/25th Inf. Promoted to corporal. SOURCE: *ANR* 38 (29 Jun 1905): 21.

Dishonorable discharge as private, C/25th Infantry, Brownsville. SOURCE: SO 266, AGO, 9 Nov 1906.

PERKINS, Henry; Private; A/10th Cav. Stole three plugs of government tobacco, Ft Cummings, NM, 1868. SOURCE: Billington, *New Mexico's Buffalo Soldiers*, 36.

PERKINS, John; Corporal; F/25th Inf. Tenth best infantry rifleman, Department of Dakota, and on departmental rifle team. SOURCE: *ANJ* 35 (25 Sep 1897): 55.

PERKINS, Thomas; Private; A/10th Cav. Arrived from Jefferson Barracks, MO, at Ft Leavenworth, KS, Oct 1866.

Original member of A/10th Cavalry; in troop when organized, Ft Leavenworth, KS, 18 Feb 1867. SOURCE: McMiller, "Buffalo Soldiers," 68.

PERNELL, Eleven; Private; K/9th Cav. On daily duty at post garden, Ft Robinson, NE. SOURCE: Order 48, 10 Mar 1890, Post Orders, Ft Robinson.

PERRIN, William H.; Private; A/10th Cav. Cook, K/9th Cavalry, at Ft Robinson, NE, 1887. *See* **JONES**, George F., Private, F/9th Cavalry

Served in 10th Cavalry, 1898; remained in U.S. during war with Spain. SOURCE: Cashin, *Under Fire with the Tenth Cavalry*, 337.

PERRY, Charles; QM Sgt; L/10th Cav. Born in Missouri; private, corporal, sergeant, first sergeant, B/10th Cavalry, 26 Feb 1877–25 Feb 1892; private, E/10th Cavalry, 26 Feb 1892; corporal, 16 Apr 1892. SOURCE: Baker, Roster.

Sergeant, 10th Cavalry, led patrol at Ojo Caliente, TX, 28 Oct 1880, in which five enlisted men were killed. SOURCE: Leckie, *The Buffalo Soldiers*, 230.

First sergeant, B/10th Cavalry, at Ft Apache, AZ, 1890, subscribed $.50 to testimonial to General Grierson. SOURCE: List of subscriptions, 23 Apr 1890, 10th Cavalry papers, MHI.

Served as first sergeant, L/10th Cavalry, 1898; remained in U.S. during war with Spain. SOURCE: Cashin, *Under Fire with the Tenth Cavalry*, 350.

Appointed from sergeant, E/10th Cavalry, to first lieutenant, 49th Infantry; to report at New York City. SOURCE: *ANJ* 37 (7 Oct 1899): 122.

First lieutenant as of 9 Sep 1899; to report for duty at Jefferson Barracks, MO. SOURCE: *ANJ* 37 (14 Oct 1899): 147.

As first lieutenant, E/49th Infantry, led detachment of twenty that wounded an insurgent and captured him and another at Laguna de Bay, Philippines, Feb 1900; first capture by 49th Infantry. SOURCE: Cleveland *Gazette*, 24 Mar 1900.

Twenty-four years' continuous service; police officer on board U.S. Army Transport *Warren*, 10 Dec 1899–11 Jan 1900, and on board U.S. Army Transport *Thomas*, 27 May 1901; commander of detachment that captured insurgent outpost near Laguna de Bay, and detachment which repulsed and captured insurgents who assaulted Alamines, Philippines, 2 Jan 1901. SOURCE: Descriptive Book, E/49 Inf.

Rejoined his troop of 10th Cavalry as quartermaster sergeant after discharge from 49th Infantry. SOURCE: Fletcher, "The Negro Soldier in the United States Army," 297.

Dance given in his honor, Ft Robinson, NE, 25 Jul 1904. SOURCE: Crawford *Tribune*, 29 Jul 1904.

PERRY, Charles; Private; K/9th Cav. Killed in action against Nana, Carrizo Canyon, NM, 12 Aug 1881.

SOURCE: Leckie, *The Buffalo Soldiers*, 232; Billington, *New Mexico's Buffalo Soldiers*, 105.

PERRY, Charles; Wagoner; C/9th Cav. At Ft Robinson, NE, 1885–86. *See* **DIGGS**, James, Private, C/9th Cavalry

PERRY, Charles E.; G/10th Cav. Original member of 10th Cavalry; in troop when organized, Ft Leavenworth, KS, 5 Jul 1867. SOURCE: McMiller, "Buffalo Soldiers," 74.

PERRY, Frank; Private; C/9th Cav. Authorized furlough from Ft McKinney, WY, to Sheridan, WY, 16 Aug– 4 Sep 1894.

PERRY, George; Private; I/9th Cav. At Ft Concho, TX, 1874; sentenced to dishonorable discharge and one year's confinement for theft of jar of candy from saloon. SOURCE: Leckie, *The Buffalo Soldiers*, 98.

PERRY, Henry; Recruit; Colored Detachment/ Mounted Service. Convicted by general court martial, Jefferson Barracks, MO, of desertion 17 Oct–14 Nov 1882; sentenced to dishonorable discharge and four years; sentence reduced to two years by Gen. William Sherman. SOURCE: GCMO 83, AGO, 21 Dec 1882.

PERRY, James; Wagoner; H/24th Inf. Recruit, Colored Detachment, Company C of Instruction, General Service, at Columbus Barracks, OH, 1890. *See* **BURSE**, Jet, Recruit, Colored Detachment/General Service

Enlisted Ft Douglas, UT, 16 Dec 1897. SOURCE: Muster Roll, H/24 Inf, May–Jun 1899.

Tenth year of continuous service began 16 Dec 1898. SOURCE: Muster Roll, H/24 Inf, Nov–Dec 1898.

Sick in hospital since 21 Feb 1899, disease contracted in line of duty. SOURCE: Muster Roll, H/24 Inf, Jan–Feb 1899.

PERRY, James; Private; C/25th Inf. Dishonorable discharge, Brownsville. SOURCE: SO 266, AGO, 9 Nov 1906.

PERRY, Jerry; D/10th Cav. Original member of 10th Cavalry; in troop when organized, Ft Leavenworth, KS, 1 Jun 1867. SOURCE: McMiller, "Buffalo Soldiers," 71.

PERRY, John W.; Private; H/24th Inf. Fined $6 by summary court, San Isidro, Philippines, for failure to obey noncommissioned officer while in ranks, 24 Jan 1902, third conviction; fined $2 for absence from eleven P.M. bed check, 2 Apr 1902. SOURCE: Register of Summary Court, San Isidro.

PERRY, W. M.; A/10th Cav. Died 10 Nov 1898; buried at Ft Douglas, UT. SOURCE: Clark, "A History of the Twenty-fourth," appendix A.

PERSINGER, Mason; K/10th Cav. Original member of 10th Cavalry; in troop when organized, Ft Riley, KS, 1 Sep 1867. SOURCE: McMiller, "Buffalo Soldiers," 77.

PETER, Major H.; Sergeant; I/10th Cav. Served in 10th Cavalry in Cuba, 1898. SOURCE: Cashin, *Under Fire with the Tenth Cavalry*, 347.

PETER, Simon; H/10th Cav. Original member of 10th Cavalry; in troop when organized, Ft Leavenworth, KS, 21 Jul 1867. SOURCE: McMiller, "Buffalo Soldiers," 75.

PETERS, Albert; Private; H/9th Cav. Deposited $47 with paymaster, Ft Robinson, NE, 1896–97.

PETERS, Dorsie; Private; M/10th Cav. Served in 10th Cavalry, 1898; remained in U.S. during war with Spain. SOURCE: Cashin, *Under Fire with the Tenth Cavalry*, 352.

PETERS, Elmer; Private; D/25th Inf. Dishonorable discharge, Brownsville. SOURCE: SO 266, AGO, 9 Nov 1906.

PETERS, Isaac; Private; C/9th Cav. At Ft Cummings, NM, 1881; on detached service in field, New Mexico, 30 Jan–3 Feb 1881. SOURCE: Regt Returns, 9 Cav, Feb 1881.

PETERS, James; Private; A/10th Cav. Served in 10th Cavalry in Cuba, 1898. SOURCE: Cashin, *Under Fire with the Tenth Cavalry*, 336.

PETERS, Michael; Corporal; A/10th Cav. At Ft Apache, AZ, 1890, subscribed $.50 to testimonial to General Grierson. SOURCE: List of subscriptions, 23 Apr 1890, 10th Cavalry papers, MHI.

PETERS, Richard; K/9th Cav. Authorized to enlist by letter, Adjutant General's Office, 23 May 1895.

PETERS, Richard W.; Sergeant; E/9th Cav. Veteran of Spanish-American War and Philippine Insurrection; at Ft D. A. Russell, WY, in 1910; sharpshooter. SOURCE: *Illustrated Review: Ninth Cavalry*.

PETERSON, Allen; Private; K/10th Cav. At Ft Robinson, NE, 1904.

Ranked number 543 among rifle experts with 68 percent, 1905. SOURCE: GO 101, AGO, 31 May 1906.

PETERSON, Arthur E.; Corporal; 48th Inf. Letter from Sanopan, Philippines, 3 May 1900. SOURCE: Gatewood, *"Smoked Yankees"*, 277.

PETERSON, George; Private; G/9th Cav. Discharged from Ft Stanton, NM, 27 Jan 1881, in accordance with General Court Martial Order 8, Department of the Missouri, 1881.

PETERSON, George; Recruit; Colored Recruits. Acquitted by general court martial, Columbus Barracks, OH, of assault on Recruit Moses Fishback, Colored Recruits, with dirk knife with intent to do bodily injury, Columbus Barracks, 10 May 1885. SOURCE: GCMO 58, AGO, 1 Jul 1885.

PETERSON, Willie A.; Sergeant; K/10th Cav. Corporal, served in 10th Cavalry, 1898; remained in U.S. during war with Spain. SOURCE: Cashin, *Under Fire with the Tenth Cavalry*, 349.

    Sergeant, at Ft Robinson, NE, 1904.

PETINO, William; B/10th Cav. Original member of 10th Cavalry; in troop when organized, Ft Leavenworth, KS, 1 Apr 1867. SOURCE: McMiller, "Buffalo Soldiers," 69.

PETTES, Charles M.; Private; E/9th Cav. Recruit from depot, arrived at Ft Robinson, NE, for K/9th Cavalry, 1 Mar 1887.

    Private, E/9th Cavalry, on special duty at post garden, Ft Robinson, Aug 1892. SOURCE: Order 131, 10 Aug 1892, and Order 145, 31 Aug 1892, Post Orders, Ft Robinson.

    Private, E/9th Cavalry, at Ft Robinson, 1894. SOURCE: Court Martial Records, Plummer.

PETTES, John; Private; G/10th Cav. Application for certificate, attesting to wound incurred in line of duty, to be used to apply for pension referred by Adjutant General to commander, G/10th Cavalry, 12 Dec 1868. SOURCE: ES, 10 Cav, 1866–71.

PETTIE, Samuel; QM Sgt; B/9th Cav. Appointed corporal, B/9th Cavalry, 16 Dec 1891. SOURCE: Roster, 9 Cav.

    Promoted to sergeant, B/9th Cavalry, Ft Duchesne, UT, Dec 1894. SOURCE: ANJ 32 (15 Dec 1894): 262.

    First sergeant, B/9th Cavalry, second in competition of Pacific Division cavalry team, Ord Barracks, CA, 1904. SOURCE: GO 167, AGO, 28 Oct 1904.

    Ranked sixth in Northern Division cavalry competition, Ft Riley, KS, 1905; silver medal. SOURCE: GO 173, AGO, 20 Oct 1905.

    Ranked number 474 among rifle experts with 68.67 percent, 1905. SOURCE: GO 101, AGO, 31 May 1906.

    Distinguished marksman, ranked second, Division of the Pacific, 1904; ranked sixth, Northern Division, 1905; ranked number 13, Division of the Philippines, 1908. SOURCE: GO 207, AGO, 19 Dec 1908.

    Expert rifleman and veteran of Spanish-American War and Philippine Insurrection; quartermaster sergeant, B/9th Cavalry, at Ft D. A. Russell, WY, in 1910. SOURCE: *Illustrated Review: Ninth Cavalry*, with picture.

PETTIE, William; Private; B/10th Cav. Served in 10th Cavalry, 1898; remained in U.S. during war with Spain. SOURCE: Cashin, *Under Fire with the Tenth Cavalry*, 333.

PETTIS, Nathaniel; Private; K/48th Inf. Wounded in head in the Philippines, 6 May 1900. SOURCE: *ANJ* 37 (9 Jun 1900): 975.

PHELPS, Allen; I/10th Cav. Original member of 10th Cavalry; in troop when organized, Ft Riley, KS, 15 Aug 1867. SOURCE: McMiller, "Buffalo Soldiers," 76.

PHELPS, James; Sergeant; F/25th Inf. Served 1875–80, 1881–89; campaigned against Sioux, 1881–82; guarded Sitting Bull, Ft Randall, ND; now age 80. SOURCE: *Winners of the West* 12 (Jul 1935): 3.

    To be discharged in accordance with special order, Adjutant General's Office, 16 Oct 1889. SOURCE: *ANJ* 27 (19 Oct 1889): 142.

PHELPS, John B.; Private; D/25th Inf. Killed in action, Cuba, 1898. SOURCE: Scipio, *Last of the Black Regulars*, 29.

    Killed in action at El Caney, 1 Jul 1898; buried one mile south of El Caney, with wooden headboard with his name cut into it, stones around headboard; name in tightly corked bottle, buried at head of grave. SOURCE: Scrapbook, 25 Inf, II.

    Died in Cuba, 1 Jul 1898. SOURCE: *ANJ* 36 (18 Feb 1898): 590.

PHELPS, Mack; Private; F/9th Cav. At Ft D. A. Russell, WY, in 1910; sharpshooter; resident of Evansville, IN. SOURCE: *Illustrated Review: Ninth Cavalry*, with picture.

PHELPS, W. H.; Private; C/9th Cav. On detached service in field, New Mexico, 25 Jan–3 Feb 1881. SOURCE: Regt Returns, 9 Cav, Feb 1881.

PHIFER, Ernest; Private; I/24th Inf. Participant in Houston riot, 1917. SOURCE: Haynes, *A Night of Violence*, 166.

PHILIPS, James; G/10th Cav. Mentioned as Indian war survivor. SOURCE: *Winners of the West* 3 (Jun 1926): 7.

PHILIPS, Stewart W.; 24th Inf. Sentenced to life in prison for part in Houston riot, 1917; escaped from Leavenworth and recaptured, released 5 Apr 1938, last Houston prisoner to be paroled. SOURCE: Haynes, *A Night of Violence*, 314.

PHILLIPS, Albert; Private; Band/25th Inf. Born Norfolk, VA; Ht 5'9", dark brown complexion, age 29; enlisted Ft Missoula, MT, 5 Jun 1893, third enlistment; last served in Band/10th Cavalry, discharged 5 Apr 1898, character good, with eight years and three months in 10th Cavalry. SOURCE: Descriptive Cards, 25 Inf.

PHILLIPS, Andrew; G/10th Cav. Original member of 10th Cavalry; in troop when organized, Ft Leavenworth, KS, 5 Jul 1867. SOURCE: McMiller, "Buffalo Soldiers," 74.

PHILLIPS, Frank B.; Private; G/9th Cav. At Ft D. A. Russell, WY, in 1910. SOURCE: *Illustrated Review: Ninth Cavalry*, with picture.

PHILLIPS, Henry; Private; L/9th Cav. At Ft D. A. Russell, WY, in 1910; resident of Madison, IN. SOURCE: *Illustrated Review: Ninth Cavalry*, with picture.

PHILLIPS, J. H.; Private; A/9th Cav. At Ft Stanton, NM, 1881. SOURCE: Regt Returns, 9 Cav, Jan 1881.

PHILLIPS, Jacob P.; Private; E/24th Inf. Died of yellow fever at Siboney, Cuba, 13 Aug 1898. SOURCE: *ANJ* 36 (18 Feb 1899): 590; AG, *Correspondence Regarding the War with Spain*, I:228.

Died of yellow fever at Siboney, 14 Aug 1898. SOURCE: Hospital Papers, Spanish-American War.

PHILLIPS, James; Private; M/24th Inf. Enlisted Chicago, 14 Aug 1893. SOURCE: Muster Roll, H/24 Inf, May–Jun 1898.

In B/24th Infantry at Ft Huachuca, AZ, 1893. *See* **FOX**, William, Private, B/24th Infantry

Discharged from H/24th Infantry, end of term, character excellent, Siboney, Cuba, 13 Aug 1898, with $160 deposits, $55.50 retained, $3.41 clothing. SOURCE: Muster Roll, H/24 Inf, Jul–Aug 1898.

Enlisted Ft Douglas, UT, 26 Sep 1898; on special duty as laborer, Subsistence Department, since 2 Oct 1898. SOURCE: Muster Roll, H/24 Inf, Sep–Oct 1898.

Discharged Ft Douglas, character good, single, 29 Jan 1899, with $138 deposits, $16.76 clothing; enlisted, 30 Jan 1899; on special duty as laborer, Subsistence Department, since 2 Oct 1898. SOURCE: Muster Roll, H/24 Inf, Jan–Feb 1899.

Private, M/24th Infantry, ranked number 51 among rifle experts with 76 percent, 1905. SOURCE: GO 101, AGO, 31 May 1906.

PHILLIPS, James D.; Private; I/9th Cav. Deserted from Ft Wingate, NM, 30 Jan 1881. SOURCE: Regt Returns, 9 Cav, Jan 1881.

PHILLIPS, Joseph; Sergeant; L/9th Cav. Veteran of Philippine Insurrection; at Ft D. A. Russell, WY, in 1910; marksman; resident of Millidgeville, GA. SOURCE: *Illustrated Review: Ninth Cavalry*, with picture.

PHILLIPS, Marshall; I/9th Cav. Clothing destroyed when fighting fire, Ft Wingate, NM, 15 Dec 1876. SOURCE: Billington, *New Mexico's Buffalo Soldiers*, 110.

PHILLIPS, Stephen F.; Private; 10th Cav. Unassigned private, deceased, Nov 1875. SOURCE: ES, 10 Cav, 1873–83.

PHILLIPS, Thomas; Private; C/9th Cav. Enlisted Ft Robinson, NE, 16 Aug 1898.

PHILLIPS, Willie; Private; E/10th Cav. Served in 10th Cavalry in Cuba, 1898. SOURCE: Cashin, *Under Fire with the Tenth Cavalry*, 342.

PICKENS, Peter; F/10th Cav. Original member of 10th Cavalry; in troop when organized, Ft Leavenworth, KS, 21 Jun 1867. SOURCE: McMiller, "Buffalo Soldiers," 73.

PICKINS, George; Private; F/10th Cav. Served in 10th Cavalry, 1898; remained in U.S. during war with Spain. SOURCE: Cashin, *Under Fire with the Tenth Cavalry*, 344.

PICKETT; Private; B/10th Cav. At Ft Apache, AZ, 1890, subscribed $.50 to testimonial to General Grierson. SOURCE: List of subscriptions, 23 Apr 1890, 10th Cavalry papers, MHI.

PICKETT, Sonny; D/9th Cav. Served 1875–80; subscribes to *Winners of the West*; age 84. SOURCE: *Winners of the West* 10 (Jan 1933): 3.

PICKETT, W. E.; Private; G/9th Cav. On detached service at Ft Craig, NM, 12 Jan–6 Feb 1881. SOURCE: Regt Returns, 9 Cav, Feb 1881.

PIERCE, J. M.; 9th Ohio Inf. Young lawyer; letters from Camp Alger, VA, 27 Jun, 26 Jul, 2 Aug 1898, and Camp Meade, PA. SOURCE: Gatewood, *"Smoked Yankees"*, 111–14.

PIERCE, James; F/10th Cav. Original member of 10th Cavalry; in troop when organized, Ft Leavenworth, KS, 21 Jun 1867. SOURCE: McMiller, "Buffalo Soldiers," 73.

PIERCE, John; Private; M/10th Cav. Served in 10th Cavalry, 1898; remained in U.S. during war with Spain. SOURCE: Cashin, *Under Fire with the Tenth Cavalry*, 352.

PIERCE, William; H/10th Cav. Original member of 10th Cavalry; in troop when organized, Ft Leavenworth, KS, 21 Jul 1867. SOURCE: McMiller, "Buffalo Soldiers," 75.

PIERCE, William P.; E/10th Cav. Original member of 10th Cavalry; in troop when organized, Ft Leavenworth, KS, 15 Jun 1867. SOURCE: McMiller, "Buffalo Soldiers," 72.

PIERSAUL, Leonidas; Private; I/10th Cav. Served in 10th Cavalry in Cuba, 1898. SOURCE: Cashin, *Under Fire with the Tenth Cavalry*, 348.

Heroism in Cuba mentioned. SOURCE: Cashin, *Under Fire with the Tenth Cavalry*, 185.

PIERSON, David; A/25th Inf. Reports that garrison of Ft Custer, MT, organized a "Regular Army and Navy Union," 15 Aug 1891; thirteen charter members, now sixty-five; meets twice a month; designed to protect old soldiers; admission contingent on honorable discharge and five years' service. SOURCE: Cleveland *Gazette*, 27 Feb 1892.

PILLOW, Alexander; Ord Sgt; U.S. Army. Sergeant, G/25th Infantry, examined for ordnance sergeant, Ft Missoula, MT, 1893. SOURCE: *ANJ* 30 (1 Jul 1893): 745.

Promoted to ordnance sergeant. SOURCE: *ANJ* 32 (27 Oct 1894): 141.

PINCHBACK, Walter A.; Lieutenant; M/9th Inf USV. Born New Orleans, 21 Oct 1871; youngest son of P. B. S. Pinchback; attended school in Andover, MA, and Southern and Columbia Universities; clerk, recorder's office, Washington, DC, until resigned to accept commission; post adjutant, Songo, Cuba. SOURCE: Coston, *The Spanish-American War Volunteer*, 82.

PINKETT, Leroy; Private; I/24th Inf. Served in Houston, 1917; involved in riot. SOURCE: Haynes, *A Night of Violence*, 99, 167.

PINKLE, Scott; H/10th Cav. Original member of 10th Cavalry; in troop when organized, Ft Leavenworth, KS, 21 Jul 1867. SOURCE: McMiller, "Buffalo Soldiers," 75.

PINKSTON; Private; B/10th Cav. At Ft Apache, AZ, 1890, subscribed $.50 to testimonial to General Grierson. SOURCE: List of subscriptions, 23 Apr 1890, 10th Cavalry papers, MHI.

PINKSTON, Alfred; Private; M/10th Cav. Killed a Kiowa in hand-to-hand combat in skirmish with Comanches, 24 Oct 1874. SOURCE: Leckie, *The Buffalo Soldiers*, 131–32.

Killed Kiowa Chief Silver Moon in personal combat, 29 Oct 1874. SOURCE: Baker, Roster.

PINKSTON, Edward; Private; M/9th Cav. Veteran of Philippine Insurrection; at Ft D. A. Russell, WY, in 1910. SOURCE: *Illustrated Review: Ninth Cavalry*, with picture.

PINKSTON, Irvin; Private; A/9th Cav. Ranked number nine in Army pistol competition and 15 in Northern Division pistol competition, both at Ft Sheridan, IL, 1906. SOURCE: GO 198, AGO, 6 Dec 1906.

PINKSTON, Samuel; Private; K/9th Cav. On extra duty as assistant baker, Ft Robinson, NE. SOURCE: Special Order 84, 3 Aug 1896, Post Orders, Ft Robinson.

Discharged on certificate of disability with constitutional syphilis, Ft Robinson, 5 Aug 1897. SOURCE: Certificates of Disability, Ft Robinson.

PINER, Albert W.; Private; E/24th Inf. In the Philippines, 1906. *See* **HARRIS**, William C., Sergeant, E/24th Infantry

PIPES, Nelson; Private; E/10th Cav. Unassigned recruit, 10th Cavalry, on temporary duty for training at Ft Bascom, NM. SOURCE: SO 3, District of NM, 23 Jan 1867.

Original member of E/10th Cavalry; in troop when organized, Ft Leavenworth, KS, 15 Jun 1867. SOURCE: McMiller, "Buffalo Soldiers," 72.

PITMAN, Silas; Private; E/10th Cav. Served in 10th Cavalry, 1898; remained in U.S. during war with Spain. SOURCE: Cashin, *Under Fire with the Tenth Cavalry*, 343.

PITTER, Charles; Corporal; I/10th Cav. To proceed from Ft Apache, AZ, to Ft Grant, AZ, to be appointed regimental quartermaster sergeant. SOURCE: *ANJ* 29 (16 Apr 1892): 588.

PITTER, Richard; Corporal; I/10th Cav. At Ft Apache, AZ, 1890, subscribed $.50 to testimonial to General Grierson. SOURCE: List of subscriptions, 23 Apr 1890, 10th Cavalry papers, MHI.

PITTMAN; Sergeant; 38th Inf. Led twenty-five mounted men of 38th Infantry to reinforce F/10th Cavalry, Aug 1867, but arrived too late to meet them before they took field from Ft Hays, KS. SOURCE: Armes, *Ups and Downs*, 240.

PITTS, Ephriam R.; Private; F/10th Cav. Transferred to Hospital Corps in accordance with Special Order 2, Department of the Missouri, 4 Jan 1904.

Fought Lightning Murray for Ft Robinson, NE, lightweight championship, 2 Mar 1906. SOURCE: Crawford *Tribune*, 2 Mar 1906.

PITTS, Lonnie; Trumpeter; A/9th Cav. Served as private, K/10th Cavalry, 1898; remained in U.S. during war with Spain. SOURCE: Cashin, *Under Fire with the Tenth Cavalry*, 349.

Private, K/10th Cavalry, released to duty from treatment for acute gonorrhea, Ft Robinson, NE, 25 Nov 1903. SOURCE: Post Surgeon to CO, K/10, 25 Nov 1903, LS, Post Surgeon, Ft Robinson.

Private, K/10th Cavalry, at Ft Robinson, 1904.

Trumpeter, A/9th Cavalry, at Ft D. A. Russell, WY, in 1910. SOURCE: *Illustrated Review: Ninth Cavalry*, with picture.

PLEASANT, Harry R.; Private; Band/10th Cav. At Ft Apache, AZ, 1890, subscribed $.50 to testimonial to General Grierson. SOURCE: List of subscriptions, 23 Apr 1890, 10th Cavalry papers, MHI.

Served in 10th Cavalry in Cuba, 1898. SOURCE: Cashin, *Under Fire with the Tenth Cavalry*, 359.

PLEASANT, John; Private; F/25th Inf. Died of malaria in the Philippines, 11 Jan 1900. SOURCE: *ANJ* 37 (10 Feb 1900): 562.

PLEASANTS, H.; Sergeant; M/10th Cav. At Ft Apache, AZ, 1890, subscribed $.50 to testimonial to General Grierson. SOURCE: List of subscriptions, 23 Apr 1890, 10th Cavalry papers, MHI.

PLEDGER, William A., Jr.; Private; H/24th Inf.
Enlisted Camp Tampa, FL, 16 May 1898. SOURCE: Muster Roll, H/24 Inf, May–Jun 1898.

Sick, disease contracted in line of duty; returned to U.S. SOURCE: Muster Roll, H/24 Inf, Jul–Aug 1898.

Transferred from Reserve Divisional Hospital, Siboney, Cuba, to Fortress Monroe, VA, on U.S. Army Transport *Concho* with yellow fever, 24 Jul 1898. SOURCE: Hospital Papers, Spanish-American War.

On furlough authorized by surgeon's certificate, 11 Aug–10 Sep 1898; on special duty, Quartermaster Department, since 5 Oct 1898. SOURCE: Muster Roll, H/24 Inf, Sep–Oct 1898.

On special duty as clerk, Quartermaster Department. SOURCE: Muster Roll, H/24 Inf, Nov–Dec 1898.

Discharged Ft Douglas, character good, single, 27 Jan 1899; due U.S. for clothing $16.03. SOURCE: Muster Roll, H/24 Inf, Jan–Feb 1899.

PLOWDEN, Jesse; Farrier; G/9th Cav. Recruit, Colored Detachment, Mounted Service, at Jefferson Barracks, MO, 1887. *See* **PORTERFIELD**, Henry, Recruit, Colored Detachment/Mounted Service

Buried, Ft Robinson, NE, 28 Jan 1895. SOURCE: List of Interments, Ft Robinson.

Funeral, Ft Robinson, 30 Jan 1895. SOURCE: Order 6, 29 Jan 1895, Post Orders, Ft Robinson.

PLUMER, Darrel; L/10th Cav. Original member of 10th Cavalry; in troop when organized, Ft Riley, KS, 21 Sep 1867. SOURCE: McMiller, "Buffalo Soldiers," 78.

PLUMER, Joseph P.; L/10th Cav. Original member of 10th Cavalry; in troop when organized, Ft Riley, KS, 21 Sep 1867. SOURCE: McMiller, "Buffalo Soldiers," 78.

PLUMER, William; M/10th Cav. Original member of 10th Cavalry; in troop when organized, Ft Riley, KS, 15 Oct 1867. SOURCE: McMiller, "Buffalo Soldiers," 79.

PLUMMER, Ellert C.; A/10th Cav. Now out of service; cited for distinguished service. SOURCE: *ANJ* 37 (24 Feb 1900): 611.

PLUMMER, Henry Vinton; Chaplain; 9th Cav. Family biography. SOURCE: Nellie Arnold Plummer, *Out of the Depths.*

During Civil War, served in U.S. Navy, aboard gunboat U.S.S. *Coeur de Leon* of Potomac Flotilla and at Washington Navy Yard; married to Julia Lomax by Sandy Alexander, minister of Second Baptist Church, Washington, DC, at Hyattsville, MD, 22 Jun 1867. SOURCE: VA File WC 17458, Henry V. Plummer.

Not accompanying regimental headquarters from Ft McKinney, WY, to Ft Robinson, NE, because of scarcity of quarters. SOURCE: *ANJ* 24 (30 Apr 1887): 794.

Mentioned as first African-American chaplain. SOURCE: Cleveland *Gazette*, 29 Aug 1891.

Resides at Ft Robinson with wife, sister, four of his six children, two servants, Aug 1893; married twenty-eight years. SOURCE: Medical History, Ft Robinson; Court Martial Records, Plummer.

Editor of Fort Robinson *Weekly Bulletin*, four pages, one folded sheet, $.05 per issue.

Author of "Resident Manager," "Fort Robinson Department," Omaha *Progress*, 1893.

Convicted by general court martial, Ft Robinson, of conduct unbecoming an officer and a gentleman, Sep 1894; sentenced to dishonorable discharge. SOURCE: Stover, "Chaplain Henry V. Plummer, His Ministry and His Court Martial."

Charles R. Lee and James A. Lee of Kansas City, KS, testify to Plummer's heart trouble, indigestion, lumbago, all of which incapacitate him for manual labor; also testify to Plummer's lack of any other means of support except daily labor, 11 Feb 1895; applied for invalid pension through Attorney Allan Rutherford, Washington, DC, 23 Feb 1895; granted $8 per month from 21 Jun 1899, approved 24 Mar 1900, based on "partial inability to earn a support by manual labor." SOURCE: VA File WC 17458, Henry V. Plummer.

Pastor, Second Baptist Church, 533 North Wichita, Wichita, KS, 1901–1902; resided at 911 Washington Avenue, Kansas City.

Picture in uniform. SOURCE: Wichita *Searchlight*, 2 Nov 1901.

Living children, 1903: Adam F. Plummer, born 30 Sep 1868; Charles Sumner Plummer, born 8 Feb 1872; Henry V. Plummer, Jr., born 7 Dec 1879; Ulysses S. G. Plummer, born 16 Mar 1881; Ferdinand G. H. Plummer, born 3 Apr 1887; Hannibal L. Plummer, born 18 Mar 1889. SOURCE: VA File WC 17458, Henry V. Plummer.

Seriously ill. SOURCE: Kansas City (KS) *American Citizen*, 3 Feb 1905.

Died in Kansas City, 10 Feb 1905. SOURCE: Kansas City *American Citizen*, 17 Feb 1905.

Undertaker W. B. Raymond, 431 Minnesota Avenue, Kansas City, shipped Plummer's remains to Washington, DC, 12 Feb 1905. SOURCE: VA File WC 17458, Henry V. Plummer.

Brother Elias Plummer, Hutchinson, Reno Co., KS, resided in Washington DC, 1867; resided with brother until latter died; African Methodist Episcopal minister for twenty years; address Box 328B, East Hutchinson, KS. SOURCE: VA File WC 17458, Henry V. Plummer.

Widow Julia (Lomax) Plummer filed application for widow's pension from 911 Washington Avenue, Kansas City, 27 Feb 1905; pension of $8 per month began 27 Feb 1905; increased to $12 per month 19 Apr 1908; widow resided at 1313 T Street, NW, Washington, DC, when she died of bronchial pneumonia, 4 Oct 1915, with $540 equity in real estate; Henry V. Plummer, Jr., age 38, resided in Washington DC, 1915. SOURCE: VA File WC 17458, Henry V. Plummer.

Biographical sketch. SOURCE: Logan and Winston, eds., *Dictionary of American Negro Biography*, 15–16.
See AGO File 6474 ACP 81.

PLUMMER, Solomon; Sergeant; D/9th Cav. Appointed sergeant 3 Feb 1888. SOURCE: Roster, 9 Cav.

On special duty as exchange steward, Ft Robinson, NE, vice Sergeant James Donohue, C/8th Infantry. SOURCE: Order 12, 4 Feb 1893, Post Orders, Ft Robinson.

In M/9th Cavalry; reenlistment for third term celebrated with dinner and hop, Ft Duchesne, UT. SOURCE: *ANJ* 36 (16 Mar 1899): 572.

Granted four-month furlough. SOURCE: *ANJ* 36 (30 Mar 1899): 619.

With detachment of nineteen men of D/9th Cavalry that engaged insurgents, captured a Remington rifle; stationed at San Fernando, Philippines. SOURCE: Hamilton, "History of the Ninth Cavalry," 106; Manila *Times*, 11 Feb 1901; *Illustrated Review: Ninth Cavalry*.

PLUMO, William; Private; H/10th Cav. Served in 10th Cavalry, 1898; remained in U.S. during war with Spain. SOURCE: Cashin, *Under Fire with the Tenth Cavalry*, 346.

POGUE, John; Cook; K/9th Cav. Retired Mar 1902. SOURCE: *ANJ* 39 (5 Apr 1902): 776.

POGUE, Peter C.; Corporal; Band/25th Inf. Private, K/25th Infantry; letter from Bamban, Philippines, 24 Nov 1899. SOURCE: Gatewood, *"Smoked Yankees"*, 258–59.

Letter from LaLoma, Luzon, Philippines. SOURCE: Cleveland *Gazette*, 18 Nov 1899.

Letter from Bamban, Philippines, 5 Dec 1899. SOURCE: Cleveland *Gazette*, 3 Feb 1900.

Letter from Cabangan, Philippines, 26 Jul 1900; received paper regularly. SOURCE: Cleveland *Gazette*, 15 Sep 1900.

Transferred to Band/25th Infantry. SOURCE: SO 99, 25 Inf, Iba, Zambales, Philippines, 1 Nov 1900, Misc Records, 25 Inf.

Promoted to corporal. SOURCE: *ANR* 38 (22 Jul 1905): 21.

POINDEXTER; Sergeant; K/9th Cav. Returned to duty as private, in accordance with letter, Department of the Platte, 25 Oct 1890.

POINDEXTER, Horace; Private; D/9th Cav. At Ft D. A. Russell, WY, in 1910; resident of New Castle, IN. SOURCE: *Illustrated Review: Ninth Cavalry*, with picture.

POINDEXTER, James; Private; 48th Inf. Sick in the Philippines, Feb 1900. SOURCE: Richmond *Planet*, 14 Apr 1900.

POINDEXTER, James A.; Private; G/9th Cav. At Ft D. A. Russell, WY, in 1910; marksman. SOURCE: *Illustrated Review: Ninth Cavalry*, with picture.

POINTNEY, Peter; Private; K/10th Cav. Sentence for desertion, which began 1 Oct 1875, reduced to eighteen months. SOURCE: GCMO 22, AGO, 23 Feb 1877.

POLK, Edward; Private; Band/25th Inf. Born Prentiss Co., MS; Ht 5'11", light brown complexion; third enlistment, single, character excellent, Ft Missoula, MT, age 29, 9 Jan 1896; previous service three years, three months in Band/9th Cavalry, and three years, three months in Band/25th Infantry. SOURCE: Descriptive Cards, 25 Inf.

Deserted, San Francisco, 13 Jul 1899. SOURCE: Regt Returns, 25 Inf, Jul 1899.

POLK, Holmes; Corporal; G/10th Cav. Promoted from wagoner. SOURCE: SO 93, 10 Cav, Ft Ethan Allen, VT, 11 Dec 1909.

POLK, Marshall; E/24th Inf. At Ft Bayard, NM, 1891. SOURCE: *ANJ* 29 (17 Oct 1891): 133.

POLK, Thomas; Cook; A/9th Cav. Sergeant, C/9th Cavalry, at Ft Robinson, NE, 1886; deposited $231 with paymaster.

Discharged, end of term, character excellent, Mar 1887.

Saddler, A/9th Cavalry, reenlistment as married authorized by letter, Adjutant General's Office, 4 Aug 1893.

Veteran of Indian wars and Philippine Insurrection; cook, A/9th Cavalry, at Ft D. A. Russell, WY, in 1910; marksman. SOURCE: *Illustrated Review: Ninth Cavalry*, with picture.

Subscriber; served 1882–92. SOURCE: *Winners of the West* 9 (Nov 1932): 1.

Reader since 1932; member, Camp 11, National Indian War Veterans; died Eden, MD, 24 Jun 1940. SOURCE: *Winners of the West* 17 (Jul 1940): 2.

POLK, William; Chief Musician; 24th Inf. Succeeds white Warrant Officer Thompson; "this gives the race three of the four bandmasters provided for our regiments in the army." SOURCE: Cleveland *Gazette*, 12 Jun 1909.

POLLARD, Budd; Private; B/10th Cav. Served in 10th Cavalry, 1898; remained in U.S. during war with Spain. SOURCE: Cashin, *Under Fire with the Tenth Cavalry*, 333.

POLSON, Dillon; Corporal; 9th Cav. One of two African-American Army musicians to win one of five scholarships to the New York Institute of Musical Art. SOURCE: Cleveland *Gazette*, 10 Jun 1916.

POOL, Henry Green; B/9th Cav. Mentioned as surviving Indian war veteran. SOURCE: *Winners of the West* 3 (Jun 1926): 7.

POOL, Robert L.; Private; K/25th Inf. At Ft Niobrara, NE, 1904. SOURCE: Wilson, "History of Fort Niobrara."

POOLE, John E.; Private; H/24th Inf. Enlisted Ft McPherson, GA, 26 Mar 1896; on special duty as company clerk, 1 Jun 1897–1 May 1898. SOURCE: Muster Roll, H/24 Inf, May–Jun 1898.

Absent sick, disease contracted in line of duty, 15 Sep–1 Nov 1898. SOURCE: Muster Roll, H/24 Inf, Sep–Oct and Nov–Dec 1898.

On special duty as clerk, adjutant's office. SOURCE: Muster Roll, H/24 Inf, Jan–Feb 1899.

Sharpshooter and scout. SOURCE: Indianapolis *Freeman*, 18 Mar 1899, with picture.

Drowned with a white private of the 4th Cavalry, 21 Aug 1899, while trying to rescue nine men of 24th Infantry, who drowned in San Mateo River, Philippines. SOURCE: Richmond *Planet*, 2 Sep 1899.

POPE, Charles F.; Private; A/24th Inf. Wounded in action at Santiago, Cuba, 1898, SOURCE: SecWar, *AR 1898*, 437; Muller, *The Twenty Fourth Infantry*, 16.

POPE, David F.; C/10th Cav. Served five years; subscriber; now seventy-seven years old. SOURCE: *Winners of the West* 10 (Aug 1933): 3.

Served 1881–86; died at Toronto, Canada. SOURCE: *Winners of the West* 11 (Mar 1934): 3.

POPE, Henry; Cook; D/24th Inf. At Cabanatuan, Philippines, 1901. *See* **TATES**, Rollins, Private, D/24th Infantry

POPE, Malachi G.; Private; K/9th Cav. Thrown into cold stream by Capt. J. Lee Humfreville, Ft Richardson, TX, 15 Dec 1872, and forced into hospital by subsequent illness. SOURCE: GCMO 23, AGO, 3 Apr 1874.

POPE, Thomas; Private; F/9th Cav. At Ft D. A. Russell, WY, in 1910; sharpshooter; resident of Huntsville, AL. SOURCE: *Illustrated Review: Ninth Cavalry*, with picture.

POPE, Zachariah; 1st Sgt; C/25th Inf. Original member of B/10th Cavalry; in troop when organized, Ft Leavenworth, KS, 1 Apr 1867. SOURCE: McMiller, "Buffalo Soldiers," 69.

Mentioned as having served in 1867. SOURCE: Baker, Roster.

Retires as first sergeant, C/25th Infantry, from Tampa, FL. SOURCE: *ANJ* 35 (11 Jun 1898): 816.

POPER, William; E/10th Cav. Original member of 10th Cavalry; in troop when organized, Ft Leavenworth, KS, 15 Jun 1867. SOURCE: McMiller, "Buffalo Soldiers," 72.

PORTER, C. C.; Private; F/10th Cav. Died of tuberculosis complicated by pneumonia, Ft Washakie, WY, 26 Dec 1905.

PORTER, Edward B.; Private; L/10th Cav. Served in 10th Cavalry, 1898; remained in U.S. during war with Spain. SOURCE: Cashin, *Under Fire with the Tenth Cavalry*, 350.

PORTER, Harrison; Private; L/9th Cav. Promoted from private to sergeant, F/10th Cavalry, 1 Mar 1898. SOURCE: *ANJ* 12 (Mar 1898): 518.

Served as private, F/10th Cavalry in Cuba, 1898. SOURCE: Cashin, *Under Fire with the Tenth Cavalry*, 343.

Veteran of Spanish-American War and Philippine Insurrection; private, L/9th Cavalry, at Ft D. A. Russell, WY, in 1910; resident of St. Louis. SOURCE: *Illustrated Review: Ninth Cavalry*, with picture.

PORTER, Harry; Private; I/10th Cav. Served in 10th Cavalry, 1898; remained in U.S. during war with Spain. SOURCE: Cashin, *Under Fire with the Tenth Cavalry*, 348.

PORTER, Issac; G/10th Cav. Original member of 10th Cavalry; in troop when organized, Ft Leavenworth, KS, 5 Jul 1867. SOURCE: McMiller, "Buffalo Soldiers," 74.

PORTER, James E.; I/25th Inf. Born New Orleans, 1882; resides in Denver; enlisted Ft Logan, CO, 1898; served in Cuba and thirty-two months in Philippines; honorable discharge in California, Apr 1902. SOURCE: *Colored American Magazine* 6 (Aug 1903): 602.

PORTER, John H.; C/25th Inf. Letter from Mr. and Mrs. Alonzo Miller, El Paso, TX, reports that Porter died, at age 71, fourteen months ago at Miller home after living with them eighteen years. SOURCE: *Winners of the West* 5 (Apr 1928): 2.

PORTER, John L.; Musician; H/24th Inf. Enlisted Ft Douglas, UT, 14 May 1898; assigned to H/24th Infantry, 16 Sep 1898; musician, 17 Sep 1898. SOURCE: Muster Roll, H/24 Inf, Sep–Oct 1898.

Fined $1 by summary court, 18 Nov 1898. SOURCE: Muster Roll, H/24 Inf, Nov–Dec 1898.

Discharged, character good, single, 29 Jan 1899; due soldier $2.48 for clothing; reenlisted Ft Douglas, 30 Jan 1899; appointment as musician continued; fined $.50 by summary court, 15 Feb 1899. SOURCE: Muster Roll, H/24 Inf, Jan–Feb 1899.

Wounded in action in the Philippines, 7 Dec 1899. SOURCE: Muller, *The Twenty Fourth Infantry*, 35.

Died of diphtheria in the Philippines, 2 Jan 1900. SOURCE: *ANJ* 37 (20 Jan 1900): 488.

PORTER, Johnson; C/10th Cav. Original member of 10th Cavalry; in troop when organized, Ft Leavenworth, KS, 14 May 1867. SOURCE: McMiller, "Buffalo Soldiers," 70.

PORTER, Loyd T.; Private; M/10th Cav. Served in 10th Cavalry, 1898; remained in U.S. during war with Spain. SOURCE: Cashin, *Under Fire with the Tenth Cavalry*, 352.

PORTER, R. A.; Sergeant; K/24th Inf. At San Carlos, AZ, 1890. *See* **HARDEE**, James A., Private, K/24th Infantry

PORTER, Richard; Comsy Sgt; 9th Cav. Veteran of Philippine Insurrection; at Ft D. A. Russell, WY. SOURCE: *Illustrated Review: Ninth Cavalry*, with picture.

PORTER, Wesley; Sergeant; Band/9th Cav. Private, reenlistment authorized by letter, Adjutant General's Office, 17 Jan 1896.

Retires as sergeant, Dec 1900. SOURCE: *ANJ* 38 (29 Dec 1900): 431.

PORTER, Will; Private; 24th Inf. Sentenced to seven years for part in Houston riot, 1917. SOURCE: Cleveland *Gazette*, 5 Jan 1917.

PORTER, William K.; Private; A/10th Cav. Served in H/10th Cavalry, 1898; remained in U.S. during war with Spain. SOURCE: Cashin, *Under Fire with the Tenth Cavalry*, 347.

Corporal, A/9th Cavalry, on special duty as troop clerk since 24 Nov 1900. SOURCE: SD List, A/9 Cav, 24 May 1902, Nueva Caceres, Philippines.

Private, A/10th Cavalry, transferred to General Recruiting Service from Ft Robinson, NE, Jun 1903; departed for Charlotte, NC, 1 Jul 1903.

PORTER, Willie; Private; C/9th Cav. Discharged on surgeon's certificate with constitutional syphilis from Ft Robinson, NE, 24 Jan 1898. SOURCE: Certificates of Disability, Ft Robinson.

PORTERFIELD, Henry; Recruit; Colored Detachment/Mounted Service. Acquitted by general court martial, Jefferson Barracks, MO, of theft from Recruit Jesse Plowden, Colored Detachment/Mounted Service, of pocketbook with $1.55. SOURCE: GCMO 85, AGO, 25 Nov 1887.

POSEY, Abner; Private; F/10th Cav. Relieved of duty in hospital. SOURCE: SO 21, Det 10 Cav, Camp near Ft Dodge, KS, 18 Apr 1869, Orders, Det 10 Cav, 1868–69.

POSEY, John; Private; F/24th Inf. Died of abscess of liver, Dagupan, Luzon, Philippines, 2 Jul 1901. SOURCE: *ANJ* 38 (24 Aug 1901): 1256.

POSEY, Moure; F/10th Cav. Original member of 10th Cavalry; in troop when organized, Ft Leavenworth, KS, 21 Jun 1867. SOURCE: McMiller, "Buffalo Soldiers," 73.

POSTLEY, John; G/10th Cav. Original member of 10th Cavalry; in troop when organized, Ft Leavenworth, KS, 5 Jul 1867. SOURCE: McMiller, "Buffalo Soldiers," 74.

POTTER; Private; A/24th Inf. At Ft Bayard, NM, 1888; his request to have regimental band accompany his minstrel troupe to Silver City, NM, denied. SOURCE: Billington, *New Mexico's Buffalo Soldiers*, 157.

POTTER, Bradford; Private; H/24th Inf. Enlisted Ft Douglas, UT, 10 Dec 1897; corporal, with fourteen years' continuous service. SOURCE: Muster Roll, H/24 Inf, May–Jun 1898.

Transferred from Reserve Divisional Hospital, Siboney, Cuba, to U.S. on U.S. Army Transport *Santiago* with dysentery, 25 Jul 1898. SOURCE: Hospital Papers, Spanish-American War.

Sick in U.S., disease contracted in line of duty. SOURCE: Muster Roll, H/24 Inf, Jul–Aug 1898.

Rejoined from absence caused by sickness, 2 Oct 1898. SOURCE: Muster Roll, H/24 Inf, Sep–Oct 1898.

On special duty as overseer of laborers since 31 Oct 1898; promoted to sergeant, 7 Nov 1898. SOURCE: Muster Roll, H/24 Inf, Nov–Dec 1898 and Jan–Feb 1899.

Private, fined $1.50 by summary court, San Isidro, for being absent without leave overnight, 25–26 Nov 1901, second conviction. SOURCE: Register of Summary Court, San Isidro.

See **TURNER**, William, Private, H/24th Infantry

POTTER, Cain; Private; B/9th Cav. Reprimanded for insubordination to Cpl. John Downey, B/9th Cavalry. SOURCE: Order 40, 18 Feb 1889, Post Orders, Ft Robinson.

POTTER, Dennis; Corporal; K/24th Inf. Enlisted Ft Myer, VA, 7 Aug 1897; promoted from private, H/24th Infantry, 10 May 1898; six years' continuous service. SOURCE: Muster Roll, H/24 Inf, May–Jun 1898.

On detached service at Ft McPherson, GA, since 15 May 1898. SOURCE: Muster Roll, H/24 Inf, Jul–Aug 1898.

Transferred to K/24th Infantry, 7 Oct 1898; due soldier $30 deposits; due U.S. $2.25 for clothing. SOURCE: Muster Roll, H/24 Inf, Sep–Oct 1898.

POTTER, Ewing; B/10th Cav. Original member of 10th Cavalry; in troop when organized, Ft Leavenworth, KS, 1 Apr 1867. SOURCE: McMiller, "Buffalo Soldiers," 69.

POTTER, Thomas; 10th Cav. Father of Sgt. Thomas H. Allsup's first wife Lulu (Lovett), took up preaching in vicinity of Ft Concho, TX. SOURCE: Affidavit, Potter, Millwood, VA, 23 Apr 1926, VA File XC 2659797, Thomas H. Allsup.

POTTER, William; K/10th Cav. Served five years; recent subscriber. SOURCE: *Winners of the West* 4 (Mar 1927): 8.

Served 1872–77; age 78; gets $50 per month pension. SOURCE: *Winners of the West* 6 (Apr 1929): 3.

POTTS, Benjamin F.; QM Sgt; 10th Cav. Private, I/10th Cavalry, at Ft Apache, AZ, 1890, subscribed $.25 to testimonial to General Grierson. SOURCE: List of subscriptions, 23 Apr 1890, 10th Cavalry papers, MHI.

Served as sergeant, I/10th Cavalry, in Cuba, 1898. SOURCE: Cashin, *Under Fire with the Tenth Cavalry*, 347.

Retired Jan 1901. SOURCE: *ANJ* 38 (2 Feb 1901): 547.

POTTS, Samuel; Private; H/10th Cav. Dishonorably discharged from Ft Apache, AZ, for false accusations against his troop commander; two years' confinement remitted. SOURCE: *ANJ* 28 (25 Apr 1891): 593.

POWELL, Charles; Private; Band/9th Cav. At Ft D. A. Russell, WY, in 1910; resident of Xenia, OH. SOURCE: *Illustrated Review: Ninth Cavalry*, with picture.

POWELL, David; Corporal; D/25th Inf. Dishonorable discharge, Brownsville. SOURCE: SO 266, AGO, 9 Nov 1906.

POWELL, George D.; Sgt Maj; 24th Inf. Sergeant, C/24th Infantry, at Ft Grant, AZ, 1890. *See* **BERRY**, Edward, Sergeant, H/24th Infantry

Authorized six-month furlough from San Carlos, AZ. SOURCE: *ANJ* 28 (13 Dec 1890): 262.

See **HARDEE**, James A., Private, K/24th Infantry

Enlisted Tampa, FL, 27 May 1898; fourteen years' continuous service. SOURCE: Muster Roll, I/24 Inf, Jan–Feb 1899.

Corporal, C/24th Infantry, wounded in action, Cuba, 1898. SOURCE: Muller, *The Twenty Fourth Infantry*, 18.

Resided at 1130 East Third South, Salt Lake City, 1898. SOURCE: Clark, "A History of the Twenty-fourth," appendix E.

Discharged, 31 Dec 1899, with $690 deposits and $29.05 clothing. SOURCE: Muster Roll, H/24 Inf, Nov–Dec 1899.

Ranked number seven, Northern Division infantry team competition, Ft Sheridan, IL, 1904. SOURCE: GO 167, AGO, 28 Oct 1904.

First sergeant, I/24th Infantry, at Ft Missoula, MT, 1905; member of division rifle team, Ft Sheridan competition, 1905. SOURCE: Muller, *The Twenty Fourth Infantry*, 42.

Ranked number 11, Northern Division infantry competition, Ft Sheridan, bronze medal, 1905; Northern Division silver medal, 1904; Northern Division bronze medal, 1905. SOURCE: GO 173, AGO, 20 Oct 1905.

Promoted from first sergeant, I/24th Infantry, to regimental sergeant major. SOURCE: Order 12, 24 Inf, Warwick Barracks, Cebu, Philippines, 1 Nov 1906, Name File, 24 Inf.

Resident of Washington, DC; retired in 1916 after thirty years, as regimental sergeant major; participated in all of 24th Infantry's military campaigns. SOURCE: *Crisis* 12 (Jun 1916): 67.

In C/24th Infantry Feb 1879–May 1898; knew Barney McKay when he arrived at Ft Sill, Indian Territory; saw McKay again when he came to Washington, DC, in 1907; now age 69, messenger, Quartermaster Department, resides at 14 D Street, SE, Washington, DC. SOURCE: Affidavit, Powell, 9 Nov 1925, VA File XC 2659455, Barney McKay.

POWELL, Herbert; Private; F/9th Cav. At Ft D. A. Russell, WY, in 1910; resident of Paris, TX. SOURCE: *Illustrated Review: Ninth Cavalry*.

POWELL, James F.; 1st Lt; C/48th Inf. Indianan, previously served in 1st Indiana Infantry; commissioned in volunteer infantry for Philippine Insurrection. SOURCE: Gatewood, "Indiana Negroes and the Spanish-American War," 138.

Recruiting enlisted men for his regiment. SOURCE: Indianapolis *Freeman*, 30 Sep 1899.

Mentioned. SOURCE: Beasley, *Negro Trailblazers*, 285.

POWELL, Samuel; I/10th Cav. Served 1879–84, at Fts Davis, Stockton, Concho, and Camp Presidio, TX; wants to hear from old boys. SOURCE: *Winners of the West* 9 (Mar 1932): 9.

Former member of Camp 20, National Indian War Veterans; died in Chicago. SOURCE: *Winners of the West* 13 (Feb 1936): 3.

POWELL, Thomas R.; Private; G/24th Inf. Transferred from Reserve Divisional Hospital, Siboney, Cuba, to U.S. on U.S. Army Transport *Santiago* with remittent malarial fever, 25 Jul 1898. SOURCE: Hospital Papers, Spanish-American War.

Deserted from Cabanatuan, Philippines, 21 Jan 1900; "steps of apprehension unsuccessful up to date." SOURCE: Regt Returns, 24 Inf, Feb 1900.

See AGO File 380893.

POWELL, William; Cook; K/25th Inf. At Ft Niobrara, NE, 1904. SOURCE: Wilson, "History of Fort Niobrara."

POWELL, William; Private; A/9th Cav. Veteran of Philippine Insurrection; at Ft D. A. Russell, WY, in 1910; sharpshooter. SOURCE: *Illustrated Review: Ninth Cavalry*, with picture.

POWELL, William; H/9th Cav. Only African-American in picture of twenty-three members of Newark, NJ, Camp No. 6, National Indian War Veterans. SOURCE: *Winners of the West* 7 (May 1930): 1.

POWER; Private; Band/10th Cav. At Ft Apache, AZ, 1890, subscribed $.50 to testimonial to General Grierson. SOURCE: List of subscriptions, 23 Apr 1890, 10th Cavalry papers, MHI.

POWERS, Alfred; D/10th Cav. Original member of 10th Cavalry; in troop when organized, Ft Leavenworth, KS, 1 Jun 1867. SOURCE: McMiller, "Buffalo Soldiers," 71.

PRANN, Charles W.; Corporal; E/9th Cav. As recruit in Colored Detachment/Mounted Service, convicted by general court martial, Jefferson Barracks, MO, of sleeping on post while in charge of general prisoner at work, 15 Jul 1887; sentenced to three months in jail and loss of three months' pay. SOURCE: GCMO 65, AGO, 25 Aug 1887.

At Ft Robinson, NE, 1889. *See* **JOHNSON**, Charles W., Private, F/9th Cavalry

Appointed corporal, 8 Jun 1893. SOURCE: Roster, 9 Cav.

PRATER, Jacob P.; Private; B/9th Cav. At Ft Robinson, NE, Dec 1892–3 Jan 1893 awaiting transportation to his proper station.

PRATHER, John; Private; H/9th Cav. Deposited $13 with paymaster, Ft Robinson, NE, 1898.

PRATHER, John; Private; B/10th Cav. Died at Ft Robinson, NE, 22 May 1905, at age 29 with three years and nine months' service. SOURCE: Monthly Report, Chaplain Anderson, 1 Jun 1905.

PRATHER, W. H.; Private; 9th Cav. Poem regarding Pine Ridge campaign, 1891. SOURCE: Foner, *The United States Soldier*, 135.

PRATT, Charles; 24th Inf. Resided at 321 South 13th East, Salt Lake City, in 1898. SOURCE: Clark, "A History of the Twenty-fourth," appendix E.

PRATT, R. H.; Corporal; H/9th Cav. In hands of civil authorities, Buffalo, WY, 30 Aug–2 Nov 1886. SOURCE: Regt Returns, 9 Cav.

PRATT, Walter A.; Private; C/9th Cav. At Ft D. A. Russell, WY, in 1910; resident of Chester, SC. SOURCE: *Illustrated Review: Ninth Cavalry*, with picture.

Escaped military prisoner from Ft D. A. Russell, who shot lieutenant leading pursuers and went into hiding in Cheyenne, WY. SOURCE: Cheyenne *State Leader*, 20 Jul 1910.

PRAYER, James J.; Private; 24th Inf. Near death; "a true and faithful soldier and loved by all his soldier brothers." SOURCE: Richmond *Planet*, 14 Apr 1900.

PREAR, Wilson; Sergeant; D/24th Inf. At Cabanatuan, Philippines, 1900–1901. *See* **BUFORD**, James J., Private, D/24th Infantry; **FAGGINS**, John H., Private, K/24th Infantry; **JOHNSON**, Otto, Private, D/24th Infantry; **MOORE**, Simon, Private, D/24th Infantry; **TATES**, Rollins, Private, D/24th Infantry

Acquitted of disobeying order of battalion sergeant major, Cabanatuan, 4 Dec 1900; witness: 1st Sgt. M. H. Ellis, D/24th Infantry. SOURCE: Name File, 24 Inf.

Fined for failure to repair for guard duty, Cabanatuan, 11 Apr 1901. SOURCE: Name File, 24 Inf.

PREDUM, Albert P.; Private; D/9th Cav. Deserted at Monterey, CA, 13 Jan 1903. SOURCE: Regt Returns, 9 Cav, Jan 1903.

PRENDERGAST, Julian; Private; H/10th Cav. Commander, H/10th Cavalry asks discharge of Prendergast, also known as Billings, "as a worthless character," 24 Nov 1876. SOURCE: ES, 10 Cav, 1873–83.

PRESSLEY, William; Private; A/9th Cav. At Ft D. A. Russell, WY, in 1910. SOURCE: *Illustrated Review: Ninth Cavalry*, with picture.

PRESTON, Benjamin N.; Sqdn Sgt Maj; 10th Cav. Commissioned second lieutenant of cavalry, camp at Leon Springs, TX, 27 Sep 1918. SOURCE: Glass, *History of the Tenth Cavalry*, appendix M.

PRESTON, Charles R.; Private; K/24th Inf. Enlisted Camp Tampa, FL, 6 May 1898. SOURCE: Muster Roll, H/24 Inf, May–Jun 1898.

Sick in hospital, Siboney, Cuba, 22–25 Aug 1898, and en route to U.S., 25–31 Aug 1898; disease contracted in line of duty. SOURCE: Muster Roll, H/24 Inf, Jul–Aug 1898.

Transferred to K/24th Infantry, 16 Sep 1898; due U.S. for clothing $11.42. SOURCE: Muster Roll, H/24 Inf, Sep–Oct 1898.

PRESTON, Emmet; Corporal; E/10th Cav. Served in 10th Cavalry in Cuba, 1898. SOURCE: Cashin, *Under Fire with the Tenth Cavalry*, 342.

PRESTON, Lee; Private; B/9th Cav. At Ft D. A. Russell, WY, in 1910. SOURCE: *Illustrated Review: Ninth Cavalry*, with picture.

PRESTON, Lloyd; Corporal; B/10th Cav. Served in 10th Cavalry in Cuba, 1898. SOURCE: Cashin, *Under Fire with the Tenth Cavalry*, 337-38.

PRESTON, W.; Corporal; D/9th Cav. With detachment scouting Utah Territory from Ft Lewis, CO, Sep–Oct 1883. SOURCE: Regt Returns, 9 Cav.

PRESTON, William; Corporal; A/24th Inf. Distinguished marksman with rifle as corporal, H/24th Infantry, 1885, and as private, C/24th Infantry, 1892 and 1893. SOURCE: GO 82, AGO, 24 Oct 1893.

Corporal, H/24th Infantry, at Ft Supply, Indian Territory; sharpshooter. SOURCE: *ANJ* 24 (21 Aug 1886): 70.

Private, C/24th Infantry, at Ft Huachuca, AZ; designated to participate in Department of Arizona rifle meet. SOURCE: Order 119, Ft Huachuca, 10 Aug 1893, Letters and Orders Received, 24 Inf, 1893.

Corporal, A/24th Infantry, mortally wounded at Lupao, Philippines, 3 Jul 1900; died later same day at Huningan. SOURCE: *ANJ* 38 (1 Sep 1900): 19; Muller, *The Twenty Fourth Infantry*, 19.

PRESTON, Willis; Sergeant; E/24th Inf. At Ft D. A. Russell, WY; accidentally shot and killed, Cheyenne, WY, 13 Jan 1899.

PRETTY, Augustus; Corporal; M/10th Cav. Original member of 10th Cavalry; in troop when organized, Ft Riley, KS, 15 Oct 1867. SOURCE: McMiller, "Buffalo Soldiers," 79.

Mentioned Oct 1870. SOURCE: ES, 10 Cav, 1866–71.

PREYER, William; Private; L/10th Cav. Served in 10th Cavalry, 1898; remained in U.S. during war with Spain. SOURCE: Cashin, *Under Fire with the Tenth Cavalry*, 350.

PRICE; Private; G/10th Cav. At Ft Apache, AZ, 1890, subscribed $.50 to testimonial to General Grierson. SOURCE: List of subscriptions, 23 Apr 1890, 10th Cavalry papers, MHI.

PRICE, A. W.; Private; B/9th Cav. Sick at Ft Bayard, NM. SOURCE: Regt Returns, 9 Cav, Jan 1881.

Discharged from Ft Bayard, 16 Feb 1881, in accordance with General Court Martial Order 15, Department of the Missouri. SOURCE: Regt Returns, 9 Cav, Feb 1881.

PRICE, Charles; Private; I/9th Cav. Deserted from San Francisco, 9 Nov 1902. SOURCE: Regt Returns, 9 Cav, Nov 1902.

PRICE, Charles E.; 9th Cav. Resides in Crawford, NE, age 57, engaged in real estate business; met Henry McClain at Ft Robinson, NE, in 1893 and has known him ever since. SOURCE: Affidavit, Price, 26 May 1921, VA File XC 2705872, Henry McClain.

Well known, considered reliable locally, wealthy, "has some influence in the community . . . a large real estate owner." SOURCE: Report, Special Investigator C. R. Franks, 28 May 1921, VA File XC 2705872, Henry McClain.

Personal property appraised at $30 and taxed at $3 in 1907, appraised at $194 and taxed at $15 in 1912, and appraised at $228 and taxed at $25 in 1917. SOURCE: Dawes County tax records.

"The local vice king and something of a legend." SOURCE: Schubert, *Buffalo Soldiers, Braves, and the Brass*, 154.

No Veterans Administration pension file.

PRICE, Edward; Private; F/24th Inf. Enlisted in H/24th Infantry, Ft McPherson, GA, 3 Jun 1896. SOURCE: Muster Roll, H/24 Inf, May–Jun 1898.

Absent sick, disease contracted in line of duty, since 14 Sep 1898. SOURCE: Muster Roll, H/24 Inf, Sep–Oct 1898.

On furlough 8 Oct–6 Dec 1898; sick in hospital, Ft McPherson, 6–16 Dec 1898; absent sick until 22 Dec 1898; rejoined company, 22 Dec 1898; sick in quarters since 30 Dec 1898. SOURCE: Muster Roll, H/24 Inf, Nov–Dec 1898.

On special duty as assistant company clerk since 30 Jan 1899. SOURCE: Muster Roll, H/24 Inf, Jan–Feb 1899.

Died of dysentery in the Philippines, 4 Mar 1901. SOURCE: *ANJ* 38 (16 Mar 1901): 703.

PRICE, George; Private; E/10th Cav. Served in 10th Cavalry, 1898; remained in U.S. during war with Spain. SOURCE: Cashin, *Under Fire with the Tenth Cavalry*, 343.

PRICE, Henry; Private; K/9th Cav. Apprehended, following desertion, at Indianapolis, 13 Jan 1881. SOURCE: Regt Returns, 9 Cav, Jan 1881.

Convicted by general court martial, Columbus Barracks, OH, of desertion, 6 Aug 1879–12 Jan 1881; sentenced to dishonorable discharge and two years. SOURCE: GCMO 13, AGO, 17 Feb 1881.

PRICE, Henry; Saddler; D/9th Cav. At Ft D. A. Russell, WY, in 1910; resident of Franklin, TN. SOURCE: *Illustrated Review: Ninth Cavalry*, with picture.

PRICE, James; Artificer; G/24th Inf. Wounded in action in Cuba, 1898. SOURCE: Clark, "A History of the Twenty-fourth," 100; Muller, *The Twenty Fourth Infantry*, 19.

PRICE, James; E/10th Cav. Died of consumption, age 28, at U.S. Soldiers Home, 8 Jun 1901. SOURCE: SecWar, *AR 1901*, 1:489.

PRICE, James; Corporal; B/9th Cav. Retired Aug 1901. SOURCE: *ANJ* 38 (10 Aug 1901): 1211.

PRICE, James; C/49th Inf. Released from confinement at Leavenworth, KS, in accordance with Supreme Court decision in Deming case, 19 May 1902. SOURCE: *ANJ* 39 (7 Jun 1902): 1005.

PRICE, John D.; Sergeant; H/10th Cav. Original member of 10th Cavalry; in troop when organized, Ft Leavenworth, KS, 21 Jul 1867. SOURCE: McMiller, "Buffalo Soldiers," 75.

Commander, H/10th Cavalry, camp near Ft Wallace, KS, asks that Price be detailed to duty with commissary department, 9 Jun 1869. SOURCE: LR, Det 10 Cav, 1868–69.

PRICE, John M.; Sergeant; K/9th Cav. Recruit from depot, arrived at Ft Robinson, NE, 1 Mar 1887.

Ranked number five in revolver competition, Departments of Dakota and the Platte, Bellevue, NE, 4–9 Aug 1890. SOURCE: GO 112, AGO, 2 Oct 1890.

Appointed sergeant 11 Dec 1891. SOURCE: Roster, 9 Cav.

Ranked number five in carbine competition and number five in revolver competition, Departments of the East, the Platte, and California, Bellevue, 15–20 Aug 1892; ranked number seven in Army carbine team competition, 1892; distinguished marksman, revolver, 1890, and revolver and carbine, 1892. SOURCE: GO 75, AGO, 3 Nov 1892.

On Department of the Platte rifle and carbine team, 1892. SOURCE: *ANJ* 30 (27 Aug 1892): 5.

Ordered from station at Ft Myer, VA, to Bellevue Rifle Range, to enter cavalry competition as distinguished marksman. SOURCE: *ANJ* 30 (12 Aug 1893): 843.

PRICE, Joseph; Private; G/9th Cav. On daily duty at post garden, Ft Robinson, NE. SOURCE: Order 48, 10 Mar 1890, Post Orders, Ft Robinson.

At Ft Robinson, 1892.

Continues on special duty as post lamplighter, Ft Robinson. SOURCE: Special Order 85, 6 Aug 1896, Post Orders, Ft Robinson.

PRICE, L. B.; Corporal; E/24th Inf. Wounded in foot at Deposito, Philippines, summer 1899. SOURCE: *ANJ* 36 (19 Aug 1899): 1223; Richmond *Planet*, 19 Aug 1899.

PRICE, Robert; Private; M/10th Cav. Served in 10th Cavalry, 1898; remained in U.S. during war with Spain. SOURCE: Cashin, *Under Fire with the Tenth Cavalry*, 352.

PRIDE, Alfred; Private; K/9th Cav. Born and reared at Amelia Court House, VA, near Richmond; occupation laborer; ran away from home at age 16; enlisted Washington, DC, 1865; appointed sergeant, Ft Robinson, NE, K/9th Cavalry, 1 Jul 1888; married Matilda Hawkins of Washington, age 32, in Washington, 5 May 1898; first marriage for both; resided in Washington thirty years. SOURCE: VA File WC 10020, Alfred Pride.

Private, B/10th Cavalry, transferred to Ft Sill, Indian Territory. SOURCE: Special Order 57, HQ, Det 10 Cav, Camp Supply, Indian Territory, 10 Aug 1869.

Sergeant, K/9th Cavalry, and sergeant of guard, Ft Robinson, when he allowed prisoner to escape and was reduced to private and fined $20: "But for his long service and good character the sentence would have been more severe." SOURCE: *ANJ* 28 (8 Nov 1890): 120.

Retires as private, K/9th Cavalry. SOURCE: SO 70, AGO, 25 Mar 1898.

Widow Matilda Pride received $12 per month pension as of 4 Mar 1917; resided at 2600 I Street, NW, Washington, when she died 20 Mar 1928, with a pension of $30 per month; late husband served in B/10th Cavalry, F/24th Infantry, 1878-83, and K/9th Cavalry, 1883-98; he died of apoplexy in Washington, 2 Aug 1910; buried Arlington Cemetery, 5 Aug 1910. SOURCE: VA File WC 10020, Alfred Pride.

Survived by brother George Allen Pride, messenger, Department of the Treasury, 1237 22nd Street, NW, Washington; also brother John Henry Pride, blacksmith, Amelia Court House; brother Moses, laborer, 1411 Massachusetts Avenue, NW, Washington; sister Marcella, wife of laborer Charles Helm, U.S. Navy Yard, Washington; sister Mary Ann, wife of farmer Eugene Morton, Rumney, NH. SOURCE: VA File WC 10020, Alfred Pride.

PRIDE, Wheeler; Private; D/24th Inf. Fined $2, Cabanatuan, Philippines, 13 Dec 1900, for entering home of Ymiela Cuevas, resident of Cabanatuan, and assaulting her by striking her with a yard stick. SOURCE: Name File, 24 Inf.

Fined $5, Cabanatuan, 16 Jan 1901, for failure to obey lawful order of Cpl. Squire Williams, D/24th Infantry, to go to quarters, after having been sent there by doctor; witnesses: Corporal Williams; Pvt. James H. Young, D/24th Infantry. SOURCE: Name File, 24 Inf.

Fined $10 and confined for twenty days, Cabanatuan, 17 Feb 1901, for being drunk and disorderly in quarters,

disobeying Cpl. Thomas Johnson's order to be still: he "didn't give a damn for thirty days in the guard house. Nothing would hurt me but Bilibid"; witnesses: Sgt. Pat Keys, D/24th Infantry; Corporal Johnson; Cpl. Walter B. Jackson.

See **BROWN**, Philip, Private, D/24th Infantry; **JACKSON**, Frank, Private, B/24th Infantry

PRIESTLY, Joseph A.; Private; L/10th Cav. Served in 10th Cavalry, 1898; remained in U.S. during war with Spain. SOURCE: Cashin, *Under Fire with the Tenth Cavalry*, 350.

PRIM, John; Private; B/10th Cav. Served in 10th Cavalry in Cuba, 1898; wounded in action. SOURCE: Cashin, *Under Fire With the Tenth Cavalry*, 338–39.

PRINCE; Private; B/10th Cav. At Ft Apache, AZ, 1890, subscribed $.50 to testimonial to General Grierson. SOURCE: List of subscriptions, 23 Apr 1890, 10th Cavalry papers, MHI.

PRINCE, George; Private; M/10th Cav. Served in 10th Cavalry, 1898; remained in U.S. during war with Spain. SOURCE: Cashin, *Under Fire with the Tenth Cavalry*, 352.

PRINCE, Noah; Private; H/9th Cav. Born Manhattan, KS; Ht 5'6 1/2"; served in C/9th Cavalry, 1891–96; joined H/9th Cavalry, Ft Robinson, NE, age 26, 17 Oct 1896; fined $3 by summary court, Ft Robinson, 7 May 1897; fined $4 and jailed for eight days by summary court martial, Ft Robinson, 2 Jul 1897; wounded in action, Santiago, Cuba, 1 Jul 1898; died of wounds, 1st Division Hospital, Siboney, Cuba, 8 Jul 1898. SOURCE: Descriptive Book, H/9 Cav.

Wounded in action at San Juan, Cuba, 2 Jul 1898. SOURCE: SecWar, *AR 1898*, 707.

PRIOLEAU, George W.; Chaplain; U.S. Army. Born Charleston, SC; educated at Claflin College; taught in public schools; graduated from Wilberforce University in 1884; entered Army as captain, 9th Cavalry, 1895; transferred to 10th Cavalry, 1915; transferred to 25th Infantry, 1916; promoted to major, 9 Aug 1917. SOURCE: *Crisis* 16 (May 1918): 15.

Born a slave in Charleston, 15 May 1856; now on second tour of duty in Philippines, Camp McGrath, Batangas. SOURCE: *Colored American Magazine* 16 (Apr 1909): 224.

Parents L. S. and Susan Prioleau, slaves; educated in public schools of Charleston and Avery Institute; attended Claflin College, Orangeburg, SC, 1875; taught primary public school, Lyons township, Orangeburg Co., SC; joined African Methodist Episcopal Church, of which father was pastor, St Mathews, SC; joined Columbia, SC, conference, Dec 1879; sent to Wilberforce, Dec 1880; retired as oldest ranking chaplain in Army. SOURCE: Beasley, *Negro Trailblazers*, 292–93.

Taught in public schools, Selma, OH, Sep 1884–Sep 1885; pastor, Hamilton, OH, 1885, and Troy, OH, 1887;

organized William H. Carney Lodge, No. 89, Grand Union of Odd Fellows; doctor of divinity, Payne Theological Seminary, 1895, which he disclaimed before preaching baccalaureate sermon at Wilberforce, 1910, due to his high conception of meaning of degree and prevailing abuse of it. SOURCE: Wright, *Centennial Encyclopedia of the AME Church*, 181.

Under administration of President B. F. Lee, Wilberforce University graduated a "brilliant galaxy of cultured young men and women," including Prioleau, now chaplain of 9th Cavalry. SOURCE: Richings, *Evidences of Progress Among Colored People*, 107.

"Among the many [Wilberforce graduates] who have reached eminence." SOURCE: Hartshorne, *An Era of Progress and Promise*, 281.

Troy minister, just returned from "very pleasant" visit to Indianapolis. SOURCE: Cleveland *Gazette*, 2 Jun 1888.

Wife Anna L. Scovell, B.S., Wilberforce, 1885; earned diploma from Wilberforce Normal Department, 1890. SOURCE: Cleveland *Gazette*, 28 Jun 1890.

Professor of Theology and Homiletics, Wilberforce; taught historical and pastoral theology in Payne Theological Seminary, formerly Theology Department, Wilberforce, 1890–94; resigned to take chaplaincy. SOURCE: McGinnis, *A History and an Interpretation of Wilberforce University*, 143–44.

In Wilberforce, OH, after extended tour of the South. SOURCE: Cleveland *Gazette*, 16 Dec 1892.

Preached sermon from Judges, Chapter 14, Verse 14, at Congregational Church, Crawford, NE, Sunday, 24 Jan 1897, "most ably and eloquently." SOURCE: Crawford *Tribune*, 29 Jan 1897.

Letter from Ft Robinson, NE, 8 Feb 1897, states pay and benefits. SOURCE: Cleveland *Gazette*, 20 Feb 1897.

Authorized one and one-half month's leave from Ft Robinson as of 15 Jul 1897. SOURCE: *ANJ* 34 (10 Jul 1897): 838.

Author of "Is the Chaplain's Work in the Army a Necessity?" in Steward, *Active Service*. SOURCE: Indianapolis *Freeman*, 11 Sep 1897.

Letter from Ft Robinson describes military routine and opportunities for black men. SOURCE: Cleveland *Gazette*, 5 Mar 1898.

Letters from Tampa, FL, 13 May 1898, regarding racism there; from Montauk, NY, Sep 1898; from Ft Grant, AZ, Oct 1898, on spread of Negrophobia. SOURCE: Gatewood, *"Smoked Yankees"*, 27–29, 74–75, 82–84.

Bed-ridden with malaria and remained in Tampa when 9th Cavalry went to Cuba (SOURCE: SO 55, 9 Cav, 13 May 1898); on regimental recruiting duty, Orangeburg (SOURCE: SO 14, 9 Cav, 14 May 1898). SOURCE: Cashin, *Under Fire with the Tenth Cavalry*, 110.

Relieved of regimental recruiting duty, Charleston, and directed to join portion of regiment in Florida. SOURCE: *ANJ* 35 (6 Aug 1898): 1009.

Letter from Ft Grant, AZ, Nov 1898, praises *Gazette*'s consistent stand against "lynching and mobocracy." SOURCE: Cleveland *Gazette*, 26 Nov 1898.

On leave in New Orleans: "We glory in the prestige won by our regiments." SOURCE: *ANJ* 36 (29 Jul 1899): 1138

Letter from New Orleans, no date: went there on leave from Ft Grant; at El Paso, TX, forced onto Jim Crow car with "greasy Mexicans"; Southern Pacific Railroad yielded to his demand to travel without such company and hitched a separate car on the train for him. SOURCE: Cleveland *Gazette*, 19 Aug 1899.

Letter, New Orleans, no date: regarding subjugation of black Americans, wrote: "Strange that the American people fail to learn the lesson of their own independence." SOURCE: Cleveland *Gazette*, 26 Aug 1899.

Letter, dated "Jim Crow Car, Texas," 25 Aug 1899: wife not well enough to leave New Orleans; has railroad car all to himself on return to Ft Grant; breakfasted with whites in Alpine, TX, this morning. SOURCE: Cleveland *Gazette*, 9 Sep 1899.

Letter, Ft Grant, 21 May 1900, informs of new law authorizing thirty dentists for regular Army, at least four of whom should be black; War Department should know "we are up again for recognition in the Army." SOURCE: Cleveland *Gazette*, 2 Jun 1900.

As of 31 Dec 1900 on duty with regiment, Nueva Caceres, Philippines. SOURCE: Hamilton, "History of the Ninth Cavalry," 100.

En route home to New Orleans from Philippines, writes that "there is greater pacification among the Filipinos where our troops are stationed and that the natives will fight most fiercely white troops but will welcome our troops without resistance." SOURCE: Cleveland *Gazette*, 12 Apr 1902.

First wife, Annie L. Prioleau, race mixed, born in New Orleans to Noah Scovell and Lucy A. Flowers, 18 Dec 1862, occupation teacher, died of uremia, 26 Feb 1903. SOURCE: VA File C 1392575, George W. Prioleau.

Wife died at Ft Walla Walla, WA, 26 Feb 1903; to be buried at New Orleans. SOURCE: Cleveland *Gazette*, 21 Mar 1903.

Aaron R. Prioleau, defrauded out of Congressional seat, 1st District, South Carolina, by George S. Legare; "though a Negro, is the rightful claimant." SOURCE: Indianapolis *Freeman*, 20 Feb 1904.

Aaron R. Prioleau is related to Chaplain Prioleau and "a successful farmer, merchant, & miller." SOURCE: Indianapolis *Freeman*, 12 Aug 1905.

Married Miss Ethel Stafford of Kansas City, KS, 20 Feb 1905; three children; first wife died 27 Feb 1902 [*sic*]; thirty-third degree Mason and member of Odd Fellows and Knights of Pythias; owns "an elegant modern home" at Raymond and West 35th Place, Los Angeles, where he will reside, and other valuable properties. SOURCE: Beasley, *Negro Trailblazers*, 293.

To conduct service, Cheyenne, WY, African Methodist Episcopal Church, Sunday, 15 Aug 1909. SOURCE: Cheyenne *Daily Leader*, 15 Aug 1909.

Veteran of Philippine Insurrection; at Ft D. A. Russell, WY, in 1910; sharpshooter. SOURCE: *Illustrated Review: Ninth Cavalry*, with picture.

Mentioned. SOURCE: Work, *Negro Year Book, 1912,* 77, and *Negro Yearbook, 1918–1919,* 228.

To be transferred from 10th Cavalry to 25th Infantry and stationed in Hawaii. SOURCE: Cleveland *Gazette,* 10 Jun 1916.

Promoted to major as of 9 Aug 1917; reports that 25th Infantry has collected $3,200 for National Association for the Advancement of Colored People, $325 of that amount for refugees from East St. Louis, IL. SOURCE: Cleveland *Gazette,* 6 Oct 1917.

Retired chaplain, resides in Los Angeles. SOURCE: Work, *The Negro Yearbook, 1925–1926,* 253.

Organized Bethel African Methodist Episcopal Church, Los Angeles. SOURCE: *Encyclopedia of African Methodism,* 175.

Daughter Ethel Suzanna born 21 Jun 1914; son George Wesley born 18 Mar 1917, Kapiolani Maternity Home, Honolulu, HI; daughter Lois Emma born 18 Jun 1924, Los Angeles; retired as major on 15 May 1920 with continuous service since 29 Apr 1895; resided at 1311 West 35th Street, Los Angeles, when died in Jul 1927; on death, widow received $8,018 in U.S. Government Life Insurance; widow's pension $22.50 per month in 1934, with $4.50 additional for one minor child. SOURCE: VA File C 1392575, George W. Prioleau.

Biographical sketch. SOURCE: Logan and Winston, eds., *Dictionary of American Negro Biography,* 13–14; Stover, *Up from Handymen,* 53–57.

PRIOR; Private; E/10th Cav. At Ft Apache, AZ, 1890, subscribed $.50 to testimonial to General Grierson. SOURCE: List of subscriptions, 23 Apr 1890, 10th Cavalry papers, MHI.

PRITCHARD, William D.; 1st Lt; 49th Inf. One of twenty-three officers of 49th Infantry recommended as regular Army second lieutenants. SOURCE: CG, DivPI, Manila, 8 Feb 1901, to AGO, AGO File 355163.

PROCTOR, Alexander; Private; I/9th Cav. Discharged on certificate of disability with syphilis, Ft Robinson, NE, 1887. SOURCE: Certificates of Disability, Ft Robinson.

PROCTOR, Clarence L.; Sergeant; L/10th Cav. Born in Virginia; private, F/10th Cavalry, 10 Dec 1886–11 Dec 1891; in G/10th Cavalry, 12 Dec 1891; corporal, 15 Dec 1895; sergeant, 26 Dec 1895; at Ft Assiniboine, MT, 1897. SOURCE: Baker, Roster.

Sergeant, G/10th Cavalry, reduced to ranks. SOURCE: *ANJ* 35 (20 Nov 1897): 212.

To be tried by general court martial for manslaughter, Ft Assiniboine. SOURCE: *ANJ* 35 (25 Dec 1897): 310–11.

Served as sergeant, L/10th Cavalry, 1898; remained in U.S. during war with Spain. SOURCE: Cashin, *Under Fire with the Tenth Cavalry,* 350.

Killed himself, Phoenix, AZ, 28 Mar 1900, while in last stage of consumption; thirteen-year veteran; contracted consumption in Cuba and discharged for disability one year ago. SOURCE: San Francisco *Chronicle,* 29 Mar 1900.

PROCTOR, John C.; Color Sgt; 9th Cav. Born Prince Georges Co., MD; occupation laborer, yellow complexion; enlisted in L/10th Cavalry, age 21, 6 Dec 1881; reenlisted 13 Dec 1886; transferred to A/10th Cavalry, 15 Feb 1891; reenlisted as sergeant, I/9th Cavalry, 17 Dec 1891; reenlisted 17 Dec 1896; discharged as first sergeant, I/9th Cavalry, 19 Jul 1898; first lieutenant, 8th Volunteer Infantry, 4 Aug 1898–6 Mar 1899; enlisted as corporal, I/9th Cavalry, 14 Jun 1899; enlisted as first sergeant, E/24th Infantry, 16 Jun 1902; reenlisted as sergeant, C/9th Cavalry, 17 Jun 1905; reenlisted 18 Feb 1907; appointed color sergeant, 9th Cavalry, 14 Jun 1908; retired 17 Sep 1908; resided at 113 Howard Avenue, Anacostia, Washington, DC; died 24 Jun 1917. SOURCE: VA File XC 2659372, John C. Proctor.

Appointed sergeant, I/9th Cavalry, 13 Oct 1892. SOURCE: Roster, 9 Cav.

Resides with wife, one white adopted child, and Ella Johnson, on laundress row, Ft Robinson, NE, Aug 1893. SOURCE: Medical History, Ft Robinson.

Ranked number four in revolver competition, Departments of the East, the Platte, and California, Bellevue, NE, as sergeant, I/9th Cavalry. SOURCE: GO 82, AGO, 24 Oct 1893.

Mrs. Proctor "has been a trouble to the commanding officer" on several occasions; this time hid a woman of bad character in her quarters. SOURCE: CO, Ft Robinson, to CO, I/9, Ft Robinson, 23 Dec 1894, LS, Ft Robinson.

First sergeant, I/9th Cavalry, at Ft Robinson, for cavalry competition, Sep 1897.

First sergeant, A/9th Cavalry, commissioned first lieutenant, 8th Volunteer Infantry, after Spanish-American War. SOURCE: Cashin, *Under Fire with the Tenth Cavalry,* 360, with picture, 356.

Commissioned for gallantry and meritorious service around Santiago, Cuba, 1–2 Jul 1898. SOURCE: Thweatt, *What the Newspapers Say,* 9; Richmond *Planet,* 13 Aug 1898; Johnson, *History of Negro Soldiers,* 50.

Lieutenant, 8th Volunteer Infantry; had a white "hill billy" put in guardhouse for failure to salute, Chickamauga, TN. SOURCE: Indianapolis *Freeman,* 24 Dec 1898.

To report for duty as captain, F/49th Infantry, at Jefferson Barracks, MO. SOURCE: *ANJ* 37 (30 Sep 1899): 101.

Private, saddler, farrier, corporal, sergeant, L and A/10th Cavalry, 6 Dec 1881–12 Dec 1891; private, farrier, corporal, sergeant, and first sergeant, I/9th Cavalry; first lieutenant, 8th Volunteer Infantry, 29 Jul 1898–6 Mar 1899; private, sergeant, first sergeant, I/9th Cavalry, 14 Jun 1899–present, on furlough; captain, 49th Infantry, 9 Sep 1899. SOURCE: Descriptive Book, F/49 Inf.

One of twenty-three officers of 49th Infantry recommended as regular Army second lieutenants. SOURCE: CG, DivPI, Manila, 8 Feb 1901, to AGO, AGO File 355163.

Quartermaster sergeant, E/24th Infantry, ranked number one, Northern Division rifle team, Ft Sheridan, IL, 1904; awarded gold medal. SOURCE: GO 167, AGO, 28 Oct 1904.

Resided at 1019 North 21st Street, Omaha, NE, in 1904.

Louisa Proctor, age 59, resided at 2124 North 27th Avenue, Omaha, in 1920, was twice married to John Proctor: "I am not going to tell why I married him twice"; first married him, Crawford, NE, around 1900; last saw Proctor in Omaha, Dec 1909; divorced at Washington, DC, 1912; had no children; raised boy named Claude who died 15 Oct 1919; previously married at age 16 to Henry Chambers, F/24th Infantry, Ft Elliott, TX; resided together seven to eight years; he got divorce. SOURCE: Affidavit, Louisa Proctor, 28 May 1920, VA File XC 2659372, John C. Proctor.

Widow Martha E. Proctor born Oxon Hill, MD, 22 Aug 1878; parents Alexander Butler and Georgianna Locker; no previous marriages; resided at 1055 Sumner Road, Anacostia, Washington, DC, and worked as laborer in 1920; resided at 2603 12th Place, SE, Washington, DC, in 1957; pension increased from $40 to $48 per month, 19 Feb 1951; died 18 Jun 1957; survived by sister, Sarah Waters. SOURCE: VA File SC 2659372, John C. Proctor.

See **SMITH**, Jacob Clay, Sergeant, 10th Cavalry; **WATKINS**, James M., Quartermaster Sergeant, C/10th Cavalry

PROFFETT, Shannon; Private; I/25th Inf. Murdered by comrade in the Philippines, 22 Jul 1900. SOURCE: *ANJ* 37 (4 Aug 1900): 1166.

Killed with .45-caliber pistol by Pvt. John H. Smith, H/25th Infantry, San Felipe, Zambales, Philippines, 23 Jul 1900. SOURCE: Manila *Times*, 31 Jul 1900.

Native of Xenia, OH; shot and killed by Private Smith, H/25th Infantry; both "noted for reckless bravery and daring," got into gambling dispute. SOURCE: Richmond *Planet*, 20 Oct 1900.

PROPHET, Harry R.; Private; G/9th Cav. At Ft D. A. Russell, WY, in 1910; resident of Beloit, WI. SOURCE: *Illustrated Review: Ninth Cavalry*, with picture.

PROWL; Sergeant; C/9th Cav. With detachment engaged against insurgents near Tinambac, Philippines, 18 and 20 Mar 1901. SOURCE: Hamilton, "History of the Ninth Cavalry," 106; *Illustrated Review: Ninth Cavalry*.

PRYOR, Frank M.; Private; K/25th Inf. Sick in battalion hospital, Castillejos, Philippines, May 1900. SOURCE: Richmond *Planet*, 30 Jun 1900.

PRYOR, James; Private; 24th Inf. Drowned in the Philippines, 28 Feb 1900. SOURCE: *ANJ* 37 (10 Mar 1900): 659.

PRYOR, Lee; Private; I/10th Cav. Served in 10th Cavalry in Cuba, 1898. SOURCE: Cashin, *Under Fire with the Tenth Cavalry*, 348.

PUGH, Alvin; Pvt 1st Cl; 24th Inf. Served in Houston, 1917; tried unsuccessfully at court martial to establish alibi for being off post during riot; sentenced to two years. SOURCE: Haynes, *A Night of Violence*, 268, 271.

PUGH, Charles; Corporal; I/9th Cav. Resigned warrant as corporal, Ft Duchesne, UT, Mar 1896. SOURCE: *ANJ* 33 (28 Mar 1896): 541.

PULLEN, Frank W., Jr.; Sgt Maj; 25th Inf. Born Halifax Co., NC; Ht 6'1", dark brown complexion; enlisted in B/25th Infantry, 16 Oct 1890; transferred to noncommissioned staff, 25th Infantry, 24 Jul 1895; discharged, single, character excellent, 15 Oct 1895; reenlisted as regimental sergeant major, age 29, Ft Missoula, MT, 16 Oct 1895. SOURCE: Descriptive Cards, 25 Inf.

Appointed sergeant major from sergeant, B/25th Infantry, vice Johnson, retired, 22 Jun 1894. SOURCE: *ANJ* 31 (28 Jul 1894): 843.

Born Enfield, NC; provided narrative of 25th Infantry history from Ft Assiniboine, MT, to Cuba. SOURCE: Johnson, *History of Negro Soldiers*, 20–32, with picture.

"A splendid specimen of the soldier-man—tall, well-proportioned, and judging from his conversation and history, intelligent and well educated" said a former schoolteacher in North Carolina. SOURCE: Cleveland *Gazette*, 23 Apr 1898.

PULLIAM, Fealex B; Private; M/9th Cav. At Ft D. A. Russell, WY, in 1910; resident of Edmonton, KY. SOURCE: *Illustrated Review: Ninth Cavalry*, with picture.

PULLIAMS, Alfred; B/10th Cav. Original member of 10th Cavalry; in troop when organized, Ft Leavenworth, KS, 1 Apr 1867. SOURCE: McMiller, "Buffalo Soldiers," 69.

PULLUM, Marvin; Private; B/9th Cav. At Ft D. A. Russell, WY, in 1910. SOURCE: *Illustrated Review: Ninth Cavalry*.

PULPRESS, Walter T.; Private; F/9th Cav. Private, A/10th Cavalry, at Ft Apache, AZ, 1890, subscribed $.50 to testimonial to General Grierson. SOURCE: List of subscriptions, 23 Apr 1890, 10th Cavalry papers, MHI.

Private, F/9th Cavalry; teacher, Ft Robinson, NE, schools, 1 Nov 1892–30 Apr 1893, 15 Sep 1893–30 Apr 1894, 15 Sep 1894–30 Apr 1895. SOURCE: Reports of Schools, Ft Robinson.

Relieved from extra duty as schoolteacher, Ft Robinson children's school, at end of term. SOURCE: Order 54, 1 Jul 1893, Post Orders, Ft Robinson.

Teacher, Ft Robinson Sunday School, 1894. SOURCE: Investigation of Charges against Chaplain Plummer.

Private, Hospital Corps, asks transfer from Ft Robinson to Ft Grant, AZ, or other station of 9th Cavalry, "states that he is a colored man and would prefer to serve with colored troops." SOURCE: Pulpress to Post Surgeon, 5 Apr 1899, Register of Correspondence, Post Surgeon, Ft Robinson.

PUMPHREY, George W.; Sergeant; H/9th Cav. Recognized as deserter from B/9th Cavalry while serving with K/9th Cavalry, Ft Robinson, NE, as George Hunter and confined, Jan 1886. SOURCE: Post Returns, Ft Robinson.

Restored to duty in accordance with General Court Martial Order 7, Department of the Platte, 22 Jan 1886.

Transferred to K/9th Cavalry by Special Order 102, Adjutant General's Office, 1 May 1886.

Complains that his captain curses and abuses the men and that they are poorly fed, seldom having more than coffee and bread for supper. SOURCE: Report of Inspection, Ft Robinson, 2 Aug 1888, Reports of Inspections, DP, I.

Private, H/9th Cavalry; authorized to reenlist as married soldier by letter, Adjutant General's Office, 16 Feb 1897.

Deposited with paymaster, Ft Robinson, $167 in 1897 and $40 in 1898.

Cited for gallantry in action, Cuba, 1 Jul 1898. SOURCE: SecWar, *AR 1898*, 708

Awarded certificate of merit for gallantry as corporal, H/9th Cavalry, 1 Jul 1898. SOURCE: GO 16, AGO, 13 Feb 1900; *ANJ* 37 (24 Feb 1900): 611; Steward, *The Colored Regulars*, 280.

Born Anne Arundel Co., MD; awarded distinguished service medal for gallantry, Santiago, Cuba, 1 Jul 1898. SOURCE: Koger, *The Maryland Negro in Our Wars*, 23.

PUMPHREY, J. H.; Lance Cpl; K/9th Cav. Saddler, B/10th Cavalry, at Ft Apache, AZ, 1890, subscribed $.50 to testimonial to General Grierson. SOURCE: List of subscriptions, 23 Apr 1890, 10th Cavalry papers, MHI.

Promoted from private, Ft Robinson, NE, Feb 1895. SOURCE: *ANJ* 32 (9 Mar 1895): 454.

PURDY; Private; C/10th Cav. Absent without leave from Ft Robinson, NE, in Crawford, NE, 25 Dec 1903; shot in right arm while on sick report. SOURCE: Post Surgeon to CO, 26 Dec 1903, Register of LR, Ft Robinson.

Commander, 10th Cavalry, directs commander, C/10th Cavalry, to prefer charges against Purdy. SOURCE: Endorsement, 28 Dec 1903, on Post Surgeon to CO, Ft Robinson, 26 Dec 1903, Register of LR, Ft Robinson.

PURKINS, Louis; Private; H/9th Cav. Born Alexandria, VA; enlisted in H/9th Cavalry, Ht 5'6", age 27, in camp near Mary's Vale Post Office, WY, 13 Aug 1897; five years' previous service in H/9th Cavalry; discharged from Ft Robinson, NE, on surgeon's certificate, totally blind, single, character very good, 19 Nov 1897; $100 deposits, $20.01 clothing, $7.10 retained. SOURCE: Descriptive Book, H/9 Cav.

PURNELL, George; Private; M/9th Cav. At Ft D. A. Russell, WY, in 1910. SOURCE: *Illustrated Review: Ninth Cavalry*, with picture.

PURNELL, William Whipple; Captain; 48th Inf. Born Philadelphia, 25 Jan 1869; son of James W. and Julia A. Purnell; attended Howard University Normal and Preparatory Departments, 1880–85; graduated from pharmacy school, Howard University, 1890, and medical school, Howard University, 1893; assistant instructor, eyes, ears, nose, and throat, Howard University, 1893–98; first lieutenant and assistant surgeon, 8th Volunteer Infantry, and captain, surgeon, 48th Infantry; a leading Negro physician of San Francisco area with "a rapidly growing practice among Italians, Spanish and members of his own race"; married Miss Theodora Lee of Chicago, granddaughter of late John Jones, 1895; son Lee Julian educated at Berkeley, CA, high school and University of California, will graduate as electrical engineer, 1914; member of Oakland Chamber of Commerce; an organizer of Elks Lodge, director of Knights of Pythias, member of Foresters and Masons; wife an organizer of Florence Nightingale Auxiliary, Oakland Red Cross, "devoted member" of St Augustin Mission of Episcopal Church and on Old Folks Home executive board. SOURCE: Beasley, *Negro Trailblazers*, 300.

Resident of Omaha, NE. SOURCE: Indianapolis *Freeman*, 30 Sep 1899.

Mentioned in San Francisco *Chronicle*, 15 Nov 1899.

PYE, Lewis; Corporal; I/9th Cav. Appointed corporal 1 Sep 1891. SOURCE: Roster, 9 Cav.

Q

QUANDER, James A.; Sergeant; C/24th Inf. Died of bichloride of mercury poisoning in the Philippines, 4 Jan 1902. SOURCE: *ANJ* 39 (1 Mar 1902): 645.

QUANDER, Richard I.; Private; H/24th Inf. Fined $2 by summary court, San Isidro, Philippines, for going on sentinel duty with blouse unbuttoned, 11 Jan 1902, second conviction. SOURCE: Register of Summary Court, San Isidro.

QUARLES, Ennis; Private; I/25th Inf. Sent to Manila, Philippines, Jan 1900, temporarily insane, due to mule kick received while at Ft Logan, CO. SOURCE: Richmond *Planet*, 17 Mar 1900.

QUARLES, James T.; Private; L/25th Inf. Wounded in ankle, Camanzi, Philippines, 3 Jan 1900. SOURCE: *ANJ* 37 (20 Jan 1900): 499.

Born Richmond, VA; reared in Boston; wounded in both feet in ambush near Mount Ararat, Philippines, early Jan 1900; recovering well. SOURCE: Richmond *Planet*, 17 Feb 1900.

QUARLES, John; Private; G/24th Inf. Missing in action, Talavero, Philippines, 28 Dec 1899. SOURCE: Muller, *The Twenty Fourth Infantry*, 36.

QUARLES, William M.; Private; D/9th Cav. At Ft D. A. Russell, WY, in 1910; resident of Oak Grove, KY. SOURCE: *Illustrated Review: Ninth Cavalry*, with picture.

QUEEN, Edgar; Private; H/9th Cav. Born Prince William Co., VA; Ht 5'7"; enlisted Washington, DC, age 26, 28 Jul 1892; five years' previous service in K/9th Cavalry; joined H/9th Cavalry, Ft Duchesne, UT, 10 Oct 1892; deserted from Ft Robinson, NE, 30 Dec 1894; surrendered Omaha, NE, 5 Mar 1895; sentenced by general court martial to six months' confinement and loss of pay; fined twice by summary courts, Ft Robinson, 1896; discharged without character, end of term, single, Ft Robinson, NE, 2 Oct 1897. SOURCE: Descriptive Book, H/9 Cav.

Letter, Department of the Platte, 25 Mar 1895, concerns charges against Queen.

Returned to duty at Ft Robinson from furlough, 24 Sep 1898.

QUEEN, Emanuel; Private; F/24th Inf. Transferred from Reserve Divisional Hospital, Siboney, Cuba, to U.S. on U.S. Army Transport *Vigilancia* with remittent malarial fever, 6 Sep 1898. SOURCE: Hospital Papers, Spanish-American War.

QUEEN, Howard D.; Sergeant; K/10th Cav. Enlisted Ft Ethan Allen, VT, 13 Apr 1911; captain, 14 Oct 1917; served with 368th Infantry, World War I, in battles at Vosges Mountains, Meuse-Argonne, Metz; served in World War II as colonel, 366th Infantry, in Africa, Sicily, Italy; attached to 15th Air Force, Apr–Nov 1944, guarding bases in Italy, Corsica, Sardinia; attached to Fifth Army Nov 1944–Feb 1945, in Rome-Arno campaign; retired as colonel, 30 Nov 1953 with over thirty-six years' service; bachelor of science in electrical engineering from Howard University, 1925; head, mathematics department, Downington (PA) Industrial and Agricultural School, 1953–54; resources examiner, Revenue Department, State of Pennsylvania, as of 1965. SOURCE: Wharfield, *10th Cavalry and Border Fights*, 39.

On Carrizal, Mexico, expedition 1916; en route to Villa Ahumade, "our orders were that the troops would move into the town in a column of twos at the gallop, and if fired upon we would use our pistols, the men on the right firing to the right and the men on the left firing to the left"; retired as colonel, U.S. Army Reserve. SOURCE: Clendenen, *Blood on the Border*, 305.

Sergeant, K/10th Cavalry, commissioned captain at Camp Des Moines, IA, 15 Oct 1917. SOURCE: Glass, *History of the Tenth Cavalry*, appendix M.

See **HOUSTON**, Henry C., Corporal, K/10th Cavalry

QUEEN, John; Private; H/24th Inf. Enlisted Ft Douglas, UT, 15 Feb 1896, with fourteen years' continuous service. SOURCE: Muster Roll, H/24 Inf, May–Jun 1898.

Sick in hospital, Siboney, Cuba, 1–25 Aug 1898, and en route to U.S., 25–31 Aug 1898, disease contracted in line of duty. SOURCE: Muster Roll, H/24 Inf, Jul–Aug 1898.

Resided at 315 South 13th East, Salt Lake City, with Raymond Richard, 1898. SOURCE: Clark, "A History of the Twenty-fourth," appendix E.

On furlough authorized by surgeon's certificate, 20 Sep–19 Oct 1898; on special duty as blacksmith, Quartermaster Department, Ft Douglas, since 19 Oct 1898. SOURCE: Muster Roll, H/24 Inf, Sep–Oct 1898.

On special duty as blacksmith. SOURCE: Muster Roll, H/24 Inf, Nov–Dec 1898 and Jan–Feb 1899.

QUEEN, William; Private; I/10th Cav. Served in 10th Cavalry in Cuba, 1898. SOURCE: Cashin, *Under Fire with the Tenth Cavalry*, 348.

Ex-soldier, bartender for Darby Ford outside of Ft Bliss, TX. SOURCE: *ANJ* 37 (24 Mar 1900): 704.

QUEENER, William; Private; A/10th Cav. Served in 10th Cavalry in Cuba, 1898. SOURCE: Cashin, *Under Fire with the Tenth Cavalry*, 336.

QUICKLEY, William H.; Private; G/10th Cav. Served in 10th Cavalry in Cuba, 1898. SOURCE: Cashin, *Under Fire with the Tenth Cavalry*, 345.

QUINN, Floyd; Private; B/9th Cav. Deserted with government horse, Jun 1880; captured and imprisoned. SOURCE: Billington, *New Mexico's Buffalo Soldiers*, 131.

QUIVERS, Thomas P.; Private; D/9th Cav. At Ft D. A. Russell, WY, in 1910; resident of Washington, DC. SOURCE: *Illustrated Review: Ninth Cavalry*, with picture.

R

RACKS, George H.; Corporal; I/10th Cav. Served in 10th Cavalry in Cuba, 1898. SOURCE: Cashin, *Under Fire with the Tenth Cavalry*, 347.

RACKS, Washington H.; Corporal; A/9th Cav. Served as corporal, G/10th Cavalry in Cuba, 1898. SOURCE: Cashin, *Under Fire with the Tenth Cavalry*, 345.

Corporal, A/9th Cavalry, at Ft D. A. Russell, WY, in 1910; sharpshooter. SOURCE: *Illustrated Review: Ninth Cavalry,* with picture.

RAFEN, Robert; Private; G/24th Inf. Transferred to Hospital Corps, Ft Bayard, NM. SOURCE: *ANJ* 32 (13 Oct 1894): 103.

RAGAN, John; Private; C/9th Cav. Authorized to reenlist as married by letter, Adjutant General's Office, 30 Jul 1897.

RAGLAND, Shelton; Private; A/9th Cav. At Ft D. A. Russell, WY, in 1910. SOURCE: *Illustrated Review: Ninth Cavalry,* with picture.

RAGLIN, Thomas; Saddler; G/10th Cav. Regiment commander refuses his request for discharge to care for his three minor children because he has already abdicated his role in their care—only one is really his, he has contributed nothing to their support, and he is needed as saddler. SOURCE: CO, 10 Cav, to AG, USA, 9 Mar 1877, ES, 10 Cav, 1873–83.

RAINE, Hazel L.; Sergeant; F/10th Cav. Commissioned first lieutenant at Camp Des Moines, IA, 15 Oct 1917. SOURCE: Glass, *History of the Tenth Cavalry,* appendix M.

RAINEY, William; 1st Sgt; F/24th Inf. Led his company up San Juan Hill, Cuba. SOURCE: Steward, *The Colored Regulars,* 216.

With all of his officers wounded, he "bravely conducted the company to the top of San Juan Hill, aided by the other non-commissioned officers." SOURCE: Coston, *The Spanish-American War Volunteer,* 52.

RAINS, J. C.; Private; H/10th Cav. At Ft Mackenzie, WY; on furlough in Sheridan, WY, 10–17 Apr 1903.

RALLS, Henry; Private; A/10th Cav. Served in 10th Cavalry, 1898; remained in U.S. during war with Spain. SOURCE: Cashin, *Under Fire with the Tenth Cavalry,* 337.

RAMBER, E.; Sergeant; D/24th Inf. At Ft Bayard, NM, 1888. *See* **COX**, Richard, Private, D/24th Infantry

RAMSAY, Robert; Private; C/24th Inf. Died of yellow fever in Cuba, 6 Aug 1898. SOURCE: *ANJ* 36 (18 Feb 1898): 590; AG, *Correspondence Regarding the War with Spain,* I:209.

RAMSEY, Crawford; Private; B/9th Cav. At Ft D. A. Russell, WY, in 1910. SOURCE: *Illustrated Review: Ninth Cavalry,* with picture.

RAMSEY, George; Private; D/10th Cav. Served in 10th Cavalry, 1898; remained in U.S. during war with Spain. SOURCE: Cashin, *Under Fire with the Tenth Cavalry,* 341.

RAMSEY, Henry; Corporal; H/9th Cav. Ranked number 412 among rifle experts with 69 percent in 1905. SOURCE: GO 101, AGO, 31 May 1906.

RAMSEY, Horace W.; Private; F/9th Cav. Recruit from depot, arrived Ft Robinson, NE, and assigned to F/9th Cavalry, 1 Mar 1887.

Attached to Band/9th Cavalry for instruction in music. SOURCE: Order 15, 9 Cav, 25 May 1887.

Returned to duty with Band/9th Cavalry, in accordance with letter, Department of the Platte, 20 Mar 1891.

In F/9th Cavalry, leader of troop band, Ft Duchesne, UT. SOURCE: *ANJ* 34 (29 May 1897): 733.

RAND, Carlton F.; Private; C/10th Cav. Born in North Carolina; died at Ft Robinson, NE, age 24, with eighteen months' service, 8 Sep 1902, from injuries received at Ardmore, SD. SOURCE: Monthly Report, Chaplain Anderson, 1 Oct 1902.

Buried at Ft Robinson, 8 Sep 1902. SOURCE: List of Interments, Ft Robinson.

RANDALL, Edward; H/25th Inf. Died of consumption at U.S. Soldiers Home, 11 Nov 1893. SOURCE: SecWar, *AR 1894,* 526.

RANDALL, George; Private; A/9th Cav. At Ft D. A. Russell, WY, in 1910. SOURCE: *Illustrated Review: Ninth Cavalry,* with picture.

RANDALL, John; Private; G/10th Cav. Original member of 10th Cavalry; in troop when organized, Ft Leavenworth, KS, 5 Jul 1867. SOURCE: McMiller, "Buffalo Soldiers," 74.

Wounded in action while guarding railroad camp forty-five miles west of Ft Hays, KS, Aug 1867. SOURCE: Leckie, *The Buffalo Soldiers*, 25.

Cited for heroism against Cheyennes, on line of Union Pacific Railroad, 45 miles west of Ft Hays, autumn 1867. SOURCE: Baker, Roster; Cashin, *Under Fire with the Tenth Cavalry*, 28.

See **FORD**, George W., Quartermaster Sergeant, 10th Cavalry

RANDELL, George; Private; L/10th Cav. Served in 10th Cavalry, 1898; remained in U.S. during war with Spain. SOURCE: Cashin, *Under Fire with the Tenth Cavalry*, 350.

RANDOLPH, James; Sergeant; L/9th Cav. Attacked twenty-four cattle thieves near Havana Ranch, TX, capturing one and scattering rest, Nov 1874. SOURCE: Hamilton, "History of the Ninth Cavalry," 21.

RANDOLPH, John; Private; B/24th Inf. Chosen to compete for place on Department of Arizona rifle team; marksman. SOURCE: CO, B/24th Inf to Adj, Ft Huachuca, AZ, 13 Jul 1893, Name File, 24 Inf.

Designated to participate in Department of Arizona rifle meet. SOURCE: Order 119, Ft Huachuca, 10 Aug 1893, Letters and Orders Received, 24 Inf, 1893.

RANDOLPH, Ruford; Private; C/24th Inf. Now military convict. SOURCE: Order 178, Ft Huachuca, AZ, 3 Dec 1893, Orders Received, 24 Inf.

RANDOLPH, Walter; Private; K/25th Inf. "Prof. Walter Randolph" sends greetings to his mother. SOURCE: Richmond *Planet*, 20 Jan 1900.

At Ft Niobrara, NE, 1904. SOURCE: Wilson, "History of Fort Niobrara."

RANKIN, Frank; Sergeant; F/10th Cav. Served in 10th Cavalry in Cuba, 1898; died of fever. SOURCE: Cashin, *Under Fire with the Tenth Cavalry*, 343.

Wounded in action, Santiago, Cuba, 1 Jul 1898. SOURCE: SecWar, *AR 1898*, 324.

Died of typhoid at Camp Wikoff, NY, 31 Aug 1898. SOURCE: Hospital Papers, Spanish-American War.

Body transferred from Montauk Point, NY, to national cemetery, Cypress Hills, NY. SOURCE: *ANJ* 36 (21 Jan 1899): 480.

RANKINS, George; Private; C/10th Cav. Served in 10th Cavalry, 1898; remained in U.S. during war with Spain. SOURCE: Cashin, *Under Fire with the Tenth Cavalry*, 340.

RANN, Price; A/25th Inf. Admitted to Soldiers Home with disability, age 28, after five years' service, 20 Aug 1889. SOURCE: SecWar, *AR 1889*, 1014.

RANN, William; Private; G/24th Inf. Convicted by general court martial, Ft Brown, TX, of failure to parade with his company for morning drill and of being "beastly drunk; and was contumacious, violent, insubordinate, and disrespectful" to noncommissioned officers, carelessly loading his musket and threatening to shoot, 22 Nov 1872; sentence of six months' confinement and loss of pay reduced to one month by commanding general, Department of Texas. SOURCE: GCMO 11, Department of Texas, 11 Jan 1873.

RANSOM, Arthur E.; Sergeant; G/9th Cav. Appointed sergeant 27 Aug 1890. SOURCE: Roster, 9 Cav.

Replaced as provost sergeant, Ft Robinson, NE, by Sgt. Nathan Fletcher, F/9th Cavalry. SOURCE: Order 5, 16 Jan 1893, Post Orders, Ft Robinson.

Witness for prosecution in court martial of Sgt. Barney McKay, G/9th Cavalry, Ft Robinson. SOURCE: Court Martial Records, McKay.

RANSOM, Henry; Private; D/24th Inf. Acquitted of wasting one round of ammunition, Cabanatuan, Philippines, 24 Nov 1900; witness: 1st Sgt. M. H. Ellis, D/24th Infantry. SOURCE: Name File, 24 Inf.

RANSOM, James; D/10th Cav. Original member of 10th Cavalry; in troop when organized, Ft Leavenworth, KS, 1 Jun 1867. SOURCE: McMiller, "Buffalo Soldiers," 71.

RANSOM, Robert; Private; C/10th Cav. Served in 10th Cavalry in Cuba, 1898. SOURCE: Cashin, *Under Fire with the Tenth Cavalry*, 340.

RAPER, Henry; Private; E/10th Cav. Mentioned 1873. SOURCE: ES, 10 Cav, 1873-83.

RASH, John; Private; B/10th Cav. Served in 10th Cavalry, 1898; remained in U.S. during war with Spain. SOURCE: Cashin, *Under Fire with the Tenth Cavalry*, 333.

RASH, William; Private; D/10th Cav. Sentenced to dishonorable discharge and confinement, Ft Robinson, NE, by general court martial, Jul 1904.

RATCLIFF, Tony; E/10th Cav. Original member of 10th Cavalry; in troop when organized, Ft Leavenworth, KS, 15 Jun 1867. SOURCE: McMiller, "Buffalo Soldiers," 72.

RATCLIFFE, Eddie; Private; G/10th Cav. Served in M/10th Cavalry, 1898; remained in U.S. during war with Spain. SOURCE: Cashin, *Under Fire with the Tenth Cavalry*, 352.

At Ft Robinson, NE, guarding prisoners, as of 29 Nov 1904.

RATCLIFFE, George R.; Private; H/10th Cav. Served in 10th Cavalry, 1898; remained in U.S. during war with Spain. SOURCE: Cashin, *Under Fire with the Tenth Cavalry*, 347.

At Camp Forse, AL, Nov 1898. SOURCE: Richmond *Planet*, 3 Dec 1898.

RATLIFFE, Benjamin; F/25th Inf. Served 1870–75. SOURCE: *Winners of the West* 1 (Jan 1924): 8.

Letter from Danville, IL: "I was engaged in guarding and protecting the mail station and I was out here and there and yonder, in the seething hot days of summer as well as the severe cold of winter, often in momentary danger of attack by the savages." SOURCE: *Winners of the West* 1 (Sep 1924): 1.

Granted $50 per month pension; seeks letters from old comrades. SOURCE: *Winners of the West* 4 (Dec 1927): 3.

Died in Chicago; was member of Camp 11, National Indian War Veterans, St. Joseph, MO. SOURCE: *Winners of the West* 7 (May 1930): 6.

RAY, Albert; 1st Sgt; F/25th Inf. At Ft Shaw, MT; to be discharged in accordance with Special Order, Adjutant General's Office, 2 Jun 1890. SOURCE: *ANJ* 27 (7 Jun 1890): 775.

RAY, Albert E.; 1st Sgt; 10th Cav. Private, K/25th Infantry, at Ft Niobrara, NE, 1904. SOURCE: Wilson, "History of Fort Niobrara."

Retired from Second Squadron, 10th Cavalry, at U.S. Military Academy, West Point, NY, 1932. SOURCE: *Cavalry Journal* 41 (Jul 1932): 62.

RAY, Alfred M.; 1st Lt; H/49th Inf. Born in Tennessee; private, saddler, sergeant, first sergeant, F/10th Cavalry, 17 May 1872–16 May 1882; private, 13 Feb 1885; corporal, 1 Jul 1885; sergeant, 15 Dec 1885; at Ft Assiniboine, MT, 1897. SOURCE: Baker, Roster.

Born Washington Co., TN, 16 May 1856; in 10th Cavalry, 1872–82, 1885–98; first lieutenant, 10th Volunteer Infantry, 2 Aug 1898–8 Mar 1899; color sergeant, 10th Cavalry, in Cuba, 1898; second lieutenant, L/49th Infantry, 9 Sep 1899; first lieutenant, 10 Oct 1900; transferred to H/49th Infantry, 20 Dec 1900; wife resides in Jonesboro, TN. SOURCE: Descriptive Book, L/49 Inf.

Color sergeant, 10th Cavalry, 1897; quartermaster sergeant, F/10th Cavalry, 1898; commissioned first lieutenant, 10th Volunteer Infantry, after Spanish-American War; served in regiment, Aug 1898–Mar 1899. SOURCE: *ANJ* 37 (4 Nov 1899): 219; Cashin, *Under Fire with the Tenth Cavalry*, 360.

Color sergeant, 10th Cavalry. SOURCE: *ANJ* 35 (19 Feb 1898): 458.

Capt. John Bigelow arrived at Chattanooga, TN, from Washington, en route to join his troop at Chickamauga: "At the station I saw a tall, fine-looking cavalryman, whom I recognized as Sergeant Ray, Color Sergeant of the Tenth Cavalry, and learned from him that there was no train to Lytle that would get me there much before midnight." SOURCE: Bigelow, *Reminiscences of Santiago*, 7.

Served in F/10th Cavalry in Cuba, 1898. SOURCE: Cashin, *Under Fire with the Tenth Cavalry*, 343.

Had twenty-six [*sic*] years in 10th Cavalry and 10th Volunteer Infantry when commissioned in 49th Infantry. SOURCE: Fletcher, *The Black Soldier*, 64.

To report to Jefferson Barracks, MO, as second lieutenant, 49th Infantry. SOURCE: *ANJ* 37 (7 Oct 1899): 123.

Picture. SOURCE: Indianapolis *Freeman*, 21 Oct 1899.

Went to Philippines with L/49th Infantry on U.S. Army Transport *Sherman*, Dec 1899.

RAY, Edward M.; Private; E/24th Inf. Transferred from Reserve Divisional Hospital, Siboney, Cuba, to U.S. on U.S. Army Transport *Santiago* with remittent yellow fever, 25 Jul 1898. SOURCE: Hospital Papers, Spanish-American War.

RAY, John I.; Corporal; G/10th Cav. Served in 10th Cavalry in Cuba, 1898. SOURCE: Cashin, *Under Fire with the Tenth Cavalry*, 345.

RAYMOND, H. C.; Private; D/10th Cav. Served in 10th Cavalry, 1898; remained in U.S. during war with Spain. SOURCE: Cashin, *Under Fire with the Tenth Cavalry*, 341.

RAYMOND, Ira Curtis; Musician; B/8th Ill Inf. Born Jacksonville, IL; died in Minnesota, 3 Aug 1948. SOURCE: Taylor, "Minnesota Black Spanish-American War Veterans."

RAYMOND, Jacob; Trumpeter; K/9th Cav. Veteran of Philippine Insurrection; at Ft D. A. Russell, WY, in 1910; sharpshooter, resident of Nashville. SOURCE: *Illustrated Review: Ninth Cavalry,* with picture.

RAYNOR, Isaiah; Private; B/25th Inf. Dishonorable discharge, Brownsville. SOURCE: SO 266, AGO, 9 Nov 1906.

RAYSON, Benjamin; 10th Cav. Served in H and K/10th Cavalry, 1887–92; member, Camp 11, National Indian War Veterans, St. Joseph, MO; died at age 76, Branchville, SC. SOURCE: *Winners of the West* 12 (Apr 1935): 2.

READ; Private; I/10th Cav. At Ft Apache, AZ, 1890, subscribed $.25 to testimonial to General Grierson. SOURCE: List of subscriptions, 23 Apr 1890, 10th Cavalry papers, MHI.

READ; Sergeant; 25th Inf. Returned to Iba, Philippines, after scout in which he and Sergeant Thompson found insurgent rendezvous, destroyed it, and captured two. SOURCE: Manila *Times*, 26 Sep 1900.

READ, Job; Private; A/24th Inf. Deserted from Ft Selden, NM, Nov 1889. SOURCE: Billington, *New Mexico's Buffalo Soldiers*, 169.

REAVES, Transum; A/9th Cav. Mrs. Rozetta W. Reaves, widow, 3824 Clay Avenue, San Diego, wants to hear from veterans who knew her husband in the service,

1875–85, to help make good her claim for pension. SOURCE: *Winners of the West* 7 (Sep 1930): 9.

RECKETTS, James; Private; I/10th Cav. Served in 10th Cavalry, 1898; remained in U.S. during war with Spain. SOURCE: Cashin, *Under Fire with the Tenth Cavalry*, 348.

RECTOR, William L.; M/10th Cav. Original member of 10th Cavalry; in troop when organized, Ft Riley, KS, 15 Oct 1867. SOURCE: McMiller, "Buffalo Soldiers," 79.

REDD, John; Private; G/10th Cav. Served in 10th Cavalry, 1898; remained in U.S. during war with Spain. SOURCE: Cashin, *Under Fire with the Tenth Cavalry*, 346.

REDD, Kid; Private; I/9th Cav. At Ft D. A. Russell, WY, in 1910; resident of Louisville. SOURCE: *Illustrated Review: Ninth Cavalry,* with picture.

REDD, McClellen; Private; M/10th Cav. Served in 10th Cavalry, 1898; remained in U.S. during war with Spain. SOURCE: Cashin, *Under Fire with the Tenth Cavalry*, 352.

REDD, Samuel; Private; I/10th Cav. Enlisted Washington, DC; wounded in action at Santiago, Cuba, 1898. SOURCE: Cleveland *Gazette*, 2 Jul 1898.

Served in 10th Cavalry in Cuba, 1898. SOURCE: Cashin, *Under Fire with the Tenth Cavalry*, 348.

REDDICK, Charles; 1st Sgt; I/25th Inf. Served with William Branch at Ft Sill, Indian Territory, as sergeant, I/25th Infantry. SOURCE: Affidavit, Reddick, Bedford City, VA, VA File C2581520, William Branch.

Authorized four-month furlough from Ft Missoula, MT. SOURCE: *ANJ* 27 (17 May 1890): 719.

Retires. SOURCE: *ANJ* 28 (17 Jan 1891): 349.

REDDICK, P. A.; Private; E/9th Cav. On detached service in field, New Mexico, 27 Jan–1 Feb 1881. SOURCE: Regt Returns, 9 Cav, Feb 1881.

REDDIE, Charles; Corporal; D/9th Cav. Served as private, E/10th Cavalry in Cuba, 1898. SOURCE: Cashin, *Under Fire with the Tenth Cavalry*, 342.

Promoted to corporal, Sep 1899. SOURCE: *ANJ* 37 (7 Oct 1899): 122.

Corporal, D/9th Cavalry, at Ft D. A. Russell, WY, in 1910; resident of Pittsburgh. SOURCE: *Illustrated Review: Ninth Cavalry,* with picture.

REDDIE, Isaac C.; Private; K/10th Cav. Served in 10th Cavalry, 1898; remained in U.S. during war with Spain. SOURCE: Cashin, *Under Fire with the Tenth Cavalry*, 349.

REDDING, Willie; Private; K/25th Inf. Married Senorita Senung Marcalina, daughter of Don Antucaio Marcalina, former Captain, Municipality of Castillejos, San Marcelina, Philippines, 15 Apr 1900. SOURCE: Richmond *Planet*, 16 Jun 1900.

REDMAN, Charles; Private; H/24th Inf. Jailed for fifteen days and fined one month's pay by summary court, San Isidro, Philippines, for being drunk, abusive, and insubordinate to Cpl. James Morrissay, E/Engineer Corps and Corporal of the Guard, Cabaio, Nueva Ecija, Philippines, 5 Dec 1901. SOURCE: Register of Summary Court, San Isidro.

REDMAN, Jesse I.; Saddler; H/9th Cav. Veteran of Philippine Insurrection; at Ft D. A. Russell, WY, in 1910; sharpshooter; resident of Pleasantville, NJ. SOURCE: *Illustrated Review: Ninth Cavalry,* with picture.

REDMOND, Francis; Private; K/9th Cav. Assigned duty as clerk, regiment headquarters, Santa Fe, NM. SOURCE: Regimental Order 48, 9 Cav, 29 Sep 1879.

Convicted by garrison court martial, Ft Robinson, NE, of conduct to prejudice of good order and discipline; jailed for ten days and fined $5. SOURCE: Order 4, 9 Jan 1886, Post Orders, Ft Robinson.

Applied for copy of proceedings of general court martial in his case, as reported in General Court Martial Order 29, Department of the Platte, 25 Mar 1886, but received no response; inspector general says he has legitimate complaint. SOURCE: Report of Inspection, Ft Robinson, 15 Nov 1886, Reports of Inspection, DP, I.

On daily duty as clerk for post adjutant, Ft Robinson. SOURCE: Order 214, 31 Oct 1887, Post Orders, Ft Robinson.

REDMOND, Washington; Recruit; L/10th Cav. Mentioned Jan 1873 as sent to L/10th Cavalry from Ft Gibson, Indian Territory. SOURCE: LS, 10 Cav, 1873–83.

REED; Private; H/10th Cav. At Ft Apache, AZ, 1890, subscribed $.50 to testimonial to General Grierson. SOURCE: List of subscriptions, 23 Apr 1890, 10th Cavalry papers, MHI.

REED, Amos B.; Private; I/10th Cav. Served in 10th Cavalry in Cuba, 1898. SOURCE: Cashin, *Under Fire with the Tenth Cavalry*, 348.

Wounded in action, Cuba, 24 Jun 1898. SOURCE: SecWar, *AR 1898*, 349.

Promoted to corporal after war; cited for heroism in Cuba. SOURCE: Cashin, *Under Fire with the Tenth Cavalry*, 185.

REED, Charles; G/24th Inf. Age 70; served 1884–94. SOURCE: *Winners of the West* 12 (Nov 1935): 3.

REED, Cosley; Private; A/24th Inf. Died en route to the Philippines, 1899; buried at sea. SOURCE: Alexander, *Battles and Victories*, 392.

REED, George; B/10th Cav. Original member of 10th Cavalry; in troop when organized, Ft Leavenworth, KS, 1 Apr 1867. SOURCE: McMiller, "Buffalo Soldiers," 69.

REED, George; Recruit; Mounted Service. Served in 1876. *See* **BRITTON**, William H., Recruit, Mounted Service

REED, George; Corporal; D/9th Cav. Veteran of Philippine Insurrection; at Ft D. A. Russell, WY, in 1910; resident of Huntsville, AL. SOURCE: *Illustrated Review: Ninth Cavalry,* with picture.

REED, James; Private; B/10th Cav. Original member of 10th Cavalry; in troop when organized, Ft Leavenworth, KS, 1 Apr 1867. SOURCE: McMiller, "Buffalo Soldiers," 69.

Caught and arrested, Hays City, KS, trying to board eastbound train, by Mr. Warren with help of Sergeant Johnson and Pvt. Dock Burks, I/10th Cavalry, 25 May 1868. SOURCE: LR, Det 10 Cav, 1868–69.

REED, James; Private; A/9th Cav. At Ft Stanton, NM, 1881. SOURCE: Regt Returns, 9 Cav, Jan 1881.

REED, James T.; Private; K/10th Cav. Arrived at Ft Leavenworth, KS, from Jefferson Barracks, MO, Oct 1866.

Relieved from duty in hospital. SOURCE: SO 5, Det 10 Cav, Ft Lyon, CO, 6 Mar 1869.

REED, John; G/24th Inf. Served 1871–76; *Winners of the West* reminds him of old days in Army. SOURCE: *Winners of the West* 7 (Dec 1929): 5.

Died at Jericho, KY, 28 May 1931; member, Camp 11, National Indian War Veterans, St. Joseph, MO. SOURCE: *Winners of the West* 8 (Jun 1931): 8.

REED, John; Corporal; I/10th Cav. Honorably discharged with eight years and three months' service, Feb 1897.

Resides in Lynchburg, VA; requests authority to enlist company of colored volunteers to be placed at disposal of Army in case of war with Spain, 24 Apr 1898.

Adjutant General advises that law specifies that volunteers are raised by states and that Reed should apply to governor of Virginia, 4 Jun 1898.

REED, John G.; Private; 24th Inf. Served in Houston, 1917; did not participate in riot. SOURCE: Haynes, *A Night of Violence,* 85, 185.

REED, Kirby; Private; C/24th Inf. Wounded in action in Cuba, 1898. SOURCE: Muller, *The Twenty Fourth Infantry,* 18.

REED, Miller; Private; M/9th Cav. Promoted to corporal at Ft Assiniboine, MT, 1 Apr 1898. SOURCE: *ANJ·* 35 (16 Apr 1898): 624; SO 16, 10 Cav, 1 Apr 1898.

Served as corporal, I/10th Cavalry in Cuba, 1898. SOURCE: Cashin, *Under Fire with the Tenth Cavalry,* 347.

Veteran of Spanish-American War; private, M/9th Cavalry, at Ft D. A. Russell, WY, in 1910; resident of Fredway, VA. SOURCE: *Illustrated Review: Ninth Cavalry,* with picture.

REED, Oscar W.; Private; C/25th Inf. Dishonorable discharge, Brownsville. SOURCE: SO 266, AGO, 9 Nov 1906.

Has sued President of United States to recover moneys due him "by virtue of illogical discharge from the United States Army." SOURCE: Washington *Bee,* 11 Jan 1908.

REED, Richard; Private; Band/24th Inf. First enlistment, Band/9th Cavalry, ended 7 Dec 1877; second enlistment, Band/9th Cavalry, ended 6 Dec 1882; enlisted in B/24th Infantry, age 31, Ht 5'7", black eyes, hair, and complexion, Ft Leavenworth, KS, 12 Dec 1882; transferred to Band/24th Infantry at Ft Supply, Indian Territory, 18 Jan 1883; discharged, end of term, Ft Sill, Indian Territory, character excellent, single, 11 Dec 1887, with $65 deposits, $60 retained, $86.42 clothing. SOURCE: Descriptive Book, 24 Inf NCS & Band.

Private, Band/9th Cavalry; with band on detached service at headquarters, District of New Mexico, Santa Fe, 1880; played first tenor. SOURCE: Billington, *New Mexico's Buffalo Soldiers,* 226.

REED, Rufus; Corporal; B/9th Cav. At Ft D. A. Russell, WY, in 1910; sharpshooter. SOURCE: *Illustrated Review: Ninth Cavalry,* with picture.

REED, Samuel; F/9th Cav. Served 1881; member Camp 11, National Indian War Veterans, St. Joseph, MO; died in Bethesda, MD. SOURCE: *Winners of the West* 15 (Sep 1838): 4.

REED, William; I/10th Cav. Original member of 10th Cavalry; in troop when organized, Ft Riley, KS, 15 Aug 1867. SOURCE: McMiller, "Buffalo Soldiers," 76.

REED, William; Private; H/9th Cav. Convicted by general court martial, Jefferson Barracks, MO, of desertion, from 12 May 1884 until surrendered 19 Sep 1884; sentenced to dishonorable discharge and two years. SOURCE: GCMO 49, AGO, 3 Nov 1884.

REED, William; Private; D/9th Cav. Post commander, Ft Robinson, NE, directs that Military Convict Reed, formerly of D/9th Cavalry, be placed in irons. SOURCE: CO, Ft Robinson, to Officer of the Day, 17 May 1894, LS, Ft Robinson.

REES, Ed; Private; F/9th Cav. At Ft D. A. Russell, WY, in 1910; resident of Coulterville, IL. SOURCE: *Illustrated Review: Ninth Cavalry,* with picture.

REESE, Manning H.; Corporal; M/10th Cav. Private, F/24th Infantry, transferred from Reserve Divisional Hospital, Siboney, Cuba, to U.S. on U.S. Army Transport *Santiago* with remittent yellow fever, 25 Jul 1898. SOURCE: Hospital Papers, Spanish-American War.

Third best pistol shot, Departments of Texas and the Missouri, 1903; ninth best pistol shot in U.S. Army, 1903;

distinguished marksman. SOURCE: SecWar, *AR 1903*, 1:428; *History of the Tenth Cavalry*, 43; GO 198, AGO, 6 Dec 1906.

Ranked number 11, bronze medal, Northern Division pistol competition, Ft Sheridan, IL, 1906. SOURCE: GO 198, AGO, 6 Dec 1906.

Northern Division distinguished pistol shot, 1907. SOURCE: GO 213, AGO, 19 Oct 1907.

REESE, Thomas; Private; 9th Cav. Resides with wife and child at Ft Robinson, NE, Aug 1893. SOURCE: Medical History, Ft Robinson.

At Ft Robinson, 1894; twice chastised by Chaplain Plummer for failure to salute him. SOURCE: Investigation of Charges against Chaplain Plummer.

REEVES, Finous; Private; A/9th Cav. At Ft D. A. Russell, WY, in 1910. SOURCE: *Illustrated Review: Ninth Cavalry,* with picture.

REEVES, Isaac; Saddler; H/9th Cav. Died of pneumonia at Ft McKinney, WY, 15 Jan 1889.

REEVES, Isaac; Private; B/48th Inf. Died in the Philippines, 26 Nov 1900. SOURCE: *ANJ* 38 (8 Dec 1900): 355.

REEVES, Jerry E.; Sergeant; D/25th Inf. Dishonorable discharge, Brownsville. SOURCE: SO 266, AGO, 9 Nov 1906.

REEVES, Len; Private; D/25th Inf. Dishonorable discharge, Brownsville. SOURCE: SO 266, AGO, 9 Nov 1906.

REEVES, Thornton; Sergeant; A/38th Inf. Implicated in soldiers' revolt at Ft Cummings, NM, autumn 1867; acquitted by court martial of involvement. SOURCE: Billington, *New Mexico's Buffalo Soldiers*, 39, 42.

REEVES, Walter; Private; G/24th Inf. Died in Cuba 8 Aug 1898. SOURCE: *ANJ* 36 (18 Feb 1899): 590.

Cause of death not stated. SOURCE: AG, *Correspondence Regarding the War with Spain*, I:214.

REID, Arthur; Farrier; L/9th Cav. Veteran of Philippine Insurrection; at Ft D. A. Russell, WY, in 1910; resident of Sandersville, GA. SOURCE: *Illustrated Review: Ninth Cavalry,* with picture.

REID, Augustus; Corporal; F/9th Cav. Veteran of Spanish-American War and Philippine Insurrection; at Ft D. A. Russell, WY, in 1910; resident of Eatonton, GA. SOURCE: *Illustrated Review: Ninth Cavalry,* with picture.

REID, Edward C.; Sergeant; E/9th Cav. Veteran of Philippine Insurrection; at Ft D. A. Russell, WY, in 1910. SOURCE: *Illustrated Review: Ninth Cavalry,* with picture.

REID, James R.; Sergeant; B/25th Inf. Dishonorable discharge, Brownsville. SOURCE: SO 266, AGO, 9 Nov 1906.

REID, John; Sergeant; B/10th Cav. Fined $10 and $5.80 costs for carrying concealed weapon, Crawford, NE, 30 Jan 1904; paid $14.30 and spent one day in jail. SOURCE: Police Court Records, Crawford.

Sergeant; request dated 10 Dec 1905 for four-month furlough to visit relatives in Omaha, NE, approved; only one furlough in seven years' previous service. SOURCE: AG File 1206256.

In hands of civil authorities 13 May 1906; reduced to private 5 Jun 1906. SOURCE: AG File 1206256.

Sentenced to seven years' confinement by Dawes County, NE, court for manslaughter; killed deputy marshal Art Moss of Crawford, May 1906; Department of the Missouri commander approved request of commander, Ft Robinson, for authority to discharge Reid without honor, 1 Feb 1907. SOURCE: AG File 1206256.

REID, William, Jr.; Corporal; D/9th Cav. Veteran of Philippine Insurrection; at Ft D. A. Russell, WY, in 1910; resident of Oakwood, SC. SOURCE: *Illustrated Review: Ninth Cavalry,* with picture.

REILLY, John; K/10th Cav. Original member of 10th Cavalry; in troop when organized, Ft Riley, KS, 1 Sep 1867. SOURCE: McMiller, "Buffalo Soldiers," 77.

RENFRO, Golden E.; Private; K/9th Cav. At Ft D. A. Russell, WY, in 1910; sharpshooter; resident of Sharpsburg, KY. SOURCE: *Illustrated Review: Ninth Cavalry,* with picture.

RENNER, W. O.; Corporal; 9th Cav. On Department of the Platte rifle team, 1892. SOURCE: *ANJ* 30 (27 Aug 1892): 5.

RESTON, James; Corporal; K/24th Inf. Promoted from private, Apr 1900. SOURCE: *ANJ* 37 (5 May 1900): 851.

Leader of mounted scouts. SOURCE: Manila *Times*, 15 Aug 1900.

REVERE, Robert; Cook; L/9th Cav. At Ft D. A. Russell, WY, in 1910; resident of Doraville, GA. SOURCE: *Illustrated Review: Ninth Cavalry,* with picture.

REYNOLDS, Eleazer N.; Corporal; H/9th Cav. Appointed corporal 21 Jun 1893. SOURCE: Roster, 9 Cav.

At Ft Robinson, NE, 1895; member of permanent color guard. SOURCE: *ANJ* 32 (3 Aug 1895): 807. *See* **LYMAN**, George, Color Sergeant, 9th Cavalry

Alternate, regimental color guard, Ft Robinson, Mar 1896. SOURCE: *ANJ* 33 (28 Mar 1896): 540.

REYNOLDS, Elijah; 1st Sgt; 25th Inf. Brother of T. H. Reynolds and Mrs. Aaron Bankett; Washington, DC, native; just promoted from quartermaster sergeant of his company, now in the Philippines. SOURCE: Washington *Bee*, 30 May 1908.

REYNOLDS, Henry; K/10th Cav. Original member of 10th Cavalry; in troop when organized, Ft Riley, KS, 1 Sep 1867. SOURCE: McMiller, "Buffalo Soldiers," 77.

REYNOLDS, M. E.; F/25th Inf. At Ft Reno, OK, 1903. SOURCE: Indianapolis *Freeman*, 21 Feb 1903.

REYNOLDS, Moses; Musician; D/24th Inf. At Cabanatuan, Philippines, 1901. *See* **JOHNSON**, Jason, Corporal, D/24th Infantry

REYNOLDS, Noah; H/49th Inf. Convicted of assisting in assaulting natives, Jul 1900; sentenced to six months' confinement and loss of pay.

REYNOLDS, Robert; Private; K/10th Cav. Served in 10th Cavalry, 1898; remained in U.S. during war with Spain. SOURCE: Cashin, *Under Fire with the Tenth Cavalry*, 349.

REYNOLDS, William; Private; G/9th Cav. Discharged by purchase, in accordance with Special Order 189, Adjutant General's Office, 12 Aug 1892.

REYNOLDS, William; Captain; A/23rd Kans Inf. Born Williams Co., TN; migrated to Topeka, KS, with parents at age 4; educated in Topeka public schools; served as volunteer in Spanish-American War, 1898; organized first company of 23rd Kansas and was commander; commanded second battalion in Cuba during absence of Maj. George W. Ford; on way home, lectured on Spanish-American War at Quindaro University, where brother A. L. Reynolds was professor; organized three companies of black home guard in Los Angeles and Pasadena, CA, 1917, all of Spanish-American War veterans. SOURCE: Beasley, *Negro Trailblazers*, 293.

Expert marksman; member, Friendship Baptist Church, Pasadena; son Cpl. Raoul Reynolds, I/365th Infantry, served in France during World War I; member Knights Templar; married to Miss Maggie E. Russel, native of Topeka, for over 25 years; she is "very interested in everything for the uplift of our race," member, Federated Women's Clubs, Past Matron, Eastern Star, and member, community auxiliary of Red Cross. SOURCE: Beasley, *Negro Trailblazers*, 294.

RHEA, John S.; Trumpeter; K/10th Cav. Served in 10th Cavalry, 1898; remained in U.S. during war with Spain. SOURCE: Cashin, *Under Fire with the Tenth Cavalry*, 349.

RHEA, Samuel; Private; H/9th Cav. Born Bristol, TN; Ht 5'9", occupation miner; enlisted, age 25, Bristol, 7 Dec 1894; discharged, end of term, single, character

excellent, 6 Dec 1897; deposits $54, retained $9, clothing $44. SOURCE: Descriptive Book, H/9 Cav.

Relieved from extra duty as packer, Quartermaster Department, Ft Robinson, NE. SOURCE: SO 90, 20 Aug 1896, Post Orders, Ft Robinson.

RHOADES, Peter; Private; D/9th Cav. At Ft D. A. Russell, WY, in 1910; resident of Austin, TX. SOURCE: *Illustrated Review: Ninth Cavalry,* with picture.

RHODES, Addison G.; Private; M/9th Cav. At Ft D. A. Russell, WY, in 1910; marksman; resident of Buxton, IA. SOURCE: *Illustrated Review: Ninth Cavalry,* with picture.

RHODES, Dorsey; Sergeant; 10th Cav. One of two African-American Army musicians to win scholarships to New York Institute of Musical Art; total of five awarded. SOURCE: Cleveland *Gazette*, 10 Jun 1916.

RHODES, H. H.; Musician; K/24th Inf. At San Carlos, AZ, 1890. *See* **HARDEE**, James A., Private, K/24th Infantry

RHODES, Harry A.; QM Sgt; F/9th Cav. Veteran of Philippine Insurrection; at Ft D. A. Russell, WY, in 1910; sharpshooter; resident of Harrisburg, PA. SOURCE: *Illustrated Review: Ninth Cavalry,* with picture.

RICE; Private; B/10th Cav. At Ft Apache, AZ, 1890, subscribed $.50 to testimonial to General Grierson. SOURCE: List of subscriptions, 23 Apr 1890, 10th Cavalry papers, MHI.

RICE; Private; K/9th Cav. General court martial sentence published in Special Order 2, Military Division of the Missouri, 21 Mar 1898.

RICE, Ernest; Private; A/48th Inf. Died of typhoid in the Philippines, 21 Aug 1901. SOURCE: *ANJ* 38 (1 Sep 1900): 19.

RICE, Harry; Private; D/9th Cav. Served as guard accompanying 1st Sgt. George Tracy in conducting Military Convicts Herman Hactor and George Washington, 9th Cavalry, from Ft Robinson to Ft Omaha, NE. SOURCE: Order 77, Ft Robinson, 3 Oct 1894.

RICE, John; Recruit; Colored Detachment/ General Service. Convicted by general court martial, Columbus Barracks, OH, 5 Aug 1889, of refusing to halt for sentry and of assaulting him by biting him on the arm and hand; jailed for three months. SOURCE: GCMO 54, AGO, 5 Sep 1889.

RICE, John K.; 2nd Lt; G/48th Inf. Mentioned. SOURCE: Beasley, *Negro Trailblazers*, 284.

One of nineteen officers of 48th Infantry recommended as regular Army second lieutenants. SOURCE: CG, DivPI, Manila, 8 Feb 1901, to AGO, AGO File 355163.

RICE, John L.; Private; 24th Inf. Unassigned; fined $6 by summary court, San Isidro, Philippines, for carelessly discharging weapon on provost guard, 18 Mar 1902.

RICE, Levi; Corporal; I/24th Inf. Enlisted Philadelphia, 22 Jul 1897. SOURCE: Muster Roll, I/24 Inf, Jan–Feb 1899.

Reenlisted 28 May 1899; went on thirty-day furlough 31 May 1899; company sailed for Manila, Philippines, 22 Jun 1899. SOURCE: Muster Roll, I/24 Inf, May–Jun 1899.

Allotted $10 per month for three months to Florence Rice. SOURCE: Muster Roll, H/24 Inf, Nov–Dec 1899.

RICE, Robert; I/10th Cav. Original member of 10th Cavalry; in troop when organized, Ft Riley, KS, 15 Aug 1867. SOURCE: McMiller, "Buffalo Soldiers," 76.

RICH, Frederick; Private; C/9th Cav. Veteran of Indian wars and Philippine Insurrection; at Ft D. A. Russell, WY, in 1910. SOURCE: *Illustrated Review: Ninth Cavalry*, with picture.

RICHARD, Raymond; 9th Cav. Enlisted in 9th Cavalry band from Georgia, age 13, 1887; lived to be 91 in Oakland, CA, area. SOURCE: Clark, "A History of the Twenty-fourth," 95.

Resided at 315 South 13th East, Salt Lake City, with John Queen. SOURCE: Clark, "A History of the Twenty-fourth," appendix E.

RICHARDS; Private; A/10th Cav. At Ft Apache, AZ, 1890, subscribed $.50 to testimonial to General Grierson. SOURCE: List of subscriptions, 23 Apr 1890, 10th Cavalry papers, MHI.

RICHARDS, Alfred; Private; Band/10th Cav. Original member of M/10th Cavalry; in troop when organized, Ft Riley, KS, 15 Oct 1867. SOURCE: McMiller, "Buffalo Soldiers," 79.

To be discharged with certificate of disability, Feb 1877. SOURCE: LS, 10 Cav, 1873–83.

Discharged today. SOURCE: CO, 10 Cav, to AG, USA, 18 Feb 1877, LS, 10 Cav, 1873–83.

RICHARDS, Fleming; Sergeant; G/10th Cav. Honorable mention for bravery against Comanches, Double Mountains Fork, Brazos River, TX, 5 Feb 1874. SOURCE: Baker, Roster.

RICHARDS, H.; Private; H/9th Cav. On detached service at Ft Bayard, NM, 16 Jan–10 Feb 1881. SOURCE: Regt Returns, 9 Cav, Feb 1881.

RICHARDS, Hayden; Sergeant; D/25th Inf. Wounded in action at El Caney, Cuba, 1 Jul 1898. SOURCE: Nankivell, *History of the Twenty-fifth Infantry*, 83.

Transferred from Reserve Divisional Hospital, Siboney, Cuba, to U.S. on U.S. Army Transport *Santiago* with yellow fever, 25 Jul 1898. SOURCE: Hospital Papers, Spanish-American War.

RICHARDS, James A.; Signal Sgt; U.S. Army. Born in England; resident of Jamaica from age 12; veteran of twelve years in U.S. Navy; enlisted at age 15 and discharged as signal quartermaster petty officer; served in D/10th Cavalry as telegraph operator, 1885–89; then 24th Infantry until 13 May 1897, when transferred to Signal Corps; in war with Spain, went to Tampa, FL, with balloon corps; promoted to sergeant 16 May 1899; now stationed in Cuba. SOURCE: Cleveland *Gazette*, 28 Oct 1899.

RICHARDS, John; Private; C/24th Inf. Died in Cuba on 21 Aug 1898. SOURCE: *ANJ* 36 (3 Sep 1898): 3; *ANJ* 36 (18 Feb 1899): 590.

Died of yellow fever. SOURCE: AG, *Correspondence Regarding the War with Spain*, I:248.

RICHARDS, S.; Private; C/9th Cav. At Ft Cummings, NM, 1881; on detached service in field, 30 Jan–3 Feb 1881.

RICHARDSON; Private; F/9th Cav. Child, R. C., buried at Ft Robinson, NE, 18 Feb 1892. SOURCE: List of Interments, Ft Robinson.

RICHARDSON, Alexander; Comsy Sgt; 24th Inf. Born Gallatin, TN, 13 Dec 1858; six months' formal schooling; left home at age 16; enlisted in B/24th Infantry, 10 Mar 1876; corporal, 1 May 1877; sergeant, 28 Jul 1880; first sergeant, 31 Mar 1889; sergeant until appointed first lieutenant, 9th Volunteer Infantry, 26 Oct 1898. SOURCE: Coston, *The Spanish-American War Volunteer*, 82.

On four-month furlough from Ft Elliott, TX. SOURCE: *ANJ* 24 (9 Oct 1886): 210.

First sergeant, A/24th Infantry; commissioned first lieutenant, 9th Volunteer Infantry, after Spanish-American War. SOURCE: Cashin, *Under Fire with the Tenth Cavalry*, 360.

Mentioned as captain, 48th Infantry. SOURCE: *ANJ* 37 (9 Dec 1899): 345b.

Mentioned as captain, B/48th Infantry. SOURCE: Beasley, *Negro Trailblazers*, 285.

Captain, B/48th Infantry; twenty-six-year veteran [*sic*]; sergeant at San Juan Hill, Cuba, 1898. SOURCE: San Francisco *Chronicle*, 15 Nov 1899.

Ranked number 342 among rifle experts with 69.67 percent in 1905. SOURCE: GO 101, AGO, 31 May 1906.

Retires as commissary sergeant, 24th Infantry. SOURCE: *ANR* 38 (7 Oct 1905): 21.

RICHARDSON, Artie; Private; C/10th Cav. Released to duty from treatment for acute gonorrhea, Ft Robinson, NE, 4 Dec 1903. SOURCE: Post Surgeon to CO, C/10, 4 Dec 1903, LS, Post Surgeon, Ft Robinson.

RICHARDSON, Dick; Private; 24th Inf. Involved in fight with Pvt. Lee Chisholm, 24th Infantry, Ft Bayard, NM, Christmas, 1889. SOURCE: Billington, *New Mexico's Buffalo Soldiers*, 164.

RICHARDSON, Harry; Private; I/24th Inf. Served in Houston, 1917; threatened with jail term by military investigators after riot; tried unsuccessfully at court martial to establish alibi for being off post during riot. SOURCE: Haynes, *A Night of Violence*, 247, 268.

RICHARDSON, Henry; Private; K/24th Inf. At San Carlos, AZ, 1890. *See* **HARDEE**, James A., Private, K/24th Infantry

RICHARDSON, Jefferson; D/10th Cav. Original member of 10th Cavalry; in troop when organized, Ft Leavenworth, KS, 1 Jun 1867. SOURCE: McMiller, "Buffalo Soldiers," 71.

RICHARDSON, John; 24th Inf. Enlisted 1 Oct 1879; served five years in 10th Cavalry and 2 1/2 years in 24th Infantry; discharged with disability; "I never see anything in your paper concerning the colored soldiers." SOURCE: *Winners of the West* 16 (Dec 1938): 2.

RICHARDSON, N.; Private; E/9th Cav. On detached service in field, New Mexico, 27 Jan–1 Feb 1881. SOURCE: Regt Returns, 9 Cav, Feb 1881.

RICHARDSON, Robert; Private; D/24th Inf. Transferred from Reserve Divisional Hospital, Siboney, Cuba, to U.S. on U.S. Army Transport *Santiago* with remittent malarial fever, 25 Jul 1898. SOURCE: Hospital Papers, Spanish-American War.

RICHARDSON, Sylvester L.; Private; B/10th Cav. Served in 10th Cavalry, 1898; remained in U.S. during war with Spain. SOURCE: Cashin, *Under Fire with the Tenth Cavalry*, 333.

RICHARDSON, Will H.; Private; F/9th Cav. At Ft D. A. Russell, WY, in 1910; sharpshooter; resident of Selma, AL. SOURCE: *Illustrated Review: Ninth Cavalry*.

RICHARDSON, William; Sergeant; F/10th Cav. Original member of 10th Cavalry; in troop when organized, Ft Leavenworth, KS, 21 Jun 1867. SOURCE: McMiller, "Buffalo Soldiers," 73.

Private, detailed to daily duty with Quartermaster Department. SOURCE: SO 14, Det 10 Cav, in field, camp near Ft Dodge, KS, 9 Apr 1869, Orders, Det 10 Cav, 1868–69.

Relieved. SOURCE: SO 21, Det 10 Cav, Ft Dodge, 18 Apr 1869, Orders, Det 10 Cav, 1868–69.

Sergeant, with twelve dismounted men of battalion, to escort train now about to start to Camp Supply, Indian Territory; each man to have forty rounds and five days' rations; to return with five days' fresh rations without delay. SOURCE: SO 41, Det 10 Cav, Ft Dodge, 16 May 1869.

On daily duty as police sergeant. SOURCE: SO 41, Det 10 Cav, Camp Supply, 24 Jun 1869.

Resided at 538 First Avenue, Clinton, IA, in 1912. SOURCE: VA File SC 11405, John Taylor.

RICHARDSON, William; Private; D/9th Cav. Deserted from Ft Craig, NM, Nov 1881, after breaking into his sergeant's locker and stealing $550 belonging to three men of company; tracked by detachment under Sergeant Dickerson, and found by Pvt. Edward Kelsey; killed Kelsey and swam across Rio Grande; found and disarmed by Sergeant Stewart and Private West, who recovered $180 and killed him when he tried to escape. SOURCE: Billington, *New Mexico's Buffalo Soldiers*, 131.

RICHARDSON, William; Private; A/10th Cav. Served in 10th Cavalry in Cuba, 1898. SOURCE: Cashin, *Under Fire with the Tenth Cavalry*, 336.

RICHARDSON, William; Private; I/10th Cav. Served in 10th Cavalry, 1898; remained in U.S. during war with Spain. SOURCE: Cashin, *Under Fire with the Tenth Cavalry*, 348.

RICHMOND, Francis; Private; C/10th Cav. Sentence for desertion, which began 1 Jun 1875, reduced to two years. SOURCE: GCMO 22, AGO, 23 Feb 1877.

RICHMOND, John; D/24th Inf. Died in Lebanon, TN. SOURCE: *Winners of the West* 8 (Oct 1931): 8.

RICHTER, William J.; B/9th Cav. Enlisted 1872; discharged 1877, Ft Bayard, NM; first sergeant was Thomas Shaw; renews subscription; wants to hear from old comrades. SOURCE: *Winners of the West* 8 (Feb 1931): 9.

"I would be in a deplorable condition if it was not for my pension of $50.00 per month." SOURCE: *Winners of the West* 8 (Sep 1931): 2.

Served 1872–77; resided at 604 Sumer Street, Media, PA; died 6 Apr 1932. SOURCE: *Winners of the West* 9 (May 1932): 8.

RICKETTS, Marcelius J.; Recruit; Colored Detachment/General Service. Convicted by general court martial, Columbus Barracks, OH, of engaging in personal altercation with William Boyd, Company D of Instruction, threatening to kill Sgts. Patrick Reilly and William L. Wilson, Company B of Instruction, when they separated them, and drawing knife and having to be forcibly restrained and disarmed, 4 Dec 1886; sentenced to dishonorable discharge and four months. SOURCE: GCMO 106, AGO, 28 Dec 1886.

RICKS, William Nauns; A/24th Inf. Born Wytheville, VA, of mixed Indian parents; mother's great-grandfather "of Indian and Royal African blood," a direct descendant of Powhattan; on father's side "of Royal English and Indian blood"; vowed after seeing lynching to "honor these drops of African blood by rendering service to the negro race"; worked on steamers to England at age 16; at 18 joined Odd Fellows, Roanoke, VA; enlisted in A/24th Infantry, 1898, and served ten months; reenlisted for twenty-seven months in Philippines; returned as invalid; became contracting plasterer; a founder of Los Angeles Forum Club. SOURCE: Beasley, *Negro Trailblazers*, 295–96.

Moved to San Francisco, 1904; married then; wife died 1908; worked for California Packing Company and attended business school at night, which resulted in eleven consecutive raises; recently head of a department; moved to Oakland, after 1906 fire; member, U.S. Spanish War Veterans; member, 15th Street African Methodist Episcopal Church, and of executive board, Northern California National Association for the Advancement of Colored People; teacher, and founder, Sunday School Improvement Club; provisional captain, C Company, Home Defense Club, which was to be nucleus of "First Colored California Volunteer Regiment"; past member, State Republican Committee, and election judge, San Francisco; poet since a boy; first published in California in Pasadena *Daily News-Star*, 1902; also published in New York *Journal*, *Sunset*, and *Overland Monthly* and completed one book of poems, *The Whistle Maker*. SOURCE: Beasley, *Negro Trailblazers*, 296.

Born Wytheville, VA; enlisted in 24th Infantry in 1898; after service worked for Smith Packing Company, San Francisco; member of California State Republican Committee. SOURCE: Clark, "A History of the Twenty-fourth," 81.

RIDDELL, Houston; Private; I/10th Cav. Served in 10th Cavalry in Cuba, 1898. SOURCE: Cashin, *Under Fire with the Tenth Cavalry*, 348.

Wounded in action at Santiago, Cuba, 1 Jul 1898. SOURCE: SecWar, *AR 1898*, 324.

RIDDLE, Alfred; Private; H/24th Inf. Private, E/24th Infantry, wounded in action in Cuba, 1898. SOURCE: Muller, *The Twenty Fourth Infantry*, 18.

Twenty-eight-year veteran shot in abdomen at San Juan Hill, Cuba; is in St. Peter's Hospital, Brooklyn, NY. SOURCE: *ANJ* 35 (30 Jul 1898): 985.

Enlisted New York City, 9 Nov 1898; twenty-nine years' continuous service. SOURCE: Muster Roll, H/24 Inf, Nov–Dec 1898.

Sick in hospital since 18 Feb 1899, "wound in line of duty." SOURCE: Muster Roll, H/24 Inf, Jan–Feb 1899.

RIDEOUT, Albert; Private; L/25th Inf. Died of dysentery in the Philippines, 10 Nov 1901. SOURCE: *ANJ* 39 (18 Jan 1902): 503.

RIDEOUT, Grant; Corporal; H/9th Cav. Private, D/9th Cavalry, in hands of civil authorities, Buffalo, WY, 1–18 May 1890. SOURCE: Regt Returns, 9 Cav, May 1890.

Appointed corporal, H/9th Cavalry, 22 Aug 1892. SOURCE: Roster, 9 Cav.

RIDGELY; Private; 9th Cav. Cited for gallantry against Victorio, Jun 1879, by Capt. Charles D. Beyer. SOURCE: Billington, "Black Cavalrymen," 64; Billington, *New Mexico's Buffalo Soldiers*, 88–89.

RIDGELY, Edward A.; Private; D/24th Inf. In Cabanatuan, Philippines, 1900–1901. *See* **LEAVELL**, William, Private, D/24th Infantry; **MOORE**, Cato, Private, D/24th Infantry; **SIMPSON**, James A., Private, D/24th Infantry

RIDGELY, Frank; Private; C/10th Cav. Served in 10th Cavalry in Cuba, 1898. SOURCE: Cashin, *Under Fire with the Tenth Cavalry*, 340.

Wounded in action, Santiago, Cuba, 1 Jul 1898. SOURCE: SecWar, *AR 1898*, 324.

RIDGLEY, Noah; Corporal; L/10th Cav. Served in 10th Cavalry, 1898; remained in U.S. during war with Spain. SOURCE: Cashin, *Under Fire with the Tenth Cavalry*, 350.

RIDLEY, Albert; Corporal; L/10th Cav. Served in 1879. *See* **THOMAS**, Benedict, Sergeant, L/10th Cavalry

RIDLEY, Charles; Trumpeter; L/10th Cav. Jailed for drunkenness, Ft Bayard, NM, Mar 1890. SOURCE: Billington, *New Mexico's Buffalo Soldiers*, 165.

RIGGS, George; Private; I/9th Cav. Convicted by general court martial, Columbus Barracks, OH, of desertion 9 Sep–4 Dec 1885; sentenced to dishonorable discharge and three years. SOURCE: GCMO 9, AGO, 6 Feb 1886.

RILEY, Ben J.; Private; B/9th Cav. Veteran of Philippine Insurrection; at Ft D. A. Russell, WY, in 1910. SOURCE: *Illustrated Review: Ninth Cavalry*.

RILEY, Thomas; 10th Cav. Served 1877–81; age 78; subscriber. SOURCE: *Winners of the West* 97 (Apr 1932): 2.

RIVERS, John A.; Private; K/10th Cav. At Ft Robinson, NE, 1904.

RIVERS, Richard; L/10th Cav. Original member of 10th Cavalry; in troop when organized, Ft Riley, KS, 21 Sep 1867. SOURCE: McMiller, "Buffalo Soldiers," 78.

RIVERS, Robert; Private; K/9th Cav. Authorized to reenlist as married by letter, Adjutant General's Office, 19 Aug 1896.

Transferred from Reserve Divisional Hospital, Siboney, Cuba, to U.S. on U.S. Army Transport *Santiago* with yellow fever, 25 Jul 1898. SOURCE: Hospital Papers, Spanish-American War.

RIVERS, Samuel; Private; G/9th Cav. At Ft Robinson, NE, 1893. *See* **GILLENWATER**, Walter, Corporal, Band/25th Infantry

RIVERS, William; D/10th Cav. Original member of 10th Cavalry; in troop when organized, Ft Leavenworth, KS, 1 Jun 1867. SOURCE: McMiller, "Buffalo Soldiers," 71.

RIZ, Charles; Color Sgt; 24th Inf. Corporal, B/24th Infantry, in Cabanatuan, Philippines, 1900. *See* **LEAVELL,** William, Private, D/24th Infantry

In Cabanatuan, Philippines, 1901. *See* **COLE,** James E, Private, B/24th Infantry

Retired as color sergeant, 24th Infantry, Aug 1901. SOURCE: *ANJ* 38 (17 Aug 1901): 1235.

ROAN, Howard C.; Musician; Band/10th Cav. Resides in Philadelphia; plays violin and trombone; on regimental baseball team. SOURCE: Lowe, "Camp Life," 205–06.

ROBARDS, Charles F.; Private; G/9th Cav. At Ft D. A. Russell, WY, in 1910; resident of Nashville. SOURCE: *Illustrated Review: Ninth Cavalry,* with picture.

ROBB; Private; E/10th Cav. At Ft Apache, AZ, 1890, subscribed $.50 to testimonial to General Grierson. SOURCE: List of subscriptions, 23 Apr 1890, 10th Cavalry papers, MHI.

ROBERTS; Private; E/10th Cav. At Ft Apache, AZ, 1890, subscribed $.50 to testimonial to General Grierson. SOURCE: List of subscriptions, 23 Apr 1890, 10th Cavalry papers, MHI.

ROBERTS; Color Sgt; 24th Inf. Retires from Ft Harrison, MT, Nov 1904; will move east with his family; "all wish him a bright future." SOURCE: Indianapolis *Freeman,* 17 Dec 1904.

ROBERTS, Amos; Private; M/10th Cav. Served in 10th Cavalry, 1898; remained in U.S. during war with Spain. SOURCE: Cashin, *Under Fire with the Tenth Cavalry,* 352.

ROBERTS, Clyde; Sergeant; G/10th Cav. Commissioned second lieutenant at Camp Des Moines, IA, 15 Oct 1917. SOURCE: Glass, *History of the Tenth Cavalry,* appendix M.

ROBERTS, Daniel; Trumpeter; F/9th Cav. At Ft D. A. Russell, WY, in 1910; sharpshooter; resident of Puerto Rico. SOURCE: *Illustrated Review: Ninth Cavalry,* with picture.

ROBERTS, Filmore; L/10th Cav. Original member of 10th Cavalry; in troop when organized, Ft Riley, KS, 21 Sep 1867. SOURCE: McMiller, "Buffalo Soldiers," 78.

Assigned to Ft Arbuckle-Ft Gibson, Indian Territory, mail route, winter of 1867–68; drowned en route. SOURCE: Leckie, *The Buffalo Soldiers,* 29.

See **FORD,** George W., Quartermaster Sergeant, 10th Cavalry

ROBERTS, George; Private; B/10th Cav. Sentenced to dishonorable discharge and jail, Ft Robinson, NE, in accordance with Special Order 20, Department of the Missouri, Feb 1903; escaped Oct 1903.

ROBERTS, George E.; Private; M/24th Inf. Died at Ft Douglas, UT, hospital; buried on post with honors. SOURCE: *ANJ* 36 (18 Feb 1899): 588.

ROBERTS, Henry; Private; F/9th Cav. Murdered, Ft Robinson, NE, 7 Dec 1886, by Pvt. Alfred Mace, C/9th Cavalry; born in Harrison Co., OH, and had friends in Fremont, OH; would have been eligible for discharge 21 Feb 1887. SOURCE: Cleveland *Gazette,* 1 Jan 1887.

Died of pistol wound while absent without leave, 6 Dec 1886. SOURCE: Post Returns, Ft Robinson, Dec 1886.

Buried Ft Robinson, 6 Dec 1886. SOURCE: List of Interments, Ft Robinson.

ROBERTS, John; Private; G/10th Cav. Served in 10th Cavalry, 1898; remained in U.S. during war with Spain. SOURCE: Cashin, *Under Fire with the Tenth Cavalry,* 346.

ROBERTS, Less; Private; A/10th Cav. Private, A/10th Cavalry, at Ft Apache, AZ, 1890, subscribed $.50 to testimonial to General Grierson. SOURCE: List of subscriptions, 23 Apr 1890, 10th Cavalry papers, MHI.

Served in 10th Cavalry, 1898; remained in U.S. during war with Spain. SOURCE: Cashin, *Under Fire with the Tenth Cavalry,* 337.

ROBERTS, Phillip; Sergeant; I/10th Cav. Born in Maryland; private, I/10th Cavalry, 21 Mar 1882–20 Mar 1887; private, general mounted service and I/10th Cavalry, 18 Apr 1887; corporal, 7 Aug 1889; sergeant, 14 Oct 1893; ranked number 10 with revolver, Department of the Missouri, with bronze medal, 1893; at Ft Assiniboine, MT, 1897. SOURCE: Baker, Roster.

Served in 10th Cavalry, 1898; remained in U.S. during war with Spain. SOURCE: Cashin, *Under Fire with the Tenth Cavalry,* 348.

ROBERTS, Robert; Private; M/10th Cav. Served as farrier, M/10th Cavalry, 1898; remained in U.S. during war with Spain. SOURCE: Cashin, *Under Fire with the Tenth Cavalry,* 351.

Killed by fall, Cauto, Santiago, Cuba, 16 Sep 1899. SOURCE: Richmond *Planet,* 23 Sep 1899.

ROBERTS, Robert W.; Corporal; B/24th Inf. Wounded in action, Cuba, 1898. SOURCE: Muller, *The Twenty Fourth Infantry,* 18.

Died in Cuba, 1 Jul 1898. SOURCE: *ANJ* 36 (18 Feb 1898): 590.

ROBERTS, Robert W.; 24th Inf. Wounded in action in Cuba, 1898; returned to Salt Lake City with regiment; promoted. SOURCE: Clark, "A History of the Twenty-fourth," 100–101.

ROBERTS, Stansberry; Private; B/25th Inf. Dishonorable discharge, Brownsville. SOURCE: SO 266, AGO, 9 Nov 1906.

ROBERTS, W. B.; Captain; 23rd Kans Inf. Letter from San Luiz, Cuba, 15 Oct 1898. SOURCE: Gatewood, *"Smoked Yankees"*, 190–92.

ROBERTS, W. H.; Private; D/10th Cav. Served in 10th Cavalry, 1898; remained in U.S. during war with Spain. SOURCE: Cashin, *Under Fire with the Tenth Cavalry*, 341.

ROBERTS, William; Private; C/9th Cav. Sentenced to dishonorable discharge and jail, Ft Robinson, NE, in accordance with General Court Martial Order 28, Department of the Platte, 9 Apr 1887.

ROBERTSON, Charles; Blacksmith; F/10th Cav. Served as blacksmith, F/10th Cavalry in Cuba, 1898; wounded in action. SOURCE: Cashin, *Under Fire With the Tenth Cavalry*, 343.

    Wounded in action at Santiago, Cuba, 1 Jul 1898. SOURCE: SecWar, *AR 1898*, 324.

ROBERTSON, Charles W.; Corporal; L/10th Cav. Served in 10th Cavalry, 1898; remained in U.S. during war with Spain. SOURCE: Cashin, *Under Fire with the Tenth Cavalry*, 350.

ROBERTSON, Henry; Sergeant; C/10th Cav. Served in 10th Cavalry in Cuba, 1898. SOURCE: Cashin, *Under Fire with the Tenth Cavalry*, 339.

ROBERTSON, Silas W.; Cook; A/25th Inf. Drowned in the Philippines, body recovered, 7 Jan 1902. SOURCE: *ANJ* 39 (8 Mar 1902): 680.

ROBERTSON, Tom; Corporal; B/24th Inf. Private, at Ft Huachuca, AZ, 1893. *See* **HAM**, James, Sergeant, B/24th Infantry

    Died in Cuba, 27 Jul 1898. SOURCE: *ANJ* 36 (18 Feb 1898): 590.

ROBESIN, Peter; Private; H/9th Cav. At Ft D. A. Russell, WY, in 1910; resident of Baltimore. SOURCE: *Illustrated Review: Ninth Cavalry*, with picture.

ROBINSON; Private; A/10th Cav. At Ft Apache, AZ, 1890, subscribed $.50 to testimonial to General Grierson. SOURCE: List of subscriptions, 23 Apr 1890, 10th Cav papers, MHI.

ROBINSON; Corporal; E/9th Cav. Reenlistment, married, authorized by letter, Adjutant General's Office, 29 Aug 1896.

ROBINSON; Private; K/24th Inf. At Cabanatuan, Philippines, 1901. *See* **STEVENS**, Samuel, Private, D/24th Infantry

ROBINSON; Private; M/24th Inf. At Ft Assiniboine, MT, 1902. *See* **GANTZ**, Frank, 24th Infantry

ROBINSON, A.; Private; G/9th Cav. On detached service at Ft Stanton, NM, 29 Jan–5 Feb 1881. SOURCE: Regt Returns, 9 Cav, Feb 1881.

ROBINSON, Alexander; Private; Band/9th Cav. With band on detached service at headquarters, District of New Mexico, Santa Fe, 1880; played third B-flat cornet. SOURCE: Billington, *New Mexico's Buffalo Soldiers*, 226.

ROBINSON, Alexander; Horseshoer; L/9th Cav. Veteran of Philippine Insurrection; at Ft D. A. Russell, WY, in 1910; resident of Jellico, TN. SOURCE: *Illustrated Review: Ninth Cavalry,* with picture.

ROBINSON, Alvin H.; Private; C/9th Cav. At Ft D. A. Russell, WY, in 1910; resident of Flemmingburg, KY. SOURCE: *Illustrated Review: Ninth Cavalry,* with picture.

ROBINSON, Arthur J.; Private; 24th Inf. Harassed and arrested by Manila police, 19 Jun 1902. SOURCE: Letter, CO, 24 Inf, to Chief of Police, Manila, 21 Jun 1902.

ROBINSON, Benjamin; Private; F/9th Cav. Detailed for duty with regimental headquarters, Santa Fe, NM. SOURCE: RO 25, 9 Cav, Santa Fe, 11 May 1897.

ROBINSON, Benjamin; Private; D/10th Cav. Served in 10th Cavalry in Cuba, 1898. SOURCE: Cashin, *Under Fire with the Tenth Cavalry*, 341.

ROBINSON, Berry; Blacksmith; G/9th Cav. Private, H/9th Cavalry; served in Lincoln, NM, Jul 1878. SOURCE: Billington, *New Mexico's Buffalo Soldiers*, 78–79.

    Reenlistment authorized by telegram, Adjutant General's Office, 18 Feb 1897.

    Retired, Dec 1901. SOURCE: *ANJ* 39 (21 Dec 1901): 394.

ROBINSON, Bill; Sergeant; F/10th Cav. Original member of 10th Cavalry; in troop when organized, Ft Leavenworth, KS, 21 Jun 1867. SOURCE: McMiller, "Buffalo Soldiers," 73.

    Commander, 10th Cavalry, thinks Capt. George F. Armes's course of action regarding Sergeant Robinson "rather hasty"; Robinson was three-year veteran as sergeant of cavalry under excellent commander. SOURCE: Adj, 10 Cav, to Capt Armes, F/10th Cavalry, Ft Harker, KS, 18 Jul 1867, LS, 10 Cav, 1866–67.

ROBINSON, Cecil; Private; L/9th Cav. At Ft D. A. Russell, WY, in 1910; resident of Waters Park, TX. SOURCE: *Illustrated Review: Ninth Cavalry.*

ROBINSON, Charles; H/25th Inf. Admitted to Soldiers Home with disability, age 37, after twelve years and eleven months' service, 24 Aug 1889. SOURCE: SecWar, *AR 1889*, 1014.

ROBINSON, Charles; Private; L/10th Cav. Served in 10th Cavalry, 1898; remained in U.S. during war with Spain. SOURCE: Cashin, *Under Fire with the Tenth Cavalry*, 350.

ROBINSON, Charles; Farrier; F/9th Cav. Funeral, Ft Robinson, NE, 6 Mar 1890. SOURCE: Order 43, 5 Mar 1890, Post Orders, Ft Robinson.

   Buried, Ft Robinson, 4 Mar 1890. SOURCE: List of Interments, Ft Robinson.

ROBINSON, Charles A.; Private; F/9th Cav. Deserted, San Francisco, 16 Aug 1900. SOURCE: Regt Returns, 9 Cav, Nov 1900.

ROBINSON, Charles C.; Private; K/9th Cav. Discharged on surgeon's certificate with typhoid fever, Ft Robinson, NE, 14 Sep 1887.

ROBINSON, Clem; F/10th Cav. Died 13 Mar 1920. SOURCE: VA File SC 11405, John Taylor.

ROBINSON, Daniel S.; Sgt Maj; 9th Cav. Retires May 1901. SOURCE: *ANJ* 38 (11 May 1901): 895.

ROBINSON, David; Sergeant; I/10th Cav. Original member of L/10th Cavalry; in troop when organized, Ft Riley, KS, 21 Sep 1867. SOURCE: McMiller, "Buffalo Soldiers," 78.

   In L/10th Cavalry, authorized two-month furlough from Ft Grant, AZ. SOURCE: *ANJ* 24 (16 Jun 1887): 1012.

   Retires from I/10th Cavalry, Ft Leavenworth, KS, 7 Aug 1893. SOURCE: *ANJ* 30 (5 Aug 1893): 827; Baker, Roster.

   Recently retired from I/10th Cavalry; before he went home to Little Rock, AR, comrades presented him with silver-headed cane as token of their regard. SOURCE: *ANJ* 30 (19 Aug 1893): 858.

ROBINSON, David; Recruit; 10th Cav. Mentioned Jan 1877 as unassigned. SOURCE: ES, 10 Cav, 1873–83.

ROBINSON, Edward; Private; D/25th Inf. Dishonorable discharge, Brownsville. SOURCE: SO 266, AGO, 9 Nov 1906.

ROBINSON, Forrest; Private; C/10th Cav. Served in 10th Cavalry in Cuba, 1898. SOURCE: Cashin, *Under Fire with the Tenth Cavalry*, 340.

ROBINSON, Frank; Private; H/10th Cav. Served in 10th Cavalry, 1898; remained in U.S. during war with Spain. SOURCE: Cashin, *Under Fire with the Tenth Cavalry*, 347.

   At Camp Forse, AL, Nov 1898. SOURCE: Richmond *Planet*, 3 Dec 1898.

ROBINSON, Fred A.; Private; D/9th Cav. Died in the Philippines, 13 Apr 1901. SOURCE: *ANJ* 38 (4 May 1901): 876.

ROBINSON, George; Private; K/25th Inf. Sang in K/25th Infantry's "Imperial Quartette" in the Philippines. SOURCE: Richmond *Planet*, 16 Dec 1899.

ROBINSON, George R.; Private; D/25th Inf. Deserted from Ft Niobrara, NE, 31 Mar 1902. SOURCE: Regt Returns, 25 Inf, Mar 1902; Descriptive Book, D/25 Inf.

ROBINSON, Harry; Corporal; E/49th Inf. Died of dysentery at Calamba, Luzon, Philippines, 25 May 1901. SOURCE: *ANJ* 38 (27 Jul 1901): 1169.

ROBINSON, Henry; QM Sgt; C/10th Cav. Born in Kentucky; private, corporal, sergeant, first sergeant, C/10th Cavalry, 5 Mar 1867–4 Mar 1882; private, 15 Mar 1886; sergeant, 1 May 1886. SOURCE: Baker, Roster.

   Original member of C/10th Cavalry; in troop when organized, Ft Leavenworth, KS, 14 May 1867. SOURCE: McMiller, "Buffalo Soldiers," 70.

   Honorable mention for gallantry against Kiowas and Comanches, Wichita Agency, Indian Territory, 22–23 Aug 1874. SOURCE: Baker, Roster.

   Authorized two-month furlough from Ft Apache, AZ. SOURCE: *ANJ* 24 (12 Mar 1887): 650.

   At Ft Apache, 1890, subscribed $.25 to testimonial to General Grierson. SOURCE: List of subscriptions, 23 Apr 1890, 10th Cavalry papers, MHI.

   Retired from the Presidio of San Francisco, CA, as quartermaster sergeant, C/10th Cavalry. SOURCE: *ANJ* 37 (28 Jul 1900): 1143.

ROBINSON, Henry; Private; K/9th Cav. Served in 1872–73. *See* **SLAUGHTER**, Rufus, Private, K/9th Cavalry

ROBINSON, Henry; Sergeant; E/9th Cav. Attacked by Victorio, 28 Sep 1879, while commanding four-man mail escort near Ojo Caliente, NM; rescued by arrival of hunting party under Sgt. James Williams, E/9th Cavalry. SOURCE: Billington, *New Mexico's Buffalo Soldiers*, 91.

ROBINSON, Henry; Private; 25th Inf. Born Charleston, SC; occupation fisherman; age 26, Ht 5'5"; enlisted 1 Jun 1881. SOURCE: Descriptive & Assignment Rolls, 25 Inf.

ROBINSON, Henry; C/9th Cav. Served 1888–91; renews subscription. SOURCE: *Winners of the West* 14 (Mar 1937): 8.

ROBINSON, Henry; Private; B/10th Cav. Served in 10th Cavalry, 1898; remained in U.S. during war with Spain. SOURCE: Cashin, *Under Fire with the Tenth Cavalry*, 333.

ROBINSON, Henry; Private; D/25th Inf. Letter from Presidio of San Francisco, CA, 9 Jun 1900, asks friends to write often and send *Searchlight*; en route to the Philippines. SOURCE: Wichita *Searchlight*, 29 Dec 1900.

Dishonorable discharge, Brownsville. SOURCE: SO 266, AGO, 9 Nov 1906.

ROBINSON, Henry; Sergeant; L/24th Inf. With twelve enlisted men sent to Haines Mission, AK, to prevent trouble between citizens and Indians, Jul 1900. SOURCE: Fletcher, "The Negro Soldier," 70.

ROBINSON, Hoytt; Musician; D/25th Inf. Dishonorable discharge, Brownsville. SOURCE: SO 266, AGO, 9 Nov 1906.

ROBINSON, Ira; Private; L/9th Cav. Veteran of Spanish-American War and Philippine Insurrection; at Ft D. A. Russell, WY, in 1910; resident of Cassopolis, MI. SOURCE: *Illustrated Review: Ninth Cavalry*, with picture.

ROBINSON, J. A.; D/24th Inf. At Ft Bayard, NM; will have five years on 9 May 1891; "Mr. Robinson has saved hundreds in cash during his term of service." SOURCE: Cleveland *Gazette*, 9 May 1891.

ROBINSON, James; Sergeant; G/9th Cav. With detachment attacked by Indians at Agua Chiquita, NM; two privates, Robert Smith and Daniel Stanton, killed in action; stationed at Ft Stanton, NM. SOURCE: Hamilton, "History of the Ninth Cavalry," 53; *Illustrated Review: Ninth Cavalry*.

Attacked by Apaches, Agua Chiquita Canyon, NM, while in command of detachment, Sep 1880; praised by commander for gallant conduct. SOURCE: Billington, *New Mexico's Buffalo Soldiers*, 97–98.

On detached service at Ft Stanton, 29 Jan–5 Feb 1881. SOURCE: Regt Returns, 9 Cav, Feb 1881.

ROBINSON, James; F/25th Inf. Admitted to Soldiers Home with disability, age 41, after twelve years and one month's service, 19 May 1890. SOURCE: SecWar, *AR 1890*, 1042.

ROBINSON, James; Corporal; L/49th Inf. Died of tuberculosis in the Philippines, 2 Oct 1900. SOURCE: *ANJ* 38 (20 Oct 1900): 187.

Stationed at Claveria, Philippines; died in hospital of "acute tuberculosis of both lungs," Aparri, Philippines, 30 Nov 1900. SOURCE: Regt Returns, 49th Infantry.

ROBINSON, James; Private; B/25th Inf. Died of tuberculosis in the Philippines, 14 Nov 1901. SOURCE: *ANJ* 39 (18 Jan 1902): 502.

ROBINSON, James; Private; I/24th Inf. Mechanic, sentenced to death for part in Houston riot. SOURCE: Haynes, *A Night of Violence*, 135, 277–78.

To be hanged for his role in Houston riot. SOURCE: Cleveland *Gazette*, 5 Jan 1918.

ROBINSON, Jeremiah; K/10th Cav. Original member of 10th Cavalry; in troop when organized, Ft Riley, KS, 1 Sep 1867. SOURCE: McMiller, "Buffalo Soldiers," 77.

ROBINSON, John; G/10th Cav. Original member of 10th Cavalry; in troop when organized, Ft Leavenworth, KS, 5 Jul 1867. SOURCE: McMiller, "Buffalo Soldiers," 74.

ROBINSON, John; Corporal; E/24th Inf. Killed in action, Cuba, 1898. SOURCE: Scipio, *Last of the Black Regulars*, 29.

ROBINSON, John; Private; C/9th Cav. Transferred from A/10th Cavalry, Ft Robinson, NE, Jun 1903, to C/9th Cavalry, Monterey, CA.

ROBINSON, John H.; Artificer; K/25th Inf. At Ft Niobrara, NE, 1904. SOURCE: Wilson, "History of Fort Niobrara."

ROBINSON, John Henry; Private; A/10th Cav. Served in 10th Cavalry, 1898; remained in U.S. during war with Spain. SOURCE: Cashin, *Under Fire with the Tenth Cavalry*, 337.

ROBINSON, John W.; Corporal; F/10th Cav. Born in Virginia; private, corporal, sergeant, F/10th Cavalry, 7 Mar 1882–6 Mar 1887; private, corporal, sergeant, first sergeant, 14 Mar 1887–13 Mar 1892; private and sergeant, general recruiting service, 2 Apr 1892–21 Apr 1894; private, F/10th Cavalry, 14 Sep 1894; corporal, 25 Feb 1895. SOURCE: Baker, Roster.

Original member of F/10th Cavalry; in troop when organized, Ft Leavenworth, KS, 21 Jun 1867. SOURCE: McMiller, "Buffalo Soldiers," 73.

Wounded in action against Indians, KS, 21 Sep 1867. SOURCE: Armes, *Ups and Downs*, 248.

ROBINSON, John W.; Private; K/10th Cav. Mentioned Mar 1873. SOURCE: LS, 10 Cav, 1873–83.

ROBINSON, Lee; Private; K/10th Cav. At Ft Robinson, NE, 1904.

ROBINSON, Mansfield; 24th Inf. Served 1889–1913. SOURCE: Interview by Edward M. Coffman, 8 Apr 1955, in Coffman, "Army Life on the Frontier," 193–201; Louisville, *Courier-Journal*, 2 Dec 1956.

Picture. SOURCE: Billington, *New Mexico's Buffalo Soldiers*, 171.

ROBINSON, Mason; Private; D/24th Inf. Wounded in the back, Santiago, Cuba, 1 Jul 1898. SOURCE: SecWar, *AR 1898*, 346; Muller, *The Twenty Fourth Infantry*, 18.

Fined $10 for willful disobedience of order to stop swearing and raising disturbance around quarters, Cabanatuan, Philippines, 14 Apr 1901; witnesses: First Sergeant Ellis; QM Sgt. R. L. Duvall, D/24th Infantry; Pvt. James A. Simpson, D/24th Infantry. SOURCE: Name File, 24 Inf.

ROBINSON, Michael H., Jr.; Private; F/25th Inf.
Letter from Iba, Philippines, 1 Feb 1900, in Gatewood, *"Smoked Yankees"*, 264.

Deserted from Iba, 2 Jan 1901, "cause unknown." SOURCE: Regt Returns, 25 Inf, Jan 1901.

"Private Michael Robinson, Company F, 25th Infantry, a trusted clerk of the commissary at Iba and having charge of the sales department of the same, appropriated the proceeds of a few days sales to his personal use, amounting to $65.00 or $70.00 in gold, and making deliberate preparations he deserted his command and joined a band of roaming insurgents in the mountains near Iba." SOURCE: Letter, Pvt. Rienzi Lemus, K/25th Infantry, Castillejos, Philippines, 20 Feb 1901, Richmond *Planet*, 23 Mar 1901.

"According to a letter to *la Democraci's* from Poteaciano Lesaca, of Iba, Zambales, the police of that place succeeded in capturing in the barrio of Baugatalinga, the negro renegade Robinson, formerly of F company of the 25th Infantry, who was a member of the command of Captain Joaquin Serrano, now the only insurrecto chief who is marauding in that neighborhood. On the next day the local police captured in the barrio of Bancal, pueblo of Botolan, the notorious negro renegade Wilmore, who had joined the insurgent forces after escaping from the guardhouse where he had been confined for military offenses. 'This important service,' the letter says, 'was rendered by the teniente of the barrio, ably seconded by the police of Botolan.' " SOURCE: Manila *Times*, 3 Mar 1901.

Commander, 25th Infantry, forwarded charges against Robinson, for desertion, treason, and violation of the laws of war, to the adjutant general, Third District, Philippines, 16 Apr 1901. SOURCE: LR, 25 Inf.

Robinson sentenced to hang for desertion; sentence commuted to life in prison. SOURCE: Crawford *Tribune*, 25 Oct 1901.

"Private Michael H. Robinson, Co. F, 25th Inf., having been tried and found guilty of desertion, having entered the armed forces of insurrection against the United States about Jan. 2, 1901, and remaining absent in desertion and in the service of the insurrectionists until apprehended about Feb. 20, 1901, by a G. C. M. convened at San Marcelino, Zambales, P.I., was sentenced to be dishonorably discharged from the service, forfeiting all pay and allowances, and to be hung by the neck. President Roosevelt has commuted the sentence of Robinson to dishonorable discharge, forfeiture of all pay and allowances, and confinement at hard labor for the period of his natural life." SOURCE: *ANJ* 39 (26 Oct 1901): 182.

ROBINSON, Oscar G.; Sergeant; D/9th Cav.
Served as private, K/10th Cavalry, 1898; remained in U.S. during war with Spain. SOURCE: Cashin, *Under Fire with the Tenth Cavalry*, 349.

Trumpeter, D/9th Cavalry; best pistol shot in Army pistol competition, with gold medal, Ft Riley, KS, 1905; ranked number 5 in Northern Division pistol competition, Ft Riley, 1905. SOURCE: GO 173, AGO, 20 Oct 1905.

Corporal, D/9th Cavalry; best pistol shot in Army pistol competition, Ft Sheridan, IL, 1906; ranked number 2 in Northern Division pistol competition, Ft Sheridan, 1906. SOURCE: GO 198, AGO, 6 Dec 1906.

Corporal, second best noncommissioned officer pistol shot in Army. SOURCE: Indianapolis *Freeman*, 26 Jan 1907.

Sergeant, ranked number 7, Army pistol competition, Ft Sheridan, 1909, distinguished pistol shot. SOURCE: GO 228, AGO, 12 Nov 1909.

Distinguished marksman and veteran of Spanish-American War; sergeant, D/9th Cavalry, at Ft D. A. Russell, WY, in 1910; resident of Fayett Co., WY. SOURCE: *Illustrated Review: Ninth Cavalry,* with picture.

ROBINSON, Richard; Corporal; H/25th Inf. Shot dead through head with Springfield rifle, while asleep on bunk, Ft Davis, TX, Sep 1878, by Sgt. Moses Marshall. SOURCE: Carroll, *The Black Military Experience*, 276.

ROBINSON, Richard E.; Wagoner; K/10th Cav.
Served in 10th Cavalry, 1898; remained in U.S. during war with Spain. SOURCE: Cashin, *Under Fire with the Tenth Cavalry*, 349.

ROBINSON, Robert; Private; 25th Inf. Lynched at Sun River, MT, by a group of masked men, after he beat Private Matchett, 3rd Infantry, for being with his mistress, Queeny Montgomery, who had followed him from Ft Sisseton, Dakota Territory, to Ft Shaw, MT, 10 Jun 1888. SOURCE: Fowler, *The Black Infantry*, 61–62.

ROBINSON, Robert W.; Color Sgt; 9th Cav.
Sergeant, K/9th Cavalry; ranked number 440 among rifle experts with 68.87 percent in 1905. SOURCE: GO 101, AGO, 31 May 1906.

Expert rifleman and veteran of Spanish-American War and Philippine Insurrection; color sergeant, 9th Cavalry, at Ft D. A. Russell, WY, in 1910; resident of St. Louis. SOURCE: *Illustrated Review: Ninth Cavalry,* with picture.

ROBINSON, Ross; Private; Band/9th Cav. At Ft D. A. Russell, WY, in 1910; resident of Fredericksburg, VA. SOURCE: *Illustrated Review: Ninth Cavalry,* with picture.

ROBINSON, Samuel; Blacksmith; C/10th Cav.
Deceased by Nov 1875. SOURCE: ES, 10 Cav, 1873–83.

ROBINSON, Samuel; Private; B/9th Cav. At Ft D. A. Russell, WY, in 1910. SOURCE: *Illustrated Review: Ninth Cavalry.*

ROBINSON, Sherman; Private; F/10th Cav. Served in 10th Cavalry, 1898; remained in U.S. during war with Spain. SOURCE: Cashin, *Under Fire with the Tenth Cavalry*, 344.

ROBINSON, Stephen V.; L/9th Cav. Served 1879–84; died at Baltimore, age 80. SOURCE: *Winners of the West* 11 (Jun 1934): 3.

ROBINSON, W. H.; 1st Lt; 9th Inf USV. Born New Orleans, LA, 24 Jan 1866; educated there and partly completed course at Straight University, New Orleans; promoted to first lieutenant, 13 Apr 1899. SOURCE: Coston, *The Spanish-American War Veteran*, 51.

ROBINSON, Wilbarn; Private; L/10th Cav. Served in 10th Cavalry, 1898; remained in U.S. during war with Spain. SOURCE: Cashin, *Under Fire with the Tenth Cavalry*, 350.

ROBINSON, Wiley; G/24th Inf. Remained in Bautista, Philippines, after service; died 1903. SOURCE: Funston papers, KSHS.

ROBINSON, William; Sergeant; B/9th Cav. Authorized four-month furlough from Ft Duchesne, UT. SOURCE: *ANJ* 24 (5 Mar 1887): 630.

ROBINSON, William; Private; I/24th Inf. Enlisted St Francis Barracks, FL, 10 Oct 1898. SOURCE: Muster Roll, I/24 Inf, Jan–Feb 1899.

Discharged, character good, 31 Dec 1899; $50 deposits, $8.80 clothing. SOURCE: Muster Roll, I/24 Inf, Nov–Dec 1899.

ROBINSON, William; Private; I/10th Cav. Released to duty from treatment for gonorrhea, Ft Robinson, NE, 16 Aug 1903. SOURCE: Post Surgeon to CO, I/10, 16 Aug 1903, LS, Post Surgeon, Ft Robinson.

ROBINSON, William H.; G/10th Cav. Original member of 10th Cavalry; in troop when organized, Ft Leavenworth, KS, 5 Jul 1867. SOURCE: McMiller, "Buffalo Soldiers," 74.

ROCK, Pierre; Sergeant; C/9th Cav. Appointed sergeant 3 Sep 1892. SOURCE: Roster, 9 Cav.

Retires from Ft Robinson, NE, Dec 1894. SOURCE: *ANJ* 32 (22 Dec 1894): 278.

RODGERS, A. N.; Corporal; B/10th Cav. At Ft Apache, AZ, 1890, subscribed $.50 to testimonial to General Grierson. SOURCE: List of subscriptions, 23 Apr 1890, 10th Cavalry papers, MHI.

RODGERS, Henry R.; Private; B/9th Cav. Transferred to Reserve Divisional Hospital, Siboney, Cuba, with remittent yellow fever, 22 Jul 1898. SOURCE: Hospital Papers, Spanish-American War.

RODGERS, Joseph; Private; M/10th Cav. Served in 10th Cavalry, 1898; remained in U.S. during war with Spain. SOURCE: Cashin, *Under Fire with the Tenth Cavalry*, 352.

RODGERS, Ollie; Private; H/10th Cav. Served in 10th Cavalry, 1898; remained in U.S. during war with Spain. SOURCE: Cashin, *Under Fire with the Tenth Cavalry*, 347.

RODGERS, William; Private; B/24th Inf. On special duty, target range, Ft Huachuca, AZ, 30 Apr–10 Aug 1893. SOURCE: Name File, 24 Inf.

Commander, E/2nd Cavalry, to send detachment of one noncommissioned officer and three privates with one Indian scout in search of Rodgers, supposed to have deserted. SOURCE: Order 144, Ft Huachuca, 30 Sep 1893, Letters and Orders Received, 24 Inf.

RODGERS, Willie J.; Private; H/9th Cav. At Ft D. A. Russell, WY, in 1910; resident of Macon, GA. SOURCE: *Illustrated Review: Ninth Cavalry,* with picture.

ROE, John W.; I/25th Inf. Saw William Branch injured at Ft Sill, Indian Territory, 1874. SOURCE: Affidavit, Roe, Van Avery, Bexar Co., TX, 18 Sep 1891, VA File C 2581520, William Branch.

ROES, George; B/10th Cav. Original member of 10th Cavalry; in troop when organized, Ft Leavenworth, KS, 1 Apr 1867. SOURCE: McMiller, "Buffalo Soldiers," 69.

ROGAN, Robert L.; Private; D/25th Inf. Dishonorable discharge, Brownsville. SOURCE: SO 266, AGO, 9 Nov 1906.

ROGAN, Wilbur; 25th Inf. Born Kansas City, KS; served 1911–19; played for Kansas City Monarchs as "Bullet" Rogan, 1919–38; then had civil service job in Kansas City and umpired Negro National League games. SOURCE: Peterson, *Only the Ball Was White*, 214–15, with picture, 215.

ROGERS; Corporal; C/10th Cav. Guest with wife at K/10th Cavalry Thanksgiving dinner, Ft Robinson, NE, 1904. SOURCE: Simmons, "Thanksgiving Day in the Tenth Cavalry," 664.

ROGERS, David L.; H/23rd Kans Inf. Died in Minnesota, 24 Jul 1937. SOURCE: Taylor, "Minnesota Black Spanish-American War Veterans."

ROGERS, Edward; Private; D/9th Cav. At Ft D. A. Russell, WY, in 1910; marksman; resident of Louisville. SOURCE: *Illustrated Review: Ninth Cavalry.*

ROGERS, Frederick; H/10th Cav. Original member of 10th Cavalry; in troop when organized, Ft Leavenworth, KS, 21 Jul 1867. SOURCE: McMiller, "Buffalo Soldiers," 75.

ROGERS, John; Trumpeter; I/9th Cav. Corporal, clothing destroyed when fighting fire, Ft Wingate, NM, 15 Dec 1876. SOURCE: Billington, *New Mexico's Buffalo Soldiers*, 110.

Trumpeter, I/9th Cavalry, volunteered to carry message seeking reinforcements when detachment ambushed by Apaches, Cuchillo Negro Mountains, NM, 16 Aug 1881. SOURCE: Billington, *New Mexico's Buffalo Soldiers*, 106.

Trumpeter, I/9th Cavalry, in action against Apache Nana, Aug 1881. SOURCE: Leckie, *The Buffalo Soldiers*, 232.

Cited for heroic action, Cuchilla Negro Mountains, in carrying message under heavy fire to commander, Lt. Gustavus Valois, Aug 1881. SOURCE: Carroll, *The Black Military Experience*, 367.

Corporal, I/9th Cavalry; family put out of quarters and off Ft Robinson, NE, reservation, for engaging in row, May 1891. SOURCE: LS, Ft Robinson.

Asked other enlisted men of I/9th Cavalry to sign petition for transfer of Capt. John Guilfoyle from command of troop. SOURCE: CO, Ft Robinson, to AAG, DP, 26 Jun 1891, LS, Ft Robinson.

Trumpeter, G/9th Cavalry, ordered by post commander, Ft Robinson, to see that his children attended school and did not loiter around barracks during school hours. SOURCE: CO, Ft Robinson, to Rogers, 22 Mar 1893, LS, Ft Robinson.

Resides with wife, two children, and brother-in-law in old barrack, Ft Robinson, Aug 1893. SOURCE: Medical History, Ft Robinson.

Trumpeter, G/9th Cavalry, with quarters on post with wife, Ft Robinson, 1894. SOURCE: Court Martial Records, Dillon.

Trumpeter, I/9th Cavalry; Ft Robinson commander disapproves his request; does not consider it in best interest of service to allow Mrs. Rogers to return to post. SOURCE: CO, Ft Robinson, to Rogers, 9 Oct 1895, LS, Ft Robinson.

ROGERS, John; Private; Band/9th Cav. Expert rifleman at Ft D. A. Russell, WY, in 1910; resident of Houston. SOURCE: *Illustrated Review: Ninth Cavalry*, with picture.

ROGERS, Joseph; Private; C/25th Inf. Dishonorable discharge, Brownsville. SOURCE: SO 266, AGO, 9 Nov 1906.

ROGERS, Lemuel J.; Private; Hospital Corps. At Cabanatuan, Philippines, 1901. *See* **MOORE**, Cato, Private, D/24th Infantry

ROGERS, Samuel; D/10th Cav. Original member of 10th Cavalry; in troop when organized, Ft Leavenworth, KS, 1 Jun 1867. SOURCE: McMiller, "Buffalo Soldiers," 71.

ROLAND, Albert; Corporal; D/25th Inf. Dishonorable discharge, Brownsville. SOURCE: SO 266, AGO, 9 Nov 1906.

ROLAND, Samuel; C/10th Cav. Original member of 10th Cavalry; in troop when organized, Ft Leavenworth, KS, 14 May 1867. SOURCE: McMiller, "Buffalo Soldiers," 70.

ROLLAR, Alfred; Private; L/10th Cav. Served in 10th Cavalry, 1898; remained in U.S. during war with Spain. SOURCE: Cashin, *Under Fire with the Tenth Cavalry*, 350.

ROLLER; Private; B/24th Inf. Second in 16-pound shot put, Department of Colorado, while at Ft Douglas, UT. SOURCE: Clark, "A History of the Twenty-fourth," 70.

ROLLINS, Green; A/10th Cav. Original member of 10th Cavalry; in troop when organized, Ft Leavenworth, KS, 18 Feb 1867. SOURCE: McMiller, "Buffalo Soldiers," 68.

ROLLINS, Horace; Trumpeter; C/10th Cav. At Ft Apache, AZ, 1890, subscribed $.25 to testimonial to General Grierson. SOURCE: List of subscriptions, 23 Apr 1890, 10th Cavalry papers, MHI.

ROLLINS, John; Private; F/24th Inf. 2nd Lt. Theodore Decker, 24th Infantry, visited Rollins's mistress, a Mexican prostitute named Refugia Estrada, town of Eagle Pass, TX, 12 Apr 1880, and engaged in disgraceful shooting fray with Rollins, in which Estrada was killed and Decker shot in face and shoulder; Decker dismissed from service. SOURCE: GCMO 50, AGO, 23 Aug 1880.

ROLLINS, Ramie; Private; L/10th Cav. Served in 10th Cavalry, 1898; remained in U.S. during war with Spain. SOURCE: Cashin, *Under Fire with the Tenth Cavalry*, 350.

ROLLINS, Walker S.; Private; F/10th Cav. Born in Virginia; private, F/10th Cavalry, 3 Aug 1889; corporal, 20 Apr 1892; sergeant, 5 Dec 1892; at Ft Assiniboine, MT, 1897. SOURCE: Baker, Roster.

Served as private, F/10th Cavalry, in Cuba, 1898. SOURCE: Cashin, *Under Fire with the Tenth Cavalry*, 343.

ROLLINS, William; Private; B/24th Inf. First in standing broad jump, 10'3", Department of Colorado, while at Ft Douglas, UT. SOURCE: Clark, "A History of the Twenty-fourth," 70.

ROLLY, J.; Private; E/9th Cav. On detached service in field, New Mexico, 27 Jan–1 Feb 1881. SOURCE: Regt Returns, 9 Cav, Feb 1881.

ROMONS, Isaac W.; Recruit; Colored Detachment/Mounted Service. At Jefferson Barracks, MO, 1886. *See* **MILLER**, Charles, Recruit, Colored Detachment/Mounted Service

RONSON, E. A.; Sergeant; G/9th Cav. Reenlistment, married, approved by letter, Adjutant General's Office, 26 Aug 1893.

ROPER, Charles H.; 1st Sgt; D/9th Cav. Private, C/9th Cavalry; application for transfer disapproved by letter, Adjutant General's Office, 24 Apr 1894.

Lance corporal, I/9th Cavalry, promoted to corporal, Ft Duchesne, UT, Jan 1896. SOURCE: *ANJ* 33 (18 Jan 1896): 348.

First sergeant, D/9th Cavalry, killed by accident in the Philippines, 2 Mar 1901. SOURCE: *ANJ* 38 (30 Mar 1901): 755.

ROPER, Neil; Private; D/10th Cav. At Ft Apache, AZ, 1890, subscribed \$.50 to testimonial to General Grierson. SOURCE: List of subscriptions, 23 Apr 1890, 10th Cavalry papers, MHI.

Served in 10th Cavalry, 1898; remained in U.S. during war with Spain. SOURCE: Cashin, *Under Fire with the Tenth Cavalry*, 341.

Buried at Cypress Hills Cemetery in New York, 15 Sep 1899. SOURCE: *ANJ* 37 (23 Sep 1899): 80.

ROPER, William; Private; 10th Cav. Apprehended from desertion in Department of the Lakes. SOURCE: Chief QM, Department of the Lakes to AAG, Department of the Lakes, 17 Aug 1887, Misc Records, 10 Cav.

ROSANO, Dell; Private; Band/25th Inf. Fined \$1 for neglect of duty, Iba, Zambales, Philippines. SOURCE: Misc Records, 25 Inf.

ROSE, Alexander; 1st Sgt; K/25th Inf. At Ft Missoula, MT, 1887–88.

ROSE, Amos; H/10th Cav. Original member of 10th Cavalry; in troop when organized, Ft Leavenworth, KS, 21 Jul 1867. SOURCE: McMiller, "Buffalo Soldiers," 75.

ROSE, Charles P.; Private; F/25th Inf. Deserted from San Francisco, 18 Aug 1902. SOURCE: Regt Returns, 25 Inf, Aug 1902.

ROSE, D.; Private; B/9th Cav. On detached service, Ft Bayard, NM, 16–31 Jan 1881. SOURCE: Regt Returns, 9 Cav, Jan 1881.

ROSE, John W.; Private; A/10th Cav. Released to duty from treatment for acute gonorrhea, Ft Robinson, NE, 4 Feb 1903. SOURCE: Post Surgeon to CO, A/10, 4 Feb 1903, LS, Post Surgeon, Ft Robinson.

With 106 sick days in last year, seven of them in line of duty. SOURCE: Post Surgeon to CO, A/10, 15 May 1903, LS, Post Surgeon, Ft Robinson.

Treated at Ft Robinson for chancroids and gonorrhea, 29 Apr–30 May 1903. SOURCE: Post Surgeon to CO, A/10, 10 Jul 1903, LS, Post Surgeon, Ft Robinson.

Released to duty from treatment for gonorrhea, Ft Robinson, 29 May 1903. SOURCE: Post Surgeon to CO, A/10, 29 May 1903, LS, Post Surgeon, Ft Robinson.

ROSE, William; Ord Sgt; U.S. Army. At Ft Elliott, TX, 1885. SOURCE: Cleveland *Gazette*, 9 Jan 1886.

At Ft Elliott, 1886. *See* **SMITH**, Jacob Clay, Sergeant, 10th Cavalry

Reduced from first sergeant to private, fined \$60, confined for six months by general court martial, Ft Elliott, for allowing and participating in 15 Dec 1886 protest meeting. SOURCE: *ANJ* 24 (26 Mar 1887): 695.

Sergeant, F/24th Infantry, authorized four-month furlough from Ft Bayard, NM. SOURCE: *ANJ* 26 (6 Jul 1889): 923.

First sergeant, F/24th Infantry, sharpshooter, Ft Bayard. SOURCE: *ANJ* 28 (27 Sep 1890): 70.

Sergeant, F/24th Infantry, examined for ordnance sergeant, Ft Bayard. SOURCE: *ANJ* 30 (8 Jul 1893): 767.

First sergeant, F/24th Infantry, promoted to ordnance sergeant. SOURCE: *ANJ* 32 (27 Oct 1894): 141.

ROSS; Private; A/25th Inf. Transferred to 9th Cavalry, in accordance with Special Order 173, Adjutant General's Office, 26 Jul 1890.

ROSS, Alfred; Private; C/9th Cav. At Ft Sill, Indian Territory, 1883–88. *See* **COLE**, Private, C/9th Cavalry

Discharged on surgeon's certificate, 1 Feb 1887.

Admitted to Soldiers Home with disability, age 36, after five years' service, 21 May 1888. SOURCE: SecWar, *AR 1888*, 903.

ROSS, Charlie; Trumpeter; A/10th Cav. General court martial sentence in Special Order 130, Adjutant General's Office, 10 Jul 1903.

ROSS, Edward; E/10th Cav. On temporary duty for training, Ft Bascom, NM. SOURCE: SO 8, HQ, District of New Mexico, 8 Mar 1867.

Original member of E/10th Cavalry; in troop when organized, Ft Leavenworth, KS, 15 Jun 1867. SOURCE: McMiller, "Buffalo Soldiers," 72.

ROSS, Edward; Private; G/9th Cav. Private, F/9th Cavalry; convicted by summary court, Ft Robinson, NE, 13 May 1891, of creating disturbance in barracks, being insubordinate and disrespectful to 1st Sgt. John Turner; when ordered to guardhouse, struck Sgt. Edward Fletcher, called him "damned son of a bitch," 10 May 1891; sentenced to thirty days and fined \$12. SOURCE: Summary Court Record, Ft Robinson.

Appointed corporal, E/9th Cavalry, 7 Mar 1893. SOURCE: Roster, 9 Cav.

Private, G/9th Cavalry, at Ft D. A. Russell, WY, in 1910; resident of Muskogee, OK. SOURCE: *Illustrated Review: Ninth Cavalry*.

ROSS, Harry H.; Corporal; 8th Ill Inf. Letter from San Luis, Cuba, 22 Oct 1898. SOURCE: Gatewood, *"Smoked Yankees"*, 197.

ROSS, Hercules; G/10th Cav. Original member of 10th Cavalry; in troop when organized, Ft Leavenworth, KS, 5 Jul 1867. SOURCE: McMiller, "Buffalo Soldiers," 74.

ROSS, James L.; Private; B/24th Inf. Died of dysentery at Tayug, Luzon, Philippines, 7 Aug 1901. SOURCE: *ANJ* 39 (12 Oct 1901): 140.

ROSS, James R.; Corporal; F/24th Inf. Wounded in action in Cuba, 1898. SOURCE: Muller, *The Twenty Fourth Infantry*, 18.

ROSS, John; Private; 24th Inf. Organist at church, Ft Apache, AZ, 1888. SOURCE: *ANJ* 25 (7 Jul 1888): 995.

ROSS, John H.; Private; L/9th Cav. At Ft D. A. Russell, WY, in 1910; resident of Cherokee, OK. SOURCE: *Illustrated Review: Ninth Cavalry,* with picture.

ROSS, Major S.; Private; H/24th Inf. Enlisted Ft Bliss, TX, 22 Feb 1899, with four years' continuous service. SOURCE: Muster Roll, H/24 Inf, Jan–Feb 1899.

ROSS, Milton; Sergeant; D/10th Cav. Resides at 405 Pontiac, Dayton, OH; remembers his first sergeant, Thomas Allsup. SOURCE: Affidavit, Ross, 28 Apr 1926, VA File XC 2659797, Thomas H. Allsup.

Surviving Indian war veteran. SOURCE: *Winners of the West* 3 (Jun 1926): 7.

Served 26 Apr 1879–25 Apr 1889 in Texas, New Mexico, and Arizona in hard campaigns, including against Geronimo; "Many times we were without water for two and three days, eating our hardtack and fat bacon"; developed rheumatism, heart trouble, asthma, and catarrh since feet froze and skin came off; now over 72 and trying to live on small pension with wife. SOURCE: *Winners of the West* 4 (Feb 1927): 8.

Stationed at Ft Bayard, NM; while on detached service at Ft Cummings, NM, Dec 1888, allowed women of ill repute on post for night. SOURCE: Billington, *New Mexico's Buffalo Soldiers,* 166.

Recent subscriber. SOURCE: *Winners of the West* 4 (Mar 1927): 8.

Grateful and happy with new $40 per month pension. SOURCE: *Winners of the West* 5 (Dec 1927): 3.

Renews subscription; pension increased; "very feeble at times." SOURCE: *Winners of the West* 15 (Apr 1938): 5.

ROSS, Robert H.; Private; G/9th Cav. At Ft D. A. Russell, WY, in 1910; resident of Washington, DC. SOURCE: *Illustrated Review: Ninth Cavalry,* with picture.

ROSS, W. C.; Private; K/9th Cav. On detached service in field, New Mexico, 21 Jan–8 Feb 1881. SOURCE: Regt Returns, 9 Cav, Feb 1881.

ROSS, William; Private; H/10th Cav. On extra duty in hospital, Ft Dodge, KS. SOURCE: SO 30, Det 10 Cav, 20 May 1869, Orders, Det 10 Cav, 1868–69.

ROSS, William; Private; G/9th Cav. Certificate of disability returned by letter, Department of the Platte, 29 Jun 1895.

ROSS, William; Private; I/24th Inf. Enlisted Louisville, 3 Feb 1899; on special duty as teamster 24 Feb 1899. SOURCE: Muster Roll, I/24 Inf, Jan–Feb 1899.

Fined $.50 by garrison court martial, Presidio of San Francisco, CA, 21 Apr 1899. SOURCE: Muster Roll, I/24 Inf, Mar–Apr 1899.

Absent sick in hospital, Manila, Philippines, from 11 Aug 1899; disease contracted in line of duty. SOURCE: Muster Roll, I/24 Inf, Jul–Aug 1899.

Absent sick in Manila since 11 Aug 1899; fined $1 by summary court, 26 Aug 1899. SOURCE: Muster Roll, I/24 Inf, Sep–Oct 1899.

ROSTON, James; Corporal; K/24th Inf. At Cabanatuan, Philippines, 1901. *See* **MORRIS**, Thomas, Private, K/24th Infantry

ROUNSVILLE, Robert; Private; I/25th Inf. Fined $1.50 by summary court, San Isidro, Philippines, for missing reveille, 30 Mar 1902, first conviction. SOURCE: Register of Summary Court, San Isidro.

ROUNTREE, William; Corporal; I/9th Cav. At Ft D. A. Russell, WY, in 1910; resident of Xenia, OH. SOURCE: *Illustrated Review: Ninth Cavalry,* with picture.

ROUSE, Curtis; Private; G/9th Cav. Sergeant, I/9th Cavalry, authorized thirty-day absence from Ft Robinson, NE, hunting with one corporal and four privates of I/9th Cavalry. SOURCE: Order 216, 9 Oct 1890, Post Orders, Ft Robinson.

Sergeant, I/9th Cavalry, asked other men of troop to sign petition to transfer commander, Capt. John Guilfoyle. SOURCE: CO, Ft Robinson, to AAG, DP, 26 Jun 1891, LS, Ft Robinson.

Private, G/9th Cavalry, witness for defense in Barney McKay court martial, Ft Robinson, 1893. SOURCE: Court Martial Records, McKay.

ROUSEY, Joseph; Private; H/10th Cav. Honorable mention for services rendered in capture of Mangas and his Apache band, Rio Bonito, AZ, 18 Oct 1886. SOURCE: Baker, Roster.

ROWAN; Private; M/9th Cav. Jailed for attempted rape of Helen Stevens, Cheyenne, WY. SOURCE: Cheyenne *Daily Leader,* 18 Sep 1909.

ROWAN, Clarence F.; Private; M/9th Cav. At Ft D. A. Russell, WY, in 1910; resident of McMinnersville, TN. SOURCE: *Illustrated Review: Ninth Cavalry,* with picture.

ROWAN, Eugene S.; Private; M/9th Cav. At Ft D. A. Russell, WY, in 1910; resident of McMinnersville, TN. SOURCE: *Illustrated Review: Ninth Cavalry.*

ROWENS, Chester R.; Private; E/10th Cav. Transferred to Hospital Corps, Ft Custer, MT, 15 Dec 1895. SOURCE: *ANJ* 33 (14 Dec 1895): 256.

ROWLAND, Ernest; Corporal; A/24th Inf. Drunk and boisterous at theatrical presentation, Ft Bayard, NM, theater, date unknown. SOURCE: Billington, *New Mexico's Buffalo Soldiers,* 165.

ROWLETT, Tillman; Private; E/10th Cav. Served in 10th Cavalry, 1898; remained in U.S. during war with Spain. SOURCE: Cashin, *Under Fire with the Tenth Cavalry*, 343.

ROWLETT, Virgil; Private; A/10th Cav. Served in 10th Cavalry in Cuba, 1898. SOURCE: Cashin, *Under Fire with the Tenth Cavalry*, 336.

ROWNE, George; Private; E/9th Cav. Convicted by general court martial, Columbus Barracks, OH, of desertion, 5 Aug 1884–30 Dec 1885; sentenced to dishonorable discharge and three years. SOURCE: GCMO 9, AGO, 6 Feb 1886.

Received at U.S. Military Prison, Leavenworth, KS, 14 Mar 1886; discharged on certificate of disability with chronic spasmodic asthma, 10 Sep 1886. SOURCE: Certificates of Disability, DivMo.

ROYSTER, George; B/10th Cav. Original member of 10th Cavalry; in troop when organized, Ft Leavenworth, KS, 1 Apr 1867. SOURCE: McMiller, "Buffalo Soldiers," 69.

ROYSTER, Henry; Private; F/9th Cav. Fined $10 and jailed for ten days for defiance of 1st Sgt. Emanuel Stance, Ft Robinson, NE, Jul 1887. SOURCE: Order 130, 4 Jul 1887, Post Orders, Ft Robinson.

ROYSTON, Jim; H/10th Cav. Original member of 10th Cavalry; in troop when organized, Ft Leavenworth, KS, 21 Jul 1867. SOURCE: McMiller, "Buffalo Soldiers," 75.

RUCKER, Alfred; Sergeant; 24th Inf. His children attended Wasatch School, Salt Lake City, while at Ft Douglas, UT; retired there in 1900, drove wagon for officers' wives; met President Harding when he visited. SOURCE: Clark, "A History of the Twenty-fourth," 78–79.

See **JACKSON**, Thornton, Corporal, C/24th Infantry

RUCKER, Clarence; Private; E/24th Inf. Wounded in forearm, Deposito, Philippines, summer 1899. SOURCE: *ANJ* 36 (19 Aug 1899): 1223; Richmond *Planet*, 19 Aug 1899.

RUCKER, DeWitt; Private; K/10th Cav. Killed in action at Carrizal, Mexico, 21 Jun 1916; buried at home in Hartwell, GA. SOURCE: Wharfield, *10th Cavalry and Border Fights*, 30, 40.

RUCKER, Henry; Private; F/10th Cav. Confined for trial, Ft Robinson, NE, 30 Jan 1906; dishonorably discharged, 4 Mar 1906.

RUCKER, Julius B.; Private; K/10th Cav. Served in 10th Cavalry in Cuba, 1898. SOURCE: Cashin, *Under Fire with the Tenth Cavalry*, 350.

RUCKER, William; Private; I/9th Cav. At Ft D. A. Russell, WY, in 1910; resident of Lynchburg, VA. SOURCE: *Illustrated Review: Ninth Cavalry*, with picture.

RUDD, R. R.; Captain; I/48th Inf. Mentioned. SOURCE: Beasley, *Negro Trailblazers*, 284.

RUDY, Charles E.; Artificer; C/25th Inf. Dishonorable discharge, Brownsville. SOURCE: SO 266, AGO, 9 Nov 1906.

RUFFIN, James; Private; I/24th Inf. Enlisted 29 Jun 1899; joined company 14 Aug 1899; sick in hospital, disease contracted in line of duty. SOURCE: Muster Roll, I/24 Inf, Jul–Aug 1899.

Drowned about 1:30 P.M., 1 Oct 1899, at San Fernando, Philippines, while bathing in Rio San Fernando. SOURCE: Muster Roll, H/24 Inf, Sep–Oct 1899; *ANJ* 37 (14 Oct 1899): 155.

Drowned while bathing, San Fernando, 2 Oct 1899; to be buried 3 Oct 1899 at First Reserve Hospital. SOURCE: Manila *Times*, 3 Oct 1899.

RUFFING, William; C/10th Cav. Original member of 10th Cavalry; in troop when organized, Ft Leavenworth, KS, 14 May 1867. SOURCE: McMiller, "Buffalo Soldiers," 70.

RUGER, Alfred; Sergeant; C/24th Inf. Retires from Ft Douglas, UT. SOURCE: *ANJ* 34 (24 Jul 1897): 873.

RUGER, William; Sergeant; C/24th Inf. Detailed provost sergeant in charge of post police, Ft Huachuca, AZ, Apr 1893. SOURCE: Order 49, Ft Huachuca, 4 Apr 1893, Name File, 24 Inf.

RUMPF, Daniel; Corporal; 24th Inf. Five-year veteran; placed in stockade at Bliss, TX, by judge advocate in Houston riot trial, 1917, to gather evidence. SOURCE: Haynes, *A Night of Violence*, 286.

RUMPF, William; Private; L/10th Cav. Discharged in accordance with Special Order 162, Department of the Missouri, 26 Aug 1904.

RUNELL, Berry H.; Private; A/10th Cav. Served in 10th Cavalry, 1898; remained in U.S. during war with Spain. SOURCE: Cashin, *Under Fire with the Tenth Cavalry*, 337.

RUSH, Wash; Private; H/9th Cav. At Ft D. A. Russell, WY, in 1910; sharpshooter; resident of Chicago. SOURCE: *Illustrated Review: Ninth Cavalry*, with picture.

RUSHINGBO, William B.; Private; G/9th Cav. Private, E/9th Cavalry; wounded in leg above knee, Camalig, Philippines, 24 Nov 1900. SOURCE: *ANJ* 38 (5 Jan 1901): 455.

Wounded in action at Bantonan, Philippines, 25 Nov 1900. SOURCE: *Illustrated Review: Ninth Cavalry*.

Veteran of Spanish-American War and Philippine Insurrection; private, G/9th Cavalry, at Ft D. A. Russell, WY, in 1910; resident of Xenia, OH. SOURCE: *Illustrated Review: Ninth Cavalry.*

RUSSEL, Jesse; Private; M/10th Cav. Served in 10th Cavalry, 1898; remained in U.S. during war with Spain. SOURCE: Cashin, *Under Fire with the Tenth Cavalry*, 352.

RUSSELL, Alonzo; Musician; C/24th Inf. At Ft D. A. Russell, WY; in hands of civil authorities, Cheyenne, WY, 24 Dec 1898 and 29 Dec 1898–11 Jan 1899.

RUSSELL, Anthony; K/10th Cav. Original member of 10th Cavalry; in troop when organized, Ft Riley, KS, 1 Sep 1867. SOURCE: McMiller, "Buffalo Soldiers," 77.

RUSSELL, Benjamin F.; Private; H/24th Inf. Fined $6 by summary court, San Isidro, Philippines, for failure to obey noncommissioned officer while in ranks, 24 Jan 1902, second conviction; fined $7 for lying out of quarters, 25 Mar 1902, and absence from 11 P.M. inspection, 25 Mar 1902. SOURCE: Register of Summary Court, San Isidro.

RUSSELL, Edward; Private; E/9th Cav. Convicted by general court martial, Jefferson Barracks, MO, of desertion, 23 May–8 Nov 1884; sentenced to dishonorable discharge and three years. SOURCE: GCMO 62, AGO, 29 Dec 1884.

RUSSELL, Edward; Private; F/10th Cav. Confined at Ft Robinson, NE, 4 Jan 1906, awaiting result of trial; dishonorably discharged in accordance with Special Order 73, Department of the Missouri, 1 Feb 1906.

RUSSELL, Henry H.; Private; F/9th Cav. At Ft D. A. Russell, WY, in 1910; resident of Washington, DC. SOURCE: *Illustrated Review: Ninth Cavalry,* with picture.

RUSSELL, J.; Private; G/9th Cav. On detached service at Ft Stanton, NM, 29 Jan–5 Feb 1881. SOURCE: Regt Returns, 9 Cav, Feb 1881.

RUSSELL, James; Private; B/10th Cav. Served in 10th Cavalry in Cuba, 1898; wounded in action. SOURCE: Cashin, *Under Fire with the Tenth Cavalry*, 338.

Enlisted in Cleveland; wounded in action at Santiago, Cuba. SOURCE: Cleveland *Gazette*, 2 Jul 1898.

RUSSELL, John; Sergeant; F/10th Cav. Discharged, end of term, Ft Robinson, NE, 6 Sep 1885. SOURCE: Post Returns, Ft Robinson, Sep 1885.

RUSSELL, John; Private; A/24th Inf. Transferred from Reserve Divisional Hospital, Siboney, Cuba, to U.S. on

U.S. Army Transport *Santiago* with yellow fever, 25 Jul 1898. SOURCE: Hospital Papers, Spanish-American War.

RUSSELL, Lemuel; 1st Sgt; E/9th Cav. Retired 31 Dec 1938, with thirty years' service. SOURCE: *Cavalry Journal* 48 (Jan–Feb 1939): 91.

RUSSELL, Lewis; Private; E/9th Cav. *See* DuBOSE, Edmond, Private, E/9th Cavalry

RUSSELL, Macon; 1st Lt; L/49th Inf. Born Mecklinburg Co., VA, 17 Jul 1858; in F/24th Infantry, 4 Jul 1881–3 Jul 1886; in H/25th Infantry, 20 Sep 1887–8 Sep 1898; second lieutenant, 8th Volunteer Infantry, 15 Sep 1898–6 Mar 1899; in H/25th Infantry, 21 Mar–21 Sep 1899; first lieutenant, 9 Sep 1899; lieutenant, H/25th Infantry, 21 Sep 1899–9 Feb 1900; mother Mrs. Clarisa Russell, Sugar Creek, NC. SOURCE: Descriptive Book, L/49 Inf.

First sergeant, H/25th Infantry; transferred from Reserve Divisional Hospital, Siboney, Cuba, to U.S. on U.S. Army Transport *Santiago* with yellow fever, 25 Jul 1898. SOURCE: Hospital Papers, Spanish-American War.

To proceed to Ft Thomas, KY, to receive commission in 8th U.S. Volunteer Infantry. SOURCE: *ANJ* 36 (17 Sep 1898): 69.

Commissioned second lieutenant, 8th Volunteer Infantry, after Spanish-American War. SOURCE: Cashin, *Under Fire with the Tenth Cavalry*, 360.

Won commission for gallantry and meritorious service around Santiago, Cuba. SOURCE: Thweatt, *What the Newspapers Say*, 4.

Commissioned for gallantry at Santiago, 1–2 Jul 1898. SOURCE: Richmond *Planet*, 13 Aug 1898.

Commissioned for bravery at El Caney, Cuba. SOURCE: Johnson, *History of Negro Soldiers*, 32.

Joined L/49th Infantry after it arrived in the Philippines; was already in Manila when 49th Infantry departed San Francisco, Dec 1899. SOURCE: Regt Returns, 49 Inf.

Mentioned. SOURCE: *ANJ* 38 (6 Oct 1900): 131.

Service in the Philippines mentioned. SOURCE: Villard, "The Negro in the Regular Army," 726.

RUSSELL, Moses; B/10th Cav. Original member of 10th Cavalry; in troop when organized, Ft Leavenworth, KS, 1 Apr 1867. SOURCE: McMiller, "Buffalo Soldiers," 69.

RUSSELL, Thomas; Private; 10th Cav. Formerly in F/25th Infantry; reenlistment in 10th Cavalry approved by regimental commander, Aug 1876. SOURCE: ES, 10 Cav, 1873–83.

RUSSELL, Thomas; Private; 24th Inf. Drowned crossing San Mateo River, Philippines, 21 Aug 1899. SOURCE: Richmond *Planet*, 2 Sep 1899.

RUSSELL, William H.; Private; F/38th Inf. At Ft Bayard, NM, 1868, stole trousers worth $3 from Sgt. Charles Southerner; also stole a government stable frock. SOURCE: Billington, *New Mexico's Buffalo Soldiers*, 36.

RUSSUM, Louis H.; Private; D/10th Cav. Convicted by general court martial, Jefferson Barracks, MO, of theft of diamond ring worth around $200 from 2nd Lt. Charles H. Grierson, 10th Cavalry, Jefferson Barracks, 3 Jun 1886; sentenced to dishonorable discharge and one year. SOURCE: GCMO 46, AGO, 15 Jun 1886.

RUTLEDGE, William; Sergeant; B/9th Cav. Died of typhoid fever in the Philippines, 11 Mar 1901. SOURCE: *ANJ* 38 (13 Apr 1901): 803.

S

SADDLER, David; Private; D/10th Cav. Casualty in fight at Cheyenne Agency, Indian Territory, 6 Apr 1875. SOURCE: Leckie, *The Buffalo Soldiers*, 139.

SADDLER, John; Private; E/25th Inf. Wounded in action, El Caney, Cuba, 1 Jul 1898. SOURCE: Muller, *The Twenty Fourth Infantry*, 83.

SADDLER, Louis; Private; I/24th Inf. Enlisted Philadelphia, 30 Mar 1899. SOURCE: Muster Roll, I/24 Inf, Mar–Apr 1899.

On detached service at Arayat, Philippines, as of 31 Oct 1899, and then at Tarlac, from 29 Dec 1899. SOURCE: Muster Roll, I/24 Inf, Sep–Oct and Nov–Dec 1899.

SADDLER, Middleton W.; Comsy Sgt; U.S. Army. Born Marietta, twelve miles from Atlanta, GA, 1873; spent youth in Alabama and Kentucky; attended public schools, Sheffield, AL; attended University of Kentucky, 1891; enlisted in 25th Infantry, 1892; commended for gallantry, El Caney, Cuba, 1 Jul 1898; decorated with medal by Miss Helen Gould in New York City on recommendation of regimental commander; with regiment in the Philippines, in twenty-two battles and skirmishes; at Ft Niobrara, NE, with regiment until promoted to post noncommissioned staff, May 1905; served as post commissary sergeant, Philippines, 1905–08; returned via Suez Canal, circumnavigating globe; served in New York, 1908–12; in the Philippines, 1912–15; in KS, 1915–17; on Mexican border, 1917; retired, Apr 1917, with twenty-five years' service; never a court martial or reprimand; resides with wife in Oakland; both active in 15th Street African Methodist Episcopal Church and "deeply interested in the uplift of the race." SOURCE: Beasley, *Negro Trailblazers*, 291–92.

His description of battle at El Caney, in which he participated as first sergeant, D/25th Infantry. SOURCE: New York *Age*, in Lynk, *The Black Troopers*, 79.

Letters from Santiago, Cuba, 30 Jul 1898, and Manila, Philippines, Sep 1899. SOURCE: Gatewood, *"Smoked Yankees"*, 55–57, 247.

Mentioned as sergeant major, first battalion, 25th Infantry, in the Philippines, 1900. SOURCE: Richmond *Planet*, 28 Jul 1900.

Mentioned as former first sergeant, D/25th Infantry, and former sergeant, K/25th Infantry. SOURCE: Richmond *Planet*, 18 Aug 1900.

Rumored to have commission in Filipino regiment. SOURCE: Richmond *Planet*, 22 Jun 1901.

ST. CLAIR, Aron; F/10th Cav. Original member of 10th Cavalry; in troop when organized, Ft Leavenworth, KS, 21 Jun 1867. SOURCE: McMiller, "Buffalo Soldiers," 73.

ST. CLAIR, Charles H.; Recruit; Mounted Service. Tried by general court martial, St. Louis Barracks, MO, for desertion until apprehended at St. Louis Barracks, 31 Jan 1874; convicted of absence without leave, and sentenced to one month's confinement with first fourteen days in solitary confinement on bread and water; solitary confinement portion remitted. SOURCE: GCMO 16, AGO, 24 Feb 1874.

ST. JOHN, Henry R.; M/10th Cav. Original member of 10th Cavalry; in troop when organized, Ft Riley, KS, 15 Oct 1867. SOURCE: McMiller, "Buffalo Soldiers," 79.

SALAS, Benito; Musician; I/24th Inf. Subscriber. SOURCE: *Winners of the West* 10 (Aug 1933): 3.

SALES, Clarence; Private; K/24th Inf. Letter from San Quentin, Philippines, 1 Nov 1900. SOURCE: Richmond *Planet*, 29 Dec 1900.

Fined $5 for absence without leave from pay table, Cabanatuan, Philippines, 17 May 1901; witness: 1st Sgt. J. Stevens, K/24th Infantry. SOURCE: Name File, 24 Inf.

Jailed for twenty days and fined $10 for altercation at Cabanatuan with Pvt. Samuel Stevens, D/24th Infantry, and for abusive and threatening language toward Stevens, 28 May 1901; also took rifle from barracks to use against Stevens. SOURCE: Name File, 24 Inf.

Letter from Manila, Philippines, 12 Oct 1901, reports that he is in Manila prison serving ten-year sentence for murder of native at Cabanatuan on 7 Jul 1901; claims self-defense; born Richmond, VA, and member of Reverend Evans Payne's 4th Baptist Church. SOURCE: Richmond *Planet*, 7 Dec 1901.

SALLEY, Coleman; B/10th Cav. Original member of 10th Cavalry; in troop when organized, Ft Leavenworth, KS, 1 Apr 1867. SOURCE: McMiller, "Buffalo Soldiers," 69.

SALTER; Private; A/10th Cav. At Ft Apache, AZ, 1890, subscribed $.50 to testimonial to General Grierson. SOURCE: List of subscriptions, 23 Apr 1890, 10th Cavalry papers, MHI.

SALTER, Emory; Private; C/10th Cav. Served in 10th Cavalry in Cuba, 1898. SOURCE: Cashin, *Under Fire with the Tenth Cavalry*, 340.

SALTON, Armp; Private; E/24th Inf. Born Grant Co., KY; brown complexion, Ht 5'8"; occupation musician; completed first enlistment in Band/9th Cavalry, 8 Apr 1884; reenlisted Chicago, 8 May 1884; joined Band/24th Infantry, 8 Jun 1884; principal musician, 24th Infantry, 27 Oct 1888; reduced to private, 29 Jan 1889; transferred to E/24th Infantry, 9 Feb 1889; character: "A good musician. A chronic growler." SOURCE: Descriptive Book, 24 Inf NCS & Band.

Served ten years; died at Council Bluffs, IA. SOURCE: *Winners of the West* 10 (Aug 1933): 3.

SAMMONS, William H.; Private; H/24th Inf. Enlisted Ft Douglas, UT, 20 Oct 1897, with five years' continuous service; formerly corporal, F/24th Infantry; transferred to H/24th Infantry as private, 6 Oct 1898; on special duty as clerk, Subsistence Department, 12 Oct 1898. SOURCE: Muster Roll, H/24 Inf, Sep–Oct 1898.

Private, F/24th Infantry; transferred from Reserve Divisional Hospital, Siboney, Cuba, to U.S. on U.S. Army Transport *Santiago* with remittent yellow fever, 25 Jul 1898. SOURCE: Hospital Papers, Spanish-American War.

Promoted to corporal, 7 Nov 1898. SOURCE: Muster Roll, H/24 Inf, Nov–Dec 1898.

On special duty as clerk, Subsistence Department, through February 1899. SOURCE: Muster Roll, H/24 Inf, Jan–Feb 1899.

SAMPLE, John; Sgt Maj; 24th Inf. Born Fredericksburg, VA; yellow complexion, Ht 5'5"; private, I/108th U.S. Colored Troops, 8 Jul 1864–21 Mar 1866, character good; private, E/40th Infantry, 9 Jan 1867–9 Jan 1870, character excellent; private, E/25th Infantry, 27 Apr 1870–27 Apr 1875, character: "A good soldier"; private, K/25th Infantry, 13 May 1875–12 May 1880, character very good; private, E/24th Infantry, San Antonio, TX, 22 Jul 1880; corporal, 10 Jan 1881; sergeant, 23 Jul 1882; sergeant major, 1 May 1884; stationed at Ft Supply, Indian Territory, 21 Jul 1885; single; additional pay $2 per month; retained $60, clothing $6.19, character excellent. SOURCE: Descriptive Book, 24 Inf NCS & Band.

SAMPSON, Charles; H/10th Cav. Original member of 10th Cavalry; in troop when organized, Ft Leavenworth, KS, 21 Jul 1867. SOURCE: McMiller, "Buffalo Soldiers," 75.

SAMPSON, J.; Private; F/9th Cav. Troop commander directed to prefer charges against Sampson for running and abusing his horse on Sunday, 16 Jul 1893, Crawford, NE; witnesses Sgt. Madison Ingoman and Pvt. William Tilton, D/9th Cavalry. SOURCE: CO, Ft Robinson, to CO, F/9, 18 Jul 1893, LS, Ft Robinson.

Returned to duty in accordance with telegram, Department of the Platte, 5 Aug 1893. SOURCE: Regt Returns, 9 Cav, Aug 1893.

SAMPSON, John W.; Corporal; F/9th Cav. Enlisted Cincinnati, 16 Jan 1899, for I/24th Infantry, with four years' continuous service. SOURCE: Muster Roll, I/24 Inf, Jan–Feb 1899.

Promoted to corporal, 12 Apr 1899. SOURCE: Muster Roll, I/24 Inf, Mar–Apr 1899.

Sick in hospital, El Deposito, Philippines, disease contracted in line of duty. SOURCE: Muster Roll, I/24 Inf, Jul–Aug 1899.

Veteran of Spanish-American War and Philippine Insurrection; expert rifleman and corporal, F/9th Cavalry, at Ft D. A. Russell, WY, in 1910; resident of Shamburburg, OH. SOURCE: *Illustrated Review: Ninth Cavalry*, with picture.

SAMUEL, George; Private; M/9th Cav. At Ft McKavett, TX, 1872–73. *See* **STANCE**, Emanuel, First Sergeant, F/9th Cavalry

SANDERS, Alexander; H/25th Inf. Resides in Phoebus, VA; "What has become of the boys of Company H, 25th U.S. Infantry, 1870 to 1875?"; encloses subscription order. SOURCE: *Winners of the West* 5 (May 1928): 5.

Wants to hear from old comrades. SOURCE: *Winners of the West* 6 (Aug 1929): 2.

SANDERS, Braxton; Private; B/10th Cav. Recruit arrived at Ft Leavenworth, KS, from Jefferson Barracks, MO. SOURCE: Adj, Ft Leavenworth, to HQ, Jefferson Barracks, 9 Oct 1866, LS, 10 Cav, 1866–67.

Regimental commander asks remission of unexpired portion of Sanders's sentence, imposed in accordance with General Order 5, Department of the Missouri, 1867, so Sanders can be assigned to B Troop and march with it to Ft Riley, KS, at once; he was confined to hard labor two months before sentence and was acquitted of greatest portion of specifications against him. SOURCE: CO, 10 Cav, to AAG, DeptMo, 2 May 1867, LS, 10 Cav, 1866–67.

General Order 73, Department of the Missouri, 3 May 1867, remits unexecuted portion of sentence against Private Sanders. SOURCE: ES, 10 Cav, 1866–71.

SANDERS, Chester; Sergeant; I/24th Inf. Ranked number eight, Northern Division infantry competition, Ft Sheridan, IL, with bronze medal. SOURCE: GO 173, AGO, 20 Oct 1905.

Member, division infantry rifle team, Ft Sheridan, 1905. SOURCE: Muller, *The Twenty Fourth Infantry*, 42.

Ranked number 24, Philippine Division infantry competition, Malabang, Mindanao, Philippines, 1906. SOURCE: GO 198, AGO, 6 Dec 1906.

Commissioned captain at Camp Des Moines, IA, Oct 1917. SOURCE: Sweeney, *History of the American Negro*, 128.

SANDERS, Edward; Private; G/24th Inf. Missing in action, Talavero, Philippines, 28 Dec 1899. SOURCE: Muller, *The Twenty Fourth Infantry*, 36.

SANDERS, George; I/10th Cav. Original member of 10th Cavalry; in troop when organized, Ft Riley, KS, 15 Aug 1867. SOURCE: McMiller, "Buffalo Soldiers," 76.

SANDERS, Isaiah; Private; L/10th Cav. Served in 10th Cavalry, 1898; remained in U.S. during war with Spain. SOURCE: Cashin, *Under Fire with the Tenth Cavalry*, 351.

SANDERS, J. H.; Private; D/10th Cav. Served in 10th Cavalry, 1898; remained in U.S. during war with Spain. SOURCE: Cashin, *Under Fire with the Tenth Cavalry*, 341.

SANDERS, James; Private; B/24th Inf. At Ft McIntosh, TX, 1877. *See* **GRAYSON**, Charles H., Private, G/24th Infantry

SANDERS, James; Private; K/48th Inf. Drowned in the Philippines, 18 Aug 1900. SOURCE: *ANJ* 38 (8 Sep 1900): 43.

SANDERS, James C.; Cook; F/10th Cav. Served in 10th Cavalry in Cuba, 1898. SOURCE: Cashin, *Under Fire with the Tenth Cavalry*, 343.

SANDERS, John C.; Sergeant; D/10th Cav. Commissioned second lieutenant of cavalry, 27 Sep 1918. SOURCE: Glass, *History of the Tenth Cavalry*, appendix M.

SANDERS, John H.; Private; E/9th Cav. Awaiting transport at Santa Fe, NM, to join his unit, I/9th Cavalry. SOURCE: RO 10, 9 Cav, 22 Mar 1879, Regimental Orders, 9 Cav.

Buried at Ft Robinson, NE, 17 Mar 1897. SOURCE: List of Interments, Ft Robinson.

SANDERS, Mingo; 1st Sgt; B/25th Inf. Born Marion, SC; attended school there until learned to read and write; enlisted Charleston, SC, 16 May 1881, after seeing advertisement for soldiers in Marion newspaper; in Dakota for considerable period; one-fourth blind after being hit in eye by exploding soda bottle; at El Caney, Cuba, with party that cut wire under heavy fire, 1 Jul 1898; at Santiago, Cuba, 2–3 and 10–11 Jul 1898; he and his company gladly shared their hardtack with Theodore Roosevelt's regiment in Cuba at Roosevelt's request; served in the Philippines at La Loma, 9 Oct 1899, at O'Donnell, 18 Oct 1899, at Commizi, 5 Jan 1900, at Subig, 29 Jan, 9–10 Feb, 21 and 23 Sep 1900; led two men through insurrectionist lines from Bam Bam to O'Donnell, 28 Nov 1899, with message from Gen. Andrew Burt to the commander, 9th Infantry; captured several insurgents and weapons while in the Philippines as first sergeant, B/25th Infantry; General Burt wrote Mary Church Terrell that "Mingo Sanders is the best non-commissioned officer I have ever known." SOURCE: Terrell, "A Sketch of Mingo Sanders," 128–31.

Recruit, age 24, occupation cotton hand, Ht 5'7"; enlisted 16 May 1881; en route from depot, David's Island, NY, to Ft Randall, Dakota Territory, 2–7 Jul 1881. SOURCE: Descriptive & Assignment Rolls, 25 Inf.

Enlisted 16 May 1881; served in Cuba and the Philippines. SOURCE: *Colored American Magazine* 12 (Feb 1907): 147.

Authorized to reenlist as married soldier, with defective vision, 23 Apr 1896. SOURCE: AGO File 36224.

Returned to unit from furlough in the U.S.; arrived at La Loma in time to take part in battle, 9 Oct 1900. SOURCE: Richmond *Planet*, 20 Jan 1900.

Located enemy outpost near Cabangan, Philippines, and captured enemy first sergeant and his rifle there. SOURCE: Richmond *Planet*, 23 Mar 1901.

Dishonorable discharge, Brownsville. SOURCE: SO 266, AGO, 9 Nov 1906.

Sanders "has the respect and esteem of every officer in his regiment, and now, in his old age, blind of an eye, and within a few months of . . . a pension, he is cast out 'without honor' from the service he loves and the flag he fought for, to make a struggle in civil life for his bread and butter. The old soldier divided the bread of his company with the hungry Rough Riders at El Caney, upon the request of him whose order now drives him out to beg." SOURCE: Cleveland *Gazette*, 1 Dec 1906.

At discharge had one year, five months, and twenty-three days to serve before retirement. SOURCE: Cleveland *Gazette*, 23 Feb 1907.

2nd Lt. George C. Lawrason, 25th Infantry, Ft Reno, Oklahoma, believes Sanders was totally innocent of participation in or knowledge of Brownsville affray, 17 Dec 1906. SOURCE: AGO File 1192148.

Maj. G. W. Penrose, 25th Infantry, Ft Reno, makes statement regarding Brownsville that tends to exonerate Sanders, 20 Dec 1906. SOURCE: AGO File 1193156.

Poem "Sergeant Mingo Sanders," by R. L., published in New York *Sun* and reprinted in Indianapolis *Freeman*, 12 Jan 1907.

Applied for reenlistment; went to Judge Advocate General to make statement but his attorney kept him from taking oath; they fear Army plans to reenlist him to send him to the Philippines or Alaska to keep him from testifying before Senate. SOURCE: Washington *Post*, 25 Jan 1907.

Honorable Henry Cabot Lodge makes telephone request for information regarding his service, 8 Jun 1907. SOURCE: AGO File 1250511.

Honorable Joseph B. Foraker requests record of one conviction against him, 8 Jul 1907. SOURCE: AGO File 1250511.

Address in October 1908: 146 M Street, SE, Washington, DC. SOURCE: VA File XC 2625648 Mingo Sanders (kept by Veterans Administration and not turned over to National Archives).

Letter to President Roosevelt asks reinstatement; his savings have vanished and his wife's health is failing; first two discharges with character very good; next four discharges with character excellent. SOURCE: Cleveland *Gazette*, 31 Oct 1908.

President of U.S. instructs that he never be allowed to return to Army, 7 Feb 1909. SOURCE: AGO File 1763692.

Entered Freedmen's Hospital, Howard University, Washington, DC, with diabetic gangrenous infection of foot, 12 Aug 1929; died 15 Aug 1929. SOURCE: Pittsburgh *Courier*, 31 Aug 1929.

Died after leg amputated; employed with Interior Department until death; resided at 463 New York Avenue, NW, Washington, DC. SOURCE: New York *Age*, 31 Aug 1929.

Leaves wife Luella and "a host of other relatives and friends"; remains are at John T. Rhines funeral chapel, Third and I Streets, SW, Washington, DC. SOURCE: Washington *Star*, 23 Aug 1929.

Former member and past patron, Ada Chapter, No. 2, Order of the Eastern Star. SOURCE: Washington *Star*, 24 Aug 1929.

Former Masonic grand master; members of Grand Lodge met at Masonic Temple, 1111 19th Street, NW, Washington, DC, 24 Aug 1929, to arrange funeral, which is scheduled for 26 Aug 1929. SOURCE: Washington *Star*, 24 Aug 1929.

Funeral scheduled for 1 P.M., 26 Aug 1929, with interment at Arlington National Cemetery. SOURCE: Washington *Star*, 25 Aug 1929.

Buried at Arlington Cemetery; survived by widow, Luella M. Sanders. SOURCE: Chicago *Defender*, 31 Aug 1929.

Biographical information. SOURCE: Weaver, *The Brownsville Raid*, 37, 95, 108, 121, 141, 242–45.

SANDERS, Sidney; H/10th Cav. Original member of 10th Cavalry; in troop when organized, Ft Leavenworth, KS, 21 Jul 1867. SOURCE: McMiller, "Buffalo Soldiers," 75.

SANDERS, Walter P.; 1st Sgt; A/10th Cav. Commissioned captain, Camp Des Moines, IA, 15 Oct 1917. SOURCE: Glass, *History of the Tenth Cavalry*, appendix M.

Retired as warrant officer and resides at 105-A Humboldt Avenue, Roxbury, MA, 1930. SOURCE: Work, *The Negro Yearbook, 1931–1932*, 334.

SANDRIDGE, Clifford A.; 1st Sgt; H/10th Cav. Served as private, H/10th Cavalry, 1898; remained in U.S. during war with Spain. SOURCE: Cashin, *Under Fire with the Tenth Cavalry*, 347.

First sergeant, H/10th Cavalry; commissioned captain at Camp Des Moines, IA, 15 Oct 1917. SOURCE: Glass, *History of the Tenth Cavalry*, appendix M.

SANDS; Private; A/24th Inf. Arrested by guard at 4 A.M., returning to Ft Huachuca, AZ, from direction of "hog ranch." SOURCE: Post Adj, Ft Huachuca, to CO, A/24, 1 Apr 1893, Letters & Orders Received, 24 Inf.

SANFORD, Joseph H.; Private; A/9th Cav. Veteran of Philippine Insurrection; at Ft D. A. Russell, WY, in 1910. SOURCE: *Illustrated Review: Ninth Cavalry*, with picture.

SANFORD, Pelm; Private; C/9th Cav. At Ft D. A. Russell, WY, in 1910; sharpshooter; resident of 902 W. Pearl St., Jackson, MS. SOURCE: *Illustrated Review: Ninth Cavalry*, with picture.

SANFORD, Sol; Wagoner; H/9th Cav. Veteran of Philippine Insurrection; at Ft D. A. Russell, WY, in 1910;

sharpshooter; resident of Milledgeville, GA. SOURCE: *Illustrated Review: Ninth Cavalry*, with picture.

SAPP, Wiliam B.; Private; L/9th Cav. At Ft D. A. Russell, WY, in 1910; resident of Savannah, GA. SOURCE: *Illustrated Review: Ninth Cavalry*.

SARVER, Ed; Private; H/9th Cav. At Ft D. A. Russell, WY, in 1910; sharpshooter; resident of Plano, KY. SOURCE: *Illustrated Review: Ninth Cavalry*.

SARVER, John; Private; H/24th Inf. Fined $10 by summary court, San Isidro, Philippines, for disrespect to noncommissioned officer, 19 Nov 1901, second conviction. SOURCE: Register of Summary Court, San Isidro.

SASSDESS, Bass; G/10th Cav. Original member of 10th Cavalry; in troop when organized, Ft Leavenworth, KS, 5 Jul 1867. SOURCE: McMiller, "Buffalo Soldiers," 74.

SATCHEL, Samuel; M/10th Cav. Admitted to Soldiers Home with disability, age 28, after three years and eight months' service, 21 Mar 1884. SOURCE: SecWar, *AR 1884*, 804.

SATCHELL, J.; Private; C/9th Cav. Ranked number six in carbine competition and number one in revolver competition, Department of the Missouri, Ft Leavenworth, KS, 17–22 Aug 1891. SOURCE: GO 81, AGO, 6 Oct 1891.

SATCHELL, James; QM Sgt; K/24th Inf. Commended for distinguished service as sergeant, A/24th Infantry, at battle of Santiago, Cuba, 1 Jul 1898, and awarded certificate of merit. SOURCE: GO 15, AGO, 13 Feb 1900.

Awarded certificate of merit for service in Cuban campaign, 1898. SOURCE: Scipio, *Last of the Black Regulars*, 130; Steward, *The Colored Regulars*, 280; *ANJ* 37 (24 Feb 1900): 611.

Quartermaster sergeant, A/24th Infantry; ranked number 185 among rifle experts with 68.67 percent in 1904. SOURCE: GO 79, AGO, 1 Jun 1905.

Quartermaster sergeant, K/24th Infantry, and distinguished marksman. SOURCE: GO 173, AGO, 20 Oct 1905.

SAUNDERS; Sergeant; 9th Cav. Arrested in Buffalo, WY, Mar 1886, for "walking through a bay-window with a brace of rocks"; acquitted. SOURCE: *Big Horn Sentinel*, 26 Mar 1886.

SAUNDERS, George I.; Private; K/24th Inf. Fined $5 for being drunk and disorderly in quarters, Cabanatuan, Philippines, 22 Feb 1901. SOURCE: Name File, 24 Inf.

SAUNDERS, Henry B.; I/10th Cav. Fined $10 and $4.80 costs for carrying concealed weapon, Crawford, NE, 12 Mar 1903.

SAUNDERS, James; K/48th Inf. Died in the Philippines, 18 Aug 1900. SOURCE: Richmond *Planet*, 8 Sep 1900.

SAUNDERS, Peter; Private; B/10th Cav. Served in 10th Cavalry in Cuba, 1898; wounded in action. SOURCE: Cashin, *Under Fire with the Tenth Cavalry*, 338.

Wounded in action at Santiago, Cuba, 1 Jul 1898, while on duty with Hotchkiss guns; helped drag wounded corporal of 3rd Cavalry from San Juan Creek to hospital under heavy artillery fire. SOURCE: SecWar, *AR 1898*, 324, 335.

SAVAGE, Jesse; F/25th Inf. Served in 1881–97; recent subscriber. SOURCE: *Winners of the West* 4 (Mar 1927): 8.

SAWYER, Henry; Private; B/10th Cav. Served in 10th Cavalry in Cuba, 1898; died of typhoid fever, General Hospital, Montauk Point, NY, 4 Sep 1898. SOURCE: Cashin, *Under Fire with the Tenth Cavalry*, 338.

Died of typhoid at Camp Wikoff, NY, 4 Sep 1898. SOURCE: Hospital Papers, Spanish-American War.

SAWYER, Joseph; C/10th Cav. Original member of 10th Cavalry; in troop when organized, Ft Leavenworth, KS, 14 May 1867. SOURCE: McMiller, "Buffalo Soldiers," 70.

SAXTON, Sam; A/10th Cav. Arrived at Fort Leavenworth, KS, from Jefferson Barracks, MO, Oct 1866. SOURCE: LS, 10 Cav, 1866–67.

Original member of 10th Cavalry; in troop when organized, Ft Leavenworth, KS, 18 Feb 1867. SOURCE: McMiller, "Buffalo Soldiers," 68.

SAYERS, Willie; Private; D/49th Inf. Deserted from Jefferson Barracks, MO, 10 Nov 1899; apprehended and discharged 7 Dec 1899. SOURCE: Descriptive Book, D/49 Inf.

SAYRE, Benjamin F.; 1st Lt; 9th Inf USV. Sergeant, C/24th Infantry; commissioned first lieutenant, 9th Volunteer Infantry, after Spanish-American War. SOURCE: Cashin, *Under Fire with the Tenth Cavalry*, 360.

Promoted from sergeant, C/24th Infantry, to sergeant major for gallantry at San Juan Hill, Santiago, Cuba, then commissioned in volunteers. SOURCE: Steward, *The Colored Regulars*, 360.

Promoted from corporal, C/24th Infantry, to sergeant major; reminiscences of battle of Santiago reprinted from New York *Age*. SOURCE: Lynk, *The Black Troopers*, 67, 72–73, with picture.

SCARSCE, Henry; Corporal; K/24th Inf. Enlistment authorized by letter, Adjutant General, to commander, Ft Robinson, NE, 11 May 1902. SOURCE: Register of LR, Ft Robinson.

Outshot "all his white associates and competitors" with 176 out of 200 at Fort Sheridan, IL, target practice. SOURCE: Chicago *Broadax*, 29 Jun 1904.

Private; ranked number 19 in Northern Division infantry team competition, Ft Sheridan, 1904. SOURCE: GO 167, AGO, 28 Nov 1904.

Corporal; ranked number 20 in Northern Division infantry team competition, Ft Sheridan, 1905, and awarded bronze medal; ranked number 225 among rifle experts with 71.33 percent. SOURCE: GO 101, AGO, 31 May 1906.

On division infantry rifle team at Ft Sheridan, 1905; stationed at Ft Missoula, MT. SOURCE: Muller, *The Twenty Fourth Infantry*, 42.

Ranked number 23 in Division of the Philippines infantry competition, Malabang, Mindanao, Philippines, 1906; distinguished marksman, 1904, 1905, 1906. SOURCE: GO 198, AGO, 6 Dec 1906.

SCEAR, William; M/10th Cav. Original member of 10th Cavalry; in troop when organized, Ft Riley, KS, 15 Oct 1867. SOURCE: McMiller, "Buffalo Soldiers," 79.

SCHLADE, James W.; Private; I/24th Inf. Enlisted Baltimore, 7 Feb 1899. SOURCE: Muster Roll, I/24 Inf, Jan–Feb 1899.

Fined $.50 by summary court, 19 Jun 1899. SOURCE: Muster Roll, I/24 Inf, May–Jun 1899.

Fined $3 by summary court, 8 Sep 1899; on detached service at Arayat, Philippines. SOURCE: Muster Roll, I/24 Inf, Sep–Oct 1899.

On detached service at Tarlac, Philippines, since 29 Dec 1899. SOURCE: Muster Roll, I/24 Inf, Nov–Dec 1899.

SCHLASS, Columbus; C/10th Cav. Original member of 10th Cavalry; in troop when organized, Ft Leavenworth, KS, 14 May 1867. SOURCE: McMiller, "Buffalo Soldiers," 70.

SCHOCKLEY, Alexander; Private; D/10th Cav. Served in 10th Cavalry in Cuba, 1898. SOURCE: Cashin, *Under Fire with the Tenth Cavalry*, 341.

SCHULLER, Charles F. L.; Private; C/25th Inf. Convicted by general court martial, Columbus Barracks, OH, of desertion, from 29 May 1883 until surrender, 29 Jun 1883; sentenced to dishonorable discharge and two years. SOURCE: GCMO 39, AGO, 27 Aug 1883.

SCHUMAN, James; Private; I/24th Inf. Enlisted Cleveland, OH, 11 Feb 1899. SOURCE: Muster Roll, I/24 Inf, Jan–Feb 1899.

Fined $.50 by summary court, 13 Jun 1899. SOURCE: Muster Roll, I/24 Inf, May–Jun 1899.

SCHWATZ, Charles; Private; H/10th Cav. Served in 10th Cavalry, 1898; remained in U.S. during war with Spain. SOURCE: Cashin, *Under Fire with the Tenth Cavalry*, 347.

At Camp Forse, AL, Nov 1898. SOURCE: Richmond *Planet*, 3 Dec 1898.

SCIPIO, David; Private; Band/9th Cav. Buried at Ft Robinson, NE, 2 Mar 1892. SOURCE: Order 35, 1 Mar 1892, Post Orders, Ft Robinson.

SCOTT; Private; G/9th Cav. 1st Lt. Francis S. Davidson, 9th Cavalry, acquitted by general court martial of visiting gambling house with Privates Scott and White of G/9th Cavalry. SOURCE: GCMO 93, AGO, 15 Nov 1878.

SCOTT, Alexander; M/10th Cav. Original member of 10th Cavalry; in troop when organized, Ft Riley, KS, 15 Oct 1867. SOURCE: McMiller, "Buffalo Soldiers," 79.

SCOTT, Alonzo; Private; E/24th Inf. At Ft Douglas, UT, not permitted to run in competition because he was so much faster than rest of men. SOURCE: Clark, "A History of the Twenty-fourth," 70.

SCOTT, Andrew; Private; I/9th Cav. At Ft D. A. Russell, WY, in 1910; resident of King Co., VA. SOURCE: *Illustrated Review: Ninth Cavalry*, with picture.

SCOTT, Beverly; Private; D/10th Cav. Commander, 10th Cavalry, forwarded final statement and inventory of personal effects regarding Scott, formerly stationed at Camp Supply, Indian Territory, to Adjutant General, 2 Apr 1873. SOURCE: ES, 10 Cav, 1873–83.

SCOTT, Burley; Private; K/25th Inf. Born Maringo, AL; Ht 5'6", dark complexion, black hair and eyes, occupation laborer; enlisted New Orleans, age 24, 1 Oct 1866; initially assigned to A/39th Infantry; discharged, end of term, Jackson Barracks, LA, 1 Oct 1869. SOURCE: Register of Enlistments.

SCOTT, Charles; Private; C/10th Cav. Served in 10th Cavalry in Cuba, 1898. SOURCE: Cashin, *Under Fire with the Tenth Cavalry*, 340.

SCOTT, Charles; Sergeant; I/24th Inf. Ranked number 178 among rifle experts with 72 percent in 1905. SOURCE: GO 101, AGO, 31 May 1906.

SCOTT, David; Private; K/24th Inf. Left Mexico, Philippines, with Pvt. John Edwards of K/24th Infantry, without authority, 27 Sep 1899; captured by insurgents; released and rejoined troop; Edwards died while prisoner. SOURCE: Muller, *The Twenty Fourth Infantry*, 34.

Deserted at Mexico, 8 Oct 1899. SOURCE: Regt Returns, 24 Inf, Oct 1899.

SCOTT, David; Private; B/10th Cav. At Ft Robinson, NE, 1903; to be tried in U.S. Court, Crawford, NE. SOURCE: AG, DeptMo, to CO, Ft Robinson, 10 Feb 1903, Register of LR, Ft Robinson.

SCOTT, Edward; Private; F/10th Cav. Original member of 10th Cavalry; in troop when organized, Ft Leavenworth, KS, 21 Jun 1867. SOURCE: McMiller, "Buffalo Soldiers," 73.

SCOTT, Edward; Corporal; K/10th Cav. Wounded in action against Geronimo, Pineto Mountains, Mexico, 3 May 1886. SOURCE: Baker, Roster.

Admitted to Soldiers Home with disability, age 30, after eight years and four months' service, 27 May 1886. SOURCE: SecWar, *AR 1884*, 748.

SCOTT, Edward; Private; D/9th Cav. Resided at Forest Glen, Montgomery Co., MD, in 1895. SOURCE: VA File C 2363092, Henry Dent.

SCOTT, Edward; Private; K/25th Inf. At Ft Niobrara, NE, 1904. SOURCE: Wilson, "History of Fort Niobrara."

SCOTT, Frank; Private; 10th Cav. Killed in action against Apaches. *See* **KELLY**, William H., K/10th Cavalry

SCOTT, George W.; Sergeant; F/9th Cav. Veteran of Philippine Insurrection; at Ft D. A. Russell, WY, in 1910; sharpshooter; resident of Thompson, GA. SOURCE: *Illustrated Review: Ninth Cavalry*, with picture.

SCOTT, H.; Private; K/9th Cav. On detached service in field, New Mexico, 21 Jan–8 Feb 1881. SOURCE: Regt Returns, 9 Cav, Feb 1881.

SCOTT, Henry; Private; G/10th Cav. Served in 10th Cavalry, 1898; remained in U.S. during war with Spain. SOURCE: Cashin, *Under Fire with the Tenth Cavalry*, 346.

SCOTT, Hugh C.; Master Sgt; HQ Troop/10th Cav. Pictured on horseback. SOURCE: *Cavalry Journal* 40 (Sep–Oct 1931): 59.

Retired from Ft Leavenworth, KS, with thirty years' service. SOURCE: *Cavalry Journal* 41 (Jul 1932): 61.

SCOTT, Isaac; G/10th Cav. Original member of 10th Cavalry; in troop when organized, Ft Leavenworth, KS, 5 Jul 1867. SOURCE: McMiller, "Buffalo Soldiers," 74.

SCOTT, Jacob; I/10th Cav. Original member of 10th Cavalry; in troop when organized, Ft Riley, KS, 15 Aug 1867. SOURCE: McMiller, "Buffalo Soldiers," 76.

SCOTT, John; I/10th Cav. Original member of 10th Cavalry; in troop when organized, Ft Riley, KS, 15 Aug 1867. SOURCE: McMiller, "Buffalo Soldiers," 76.

Mentioned as Indian war survivor. SOURCE: *Winners of the West* 3 (Jun 1926): 7.

SCOTT, John; Private; I/9th Cav. Wounded slightly in action against Victorio, Jun 1879. SOURCE: Billington, "Black Cavalrymen," 64; Billington, *New Mexico's Buffalo Soldiers*, 89.

SCOTT, John; Sergeant; E/24th Inf. Resident of Boston; to be discharged at end of term, Ft Bayard, NM, 8 Dec 1891. SOURCE: Cleveland *Gazette*, 12 Dec 1891.

SCOTT, John; Private; H/24th Inf. Enlisted Louisville, 7 Jun 1898; assigned to H Company 16 Sep but never joined; absent sick, disease contracted in line of duty, Ft McPherson, GA, since 16 Sep 1898. SOURCE: Muster Roll, H/24 Inf, Sep–Oct 1899.

Absent, sick, at Ft McPherson, until 8 Nov; on furlough, sick, 8 Nov–7 Dec 1898; rejoined 11 Dec 1898. SOURCE: Muster Roll, H/24 Inf, Nov–Dec 1898.

Discharged, Ft Douglas, UT, character good, single, 27 Jan 1899; due U.S. for clothing $21.18. SOURCE: Muster Roll, H/24 Inf, Jan–Feb 1899.

SCOTT, John H.; I/10th Cav. Original member of 10th Cavalry; in troop when organized, Ft Riley, KS, 15 Aug 1867. SOURCE: McMiller, "Buffalo Soldiers," 76.

SCOTT, Joseph; Private; G/9th Cav. Veteran of Philippine Insurrection; at Ft D. A. Russell, WY, in 1910; resident of Washington, DC. SOURCE: *Illustrated Review: Ninth Cavalry*, with picture.

SCOTT, Levi; A/25th Inf. Resides in Nobleville, IN; served in 1872–77; would be glad to hear from comrades; applies for membership in Camp 11, National Indian War Veterans. SOURCE: *Winners of the West* 5 (Jun 1928): 3.

SCOTT, Miller; Private; E/49th Inf. Wounded in hip in the Philippines, Feb 1901. SOURCE: *ANJ* 38 (23 Feb 1901): 631.

SCOTT, Nelson; Lance Cpl; G/9th Cav. Private, B/9th Cavalry, at Ft Duchesne, UT; teacher in post school, 1 Nov 1891–31 Jan 1892, 14 Dec 1892–30 Apr 1893. SOURCE: Reports of Schools, Fort Duchesne.

Assigned to extra duty as teacher, Ft Robinson, NE. SOURCE: Order 67, 24 Sep 1895, Post Orders, Ft Robinson.

At Ft Robinson; teacher in post school, Sep 1895–Feb 1896. SOURCE: Reports of Schools, Fort Duchesne.

Lance corporal, G/9th Cavalry; relieved from extra duty as schoolteacher, Ft Robinson. SOURCE: SO 14, 2 Feb 1897, Post Orders, Ft Robinson.

SCOTT, Oliver; Private; D/10th Cav. Sentenced to dishonorable discharge and nine months in prison, Ft Robinson, NE, 2 Jul 1902; released 16 Feb 1903. SOURCE: Post Returns, Ft Robinson.

SCOTT, Oscar; Private; C/10th Cav. Served in 10th Cavalry in Cuba, 1898. SOURCE: Cashin, *Under Fire with the Tenth Cavalry*, 340.

SCOTT, Oscar J. W.; Chaplain; U.S. Army. Born Gallipolis, OH, 31 Jul 1867; bachelor's and master's degrees from Ohio Wesleyan University; bachelor of divinity from Drew Theological Seminary; doctorate of divinity from Payne Theological Seminary; as minister of Metropolitan African Methodist Episcopal Church reduced church debt from $31,000 to $19,000 in six months; wife accomplished on piano and organ and is assistant chorus director, Ohio Institute for the Blind. SOURCE: Talbert, *The Sons of Allen*, 168–69, with picture.

Minister at Shorter Chapel, African Methodist Episcopal Church, Denver; elected president of Alumni Association, Denver University Theological Seminary; other officers are white; wife Nellie Poindexter of Columbus, OH, a skilled pianist who once taught music at Ohio State Hospital for the Blind. SOURCE: Cleveland *Gazette*, 17 Jun 1899.

Former resident of Columbus and Delaware, OH; received bachelor of oratory degree from University of Denver. SOURCE: Cleveland *Gazette*, 1 Jun 1899.

Minister of African Methodist Episcopal Church, Denver; appointed to replace Reverend Jesse F. Peck at Allen Chapel, Kansas City, MO. SOURCE: Wichita *Searchlight*, 22 Dec 1900.

Members of Metropolitan African Methodist Episcopal Zion Church, Washington, DC, gave reception for him as he left after four-year tenure to be chaplain, U.S. Army. Thursday, 16 May 1907. SOURCE: Washington *Bee*, 25 May 1907.

Graduate of Theological and Oratorical Departments, University of Denver, as well as Ohio Wesleyan and Drew Universities; doctor of divinity; pastor, Shorter Chapel, African Methodist Episcopal Church, Denver; appointed first lieutenant, 17 Apr 1907; now with regiment in Mindanao, Philippines. SOURCE: *Colored American Magazine* 16 (Apr 1909): 224.

Passed through Cleveland, OH, with his wife Saturday, 6 Aug 1910, en route from Niagara Falls to Columbus; graduate of Ohio Wesleyan University; wife is Nellie Poindexter of Columbus. SOURCE: Cleveland *Gazette*, 13 Aug 1910.

Mentioned as chaplain and first lieutenant. SOURCE: Work, *The Negro Year Book, 1912*, 77.

Recently promoted to captain; stationed in Hawaii. SOURCE: Cleveland *Gazette*, 1 Aug 1914.

Previously pastor at Madison, NJ, Kansas City, Denver, Washington, DC; appointed chaplain, 25th Infantry, 17 Apr 1907; served in Texas, the Philippines, Washington, now in Hawaii; organized and maintains Young Men's Bible Study Class and Scott Literary Association. SOURCE: Wright, *The Centennial Encyclopedia of the AME Church*, 196, with picture.

En route home from Hawaii. SOURCE: Cleveland *Gazette*, 24 Jun 1916.

Delivered invocation at Wilberforce University commencement. SOURCE: Cleveland *Gazette*, 6 Jul 1918.

Mentioned as captain and chaplain, 10th Cavalry. SOURCE: Work, *The Negro Yearbook, 1918–1919*, 228.

Mentioned in acknowledgements. SOURCE: Mary Curtis, *The Black Soldiers*.

Mentioned as retired major, residing in Washington, DC. SOURCE: Work, *The Negro Yearbook, 1925–1926*, 253.

SCOTT, Raleigh A.; Private; F/24th Inf. Born Knoxville, TN; occupation musician; Ht 5'9", yellow complexion, brown eyes, black hair; enlisted, age 32, Ft Bayard, NM, 17 Oct 1892; transferred to F/24th Infantry, single, character good, 16 Mar 1894; retained $48, clothing $6.45. SOURCE: Descriptive Book, 24 Inf NCS & Band.

SCOTT, Richard; Private; K/24th Inf. At San Carlos, AZ, 1890. *See* **HARDEE**, James A., Private, K/24th Infantry

SCOTT, Richard; Private; G/25th Inf. Died in brawl at "disreputable saloon" near Ft Missoula, MT; shot on evening of 24 May 1896; second such death this year. SOURCE: Monthly Report, Chaplain Steward, 1 Jun 1896, Steward ACP file.

SCOTT, Robert; D/10th Cav. Original member of 10th Cavalry; in troop when organized, Ft Leavenworth, KS, 1 Jun 1867. SOURCE: McMiller, "Buffalo Soldiers," 71.

SCOTT, Robert; Private; G/24th Inf. Transferred from Reserve Divisional Hospital, Siboney, Cuba, to U.S. on U.S. Army Transport *Santiago* with yellow fever, 25 Jul 1898. SOURCE: Hospital Papers, Spanish-American War.

SCOTT, Robert; Corporal; E/10th Cav. Served as private, E/10th Cavalry, 1898; remained in U.S. during war with Spain. SOURCE: Cashin, *Under Fire with the Tenth Cavalry*, 343.

Promoted to corporal, Sep 1899. SOURCE: *ANJ* 37 (7 Oct 1899): 122.

SCOTT, Rufus; Corporal; K/25th Inf. After ambush in the Philippines, 29 Jan 1900, with ten privates protected wounded and medical detail. SOURCE: Richmond *Planet*, 17 Mar 1900.

Captured by insurgents at Subig, Philippines, 23 Feb 1900; escaped 21 Mar 1900. SOURCE: Manila *Times*, 27 Mar 1900.

SCOTT, Samuel E.; Private; D/25th Inf. Dishonorable discharge, Brownsville. SOURCE: SO 266, AGO, 9 Nov 1906.

One of fourteen cleared of involvement in Brownsville raid by court, 1910; authorized to reenlist. SOURCE: Weaver, *The Brownsville Raid*, 248.

SCOTT, Samuel J.; Sergeant; B/9th Cav. "One of the heroes of the Black Hills." SOURCE: Guthrie, *Camp-Fires of the Afro-American*, 646.

SCOTT, Solomon; Private; B/24th Inf. At Ft Huachuca, AZ, 1893. *See* **BROWN**, Alfred, First Sergeant, H/24th Infantry

Transferred from Reserve Divisional Hospital, Siboney, Cuba, to U.S. on U.S. Army Transport *Concho* with yellow fever, 23 Jul 1898. SOURCE: Hospital Papers, Spanish-American War.

SCOTT, Thomas J.; Private; M/9th Cav. Died of "saritonitis" at Ft Washakie, WY, 24 Mar 1887. SOURCE: Regt Returns, 9 Cav, Mar 1887.

SCOTT, W. C.; Private; H/9th Cav. On detached service at Ft Bayard, NM, 16 Jan–10 Feb 1881. SOURCE: Regt Returns, 9 Cav, Feb 1881.

SCOTT, Walker; Private; A/9th Cav. On special duty as stable orderly since 10 May 1902. SOURCE: SD List, A/9, 24 May 1902.

SCOTT, Washington; Corporal; L/10th Cav. Farrier, L/10th Cavalry, 1898; remained in U.S. during war with Spain. SOURCE: Cashin, *Under Fire with the Tenth Cavalry*, 350.

Released to duty from treatment for gonorrhea, Ft Robinson, NE, 9 Oct 1903. SOURCE: Post Surgeon to CO, Det 10, 9 Oct 1903, LS, Post Surgeon, Ft Robinson.

SCOTT, William; Private; D/9th Cav. Married to Julia Nelson, 1894; divorced, 1908; five children, of whom only William, Jr., was alive in 1915. SOURCE: VA File C 2581520, William Branch.

SCOTT, William; G/10th Cav. Original member of 10th Cavalry; in troop when organized, Ft Leavenworth, KS, 5 Jul 1867. SOURCE: McMiller, "Buffalo Soldiers," 74.

SCOTT, William F.; Tech Sgt; HQ Troop/10th Cav. Squadron sergeant major, 10th Cavalry, commissioned captain at Camp Des Moines, IA, 15 Oct 1917. SOURCE: Glass, *History of the Tenth Cavalry*, appendix M.

Won Shipp Cup as outstanding soldier in regiment, Organization Day, 1931. SOURCE: *Cavalry Journal* 40 (Sep–Oct 1931): 59.

SCOTT, Winfield; Sergeant; B/25th Inf. Born in Pennsylvania; private and blacksmith, M/10th Cavalry, 7 Jan 1870–7 Jan 1875; blacksmith and sergeant, 16 Jan 1875–15 Jan 1885; private, corporal, sergeant, D/10th Cavalry, 19 Jan 1885–18 Jan 1890; private, corporal, sergeant, 22 Jan 1890–21 Jan 1895; private, 2 Feb 1895; sergeant, 6 Feb 1896; at Ft Assiniboine, MT, 1897. SOURCE: Baker, Roster.

Sergeant, M/10th Cavalry, wounded in action, along with Pvt. Augustus Dover, while attempting to arrest desperado W. W. Alexander on military reservation, Pena Colorado, TX, Jul 1882; Alexander killed. SOURCE: Leckie, *The Buffalo Soldiers*, 238.

Discharged as sergeant, D/10th Cavalry. SOURCE: *ANJ* 35 (26 Feb 1898): 478.

Retires as sergeant, B/25th Infantry, in the Philippines, Feb 1900. SOURCE: *ANJ* 37 (24 Feb 1900): 603.

SCROGGINS, William H.; Sgt Maj; 24th Inf. Born Lexington, KY; Ht 5'9", black complexion; enlisted, Cincinnati, age 23, 26 Jul 1883; joined G/24th Infantry, Ft Supply, Indian Territory, 27 Nov 1883; corporal, 22 Dec 1884; private, 28 May 1885; regimental clerk, 20 Aug 1885–17 Oct 1887; sergeant major, 24th Infantry, 19 Dec 1887; sent to Army and Navy General Hospital, Hot Springs, AR, 23 Jun 1888; discharged there, end of term, single, character excellent, 25 Jul 1888. SOURCE: Descriptive Book, 24 Inf NCS & Band.

SCRUGGS, Gilbert; Corporal; Band/9th Cav. Born Bradford, TN; Ht 5'9", black complexion; enlisted for Band/24th Infantry, age 31, Ft Leavenworth, KS, 23 Aug 1893; two previous enlistments in L, I, Band, and G/9th Cavalry; transferred to H/24th Infantry, Ft Bayard, NM, single, character good, 5 Mar 1895; retained $18, clothing $5; owes U.S. $3 for subsistence stores. SOURCE: Descriptive Book, 24 Inf NCS & Band.

Private, G/9th Cavalry, transferred to Band/9th Cavalry, Ft Robinson, NE. SOURCE: *ANJ* 33 (28 Mar 1896): 540.

Corporal, Band/9th Cavalry; died of typhoid, Nueva Caceres, Luzon, Philippines, 22 Jul 1901.

SCRUGGS, William; Private; A/49th Inf. Convicted of robbery in the Philippines and sentenced to two years, Apr 1900.

SEABRON, Emerson; Private; L/9th Cav. At Ft D. A. Russell, WY, in 1910; resident of Asheville, NC. SOURCE: *Illustrated Review: Ninth Cavalry*, with picture.

SEALS, Abraham; Private; M/9th Cav. Veteran of Philippine Insurrection; at Ft D. A. Russell, WY, in 1910. SOURCE: *Illustrated Review: Ninth Cavalry*.

SEALS, Benjamin; Sergeant; H/24th Inf. Sergeant, Band/9th Cavalry, on detached service at headquarters, District of New Mexico, Santa Fe, 1880; played third alto. SOURCE: Billington, *New Mexico's Buffalo Soldiers*, 226.

Private, H/24th Infantry; on extra duty as laborer, Quartermaster Department. SOURCE: Order 165, Ft Huachuca, AZ, 10 Nov 1893, Name File, 24 Inf.

Enlisted Ft Douglas, UT, 31 Jan 1898; nineteen years' continuous service; promoted from corporal to sergeant, 10 May 1898. SOURCE: Muster Roll, H/24 Inf, May–Jun 1898.

On furlough, authorized by surgeon's certificate, 24 Sep–6 Nov 1898, disease contracted in line of duty; discharged in accordance with paragraphs 145 and 146, Army Regulations, single, character excellent, 6 Nov 1898; deposits $521.86, clothing $49.85. SOURCE: Muster Roll, H/24 Inf, Sep–Oct and Nov–Dec 1898.

SEALS, Dock; Recruit; Colored Detachment/ Mounted Service. Convicted by general court martial, Jefferson Barracks, MO, of desertion, 6–20 Sep 1887; sentenced to dishonorable discharge and four years. SOURCE: GCMO 79, AGO, 7 Nov 1887.

SEALS, Joseph; Private; C/10th Cav. Served in 10th Cavalry, 1898; remained in U.S. during war with Spain. SOURCE: Cashin, *Under Fire with the Tenth Cavalry*, 340.

SEALS, Wallace D.; 2nd Lt; 9th Inf USV. Born Cherokee, Cherokee Co., TX, 5 Dec 1862; moved to Galveston, TX, with parents, 1868; worked in freight department, Gulf Coast and Santa Fe Railroads, for fifteen years; then worked as cotton clerk and paymaster; first sergeant of "Lincoln Guards," Galveston, for four years, then second lieutenant. SOURCE: Coston, *The Spanish-American War Volunteer*, 52–55.

SEARCY, Fred; Private; B/10th Cav. Served in 10th Cavalry, 1898; remained in U.S. during war with Spain. SOURCE: Cashin, *Under Fire with the Tenth Cavalry*, 333.

SEARIGHT, Albert; Private; G/10th Cav. Served in 10th Cavalry, 1898; remained in U.S. during war with Spain. SOURCE: Cashin, *Under Fire with the Tenth Cavalry*, 345.

SEARS, Elijah; Private; H/48th Inf. Died of variola in the Philippines, 3 May 1900. SOURCE: *ANJ* 37 (19 May 1900): 903.

SEARS, Richard; Private; H/24th Inf. Enlisted Louisville, 8 Jul 1898; sick, disease contracted in line of duty, 17 Sep–27 Oct 1898. SOURCE: Muster Roll, H/24 Inf, Sep–Oct 1898.

Assistant cook since 19 Nov 1898. SOURCE: Muster Roll, H/24 Inf, Nov–Dec 1898.

Discharged, single, character good, Ft Douglas, UT, 27 Jan 1899; clothing $1.87. SOURCE: Muster Roll, H/24 Inf, Jan–Feb 1899.

SEATON, Loss; Private; B/24th Inf. At Ft McIntosh, TX, 1877. *See* **GRAYSON**, Charles H., Private, G/24th Infantry

SEDDEN, James R.; Private; A/24th Inf. Died in Cuba, 18 Aug 1898. SOURCE: *ANJ* 36 (18 Feb 1899): 590.

SELFT, Henry; Private; H/24th Inf. Fined $1 by summary court, San Isidro, Philippines, for failure to challenge commander within twenty paces while sentry, 21 Feb 1902. SOURCE: Register of Summary Court, San Isidro.

SELTRY, Jerry; L/10th Cav. Original member of 10th Cavalry; in troop when organized, Ft Riley, KS, 21 Sep 1867. SOURCE: McMiller, "Buffalo Soldiers," 78.

SEMLER, James; Private; 9th Cav. Wounded in thumb, Naco, AZ, 20 Nov 1914. SOURCE: Cleveland *Gazette*, 13 May 1916.

SENOR, Mack; Private; G/9th Cav. At Ft D. A. Russell, WY, in 1910; resident of St. Louis. SOURCE: *Illustrated Review: Ninth Cavalry*, with picture.

SENTERS, Charles C.; Private; C/10th Cav. Served in 10th Cavalry in Cuba, 1898. SOURCE: Cashin, *Under Fire with the Tenth Cavalry*, 340.

SETPHEIN, Benjamin; Corporal; H/24th Inf. Enlisted with ten years' continuous service, Ft Tampa, FL, 12 Jun 1898. SOURCE: Muster Roll, H/24 Inf, May–Jun 1898.

Promoted to corporal 16 Sep 1898; due U.S. for lost ordnance (oiler) $.25. SOURCE: Muster Roll, H/24 Inf, Sep–Oct 1898.

Discharged, single, character excellent, 29 Jan 1899; reenlisted 30 Jan 1899; warrant as corporal continued since 16 Sep 1898; deposits $135, clothing $26.21. SOURCE: Muster Roll, H/24 Inf, Jan–Feb 1899.

SETTLERS, James; Private; G/25th Inf. Mentioned in orders among men who distinguished themselves in 1889 for meritorious conduct while private, E/9th Cavalry; saved his commander from drowning while crossing Wind River, WY, at risk of his own life, 19 Jul 1889. SOURCE: GO 18, AGO, 1891.

Private, F/9th Cavalry; relieved of extra duty with Quartermaster Department, Ft Robinson, NE. SOURCE: Order 181, 25 Oct 1892, Post Orders, Ft Robinson.

Transferred from 9th Cavalry to 25th Infantry. SOURCE: SO 244, AGO, 23 Oct 1893.

Certificate of merit for 1889 rescue awarded 16 Jan 1900; discharged 29 Sep 1900. SOURCE: *ANJ* 39 (2 Aug 1902): 1219; GO 86, AGO, 24 Jul 1902.

SEWALL, B.; Private; L/9th Cav. On detached service in field, New Mexico, 21 Jan–24 Feb 1881. SOURCE: Regt Returns, 9 Cav, Feb 1881.

SEWARD, William; G/9th Cav. Born Harden Co., KY; occupation farmer; Ht 5'7 1/2", black complexion, hair, and eyes; enlisted Louisville, age 25, 24 Nov 1871; discharged, end of term, Ft Ringgold, TX, 23 Sep 1874. SOURCE: Register of Enlistments.

SEWELL, Fletcher; QM Sgt; A/10th Cav. Commissioned captain at Camp Des Moines, IA, 15 Oct 1917. SOURCE: Glass, *History of the Tenth Cavalry*, appendix M.

SEWELL, George; E/24th Inf. Remained in San Isidro, Nueva Ecija, Philippines, after service; occupation cook. SOURCE: Funston papers, KSHS.

SEXTON; Private; B/25th Inf. Wounded in ambush in the Philippines, 29 Jan 1900. SOURCE: Richmond *Planet*, 17 Mar 1900.

SHAFTER, Sweeney; Private; F/10th Cav. Mentioned in Mar 1877 as enlisting in F/10th Cavalry. SOURCE: ES, 10 Cav, 1873–83.

SHANKLIN, Greenfer; Private; H/10th Cav. Sentence for desertion, which began on 23 Mar 1876, reduced to eighteen months. SOURCE: GCMO 22, AGO, 23 Feb 1877.

SHANKS, Joseph; Private; D/25th Inf. Dishonorable discharge, Brownsville. SOURCE: SO 266, AGO, 9 Nov 1906.

SHANNAN, Jack; Private; L/10th Cav. Served in 10th Cavalry, 1898; remained in U.S. during war with Spain. SOURCE: Cashin, *Under Fire with the Tenth Cavalry*, 351.

SHANNON; Private; L/25th Inf. Wounded and then killed in ambush in the Philippines, 29 Jan 1900; "one of the most industrious men in the army, a quiet and unassuming man." SOURCE: Richmond *Planet*, 17 Mar 1900.

SHANNON, George; Private; D/9th Cav. Distinguished marksman and sharpshooter at Ft D. A. Russell, WY, in 1910; resident of Forsyth, GA. SOURCE: *Illustrated Review: Ninth Cavalry*, with picture.

SHANNON, James; M/10th Cav. Original member of 10th Cavalry; in troop when organized, Ft Riley, KS, 15 Oct 1867. SOURCE: McMiller, "Buffalo Soldiers," 79.

SHARP, Charles E.; Private; B/10th Cav. Sentenced to dishonorable discharge and confinement by general court martial, Ft Robinson, NE, Sep 1902; released Nov 1902. SOURCE: SO 166, DeptMo, 2 Sep 1902; Regt Returns, 10 Cav, Nov 1902.

SHARP, James; F/25th Inf. Knew George Crockett while serving in F/25th Infantry; resided in Knoxville, TN, 1890, age 48. SOURCE: Affidavit, Sharp, 7 Jul 1890, VA File XC 2624113, George D. Crockett.

SHARPE, William; Private; K/9th Cav. Killed in action, 26 Dec 1867. SOURCE: Leckie, *The Buffalo Soldiers*, 85; *Illustrated Review: Ninth Cavalry*. See **BOWERS**, Edward, Private, K/9th Cavalry; **TRIMBLE**, Anderson, Private, K/9th Cavalry

SHARPS, Joseph; K/10th Cav. Original member of 10th Cavalry; in troop when organized, Ft Riley, KS, 1 Sep 1867. SOURCE: McMiller, "Buffalo Soldiers," 77.

SHAVER, Lee; Private; K/24th Inf. Fined $5 for failure to clean rifle properly for guard duty, Cabanatuan, Philippines, 30 Mar 1901. SOURCE: Name File, 24 Inf.

Fined $5 for being too drunk to fall in for pay, Cabanatuan, 17 May 1901; witness: 1st Sgt. Jacob Stevens, K/24th Infantry. SOURCE: Name File, 24 Inf.

Fined $10 and confined for twenty days for being drunk and disorderly in camp and for having loud and disorderly conversation with native woman, with his arrest required to prevent serious trouble; witness: Cpl. Hugh Fortner, K/24th Infantry. SOURCE: Name File, 24 Inf.

SHAW; Private; M/9th Cav. Wounded in action, 17 Jan 1880. *See* **STOUT**, Albert, Ordnance Sergeant, U.S. Army

SHAW, Harry A.; Corporal; F/24th Inf. Died in Cuba, 31 Jul 1898. SOURCE: *ANJ* 36 (18 Feb 1899): 590.

Cause of death not reported. SOURCE: AG, *Correspondence Regarding the War with Spain*, I:202.

SHAW, James N.; Private; L/10th Cav. Served in 10th Cavalry, 1898; remained in U.S. during war with Spain. SOURCE: Cashin, *Under Fire with the Tenth Cavalry*, 351.

SHAW, Perry; Private; M/10th Cav. At Ft McDowell, AZ, 1887. SOURCE: Misc Records, 10 Cav.

At Ft Apache, AZ, 1890, subscribed $.50 to testimonial to General Grierson. SOURCE: List of subscriptions, 23 Apr 1890, 10th Cavalry papers, MHI.

SHAW, Thomas; Sergeant; K/9th Cav. Born Covington, KY; awarded Medal of Honor for heroism against Apache Nana, while sergeant, K/9th Cavalry, Carrizo Canyon, NM, 19 Jul 1881. SOURCE: Carroll, *The Black Military Experience*, 397–98; Leckie, *The Buffalo Soldiers*, 232.

Medal of Honor for heroism in action against Nana, Carrizo Canyon, 12 Aug 1881. SOURCE: Billington, *New Mexico's Buffalo Soldiers*, 105.

First sergeant, B/9th Cavalry, at Ft Bayard, NM, 1877. *See* **RICHTER**, William J., B/9th Cavalry

On furlough from Ft Cummings, NM, 20 Dec 1880–18 Feb 1881. SOURCE: Regt Returns, 9 Cav, Dec 1880–Feb 1881.

Enlisted as private, Ft Robinson, NE, 7 Dec 1886. SOURCE: Post Returns, Ft Robinson, Dec 1886.

Date of rank as sergeant 10 Dec 1886. SOURCE: Roster, 9 Cav.

At Ft Robinson, 1888; wife visiting in Kansas City, MO. SOURCE: Cleveland *Gazette*, 12 Jan 1889.

Treasurer of Diamond Club, K/9th Cavalry, as sergeant, Ft Robinson. SOURCE: *ANJ* 28 (2 May 1891): 620.

SHAWES, Dick; Private; K/9th Cav. On daily duty in post garden, Ft Robinson, NE. SOURCE: Order 48, 10 Mar 1890, Post Orders, Ft Robinson.

SHAWN, Edward; D/10th Cav. Original member of 10th Cavalry; in troop when organized, Ft Leavenworth, KS, 1 Jun 1867. SOURCE: McMiller, "Buffalo Soldiers," 71.

SHEAFF, Joseph E.; Corporal; G/9th Cav. With troop in Pine Ridge campaign, winter of 1890–91; camped at Rosebud Agency, 22 Nov 1890, and experienced very hard weather and shortage of tents, and had to do twenty-four-hour guard duty without shelter; bunked with Joseph Blew; in blizzard during late December "we suffered untold agony" after which Blew's joints stiffened. SOURCE: Affidavit, Sheaff, age 33, 222 River Street, Cambridge, MA, 26 Dec 1893, VA File XC 970422, Joseph Blew.

SHEAR, Robert; Recruit; L/10th Cav. Mentioned Jan 1873 as recruit sent to L/10th Cavalry, from Ft Gibson, Indian Territory. SOURCE: LS, 10 Cav, 1873–83.

SHEARS, William H.; Private; I/10th Cav. On daily duty as company baker, Camp Supply, Indian Territory.

SOURCE: Special Order 59, Det 10 Cav, 26 Aug 1869, Orders, Det 10 Cav, 1868–69.

SHEFFIELD, Frederick; Private; B/10th Cav. Served in 10th Cavalry in Cuba, 1898. SOURCE: Cashin, *Under Fire with the Tenth Cavalry*, 338.

SHELL, Robert L.; Private; H/10th Cav. Served in 10th Cavalry, 1898; remained in U.S. during war with Spain. SOURCE: Cashin, *Under Fire with the Tenth Cavalry*, 347.

SHELLINGTON, Isaac; Private; B/10th Cav. Served in 10th Cavalry, 1898; remained in U.S. during war with Spain. SOURCE: Cashin, *Under Fire with the Tenth Cavalry*, 333.

SHELLY, James W.; Private; M/9th Cav. At Ft D. A. Russell, WY, in 1910; resident of Macon, GA. SOURCE: *Illustrated Review: Ninth Cavalry*, with picture.

SHELTON, Joseph; Private; I/24th Inf. Enlisted Huntington, WV, 25 Mar 1899. SOURCE: Muster Roll, I/24 Inf, Mar–Apr 1899.

Died of dysentery, Bangued, Luzon, Philippines, 10 Jul 1901. SOURCE: *ANJ* 39 (7 Sep 1901): 17.

SHELTON, Thomas D.; 1st Sgt; K/9th Cav. Private, sick in Ft Robinson, NE, hospital, 22 May–Jun 1891. SOURCE: Regt Returns, 9 Cav, May–Jun 1891.

Corporal as of 4 Oct 1893; at Ft Robinson, 1895. SOURCE: *ANJ* 32 (1 Jun 1895): 658.

Reenlistment as married soldier authorized by letter, Adjutant General's Office, 1 May 1895.

Veteran of Indian wars, Spanish-American War, and Philippine Insurrection; first sergeant, at Ft D. A. Russell, WY, in 1910; marksman; resident of Albemarle Co., VA. SOURCE: *Illustrated Review: Ninth Cavalry*, with picture.

SHELVIN, Robert. Spanish-American War veteran; died in Minnesota. SOURCE: Taylor, "Minnesota Black Spanish-American War Veterans."

SHEPARD, Thomas; Corporal; F/10th Cav. Original member of 10th Cavalry; in troop when organized, Ft Leavenworth, KS, 21 Jun 1867. SOURCE: McMiller, "Buffalo Soldiers," 73.

Wounded in action against Indians in Kansas, 21 Aug 1867. SOURCE: Armes, *Ups and Downs*, 247.

SHEPARDSON, George; Private; A/49th Inf. Deserted from Cordin, Philippines, 24 Dec 1900, after trying to kill 1st Sgt. Peter G. Gibson and killing a native. SOURCE: Descriptive Book, A/49 Inf.

SHEPERD, Frank; Private; M/9th Cav. Assaulted with pistol by Private Edwards, G/9th Cavalry, at Bellevue, NE, rifle range; Edwards, previously arrested for stabbing soldier at Ft Sill, Indian Territory, was sentenced to two years and escorted to prison by Sergeant Simons, 9th Cavalry. SOURCE: Omaha *Bee*, 16 Aug 1886.

SHEPHARD, Henry; Private; H/9th Cav. Veteran of Philippine Insurrection; at Ft D. A. Russell, WY, in 1910; sharpshooter; resident of Pensacola, FL. SOURCE: *Illustrated Review: Ninth Cavalry*, with picture.

SHEPHERD, S. J.; Private; D/9th Cav. Discharged by general court martial, Ft Cummings, NM, 31 Jan 1881. SOURCE: Regt Returns, 9 Cav, Feb 1881.

SHEPPARD, Bernhard; A/10th Cav. Original member of 10th Cavalry; in troop when organized, Ft Leavenworth, KS, 18 Feb 1867. SOURCE: McMiller, "Buffalo Soldiers," 68.

SHEPPARD, King W.; Private; F/25th Inf. Deserted from San Francisco, 25 Aug 1902. SOURCE: Regt Returns, 25 Inf, Aug 1902.

SHEPPARD, Marshall; Corporal; C/9th Cav. Private, C/9th Cavalry, commended for gallantry in charge on San Juan Hill, battle of Santiago, Cuba, 1 Jul 1898. SOURCE: GO 15, AGO, 13 Feb 1900; *ANJ* 37 (24 Feb 1900): 611.

Veteran of Spanish-American War and Philippine Insurrection; corporal, L/9th Cavalry, at Ft D. A. Russell, WY, in 1910; marksman; resident of Caroline Co., VA. SOURCE: *Illustrated Review: Ninth Cavalry*, with picture.

SHEPPARD, Sherman; Private; F/25th Inf. "Foully murdered" in the Philippines by native while searching for fruit without weapon, Jan 1900. SOURCE: Richmond *Planet*, 10 Mar 1900.

Killed in action at Iba, Philippines, 3 Jan 1900. SOURCE: *ANJ* 37 (10 Feb 1900): 562.

SHEPPARD, William; C/10th Cav. Original member of 10th Cavalry; in troop when organized, Ft Leavenworth, KS, 14 May 1867. SOURCE: McMiller, "Buffalo Soldiers," 70.

SHERIDAN, David; Recruit; Colored Inf. Convicted by general court martial, Jefferson Barracks, MO, of desertion, 1 Mar 1880–11 Aug 1882; sentenced to dishonorable discharge and four years. SOURCE: GCMO 10, AGO, 27 Jan 1883.

SHERIDAN, Jeremiah H.; Private; M/10th Cav. Served in 10th Cavalry, 1898; remained in U.S. during war with Spain. SOURCE: Cashin, *Under Fire with the Tenth Cavalry*, 352.

SHERRELL, Moses; Private; I/24th Inf. Enlisted Mobile, AL, 11 Jan 1899. SOURCE: Muster Roll, I/24 Inf, Jan–Feb 1899.

Allotted $12 per month for twelve months to Dollie Sherrell. SOURCE: Muster Roll, I/24 Inf, Sep–Oct 1899.

On detached service at Cabanatuan, Philippines, since 30 Dec 1899. SOURCE: Muster Roll, I/24 Inf, Nov–Dec 1899.

SHERWOOD, Edward; D/10th Cav. Original member of 10th Cavalry; in troop when organized, Ft Leavenworth, KS, 1 Jun 1867. SOURCE: McMiller, "Buffalo Soldiers," 71.

SHERWOOD, James H.; Recruit; Colored Detachment/Mounted Service. Acquitted by general court martial, Jefferson Barracks, MO, of theft of government boots from Recruit Clem Henson, Colored Detachment, 5 Jan 1889, and of theft of government shirt from Recruit Hurley Porter, Company D of Instruction, 31 Jan 1889. SOURCE: GCMO 13, AGO, 6 Mar 1889.

SHIDELL, John J.; Private; B/9th Cav. In hands of civil authorities, Price, UT, and Salt Lake City, 2 Oct 1897–18 Apr 1898. SOURCE: Regt Returns, 9 Cav, Oct 1897–Apr 1898.

SHIELDS, James; M/10th Cav. Original member of 10th Cavalry; in troop when organized, Ft Riley, KS, 15 Oct 1867. SOURCE: McMiller, "Buffalo Soldiers," 79.

SHINEHOUSE, James; Corporal; C/9th Cav. Private, at Ft Robinson, NE, 1886. SOURCE: Regt Returns, 9 Cav.

Corporal, discharged from Ft Robinson, end of term, 15 Feb 1887. SOURCE: Regt Returns, 9 Cav, Feb 1887

SHIPLEY, John; Sergeant; A/9th Cav. Private, H/9th Cavalry, at Ft McKinney, WY, 1888. SOURCE: Regt Returns, 9 Cav.

Reenlisted as private, H/9th Cavalry, Ft Robinson, NE, and requests retirement, 14 Aug 1898; discharge at end of previous term was with character good. SOURCE: Regt Returns, 9 Cav, Aug 1898.

Retired as sergeant, A/9th Cavalry, Ft Grant, AZ, Dec 1899. SOURCE: *ANJ* 37 (23 Dec 1899): 395.

No Veterans Administration pension file.

SHIPLEY, John; Cook; D/25th Inf. Retired Jun 1902. SOURCE: *ANJ* 39 (28 Jun 1902): 1091.

SHIPLEY, Lee; Private; A/24th Inf. Born a slave, Lincoln Co., KY, around 1840; enlisted in 124th U.S. Colored Troops, Lexington, KY, 21 Feb 1865; rose to sergeant and reduced back to private; served eight enlistments in 24th Infantry; retired 31 Mar 1897; remained in Salt Lake City; died three months later and buried at Ft Douglas, UT. SOURCE: Clark, "A History of the Twenty-fourth," 76–77.

Died with thirty years and three months' service, at Ft Douglas; memorial service held for him. SOURCE: *ANJ* 34 (19 Jun 1897): 776.

SHIPMAN; Private; I/9th Cav. Discharged in accordance with Special Order 100, Adjutant General's Office, 2 May 1891.

SHOBE, Hughes F.; Private; G/10th Cav. Served in 10th Cavalry, 1898; remained in U.S. during war with Spain. SOURCE: Cashin, *Under Fire with the Tenth Cavalry*, 346.

SHOBE, Robert T.; Sergeant; C/10th Cav. Served as private, C/10th Cavalry, 1898; remained in U.S. during war with Spain. SOURCE: Cashin, *Under Fire with the Tenth Cavalry*, 340.

Commissioned first lieutenant, Camp Des Moines, IA, 15 Oct 1917. SOURCE: Glass, *History of the Tenth Cavalry*, appendix M.

SHOCKLEY, Fred; Private; D/10th Cav. Served in 10th Cavalry in Cuba, 1898. SOURCE: Cashin, *Under Fire with the Tenth Cavalry*, 341.

Wounded in action at Santiago, Cuba, 1898. SOURCE: SecWar, *AR 1898*, 711; Bigelow, *Reminiscences of Santiago*, 133.

SHOECRAFT, Charles; Private; H/9th Cav. Deposited $79 with paymaster, Ft Robinson, NE, 1896–98.

On special duty as assistant librarian, Fort Robinson. SOURCE: SO 156, 26 Nov 1897, Post Orders, Ft Robinson.

SHOECRAFT, William H.; Private; I/10th Cav. Served in 10th Cavalry in Cuba, 1898. SOURCE: Cashin, *Under Fire with the Tenth Cavalry*, 348.

SHORES, Garth; Private; H/9th Cav. Born Lima, OH; Ht 5'7", medium complexion, brown eyes, black hair; occupation laborer; enlisted Wapakaneta, OH, age 18 1/2, 5 Apr 1900; absent with full equipment, 6 Oct 1900; dropped from rolls as killed, captured, or deserted, 19 Oct 1900. SOURCE: Descriptive Book, H/9 Cav.

Deserted at Albay, Luzon, the Philippines (listed as missing in action): "Absent since 6 Oct 1900 with full equipment, supposed to have deserted to the enemy or captured or killed." SOURCE: Regt Returns, 9 Cav, Dec 1901.

Missing at Albay, 6 Oct 1900. SOURCE: Hamilton, "History of the Ninth Cavalry," 104; *Illustrated Review: Ninth Cavalry*.

"Private Garth Shores, Troop H, 9th Cavalry, who is supposed to have deserted on the 9th instant with carbine and revolver and 100 rounds of ammunition is reported a prisoner at Jovellar. This comes from a friendly native who ascertained the fact. Shores was warned by his comrades but he laughed at them and was taken an alleged prisoner. He was dealing Monte among the Phillippinos [sic], and allowed one of them to hold his carbine." SOURCE: Maj. W. C. Forbush, CO, 2nd Squadron, 9 Cav, Albay, to AAG, 3rd District, Department of Southern Luzon, Nueva Caceres, Philippines, 21 Oct 1900, Orders, 2nd Battalion, 9 Cav.

Shores reported a prisoner at Jovellar by Major Forbush, 9th Cavalry, commander at Guinobatan, Albay. SOURCE: Manila *Times*, 27 Dec 1900.

Surrendered with insurgent force at Legaspi, Philippines, 5 Jul 1901, along with deserters Fred Hunter and William Victor. SOURCE: Descriptive Book, H/9 Cav.

Delivered by General Belarmino to U.S. Army with request for leniency as special favor to Belarmino. SOURCE: SecWar, *AR 1902*, 346.

"Gus Shores a deserter from Troop H 9th Cavalry was brought in wounded yesterday and surrendered to Colonel Wint by General Rober of General Belarmino's Staff, he did not bring his carbine, but claims it was turned in with other arms on the 5th inst." SOURCE: Manila *Times*, 11 Jul 1901.

Acquitted by Military Commission at Albay of treason. SOURCE: Descriptive Book, H/9 Cav.

Sentenced by summary court to ten days' confinement at Guinobatan, 5 Feb 1902. SOURCE: Descriptive Book, H/9 Cav.

Sentenced to hang for desertion by general court martial at Guinobatan; sentence reduced to three years by President Roosevelt. SOURCE: *ANJ* 39 (28 Jun 1902): 1091.

Sentenced to three years' confinement, 3 Oct 1902. SOURCE: Descriptive Book, H/9 Cav.

SHORT, David; Private; D/24th Inf. At Cabanatuan, Philippines, 1900. *See* **LEAVELL**, William, Private, D/24th Infantry

SHORTER, Charles; Private; Band/9th Cav. At Ft D. A. Russell, WY, in 1910; resident of Atlanta. SOURCE: *Illustrated Review: Ninth Cavalry*.

SHORTER, Lloyd; Private; I/24th Inf. Age 19; testified at Houston riot court martial under grant of immunity; reared by doctor's family, Alexandria, LA. SOURCE: Haynes, *A Night of Violence*, 264, 293.

SHROPSHIRE, Shelvin; 1st Sgt; H/10th Cav. Born in Alabama; private and corporal, F/15th U.S. Colored Troops, 18 Jan 1864–13 May 1866; private, corporal, sergeant, first sergeant, C/10th Cavalry, and regimental quartermaster sergeant, 10th Cavalry, 1 Mar 1867–1 Mar 1882; private, B/10th Cavalry, 8 Aug 1883; corporal, 1 Nov 1883; transferred to L/10th Cavalry, 5 Nov 1884; sergeant, 1 Mar 1888; first sergeant, 23 Jun 1888; transferred to H/10th Cavalry, 23 Oct 1890; at Ft Assiniboine, MT, 1897. SOURCE: Baker, Roster.

Constituent member of C/10th Cavalry when organized at Ft Leavenworth, 16 May 1867, and "a conspicuous figure in regimental history since"; first Indian action against Cheyennes, at Great Bend of Arkansas River; at Galestee, NM, disarmed a second lieutenant of regiment who had already shot and killed two men and thus prevented mutiny; mentioned for bravery in action against Kiowas and Comanches at Wichita Agency, Indian Territory, 22–23 Aug 1874; "rendered excellent service through the Geronimo campaign of 1885–86." SOURCE: Baker, Roster.

At Ft Bayard, NM, 1891. *See* **STARGALL**, Charlie, Private, 10th Cavalry

Conversation with Frederick Remington reported. SOURCE: Remington, "Vagabonding with the Tenth," *Cosmopolitan Magazine* 22 (Feb 1897).

Served in 10th Cavalry, 1898; remained in U.S. during war with Spain. SOURCE: Cashin, *Under Fire with the Tenth Cavalry*, 346.

At Camp Forse, AL, Nov 1898; feet were so sore he could not attend Thanksgiving dinner and was served in his tent.

By 1898 soldiers were relatively well educated and frequently resented discipline by noncommissioned officers who could barely read and write, such as Shropshire. SOURCE: Fletcher, "The Negro Soldier," 31.

Retirement with thirty-three years' service celebrated by regimental parade; elaborate dinner dance held in his honor by his troop on following day. SOURCE: Fletcher, "The Negro Soldier," 95.

No Veterans Administration pension file.

SIDNEY, S.; Private; G/9th Cav. On detached service, Ft Stanton, NM, 29 Jan–5 Feb 1881. SOURCE: Regt Returns, 9 Cav, Feb 1881.

SIGALLS, Allen K.; Corporal; L/10th Cav. Stationed at Ft Stockton, TX; led detachment of L/10th Cavalry, on scout of one hundred miles, from camp at Escondidos, TX, south of old mail station, in search of water holes, 25–27 Sep 1879. SOURCE: SecWar, *AR 1880*, 145.

See **COLLINS**, George, Private, L/10th Cavalry

SILBERT, William; Sergeant; F/10th Cav. Corporal, at Ft Robinson, NE, as witness in general court martial, 30 Jan–14 Feb 1906. SOURCE: Regt Returns, 10 Cav, Feb 1906.

Promoted to sergeant. SOURCE: SO 93, 10 Cav, Ft Ethan Allen, VT, 11 Dec 1909, Special Orders, 10 Cav.

SILLS, H.; Private; B/9th Cav. On detached service, Ft Bliss, TX, 8 Jan–9 Feb 1881. SOURCE: Regt Returns, 9 Cav, Feb 1881.

SILVERS, George; Private; E/10th Cav. Witness in general court martial at Ft Robinson, NE, 26 Jan–21 Feb 1906. SOURCE: Regt Returns, 10 Cav, Feb 1906.

SILVEY, Jerry; L/10th Cav. *See* **ANDERSON**, Henry, Private, L/10th Cavalry

SIMES, James W.; Corporal; D/24th Inf. At Cabanatuan, Philippines, 1901. *See* **COOK**, Julius, Private, B/24th Infantry

SIMMINS, George; C/10th Cav. Original member of 10th Cavalry; in troop when organized, Ft Leavenworth, KS, 14 May 1867. SOURCE: McMiller, "Buffalo Soldiers," 70.

SIMMONS; Private; E/10th Cav. At Ft Apache, AZ, 1890, subscribed $.50 to testimonial to General Grierson. SOURCE: List of subscriptions, 23 Apr 1890, 10th Cavalry papers, MHI.

SIMMONS, Anderson; C/10th Cav. Original member of 10th Cavalry; in troop when organized, Ft Leavenworth, KS, 14 May 1867. SOURCE: McMiller, "Buffalo Soldiers," 70.

SIMMONS, Charles; Recruit; 9th Cav. Enlisted at Ft Robinson, NE, 18 Aug 1885.

SIMMONS, Charles; Corporal; K/10th Cav. At Ft Robinson, NE, 1904; author of "Thanksgiving Day in the Tenth Cavalry," *The Voice of the Negro* 2 (Jan 1905).

SIMMONS, Frank; Private; 10th Cav. Arrived at Ft Leavenworth, KS, from Jefferson Barracks, MO. SOURCE: LS, 10 Cav, 1866–67.

SIMMONS, Harry; Corporal; H/9th Cav. At Ft D. A. Russell, WY, in 1910; sharpshooter; resident of Augusta, GA. SOURCE: *Illustrated Review: Ninth Cavalry*, with picture.

SIMMONS, James; B/10th Cav. Fined $10 and $4.70 costs for carrying concealed weapon, Crawford, NE, 23 May 1904.

SIMMONS, James A.; Private; A/25th Inf. Dishonorable discharge, Brownsville. SOURCE: SO 266, AGO, 9 Nov 1906.

SIMMONS, John W.; Private; Band/24th Inf. Born Palestine, TX; occupation railroad porter; Ht 5'7", black complexion, Negro hair and eyes; enlisted, age 22, Ft Sam Houston, TX, 26 Jun 1893; transferred to G/24th Infantry, single, character very good, 28 Aug 1893; transferred to Band/24th Infantry, single, character excellent, 10 Jan 1894; deposits (1897) $26. SOURCE: Descriptive Book, 24 Inf NCS & Band.

SIMMONS, Marcus; Private; 25th Inf. Born Charleston, SC; occupation laborer; Ht 5'8 1/2", dark complexion, black hair and eyes; enlisted, age 20, Charleston, 5 Jul 1881. SOURCE: Descriptive & Assignment Rolls, 25 Inf.

SIMMONS, Robert; K/10th Cav. Original member of 10th Cavalry; in troop when organized, Ft Riley, KS, 1 Sep 1867. SOURCE: McMiller, "Buffalo Soldiers," 77.

SIMMONS, William; Private; F/10th Cav. Original member of 10th Cavalry; in troop when organized, Ft Leavenworth, KS, 21 Jun 1867. SOURCE: McMiller, "Buffalo Soldiers," 73.

On daily duty as blacksmith, Camp Supply, Indian Territory. SOURCE: SO 38, Det 10 Cav, 21 Jun 1869, Orders, Det 10 Cav, 1868–69.

Mentioned Mar 1874. SOURCE: ES, 10 Cav, 1873–83.

SIMMONS, William; Trumpeter; L/10th Cav. Excused from duty, Camp Santa Rosa, TX, by Assistant Surgeon M. F. Price because of dysentery, May 1879, but kept at menial tasks by Capt. George A. Armes, 10th Cavalry; locked in barracks by Pvt. John W. Woods on orders of Armes, 11 Jun 1879, Ft Stockton, TX, in defiance of post commander's orders that Simmons be hospitalized; due to Armes's actions, disease worsened and Simmons died, Ft Stockton, 7 Sep 1879. SOURCE: GCMO 36, AGO, 27 May 1880.

See **COLLINS**, George, Private, L/10th Cavalry

SIMMONS, William H.; E/10th Cav. Original member of 10th Cavalry; in troop when organized, Ft Leavenworth, KS, 15 Jun 1867. SOURCE: McMiller, "Buffalo Soldiers," 72.

SIMMS, A.; Private; H/9th Cav. On detached service, Ft Bayard, NM, 16 Jan–10 Feb 1881. SOURCE: Regt Returns, 9 Cav, Feb 1881.

SIMMS, Charles; D/25th Inf. Enlisted 14 Feb 1888; discharged 13 Feb 1893; now age 61 with $25 per month pension; *Winners of the West* is "quite an inspiration to me." SOURCE: *Winners of the West* 6 (Apr 1929): 3.
    Letter. SOURCE: *Winners of the West* 6 (Oct 1929): 3.

SIMMS, Elsie; Corporal; I/10th Cav. Served in 10th Cavalry in Cuba, 1898. SOURCE: Cashin, *Under Fire with the Tenth Cavalry*, 347.

SIMMS, Henry; Private; I/10th Cav. On daily duty as company clerk, Camp Supply, Indian Territory. SOURCE: SO 10, Det 10 Cav, 26 Aug 1869, Orders, Det 10 Cav, 1868–69.

SIMMS, J. D.; Private; H/9th Cav. On detached service, Ft Bayard, NM, 16 Jan–10 Feb 1881. SOURCE: Regt Returns, 9 Cav, Feb 1881.

SIMMS, John W.; Private; I/10th Cav. Served in 10th Cavalry in Cuba, 1898. SOURCE: Cashin, *Under Fire with the Tenth Cavalry*, 348.

SIMMS, Squire; Private; C/24th Inf. Born Prince Georges Co., MD; Ht 5'6", brown complexion, eyes, and hair; second enlistment, age 29, Washington DC, 31 Oct 1881; discharged, end of term, Ft Sill, Indian Territory, 30 Dec 1886. SOURCE: Register of Enlistments,

SIMON, John J.; Private; C/9th Cav. Transferred from L/9th Cavalry, to Hospital Corps, Ft Leavenworth, KS. SOURCE: *ANJ* 25 (7 Apr 1888): 734.
    Private, C/9th Cavalry; schoolteacher, Ft Robinson, NE, 15 Nov 1894–30 Apr 1895. SOURCE: Reports of Schools, Ft Robinson.
    Request for discharge disapproved by letter, Department of the Platte, 8 Aug 1895.
    Relieved from extra duty as schoolteacher, Ft Robinson. SOURCE: Order 67, 24 Sep 1895, Post Orders, Ft Robinson.
    On extra duty as schoolteacher, Ft Robinson. SOURCE: SO 125, 6 Nov 1896, Post Orders, Ft Robinson.

SIMONDS; A/24th Inf. Remained in Bautista, Philippines after service; occupation businessman. SOURCE: Funston papers, KSHS.

SIMONS; Sergeant; 9th Cav. At Bellevue, NE, rifle range, 1886. See **SHEPERD**, Frank, Private, M/9th Cavalry

SIMONS, Benjamin; L/10th Cav. Original member of 10th Cavalry; in troop when organized, Ft Riley, KS, 21 Sep 1867. SOURCE: McMiller, "Buffalo Soldiers," 78.

SIMONS, David; Private; A/24th Inf. At Ft Reno, Indian Territory, 1886. *See* **WEBSTER**, Porter, Sergeant, A/24th Infantry

SIMONS, Frank; Wagoner; I/9th Cav. At Ft D. A. Russell, WY, in 1910; sharpshooter; resident of Mound City, KS. SOURCE: *Illustrated Review: Ninth Cavalry*, with picture.

SIMPSON; Private; 10th Cav. Transferred from B/25th Infantry in accordance with Special Order 134, Adjutant General's Office, 9 Jun 1903.

SIMPSON, Ambrose; Sergeant; F/10th Cav. Resided at 325 Ruiz Street, San Antonio, TX, in 1922. SOURCE: VA File SC 11405, John Taylor.

SIMPSON, Anthony; Private; C/9th Cav. Died at Camp Wikoff, NY, 28 Aug 1898, cause unstated. SOURCE: Hospital Papers, Spanish-American War.

SIMPSON, J. T.; Private; D/10th Cav. Served in 10th Cavalry, 1898; remained in U.S. during war with Spain. SOURCE: Cashin, *Under Fire with the Tenth Cavalry*, 341.

SIMPSON, James A.; Private; D/24th Inf. Fined $8 at Cabanatuan, Philippines, for four-hour absence from duty, 11 Feb 1901; witnesses: 1st Sgt. M. H. Ellis, Pvt. Charles F. Mitchell, and Pvt. Edward A. Ridgely, all of D/24th Infantry. SOURCE: Name File, 24 Inf.
    Fined $8 and jailed for ten days at Cabanatuan for failure to challenge properly after taps and replying disrespectfully to officer of day while on guard duty, 27 Apr 1901. SOURCE: Name File, 24 Inf.
    See **ROBINSON**, Mason, Private, D/24th Infantry

SIMPSON, James S.; Private; E/10th Cav. Served in 10th Cavalry in Cuba, 1898. SOURCE: Cashin, *Under Fire with the Tenth Cavalry*, 342.

SIMPSON, James T.; Private; K/10th Cav. At Ft Robinson, NE, 1904.

SIMPSON, James Thomas; Bn Sgt Maj; 25th Inf. Retired and employed as clerk, Quartermaster Department; reviewed Theophilus G. Steward's *The Colored Regulars in the United States Army* in *The Colored American Magazine* 8 (Jun 1905): 299–303.

SIMPSON, John; Private; D/9th Cav. At Ft D. A. Russell, WY, in 1910; sharpshooter; resident of Alton, IL. SOURCE: *Illustrated Review: Ninth Cavalry*, with picture.

SIMPSON, Richard; Private; M/10th Cav. Served in 10th Cavalry, 1898; remained in U.S. during war with

Spain. SOURCE: Cashin, *Under Fire with the Tenth Cavalry*, 352.

SIMPSON, Williams; G/10th Cav. Original member of 10th Cavalry; in troop when organized, Ft Leavenworth, KS, 5 Jul 1867. SOURCE: McMiller, "Buffalo Soldiers," 74.

SIMS, Albert; G/24th Inf. Remained in San José, Philippines, after service; occupation farmer. SOURCE: Funston papers, KSHS.

SIMS, Charles M.; C/25th Inf. Convicted of assault on native policeman in the Philippines, 14 Apr 1901; sentenced to six months' confinement.

SIMS, Henry W.; Private; I/24th Inf. Enlisted Louisville, 7 Feb 1899. SOURCE: Muster Roll, I/24 Inf, Jan–Feb 1899.

    Fined $10 by summary court, 22 Jul 1899. SOURCE: Muster Roll, I/24 Inf, Jul–Aug 1899.

SIMS, Lewis; Private; K/25th Inf. At Ft Niobrara, NE, 1904. SOURCE: Wilson, "History of Fort Niobrara."

SIMS, Robert; H/9th Cav. Died of consumption at age 36 in Soldiers Home, 16 Jul 1896. SOURCE: SecWar, *AR 1896*, 640.

SIMS, Sprague; Trumpeter; A/10th Cav. At Ft Apache, AZ, 1890, subscribed $.50 to testimonial to General Grierson. SOURCE: List of subscriptions, 23 Apr 1890, 10th Cavalry papers, MHI.

    Served in 10th Cavalry in Cuba, 1898. SOURCE: Cashin, *Under Fire with the Tenth Cavalry*, 341.

SINCLAIR, Thomas; Private; B/9th Cav. Wounded in battle of El Caney, Cuba, 1898. SOURCE: Cashin, *Under Fire with the Tenth Cavalry*, 117.

SINGLETARY, N.; 2nd Lt; 23rd Kans Inf. Mentioned. SOURCE: Beasley, *Negro Trailblazers*, 285.

SINGLETON; Sergeant; L/25th Inf. Wounded in hip during ambush in the Philippines, 29 Jan 1900; hid in sugar cane until rescued. SOURCE: Richmond *Planet*, 17 Mar 1900.

SINGLETON, George A.; Private; 24th Inf. Acting battalion chaplain, Houston, 1917. SOURCE: Haynes, *A Night of Violence*, 45.

    Organized relief committee and collected money for black victims of East St. Louis, IL, Jul 1917. SOURCE: Haynes, *A Night of Violence*, 59.

    "Most forceful defender" of soldiers' conduct while in Houston. SOURCE: Haynes, *A Night of Violence*, 240.

SINGLETON, George C.; Private; I/10th Cav. Served in 10th Cavalry, 1898; remained in U.S. during war with Spain. SOURCE: Cashin, *Under Fire with the Tenth Cavalry*, 348.

SINGLETON, Isaac; Private; E/10th Cav. Served in 10th Cavalry in Cuba, 1898. SOURCE: Cashin, *Under Fire with the Tenth Cavalry*, 342.

SINGLETON, William; Private; H/9th Cav. Deposited $30 with paymaster, Ft Robinson, NE, 1897–98.

SINKLER, James; Private; C/25th Inf. Dishonorable discharge, Brownsville. SOURCE: SO 266, AGO, 9 Nov 1906.

SISBY, Frank A.; Private; H/10th Cav. Recently deceased; final statement sent to Adjutant General. SOURCE: CO, 10 Cav, to AG, 3 Sep 1877, ES, 10 Cav, 1873–83.

SISUES, Henry L.; I/10th Cav. Original member of 10th Cavalry; in troop when organized, Ft Riley, KS, 15 Aug 1867. SOURCE: McMiller, "Buffalo Soldiers," 76.

SIVEL, Alexander; Private; I/10th Cav. Served in 10th Cavalry, 1898; remained in U.S. during war with Spain. SOURCE: Cashin, *Under Fire with the Tenth Cavalry*, 348.

SKELTON, Newton J.; Private; C/9th Cav. Discharged on certificate of disability, Ft Robinson, NE, 4 Jun 1898. SOURCE: Certificates of Disability, Ft Robinson.

SKELTON, William; Private; L/10th Cav. Served in 10th Cavalry, 1898; remained in U.S. during war with Spain. SOURCE: Cashin, *Under Fire with the Tenth Cavalry*, 351.

SKIDAISK, Fredrick; I/10th Cav. Original member of 10th Cavalry; in troop when organized, Ft Riley, KS, 15 Aug 1867. SOURCE: McMiller, "Buffalo Soldiers," 76.

SKIDRICK, Frank; Sergeant; D/10th Cav. Died of accidental gunshot wound late 1870. SOURCE: Leckie, *The Buffalo Soldiers*, 56.

    Final statement sent to Adjutant General. SOURCE: CO, 10 Cav, to AG, 21 Aug 1870, ES, 10 Cav, 1866–71.

SKINIER, James T.; B/10th Cav. Original member of 10th Cavalry; in troop when organized, Ft Leavenworth, KS, 1 Apr 1867. SOURCE: McMiller, "Buffalo Soldiers," 69.

SKINNER, Edward; Private; I/24th Inf. Enlisted Washington Barracks, Washington, DC, 18 Feb 1899. SOURCE: Muster Roll, I/24 Inf, Jan–Feb 1899.

    Allotted $8 per month for ten months to Emma Ross; on detached service at Arayat, Philippines, since 31 Oct 1899. SOURCE: Muster Roll, I/24 Inf, Sep–Oct 1899.

    Wounded in action (thigh) at Munes, Luzon, Philippines, 10 Oct 1900. SOURCE: *ANJ* 38 (3 Nov 1900): 235.

    Wounded and captured, 10 Oct 1900. *See* **BURNS**, William J., Corporal, I/24th Infantry

SKINNER, James; Private; H/9th Cav. Deposited $25 with paymaster, Ft Robinson, NE, 1898.

SLANTER, William; Color Sgt; 9th Cav. Enlisted at Lexington, KY, 21 Dec 1871, and assigned to G/9th Cavalry; participated in Pine Ridge campaign, 1890–91; served in Philippines, 16 Sep 1900–16 Sep 1902 and 31 May 1907–15 May 1909; at Ft D. A. Russell, WY, in 1910; resident of St. Louis. SOURCE: *Illustrated Review: Ninth Cavalry*, with picture.

SLAUGHTER, Clarence; Private; H/24th Inf. Enlisted Louisville, 9 Jul 1898; assigned to H/24th Infantry 16 Sep 1898; due U.S. for lost ordnance (tin cup) $.15. SOURCE: Muster Roll, H/24 Inf, Sep–Oct 1898.

Discharged, single, character good, Ft Douglas, UT, 27 Jan 1899; due U.S. for clothing $11.60 and for ordnance (fifty .30 cartridges) $1.25. SOURCE: Muster Roll, H/24 Inf, Jan–Feb 1899.

SLAUGHTER, Rufus; Private; K/9th Cav. Served in E/13th Artillery, Mar 1864–Nov 1865; served continuously from 1866 to 1886; got rheumatism in right shoulder, hip, knees, from explosion, Ft Supply, Indian Territory, Jul 1884; filed claim for invalid pension from Crawford, NE, at age 54, 8 Apr 1891; at time of death on 12 Oct 1907, former wife Ella Slaughter resided at 119 Sweetwater Street, Hot Springs, SD. SOURCE: VA File XC 2648848, Rufus Slaughter.

Capt. Lee Humfreville, 9th Cavalry, convicted by general court martial of handcuffing in pairs Slaughter and Pvts. James Imes, Jerry Williams, Levi Comer, Henry Robinson, and Jim Wade, and Farrier E. Tucker, pulling them 450 miles by a rope hitched to an Army wagon, from Ft Richardson to Ft McKavett, TX, in a nineteen-day period, allowing them only bread and meat and no fire in their camp, 15 Dec 1872–20 Jan 1873. SOURCE: GCMO 23, AGO, 3 Apr 1874.

Wife Ella is visiting sister-in-law in Louisville. SOURCE: Cleveland *Gazette*, 14 Aug 1886.

Discharged as trumpeter, K/9th Cavalry, end of term, Ft Robinson, NE, 25 Dec 1886.

Completed twenty years in regular Army on 29 Dec 1886; has joined his family on a farm three miles from Ft Robinson, where he will try civilian life. SOURCE: Cleveland *Gazette*, 1 Jan 1887.

Unmarried, divorced from Ella Slaughter of Hot Springs, SD, 1892; two children: Gertrude, born 1876, and Sam, born 1878. SOURCE: Bureau of Pensions Questionnaire, 27 Jun 1898, VA File XC 2648848, Rufus Slaughter.

"Resented the carving up of his coat Saturday night by Brooks," and knocked down and chastised Brooks. SOURCE: Crawford *Tribune*, 27 Dec 1901.

Lived alone in 1904, but nursed through difficult attack of rheumatism by former comrade Henry Wilson, Crawford, 1904. SOURCE: Schubert, *Buffalo Soldiers, Braves, and the Brass*, 155.

Resident of Crawford, 1905, with personal property assessed at $51, on which he paid $2 tax. SOURCE: Dawes County tax records.

Died at Alliance, NE, Oct 1907, an "old colored pioneer" of Crawford. SOURCE: Crawford *Tribune*, 18 Oct 1907.

Pension at time of death was $6 per month. SOURCE: VA File XC 2648848, Rufus Slaughter.

Son Sam resided in Crawford, 1907, with no assessed personal property of value. SOURCE: Dawes County tax records.

See **JORDAN**, George, First Sergeant, K/9th Cavalry; **WASHINGTON**, William, 9th Cavalry; **WRIGHT**, Daniel, Sergeant, K/9th Cavalry

SLAUGHTER, William H.; Private; G/10th Cav. Killed in action, Santiago, Cuba, 1 Jul 1898. SOURCE: Scipio, *Last of the Black Regulars*, 29; SecWar, *AR 1898*, 323; *ANJ* 36 (18 Feb 1899): 590.

SLAUTER, William; Corporal; G/9th Cav. Appointed corporal 23 Oct 1891. SOURCE: Roster, 9 Cav.

Post gardener, Ft Robinson, NE. SOURCE: Order 54, 16 Aug 1895, Post Orders, Ft Robinson.

Discharged at Ft Robinson, Oct 1895. SOURCE: *ANJ* 33 (12 Oct 1895): 87.

SLIDELL; Private; C/9th Cav. Child Willie died and buried at Ft Robinson, NE, 3 Apr 1886. SOURCE: List of Interments, Ft Robinson.

SLIMP, Jacob; Private; D/10th Cav. Casualty in fight at Cheyenne Agency, Indian Territory, 6 Apr 1875. SOURCE: Leckie, *The Buffalo Soldiers*, 139.

SLOW, John; Private; D/25th Inf. Dishonorable discharge, Brownsville. SOURCE: SO 266, AGO, 9 Nov 1906.

SMALL, Dennis; Private; H/24th Inf. Fined $10 by summary court, San Isidro, Philippines, for disrespect to noncommissioned officer, 3 Mar 1902, second conviction. SOURCE: Register of Summary Court, San Isidro.

SMALL, George; Private; L/9th Cav. Killed in saloon shootout along with Pvts. John Hanson and Anthony Harvey, L/9th Cavalry, Cimarron, NM, Apr 1876; buried at Ft Union, NM. SOURCE: Billington, *New Mexico's Buffalo Soldiers*, 67.

SMALL, Thomas; Private; I/10th Cav. Original member of 10th Cavalry; in troop when organized, Ft Riley, KS, 15 Aug 1867. SOURCE: McMiller, "Buffalo Soldiers," 76.

Final statement and inventories of effects of Pvts. Small and Augustus James, I/10th Cavalry, forwarded to Adjutant General by commander, 10th Cavalry, Mar 1870. SOURCE: ES, 10 Cav, 1866–71.

SMALL, Thomas H.; Corporal; M/10th Cav. Promoted from private, 30 May 1901. SOURCE: *ANJ* 38 (15 Jun 1901): 1019.

SMALLGOOD, Eli; Private; G/25th Inf. Born Frederick, MD; occupation laborer; Ht 5'10", dark complexion, black hair and eyes; enlisted, age 22, Norfolk, VA, 17 Oct 1866; initially served in A/40th Infantry; discharged, end of term, Jackson Barracks, LA, 14 Oct 1869. SOURCE: Register of Enlistments.

SMALLOW, George; Private; L/9th Cav. Killed at Cimarron, NM, 24 Jan 1876. SOURCE: *Illustrated Review: Ninth Cavalry. See* **HARVEY**, Anthony, Private, L/9th Cavalry

SMALLS; Private; B/10th Cav. At Ft Apache, AZ, 1890, subscribed $.50 to testimonial to General Grierson. SOURCE: List of subscriptions, 23 Apr 1890, 10th Cavalry papers, MHI.

SMALLS, Cyrus; Private; H/24th Inf. Enlisted Camp Tampa, FL, 1 Jun 1898. SOURCE: Muster Roll, H/24 Inf, May–Jun 1898.

Sick in hospital, Siboney, Cuba, 23–25 Aug 1898, and en route to U.S., 25–31 Aug, disease contracted in line of duty. SOURCE: Muster Roll, H/24 Inf, Jul–Aug 1898.

Discharged, end of term, single, character good, Ft Douglas, UT, 28 Jan 1899; deposits $40, clothing $1.43. SOURCE: Muster Roll, H/24 Inf, Jan–Feb 1899.

SMALLS, George W.; G/10th Cav. Original member of 10th Cavalry; in troop when organized, Ft Leavenworth, KS, 5 Jul 1867. SOURCE: McMiller, "Buffalo Soldiers," 74.

SMALLWOOD; Sergeant; 9th Cav. Stationed at Ord Barracks, Monterey, CA, 1903; sergeant-at-arms of Literary and Social Club organized with civilians of Pacific Grove, CA. SOURCE: Indianapolis *Freeman*, 5 Dec 1903.

SMALLWOOD, T. L.; Private; G/9th Cav. On detached service, Ft Stanton, NM, 29 Jan–5 Feb 1881. SOURCE: Regt Returns, 9 Cav, Feb 1881.

SMART, Charles H.; Private; 10th Cav. Transferred from L/25th Infantry, in accordance with Special Order 45, Adjutant General's Office, 24 Feb 1903.

SMART, G. H.; Sergeant; 10th Cav. Wounded in toe of left foot, Naco, AZ, 16 Dec 1914. SOURCE: Cleveland *Gazette*, 13 May 1916.

SMART, Hugh M.; Private; H/24th Inf. Enlisted Louisville, 9 Jul 1898; joined company 16 Sep 1898; due U.S. for lost ordnance (oiler, screwdriver, spoon, knife) $.45. SOURCE: Muster Roll, H/24 Inf, Sep–Oct 1898.

Discharged, single, character good, Ft Douglas, UT, 27 Jan 1899; deposits $9, due U.S. for clothing $23.88. SOURCE: Muster Roll, H/24 Inf, Jan–Feb 1899.

SMELLY, Dock; Sergeant; L/9th Cav. Veteran of Philippine Insurrection; at Ft D. A. Russell, WY, in 1910; resident of Randolph, AL. SOURCE: *Illustrated Review: Ninth Cavalry*, with picture.

SMISH, John; A/10th Cav. Original member of 10th Cavalry; in troop when organized, Ft Leavenworth, KS, 18 Feb 1867. SOURCE: McMiller, "Buffalo Soldiers," 68.

SMITH; Private; C/10th Cav. At Ft Apache, AZ, 1890, subscribed $.25 to testimonial to General Grierson. SOURCE: List of subscriptions, 23 Apr 1890, 10th Cavalry papers, MHI.

SMITH; Private; E/10th Cav. At Ft Apache, AZ, 1890, subscribed $.50 to testimonial to General Grierson. SOURCE: List of subscriptions, 23 Apr 1890, 10th Cavalry papers, MHI.

SMITH; Private; H/24th Inf. At Ft Huachuca, AZ, 1893. *See* **HAM**, James, Sergeant, B/24th Infantry

SMITH; Sergeant; K/24th Inf. Involved in brawl at Winnemucca, NV, 29 Jul 1899. SOURCE: San Francisco *Chronicle*, 30 Jun 1899.

SMITH, A.; Private; H/9th Cav. In hands of civil authorities, Buffalo, WY, 30 Aug 1886–28 Mar 1887. SOURCE: Regt Returns, 9 Cav.

Sentenced to six months for assault on city marshal, Buffalo. SOURCE: *Big Horn Sentinel*, 6 Nov 1886.

SMITH, Adam T.; Private; A/10th Cav. Commander, 10th Cavalry, forwards final statement of late Private Smith to Adjutant General, 8 Dec 1873. SOURCE: ES, 10 Cav, 1873–83.

SMITH, Albert; Private; D/10th Cav. Original member of 10th Cavalry; in troop when organized, Ft Leavenworth, KS, 1 Jun 1867. SOURCE: McMiller, "Buffalo Soldiers," 71.

Transferred from Camp Supply, Indian Territory, to Ft Sill, Indian Territory. SOURCE: SO 57, Det 10 Cav, 10 Aug 1869, Orders, Det 10 Cav.

SMITH, Albert; Trumpeter; G/10th Cav. At Ft Apache, AZ, 1890, subscribed $.50 to testimonial to General Grierson. SOURCE: List of subscriptions, 23 Apr 1890, 10th Cavalry papers, MHI.

SMITH, Albert; Private; L/10th Cav. Served in 10th Cavalry, 1898; remained in U.S. during war with Spain. SOURCE: Cashin, *Under Fire with the Tenth Cavalry*, 351.

SMITH, Alexander; B/10th Cav. Original member of 10th Cavalry; in troop when organized, Ft Leavenworth, KS, 1 Apr 1867. SOURCE: McMiller, "Buffalo Soldiers," 69.

SMITH, Alonzo W.; A/24th Inf. Served 1872–82; subscriber; died 20 Jul 1932. SOURCE: *Winners of the West* 10 (Feb 1933): 3.

SMITH, Andrew; Private; A/10th Cav. Sentenced to two years in military prison for desertion in accordance with General Court Martial Order 55, 1879; escaped from guard en route from Ft Davis, TX, at Leon Springs, TX, 4 Jul 1879. SOURCE: Report of Trials, Department of Texas.

SMITH, Andrew J.; Drum Maj; Band/25th Inf. Private, C/10th Cavalry, 1869. SOURCE: Baker, Roster.

Sergeant, C/10th Cavalry, cited for gallantry against Kiowas and Comanches, Wichita Agency, Indian Territory, 22–23 Aug 1874. SOURCE: Baker, Roster.

First sergeant, B/25th Infantry, authorized fifty-day furlough from Ft Snelling, MN. SOURCE: *ANJ* 24 (20 Nov 1886): 230.

First sergeant, B/25th Infantry, at Ft Buford, ND; examined for ordnance sergeant. SOURCE: *ANJ* 30 (1 Jul 1893): 745.

North Carolinian commissioned for bravery at El Caney, Cuba, 1898. SOURCE: Johnson, *History of Negro Soldiers*, 32.

Commissioned in volunteers for gallantry at Santiago, Cuba, 1–2 Jul 1898. SOURCE: Richmond *Planet*, 13 Aug 1898; Thweatt, *What the Newspapers Say*, 10.

Sergeant, B/25th Infantry, commissioned second lieutenant, 8th Volunteer Infantry, after Spanish-American War. SOURCE: Cashin, *Under Fire with the Tenth Cavalry*, 360, with picture, 133.

In the Philippines, 1900. SOURCE: Richmond *Planet*, 28 Jul 1898.

Drum major, Band/25th Infantry, transferred from Manila, Philippines, to San Francisco. SOURCE: *ANJ* 38 (8 Dec 1900): 355.

SMITH, Anis; H/10th Cav. Original member of 10th Cavalry; in troop when organized, Ft Leavenworth, KS, 21 Jul 1867. SOURCE: McMiller, "Buffalo Soldiers," 75.

SMITH, Archie M.; Private; K/10th Cav. Served in 10th Cavalry, 1898; remained in U.S. during war with Spain. SOURCE: Cashin, *Under Fire with the Tenth Cavalry*, 349.

SMITH, Arthur; Private; E/10th Cav. Mentioned Feb 1875. SOURCE: ES, 10 Cav, 1873–83.

Mentioned as survivor of Indian wars. SOURCE: *Winners of the West* 3 (Jun 1926): 7.

SMITH, Arthur; B/9th Cav. Born Bristol, VA; Protestant; enlisted Greenville, TN; served 14 Jun 1898–28 Jan 1899; discharged Ft Grant, AZ; civilian occupation cook; earned about $20 per week as cook until third marriage; several times cooked for circuses and left town with them; married first wife, born Lemmie Peters, Sep 1901; she died Dec 1910; second wife, born Mary Waterson, at Surgeonsville, TN, 8 Nov 1875, died of stomach cancer, Appalachia, VA, 8 Dec 1917; married third wife Sallie Smith 17 Aug 1918; deserted her in 1925; in 1935 moved from Mountain Home Veterans Hospital in Tennessee, to Danville, IL, with "dementia precox, paranoid"; in 1936 had $17.50 per month disability pension; died in Illinois, 21 Apr 1936; unremarried widow Sallie, formerly married in 1913 to Rush McCormack, resided at 403 Patton, Knoxville, TN, after his death. SOURCE: VA File C 2410890, Arthur Smith.

Contracted yellow fever while tending troop horses, Port Tampa, FL; still suffers from effects of same. SOURCE: Affidavit, Smith, 9 Nov 1922, VA File C 2410890, Arthur Smith.

SMITH, Arthur; Private; L/10th Cav. Stabbed sixteen-year-old hack driver Ray Matney "without apparent cause," while he was blanketing his team at Ft Robinson, NE; arrested. SOURCE: Crawford *Tribune*, 12 Feb 1904.

Sent to Federal prison, Omaha, NE, to await trial; did not have $500 for bail. SOURCE: Crawford *Bulletin*, 26 Feb 1904.

In hands of civil authorities as of 20 Feb 1904. SOURCE: Regt Returns, 10 Cav, Feb 1904.

Discharged in accordance with Special Order 170, Adjutant General's Office, 21 Jul 1904.

SMITH, Arthur R. D.; Private; L/25th Inf. In K/25th Infantry at San Marcelino, Philippines, 1899. SOURCE: Richmond *Planet*, 19 Jan 1900.

In K/25th Infantry; president of regimental branch of Y.M.C.A., San Marcelino. SOURCE: Richmond *Planet*, 20 Oct 1900.

Wounded in thigh at Subig, Luzon, Philippines, 10 Nov 1900. SOURCE: *ANJ* 38 (1 Dec 1900): 331.

Led advance guard of five which was ambushed at Subig Pass, 10 Nov 1900; captured 10 Nov with Private Edwards, L/25th Infantry; Private McCormick, L/25th Infantry, killed in action; returned at Subig with bad flesh wounds in leg; treated well by enemy; died of exposure and blood poisoning, 29 Nov 1900; thirty-year-old native of Nashville, and member of African Methodist Episcopal Church; "gentle nature and a robust constitution"; an organizer of Y.M.C.A. and its president at San Marcelino; survived by mother and brother. SOURCE: Richmond *Planet*, 12 Jan 1901.

SMITH, Augustus; Sergeant; I/24th Inf. Original member of E/10th Cavalry; in troop when organized, Ft Leavenworth, KS, 15 Jun 1867. SOURCE: McMiller, "Buffalo Soldiers," 72.

Recruit, 10th Cavalry, assigned to E Troop, Jun 1867. SOURCE: LS, 10 Cav, 1866–67.

Sergeant, I/24th Infantry, to be sent from station at Ft Grant, AZ, to Ft Mason, CA, for hospital treatment. SOURCE: *ANJ* 27 (8 Mar 1890): 525.

Admitted to Soldiers Home, age 47, with twenty-five years and nine months' service. SOURCE: SecWar, *AR 1890*, 1043.

Died of interstitial nephritis at Soldiers Home, 23 Feb 1903. SOURCE: SecWar, *AR 1903* 4:257.

SMITH, Beauford; Private; H/9th Cav. At Ft D. A. Russell, WY, in 1910; sharpshooter; resident of Austin, TX. SOURCE: *Illustrated Review: Ninth Cavalry*, with picture.

SMITH, Benjamin; Private; D/10th Cav. Original member of G/10th Cavalry; in troop when organized, Ft Leavenworth, KS, 5 Jul 1867. SOURCE: McMiller, "Buffalo Soldiers," 74.

On daily duty with Commissary Department at camp near Ft Dodge, KS, 9–16 Apr 1869. SOURCE: SO 14, Det 10 Cav, 9 Apr 1869, and SO 20, Det 10 Cav, 16 Apr 1869, Orders, Det 10 Cav.

In D/10th Cavalry; casualty in fight at Cheyenne Agency, Indian Territory, 6 Apr 1875. SOURCE: Leckie, *The Buffalo Soldiers*, 139.

SMITH, Benjamin; Saddler; C/10th Cav. Served in 10th Cavalry in Cuba, 1898. SOURCE: Cashin, *Under Fire with the Tenth Cavalry*, 340.

SMITH, Bursh L.; Private; 24th Inf. Served in Houston, 1917; convinced court martial he remained in camp during riot. SOURCE: Haynes, *A Night of Violence*, 268.

SMITH, Byrd; Private; I/24th Inf. Enlisted Charleston, WV, 1 Jul 1899. SOURCE: Muster Roll, I/24 Inf, Jul–Aug 1899.

On detached service at Cabanatuan, Philippines, since 30 Sep 1899. SOURCE: Muster Roll, I/24 Inf, Nov–Dec 1899.

SMITH, C. H.; Sergeant; I/24th Inf. Killed in action near Talavera, Philippines, 31 Jul 1900, while leading detachment that was ambushed by insurgents; his men were Pvts. Elijah Bethel (killed), Eddie Fields (killed), George Bivens (wounded), Lawrence Buchanan (wounded), G. W. Jackson (captured), and Robert H. Brooks (captured). SOURCE: Muller, *The Twenty Fourth Infantry*, 39.

SMITH, Calton; I/10th Cav. Original member of 10th Cavalry; in troop when organized, Ft Riley, KS, 15 Aug 1867. SOURCE: McMiller, "Buffalo Soldiers," 76.

SMITH, Calvin; Private; C/25th Inf. Dishonorable discharge, Brownsville. SOURCE: SO 266, AGO, 9 Nov 1906.

One of fourteen men cleared of involvement in Brownsville raid by court, 1910, and authorized to reenlist. SOURCE: Weaver, *The Brownsville Raid*, 248.

SMITH, Carter; Sergeant; A/10th Cav. Born in Mississippi; private, A/10th Cavalry, 12 Jul 1882; corporal, 1 Sep 1889; sergeant, 1 Feb 1892; at Ft Custer, MT, 1897. SOURCE: Baker, Roster.

Ranked number nine in revolver competition, Departments of California and Arizona, Ft Wingate, NM, 1889, bronze medal. SOURCE: GO 78, AGO, 12 Oct 1889; Baker, Roster.

Corporal, A/10th Cavalry, at Ft Apache, AZ, 1890, subscribed $.50 to testimonial to General Grierson. SOURCE: List of subscriptions, 23 Apr 1890, 10th Cavalry papers, MHI.

Served as quartermaster sergeant, A/10th Cavalry in Cuba, 1898. SOURCE: Cashin, *Under Fire with the Tenth Cavalry*, 333.

Acting first sergeant; a noncommissioned officer whose heroism has been slighted and who should be commissioned,

according to unsigned and undated letter. SOURCE: Gatewood, *"Smoked Yankees"*, 77.

Narrates Spanish-American War experience. SOURCE: Cashin, *Under Fire with the Tenth Cavalry*, 266.

Sergeant, A/10th Cavalry, detailed to color guard, Ft Robinson, NE. SOURCE: SO 67, 10 Cav, 24 Jun 1902.

Died Ft Robinson, 3 Oct 1903, at age 43; born Gubtown, Dippert Co., MS. SOURCE: Monthly Report, Chaplain Anderson, 1 Nov 1903; List of Interments, Ft Robinson.

SMITH, Charles; B/10th Cav. Original member of 10th Cavalry; in troop when organized, Ft Leavenworth, KS, 1 Apr 1867. SOURCE: McMiller, "Buffalo Soldiers," 69.

SMITH, Charles; Private; C/10th Cav. Killed in 1871. *See* **JOHNSON**, York, Private, C/10th Cavalry

SMITH, Charles; Private; L/10th Cav. Served in 10th Cavalry, 1898; remained in U.S. during war with Spain. SOURCE: Cashin, *Under Fire with the Tenth Cavalry*, 351.

SMITH, Charles; Private; F/9th Cav. At Ft D. A. Russell, WY, in 1910; resident of Farmington, MO. SOURCE: *Illustrated Review: Ninth Cavalry*, with picture.

SMITH, Charles H.; Sergeant; I/24th Inf. Enlisted Ft D. A. Russell, WY, 14 Sep 1899, with seven years' continuous service. SOURCE: Muster Roll, I/24 Inf, Jan–Feb 1899.

Allotted $5 per month for twelve months to Clara Harris. SOURCE: Muster Roll, I/24 Inf, Nov–Dec 1899.

SMITH, Charles P.; Private; C/10th Cav. Discharged on certificate of disability with gonorrhea from Ft Robinson, NE, 5 Jan 1905. SOURCE: Certificates of Disability, Ft Robinson.

SMITH, Daniel; Private; A/10th Cav. Served in 10th Cavalry in Cuba, 1898. SOURCE: Cashin, *Under Fire with the Tenth Cavalry*, 336.

SMITH, Daniel; Private; G/9th Cav. Veteran of Philippine Insurrection; at Ft D. A. Russell, WY, in 1910. SOURCE: *Illustrated Review: Ninth Cavalry*.

SMITH, Daniel; 1st Sgt; C/10th Cav. Commissioned captain at Camp Des Moines, IA, 15 Oct 1917. SOURCE: Glass, *History of the Tenth Cavalry*, appendix M.

SMITH, David J.; D/24th Inf. Wants to hear from old comrades of D/24th Infantry, 1889–94. SOURCE: *Winners of the West* 7 (Oct 1930): 7.

Renews subscription. SOURCE: *Winners of the West* 8 (Dec 1931): 6.

SMITH, Dee; Corporal; D/25th Inf. Fined $10 by summary court, San Isidro, Philippines, for going off limits without authorization, 20 May 1902, second conviction. SOURCE: Register of Summary Court, San Isidro.

SMITH, Dennis A.; Private; E/24th Inf. Transferred from Reserve Divisional Hospital, Siboney, Cuba, to U.S. on U.S. Army Transport *Vigilancia* with remittent malarial fever, 6 Sep 1898. SOURCE: Hospital Papers, Spanish-American War.

Ranked number 395 among rifle experts with 69.33 percent, 1905. SOURCE: GO 101, AGO, 31 May 1906.

SMITH, E.; Private; L/9th Cav. On detached service in field, New Mexico, 21 Jan–24 Feb 1881. SOURCE: Regt Returns, 9 Cav, Feb 1881.

SMITH, Edward; Private; E/10th Cav. Served in 10th Cavalry, 1898; remained in U.S. during war with Spain. SOURCE: Cashin, *Under Fire with the Tenth Cavalry*, 343.

SMITH, Edward; Corporal; K/25th Inf. While leading detachment of sixteen, captured group of native bandits near San Marcelino, Philippines, Jun 1900. SOURCE: Richmond *Planet*, 18 Aug 1900.

SMITH, Elijah; Private; A/10th Cav. Served in 10th Cavalry, 1898; remained in U.S. during war with Spain. SOURCE: Cashin, *Under Fire with the Tenth Cavalry*, 337.

SMITH, Elijah; Private; H/24th Inf. Enlisted Louisville, 13 Jul 1898; due U. S. for lost ordnance (canteen, canteen strap, and oiler) $1.10. SOURCE: Muster Roll, H/24 Inf, Sep–Oct 1898.

Discharged, Ft Douglas, UT, single, character good, 27 Jan 1899; deposits $10; due U.S. for clothing $8.38. SOURCE: Muster Roll, H/24 Inf, Jan–Feb 1899.

SMITH, Elmer; 1st Sgt; 9th Cav. Retired with rank of second lieutenant, 31 Dec 1937. SOURCE: *Cavalry Journal* 47 (Jan–Feb 1938): 88.

SMITH, Emile; Private; E/9th Cav. On special duty as clerk, Adjutant's Office, Ft Robinson, NE. SOURCE: Order 71, 30 Apr 1892, Post Orders, Ft Robinson.

Involved in affray at Suggs, WY, Jun 1892. SOURCE: Schubert, "The Suggs Affray," 63.

On special duty as post librarian, Ft Robinson. SOURCE: Order 161, 23 Sep 1892, Post Orders, Ft Robinson.

Teacher, Ft Robinson school, 9 Dec 1892–1 Feb 1893. SOURCE: Reports of Schools, DP.

Acquitted by garrison court martial, Ft Robinson, of disobeying order issued by commander through 1st Sgt. William Clay. SOURCE: Order 16, 23 Feb 1893, Post Orders, Ft Robinson.

SMITH, Ephriam; Private; D/10th Cav. Casualty in fight at Cheyenne Agency, Indian Territory, 6 Apr 1875. SOURCE: Leckie, *The Buffalo Soldiers*, 139.

SMITH, Eugene; Private; I/24th Inf. Enlisted Pittsburgh, PA, 5 Aug 1898. SOURCE: Muster Roll, I/24 Inf, Jan–Feb 1899.

On detached service at Three Rivers, CA, 3 May–21 Jun 1899, and at Presidio of San Francisco, CA, from 22 Jun 1899. SOURCE: Muster Roll, I/24 Inf, May–Jun 1899.

Rejoined company, 26 Jul 1899; fined $3 by summary court, 7 Jun 1899. SOURCE: Muster Roll, I/24 Inf, Jul–Aug 1899.

Allotted $10 per month for nine months to Georgiana Smith. SOURCE: Muster Roll, I/24 Inf, Sep–Oct 1899.

Discharged, character good, 31 Dec 1899; deposits $10 and clothing $40.48. SOURCE: Muster Roll, I/24 Inf, Nov–Dec 1899.

SMITH, Ewing; C/10th Cav. Original member of 10th Cavalry; in troop when organized, Ft Leavenworth, KS, 14 May 1867. SOURCE: McMiller, "Buffalo Soldiers," 70.

SMITH, F.; Private; F/10th Cav. Wounded in battle, Kansas, 21 Aug 1867. SOURCE: Armes, *Ups and Downs*, 248.

SMITH, F.; Private; G/9th Cav. On detached service at Ft Craig, NM, 12 Jan–6 Feb 1881. SOURCE: Regt Returns, 9 Cav, Feb 1881.

SMITH, Frank; Private; M/10th Cav. Mentioned as having enlisted on 19 Feb 1873. SOURCE: ES, 10 Cav, 1873–83.

SMITH, Frank; Private; G/9th Cav. Convicted of desertion, 22 Jul–30 Dec 1884, by general court martial at David's Island, NY; sentenced to dishonorable discharge and five years. SOURCE: GCMO 12, AGO, 31 Jan 1885.

SMITH, Frank; Private; I/24th Inf. Enlisted Baltimore, 17 Feb 1899. SOURCE: Muster Roll, I/24 Inf, Jan–Feb 1899.

On detached service at Benicia Barracks, CA, as of 8 Apr 1899. SOURCE: Muster Roll, I/24 Inf, Mar–Apr 1899.

Fined $2 by summary court, 10 May 1899. SOURCE: Muster Roll, I/24 Inf, May–Jun 1899.

Fined $10 by summary court, 26 Sep 1899. SOURCE: Muster Roll, I/24 Inf, Sep–Oct 1899.

SMITH, Frank; Private; L/25th Inf. Fined $3 by summary court for absence from reveille, San Isidro, Philippines, 21 Jun 1902, first conviction. SOURCE: Register of Summary Court, San Isidro.

SMITH, Franklin; M/10th Cav. Original member of 10th Cavalry; in troop when organized, Ft Riley, KS, 15 Oct 1867. SOURCE: McMiller, "Buffalo Soldiers," 79.

SMITH, Fred; Private; L/10th Cav. At Ft Robinson, NE, 1903; in good physical condition except for chronic gonorrhea. SOURCE: Post Surgeon to Post Adjutant, Ft Robinson, 18 Jan 1903, LS, Post Surgeon, Ft Robinson.

Sentenced to dishonorable discharge and confinement at Ft Robinson, Feb 1903, in accordance with Special Order 39, Department of the Missouri; escaped 26 Mar 1903. SOURCE: Regt Returns, 10 Cav, Feb–Mar 1903.

SMITH, Fred; Private; L/9th Cav. At Ft D. A. Russell, WY, in 1910; resident of Oakdale, TN. SOURCE: *Illustrated Review: Ninth Cavalry*, with picture.

SMITH, Frederick (1); C/10th Cav. Original member of 10th Cavalry; in troop when organized, Ft Leavenworth, KS, 14 May 1867. SOURCE: McMiller, "Buffalo Soldiers," 70.

SMITH, Frederick (2); C/10th Cav. Original member of 10th Cavalry; in troop when organized, Ft Leavenworth, KS, 14 May 1867. SOURCE: McMiller, "Buffalo Soldiers," 70.

SMITH, Frederick; K/10th Cav. Original member of 10th Cavalry; in troop when organized, Ft Riley, KS, 1 Sep 1867. SOURCE: McMiller, "Buffalo Soldiers," 77.

SMITH, Frederick M.; 1st Lt; 48th Inf. One of nineteen officers of 48th Infantry recommended as regular Army second lieutenants. SOURCE: CG, DivPI, Manila, 8 Feb 1901, to AGO, AGO File 355163.

SMITH, G. R. S.; 1st Sgt; H/10th Cav. At Ft Apache, AZ, 1886; in letter of 23 Aug 1886 voices approval of monument to black soldiers killed in action and claims other troops agree. SOURCE: Cleveland *Gazette*, 14 Aug 1886.

SMITH, G. W.; Sergeant; L/25th Inf. As corporal, G/25th Infantry, assisted Lt. John McMartin in shutting down saloons in Coeur d'Alene, ID. SOURCE: Richmond *Planet*, 28 Jul 1900.

Did comic recitation at Y.M.C.A., Marcelinas, Philippines, 24 Aug 1900. SOURCE: Richmond *Planet*, 20 Oct 1900.

Retired as sergeant with thirty years of honorable service, 1910; resides in Pacific Grove, CA. SOURCE: *Crisis* 40 (Aug 1930): 278.

SMITH, George; I/10th Cav. Original member of 10th Cavalry; in troop when organized, Ft Riley, KS, 15 Aug 1867. SOURCE: McMiller, "Buffalo Soldiers," 76.

SMITH, George; K/10th Cav. Original member of 10th Cavalry; in troop when organized, Ft Riley, KS, 1 Sep 1867. SOURCE: McMiller, "Buffalo Soldiers," 77.

SMITH, George; Private; G/10th Cav. Served in 10th Cavalry, 1898; remained in U.S. during war with Spain. SOURCE: Cashin, *Under Fire with the Tenth Cavalry*, 346.

SMITH, George; Corporal; I/10th Cav. Served in 10th Cavalry in Cuba, 1898. SOURCE: Cashin, *Under Fire with the Tenth Cavalry*, 347.

Heroism in Cuba mentioned. SOURCE: Cashin, *Under Fire with the Tenth Cavalry*, 185.

SMITH, George; Color Sgt; 10th Cav. Reduced to ranks from corporal, I/10th Cavalry, Ft Assiniboine, MT, Apr 1899. SOURCE: SO 16, 10 Cav, 1 Apr 1898.

Served as trumpeter in M/10th Cavalry in Cuba, 1898. SOURCE: Cashin, *Under Fire with the Tenth Cavalry*, 352.

First sergeant, M/10th Cavalry, at Ft Robinson, NE; age 36, married on 13 Jul 1904 to Ambrosina Quallo, age 29, born Kingston, Jamaica. SOURCE: Medical History, Ft Robinson; Monthly Report, Chaplain Anderson, 1 Aug 1904.

Promoted to regimental color sergeant, Ft Huachuca, AZ, 1 Mar 1915. SOURCE: GO 2, 10 Cav, 1 Mar 1915.

SMITH, George; Private; C/25th Inf. Dishonorable discharge, Brownsville. SOURCE: SO 266, AGO, 9 Nov 1906.

SMITH, George A.; Private; M/9th Cav. Private, F/10th Cavalry, at Ft Robinson, NE, 11 Jan–14 Feb 1906, as witness in general court martial. SOURCE: Regt Returns, 10 Cav, Jan–Feb 1906.

Veteran of Spanish-American War; at Ft D. A. Russell, WY, in 1910. SOURCE: *Illustrated Review: Ninth Cavalry*, with picture.

SMITH, George H.; Private; H/10th Cav. Served in 10th Cavalry, 1898; remained in U.S. during war with Spain. SOURCE: Cashin, *Under Fire with the Tenth Cavalry*, 347.

SMITH, George W.; Private; M/24th Inf. In the Philippines, 1906. *See* **TAYLOR**, William, Quartermaster Sergeant, M/24th Infantry

SMITH, Gilbert; Private; E/24th Inf. Born in Kentucky; died of typhoid in the Philippines, 7 Aug 1899. SOURCE: Manila *Times*, 8 Aug 1899.

Died in the Philippines of erysipelas. SOURCE: *ANJ* 36 (19 Aug 1899): 1223; Richmond *Planet*, 19 Aug 1899.

SMITH, Gilbert C.; Captain; 49th Inf. One of twenty-three officers of 49th Infantry recommended as regular Army second lieutenants. SOURCE: CG, DivPI, Manila, 8 Feb 1901, to AGO, AGO File 355163.

SMITH, Gloster; Private; B/10th Cav. Sentenced by general court martial, Ft Robinson, NE, to dishonorable discharge and confinement, in accordance with Special Order 93, Department of the Missouri; released Aug 1904. SOURCE: Regt Returns, 10 Cav, May–Aug 1904.

SMITH, Gus; Sergeant. At Ft Riley, KS; mentioned. SOURCE: Acknowledgements to Mary Curtis, *The Black Soldier*.

SMITH, Harry; Private; M/10th Cav. Served in 10th Cavalry, 1898; remained in U.S. during war with Spain. SOURCE: Cashin, *Under Fire with the Tenth Cavalry*, 352.

SMITH, Henry; M/10th Cav. Original member of 10th Cavalry; in troop when organized, Ft Riley, KS, 15 Oct 1867. SOURCE: McMiller, "Buffalo Soldiers," 79.

SMITH, Henry; Private; G/24th Inf. Deserted from Presidio of San Francisco, CA, 22 Jun 1899. SOURCE: Regt Returns, 24 Inf, Jul 1899.

SMITH, Henry; Horseshoer; G/9th Cav. Veteran of Philippine Insurrection; at Ft D. A. Russell, WY, in 1910. SOURCE: *Illustrated Review: Ninth Cavalry.*

SMITH, Henry C.; Private; L/48th Inf. Born Morlin, IL; died in Minnesota, 21 Apr 1929. SOURCE: Taylor, "Minnesota Black Spanish-American War Veterans."

SMITH, Henry N.; Private; M/10th Cav. Recently deceased; final statement transmitted. SOURCE: CO, 10 Cav, to AG, USA, 2 Sep 1877, ES, 10 Cav, 1873–83.

SMITH, Henry W.; Private; E/10th Cav. On temporary duty for training, Ft Bascom, NM. SOURCE: SO 8, HQ, District of NM, 8 Mar 1867, Name File, 10 Cav.

Original member of E/10th Cavalry; in troop when organized, Ft Leavenworth, KS, 15 Jun 1867. SOURCE: McMiller, "Buffalo Soldiers," 72.

SMITH, Herbert; Private; K/9th Cav. At Ft D. A. Russell, WY, in 1910; resident of Rockym Co., KY. SOURCE: *Illustrated Review: Ninth Cavalry*, with picture.

SMITH, Hezekiah K.; Corporal; E/9th Cav. Private, E/9th Cavalry, at Ft D. A. Russell, WY, in 1910; sharpshooter; resident of Darlington, SC. SOURCE: *Illustrated Review: Ninth Cavalry.*

Corporal, E/9th Cavalry, at Douglas, AZ, 1915. See **WASHINGTON**, Ernest S., Sergeant, G/10th Cavalry

SMITH, Homer; Trumpeter; B/9th Cav. At Ft D. A. Russell, WY, in 1910. SOURCE: *Illustrated Review: Ninth Cavalry.*

SMITH, Horace J.; Private; D/24th Inf. Acquitted of sleeping on guard duty at Cabanatuan, Philippines, 8 Dec 1900; witnesses: Pvts. Henry Taggart and Joseph Moranders, D/24th Infantry. SOURCE: Name File, 24 Inf.

Fined $5 for being drunk and disorderly in streets of Cabanatuan, 13 Jul 1901. SOURCE: Name File, 24 Inf.

SMITH, Howard; Private; H/24th Inf. Enlisted Ft Douglas, UT, with three years' continuous service, 10 May 1898. SOURCE: Muster Roll, H/24 Inf, Sep–Oct 1898.

Discharged Ft Douglas, character good, single, 29 Jan 1899; clothing $2.60. SOURCE: Muster Roll, H/24 Inf, Jan–Feb 1899.

SMITH, J. P.; Sergeant; I/24th Inf. Sentenced to dishonorable discharge and eleven months' confinement for falsifying target scores, Ft Sill, Indian Territory. SOURCE: *ANJ* 25 (19 Nov 1887): 323.

SMITH, Jacob; I/10th Cav. Original member of 10th Cavalry; in troop when organized, Ft Riley, KS, 15 Aug 1867. SOURCE: McMiller, "Buffalo Soldiers," 76.

SMITH, Jacob Clay; Sergeant; 10th Cav. Born Taylorsville, KY, 25 Jun 1857; enlisted 20 Jan 1880; joined I/24th Infantry, Ringgold Barracks, TX, 16 Mar 1880; transferred to F/24th Infantry, 31 Mar 1881; corporal, 4 Aug 1882; sergeant, 23 Feb 1883; transferred to 10th Cavalry, Oct 1887; private, M/10th Cavalry and E/10th Cavalry, 5 Nov 1887–20 Jan 1890; transferred to C/10th Cavalry, 6 Feb 1890; sergeant, 1 Apr 1890; saddler sergeant, 5 Oct 1894; commissioned second lieutenant, K/9th Volunteer Infantry, 27 Oct 1898; served with 9th Infantry, Cruisto, Cuba, Jan 1899. SOURCE: Baker, Roster; Coston, *The Spanish-American War Volunteer*, 77.

Letters, Ft Elliott, TX, 26 Oct and 29 Dec 1885. SOURCE: Cleveland *Gazette*, 2 Nov 1885 and 9 Jan 1886, respectively.

Called meeting at Ft Elliott, 15 Dec 1886, which condemned ineptitude of Sgt. Charles Connor and two privates who allowed prisoner to escape en route to Ft Leavenworth, KS; Smith served as secretary of meeting; chaired first by temporary chairman Sgt. M. Wilcox, then chairman Sgt. William Wilkes; committee which drafted resolution: 1st Sgt. William Rose, Pvt. Asa L. Lewis, and Sgt. Spurling, all of F/24th Infantry. SOURCE: *ANJ* 24 (25 Dec 1886): 43.

Made speech at picnic of E/24th Infantry band, Ft Grant, AZ, Jun 1890. SOURCE: Cleveland *Gazette*, 28 Jun 1890.

To report to regiment commander, Ft Custer, MT, as saddler sergeant. SOURCE: *ANJ* 32 (13 Oct 1894): 102.

Examined at Ft Assiniboine, MT, for post quartermaster sergeant, Jan 1896. SOURCE: *ANJ* 33 (18 Jan 1896): 349.

Met a little black boy who needed clothes at Chattanooga, 1898; took him to clothing store, bought him complete outfit, hat to shoes, for $10. SOURCE: Fletcher, "The Negro Soldier," 189.

Served as saddler sergeant, 10th Cavalry, in Cuba, 1898. SOURCE: Cashin, *Under Fire with the Tenth Cavalry*, 352.

Commissioned second lieutenant, 9th Volunteer Infantry, after Spanish-American War. SOURCE: Cashin, *Under Fire with the Tenth Cavalry*, 360.

Lieutenant, 48th Infantry, and Cuba veteran. SOURCE: San Francisco *Chronicle*, 15 Nov 1899.

First lieutenant, K/48th Infantry. SOURCE: Beasley, *Negro Trailblazers*, 284.

Real estate agent, age 62, resided at 1117 N Street, SE, Washington, DC, in 1920; knew Martha C. Proctor, wife of John C. Proctor, at least ten years and her late husband from 1882; Louisa Proctor's first husband, Henry Chambers, was in F/24th Infantry; was best man in Chambers-Proctor wedding, Mobeetie, TX, c. 1884–1885; Chambers later remarried; Peter McCown married sister of Henry Chambers's second wife. SOURCE: Affidavit, Smith, 1920, VA File XC 2659372, John C. Proctor.

Resided at 1117 N Street in 1926; knew Thomas H. Allsup well, from 1880 until 1905; retired in 1908. SOURCE: Affidavit, Smith, 24 Jan 1926, VA File XC 2659797, Thomas H. Allsup.

Picture. SOURCE: Mary Curtis, *The Black Soldier*, opposite 52.

SMITH, James; Private; D/10th Cav. Enlisted Little Rock, AR, 27 Mar 1867; at Ft Gibson, Indian Territory, Jun 1867. SOURCE: LS, 10 Cav, 1866–67.

SMITH, James; Private; 10th Cav. Enlisted Tuscumbia, AL, 4 Apr 1867. SOURCE: LS, 10 Cav, 1866–67.

SMITH, James; Private; 10th Cav. Enlisted Memphis, 13 May 1867. SOURCE: LS, 10 Cav, 1866–67.

SMITH, James (1); D/10th Cav. Original member of 10th Cavalry; in troop when organized, Ft Leavenworth, KS, 1 Jun 1867. SOURCE: McMiller, "Buffalo Soldiers," 71.

SMITH, James (2); D/10th Cav. Original member of 10th Cavalry; in troop when organized, Ft Leavenworth, KS, 1 Jun 1867. SOURCE: McMiller, "Buffalo Soldiers," 71.

SMITH, James; Private; C/10th Cav. Mentioned Jan 1873 as having enlisted in Washington, DC, 23 Sep 1867; discharged. SOURCE: LS, 10 Cav, 1873–83.

SMITH, James; Private; C/10th Cav. Mentioned Jan 1873 as having enlisted in Philadelphia, 12 Dec 1867. SOURCE: LS, 10 Cav, 1873–83.

SMITH, James; B/9th Cav. Born Shreveport, LA; occupation laborer, Ht 5'7", black hair, eyes, and complexion; enlisted, age 21, Pittsburgh, 21 Nov 1871; deserted 16 Feb 1872. SOURCE: Register of Enlistments.

SMITH, James; Private; 10th Cav. Served in 1891. *See* **CHESTER**, Stanley, Private, 10th Cavalry

SMITH, James; Private; F/24th Inf. Wounded in action at Santa Anna, Philippines, 7 Oct 1899. SOURCE: *ANJ* 37 (21 Oct 1899): 178; Muller, *The Twenty Fourth Infantry*, 30.

SMITH, James; Corporal; I/25th Inf. Acquitted by summary court, San Isidro, Philippines, of failure to report assault by soldier on native, 18 Apr 1902; no previous convictions. SOURCE: Register of Summary Court, San Isidro.

SMITH, James E.; Captain; D/48th Inf. Resides in Xenia, OH; an exceptionally competent officer, according to Cpl. Walter E. Merchant, 48th Infantry, in letter of 12 Jun 1900. SOURCE: Gatewood, *"Smoked Yankees"*, 282.

Mentioned. SOURCE: Beasley, *Negro Trailblazers*, 284.

Led expedition against insurgents at Sodipan, small mountain town in the Philippines. SOURCE: Cleveland *Gazette*, 1 Sep 1900.

SMITH, James W.; Private; A/10th Cav. Released to duty from treatment for acute gonorrhea, Ft Robinson, NE, 1 Dec 1903. SOURCE: Post Surgeon to CO, A/10, 1 Dec 1903, LS, Post Surgeon, Ft Robinson.

SMITH, James W.; Private; M/9th Cav. At Ft D. A. Russell, WY, in 1910; resident of Denver. SOURCE: *Illustrated Review: Ninth Cavalry.*

SMITH, Jeff; Recruit; Colored Detachment/ Mounted Service. Tried by general court martial, Jefferson Barracks, MO, for desertion, 24–26 Dec 1886. SOURCE: GCMO 11, AGO, 2 Feb 1887.

SMITH, Jeff; 24th Inf. Ex-soldier, shot by native policeman while trying to escape arrest for fight with Pvt. Louis Conway, 24th Infantry; now near death. SOURCE: Manila *Times*, 19 Mar 1902.

SMITH, Jesse B.; Private; K/25th Inf. Accidentally shot and killed by Sgt. H. T. Henry, K/25th Infantry, at Castillejos, Philippines, 31 Dec 1900; was twenty-two-year-old native of Kentucky and "fine speciman of physical manhood." SOURCE: Richmond *Planet*, 9 Mar 1901; *ANJ* 38 (30 Mar 1901): 753.

SMITH, John; Private; A/10th Cav. Served against Cheyennes and Kiowas, 1866 [*sic*]; died 1900; widow Mary Smith, Indianapolis, has $12 per month pension after fifteen years of effort, which is her total income. SOURCE: *Winners of the West* 1 (Nov 1924): 2, 5.

SMITH, John; D/10th Cav. Original member of 10th Cavalry; in troop when organized, Ft Leavenworth, KS, 1 Jun 1867. SOURCE: McMiller, "Buffalo Soldiers," 71.

SMITH, John; G/10th Cav. Original member of 10th Cavalry; in troop when organized, Ft Leavenworth, KS, 5 Jul 1867. SOURCE: McMiller, "Buffalo Soldiers," 74.

SMITH, John; Private; 38th Inf. Died of pneumonia at Ft Cummings, NM, Sep 1867. SOURCE: Billington, *New Mexico's Buffalo Soldiers*, 34.

SMITH, John; Private; H/24th Inf. Convicted by general court martial, Ft Brown, TX, of refusing to accompany Sgt. William Haines, G/24th Infantry, to guardhouse when ordered and fleeing until brought back by force, of disrespect and insolence to Capt. L. Johnson's questions regarding unauthorized visit to Brownsville, 11 Dec 1872, and of disturbance and resisting arrest, Brownsville, 11 Dec 1872; sentence of six months reduced to four months by commanding general, Department of Texas. SOURCE: GCMO 1, Department of Texas, 11 Jan 1873.

SMITH, John; Private; I/10th Cav. Mentioned Jun 1875 as having reenlisted. SOURCE: ES, 10 Cav, 1873–83.

SMITH, John; Private; Band/9th Cav. With band on detached service at headquarters, District of New Mexico, Santa Fe, 1880; played first B-flat cornet. SOURCE: Billington, *New Mexico's Buffalo Soldiers*, 226.

SMITH, John; Trumpeter; A/9th Cav. Letter, Adjutant General's Office, 1 May 1896, concerns his enlistment papers.

Ordered to Ft Crook, NE, for medical treatment by Special Order 52, Adjutant General's Office, 5 Mar 1897.

SMITH, John; Private; D/24th Inf. At Cabanatuan, Philippines, 1901. *See* **JOHNSON**, Otto, Private, D/24th Infantry

SMITH, John; Corporal; E/24th Inf. Certificate of merit awarded 8 Dec 1903 for conspicuous bravery in rescue of comrade from drowning, Rio Grande, near Cabanatuan, Philippines, 22 Nov 1899, when private, E/24th Infantry; discharged 16 Jan 1902. SOURCE: GO 32, AGO, 6 Feb 1904.

SMITH, John; Private; F/25th Inf. Born Martinsburg, WV, 1872; occupation stonecutter, Ht 5'8"; brown eyes, curly brown hair, colored complexion; enlisted Carlisle, PA, Jun 1899; joined regiment, Presidio of San Francisco, CA, 28 Jun 1899; discharged, end of term, Iba, Zambales, Philippines, 18 Jan 1902, "service not honest and faithful . . . mentally and physically incapacitated for service by excessive use of *vino*." SOURCE: Descriptive Book, F/25 Inf.

Deserted at Iba, Zambales, Philippines, 20 Mar 1902; dropped from rolls, 30 Mar 1902; apprehended by civil authorities, Botolan, Philippines, 2 Apr 1902. SOURCE: Regt Returns, 25 Inf, Mar 1902; Descriptive Book, F/25 Inf.

SMITH, John; Private; C/25th Inf. Dishonorable discharge, Brownsville. SOURCE: SO 266, AGO, 9 Nov 1906.

One of fourteen cleared of involvement in Brownsville raid by court, 1910, and authorized to reenlist. SOURCE: Weaver, *The Brownsville Raid*, 248.

SMITH, John; Private; K/9th Cav. At Ft D. A. Russell, WY, in 1910; sharpshooter; resident of Dunn, NC. SOURCE: *Illustrated Review: Ninth Cavalry*, with picture.

SMITH, John; Private; 24th Inf. Sentenced to seven years for part in Houston riot. SOURCE: Cleveland *Gazette*, 5 Jan 1918.

SMITH, John E.; Private; A/10th Cav. Served in 10th Cavalry in Cuba, 1898. SOURCE: Cashin, *Under Fire with the Tenth Cavalry*, 336.

SMITH, John E. (1); Private; E/10th Cav. Served in 10th Cavalry in Cuba, 1898. SOURCE: Cashin, *Under Fire with the Tenth Cavalry*, 342.

SMITH, John E. (2); Private; E/10th Cav. Served in 10th Cavalry in Cuba, 1898. SOURCE: Cashin, *Under Fire with the Tenth Cavalry*, 342.

SMITH, John H.; Private; H/25th Inf. Shot and killed Pvt. Shannon Proffett, I/25th Infantry, with service pistol, after quarrel at San Felipe, Zambales, Philippines, 23 Jul 1900. SOURCE: Manila *Times*, 31 Jul 1900.

Native of West Philadelphia, PA. SOURCE: Richmond *Planet*, 20 Oct 1900.

SMITH, John H.; Private; K/9th Cav. Deserted at Monterey, CA, 25 Dec 1902. SOURCE: Regt Returns, 9 Cav, Jan 1903.

SMITH, John W.; Private; C/10th Cav. Served in 10th Cavalry, 1898; remained in U.S. during war with Spain. SOURCE: Cashin, *Under Fire with the Tenth Cavalry*, 340.

SMITH, Johnson; Sergeant; E/9th Cav. Served in 1867. *See* **DOUGLAS**, Joseph, First Sergeant, E/9th Cavalry

SMITH, Joseph; Private; I/24th Inf. Sentenced to death for role in Houston riot. SOURCE: Haynes, *A Night of Violence*, 277–78; Cleveland *Gazette*, 5 Jan 1918.

SMITH, Joseph C.; Corporal; G/25th Inf. Musician, E/25th Infantry, Ft Buford, ND, 1893; catcher, regimental baseball team, "one of the gamiest [*sic*] and scrappiest players that ever donned a baseball suit," according to Sergeant D. P. Green. SOURCE: Nankivell, *History of the Twenty-fifth Infantry*, 164.

Corporal, G/25th Infantry, second best infantry marksman, Department of the Missouri, 1903. SOURCE: SecWar, *AR 1903*, 1:427.

Ranked first with gold medal, Southern Division infantry team competition, Ft Reno, OK, 1904. SOURCE: GO 167, AGO, 28 Oct 1904.

Distinguished marksman, with Department of Missouri silver medal, 1903, and Southwestern Division gold medals, 1904 and 1905. SOURCE: GO 173, AGO, 20 Oct 1905.

Ranked number 180 among rifle experts, 1904, with 68.67 percent. SOURCE: GO 79, AGO, 1 Jun 1905.

First place at Army's Ft Sheridan, IL, rifle competition, 3 Aug 1905; broke all records with 181 out of 200 slow fire and 97 of 100 rapid fire. SOURCE: New York *Age*, 10 Aug 1905.

Ranked number 358 among rifle experts, 1905, with 69.67 percent. SOURCE: GO 101, AGO, 31 May 1906.

SMITH, Joseph M.; Private; E/9th Cav. Died in Cuba, 9 Aug 1898. SOURCE: *ANJ* 36 (18 Feb 1899): 590.

SMITH, Keith H.; G/10th Cav. Original member of 10th Cavalry; in troop when organized, Ft Leavenworth, KS, 5 Jul 1867. SOURCE: McMiller, "Buffalo Soldiers," 74.

SMITH, Lamb; Private; F/9th Cav. Sentenced to thirty days' confinement by garrison court martial, Ft Robinson, NE, 20 Jun 1887, for insubordination to 2nd Lt. William D. McAnaney. SOURCE: Order 123, 20 Jun 1887, Post Orders, Ft Robinson.

SMITH, Lawson; Private; M/10th Cav. Born Hopkinsville, KY; died in Minnesota, 7 Nov 1947. SOURCE: Taylor, "Minnesota Black Spanish-American War Veterans."

Served in 10th Cavalry, 1898; remained in U.S. during war with Spain. SOURCE: Cashin, *Under Fire with the Tenth Cavalry*, 352.

SMITH, Leonard; Private; H/24th Inf. Enlisted New York City, 27 Jun 1898; assigned and joined 16 Sep 1898; due U.S. for ordnance (meat can, oiler, screwdriver) $.63. SOURCE: Muster Roll, H/24 Inf, Sep–Oct 1898.

Discharged, end of term, character good, Ft Douglas, UT, 28 Jan 1899; due U.S. for clothing $21.25. SOURCE: Muster Roll, H/24 Inf, Jan–Feb 1899.

SMITH, Levi; Private; I/9th Cav. Recruit, arrived at Ft Robinson, NE, from depot, 1 Mar 1887, and assigned to C/9th Cavalry. SOURCE: Regt Returns, 9 Cav, 1 Mar 1887.

At Ft D. A. Russell, WY, in 1910; sharpshooter; resident of New Berne, NC. SOURCE: *Illustrated Review: Ninth Cavalry*, with picture.

SMITH, Lewis; Private; C/9th Cav. At Ft D. A. Russell, WY, in 1910; resident of 407 E. 6th St., Chattanooga, TN. SOURCE: *Illustrated Review: Ninth Cavalry*, with picture.

SMITH, Lewis M.; 1st Sgt; M/10th Cav. Born in Virginia; private, I/10th Cavalry, 28 Apr 1875–27 Apr 1880; private, C/24th Infantry, 13 May 1880–13 Jul 1881; private, E/10th Cavalry, 13 Jul 1881; corporal, 1 Jul 1882; sergeant, 1 Feb 1884; first sergeant, 1 Apr 1894; at Ft Custer, MT, 1897. SOURCE: Baker, Roster.

Born Warrenton, VA, 15 Jul 1854; enlisted at age 21 for I/10th Cavalry; Indian campaigns in Arizona, Idaho, Texas, and Indian Territory; commanded company in battle in Cuba. SOURCE: Lynk, *The Black Troopers*, 52.

Authorized six-month furlough from Ft Apache, AZ. SOURCE: *ANJ* 27 (15 Mar 1890): 542.

Sergeant, E/10th Cavalry; at Ft Apache, 1890, subscribed $.50 to testimonial to General Grierson. SOURCE: List of subscriptions, 23 Apr 1890, 10th Cavalry papers, MHI.

At Ft Apache, AZ, 1891; sharpshooter. SOURCE: *ANJ* 31 (4 Jul 1891): 765.

Ranked number two with revolver, Departments of Arizona and Texas, 1891, silver medal; ranked number six with revolver, Departments of Dakota and Columbia, 1894, silver medal. SOURCE: Baker, Roster.

Ranked number two in revolver competition, Departments of Texas and Arizona, Ft Wingate, NM, 17–22 Aug 1891. SOURCE: GO 81, AGO, 6 Oct 1891.

Ranked number 17 among carbine sharpshooters with over 72 percent, 1891. SOURCE: GO 1, AGO, 2 Jan 1892.

Ranked number six in revolver competition, Departments of Dakota and Columbia, Ft Keogh, MT, 18–27 Sep 1897. SOURCE: GO 62, AGO, 15 Nov 1894.

First sergeant, E/10th Cavalry, at Ft Robinson, NE, for cavalry competition, Sep 1897. SOURCE: Monthly Returns, Ft Robinson, Sep 1897.

Served as first sergeant, M/10th Cavalry in Cuba, 1898. SOURCE: Cashin, *Under Fire with the Tenth Cavalry*, 352.

First lieutenant, 48th Infantry, as of 9 Sep 1899, and ordered to Ft Thomas, KY. SOURCE: *ANJ* 37 (14 Oct 1899): 147.

Mentioned as first lieutenant, I/48th Infantry. SOURCE: Beasley, *Negro Trailblazers*, 284.

Stationed at San Fernand de la Union, Philippines; led detachment of I/48th Infantry that captured thirty of enemy, Jun 1900; Corporal Daniel Lee, I/48th Infantry, cited for gallantry in this action. SOURCE: Richmond *Planet*, 28 Jul 1900.

Retires as first sergeant, M/10th Cavalry, in accordance with Special Order 272, Adjutant General's Office, 19 Nov 1902.

Widow Jennie remarried in Alexandria, VA, 1907, resided at 132 S. Newberry, York, PA. SOURCE: Chief, Bureau of Pensions, to Commissioner of Pensions, 7 Apr 1926, VA File XC 2659797, Thomas H. Allsup.

See **HOUSTON**, Adam, Quartermaster Sergeant, 10th Cavalry

SMITH, Luchious; Private; D/10th Cav. Served as corporal, D/10th Cavalry in Cuba, 1898. SOURCE: Cashin, *Under Fire with the Tenth Cavalry*, 341.

Distinguished himself at San Juan Hill and promoted to corporal. SOURCE: SecWar, *AR 1898*, 710.

In going up San Juan Hill, three men of D/10th Cavalry distinguished themselves: Smith, Cpl. John Walker, and Sergeant Elliot; Smith and Elliot "were during the ascent of the hill constantly among the bolder few who voluntarily made themselves ground-scouts, drawing the attention of the enemy from the main line upon themselves." SOURCE: Bigelow, *Reminiscences of Santiago*, 130–31.

Commended for distinguished service in battle of Santiago, Cuba, 1 Jul 1898; now out of service. SOURCE: GO 15, AGO, 13 Feb 1900.

Certificate of merit mentioned. SOURCE: Steward, *The Colored Regulars*, 280; *ANJ* 37 (24 Feb 1900): 611.

Corporal; heroism in Cuba mentioned. SOURCE: Gatewood, *"Smoked Yankees"*, 80.

Private, D/10th Cavalry, at Ft Robinson, NE; in hands of civil authorities, Crawford, NE, 15–17 May 1903. SOURCE: Regt Returns, 10 Cav, May 1903.

SMITH, Mason; C/10th Cav. Original member of 10th Cavalry; in troop when organized, Ft Leavenworth, KS, 14 May 1867. SOURCE: McMiller, "Buffalo Soldiers," 70.

SMITH, Mathew; C/10th Cav. Original member of 10th Cavalry; in troop when organized, Ft Leavenworth, KS, 14 May 1867. SOURCE: McMiller, "Buffalo Soldiers," 70.

SMITH, Myles Y.; Private; D/9th Cav. In F/9th Cavalry; in hands of civil authorities, Chadron, NE, 13 Dec 1891–18 Mar 1892. SOURCE: Regt Returns, 9 Cav, Dec 1891–Mar 1892.

Restored to duty in accordance with letter, Department of the Platte, 19 Dec 1893.

To be released and restored to duty in accordance with telegram, Department of the Platte, 20 Oct 1894.

Deserter picked up from city marshal, Douglas, WY, by Sgt. John Jackson, D/9th Cavalry, and returned to Ft Robinson, NE. SOURCE: Order 89, 30 Nov 1894, Post Orders, Ft Robinson.

1st Lt. John M. McBlaine directed to be counsel for defense in trial before general court martial of Myles Smith for desertion. SOURCE: CO, Ft Robinson, to Lt McBlaine, 7 Dec 1894, LS, Ft Robinson.

Convicted of desertion and sentenced to dishonorable discharge and eighteen months in accordance with General Court Martial Order 142, Department of the Platte, 23 Dec 1894; released in Jun 1895.

Clemency denial by President Arthur reported in letter, Adjutant General's Office, 21 Feb 1895.

Nineteen years' service before deserted; his captain says he has become a "trifling and worthless man"; deliberately deserted and obtained job as hotel waiter; put in irons because post had had trouble some time ago with a man escaping twice; serves as guardhouse room orderly and does not work outside with prisoners; instead is safe from cold, rain, and wind. SOURCE: CO, Ft Robinson, to AGO, 31 Jan 1895, LS, Ft Robinson.

Iron shackles to be removed in accordance with telegram, Department of the Platte, 20 Feb 1895.

Now out of irons for ten days; has easiest work of any prisoner in guardhouse. SOURCE: CO, Ft Robinson, to AAG, DP, 21 Feb 1895, LS, Ft Robinson.

SMITH, O.; Private; H/9th Cav. On detached service at Ft Bayard, NM, 16 Jan–10 Feb 1881. SOURCE: Regt Returns, 9 Cav, Feb 1881.

SMITH, Oliver; Private; D/49th Inf. Died of dysentery in the Philippines, 27 Dec 1900. SOURCE: *ANJ* 38 (5 Jan 1901): 455.

SMITH, P.; Private; B/9th Cav. On detached service at Santa Fe, NM, Sep 1880–Jan 1881. SOURCE: Regt Returns, 9 Cav, Sep 1880–Jan 1881.

SMITH, Richard; Private; E/24th Inf. Resident of Cincinnati; to be discharged at end of term from Ft Bayard, NM, 6 Dec 1891. SOURCE: Cleveland *Gazette*, 12 Dec 1891.

SMITH, Richard; Private; A/10th Cav. Served in 10th Cavalry, 1898; remained in U.S. during war with Spain. SOURCE: Cashin, *Under Fire with the Tenth Cavalry*, 337.

SMITH, Richard; Corporal; I/24th Inf. Enlisted Ft D. A. Russell, WY, 16 Dec 1897, with three years' service. SOURCE: Muster Roll, I/24 Inf, Jan–Feb 1899.

Fined one month's pay by garrison court martial, 23 Mar 1899. SOURCE: Muster Roll, I/24 Inf, Mar–Apr 1899.

SMITH, Richard; Private; E/9th Cav. At Ft D. A. Russell, WY, in 1910; resident of Cincinnati. SOURCE: *Illustrated Review: Ninth Cavalry*, with picture.

SMITH, Robert; Private; G/9th Cav. 1st Lt. Francis S. Davidson acquitted by general court martial, Ft Brown, TX, 22 Jul 1875, of failure to equip Smith with serviceable cartridge box. SOURCE: GCMO 93, AGO, 15 Nov 1875.

Killed in action in New Mexico, 1 Sep 1886. *See* **ROBINSON**, James, Sergeant, G/9th Cavalry

SMITH, Robert A.; Private; L/10th Cav. Confined at Ft Leavenworth, KS, not Ft Gibson, Indian Territory, Dec 1872. SOURCE: ES, 10 Cav, 1873–83.

SMITH, Robert V.; Private; A/10th Cav. Served in 10th Cavalry, 1898; remained in U.S. during war with Spain. SOURCE: Cashin, *Under Fire with the Tenth Cavalry*, 337.

SMITH, Roy; Private; C/10th Cav. Served in 10th Cavalry in Cuba, 1898. SOURCE: Cashin, *Under Fire with the Tenth Cavalry*, 340.

SMITH, Russell; Sergeant; B/10th Cav. Commissioned first lieutenant at Camp Des Moines, IA, 15 Oct 1917. SOURCE: Glass, *History of the Tenth Cavalry*, appendix M.

SMITH, Samuel; Private; M/10th Cav. Original member of 10th Cavalry; in troop when organized, Ft Riley, KS, 15 Oct 1867. SOURCE: McMiller, "Buffalo Soldiers," 79.

Mentioned Jan 1873 as having enlisted in Sep 1867. SOURCE: LS, 10 Cav, 1873–83.

SMITH, Sandy; Private; H/24th Inf. Enlisted Ft Douglas, UT, 15 Mar 1897, with six years' service. SOURCE: Muster Roll, H/24 Inf, May–Jun 1898.

Died of yellow fever contracted in line of duty, at field hospital, Siboney, Cuba, 21 Aug 1898; deposits $5; due U.S. for clothing $38.97. SOURCE: Muster Roll, H/24 Inf, Jul–Aug 1898; *ANJ* 36 (3 Sep 1898): 19, and *ANJ* 36 (18 Feb 1899): 590; AG, *Correspondence Regarding the War with Spain*, I:248.

SMITH, Sidney; Private; F/10th Cav. Resided in Kentucky; enlisted Cincinnati, 1869; served five years; discharged in Indian Territory; employed as janitor, immigration office, and resided at 530 N. 9th, Tucson, AZ, in 1922. SOURCE: VA File SC 11405, John Taylor.

SMITH, Solomon; Private; H/24th Inf. Enlisted Camp G. H. Thomas, GA, 29 Apr 1898. SOURCE: Muster Roll, H/24 Inf, May–Jun 1898.

Sick, disease contracted in line of duty, and returned to U.S. for treatment. SOURCE: Muster Roll, H/24 Inf, Sep–Oct 1898.

Transferred from Reserve Divisional Hospital, Siboney, Cuba, to U.S. on U.S. Army Transport *Santiago* with remittent malarial fever, 25 Jul 1898. SOURCE: Hospital Papers, Spanish-American War.

Authorized furlough on surgeon's certificate, 19 Sep–18 Oct 1898. SOURCE: Muster Roll, H/24 Inf, Sep–Oct 1898.

Discharged, end of term, character good, single, Ft Douglas, UT, 27 Jan 1899; deposits $45; due U.S. for clothing $38.69. SOURCE: Muster Roll, H/24 Inf, Jan–Feb 1899.

Youngest soldier in regular Army. SOURCE: Indianapolis *Freeman*, 4 Feb 1899, with picture.

SMITH, T. Clay; Sgt Maj; 24th Inf. Letter from Ft Assiniboine, MT, Oct 1902. SOURCE: Gatewood, *"Smoked Yankees"*, 316.

SMITH, Terry; Private; M/24th Inf. Participated in Houston riot, 1917; acquitted. SOURCE: Haynes, *A Night of Violence*, 192, 271–72.

SMITH, Theodore H.; Private; C/9th Cav. At Ft D. A. Russell, WY, in 1910; sharpshooter; resident of Jefferson Co., KY. SOURCE: *Illustrated Review: Ninth Cavalry*, with picture.

SMITH, Thomas; F/10th Cav. Original member of 10th Cavalry; in troop when organized, Ft Leavenworth, KS, 21 Jun 1867. SOURCE: McMiller, "Buffalo Soldiers," 73.

SMITH, Thomas; Private; 25th Inf. Served five years in E/25th Infantry and ten years in I/25th Infantry; now age 75. SOURCE: *Winners of the West* 10 (Jan 1933): 3.

SMITH, Thomas; Saddler; K/9th Cav. Tried by general court martial, Jefferson Barracks, MO, for desertion from St. Louis Barracks, MO, 4 Oct 1876, until apprehended in Baltimore, 16 Nov 1878; convicted of absence without leave and sentenced to dishonorable discharge. SOURCE: GCMO 55, AGO, 16 Dec 1878.

SMITH, Thomas; Private; A/10th Cav. Born Columbia, SC; occupation butler; enlisted at age 23 in A/10th Cavalry 13 Jan 1876; contracted gonorrhea in 1884; married Suzie Hunter Dickinson, age 20, of North Dakota, 29 Dec 1896; she had previously been married to Joseph Dickinson and divorced at Miles City, MT, 15 Jan 1896; spent entire career in A/10th Cavalry; retired as private from Ft Robinson, NE, 27 Oct 1902; died at Miles City of disease contracted in service, 8 Aug 1903; widow filed pension application 20 Nov 1906. SOURCE: VA File WC 858864, Thomas Smith.

At Ft Apache, AZ, 1890, subscribed $.50 to testimonial :o General Grierson. SOURCE: List of subscriptions, 23 Apr 1890, 10th Cavalry papers, MHI.

Served in 10th Cavalry in Cuba, 1898. SOURCE: Cashin, *Under Fire with the Tenth Cavalry*, 336.

Retired Aug 1902, in accordance with Special Order 202, Adjutant General's Office, 27 Aug 1902. SOURCE: *ANJ* 39 (30 Aug 1902): 1315.

SMITH, Thomas; Private; M/10th Cav. Served in 10th Cavalry, 1898; remained in U.S. during war with Spain. SOURCE: Cashin, *Under Fire with the Tenth Cavalry*, 352.

SMITH, Thompson W.; Private; E/10th Cav. Lieutenant Wallace, 6th Cavalry, Recruiting Officer, Baltimore, notifies commander, Ft Concho, TX, of apprehension of Smith from desertion in Washington, DC, 4 Jan 1876. SOURCE: ES, 10 Cav, 1873–83.

Convicted of desertion by general court martial, St. Louis Barracks, MO; sentenced to dishonorable discharge and three years. SOURCE: GCMO 30, AGO, 16 Mar 1876.

Prisoner number 331, U.S. Military Prison, Ft Leavenworth, KS; married, age 24, resident of Washington, DC, before enlistment; died 15 Sep 1876 of gunshot wound received while trying to escape from guard. SOURCE: Certificates of Disability, DivMo, 1875–87.

SMITH, Tom; Private; B/10th Cav. Died of gunshot wound, Holguin, Cuba, 7 Jan 1902. SOURCE: *ANJ* 39 (18 Jan 1902): 502.

SMITH, Tom; Private; B/9th Cav. At Ft D. A. Russell, WY, in 1910. SOURCE: *Illustrated Review: Ninth Cavalry*, with picture.

SMITH, W. E.; Private; I/10th Cav. Court martial sentence published in Special Order 4, Department of the Missouri, 6 Jan 1903.

Fined $10 and $13.75 costs for carrying concealed weapon, Crawford, NE, 12 Mar 1903. SOURCE: Police Court Records, Crawford.

SMITH, W. T.; Private; L/9th Cav. On detached service in field, New Mexico, 21 Jan–24 Feb 1881. SOURCE: Regt Returns, 9 Cav, Feb 1881.

SMITH, Walter; Private; F/9th Cav. Fined $10 by garrison court martial, Ft Robinson, NE, for disrespect to Sergeant Fletcher, F/9th Cavalry; "the court is thus lenient on account of the apparent want of intelligence on the part of the accused." SOURCE: Order 122, 28 Jun 1888, Post Orders, Ft Robinson.

SMITH, Walter; Private; F/10th Cav. Served in 10th Cavalry in Cuba, 1898. SOURCE: Cashin, *Under Fire with the Tenth Cavalry*, 344.

Second best running broad jump, Department of Colorado competition, Ft Washakie, WY, and third in Army, with 20'11"; fourth best standing broad jump in Army, with 10'0", 1903. SOURCE: SecWar, *AR 1903*, 1:430.

SMITH, Walter E.; Comsy Sgt; U.S. Army. Born Bradford Co., VA, 1869; Ht 5'8", brown eyes, black hair, "L Choc" complexion; served three years and three months in 10th Cavalry, until 9 Jan 1896; served three years in H/24th Infantry, until 22 Mar 1899; promoted to sergeant major, 24th Infantry, 24 Aug 1898 for soldierly conduct at Santiago, Cuba; mentioned for gallantry at San Juan, Cuba, in General Order 14, 1898; transferred from M/10th Cavalry to non-commissioned staff, character excellent, 21 Jun 1899; promoted to drum major, 1 Jul 1899; promoted to regimental commissary sergeant, 4 Oct 1899; promoted to post commissary sergeant, character excellent, 9 Dec 1901; mother: Mrs. Ruth Smith, 524 N. 18th Street, Philadelphia. SOURCE: Descriptive Book, 10 Cav Officers & NCOs.

Enlisted Philadelphia, 23 Mar 1896; promoted to corporal, Tampa, FL, 23 May 1898. SOURCE: Muster Roll, H/24 Inf, May–Jun 1898.

Transferred to 24th Infantry noncommissioned staff as regimental sergeant major, character excellent, 24 Aug 1898, with $15.89 clothing. SOURCE: Muster Roll, H/24 Inf, Jul–Aug 1898.

Reduced to private "upon his own application" and joined H/24th Infantry 30 Nov 1898; on special duty as clerk, Quartermaster Department, since 1 Dec 1898. SOURCE: Muster Roll, H/24 Inf, Nov–Dec 1898 and Jan–Feb 1899.

SMITH, Wesse B.; Private; K/25th Inf. Died in the Philippines, 31 Dec 1900. SOURCE: *ANJ* 38 (19 Jan 1901): 503.

SMITH, William; Private; A/40th Inf. Born Accomack Co., VA; occupation waiter; Ht 5'7 1/2"; black eyes, hair, and complexion; enlisted age 20, Norfolk, VA, 16 Oct 1866; killed accidentally, Goldsboro, NC, 11 Jul 1868. SOURCE: Register of Enlistments.

SMITH, William; Private; D/10th Cav. Enlisted Little Rock, AR, 5 Feb 1867; at Ft Gibson, Indian Territory, Jun 1867. SOURCE: LS, 10 Cav, 1866–67.

Original member of 10th Cavalry; in troop when organized, Ft Leavenworth, KS, 1 Jun 1867. SOURCE: McMiller, "Buffalo Soldiers," 71.

SMITH, William; K/10th Cav. Original member of 10th Cavalry; in troop when organized, Ft Riley, KS, 1 Sep 1867. SOURCE: McMiller, "Buffalo Soldiers," 77.

SMITH, William; Corporal; M/10th Cav. Original member of 10th Cavalry; in troop when organized, Ft Riley, KS, 15 Oct 1867. SOURCE: McMiller, "Buffalo Soldiers," 79.

Mentioned Dec 1876 as having enlisted at Ft Davis, TX, 1875. SOURCE: LS, 10 Cav, 1873–83.

SMITH, William; Private; M/9th Cav. Served 1871–76; resident of U.S. Soldiers Home, Washington, DC, until recent death. SOURCE: *Winners of the West* 11 (Feb 1934): 3.

At Ft McKavett, TX, 1872–73. *See* **STANCE**, Emanuel, First Sergeant, F/9th Cavalry

Member of Col. Charles Young Camp, National Indian War Veterans, Washington, DC. SOURCE: *Winners of the West* 6 (Jun 1929): 4.

SMITH, William; Farrier; C/9th Cav. At Ft Robinson, NE, 1885–87. *See* **DIGGS**, James, Private, C/9th Cavalry

SMITH, William; Private; F/9th Cav. At Ft Robinson, NE, 1887. *See* **KENDRICK**, David, Private, F/9th Cavalry

SMITH, William; Lance Cpl; I/9th Cav. Promoted to corporal, Ft Robinson, NE, May 1895. SOURCE: *ANJ* 32 (18 May 1895): 626.

SMITH, William; Private; E/9th Cav. Deserter to be picked up at Hot Springs, SD, by Sgt. William N. Penn, K/9th Cavalry. SOURCE: Special Order 129, 21 Nov 1896, Post Orders, Ft Robinson.

SMITH, William; Private; H/10th Cav. Served in 10th Cavalry, 1898; remained in U.S. during war with Spain. SOURCE: Cashin, *Under Fire with the Tenth Cavalry*, 347.

SMITH, William; Private; B/24th Inf. Transferred from Reserve Divisional Hospital, Siboney, Cuba, to Fortress Monroe, VA, on U.S. Army Transport *Concho* with yellow fever, 23 Jul 1898. SOURCE: Hospital Papers, Spanish-American War.

SMITH, William; Sergeant; K/25th Inf. Retired from Ft Logan, CO, Jul 1899. SOURCE: *ANJ* 36 (22 Jul 1899): 1127.

Retired from Army with thirty-three years' service in D, B, and K/25th Infantry; over fifty years old and resides with mother, Washington, DC. SOURCE: Richmond *Planet*, 28 Jul 1899.

SMITH, William; Private; I/25th Inf. Shot and killed in the Philippines by sergeant of guard in self-defense, 14 Apr 1900. SOURCE: *ANJ* 37 (14 Apr 1900): 803.

SMITH, William; Private; I/48th Inf. Died of pneumonia in the Philippines, 22 Aug 1900. SOURCE: *ANJ* 38 (8 Sep 1900): 43.

Died in the Philippines, 31 Aug 1900. SOURCE: Richmond *Planet*, 8 Sep 1900.

SMITH, William; Farrier; H/9th Cav. Died of cholera in the Philippines, 11 Jun 1902. SOURCE: *ANJ* 39 (9 Aug 1902): 1248.

SMITH, William; Private; B/25th Inf. Dishonorable discharge, Brownsville. SOURCE: SO 266, AGO, 9 Nov 1906.

SMITH, William; L/24th Inf. Killed in action in the Philippines. SOURCE: Cleveland *Gazette*, 29 Dec 1906.

SMITH, William; Sergeant; L/9th Cav. Veteran of Philippine Insurrection; at Ft D. A. Russell, WY, in 1910; sharpshooter; resident of Vienna, VA. SOURCE: *Illustrated Review: Ninth Cavalry*, with picture.

SMITH, William D.; Sergeant; L/24th Inf. Ranked number 218 among rifle experts in 1905 with 71.33 percent. SOURCE: GO 101, AGO, 31 May 1906.

SMITH, William E.; Farrier; B/9th Cav. Veteran of Philippine Insurrection; at Ft D. A. Russell, WY, in 1910; marksman. SOURCE: *Illustrated Review: Ninth Cavalry*, with picture.

SMITH, William E.; Sergeant; M/9th Cav. At Ft D. A. Russell, WY, in 1910; sharpshooter; resident of Chicago. SOURCE: *Illustrated Review: Ninth Cavalry*, with picture.

SMITH, William H.; Private; 40th Inf. Born Great Barrington, MA; occupation shoemaker; Ht 5'11 1/2", black hair, dark complexion; enlisted Norfolk, VA, age 24, 24 Oct 1866; "Held in arrest by Civil Authorities at Norfolk, Va., Dec. 1, 1866. Nothing further known." SOURCE: Register of Enlistments.

SMITH, William H.; Private; D/25th Inf. Born Montreal, Canada; occupation musician; Ht 5'9", black hair and eyes, dark skin; enlisted Boston, age 21, 19 Mar 1880; arrived Ft Snelling, MN, 28 Aug 1880, and assigned to regimental band. SOURCE: Misc Records, 25 Inf.

SMITH, William H.; Corporal; F/25th Inf. Appreciates efforts of editor and magazine on behalf of Indian war veterans' pensions. SOURCE: *Winners of the West* 1 (Oct 1924): 15.

SMOOT, John H.; Private; A/10th Cav. Killed in action, Santiago, Cuba, 1 Jul 1898. SOURCE: Scipio, *Last of the Black Regulars*, 29; Cashin, *Under Fire with the Tenth Cavalry*, 337; SecWar, *AR 1898*, 323; *ANJ* 36 (18 Feb 1899): 590.

SMOTHERS, Isaac; Private; H/24th Inf. Convicted of selling greatcoat; sentence disapproved because of defects in trial. SOURCE: Report of Trials, Department of Texas, 1878–79.

SNAPP, Peter; Wagoner; B/9th Cav. Veteran of Philippine Insurrection; at Ft D. A. Russell, WY, in 1910. SOURCE: *Illustrated Review: Ninth Cavalry*, with picture.

SNEED; Private; F/10th Cav. Served in 1876. *See* **JOHNSON**, William, Private, Band/10th Cavalry

SNEED, John; Private; E/25th Inf. Born Accomack Co., VA; occupation hostler; Ht 5'7 1/2"; brown eyes, black hair, brown complexion; enlisted Baltimore, age 22, 14 Dec 1886; discharged, end of term, character excellent, Ft Buford, ND, 31 Dec 1891. SOURCE: Register of Enlistments.

Resident of Baltimore; to be discharged at end of term from Ft Bayard, NM, 3 Dec 1891. SOURCE: Cleveland *Gazette*, 12 Dec 1891.

SNELLY; Sergeant; L/9th Cav. Won Roman race, Frontier Days, Cheyenne, WY, 1912. SOURCE: Cheyenne *State Leader*, 14 Aug 1912.

SNODGRASS, Carlos; Private; I/24th Inf. Sentenced to death for part in Houston riot, 1917. SOURCE: Haynes, *A Night of Violence*, 271.

Hanged for part in Houston riot, Ft Sam Houston, TX, 13 Dec 1917. SOURCE: Cleveland *Gazette*, 15 Dec 1917.

SNOTEN, Augustus; Private; C/24th Inf. On special duty at target range, Ft Huachuca, AZ. SOURCE: Order 62, Ft Huachuca, 30 Apr 1893, Name File, 24 Inf.

Relieved of special duty at target range. SOURCE: Order 96, Ft Huachuca, 30 Jun 1893, Name File, 24 Inf.

On extra duty as teamster, Quartermaster Department. SOURCE: Order 119, Ft Huachuca, 10 Aug 1893, Name File, 24 Inf.

Relieved of extra duty as teamster, Quartermaster Department. SOURCE: Order 163, Ft Huachuca, 2 Nov 1893, Name File, 24 Inf.

Wounded in action at San Juan, Cuba, 1 Jul 1898. SOURCE: Muller, *The Twenty Fourth Infantry*, 18; SecWar, *AR 1898*, 438.

See VA File WC 1218572, Augustus Snoten.

SNOTEN, Peter; Sergeant; G/9th Cav. Born Somers Co., TN; parents unknown; occupation laborer; Ht 5'11", black complexion; enlisted in A/24th Infantry, 8 Apr 1876; transferred to G/9th Cavalry, 5 May 1885; transferred to L/9th Cavalry, 26 Jul 1900; transferred to G/9th Cavalry, 20 Aug 1902; retired as sergeant, G/9th Cavalry, 14 Jun 1905; wife Fannie, 516 E. 1st Street, Los Angeles, died 14 Apr 1923; then married Sarah B. Snoten, divorced from Sam Skinner, Beaumont, TX, 15 Aug 1910; died at age 72, at Soldiers Home, Sawtelle, CA; Sarah Snoten's attorney without fee C. W. Cordin of National Military Home, CA, 1927; after Snoten's death, she married Coleman Moore, late private, D/3rd North Carolina Infantry; she sold eggs on street and chickens door-to-door for eight years, could find no stable work, pleaded for help from Mrs. Franklin Roosevelt, 30 Nov 1936: lived "with not even enough shoes and stockings to meet the winter." SOURCE: VA File XC 978555, Peter Snoten.

Veteran of Spanish-American War; wife Fannie resided in Crawford, NE, 1899. SOURCE: Crawford *Tribune*, 27 Jan 1899.

Resided at 1326 E. 28th Street, Los Angeles, from 1905 until 1926; was in G/9th Cavalry in 1891 on detached service at Ft Custer, MT, when he met Sergeant and Mrs. Thomas H. Allsup. SOURCE: Affidavit, Snoten, 15 Apr 1926, VA File XC 2659797, Thomas H. Allsup.

SNOW, James; Private; I/9th Cav. Reenlistment as married soldier authorized by letter, Adjutant General's Office, 12 Mar 1895.

SNOWDEN, James; A/10th Cav. Mentioned as surviving Indian war veteran. SOURCE: *Winners of the West* 3 (Jun 1926): 7.

SNOWDEN, Joseph; Private; I/24th Inf. Enlisted Baltimore, 20 Feb 1899. SOURCE: Muster Roll, I/24 Inf, Jan–Feb 1899.

Sentenced to twenty days by summary court, 18 May 1899. SOURCE: Muster Roll, I/24 Inf, May–Jun 1899.

SNOWDEN, William E.; Private; G/10th Cav. Served in 10th Cavalry in Cuba, 1898. SOURCE: Cashin, *Under Fire with the Tenth Cavalry*, 345.

SNYDER, George; Private; D/10th Cav. At Ft Robinson, NE, for cavalry competition, Sep 1897. SOURCE: Post Returns, Ft Robinson, Sep 1897.

SNYDER, James W.; Private; D/24th Inf. Assaulted Nora Basshe, cook at teamsters' mess, Ft Bayard, NM, when she resisted his advances, Ft Bayard, Sep 1890. SOURCE: Billington, *New Mexico's Buffalo Soldiers*, 166.

SOLLY, Ross; Sergeant; 10th Cav. Son born to wife at Ft Robinson, NE, 1 Sep 1905. SOURCE: Monthly Report, Chaplain Anderson, 1 Nov 1905.

SOLOMON, Abraham; Private; B/10th Cav. Enlisted Memphis, spring 1867. SOURCE: LS, 10 Cav, 1866–67.

Original member of 10th Cavalry; in troop when organized, Ft Leavenworth, KS, 1 Apr 1867. SOURCE: McMiller, "Buffalo Soldiers," 69.

Commander, B/10th Cavalry, asks his release from confinement in the guardhouse, where he has been held too long without charges. SOURCE: CO, B/10, to Adj, Det 10 Cav, 20 Jul 1868, LR, Det 10 Cav, 1868–69.

SOMMERVILLE, Edward; F/25th Inf. Died at U.S. Soldiers Home of heart disease, age 51, 25 Mar 1896. SOURCE: SecWar, *AR 1896*, 640.

SOROSORI, Robert; I/10th Cav. Original member of 10th Cavalry; in troop when organized, Ft Riley, KS, 15 Aug 1867. SOURCE: McMiller, "Buffalo Soldiers," 76.

SORRIE, Morris A.; M/10th Cav. Original member of 10th Cavalry; in troop when organized, Ft Riley, KS, 15 Oct 1867. SOURCE: McMiller, "Buffalo Soldiers," 79.

SOUTHALL, James; L/10th Cav. Accidentally shot in mouth by ex-soldier Miller, Crawford, NE, 30 Apr 1903. SOURCE: Crawford *Tribune*, 1 May 1903.

No Veterans Administration pension file.

SOUTHERNER, Charles; Sergeant; F/38th Inf. At Ft Bayard, NM, 1868. *See* **RUSSELL**, William H., Private, F/38th Infantry

SOYSERN, Shelson; C/10th Cav. Original member of 10th Cavalry; in troop when organized, Ft Leavenworth, KS, 14 May 1867. SOURCE: McMiller, "Buffalo Soldiers," 70.

SPAIN, Fred; Private; B/10th Cav. Fined $3 and $4.80 costs for riding horse on sidewalk, Crawford, NE, 28 Jun 1902; paid $5.80. SOURCE: Police Court Records, Crawford.

Sentenced to dishonorable discharge and confinement, Ft Robinson, NE, Feb 1903; released 25 Apr 1903. SOURCE: Regt Returns, 10 Cav, Feb–Apr 1903.

SPANKLER, Robert; Private; H/24th Inf. Enlisted Washington, DC, 28 Apr 1898. SOURCE: Muster Roll, H/24 Inf, May–Jun 1898.

Sick in hospital, Siboney, Cuba, 2–25 Aug and en route to U.S. 25–31 Aug 1898; disease contracted in line of duty. SOURCE: Muster Roll, H/24 Inf, Jul–Aug 1898.

Absent, sick, Ft Wadsworth, NY, 31 Aug–24 Dec 1898; on furlough 24 Dec 1898–23 Jan 1899; discharged, Ft Douglas, UT, character good, single, 29 Jan 1899; clothing $54.70. SOURCE: Muster Roll, H/24 Inf, Sep–Oct 1898, Nov–Dec 1898, Jan–Feb 1899.

SPARKS, Asberry; Private; A/9th Cav. At Ft D. A. Russell, WY, in 1910; resident of Columbus, GA. SOURCE: *Illustrated Review: Ninth Cavalry*, with picture.

SPARKS, Augustus; Corporal; H/10th Cav. Ranked number eight in revolver competition, Departments of California and Arizona, Ft Wingate, NM, 1889, bronze medal. SOURCE: GO 78, AGO, 12 Oct 1889; Baker, Roster.

At Ft Apache, AZ, 1890, subscribed $.50 to testimonial to General Grierson. SOURCE: List of subscriptions, 23 Apr 1890, 10th Cavalry papers, MHI.

SPARKS, Zachariah; Private; D/25th Inf. Dishonorable discharge, Brownsville. SOURCE: SO 266, AGO, 9 Nov 1906.

SPARLING, John D.; Private; F/24th Inf. At Ft Bayard, NM, Oct 1888; convicted of allowing prisoners in guardhouse to drink and gamble while he was sergeant of the guard. SOURCE: Billington, *New Mexico's Buffalo Soldiers*, 163–64.

SPEAKS, James; E/10th Cav. Original member of 10th Cavalry; in troop when organized, Ft Leavenworth, KS, 15 Jun 1867. SOURCE: McMiller, "Buffalo Soldiers," 72.

SPEAKS, Perry E.; Private; I/24th Inf. Enlisted Washington, DC, 20 Feb 1899. SOURCE: Muster Roll, I/24 Inf, Jan–Feb 1899.

On detached service at Three Rivers, CA, 3 May–21 Jun 1899; on detached service at Presidio of San Francisco, CA, 22 Jun–26 Jul 1899. SOURCE: Muster Roll, I/24 Inf, May–Jun and Jul–Aug 1899.

Allotted $10 per month for twelve months to Sarah Speaks. SOURCE: Muster Roll, I/24 Inf, Sep–Oct 1899.

SPEAR, James; Sergeant; E/10th Cav. Authorized two-month furlough from Ft Thomas, AZ. SOURCE: *ANJ* 26 (12 Jan 1888): 386.

At Ft Apache, AZ, 1890, subscribed $.50 to testimonial to General Grierson. SOURCE: List of subscriptions, 23 Apr 1890, 10th Cavalry papers, MHI.

SPEARMAN, Edward W.; Sqdn Sgt Maj; 10th Cav. Squadron sergeant major, commissioned captain at Camp Des Moines, IA, 15 Oct 1917. SOURCE: Glass, *History of the Tenth Cavalry*, appendix M.

Warrant officer, stationed at Ft Benning, GA, 1930. SOURCE: Work, *The Negro Yearbook, 1931–1932*, 334.

SPEARS, William H.; Private; H/24th Inf. Fined $1.50 by summary court, San Isidro, Philippines, for absence from check roll call, 24 Dec 1901, second conviction. SOURCE: Register of Summary Court, San Isidro.

Died of aortic aneurism and fibroid tuberculosis in right lung aboard U.S. Army Transport *Thomas* en route to San Francisco, 24 Jul 1902. SOURCE: *ANJ* 39 (9 Aug 1902): 1249.

SPENCE, William; Band/24th Inf. Remained in Tayug, Philippines, after service. SOURCE: Funston papers, KSHS.

SPENCER; Private; B/10th Cav. At Ft Apache, AZ, 1890, subscribed $.50 to testimonial to General Grierson. SOURCE: List of subscriptions, 23 Apr 1890, 10th Cavalry papers, MHI.

SPENCER, Herbert F.; Private; H/24th Inf. Enlisted Baltimore, 23 Jun 1898; assigned and joined 16 Sep 1898. SOURCE: Muster Roll, H/24 Inf, Sep–Oct 1898.

Discharged Ft Douglas, UT, 28 Jan 1899, character good, single; due U.S. for clothing $16.47. SOURCE: Muster Roll, H/24 Inf, Jan–Feb 1899.

SPENCER, Jeremiah; Private; H/9th Cav. Convicted of desertion by general court martial, Jefferson Barracks, MO; sentenced to dishonorable discharge and four years. SOURCE: GCMO 7, AGO, 16 Jan 1883.

SPENCER, Mortimer E.; Private; H/24th Inf. Enlisted Ft McPherson, GA, 3 Jun 1896; sick in quarters, disease contracted in line of duty. 26 Apr–3 May 1898. SOURCE: Muster Roll, H/24 Inf, May–Jun 1898.

Sick at Siboney, Cuba, 20 Aug–5 Oct 1898; died of typhoid and diarrhea at Siboney, 5 Oct 1898; clothing $5.04, deposits $26.62. SOURCE: Muster Roll, H/24 Inf, Sep–Oct and Nov–Dec 1899.

Died in Cuba, 5 Oct 1898. SOURCE: *ANJ* 36 (18 Feb 1899): 590.

SPRIDDLES, Hamilton O.; Private; G/10th Cav. Served in 10th Cavalry in Cuba, 1898. SOURCE: Cashin, *Under Fire with the Tenth Cavalry*, 345.

SPRIGG; Private; F/9th Cav. Discharged in accordance with Special Order 257, Adjutant General's Office, 4 Nov 1889.

SPRIGGS, Eliord; F/10th Cav. Original member of 10th Cavalry; in troop when organized, Ft Leavenworth, KS, 21 Jun 1867. SOURCE: McMiller, "Buffalo Soldiers," 73.

SPRIGGS, John H.; Private; H/24th Inf. Relieved from extra duty as painter, Quartermaster Department, Ft Huachuca, AZ. SOURCE: Order 9, Ft Huachuca, 30 Jan 1893, Letters & Orders Received, 24 Inf, 1893.

On extra duty as painter, Quartermaster Department. SOURCE: Order 81, Ft Huachuca, 6 Jun 1893, Letters & Orders Received, 24 Inf, 1893.

On extra duty as painter, Quartermaster Department. SOURCE: Order 139, Ft Huachuca, 20 Sep 1893, Letters & Orders Received, 24 Inf, 1893.

Fined $5 by summary court, San Isidro, Philippines, for disrespect to commissioned officer in presence of officer and several enlisted men, 18 Nov 1901, first conviction. SOURCE: Register of Summary Court, San Isidro.

SPRIGGS, Stephen; Private; L/9th Cav. Discharged at Ft Bliss, TX, in accordance with General Court Martial Order 1, Department of the Missouri. SOURCE: Regt Returns, 9 Cav, Jan 1881.

SPRINGFIELD, Fletcher S.; Private; H/24th Inf. On extra duty as laborer, Quartermaster Department. SOURCE: Order 139, Ft Huachuca, 20 Sep 1893, Letters & Orders Received, 24 Inf, 1893.

Relieved from extra duty as laborer, Quartermaster Department. SOURCE: Order 162, Ft Huachuca, 1 Nov 1893, Letters & Orders Received, 24 Inf, 1893.

SPRINGFIELD, Herman; Private; H/9th Cav. At Ft D. A. Russell, WY, in 1910; resident of Madisonville, KY. SOURCE: *Illustrated Review: Ninth Cavalry*, with picture.

SPRUEIL, James; Corporal; E/9th Cav. At Ft D. A. Russell, WY, in 1910; sharpshooter. SOURCE: *Illustrated Review: Ninth Cavalry*, with picture.

SPURLING, John D.; Corporal; F/24th Inf. Sergeant, at Ft Elliott, TX, 1886. *See* **SMITH**, Jacob Clay, Sergeant, 10th Cavalry

Retires from Ft Bayard, NM, May 1895. SOURCE: *ANJ* 32 (18 May 1895): 627.

SPURLOCK, Charles; 1st Lt; G/49th Inf. Born in Virginia; private, K/10th Cavalry, 22 Nov 1882; corporal, 10 May 1888; sergeant, 17 Nov 1892; at Ft Custer, MT, 1897. SOURCE: Baker, *Roster*.

Served in Geronimo campaign with K/10th Cavalry; transferred to E/9th Cavalry, 1897; lance corporal, corporal, and sergeant, 1898; served at San Juan Hill, Santiago, Cuba, Jul 1898. SOURCE: *ANJ* 37 (4 Nov 1899): 219.

Corporal, K/10th Cavalry, at Ft Apache, AZ, 1890, subscribed $.50 to testimonial to General Grierson. SOURCE: List of subscriptions, 23 Apr 1890, 10th Cavalry papers, MHI.

Acquitted by general court martial, Ft Custer, of conduct prejudicial to good order and discipline. SOURCE: *ANJ* 33 (22 Aug 1896): 919.

First lieutenant, G/49th Infantry, as of 9 Sep 1899; in K/10th Cavalry 23 Nov 1882–23 Nov 1897; transferred to E/9th Cavalry; commander in engagement at Zapote Bridge, Philippines, 2 Aug 1900; participated in midnight attack, Las Pinas, Philippines, 24 Sep 1900, and at Barrio, San Ignacio, Philippines, 18 Dec 1900. SOURCE: Descriptive Book, G/49 Inf.

One of twenty-three officers of 49th Infantry recommended as regular Army second lieutenants. SOURCE: CG, DivPI, Manila, 8 Feb 1901, to AGO, AGO File 355163.

SPURLOCK, Ed; Private; M/9th Cav. At Ft D. A. Russell, WY, in 1910; marksman; resident of Chattanooga, TN. SOURCE: *Illustrated Review: Ninth Cavalry*, with picture.

SPUVEY; Private; K/25th Inf. Wounded in ambush in the Philippines, 29 Jan 1900. SOURCE: Richmond *Planet*, 17 Mar 1900.

SQUIRES, Albert H.; Trumpeter; F/10th Cav. Private, K/24th Infantry, at San Carlos, AZ, 1890. *See* HARDEE, James A., Private, K/24th Infantry

Served in 10th Cavalry in Cuba, 1898. SOURCE: Cashin, *Under Fire with the Tenth Cavalry*, 344.

STACY, Julius; Private; K/10th Cav. Served in 10th Cavalry, 1898; remained in U.S. during war with Spain. SOURCE: Cashin, *Under Fire with the Tenth Cavalry*, 349.

STAFF, Edward; Corporal; C/9th Cav. Appointed corporal 3 Sep 1898. SOURCE: Roster, 9 Cav.

Died of abscess on brain, Ft McKinney, WY, 26 Oct 1893. SOURCE: Regt Returns, 9 Cav, Oct 1893.

Killed recently at Buffalo, WY, and buried with honors at National Cemetery, Ft Leavenworth, KS. SOURCE: *ANJ* 31 (11 Nov 1893): 191.

STAFF, William R.; Captain; B/49th Inf. Born Washington, DC, 1 Jan 1873; educated and enlisted at Leavenworth, KS; mentioned for gallantry at San Juan, Cuba, 1 Jul 1898. SOURCE: *ANJ* 37 (20 Jan 1900): 478.

Private, corporal, sergeant, C/24th Infantry, 30 Jun 1892–25 Mar 1899; battalion sergeant major, 24th Infantry, 25 Mar 1899; participated in battles of San Juan and Santiago, Cuba, 1–15 Jul 1898; at yellow fever camp, Siboney, Cuba, 16 Jul–25 Aug 1898; arrived in the Philippines 2 Jan 1900; participated in engagements at Las Pinas, Philippines, 24 and 26 Sep 1900. SOURCE: Descriptive Book, B/49 Inf.

Private, C/24th Infantry, on extra duty as painter, Quartermaster Department, Ft Huachuca, AZ. SOURCE: Order 81, Ft Huachuca, 6 Jun 1893, Name File, 24 Inf.

Relieved of extra duty as painter, Quartermaster Department, Ft Huachuca. SOURCE: Order 96, Ft Huachuca, 30 Jun 1893, Name File, 24 Inf.

Relieved of extra duty as painter, Quartermaster Department, Ft Huachuca. SOURCE: Order 165, Ft Huachuca, 10 Nov 1893, Name File, 24 Inf.

Stationed at Vancouver Barracks, WA, 1899. SOURCE: San Francisco *Chronicle*, 15 Sep 1899.

Engaged insurgents at Zapote Bridge, Las Pinas, Philippines, 24 Sep 1900. SOURCE: *ANJ* 38 (1 Dec 1900): 333.

Won victory over insurgents, San Pueblo, Philippines, Jan 1901. SOURCE: *ANJ* 38 (30 Mar 1901): 753.

Mentioned as captain, B/49th Infantry. SOURCE: Beasley, *Negro Trailblazers*, 217.

STAFFORD, Haywood M.; Corporal; K/9th Cav. Expert rifleman at Ft D. A. Russell, WY, in 1910; resident of Aleman, MI. SOURCE: *Illustrated Review: Ninth Cavalry*, with picture.

STAFFORD, James N.; Private; H/24th Inf. Enlisted Chicago, 23 Nov 1896, with five years' service. SOURCE: Muster Roll, H/24 Inf, May–Jun 1898.

Wounded in action on San Juan Hill, Santiago, Cuba, 1 Jul 1898; returned to U.S. for treatment. SOURCE: Muster Roll, H/24 Inf, Sep–Oct 1898.

Wounded in Cuba, 1898. SOURCE: Muller, *The Twenty Fourth Infantry*, 19.

On furlough authorized by surgeon's certificate, 24 Sep–23 Oct 1898. SOURCE: Muster Roll, H/24 Inf, Sep–Oct 1898.

On special duty as laborer with Quartermaster Department, 18 Nov 1898–28 Feb 1899. SOURCE: Muster Roll, H/24 Inf, Nov–Dec 1898 and Jan–Feb 1899.

STAFFORD, Lloyd A.; Corporal; H/10th Cav. Promoted from private, May 1902. SOURCE: *ANJ* 39 (19 Jul 1902): 1168.

Tied for second best in 220-yard run, Department of Colorado competition, Ft Mackenzie, WY, 1903. SOURCE: SecWar, *AR 1903*, 1:429.

Commissioned captain at Camp Des Moines, IA, Oct 1917. SOURCE: Sweeney, *History of the American Negro*, 129.

STAFFORD, William; Private; L/10th Cav. Served in 10th Cavalry, 1898; remained in U.S. during war with Spain. SOURCE: Cashin, *Under Fire with the Tenth Cavalry*, 351.

STALEY, Edward; Private; M/10th Cav. Served in 10th Cavalry, 1898; remained in U.S. during war with Spain. SOURCE: Cashin, *Under Fire with the Tenth Cavalry*, 352.

STANCE, Emanuel; 1st Sgt; F/9th Cav. Born Carroll Parish, LA; occupation farmer; Ht 5'1 1/2", black complexion; enlisted, age 19, 2 Oct 1866; reenlisted, Ht 5'5 1/2", 1876. SOURCE: Register of Enlistments.

Enlisted 1867 [*sic*]; scarcely five feet tall; native of Charleston, SC; stationed at Ft McKavett, TX, 1870; had five successful encounters with Indians in two years; received Medal of Honor. SOURCE: Leckie, *The Buffalo Soldiers*, 10.

With five enlisted men of F/9th Cavalry, surprised and attacked small village at Kickapoo Springs, TX, about fourteen miles from Ft McKavett, wounded four Indians, recaptured two white boys and fifteen horses, 19–20 May 1870. SOURCE: Hutcheson, "The Ninth Regiment of Cavalry"; Hamilton, "History of the Ninth Cavalry," 12; *Illustrated Review: Ninth Cavalry*.

Mentioned. SOURCE: Carroll, *The Black Military Experience in the American West*, 72, 403.

Expressed appreciation for Medal of Honor in letter to Adjutant General, U.S. Army, 24 Jul 1870: "I will cherish the gift as a thing of priceless value and endeavor by my future conduct to merit the high honor conferred upon me." SOURCE: Lee, *Negro Medal of Honor Men*, 59, 61.

While sergeant, M/9th Cavalry, convicted by general court martial, Ft McKavett, 3 Jan 1873, of being drunk to prejudice of good order and discipline, at stables, Ft McKavett, 26 Dec 1872, of telling 1st Sgt. Henry Green, "If you reported that I was drunk you reported a God-damned lie and God-damn you you can't whip me," and of "Mayhem, to the prejudice of good order and discipline," assaulting Sgt. Green and biting off a portion of his lower lip, all on same day; prosecution witnesses: 1st Sgt. Green, Sgt. Horace Johnson, Sgt. Monroe Johnson, and Pvt. William Smith, all of M/9th Cavalry; defense witnesses: Pvt. George Samuel and Cpl. Lawrence Johnson, M/9th Cavalry; sentenced to reduction to private and six months' confinement and loss of pay. SOURCE: GCMO 1, Department of Texas, 11 Jan 1873, appended to Court Martial Records, Stance.

Fined $10 by garrison court martial, Ft Robinson, NE. SOURCE: Order 6, 12 Jan 1886, Post Orders, Ft Robinson.

Authorized four-month furlough by Special Order 136, Division of the Missouri, 6 Sep 1886.

Completed twenty years of service on 25 Dec 1886; unit will give dinner and dance in his honor. SOURCE: Cleveland *Gazette*, 1 Jan 1887.

Reenlisted Ft Robinson, 26 Dec 1886. SOURCE: Post Returns, Ft Robinson, Dec 1886.

With detachment from Ft Robinson "scouting for robbers," 11–12 Jan 1887. SOURCE: Monthly Returns, 9 Cav, Jan 1887.

Regarding Stance at Ft Robinson in 1887, *see* **GLENN**, Louis, Private, F/9th Cavalry; **ROYSTER**, Henry, Private, F/9th Cavalry; **WATERFORD**, George, Blacksmith, F/9th Cavalry

Found dead on public highway between Ft Robinson and Crawford, NE, with four gunshot wounds, between 7:30 and 8:30 in the morning, 25 Dec 1887. SOURCE: Medical History, Ft Robinson.

Pvt. Simpson Mann heard that just before his 1888 arrival at Ft Robinson two or three soldiers had killed a sergeant who had beaten soldiers and told their captain lies about them; sergeant had been "dirty mean." SOURCE: Rickey, Mann interview.

Died at post hospital, Ft Robinson; funeral scheduled for 2 P.M., 27 Dec 1887. SOURCE: Post Surgeon to CO, Ft Robinson, 26 Dec 1887, Register of Correspondence, Post Surgeon, Ft Robinson.

Funeral scheduled for 10 A.M., 28 Dec 1887. SOURCE: Order 253, 27 Dec 1887, Post Orders, Ft Robinson.

Buried at Ft Robinson, 25 Dec 1887. SOURCE: List of Interments, Ft Robinson.

See Schubert, "The Violent World of Emanuel Stance."

"As he was a very strict disciplinarian, it is believed he was killed by one of his own men. He stood high in the esteem of his superiors and wore a medal awarded by Congress for bravery in rescuing children from Indians." SOURCE: *ANJ* 25 (31 Dec 1887): 442.

"He was a Congressional medal man and left it and a manuscript of his life, with drawings, which should go to the Army Museum. Great effort has been made to discover the perpetrators of this villainous murder by members of this garrison. Stance was very strict. But his troop needed a strong hand, and it took a pretty nervy man to be 1st sergeant." SOURCE: *ANJ* 25 (14 Jan 1888): 482.

Biographical sketch. SOURCE: Logan and Winston, eds., *Dictionary of American Negro Biography*, 568–69.

STANDEMIRE, Taylor; Private; 9th Cav. Discharged without honor from Ft Riley, KS; was at Ft Brown, TX, with 25th Infantry during Brownsville raid. SOURCE: Cleveland *Gazette*, 1 Dec 1906.

STANDFIELD, Percy; Private; K/10th Cav. Served in 10th Cavalry, 1898; remained in U.S. during war with Spain. SOURCE: Cashin, *Under Fire with the Tenth Cavalry*, 349.

STANDLEY, Charles; Private; E/24th Inf. Born New York City; occupation coachman; Ht 5'9 1/2", black eyes, hair, and complexion; enlisted New York, age 22, 14 Nov 1871; deserted 15 Mar 1873. SOURCE: Register of Enlistments.

STANFIELD, Mack; QM Sgt; B/24th Inf. Wounded in action, Cuba, 1898. SOURCE: Muller, *The Twenty Fourth Infantry*, 18.

STANFORD, John G.; Private; K/24th Inf. Native Leon Carig convicted of his murder with bolo near San

Vicente, Philippines, Feb 1900, reversed for lack of evidence; Stanford had been left near highway drunk by comrades. SOURCE: Manila *Times*, 1 Feb 1901.

STANLEY; Corporal; H/10th Cav. Jailed in Cheyenne, WY, for attempted assault on prostitute. SOURCE: Cheyenne *Daily Leader*, 22 Feb 1907.

STANLEY, Benjamin; Private; G/48th Inf. Convicted by general court martial, San Fernando de la Union, Philippines, of rape and desertion; death sentence commuted to twenty years at Ft Leavenworth, KS, military prison by President McKinley. SOURCE: *ANJ* 38 (22 Dec 1900): 407.

Released from confinement at Leavenworth in accordance with Supreme Court decision in Deming case, 19 May 1902. SOURCE: *ANJ* 39 (7 Jun 1902): 1005.

STANLEY, James; Private; K/10th Cav. Killed in action, Ojo Caliente, TX, 29 Oct 1880. SOURCE: Baker, Roster; Leckie, *The Buffalo Soldiers*, 230.

STANLEY, William; Sergeant; B/10th Cav. Born Newbern, NC; black complexion; enlisted San Antonio, TX, 13 Jan 1880, with five years' continuous service; trumpeter as of 1880 enlistment; does not write his name; retained $60, clothing $24.15, deposits, 1880–83, $50; reenlisted Ft Davis, TX, 13 Jan 1885, unmarried, trumpeter, retained $60 and clothing $59; enlisted Ft Apache, AZ, 13 Jan 1990, single; marksman, 1883–85, 1888, 1890–91; sharpshooter, 1884–85; discharged, character excellent, Ft Custer, MT, 12 Jan 1895; retained $60, clothing $85, deposits $40; enlisted 13 Jan 1895. SOURCE: Descriptive Book, B/10 Cav.

Trumpeter, B/10th Cavalry, at Ft Apache, AZ, 1890, subscribed $.50 to testimonial to General Grierson. SOURCE: List of subscriptions, 23 Apr 1890, 10th Cavalry papers, MHI.

Served as trumpeter, B/10th Cavalry in Cuba, 1898. SOURCE: Cashin, *Under Fire with the Tenth Cavalry*, 338.

Retired Mar 1902 as sergeant, B/10th Cavalry. SOURCE: *ANJ* 39 (8 Mar 1902): 671.

STANTFORD, Moses; Private; Band/10th Cav. Mentioned Jan 1874 as not being absent without leave. SOURCE: LS, 10 Cav, 1873–83.

STANTON, Daniel; Private; G/9th Cav. Killed in action in New Mexico, 1 Sep 1880. *See* **ROBINSON,** James, Sergeant, G/9th Cavalry

STANTON, James; Private; K/10th Cav. Served in 10th Cavalry, 1898; remained in U.S. during war with Spain. SOURCE: Cashin, *Under Fire with the Tenth Cavalry*, 349.

STANTON, Nathaniel; Private; F/9th Cav. Born Charleston, SC; Ht 5'9", black eyes, hair, and complexion; occupation farmer; enlisted, age 27, 1 Oct 1866; discharged 18 Mar 1867. SOURCE: Register of Enlistments.

STAPLES, Hamilton; Private; M/10th Cav. Released to duty from treatment for acute gonorrhea, Ft Robinson, NE, 16 Oct 1903. SOURCE: Post Surgeon to CO, M/10, 16 Oct 1903, LS, Post Surgeon, Ft Robinson.

STARGALL, Charlie; Private; 10th Cav. Drunk, Ft Bayard, NM, Nov 1891; jailed after refusing to obey order to desist from Sgt. Shelvin Shropshire, 10th Cavalry. SOURCE: Billington, *New Mexico's Buffalo Soldiers*, 165.

STARKEY, George; Private; D/10th Cav. Served in 10th Cavalry in Cuba, 1898. SOURCE: Cashin, *Under Fire with the Tenth Cavalry*, 341.

STARLING, Eli; Private; H/24th Inf. Enlisted Ft McPherson, GA, 18 Dec 1895. SOURCE: Muster Roll, H/24 Inf, May–Jun 1898.

Sick at Siboney, Cuba, disease contracted in line of duty, since 20 Aug 1898. SOURCE: Muster Roll, H/24 Inf, Jul–Aug 1898.

Furlough authorized by surgeon's certificate, 19 Sep–7 Oct 1898; present, sick, since 8 Oct 1898. SOURCE: Muster Roll, H/24 Inf, Sep–Oct 1898.

Sick until 14 Dec 1898; discharged 17 Dec 1898, end of term, character excellent, single; deposits $10, due U.S. for clothing $7.39. SOURCE: Muster Roll, H/24 Inf, Nov–Dec 1898.

Enlisted Ft McPherson, GA, 16 Jan 1899. SOURCE: Muster Roll, H/24 Inf, Jan–Feb 1899.

Deserted from Presidio of San Francisco, CA, 23 Jun 1899. SOURCE: Regt Returns, 24 Inf, Jul 1899.

STARR, Joseph; Private; L/10th Cav. Served in 10th Cavalry, 1898; remained in U.S. during war with Spain. SOURCE: Cashin, *Under Fire with the Tenth Cavalry*, 351.

STARR, Stephen G.; Sergeant; Band/24th Inf. Born Helena, AR, 1845; Ht 6'2", yellow complexion; in C/24th Infantry, 16 Jul 1870; corporal, 1 Jan 1871; transferred to Band/24th Infantry and resigned as corporal, 1 May 1871; discharged 16 Jul 1875; discharged from E/24th Infantry, 20 Sep 1882; reduced to private at own request and transferred to H/24th Infantry, 1 Nov 1885; principal musician, Band/24th Infantry, Ft Supply, Indian Territory, character excellent, 13 Nov 1885. SOURCE: Descriptive Book, 24 Inf NCS & Band.

Sergeant, resides with wife at Ft Supply, Christmas 1885. SOURCE: Cleveland *Gazette*, 9 Jan 1886.

Born Buena Vista, Mexico, of African-Mexican parentage, 5 Feb 1845; between ages 10 and 16 sheepherder and cowboy; moved to U.S. in 1863; enlisted in 65th Volunteer Infantry, 9 Dec 1864; wounded in action at Port Hudson, LA, 29 Dec 1864; discharged 14 Sep 1865; in 41st Infantry 7 Jan 1867–6 Jan 1870; in 24th Infantry 16 Jul 1870–15 Jul 1875, 20 Sep 1877–19 Sep 1882, 16 Oct 1882–15 Oct 1887; in General Service/Detachment of Messengers, 16 Oct 1887–6 Aug 1894, when discharged by act of Congress; in 24th Infantry, 5 Nov 1894–4 Nov 1897; reenlisted 5 Nov 1897; in action at San Juan Hill, Santiago, Cuba, 1898; commissioned second lieutenant, 9th Infantry, U.S. Volunteers, 28 Nov 1898; only education in post schools. SOURCE: Coston, *The Spanish-American War Volunteer*, 57.

Sergeant, D/24th Infantry, wounded in Cuba, 1898. SOURCE: Muller, *The Twenty Fourth Infantry*, 18.

Enlisted in 41st Infantry in 1867; wounded at San Juan Hill in 1898. SOURCE: San Francisco *Chronicle*, 15 Nov 1899.

Resided at 150 South 4th East, Salt Lake City, in 1898. SOURCE: Clark, "A History of the Twenty-fourth," 70.

Sergeant, D/24th Infantry, commissioned second lieutenant, 9th Volunteer Infantry, after Spanish-American War. SOURCE: Cashin, *Under Fire with the Tenth Cavalry*, 360.

Promotion to 9th Infantry and career mentioned. SOURCE: *Wyoming State Tribune*, 18 Dec 1898.

Ordered to report to 48th Infantry at Ft Thomas, KY. SOURCE: *ANJ* 37 (23 Sep 1899): 81.

Mentioned as captain, C/48th Infantry. SOURCE: Beasley, *Negro Trailblazers*, 284.

Retired as sergeant, Band/24th Infantry, 1900. SOURCE: *ANJ* 38 (15 Dec 1900): 373.

STATON, Governor; Corporal; G/25th Inf. Wounded in action at El Caney, Cuba, 1 Jul 1898. SOURCE: Nankivell, *History of the Twenty-fifth Infantry*, 83.

STATON, Samuel; Private; C/24th Inf. Transferred from Reserve Divisional Hospital, Siboney, Cuba, to U.S. on U.S. Army Transport *Santiago* with remittent malarial fever, 25 Jul 1898. SOURCE: Hospital Papers, Spanish-American War.

STEAD, Eugene; Private; F/9th Cav. Died of cholera in the Philippines, 15 Jun 1902. SOURCE: *ANJ* 39 (9 Aug 1902): 1248.

STEED, Albert; Corporal; K/24th Inf. On detached service as scorer, Department Rifle Meet, Ft Bayard, NM. SOURCE: Order 118, Ft Huachuca, AZ, 9 Aug 1893, Name File, 24 Inf.

Enlisted Ft Huachuca, AZ, with eleven years' continuous service, in H/24th Infantry; promoted from private at Tampa, FL, 10 May 1898. SOURCE: Muster Roll, H/24 Inf, May–Jun 1899.

On detached service at Ft McPherson, GA, SOURCE: Muster Roll, H/24 Inf, Jul–Aug 1898.

Transferred to K/24th Infantry, 16 Sep 1898; retained $22.63, deposits $5. SOURCE: Muster Roll, H/24 Inf, Sep–Oct 1898.

STEED, Luke; Private; D/9th Cav. Certificates of final statements of Pvts. Luke Steed and Oscar McGhee, D/9th Cavalry, Ft Washakie, WY, transmitted by chief paymaster, Department of the Platte, to Maj. John S. Loud, Ft Washakie, 20 Jul 1897. SOURCE: Misc Records, DP.

STEEL, Elder; G/10th Cav. Original member of 10th Cavalry; in troop when organized, Ft Leavenworth, KS, 5 Jul 1867. SOURCE: McMiller, "Buffalo Soldiers," 74.

STEEL, Max K.; Private; H/10th Cav. Served in 10th Cavalry, 1898; remained in U.S. during war with Spain. SOURCE: Cashin, *Under Fire with the Tenth Cavalry*, 347.

STEELE, John W.; Private; D/25th Inf. Killed in action, Cuba, 1898. SOURCE: Scipio, *Last of the Black Regulars*, 29; *ANJ* 36 (18 Feb 1899): 590.

Killed in action at El Caney, Cuba, 1 Jul 1898; buried one mile south of El Caney; wood headboard, surrounded by stones, has name cut into it; name enclosed in tightly corked bottle buried at head of grave. SOURCE: Scrapbook, 25 Inf, II.

STEELE, Waddell C.; Corporal; E/10th Cav. Commissioned first lieutenant at Camp Des Moines, IA, 15 Oct 1917. SOURCE: Glass, *History of the Tenth Cavalry*, appendix M.

STEFY, William; Private; M/10th Cav. Served in 10th Cavalry, 1898; remained in U.S. during war with Spain. SOURCE: Cashin, *Under Fire with the Tenth Cavalry*, 352.

STEINTON, Elijah; M/10th Cav. Original member of 10th Cavalry; in troop when organized, Ft Riley, KS, 15 Oct 1867. SOURCE: McMiller, "Buffalo Soldiers," 79.

STEPHEN, H.; Corporal; E/24th Inf. Promoted from private, Ft Bayard, NM, May 1891. SOURCE: Cleveland *Gazette*, 9 May 1891.

STEPHENS, William; Private; K/25th Inf. At Ft Niobrara, NE, 1904. SOURCE: Wilson, "History of Fort Niobrara."

STEPHENSON, Frank J.; Private; C/9th Cav. At Ft D. A. Russell, WY, in 1910; resident of 319 E. Hall St., Charlotte, NC. SOURCE: *Illustrated Review: Ninth Cavalry*, with picture.

STEPHENSON, Henry; F/10th Cav. Original member of 10th Cavalry; in troop when organized, Ft Leavenworth, KS, 21 Jun 1867. SOURCE: McMiller, "Buffalo Soldiers," 73.

STEPHENSON, James; Sergeant; F/10th Cav. At Camp Supply, Indian Territory, 1870. See **TAYLOR**, John, Private, F/10th Cavalry

STEPNEY, Alexander; Private; 9th Cav. Born Anne Arundel Co., MD; pension of $2 per month as of Apr 1891 based on injury to left knee; wife Fannie (Butler) previously married to Seth Jonas, formerly of A/9th Cavalry; pension of $12 per month in 1913, at which time employed on contract carrying mail from depot to Ft Robinson, NE. SOURCE: VA File SC 874522, Alexander Stepney.

Former slave; during Civil War was servant to Confederate officer; after discharge in 1891 found employment at ranch in western Nebraska as bunkhouse cook; then moved to Crawford, NE, and worked as mail carrier until death. SOURCE: Schubert, *Buffalo Soldiers, Braves and the Brass*, 153.

Buried at Ft Robinson, 18 May 1918. SOURCE: List of Interments, Ft Robinson.

STEPP, Thaddeus W.; 2nd Lt; D/8th Ill Inf. Died in Minnesota. SOURCE: Taylor, "Minnesota Black Spanish-American War Veterans."

STEVENS, Albert; Private; A/10th Cav. Commander, 10th Cavalry, forwards final statement and inventory of effects of deceased Private Stevens to Adjutant General, 3 Jan 1876. SOURCE: ES, 10 Cav, 1873–83.

STEVENS, Jacob W.; 1st Sgt; K/24th Inf. Born Baltimore; awarded distinguished service medal for role in engagement near Santa Ana, Philippines, 6 Oct 1899. SOURCE: Koger, *The Maryland Negro in Our Wars*, 23.

Certificate of merit awarded 8 Dec 1903 for coolness and good judgment under fire as first sergeant, K/24th Infantry, in engagement at Santa Ana, 6 Oct 1899. SOURCE: GO 32, AGO, 6 Feb 1904.

At Cabanatuan, Philippines, 1900–1901. *See* **COOK**, Isaiah, Private; **FAGGINS**, John H., Private; **HARGRAVES**, John C., Private; **HARRIS**, Thomas M., Private; **INGMAN**, James, Sergeant; **LEE**, William, Private; **McHENRY**, Joseph, Private; **MORRIS**, Thomas, Private; **MYERS**, Frank, Private; **SALES**, Clarence, Private; and **SHAVER**, Lee, Private, all K/24th Infantry

STEVENS, John; QM Sgt; B/10th Cav. Original member of 10th Cavalry; in troop when organized, Ft Leavenworth, KS, 1 Apr 1867. SOURCE: McMiller, "Buffalo Soldiers," 69.

On daily duty with Quartermaster Department, camp near Ft Dodge, KS, 9–16 Apr 1869. SOURCE: SO 14, Det 10 Cav, 9 Apr 1869, and SO 16, Det 10 Cav, 16 Apr 1869, Orders, Det 10 Cav.

STEVENS, John F.; Private; L/9th Cav. Veteran of Philippine Insurrection; at Ft D. A. Russell, WY, in 1910; resident of St. Mary's Co., MD. SOURCE: *Illustrated Review: Ninth Cavalry*, with picture.

STEVENS, Joseph; Private; H/10th Cav. Served in 10th Cavalry, 1898; remained in U.S. during war with Spain. SOURCE: Cashin, *Under Fire with the Tenth Cavalry*, 347.

STEVENS, Joseph J.; Private; B/10th Cav. Served in 10th Cavalry, 1898; remained in U.S. during war with Spain. SOURCE: Cashin, *Under Fire with the Tenth Cavalry*, 333.

STEVENS, Milton; Sergeant; C/10th Cav. Corporal, mentioned for gallantry against Kiowas and Comanches, Wichita Agency, Indian Territory, 22–23 Aug 1874. SOURCE: Baker, Roster.

Former sergeant; commander, 10th Cavalry, approves his request to have his sentence mitigated to two years. SOURCE: CO, 10 Cav, to AAG, Department of Texas, 18 Sep 1877, ES, 10 Cav, 1872–81.

STEVENS, Samuel; Private; D/24th Inf. Convicted by court martial, Cabanatuan, Philippines, 28 May 1901, of having altercation with Pvt. Clarence Sales, K/24th Infantry, using abusive language, and carrying revolver contrary to post orders; sentenced to $10 fine and twenty days; witnesses: Sergeant Brice and Private Willis, D/24th Infantry, Private Robinson and Corporal Camp, K/24th Infantry. SOURCE: Name File, 24 Inf.

STEVENSON, Guy; Private; M/9th Cav. Sentenced to death by general court martial, Catbalogan, Samar, Philippines, for criminal assault (rape); sentence commuted by President Roosevelt to dishonorable discharge and fifteen years at military prison, Ft Leavenworth, KS. SOURCE: *ANJ* 39 (26 Jul 1902): 1194; San Francisco *Chronicle*, 26 Jul 1902.

STEVENSON, James; Sergeant; B/10th Cav. At Ft Lyon, CO, Mar 1869. SOURCE: LR, Det 10 Cav, 1868–69.

STEVENSON, John T.; Private; E/10th Cav. Formerly with A/10th Cavalry, reenlists in E/10th Cavalry; both units at Ft Griffin, TX, Jun 1875. SOURCE: LS, 10 Cav, 1873–83.

STEVENSON, William; C/10th Cav. Original member of 10th Cavalry; in troop when organized, Ft Leavenworth, KS, 14 May 1867. SOURCE: McMiller, "Buffalo Soldiers," 70.

STEVESON, James W.; F/10th Cav. Original member of 10th Cavalry; in troop when organized, Ft Leavenworth, KS, 21 Jun 1867. SOURCE: McMiller, "Buffalo Soldiers," 73.

STEWARD; Private; B/10th Cav. At Ft Apache, AZ, 1890, subscribed $.50 to testimonial to General Grierson. SOURCE: List of subscriptions, 23 Apr 1890, 10th Cavalry papers, MHI.

STEWARD, Frank R.; Captain; G/49th Inf. Son of Chaplain Theophilus G. Steward; born Wilmington, DE, 3 Mar 1872; graduated from Harvard College, 1896, "prominent in debating, representing Harvard in joint debate with both Princeton and Yale"; president, Harvard Forum; Harvard Law, 1899; private and second lieutenant, 8th Volunteer Infantry, 1898. SOURCE: *ANJ* 37 (18 Nov 1899): 278.

To represent Harvard in upcoming debate with Yale. SOURCE: Cleveland *Gazette*, 2 May 1896.

Private, corporal, sergeant, M and A/8th Volunteer Infantry, 12 Aug 1898–27 Jun 1899; second lieutenant, 8th Infantry, 10 Jan–6 Mar 1899; summary court officer, Paranaque, Philippines, 3–21 Mar 1900; judge, San Pablo, Philippines, 17 Oct 1900–16 May 1901; commander, detachment, Las Pinas, Philippines, which repelled midnight attack, 24 Sep 1900; commander in engagement at Barrio San Ignacio, San Pablo, Laguna, Philippines, 18 Dec 1900; commanded following stations in the Philippines: Zapote Bridge, 22 Mar–3 Jun 1900; Las Pinas, 4 Jun–10 Oct 1900; San Pablo, 25 Jan–8 Apr 1901; Alaminas, 9 Apr–16 May 1901. SOURCE: Descriptive Book, G/49 Inf.

Passed through town Tuesday night with ten recruits en route to Jefferson Barracks, MO; was in Harvard Law when volunteered and has A.B. degree from Harvard; "Captain Steward travels in a Pullman." SOURCE: Richmond *Planet*, 14 Oct 1899.

Letters from headquarters, 49th Infantry, Paranaque, Philippines, early 1900, and from San Pablo, 22 Jan 1901. SOURCE: Gatewood, *"Smoked Yankees"*, 263, 294.

His company engaged insurgents at Zapote Bridge and Las Pinas, 24 Sep 1900. SOURCE: *ANJ* 38 (1 Dec 1900): 333.

Graduate of Washington Colored High School and Harvard; lawyer, Pittsburgh, PA. SOURCE: *The Voice of the Negro* 1 (Jun 1904): 222, with picture, 221.

Biography and picture. SOURCE: *Colored American Magazine* 2 (Jan 1901): 199, 202.

Author of "Pepe's Anting-Anting," *Colored American Magazine* 5 (Sep 1902): 358–62; "Starlik," *Colored American Magazine* 6 (May 1903): 387–91; "The Men Who Prey," *Colored American Magazine* 6 (Oct 1903): 720–24; chapter 12, "Colored Officers," in T. G. Steward, *The Colored Regulars*.

Biographical sketch. SOURCE: Logan and Winston, eds., *Dictionary of American Negro Biography*, 569.

STEWARD, George; Private; K/24th Inf. At San Carlos, AZ, 1890. *See* **HARDEE**, James A., Private, K/24th Infantry

STEWARD, Isaiah; Private; M/10th Cav. Original member of 10th Cavalry; in troop when organized, Ft Riley, KS, 15 Oct 1867. SOURCE: McMiller, "Buffalo Soldiers," 79.

Mentioned as reenlisting, Sep 1877. SOURCE: ES, 10 Cav, 1873–83.

STEWARD, James; Private; I/10th Cav. Served in 10th Cavalry in Cuba, 1898. SOURCE: Cashin, *Under Fire with the Tenth Cavalry*, 348.

STEWARD, Lewis; Private; G/25th Inf. Born Baltimore; occupation laborer; Ht 5'6", black eyes, hair, complexion; enlisted New Orleans, age 24, 11 Oct 1866; assigned to B/39th Infantry; discharged from G/25th Infantry, 1 May 1869. SOURCE: Register of Enlistments.

STEWARD, Lewis; Private; F/9th Cav. Buried at Ft Robinson, NE, 17 Aug 1890. SOURCE: List of Interments, Ft Robinson.

STEWARD, Samuel; Private; A/10th Cav. Received at U.S. Military Prison, Ft Leavenworth, KS, 22 May 1884; discharged on certficate of disability with enlarged heart and extensive valvular disease of heart, incurable, 16 Oct 1884. SOURCE: Certificates of Disability, DivMo, 1875–87.

STEWARD, Theophilus G.; Chaplain; 25th Inf. Belongs to old colored family which goes back to pre-Revolutionary War New Jersey freemen; chaplain since 1891; wife a medical doctor at Wilberforce University; six sons: two Harvard graduates, one in medical school at University of Minnesota, three at Wilberforce. SOURCE: San Francisco *Chronicle*, 22 Oct 1899.

Career abstract: taught school, 1863–64; entered ministry; taught school, Marion, SC, and Stewart Co., GA, while in south; cashier, Freedmen's Bank, Macon, GA; in Delaware, 1871–73; in Haiti, Dec 1874; pastor of Bridge Street African Methodist Episcopal Church, Brooklyn, NY, 1875–77; in West Philadelphia, PA, Divinity School of Protestant Episcopal Church, 1877–80, graduating at head of class; one year in Frankford, PA; two years in Delaware; two years in Union Church, Philadelphia; then Metropolitan African Methodist Episcopal Church, Washington, DC. SOURCE: AGO File 4634 ACP 91, T. G. Steward.

Spent 1865–67 in South Carolina and Georgia "doing missionary work"; large brick church in Macon, built during his management and named Steward's Church over his protest; registrar and elections judge, Stewart Co., GA; wrote Republican platform in Delaware, 1872–73; member of state central committee, Brooklyn, NY, 1875–78, when knew Dr. Susan McKinney; now one of few delegates of African Methodist Episcopal Church in Ecumenical Conference planned for Washington, DC, this November. SOURCE: Steward, 1410 Pierce Place, Washington, DC, to John R. Lynch, 2 Jun 1891, AGO File 4634 ACP 91, T. G. Steward.

Accompanied Bishop D. A. Payne and sailed from New York to Charleston, SC, on U.S. government vessel *Arago*, 9 May 1865; then "itinerant licentiate," became deacon of South Carolina Conference, organized 16 May 1865 at colored Presbyterian Church, Calhoun Street (then Boundary Street) at northern limit of Charleston near King Street. SOURCE: Payne, *History of the African Methodist Episcopal Church*, 469.

At opening session of African Methodist Episcopal Conference, Charleston, Zion Presbyterian Church, May 1865, Steward assigned to Beaufort, SC. SOURCE: Taylor, *The Negro in South Carolina*, 113–14.

President B. F. Lee of Wilberforce University resigned 1884; teachers' committee endorsed Steward as successor; in election John G. Mitchell got seventeen of thirty-one votes; Steward followers protested; on next vote Mitchell's brother, S. T. Mitchell, elected. SOURCE: McGinnis, *A History and an Interpretation of Wilberforce University*, 55–56.

For last seventeen months minister of Metropolitan African Methodist Episcopal Church, Washington, DC; has reduced debt by $4,000. SOURCE: Cleveland *Gazette*, 3 Dec 1887.

Letter from Col. James Biddle, commander, 9th Cavalry, Ft Robinson, NE, to Steward, 31 Jan 1893, says Biddle has never been in action with his regiment but has with colored soldiers, whose casualties wholly equalled whites: "in garrison my soldiers are the peers of any, and I doubt not in action would prove the same." SOURCE: LS, Ft Robinson.

Letter from Lt. Gen. Nelson Miles to Steward, 5 Aug 1893, praises 40th Infantry, which Miles commanded after Civil War. SOURCE: Nankivell, *History of the Twenty-fifth Infantry*, 9.

"One of the most scholarly ministers of the A.M.E. Church," recently appointed chaplain. SOURCE: Cleveland *Gazette*, 8 Aug 1891.

Mentioned as third Afro-American chaplain. SOURCE: Cleveland *Gazette*, 29 Aug 1891.

Son Benjamin visited him at Ft Missoula, MT, Christmas 1891. SOURCE: *ANJ* 29 (9 Jan 1891): 347.

Efficiency Report, Ft Missoula, MT, 16 Feb 1893, notes that Steward knows French, German, Hebrew, and Greek. SOURCE: AGO File 4634 ACP 91, T. G. Steward.

Authorized one-month leave from Ft Missoula. SOURCE: *ANJ* 30 (18 Mar 1893): 495.

Andrew S. Burt, Efficiency Report, 12 Feb 1894, calls Steward "the most conscientious chaplain in the discharge of his duties I have ever served with. I deem him an ornament to the service." SOURCE: AGO File 4634 ACP 91, T. G. Steward.

Author of "Mortality of Negro," *Social Economist* 9 (1895): 204.

Expected to leave Ft Missoula this week to go East for Christmas. SOURCE: *ANJ* 34 (14 Nov 1896): 174.

Student at University of Montana, 1897–98. SOURCE: Joiner, *A Half Century of Freedom*, 51.

Author of "a little publication titled, 'Active Service or Gospel Work among the U.S. Soldiers.'" SOURCE: Indianapolis *Freeman*, 11 Sep 1897.

At Chattanooga, TN, with regiment; his wife a practicing physician "and a thorough scholar . . . also a musician." SOURCE: Indianapolis *Freeman*, 30 Apr 1898.

Letters from Chickamauga, GA, 28 May 1898, and Manila, Philippines, 19 Jan 1900, in Gatewood, *"Smoked Yankees"*, 25–26, 262–63.

At Chickamauga forced with family "to travel to and from the park, with the common herd and not permitted to travel as a United States officer." SOURCE: Indianapolis *Freeman*, 24 Dec 1898.

Author of "The New Colored Soldier," *The Independent* 50 (13 Jun 1898): 782–83.

Speaker at Peace Jubilee, Bridge Street Church, Brooklyn, sponsored by Montauk Soldiers Relief Association, Dr. Susan McKinney Steward, president; praised black troops as "reserved, obedient and . . . good soldiers . . . filled with a stock of good humor and good cheer." SOURCE: Cleveland *Gazette*, 24 Sep 1898.

Desiring to preserve for future and state to present generation of Negroes history of "the valorous conduct of the four black regiments in Cuba," and to further justify policy which keeps blacks in Army, asks for four months on detached service, including one month in Cuba, to gather data, write, publish, especially while Chaplain McCleery is available to replace him, all "for the cause of my race and my country." SOURCE: Steward, Ft Logan, CO, to AG, USA, 19 Dec 1898, AGO File 4634 ACP 91, T. G. Steward.

Authorized one-month leave by Special Order 122, Department of Colorado, 22 Dec 1898.

Three months of leave approved by memorandum, Adjutant General's Office, 14 Jan 1899.

Leave extended two months by Special Order 12, Adjutant General's Office, 16 Jan 1899.

Transferred to Ft Apache, AZ, at end of leave in accordance with Special Order 44, Adjutant General's Office, 23 Feb 1899.

Ordered to Ft Apache. SOURCE: *ANJ* 36 (4 Mar 1899): 631.

Bishop Benjamin Arnett, Wilberforce University, endorsed his plan to write history of colored regiments and asked President McKinley for approval, 23 Feb 1899. SOURCE: AGO File 4634 ACP 91, T. G. Steward.

The War Department agreed with Bishop Arnett that Steward was "a very suitable man to write the proposed history and that every facility will be accorded him for the prosecution of this task," in letter from Adjutant General, 1 Mar 1899. SOURCE: AGO File 4634 ACP 91, T. G. Steward.

L. J. Coppin, pastor, Bethel African Methodist Episcopal Church, Philadelphia, wrote President McKinley, 7 Mar 1899, expressing regret of Philadelphia African Methodist Episcopal pastors regarding Steward's assignment to Ft Apache. SOURCE: AGO File 4634 ACP 91, T. G. Steward.

Gen. Miles rescinded Steward's transfer to Ft Apache because chaplain should be on duty with his regiment, 8 Mar 1899. SOURCE: AGO File 4634 ACP 91, T. G. Steward.

"The well-known author" has undertaken important work of an accurate, complete history of the four black regiments in Cuba; now has a novel in press; "he will bring to the work wide literary experience, a painstaking regard to accuracy, as well as an enthusiastic admiration for the black soldier." SOURCE: Indianapolis *Freeman*, 18 Mar 1899.

Ordered on temporary duty to Wilberforce. SOURCE: *ANJ* 36 (25 Mar 1899): 710.

To write history of black regular regiments after visit to Cuba to go over battlefield where they distinguished themselves. SOURCE: Cleveland *Gazette*, 15 Apr 1899.

His most important theological works are *Death, Hades, and the Resurrection*, *Divine Attributes*, *End of the World*, and *Genesis Re-Read*, which examines latest conclusions of science and their bearing on Old Testament; this book "extensively read, highly endorsed by press and clergy," and used as reference book at Wilberforce; also wrote *Religious Life in the U.S. Army*. SOURCE: Indianapolis *Freeman*, 20 May 1899.

Author of pamphlet on "how the Black St. Domingo Legion saved the patriot army in the siege of Savanna in 1779." SOURCE: Cleveland *Gazette*, 1 Jul 1899.

To proceed to the Philippines on U.S. Army Transport *Newport* on or about 23 Oct 1899. SOURCE: *ANJ* 37 (28 Oct 1899): 195.

Arrived in Manila from detached service; appointed by Secretary of War to write complete history of colored troops in war with Spain, which he just finished; will preach at Soldiers Institute tomorrow. SOURCE: Manila *Times*, 25 Nov 1899.

Arrived in the Philippines, early Dec 1899; "the boys were glad to welcome him as his literary work is a rare treat and his presence is much enjoyed after an extended absence." SOURCE: Private Rienzi Lemus in Richmond *Planet*, 27 Jan 1900.

Letter. SOURCE: *The Independent* 52 (1 Feb 1900): 312–14.

Letter from Manila, no date, comments on sins of Americans in the Philippines and immorality of open door policy. SOURCE: Cleveland *Gazette*, 29 Dec 1900.

Poem "The Aged Patriot's Lament," in Manila *Times*, 6 Feb 1901.

Visiting regimental garrisons, Philippines, Dec 1900. SOURCE: Richmond *Planet*, 16 Feb 1901.

Author of articles "Holy Week in Manila," *Colored American Magazine* 2 (Apr 1901): 446–48; "Two Years in Luzon," *Colored American Magazine* 4 (Nov 1901): 4–10, 4 (Jan–Feb 1902): 164–70, 5 (Aug 1902): 244–49.

Granted three-month furlough, May 1901, "in view of exceptional circumstances." SOURCE: *ANJ* 38 (22 Jun 1901): 1043.

Just back from twelve months in the Philippines; delivered lecture at Wilberforce Chapel last Tuesday on "the Philippines," with Mrs. Steward appearing on platform "in full Philippino costume, the dress having been presented to her through the chaplain, by the distinguished sister of the great Philippine scholar, author, and statesman, Don Pedro A. Paterno, late chief of Aguinaldo's cabinet." SOURCE: Indianapolis *Freeman*, 27 Jul 1901.

Visited General Hospital, Presidio of San Francisco, CA, then went to Philippines with son on 1 Oct 1901 to resume duty after four-month leave. SOURCE: Cleveland *Gazette*, 26 Oct 1901.

25th Infantry band recently gave concert to Mrs. Steward, visiting husband at Ft Niobrara, NE. SOURCE: Indianapolis *Freeman*, 15 Nov 1903.

Lt. Gen. Adna R. Chaffee thanks Steward for sending translation of French "Military Education and Instruction" from Ft Niobrara, 3 Feb 1904. SOURCE: AGO File 4634 ACP 91, T. G. Steward.

Praise for his just-published *The Colored Regulars in the United States Army*, with editorial against prejudice against blacks in the Army; claims Steward seeks to arouse American people to proper sense of gratitude and win open door to promotion for blacks. SOURCE: New York *Age*, 8 Jun 1905.

Undated letter from Ft Niobrara advocates military education. SOURCE: Indianapolis *Freeman*, 19 Aug 1905.

On recent trip to Mexico observed that Mexican army had no color distinction; in New York City and Philadelphia saw that blacks' hold on labor market for common labor was improving as compared to "Pat and Antonio." SOURCE: Cleveland *Gazette*, 22 Dec 1906.

Steward, Bridgeton, NJ, 12 Jan 1907, requests retirement to Wilberforce, OH, as soon as possible. SOURCE: AGO File 4634 ACP 91, T. G. Steward.

Retires in Apr to home at Wilberforce on reaching mandatory retirement age; born Apr 1843. SOURCE: Cleveland *Gazette*, 23 Feb 1907.

Marriage of son, Dr. Charles G. Steward, to Maude A. Trotter, reported. SOURCE: Washington *Bee*, 2 Mar 1907.

African Methodist Episcopal clergyman, retired from service Apr 1907, after twenty-five years. SOURCE: *Colored American Magazine* 12 (May 1907): 391.

Elected vice president of Wilberforce University in 1908. SOURCE: Joiner, *A Half Century of Freedom*, 47.

B. F. Lee, Secretary, Council of Bishops, African Methodist Episcopal Church, Wilberforce, informs President Taft, 8 Feb 1911, that he has commissioned Steward to represent his church at the Universal Races Conference, London, England, Jul 1911. SOURCE: AGO File 4634 ACP 91, T. G. Steward.

Resident of Wilberforce; will preach at St. John's African Methodist Episcopal Church, Cleveland, OH, on 3 May, and give his famous lecture, "Our Civilization," on 4 May. SOURCE: Cleveland *Gazette*, 2 May 1914.

Author of *The Haitian Revolution, 1791 to 1804, or, Sidelights on the French Revolution* (New York: Neale Publishing Co., 1914).

Advertisement: *The Army and Navy Register* says of his new book, *The Haitian Revolution*, "No more interesting book has ever been written"; Albert Bushnell Hart says, "It cannot fail to be serviceable both for the understanding of the Negro race and the relations of France with the West Indies." SOURCE: Cleveland *Gazette*, 10 Jul 1915.

Vice president of Wilberforce University, in charge of "Wilberforce Week" campaign to interest people of Cleveland in the university; will deliver principal address at mass meeting, St. John's African Methodist Episcopal Church, 30 Jul 1916; goal is $50,000; Steward and others will take campaign to Indianapolis, Louisville, and elsewhere. SOURCE: Cleveland *Gazette*, 29 Jul 1916.

"A master of controversy," according to Cromwell, *The Negro in American History*.

Dr. S. Maria Steward, wife of Chaplain Steward, born Brooklyn, NY, 1845, to Sylvanus and Anna Smith; valedictorian, New York Homeopathic College for Women; practiced medicine in New York State for many years; member, King's Co. Homeopathic Society and New York State Medical Society; organist at Bridge Street African Methodist Episcopal Church for 28 years; mother of two and lately resident physician at Wilberforce University; "a woman of rare charm and ability." SOURCE: "Men of the Month," *Crisis* 18 (May 1918): 15.

Susan Maria Steward, Resident Physician, College of Arts and Sciences, Wilberforce, 1900–1908. SOURCE:

McGinnis, *A History and an Interpretation of Wilberforce University*, 151.

Susan Steward was author and publisher of *Woman in Medicine*, 1915.

Family history. SOURCE: Steward and Steward, *Gouldtown*; Broadstone, *History of Greene County*, 968–73.

Listed with publications. SOURCE: Coyle, *Ohio Authors and Their Books*, 599.

Biographical article. SOURCE: Indianapolis *Freeman*, 20 May 1899.

Biographical sketch. SOURCE: Logan and Winston, eds., *Dictionary of American Negro Biography*, 570–71.

Pictures. SOURCE: Cashin, *Under Fire with the Tenth Cavalry*, 141; Nankivell, *History of the Twenty-fifth Infantry*, 55.

Biographical sketch of wife Susan McKinney Steward. SOURCE: Hine et al., eds., *Black Women in America*, 1109–12.

Mentioned. SOURCE: Acknowledgements to Mary Curtis, *The Black Soldier*.

Biography of son Gustavus A. Steward. SOURCE: Boris, ed., *Who's Who in Colored America*, 192.

STEWARD, Zachariah; Trumpeter; G/10th Cav. Served with distinction in 10th Cavalry in Cuba, 1898. SOURCE: Cashin, *Under Fire with the Tenth Cavalry*, 178, 345.

STEWART; Sergeant; 9th Cav. At Ft Craig, NM, 1881. *See* **RICHARDSON**, William, Private, D/9th Cavalry

STEWART, Anderson F.; Private; K/10th Cav. Served in 10th Cavalry, 1898; remained in U.S. during war with Spain. SOURCE: Cashin, *Under Fire with the Tenth Cavalry*, 349.

STEWART, Charles A.; Corporal; M/9th Cav. Convicted by general court martial, Columbus Barracks, OH, of desertion, 5 Sep–3 Oct 1881; sentenced to dishonorable discharge and two years. SOURCE: GCMO 66, AGO, 9 Nov 1881.

STEWART, Charlie; Private; I/24th Inf. Enlisted Nashville, 27 Feb 1899. SOURCE: Muster Roll, I/24 Inf, Mar–Apr 1899.

Fined $3 by summary court, 4 May 1899. SOURCE: Muster Roll, I/24 Inf, May–Jun 1899.

Allotted $10 per month for six months to Fannie Stewart. SOURCE: Muster Roll, I/24 Inf, Sep–Oct 1899.

STEWART, Daniel; Private; F/24th Inf. Deserted from Camp McKinley, Philippines, 1 Aug 1899. SOURCE: Regt Returns, 24 Inf, Sep 1899.

STEWART, Edward J.; Private; L/24th Inf. Enlisted in H/24th Infantry, Columbus Barracks, OH, with three years' service, 17 Nov 1897; absent sick, disease contracted in line of duty, Ft Douglas, UT, 20 Apr–30 Aug 1898. SOURCE: Muster Roll, H/24 Inf, May–Jun and Jul–Aug 1898.

Transferred to L/24th Infantry, 7 Oct 1898; deposits $18, clothing $3.86. SOURCE: Muster Roll, H/24 Inf, Sep–Oct 1898.

STEWART, Frank; 24th Inf. Served in 38th Infantry and 24th Infantry; age 84 and new subscriber. SOURCE: *Winners of the West* 10 (Nov 1933): 2.

STEWART, Frank; Private; K/10th Cav. At Ft Robinson, NE, 1904; member of troop orchestra. SOURCE: Barrow, "Christmas in the United States Army," 96.

STEWART, Frank H.; Private; A/9th Cav. At Ft Robinson, NE, 1894. SOURCE: Court Martial Records, Plummer.

STEWART, Harmon; Private; K/9th Cav. At Ft D. A. Russell, WY, in 1910; sharpshooter; resident of Berkeley Springs, WV. SOURCE: *Illustrated Review: Ninth Cavalry*, with picture.

STEWART, John; I/10th Cav. Served 1881–86; died in Baltimore. SOURCE: *Winners of the West* 10 (Sep 1933): 3.

STEWART, John; Sergeant; B/10th Cav. Blacksmith, at Ft Apache, AZ, 1890, subscribed $.50 to testimonial to General Grierson. SOURCE: List of subscriptions, 23 Apr 1890, 10th Cavalry papers, MHI.

Served as blacksmith in 10th Cavalry in Cuba, 1898. SOURCE: Cashin, *Under Fire with the Tenth Cavalry*, 338.

Retired as sergeant, Apr 1900. SOURCE: *ANJ* 37 (5 May 1900): 851.

STEWART, John; Private; B/9th Cav. Veteran of Philippine Insurrection; at Ft D. A. Russell, WY, in 1910. SOURCE: *Illustrated Review: Ninth Cavalry*.

STEWART, Johnie; Private; B/10th Cav. Served in 10th Cavalry in Cuba, 1898. SOURCE: Cashin, *Under Fire with the Tenth Cavalry*, 338.

STEWART, Leon; Private; L/9th Cav. At Ft D. A. Russell, WY, in 1910; marksman; resident of St. Louis. SOURCE: *Illustrated Review: Ninth Cavalry*, with picture.

STEWART, Moses; Private; 24th Inf. Died of chronic pulmonary tuberculosis on board U.S. Army Transport *Kilpatrick* bound for San Francisco, 22 Mar 1902. SOURCE: *ANJ* 39 (5 Apr 1902): 786.

STEWART, William; B/10th Cav. Original member of 10th Cavalry; in troop when organized, Ft Leavenworth, KS, 1 Apr 1867. SOURCE: McMiller, "Buffalo Soldiers," 69.

STEWART, William; Private; C/10th Cav. At Ft Robinson, NE; post surgeon recommends discharge of six-year veteran because venereal disease makes him unfit for service. SOURCE: Post Surgeon to Post Adj, 10 Feb 1904, LS, Post Surgeon, Ft Robinson.

STEWART, William; Private; B/9th Cav. Veteran of Philippine Insurrection; at Ft D. A. Russell, WY, in 1910. SOURCE: *Illustrated Review: Ninth Cavalry.*

STEWART, William G.; Private; A/10th Cav. Served in 10th Cavalry, 1898; remained in U.S. during war with Spain. SOURCE: Cashin, *Under Fire with the Tenth Cavalry*, 337.

STILL, Revere N.; Corporal; K/10th Cav. Trumpeter, at Ft Robinson, NE, 1904; ranked number 229 among rifle experts with 67.33 percent. SOURCE: GO 79, AGO, 1 Jun 1905.

Ranked number 466 among rifle experts with 68.67 percent, 1906. SOURCE: GO 101, AGO, 31 May 1906.

Ranked number one in Northern Division pistol competition, Ft Sheridan, IL, 1906. SOURCE: GO 198, AGO, 6 Dec 1906; Glass, *History of the Tenth Cavalry*, 15.

Corporal, K/10th Cavalry; ranked number seven, Division of the Philippines pistol competition, Ft William McKinley, Rizal, Philippines, 1907.

STITH; Private; B/10th Cav. At Ft Apache, AZ, 1890, subscribed $.50 to testimonial to General Grierson. SOURCE: List of subscriptions, 23 Apr 1890, 10th Cavalry papers, MHI.

STITH, Nathan; Sergeant; 10th Cav. Private, M/10th Cavalry, assigned to Ft Riley, KS, in accordance with Special Order 252, Department of the Missouri, 28 Dec 1903.

Sergeant, wounded in action at Naco, AZ, 17 Oct 1914. SOURCE: Cleveland *Gazette*, 13 May 1916.

STITH, William A.; Sergeant; M/10th Cav. Commissioned first lieutenant, Camp Des Moines, IA, 15 Oct 1917. SOURCE: Glass, *History of the Tenth Cavalry*, appendix M.

STOCKTON, James; Private; C/10th Cav. Served in 10th Cavalry, 1898; remained in U.S. during war with Spain. SOURCE: Cashin, *Under Fire with the Tenth Cavalry*, 340.

STOKES, Cornelius; E/48th Inf. Convicted of entering native house in violation of standing orders, Aug 1900; sentenced to five years.

STOKES, Earnest; Private; F/24th Inf. Recommended for certificate of merit for gallantry, Naguilian, Luzon, Philippines, 7 Dec 1899. SOURCE: *ANJ* 39 (15 Feb 1902): 594–95.

Awarded certificate of merit for distinguished gallantry, Naguilian, 7 Dec 1899, on 10 Mar 1902. SOURCE: GO 86, AGO, 24 Jul 1902.

STOKES, Elwood; M/10th Cav. Original member of 10th Cavalry; in troop when organized, Ft Riley, KS, 15 Oct 1867. SOURCE: McMiller, "Buffalo Soldiers," 79.

STOKES, Harry D.; Farrier; I/10th Cav. At Ft Apache, AZ, 1890, subscribed $.50 to testimonial to General Grierson. SOURCE: List of subscriptions, 23 Apr 1890, 10th Cavalry papers, MHI.

STOKES, Henry A.; Corporal; C/9th Cav. Assisted Sgt. Julius LeSage, D/8th Infantry, along with Musician Frank Mayers, L/8th Infantry, and Pvt. John Thomas, F/9th Cavalry, in getting Pvt. Joseph Schwartzentroup, K/8th Infantry, to guardhouse, Ft Robinson, NE, 4 Sep 1887; Schwartzentroup protested that he "would not go with a damned black nigger son of a bitch." SOURCE: Order 182, 12 Sep 1887, Post Orders, Ft Robinson.

STOKES, Marshal; Sergeant; H/24th Inf. Enlisted Chicago, 27 Jul 1895; on detached service at Ft Douglas, UT, since 20 Apr 1898, in charge of company property. SOURCE: Muster Roll, H/24 Inf, May–Jun 1898.

Discharged, end of term, Ft Douglas, 26 Jul 1898; character excellent, single; deposits $699.13, retained $7.66, clothing $41.91. SOURCE: Muster Roll, H/24 Inf, Jul–Aug 1898.

STOKES, Sheppard; QM Sgt; I/24th Inf. Enlisted Ft D. A. Russell, WY, 7 Jan 1899, with twenty-five years' service; appointed wagoner, 17 Jan 1899. SOURCE: Muster Roll, I/24 Inf, Jan–Feb 1899.

On furlough in Cheyenne, WY, 24 Jan–12 Feb 1899.

Promoted to corporal from artificer, 10 Apr 1899. SOURCE: Muster Roll, I/24 Inf, Mar–Apr 1899.

Promoted to sergeant, 4 May 1899; appointed quartermaster sergeant, 5 May 1899. SOURCE: Muster Roll, I/24 Inf, May–Jun 1899.

In the Philippines, on detached service since 30 Sep 1899. SOURCE: Muster Roll, I/24 Inf, Nov–Dec 1899.

STONE, Arthur; D/10th Cav. Original member of 10th Cavalry; in troop when organized, Ft Leavenworth, KS, 1 Jun 1867. SOURCE: McMiller, "Buffalo Soldiers," 71.

STONE, George; Private; E/9th Cav. At Ft D. A. Russell, WY, in 1910; marksman; resident of Talladega, AL. SOURCE: *Illustrated Review: Ninth Cavalry*, with picture.

STONE, John H.; Private; D/24th Inf. Fined $5 by summary court, Cabanatuan, Philippines, 21 May 1901, for disobeying order of Sgt. George Driscoll, D/24th Infantry, to stop using obscene language at dinner table; witnesses: Sergeant Driscoll, Cpl. Walter B. Jackson, and Pvt. William Workman, D/24th Infantry. SOURCE: Name File, 24 Inf.

STONE, Minor; Private; L/9th Cav. On detached service in field, New Mexico, 21 Jan–24 Feb 1881. SOURCE: Regt Returns, 9 Cav, Feb 1881.

STONE, Thomas; Private; C/9th Cav. Veteran of Philippine Insurrection; at Ft D. A. Russell, WY, in 1910; resident of Chatham, VA. SOURCE: *Illustrated Review: Ninth Cavalry*, with picture.

STOREY, Charles J.; Private; K/9th Cav. At Ft D. A. Russell, WY, in 1910; resident of Luray, VA. SOURCE: *Illustrated Review: Ninth Cavalry*, with picture.

STORGEN, Albert; Private; I/24th Inf. Enlisted Ft D. A. Russell, WY, 6 Feb 1899. SOURCE: Muster Roll, I/24 Inf, Jan–Feb 1899.

Fined $2 by summary court, 13 Aug 1899. SOURCE: Muster Roll, I/24 Inf, Jul–Aug 1899.

Absent sick at Cabanatuan, Philippines, since 16 Dec 1899. SOURCE: Muster Roll, I/24 Inf, Nov–Dec 1899.

STOUT, Albert; Ord Sgt; U.S. Army. Sergeant, M/9th Cavalry, wounded in action in San Mateo Mountains, NM, 17 Jan 1880, along with Privates Bolt and Shaw. SOURCE: Hamilton, "History of the Ninth Cavalry," 54.

Appointed ordnance sergeant from sergeant, M/9th Cavalry, 24 Jun 1887. SOURCE: Roster, 9 Cav.

STOUT, Blair; Private; B/10th Cav. Served in 10th Cavalry, 1898; remained in U.S. during war with Spain. SOURCE: Cashin, *Under Fire with the Tenth Cavalry*, 333.

STOVALL, George; Private; D/10th Cav. Killed in action, Santiago, Cuba, 1 Jul 1898. SOURCE: Scipio, *Last of the Black Regulars*, 29; *ANJ* 36 (18 Feb 1899): 590; SecWar, *AR 1898*, 323.

Details of death. SOURCE: Bigelow, *Reminiscences of Santiago*, 114.

STOW, Benjamin; Sergeant; 25th Inf. At Ft Stockton, TX, 1883. SOURCE: Fowler, *The Black Infantry in the West*, 25.

STRAIN, Debret; Private; H/9th Cav. At Ft D. A. Russell, WY, in 1910; resident of Paducah, KY. SOURCE: *Illustrated Review: Ninth Cavalry*.

STRANGE, Edward R.; Private; H/24th Inf. Enlisted Pittsburgh, 18 Apr 1896. SOURCE: Muster Roll, H/24 Inf, May–Jun 1898.

Sick en route to U.S., date of departure unknown, disease contracted in line of duty. SOURCE: Muster Roll, H/24 Inf, Jul–Aug 1898.

Rejoined company from treatment of sickness, 25 Sep 1898; sick in hospital, 29 Oct–26 Dec 1898. SOURCE: Muster Roll, H/24 Inf, Sep–Oct and Nov–Dec 1898.

In hands of civil authorities, Salt Lake City, for drunkenness, 26 Jan–14 Feb 1899; fined $1 by summary court, 15 Feb 1899. SOURCE: Muster Roll, H/24 Inf, Jan–Feb and May–Jun 1899.

See **WILLIAMS**, Walter B., Sergeant Major, 24th Infantry

STRATTON, George; Private; A/38th Inf. Arrested for part in soldiers' revolt at Ft Cummings, NM, autumn 1867; acquitted by court martial. SOURCE: Billington, *New Mexico's Buffalo Soldiers*, 40, 42.

STRATTON, John H.; QM Sgt; D/10th Cav. Born in Pennsylvania; private, L/10th Cavalry, 25 Mar 1883–24 Mar 1888; private and corporal, L/10th Cavalry, and sergeant, C/10th Cavalry, 9 Apr 1888–8 Apr 1893; private, D/10th Cavalry, 27 Apr 1893; corporal, 20 Aug 1893; sergeant, 22 Aug 1896; at Ft Assiniboine, MT, 1897. SOURCE: Baker, Roster.

Served in 10th Cavalry in Cuba, 1898. SOURCE: Cashin, *Under Fire with the Tenth Cavalry*, 341.

Accompanied Capt. John Bigelow to shore from transport in Tampa Harbor to obtain meat for troop rations while serving as quartermaster sergeant, D/10th Cavalry, summer 1898. SOURCE: Bigelow, *Reminiscences of Santiago*, 65.

Died in Minnesota. SOURCE: Taylor, "Minnesota Black Spanish-American War Veterans."

STRATTON, Robert H.; Private; I/9th Cav. At Ft D. A. Russell, WY, in 1910; resident of Nashville. SOURCE: *Illustrated Review: Ninth Cavalry*.

While on guard, Ft D. A. Russell, WY, shot and killed Pvt. Robert Wooden, I/9th Cavalry; now in guardhouse. SOURCE: *Wyoming State Tribune*, 16 Dec 1910.

STRAW, Patrick; Private; Band/9th Cav. With band on detached service at headquarters, District of New Mexico, Santa Fe, 1880; played first alto. SOURCE: Billington, *New Mexico's Buffalo Soldiers*, 226.

STRAWDER, M.; Private; G/9th Cav. Transferred to Ft Crook, NE, in accordance with Special Order 12, Adjutant General's Office, 15 Jan 1897.

STRAYHORN, William M.; Private; H/10th Cav. Served in 10th Cavalry, 1898; remained in U.S. during war with Spain. SOURCE: Cashin, *Under Fire with the Tenth Cavalry*, 347.

STREATER, John; Private; C/25th Inf. Dishonorable discharge, Brownsville. SOURCE: SO 266, AGO, 9 Nov 1906.

STREATER, John J.; Private; C/10th Cav. Served in 10th Cavalry, 1898; remained in U.S. during war with Spain. SOURCE: Cashin, *Under Fire with the Tenth Cavalry*, 340.

STREET, William; Private; C/10th Cav. Served in 10th Cavalry in Cuba, 1898. SOURCE: Cashin, *Under Fire with the Tenth Cavalry*, 340.

Died of valvular heart disease aboard U.S. Army Transport *Thomas*, bound for San Francisco, 29 Jun 1902; buried at Nagasaki, Japan, due to defective casket. SOURCE: *ANJ* 39 (9 Aug 1902): 1249.

STREETER, Wallace; Private; D/24th Inf. At Cabanatuan, Philippines, 1900. *See* **LEAVELL**, William, Private, D/24th Infantry

STREETER, William; Cook; A/10th Cav. Deserter; examined and found to be in good physical condition at Ft Robinson, NE. SOURCE: Post Surgeon to Post Adj, 18 Jan 1903, LS, Post Surgeon, Ft Robinson.

Sentenced at Ft Robinson to dishonorable discharge and confinement, in accordance with Special Order 39, Department of the Missouri, 1903; escaped confinement, 20 May 1903. SOURCE: Regt Returns, 10 Cav, Feb–May 1903.

STREETS, Deleware; Private; K/9th Cav. Veteran of Philippine Insurrection; at Ft D. A. Russell, WY, in 1910; resident of Lexington, KY. SOURCE: *Illustrated Review: Ninth Cavalry*, with picture.

STRICKLAND, John; Private; H/10th Cav. Served in 10th Cavalry, 1898; remained in U.S. during war with Spain. SOURCE: Cashin, *Under Fire with the Tenth Cavalry*, 347.

STRICKLAND, Joseph; Private; H/48th Inf. Died of variola in the Philippines, 20 Mar 1900. SOURCE: *ANJ* 37 (31 Mar 1900): 731.

STRICKLAND, Morgan; Corporal; I/25th Inf. Lance corporal, I/25th Infantry, 1901. *See* **THOMPSON,** Sergeant, M/25th Infantry

Private, I/25th Infantry, fined $7 for lying out of quarters and going off limits, San Isidro, Philippines, 21 May 1902, first conviction. SOURCE: Register of Summary Court, San Isidro.

Private, I/25th Infantry, promoted to corporal. SOURCE: *ANR* 38 (5 Aug 1905): 21.

STRONG, Christopher; A/10th Cav. Original member of 10th Cavalry; in troop when organized, Ft Leavenworth, KS, 18 Feb 1867. SOURCE: McMiller, "Buffalo Soldiers," 68.

Resided in Austin, TX, 1926; remembered Thomas Allsup's marriage to Lulu, Ft Concho, TX, around 1874. SOURCE: Affidavit, Strong, 23 Apr 1926, VA File XC 2659797, Thomas H. Allsup.

STRONG, Wiley L.; Private; M/24th Inf. Shot in abdomen while in camp, night of Houston riot, 1917; remarkably, only soldier in camp wounded; later died. SOURCE: Haynes, *A Night of Violence*, 124, 169.

STROTHER; Private; D/9th Cav. Released from confinement in accordance with telegram, Department of the Platte, 6 Oct 1890.

STROTHER, Albert; Private; H/25th Inf. Died in Cuba, 1 Jul 1898. SOURCE: *ANJ* 36 (18 Feb 1899): 590.

Killed in action at El Caney, Cuba, 1 Jul 1898; buried one mile south of El Caney; wood headboard, surrounded by stones, has name cut into it; name enclosed in tightly corked bottle buried at head of grave. SOURCE: Scrapbook, 25 Inf, II.

STROTHER, Alonzo W.; Private; E/9th Cav. Ranked number one at revolver competition, Departments of the East, the Platte, and California, Bellevue, NE, 17–22 Aug 1891. SOURCE: GO 81, AGO, 6 Oct 1891.

Ranked number one at revolver competition, Departments of the East, the Platte, and California, Bellevue, 15–20 Aug 1892. SOURCE: GO 75, AGO, 3 Nov 1892.

Appointed corporal, F/9th Cavalry, 4 Sep 1892. SOURCE: Roster, 9 Cav.

Distinguished marksman with revolver as private, F/9th Cavalry, 1891, and as corporal, F/9th Cavalry, 1892; ranked first in revolver competition, Departments of the East, the Platte, and California, Bellevue, 14–19 Aug 1893. SOURCE: GO 82, AGO, 24 Oct 1894.

Promoted to sergeant as of 22 Jul 1894, Ft Duchesne, UT. SOURCE: *ANJ* 31 (4 Aug 1894): 858.

Sergeant, F/9th Cavalry, transferred to E/9th Cavalry as private in accordance with Special Order 256, Adjutant General's Office, 30 Oct 1896. SOURCE: *ANJ* 34 (7 Nov 1896): 156.

STROTHER, Edward; Sergeant; C/9th Cav. Commended for gallantry in charge on San Juan Hill, battle of Santiago, Cuba, 1 Jul 1898, while wagoner, C/9th Cavalry. SOURCE: GO 15, AGO, 13 Feb 1900; *ANJ* 37 (24 Feb 1900): 611.

Retired from Ft Douglas, UT, as sergeant, C/9th Cavalry. SOURCE: *ANJ* 37 (11 Nov 1899): 247.

STROUP, Henry; Sergeant; A/10th Cav. Served five years; participated in Geronimo campaign, 1885, while stationed at Ft Apache, AZ; claims Indian war veterans are overlooked and discriminated against regarding pensions. SOURCE: *Winners of the West* 37 (Mar 1926): 8.

Grateful for $30 per month pension; will renew subscription; "I am very lonesome without it [*Winners of the West*]." SOURCE: *Winners of the West* 4 (Aug 1927): 4.

STROUTHER, Charles; Private; G/49th Inf. Former soldier, died in the Philippines of empyema, 9 Jul 1901. SOURCE: *ANJ* 38 (24 Aug 1901): 1256.

STRUTTER, Joshua; Private; H/9th Cav. At Ft Robinson, NE, 1898; deposited $10 with paymaster.

STUART, Will; Private; I/9th Cav. Veteran of Philippine Insurrection; at Ft D. A. Russell, WY, in 1910; resident of Blunt Co., TN. SOURCE: *Illustrated Review: Ninth Cavalry*.

STUCKEY, Amos H.; Private; H/24th Inf. Fined $2 by summary court, San Isidro, Philippines, for appearing at inspection with dirty rifle, 8 Feb 1902, fourth conviction. SOURCE: Register of Summary Court, San Isidro.

Recommended for certificate of merit for gallantry at Naguilian, Luzon, Philippines, 7 Dec 1899. SOURCE: *ANJ* 39 (15 Feb 1902): 594–95.

Awarded certificate of merit for gallantry in the Philippines, 7 Dec 1899; already discharged when award made, 10 Mar 1902. SOURCE: GO 86, AGO, 24 Jul 1902.

STURGIS, Harry; Private; D/10th Cav. Served in 10th Cavalry in Cuba, 1898. SOURCE: Cashin, *Under Fire with the Tenth Cavalry*, 341.

Wounded in action at Santiago, Cuba, 1898. SOURCE: SecWar, *AR 1898*, 711; Bigelow, *Reminiscences of Santiago*, 133.

SULDER, Alexander; Trumpeter; C/10th Cav. Served in 1896. *See* **JOHNSON**, William, Cook, C/10th Cavalry

Served in 10th Cavalry in Cuba, 1898. SOURCE: Cashin, *Under Fire with the Tenth Cavalry*, 339–40.

SULLIVAN, Allen; Private; H/10th Cav. At Ft Robinson, NE, guarding prisoners, as of 29 Nov 1904. SOURCE: Regt Returns, 10 Cav, Nov 1904.

SULLIVAN, George; Private; H/24th Inf. Enlisted Ft Douglas, UT, 19 Dec 1896, with five years' service; sick in quarters, injured in line of duty, 26 Apr–9 May 1898. SOURCE: Muster Roll, H/24 Inf, Mar–Apr and May–Jun 1898.

Sick in hospital, Siboney, Cuba, 13–25 Aug 1898, and en route to U.S., 25–31 Aug 1898, disease contracted in line of duty. SOURCE: Muster Roll, H/24 Inf, Jul–Aug 1898.

Returned to duty, 12 Sep 1898. SOURCE: Muster Roll, H/24 Inf, Sep–Oct 1898.

Present. SOURCE: Muster Roll, H/24 Inf, Nov–Dec 1898 and Jan–Feb 1899.

SULLIVAN, Jermiah; M/10th Cav. Original member of 10th Cavalry; in troop when organized, Ft Riley, KS, 15 Oct 1867. SOURCE: McMiller, "Buffalo Soldiers," 79.

SULLIVAN, Melvin; Private; E/9th Cav. Deserted in New Mexico, 14 Jan 1881. SOURCE: Regt Returns, 9 Cav, Feb 1881.

SULLIVAN, R. E. Commander, Col. Charles Young Camp No. 24, Washington, DC, National Indian War Veterans. SOURCE: *Winners of the West* 6 (Jun 1929): 4.

SULLIVAN, Wallace W.; Trumpeter; K/9th Cav. Ranked number 406 among rifle experts with 69.00 percent. SOURCE: GO 101, AGO, 31 May 1906.

SULLIVANT; Comsy Sgt; U.S. Army. Served 1879. *See* **JEFFERS**, David B., First Lieutenant, E/48th Infantry

SULLIVEN, George; Private; K/24th Inf. At San Carlos, AZ, 1890. *See* **HARDEE**, James A., Private, K/24th Infantry

SUMMERS, Charles A.; Private; M/9th Cav. At Ft D. A. Russell, WY, in 1910; marksman; resident of Rock Springs, KY. SOURCE: *Illustrated Review: Ninth Cavalry*, with picture.

SUMMERS, John; Private; H/24th Inf. Fined $3 by summary court, San Isidro, Philippines, for lying out of quarters without permission, 8 Apr 1902, second conviction. SOURCE: Register of Summary Court, San Isidro.

SUMMERS, Matthew; Private; 10th Cav. Arrived from Jefferson Barracks, MO, at Ft Leavenworth, KS. SOURCE: Adj, Ft Leavenworth, to HQ, Jefferson Barracks, LS, 10 Cav, 1866–67.

SUMMERS, Michael; A/10th Cav. Original member of 10th Cavalry; in troop when organized, Ft Leavenworth, KS, 18 Feb 1867. SOURCE: McMiller, "Buffalo Soldiers," 68.

SURDY, Allen; Private; K/10th Cav. Released to duty from treatment for acute chancroids, Ft Robinson, NE, 31 Jan 1903. SOURCE: Post Surgeon to CO, K/10, 31 Jan 1903, LS, Post Surgeon, Ft Robinson.

SURGEON, Forester; Corporal; C/9th Cav. At Ft Cummings, NM, 1876. SOURCE: Billington, *New Mexico's Buffalo Soldiers*, 113.

SUTER, George; Private; I/10th Cav. Sentence of dishonorable discharge and five years for conduct to prejudice of good order and discipline reduced to dishonorable discharge by General Brooke; Suter's "moral degradation" makes him unfit for confinement in a military guardhouse. SOURCE: *ANJ* 34 (20 Feb 1897): 444.

SUTPHIN, William; 24th Inf. Ninety-three-year-old resident of South Boston, VA, enlisted in 24th Infantry at Pittsburgh; marched from Pittsburgh to Arizona, averaging twenty-five miles per day; one dark night fought Indians hand-to-hand: "I hit two or three on the head and the others ran away." SOURCE: *Army Digest* 21 (Dec 1966): 63.

SUTTON; Private; E/9th Cav. To be returned to infantry, in accordance with telegram, Department of the Platte, 13 Aug 1897.

SUTTON, Edward; Private; G/9th Cav. Died of malaria in Cuba, 30 Jul 1898. SOURCE: *ANJ* 36 (18 Feb 1899): 590; AG, *Correspondence Regarding the War with Spain*, I:195.

SUTTON, Harry; Private; E/9th Cav. Veteran of Philippine Insurrection; at Ft D. A. Russell, WY, in 1910; marksman; resident of Washington, DC. SOURCE: *Illustrated Review: Ninth Cavalry*, with picture.

SUTTON, James; Private; D/10th Cav. Served in 10th Cavalry in Cuba, 1898. SOURCE: Cashin, *Under Fire with the Tenth Cavalry*, 341.

SUTTON, William R.; G/24th Inf. Convicted of larceny in the Philippines, Dec 1900; sentenced to four months and $40 fine.

SWAN, E.; Private; L/9th Cav. On detached service in field, New Mexico, 21 Jan–24 Feb 1881. SOURCE: Regt Returns, 9 Cav, Feb 1881.

SWAN, Harry; Private; D/10th Cav. Served in 10th Cavalry in Cuba, 1898. SOURCE: Cashin, *Under Fire with the Tenth Cavalry*, 341.

SWAN, John R.; Corporal; E/10th Cav. Served in 10th Cavalry in Cuba, 1898. SOURCE: Cashin, *Under Fire with the Tenth Cavalry*, 342.

SWANN; Private; F/10th Cav. At Ft Apache, AZ, 1890, subscribed $.50 to testimonial to General Grierson. SOURCE: List of subscriptions, 23 Apr 1890, 10th Cavalry papers, MHI.

SWANN, Hugh; Private; E/25th Inf. Wounded in action at El Caney, Cuba, 1 Jul 1898. SOURCE: Nankivell, *History of the Twenty-fifth Infantry*, 83.

SWEAT, G. W.; Private; B/10th Cav. Served as striker (personal servant) to Lt. L. H. Orleans, Ft Stockton, TX, 1879. SOURCE: Stallard, *Glittering Misery*, 119–20.

SWEENEY; Private; F/10th Cav. At Ft Apache, AZ, 1890, subscribed $.50 to testimonial to General Grierson. SOURCE: List of subscriptions, 23 Apr 1890, 10th Cavalry papers, MHI.

SWEENEY, Alfred; Private; B/9th Cav. Veteran of Philippine Insurrection; at Ft D. A. Russell, WY, in 1910; sharpshooter. SOURCE: *Illustrated Review: Ninth Cavalry*, with picture.

SWEENEY, Robert; Sergeant; B/10th Cav. Original member of 10th Cavalry; in troop when organized, Ft Leavenworth, KS, 1 Apr 1867. SOURCE: McMiller, "Buffalo Soldiers," 69.

Detailed detachment sergeant major, Ft Lyon, CO, 22 Dec 1869. SOURCE: Special Order 1, Det 10 Cav, 22 Feb 1869, Orders, Det 10 Cav, 1868–69.

Sergeant, B/10th Cavalry, relieved of duty with this headquarters. SOURCE: Special Order 20, Det 10 Cav, Ft Dodge, KS, 16 Apr 1869.

Commander of regiment asks authority to reenlist Sweeney, sergeant for ten years in B/10th Cavalry, in F/10th Cavalry. SOURCE: CO, 10 Cav, to AAG, Department of Texas, 23 May 1877, LS, 10 Cav, 1873–83.

SWENTON, Norman E.; Private; K/25th Inf. At Ft Niobrara, NE, 1904. SOURCE: Wilson, "History of Fort Niobrara."

SWIFT, Thomas; Private; E/24th Inf. Wounded in action in Cuba, 1898. SOURCE: Muller, *The Twenty Fourth Infantry*, 18.

Died in Cuba, 5 Jul 1898. SOURCE: *ANJ* 36 (18 Feb 1899): 590.

SYKES, Zekiel; Corporal; E/9th Cav. Enlisted New Orleans, 4 Oct 1866; reenlisted Ft Clark, TX, 4 Oct 1871; discharged 25 Oct 1876, character good; enlisted Ft Union, NM, 24 Nov 1876; discharged 12 Dec 1881, character very good; enlisted in B/9th Cavalry, Ft Hays, KS, 22 Dec 1881; discharged 21 Dec 1886, character excellent; enlisted Ft Duchesne, UT, 22 Dec 1886; discharged 21 Dec 1891, character excellent; enlisted Ft Duchesne, 22 Dec 1891; discharged 21 Dec 1896, character excellent. VA File XC 2650122, Zekiel Sykes.

Occupation servant; Ht 5'6", yellow complexion; second enlistment, age 25, Ft Clark, 4 Oct 1871; discharged Ft Wingate, NM, 25 Oct 1876, character good. SOURCE: Register of Enlistments.

Sergeant, B/9th Cavalry, authorized six-month furlough from Ft Duchesne. SOURCE: *ANJ* 24 (4 Dec 1886): 370.

Born Corinth, LA; fifth enlistment, as sergeant, B/9th Cavalry, Ft Duchesne, 22 Dec 1886; discharged Ft Duchesne, 21 Dec 1891, character excellent. SOURCE: Register of Enlistments.

Corporal, E/9th Cavalry, authorized to reenlist as married soldier, by letter, Adjutant General's Office, 21 Nov 1896.

Retires from Ft Robinson, NE, as corporal, E/9th Cavalry, in accordance with Special Order 16, Adjutant General's Office, 29 Jan 1897. SOURCE: *ANJ* 34 (30 Jan 1897): 384.

Married Margaret, 14 Apr 1890; divorced Nov 1912 for desertion, Cook Co., IL; married Lucinda Hurd, Crown Point, IN, 12 Dec 1912; resided in Chicago, 1905–1926; retired pay $56 per month in 1923; death benefits $335 from Metropolitan Life Insurance Co. SOURCE: VA File XC 2650122, Zekiel Sykes.

Died 13 Jul 1926; unremarried widow Lucinda resided at 4213 Champlain, Chicago, in 1933, received $40 per month pension as of 8 Jun 1944, died at age 92 on 7 Mar 1948. SOURCE: VA File XC 2650122, Zekiel Sykes.

τ

TABER, Claude; Private; A/24th Inf. Died of cholera in the Philippines, 16 Jul 1900. SOURCE: *ANJ* 37 (4 Aug 1900): 1166.

TAGGART, Henry; Private; D/24th Inf. Acquitted of wasting one round of ammunition, Cabanatuan, Philippines, 24 Nov 1900; witness: 1st Sgt. M. E. Ellis, D/24th Infantry. SOURCE: Name File, 24 Inf.

Fined $1 for fighting and abusive language with Pvt. Rollins Tates, D/24th Infantry, Cabanatuan, 11 Dec 1900. SOURCE: Name File, 24 Inf.

See **SMITH**, Horace J., Private, D/24th Infantry; **TATES**, Rollins, Private, D/24th Infantry

TALBERT, Frank; Private; H/24th Inf. Fined $3 by summary court, San Isidro, Philippines, for absence from check roll call, 16 Jan 1902, first conviction. SOURCE: Register of Summary Court, San Isidro.

TALBERT, Willie P.; Private; B/9th Cav. Funeral, Ft Robinson, NE, 15 Jun 1890. SOURCE: Order 123, 14 Jun 1890, Post Orders, Ft Robinson.

Died Ft Robinson, 14 Jan 1890. SOURCE: List of Interments, Ft Robinson.

TALBOT, John; Private; L/10th Cav. Served in 10th Cavalry, 1898; remained in U.S. during war with Spain. SOURCE: Cashin, *Under Fire with the Tenth Cavalry*, 350.

TALBOT, Richard; Private; I/10th Cav. At Ft Concho, TX, 1874; sentenced to dishonorable discharge and one year's confinement for theft of $1 from civilian. SOURCE: Leckie, *The Buffalo Soldiers*, 98.

TALBOTT, Lee; Blacksmith; C/10th Cav. Killed in action, Carrizal, Mexico, 21 Jun 1916; remains not recovered and Talbott initially reported missing in action. SOURCE: Wharfield, *10th Cavalry and Border Fights*, 30, 40.

TALEY, McCulloh; Private; C/10th Cav. Served in 10th Cavalry, 1898; remained in U.S. during war with Spain. SOURCE: Cashin, *Under Fire with the Tenth Cavalry*, 340.

TALIAFERRO, Charles L.; Private; H/25th Inf. Died in Cuba, 30 Jul 1898. SOURCE: *ANJ* 36 (18 Feb 1899): 590.

Died in camp, 30 Jul 1898; buried two miles north of Santiago; wood headboard, surrounded by stones, has name cut into it; name enclosed in tightly corked bottle buried at head of grave. SOURCE: Scrapbook, 25 Inf, II.

TALIAFERRO, Spottswood W.; Sgt Maj; 25th Inf. First sergeant, C/25th Infantry; speaker at peace jubilee, Bridge Street Church, Brooklyn, NY, sponsored by Montauk Soldiers Relief Association; told of his regiment's moves from Tampa, FL, 7 Jun 1898, to Cuba, 22 Jun 1898; he led second battalion at El Caney after Lieutenant Burdick was wounded in action. SOURCE: Cleveland *Gazette*, 24 Sep 1898.

Virginian, educated in Lynchburg; "quiet, well-behaved and respectful" boy, bright student; years ago had highest qualifying score for U.S. Military Academy but was kept out because he was black; secretary of Y.M.C.A. and founder-editor of Lynchburg *Southern Forge*, which failed through no fault of his own. SOURCE: Cleveland *Gazette*, 1 Oct 1898.

First sergeant, C/25th Infantry, rumored to have commission in native regiment. SOURCE: Richmond *Planet*, 27 Jun 1901.

Sergeant major, 25th Infantry, Ft Brown, TX, 1906. SOURCE: Weaver, *The Brownsville Raid*, 26.

TALLIFORRO, Daniel; Corporal; 9th Cav. Shot and killed by wife of Lt. Frederic Kendall, Ft Davis, TX, 21 Nov 1872, while climbing in her bedroom window. SOURCE: Stallard, *Glittering Misery*, 38; Carroll, *The Black Military Experience*, 262.

TANNER, Charles D.; Private; L/9th Cav. At Ft D. A. Russell, WY, in 1910; resident of Chicago. SOURCE: *Illustrated Review: Ninth Cavalry*, with picture.

TAPER, Charles; Farrier; F/10th Cav. Served in 10th Cavalry in Cuba, 1898. SOURCE: Cashin, *Under Fire with the Tenth Cavalry*, 343.

TARY, Saint; Private; C/9th Cav. Discharged from Ft Robinson, NE, on surgeon's certificate, Mar 1888.

TASKER, Lyman; Private; M/10th Cav. Original member of 10th Cavalry; in troop when organized, Ft Riley, KS, 15 Oct 1867. SOURCE: McMiller, "Buffalo Soldiers," 79.

Mentioned Jan 1873 as having enlisted Sep 1867. SOURCE: LS, 10 Cav, 1873–83.

TATE, Albert; Private; K/10th Cav. Served in 10th Cavalry, 1898; remained in U.S. during war with Spain. SOURCE: Cashin, *Under Fire with the Tenth Cavalry*, 351.

TATE, John; Private; M/10th Cav. Died at Ft Robinson, NE, 14 Jan 1905, age 21; frozen to death while orderly to commander, M/10th Cavalry. SOURCE: Monthly Report, Chaplain Anderson, 1 Feb 1905; List of Interments, Ft Robinson.

TATE, Rufus; Private; F/9th Cav. Died at Ft Robinson, 5 Nov 1890. SOURCE: List of Interments, Ft Robinson.

Funeral at Ft Robinson, NE, 6 Nov 1890. SOURCE: Order 237, 6 Nov 1890, Post Orders, Ft Robinson.

TATE, William; Sergeant; L/25th Inf. Corporal, A/24th Infantry; distinguished marksman with Department of Colorado bronze medal, 1897. SOURCE: GO 11, AGO, 27 Jan 1905.

Corporal, A/24th Infantry; wounded in action at Santiago, Cuba, 1898. SOURCE: SecWar, *AR 1898*, 437; Muller, *The Twenty Fourth Infantry*, 16.

Wounded in action in Cuba, 1898; returned to Ft Douglas, UT; transferred to unit at Ft Harrison, MT, 1899. SOURCE: Clark, "A History of the Twenty-fourth," 100.

Corporal, K/25th Infantry, ranked number four among infantry marksmen, Department of the Missouri, 1903. SOURCE: SecWar, *AR 1903*, 1:427.

Corporal, K/25th Infantry, distinguished marksman, 1903, with Department of the Missouri bronze medal. SOURCE: GO 11, AGO, 27 Jan 1905.

Ranked number 41 among expert riflemen, 1903, with 69.67 percent. SOURCE: GO 52, AGO, 19 Mar 1904.

Distinguished marksman; ranked number three in competition of Northern Division infantry rifle team, Ft Sheridan, IL, 1904, with silver medal. SOURCE: GO 167, AGO, 28 Oct 1904; GO 11, AGO, 27 Jan 1905.

Sergeant, L/25th Infantry; distinguished marksman, ranked number five among Army marksmen, National Individual Rifle Competition, Sea Girt, NJ; silver medal and $40. SOURCE: SecWar, *AR 1905*, 1:159; GO 173, AGO, 20 Oct 1905; GO 179, AGO, 25 Oct 1905.

Sergeant, L/25th Infantry, included in picture of U.S. Army infantry rifle team. SOURCE: *ANR* 38 (16 Sep 1905): 3.

Sergeant, 25th Infantry, age 28, married Miss Fannie Turner, age 26, Ft Niobrara, NE, 14 Jan 1906. SOURCE: Monthly report, Chaplain Steward, 31 Jan 1906.

Ranked number four on first place Army infantry team, National Rifle Matches, Sea Girt, 1906; national trophy, $300, and medal to each man; ranked number 21 in National Individual Match, $10. SOURCE: GO 190, AGO, 15 Nov 1906.

TATE, Willie L.; Private; C/9th Cav. At Ft D. A. Russell, WY, in 1910; resident of Patton, McDowell Co., NC. SOURCE: *Illustrated Review: Ninth Cavalry*, with picture.

TATES, Rollins; Private; D/24th Inf. Fined $5 for leaving rifle outside of quarters, 6–8 P.M., 10 Dec 1900, Cabanatuan, Philippines; witnesses: QM Sgt. Robert Duvall, D/24th Infantry; Cook Henry Pope, D/24th Infantry; Pvt. William Collins, D/24th Infantry. SOURCE: Name File, 24 Inf.

Fined $1 for fight in quarters and abusive language with Pvt. Henry Taggart, D/24th Infantry, Cabanatuan, 11 Dec 1900; witnesses: Sgt. Wilson Prear, D/24th Infantry; Pvt. Henry Taggart, D/24th Infantry. SOURCE: Name File, 24 Inf.

Fined $10 and jailed for twenty days for refusal to obey lawful order of 1st Sgt. M. E. Ellis, Cabanatuan, 9 Feb 1901; witnesses: First Sergeant Ellis; Sgt. George Driscoll, D/24th Infantry; Pvt. Charles F. Mitchell, D/24th Infantry. SOURCE: Name File, 24 Inf.

See **TAGGART**, Henry, Private, D/24th Infantry

TATUM; Private; G/10th Cav. At Ft Apache, AZ, 1890, subscribed $.50 to testimonial to General Grierson. SOURCE: List of subscriptions, 23 Apr 1890, 10th Cavalry papers, MHI.

TAYLOR; Sergeant; F/10th Cav. Actions of Capt. George F. Armes, at Ft Harker, KS, in case of Sergeant Taylor approved by regiment commander; noncommissioned officers must be good examples to men regarding care of horses. SOURCE: Adj, 10 Cav, to CO, F/10, Ft Harker, 18 Jul 1867, LS, 10 Cav, 1866–67.

TAYLOR; C/10th Cav. Shot and killed by Walker, K/10th Cavalry, Crawford, NE, 31 May 1904, after rumpus in West Elm Street dive. SOURCE: Crawford *Bulletin*, 3 Jun 1904.

TAYLOR, Addison; Private; D/10th Cav. Ranked number three in revolver competition, Departments of Dakota and Columbia, Ft Keogh, MT, 15–23 Aug 1892; silver medal. SOURCE: GO 75, AGO, 3 Nov 1902; Baker, Roster.

TAYLOR, Albert; Private; M/10th Cav. Original member of 10th Cavalry; in troop when organized, Ft Riley, KS, 15 Oct 1867. SOURCE: McMiller, "Buffalo Soldiers," 79.

Mentioned Oct 1870. SOURCE: ES, 10 Cav, 1866–71.

TAYLOR, Albert B.; Private; K/24th Inf. Jailed for ten days and fined $5 for being drunk and disorderly in native house after taps, Cabanatuan, Philippines, 17 May 1901; witness: Sgt. William H. Brice, D/24th Infantry. SOURCE: Name File, 24 Inf.

TAYLOR, Alex; Private; K/9th Cav. Veteran of Philippine Insurrection; at Ft D. A. Russell, WY, in 1910; resident of Madison, AL. SOURCE: *Illustrated Review: Ninth Cavalry*, with picture.

TAYLOR, Alexander; Private; I/9th Cav. Served with Cpl. James F. Jackson, G/9th Cavalry, at Ft Niobrara, NE, in March 1887; was in G/9th Cavalry when Jackson was exposed to cold and snow and became rheumatic in 1887; resided at 2501 South 25th Street, South Omaha, NE, in 1898, at age 35. SOURCE: VA File C 2555351, James F. Jackson.

Private, I/9th Cavalry, discharged from Ft Robinson, NE, on surgeon's certificate with syphilis, Jul 1888. SOURCE: Regt Returns, 9 Cav, Jul 1888.

Served as blacksmith of G/9th Cavalry; letter, Adjutant General's Office, 24 May 1897, concerns his claim.

TAYLOR, Alexander; Private; L/10th Cav. Served in 10th Cavalry, 1898; remained in U.S. during war with Spain. SOURCE: Cashin, *Under Fire with the Tenth Cavalry*, 351.

TAYLOR, Alonzo; Recruit; Colored Detachment/ Mounted Service. Convicted by general court martial, Jefferson Barracks, MO, of drawing knife on Recruit Minor Williams, Colored Detachment, and threatening his life, saying "I'll cut your God damn guts out," at Jefferson Barracks, 9 Aug 1885; sentenced to two months' confinement and loss of $10 per month for two months. SOURCE: GCMO 90, AGO, 7 Sep 1885.

TAYLOR, Anderson; K/10th Cav. Original member of 10th Cavalry; in troop when organized, Ft Riley, KS, 1 Sep 1867. SOURCE: McMiller, "Buffalo Soldiers," 77.

TAYLOR, Arthur; Private; E/10th Cav. Served in 10th Cavalry, 1898; remained in U.S. during war with Spain. SOURCE: Cashin, *Under Fire with the Tenth Cavalry*, 343.

TAYLOR, Belford; Private; D/10th Cav. Served 1884–89. SOURCE: *Winners of the West* 12 (Nov 1935): 3.

Knew Thomas H. Allsup as first sergeant, D/10th Cavalry; Allsup's wife was "a perfect lady"; resides at 1108 East 11th rear, Los Angeles, in 1925. SOURCE: Taylor, Affidavit, VA File XC 2659797, Thomas H. Allsup.

TAYLOR, Benjamin; F/10th Cav. Original member of 10th Cavalry; in troop when organized, Ft Leavenworth, KS, 21 Jun 1867. SOURCE: McMiller, "Buffalo Soldiers," 73.

TAYLOR, C. S.; Lt Col; 3rd NC Inf. Born of slave parents; member of militia from 1887; barber and musician before joining 3rd North Carolina Infantry; two sons in 10th Cavalry. SOURCE: Fletcher, "The Negro Soldier and Officer," 237.

TAYLOR, Charles; Private; I/10th Cav. Honorable mention for conspicuous bravery against Apaches, Salt River, AZ, 7 Mar 1890. SOURCE: Baker, Roster.

TAYLOR, Charles; Corporal; F/10th Cav. Born in Kentucky; private, F/10th Cavalry, 24 Aug 1892; corporal, 10 Feb 1896; at Ft Assiniboine, MT, 1897. SOURCE: Baker, Roster.

TAYLOR, Charles E.; Private; H/9th Cav. At Ft D. A. Russell, WY, in 1910; resident of West Middleton, PA. SOURCE: *Illustrated Review: Ninth Cavalry*, with picture.

TAYLOR, Charles I.; Private; H/10th Cav. Born in North Carolina; lived 1872–1922; educated at Clark College, Atlanta; served in Spanish-American War; manager in Negro baseball leagues from 1904 until death on 9 Mar 1922, including Indianapolis ABC, 1915–22. SOURCE: Peterson, *Only the Ball Was White*, 251.

Served in 10th Cavalry, 1898; remained in U.S. during war with Spain. SOURCE: Cashin, *Under Fire with the Tenth Cavalry*, 347.

TAYLOR, Daniel T.; Sergeant; G/9th Cav. Veteran of Philippine Insurrection; at Ft D. A. Russell, WY, in 1910; marksman. SOURCE: *Illustrated Review: Ninth Cavalry*, with picture.

TAYLOR, Elijah; Sergeant; C/9th Cav. Corporal, C/9th Cavalry, commended for gallantry in charge on San Juan Hill, Cuba, 1 Jul 1898, as private, C/9th Cavalry. SOURCE: GO 15, AGO, 13 Feb 1900.

Sergeant, C/9th Cavalry, cited for distinguished service, 1 Jul 1898. SOURCE: *ANJ* 37 (24 Dec 1900): 611.

TAYLOR, Eugene; Private; B/24th Inf. Fined $10 for going to guardhouse to engage in fight with Pvt. James Cole, B/24th Infantry, member of guard, Cabanatuan, Philippines, 3 Jan 1900. SOURCE: Name File, 24 Inf.

See **COLE**, James E., Private, B/24th Infantry

TAYLOR, Eugene B.; Private; 24th Inf. Sentenced to seven years for part in Houston riot. SOURCE: Cleveland *Gazette*, 5 Jan 1918.

TAYLOR, Evans; Private; D/10th Cav. Served in 10th Cavalry, 1898; remained in U.S. during war with Spain. SOURCE: Cashin, *Under Fire with the Tenth Cavalry*, 341.

TAYLOR, Frank; Private; K/49th Inf. In the Philippines, 1900. See **BLUNT**, Hamilton H., Captain, K/49th Infantry

TAYLOR, G. W.; 2nd Lt; D/48th Inf. Mentioned. SOURCE: Beasley, *Negro Trailblazers*, 284.

TAYLOR, George; Private; C/9th Cav. Recruit arrived at Ft Robinson, NE, from depot, 1 Mar 1887. SOURCE: Regt Returns, 9 Cav, Mar 1887.

Fined $5 by garrison court martial, Ft Robinson, for use of vulgar language in troop dining room and assault with knife on Pvt. Willis Huff, C/9th Cavalry, without provocation. SOURCE: Order 219, 10 Nov 1887, Post Orders, Ft Robinson.

TAYLOR, George N.; Private; K/24th Inf. Convicted of being drunk and disorderly in camp, making it necessary to take his rifle due to threats to shoot Private Kibby, D/24th Infantry, Cabanatuan, Philippines, 21 Apr 1901; sentenced to thirty days' confinement and loss of pay; witnesses: Sgt. Samuel Cook, K/24th Infantry; Private Kibby, D/24th Infantry. SOURCE: Name File, 24 Inf.

Convicted of being drunk and disorderly in quarters and fighting with Pvt. John N. Faggins, K/24th Infantry, Cabanatuan, 12 Jun 1901; sentenced to ten days and $7 fine; witnesses: Corporal Jackson, K/24th Infantry; Private Gibson, K/24th Infantry. SOURCE: Name File, 24 Inf.

TAYLOR, George R.; Sergeant; A/10th Cav. Promoted from private to corporal, 4 Dec 1897. SOURCE: *ANJ* 35 (25 Dec 1897): 310.

Promoted from corporal to sergeant, Ft Keogh, MT, 3 Mar 1898. SOURCE: *ANJ* 35 (12 Mar 1898): 518.

Served with A/10th Cavalry in Cuba, 1898. SOURCE: Cashin, *Under Fire with the Tenth Cavalry*, 336.

Narrates Spanish-American War experience. SOURCE: Cashin, *Under Fire with the Tenth Cavalry*, 265.

A noncommissioned officer who should be commissioned, according to unsigned [probably John E. Lewis] letter from Montauk, NY. SOURCE: Gatewood, *"Smoked Yankees"*, 77.

Transferred to General Recruiting Service in accordance with Special Order 133, Adjutant General's Office, 7 Jun 1904.

TAYLOR, Henry; Private; A/10th Cav. Served in 10th Cavalry in Cuba, 1898. SOURCE: Cashin, *Under Fire with the Tenth Cavalry*, 336.

TAYLOR, Henry; 2nd Lt; 23rd Kans Inf. Mentioned. SOURCE: Beasley, *Negro Trailblazers*, 285.

TAYLOR, Herbert; Recruit; Colored Detachment/ Mounted Service. Convicted by general court martial, Jefferson Barracks, MO, of disposing of about $20 worth of military clothing, Jefferson Barracks, 8 Apr 1886; sentenced to six months' confinement, half pay, and reimbursement of government for $25.20. SOURCE: GO 33, AGO, 8 May 1886.

TAYLOR, Isom; Private; F/10th Cav. Served in 10th Cavalry in Cuba, 1898; wounded in action. SOURCE: Cashin, *Under Fire with the Tenth Cavalry*, 344.

Wounded in action, Santiago, Cuba, 1 Jul 1898. SOURCE: SecWar, *AR 1898*, 324.

TAYLOR, James; G/10th Cav. Original member of 10th Cavalry; in troop when organized, Ft Leavenworth, KS, 5 Jul 1867. SOURCE: McMiller, "Buffalo Soldiers," 74.

TAYLOR, James; Private; K/24th Inf. At San Carlos, AZ, 1890. *See* **HARDEE**, James A., Private, K/24th Infantry

TAYLOR, James; Private; G/10th Cav. Served in 10th Cavalry, 1898; remained in U.S. during war with Spain. SOURCE: Cashin, *Under Fire with the Tenth Cavalry*, 345.

TAYLOR, James F.; Private; D/10th Cav. Served in 10th Cavalry in Cuba, 1898. SOURCE: Cashin, *Under Fire with the Tenth Cavalry*, 341.

Wounded in action at Santiago, Cuba, 1898. SOURCE: SecWar, *AR 1898*, 711; Bigelow, *Reminiscences of Santiago*, 133.

TAYLOR, James H.; Private; H/24th Inf. Enlisted Richmond, VA, 30 Jul 1898; assigned and joined company, 16 Sep 1898; credit sales from Subsistence Department, $1.42. SOURCE: Muster Roll, H/24 Inf, Sep–Oct 1898.

Discharged Ft Douglas, UT, 28 Jan 1899, character good, single; deposits $25, due U.S. for clothing $30.03. SOURCE: Muster Roll, H/24 Inf, Jan–Feb 1899.

TAYLOR, John; Private; A/10th Cav. Arrived from Jefferson Barracks, MO, at Ft Leavenworth, KS. SOURCE: Adj, Ft Leavenworth, to HQ, Jefferson Barracks, 9 Oct 1866, LS, 10 Cav, 1866–67.

Original member of 10th Cavalry; in troop when organized, Ft Leavenworth, KS, 18 Feb 1867. SOURCE: McMiller, "Buffalo Soldiers," 68.

TAYLOR, John; Private; F/10th Cav. Born 4 Jan 1840; reared in Lowell, MA, by white Mary Watts Moran, until Civil War; father Charley Taylor, whaler, died at sea; occupation livery driver; enlisted Boston. 6 Dec 1868; First Sergeant Edmondson of Maryland succeeded 1st Sgt. Jake Thornton, who was discharged with wound in knee inflicted by arrow and went home to Dayton, OH; thrown by horse and got hernia; served in Texas, 1874–75, carrying Ft Griffin-Ft Elliot mail; resided in Mobeetie, TX, where owned four lots and a shack, until 1889; resided in Elk City, KS, from 1 Feb 1889 to 1922; never married; granted $20 per month pension on 4 Mar 1917. SOURCE: VA File SC 11405, John Taylor.

Injured at Camp Supply, Indian Territory, 1870; first sergeant was John Edmondson; sergeants were John B. Miles, James Stephenson, and Emanuel Jones; corporals were William Burley and Louis Butler. SOURCE: Edwin L. Wyatt to Commissioner of Pensions, 22 Sep 1915, VA File SC 11405, John Taylor.

Resided in same shack in Elk City for thirty-three years; only colored resident of town ever; claims to be from Boston; "He is old and decrepit but seems to have an intelligence away above most of the colored persons who served in the Civil War"; insists he horsed with 54th Massachusetts Infantry in Civil War. SOURCE: Report of Special Examiner, 12 Jul 1922, VA File SC 11405, John Taylor.

TAYLOR, John H.; Corporal; H/24th Inf. Promoted from private. SOURCE: *ANR* 38 (29 Jul 1905): 21.

TAYLOR, John J. L.; 1st Sgt; E/10th Cav. Born in North Carolina; private, E/10th Cavalry, 9 May 1894; corporal, 14 Feb 1896; at Ft Custer, MT, 1897. SOURCE: Baker, Roster.

Served as private, E/10th Cavalry in Cuba, 1898; wounded in action. SOURCE: Cashin, *Under Fire with the Tenth Cavalry*, 342.

Wounded in action while on duty with Hotchkiss guns, Santiago, Cuba, 1 Jul 1898. SOURCE: SecWar, *AR 1898*, 324.

Promoted to corporal, Sep 1899. SOURCE: *ANJ* 37 (23 Sep 1899): 80.

Promoted to sergeant, Sep 1899. SOURCE: *ANJ* 37 (7 Oct 1899): 122.

Reenlisted. SOURCE: *ANJ* 39 (9 Aug 1902): 1242.

Just promoted to first sergeant at Ft Washakie, WY, vice William H. Johnson, retired. SOURCE: Fremont *Clipper*, 30 Nov 1906.

Picture as first sergeant, 10th Cavalry. SOURCE: Mary Curtis, *The Black Soldier*, opposite 35.

Retired with twenty-six years' continuous service. SOURCE: *Crisis* 21 (Mar 1921): 226.

Thirty-year veteran retired in 1921; veteran of Spanish-American War; widow Ida Smith, age 49 in 1927, lived with him 20 years in Army, resided at 1649 West 35th Place, Los Angeles; knew Chaplain Prioleau at Nogales, AZ, with 25th Infantry. SOURCE: Affidavit, Ida Smith, 26 Jul 1927, VA File C 1392575, George W. Prioleau.

TAYLOR, John P.; Private; G/9th Cav. At Ft D. A. Russell, WY, in 1910. SOURCE: *Illustrated Review: Ninth Cavalry*, with picture.

In Texas when wife Bessie Taylor was shot and killed by Carrie Sandford, colored prostitute at whist party at Taylor home, 1719 Eddy, Cheyenne, WY; her remains shipped home to Atchison, KS. SOURCE: Cheyenne *State Leader*, 5 and 10 May 1911.

TAYLOR, Jordan; Private; B/10th Cav. Born in Alabama; served five years; died at Ft Robinson, NE, age 26, 13 May 1906; full military burial. SOURCE: Monthly Report, Chaplain Anderson, 1 Jun 1906; List of Interments, Ft Robinson.

TAYLOR, Joseph; Corporal; M/25th Inf. Promoted from private. SOURCE: *ANR* 38 (1 Jul 1905): 21.

TAYLOR, Julius; Private; F/10th Cav. Served in 10th Cavalry in Cuba, 1898. SOURCE: Cashin, *Under Fire with the Tenth Cavalry*, 344.

TAYLOR, Levi J.; Recruit; Colored Recruits/ General Service. Tried by general court martial, David's Island, NY, for desertion, failure to return to company on expiration of furlough, 11–16 Mar 1880, until apprehended in South Bethlehem, PA, 23 Jun 1880; convicted of absence without leave; sentenced to thirty days plus payment of $30 cost of reward; sentence approved except for repayment of reward. SOURCE: GCMO 44, AGO, 23 Jul 1880.

TAYLOR, Lewis; Private; F/10th Cav. Original member of 10th Cavalry; in troop when organized, Ft Leavenworth, KS, 21 Jun 1867. SOURCE: McMiller, "Buffalo Soldiers," 73.

Drowned in Texas in Brazos River, 6 Jan 1874. SOURCE: ES, 10 Cav, 1873–83.

TAYLOR, Lewis; Corporal; D/9th Cav. Appointed corporal 23 Apr 1891. SOURCE: Roster, 9 Cav.

In Lander, WY, publicizing appearance of minstrels from Ft Washakie, WY. SOURCE: *Fremont Clipper*, 9 Apr 1897.

TAYLOR, Lewis N.; Private; H/9th Cav. At Ft Robinson, NE, deposited $118.25 with paymaster, 1897–98.

TAYLOR, Lewis W.; Private; H/24th Inf. Enlisted Dallas, 7 Jun 1898; assigned and joined company 6 Sep 1898. SOURCE: Muster Roll, H/24 Inf, Sep–Oct 1898.

Discharged Ft Douglas, UT, 26 Jan 1899, character good, single; clothing $2.61. SOURCE: Muster Roll, H/24 Inf, Jan–Feb 1899.

TAYLOR, Maston; Private; H/24th Inf. Witness in trial of Pvt. George Washington's assailant, San Francisco. SOURCE: San Francisco *Chronicle*, 30 Jun 1899.

Fined $10.50 by summary court, San Isidro, Philippines, for being drunk and disorderly in quarters, 17 Nov 1901. SOURCE: Register of Summary Court, San Isidro.

TAYLOR, Morris; Private; D/9th Cav. In hands of civil authorities, Buffalo, WY, 30 Oct–9 Nov 1890, and Crawford, NE, 28–30 Mar 1893. SOURCE: Regt Returns, 9 Cav, Oct–Nov 1890 and Mar 1893.

TAYLOR, Oliver; Private; A/8th Ill Inf. Died in Minnesota. SOURCE: Taylor, "Minnesota Black Spanish-American War Veterans."

TAYLOR, P.; Saddler; K/9th Cav. Reenlistment as married soldier authorized by letter, Adjutant General's Office, 18 Dec 1896.

TAYLOR, Peter; Private; I/24th Inf. Enlisted Nashville, 17 Dec 1896, with three years' service; sick since 17 Jan 1899, disease contracted in line of duty. SOURCE: Muster Roll, I/24 Inf, Jan–Feb 1899.

Authorized furlough in Cheyenne, WY, from Ft D. A. Russell, WY, 24–30 Dec 1898. SOURCE: Regt Returns, 24 Inf, Dec 1898.

TAYLOR, Robert; Private; C/24th Inf. Relieved of special duty as fireman, post ice factory, Ft Huachuca, AZ. SOURCE: Order 104, Ft Huachuca, 20 Jul 1893, Name File, 24 Inf.

Relieved of special duty as fireman, post ice factory, Ft Huachuca, and ordered to report to unit for duty, Ft Huachuca. SOURCE: Order 123, Ft Huachuca, 17 Aug 1893, Name File, 24 Inf.

TAYLOR, Samuel; Sergeant; K/48th Inf. Died of variola in the Philippines, 14 Jul 1900. SOURCE: *ANJ* 37 (28 Jul 1900): 1142.

TAYLOR, Stephen; Chief Trumpeter; 9th Cav. With band on detached service at headquarters, District of New Mexico, Santa Fe, 1880; played E-flat cornet. SOURCE: Billington, *New Mexico's Buffalo Soldiers*, 226.

Authorized four-month furlough from Ft Robinson, NE. SOURCE: *ANJ* 25 (25 Feb 1888): 605.

Appointed chief trumpeter, 15 Mar 1888. SOURCE: Roster, 9 Cav.

With regiment on practice march from Ft Robinson, Aug 1890.

Retires from Ft Robinson. SOURCE: *ANJ* 35 (9 Apr 1898): 603.

TAYLOR, Thomas; Private; K/10th Cav. Unexecuted portion of sentence promulgated in General Court Martial Order 37, Department of Texas, 1 Oct 1875, remitted; prisoner to be released and set at liberty. SOURCE: GCMO, AGO, 27 May 1876.

TAYLOR, Thomas; Private; B/10th Cav. Served in 10th Cavalry, 1898; remained in U.S. during war with Spain. SOURCE: Cashin, *Under Fire with the Tenth Cavalry*, 333.

TAYLOR, Thomas; Private; D/10th Cav. Promoted from private to corporal, 5 Nov 1897. SOURCE: *ANJ* 35 (20 Nov 1897): 212.

Served as private, D/10th Cavalry, 1898; remained in U.S. during war with Spain. SOURCE: Cashin, *Under Fire with the Tenth Cavalry*, 341.

TAYLOR, Thomas; Private; B/25th Inf. Dishonorable discharge, Brownsville. SOURCE: SO 266, AGO, 9 Nov 1906.

TAYLOR, Thomas W.; 24th Inf. Born Freetown, Sierra Leone, 17 Jan 1870; claimed to be Zulu prince; enlisted 12 Mar 1896; fought at San Juan Hill, Santiago, Cuba, 1898, and accompanied regiment to San Francisco. SOURCE: Clark, "A History of the Twenty-fourth," 79–81.

TAYLOR, Thomas W.; Private; H/24th Inf. Enlisted Louisville, 23 Apr 1898; transferred from E/24th Infantry, 18 Oct 1898; on special duty as company tailor since 20 Oct 1898. SOURCE: Muster Roll, H/24 Inf, Sep–Oct 1898.

On special duty as company tailor, Nov–Dec 1898. SOURCE: Muster Roll, H/24 Inf, Nov–Dec 1898.

On special duty as tailor; discharged Ft Douglas, UT, 29 Jan 1899, character good, single, $30.60 deposits and $42.23 due U.S. for clothing; reenlisted 30 Jan 1899. SOURCE: Muster Roll, H/24 Inf, Jan–Feb 1899.

Fined $5 by summary court, San Isidro, Philippines, for being drunk and disorderly in street, 11 Jan 1902, first conviction. SOURCE: Register of Summary Court, San Isidro.

TAYLOR, W.; Private; D/9th Cav. In hands of civil authorities, Buffalo, WY, 19 Nov–16 Dec 1890. SOURCE: Regt Returns, 9 Cav, Dec 1890.

TAYLOR, Walker; B/10th Cav. Original member of 10th Cavalry; in troop when organized, Ft Leavenworth, KS, 1 Apr 1867. SOURCE: McMiller, "Buffalo Soldiers," 69.

TAYLOR, William; A/10th Cav. Original member of 10th Cavalry; in troop when organized, Ft Leavenworth, KS, 18 Feb 1867. SOURCE: McMiller, "Buffalo Soldiers," 68.

TAYLOR, William; D/10th Cav. Original member of 10th Cavalry; in troop when organized, Ft Leavenworth, KS, 1 Jun 1867. SOURCE: McMiller, "Buffalo Soldiers," 71.

TAYLOR, William; Private; F/10th Cav. Killed in action, in canyon north of Bowen Springs, Guadalupe Mountains, TX, 4 Aug 1880. SOURCE: Baker, Roster.

TAYLOR, William; Corporal; H/24th Inf. Private, C/24th Infantry, on extra duty as painter, Quartermaster Department, Ft Huachuca, AZ. SOURCE: Order 68, Ft Huachuca, 12 May 1893, Name File, 24 Inf.

Enlisted Ft Huachuca, 25 Jul 1896, with five years' service. SOURCE: Muster Roll, H/24 Inf, May–Jun 1898.

Wounded in action on San Juan Hill, Santiago, Cuba, 1 Jul 1898, and returned to U.S. for treatment. SOURCE: Muster Roll, H/24 Inf, Jul–Aug 1898; Muller, *The Twenty Fourth Infantry*, 19.

Rejoined company 16 Oct 1898; promoted to corporal, 27 Oct 1898. SOURCE: Muster Roll, H/24 Inf, Sep–Oct 1898.

On special duty as painter, Quartermaster Department, since 23 Jan 1899. SOURCE: Muster Roll, H/24 Inf, Jan–Feb 1899.

TAYLOR, William; Corporal; I/9th Cav. At Ft Sheridan, IL, 1906. *See* **GRIFFIN**, John, Sergeant, I/9th Cavalry

TAYLOR, William; QM Sgt; M/24th Inf. Tried by general court martial for "shooting his superior officer in violation of the 21st Article of War," Iloilo, Panay, Philippines, shooting 1st Lt. Robert B. Calvert, 24th Infantry, in the right shoulder, abdomen, back, head, and scrotum, with .38-caliber Colt revolver, at Albuern, Leyte, Philippines, 16 Oct 1906; also charged with conduct to prejudice of good order and discipline, threatening Pvt. George W. Smith, M/24th Infantry, "If you don't pay me eight pesos and ten cents Mex by nine o'clock tomorrow morning I am going to kill you," Albuern, 14 Oct 1906, and insubordinate reply to Lieutenant Calvert, who said "Sergeant, you are trying my patience," to which Taylor replied, "Yes, and you are trying mine"; convicted and sentenced to death by hanging; sentence approved by President Theodore Roosevelt. SOURCE: GO 122, AGO, 6 Jun 1907.

At Camp Downes, Leyte, shot and killed First Lieutenant Calvert, 24th Infantry, at Calvert's quarters due to Calvert's relations with Taylor's wife; Taylor is twenty-one-year veteran of San Juan Hill and Siboney yellow fever camp, Cuba. SOURCE: Cleveland *Gazette*, 22 Dec 1906.

TAYLOR, Willie; Trumpeter; E/10th Cav. Served in 10th Cavalry, 1898; remained in U.S. during war with Spain. SOURCE: Cashin, *Under Fire with the Tenth Cavalry*, 343.

TAYLOR, Woods S.; H/10th Cav. Original member of 10th Cavalry; in troop when organized, Ft Leavenworth, KS, 21 Jul 1867. SOURCE: McMiller, "Buffalo Soldiers," 75.

TEAGLE, James; Private; A/24th Inf. Asks that he be relieved from extra duty as teamster, Quartermaster Department, Ft Huachuca, AZ, as of 20 Jul 1893. SOURCE: CO, A/24, to Adj, Ft Huachuca, 24 Jul 1893, Name File, 24 Inf.

On extra duty as teamster, Quartermaster Department. SOURCE: Order 163, Ft Huachuca, 2 Nov 1893, Name File, 24 Inf.

With fourteen-mule team and escort wagon (ambulance), will report to assistant surgeon. SOURCE: Order 175, Ft Huachuca, 28 Nov 1893, Name File, 24 Inf.

Retires from Ft Huachuca, AZ, Aug 1894.

TEBLE, George; Private; D/10th Cav. Served in 10th Cavalry, 1898; remained in U.S. during war with Spain. SOURCE: Cashin, *Under Fire with the Tenth Cavalry*, 341.

TEDDER, John; E/10th Cav. Original member of 10th Cavalry; in troop when organized, Ft Leavenworth, KS, 15 Jun 1867. SOURCE: McMiller, "Buffalo Soldiers," 72.

TELL, John; Private; I/10th Cav. Served in 10th Cavalry, 1898; remained in U.S. during war with Spain. SOURCE: Cashin, *Under Fire with the Tenth Cavalry*, 348.

TELLIES, Robert; Private; Band/25th Inf. Born Williamson Co., TN; Ht 5'8"; in B and F/25th Infantry, 23 Mar 1886–22 Mar 1891, character good, single; reenlisted Ft Missoula, MT, 23 Mar 1891; six summary court martials and two general court martials, both of which sentenced him to two months' confinement; marksman, 1887–89, 1892–94; first class marksman, 1890; participated in expedition against strikers, Idaho, 1892, single, no character, 9 Feb 1895; enlisted in H/25th Infantry, 9 Jul 1896, single, character very good; enlisted Nashville, 19 Apr 1899. SOURCE: Descriptive & Assignment Cards of Recruits, 25 Inf.

Private, Band/25th Infantry, authorized four-month furlough from Ft Logan, CO, 24 Mar 1899. SOURCE: AAG, USA, to CG, Department of Colorado, 24 Mar 1899, Misc Records, 25 Inf.

Private, Band/25th Infantry, fined $.50 for absence from reveille, Subig, Philippines, Oct 1900. SOURCE: Misc Records, 25 Inf.

TELLIS, Wicks; Private; D/9th Cav. At Ft D. A. Russell, WY, in 1910; resident of Bledsoe, TN. SOURCE: *Illustrated Review: Ninth Cavalry*, with picture.

TEMPLE, Abraham; Private; A/10th Cav. Served in 10th Cavalry in Cuba, 1898. SOURCE: Cashin, *Under Fire with the Tenth Cavalry*, 336.

TEMPLE, Guy; Farrier; K/9th Cav. Killed in action against Nana, Carrizo Canyon, NM, 12 Aug 1881. SOURCE: Hamilton, "History of the Ninth Cavalry," 61; Leckie, *The Buffalo Soldiers*, 232; Billington, *New Mexico's Buffalo Soldiers*, 105; *Illustrated Review: Ninth Cavalry*.

TEMPER, James; M/10th Cav. Original member of 10th Cavalry; in troop when organized, Ft Riley, KS, 15 Oct 1867. SOURCE: McMiller, "Buffalo Soldiers," 79.

TERRELL, John W.; H/49th Inf. Convicted of beating natives with revolver, Jul 1900; sentenced to six months and $60 fine.

TERRELL, S. C.; Private; E/9th Cav. On detached service in field, New Mexico, 26 Jan–1 Feb 1881. SOURCE: Regt Returns, 9 Cav, Feb 1881.

TERRER, Jackson; L/10th Cav. Original member of 10th Cavalry; in troop when organized, Ft Riley, KS, 21 Sep 1867. SOURCE: McMiller, "Buffalo Soldiers," 78.

TERRY, Charles K.; Private; H/10th Cav. Born Delphi, IN; mulatto, Ht 5'6"; assigned to Band/25th Infantry, Ft Missoula, MT, 12 Apr 1897; on fourth enlistment, age 39 in 1897; most recent service in Band/10th Cavalry, discharged 16 Jan 1897, character good. SOURCE: Descriptive & Assignment Cards, 25 Inf.

Honorable mention for services rendered as private, H/10th Cavalry, in capture of Apache Mangas and his band, Rio Bonito, AZ, 18 Oct 1886. SOURCE: Baker, Roster.

Jailed for fifteen days for being absent without leave for twenty-six hours, Ft Missoula, MT, 16–17 Mar 1897, and being absent from guard duty, 17 Sep 1897. SOURCE: Descriptive & Assignment Cards, 25 Inf.

Wounded in side in Cuba, 1898; arrived at home in Indianapolis. SOURCE: Indianapolis *Freeman*, 20 Aug 1898.

TERRY, George; D/10th Cav. Original member of 10th Cavalry; in troop when organized, Ft Leavenworth, KS, 1 Jun 1867. SOURCE: McMiller, "Buffalo Soldiers," 71.

TERRY, Miles; Corporal; Band/25th Inf. Fined $.50 for absence from reveille, Subig, Philippines, Oct 1900. SOURCE: Misc Records, 25 Inf.

At Iba, Philippines, 1900, with his black American wife. SOURCE: *ANJ* 38 (1 Dec 1900): 328.

TEWELL, Frank; Private; H/24th Inf. Enlisted Louisville, 2 Aug 1898; assigned and joined 16 Sep 1898. SOURCE: Muster Roll, H/24 Inf, Sep–Oct 1898.

Discharged Ft Douglas, UT, 28 Jan 1899, character good, single; due U.S. for clothing $16.84. SOURCE: Muster Roll, H/24 Inf, Jan–Feb 1899.

THACKER, William; Sergeant; F/10th Cav. Born in Kentucky; private, F/10th Cavalry, 10 Dec 1886–9 Dec 1891; in G/10th Cavalry, 22 Dec 1891–21 Dec 1896; reenlisted 27 Dec 1896; corporal, 1 Jan 1897; at Ft Assiniboine, MT, 1897. SOURCE: Baker, Roster.

At Ft Apache, AZ, 1890, subscribed $.50 to testimonial to General Grierson. SOURCE: List of subscriptions, 23 Apr 1890, 10th Cavalry papers, MHI.

Promoted to sergeant, G/10th Cavalry, 20 Mar 1898. SOURCE: *ANJ* 36 (9 Apr 1898): 602.

Served as sergeant, F/10th Cavalry in Cuba, 1898. SOURCE: Cashin, *Under Fire with the Tenth Cavalry*, 344.

THARP, Lafayette; 2nd Lt; 9th Inf USV. Born Lafayette Co., AR; president of C. L. M.'s Alliance, an organization of 12,000 in New Orleans; on muster and acted as chaplain of regiment until arrival of Reverend T. Walker. SOURCE: Coston, *The Spanish-American War Volunteer*, 103.

THAXTON, Edward; Corporal; G/24th Inf. To be discharged at Manila, Philippines, at end of term of service, c. Jun or Jul 1902. SOURCE: Press copies of letters sent, 24 Inf.

THIBBITT, Walter; Private; C/25th Inf. Killed by shark while swimming, Philippines; body recovered. SOURCE: *ANJ* 39 (8 Feb 1902): 577.

THISTLE, James T.; H/10th Cav. Original member of 10th Cavalry; in troop when organized, Ft Leavenworth, KS, 21 Jul 1867. SOURCE: McMiller, "Buffalo Soldiers," 75.

THOMAS; Sergeant; A/9th Cav. Engaged in duel with unknown colored civilian; a good, sober soldier who will probably be exonerated. SOURCE: Cheyenne *Daily Leader*, 18 Jan 1910.

THOMAS, Albert; Private; H/24th Inf. Enlisted Baltimore, 11 Jul 1898; assigned and joined 16 Sep 1898; on special duty as janitor, post chapel, Ft Douglas, UT, since 13 Oct 1898. SOURCE: Muster Roll, H/24 Inf, Sep–Oct 1898.

On special duty as janitor. SOURCE: Muster Roll, H/24 Inf, Nov–Dec 1898.

Discharged Ft Douglas, 27 Jan 1899, character good, single; due U.S. for clothing $34.05. SOURCE: Muster Roll, H/24 Inf, Jan–Feb 1899.

THOMAS, Alfred J.; Chief Musician; Band/10th Cav. Lance corporal, H/10th Cavalry, attached to Band/10th Cavalry, Ft Robinson, NE, for study of music, Jan–Feb 1905; assigned to band 1 Mar 1905. SOURCE: Regt Returns, 10 Cav, Jan–Mar 1905.

Chief musician, 10th Cavalry; only black among five military bandsmen to win scholarships for one-year course at Institution of Musical Art, New York City. SOURCE: Cleveland *Gazette*, 26 Oct 1912.

THOMAS, Benedict; Sergeant; L/10th Cav. With Cpls. James Coxe and Albert Ridley, L/10th Cavalry, publicly degraded and arbitrarily punished by Capt. George A. Armes, 10th Cavalry, who had their chevrons cut off without just cause or trial, Pope's Crossing, Pecos River, TX, 20 May 1879; also ordered by Armes to defy Surgeon Price and require duty of all men, whether relieved on account of illness or not. SOURCE: GCMO 36, AGO 27 May 1880.

THOMAS, Benjamin F.; Corporal; E/9th Cav. Expert rifleman at Ft D. A. Russell, WY, in 1910; resident of Chicago. SOURCE: *Illustrated Review: Ninth Cavalry*, with picture.

THOMAS, Charles; F/10th Cav. Original member of 10th Cavalry; in troop when organized, Ft Leavenworth, KS, 21 Jun 1867. SOURCE: McMiller, "Buffalo Soldiers," 73.

THOMAS, Charles; Private; C/10th Cav. Ranked number ten in carbine competition and number seven in revolver competition, Departments of Dakota and Columbia, Ft Keogh, MT, 15–23 Aug 1892. SOURCE: GO 75, AGO, 3 Nov 1892.

THOMAS, Charles; Private; H/9th Cav. Discharged on surgeon's certificate, Ft Robinson, NE, 10 Dec 1896; total deposits with paymaster $5. SOURCE: CO, H/9, to PMG, USA, 10 Dec 1896, LS, H/9.

THOMAS, Clarence; Corporal; C/24th Inf. Ranked number 144 among rifle experts with 73 percent in 1905. SOURCE: GO 101, AGO, 31 May 1906.

THOMAS, Colvin C.; Private; B/10th Cav. At Ft Apache, AZ, 1890, subscribed $.50 to testimonial to General Grierson. SOURCE: List of subscriptions, 23 Apr 1890, 10th Cavalry papers, MHI.

Served in 10th Cavalry, 1898; remained in U.S. during war with Spain. SOURCE: Cashin, *Under Fire with the Tenth Cavalry*, 333.

THOMAS, Edward; Sergeant; A/9th Cav. At Ft D. A. Russell, WY, in 1910; marksman. SOURCE: *Illustrated Review: Ninth Cavalry*, with picture.

THOMAS, Eston; Private; D/10th Cav. Served in 10th Cavalry in Cuba, 1898. SOURCE: Cashin, *Under Fire with the Tenth Cavalry*, 341.

THOMAS, Frank; Private; I/10th Cav. Served in 10th Cavalry in Cuba, 1898. SOURCE: Cashin, *Under Fire with the Tenth Cavalry*, 348.

THOMAS, Frederick A.; Musician; Band/24th Inf. Harassed and arrested by Manila, Philippines, police, 19 Jun 1902.

THOMAS, Garfield; Private; G/24th Inf. While in delirium induced by fever, drowned self in San Fernando River, Philippines. SOURCE: Manila *Times*, 4 Oct 1899.

THOMAS, George; Private; C/9th Cav. Born Accomack Co., VA; black complexion; occupation laborer; enlisted Baltimore, 6 Jan 1879; discharged on certificate of disability with constitutional syphilis from U.S. Military Prison, Ft Leavenworth, KS, 28 Jun 1882. SOURCE: Certificates of Disability, DivMo.

THOMAS, George; Private; Band/24th Inf. Born Flemingsburg, KY; Ht 5'5", black eyes, hair, complexion; first enlisted in Band/9th Cavalry, discharged 23 Jan 1870; then served in Band/10th Cavalry, discharged 30 May 1880; enlisted in F/24th Infantry, 7 Jun 1880; transferred to Band/24th Infantry, 20 Jan 1881; fined one month's pay by garrison court martial, 2 Oct 1884; married, character on discharge, Ft Supply, Indian Territory, good; deposits $250, Jan 1883–Mar 1885. SOURCE: Descriptive Book, 24 Inf NCS & Band.

THOMAS, George; Sergeant; C/25th Inf. Dishonorable discharge, Brownsville. SOURCE: SO 266, AGO, 9 Nov 1906.

THOMAS, George H.; Private; G/24th Inf. Wounded in action, Bongabon, Philippines, 29 Dec 1899. SOURCE: Muller, *The Twenty Fourth Infantry*, 36.

THOMAS, H. R.; Private; F/9th Cav. On detached service from Ft Robinson, NE, at Ft McKinney, WY, Mar 1887. SOURCE: Regt Returns, 9 Cav, Mar 1887.

THOMAS, Hardin; E/10th Cav. Original member of 10th Cavalry; in troop when organized, Ft Leavenworth, KS, 15 Jun 1867. SOURCE: McMiller, "Buffalo Soldiers," 72.

THOMAS, Henry; Private; K/10th Cav. Original member of 10th Cavalry; in troop when organized, Ft Riley, KS, 1 Sep 1867. SOURCE: McMiller, "Buffalo Soldiers," 77.

On daily duty as baker, Camp Supply, Indian Territory. SOURCE: SO 47, Det 10 Cav, Camp Supply, 21 Jun 1869, Orders, Det 10 Cav, 1868–69.

THOMAS, Henry; Sergeant; A/24th Inf. Corporal, designated to participate in Department of Arizona rifle meet. SOURCE: Order 119, Ft Huachuca, 10 Aug 1893, Letters & Orders Received, 24 Inf, 1893.

Convicted by general court martial, Ft Huachuca, AZ, of assault with deadly weapon; sentenced to reduction to private and confinement for one month. SOURCE: *ANJ* 32 (22 Dec 1894): 279.

Sergeant, died in the Philippines, 27 Apr 1901. SOURCE: *ANJ* 38 (4 May 1901): 876.

THOMAS, Henry; Musician; 25th Inf. Died at Palavig, Luzon, Philippines, 2 Aug 1901. SOURCE: *ANJ* 39 (28 Sep 1901): 81.

THOMAS, Henry; Corporal; A/9th Cav. Veteran of Philippine Insurrection; at Ft D. A. Russell, WY, in 1910. SOURCE: *Illustrated Review: Ninth Cavalry*, with picture.

THOMAS, J.; Private; G/9th Cav. On detached service at Ft Stanton, NE, 29 Jan–5 Feb 1881. SOURCE: Regt Returns, 9 Cav, Feb 1881.

THOMAS, James; 1st Sgt; E/24th Inf. Granted two-month furlough from San Carlos, AZ. SOURCE: *ANJ* 26 (30 Mar 1889): 619.

THOMAS, James; Private; M/25th Inf. Died of dysentery in the Philippines, 10 Sep 1900. SOURCE: *ANJ* 38 (29 Sep 1900): 115.

THOMAS, James; G/24th Inf. Remained in San Jose, Philippines, after service; occupation sergeant of police. SOURCE: Funston papers, KSHS.

THOMAS, James E.; Corporal; H/25th Inf. Sergeant, 25th Infantry; resident of Baltimore; has five honorable discharges; blind in one eye from arrow wound. SOURCE: Guthrie, *Camp-Fires of the Afro-American*, 646.

Retires from Ft Missoula, MT, as corporal, H/25th Infantry. SOURCE: *ANJ* 34 (1 May 1897): 545.

THOMAS, James H.; Chief Trumpeter; 10th Cav. Born in Virginia; private and trumpeter, H/10th Cavalry, 7 Jun 1867–7 Jun 1872; private, Band/10th Cavalry, and trumpeter, C/10th Cavalry, 18 Jun 1872; saddler sergeant, 1 Dec 1882; quartermaster sergeant, 1 Dec 1887; chief trumpeter, 28 Jan 1891; at Ft Assiniboine, MT, 1897. SOURCE: Baker, Roster.

Original member of H/10th Cavalry; in troop when organized, Ft Leavenworth, KS, 21 Jul 1867. SOURCE: McMiller, "Buffalo Soldiers," 75.

In H/10th Cavalry, with relief force, Beecher's Island, KS, 1867; on Staked Plains, TX, scouts, 1875–77. SOURCE: Baker, Roster.

With band decimated by death, discharge, and other causes, willing to transfer James H. Thomas of C/10th Cavalry to band, with your approval. SOURCE: CO, 10 Cav, to CO, C/10, 15 Dec 1876, LS, 10 Cav, 1873–83.

Mentioned as trumpeter, C/10th Cavalry, Jan 1877. SOURCE: ES, 10 Cav, 1873–83.

Quartermaster sergeant, 10th Cavalry, at Ft Apache, AZ, 1890, subscribed $.50 to testimonial to General Grierson. SOURCE: List of subscriptions, 23 Apr 1890, 10th Cavalry papers, MHI.

Retires from Ft Assiniboine as chief trumpeter. SOURCE: *ANJ* 34 (7 Aug 1897): 909.

THOMAS, James H.; 1st Lt; D/49th Inf. Enlisted in A/1st Indiana Infantry, 28 Jun 1898; first lieutenant, 5 Jul 1898; mustered out 20 Jun 1899; first lieutenant, 49th Infantry, 9 Sep 1899; on recruiting duty at Indianapolis, 13–28 Sep 1899, and at Evansville, IN, 6–16 Oct 1899. SOURCE: Descriptive Book, D/49 Inf.

Only officer among black Indiana volunteers considered adequately educated by Inspector General Col. Marion Maus, Chickamauga, GA, Oct 1898. SOURCE: Gatewood, "Indiana Negroes and the Spanish-American War," 136, 138.

Indianapolis native on recruiting duty; last Monday he and his wife received visitors at "their elegant home" on West 14th Street; he leaves shortly to join his regiment at Jefferson Barracks, MO. SOURCE: Indianapolis *Freeman*, 30 Sep 1899.

Mentioned. SOURCE: Beasley, *Negro Trailblazers*, 284.

One of twenty-three officers of 49th Infantry recommended as regular Army second lieutenants. SOURCE: CG, DivPI, Manila, 8 Feb 1901, to AGO, AGO File 355163.

Resided at 516 West 13th Street, Indianapolis, in 1905; physically unable to write so dictated statement; was in Capt.

Floyd Crumbly's company, D/49th Infantry; Crumbly was sick in hospital, Oct–Nov 1900, and thereafter ill but "always ready and anxious to do his whole duty." SOURCE: Affidavit, Thomas, 2 May 1905, VA File XC 2624105, Floyd H. Crumbly.

THOMAS, James H.; Private; 24th Inf. Wounded in leg, Bongabon, Philippines, 28 Feb 1900. SOURCE: *ANJ* 37 (14 Apr 1900): 779.

THOMAS, Jessie; Private; L/9th Cav. At Ft D. A. Russell, WY, in 1910; resident of St. Louis. SOURCE: *Illustrated Review: Ninth Cavalry*, with picture.

THOMAS, John; Sergeant; C/10th Cav. Original member of 10th Cavalry; in troop when organized, Ft Leavenworth, KS, 14 May 1867. SOURCE: McMiller, "Buffalo Soldiers," 70.

At Ft Apache, AZ, 1890, subscribed $.50 to testimonial to General Grierson. SOURCE: List of subscriptions, 23 Apr 1890, 10th Cavalry papers, MHI.

THOMAS, John; Private; A/10th Cav. Mentioned Jan 1873 as enlisted on 4 Sep 1867. SOURCE: LS, 10 Cav, 1873–83.

THOMAS, John; L/10th Cav. Original member of 10th Cavalry; in troop when organized, Ft Riley, KS, 21 Sep 1867. SOURCE: McMiller, "Buffalo Soldiers," 78.

Camped at Camp Sill, Indian Territory, May 1868, with Grierson expedition to Wichita Mountains: "It rained several days and nights very hard. We laid in this two full weeks. All the streams and lowlands were flooded." SOURCE: *Winners of the West* 11 (May 1934): 3.

THOMAS, John; Private; F/9th Cav. At Ft Robinson, NE, 1887. *See* **STOKES**, Henry A., Corporal, C/9th Cavalry

THOMAS, John; Private; G/25th Inf. Wounded in action, El Caney, Cuba, 1898. SOURCE: Nankivell, *History of the Twenty-fifth Infantry*, 83.

THOMAS, John; Private; K/10th Cav. At Ft Robinson, NE, 1904.

THOMAS, John H.; G/10th Cav. Original member of 10th Cavalry; in troop when organized, Ft Leavenworth, KS, 5 Jul 1867. SOURCE: McMiller, "Buffalo Soldiers," 74.

THOMAS, John W.; Sergeant; G/10th Cav. At Ft Apache, AZ, 1890, subscribed $.50 to testimonial to General Grierson. SOURCE: List of subscriptions, 23 Apr 1890, 10th Cavalry papers, MHI.

THOMAS, Joseph; Private; H/10th Cav. At Ft Apache, AZ, 1890, subscribed $.50 to testimonial to General Grierson. SOURCE: List of subscriptions, 23 Apr 1890, 10th Cavalry papers, MHI.

Served in 10th Cavalry, 1898; remained in U.S. during war with Spain. SOURCE: Cashin, *Under Fire with the Tenth Cavalry*, 347.

THOMAS, Joseph; Private; K/25th Inf. At Ft Niobrara, NE, 1904. SOURCE: Wilson, "History of Fort Niobrara."

THOMAS, Lankin; C/10th Cav. Original member of 10th Cavalry; in troop when organized, Ft Leavenworth, KS, 14 May 1867. SOURCE: McMiller, "Buffalo Soldiers," 70.

THOMAS, Leonard; F/9th Cav. Admitted to Soldiers Home with disability, age 44, after three years' service, 25 Feb 1891. SOURCE: SecWar, *AR 1891*, 752.

THOMAS, Littleton; L/10th Cav. Original member of 10th Cavalry; in troop when organized, Ft Riley, KS, 21 Sep 1867. SOURCE: McMiller, "Buffalo Soldiers," 78.

THOMAS, Marcus; Private; H/24th Inf. Enlisted Louisville, 11 Jul 1898; assigned and joined company 16 Sep 1898; on special duty as carpenter with Quartermaster Department since 13 Oct 1898; due U.S. for ordnance (tin cup, fork, knife) $.27. SOURCE: Muster Roll, H/24 Inf, Sep–Oct 1898.

On special duty as carpenter. SOURCE: Muster Roll, H/24 Inf, Nov–Dec 1898.

Discharged Ft Douglas, UT, 28 Jan 1899, character good, single; due U.S. for clothing $18.42. SOURCE: Muster Roll, H/24 Inf, Jan–Feb 1899.

THOMAS, Millard; Private; F/9th Cav. At Ft D. A. Russell, WY, in 1910; resident of Indianapolis. SOURCE: *Illustrated Review: Ninth Cavalry*, with picture.

THOMAS, Moses; Private; E/48th Inf. Died of variola in the Philippines, 31 Jul 1900. SOURCE: *ANJ* 37 (11 Aug 1900): 1191.

THOMAS, P.; Private; D/9th Cav. Died of pneumonia at Ft McKinney, WY, 9 Mar 1889. SOURCE: Regt Returns, 9 Cav, Mar 1889.

THOMAS, Samuel; Private; Band/24th Inf. Born Vincennes, IN; black eyes and hair, brown complexion, Ht 5'9"; enlisted at Ft Bayard, NM, age 27, 24 Apr 1890; joined Band/24th Infantry, Ft Bayard, 17 Feb 1891; transferred to F/24th Infantry, 10 Jan 1894, character excellent, married, no children; deposits $250 in 1893, clothing $60.14, retained $44. SOURCE: Descriptive Book, 24 Inf NCS & Band.

At Ft Douglas, UT, wife Cora complained about his gambling, later shot and killed him; died 11 Jun 1897 and buried at Ft Douglas. SOURCE: Clark, "A History of the Twenty-fourth," 84, appendix A.

THOMAS, Samuel; Trumpeter; H/9th Cav. Appointed trumpeter 1 Jun 1897. SOURCE: CO, H/9, to AG, USA, 14 May 1897, LS, H/9 Cav.

THOMAS, Simon; Private; H/9th Cav. In hands of civil authorities, Buffalo, WY, 15 Nov 1888–10 Jan 1889. SOURCE: Regt Returns, 9 Cav, Nov 1888–Jan 1889.

THOMAS, Spencer H.; QM Sgt; H/9th Cav. Ranked number eight in rifle competition, Departments of the Platte and Dakota, Bellevue, NE, 4–9 Aug 1890. SOURCE: *ANJ* 27 (16 Aug 1890): 943; GO 112, AGO, 2 Oct 1890.

Private, A/9th Cavalry, on special duty at Ft Robinson, NE, canteen. SOURCE: Order 74, 10 Apr 1891, Post Orders, Ft Robinson.

Relieved from special duty at post canteen, Ft Robinson. SOURCE: Order 103, 18 May 1891, Post Orders, Ft Robinson.

Ranked number four in carbine competition and number eight in revolver competition, Departments of the East, the Platte, and California, Bellevue, 17–22 Aug 1891; distinguished marksman, revolver, 1890 and 1891, and carbine, 1891. SOURCE: GO 81, AGO, 6 Oct 1891.

Private, at rifle competition, Ft Sheridan, IL, Sep 1891. SOURCE: *ANJ* 29 (5 Sep 1891): 25.

Private, A/9th Cavalry; leave extended fifteen days in accordance with letter, Department of the Platte, 23 Sep 1893. SOURCE: Regt Returns, 9 Cav, Sep 1893.

Promoted from lance corporal to corporal, H/9th Cavalry, 22 Aug 1894. SOURCE: *ANJ* 32 (1 Sep 1894): 6.

Corporal, H/9th Cavalry, ranked number two in competition of Army carbine team, 1894. SOURCE: GO 15, AGO, 15 Nov 1894.

At Ft Robinson, 1896–1898, deposited $115 with paymaster; promoted to sergeant, 1898.

Quartermaster sergeant, H/9th Cavalry, ranked number eight among expert riflemen, 1904, with 81 percent. SOURCE: GO 79, AGO, 1 Jun 1905.

Distinguished marksman, 1905. SOURCE: GO 173, AGO, 20 Oct 1905.

Ranked number 410 among expert riflemen, 1905, with 69 percent. SOURCE: GO 101, AGO, 31 May 1906.

THOMAS, Wilber; Private; H/24th Inf. Enlisted Pittsburgh, 8 Aug 1898; assigned and joined company 16 Sep 1898; due U.S. for ordnance (canteen, canteen strap, and spoon) $.88. SOURCE: Muster Roll, H/24 Inf, Sep–Oct 1898.

In hospital since 23 Dec 1898, disease contracted in line of duty. SOURCE: Muster Roll, H/24 Inf, Nov–Dec 1898.

Discharged at Ft Douglas, UT, 29 Jan 1899, character good, single; due U.S. for clothing $8.18. SOURCE: Muster Roll, H/24 Inf, Jan–Feb 1899.

THOMAS, William; Private; 10th Cav. Recruit arrived at Ft Leavenworth, KS, from Jefferson Barracks, MO, 9 Oct 1866. SOURCE: LS, 10 Cav, 1866–67.

Commander forwarded to Adjutant General final statement and inventory of effects of Private Thomas, late recruit, 10th Cavalry, 30 Oct 1866. SOURCE: LS, 10 Cav, 1866–67.

THOMAS, William; Private; E/9th Cav. Deserted at San Antonio, TX, 9 Apr 1867. SOURCE: Hamilton, "History of the Ninth Cavalry," 5; *Illustrated Review: Ninth Cavalry*.

Deserted from confinement after participation in mutiny. SOURCE: Ninth Cavalry, *Historical and Pictorial Review*, 44.

THOMAS, William; G/10th Cav. Original member of 10th Cavalry; in troop when organized, Ft Leavenworth, KS, 5 Jul 1867. SOURCE: McMiller, "Buffalo Soldiers," 74.

THOMAS, William; Corporal; M/10th Cav. Original member of 10th Cavalry; in troop when organized, Ft Riley, KS, 15 Oct 1867. SOURCE: McMiller, "Buffalo Soldiers," 79.

Mentioned Oct 1870. SOURCE: ES, 10 Cav, 1866–71.

THOMAS, William; Private; G/10th Cav. Served in 10th Cavalry, 1898; remained in U.S. during war with Spain. SOURCE: Cashin, *Under Fire with the Tenth Cavalry*, 345.

THOMAS, William; Private; B/25th Inf. Dishonorable discharge, Brownsville. SOURCE: SO 266, AGO, 9 Nov 1906.

THOMAS, William E.; Private; H/24th Inf. Enlisted Baltimore, 26 Jul 1898; assigned and joined 16 Sep 1898; due U.S. for ordnance (cup) $.15. SOURCE: Muster Roll, H/24 Inf, Sep–Oct 1898.

Discharged Ft Douglas, UT, 28 Jan 1899, character good, single; deposits $30; due U.S. for clothing $14.45. SOURCE: Muster Roll, H/24 Inf, Jan–Feb 1899.

THOMAS, William H.; L/10th Cav. Original member of 10th Cavalry; in troop when organized, Ft Riley, KS, 21 Sep 1867. SOURCE: McMiller, "Buffalo Soldiers," 78.

THOMAS, William H.; Private; C/9th Cav. On furlough from Ft Robinson, NE, Feb 1887. SOURCE: Post Returns, Ft Robinson, Feb 1887.

Reenlistment authorized 21 Feb 1887. SOURCE: Post Returns, Ft Robinson, Feb 1887.

THOMAS, William H.; Private; H/24th Inf. Designated to participate in Department of Arizona rifle meet. SOURCE: Order 119, Ft Huachuca, 10 Aug 1893, Letters & Orders Received, 24 Inf, 1893.

To compete for position on department team, Ft Bayard, NM. SOURCE: Name File, 24 Inf.

THOMAS, William R.; Private; G/9th Cav. Private, L/9th Cavalry, on detached service in field, New Mexico, 21 Jan–24 Feb 1881. SOURCE: Regt Returns, 9 Cav, Feb 1881.

Corporal, F/9th Cavalry; reduced to private, fined $120, and confined for one year, Ft Robinson, NE, for drawing pistol on private and menacing him while on guard; "severe but just." SOURCE: *ANJ* 27 (4 Jan 1890): 368.

Private, G/9th Cavalry; at Ft Robinson, 1894. SOURCE: Court Martial Records, Plummer.

Retired as private, G/9th Cavalry, Jun 1901. SOURCE: *ANJ* 38 (22 Jun 1901): 1043.

THOMAS, Willis; Private; D/10th Cav. Enlisted Little Rock, AR, 23 Feb 1867; at Ft Gibson, Indian Territory, Jun 1867. SOURCE: LS, 10 Cav, 1866–67.

Original member of 10th Cavalry; in troop when organized, Ft Leavenworth, KS, 1 Jun 1867. SOURCE: McMiller, "Buffalo Soldiers," 71.

THOMAS, Wilson M.; Private; E/10th Cav. Served in 10th Cavalry in Cuba, 1898. SOURCE: Cashin, *Under Fire with the Tenth Cavalry*, 342.

THOMASON, Hugh; Captain; 48th Inf. One of nineteen officers of 48th Infantry recommended as regular Army second lieutenants. SOURCE: CG, DivPI, Manila, 8 Feb 1901, to AGO, AGO File 355163.

THOMPKINS, William H.; Sergeant; H/25th Inf. At Ft Robinson, NE, 1893. *See* **GILLENWATER**, Walter, Corporal, Band/25th Infantry

Born Paterson, NJ; awarded Medal of Honor on 30 Jun 1899 while on occupation duty at Manzanillo, Cuba. SOURCE: Lee, *Negro Medal of Honor Men*, 92, 98.

Private, G/10th Cavalry, promoted to corporal 18 Feb 1898. SOURCE: *ANJ* 35 (5 Mar 1898): 498.

Corporal, A/10th Cavalry; commended for distinguished gallantry while private, G/10th Cavalry, Tayabacoa, Cuba, with force that had landed and had been forced to withdraw to boats, leaving their killed and missing ashore; along with Pvt. Fitz Lee, M/10th Cavalry (now out of service), Pvt. Dennis Bell, H/10th Cavalry, and Pvt. George Wanton, M/10th Cavalry (now out of service), voluntarily returned to shore in face of enemy fire and aided in rescue of wounded comrades who otherwise would have been captured; all three awarded Medal of Honor. SOURCE: GO 15, AGO, 13 Feb 1900.

Medal of Honor mentioned. SOURCE: Steward, *The Colored Regulars*, 205.

Corporal, A/10th Cavalry; cited for distinguished service, 30 Jun 1898. SOURCE: *ANJ* 37 (24 Feb 1900): 611.

Sergeant, H/25th Infantry; commended for gallantry while private, G/10th Cavalry, saving comrade from drowning at Tayabacoa, 30 Jun 1898. SOURCE: Cleveland *Gazette*, 24 Jun 1906.

THOMPSON; Sergeant; M/25th Inf. Sergeant, returned to Iba, Zambales, Philippines, after scout in which he and Sergeant Read found insurgent rendezvous, destroyed it, and captured two. SOURCE: Manila *Times*, 26 Sep 1900.

Corporal, M/25th Infantry, and instructor of Ilocano scouts, Castillejos, Zambales, Philippines, assisted by Lance Cpls. Clemmens, K/25th Infantry, and Strickland, I/25th Infantry. SOURCE: *ANJ* 38 (16 Mar 1901): 702.

Sergeant, M/25th Infantry, organized and trained Ilocano scouts. SOURCE: Richmond *Planet*, 22 Jun 1901.

THOMPSON, Albert; Private; E/10th Cav. Served in 10th Cavalry, 1898; remained in U.S. during war with Spain. SOURCE: Cashin, *Under Fire with the Tenth Cavalry*, 343.

Now serving life sentence in Alabama state penitentiary for rape; conviction based on dubious identification. SOURCE: Indianapolis *Freeman*, 29 Apr 1899.

THOMPSON, Albert; Private; I/25th Inf. Fined $4 by summary court, San Isidro, Philippines, for involvement in street fight, 20 Jun 1902, first conviction. SOURCE: Register of Summary Court, San Isidro.

Fined $5 by summary court, San Isidro, for being drunk and disorderly in quarters after taps, 4 Jul 1902. SOURCE: Register of Summary Court, San Isidro.

THOMPSON, Albert; Private; G/9th Cav. At Ft D. A. Russell, WY, in 1910; resident of Boston. SOURCE: *Illustrated Review: Ninth Cavalry*, with picture.

THOMPSON, Aleck; Private; A/10th Cav. Original member of 10th Cavalry; in troop when organized, Ft Leavenworth, KS, 18 Feb 1867. SOURCE: McMiller, "Buffalo Soldiers," 68.

Discharge without character mentioned, Feb 1877. SOURCE: ES, 10 Cav, 1873–83.

THOMPSON, Andrew; Private; M/49th Inf. Died of dysentery in the Philippines, 8 Sep 1900. SOURCE: *ANJ* 38 (19 Jan 1901): 503.

THOMPSON, Byron; Private; A/10th Cav. Served in 10th Cavalry, 1898; remained in U.S. during war with Spain. SOURCE: Cashin, *Under Fire with the Tenth Cavalry*, 337.

THOMPSON, Charles A.; Hospital Corps. Left Cleveland, OH, May 1911; now stationed in New Mexico: "My time in the army will soon expire and I am going to try for the position of embalmer in the (Panama) Canal Zone. You know me, my mother, sisters and brothers well, and a letter of recommendation from you would go a long way toward helping me get this position. I am trying to climb. Please help me. Hoping I may hear from you at your earliest convenience." SOURCE: Letter, Hachita, NM, 4 Dec 1913, in Cleveland *Gazette*, 14 Jan 1914.

Stationed with A/9th Cavalry, commanded by Lieutenant Rothwell. SOURCE: Letter, Alamo Hueco, NM, 16 Mar 1914, in Cleveland *Gazette*, 28 Mar 1914.

THOMPSON, Charles H.; Private; C/49th Inf. Died of chronic dysentery aboard U.S. Army Transport *Grant* bound for San Francisco, 22 Jun 1901.

THOMPSON, Charles N.; Private; I/24th Inf. Enlisted Louisville, 15 Feb 1899. SOURCE: Muster Roll, I/24 Inf, Jan–Feb 1899.

Sick since 18 Apr 1899, disease contracted in line of duty. SOURCE: Muster Roll, I/24 Inf, Mar–Apr 1899.

Discharged on surgeon's certificate, 19 Jun 1899, character good, clothing $17.02. SOURCE: Muster Roll, I/24 Inf, May–Jun 1899.

THOMPSON, David; Private; C/9th Cav. Transferred from B/9th Cavalry and attached to Band/9th Cavalry for instruction in music. SOURCE: Order 16, 9 Cav, 26 May 1887.

THOMPSON, Fred F.; Private; K/9th Cav. At Ft D. A. Russell, WY, in 1910; resident of Hamilton, MO. SOURCE: *Illustrated Review: Ninth Cavalry*, with picture.

THOMPSON, Garfield; Private; G/24th Inf. Served as private, G/10th Cavalry, 1898; remained in U.S. during war with Spain. SOURCE: Cashin, *Under Fire with the Tenth Cavalry*, 345.

Accidentally drowned in the Philippines, 3 Oct 1899. SOURCE: *ANJ* 37 (14 Oct 1899): 155.

THOMPSON, General S.; Private; H/24th Inf. Enlisted Nashville, 23 Jul 1898; assigned and joined company 16 Sep 1898; on furlough authorized by surgeon's certificate, 20 Sep–18 Oct 1898; on detached service en route to join company, 23–28 Oct 1898; fined $.75 by summary court. SOURCE: Muster Roll, H/24 Inf, Sep–Oct 1898.

Fined $2 by summary court, 23 Nov 1898; dishonorable discharge, Ft Douglas, UT, 24 Jan 1899, not entitled to travel pay; deposits $30; due U.S. for clothing $57.70. SOURCE: Muster Roll, H/24 Inf, Nov–Dec 1898 and Jan–Feb 1899.

THOMPSON, George; Private; E/9th Cav. *See* **BARD**, Benjamin, Private, H/10th Cavalry

THOMPSON, George S.; 1st Lt; Philippine Scouts. Born Clinton, IA; occupation waiter; Ht 5'8", yellow complexion; enlisted, age 22, Fort Sill, Indian Territory; marksman, 1887 and 1888; learning music, 21 Sep 1888; fined $10 by garrison court martial, 1889; discharged, end of term, Ft Bayard, NM, 4 Nov 1889, character very good, single; due U.S. for clothing $22; retained $72. SOURCE: Descriptive Book, 24 Inf NCS & Band.

Private and musician, K/24th Infantry and Band/24th Infantry, 5 Nov 1884–4 Nov 1889. SOURCE: Baker, Roster.

Leader of Ft Reno, Indian Territory, band, "entirely self-learned [and] a remarkable band-leader." SOURCE: Cleveland *Gazette*, 23 Apr 1887.

Private, Band/10th Cavalry, 7 Nov 1889; sergeant, 18 Jun 1893; at Ft Assiniboine, MT, 1897. SOURCE: Baker, Roster.

Private, Band/10th Cavalry, at Fort Apache, AZ, 1890, subscribed $.50 to testimonial to General Grierson. SOURCE: List of subscriptions, 23 Apr 1890, 10th Cavalry papers, MHI.

Sergeant, Band/25th Infantry, led detachment from San Marcelino, Philippines, after insurgents, Apr 1900. SOURCE: Richmond *Planet*, 16 Jan 1900.

Promoted to first sergeant of scouts. SOURCE: Richmond *Planet*, 27 Jan 1900.

Wounded in action (knee), Palavig, Luzon, Philippines, 13 May 1900. SOURCE: *ANJ* 37 (9 Jun 1900): 975.

Principal musician, 25th Infantry, rumored to have commission in native regiment. SOURCE: Richmond *Planet*, 22 Jun 1901.

Led scouting detachment from San Felipe, Philippines, which had lively one-to-two-hour engagement with enemy in mid-August 1900 between San Felipe and San Narciso. SOURCE: Richmond *Planet*, 20 Oct 1900.

Appointed second lieutenant of Philippine Scouts from Ft Niobrara, NE; previously commended for heroism in the Philippines; "one of the crack shots in the army." SOURCE: Indianapolis *Freeman*, 1 Apr 1905.

Commissioned second lieutenant in Philippine Scouts; outstanding marksman; served in insurrection with "heroism and efficiency." SOURCE: Cleveland *Gazette*, 1 Apr 1905.

See **GILMER**, David J., First Lieutenant, Philippine Scouts; **GREEN**, Dalbert P., Master Sergeant, 25th Infantry

Convicted by general court martial, Camp Daraga, Albay, Philippines, of conduct unbecoming an officer and gentleman, immorality with native woman, allowing enlisted men to violate quarantine, and borrowing money from his first sergeant, 48th Company, Philippine Scouts; sentenced to dismissal from service; sentence approved by President Roosevelt. SOURCE: GO 29, AGO, 21 Feb 1910.

Dismissed from Army at Ft Lawton, WA. SOURCE: Cleveland *Gazette*, 9 Apr 1910.

Age 63 in 1929, resided at Apache Junction, AZ; served twenty-six years, and had scars from eleven bullet wounds, a dozen bolo cuts, and many arrow and spear wounds; had confrontation with Theodore Roosevelt over slapjacks he made near Siboney, Cuba, while serving as messenger-interpreter, 2nd Brigade, 2nd Division, 24 Jun 1898; in the Philippines, led scouts for 3rd Battalion, 25th Infantry, then all regimental scouts; with help of buddy who was coachman to Senator John Spooner of Wisconsin got interview with President Roosevelt and then commission in Philippine Scouts. SOURCE: "Colored Doughboy Reprimands Roosevelt," *US Army Recruiting News* 11 (1 Aug 1929); 9, based on material first published in 25th Infantry's weekly *The Bullet*.

THOMPSON, Harvey A.; 9th Cav. Letter from Ft McKinney, WY, 20 Sep 1886, informs of establishment of Clear Creek Lodge, Grand Union of Odd Fellows, with Pvt. H. B. King, Band/9th Cavalry, serving as president. SOURCE: Cleveland *Gazette*, 2 Oct 1886.

THOMPSON, Isaac; E/10th Cav. Original member of 10th Cavalry; in troop when organized, Ft Leavenworth, KS, 15 Jun 1867. SOURCE: McMiller, "Buffalo Soldiers," 72.

THOMPSON, James; QM Sgt; B/10th Cav. Born in Maryland; private, B/10th Cavalry, 22 Nov 1888; corporal, 6 Aug 1893; sergeant, 28 Jan 1895; stationed at Ft Custer, MT, 1897. SOURCE: Baker, Roster.

Private, B/10th Cavalry, at Ft Apache, AZ, 1890, subscribed $.50 to testimonial to General Grierson. SOURCE: List of subscriptions, 23 Apr 1890, 10th Cavalry papers, MHI.

Served in 10th Cavalry in Cuba, 1898. SOURCE: Cashin, *Under Fire with the Tenth Cavalry*, 337.

THOMPSON, James; Private; D/48th Inf. Died of appendicitis in the Philippines, 10 Mar 1900. SOURCE: *ANJ* 37 (17 Mar 1900): 682.

THOMPSON, James A.; Private; Band/9th Cav. Private, D/9th Cavalry, in hands of civil authorities, Crawford, NE, 15–20 Feb 1891. SOURCE: Regt Returns, 9 Cav, Feb 1891.

Private, Band/9th Cavalry, in hands of civil authorities, Chadron, NE, 5–7 Nov 1896. SOURCE: Regt Returns, 9 Cav, Nov 1896.

THOMPSON, John; E/10th Cav. Original member of 10th Cavalry; in troop when organized, Ft Leavenworth, KS, 15 Jun 1867. SOURCE: McMiller, "Buffalo Soldiers," 72.

THOMPSON, John; H/10th Cav. Original member of 10th Cavalry; in troop when organized, Ft Leavenworth, KS, 21 Jul 1867. SOURCE: McMiller, "Buffalo Soldiers," 75.

THOMPSON, John; Private; L/10th Cav. At Ft Stockton, TX, 1879. *See* **WOODS**, John W., Private, L/10th Cavalry

THOMPSON, John R.; Private; L/9th Cav. At Ft D. A. Russell, WY, in 1910; resident of Chicago. SOURCE: *Illustrated Review: Ninth Cavalry*, with picture.

THOMPSON, John T.; Private; I/10th Cav. Served in 10th Cavalry, 1898; remained in U.S. during war with Spain. SOURCE: Cashin, *Under Fire with the Tenth Cavalry*, 348.

THOMPSON, Joseph; Corporal; I/10th Cav. Private, I/10th Cavalry, at Ft Robinson, NE, for cavalry competition, Sep 1897. SOURCE: Post Returns, Ft Robinson, Sep 1897.

Served in 10th Cavalry in Cuba, 1898. SOURCE: Cashin, *Under Fire with the Tenth Cavalry*, 347.

THOMPSON, Joseph; Private; I/24th Inf. Enlisted Mobile, AL, 28 Mar 1899. SOURCE: Muster Roll, I/24 Inf, Mar–Apr 1899.

Allotted $7 per month for twelve months to Lucy Thompson. SOURCE: Muster Roll, I/24 Inf, Sep–Oct 1899.

On detached service at Cabanatuan, Philippines, since 30 Dec 1899. SOURCE: Muster Roll, I/24 Inf, Nov–Dec 1899.

THOMPSON, Joseph; Corporal; G/9th Cav. Veteran of Philippine Insurrection; at Ft D. A. Russell, WY, in 1910; sharpshooter. SOURCE: *Illustrated Review: Ninth Cavalry*, with picture.

THOMPSON, King D.; Private; H/24th Inf. Enlisted Cincinnati, 21 Jun 1898; assigned and joined company 16 Sep 1898. SOURCE: Muster Roll, H/24 Inf, Sep–Oct 1898.

Discharged Ft Douglas, UT, 28 Jan 1899, character good, single; deposits $50; due U.S. for clothing $16.48. SOURCE: Muster Roll, H/24 Inf, Jan–Feb 1899.

THOMPSON, Lorenzo; K/10th Cav. Original member of 10th Cavalry; in troop when organized, Ft Riley, KS, 1 Sep 1867. SOURCE: McMiller, "Buffalo Soldiers," 77.

THOMPSON, Maryland; Private; G/10th Cav. Served in 10th Cavalry in Cuba, 1898. SOURCE: Cashin, *Under Fire with the Tenth Cavalry*, 345.

Died of yellow fever in Cuba, 10 Aug 1898. SOURCE: AG, *Correspondence Regarding the War with Spain*, I:218.

THOMPSON, Montague; Private; K/24th Inf. Sentenced to ten days' confinement, Cabanatuan, Philippines, for conversing with prisoners he guarded and permitting them to engage in loud, boisterous conversation, 10 Apr 1901. SOURCE: Name File, 24 Inf.

THOMPSON, Murry; Corporal; C/10th Cav. Served in 10th Cavalry in Cuba, 1898. SOURCE: Cashin, *Under Fire with the Tenth Cavalry*, 339.

THOMPSON, O.; Private; L/9th Cav. On detached service in field, New Mexico, 21 Jan–24 Feb 1881. SOURCE: Regt Returns, 9 Cav, Feb 1881.

THOMPSON, Richard; Corporal; I/9th Cav. Clothing destroyed when fighting fire, Ft Wingate, NM, 15 Dec 1876. SOURCE: Billington, *New Mexico's Buffalo Soldiers*, 110.

THOMPSON, Robert; Private; E/9th Cav. Transferred to Hospital Corps in accordance with Special Order 66, Adjutant General's Office, 19 Mar 1896.

THOMPSON, Samuel; Private; 10th Cav. Enlisted Helena, AR, 27 Apr 1867. SOURCE: LS, 10 Cav, 1866–67.

THOMPSON, Samuel; Recruit; I/9th Cav. Convicted by general court martial, Jefferson Barracks, MO, of desertion, 25 Jun 1883; sentenced to dishonorable discharge and two years. SOURCE: GCMO 52, AGO, 14 Nov 1883.

THOMPSON, W. M.; Private; K/24th Inf. At San Carlos, AZ, 1890. *See* **HARDEE**, James A., Private, K/24th Infantry

THOMPSON, Wallace; I/24th Inf. Admitted to Soldiers Home with disability, age 36, after thirteen years and two months' service, 20 Feb 1888. SOURCE: SecWar, *AR 1888*, 902.

THOMPSON, Walter; Private; A/10th Cav. Served in 10th Cavalry, 1898; remained in U.S. during war with Spain. SOURCE: Cashin, *Under Fire with the Tenth Cavalry*, 337.

THOMPSON, William; Private; B/10th Cav. At Ft Apache, AZ, 1890, subscribed $.50 to testimonial to General Grierson. SOURCE: List of subscriptions, 23 Apr 1890, 10th Cavalry papers, MHI.

THOMPSON, William; Corporal; F/24th Inf. Authorized six-month furlough from Ft Bayard, NM, upon reenlistment. SOURCE: *ANJ* 28 (18 Apr 1891): 577.

Retires from Ft Douglas, UT. SOURCE: *ANJ* 35 (23 Apr 1898): 649.

THOMPSON, William; QM Sgt; L/25th Inf. Back on duty after three-month illness. SOURCE: Richmond *Planet*, 20 Jan 1900.

Led detachment from San Marcelino, Philippines, in pursuit of bandits, Apr 1900. SOURCE: Richmond *Planet*, 16 Jun 1900.

THOMPSON, William W.; QM Sgt; 10th Cav. Picture. SOURCE: Mary Curtis, *The Black Soldier*, opposite 37.

Commissary sergeant, passed examination for commission, Ft Huachuca, AZ, Nov 1914. SOURCE: *Crisis* 8 (May 1914): 14.

Regimental quartermaster sergeant, 10th Cavalry, commissioned captain at Camp Des Moines, IA, 15 Oct 1917. SOURCE: Glass, *History of the Tenth Cavalry*, appendix M.

THORNTON; Private; M/10th Cav. At Ft Apache, AZ, 1890, subscribed $.50 to testimonial to General Grierson. SOURCE: List of subscriptions, 23 Apr 1890, 10th Cavalry papers, MHI.

THORNTON, Beverly F.; Cook; K/10th Cav. Corporal, K/10th Cavalry; served in regiment, 1898; remained in U.S. during war with Spain. SOURCE: Cashin, *Under Fire with the Tenth Cavalry*, 349.

Age 43, married Miss Sallie A. Conley of Huntsville, AL, age 42, at Ft Robinson, NE, 21 Apr 1904. SOURCE: Monthly Report, Chaplain Anderson, 1 May 1904; Medical History, Ft Robinson.

Guest with wife at K/10th Cavalry Thanksgiving dinner, Ft Robinson. SOURCE: Simmons, "Thanksgiving Day in the Tenth Cavalry," 664.

Read paper entitled "Economy" at Y.M.C.A., Ft Robinson, 4 Jan 1905, published in *Colored American Magazine* 9 (Mar 1905): 150–51.

Deposition, 11 Jul 1906, supports pension claim of Caleb Benson. SOURCE: VA File XC 2499129, Caleb Benson.

THORNTON, Charles E.; Private; H/9th Cav. Enlisted Washington, DC, 29 Mar 1887; in hands of civil authorities, Buffalo, WY, since 5 Aug 1890, charged with theft and sale of government property; absent without leave 29 Jul–5 Aug 1890; released by civil authorities 22 Apr 1891 and now in confinement at Ft McKinney, WY. SOURCE: Muster Roll, Det 9 Cav, 28 Feb–30 Apr 1891.

In hands of civil authorities, Buffalo, WY, 5 Jul 1890–22 Apr 1891. SOURCE: Regt Returns, 9 Cav.

THORNTON, Cliff; Private; G/10th Cav. Served in 10th Cavalry in Cuba, 1898. SOURCE: Cashin, *Under Fire with the Tenth Cavalry*, 345.

THORNTON, Jake; 1st Sgt; F/10th Cav. Adjutant, 10th Cavalry, informed Capt. George F. Armes, F/10th Cavalry, Ft Harker, KS, 18 Jul 1867, that his first sergeant was Thornton, not Thorn, as Armes referred to him. SOURCE: LS, 10 Cav, 1866–67.

Shot through left leg below knee in engagement with Indians at Camp Price, on Beaver Creek, KS, 21 Aug 1867; broke leg so he could not stand. SOURCE: Armes, *Ups and Downs*, 244, 247.

Wounded in knee by arrow, discharged, and returned to home in Dayton, OH. *See* **TAYLOR**, John, Private, F/10th Cavalry

THORNTON, James; Private; G/10th Cav. Charges of petty larceny against Thornton referred for trial to Field Officers Court by commander, 10th Cavalry, 19 Jun 1873. SOURCE: ES, 10 Cav, 1873–83.

THORNTON, John; Corporal; D/10th Cav. Original member of 10th Cavalry; in troop when organized, Ft Leavenworth, KS, 1 Jun 1867. SOURCE: McMiller, "Buffalo Soldiers," 71.

Served in 10th Cavalry in Cuba, 1898. SOURCE: Cashin, *Under Fire with the Tenth Cavalry*, 341.

THORNTON, Luther G.; Sergeant; B/25th Inf. Dishonorable discharge, Brownsville. SOURCE: SO 266, AGO, 9 Nov 1906.

THORNTON, Luther T.; Private; L/10th Cav. Served in 10th Cavalry, 1898; remained in U.S. during war with Spain. SOURCE: Cashin, *Under Fire with the Tenth Cavalry*, 351.

THORNTON, Magager; Private; H/9th Cav. At Ft D. A. Russell, WY, in 1910; resident of Alchie, VA. SOURCE: *Illustrated Review: Ninth Cavalry*, with picture.

THORNTON, Temple; Corporal; D/25th Inf. Dishonorable discharge, Brownsville. SOURCE: SO 266, AGO, 9 Nov 1906.

THORNTON, William; Sergeant; E/25th Inf. At Ft Buford, ND, 1893. SOURCE: Nankivell, *History of the Twenty-fifth Infantry*, 50 (picture).

THORNTON, William; Comsy Sgt; U.S. Army. Born Washington Court House, OH; enlisted from residence at Great Falls, MT; awarded Distinguished Service Cross in lieu of certificate of merit for distinguished service, Santiago, Cuba, 1 Jul 1898. SOURCE: *Decorations. US Army. Supplement I*, 30; GO 15, AGO, 13 Feb 1900.

Corporal, G/24th Infantry; led detachment of four that was first group of U.S. troops to enter blockhouse on San Juan Hill, 1 Jul 1898; awarded certificate of merit. SOURCE: Scipio, *Last of the Black Regulars*, 29, 130; Steward, *The Colored Regulars*, 280.

Commissary sergeant, 1900; certificate of merit mentioned. SOURCE: *ANJ* 37 (24 Feb 1900): 611.

THORTON, Moses; Private; I/24th Inf. Enlisted Mobile, AL, 8 Apr 1899. SOURCE: Muster Roll, I/24 Inf, Mar–Apr 1899.

Absent sick in Manila, Philippines since 29 Sep 1899; disease contracted in line of duty. SOURCE: Muster Roll, I/24 Inf, Sep–Oct 1899.

THRASH, Robert; H/10th Cav. Original member of 10th Cavalry; in troop when organized, Ft Leavenworth, KS, 21 Jul 1867. SOURCE: McMiller, "Buffalo Soldiers," 75.

THRASHER, George; 1st Sgt; G/10th Cav. Private, M/10th Cavalry; at Ft Apache, AZ, 1890, subscribed $.50 to testimonial to General Grierson. SOURCE: List of subscriptions, 23 Apr 1890, 10th Cavalry papers, MHI.

Served as private, G/10th Cavalry, in Cuba, 1898. SOURCE: Cashin, *Under Fire with the Tenth Cavalry*, 345.

Private, G/10th Cavalry; sick at hospital, Ft Robinson, NE, 29 Sep–20 Oct 1904. SOURCE: Regt Returns, 10 Cav, Sep–Oct 1904.

First sergeant, G/10th Cavalry; retiring from Ft Mackenzie, WY, after thirty years with fine service record. SOURCE: Sheridan *Post*, 27 Jan 1905.

Squadron review held in his honor at Ft Mackenzie, 1 Mar 1905: "The government has had few more worthy soldiers." SOURCE: Sheridan *Post*, 3 Mar 1905.

THREAT; Private; B/24th Inf. At Madison Barracks, NY, 1908. *See* **WHITE**, George W., Cook, C/24th Infantry

THROWER, Jesse; Sergeant; B/9th Cav. Promoted from corporal to sergeant, Ft Duchesne, UT, Nov 1895. SOURCE: *ANJ* 33 (7 Dec 1895): 236.

First sergeant, seriously wounded in leg during attack by insurgents, Lupi, Luzon, Philippines, 13 May 1901. SOURCE: *ANJ* 38 (1 Jun 1901): 967; Hamilton, "History of the Ninth Cavalry," 105.

Veteran of Philippine Insurrection; sergeant, B/9th Cavalry, at Ft D. A. Russell, WY, in 1910; sharpshooter. SOURCE: *Illustrated Review: Ninth Cavalry*, with picture.

Sergeant and Mrs. Thrower of Cleveland, OH, recently had dinner in honor of their niece and nephews from Atlanta. SOURCE: Cleveland *Gazette*, 8 Sep 1917.

THURMAN, Harry; Musician; K/24th Inf. Musician, K/24th Infantry, fined $5, Cabanatuan, Philippines, 5 Jun 1901, for neglecting to deliver order to quartermaster while orderly. SOURCE: Name File, 24 Inf.

Fined one month's pay and confined for thirty days, Cabanatuan, Philippines, for taking a bottle of native *vino* to guardhouse and delivering it to Sergeant of the Guard James Ingman, K/24th Infantry. SOURCE: Name File, 24 Inf.

Stationed at Houston, 1917; did not participate in mutiny. SOURCE: Haynes, *A Night of Violence*, 259.

THURMAN, John A.; Private; I/24th Inf. Enlisted Louisville, 8 Feb 1899. SOURCE: Muster Roll, I/24 Inf, Jan–Feb 1899.

Fined $1 by summary court, 5 May 1899. SOURCE: Muster Roll, I/24 Inf, May–Jun 1899.

Fined $3 by summary court, 25 Sep 1899. SOURCE: Muster Roll, H/24 Inf, Sep–Oct 1899.

THURSTON, Jacob; F/10th Cav. Original member of 10th Cavalry; in troop when organized, Ft Leavenworth, KS, 21 Jun 1867. SOURCE: McMiller, "Buffalo Soldiers," 73.

THURSTON, William T.; Private; B/23rd Kans Inf. Born Lawrence, KS; died in Minnesota, 23 Oct 1942. SOURCE: Taylor, "Minnesota Black Spanish-American War Veterans."

TIGLES, John J.; Private; Band/9th Cav. At Ft D. A. Russell, WY, in 1910; resident of Pittsburgh. SOURCE: *Illustrated Review: Ninth Cavalry*, with picture.

TILLEY, James D.; Corporal; K/10th Cav. Born in Kentucky; private, L/10th Cavalry, 12 Sep 1888; transferred to K/10th Cavalry, 25 Aug 1890; trumpeter, 1 May 1891; blacksmith, 1 Sep 1894; corporal, 7 Apr 1895; at Ft Custer, MT, 1897. SOURCE: Baker, Roster.

TILLIMON, Britton; H/10th Cav. Original member of 10th Cavalry; in troop when organized, Ft Leavenworth, KS, 21 Jul 1867. SOURCE: McMiller, "Buffalo Soldiers," 75.

TILLISON, Samuel; Private; I/24th Inf. Enlisted Baltimore, 26 Jul 1899; fined $3 by summary court, 28 Jul 1899. SOURCE: Muster Roll, I/24 Inf, Jul–Aug 1899.

TILLMAN, Charles W.; Private; I/10th Cav. Convicted by general court martial, Jefferson Barracks, MO, of desertion, 13 Mar–15 Sep 1883; sentenced to dishonorable discharge and three years. SOURCE: GCMO 52, AGO, 14 Nov 1883.

TILLMAN, Lafayette A.; 1st Lt; 49th Inf. Born Evansville, IN, 15 Mar 1860; educated in Evansville public schools, Wayland Seminary, Washington, DC, and Kansas City School of Law; served as private and quartermaster sergeant, 7th Volunteer Infantry, until discharged 28 Feb 1899 with excellent record; now in F/49th Infantry. SOURCE: *ANJ* 37 (14 Oct 1899): 145.

Served in 9th Volunteer Infantry, 5 Jul 1898–28 Feb 1899; commissioned first lieutenant, 49th Infantry, 9 Sep 1899; now with I/49th Infantry. SOURCE: Descriptive Book, I/49 Inf.

One of twenty-three officers of 49th Infantry recommended as regular Army second lieutenants. SOURCE: CG, DivPI, Manila, 8 Feb 1901, to AGO, AGO File 355163.

TILLMAN, Robert; Corporal; 24th Inf. Accused of role in Houston riot, 1917; sentenced to death; commuted to life in prison; reduced to twenty years in 1922. SOURCE: Haynes, *A Night of Violence*, 287, 294, 302, 312–13.

TILMAN, George; Private; D/24th Inf. At Ft Bayard, NM, Aug 1890. *See* **ANDERSON**, Charles L., Private, D/24th Infantry

TILTON, William; Private; D/9th Cav. In hands of civil authorities, Chadron, NE, 6 Aug 1891–16 Mar 1892. SOURCE: Regt Returns, 9 Cav.

Commander, Ft Robinson, NE, forwards letter from city marshal, Crawford, NE, complaining about Tilton, and directs commander of D/9th Cavalry to prepare charges. SOURCE: CO, Ft Robinson, to CO, D/9, 17 Jun 1893, LS, Ft Robinson.

TIMBERLAKE, David; Private; B/10th Cav. Served in 10th Cavalry, 1898; remained in U.S. during war with Spain. SOURCE: Cashin, *Under Fire with the Tenth Cavalry*, 333.

TIMBERS, John; Private; H/10th Cav. Served in 10th Cavalry, 1898; remained in U.S. during war with Spain. SOURCE: Cashin, *Under Fire with the Tenth Cavalry*, 347.

TIMOS, James T.; Private; F/9th Cav. Died in the Philippines, 15 Feb 1901. SOURCE: *ANJ* 38 (23 Feb 1901): 631.

TINSLEY, George; Sergeant; F/9th Cav. Veteran of Philippine Insurrection; at Ft D. A. Russell, WY, in 1910; resident of Pittsburg, KY. SOURCE: *Illustrated Review: Ninth Cavalry*, with picture.

TIPTON, C.; Private; L/9th Cav. On detached service in field, New Mexico, 21 Jan–24 Feb 1881.

TITUS, Joseph; Private; B/10th Cav. Drowned in the Rio Grande, Aug 1876. SOURCE: Leckie, *The Buffalo Soldiers*, 151.

TOAST, Sam; Cook; K/25th Inf. Private, sang with K/25th Infantry's "Imperial Quartette" in the Philippines. SOURCE: Richmond *Planet*, 16 Dec 1899.

Cook, at Ft Niobrara, NE, 1904. SOURCE: Wilson, "History of Fort Niobrara."

TODD, Arthur J.; Private; A/23rd Kans Inf. Died in Minnesota. SOURCE: Taylor, "Minnesota Black Spanish-American War Veterans."

TOLBERT, Thomas; Private; K/48th Inf. Died of variola in the Philippines, 19 Jul 1900. SOURCE: *ANJ* 37 (28 Jul 1900): 1142.

TOLBERT, Walter; Private; F/10th Cav. Served in 10th Cavalry in Cuba, 1898. SOURCE: Cashin, *Under Fire with the Tenth Cavalry*, 344.

TOLER, George; Recruit; Colored Detachment/Mounted Service. Convicted by general court martial, Jefferson Barracks, MO, of allowing prisoner, Recruit McMennus of Company C of Instruction, Mounted Service, to escape, 3 Sep 1889; sentenced to six months' confinement and loss of pay; sentence remitted by Maj. Gen. John M. Schofield on unanimous recommendation of court for clemency. SOURCE: GCMO 59, AGO, 14 Oct 1889.

TOLER, M.; Sergeant; D/9th Cav. Appointed corporal 13 Sep 1888. SOURCE: Roster, 9 Cav.

Corporal, ranked number four in carbine competition, Departments of Dakota and the Platte, Bellevue, NE, 4–9 Aug 1890. SOURCE: GO 112, AGO, 2 Oct 1890.

Corporal, D/9th Cavalry, ranked fourth in rifle competition, Departments of the Platte and Dakota, Bellevue. SOURCE: *ANJ* 27 (16 Aug 1890): 943.

Corporal, D/9th Cavalry; reenlistment as married soldier authorized by telegram, Adjutant General's Office, 8 Aug 1891.

Corporal, ranked number five in revolver competition, Departments of the East, the Platte, and California, Bellevue, 17–22 Aug 1891. SOURCE: GO 81, AGO, 6 Oct 1891.

Sergeant, ranked number four in revolver competition and number six in carbine competition, Departments of the East, the Platte, and California, Bellevue, 18–25 Aug 1894; distinguished marksman, 1890, 1891, 1894. SOURCE: GO 62, AGO, 15 Nov 1894.

Distinguished marksman, 1906. SOURCE: GO 198, AGO, 6 Dec 1906.

TOLIVER, Charles; Private; D/10th Cav. Served in 10th Cavalry, 1898; remained in U.S. during war with Spain. SOURCE: Cashin, *Under Fire with the Tenth Cavalry*, 341.

TOLIVER, Frederick; Sergeant; E/25th Inf. Acquitted by general court martial, Ft Buford, ND, and returned to duty. SOURCE: *ANJ* 32 (22 Sep 1894): 55.

TOLIVER, Lewis; 9th Cav. Cook at post exchange lunch counter, Ft Robinson, NE, with wage of $15 per month, Sep 1894. SOURCE: Reports of Inspections, DP, II.

Died at Ft Robinson, 25 Sep 1903. SOURCE: List of Interments, Ft Robinson.

No Veterans Administration pension file.

TOLLIVER; Private; K/9th Cav. Transferred to 24th Infantry in accordance with Special Order 50, Adjutant General's Office, 2 Mar 1897.

TOLLIVER, William; Private; A/9th Cav. Napped on guard duty, Ft Concho, TX, 1874; sentenced to six months in guardhouse. SOURCE: Leckie, *The Buffalo Soldiers*, 98.

TOLSON; Blacksmith; G/9th Cav. At Ft Robinson, NE, 1894. SOURCE: Court Martial Proceedings, Plummer.

TOLSON, Charles; Farrier; F/10th Cav. At Ft Robinson, NE, for cavalry competition, Sep 1897. SOURCE: Post Returns, Ft Robinson, Sep 1897.

TOLSON, E. L.; Private; C/9th Cav. Authorized furlough at Rock Springs, WY, Jul 1888. SOURCE: Regt Returns, 9 Cav, Jul 1888.

TOLSON, Marion; Private; H/9th Cav. At Ft D. A. Russell, WY, in 1910; resident of Kansas City, MO. SOURCE: *Illustrated Review: Ninth Cavalry*, with picture.

TOMPKINS, William; Private; G/9th Cav. *See* **THOMPKINS**, William H., Sergeant, H/25th Infantry

TONEY, Hart; Private; D/9th Cav. At Ft D. A. Russell, WY, in 1910; resident of Huntsville, AL. SOURCE: *Illustrated Review: Ninth Cavalry*.

TORTE, John; C/10th Cav. Original member of 10th Cavalry; in troop when organized, Ft Leavenworth, KS, 14 May 1867. SOURCE: McMiller, "Buffalo Soldiers," 70.

TOUNG, Eugene; Private; I/24th Inf. Missing in action, probably killed in action, 10 Oct 1900. *See* **BURNS**, William J., Corporal, I/24th Infantry

TOURNAGE, Sandy; Private; A/9th Cav. Ex-soldier working for livery stable, Crawford, NE, when killed, May 1897; found on floor outside bedroom by white Mrs. Fuller. SOURCE: Crawford *Tribune*, 14 May 1897.
    See **WALKER**, Robert H., Private, G/9th Cavalry
    Buried at Ft Robinson, NE. SOURCE: List of Interments, Ft Robinson.
    No Veterans Administration pension file.

TOWNES, Homer M.; Private; M/49th Inf. Engaged against enemy, Tuao, Cagayan, Philippines, 18 Oct 1900. SOURCE: *ANJ* 38 (11 May 1901): 901.

TOWNSEND, Allen; Private; F/38th Inf. Stole trousers from Pvt. William Herron and flannel sack coat from Pvt. Robert Berry, both of F/38th Infantry, at Ft Cummings, NM, 1868. SOURCE: Billington, *New Mexico's Buffalo Soldiers*, 36.

TOWNSEND, Edward; Sergeant; E/10th Cav. Honorable mention for gallantry against Kiowas and Comanches, Wichita Agency, Indian Territory, 22–23 Aug 1874. SOURCE: Baker, Roster.

TOWNSEND, William J.; Private; Band/24th Inf. Enlisted New York City, with three years' service, 14 Apr 1898; transferred from A/24th Infantry to H/24th Infantry, 21 Sep 1898; corporal, 17–21 Sep 1898; transferred to Band/24th Infantry, 13 Oct 1898. SOURCE: Muster Roll, H/24, Sep–Oct 1898.

TOWSEY, Arthur J.; Private; I/24th Inf. Enlisted Cincinnati, 16 Jan 1899. SOURCE: Muster Roll, I/24 Inf, Jan–Feb 1899.
    Dishonorably discharged 25 Aug 1899, in accordance with Special Order 102, 1st Division, 8th Army Corps, Manila, Philippines, 21 Aug 1899; due U.S. for ordnance and clothing $7.45. SOURCE: Muster Roll, I/24 Inf, Jul–Aug 1899.

TRACY, George; 1st Sgt; D/9th Cav. Private, K/9th Cavalry, on detached service in field, New Mexico, 30 Jan–2 Feb 1881; discharged, end of term, Ft Cummings, NM, 22 Feb 1881. SOURCE: Regt Returns, 9 Cav, Feb 1881.
    Appointed first sergeant, D/9th Cavalry, 16 Sep 1889; sergeant since 31 Mar 1886. SOURCE: Roster, 9 Cav.
    First sergeant, I/9th Cavalry, Ft Robinson, NE, 1891. *See* **JEMSON**, Joe, Private, I/9th Cavalry
    Son Clarence Ernest Tracy buried at Ft Robinson, 15 Mar 1893. SOURCE: List of Interments, Ft Robinson.
    First sergeant, D/9th Cavalry; examined for position of ordnance sergeant, Ft Robinson. SOURCE: *ANJ* 30 (1 Jul 1893): 745.
    Sergeant, D/9th Cavalry, resides at Ft Robinson with wife and child, Aug 1893. SOURCE: Medical History, Ft Robinson.
    First sergeant, D/9th Cavalry; conducted military convicts Herman Hector and George Washington, 9th Cavalry, from Ft Robinson to Ft Omaha, with guard, Pvt. Harry Rice, D/9th Cavalry. SOURCE: Order 77, 3 Oct 1894, Post Orders, Ft Robinson.
    First sergeant, D/9th Cavalry, at Ft Washakie, WY, 1897. *See* **JONES**, Lewis, Private, D/9th Cavalry

TRAVILLION, Thomas; Sergeant; M/10th Cav. Born in Mississippi; private, F/10th Cavalry, 30 Jul 1892–29 Oct 1895; private, A/10th Cavalry, 8 Jan 1896; corporal, 8 Sep 1896; at Ft Custer, MT, 1897. SOURCE: Baker, Roster.
    Sergeant, M/10th Cavalry; served in 10th Cavalry in Cuba, 1898. SOURCE: Cashin, *Under Fire with the Tenth Cavalry*, 352.
    Sergeant, M/10th Cavalry; died, age 31, with twelve years' service, Ft Robinson, NE, 26 Apr 1904; born Port Gibson, MS. SOURCE: Monthly Report, Chaplain Anderson, 1 May 1904.
    Buried at Ft Robinson. SOURCE: List of Interments, Ft Robinson.

TRENT, Arthur; Private; G/9th Cav. On detached service at South Fork, NM, 17 Nov 1880–12 Jan 1881. SOURCE: Regt Returns, 9 Cav, Jan 1881.

TRENT, Leonidas B.; Lance Sgt; Colored Detachment/Mounted Service. At Jefferson Barracks, MO, May 1885. *See* **WAXWOOD**, Harvy, Recruit, Colored Detachment/Mounted Service

Convicted by general court martial, Jefferson Barracks, of desertion, 9 Sep 1885, until apprehended at Memphis, 4 Nov 1885; pled guilty to absence without leave; sentenced to dishonorable discharge and three years. SOURCE: GCMO 3, AGO, 12 Jan 1886.

TRICE, Edward; Private; 24th Inf. Harassed and arrested by police, Manila, Philippines, 19 Jun 1902. SOURCE: CO, 24 Inf, to Chief of Police, Manila, 21 Jun 1902.

TRICE, Green; Private; L/10th Cav. Former soldier, age 28; saw horse fall on John Howerton, Ft Stockton, TX, Apr 1884. SOURCE: Affidavit, Trice, Hiram, OH, 19 Feb 1894, VA File XC 896871, John C. Howerton.

TRICE, Robert; Corporal; K/25th Inf. Private, I/25th Infantry; fined $5 by summary court, San Isidro, Philippines, for absence from eleven P.M. check roll call, 21 Apr 1902, and reveille, 22 Apr 1902, second conviction.

Corporal, K/25th Infantry, at Ft Niobrara, NE, 1904. SOURCE: Wilson, "History of Fort Niobrara."

TRICKLER, Joyner; G/10th Cav. Original member of 10th Cavalry; in troop when organized, Ft Leavenworth, KS, 5 Jul 1867. SOURCE: McMiller, "Buffalo Soldiers," 74.

TRIMBLE, Anderson; Private; K/9th Cav. Killed in action against force of 900 Kickapoos, Navahos, Mexicans, and white renegades, Ft Lancaster, TX, along with Pvts. William Sharpe and Edward Bowers, K/9th Cavalry, 26 Dec 1867. SOURCE: Hamilton, "History of the Ninth Cavalry," 7; *Illustrated Review: Ninth Cavalry.*

TRIMBLE, Andrew; Private; K/9th Cav. *See* **TRIMBLE**, Anderson, Private, K/9th Cavalry

TRIPP, William; Private; H/24th Inf. Enlisted Baltimore, 11 Jul 1898; assigned and joined 16 Sep 1898; due U.S for ordnance (meat can, blanket bag, tin cup, spoon, knife, blanket bag shoulder strap, coat straps, haversack and straps) $4.31. SOURCE: Muster Roll, H/24 Inf, Sep–Oct 1898.

Discharged Ft Douglas, UT, 28 Jan 1899, character good, single; deposits $8; due U.S. for clothing $13.70. SOURCE: Muster Roll, H/24 Inf, Jan–Feb 1899.

TROTMAN, Albert R.; Corporal; Band/9th Cav. Private B/10th Cavalry, attached to Band/10th Cavalry for duty. SOURCE: Crawford *Tribune*, 19 Jan 1906.

Corporal, Band/9th Cavalry, at Ft D. A. Russell, WY, in 1910; resident of Bridgetown, Barbados. SOURCE: *Illustrated Review: Ninth Cavalry*, with picture.

TROTT, Robert D.; Private; H/24th Inf. Enlisted Ft Columbus, NY, 7 Jan 1899. SOURCE: Muster Roll, H/24 Inf, Jan–Feb 1899.

TROUT, Henry; Private; E/9th Cav. Retires from Ft Robinson, NE. SOURCE: *ANJ* 34 (24 Jul 1897): 873.

Thirty years in Army; retired to Crawford, NE; died at post hospital, Ft Robinson, 14 Aug 1908. SOURCE: Crawford *Tribune*, 21 Aug 1908.

Buried at Ft Robinson, 15 Aug 1908. SOURCE: List of Interments, Ft Robinson.

No Veterans Administration pension file.

TROUTMAN, Edward; Sergeant; G/9th Cav. On patrol from Ft Ringgold, TX, with four privates, Jan 1875, when ambushed by civilians; Pvts. Jerry Owsley and Moses Turner killed; Pvts. Charley Blackstone and John Fredericks escaped. SOURCE: Leckie, *The Buffalo Soldiers*, 108.

TRUE, Otto; Private; D/10th Cav. Served in 10th Cavalry, 1898; remained in U.S. during war with Spain. SOURCE: Cashin, *Under Fire with the Tenth Cavalry*, 341.

Fined $1 for disturbing the peace, Crawford, NE, Oct 1906. SOURCE: Police Court Docket, Crawford.

Discharged from Ft Robinson, NE, end of term, character good. SOURCE: Regt Returns, 10 Cav, Nov 1902.

Veterans Administration Pension file C 2333113 not located at National Archives.

TRUMAN; Private; M/10th Cav. At Ft Apache, AZ, 1890, subscribed $.50 to testimonial to General Grierson. SOURCE: List of subscriptions, 23 Apr 1890, 10th Cavalry papers, MHI.

TRUMAN, Isaac W.; Private; A/9th Cav. Post librarian, Ft Robinson, NE, 10 Sep–15 Dec 1894. SOURCE: Order 69, 10 Sep 1894, and Order 92, 15 Dec 1894, Post Orders, Ft Robinson.

Post librarian, Ft Robinson, 27 Sep–9 Oct 1895. SOURCE: Order 69, 27 Sep 1895, and Order 74, 9 Oct 1895, Post Orders, Ft Robinson.

Reenlistment as married soldier authorized by letter, Adjutant General's Office, 23 Oct 1897.

TRUMAN, John; 25th Inf. Pallbearer at funeral of Col. Andrew W. Burt, 25th Infantry. SOURCE: Curtis, *The Black Soldier*, 49.

TUBEMAN, Josiah G.; Corporal; E/10th Cav. Born in Maryland; private, corporal, sergeant, L and A/10th Cavalry, 3 Nov 1884–2 Nov 1894; private, B/10th Cavalry, 20 Nov 1894; corporal, 24 Jul 1896; at Ft Custer, MT, 1897. SOURCE: Baker, Roster.

Sergeant, G/10th Cavalry, furlough from Ft Bayard, NM, extended to 28 Feb 1890. SOURCE: *ANJ* 26 (14 Dec 1889): 310.

Served as corporal, E/10th Cavalry, 1898; remained in U.S. during war with Spain. SOURCE: Cashin, *Under Fire with the Tenth Cavalry*, 343.

TUCKER, Charles; Blacksmith; K/10th Cav. At Ft Robinson, NE, 1904.

TUCKER, Daniel; D/10th Cav. Original member of 10th Cavalry; in troop when organized, Ft Leavenworth, KS, 1 Jun 1867. SOURCE: McMiller, "Buffalo Soldiers," 71.

TUCKER, E.; Farrier; K/9th Cav. Served 1872–73. *See* **SLAUGHTER**, Rufus, Private, K/9th Cavalry

TUCKER, George C.; G/9th Cav. Mentioned as surviving veteran of Indian wars. SOURCE: *Winners of the West* 3 (Jun 1926): 7.

Age 66, resided at 3417 Madison, South Omaha, NE, 1929; served in Army with Joseph Blew. SOURCE: Affidavit, Tucker, 18 Feb 1829, VA File XC 970422, Joseph Blew.

TUCKER, James; Private; G/10th Cav. Mentioned Oct 1874. SOURCE: LS, 10 Cav, 1873–83.

TUCKER, James; Private; B/10th Cav. Served in 10th Cavalry, 1898; remained in U.S. during war with Spain. SOURCE: Cashin, *Under Fire with the Tenth Cavalry*, 333.

TUCKER, Joseph H.; Private; H/24th Inf. Private, A/24th Infantry; on special duty as fireman, post ice house, Ft Huachuca, AZ; ordered to report to post surgeon. SOURCE: Order 123, Ft Huachuca, 17 Aug 1893, Name File, 24 Inf.

Relieved as fireman, post ice house, Ft Huachuca. SOURCE: Order 125, Ft Huachuca, 21 Aug 1893.

Enlisted Ft Crook, NE, 13 Jun 1898; joined company at San Juan, Cuba, 12 Jul 1898; sick in hospital, Siboney, Cuba, 1–25 Aug 1898 and en route to U.S. 25–31 Aug; disease contracted in line of duty. SOURCE: Muster Roll, H/24 Inf, Jul–Aug 1898.

On furlough authorized by surgeon's certificate, 6 Sep–5 Oct 1898; on special duty as assistant printer since 13 Oct 1898. SOURCE: Muster Roll, H/24 Inf, Sep–Oct 1898.

On special duty as assistant printer; fined $4 by summary court, 28 Nov 1898. SOURCE: Muster Roll, H/24 Inf, Nov–Dec 1898.

Fined $2 by summary court, 24 Jan 1899; discharged Ft Douglas, UT, 29 Jan 1899, character good, single; reenlisted 30 Jan 1899; due U.S. for clothing $20.77; on special duty as assistant printer; sick in hospital, disease contracted in line of duty, since 25 Feb 1899. SOURCE: Muster Roll, H/24 Inf, Jan–Feb 1899.

In H/24th Infantry; letter to editor from Manila, Philippines, 18 Aug 1899. SOURCE: Indianapolis *Freeman*, 14 Oct 1899. *See* **WILLIAMS**, Walter B., Sergeant Major, 24th Infantry

Fined $1 for being in street, San Isidro, Philippines, with blouse unbuttoned, 3 Nov 1901, third conviction. SOURCE: Register of Summary Court, San Isidro.

TUCKER, Turner; Private; L/9th Cav. At Ft D. A. Russell, WY, in 1910; resident of Hopkinsville, KY. SOURCE: *Illustrated Review: Ninth Cavalry.*

TUCKER, Walter B.; Private; 24th Inf. Served in Houston, 1917; tried unsuccessfully at court martial to establish alibi for being off post during riot; sentenced to two years. SOURCE: Haynes, *A Night of Violence*, 268, 271.

TUDOR, Charles; Private; E/10th Cav. Served in 10th Cavalry, 1898; remained in U.S. during war with Spain. SOURCE: Cashin, *Under Fire with the Tenth Cavalry*, 343.

TUDOR, Gus; Private; E/10th Cav. Served in 10th Cavalry, 1898; remained in U.S. during war with Spain. SOURCE: Cashin, *Under Fire with the Tenth Cavalry*, 343.

TULL, John; Private; H/24th Inf. Enlisted Washington Barracks, Washington, DC, 25 Jul 1898; never joined company; absent sick, disease contracted in line of duty, since 16 Sep 1898. SOURCE: Muster Roll, H/24 Inf, Sep–Oct 1898.

Absent sick until 15 Nov 1898; present sick 15 Nov–22 Dec 1898; disability, cause unknown, since enlistment: chronic rheumatism in both knees, varicose veins, cyst on left testicle, corns on both feet; disability 50 percent; discharged 22 Dec 1898, character good; due U.S. for clothing $11.35. SOURCE: Muster Roll, H/24 Inf, Nov–Dec 1898.

TULL, Joseph; Private; E/9th Cav. Relieved from extra duty as teamster with Quartermaster Department, Ft Robinson, NE. SOURCE: SO 86, 8 Aug 1896, Post Orders, Ft Robinson.

Wounded in action at San Juan, Cuba, 1 Jul 1898. SOURCE: *Illustrated Review: Ninth Cavalry.*

Discharged end of term, Ft Robinson, 23 Sep 1898, character good, no children; reenlisted 5 Oct 1898. SOURCE: Regt Returns, 9 Cav, Sep–Oct 1898.

TUMPKIN, Hezekiah; Private; E/9th Cav. At Ft D. A. Russell, WY, in 1910; resident of Mellon, IN. SOURCE: *Illustrated Review: Ninth Cavalry*, with picture.

TURKIN, Edward; F/10th Cav. Original member of 10th Cavalry; in troop when organized, Ft Leavenworth, KS, 21 Jun 1867. SOURCE: McMiller, "Buffalo Soldiers," 73.

TURLEY; Private; D/10th Cav. Released to duty from treatment for acute gonorrhea, Ft Robinson, NE, 9 Oct 1903. SOURCE: Post Surgeon to CO, D/10 Cav, 9 Oct 1903, LS, Post Surgeon, Ft Robinson.

TURLEY, Albert H.; Private; G/10th Cav. Served in 10th Cavalry, 1898; remained in U.S. during war with Spain. SOURCE: Cashin, *Under Fire with the Tenth Cavalry*, 345.

TURNER; Private; C/9th Cav. At Ft Sill, Indian Territory, 1883–84. *See* **COLE**, Private, C/9th Cavalry

TURNER; Private; H/10th Cav. At Ft Apache, AZ, 1890, subscribed $.50 to testimonial to General Grierson. SOURCE: List of subscriptions, 23 Apr 1890, 10th Cavalry papers, MHI.

TURNER; Private; I/10th Cav. At Ft Apache, AZ, 1890, subscribed $.25 to testimonial to General Grierson. SOURCE: List of subscriptions, 23 Apr 1890, 10th Cavalry papers, MHI.

TURNER; Private; D/9th Cav. Wounded in action at San Juan, Cuba, 1 Jul 1898. SOURCE: *Illustrated Review: Ninth Cavalry.*

TURNER; Private; A/10th Cav. Best half-mile run, Department of the Missouri, Ft Robinson, NE, at 2 minutes, 13.4 seconds. SOURCE: SecWar, *AR 1903*, 1:429.

TURNER, Abram; Private; Band/10th Cav. Deposited $10 with paymaster, Ft Concho, TX, Sep 1881. SOURCE: Adj, 10 Cav, to PMG, 12 Sep 1881, LS, 10 Cav, 1873–83.

TURNER, Andrew; Private; E/9th Cav. At Ft D. A. Russell, WY, in 1910. SOURCE: *Illustrated Review: Ninth Cavalry.*

TURNER, Charles B.; Sgt Maj; 2nd Sqdn/10th Cav. Born in Wisconsin; private, E/10th Cavalry, 15 Nov 1875; corporal, 20 Nov 1879; sergeant, 1 Jan 1882; first sergeant, 5 Aug 1890; sergeant, 1 Jan 1891; at Ft Custer, MT, 1897. SOURCE: Baker, Roster.

Born Mineral Point, WI; Ht 5'8", mulatto; promoted from corporal, E/10th Cavalry, to sergeant major, 2nd Squadron/10th Cavalry, 27 Dec 1902; assigned to Ft Mackenzie, WY, 2 Jan 1903; retired to Louisville, 21 Sep 1903; campaigns: Lipans, 1876, Victorio, 1880, disarming Kiowas and Comanches, 1881, Geronimo, 1885–86, Philippines, 1900–1901; character on retirement excellent; married to Clara B. Turner; clothing not drawn $51.99. SOURCE: Descriptive Book, 10 Cav Officers & NCOs.

Born 25 Jan 1859; early education in Cincinnati; enlisted Indianapolis, age 16, 15 Nov 1875; delegate to national convention of Regular Army and Navy Union, St Louis, 1893; on recruiting duty in Kentucky during Cuban campaign, 1898; Odd Fellow and Mason; sergeant major as of 6 Nov 1898. SOURCE: Cashin, *Under Fire with the Tenth Cavalry*, 314–16, with picture, 315.

Sergeant, E/10th Cavalry, Ft Grant, AZ, to be examined for regimental quartermaster sergeant. SOURCE: *ANJ* 25 (29 Oct 1887): 262.

Sergeant, E/10th Cavalry, Ft Grant, to be examined for post quartermaster sergeant. SOURCE: *ANJ* 25 (7 Jan 1888): 462.

Sergeant, E/10th Cavalry, Ft Apache, AZ, 1890, subscribed $.50 to testimonial to General Grierson. SOURCE: List of subscriptions, 23 Apr 1890, 10th Cavalry papers, MHI.

First sergeant, E/10th Cavalry, authorized six-month furlough from Ft Apache. SOURCE: *ANJ* 28 (8 Nov 1890): 170.

Sergeant, E/10th Cavalry, on furlough at New Orleans, to be furnished transportation back to Ft Apache by Quartermaster Department. SOURCE: *ANJ* 28 (6 Jun 1891): 692.

Sergeant, E/10th Cavalry, examined for post commissary sergeant, Ft Custer, MT. SOURCE: *ANJ* 29 (6 Aug 1892): 863.

Served as first sergeant, E/10th Cavalry, 1898; remained in U.S. during war with Spain. SOURCE: Cashin, *Under Fire with the Tenth Cavalry*, 343.

Commissioned from 10th Cavalry as second lieutenant, 48th Infantry, and ordered to report to New York. SOURCE: *ANJ* 37 (7 Oct 1899): 122.

Second lieutenant, 48th Infantry, as of 9 Sep 1899; to report at Ft Thomas, KY. SOURCE: *ANJ* 37 (14 Oct 1899): 147.

Mentioned as second lieutenant, K/48th Infantry. SOURCE: Beasley, *Negro Trailblazers*, 284.

Appointed sergeant major, 2nd Squadron/10th Cavalry, from corporal, E/10th Cavalry, 27 Dec 1902; arrived 4 Jan 1903. SOURCE: Muster Roll, Det Field and Staff, 2nd Sqdn, 10 Cav, Dec 1902–Feb 1903.

Retires from Ft Mackenzie, 2 Oct 1903; transport furnished to his home, Louisville. SOURCE: Muster Roll, Det Field and Staff, 2nd Sqdn, 10 Cav, Aug–Oct 1903.

TURNER, Charles B.; I/24th Inf. Wounded seriously in neck at Arayat, Philippines, 12 Oct 1899. SOURCE: Cleveland *Gazette*, 2 Dec 1899.

TURNER, Daniel; Corporal; K/38th Inf. With small detachment at Wilson Creek, KS, repulsed large Indian party and killed five. SOURCE: Rickey, "The Negro Regulars," 5.

TURNER, Daniel; M/10th Cav. Original member of 10th Cavalry; in troop when organized, Ft Riley, KS, 15 Oct 1867. SOURCE: McMiller, "Buffalo Soldiers," 79.

TURNER, Daniel; Private; C/9th Cav. Sentenced to thirty days' confinement by garrison court martial, Ft Robinson, NE, for insubordination to 1st Lt. B. S. Humphreys and striking Pvt. Robert Turner, C/9th Cavalry. SOURCE: Order 123, 20 Jun 1887, Post Orders, Ft Robinson.

TURNER, David; Sergeant; Band/25th Inf. Private, Band/10th Cavalry, discharged in accordance with General Order 48, Adjutant General's Office, 1904.

Promoted from corporal. SOURCE: *ANR* 38 (22 Jun 1905): 21.

TURNER, Ernest E.; Private; H/9th Cav. At Ft D. A. Russell, WY, in 1910; resident of Chicago. SOURCE: *Illustrated Review: Ninth Cavalry*, with picture.

TURNER, George; Private; C/10th Cav. At Carrizal, Mexico, 1916; testified before Senate investigative committee regarding battle. SOURCE: Clendenen, *Blood on the Border*, 314.

TURNER, George C.; Private; C/9th Cav. At Ft D. A. Russell, WY, in 1910; resident of 412 Madison Ave., Madison, IN. SOURCE: *Illustrated Review: Ninth Cavalry*, with picture.

TURNER, George H.; Corporal; H/10th Cav. Served in 10th Cavalry, 1898; remained in U.S. during war with Spain. SOURCE: Cashin, *Under Fire with the Tenth Cavalry*, 346.

TURNER, George W.; Private; C/10th Cav. Mentioned Jul 1874. SOURCE: LS, 10 Cav, 1873–83.

TURNER, Goodricks; Private; I/24th Inf. Enlisted Baltimore, 20 Feb 1899. SOURCE: Muster Roll, I/24 Inf, Jan–Feb 1899.

Sick since 28 Apr 1899, disease contracted in line of duty. SOURCE: Muster Roll, I/24 Inf, Mar–Apr 1899.

Fined one month's pay by summary court, 8 Aug 1899. SOURCE: Muster Roll, I/24 Inf, Jul–Aug 1899.

Fined $3 by summary court, 25 Sep 1899. SOURCE: Muster Roll, I/24 Inf, Sep–Oct 1899.

On detached service at Cabanatuan, Philippines, since 30 Dec 1899. SOURCE: Muster Roll, I/24 Inf, Nov–Dec 1899.

TURNER, Harrison; Private; F/24th Inf. Deserted from Penanauda, Philippines, 9 May 1902. SOURCE: Regt Returns, 24 Inf, May 1902.

TURNER, Henry; A/10th Cav. Original member of 10th Cavalry; in troop when organized, Ft Leavenworth, KS, 18 Feb 1867. SOURCE: McMiller, "Buffalo Soldiers," 68.

TURNER, Hezekiah; Private; I/24th Inf. Participated in Houston riot, 1917. SOURCE: Haynes, *A Night of Violence*, 163.

TURNER, James; Private; E/10th Cav. Served in 10th Cavalry, 1898; remained in U.S. during war with Spain. SOURCE: Cashin, *Under Fire with the Tenth Cavalry*, 343.

TURNER, James; Corporal; L/9th Cav. At Ft D. A. Russell, WY, in 1910; sharpshooter; resident of Savannah, GA. SOURCE: *Illustrated Review: Ninth Cavalry*, with picture.

TURNER, James B.; Private; I/24th Inf. Enlisted Philadelphia, 28 Jun 1899. SOURCE: Muster Roll, I/24 Inf, Jul–Aug 1899.

Wounded through neck in advance on Arayat, Philippines, 12 Oct 1899; in hospital in Manila, Philippines, 14 Oct–31 Dec 1899. SOURCE: Muster Roll, I/24 Inf, Sep–Oct and Nov–Dec 1899.

Wounded in neck near Arayat, 12 Oct 1899. SOURCE: *ANJ* 37 (18 Nov 1899): 276; Muller, *The Twenty Fourth Infantry*, 30.

TURNER, James E.; A/23rd Kans Inf. Died in Minnesota. SOURCE: Taylor, "Minnesota Black Spanish-American War Veterans."

TURNER, John; M/10th Cav. Original member of 10th Cavalry; in troop when organized, Ft Riley, KS, 15 Oct 1867. SOURCE: McMiller, "Buffalo Soldiers," 79.

TURNER, John; 1st Sgt; F/9th Cav. At Ft Robinson, NE; reduced to private, fined $60, and confined for six months for being drunk on duty and other offenses. SOURCE: *ANJ* 26 (22 Jun 1889): 882.

First sergeant, at Ft Robinson, 1891. *See* **ROSS**, Edward, Private, G/9th Cavalry

TURNER, John C.; Private; Band/25th Inf. Born Baltimore; Ht 5'4", black complexion, third enlistment, age 32, Baltimore, 14 Jun 1894; transferred from Band/9th Cavalry, 27 Jan 1896, character fair. SOURCE: Descriptive Cards, 25 Inf.

Transferred from Band/9th Cavalry, in accordance with Special Order 24, Adjutant General's Office, 29 Jan 1896.

TURNER, John M.; Comsy Sgt; 25th Inf. To report to Seattle for duty in Alaska. SOURCE: *ANJ* 36 (1 Apr 1899): 727.

TURNER, Joseph B.; Private; I/24th Inf. Captured in the Philippines, 10 Oct 1900. *See* **BURNS**, William J., Corporal, I/24th Infantry

TURNER, Matthew; Private; A/24th Inf. Transferred from Reserve Divisional Hospital, Siboney, Cuba, to U.S. on U.S. Army Transport *Santiago* with yellow fever, 25 Jul 1898. SOURCE: Hospital Papers, Spanish-American War.

TURNER, Moses; Private; G/9th Cav. Murdered 1875. *See* **OWSLEY**, Jeremiah, Private, G/9th Cavalry; **TROUTMAN**, Edward, Sergeant, G/9th Cavalry

TURNER, P.; Private; G/9th Cav. On detached service at Ft Stanton, NM, 29 Jan–5 Feb 1881. SOURCE: Regt Returns, 9 Cav, Feb 1881.

TURNER, Peter H.; Blacksmith; E/9th Cav. $59 gold watch and chain that Turner had pawned to Cpl. William H. Harper, E/9th Cavalry, stolen by Pvt. Herman Hector, Ft Robinson, NE, 1894. SOURCE: Court Martial Records, Hector.

Veteran of Spanish-American War and Philippine Insurrection; at Ft D. A. Russell, WY, in 1910. SOURCE: *Illustrated Review: Ninth Cavalry*, with picture.

TURNER, Robert; 1st Sgt; H/9th Cav. Discharged on certificate of disability, Ft Bayard, NM, 16 Jan 1881. SOURCE: Regt Returns, 9 Cav, Jan 1881.

TURNER, Robert; Private; C/9th Cav. At Ft Robinson, NE, 1887. *See* **TURNER**, Daniel, Private, C/9th Cavalry

TURNER, Robert; Private; C/25th Inf. Dishonorable discharge, Brownsville. SOURCE: SO 266, AGO, 9 Nov 1906.

TURNER, Samuel; Sergeant; K/25th Inf. Private, H/24th Infantry; enlisted Presidio of San Francisco, CA, 17 Mar 1898, with ten years' service. SOURCE: Muster Roll, H/24 Inf, May–Jun 1898.

Wounded in action at San Juan Hill, Santiago, Cuba, 1 Jul 1898; returned to U.S. for treatment. SOURCE: Muster Roll, H/24 Inf, Jul–Aug 1898; Muller, *The Twenty Fourth Infantry*, 19.

On furlough authorized by surgeon's certificate, 17 Sep–16 Oct 1898. SOURCE: Muster Roll, H/24 Inf, Sep–Oct 1898.

Present for duty. SOURCE: Muster Roll, H/24 Inf, Nov–Dec 1898 and Jan–Feb 1899.

Sergeant, K/25th Infantry, at Ft Niobrara, NE, 1904. SOURCE: Wilson, "History of Fort Niobrara."

Commissioned second lieutenant at Camp Des Moines, IA, Oct 1917. SOURCE: Sweeney, *History of the American Negro*, 129.

TURNER, Simon; L/10th Cav. Original member of 10th Cavalry; in troop when organized, Ft Riley, KS, 21 Sep 1867. SOURCE: McMiller, "Buffalo Soldiers," 78.

TURNER, Simon; B/10th Cav. Enlisted Baltimore in H/10th Cavalry, 7 May 1873; reenlisted in B/10th Cavalry, 1878; engaged against Kiowas, Apaches, Comanches; member of Col. R. S. Mackenzie Camp No. 13, National Indian War Veterans, Stockton, CA. SOURCE: *Winners of the West* 7 (Nov 1930): 11.

After service, resided in San Antonio, TX; was captain, A/Excelsior Guards, 1886. SOURCE: *Winners of the West* 8 (Jul 1931): 8.

Wife, Mrs. Lucy Turner, age 80, died in San Francisco. SOURCE: *Winners of the West* 11 (Aug 1934): 3.

TURNER, Tom; F/10th Cav. Resided in Chicago, 1924; served in campaigns against Cheyennes and Arapahoes, Jul 1867, on Saline River, KS; scouted between Fts Harker and Hays, KS; engaged in wagon train escorts between Ft Wallace, KS, and Ft Lyons, CO, summer 1868. SOURCE: *Winners of the West* 1 (Oct 1924): 9.

TURNER, Wallace; L/9th Cav. Private bill passed by Congress, authorizing $12 per month pension for widow Winnie Turner. SOURCE: *Winners of the West* 3 (Apr 1926): 2.

TURNER, Walter; Private; A/10th Cav. Born Middletown, DE; black complexion; occupation waiter; enlisted Baltimore, 23 Nov 1880; discharged from U.S. Military Prison, Ft Leavenworth, KS, with constitutional

syphilis, 3 Nov 1882. SOURCE: Certificates of Disability, DivMo.

TURNER, William; C/10th Cav. Original member of 10th Cavalry; in troop when organized, Ft Leavenworth, KS, 14 May 1867. SOURCE: McMiller, "Buffalo Soldiers," 70.

TURNER, William; Private; F/10th Cav. Original member of 10th Cavalry; in troop when organized, Ft Leavenworth, KS, 21 Jun 1867. SOURCE: McMiller, "Buffalo Soldiers," 73.

Wounded in battle, Kansas, 21 Aug 1867. SOURCE: Armes, *Ups and Downs*, 248.

TURNER, William; 1st Sgt; L/10th Cav. Mentioned Jan 1873 as recruit sent to L/10th Cavalry from Ft Gibson, Indian Territory. SOURCE: LS, 10 Cav, 1873–83.

First sergeant, L/10th Cavalry, at Ft Stockton, TX, 1880; refused to swear false affidavit against Capt. George A. Armes. SOURCE: Armes, *Ups and Downs*, 486.

TURNER, William; Private; C/10th Cav. Served in 10th Cavalry, 1898; remained in U.S. during war with Spain. SOURCE: Cashin, *Under Fire with the Tenth Cavalry*, 340.

TURNER, William; Corporal; K/10th Cav. Born in Maryland; private, K/10th Cavalry, 6 Jan 1881; corporal, 28 Sep 1895; at Ft Custer, MT, 1897. SOURCE: Baker, Roster.

Honorable mention for conspicuous bravery against Apaches, Salt River, AZ, 7 Mar 1890. SOURCE: Baker, Roster.

Served as corporal, K/10th Cavalry, 1898; remained in U.S. during war with Spain. SOURCE: Cashin, *Under Fire with the Tenth Cavalry*, 349.

TURNER, William; Private; H/24th Inf. Fined $6 by summary court, San Isidro, Philippines, for being disorderly in quarters, 17 Nov 1901, second conviction. SOURCE: Register of Summary Court, San Isidro.

Fined $6 for being drunk and disorderly in quarters, 12 Mar 1902, third conviction. SOURCE: Register of Summary Court, San Isidro.

Fined $2.50 for obscene and abusive language to Sgt. Bradford Potter, 5 Apr 1902; acquitted of disorderly conduct in restaurant of Stuckey and Thomas, fourth conviction. SOURCE: Register of Summary Court, San Isidro.

TURNER, William; Private; C/9th Cav. Convicted of entry, assault, and robbery, Goa, Philippines, 1 Jan 1902; sentenced to 2 1/2 months.

TURNER, William; Sergeant; C/25th Inf. Ranked number 178 among rifle experts with 68.67 percent, 1904. SOURCE: GO 79, AGO, 1 Jun 1905.

Ranked number 490 among rifle experts with 68.33 percent, 1905. SOURCE: GO 101, AGO, 31 May 1906.

Ranked number nine, Southwestern Division rifle competition, Leon Springs, TX, 1907. SOURCE: GO 213, AGO, 19 Oct 1907.

TURNER, William A.; Corporal; H/24th Inf. Fined $15 by summary court, San Isidro, Philippines, for being drunk at guard mount, 17 Nov 1901, first conviction. SOURCE: Register of Summary Court, San Isidro.

TURPIN, George B.; 9th Cav. Served in E and M Troops, 1872–82; recent subscriber. SOURCE: *Winners of the West* 4 (Mar 1927): 8.

TURPIN, P. B.; Sergeant; H/9th Cav. On detached service at Ft Bayard, NM, 16 Jan–10 Feb 1881. SOURCE: Regt Returns, 9 Cav, Feb 1881.

TUTTLE, Aleck; Private; C/24th Inf. Born Prince Georges Co., MD; three enlistments before being killed in Cuba. SOURCE: Clark, "A History of the Twenty-fourth," 100.
  Killed in action, Cuba, 1898. SOURCE: Scipio, *Last of the Black Regulars*, 29.

TWISBY, James P.; Private; F/10th Cav. Served in 10th Cavalry in Cuba, 1898; killed at Montauk Point, NY, by Pvt. Lindsey P. Holt, F/10th Cavalry. SOURCE: Cashin, *Under Fire with the Tenth Cavalry*, 344.

TWYMAN, John W. H.; Private; A/10th Cav. Served in 10th Cavalry, 1898; remained in U.S. during war with Spain. SOURCE: Cashin, *Under Fire with the Tenth Cavalry*, 337.

TYLER; Saddler; K/9th Cav. Returned to duty in accordance with letter, Department of the Platte, 15 Feb 1890.

TYLER, Andrew; Private; A/9th Cav. At Ft D. A. Russell, WY, in 1910. SOURCE: *Illustrated Review: Ninth Cavalry.*

TYLER, Benjamin F.; Private; C/10th Cav. Served in 10th Cavalry in Cuba, 1898. SOURCE: Cashin, *Under Fire with the Tenth Cavalry*, 340.
  Wounded in action at Santiago, Cuba, 2 Jul 1898. SOURCE: SecWar, *AR 1898*, 324.

TYLER, Charles; Private; M/10th Cav. Served in 10th Cavalry, 1898; remained in U.S. during war with Spain. SOURCE: Cashin, *Under Fire with the Tenth Cavalry*, 352.

TYLER, Jacob N.; Private; 9th Cav. At Ft Cummings, NM, 1881. SOURCE: Billington, *New Mexico's Buffalo Soldiers*, 130.

TYLER, Julius; Private; D/9th Cav. At Ft D. A. Russell, WY, in 1910; sharpshooter. SOURCE: *Illustrated Review: Ninth Cavalry.*

TYLER, Roy; Private; 24th Inf. Served in Houston, 1917; tried unsuccessfully at court martial to establish alibi for being off post during riot. SOURCE: Haynes, *A Night of Violence*, 268.

TYLER, Thomas S.; Private; H/24th Inf. Enlisted Ft Crook, NE, 13 Jun 1898; assigned and joined 6 Sep 1898; due U.S. for ordnance (canteen and strap) $.85. SOURCE: Muster Roll, H/24 Inf, Sep–Oct 1898.
  Discharged Ft Douglas, UT, 28 Jan 1899, character excellent, single; clothing $3.33; reenlisted 29 Jan 1899. SOURCE: Muster Roll, H/24 Inf, Jan–Feb 1899.
  Promoted to corporal. SOURCE: Indianapolis *Freeman*, 18 Mar 1899, with picture.

TYLER, William; Private; D/10th Cav. Served in 10th Cavalry in Cuba, 1898. SOURCE: Cashin, *Under Fire with the Tenth Cavalry*, 341.

TYLER, William E.; 2nd Lt; M/49th Inf. Sergeant major, 49th Infantry; commissioned second lieutenant, 6 Nov 1900. SOURCE: *ANJ* 38 (24 Nov 1900): 307.
  Assigned to M Company as of 19 Nov 1900. SOURCE: Descriptive Book, M/49 Inf.

TYNES, Edward; Private; D/9th Cav. Deserted from San Francisco, "on day of sailing for foreign service," 16 Aug 1900. SOURCE: Regt Returns, 9 Cav, Oct 1900.

TYNES, James E.; 10th Cav. Born Smithfield, VA, 22 May 1872; enlisted 25 May 1896; post schoolteacher before war with Spain; served in Cuba, 1898. SOURCE: Cashin, *Under Fire with the Tenth Cavalry*, 316.

TYREE, Charles; Private; I/25th Inf. Confined to quarters for one month and fined $8 by summary court, San Isidro, Philippines, for disobeying order to clean up waste food he had dropped on dining room floor, 1 May 1902. SOURCE: Register of Summary Court, San Isidro.

U

UICEY, Samuel; H/10th Cav. Original member of 10th Cavalry; in troop when organized, Ft Leavenworth, KS, 21 Jul 1867. SOURCE: McMiller, "Buffalo Soldiers," 75.

ULLMAN, James; Corporal; H/9th Cav. Veteran of Philippine Insurrection; at Ft D. A. Russell, WY, in 1910; marksman; resident of Richmond, VA. SOURCE: *Illustrated Review: Ninth Cavalry*, with picture.

UMBLES, William S.; Sergeant; A/10th Cav. On expedition against marauders on Staked Plains, TX, summer 1877; convicted of desertion and sentenced to dishonorable discharge and one year. SOURCE: Leckie, *The Buffalo Soldiers*, 159, 162.

Commander, 10th Cavalry, complies with request of Ferdinand Baker, constable, San Antonio, TX, 30 Jun 1877, to collect $21 from Umbles. SOURCE: ES, 10 Cav, 1873–83.

Deserter from Nolan expedition on Staked Plains. SOURCE: Sullivan, "Fort McKavett," 147.

Convicted of desertion by general court martial, Ft Clark, TX, 10 Dec 1877. SOURCE: Miles, "Fort Concho in 1877," 49.

UNDERWOOD, Charles; E/41st Inf. Served 1867–70; now age 82, with $50 per month pension; would be glad to hear from old comrades; subscriber. SOURCE: *Winners of the West* 6 (Jun 1929): 4.

UNDERWOOD, Elisha M.; Private; B/24th Inf. First place, hasty entrenchment contest, military tournament, Albany, NY, autumn 1909. SOURCE: Muller, *The Twenty Fourth Infantry*, 60.

UPSHUR, George C.; Private; E/10th Cav. Convicted by general court martial, Ft Custer, MT, of assault on noncommissioned officers, threatened to shoot another enlisted man; sentenced to dishonorable discharge and one year. SOURCE: *ANJ* 34 (19 Sep 1896): 38.

v

VADER, Louis; Corporal; K/9th Cav. Promoted from lance corporal, Ft Robinson, NE, Mar 1895. SOURCE: *ANJ* 32 (30 Mar 1895): 506.

Teacher, Ft Robinson school, 1 Nov–31 Dec 1895, 6 Jan–29 Feb 1896. SOURCE: Report of Schools, Ft Robinson.

VALDEZ, Julian; Corporal. Died before fall of Manila, Philippines, 1942; daughter Beatriz Valdez Brook, age 51, widow of black merchant marine, works as laundress to support eight-member household and resides in clean one-room hovel. SOURCE: Thompson, "Veterans Who Never Came Home," 112.

VALENTINE, Israel; Sergeant; A/9th Cav. Died at Ft Robinson, NE, 21 Jun 1892. SOURCE: *ANJ* 29 (2 Jul 1892): 782.

Buried at Ft Robinson, 21 Jun 1892. SOURCE: List of Interments, Ft Robinson.

Commander's reasons for insisting that Mrs. Valentine vacate quarters at Ft Robinson are of greater importance than sentiment that may attach Mrs. Valentine to Troop A; quarters are for married men and not widows; she must leave. SOURCE: CO, Ft Robinson, to CO, A/9, 3 Feb 1893, LS, Ft Robinson.

VALENTINE, Thomas P.; Private; I/24th Inf. Enlisted San Francisco, 19 Jun 1899. SOURCE: Muster Roll, I/24 Inf, May–Jun 1899.

On detached service at Cabanatuan, Philippines, since 30 Dec 1899. SOURCE: Muster Roll, I/24 Inf, Nov–Dec 1899.

VAN BUREN, L. M.; M/49th Inf. Served in 1900. *See* McNEAL, S. H., Private, M/49th Infantry

VANCE, S.; Trumpeter; C/9th Cav. Sergeant, 9th Cavalry, has nearly twenty years' continuous service in 9th Cavalry and is writing autobiography. SOURCE: Cleveland *Gazette*, 26 Jul 1886.

Trumpeter, C/9th Cavalry; letter, Department of the Platte, 20 Feb 1890, concerns charges against him.

VANDEBURG, Burt; Private; E/10th Cav. Served in 10th Cavalry in Cuba, 1898. SOURCE: Cashin, *Under Fire with the Tenth Cavalry*, 342.

VANDERHOST; Private; I/10th Cav. At Ft Apache, AZ, 1890, subscribed $.50 to testimonial to General Grierson. SOURCE: List of subscriptions, 23 Apr 1890, 10th Cavalry papers, MHI.

VANDYKE, John; Private; E/10th Cav. Served in 10th Cavalry, 1898; remained in U.S. during war with Spain. SOURCE: Cashin, *Under Fire with the Tenth Cavalry*, 343.

VANHOOK, William; Private; D/25th Inf. Dishonorable discharge, Brownsville. SOURCE: SO 266, AGO, 9 Nov 1906.

One of fourteen cleared of involvement in Brownsville raid by court, 1910; authorized to reenlist. SOURCE: Weaver, *The Brownsville Raid*, 248.

VANHORN, Frank; Private; E/10th Cav. Served in 10th Cavalry, 1898; remained in U.S. during war with Spain. SOURCE: Cashin, *Under Fire with the Tenth Cavalry*, 343.

VARNES, L.; Private; H/24th Inf. At Ft Grant, AZ, 1890. *See* BERRY, Edward, Sergeant, H/24th Infantry

At Ft Huachuca, AZ, 1893. *See* HAM, James, Sergeant, B/24th Infantry

VAUGHN, Louis L.; Sgt Maj; 1st Sqdn/10th Cav. Born Amelia, VA; Ht 5'7", dark complexion, brown eyes; occupation laborer; enlisted Richmond, VA, 9 Mar 1903; three years' prior service in K/10th Cavalry, until 21 Mar 1902; joined K/10th Cavalry, 13 Mar 1903; lance corporal, 3 May 1903; corporal, 1 Aug 1903; fined one month's pay by summary court, 5 Dec 1903; reduced to private by summary court, 25 Jan 1904; promoted to squadron sergeant major, 17 Oct 1904; proficient in noncommissioned officer school (Army regulations, minor tactics, drill regulations), Ft Robinson, NE, 1905; mother Mrs. Sarah Vaughn, Kemps, Amelia Co., VA; first-class marksman, 1900, 1901, 1902; marksman, 1904; discharged, end of term, 8 Mar 1906, character very good, married; clothing $12. SOURCE: Descriptive Book, 10 Cav Officers & NCOs.

Sergeant Major Vaughn and wife guests of K/10th Cavalry for Christmas, 1904. SOURCE: Barrow, "Christmas in the United States Army," 97.

Wife thrown from hack en route to Crawford, NE, from Ft Robinson. SOURCE: Crawford *Tribune*, 9 Mar 1906.

VAUGHN, Marcellus; Recruit; Colored Detachment/General Service. Convicted by general court martial, Columbus Barracks, OH, of theft of $3 worth of clothing (two scarf pins) from Recruit William B. Murray, Company B of Instruction, 10 Mar 1887; sentenced to dishonorable discharge and three months. SOURCE: GCMO 32, AGO, 8 Apr 1887.

VENABLE, Henry; Private; A/9th Cav. Private, F/9th Cavalry; commended for role in capture of escapee, Ft Robinson, NE, 24 Jan 1887. SOURCE: CO, Ft Robinson, to CO, K/9, 25 Jan 1887, LS, Ft Robinson.

Private, A/9th Cavalry, authorized to reenlist as married soldier in accordance with letter, Adjutant General's Office, 9 Aug 1897.

Died in Cuba, 24 Jul 1898. SOURCE: *ANJ* 36 (18 Feb 1899): 590.

VENSON, Ed; Private; B/9th Cav. At Ft D. A. Russell, WY, in 1910. SOURCE: *Illustrated Review: Ninth Cavalry*, with picture.

VERNON, Joseph; K/10th Cav. Original member of 10th Cavalry; in troop when organized, Ft Riley, KS, 1 Sep 1867. SOURCE: McMiller, "Buffalo Soldiers," 77.

VICTOR, William; Private; H/9th Cav. Pvt. Benjamin Davis, I/9th Cavalry, Ft Robinson, NE, threw bowl at Victor in troop dining room. SOURCE: Order 68, 22 Mar 1889, Post Orders, Ft Robinson.

Born Berlin, MD; black hair and eyes, Ht 5'4 1/2"; enlisted Ft Robinson, 16 Apr 1894; discharged Ft Duchesne, UT, 15 Apr 1899, age 32, character very good. SOURCE: Register of Enlistments, 1894.

Among casuals who arrived on post, Ft Robinson, awaiting transportation to troop, D/9th Cavalry, Ft Washakie, WY; departed 4 Oct 1895. SOURCE: Post Returns, Ft Robinson, Sep–Oct 1895.

Enlisted Denver, 10 Apr 1899; brown eyes, black complexion and hair; age 37; seventeen years' continuous service. SOURCE: Register of Enlistments.

Convicted of rape in the Philippines, 10 Jan 1901, in accordance with General Order 14, Department of Southern Luzon, 5 Feb 1901.

Sentenced to dishonorable discharge and twenty years for rape of fourteen-year-old Sebastiana Camacho, 10 Jan 1901; General Order 14, Department of Southern Luzon, 5 Feb 1901, reads, in part, "In the foregoing case of Private William Victor, Troop H, Ninth U.S. Cavalry, a considerable amount of hearsay evidence was admitted which should have been excluded." SOURCE: Senate Document 331, pt. 2, 991, pt. 3, 2107.

To serve twenty-year sentence at Bilibid Prison, Manila, Philippines. SOURCE: *ANJ* 38 (23 May 1901): 719.

Deserted at Guinobatan, Philippines, 13 Feb 1901; "escaped guard and deserted to insurrectos." SOURCE: Regt Returns, 9 Cav, Feb 1901.

"Escaped from guard and deserted to insurrectos Feb 13, 1901, at Guinobatan, P.I., taking 1 carbine from troop and 1 belt full of ammunition"; forfeited deposits of $290.15; "surrendered with Insurgent forces July 5th, 1901, at Legaspi," with deserters Fred Hunter and Garth Shores. SOURCE: Descriptive Book, H/9 Cav.

Deserters Victor and Hunter delivered by General Belarmino with request for lenient treatment as special favor to him, 7 Jul 1901. SOURCE: SecWar, *AR 1902*, 346.

"William Victor and Fred Hunter, deserters from Troop G, 9th Cavalry, with carbines, belts and ammunition were brought into Legaspi yesterday [7 Jul] by officers of Ballarmino's [*sic*] command and turned over to Colonel Wint." SOURCE: Manila *Times*, 9 Jul 1901.

See ANJ 38 (20 Jul 1901): 1147.

To be transferred from Alcatraz Island, CA, to U.S. Penitentiary, Ft Leavenworth, KS, for completion of sentence, in accordance with Special Order 80, Department of California, 16 Dec 1901. SOURCE: Orders, H/9 Cav.

VIELE, Madison; Corporal; E/10th Cav. Original member of 10th Cavalry; in G Troop when organized, Ft Leavenworth, KS, 5 Jul 1867. SOURCE: McMiller, "Buffalo Soldiers," 72.

Enlisted in 10th Cavalry 1867; sergeant, E/10th Cavalry. SOURCE: Baker, Roster.

His application for transfer to his old company, G/10th Cavalry, disapproved by regiment commander, 16 Jan 1874; if the two companies are again stationed together, he may reapply; mentioned Mar 1874 as having served in G/10th Cavalry, 10 Jun 1867–10 Jun 1872. SOURCE: ES, 10 Cav, 1873–83.

Corporal, E/10th Cavalry, at Ft Apache, AZ, 1890, subscribed $.50 to testimonial to General Grierson. SOURCE: List of subscriptions, 23 Apr 1890, 10th Cavalry papers, MHI.

Corporal, E/10th Cavalry, at Ft Apache; sharpshooter. SOURCE: *ANJ* 28 (4 Jul 1891): 765.

VINCENT, Sammy; Private; D/10th Cav. Casualty in fight at Cheyenne Agency, Indian Territory, 6 Apr 1875. SOURCE: Leckie, *The Buffalo Soldiers*, 139.

VINE, Frank A.; Wagoner; E/9th Cav. Died of meningitis in Cuba, 17 Aug 1898. SOURCE: *ANJ* 36 (18 Feb 1899): 590; AG, *Correspondence Regarding the War with Spain*, I:238.

VINEYARD, Henry; Private; C/10th Cav. Served in 10th Cavalry, 1898; remained in U.S. during war with Spain. SOURCE: Cashin, *Under Fire with the Tenth Cavalry*, 340.

VOORHEIS; Private; K/10th Cav. At Ft Apache, AZ, 1890, subscribed $.50 to testimonial to General Grierson. SOURCE: List of subscriptions, 23 Apr 1890, 10th Cavalry papers, MHI.

VROOMAN, William A.; QM Sgt; 9th Cav. Enlisted at Buffalo, NY, 18 Jun 1886; assigned to I/9th Cavalry, 22 Jan 1887; appointed sergeant, 17 Sep 1888; served in Sioux campaign, including engagement at Drexel Mission, SD, 28 Dec 1890; reenlisted and assigned to G/9th Cavalry, 10 Jul 1887; appointed sergeant, 17 Apr 1892; competitor, Departments of the Platte, the East, and Columbia rifle and pistol competitions, 1892–1894, and ranked second, third, and fifth with rifle, seventh with pistol; distinguished marksman, 1894; veteran of Indian wars, Spanish-American War, and Philippine Insurrection; appointed regimental quartermaster sergeant, 1 Jan 1909; at Ft D. A. Russell, WY, in 1910. SOURCE: *Illustrated Review: Ninth Cavalry*, with picture.

Acquitted by general court martial, Jefferson Barracks, MO, of attempting to steal raincoat from Recruit James E. Russell, Company D of Instruction, 24 Nov 1886.

Corporal, G/9th Cavalry; ranked number two, carbine competition, Departments of the Platte, the East, and California, Bellevue, NE, 15–20 Aug 1892. SOURCE: GO 75, AGO, 3 Nov 1892.

Corporal, G/9th Cavalry; witness for defense. SOURCE: Court Martial Records, McKay.

Appointed sergeant, G/9th Cavalry, 28 Jul 1893. SOURCE: Roster, 9 Cav.

Sergeant, G/9th Cavalry; ranked number seven in carbine competition, Departments of the Platte, the East, and California, Bellevue, 14–19 Aug 1893. SOURCE: GO 82, AGO, 24 Oct 1893.

Recognized for role in capturing escaping prisoner, Ft Robinson, NE, 24 Jun 1894. SOURCE: CO, Ft Robinson, to Vrooman, 25 Jun 1894, LS, Ft Robinson.

Sergeant, G/9th Cavalry; ranked number three, carbine competition, and number seven, revolver competition Departments of the Platte, the East, and Columbia, Bellevue, 18–25 Sep 1894; distinguished marksman, revolver, 1892, 1893, and 1894, and carbine, 1894. SOURCE: GO 62, AGO, 15 Nov 1894.

Lieutenant, Crispus Attucks Lodge No. 3, Knights of Pythias, State of Nebraska, Ft Robinson. SOURCE: Richmond *Planet*, 18 Dec 1897.

Retires as regimental quartermaster sergeant, 9th Cavalry, age 45, with thirty years' service and pension of $67.50 per month. SOURCE: Cleveland *Gazette*, 2 Oct 1915.

VOSS, Charles; Private; F/10th Cav. At Ft Washakie, WY, 1902; wandered from hunting camp, 13 Nov 1902; found badly frozen same day; died at DuBois, WY, 17 Nov 1902. SOURCE: Regt Returns, 10 Cav, Nov 1902.

W

WADDLETON, Albert; Private; F/9th Cav. At Ft D. A. Russell, WY, in 1910; resident of Spartanburg, SC. SOURCE: *Illustrated Review: Ninth Cavalry*, with picture.

WADE, Chester; D/10th Cav. Original member of 10th Cavalry; in troop when organized, Ft Leavenworth, KS, 1 Jun 1867. SOURCE: McMiller, "Buffalo Soldiers," 71.

WADE, Gish; Private; E/25th Inf. Wounded in action (leg), Ivo, Philippines, 19 Dec 1899. SOURCE: *ANJ* 37 (30 Dec 1899): 412.

WADE, H.; Private; H/9th Cav. Froze to death while hunting in blizzard, near Ft McKinney, WY, 16 Nov 1886. SOURCE: Regt Returns, 9 Cav, 16 Nov 1886.

WADE, Henry; A/10th Cav. Arrived at Ft Leavenworth, KS, from Jefferson Barracks, MO, 9 Oct 1866. SOURCE: LS, 10 Cav, 1866–67.

Original member of 10th Cavalry; in troop when organized, Ft Leavenworth, KS, 18 Feb 1867. SOURCE: McMiller, "Buffalo Soldiers," 68.

WADE, Jim; Private; K/9th Cav. Served in 1872–73. *See* SLAUGHTER, Rufus, Private, K/9th Cavalry

WADE, John; Private; C/24th Inf. Killed at Del Rio, TX, 8 Apr 1916, when Texas Rangers tried to arrest sixteen soldiers for a disturbance. SOURCE: Cleveland *Gazette*, 15 Apr 1916.

WADE, Lawrence; Private; M/9th Cav. At Ft D. A. Russell, WY, in 1910; resident of Chicago. SOURCE: *Illustrated Review: Ninth Cavalry*.

WADE, Randall; Private; M/49th Inf. Engaged against enemy, Tuao, Cagayan, Philippines, 18 Oct 1900. SOURCE: *ANJ* 38 (11 May 1901): 901.

WADE, Silas N.; Private; H/24th Inf. Served as private, F/10th Cavalry, in Cuba, 1898. SOURCE: Cashin, *Under Fire with the Tenth Cavalry*, 344.

Private, H/24th Infantry, fined $5 by summary court, San Isidro, Philippines, for absence from eleven P.M. inspection, 29 Jan 1902, second conviction. SOURCE: Register of Summary Court, San Isidro.

WADKINS, Henry; K/10th Cav. Original member of 10th Cavalry; in troop when organized, Ft Riley, KS, 1 Sep 1867. SOURCE: McMiller, "Buffalo Soldiers," 77.

WAGNER, Robert S.; Private; H/24th Inf. Enlisted Nashville, 9 Jun 1898; joined company at San Juan, Cuba, 12 Jun 1898. SOURCE: Muster Roll, H/24 Inf, Jul–Aug 1898.

Due U.S. for ordnance (meat can and fork) $.33. SOURCE: Muster Roll, H/24 Inf, Sep–Oct 1898.

Discharged Ft Douglas, UT, 29 Jan 1899, character good, single; reenlisted 30 Jan 1899; clothing $6.45. SOURCE: Muster Roll, H/24 Inf, Jan–Feb 1899.

WAGNER, William; Private; C/10th Cav. Served in 10th Cavalry, 1898; remained in U.S. during war with Spain. SOURCE: Cashin, *Under Fire with the Tenth Cavalry*, 340.

WAIN, William; B/10th Cav. Original member of 10th Cavalry; in troop when organized, Ft Leavenworth, KS, 1 Apr 1867. SOURCE: McMiller, "Buffalo Soldiers," 69.

WAKEFIELD, Daniel; Private; 9th Cav. Wounded in action (head), Naco, AZ, 17 Oct 1914; now blind. SOURCE: Cleveland *Gazette*, 13 May 1916.

WAKEFIELD, Samuel; Private; D/49th Inf. Deserted, St Louis, 20 Oct 1899. SOURCE: Descriptive Book, D/49 Inf.

WALDEN, John C.; Corporal; B/9th Cav. At Ft D. A. Russell, WY, in 1910. SOURCE: *Illustrated Review: Ninth Cavalry*, with picture.

WALES, Charles; Private; D/9th Cav. At Ft D. A. Russell, WY, in 1910; resident of Georgetown, Washington, DC. SOURCE: *Illustrated Review: Ninth Cavalry*, with picture.

WALEY, Thomas; E/10th Cav. Original member of 10th Cavalry; in troop when organized, Ft Leavenworth, KS, 15 Jun 1867. SOURCE: McMiller, "Buffalo Soldiers," 72.

WALKER; Private; E/10th Cav. At Ft Apache, AZ, 1890, subscribed $.50 to testimonial to General Grierson. SOURCE: List of subscriptions, 23 Apr 1890, 10th Cavalry papers, MHI.

WALKER; Private; 9th Cav. Transferred from A/24th Infantry in accordance with Special Order 105, Adjutant General's Office, 30 Apr 1890.

WALKER; Private; K/10th Cav. Involved in rumpus in dive on W. Elm Street, Crawford, NE, early 31 May 1904; shot and killed Taylor, C/10th Cavalry; has eluded capture to date. SOURCE: Crawford *Bulletin*, 3 Jun 1904.

WALKER; Blacksmith; I/9th Cav. Commander, Ft Robinson, NE, orders that his children of proper age must attend post school or some other school and must not under any circumstances loiter around barracks during school hours. SOURCE: CO, Ft Robinson, to Walker, 22 Mar 1893, LS, Ft Robinson.

Resides with wife, sister-in-law, and five children in improvised dwelling at Ft Robinson, across Soldiers Creek; shares residence with Private James, D/9th Cavalry, and his wife, Aug 1893. SOURCE: Medical History, Ft Robinson.

Walker's two daughters are both bad characters; one slashed soldier with razor, put his life in danger, and must remain off post; other is pregnant and employed by officer as servant; she may stay until her child is old enough to move. SOURCE: CO, Ft Robinson, to CO, I/9, 23 Dec 1894, LS, Ft Robinson.

WALKER, Alexander; Private; B/25th Inf. Dishonorable discharge, Brownsville. SOURCE: SO 266, AGO, 9 Nov 1906.

WALKER, Andrew; Major; 3rd NC Inf. Private, North Carolina militia, for several years, then first lieutenant, Apr 1898, before promotion to major. SOURCE: Fletcher, "The Negro Soldier," 238.

WALKER, Arthur; Private; H/24th Inf. Enlisted Camp G. H. Thomas, GA, 29 Apr 1898; on detached service at Siboney, Cuba, guarding company property since 25 June 1898. SOURCE: Muster Roll, H/24 Inf, May–Jun 1898.

On detached service at Siboney until 15 July 1898. SOURCE: Muster Roll, H/24 Inf, Jul–Aug 1898.

On furlough authorized by surgeon's certificate, 26 Sep–16 Oct 1898. SOURCE: Muster Roll, H/24 Inf, Sep–Oct 1898.

Discharged Ft Douglas, UT, 26 Jan 1899, character good, single; deposits $53; due U.S. for clothing $22.39. SOURCE: Muster Roll, H/24 Inf, Jan–Feb 1899.

WALKER, Beaman; Corporal; A/9th Cav. Ranked number five as marksman; member of Department of the Platte team. SOURCE: Omaha *Bee*, 24 Aug 1887.

WALKER, C. T.; Chaplain; 9th Inf USV. Letter from San Luis, Cuba, 15 Dec 1898. SOURCE: Gatewood, *"Smoked Yankees"*, 207.

WALKER, Charry; Recruit; Mounted Service. Served in 1876. *See* **WHITE**, Henry, Recruit, Mounted Service

WALKER, Daniel; Private; I/10th Cav. Served in 10th Cavalry, 1898; remained in U.S. during war with Spain. SOURCE: Cashin, *Under Fire with the Tenth Cavalry*, 348.

WALKER, Edward; Cook; G/9th Cav. Veteran of Spanish-American War and Philippine Insurrection; at Ft D. A. Russell, WY, in 1910. SOURCE: *Illustrated Review: Ninth Cavalry*, with picture.

WALKER, George; L/10th Cav. Original member of 10th Cavalry; in troop when organized, Ft Riley, KS, 21 Sep 1867. SOURCE: McMiller, "Buffalo Soldiers," 78.

WALKER, George; Private; I/24th Inf. Enlisted Kansas City, MO, 9 Feb 1899. SOURCE: Muster Roll, I/24 Inf, Jan–Feb 1899.

Fined $.50 by summary court, 19 Jun 1899. SOURCE: Muster Roll, I/24 Inf, May–Jun 1899.

Allotted $10 per month for six months to Bettie Walker. SOURCE: Muster Roll, I/24 Inf, Sep–Oct 1899.

WALKER, George E; Private; A/9th Cav. At Ft D. A. Russell, WY, in 1910; sharpshooter. SOURCE: *Illustrated Review: Ninth Cavalry*, with picture.

WALKER, George P.; Private; E/9th Cav. At Ft D. A. Russell, WY, in 1910; marksman; resident of 324 Wabash Ave., Chicago. SOURCE: *Illustrated Review: Ninth Cavalry*, with picture.

WALKER, Harry; Private; M/10th Cav. Charged with conduct to the prejudice of good order and discipline; general court martial recommended. SOURCE: Capt. C. P. Johnson to CO, Ft Robinson, NE, 26 Apr 1903, and endorsement to AG, DeptMo, 27 Apr 1894, Register of LR, Ft Robinson.

Court martial sentence published in Special Order 120, Department of the Missouri, 23 Jun 1903.

WALKER, Harry; Private; K/10th Cav. Buried at Ft Robinson, NE, 30 May 1904. SOURCE: List of Interments, Ft Robinson.

WALKER, Henry D.; Private; E/9th Cav. At Ft D. A. Russell, WY, in 1910; resident of La Grange, GA. SOURCE: *Illustrated Review: Ninth Cavalry*, with picture.

WALKER, James; E/10th Cav. Original member of 10th Cavalry; in troop when organized, Ft Leavenworth, KS, 15 Jun 1867. SOURCE: McMiller, "Buffalo Soldiers," 72.

WALKER, Jesse W.; Private; B/10th Cav. Served in 10th Cavalry in Cuba, 1898. SOURCE: Cashin, *Under Fire with the Tenth Cavalry*, 338.

Transferred to Reserve Divisional Hospital, Siboney, Cuba, with yellow fever, around 22 Jul 1898. SOURCE: Hospital Papers, Spanish-American War.

WALKER, John; Private; 9th Cav. Discharge revoked by telegram, Adjutant General's Office, 2 Aug 1894.

WALKER, John; Sergeant; D/10th Cav. Served as corporal, D/10th Cavalry in Cuba, 1898. SOURCE: Cashin, *Under Fire with the Tenth Cavalry*, 341.

Narrates role of 10th Cavalry on San Juan Hill. SOURCE: Cashin, *Under Fire with the Tenth Cavalry*, 267–70.

Sergeant, 1900; recommended by Capt. John Bigelow for Medal of Honor; awarded certificate of merit for heroism in Cuba; cut barbed-wire fence before San Juan Hill, 1 Jul 1898, so advance could continue. SOURCE: Steward, *The Colored Regulars*, 280; SecWar, *AR 1898*, 710; GO 15, AGO, 13 Feb 1900; Bigelow, *Reminiscences of Santiago*, 130–33, 163.

WALKER, John; Private; D/9th Cav. At Ft D. A. Russell, WY, in 1910; resident of Manchester, KY. SOURCE: *Illustrated Review: Ninth Cavalry*.

WALKER, John P.; Sergeant; E/10th Cav. Commissioned first lieutenant at Camp Des Moines, IA, 15 Oct 1917. SOURCE: Glass, *History of the Tenth Cavalry*, appendix M.

WALKER, Lorenzo; Sergeant; C/10th Cav. Honorable mention for gallantry against Kiowas and Comanches, Wichita Agency, Indian Territory, 22–23 Aug 1874. SOURCE: Baker, Roster.

WALKER, Michael; Private; C/9th Cav. Convicted of firing through door of native canteen in the Philippines, Aug 1901; sentenced to dishonorable discharge and three months.

WALKER, Neely; M/10th Cav. Original member of 10th Cavalry; in troop when organized, Ft Riley, KS, 15 Oct 1867. SOURCE: McMiller, "Buffalo Soldiers," 79.

WALKER, Otis; C/10th Cav. Served 1887–89; discharged at Ft Grant, AZ; died, age 74, at Foster, OH, 5 May 1939. SOURCE: *Winners of the West* 16 (May 1939): 2.

WALKER, Phillip E.; Private; K/24th Inf. Enlisted Baltimore, 30 May 1898; assigned to H Company at San Juan, Cuba, 12 Jul 1898. SOURCE: Muster Roll, H/24 Inf, Jul–Aug 1898.

Transferred to K/24th Infantry, 16 Sep 1898. SOURCE: Muster Roll, H/24 Inf, Sep–Oct 1898.

WALKER, Quiller; Private; K/24th Inf. Claimed he hid in privy in camp during shooting, night of Houston riot; sentenced to death; commuted to life in prison. SOURCE: Haynes, *A Night of Violence*, 125, 294, 302.

WALKER, Ralph; Private; G/9th Cav. Discharged on certificate of disability from Ft Robinson, NE, 2 Mar 1898; one of five recruits who joined with gonorrhea. SOURCE: CO, Ft Robinson, to Surgeon, Ft Robinson, 2 May 1898, LS, Ft Robinson; Certificates of Disability, Ft Robinson.

WALKER, Robert H.; Private; G/9th Cav. In hands of civil authorities, Chadron, NE, 11 May–14 Sep 1897. SOURCE: Regt Returns, 9 Cav, May–Sep 1897.

Indicted for murder of former soldier Sandy Tournage, May 1897; taken to Chadron, tried, and acquitted. SOURCE: Crawford *Tribune*, 14 May and 19 Nov 1897.

WALKER, Samuel; Private; D/9th Cav. Wounded in action escorting supplies up Bicol River, Philippines, 26 Nov 1900; died same day, Nueva Caceres, Philippines, from shock following amputation of left leg at thigh. SOURCE: Hamilton, "History of the Ninth Cavalry," 103–4; *Illustrated Review: Ninth Cavalry*.

Killed in action, Umbao, Luzon, Philippines, 26 Nov 1900. SOURCE: *ANJ* 38 (8 Dec 1900): 355.

WALKER, Samuel W.; Private; I/24th Inf. Enlisted Ft Crook, NE, 30 Jun 1899. SOURCE: Muster Roll, I/24 Inf, Jul–Aug 1899.

On detached service at Cabanatuan, Philippines, since 20 Dec 1899. SOURCE: Muster Roll, I/24 Inf, Nov–Dec 1899.

WALKER, William; Private; M/10th Cav. Served in 10th Cavalry, 1898; remained in U.S. during war with Spain. SOURCE: Cashin, *Under Fire with the Tenth Cavalry*, 352.

WALKER, William; Private; A/9th Cav. At Ft D. A. Russell, WY, in 1910. SOURCE: *Illustrated Review: Ninth Cavalry*, with picture.

WALL, Archy; Principal Musician; 24th Inf. Born Murray Co., TN; brown complexion, Ht 5'5"; first enlistment in Band/24th Infantry completed 17 Feb 1881, age 26; reenlisted Ft Supply, Indian Territory, 21 Feb 1881; discharged, end of term, Ft Bayard, NM, 20 Feb 1886, character "excellent—reliable and trustworthy. A very good baritone player," married with three children; deposits $535, 1881–86, retained $60, clothing $114.63.

Born Franklin, Williams Co., TN, 1857; enlisted in H/24th Infantry, Nashville, 18 Feb 1876; served in Victorio campaign, in Cuba, on nursing duty at Montauk Point, NY, and in the Philippines as second lieutenant, A/49th Infantry; principal musician, 24th Infantry, 15 Mar 1885; served eighteen years as principal musician with at least twenty-six men under him; charter member of Guy V. Henry Post No. 3, Spanish-American War Veterans; married Miss Fanny McKay of Louisville, 1 Jun 1885; wife "one of the most active workers in the California Federation of Colored Women's Clubs," with seven years as state treasurer, who presided over city and district work of orphanage; active in organization of Spanish-American War auxiliary and now president; president, Art and Industrial Club of Oakland; children: Clifton, Florence Wall-Murry, and Lillian Wall-Williams, all musically inclined and educated in Oakland, CA, public schools; girls attractive "leaders in society of the Bay cities, marrying befitting their station." SOURCE: Beasley, *Negro Trailblazers*, 228, 284, 297–98.

In E/24th Infantry, married, at Ft Bayard, NM. SOURCE: *ANJ* 29 (17 Oct 1891): 133.

At Ft Douglas, UT. SOURCE: Clark, "A History of the Twenty-fourth," 69.

See **BRYANT**, Ferdinand, 24th Infantry; **GOODLOE**, Thomas, First Sergeant, G/9th Cavalry

Retired from Ft Harrison, MT, 13 Jul 1903; died at age 74 as retired staff sergeant, of arteriosclerosis, Letterman

Hospital, Presidio of San Francisco, CA, 7 Apr 1931; application for hospitalization shows his race as white and color as ruddy; wife had pension of $30 per month, resided at 6114 Telegraph, Oakland, with daughter Florence Wall-White until her death 11 May 1944. SOURCE: VA File C 2643745, Archy Wall.

Mollie Green, age 72 in 1931, resided at Ft Supply in 1885 when Wall took furlough to Louisville to marry; his wife came to Ft Supply in 1886 and was entertained in Green home for several days before Walls settled in their own house; has been with or near Walls at military posts and in Oakland since. SOURCE: Affidavit, Mollie Green, 962 63rd Street, Oakland, 28 Oct 1931, VA File C 2643745, Archy Wall.

Fanny Wall's maiden name Franklin, born Sumner Co., TN; married to George McKay at age 16 in 1878; McKay died in Louisville, 1882. SOURCE: VA File C 2643745, Archy Wall.

Fanny Wall motivating spirit behind Fanny Wall Children's Home and Day Nursery, Linden near 8th, Oakland, which is "a colossal monument to the efforts of the [California Federation of Colored Women's Clubs] and to Mrs. Wall." SOURCE: Davis, *Lifting as They Climb*, 280.

WALLACE, Al; Private; K/48th Inf. Died of variola in the Philippines, 16 Jul 1900. SOURCE: *ANJ* 37 (28 Jul 1900): 1142.

WALLACE, Charles E.; 1st Sgt; F/9th Cav. Veteran of Philippine Insurrection; at Ft D. A. Russell, WY, in 1910; sharpshooter; resident of South Bend, IN. SOURCE: *Illustrated Review: Ninth Cavalry*, with picture.

WALLACE, Den; M/24th Inf. Convicted of attempting to shoot two native prisoners in the Philippines, June 1901; sentenced to one year.

WALLACE, Edward; Private; B/10th Cav. Served in 10th Cavalry, 1898; remained in U.S. during war with Spain. SOURCE: Cashin, *Under Fire with the Tenth Cavalry*, 333.

WALLACE, Edward; Private; M/10th Cav. Served in 10th Cavalry, 1898; remained in U.S. during war with Spain. SOURCE: Cashin, *Under Fire with the Tenth Cavalry*, 352.

WALLACE, Elias; Private; I/24th Inf. Enlisted Youngstown, OH, 10 Feb 1899. SOURCE: Muster Roll, I/24 Inf, Jan–Feb 1899.

Fined $.50 by garrison court martial, Presidio of San Francisco, CA, 19 Apr 1899. SOURCE: Muster Roll, I/24 Inf, Mar–Apr 1899.

Fined $2 by summary court martial, Presidio of San Francisco, 10 May 1899; fined $3 by summary court martial, Presidio of San Francisco, 23 May 1899. SOURCE: Muster Roll, I/24 Inf, May–Jun 1899.

Fined $3 by summary court martial, Presidio of San Francisco, 18 Sep 1899. SOURCE: Muster Roll, I/24 Inf, Sep–Oct 1899.

WALLACE, George; Corporal; A/9th Cav. At Ft D. A. Russell, WY, in 1910. SOURCE: *Illustrated Review: Ninth Cavalry*, with picture.

WALLACE, H.; Sergeant; L/9th Cav. Ranked number 75 among sharpshooters over 90 percent in 1886. SOURCE: GO 97, AGO, 31 Dec 1886.

WALLACE, Harry; Sergeant; C/9th Cav. Appointed sergeant, C/9th Cavalry, as of 1 Jul 1885. SOURCE: Roster, 9 Cav.

Ranked number eight in revolver competition, Departments of the East, the Platte, and California, Bellevue, NE, 14–19 Aug 1893. SOURCE: GO 82, AGO, 24 Oct 1893.

Examined for post quartermaster sergeant at Ft Robinson, NE, Aug 1895. SOURCE: *ANJ* 32 (10 Aug 1895): 823.

Ordered by post commander, Ft Robinson, to send his son to school, despite Wallace's claim that his son is out because he helps his mother. SOURCE: CO, Ft Robinson, to Superintendent, Post School, 15 Feb 1898, LS, Ft Robinson.

Two children, Gertrude, age four, and Mattie, age two, burned to death in quarters, Ft Robinson, after their mother locked them in while she went visiting, 22 Mar 1898. SOURCE: Medical History, Ft Robinson; CO, Ft Robinson, to AG, DeptMo, 23 Mar 1898, LS, Ft Robinson.

Kansas City, MO, *Times* reports that everyone in Army sympathizes with Wallace and his wife for the loss of two little children in recent fire. SOURCE: *ANJ* 35 (2 Apr 1898): 582.

WALLACE, John; Private; H/10th Cav. Served in 10th Cavalry, 1898; remained in U.S. during war with Spain. SOURCE: Cashin, *Under Fire with the Tenth Cavalry*, 347.

At Camp Forse, AL, Nov 1898. SOURCE: Richmond *Planet*, 3 Dec 1898.

WALLACE, John C.; Private; H/24th Inf. Convicted by general court martial, Ft Brown, TX, of same offenses as Pvt. John Smith, H/24th Infantry; sentence of eight months reduced to six by commanding general, Department of Texas. SOURCE: GCMO 1, Department of Texas, 11 Jan 1873.

WALLACE, Joseph; M/10th Cav. Original member of 10th Cavalry; in troop when organized, Ft Riley, KS, 15 Oct 1867. SOURCE: McMiller, "Buffalo Soldiers," 79.

WALLACE, Lewis H.; H/9th Cav. Surviving veteran of Indian wars; resides in Washington, LA; pension increased from $20 per month to $50 per month. SOURCE: *Winners of the West* 3 (Jun 1926): 7; *Winners of the West* 4 (Nov 1927): 8.

WALLACE, Lewis W.; Band/9th Cav. Corporal, M/10th Cavalry, at Ft D. A. Russell, WY, in 1910; resident of Chicago. SOURCE: *Illustrated Review: Ninth Cavalry*, with picture.

Chicago resident visited his aunt, Mrs. A. E. Stevens of Central Avenue, Cleveland, OH, last week. SOURCE: Cleveland *Gazette*, 16 Sep 1911.

Commissioned captain at Camp Des Moines, IA, Oct 1917. SOURCE: Sweeney, *History of the American Negro*, 130.

WALLACE, Robert; Private; D/10th Cav. Served in 10th Cavalry, 1898; remained in U.S. during war with Spain. SOURCE: Cashin, *Under Fire with the Tenth Cavalry*, 341.

WALLACE, Samuel; Private; C/10th Cav. Served in 10th Cavalry, 1898; remained in U.S. during war with Spain. SOURCE: Cashin, *Under Fire with the Tenth Cavalry*, 340.

WALLER, E.; Private; 10th Cav. With escort that saved Gen. E. A. Carr at Beaver Creek, KS, Oct 1868. SOURCE: Rickey, "The Negro Regulars," 6–7.

See **WALLER**, Reuben, Private, H/10th Cavalry

WALLER, John; Private; D/9th Cav. At Ft D. A. Russell, WY, in 1910; sharpshooter. SOURCE: *Illustrated Review: Ninth Cavalry.*

WALLER, John L.; Captain; 23rd Kans Inf. Prominent black Republican and former consul in Madagascar; encouraged black emigration to Cuba through his 1899 Afro-American Emigration Society; urged only blacks with capital or particular skills to go. SOURCE: Gatewood, "Kansas Negroes and the Spanish-American War," 312.

See Allison Blakeley, "The John L. Waller Affair, 1895–1896," *Negro History Bulletin* 37 (Feb–Mar 1974): 216–18.

WALLER, John L.; Sgt Maj; 49th Inf. Born in Kansas, 22 May 1882; enlisted, age 16, Jul 1898; six months after mustered out at Ft Leavenworth, KS, enlisted in 49th Infantry; served as private, corporal, and sergeant, A/49th Infantry, battalion and regimental sergeant major; on discharge hired as private secretary to governor of Isabella Province, Northern Luzon, Philippines; then clerk, headquarters, Philippine Constabulary, until 1905; clerk, office of the Quartermaster General, Washington, DC, 1906–1908; then resided in New York City for five years; returned to Manila, Philippines with Quartermaster General in 1913. SOURCE: Cleveland *Gazette*, 5 Aug 1916.

WALLER, Reuben; Private; H/10th Cav. Born a slave in 1840; servant to Confederate cavalry general in Civil War; enlisted in H/10th Cavalry, 16 Jul 1867; fought at Beecher's Island, KS; served ten years and settled at El Dorado, KS. SOURCE: Carroll, *The Black Military Experience*, 193–99.

Original member of 10th Cavalry; in troop when organized, Ft Leavenworth, KS, 21 Jul 1867. SOURCE: McMiller, "Buffalo Soldiers," 75.

Enlisted Ft Leavenworth for five years, 16 Jul 1867; drilled and trained for horse riding about two months, marched to Ft Hays, KS, under Capt. Louis H. Carpenter; near Ft Harker, KS, Indians refused to engage in battle; later five enlisted men and white scout captured while hunting; Indians scalped and burned white, stripped and beat blacks and sent them away, saying "black man's scalp no good"; resides in El Dorado. SOURCE: *Winners of the West* 1 (Jul 1924): 1.

At battle of Beaver Creek, KS, H and I/10th Cavalry, protected Gen. E. A. Carr as escort from Ft Wallace: "Our soldiers . . . scalped some of the Indians, but we soon put a stop to that kind of barbarity amongst the Tenth cavalrymen." SOURCE: *Winners of the West* 1 (Oct 1924): 3.

Now 89 years old, with $50 per month pension; to attend sixtieth anniversary commemoration of Beecher's Island fight on Republican River, to be held in Colorado, 14–16 Sep 1928: "History shows that Colonel Carpenter and his colored orderly were the first to rescue the men, and the colored orderly was myself." SOURCE: *Winners of the West* 5 (Aug 1928): 2.

Delivered opening address at Beecher's Island celebration last year to about two thousand in attendance: "My old buddies of Troop H, 10th U.S. Cavalry, if any of you are still living, do you remember on September 19, 1868, when we charged into the Indians and stampeded them, rescuing 20 men who were living out of the 51 that went into the fight? Let us hear from you." SOURCE: *Winners of the West* 6 (May 1929): 2.

Letter. SOURCE: *Winners of the West* 7 (Mar 1930): 2.

Age 94, last survivor of Beecher's Island fight. SOURCE: *Winners of the West* 10 (Nov 1933): 2, with picture.

WALLIS, Ingraham; Corporal; H/24th Inf. Enlisted Ft Douglas, UT, 17 Mar 1898, with ten years' continuous service; promoted from artificer to corporal at Tampa, FL, 10 May 1898. SOURCE: Muster Roll, H/24 Inf, May–Jun 1898.

On four-month furlough, 27 Sep 1898–26 Jan 1899. SOURCE: Muster Roll, H/24 Inf, Sep–Oct 1898 and Jan–Feb 1899.

WALLS, H. F.; 2nd Lt; A/49th Inf. Private, corporal, sergeant, D/9th Cavalry, 4 Feb 1893–3 Feb 1898; reenlisted in D/9th Cavalry, 4 Feb 1898; sergeant until 24 Nov 1898; wounded in action at San Juan, Cuba, 1 Jul 1898; in hospital, Ft McPherson, GA, 11 Jul–8 Aug 1898; saddler sergeant, 9th Cavalry, 24 Nov 1898; squadron sergeant major, 9th Cavalry, 15 Mar 1899; commissary sergeant, 9th Cavalry, 1 May 1899; second lieutenant, 49th Infantry, 13 Sep 1899. SOURCE: Descriptive Book, A/49 Inf.

Promoted from private to corporal, D/9th Cavalry, Ft Robinson, NE, 10 May 1895. SOURCE: *ANJ* 32 (25 May 1895): 642.

Relieved from special duty as assistant librarian, Ft Robinson. SOURCE: Order 30, 16 May 1895, Post Orders, Ft Robinson.

Corporal, D/9th Cavalry; ranked number five in carbine competition, Departments of the Platte, Columbia, and Dakota, Ft Robinson, 27–30 Sep 1897. SOURCE: GO 64, AGO, 18 Nov 1897.

Former commissary sergeant, 9th Cavalry, commissioned second lieutenant, 49th Infantry. SOURCE: *ANJ* 37 (9 Dec 1899): 345b.

WALLS, Henry T.; Private; 24th Inf. Served in Houston, 1917; tried unsuccessfully at court martial to establish alibi for being off post during riot; sentenced to two years. SOURCE: Haynes, *A Night of Violence*, 268, 271.

WALLS, John S.; Private; H/24th Inf. Sentenced to twenty days and fined $10 by summary court, San Isidro, Philippines, for being drunk in quarters and a nuisance, 11 Nov 1901, second conviction. SOURCE: Register of Summary Court, San Isidro.

Fined $1.50 by summary court, San Isidro, for absence from eleven P.M. check roll call, 10 Mar 1902. SOURCE: Register of Summary Court, San Isidro.

Fined $10 for carelessly discharging weapon on provost guard, San Isidro, 18 Mar 1902. SOURCE: Register of Summary Court, San Isidro.

Fined one month's pay for reporting drunk to guard duty, 20 Mar 1902. SOURCE: Register of Summary Court, San Isidro.

Fined $2 for missing eleven P.M. check roll call, 4 Apr 1902. SOURCE: Register of Summary Court, San Isidro.

WALLUS, J.; Trumpeter; E/9th Cav. On detached service in field, New Mexico, 26 Jan–1 Feb 1881. SOURCE: Regt Returns, 9 Cav, Feb 1881.

WALLY, Augustus; Sergeant; E/10th Cav. Born Reisterstown, MD; awarded Medal of Honor for heroism against Apache Nana, Cuchillo Negro Mountains, NM, while private, I/9th Cavalry, 16 Aug 1881. SOURCE: Lee, *Negro Medal of Honor Men*, 71, 74.

Awarded medal for heroism against Nana, Carrizo Canyon, NM, 12 Aug 1881. SOURCE: Carroll, *The Black Military Experience*, 365–69; Billington, *New Mexico's Buffalo Soldiers*, 106.

Medal of Honor mentioned. SOURCE: Leckie, *The Buffalo Soldiers*, 232–33; Koger, *The Maryland Negro in Our Wars*, 23.

Served as private E/10th Cavalry in Cuba, 1898. SOURCE: Cashin, *Under Fire with the Tenth Cavalry*, 342.

Narrates Spanish-American War experiences. SOURCE: Cashin, *Under Fire with the Tenth Cavalry*, 364–65.

Showed "great gallantry" before Santiago, Cuba, 24 Jun 1898; with Capt. C. G. Ayers and Privates Neal, Nelson, and White, dragged wounded Major Bell of 1st Cavalry to safety. SOURCE: SecWar, *AR 1898*, 355.

Recently promoted from cook to sergeant; has Medal of Honor; will retire with thirty years' service on 1 Feb 1907. SOURCE: Fremont *Clipper*, 14 Dec 1906.

WALSH, David; Private; L/49th Inf. In the Philippines, 1900. *See* **CLAY**, Henry, Private, L/49th Infantry

WALSH, Thomas; D/25th Inf. Convicted of assault with intent to rape in the Philippines, Mar 1901; sentenced to five months.

WALSH, William; C/10th Cav. Original member of 10th Cavalry; in troop when organized, Ft Leavenworth, KS, 18 Feb 1867. SOURCE: McMiller, "Buffalo Soldiers," 70.

WALTERS, Alfred; L/10th Cav. Original member of 10th Cavalry; in troop when organized, Ft Riley, KS, 21 Sep 1867. SOURCE: McMiller, "Buffalo Soldiers," 78.

WALTERS, Francis; Recruit; Colored Detachment/General Service. In Company B of Instruction, Columbus Barracks, OH, 1888. *See* **WILLIAMS**, John W., Recruit, Colored Detachment/General Service

WALTERS, Smith; Private; D/10th Cav. Retires from Ft Assiniboine, MT, Oct 1895. SOURCE: *ANJ* 33 (12 Oct 1895): 87.

WALTON, Frank; K/25th Inf. Admitted to Soldiers Home, age 28, after twenty years and one month's service, 15 Jun 1888. SOURCE: SecWar, *AR 1888*, 904.

WALTON, Harold F.; Private; L/9th Cav. At Ft D. A. Russell, WY, in 1910; resident of Camp Dennison, OH. SOURCE: *Illustrated Review: Ninth Cavalry*, with picture.

WALTON, William E.; Private; L/10th Cav. Served in 10th Cavalry, 1898; remained in U.S. during war with Spain. SOURCE: Cashin, *Under Fire with the Tenth Cavalry*, 351.

WAMAN, Aleck; A/10th Cav. Original member of 10th Cavalry; in troop when organized, Ft Leavenworth, KS, 18 Feb 1867. SOURCE: McMiller, "Buffalo Soldiers," 68.

WANGLE, Charles; Private; E/24th Inf. Died of yellow fever in Cuba, 26 Jun 1898. SOURCE: *ANJ* 36 (18 Feb 1899): 590; AG, *Correspondence Regarding the War with Spain*, I:183.

WANTON, George H.; Private; M/10th Cav. Born in Paterson, NJ; awarded Medal of Honor for heroism in Cuba; received medal in Paterson 30 Jun 1899. SOURCE: Lee, *Negro Medal of Honor Men*, 92, 98.

Served as corporal, M/10th Cavalry, in Cuba, 1898. SOURCE: Cashin, *Under Fire with the Tenth Cavalry*, 352.

Left service shortly after service in Cuba, for which he won medal, as private, M/10th Cavalry. SOURCE: Steward, *The Colored Regulars*, 205; *ANJ* 37 (24 Feb 1900): 611.

WARD, Edward; Private; H/10th Cav. Served in 10th Cavalry, 1898; remained in U.S. during war with Spain. SOURCE: Cashin, *Under Fire with the Tenth Cavalry*, 347.

WARD, James; Corporal; F/25th Inf. Killed in action, Cabangan, eight miles north of San Felipe, Luzon, Philippines, Jul 1900. SOURCE: *ANJ* 37 (28 Jul 1900): 1142; Richmond *Planet*, 8 Sep 1900; Cleveland *Gazette*, 15 Sep 1900.

WARD, John; Sergeant; 24th Inf. Seminole-Negro scout; awarded Medal of Honor for heroism, Pecos River, TX, with Lieutenant Bullis, 26 Apr 1875. SOURCE: Carroll, *The Black Military Experience*, 390.

WARD, Nathan; Blacksmith; A/9th Cav. At Ft Niobrara, NE, 1889. *See* **CARTER**, William H., Trumpeter, A/9th Cavalry

Veteran of Indian wars and Philippine Insurrection; at Ft D. A. Russell, WY, in 1910; marksman. SOURCE: *Illustrated Review: Ninth Cavalry*, with picture.

WARDEN, George; Private; G/9th Cav. At Ft D. A. Russell, WY, in 1910; resident of Galveston, TX. SOURCE: *Illustrated Review: Ninth Cavalry*, with picture.

WARE, Burges; Corporal; B/10th Cav. Served in 10th Cavalry in Cuba, 1898. SOURCE: Cashin, *Under Fire with the Tenth Cavalry*, 337.

WARE, Jesse; Private; M/10th Cav. Served in 10th Cavalry, 1898; remained in U.S. during war with Spain. SOURCE: Cashin, *Under Fire with the Tenth Cavalry*, 352.

WARE, John; Private; C/9th Cav. Discharged on surgeon's certificate with constitutional syphilis from Ft Robinson, NE, 29 Oct 1887. SOURCE: *Certificates of Disability*, Ft Robinson.

WARE, June; Private; H/9th Cav. Certificate of disability mentioned in letter, Department of the Platte, 25 Nov 1895.

WARE, Louden; Private; E/24th Inf. Wounded slightly in head, San Mateo, Philippines, mid-August 1899. SOURCE: Richmond *Planet*, 19 Aug 1899.

WARFIELD; Private; H/10th Cav. At Ft Apache, AZ, 1890, subscribed $.50 to testimonial to General Grierson. SOURCE: List of subscriptions, 23 Apr 1890, 10th Cavalry papers, MHI.

WARFIELD, Edward; Private; B/25th Inf. Dishonorable discharge, Brownsville. SOURCE: SO 266, AGO, 9 Nov 1906.

One of fourteen cleared of involvement in Brownsville raid by court, 1910, and authorized to reenlist. SOURCE: Weaver, *The Brownsville Raid*, 248.

WARFIELD, Kearry; L/10th Cav. Original member of 10th Cavalry; in troop when organized, Ft Riley, KS, 21 Sep 1867. SOURCE: McMiller, "Buffalo Soldiers," 78.

WARFIELD, Samuel A.; Private; E/9th Cav. Arrived Ft Robinson, NE, 28 Feb 1894. SOURCE: Regt Returns, 9 Cav, Feb 1894.

See **DILLON**, David R., Sergeant, Band/9th Cavalry

WAREFIELD, Harry; L/10th Cav. Mentioned as Indian war veteran. SOURCE: *Winners of the West* 3 (Jun 1926): 7.

Wife Ella applies for membership in Camp 11, National Indian War Veterans. SOURCE: *Winners of the West* 5 (Jun 1928): 3.

WARICK, Robert; Sergeant; Band/25th Inf. *See* **WARRICK**, Robert, Sergeant, Band/25th Infantry

WARING, Robert; B/24th Inf. Enlisted at Marietta, GA, in B/38th Infantry, 1867; discharged from B/24th Infantry, at Ft Griffin, TX, 1870. SOURCE: *Winners of the West* 8 (Feb 1931): 8.

WARN, George; Corporal; I/9th Cav. Promoted from lance corporal, Ft Duchesne, UT, Mar 1896. SOURCE: *ANJ* 33 (28 Mar 1896): 540.

Stationed at Ft Washakie, WY, late in 1896.

WARNER, F.; Trumpeter; A/9th Cav. Ranked number ten with revolver in Departments of the East, the Platte, and California, Bellevue, NE, 14–19 Aug 1893. SOURCE: GO 82, AGO, 24 Oct 1893.

WARNZER, Alonzo; Private; C/24th Inf. Relieved of extra duty with Quartermaster Department, Ft Huachuca, AZ. SOURCE: Order 162, Ft Huachuca, 1 Nov 1893, Orders & Letters Received, 24 Inf.

On extra duty as teamster with Quartermaster Department, Ft Huachuca. SOURCE: Order 177, Ft Huachuca, 30 Nov 1893, Orders & Letters Received, 24 Inf.

See **BROWN**, Benjamin, Drum Major, 24th Infantry

WARREN, Daniel; Private; C/9th Cav. At Ft McKinney, WY, 1894.

Wounded in action at San Juan, Cuba, 1 Jul 1898. SOURCE: *Illustrated Review: Ninth Cavalry*.

WARREN, George; 24th Inf. Sentenced to thirty days in jail by Salt Lake City civil court for theft of suit. SOURCE: Clark, "A History of the Twenty-fourth," 109.

WARREN, George; 1st Sgt; E/9th Cav. Veteran of Philippine Insurrection; expert rifleman at Ft D. A. Russell, WY, in 1910; resident of Riding, TN. SOURCE: *Illustrated Review: Ninth Cavalry*, with picture.

WARREN, S.; Private; G/9th Cav. On detached service, Ft Stanton, NM, 29 Jan–5 Feb 1881. SOURCE: Regt Returns, 9 Cav, Feb 1881.

WARREN, Samuel; Cook; F/9th Cav. Retired May 1902. SOURCE: *ANJ* 39 (24 May 1902): 955.

WARREN, W.; Private; F/24th Inf. At Ft Bayard, NM, 1894. *See* **CRAIG**, Thomas, Private, F/24th Infantry

WARREN, Walter; Private; I/49th Inf. Died in the Philippines, 24 Oct 1900. SOURCE: *ANJ* 38 (10 Nov 1900): 259.

WARREN, William; Private; Band/9th Cav. Born Georgetown, KY; Ht 5'6 1/2"; occupation musician; arrived Ft Robinson, NE, age 25, 12 Jan 1895; transferred from H/9th Cavalry, 3 Jun 1895. SOURCE: Descriptive Book, H/9 Cav.

WARRENT, William; Private; K/10th Cav. Honorable mention for conspicuous bravery against Apaches, Salt River, AZ, 7 Mar 1890. SOURCE: Baker, Roster.

WARRICK, Robert; Sergeant; Band/25th Inf. Born Chesapeake City, MD; Ht 5'6", brown eyes and hair, dark brown complexion; enlisted, age 29, Chicago, 13 Apr 1898, with eight years' service, five in E and Band/10th Cavalry and three in Band/25th Infantry, single. SOURCE: Descriptive & Assignment Cards, 25th Inf.

At San Marcelino, Philippines, 1900. *See* **FULBRIGHT**, William R., Private, H/25th Infantry

WASHINGTON; Private; K/10th Cav. At Ft Apache, AZ, 1890, subscribed $.50 to testimonial to General Grierson. SOURCE: List of subscriptions, 23 Apr 1890, 10th Cavalry papers, MHI.

WASHINGTON; Private; K/24th Inf. At Cabanatuan, Philippines, 1901. *See* **LEE**, William, Private, K/24th Infantry

WASHINGTON; Private; B/10th Cav. Court martial sentence published in Special Order 10, Department of the Missouri, 14 Jan 1903.

WASHINGTON, Adam; Private; B/25th Inf. At San Felipe, TX, 1878; best marksman in company and ninth in regiment. SOURCE: 25 Inf, Scrapbook, I.

WASHINGTON, Andrew; Private; I/25th Inf. Convicted by general court martial, David's Island, NY, of desertion, 18 May–4 Jul 1886; sentenced to dishonorable discharge and five years. SOURCE: GCMO 71, AGO, 19 Aug 1886.

WASHINGTON, B.; Private; D/9th Cav. Returned to duty in accordance with telegram, Department of the Platte, 13 Aug 1891.

WASHINGTON, C. S.; Private; E/9th Cav. On detached service in field, New Mexico, 27 Jan–1 Feb 1881. SOURCE: Regt Returns, 9 Cav, Feb 1881.

WASHINGTON, Claude; Private; I/24th Inf. Enlisted Huntington, WV, 24 Mar 1899. SOURCE: Muster Roll, I/24 Inf, Mar–Apr 1899.

Allotted $10 per month for eight months to Harriet Washington. SOURCE: Muster Roll, I/24 Inf, Sep–Oct 1899.

On detached service at Cabanatuan, Philippines, since 30 Dec 1899. SOURCE: Muster Roll, I/24 Inf, Nov–Dec 1899.

Captured in the Philippines, 10 Oct 1900. *See* **BURNS**, William J., Corporal, I/24th Infantry

WASHINGTON, Claude; Private; F/9th Cav. Died of cholera in the Philippines, 13 Jun 1902. SOURCE: *ANJ* 39 (9 Aug 1902): 1248.

WASHINGTON, David L; Cook; H/9th Cav. Veteran of Philippine Insurrection; at Ft D. A. Russell, WY, in 1910; marksman; resident of Leesburg, VA. SOURCE: *Illustrated Review: Ninth Cavalry*, with picture.

WASHINGTON, Edward; M/10th Cav. Original member of 10th Cavalry; in troop when organized, Ft Riley, KS, 15 Oct 1867. SOURCE: McMiller, "Buffalo Soldiers," 79.

WASHINGTON, Edward; Private; G/10th Cav. Served in 10th Cavalry, 1898; remained in U.S. during war with Spain. SOURCE: Cashin, *Under Fire with the Tenth Cavalry*, 346.

WASHINGTON, Ernest S.; Sergeant; G/10th Cav. Promoted to corporal, 20 Mar 1898. SOURCE: *ANJ* 35 (9 Apr 1898): 602.

Served as sergeant, E/10th Cavalry in Cuba, 1898; wounded in action. SOURCE: Cashin, *Under Fire with the Tenth Cavalry*, 345.

Wounded in action at Santiago, Cuba, 1 Jul 1898. SOURCE: SecWar, *AR 1898*, 324.

Reenlisted as corporal, G/10th Cavalry. SOURCE: *ANJ* 39 (9 Aug 1902): 1242.

Sergeant, E/10th Cavalry, stationed at Ft Huachuca, AZ; he and Cpl. Hezekiah K. Smith, E/9th Cavalry, Douglas, AZ, won honors in horsemanship at Ft Riley, U.S. Army Mounted Service School. SOURCE: Cleveland *Gazette*, 29 May 1915.

WASHINGTON, Genoa S.; Bn Sgt Maj; 24th Inf. Commissioned at Camp Des Moines, IA, 1917. SOURCE: Beasley, *Negro Trailblazers*, 285.

WASHINGTON, George; 1st Sgt; B/9th Cav. First man to enlist in 9th Cavalry, 5 Aug 1866; assigned to A Troop. SOURCE: Hamilton, "History of the Ninth Cavalry," 1.

"Almost as an omen of the fame to be enjoyed by the new Regiment, the first man enlisted upon its rosters was George Washington, who signed for service on August 5, 1866, and who later was assigned to Troop A." SOURCE: Ninth Cavalry, *Historical and Pictorial Review*, 44.

Appointed sergeant, B/9th Cavalry, 1 May 1882. SOURCE: Roster, 9 Cav.

Retires as first sergeant, from Ft Duchesne, UT. SOURCE: *ANJ* 34 (19 Jun 1897): 781.

WASHINGTON, George; Private; C/10th Cav. Enlisted at St Louis. SOURCE: LS, 10 Cav, 1866–67.

Original member of 10th Cavalry; in troop when organized, Ft Leavenworth, KS, 18 Feb 1867. SOURCE: McMiller, "Buffalo Soldiers," 70.

On extra duty at Ft Leavenworth, KS. SOURCE: CO, 10 Cav, to Adj, Ft Leavenworth, 15 May 1867, LS, 10 Cav, 1866–67.

WASHINGTON, George; Corporal; K/10th Cav. Commander of detachment of 10th Cavalry asked to have prisoner, Cpl. George Washington, report to court martial room tomorrow, ten A.M. SOURCE: Judge Advocate, Ft Lyon,

CO, to CO, Det 10 Cav, 14 Mar 1869, LR, Det 10 Cav, 1868–69.

Acquitted by general court martial, Ft Lyon, CO, of larceny, theft of pair of gloves from Pvt. John Myers, B/5th Cavalry, at depot camp of expedition, Suell Creek, TX, 11 Jan 1869. SOURCE: GCMO 25, DeptMo, 16 Apr 1869.

WASHINGTON, George; Private; C/9th Cav. Commander, C/9th Cavalry, requests furlough for Washington, who has thirteen years' loyal service and is a "faithful soldier" who wants to visit relatives in the East; reenlisted 25 Apr 1883; now at Ft Robinson, NE. SOURCE: CO, C/9, to AG, USA, 19 Nov 1885, LS, C/9 Cav.

Commander, C/9th Cavalry, forwards $37.25 to Washington in Washington, DC; sum includes $35.75 in pay for Nov and Dec 1885 and $1.50 owed him by Blacksmith Holiday. SOURCE: CO, C/9, to Washington, 16 Jan 1886, LS, C/9 Cav.

WASHINGTON, George; 1st Sgt; M/9th Cav. Detached from post, Ft Bayard, NM, and detailed in charge of music, Ft Cummings, NM, late 1880. SOURCE: Billington, *New Mexico's Buffalo Soldiers*, 116.

Authorized four-month furlough from Ft Washakie, WY. SOURCE: *ANJ* 24 (5 Feb 1887): 550.

Recently shot and killed at Ft Duchesne, UT, by Private Collins of M/9th Cavalry. SOURCE: *ANJ* 25 (10 Dec 1887): 382.

WASHINGTON, George; Private; B/9th Cav. On daily duty in post garden, Ft Robinson, NE. SOURCE: Order 48, 10 Mar 1890, Post Orders, Ft Robinson.

Retires from Ft Duchesne, UT, Oct 1893. SOURCE: *ANJ* 31 (21 Oct 1893): 135.

WASHINGTON, George; Private; 9th Cav. Military convict conducted from Ft Robinson, NE, with military convict Herman Hector, Jr., 9th Cavalry, by 1st Sgt. George Tracy, D/9th Cavalry, and guard, Pvt. Harry Rice, D/9th Cavalry. SOURCE: Order 77, 3 Oct 1894. Post Orders, Ft Robinson.

WASHINGTON, George; Sergeant; K/9th Cav. Appointed 10 Jul 1892. SOURCE: Roster, 9 Cav.

WASHINGTON, George; Private; L/10th Cav. Served in 10th Cavalry, 1898; remained in U.S. during war with Spain. SOURCE: Cashin, *Under Fire with the Tenth Cavalry*, 351.

WASHINGTON, George; Corporal; B/24th Inf. Born Lexington, KY; died in Minnesota, 22 Feb 1948. SOURCE: Taylor, "Minnesota Black Spanish-American War Veterans."

WASHINGTON, George; Private; H/24th Inf. Enlisted Boston, 23 Jan 1899; assigned and joined 5 Feb 1899; on special duty as painter, Quartermaster Department, since 23 Feb 1899. SOURCE: Muster Roll, H/24 Inf, Jan–Feb 1899.

Cut with razor by Eugene Sharp, 14th Infantry, in San Francisco. SOURCE: San Francisco *Chronicle*, 30 Jun 1899.

WASHINGTON, George; Private; C/9th Cav. Convicted of entry, assault, and robbery, Goa, Philippines, 1 Jan 1902; sentenced to three months.

WASHINGTON, George H.; Farrier; H/10th Cav. Served in 10th Cavalry, 1898; remained in U.S. during war with Spain. SOURCE: Cashin, *Under Fire with the Tenth Cavalry*, 346.

WASHINGTON, George W.; Corporal; A/9th Cav. Relieved from extra duty as clerk, adjutant's office, Ft Robinson, NE. SOURCE: Special Order 90, 20 Aug 1896, Post Orders, Ft Robinson.

On recruiting duty, early 1898. SOURCE: Cashin, *Under Fire with the Tenth Cavalry*, 112.

WASHINGTON, Grand G.; H/10th Cav. Original member of 10th Cavalry; in troop when organized, Ft Leavenworth, KS, 21 Jul 1867. SOURCE: McMiller, "Buffalo Soldiers," 75.

WASHINGTON, Henry F.; Private; G/25th Inf. Sergeant, E/25th Infantry, stationed at Ft Buford, ND, 1891. SOURCE: Cleveland *Gazette*, 19 Sep 1891.

Former private, G/25th Infantry; Chaplain Steward attended funeral of his child, Missoula, MT, 26 Dec 1892. SOURCE: Monthly Report, Chaplain Steward, Dec 1892.

WASHINGTON, Israel; Private; A/10th Cav. Served in 10th Cavalry in Cuba, 1898. SOURCE: Cashin, *Under Fire with the Tenth Cavalry*, 336.

WASHINGTON, J. C.; Private; D/10th Cav. Served in 10th Cavalry, 1898; remained in U.S. during war with Spain. SOURCE: Cashin, *Under Fire with the Tenth Cavalry*, 341.

WASHINGTON, James; M/10th Cav. Original member of 10th Cavalry; in troop when organized, Ft Riley, KS, 15 Oct 1867. SOURCE: McMiller, "Buffalo Soldiers," 79.

WASHINGTON, James H.; Private; A/24th Inf. Died of dysentery in the Philippines, 24 Feb 1900. SOURCE: *ANJ* 37 (10 Mar 1900): 659.

WASHINGTON, John; I/10th Cav. Original member of 10th Cavalry; in troop when organized, Ft Riley, KS, 15 Aug 1867. SOURCE: McMiller, "Buffalo Soldiers," 76.

WASHINGTON, John; M/10th Cav. Original member of 10th Cavalry; in troop when organized, Ft Riley, KS, 15 Oct 1867. SOURCE: McMiller, "Buffalo Soldiers," 79.

WASHINGTON, John; Corporal; I/24th Inf. Involved in Houston riot, 1917. SOURCE: Haynes, *A Night of Violence*, 130.

Sentenced to ten years for part in riot. SOURCE: Cleveland *Gazette*, 5 Jan 1918.

WASHINGTON, John H.; Private; E/10th Cav. Enlisted in St. Louis. SOURCE: LS, 10 Cav, 1866–67.

Original member of 10th Cavalry; in troop when organized, Ft Leavenworth, KS, 15 Jun 1867. SOURCE: McMiller, "Buffalo Soldiers," 72.

WASHINGTON, Lewis; Private; K/25th Inf. At Ft Niobrara, NE, 1904. SOURCE: Wilson, "History of Fort Niobrara."

WASHINGTON, Lewis E.; Private; I/9th Cav. At Ft D. A. Russell, WY, in 1910; marksman; resident of Leesburg, VA. SOURCE: *Illustrated Review: Ninth Cavalry*, with picture.

WASHINGTON, Lincoln; Sqdn Sgt Maj; 9th Cav. Enlisted at Baltimore, 21 Jul 1885; second lieutenant, 48th Infantry, Sep 1899–30 Jun 1901; served in Philippines Jan 1900–1 May 1901 and 31 May 1907–15 May 1909; squadron sergeant major, 9th Cavalry, and expert rifleman at Ft D. A. Russell, WY, in 1910. SOURCE: *Illustrated Review: Ninth Cavalry*.

Appointed corporal, B/9th Cavalry, 28 Dec 1891. SOURCE: Roster, 9 Cav.

Promoted from corporal to sergeant, B/9th Cavalry, Ft Duchesne, UT, Jan 1895. SOURCE: *ANJ* 32 (26 Jan 1895): 358.

Appointed second lieutenant, 48th Infantry, from squadron sergeant major, 9th Cavalry, Ft Duchesne. SOURCE: *ANJ* 37 (23 Sep 1899): 81; *ANJ* 37 (9 Dec 1899): 284.

Mentioned as second lieutenant, A/48th Infantry. SOURCE: Beasley, *Negro Trailblazers*, 284.

One of nineteen officers of 48th Infantry recommended as regular Army second lieutenants. SOURCE: CG, DivPI, Manila, 8 Feb 1901, to AGO, AGO File 355163.

Commander, 10th Cavalry, has no objection to his enlistment in 10th Cavalry, provided he distinctly understands he will not be entitled to any special privilege by reason of marriage; no vacant quarters on post for enlisted families at Ft Robinson, NE. SOURCE: Endorsement, CO, Ft Robinson, 22 Jun 1902, to request of Washington to reenlist as married, LS, 10 Cav.

Discharged as farrier, K/10th Cavalry, Jul 1905. SOURCE: Regt Returns, 10 Cav, Jul 1905.

Squadron sergeant major, 9th Cavalry; advised to seek information he wants from Adjutant General; chief clerk is not authorized to give it. SOURCE: Chief Clerk, DeptMo, to Washington, 13 Apr 1910, Misc Records, DeptMo.

WASHINGTON, Louis W.; Corporal; G/24th Inf. Wounded in action in Cuba, 1898. SOURCE: Muller, *The Twenty Fourth Infantry*, 19.

Transferred from Reserve Divisional Hospital, Siboney, Cuba, to U.S. on U.S. Army Transport *Concho* with yellow fever, 23 Jul 1898. SOURCE: Hospital Papers, Spanish-American War.

WASHINGTON, Morgan G.; Corporal; B/25th Inf. Private, C/24th Infantry; on extra duty as saddler, Quartermaster Department, Ft Huachuca, AZ, 3 Jun–20 Jul 1893. SOURCE: Order 80, Ft Huachuca, 3 Jun 1893, and Order 104, Ft Huachuca, 20 Jul 1893, Name File, 24 Inf.

Killed in action at Arayat, Philippines, in ambush, 5 Jan 1900; died of stomach wounds; thirteen-year veteran, native of Nashville; served in both 24th and 25th Infantry; "He was respected by all who knew him." SOURCE: Richmond *Planet*, 17 Feb 1900; Nankivell, *History of the Twenty-fifth Infantry*, 90.

WASHINGTON, Peter; G/10th Cav. Original member of 10th Cavalry; in troop when organized, Ft Leavenworth, KS, 5 Jul 1867. SOURCE: McMiller, "Buffalo Soldiers," 74.

WASHINGTON, Preston; Corporal; C/25th Inf. Dishonorable discharge, Brownsville. SOURCE: SO 266, AGO, 9 Nov 1906.

WASHINGTON, Richard; Sergeant; B/9th Cav. Appointed sergeant 28 Dec 1891. SOURCE: Roster, 9 Cav.

Resigned as sergeant, Ft Duchesne, UT, Jan 1895. SOURCE: *ANJ* 32 (26 Jan 1895): 358.

WASHINGTON, Samuel; Private; E/9th Cav. At Ft D. A. Russell, WY, in 1910; resident of St. Louis. SOURCE: *Illustrated Review: Ninth Cavalry*, with picture.

WASHINGTON, Scott; 1st Sgt; M/9th Cav. Veteran of Spanish-American War and Philippine Insurrection; at Ft D. A. Russell, WY, in 1910; resident of Alton, IL. SOURCE: *Illustrated Review: Ninth Cavalry*, with picture.

WASHINGTON, Walter L.; Sergeant; C/24th Inf. Wounded in action, Cuba, 1898; later promoted to sergeant. SOURCE: Clark, "A History of the Twenty-fourth," 100–101.

Transferred from Reserve Divisional Hospital, Siboney, Cuba, to U.S. on U.S. Army Transport *Concho* with remittent yellow fever, 23 Jul 1898. SOURCE: Hospital Papers, Spanish-American War.

Sergeant, attacked while on escort duty with eight men, and killed in action, Manicling, Philippines, 13 Sep 1900. SOURCE: Muller, *The Twenty Fourth Infantry*, 38; *ANJ* 38 (29 Sep 1900): 115.

WASHINGTON, William; D/10th Cav. Original member of 10th Cavalry; in troop when organized, Ft Leavenworth, KS, 1 Jun 1867. SOURCE: McMiller, "Buffalo Soldiers," 71.

WASHINGTON, William; Private; G/10th Cav. At Ft Lyon, CO, Mar 1869. SOURCE: LR, Det 10 Cav, 1868–69.

WASHINGTON, William; Sqdn Sgt Maj; 2nd Sqdn/9th Cav. Born New Orleans; occupation waiter; mulatto; enlisted in M/9th Cavalry, 12 Sep 1883; reenlisted in E/9th Cavalry, 25 Sep 1888 and 21 Oct 1893; transferred to F/9th Cavalry, 17 May 1894; commissioned first lieutenant, 8th Infantry, U.S. Volunteers, 4 Aug 1898; in F/9th Cavalry, 9 Mar 1899; cited for highly courageous conduct against enemy, Camalig, Albay, Philippines, 8 Nov 1900, by Capt. George B. Pritchard, 5th Cavalry; sergeant major, 2nd Squadron, 9th Cavalry, 1 Oct 1901; two children with first wife Marcia, who died at Ft Walla Walla, WA, Aug 1903; married Louise E. Roberts of Baltimore, age 21, single, 6 Jul 1910; kicked in head by mule just before retirement, 1910; died 1 Feb 1920 and buried in national cemetery, Baltimore; widow resided at 758 George Street, Baltimore, and remarried 14 May 1921, becoming Louise E. Johnson, 1514 12th Street, NW, Washington, DC; her claim for pension rejected because his death of cerebral hemorrhage took place nearly ten years after his retirement. SOURCE: VA File WC 894780, William Washington.

Appointed first sergeant, E/9th Cavalry, 21 Jun 1893; sergeant since 8 Dec 1888. SOURCE: Roster, 9 Cav.

Resides with wife on laundress row, Ft Robinson, NE, Aug 1893. SOURCE: Medical History, Ft Robinson.

First sergeant, E/9th Cavalry; letter from Adjutant General's Office, 7 Oct 1893, concerns his reenlistment.

Ranked number 36 among carbine sharpshooters with 75.14 percent; third qualification. SOURCE: GO 1, AGO, 2 Jan 1894.

Transfer from Hospital Corps to G/9th Cavalry disapproved by letter, Department of the Platte, 4 Oct 1895.

First sergeant, F/9th Cavalry, commissioned first lieutenant, 8th Volunteer Infantry, after Spanish-American War. SOURCE: Cashin, *Under Fire with the Tenth Cavalry*, 359–60.

Commissioned for gallantry at Santiago, Cuba, 1–2 Jul 1898. SOURCE: Richmond *Planet*, 13 Aug 1898; Thweatt, *What the Newspapers Say*, 9.

Served with 9th Cavalry in Philippines, 16 Sep 1900–16 Sep 1902 and 31 May 1907–15 May 1909; squadron sergeant major, 9th Cavalry, from 1 Oct 1901; sharpshooter, 1889–1896, 1900–1901, 1906–1909. SOURCE: *Illustrated Review: Ninth Cavalry*, with picture.

See **DEAN**, Milton T., Major, U.S. Army; **PENN**, William H., First Sergeant, K/9th Cavalry

WASHINGTON, William; 9th Cav. Resident of Crawford, NE, 1897, with personal property assessed at $29 and taxed at $2. SOURCE: Dawes County tax records.

Resident of Crawford, 1899; former soldier and former Crawford roommate of Rufus Slaughter. SOURCE: VA File XC 2648848, Rufus Slaughter.

Resident of Crawford, 1902, with personal property assessed at $17 and taxed at $1. SOURCE: Dawes County tax records.

WASHINGTON, William; Private; A/10th Cav. Served in 10th Cavalry in Cuba, 1898. SOURCE: Cashin, *Under Fire with the Tenth Cavalry*, 336.

WASHINGTON, William; Private; A/10th Cav. Served in 10th Cavalry, 1898; remained in U.S. during war with Spain. SOURCE: Cashin, *Under Fire with the Tenth Cavalry*, 337.

WASHINGTON, William; Private; K/9th Cav. Veteran of Philippine Insurrection; at Ft D. A. Russell, WY, in 1910; resident of Brookville, MD. SOURCE: *Illustrated Review: Ninth Cavalry*, with picture.

WASHINGTON, William; Bn Sgt Maj; 3rd Bn/24th Inf. Served in Houston, 1917. SOURCE: Haynes, *A Night of Violence*, 110.

Silenced when tried to warn officers of growing anger of men at treatment in Houston. SOURCE: Haynes, *A Night of Violence*, 112.

WASHINGTON, Winter; Corporal; D/25th Inf. Private, E/24th Infantry, wounded in action, Cuba, 1898. SOURCE: Muller, *The Twenty Fourth Infantry*, 18.

Dishonorable discharge, Brownsville. SOURCE: SO 266, AGO, 9 Nov 1906.

One of fourteen cleared of involvement in Brownsville raid by court, 1910, and authorized to reenlist. SOURCE: Weaver, *The Brownsville Raid*, 248.

WATERFORD, George; Blacksmith; F/9th Cav. Fined $10 for absence without leave, disturbance in troop dining room, and insubordination to 1st Sgt. Emanuel Stance, all at Ft Robinson, NE, on 22 Nov 1887. SOURCE: Order 238, 2 Dec 1887, Post Orders, Ft Robinson.

WATERS; Private; G/10th Cav. His fine paid by Maj. John E. Yard; amounts to be collected from Waters's pay and forwarded to Yard. SOURCE: Adj, Ft Hays, KS, to Adj, Det 10 Cav, Camp near Ft Hays, 8 Jun 1868, LR, Det 10 Cav, 1868–69.

WATERS, Charles; Private; L/10th Cav. Stole pair of leather gauntlets from Sgt. James H. Alexander, L/10th Cavalry, Ft Bayard, NM, Nov 1889. SOURCE: Billington, *New Mexico's Buffalo Soldiers*, 168.

Wrote indecent proposals to Ella Johnson, wife of Private James M. Johnson, A/24th Infantry, Ft Bayard. SOURCE: Billington, *New Mexico's Buffalo Soldiers*, 166–67.

WATERS, George; Private; B/9th Cav. Convicted by garrison court martial, Ft Robinson, NE, of disobedience to Cpl. John Downey, B/9th Cavalry, and resisting arrest by Corporals Downey and Gus Bailey; sentenced to thirty days. SOURCE: Order 183, 6 Jun 1889, Post Orders, Ft Robinson.

WATERS, John; Private; F/10th Cav. Served in 10th Cavalry in Cuba, 1898. SOURCE: Cashin, *Under Fire with the Tenth Cavalry*, 344.

WATERS, John C.; Private; I/9th Cav. At Ft D. A. Russell, WY, in 1910; resident of Green Co., OH. SOURCE: *Illustrated Review: Ninth Cavalry*, with picture.

WATERS, Joseph W.; Private; H/24th Inf. Enlisted Baltimore, 29 Jul 1898; on special duty as assistant post baker, Ft Douglas, UT, since 10 Oct 1898. SOURCE: Muster Roll, H/24 Inf, Sep–Oct 1898.

On special duty as assistant post baker; fined $.50 by summary court, 5 Dec 1898. SOURCE: Muster Roll, H/24 Inf, Nov–Dec 1898.

Discharged Ft Douglas, 28 Jan 1899, character good, single; due U.S. for clothing $27.57. SOURCE: Muster Roll, H/24 Inf, Jan–Feb 1899.

WATERS, Smith; Private; D/10th Cav. Retired 9 Oct 1895. SOURCE: Baker, Roster.

WATKINS; Private; H/10th Cav. Capt. John Bigelow's driver between Ft Grant and Crittenden, AZ, 1885; served in B/10th Cavalry at Ft Duncan, TX, 1877, when Bigelow first joined regiment; also served under Bigelow at Ft Stockton, TX. SOURCE: Bigelow, *On the Bloody Trail of Geronimo*, 91.

WATKINS, Allen; Sergeant; M/9th Cavalry. Promoted from private to corporal, K/10th Cavalry. SOURCE: *ANJ* 35 (19 Mar 1898): 539.

Promoted from corporal to sergeant, M/9th Cavalry, Apr 1900. SOURCE: *ANJ* 37 (5 May 1900): 843.

WATKINS, B.; Private; D/9th Cav. In hands of civil authorities, Buffalo, WY, 18 Mar–20 Jun 1890. SOURCE: Regt Returns, 9 Cav, Mar–Jun 1890.

WATKINS, Calib; C/10th Cav. Original member of 10th Cavalry; in troop when organized, Ft Leavenworth, KS, 18 Feb 1867. SOURCE: McMiller, "Buffalo Soldiers," 70.

WATKINS, Edward; Private; A/10th Cav. Murdered by civilian, Manzanillo, Cuba, 18 Mar 1902. SOURCE: *ANJ* 39 (29 Mar 1902): 752.

WATKINS, George; I/10th Cav. Original member of 10th Cavalry; in troop when organized, Ft Riley, KS, 15 Aug 1867. SOURCE: McMiller, "Buffalo Soldiers," 76.

Shot and killed by trooper, late 1870. SOURCE: Leckie, *The Buffalo Soldiers*, 56.

WATKINS, Henry; Private; A/38th Inf. Arrested for part in soldiers' revolt at Ft Cummings, NM, autumn 1867; acquitted by court martial. SOURCE: Billington, *New Mexico's Buffalo Soldiers*, 40, 42.

WATKINS, Isaac; Sergeant; H/9th Cav. Born Columbus, LA; Ht 5'9"; enlisted Ft Douglas, UT, age 23, 6 Jul 1897, with five years' previous service in E/24th Infantry; joined H Troop at Ft Robinson, NE, 10 Jul 1897; three summary court convictions, two at Ft Robinson and one at Ft Wingate, NM; discharged, end of term, Ft Wingate, Jul 1900, character excellent. SOURCE: Descriptive Book, H/9 Cav.

Veteran of Spanish-American War and Philippine Insurrection; sergeant at Ft D. A. Russell, WY, in 1910; resident of Columbus, LA. SOURCE: *Illustrated Review: Ninth Cavalry*, with picture.

WATKINS, Isom; Private; H/24th Inf. Enlisted Columbus Barracks, OH, 9 Feb 1899. SOURCE: Muster Roll, H/24 Inf, Jan–Feb 1899.

WATKINS, James; Corporal; F/24th Inf. Retires from Ft Bayard, NM, Oct 1895. SOURCE: *ANJ* 33 (19 Oct 1895): 103.

WATKINS, James M.; QM Sgt; C/10th Cav. Sergeant, at Ft Apache, AZ, 1890, subscribed $.50 to testimonial to General Grierson. SOURCE: List of subscriptions, 23 Apr 1890, 10th Cavalry papers, MHI.

Corporal, served in 10th Cavalry in Cuba, 1898. SOURCE: Cashin, *Under Fire with the Tenth Cavalry*, 339.

Quartermaster sergeant at Ft Robinson, NE, 1902; detailed to color guard. SOURCE: SO 62, 9 Jul 1902, Special Orders, 10 Cav.

Retirement address: 1514 S Street, NW, Washington, DC; knew John C. Proctor in 10th Cavalry. SOURCE: VA File XC 2659372, John C. Proctor.

WATKINS, Leroy; Corporal; F/24th Inf. Died of variola in the Philippines. SOURCE: *ANJ* 37 (3 Mar 1900): 635.

WATKINS, Major; A/10th Cav. Original member of 10th Cavalry; in troop when organized, Ft Leavenworth, KS, 18 Feb 1867. SOURCE: McMiller, "Buffalo Soldiers," 68.

WATKINS, Murray; Private; L/10th Cav. In hands of civil authorities, Sioux City, IA, 27 Nov–13 Dec 1903. SOURCE: Regt Returns, 10 Cav, Dec 1903.

Sentenced to dishonorable discharge and confinement by general court martial, Ft Robinson, NE, in accordance with Special Order 40, Department of the Missouri, 1 Mar 1904.

WATKINS, Rufus; Private; H/24th Inf. Enlisted Clarksville, TN, 6 Aug 1898; assigned and joined 16 Sep 1898; due U.S. for ordnance (canteen and strap) $.85. SOURCE: Muster Roll, H/24 Inf, Sep–Oct 1898.

On special duty in adjutant's office as assistant telegrapher since 7 Dec 1898. SOURCE: Muster Roll, H/24 Inf, Nov–Dec 1898.

Discharged Ft Douglas, UT, 28 Jan 1899, character good, single; deposits $5; due U.S. for clothing $6.62. SOURCE: Muster Roll, H/24 Inf, Jan–Feb 1899.

WATKINS, Seth; Private; 24th Inf. Convicted by general court martial, Ft Brown, TX, of sleeping on post, 8 Nov 1872; sentence of six months' confinement reduced to four by commanding general, Department of Texas. SOURCE: GCMO 1, Department of Texas, 11 Jan 1873.

WATKINS, Walter; Private; H/24th Inf. Enlisted Baltimore, 1 Sep 1898. SOURCE: Muster Roll, H/24 Inf, Sep–Oct 1898.

Discharged Ft Douglas, UT, 28 Jan 1899, character good, single; due U.S. for clothing $16.96. SOURCE: Muster Roll, H/24 Inf, Jan–Feb 1899.

WATKINS, Wesley; Corporal; F/9th Cav. Unassigned recruit at Ft Robinson, NE, awaiting assignment, Jul 1892. SOURCE: Regt Returns, 9 Cav, Jul 1892.

Reenlisted; warrant as corporal continuous since 2 Apr 1897. SOURCE: *ANJ* 34 (17 Jun 1897): 854.

WATKINS, William; Private; E/10th Cav. Killed in saloon, San Angelo, TX, Jan 1881. SOURCE: Leckie, *The Buffalo Soldiers*, 235.

WATKINS, William; A/10th Cav. Known as "Wild Bill": fined $10 and $5.80 costs in Crawford, NE, for disturbing peace on complaint of Lizzie Carr; worked eight days on city streets and paid costs, 16 Feb 1906. SOURCE: Police Court Docket, Crawford.

WATLINGTON, Wade H.; Corporal; B/25th Inf. Dishonorable discharge, Brownsville. SOURCE: SO 266, AGO, 9 Nov 1906.

WATSON, Arthur C.; Sergeant; B/10th Cav. Served in 10th Cavalry in Cuba, 1898; died of typhoid fever, Brooklyn, NY, 3 Oct 1898. SOURCE: Cashin, *Under Fire with the Tenth Cavalry*, 337–38.

Helped drag wounded corporal of 3rd Cavalry from San Juan Creek to hospital under heavy artillery fire, Cuba, 1 Jul 1898. SOURCE: SecWar, *AR 1898*, 335.

WATSON, Baxter W.; 1st Sgt; K/25th Inf. Quartermaster sergeant, K/25th Infantry, in the Philippines, 1900. SOURCE: Richmond *Planet*, 29 Dec 1900.

First sergeant, at Ft Niobrara, NE, 1904. SOURCE: Wilson, "History of Fort Niobrara."

Commissioned second lieutenant at Camp Des Moines, IA, Oct 1917. SOURCE: Sweeney, *History of the American Negro*, 130.

WATSON, Bryant; Private; K/24th Inf. Participated in Houston riot, 1917; accidently shot in back and killed by unidentified fellow trooper. SOURCE: Haynes, *A Night of Violence*, 157.

WATSON, Frank; K/10th Cav. Original member of 10th Cavalry; in troop when organized, Ft Riley, KS, 1 Sep 1867. SOURCE: McMiller, "Buffalo Soldiers," 77.

WATSON, George; I/10th Cav. Original member of 10th Cavalry; in troop when organized, Ft Riley, KS, 15 Aug 1867. SOURCE: McMiller, "Buffalo Soldiers," 76.

WATSON, Isaac; Private; F/25th Inf. Died of malaria in the Philippines, 20 Dec 1899. SOURCE: *ANJ* 37 (30 Dec 1899): 412.

WATSON, James T.; Private; H/24th Inf. Enlisted Wilmington, DE, 7 Jul 1898; assigned and joined company 16 Sep 1898; due U.S. for ordnance (tin cup and fork) $.20. SOURCE: Muster Roll, H/24 Inf, Sep–Oct 1898.

Discharged Ft Douglas, UT, 27 Jan 1899, character good, single; due U.S. for clothing $28.16. SOURCE: Muster Roll, H/24 Inf, Jan–Feb 1899.

See **WILLIAMS**, Walter B., Sergeant Major, 24th Infantry

WATSON, James T.; Private; H/25th Inf. Died of diarrhea in the Philippines, 12 Sep 1900. SOURCE: *ANJ* 38 (22 Sep 1900): 91.

WATSON, John; Private; G/9th Cav. Authorized three-month furlough from Ft Robinson, NE, by letter, Adjutant General's Office, 20 Aug 1894. SOURCE: Regt Returns, 9 Cav, Aug 1894.

WATSON, John; Corporal; F/10th Cav. Served in 10th Cavalry in Cuba, 1898. SOURCE: Cashin, *Under Fire with the Tenth Cavalry*, 343.

WATSON, John; Private; F/10th Cav. Served in 10th Cavalry in Cuba, 1898; wounded in action. SOURCE: Cashin, *Under Fire with the Tenth Cavalry*, 344.

Wounded in action at Santiago, Cuba, 1 Jul 1898. SOURCE: SecWar, *AR 1898*, 324.

WATSON, John; Private; I/24th Inf. Enlisted Raleigh, NC, 24 Mar 1899. SOURCE: Muster Roll, I/24 Inf, Mar–Apr 1899.

WATSON, Joe; Private; G/9th Cav. Died of dysentery at First Reserve Hospital, Manila, Philippines, 11 Aug 1901. SOURCE: *ANJ* 39 (12 Oct 1901): 140.

WATSON, R. B.; Private; 9th Cav. Wounded in action, Naco, AZ, 17 Oct 1914; died of wounds 20 Oct 1914. SOURCE: Cleveland *Gazette*, 13 Aug 1916.

WATSON, Samuel; Private; C/10th Cav. Sick in post hospital, Ft Riley, KS, Apr 1868. SOURCE: LR, Det 10 Cav, 1868–69.

WATSON, T. J.; Private; H/9th Cav. On detached service at Ft Bayard, NM, 16 Jan–10 Feb 1881. SOURCE: Regt Returns, 9 Cav, Feb 1881.

WATSON, William H.; Private; H/24th Inf. Enlisted Wilmington, DE, 13 Jul 1898; assigned and joined 16 Sep 1898. SOURCE: Muster Roll, H/24 Inf, Sep–Oct 1898.

Discharged Ft Douglas, UT, 27 Jan 1899, character good, single; due U.S. for clothing $12.70. SOURCE: Muster Roll, H/24 Inf, Jan–Feb 1899.

WATSON, William H.; Private; I/24th Inf. Enlisted Philadelphia, 30 Mar 1899. SOURCE: Muster Roll, I/24 Inf, Mar–Apr 1899.

Fined $4 by summary court, 15 May 1899; fined $5 by summary court, 3 Jun 1899. SOURCE: Muster Roll, I/24 Inf, May–Jun 1899.

Fined $3 by summary court, 18 Sep 1899. SOURCE: Muster Roll, I/24 Inf, Sep–Oct 1899.

Fined $5 and confined for fifteen days by summary court; on detached service at Cabanatuan, Philippines, since 30 Dec 1899. SOURCE: Muster Roll, I/24 Inf, Nov–Dec 1899.

Captured 10 Oct 1900. *See* **BURNS**, William J., Corporal, I/24th Infantry

WATSON, William S.; Private; G/10th Cav. Sick at Ft Robinson, NE, hospital, 18 Jun 1906; returned to Ft D. A. Russell, WY, 14 Oct 1906. SOURCE: Regt Returns, 10 Cav.

WATTS, David; Farrier; D/9th Cav. "Dr." Watts "is a very intelligent young colored man," who learned his trade from Veterinarian MacDonald at Ft McKinney, WY. SOURCE: Buffalo *Bulletin*, 23 Oct 1890.

WATTS, Fred; Private; F/10th Cav. At Ft Robinson, NE, as witness in general court martial, 4 Jan–7 Feb 1906. SOURCE: Regt Returns, 10 Cav, Feb 1906.

WATTS, George; Private; G/10th Cav. Honorable mention for bravery against Comanches, Double Mountain Fork, Brazos River, TX, 5 Feb 1874. SOURCE: Baker, Roster.

WATTS, Joseph; Private; L/10th Cav. Served in 10th Cavalry, 1898; remained in U.S. during war with Spain. SOURCE: Cashin, *Under Fire with the Tenth Cavalry*, 351.

WATTS, Richard H.; Private; E/9th Cav. Transferred from C/24th Infantry in accordance with Special Order 168, Adjutant General's Office, 23 Jul 1891.

Discharged in accordance with Special Order 74, Adjutant General's Office, 29 Mar 1892.

WATTS, Thomas; Private; F/25th Inf. Born Springfield, KY; Ht 5'7", black eyes, hair, and complexion; enlisted Indianapolis, IN, 18 Feb 1880; assigned to Ft Randall, Dakota Territory. SOURCE: Misc Records, 25 Inf.

WATTS, W. H.; Private; 10th Cav. Mentioned 1873. SOURCE: ES, 10 Cav, 1873–83.

WATTS, William; Corporal; M/10th Cav. Served in 10th Cavalry in Cuba, 1898. SOURCE: Cashin, *Under Fire with the Tenth Cavalry*, 352.

WATTS, William W.; Private; H/24th Inf. Enlisted Louisville, 7 Jul 1898; assigned and joined 16 Sep 1898; on furlough authorized by surgeon's certificate, 19 Sep–8 Oct 1898; present sick since 10 Oct 1898, disease contracted in line of duty. SOURCE: Muster Roll, H/24 Inf, Sep–Oct 1898.

Present sick until discharged on surgeon's certificate with 50 percent disability due to knee injury, 7 Nov 1898, character good, single; due U.S. for clothing $17.07. SOURCE: Muster Roll, H/24 Inf, Nov–Dec 1898.

WATTS, Willie; Private; M/9th Cav. At Ft D. A. Russell, WY, in 1910; resident of Joplin, MO. SOURCE: *Illustrated Review: Ninth Cavalry.*

WATTS, Willis; Private; G/24th Inf. Served in G/9th Cavalry, 29 Sep 1889–28 Sep 1894; knew James F. Jackson, corporal, G/9th Cavalry, well at Ft Robinson, NE; Jackson was in great pain, laid up in quarters with stiff arms and shoulders; age 28, resides at 202 North 18th Street, Omaha, NE, in 1898. SOURCE: VA File C 2555351, James F. Jackson.

Reenlistment in G/24th Infantry authorized by telegram, Department of the Platte, 3 Oct 1894.

WAXWOOD, Harvy; Recruit; Colored Detachment/Mounted Service. Convicted by general court martial, Jefferson Barracks, MO, of refusing order of Lance Sgt. Leonidas B. Trent, Colored Detachment/Mounted Service, to rake dirt in road, 23 May 1885, and threatening to kill him; sentenced to two months' confinement. SOURCE: GCMO 63, AGO, 15 Jun 1885.

WEAKLEY, Richard; Private; A/9th Cav. Discharged on certificate of disability with syphilis from Ft Robinson, NE, 26 Jan 1898. SOURCE: Certificates of Disability, Ft Robinson.

Discharged by Adjutant General, as stated in letter, Department of the Platte, 11 Feb 1898.

WEAKLEY, William A.; Private; I/25th Inf. Died in the Philippines, 7 Aug 1900. SOURCE: Richmond *Planet*, 8 Sep 1900.

Died in the Philippines, 27 Aug 1900, victim of homicide. SOURCE: *ANJ* 38 (8 Sep 1900): 43.

WEATHERLY, James; Corporal; F/9th Cav. Private and principal musician, F/9th Cavalry band, Ft Duchesne, UT. SOURCE: *ANJ* 34 (29 May 1897): 733.

Veteran of Indian wars and Philippine Insurrection; corporal at Ft D. A. Russell, WY, in 1910; marksman; resident of Marshall Co., MS. SOURCE: *Illustrated Review: Ninth Cavalry*, with picture.

WEATHERS, Reuben; Private; L/25th Inf. Died of malaria in the Philippines, 29 Dec 1899. SOURCE: *ANJ* 37 (13 Dec 1900): 463.

Died of spinal meningitis at Malabacat, Philippines, last week of December 1899. SOURCE: Richmond *Planet*, 10 Feb 1900.

WEAVER, Asa; Corporal; H/10th Cav. Cited for gallantry leading detachment against Victorio, 1880; promoted to sergeant, 30 Jul 1880. SOURCE: Bigelow, *On the Bloody Trail of Geronimo*, 20; Carroll, *The Black Military Experience*, 87.

WEAVER, Henry; K/10th Cav. Original member of 10th Cavalry; in troop when organized, Ft Riley, KS, 1 Sep 1867. SOURCE: McMiller, "Buffalo Soldiers," 77.

WEBB, Benjamin; Private; H/24th Inf. At Ft Supply, Indian Territory, 1888; subscriber to Cleveland *Gazette*. SOURCE: Cleveland *Gazette*, 25 Feb 1888.

At Ft Grant, AZ, 1890. *See* **BERRY**, Edward, Sergeant, H/24th Infantry

WEBB, Leartis; Private; C/25th Inf. Dishonorable discharge, Brownsville. SOURCE: SO 266, AGO, 9 Nov 1906.

WEBB, Moses; Sergeant; E/9th Cav. Veteran of Philippine Insurrection; at Ft D. A. Russell, WY, in 1910; resident of Oxford, MS. SOURCE: *Illustrated Review: Ninth Cavalry*, with picture.

WEBB, Robert; Private; I/9th Cav. At Ft D. A. Russell, WY, in 1910; resident of Roberta, GA. SOURCE: *Illustrated Review: Ninth Cavalry*, with picture.

WEBB, Will; Private; C/24th Inf. Killed in action at Manicling, Luzon, Philippines, northeast of San Isidro, 4 Jul 1900. SOURCE: Muller, *The Twenty Fourth Infantry*, 38.

Killed at Manicling, 4 Jul 1900. SOURCE: *ANJ* 37 (14 Jul 1900): 1083.

WEBB, William J.; Corporal; H/10th Cav. Wounded in action against Indians near Sulphur Springs, TX, Jul 1879, while member of Capt. M. L. Courtney's command; two Indians killed in action. SOURCE: SecWar, *AR 1879*, 106.

Private bill passed Congress authorizing pension of $30 per month for Webb. SOURCE: *Winners of the West* 3 (Apr 1926): 2.

WEBBER, George; 1st Lt; 48th Inf. To report to Ft Thomas, KY, for duty. SOURCE: *ANJ* 37 (30 Sep 1899): 101.

WEBBER, Perry M.; B/10th Cav. Original member of 10th Cavalry; in troop when organized, Ft Leavenworth, KS, 1 Apr 1867. SOURCE: McMiller, "Buffalo Soldiers," 69.

WEBSTER, F.; Private; F/9th Cav. Discharged, end of term, Ft Robinson, NE, 24 Sep 1885. SOURCE: Post Returns, Ft Robinson, Sep 1885.

WEBSTER, Francis; Corporal; G/10th Cav. Transferred from Reserve Divisional Hospital, Siboney, Cuba, to Fortress Monroe, VA, on U.S. Army Transport *Concho* with yellow fever, 23 Jul 1898. SOURCE: Hospital Papers, Spanish-American War.

WEBSTER, James H.; Private; G/9th Cav. Veteran of Philippine Insurrection; at Ft D. A. Russell, WY, in 1910; marksman. SOURCE: *Illustrated Review: Ninth Cavalry.*

WEBSTER, Joseph; Private; 9th Cav. In fight with civil authorities, Hastings, NE, Jun 1885; shot twice; left there by regiment and attended to by city physician. SOURCE: Lincoln *Daily State Journal*, 27 Jun and 9 Jul 1885.

Passed through Kearney, NE, with an orderly en route to join regiment at North Platte, NE; will be discharged with disability. SOURCE: Kearney *New Era*, 25 Jul 1885.

WEBSTER, Porter; Sergeant; A/24th Inf. Killed by Pvt. David Simons, A/24th Infantry, while trying to arrest Simons for threat to a woman's life, Ft Reno, Indian Territory. SOURCE: *ANJ* 25 (19 May 1888): 855.

WEBSTER, Samuel; Private; E/24th Inf. Wounded severely in chest during action at Deposito, Philippines, summer 1899. SOURCE: Richmond *Planet*, 19 Aug 1899; *ANJ* 36 (19 Aug 1899): 1223.

WEEDEN, Jefferson; Private; G/24th Inf. Admitted to Soldiers Home with disability, age 30, after two years and eleven months' service, 21 Mar 1891. SOURCE: SecWar, *AR 1891*, 753.

WEEDEN, McAllister; Corporal; B/9th Cav. Veteran of Philippine Insurrection; at Ft D. A. Russell, WY, in 1910. SOURCE: *Illustrated Review: Ninth Cavalry*, with picture.

Broke arm in Roman Race, Frontier Days, 1912. SOURCE: Cheyenne *State Leader*, 14 Aug 1912.

WEEKS, Henry; Private; I/24th Inf. Enlisted Philadelphia, 30 Mar 1899. SOURCE: Muster Roll, I/24 Inf, Mar–Apr 1899.

WEEKS, Henry C.; Private; H/24th Inf. Enlisted Louisville, 7 Jul 1898; assigned and joined 16 Sep 1898. SOURCE: Muster Roll, H/24 Inf, Sep–Oct 1898.

Discharged Ft Douglas, UT, 28 Jan 1899, character good, single; deposits $5; due U.S. for clothing $24.72. SOURCE: Muster Roll, H/24 Inf, Jan–Feb 1899.

WEIGHT, John; Private; L/10th Cav. Served in 10th Cavalry, 1898; remained in U.S. during war with Spain. SOURCE: Cashin, *Under Fire with the Tenth Cavalry*, 351.

WEILAND. Thomas; Corporal; G/25th Inf. Retires from Ft Missoula, MT, Apr 1894. SOURCE: *ANJ* 31 (28 Apr 1894): 609.

WEISMAN, Robert; I/10th Cav. Original member of 10th Cavalry; in troop when organized, Ft Riley, KS, 15 Aug 1867. SOURCE: McMiller, "Buffalo Soldiers," 76.

WEISS, Joseph; L/10th Cav. Original member of 10th Cavalry; in troop when organized, Ft Riley, KS, 21 Sep 1867. SOURCE: McMiller, "Buffalo Soldiers," 78.

WELBER, John; Private; G/24th Inf. Wounded in action in Cuba, 1898. SOURCE: Muller, *The Twenty Fourth Infantry*, 19.

WELCH, Alfred; Private; C/10th Cav. Served in 10th Cavalry in Cuba, 1898. SOURCE: Cashin, *Under Fire with the Tenth Cavalry*, 340.

WELCH, Raymond W.; 1st Sgt; L/25th Inf. Ranked number 146 among rifle experts with 69.33 percent in 1904. SOURCE: GO 79, AGO, 1 Jun 1905.

WELKEY, Stock; I/10th Cav. Original member of 10th Cavalry; in troop when organized, Ft Riley, KS, 15 Aug 1867. SOURCE: McMiller, "Buffalo Soldiers," 76.

WELLINGTON, William; Corporal; G/10th Cav. *See* **WETTENTON**, William, Sergeant, G/10th Cavalry

WELLS, Clarence; Private; F/10th Cav. Served in 10th Cavalry, 1898; remained in U.S. during war with Spain. SOURCE: Cashin, *Under Fire with the Tenth Cavalry*, 344.

WELLS, Henry; Private; K/10th Cav. Mentioned Oct 1873 as having deserted 12 Jan 1873. SOURCE: ES, 10 Cav, 1873–83.

WELLS, John; Private; G/10th Cav. Served in 10th Cavalry in Cuba, 1898. SOURCE: Cashin, *Under Fire with the Tenth Cavalry*, 345.

WELLS, Morgan; Corporal; K/25th Inf. In the Philippines, 1900. SOURCE: Richmond *Planet*, 16 Jan 1900.

At Ft Niobrara, NE, 1904. SOURCE: Wilson, "History of Fort Niobrara."

WELLS, Peter; Private; I/9th Cav. Dishonorably discharged in accordance with Special Order 187, Adjutant General's Office, 16 Aug 1893.

WELLS, Robert; Private; I/10th Cav. Served in 10th Cavalry in Cuba, 1898. SOURCE: Cashin, *Under Fire with the Tenth Cavalry*, 348.

WELLS, William T.; Corporal; G/10th Cav. Served in 10th Cavalry in Cuba, 1898. SOURCE: Cashin, *Under Fire with the Tenth Cavalry*, 344.

WELSH, George; Private; H/9th Cav. Born Elizabethtown, TN; occupation blacksmith; Ht 5'6 1/2"; enlisted, age 22, Bristol, TN, 6 Dec 1894; fined $.75 by summary court, Ft Robinson, NE, 1 Jun 1895; confined for six months by general court martial, Ft Robinson, Mar 1896; fined $10 by summary court, Ft Robinson, 29 Nov 1896; discharged, end of term, 5 Dec 1897, character good, single; retained $8.80, clothing $16.69, deposits $20. SOURCE: Descriptive Book, H/9 Cav.

Deposited $20 with paymaster, Ft Robinson, 1897.

WENSLOW, Nelson; M/10th Cav. Original member of 10th Cavalry; in troop when organized, Ft Riley, KS, 15 Oct 1867. SOURCE: McMiller, "Buffalo Soldiers," 79.

WESLEY, James; Private; D/9th Cav. Deserted while troop was in field scouting Blue Mountains near Ft Lewis, CO, 18 Aug 1883; stole horse. SOURCE: Regt Returns, 9 Cav, Aug 1883.

WEST, Benjamin; Private; F/10th Cav. Served in 10th Cavalry in Cuba, 1898. SOURCE: Cashin, *Under Fire with the Tenth Cavalry*, 344.

Wounded in action at Santiago, Cuba, 1 Jul 1898. SOURCE: SecWar, *AR 1898*, 324.

WEST, Charles R.; Private; E/10th Cav. Served in 10th Cavalry, 1898; remained in U.S. during war with Spain. SOURCE: Cashin, *Under Fire with the Tenth Cavalry*, 343.

WEST, Clarence; Private; E/10th Cav. Served in 10th Cavalry, 1898; remained in U.S. during war with Spain. SOURCE: Cashin, *Under Fire with the Tenth Cavalry*, 343.

WEST, F. A.; Sergeant; D/9th Cav. With detachment under 1st Lt. John A. Guilfoyle scouting Utah Territory from Ft Lewis, CO, Sep–Oct 1883. SOURCE: Regt Returns, 9 Cav, Sep–Oct 1883.

WEST, H.; Private; L/9th Cav. On detached service in field, New Mexico, 21 Jan–24 Feb 1881. SOURCE: Regt Returns, 9 Cav, Feb 1881.

At Ft Craig, NM, 1881. *See* **RICHARDSON**, William, Private, D/9th Cavalry

WEST, Henry; D/10th Cav. Original member of 10th Cavalry; in troop when organized, Ft Leavenworth, KS, 1 Jun 1867. SOURCE: McMiller, "Buffalo Soldiers," 71.

Enlisted Little Rock, AR, 24 Apr 1867; at Ft Gibson, Indian Territory, Jun 1867. SOURCE: LS, 10 Cav, 1866–67.

WEST, James; Private; 10th Cav. Enlisted Little Rock, AR, 21 Apr 1867. SOURCE: LS, 10 Cav, 1866–67.

WEST, Willie; Private; K/10th Cav. At Ft Robinson, NE, 1904.

WESTACOTT, Charles; Trumpeter; D/10th Cav. Served at Fts Buford, ND, and Assiniboine, MT, 1889–92 and 1894–96. SOURCE: *Winners of the West* 13 (Sep 1936): 16.

Renews subscription. SOURCE: *Winners of the West* 15 (Jun 1938): 8.

Writes from Los Angeles. SOURCE: *Winners of the West* 16 (Apr 1939): 2.

WESTERFIELD, George; Trumpeter; F/9th Cav. At Ft D. A. Russell, WY, in 1910; marksman; resident of Knox Co., KY. SOURCE: *Illustrated Review: Ninth Cavalry*, with picture.

WESTFALL, John E. N.; Private; H/10th Cav. Served in 10th Cavalry, 1898; remained in U.S. during war with Spain. SOURCE: Cashin, *Under Fire with the Tenth Cavalry*, 347.

Resident of New York City; troop clerk, Camp Forse, AL, Nov 1898, master of ceremonies, Thanksgiving dinner, H/10th Cavalry, 1898. SOURCE: Richmond *Planet*, 3 Dec 1898.

WESTON, Edward Y.; Private; A/10th Cav. Mentioned Feb 1877 as having enlisted Aug 1876. SOURCE: ES, 10 Cav, 1873–83.

WETHERLY, Richard; B/10th Cav. Original member of 10th Cavalry; in troop when organized, Ft Leavenworth, KS, 1 Apr 1867. SOURCE: McMiller, "Buffalo Soldiers," 69.

WETTENTON, William; Sergeant; G/10th Cav. Corporal, shot and mortally wounded Sgt. James Logan at Ft Grant, AZ, 20 Dec 1888. SOURCE: *ANJ* 26 (29 Dec 1888): 346.

Sergeant, at Ft Apache, AZ, 1890, subscribed $.50 to testimonial to General Grierson. SOURCE: List of subscriptions, 23 Apr 1890, 10th Cavalry papers, MHI.

WHALEN, Sylvester; Sergeant; H/24th Inf. Promoted from corporal. SOURCE: *ANJ* 34 (7 Jul 1897): 855.

WHARTON, Will; Private; I/9th Cav. At Ft D. A. Russell, WY, in 1910; resident of Madison Co., TN. SOURCE: *Illustrated Review: Ninth Cavalry*, with picture.

WHEAT; Private; A/9th Cav. "In regard to assigning quarters to Private Wheat, it is understood his wife is not a desirable woman." SOURCE: CO, Ft Robinson, NE, to CO, A/9, 19 Nov 1894, LS, Ft Robinson.

WHEAT, John; Private; G/9th Cav. On detached service at Ft Stanton, NM, 29 Jan–5 Feb 1881. SOURCE: Regt Returns, 9 Cav, Feb 1881.

WHEATLEY, James; Corporal; I/24th Inf. One of Sergeant Henry's "most dedicated disciples," Houston riot, 1917; sentenced to death. SOURCE: Haynes, *A Night of Violence*, 128, 271.

Hanged, Ft Sam Houston, TX, 13 Dec 1917, for part in Houston riot. SOURCE: Cleveland *Gazette*, 15 Dec 1917.

WHEATON, Horace F.; 2nd Lt; 49th Inf. Born Cleveland, OH, 17 Jan 1870; enlisted in L/6th Massachusetts Infantry, 1898; then commissioned in 49th Infantry, Jefferson Barracks, MO. SOURCE: *Colored American Magazine* 2 (Apr 1901): 471, with picture, 461.

Possessed "splendid musical education" and "a military record worthy of historical prominence"; with L/6th Massachusetts Infantry, 1898, in Puerto Rico as field hospital nurse and acting hospital steward, Hospital No. 3 for officers; second lieutenant, 49th Infantry; served mostly in northern Cagayan Province, Luzon, Philippines, including as acting commissary and quartermaster of military district; values commission very highly, especially for signature of "the martyred President, William McKinley"; after service in the Philippines, returned to Boston and medical school, which he did not finish; moved to Los Angeles, where appointed clerk at post office; musician and leader of largest concert orchestra of colored musicians ever assembled in Los Angeles, which served during colored Chautauqua, Aug 1915. SOURCE: Beasley, *Negro Trailblazers*, 298–99.

Mentioned. SOURCE: *ANJ* 37 (12 May 1900): 879.

One of twenty-three officers of 49th Infantry recommended as regular Army second lieutenants. SOURCE: CG, DivPI, Manila, 8 Feb 1901, to AGO, AGO File 355163.

Author of "A Feast with the Filipinos," in *Colored American Magazine* 3 (Jun 1903): 154–55.

WHEDBEE, Samuel; Corporal; C/24th Inf. On special duty at post exchange, Ft Huachuca, AZ, 1893. SOURCE: Order 84, Ft Huachuca, 12 Jun 1893, Name File, 24 Inf.

WHEELER; Private; F/24th Inf. Second in pole vault, Department of the Colorado, while at Ft Douglas, UT. SOURCE: Clark, "A History of the Twenty-fourth," 70.

WHEELER, Arthur G.; Private; B/10th Cav. Resident of New Milford, CT; enlisted New York City; wounded at Santiago, Cuba. SOURCE: Cleveland *Gazette*, 2 Jul 1898.

Served in 10th Cavalry in Cuba, 1898; wounded in action. SOURCE: Cashin, *Under Fire with the Tenth Cavalry*, 338.

Heroism at Las Guasimas, 24 Jun 1898, attested to by Sgts. James W. Ford and William Bell, Camp Forse, AL, 4 Dec 1898. SOURCE: Cashin, *Under Fire with the Tenth Cavalry*, 179–80.

Recommended for Medal of Honor for heroism, assault on Las Guasimas, 24 Jun 1898, by Capt. H. W. Watson, 10th Cavalry. SOURCE: Cashin, *Under Fire with the Tenth Cavalry*, 186.

WHEELER, Henry; L/10th Cav. Original member of 10th Cavalry; in troop when organized, Ft Riley, KS, 21 Sep 1867. SOURCE: McMiller, "Buffalo Soldiers," 78.

WHEELER, James; Private; G/10th Cav. Mentioned among men who distinguished themselves in 1889; received certificate of merit for gallant and meritorious conduct while escorting Maj. Joseph W. Wham, paymaster, when attacked by robbers between Fts Grant and Thomas, AZ; now out of service. SOURCE: GO 18, AGO, 1891.

At Ft Apache, AZ, 1890, subscribed $.50 to testimonial to General Grierson. SOURCE: List of subscriptions, 23 Apr 1890, 10th Cavalry papers, MHI.

Stationed at Ft Grant, 1890; certificate of merit mentioned. SOURCE: SecWar, *AR 1890*, 289

Certificate of merit for gallant conduct, 11 May 1889, mentioned. SOURCE: Baker, Roster.

WHEELER, Samuel; Private; H/9th Cav. In hands of civil authorities, Buffalo, WY, 23 Aug–10 Sep 1888. SOURCE: Regt Returns, 9 Cav, Sep 1888.

At Ft Wingate, NM, married Lizzie Hummons of Winchester, KY, by telegraph, 22 Dec 1899. SOURCE: *ANJ* 37 (30 Dec 1899): 417.

WHEELER, Samuel; Private; D/25th Inf. Dishonorable discharge, Brownsville. SOURCE: SO 266, AGO, 9 Nov 1906.

WHEELER, Thomas; Private; H/9th Cav. Born Clark Co., VA; Ht 5'11"; enlisted Ft Robinson, NE, 29 Jun 1897, with five years' prior service in both E/10th Cavalry and H/9th Cavalry; fined twice by summary courts, Ft Robinson, 1897, total $1.25; corporal, 5 Sep 1898; reduced to private, Ft Wingate, NM, 20 Jun 1899; discharged, end of term, Jun 1900. SOURCE: Descriptive Book, H/9 Cav.

WHEELER, William L.; Private; I/9th Cav. At Ft D. A. Russell, WY, in 1910; resident of Charlotte, NC. SOURCE: *Illustrated Review: Ninth Cavalry*, with picture.

WHEELER, William R.; Private; G/9th Cav. At Ft D. A. Russell, WY, in 1910. SOURCE: *Illustrated Review: Ninth Cavalry*, with picture.

WHEELOCK, Joseph M.; Corporal; K/10th Cav. Author of "Our Own Editors and Publishers," read at Y.M.C.A., Ft Robinson, NE, and published in *Colored American Magazine* 8 (Jan 1905): 29–30.

WHELDON, Samuel; F/25th Inf. Methodist; stationed at Botolen, Zambales, Philippines, Dec 1900. SOURCE: Steward, *Fifty Years in the Gospel Ministry*, 326.

WHIESNANT, Porter; Private; D/10th Cav. Served in 10th Cavalry, 1898; remained in U.S. during war with Spain. SOURCE: Cashin, *Under Fire with the Tenth Cavalry*, 341.

WHINE, Minton; C/10th Cav. Original member of 10th Cavalry; in troop when organized, Ft Leavenworth, KS, 18 Feb 1867. SOURCE: McMiller, "Buffalo Soldiers," 70.

WHITAKER, John H.; Sergeant; F/25th Inf. Retires from Ft Missoula, MT. SOURCE: *ANJ* 34 (26 Dec 1896): 291.

WHITE; Private; G/9th Cav. Served in 1875. *See* **SCOTT**, Private, G/9th Cavalry

WHITE; Private; E/10th Cav. At Ft Apache, AZ, 1890, subscribed $.50 to testimonial to General Grierson. SOURCE: List of subscriptions, 23 Apr 1890, 10th Cavalry papers, MHI.

WHITE; Private; M/10th Cav. At Ft Apache, AZ, 1890, subscribed $.50 to testimonial to General Grierson.

SOURCE: List of subscriptions, 23 Apr 1890, 10th Cavalry papers, MHI.

WHITE, Allen C.; Private; E/10th Cav. Served in 10th Cavalry in Cuba, 1898; wounded in action. SOURCE: Cashin, *Under Fire with the Tenth Cavalry*, 342.

Displayed "great gallantry" before Santiago, Cuba, 24 Jun 1898; wounded in action at Santiago, 1 Jul 1898. SOURCE: SecWar, *AR 1898*, 324, 355.

See **NEAL**, Burr, Private, E/10th Cavalry

WHITE, Andrew; Recruit; Colored Detachment/Mounted Service. Convicted by general court martial, Jefferson Barracks, MO, of assaulting and striking Recruit Marten Pedersson, Company D of Instruction, Mounted Service, with shovel, with intent to inflict severe bodily harm, in company quarters, Jefferson Barracks, 4 Feb 1889; fined $20; reviewing officer, Maj. Gen. John M. Schofield, revoked finding because no proof was presented to show he used more force than necessary to resist assault; restored to duty. SOURCE: GCMO 13, AGO, 6 Mar 1889.

WHITE, Andrew J.; Private; A/9th Cav. Deserted from Monterey, CA, 29 Nov 1902. SOURCE: Regt Returns, 9 Cav, Dec 1902.

WHITE, Burrel; Corporal; I/9th Cav. At Ft D. A. Russell, WY, in 1910; resident of St. Louis. SOURCE: *Illustrated Review: Ninth Cavalry*, with picture.

WHITE, Charles; Private; D/10th Cav. Served in 10th Cavalry in Cuba, 1898. SOURCE: Cashin, *Under Fire with the Tenth Cavalry*, 341.

WHITE, Charles Frederick; Corporal; 8th Ill Inf. Born 1876; author of *Plea of the Negro Soldier, and a Hundred Other Poems* (Easthampton, MA: Press of Enterprise Printing Company, c. 1908, reprinted by Books for Libraries Press, 1970).

WHITE, Daniel; Sergeant; A/9th Cav. Veteran of Spanish-American War and Philippine Insurrection; at Ft D. A. Russell, WY, in 1910; sharpshooter. SOURCE: *Illustrated Review: Ninth Cavalry.*

WHITE, Dillard; Corporal; K/9th Cav. Veteran of Indian wars and Philippine Insurrection; at Ft D. A. Russell, WY, in 1910; marksman; resident of Clay Co., KY. SOURCE: *Illustrated Review: Ninth Cavalry*, with picture.

WHITE, Doc; Private; I/9th Cav. At Ft D. A. Russell, WY, in 1910; marksman; resident of Elkton, VA. SOURCE: *Illustrated Review: Ninth Cavalry*, with picture.

WHITE, Fitan; C/10th Cav. Original member of 10th Cavalry; in troop when organized, Ft Leavenworth, KS, 18 Feb 1867. SOURCE: McMiller, "Buffalo Soldiers," 70.

WHITE, Fountain; Corporal; 25th Inf. Retires Jan 1901. SOURCE: *ANJ* 38 (19 Jan 1901): 495.

WHITE, George; C/10th Cav. Original member of 10th Cavalry; in troop when organized, Ft Leavenworth, KS, 18 Feb 1867. SOURCE: McMiller, "Buffalo Soldiers," 70.

WHITE, George F.; Private; F/9th Cav. Convicted by general court martial, Jefferson Barracks, MO, of desertion from 13 Jul 1886 until he surrendered, 1 Oct 1887; sentenced to dishonorable discharge and four years. SOURCE: GCMO 87, AGO, 30 Nov 1887.

WHITE, George W.; Private; F/9th Cav. Convicted of minor infraction by garrison court martial, Ft Robinson, NE. SOURCE: Order 6, 12 Jan 1886, Post Orders, Ft Robinson.

WHITE, George W.; Cook; C/24th Inf. Letter from Manila, Philippines. SOURCE: Cleveland *Gazette*, 29 Dec 1906.

Resides in Cadiz, OH; letter from Ormoc, Leyte, Philippines, 15 Apr 1907. SOURCE: Cleveland *Gazette*, 8 Jun 1907.

Reads *Gazette* in the Philippines; still at Ormoc, 23 Jul 1907. SOURCE: Cleveland *Gazette*, 14 Sep 1907.

At Madison Barracks, Sacketts Harbor, NY, 9 Apr 1908, along with two battalions of regiment; other companies at Ft Ontario, NY; all in good health and glad to be home. SOURCE: Cleveland *Gazette*, 11 Apr 1908.

Chaplain Gladden preparing for Easter at Madison Barracks; choir consists of Mesdames Robinson and Hill, Private Threat, B/24th Infantry, Corporal Jennings, A/24th Infantry, and White. SOURCE: Cleveland *Gazette*, 18 Apr 1908.

WHITE, Harry; Private; F/10th Cav. Original member of 10th Cavalry; in troop when organized, Ft Leavenworth, KS, 21 Jun 1867. SOURCE: McMiller, "Buffalo Soldiers," 63.

On detail as teamster. SOURCE: Special Order 54, HQ, Det 10 Cav, Camp Supply, 31 Jul 1869, Orders, Det 10 Cav.

WHITE, Henry; Private; 38th Inf. Tried by court martial, Ft Cummings, NM, 1869. SOURCE: Billington, *New Mexico's Buffalo Soldiers*, 37.

WHITE, Henry; Recruit; Mounted Service. Convicted by general court martial, St. Louis Barracks, MO, of stabbing without cause Recruit (colored) Charry Walker, St. Louis Barracks, 13 Dec 1876; sentenced to three months. SOURCE: GCMO 7, AGO, 23 Jan 1877.

WHITE, Henry; Private; C/10th Cav. Served in 10th Cavalry in Cuba, 1898. SOURCE: Cashin, *Under Fire with the Tenth Cavalry*, 340.

WHITE, Henry; Private; C/24th Inf. Transferred from Reserve Divisional Hospital, Siboney, Cuba, to U.S. on U.S. Army Transport *Santiago* with remittent malarial fever, 25 Jul 1898. SOURCE: Hospital Papers, Spanish-American War.

WHITE, Isaac; QM Sgt; F/25th Inf. Ranked number 179 among rifle experts with 68.67 percent in 1904. SOURCE: GO 79, AGO, 1 Jun 1905.

WHITE, J. D.; Private; K/9th Cav. Discharged in accordance with Special Order 147, Adjutant General's Office, 25 Jun 1897.

WHITE, J. E.; Private; G/24th Inf. Describes duty station, Ft Assiniboine, MT, and nearby town of Havre, which has population of two thousand, 10 percent of which is black. SOURCE: Indianapolis *Freeman*, 13 Sep 1902.

WHITE, James; Private; M/10th Cav. Served in 10th Cavalry, 1898; remained in U.S. during war with Spain. SOURCE: Cashin, *Under Fire with the Tenth Cavalry*, 352.

WHITE, James H.; Private; Band/9th Cav. With band on detached service at headquarters, District of New Mexico, Santa Fe, 1880; played second tenor. SOURCE: Billington, *New Mexico's Buffalo Soldiers*, 226.

WHITE, James M.; Private; E/24th Inf. Resident of Washington, DC; to be discharged from Ft Bayard, NM, at end of term, 8 Dec 1891. SOURCE: Cleveland *Gazette*, 12 Dec 1891.

WHITE, Janas; H/10th Cav. Original member of 10th Cavalry; in troop when organized, Ft Leavenworth, KS, 21 Jul 1867. SOURCE: McMiller, "Buffalo Soldiers," 75.

WHITE, Jerry M.; 1st Lt; 48th Inf. Mentioned as first lieutenant, 23rd Kansas Infantry. SOURCE: Beasley, *Negro Trailblazers*, 284.

One of nineteen officers of 48th Infantry recommended as regular Army second lieutenants. SOURCE: CG, DivPI, Manila, 8 Feb 1901, to AGO, AGO File 355163.

WHITE, John; A/10th Cav. Original member of 10th Cavalry; in troop when organized, Ft Leavenworth, KS, 18 Feb 1867. SOURCE: McMiller, "Buffalo Soldiers," 68.

WHITE, John; Private; K/10th Cav. Sick in post hospital, Ft Riley, KS, Apr 1868. SOURCE: LR, Det 10 Cav, 1868–69.

WHITE, John; Private; G/10th Cav. Adjutant General directs discharge of White from service, Ft Sill, Indian Territory, Dec 1872. SOURCE: ES, 21 Cav, 1873–83.

WHITE, John; Sergeant; 25th Inf. Former soldier settled on ranch above Kalispell, MT; Chaplain Steward attended his wife's funeral, 1893. SOURCE: Monthly Report, Chaplain Steward, Aug 1893.

WHITE, John; Cook; H/10th Cav. Private, H/10th Cavalry, 1898; remained in U.S. during war with Spain. SOURCE: Cashin, *Under Fire with the Tenth Cavalry*, 347.

Cook, H/10th Cavalry, at Camp Forse, AL, Nov 1898. SOURCE: Richmond *Planet*, 3 Dec 1898.

WHITE, John D.; Sergeant; K/9th Cav. Corporal, A/9th Cavalry, on special duty instructing recruits since 26 May 1902. SOURCE: SD List, A/9, Nueva Caceres, Philippines, 31 May 1902.

Veteran of Indian wars, Spanish-American War, and Philippine Insurrection; expert rifleman and sergeant, K/9th Cavalry, at Ft D. A. Russell, WY, in 1910; resident of Powhattan Co., VA. SOURCE: *Illustrated Review: Ninth Cavalry*, with picture.

WHITE, John W.; Private; I/24th Inf. Enlisted Baltimore, 17 Feb 1899. SOURCE: Muster Roll, I/24 Inf, Jan–Feb 1899.

Fined $1 by summary court, 3 Jun 1899. SOURCE: Muster Roll, I/24 Inf, Jul–Aug 1899.

Allotted $10 per month for four months to Laura Green. SOURCE: Muster Roll, I/24 Inf, Sep–Oct 1899.

WHITE, Joseph; Recruit; L/10th Cav. Mentioned Jan 1873 as having been sent to L Troop from Ft Gibson, Indian Territory. SOURCE: LS, 10 Cav, 1873–83.

WHITE, Joseph; Sergeant; B/24th Inf. Born New Orleans; Ht 6'2", black complexion; enlisted Ft Leavenworth, KS, 28 Feb 1888; transferred from G/24th Infantry to Band/24th Infantry, Ft Bayard, NM, 1 Sep 1892; discharged Ft Bayard, 27 Feb 1893, single, character very good; retained $60, clothing $65. SOURCE: Descriptive Book, 24 Inf NCS & Band.

Awarded certificate of merit for distinguished conduct in rescue of comrade from drowning, Rio Grande de la Pampagna, Cabanatuan, Philippines, 8 Nov 1900, while musician, B/24th Infantry. SOURCE: GO 32, AGO, 6 Feb 1904.

Retired as sergeant, B/24th Infantry, Jun 1902. SOURCE: *ANJ* 39 (14 Jun 1902): 1037.

Commended for rescue of comrade from Rio Grande de la Pampagna, 8 Nov 1900; now retired. SOURCE: Cleveland *Gazette*, 24 Nov 1906.

Served thirty years; Portland, OR, camp of Spanish-American War veterans named in his honor; in Nov 1900 fight, held band of insurgents at bay and saved patrol of 13th Infantry from ambush; awarded certificate of merit. SOURCE: Wharfield, *10th Cavalry and Border Fights*, 74.

WHITE, Joseph; Trumpeter; E/10th Cav. Served in 10th Cavalry in Cuba, 1898. SOURCE: Cashin, *Under Fire with the Tenth Cavalry*, 342.

WHITE, Joseph; Sergeant; M/10th Cav. Born Georgetown, SC; died Ft Robinson, NE, age 42, with twenty-three years' service, 27 Mar 1904. SOURCE: Monthly Report, Chaplain Anderson, 1 Apr 1904; List of Interments, Ft Robinson.

WHITE, Lee; Private; A/10th Cav. Served in 10th Cavalry, 1898; remained in U.S. during war with Spain. SOURCE: Cashin, *Under Fire with the Tenth Cavalry*, 337.

WHITE, Leonard; Private; D/24th Inf. Fined $5, Cabanatuan, Philippines, 17 May 1901; while on guard duty allowed prisoner Henry Black, K/24th Infantry, to become drunk; witness: Sergeant Dawson, K/24th Infantry. SOURCE: Name File, 24 Inf.

WHITE, Leslie; Private; M/10th Cav. Served in C/10th Cavalry, 1898; remained in U.S. during war with Spain. SOURCE: Cashin, *Under Fire with the Tenth Cavalry*, 340.

Authorized furlough from Ft D. A. Russell, WY, to Cheyenne, WY, Jul 1904. SOURCE: Regt Returns, 10 Cav, Jul 1904.

WHITE, Lewis; Private; C/9th Cav. At Ft Davis, TX, 1868. *See* **COLLYER**, S., Private, F/9th Cavalry

WHITE, Louis A.; Corporal; B/9th Cav. At Ft D. A. Russell, WY, in 1910. SOURCE: *Illustrated Review: Ninth Cavalry*, with picture.

WHITE, Masons A.; Private; G/10th Cav. Served in 10th Cavalry, 1898; remained in U.S. during war with Spain. SOURCE: Cashin, *Under Fire with the Tenth Cavalry*, 346.

WHITE, Matthew; Private; C/10th Cav. Served in 10th Cavalry, 1898; remained in U.S. during war with Spain. SOURCE: Cashin, *Under Fire with the Tenth Cavalry*, 340.

WHITE, Randolph F.; Hospital Steward; U.S. Army. Born Warrentown, FL, 25 Jun 1870; graduated from Howard University, Washington, DC, 1897; first position as pharmacist in People's Drug Store, Louisville; hospital steward, U.S. Army, in the Philippines, 1899–1901; opened drugstore, Owensboro, KY, 1901; married Fannie Hathaway, in Lexington, KY, 23 Jul 1901. SOURCE: Richardson, *National Cyclopedia of the Colored Race*, 177.

WHITE, Spencer; Private; B/10th Cav. Served in 10th Cavalry, 1898; remained in U.S. during war with Spain. SOURCE: Cashin, *Under Fire with the Tenth Cavalry*, 333.

WHITE, Theophilus T.; Sergeant; A/9th Cav. On special duty as post gardener, Ft Robinson, NE. SOURCE: Order 68, 25 Sep 1895, Post Orders, Ft Robinson.

Died at Ft Robinson 11 Sep 1896; buried 13 Sep 1896. SOURCE: Special Order 100, 12 Sep 1896, Post Orders, Ft Robinson; List of Interments, Ft Robinson.

WHITE, Thomas; Private; G/10th Cav. Original member of M/10th Cavalry; in troop when organized, Ft Riley, KS, 15 Oct 1867. SOURCE: McMiller, "Buffalo Soldiers," 79.

To retire from Ft Grant, AZ, 19 May 1892. SOURCE: *ANJ* 29 (30 Apr 1892): 625; Baker, Roster.

WHITE, Thomas; Private; M/9th Cav. Broke into trunk of Lt. John McBlain, Ft Cummings, NM, Nov 1881, and stole $140 belonging to Pvt. George Brown, M/9th Cavalry; deserted and captured. SOURCE: Billington, *New Mexico's Buffalo Soldiers*, 131.

WHITE, Thomas; Private; G/10th Cav. Served in 10th Cavalry, 1898; remained in U.S. during war with Spain. SOURCE: Cashin, *Under Fire with the Tenth Cavalry*, 346.

WHITE, Thomas; Private; C/10th Cav. Died of tuberculosis, Bayamo, Cuba, 23 Feb 1902. SOURCE: *ANJ* 39 (15 Mar 1902): 706.

WHITE, Thomas; F/24th Inf. Remained in San Quentin, Philippines, after service. SOURCE: Funston papers, KSHS.

WHITE, Tony; Private; E/10th Cav. Mentioned as recruit to be assigned to E Troop. SOURCE: LS, 10 Cav, 1866–67.

Original member of 10th Cavalry; in troop when organized, Ft Leavenworth, KS, 15 Jun 1867. SOURCE: McMiller, "Buffalo Soldiers," 72.

WHITE, William; K/10th Cav. Original member of 10th Cavalry; in troop when organized, Ft Riley, KS, 1 Sep 1867. SOURCE: McMiller, "Buffalo Soldiers," 77.

WHITE, William; Sergeant; F/10th Cav. Born in Mississippi; private, F/10th Cavalry, 13 Sep 1892; corporal, 25 Feb 1895; sergeant, 22 Jan 1896. SOURCE: Baker, Roster.

WHITE, William; Private; Band/10th Cav. Served in 10th Cavalry in Cuba, 1898. SOURCE: Cashin, *Under Fire with the Tenth Cavalry*, 359.

WHITE, William; Sergeant; G/9th Cav. At Ft D. A. Russell, WY, in 1910; sharpshooter. SOURCE: *Illustrated Review: Ninth Cavalry*, with picture.

WHITE, William; Corporal; L/9th Cav. Veteran of Philippine Insurrection; at Ft D. A. Russell, WY, in 1910; marksman; resident of Maysville, AL. SOURCE: *Illustrated Review: Ninth Cavalry*, with picture.

WHITE, William A.; Private; I/9th Cav. At Ft D. A. Russell, WY, in 1910; resident of Nashville. SOURCE: *Illustrated Review: Ninth Cavalry*, with picture.

WHITE, William H.; Corporal; M/10th Cav. Served in 10th Cavalry in Cuba, 1898. SOURCE: Cashin, *Under Fire with the Tenth Cavalry*, 352.

WHITE, William J.; Private; A/24th Inf. Murdered by Filipinos, 1899.

WHITE, William L.; Corporal; E/10th Cav. Served in 10th Cavalry in Cuba, 1898; killed in action. SOURCE: Cashin, *Under Fire with the Tenth Cavalry*, 342.

Killed before Santiago, Cuba, 24 Jun 1898. SOURCE: SecWar, *AR 1898*, 355; AG, *Correspondence Regarding the War with Spain*, I:61.

WHITEHEAD, Robert; Private; I/24th Inf. Enlisted Chattanooga, TN, 29 Jun 1899; never joined company, absent sick, place unknown. SOURCE: Muster Roll, I/24 Inf, Jul–Aug 1899.

Joined company, from absent sick, 2 Oct 1899. SOURCE: Muster Roll, I/24 Inf, Sep–Oct 1899.

WHITEHEAD, William; B/10th Cav. Original member of 10th Cavalry; in troop when organized, Ft Leavenworth, KS, 1 Apr 1867. SOURCE: McMiller, "Buffalo Soldiers," 69.

WHITEHEAD, William; L/25th Inf. Convicted of assault with intent to kill, Philippines, Feb 1901; sentenced to five years.

WHITELY, Benjamin B.; Corporal; I/49th Inf. Promoted from private, Sep 1900. SOURCE: *ANJ* 38 (6 Oct 1900): 131.

WHITEN, Walter J.; Private; 24th Inf. Private, I/9th Cavalry; sentenced to three days' confinement by garrison court martial, Ft Robinson, NE, for loitering around post trader's saloon when directed by 1st Sgt. Walter Green to go from target range to quarters and then to stable duty with troop. SOURCE: Order 135, 9 Jun 1889, Post Orders, Ft Robinson.

Authorized to enlist in 24th Infantry by telegram, Adjutant General's Office, 25 Sep 1896.

WHITESIDES, Alex; Cook; A/49th Inf. Died of malaria in the Philippines, 18 Sep 1900. SOURCE: *ANJ* 38 (29 Sep 1900): 115.

WHITFIELD, James; Private; F/9th Cav. Deserted from Ft Cummings, NM, 11 Feb 1881. SOURCE: Regt Returns, 9 Cav, Feb 1881.

WHITING, James; M/10th Cav. Original member of 10th Cavalry; in troop when organized, Ft Riley, KS, 15 Oct 1867. SOURCE: McMiller, "Buffalo Soldiers," 79.

WHITING, John; Private; F/9th Cav. Recruit from depot, arrived at Ft Robinson, NE, 1 Mar 1887. SOURCE: Regt Returns, Mar 1887.

Attached to Band/9th Cavalry for instruction in music. SOURCE: Order 15, 25 May 1887, Orders, 9 Cav.

Confined for ten days by garrison court martial for stabbing of Pvt. Harry Gross, C/9th Cavalry. SOURCE: Order 137, 10 Jul 1887, Post Orders, Ft Robinson.

Confined for one month by garrison court martial for felonious assault on Pvt. Samuel Farson, D/8th Infantry, by biting his index finger, right hand. SOURCE: Order 80, 5 Apr 1889, Post Orders, Ft Robinson.

WHITING, John; Private; F/10th Cav. Served in 10th Cavalry in Cuba, 1898. SOURCE: Cashin, *Under Fire with the Tenth Cavalry*, 344.

WHITLEY; Sergeant; D/24th Inf. Reenlisted for E/9th Cavalry, Ft Duchesne, UT, because he thought he had been too long in Indian Territory, according to the Kansas City, MO, *Times*. SOURCE: *ANJ* 25 (3 Mar 1888): 629.

WHITLOCK, William; Private; Band/10th Cav. Served in 10th Cavalry in Cuba, 1898. SOURCE: Cashin, *Under Fire with the Tenth Cavalry*, 359.

WHITMAN, Charles; Private; L/9th Cav. Deserted from Arizona, 23 Jul 1900. SOURCE: Regt Returns, 9 Cav, Aug 1900.

WHITMIRE, Henry; Wagoner; C/9th Cav. At Ft D. A. Russell, WY, in 1910; resident of Asheville, NC. SOURCE: *Illustrated Review: Ninth Cavalry*, with picture.

WHITMIRE, Joe; Farrier; B/10th Cav. Discharged on certificate of disability with gonorrhea from Ft Robinson, NE, 2 Mar 1905. SOURCE: Certificates of Disability, Ft Robinson.

WHITNEY, William S.; Private; A/10th Cav. At Ft Apache, AZ, 1890, subscribed $.50 to testimonial to General Grierson. SOURCE: List of subscriptions, 23 Apr 1890, 10th Cavalry papers, MHI.

To retire from Ft Grant, AZ, 21 Dec 1891. SOURCE: *ANJ* 29 (19 Dec 1891): 289; Baker, Roster.

WHITSON, Edward N.; Private; B/10th Cav. Served in 10th Cavalry in Cuba, 1898. SOURCE: Cashin, *Under Fire with the Tenth Cavalry*, 338.

WHITSON, Irvin; Private; G/10th Cav. Served in 10th Cavalry in Cuba, 1898. SOURCE: Cashin, *Under Fire with the Tenth Cavalry*, 345.

Died in Cuba, 28 Aug 1898. SOURCE: *ANJ* 36 (3 Sep 1898): 19; *ANJ* 36 (18 Feb 1899): 590.

WHITTED, Eugene R.; Private; 25th Inf. Enlisted Wichita, KS, and left for California and the Philippines, 13 Nov 1900. SOURCE: Wichita *Searchlight*, 17 Nov 1900.

WHITTINGTON, Len; Private; K/25th Inf. Enlisted in I/24th Infantry, Columbus Barracks, OH, 27 Jun 1899. SOURCE: Muster Roll, I/24 Inf, Jul–Aug 1899.

Fined one month's pay by summary court, 10 Sep 1899; fined $5 by summary court, 18 Sep 1899. SOURCE: Muster Roll, I/24 Inf, Sep–Oct 1899.

In K/25th Infantry at Ft Niobrara, NE, 1904. SOURCE: Wilson, "History of Fort Niobrara."

WHITWORTH, Judge; A/10th Cav. Original member of 10th Cavalry; in troop when organized, Ft Leavenworth, KS, 18 Feb 1867. SOURCE: McMiller, "Buffalo Soldiers," 68.

WHYTHE, Johnson; G/10th Cav. Original member of 10th Cavalry; in troop when organized, Ft Leavenworth, KS, 5 Jul 1867. SOURCE: McMiller, "Buffalo Soldiers," 74.

WICKERSHAM, Edward; Private; D/25th Inf. Dishonorable discharge, Brownsville. SOURCE: SO 266, AGO, 9 Nov 1906.

WICKERSON, W.; Private; A/9th Cav. At Ft Stanton, NM, 1881. SOURCE: Regt Returns, 9 Cav, Jan 1881.

WICKLIFF, Preston F. W.; Private; M/10th Cav. Served in 10th Cavalry, 1898; remained in U.S. during war with Spain. SOURCE: Cashin, *Under Fire with the Tenth Cavalry*, 352.

WICKS, James H.; Private; B/10th Cav. Served in 10th Cavalry, 1898; remained in U.S. during war with Spain. SOURCE: Cashin, *Under Fire with the Tenth Cavalry*, 333.

WIGFALL, Frank; Private; H/24th Inf. Enlisted Louisville, 10 Aug 1898; assigned and joined 16 Sep 1898. SOURCE: Muster Roll, H/24 Inf, Sep–Oct 1898.

Discharged Ft Douglas, UT, 29 Jan 1899, character good, single; due U.S. for clothing $18.60; reenlisted 30 Jan 1899. SOURCE: Muster Roll, H/24 Inf, Jan–Feb 1899.

WIGGINGTON, Frank B.; Private; F/25th Inf. Died in Minnesota. SOURCE: Taylor, "Minnesota Black Spanish-American War Veterans."

WIGGINS, John; Private; Band/10th Cav. Original member of I/10th Cavalry; in troop when organized, Ft Riley, KS, 15 Aug 1867. SOURCE: McMiller, "Buffalo Soldiers," 76.

"A noted character among the enlisted men"; served against Indians on Saline River, KS, and Big Sandy, CO, 1868; at Camp Supply, Indian Territory, 1870, when Indians attacked; in action against Lipans and Kickapoos, Saragosa, Mexico, Jul 1867; with Colonel Grierson when attacked by Victorio between Ft Quitman and Eagle Springs, TX, also at Rattlesnake Springs, TX; "all these years has served as cook and today hale and hearty and can be seen daily lugging his pots and pans as of yore"; private, B/10th Cavalry, in 1897. SOURCE: Baker, Roster.

Deposited $100 with paymaster, 13 Jan 1874. SOURCE: LS, 10 Cav, 1873–83.

Private, Band/10th Cavalry, deposited $62 with paymaster, 14 May 1874. SOURCE: LS, 10 Cav, 1873–83.

Son John Wesley Wiggins, age nine, died at Ft Davis, TX, Oct 1884. SOURCE: Leckie, *The Buffalo Soldiers*, 239.

Private, Band/10th Cavalry, at Ft Apache, AZ, 1890, subscribed $.50 to testimonial to General Grierson.

SOURCE: List of subscriptions, 23 Apr 1890, 10th Cavalry papers, MHI.

Served in Band/10th Cavalry in Cuba, 1898. SOURCE: Cashin, *Under Fire with the Tenth Cavalry*, 359.

WIGGINS, S. T.; Lieutenant; 8th Inf USV. Born Columbus, OH; graduated Columbus High School, 1885; taught in Appomattox, VA, 1885–87, then at Dangerfield, TX, 1887–91; graduated from law school, University of Michigan, 1893; master of arts, Ohio State University, 1894; bachelor of philosophy, Ohio State, 1897; adjutant, 9th Battalion, Ohio National Guard; moved to Texas autumn 1897; taught in Red River Co., near Clarksville, 1898; in 8th U.S. Volunteer Infantry, Ft Thomas, KY; mustered out 1899; practiced law, Coffeyville, KS, with licenses to practice before supreme courts of Michigan and Kansas; moved to Indian Territory, 1900, and admitted to bar, McAlester, OK; practiced at Wewoka and McAlester, then seven years at Ardmore, OK; admitted to practice before U.S. Supreme Court, 1905; moved to Wagner, OK, at statehood; 33rd degree Mason; visited Europe, autumn 1911; president of Interstate Oil, Gas, Mining, and Refining Company, recently organized and capitalized at $50,000. SOURCE: Wright, *The Centennial Encyclopedia of the AME Church*, 245–46.

WILBURN, Thomas G.; Musician; K/25th Inf. Native of Missouri, played trumpet, one-time student at Lincoln Institute, Jefferson City, MO; died of dysentery and appendicitis, age 21, in hospital, Castillejos, Philippines; "one of ablest young men in the service"; funeral conducted by Reverend William M. Wimms, K/25th Infantry. SOURCE: Richmond *Planet*, 8 Sep 1900.

WILCOX, Mitchell; Color Sgt; 24th Inf. At Ft Elliott, TX, 1886. *See* **SMITH**, Jacob Clay, Sergeant, 10th Cavalry

Acquitted by court martial of fighting and assaulting a private, D/24th Infantry, with knife, Ft Missoula, MT. SOURCE: *ANJ* 31 (13 Jan 1894): 359.

In the Philippines, 1899. SOURCE: Muller, *The Twenty Fourth Infantry*, 34.

Thirty-year veteran retires from Ft Assiniboine, MT, as color sergeant; whole career with F/24th Infantry. SOURCE: Indianapolis *Freeman*, 4 Jun 1903.

WILCOX, William G.; Color Sgt; 24th Inf. Picture. SOURCE: Muller, *The Twenty Fourth Infantry*, 23.

WILEY, Daniel; Sergeant; E/9th Cav. Daughter Ophelia, fourth child, born to wife, maiden name Jenny Stone, Ft Robinson, NE, 1 May 1898, and died, age 24 days, of acute bronchitis, 25 May 1898; interred at Ft Robinson. SOURCE: Medical History and List of Interments, Ft Robinson.

WILEY, Frederick; Private; A/10th Cav. Recruit from depot, assigned to 9th Cavalry, arrived at Ft Robinson, NE, 1 Mar 1887. SOURCE: Regt Returns, 9 Cav, Mar 1887.

In C/9th Cavalry, relieved as post librarian, Ft Robinson, by Pvt. John Vaughn, C/8th Infantry. SOURCE: Order 101, 24 May 1887, Post Orders, Ft Robinson.

Private, A/10th Cavalry; contributed $.25 of $3.25 sent by men of A/10th Cavalry to Richmond *Planet* for defense fund of three black women accused of murder, Lunenburg Co., VA, as reported in letter, A/10th Cavalry, Ft Keogh, MT, 9 Sep 1895, to editor. SOURCE: Richmond *Planet*, 21 Sep 1895.

WILEY, Harvey; Private; B/9th Cav. At Ft D. A. Russell, WY, in 1910; sharpshooter. SOURCE: *Illustrated Review: Ninth Cavalry*, with picture.

WILEY, Purcell; Trumpeter; D/10th Cav. Served in 10th Cavalry in Cuba, 1898. SOURCE: Cashin, *Under Fire with the Tenth Cavalry*, 341.

WILEY, Willie; Private; K/10th Cav. Served in 10th Cavalry, 1898; remained in U.S. during war with Spain. SOURCE: Cashin, *Under Fire with the Tenth Cavalry*, 350.

WILKEN, Shelly; Private; L/49th Inf. In the Philippines, 1900. *See* **CLAY**, Henry, Private, L/49th Infantry

WILKENS, Joseph B.; 24th Inf. At Ft Elliott, TX, 1887; letter to editor. SOURCE: Cleveland *Gazette*, 15 Jan 1887.

WILKERSON, Alphonse G.; Private; I/25th Inf. Died in Minnesota, 19 Nov 1939. SOURCE: Taylor, "Minnesota Black Spanish-American War Veterans."

WILKES, William; QM Sgt; 24th Inf. Born Columbia, Maury Co., TN, 29 Jun 1856; enlisted Nashville, 10 Jan 1876; sent to Columbus Barracks, OH, and then to Ft Duncan, TX; corporal, 1 Aug 1876; sergeant, 1 Jan 1877; discharged, Cantonment at North Fork, Canadian River, Indian Territory, 9 Jan 1881; enlisted in 9th Cavalry, St Louis, 4 Feb 1881; joined L/9th Cavalry, Ft Bliss, TX, 24 Mar 1881; in field on scouts, New Mexico, May–Nov 1881; transferred to Ft Riley, KS, Dec 1881; served against Utes in Colorado, 1882; corporal, 7 Aug 1883; sergeant, Ft McKinney, WY, 2 Dec 1885; discharged 3 Feb 1886; reenlisted in F/24th Infantry, Ft Leavenworth, KS, 26 Feb 1886; sergeant, 7 May 1886; at Ft Bayard, NM, 7 Jun 1888; discharged and reenlisted, 25 Feb 1891 and 25 Feb 1896; at Ft Douglas, Oct 1896; at Chickamauga, GA, and Cuba, contracted yellow fever 3 Aug 1898; at Ft Douglas, UT, Sep 1898; commissioned first lieutenant, 9th Infantry, U.S. Volunteers, 24 Oct 1898. SOURCE: Coston, *The Spanish-American War Volunteer*, 51–52.

Sergeant, F/24th Infantry, at Ft Elliott, TX, 1886. *See* **SMITH**, Jacob Clay, Sergeant, 10th Cavalry

At Ft Bayard, Jul 1888; selected for Department of Arizona rifle competition, Ft Wingate, NM. SOURCE: Billington, *New Mexico's Buffalo Soldiers*, 154.

At Ft Bayard; qualified as sharpshooter. SOURCE: *ANJ* 28 (27 Sep 1890): 70.

Sergeant, F/24th Infantry, ranked number five in competition of Army rifle team, 1892; distinguished marksman, rifle, 1890, 1891, 1892. SOURCE: GO 75, AGO, 3 Nov 1892.

Sergeant, F/24th Infantry; commissioned first lieutenant, 9th Volunteer Infantry, after Spanish-American War. SOURCE: Cashin, *Under Fire with the Tenth Cavalry*, 360.

Promoted from lance corporal to corporal, 24th Infantry, Apr 1900. SOURCE: *ANJ* 37 (5 May 1900): 851.

Retired as quartermaster sergeant, 24th Infantry, in 1904; gave talk at sixty-fourth anniversary of 9th Cavalry, Ft Leavenworth, 28 Jul 1930. SOURCE: *Cavalry Journal* 29 (Oct 1930): 616.

WILKESON, Peter; E/10th Cav. Original member of 10th Cavalry; in troop when organized, Ft Leavenworth, KS, 15 Jun 1867. SOURCE: McMiller, "Buffalo Soldiers," 72.

WILKINS, Julius; Private; B/25th Inf. Dishonorable discharge, Brownsville. SOURCE: SO 266, AGO, 9 Nov 1906.

WILKINS, Melvin A.; Private; E/9th Cav. First sergeant, E/9th Cavalry, authorized four-month furlough from Ft Duchesne, UT. SOURCE: *ANJ* 24 (1 Jan 1887): 450.

Reduced to private and fined $20 at Ft Duchesne for engaging in drunken brawl, for showing disrespect and using insubordinate language to troop commander, and for making false statements. SOURCE: *ANJ* 24 (9 Apr 1887): 734.

WILKINSON, Thomas H.; Private; G/25th Inf. Retires from Ft Missoula, MT, Aug 1894. SOURCE: *ANJ* 32 (8 Sep 1894): 23.

WILKO, Abraham; B/10th Cav. Original member of 10th Cavalry; in troop when organized, Ft Leavenworth, KS, 1 Apr 1867. SOURCE: McMiller, "Buffalo Soldiers," 69.

WILKS, Jacob; 9th Cav. At his home in San Angelo, TX, 1914, told life story to John W. Hunter: born slave around thirty miles south of Ohio River in Kentucky; escaped with parents to Ohio, while still infant; served forty-five months in 116th U.S. Colored Troops in Civil War, sergeant at Appomattox, VA; enlisted in 9th Cavalry after war; came to Ft Concho, TX, from Ft McKavett, TX, in 1874. SOURCE: Hunter, "A Negro Trooper of the Ninth Cavalry."

WILLARD, C. W.; Private; K/9th Cav. Authorized four-month furlough in accordance with Special Order 85, Division of the Missouri, 19 Jul 1887.

WILLIAMS; Private; E/10th Cav. At Ft Apache, AZ, 1890, subscribed $.50 to testimonial to General Grierson. SOURCE: List of subscriptions, 23 Apr 1890, 10th Cavalry papers, MHI.

WILLIAMS, Albert; Private; A/24th Inf. On extra duty as teamster, Quartermaster Department, Ft Huachuca, AZ, 24 Jul–10 Aug 1893. SOURCE: Name File, 24 Inf.

WILLIAMS, Alexander; L/10th Cav. Original member of 10th Cavalry; in troop when organized, Ft Riley, KS, 21 Sep 1867. SOURCE: McMiller, "Buffalo Soldiers," 78.

WILLIAMS, Alexander; 1st Sgt; A/24th Inf. Born New Bern, NC; Ht 5'9", black complexion; transferred from D/24th Infantry to Band/24th Infantry as sergeant, age 39, 29 Oct 1884; transferred to A/24th Infantry, Ft Supply, Indian Territory, 19 Mar 1887, character good, single. SOURCE: Descriptive Book, 24 Inf NCS & Band.

Sergeant, A/24th Infantry, ordered to report to camp of International Boundary Commission, taking railroad to Tucson, AZ, and stage to Arivaca, AZ, Aug 1893. SOURCE: Name File, 24 Inf.

Commissioned first lieutenant, 9th Volunteer Infantry, after Spanish-American War. SOURCE: Cashin, *Under Fire with the Tenth Cavalry*, 360.

Retired as first sergeant, A/24th Infantry, May 1900. SOURCE: *ANJ* 37 (19 May 1900): 895.

Died 16 Dec 1904; buried at Ft Douglas, UT. SOURCE: Clark, "A History of the Twenty-fourth," appendix A.

WILLIAMS, Alfred N.; Private; B/25th Inf. Dishonorable discharge, Brownsville. SOURCE: SO 266, AGO, 9 Nov 1906.

WILLIAMS, Alverse; Private; I/9th Cav. At Ft D. A. Russell, WY, in 1910; sharpshooter; resident of Avenne, AR. SOURCE: *Illustrated Review: Ninth Cavalry*, with picture.

WILLIAMS, Anderson; Private; K/24th Inf. Fined $10, Cabanatuan, Philippines, 11 Feb 1901, for failure to obey lawful order of Cpl. F. J. Monroe, K/24th Infantry, and failure to obey promptly order of First Lieutenant Keller, 24th Infantry, to stop talking in ranks. SOURCE: Name File, 24 Inf.

Fined $5 for being careless on target range, failing to mark hits properly, Cabanatuan, 5 Jun 1901. SOURCE: Name File, 24 Inf.

WILLIAMS, Arlan; D/10th Cav. Original member of 10th Cavalry; in troop when organized, Ft Leavenworth, KS, 1 Jun 1867. SOURCE: McMiller, "Buffalo Soldiers," 71.

WILLIAMS, Arthur; Private; H/9th Cav. Born Athens, GA; Ht 5'9", mulatto; first enlistment, B/9th Cavalry, completed 10 Jun 1892; enlisted Jefferson Barracks, MO, 20 Jun 1892; joined H/9th Cavalry, age 27, Ft Robinson, NE, 1 Apr 1895. SOURCE: Descriptive Book, H/9 Cav.

WILLIAMS, Arthur; Private; M/9th Cav. At Ft D. A. Russell, WY, in 1910; marksman; resident of Birmingham, AL. SOURCE: *Illustrated Review: Ninth Cavalry*, with picture.

WILLIAMS, August; Private; A/25th Inf. Dishonorable discharge, Brownsville. SOURCE: SO 266, AGO, 9 Nov 1906.

WILLIAMS, B.; Private; C/9th Cav. On detached service at Ft Bayard, NM, 6 Mar 1880–3 Feb 1881. SOURCE: Regt Returns, 9 Cav, Feb 1881.

WILLIAMS, B. W.; Private; L/10th Cav. In hands of civil authorities, Crawford, NE, 14–16 Jan 1904. SOURCE: Regt Returns, 9 Cav, Jan 1904.

WILLIAMS, Berg; I/10th Cav. Original member of 10th Cavalry; in troop when organized, Ft Riley, KS, 15 Aug 1867. SOURCE: McMiller, "Buffalo Soldiers," 76.

WILLIAMS, Brister; Private; B/25th Inf. Dishonorable discharge, Brownsville. SOURCE: SO 266, AGO, 9 Nov 1906.

WILLIAMS, Charles; A/10th Cav. Original member of 10th Cavalry; in troop when organized, Ft Leavenworth, KS, 18 Feb 1867. SOURCE: McMiller, "Buffalo Soldiers," 68.

WILLIAMS, Charles; Recruit; 10th Cav. Died in post hospital, Ft Leavenworth, KS, 31 May 1867. SOURCE: LS, 10 Cav, 1866–67.

WILLIAMS, Charles; H/10th Cav. Original member of 10th Cavalry; in troop when organized, Ft Leavenworth, KS, 21 Jul 1867. SOURCE: McMiller, "Buffalo Soldiers," 75.

WILLIAMS, Charles; Sergeant; K/25th Inf. At Grierson's Springs, TX, 1878; best marksman in company and tenth best in regiment. SOURCE: 25 Inf, Scrapbook, I.

WILLIAMS, Charles; Private; F/9th Cav. Fined $10 and confined for five days for insubordination to Sgt. Edward Fletcher, F/9th Cavalry. SOURCE: Order 55, 22 Mar 1888, Post Orders, Ft Robinson.

WILLIAMS, Charles; Private; H/9th Cav. Charges withdrawn in accordance with letter, Department of the Platte, 25 Sep 1895.

WILLIAMS, Charles; Private; H/24th Inf. Enlisted Ft Bayard, NM, 21 Apr 1896; transferred from E/24th Infantry, 8 Oct 1898. SOURCE: Muster Roll, H/24 Inf, Sep–Oct 1898.

Paid double for July–August 1898, once on E/24th Infantry payroll and once on H/24th Infantry payroll; owes U.S. for three months' pay; sick in quarters, disease contracted in line of duty, since 30 Dec 1898; eight years' continuous service. SOURCE: Muster Roll, H/24 Inf, May–Jun and Nov–Dec 1898.

Sick in hospital, 30 Dec 1898–5 Jan 1899. SOURCE: Muster Roll, H/24 Inf, Jan–Feb 1899.

WILLIAMS, Charles; Private; K/9th Cav. At Ft D. A. Russell, WY, in 1910; resident of Warthon, TX. SOURCE: *Illustrated Review: Ninth Cavalry*, with picture.

WILLIAMS, Charles; Private; M/9th Cav. Veteran of Philippine Insurrection; at Ft D. A. Russell, WY, in 1910. SOURCE: *Illustrated Review: Ninth Cavalry*.

WILLIAMS, Charley W.; Private; I/9th Cav. U.S. Marshal served writ on which Williams was turned over to U.S. District Court, Lincoln, NE, on charge of dispensing liquor to Indians, 24 Jan 1893; Williams' letter reporting that he is stranded without money in Lincoln received today; great injustice has been done; he cannot buy food or pay for transportation to post at Ft Robinson, NE. SOURCE: CO, Ft Robinson, to AAG, DP, 30 Jan 1893, LS, Ft Robinson.

In hands of civil authorities, Lincoln, 24 Jan–2 Feb 1893. SOURCE: Regt Returns, 9 Cav, Feb 1893.

Williams says he was brought to Omaha, NE, 7 Jun 1893, for trial on charge of selling whiskey to Indian scouts, Ft Robinson; tried without attorney or witnesses and fined $1 and costs; "I am loose and have no way of getting back home. I apply for transportation to my station, Ft Robinson." SOURCE: Williams to AAG, DP, 10 Jun 1893, LR, DP.

WILLIAMS, Daniel; H/10th Cav. Original member of 10th Cavalry; in troop when organized, Ft Leavenworth, KS, 21 Jul 1867. SOURCE: McMiller, "Buffalo Soldiers," 75.

WILLIAMS, Daniel; Private; K/10th Cav. Served in 10th Cavalry, 1898; remained in U.S. during war with Spain. SOURCE: Cashin, *Under Fire with the Tenth Cavalry*, 350.

WILLIAMS, Darryl; G/10th Cav. Original member of 10th Cavalry; in troop when organized, Ft Leavenworth, KS, 5 Jul 1867. SOURCE: McMiller, "Buffalo Soldiers," 74.

WILLIAMS, David; Private; H/10th Cav. Mentioned Dec 1876. SOURCE: ES, 10 Cav, 1873–83.

WILLIAMS, Doc; Private; D/10th Cav. Enlisted Columbus. KY, 8 Apr 1867; at Ft Gibson, Indian Territory, Jun 1867. SOURCE: LS, 10 Cav, 1866–67.

WILLIAMS, Edward; Private; L/9th Cav. Drowned in Pecos River, TX, in pursuit of Indians, Jun 1869. SOURCE: Hamilton, "History of the Ninth Cavalry," 11; *Illustrated Review: Ninth Cavalry*.

WILLIAMS, Edward; Recruit; Colored Detachment/Mounted Service. At Jefferson Barracks, MO, 1888. *See* **ALLEN**, Lee, Recruit, Colored Detachment/Mounted Service.

WILLIAMS, Edward; Private; 24th Cav. Drunk and abusive; taken forcibly to guardhouse, Ft Bayard, NM, Nov 1891; there assaulted Sgt. James Watkins, 24th Infantry. SOURCE: Billington, *New Mexico's Buffalo Soldiers*, 164–65.

WILLIAMS, Edward; Private; M/10th Cav. Served in 10th Cavalry in Cuba, 1898. SOURCE: Cashin, *Under Fire with the Tenth Cavalry*, 352.

WILLIAMS, Edward; 1st Sgt; L/24th Inf. Born Centerville, Hickman Co., TN; enlisted in 24th Infantry, 19 Jan 1876; private, corporal, sergeant, first sergeant, until commissioned in 9th Volunteer Infantry, 26 Oct 1898; served as first sergeant, L/24th Infantry in Cuba; twenty-three years and six months' continuous service. SOURCE: Coston, *The Spanish-American War Volunteer*, 49.

First sergeant, C/24th Infantry; commissioned first lieutenant, 9th Volunteer Infantry, after Spanish-American War. SOURCE: Cashin, *Under Fire with the Tenth Cavalry*, 360.

First sergeant, L/24th Infantry, with Sergeant O'Connor of same company directed Christmas festivities, Skagway, AK, 1901. SOURCE: Indianapolis *Freeman*, 8 Feb 1902.

WILLIAMS, Edward; Private; H/9th Cav. Relieved from extra duty as teamster, Quartermaster Department, Ft Robinson, NE. SOURCE: Special Order 90, 20 Aug 1896, Post Orders, Ft Robinson.

To be discharged from Ft Robinson, 26 May 1897, in accordance with Special Order 45, Department of the Platte, 20 Apr 1897; deposits $100; clothing $46; retained $46. SOURCE: CO, H/9, to Chief Paymaster, DP, 23 May 1897, LS, H/9 Cav.

WILLIAMS, Edward A.; Private; I/9th Cav. Deserted from San Francisco, 9 Nov 1902. SOURCE: Regt Returns, 9 Cav, Nov 1902.

WILLIAMS, Elbert; Band/10th Cav. Born Brooklyn, NY; occupation musician; Ht 5'8", black eyes, hair, and complexion; completed first enlistment in Band/9th Cavalry, 8 Aug 1889; enlisted New York City in 24th Infantry, age 26, 6 Sep 1889, and joined Band/24th Infantry, Ft Bayard, NM, 29 Sep 1889; single; deserted on furlough, 7 May 1890; dropped as deserter, 17 May 1890; surrendered at St. Francis Barracks, FL, 15 Mar 1891; general court martial sentence of dishonorable discharge and eighteen months' confinement promulgated by General Court Martial Order 21, Division of the Atlantic, 13 Apr 1891. SOURCE: Descriptive Book, 24 Inf NCS & Band.

Private, C/9th Cavalry, attached to Band/9th Cavalry, for instruction in music. SOURCE: Order 15, 9 Cav, 25 May 1887, Orders, 9 Cav.

Transferred from 9th Cavalry, Ft Robinson, NE, to 24th Infantry, Ft Missoula, MT, as private, in accordance with Special Order 122, Adjutant General's Office, 24 Mar 1894.

Composer of "Tenth U.S. Cavalry Regimental Fanfare Song," 1898. SOURCE: Cashin, *Under Fire with the Tenth Cavalry*, 280.

Sergeant, 25th Infantry, and new bandmaster, Tuskegee Institute, in Alabama. SOURCE: Indianapolis *Freeman*, 17 Oct 1903.

In 10th Cavalry band, applied for position of chief musician, 1907, after Theodore Roosevelt ordered black chief

musicians for black regiments; authorities ignored him with excuse that he had not served long enough with regiment. SOURCE: Fletcher, "The Negro Soldier," 147.

WILLIAMS, Fletcher; Corporal; K/48th Inf. Died of variola in the Philippines, 17 Jul 1900. SOURCE: *ANJ* 37 (28 Jul 1900): 1142.

WILLIAMS, Frank; A/24th Inf. Badly crippled from service on Staked Plains, TX. SOURCE: *Winners of the West* 9 (May 1932): 7.

WILLIAMS, Frank; Sergeant; A/9th Cav. Discharged on certificate of disability, Ft Stanton, NM, 11 Jan 1881. SOURCE: Regt Returns, 9 Cav, Jan 1881.

WILLIAMS, Fred; Private; F/24th Inf. Wounded in action, Cuba, 1898. SOURCE: Muller, *The Twenty Fourth Infantry*, 18.

WILLIAMS, Fred; Private; C/9th Cav. At Ft D. A. Russell, WY, in 1910; sharpshooter; resident of 137 E. Henry St., Greenville, TX. SOURCE: *Illustrated Review: Ninth Cavalry*.

WILLIAMS, Gardner; Private; M/9th Cav. At Ft D. A. Russell, WY, in 1910; resident of Marietta, GA. SOURCE: *Illustrated Review: Ninth Cavalry*, with picture.

WILLIAMS, George; 1st Sgt; A/25th Inf. Relieved of duty with Department of Dakota rifle competition and ordered to Ft Meade, Dakota Territory. SOURCE: *ANJ* 24 (2 Oct 1886): 190.

At Ft Custer, MT, 1893; examined for ordnance sergeant. SOURCE: *ANJ* 30 (1 Jul 1893): 745.

Retires as first sergeant, Apr 1901. SOURCE: *ANJ* 38 (13 Apr 1901): 795.

WILLIAMS, George; Private; C/9th Cav. Recruit, enlisted at Omaha, NE, for C/9th Cavalry; arrived at Ft Robinson, NE, Mar 1887. SOURCE: Regt Returns, 9 Cav, Mar 1887.

WILLIAMS, George; H/25th Inf. Admitted to Soldiers Home with disability, age 41, after nineteen years and eight months' service, 23 Jan 1888. SOURCE: SecWar, *AR 1888*, 902.

WILLIAMS, George; Private; D/24th Inf. *See* **NICHOLSON**, George H., Private, Band/24th Infantry

WILLIAMS, George; Chief Trumpeter; 9th Cav. Toastmaster for 9th Cavalry Band reception, held with 10th Cavalry Band 1914, with hall adorned with portraits of Booker T. Washington, Abraham Lincoln, and Frederick Douglass. SOURCE: Fletcher, "The Negro Soldier," 79.

WILLIAMS, George A.; Private; H/9th Cav. Born Ann Arbor, MI; Ht 5'8"; enlisted Ft Omaha, NE, age 25, 11 Jan 1895; joined company at Ft Robinson, NE, 16 Jan 1895;

seven summary court martial convictions for minor infractions, 1895–97; discharged, end of term, 10 Jan 1897, character fair, single. SOURCE: Descriptive Book, H/9 Cav.

WILLIAMS, George A.; 2nd Lt; 49th Inf. Born Evansville, IN; occupation teacher; enlisted in Indiana Colored Volunteers, 8 Jul 1898–Dec 1898; in 8th U.S. Volunteeer Infantry, Dec 1898–6 Mar 1899; enlisted in 49th Infantry, Evansville, 12 Oct 1899; private, sergeant, first sergeant, F/49th Infantry, and battalion sergeant major; age 32 in 1900; married to Sarah Williams of Evansville. SOURCE: Descriptive Book, 49 Inf.

Letter from Paranaqua, Philippines, 27 Jan 1900, comments on absence of racial prejudice in the Philippines; debunks atrocity stories. SOURCE: Indianapolis *Freeman*, 7 Apr 1900.

Promoted from battalion to regimental sergeant major, Sep 1900. SOURCE: *ANJ* 38 (6 Oct 1900): 131.

Commissioned second lieutenant, 17 Oct 1900. SOURCE: *ANJ* 38 (24 Nov 1900): 307.

Resides in Los Angeles, 1905; has been with Capt. Floyd Crumbly almost every day since Crumbly came to Los Angeles, spring 1903; Crumbly has been weak and sickly ever since. SOURCE: Affidavit, Williams, 9 Dec 1905, VA File XC 2654105, Floyd Crumbly.

WILLIAMS, George H.; L/24th Inf. At Skagway, AK, 1902. *See* **CASSELLE**, Nelson A., Private, L/24th Infantry

WILLIAMS, George J.; Private; A/10th Cav. At Ft Apache, AZ, 1890, subscribed $.50 to testimonial to General Grierson. SOURCE: List of subscriptions, 23 Apr 1890, 10th Cavalry papers, MHI.

WILLIAMS, George W.; L/10th Cav. Original member of 10th Cavalry; in troop when organized, Ft Riley, KS, 21 Sep 1867. SOURCE: McMiller, "Buffalo Soldiers," 78.

WILLIAMS, Glover; C/48th Inf. Convicted of attempted rape in the Philippines, Jan 1901; sentenced to five years.

WILLIAMS, Gus; Sergeant; D/10th Cav. Commissioned first lieutenant at Camp Des Moines, IA, 15 Oct 1917. SOURCE: Glass, *History of the Tenth Cavalry*, appendix M.

Retired as sergeant; won distinguished service cross for heroism at Naguilan, Luzon, Philippines, 1899. SOURCE: *Crisis* 30 (Jun 1925): 78.

WILLIAMS, H. A.; Sergeant; L/25th Inf. As corporal, G/25th Infantry, nearly drowned during Siboney, Cuba, landing, 22 Jun 1898. SOURCE: Richmond *Planet*, 28 Jul 1900.

WILLIAMS, Hamilton; Private; K/9th Cav. Discharged on certificate of disability with syphilis, Ft Robinson, NE, 23 Jan 1898. SOURCE: Certificates of Disability, Ft Robinson.

Discharged by Adjutant General as reported in letter, Department of the Platte, 12 Feb 1898.

WILLIAMS, Harrison; Private; G/9th Cav. Died at Ft Robinson, NE, 1 Oct 1897, and buried there. SOURCE: Special Order 119, 3 Oct 1898, Post Orders, Ft Robinson; List of Interments, Ft Robinson.

$30.75 due deceased Private Harrison, killed near Ft Robinson, 1 Oct 1897, forwarded to paymaster. SOURCE: CO, G/9 Cav, to Chief Paymaster, DP, 22 Nov 1897, Misc Records, DP.

WILLIAMS, Harry; Private; A/10th Cav. Transferred to Hospital Corps at San Carlos, AZ. SOURCE: *ANJ* 25 (28 Jan 1888): 526.

WILLIAMS, Harry; Farrier; G/10th Cav. Served in 10th Cavalry in Cuba, 1898. SOURCE: Cashin, *Under Fire with the Tenth Cavalry*, 345.

WILLIAMS, Harry; Private; M/10th Cav. Discharged on certificate of disability with tertiary syphilis and chronic gonorrhea, from Ft Robinson, NE, Sep 1902. SOURCE: Certificates of Disability, Ft Robinson.

WILLIAMS, Harry; Private; G/10th Cav. On furlough from Ft Mackenzie, WY, at Sheridan, WY, 3–9 Feb 1903. SOURCE: Regt Returns, 10 Cav, Feb 1903.

WILLIAMS, Harry J.; Private; L/9th Cav. Veteran of Philippine Insurrection; at Ft D. A. Russell, WY, in 1910; sharpshooter; resident of Belmont, MA. SOURCE: *Illustrated Review: Ninth Cavalry*, with picture.

WILLIAMS, Henry; Private; A/10th Cav. Arrived from Jefferson Barracks, MO, at Ft Leavenworth, KS, Oct 1866. SOURCE: LS, 10 Cav, 1866–67.

Original member of 10th Cavalry; in troop when organized, Ft Leavenworth, KS, 18 Feb 1867. SOURCE: McMiller, "Buffalo Soldiers," 68.

WILLIAMS, Henry; Private; E/10th Cav. Served in 10th Cavalry, 1898; remained in U.S. during war with Spain. SOURCE: Cashin, *Under Fire with the Tenth Cavalry*, 343.

WILLIAMS, Henry; Private; H/24th Inf. Enlisted Louisville, 8 Jul 1898; assigned and joined 16 Sep 1898; absent sick, disease contracted in line of duty, 16 Sep–25 Oct 1898. SOURCE: Muster Roll, H/24 Inf, Sep–Oct 1898.

Present sick, 25 Oct–5 Dec 1898, upper spinal cord injured in line of duty, total disability; discharged on surgeon's certificate, 5 Dec 1898; deposits $20; due U.S. for clothing $27.76. SOURCE: Muster Roll, H/24 Inf, Nov–Dec 1898.

WILLIAMS, Henry; Private; A/24th Inf. Transferred from Reserve Divisional Hospital, Siboney, Cuba, to U.S. on U.S. Army Transport *Vigilancia* with remittent malarial fever, 6 Sep 1898. SOURCE: Hospital Papers, Spanish-American War.

WILLIAMS, Henry; Sergeant; C/25th Inf. Retires from San Carlos, AZ, Jan 1899. SOURCE: *ANJ* 36 (14 Jan 1899): 471.

WILLIAMS, Henry; F/48th Inf. Convicted of robbery in the Philippines, May 1900; sentenced to six months.

WILLIAMS, Henry; Private; C/9th Cav. At Ft D. A. Russell, WY, in 1910; resident of 214 S. Skidmore St., Columbus, OH. SOURCE: *Illustrated Review: Ninth Cavalry*, with picture.

WILLIAMS, Henry H.; Private; E/10th Cav. Served in 10th Cavalry, 1898; remained in U.S. during war with Spain. SOURCE: Cashin, *Under Fire with the Tenth Cavalry*, 343.

WILLIAMS, Henry L.; Corporal; L/25th Inf. Fined $15 by summary court, San Isidro, Philippines, for interference with sergeant of guard while he was making arrest. SOURCE: Register of Summary Court, San Isidro.

WILLIAMS, Herbert; Private; C/10th Cav. Released to duty from treatment for gonorrhea, Ft Robinson, NE, 17 Aug 1903. SOURCE: Post Surgeon to CO, C/10, 17 Aug 1903, LS, Post Surgeon, Ft Robinson.

WILLIAMS, J. E.; Private; L/9th Cav. On detached service in field, New Mexico, 21 Jan–24 Feb 1881. SOURCE: Regt Returns, 9 Cav, Feb 1881.

WILLIAMS, J. W.; Private; K/38th Inf. Seriously cut on foot with ax at Ft Selden, NM, Jul 1869. SOURCE: Billington, *New Mexico's Buffalo Soldiers*, 34.

WILLIAMS, Jake; Private; M/49th Inf. Engaged against enemy, Tuao, Cagayan, Philippines, 18 Oct 1900. SOURCE: *ANJ* 38 (11 May 1901): 901.

WILLIAMS, James; D/10th Cav. Original member of 10th Cavalry; in troop when organized, Ft Leavenworth, KS, 1 Jun 1867. SOURCE: McMiller, "Buffalo Soldiers," 71.

WILLIAMS, James; G/10th Cav. Original member of 10th Cavalry; in troop when organized, Ft Leavenworth, KS, 5 Jul 1867. SOURCE: McMiller, "Buffalo Soldiers," 74.

WILLIAMS, James; Private; K/10th Cav. Commander of troop transmits inventory of effects and final statement of Private Williams to regimental commander, Apr 1870. SOURCE: ES, 10 Cav, 1866–71.

WILLIAMS, James; Sergeant; E/9th Cav. In New Mexico, 1879. *See* **ROBINSON**, Henry, Sergeant, E/9th Cavalry

With small hunting party that prevented Indians from attacking mail escort near Ojo Caliente, NM, 28 Sep 1879. SOURCE: Hamilton, "History of the Ninth Cavalry," 44; *Illustrated Review: Ninth Cavalry*.

On detached service in field, Columbus, NM, 30 Dec 1880–2 Jan 1881. SOURCE: Regt Returns, 9 Cav, Jan 1881.

WILLIAMS, James; Recruit; Colored Detachment/ Mounted Service. Convicted by general court martial, Jefferson Barracks, MO, 8 Dec 1882, of being absent without leave and disposing of issue greatcoat worth $12.36; sentenced to two months and docked $6.18 per month for two months. SOURCE: GCMO 7, AGO, 16 Jan 1883.

WILLIAMS, James; Private; 10th Cav. Former soldier, broke into corral, Ft Bayard, NM, Jan 1891, and stole two harnesses. SOURCE: Billington, *New Mexico's Buffalo Soldiers*, 168.

WILLIAMS, James; A/24th Inf. Died in Minnesota. SOURCE: Taylor, "Minnesota Black Spanish-American War Veterans."

WILLIAMS, James; Sergeant; M/10th Cav. On furlough from Ft D. A. Russell to Cheyenne, WY, Jul 1904. SOURCE: Regt Returns, 10 Cav, Jul 1904.

Killed "Pap" Henry Wilson with shotgun, Crawford, NE, 30 Jun 1907. SOURCE: Crawford *Tribune*, 5 Jul 1907.

WILLIAMS, James Clifford; 1st Sgt; M/10th Cav. Born Georgetown, KY, to Nelson Williams and Mary Chinn, 10 Jan 1874; occupation waiter; mulatto; enlisted in B/9th Cavalry, Lexington, KY, 10 Jan 1895; discharged on certificate of disability with hernia, 27 Apr 1897; injured when thrown against saddle by horse, hospitalized at Ft Robinson, NE, for right herniotomy; enlisted in M/10th Cavalry, 8 Jun 1898; contracted syphilis, 1898; honorable discharge, Ft Clark, TX, 28 Feb 1899; married Drucilla Williams, Huntsville, AL, 8 Mar 1899, divorced her 6 Mar 1919, and remarried her 20 Nov 1919; janitor, Logan School, Des Moines, IA, 1930–36; son James N. Williams, former secretary, Y.M.C.A., Montclair, NJ; son William O. Williams resided at 1012 West 12th St., Des Moines; son Richard M. Williams resided at 1233 Yesley Way, Seattle, WA; daughter Mrs. Zella M. Hudson, resided at 1012 West 12th Street, Des Moines; daughter Mrs. Suzie Thomas, resided at 120 College Street, Georgetown, KY; died Des Moines, 22 Jun 1937; widow received pension at 1334 McCormick Street, Des Moines, and at Oak Forest Hospital, Oak Forest, IL, until death 1 Jan 1970. SOURCE: VA File C 2557169, James C. Williams.

Served in Bannock campaign, 1895; stationed at Ft Robinson, 1895, Ft Washakie, WY, 1895–96, Ft Robinson, 1896, Ft Washakie, 1896–97, Lakeland, FL, and Camp Wikoff, NY, 1898, Camp Forse, AL, 1898-99, Ft Clark, TX, 1899. SOURCE: VA File C 2557169, James C. Williams.

Private, D/9th Cavalry, Ft Washakie, sick in post hospital, Ft Robinson, 1 Aug–22 Sep 1896. SOURCE: Regt Returns, 9 Cav, Sep 1896.

Served as corporal, M/10th Cavalry, 1898; remained in U.S. during war with Spain. SOURCE: Cashin, *Under Fire with the Tenth Cavalry*, 351.

First sergeant; reminiscences of war with Spain. SOURCE: Lynk, *The Black Troopers*, 52–53.

WILLIAMS, James E.; 10th Cav. VA File C 2356337 missing from Federal Records Center, Suitland, MD.

WILLIAMS, James H.; Corporal; A/10th Cav. Born in Maryland; private, E/9th Cavalry, 5 May 1886–4 May 1891; private and corporal, F/25th Infantry, 29 Jun 1891–28 Jun 1896; private, A/10th Cavalry, 3 Jul 1896; corporal, 8 Jan 1897. SOURCE: Baker, Roster.

Served as sergeant, A/10th Cavalry, in Cuba, 1898. SOURCE: Cashin, *Under Fire with the Tenth Cavalry*, 336.

A noncommissioned officer who should be commissioned according to unsigned letter from Montauk, NY, no date. SOURCE: Gatewood, *"Smoked Yankees"*, 77.

Resided at 1309 V Street, NW, Washington, DC, at age 65, with no occupation; soldiered with Thomas H. Allsup. SOURCE: VA File XC 2659797, Thomas H. Allsup.

Tenth best marksman, Departments of the Missouri and Texas, 1903. SOURCE: Glass, *History of the Tenth Cavalry*, 43.

WILLIAMS, James H.; Private; B/24th Inf. At Ft Huachuca, AZ, 1893. *See* **BROWN**, Alfred, First Sergeant, H/24th Infantry

WILLIAMS, James H.; Private; I/24th Inf. Enlisted Macon, GA, 1 Jul 1899; joined company 14 Aug 1899. SOURCE: Muster Roll, I/24 Inf, Nov–Dec 1899.

WILLIAMS, Jeremiah; Private; K/9th Cav. Recruit from depot, arrived at Ft Robinson, NE, 1 Mar 1887. SOURCE: Regt Returns, 9 Cav, Mar 1887.

WILLIAMS, Jerry; H/10th Cav. Original member of 10th Cavalry; in troop when organized, Ft Leavenworth, KS, 21 Jul 1867. SOURCE: McMiller, "Buffalo Soldiers," 75.

WILLIAMS, Jerry; Private; K/9th Cav. Served 1872–73. *See* **SLAUGHTER**, Rufus, Private, K/9th Cavalry

Struck on head with carbine by Capt. J. Lee Humfreville, while held by two noncommissioned officers, then struck with club, then suspended from tree, Ft Richardson, TX, 15 Dec 1872; Pvt. James Imes received same treatment. SOURCE: GCMO 23, AGO, 3 Apr 1874.

WILLIAMS, Joe; Corporal; I/10th Cav. Served in 10th Cavalry, 1898; remained in U.S. during war with Spain. SOURCE: Cashin, *Under Fire with the Tenth Cavalry*, 348.

WILLIAMS, John; Private; 10th Cav. Brevet 1st Lt. Daniel Flynn, St. Louis, asks abstract of proceedings of Board of Inspection concerning Recruit John Williams, 10th Cavalry, enlisted St. Louis, 7 Oct 1866. SOURCE: ES, 10 Cav, 1866–71.

WILLIAMS, John; Private; 10th Cav. Enlisted spring 1867. SOURCE: LS, 10 Cav, 1866–67.

WILLIAMS, John; B/10th Cav. Original member of 10th Cavalry; in troop when organized, Ft Leavenworth, KS, 1 Apr 1867. SOURCE: McMiller, "Buffalo Soldiers," 69.

WILLIAMS, John (1st); C/10th Cav. Original member of 10th Cavalry; in troop when organized, Ft Leavenworth, KS, 18 Feb 1867. SOURCE: McMiller, "Buffalo Soldiers," 70.

WILLIAMS, John (2nd); C/10th Cav. Original member of 10th Cavalry; in troop when organized, Ft Leavenworth, KS, 18 Feb 1867. SOURCE: McMiller, "Buffalo Soldiers," 70.

WILLIAMS, John; E/10th Cav. Original member of 10th Cavalry; in troop when organized, Ft Leavenworth, KS, 15 Jun 1867. SOURCE: McMiller, "Buffalo Soldiers," 72.

WILLIAMS, John; Corporal; L/10th Cav. Original member of 10th Cavalry; in troop when organized, Ft Riley, KS, 21 Sep 1867. SOURCE: McMiller, "Buffalo Soldiers," 78.

Mentioned Oct 1870. SOURCE: ES, 10 Cav, 1866–71.

WILLIAMS, John; 1st Sgt; E/25th Inf. At Masque Canyon, TX, 1878; best marksman in company and third in regiment. SOURCE: 25 Inf, Scrapbook, I.

WILLIAMS, John; Private; H/9th Cav. Seriously wounded in action, Gavilan Pass, Mimbres Mountains, NM, 19 Aug 1881, along with Pvt. Wesley Harris. SOURCE: Hamilton, "History of the Ninth Cavalry," 60.

WILLIAMS, John; C/10th Cav. Admitted to Soldiers Home with disability, age 29, after two years and ten months' service, 24 Apr 1888. SOURCE: SecWar, *AR 1888*, 903.

WILLIAMS, John; QM Sgt; 25th Inf. Retires from Ft Missoula, MT. SOURCE: *ANJ* 34 (20 Mar 1897): 525.

WILLIAMS, John; Private; B/8th Ill Inf. *See* **WILLIAMS**, Noah W., Private, B/8th Illinois Infantry

WILLIAMS, John; Private; I/24th Inf. Enlisted Baltimore, 26 Jun 1899; joined company 14 Aug 1899. SOURCE: Muster Roll, I/24 Inf, Jul–Aug 1899.

Fined $5 by summary court, 23 Sep 1899. SOURCE: Muster Roll, I/24 Inf, Sep–Oct 1899.

WILLIAMS, John; Private; A/24th Inf. Convicted of absence without leave, 1 Dec 1901; fined $2.

WILLIAMS, John; Private; C/9th Cav. Corporal, A/10th Cavalry, distinguished marksman, with Department of the Missouri bronze medal, 1903. SOURCE: GO 198, AGO, 6 Dec 1906.

Ranked number 15, Northern Division cavalry competition, Ft Riley, KS, 1905, with bronze medal. SOURCE: GO 173, AGO, 20 Oct 1905.

Private, C/9th Cavalry, ranked number four in Northern Division rifle competition, Ft Sheridan, IL, 1906, silver medal. SOURCE: GO 198, AGO, 6 Dec 1906.

WILLIAMS, John; Private; L/25th Inf. Fined $7 by summary court, San Isidro, Philippines, for being off limits, 14 Jun 1902, first conviction. SOURCE: Register of Summary Court, San Isidro.

WILLIAMS, John; Private; I/25th Inf. Fined $10 by summary court, San Isidro, Philippines, for being drunk and disorderly in quarters after taps and resisting arrest by Sgt. Robert Yours, I/25th Infantry, 4 Jul 1902, first conviction. SOURCE: Register of Summary Court, San Isidro.

WILLIAMS, John; Private; M/9th Cav. At Ft D. A. Russell, WY, in 1910; resident of Chicago. SOURCE: *Illustrated Review: Ninth Cavalry*, with picture.

WILLIAMS, John G.; Private; H/24th Inf. Enlisted Camp Tampa, FL, 6 May 1898. SOURCE: Muster Roll, H/24 Inf, May–Jun 1898.

Sick in hospital, Siboney, Cuba, 21–25 Aug, 1898, and en route to U.S., 25–31 Aug 1898, disease contracted in line of duty. SOURCE: Muster Roll, H/24 Inf, Jul–Aug 1898.

On special duty as laborer, Subsistence Department, since 5 Oct 1898; on furlough authorized by surgeon's certificate, 6 Sep–5 Oct 1898. SOURCE: Muster Roll, H/24 Inf, Sep–Oct 1898.

On special duty as laborer, Quartermaster Department, 12–18 Nov 1898; fined $3 by summary court, no date. SOURCE: Muster Roll, H/24 Inf, Nov–Dec 1898.

Discharged Ft Douglas, UT, 27 Jan 1899, character good, single; deposits $65; due U.S. for clothing $18.06. SOURCE: Muster Roll, H/24 Inf, Jan–Feb 1899.

WILLIAMS, John G.; 1st Sgt; F/25th Inf. Eleven-year veteran, killed by Corporal Nelson, F/25th Infantry, May 1900. SOURCE: Richmond *Planet*, 28 Jul 1900.

Died, homicide victim, in the Philippines, 19 May 1900. SOURCE: *ANJ* 37 (2 Jun 1900): 951.

WILLIAMS, John P.; Sergeant; F/24th Inf. Killed in action, Cuba, 1898. SOURCE: Scipio, *Last of the Black Regulars*, 29.

Died in Cuba, 1 Jul 1898. SOURCE: *ANJ* 36 (18 Feb 1898): 590.

WILLIAMS, John S.; Private; H/10th Cav. Served in 10th Cavalry, 1898; remained in U.S. during war with Spain. SOURCE: Cashin, *Under Fire with the Tenth Cavalry*, 347.

WILLIAMS, John S.; Private; H/25th Inf. With Pvt. Samuel Goosley, A/25th Infantry, served as orderly, Headquarters, 3rd Brigade, Encampment at Camp W. C. Sanger, KS, Oct 1903; adjutant requested permanent attachment to 3rd Brigade in letter to Adjutant General, 2nd Brigade, Provisional Division, Ft Riley, KS, 20 Oct 1903. SOURCE: Misc Records, 25 Inf.

WILLIAMS, John T.; Sergeant; G/24th Inf. Awarded certificate of merit for service in Cuban campaign, 1898. SOURCE: Scipio, *Last of the Black Regulars*, 130.

Commended for distinguished service, battle of Santiago, 1 Jul 1898; awarded certificate of merit; now out of service. SOURCE: GO 15, AGO, 13 Feb 1900.

Certificate of merit mentioned. SOURCE: Steward, *The Colored Regulars*, 280.

At Siboney, Cuba, 1898. *See* **WOODS**, Robert Gordon, Captain, I/49th Infantry

WILLIAMS, John W.; K/10th Cav. Original member of 10th Cavalry; in troop when organized, Ft Riley, KS, 1 Sep 1867. SOURCE: McMiller, "Buffalo Soldiers," 77.

WILLIAMS, John W.; Recruit; Colored Detachment/General Service. Tried by general court martial, Columbus Barracks, OH, for selling pair of campaign shoes, on or about 15 Jun 1888, and theft of pair of campaign shoes from Recruit Francis Walters, Colored Detachment, Company B of Instruction, General Service, 16 Jun 1888; convicted of first charge and acquitted of second; fined $2.64 (price of shoes) and confined for one month. SOURCE: GCMO 45, AGO, 17 Aug 1888.

WILLIAMS, Joliet W.; H/10th Cav. Original member of 10th Cavalry; in troop when organized, Ft Leavenworth, KS, 21 Jul 1867. SOURCE: McMiller, "Buffalo Soldiers," 75.

WILLIAMS, Joseph; Private; K/10th Cav. Sick in post hospital, Ft Riley, KS, Apr 1868. SOURCE: LR, Det 10 Cav, 1868–69.

WILLIAMS, Joseph; Corporal; G/10th Cav. Served in 10th Cavalry in Cuba, 1898; wounded in action. SOURCE: Cashin, *Under Fire with the Tenth Cavalry*, 345.

Wounded at Santiago, Cuba, 1 Jul 1898. SOURCE: SecWar, *AR 1898*, 324.

WILLIAMS, Joseph; Sergeant; I/10th Cav. Guest with wife at K/10th Cavalry Thanksgiving dinner, Ft Robinson, NE, 1904. SOURCE: Simmons, "Thanksgiving Day in the Tenth Cavalry," 664.

Ranked number 377 among rifle experts with 69.33 percent in 1906. SOURCE: GO 101, AGO, 31 May 1906.

Daughter Geraldine Bernice, first child, born to wife, maiden name Sarah K. Viele, at Ft Robinson, 3 Feb 1907. SOURCE: Medical History, Ft Robinson.

WILLIAMS, Joseph E.; Private; H/9th Cav. Born Coal Co., MO; occupation cook; Ht 5'6"; enlisted in C/9th Cavalry, 1891; discharged 1894; enlisted, age 38, Ft Omaha, NE, 25 Jul 1895; joined at Ft Robinson, NE, 1 Aug 1895; convicted of infractions by summary courts three times, Ft Robinson, 1896–97; discharged, Camp Wikoff, NY, 27 Aug 1898. SOURCE: Descriptive Book, H/9 Cav.

Deposited $32 with paymaster, Ft Robinson, 1897–98.

WILLIAMS, Joseph W.; H/10th Cav. Admitted to Soldiers Home with disability, age 45, after one year's service, 13 Mar 1891. SOURCE: SecWar, *AR 1891*, 753.

Died at Soldiers Home of consumption, age 51, 26 Sep 1896. SOURCE: SecWar, *AR 1896*, 640.

WILLIAMS, Levi; Private; K/24th Inf. Died of variola in the Philippines, 18 Jul 1900. SOURCE: *ANJ* 37 (4 Aug 1900): 1166.

WILLIAMS, Lewis; Private; C/25th Inf. Dishonorable discharge, Brownsville. SOURCE: SO 266, AGO, 9 Nov 1906.

WILLIAMS, Lilburn; Private; K/9th Cav. Expert rifleman at Ft D. A. Russell, WY, in 1910; resident of Saline Co., MO. SOURCE: *Illustrated Review: Ninth Cavalry*, with picture.

WILLIAMS, Livingston; Sergeant; L/10th Cav. Commissioned second lieutenant, 27 Sep 1918. SOURCE: Glass, *History of the Tenth Cavalry*, appendix M.

WILLIAMS, Lonnie; Private; K/10th Cav. Member of troop orchestra, Ft Robinson, NE, 1904. SOURCE: Barrow, "Christmas in the United States Army," 96.

WILLIAMS, Major; Sergeant; I/9th Cav. Veteran of Philippine Insurrection; at Ft D. A. Russell, WY, in 1910; sharpshooter; resident of Yorktown, VA. SOURCE: *Illustrated Review: Ninth Cavalry*, with picture.

WILLIAMS, Marshall; Private; B/9th Cav. At Ft D. A. Russell, WY, in 1910; marksman. SOURCE: *Illustrated Review: Ninth Cavalry*, with picture.

WILLIAMS, Maxwell A.; Corporal; B/25th Inf. Sergeant, Ft Buford, ND, 1893. SOURCE: Nankivell, *History of the Twenty-fifth Infantry*, 50 (picture).

Retires from Ft Missoula, MT. SOURCE: *ANJ* 35 (22 Jan 1898): 383.

WILLIAMS, Minor; Recruit; Colored Detachment/Mounted Service. At Jefferson Barracks, MO, 1885. *See* **TAYLOR**, Alonzo, Recruit, Colored Detachment/Mounted Service

WILLIAMS, Moses; Ord Sgt; U.S. Army. Born Carroll Co., PA; awarded Medal of Honor for heroism against Nana, Carrizo Canyon, NM, 12 Aug 1881. SOURCE: Carroll, *The Black Military Experience*, 279–80, 365–69; Leckie, *The Buffalo Soldiers*, 232–33; Lee, *Negro Medal of Honor Men*, 71.

Sergeant, I/9th Cavalry; Medal of Honor for heroism in action against Nana, Cuchillo Negro Mountains, NM, 16 Aug 1881, mentioned. SOURCE: Billington, *New Mexico's Buffalo Soldiers*, 106.

First Sergeant, I/9th Cavalry, Ft Niobrara, NE, appointed ordnance sergeant, U.S. Army, as of 28 Sep 1886. SOURCE: *ANJ* 24 (2 Oct 1886): 189; Roster, 9 Cav.

WILLIAMS, Moses; Private; I/9th Cav. At Ft Robinson, NE, Aug 1888, complained to inspector general that he was subjected to great deal of abuse by first sergeant and is now in confinement for drawing saber on first sergeant after latter drew pistol on him. SOURCE: Reports of Inspection, DP, I.

WILLIAMS, Noah W.; Private; B/8th Ill Inf. Born Springfield Township, IL, 25 Dec 1876; sixth of seven sons of Charles Henry and Harriett Williams; attended grammar and high schools in Springfield; joined African Methodist Episcopal Church, 1896; enlisted with brother John in B/8th Illinois Infantry, 1899; spent seven months on detached service in Cuba as chaplain's assistant; built church with soldier subscriptions and native aid; went to Tuscola, IL, to organize church, Jul 1899; attended Wilberforce University on scholarship, autumn 1900; became elder, 1901; studied at DePauw University, State Normal School, and Earlham College, while pastor at Greencastle, Terre Haute, and Richmond, IN; also pastor at Hannibal, MO, and Knoxville, Shelbyville, and most recently Clarksville, Tennessee; delegate of TN conference to centennial general conference; married Miss Hattie C. Johnson, daughter of Reverend Benjamin and Sallie Johnson of Springfield, IL, 15 Oct 1903. SOURCE: Wright, *The Centennial Encyclopedia of the AME Church*, 248–49.

WILLIAMS, Norman; E/10th Cav. Original member of 10th Cavalry; in troop when organized, Ft Leavenworth, KS, 15 Jun 1867. SOURCE: McMiller, "Buffalo Soldiers," 72.

WILLIAMS, Odia; Private; K/25th Inf. At Ft Niobrara, NE, 1904. SOURCE: Wilson, "History of Fort Niobrara."

WILLIAMS, Oliver; Private; M/48th Inf. Died of hydrophobia in the Philippines, 15 Sep 1900. SOURCE: *ANJ* 38 (29 Sep 1900): 115.

WILLIAMS, Osborne; Private; 10th Cav. At Ft Wallace, KS, Jun 1868. SOURCE: LR, Det 10 Cav, 1868–69.

WILLIAMS, Polk; Corporal; 24th Inf. Served in Houston, summer 1917. SOURCE: Haynes, *A Night of Violence*, 43.

WILLIAMS, Prince; Private; 10th Cav. Mentioned as having enlisted 19 Apr 1873. SOURCE: ES, 10 Cav, 1873–83.

WILLIAMS, Richard; Sergeant; B/24th Inf. "Worthy of especial mention for bravery and fidelity." SOURCE: SecWar, *AR 1898*, 715.

Awarded certificate of merit for service as corporal in Cuban campaign, 1 Jul 1898. SOURCE: GO 15, AGO, 13 Feb 1900; Scipio, *Last of the Black Regulars*, 130; *ANJ* 37 (24 Feb 1900): 611; Steward, *The Colored Regulars*, 280.

Sergeant, B/24th Infantry; on special duty as provost sergeant, Cabanatuan, Philippines, Jan 1901. SOURCE: Name File, 24 Inf.

WILLIAMS, Richard; Private; I/24th Inf. Enlisted Mobile, AL, 28 Mar 1899; fined $2 by summary court, 18 Apr 1899. SOURCE: Muster Roll, I/24 Inf, Mar–Apr 1899.

Fined $.50 by summary court, 19 Jun 1899. SOURCE: Muster Roll, I/24 Inf, May–Jun 1899.

Allotted $10 per month for six months to Fannie Williams. SOURCE: Muster Roll, I/24 Inf, Sep–Oct 1899.

On detached service at Cabanatuan, Philippines, since 30 Dec 1899. SOURCE: Muster Roll, I/24 Inf, Nov–Dec 1899.

WILLIAMS, Richard A.; Sqdn Sgt Maj; 10th Cav. Born Philadelphia; Ht 5'10 1/2" brown eyes, black hair, chocolate complexion; served three years in L/10th Cavalry, to 4 Sep 1901; reenlisted in L/10th Cavalry and continued as sergeant; assigned to Philippines, 1 Aug 1902; promoted to sergeant major, 2nd squadron, 10th Cavalry, 14 Nov 1903; discharged, end of term, Ft Mackenzie, WY, 4 Sep 1904, single, character excellent, with $54.52 clothing; next of kin Richard H. Williams, Lansdowne, Delaware Co., PA. SOURCE: Descriptive Book, 10 Cav Officers & NCOs.

WILLIAMS, Robert; D/10th Cav. Original member of 10th Cavalry; in troop when organized, Ft Leavenworth, KS, 1 Jun 1867. SOURCE: McMiller, "Buffalo Soldiers," 71.

WILLIAMS, Robert; Private; I/10th Cav. Mentioned Dec 1875. SOURCE: ES, 10 Cav, 1873–83.

WILLIAMS, Robert; A/24th Inf. Died in Minnesota. SOURCE: Taylor, "Minnesota Black Spanish-American War Veterans."

WILLIAMS, Robert; Cook; D/25th Inf. Dishonorable discharge, Brownsville. SOURCE: SO 266, AGO, 9 Nov 1906.

One of fourteen cleared of involvement in Brownsville raid by court, 1910; authorized to reenlist. SOURCE: Weaver, *The Brownsville Raid*, 248.

Readmitted to Army after Brownsville with back pay of $2,419.65, highest amount granted to any of the fourteen allowed back in service. SOURCE: Cleveland *Gazette*, 16 Sep 1916.

WILLIAMS, Robert E.; Farrier; G/9th Cav. Served as private, K/10th Cavalry, 1898; remained in U.S. during war with Spain. SOURCE: Cashin, *Under Fire with the Tenth Cavalry*, 349.

Veteran of Spanish-American War and Philippine Insurrection; farrier, G/9th Cavalry, at Ft D. A. Russell, WY, in 1910; resident of Steelton, PA. SOURCE: *Illustrated Review: Ninth Cavalry*, with picture.

WILLIAMS, Robert N.; Sergeant; A/24th Inf. Died of tuberculosis in the Philippines, 1 Oct 1901. SOURCE: *ANJ* 39 (7 Dec 1901): 339.

WILLIAMS, Rodney; G/10th Cav. Original member of 10th Cavalry; in troop when organized, Ft Leavenworth, KS, 5 Jul 1867. SOURCE: McMiller, "Buffalo Soldiers," 74.

WILLIAMS, Roland F.; Private; A/9th Cav. At Ft D. A. Russell, WY, in 1910. SOURCE: *Illustrated Review: Ninth Cavalry*, with picture.

WILLIAMS, Roy; Private; A/10th Cav. At Ft Apache, AZ, 1890, subscribed $.50 to testimonial to General Grierson. SOURCE: List of subscriptions, 23 Apr 1890, 10th Cavalry papers, MHI.

WILLIAMS, Rufus; 25th Inf. Enlistment authorized by telegram, Adjutant General's Office, 12 Oct 1897.

WILLIAMS, Samuel; C/10th Cav. Original member of 10th Cavalry; in troop when organized, Ft Leavenworth, KS, 18 Feb 1867. SOURCE: McMiller, "Buffalo Soldiers," 70.

WILLIAMS, Seth; Private; F/10th Cav. Served in 10th Cavalry in Cuba, 1898. SOURCE: Cashin, *Under Fire with the Tenth Cavalry*, 344.

WILLIAMS, Sidney; Private; K/10th Cav. Released to duty from treatment for gonorrhea, Ft Robinson, NE, 7 Aug 1903. SOURCE: Post Surgeon to CO, K/10, 7 Aug 1903, LS, Post Surgeon, Ft Robinson.

Released to duty from treatment for gonorrhea, Ft Robinson, NE, 24 Aug 1903. SOURCE: Post Surgeon to CO, K/10, 24 Aug 1903, LS, Post Surgeon, Ft Robinson.

Member of troop orchestra. SOURCE: Barrow, "Christmas in the United States Army," 96.

WILLIAMS, Solomon; Private; Band/10th Cav. Served in 10th Cavalry in Cuba, 1898. SOURCE: Cashin, *Under Fire with the Tenth Cavalry*, 359.

WILLIAMS, Squire; Corporal; D/24th Inf. Mentioned among men who distinguished themselves in 1889; awarded certificate of merit for gallant and meritorious conduct as escort for Maj. Joseph W. Wham, paymaster, when attacked by robbers between Fts Grant and Thomas, AZ; now in B/24th Infantry. SOURCE: GO 18, AGO, 1891.

Transferred from Reserve Divisional Hospital, Siboney, Cuba, to U.S. on U.S. Army Transport *Santiago* with yellow fever, 25 Jul 1898. SOURCE: Hospital Papers, Spanish-American War.

Corporal, D/24th Infantry, at Cabanatuan, Philippines, 1900. *See* **WORKMAN**, William, Private, D/24th Infantry

Corporal, D/24th Infantry, at Cabanatuan, Philippines, 1901. *See* **PRIDE**, Wheeler, Private, D/24th Infantry

Retired as corporal D/24th Infantry, Jun 1901. SOURCE: *ANJ* 38 (15 Jun 1901): 1019.

Served with Buford Parker; settled in Salt Lake City. SOURCE: Clark, "A History of the Twenty-fourth," 69.

Now retired; commended for gallantry, 11 May 1889, while private, K/24th Infantry, on escort duty. SOURCE: Cleveland *Gazette*, 24 Nov 1906.

WILLIAMS, Thomas; A/10th Cav. Recruit from Jefferson Barracks, MO; arrived Ft Leavenworth, KS, 9 Oct 1866; died of pneumonia in Ft Leavenworth hospital same day. SOURCE: McMiller, "Buffalo Soldiers," 45.

WILLIAMS, Thomas; Farrier; A/9th Cav. At Ft Robinson, NE, 1894. SOURCE: Investigation of Charges against Chaplain Plummer.

Enlistment authorized by letter, Adjutant General's Office, 18 Sep 1895.

WILLIAMS, Thomas; Private; F/25th Inf. Deserted in Luzon, Philippines, 27 Sep 1900. SOURCE: Regt Returns, 25 Inf, Oct 1899.

Died of syphilis in the Philippines, 3 Aug 1901. SOURCE: *ANJ* 39 (28 Sep 1901): 81.

WILLIAMS, Tony; Sergeant; C/10th Cav. Born in Arkansas; private and corporal, G/10th Cavalry, 8 Dec 1892–7 Mar 1896; private, C/10th Cavalry, 27 Apr 1896; corporal, 2 Oct 1896; at Ft Assiniboine, MT, 1897. SOURCE: Baker, Roster.

Served as sergeant, C/10th Cavalry, in Cuba, 1898. SOURCE: Cashin, *Under Fire with the Tenth Cavalry*, 339.

WILLIAMS, Underhill; I/10th Cav. Original member of 10th Cavalry; in troop when organized, Ft Riley, KS, 15 Aug 1867. SOURCE: McMiller, "Buffalo Soldiers," 76.

WILLIAMS, Van; C/10th Cav. Original member of 10th Cavalry; in troop when organized, Ft Leavenworth, KS, 18 Feb 1867. SOURCE: McMiller, "Buffalo Soldiers," 70.

WILLIAMS, Vernell; Private; B/9th Cav. At Ft D. A. Russell, WY, in 1910; sharpshooter. SOURCE: *Illustrated Review: Ninth Cavalry*, with picture.

WILLIAMS, W.; Private; H/24th Inf. At Ft Grant, AZ, 1890. *See* **BERRY**, Edward, Sergeant, H/24th Infantry

WILLIAMS, Walter; Recruit; Colored Detachment/Mounted Service. Convicted by general court martial, Jefferson Barracks, MO, of desertion, 7 Aug 1888, until apprehended 1 Jan 1889; sentenced to dishonorable discharge and five years. SOURCE: GCMO 6, AGO, 31 Jan 1889.

WILLIAMS, Walter; Private; D/9th Cav. At Ft Robinson, NE, 1892. SOURCE: Order 181, 25 Oct 1892, Post Orders, Ft Robinson.

WILLIAMS, Walter B.; Sgt Maj; 24th Inf. Private, B/24th Infantry, transferred from Reserve Divisional Hospital, Siboney, Cuba, to U.S. on U.S. Army Transport *Santiago* with yellow fever, 25 Jul 1898. SOURCE: Hospital Papers, Spanish-American War.

Leader of H/24th Infantry sextet that serenaded Governor Dole of Hawaii en route to the Philippines; other members of group: J. H. Tucker, L. J. Clark, J. T. Watson, E. R. Strange,

L. G. Carney; Williams is former member of Indianapolis *Freeman* staff. SOURCE: Letter, Joseph H. Tucker, Manila, Philippines, 18 Aug 1899, in Indianapolis *Freeman*, 14 Oct 1899.

Sergeant major, 24th Infantry, at Ft Harrison, MT, 1902; "one of the most efficient sergeant-majors of the army." SOURCE: Letter, Chaplain Allen Allensworth, 4 Oct 1902, in Indianapolis *Freeman*, 18 Oct 1902.

Sends copies of the "Knocker," weekly publication of 24th Infantry, from Ft Harrison. SOURCE: Indianapolis *Freeman*, 8 Nov 1902.

On division rifle team, Ft Sheridan, IL, 1905. SOURCE: Muller, *The Twenty Fourth Infantry*, 42.

Ranked number 13 in Northern Division Infantry competition, Ft Sheridan, 1905, with bronze medal. SOURCE: GO 173, AGO, 20 Oct 1905.

Ranked number 57 among rifle experts with 76.00 percent in 1905. SOURCE: GO 101, AGO, 31 May 1906.

Wife left Ft Harrison for Ft Leavenworth, KS. SOURCE: Indianapolis *Freeman*, 15 Jul 1905.

Ranked number 16 in Division of the Philippines rifle competition, Ft William McKinley, Rizal, Philippines, 1907. SOURCE: GO 213, AGO, 19 Oct 1907.

Ranked number 15 in marksmanship, Division of the Philippines, 1908, with bronze medal. SOURCE: Muller, *The Twenty Fourth Infantry*, 48.

Distinguished marksman: number 13, Northern Division, 1905; number 16, Division of the Philippines, 1907; number 15, Division of the Philippines, 1908. SOURCE: GO 207, AGO, 19 Dec 1908.

Commissioned captain, Camp Des Moines, IA, Oct 1917. SOURCE: Sweeney, *History of the American Negro*, 130.

Ranking noncommissioned officer in Army when commissioned at Des Moines; now resides in Pasadena, CA. SOURCE: Beasley, *Negro Trailblazers*, 285.

Pictures. SOURCE: Muller, *The Twenty Fourth Infantry*, 53, and Curtis, *The Black Soldier*, opposite 39.

WILLIAMS, Washington; Private; K/9th Cav. At Ft D. A. Russell, WY, in 1910; resident of West Point, MS. SOURCE: *Illustrated Review: Ninth Cavalry*, with picture.

WILLIAMS, William; Sergeant; H/10th Cav. At Ft Apache, AZ, 1890, subscribed $.50 to testimonial to General Grierson. SOURCE: List of subscriptions, 23 Apr 1890, 10th Cavalry papers, MHI.

WILLIAMS, William; Private; E/25th Inf. Died of variola in the Philippines, 21 Sep 1901. SOURCE: *ANJ* 39 (7 Dec 1901): 339.

WILLIAMS, William; Private; G/25th Inf. Died of heart failure in the Philippines, 10 Apr 1902. SOURCE: *ANJ* 39 (14 Jun 19021): 1046.

WILLIAMS, William H.; Private; I/25th Inf. Served at Ft Sill, Indian Territory, with William Branch; resides at 217 Starr Avenue, San Antonio, TX, age 46.

SOURCE: Affidavit, 21 Mar 1899, VA File C 2581520, William Branch.

Junior Vice Commander, Camp 30, National Indian War Veterans, San Antonio. SOURCE: *Winners of the West* 6 (Oct 1929): 7.

Picture with comrades of Camp 30, National Indian War Veterans. SOURCE: *Winners of the West* 9 (Mar 1932): 7

WILLIAMS, William H.; Staff Sgt; HQ Troop/ 10th Cav. Regimental quartermaster sergeant, 10th Cavalry, commissioned captain, Camp Des Moines, IA, 15 Oct 1917. SOURCE: Glass, *History of the Tenth Cavalry*, appendix M.

Staff sergeant, HQ Troop, won Shipp Trophy as regiment's outstanding soldier, Regiment Day, 28 Jul 1929, Ft Huachuca, AZ. SOURCE: *Cavalry Journal* 28 (Oct 1929): 608.

WILLIAMS, William J.; Captain; L/6th Mass Inf. Born in Canada, 1863; resided in Chelsea, MA; graduate of Phillips Exeter and Harvard Law School; retired as major; alderman for eighteen years; died 1924. SOURCE: *Crisis* 29 (Dec 1924): 75.

WILLIAMS, William O.; Corporal; G/9th Cav. Veteran of Philippine Insurrection; at Ft D. A. Russell, WY, in 1910; sharpshooter; resident of Chattanooga, TN. SOURCE: *Illustrated Review: Ninth Cavalry*, with picture.

WILLIAMS, Willie; Private; A/24th Inf. Transferred from Reserve Divisional Hospital, Siboney, Cuba, to U.S. on U.S. Army Transport *Santiago* with remittent malarial fever, 25 Jul 1898. SOURCE: Hospital Papers, Spanish-American War.

WILLIAMS, Willie A.; Private; K/10th Cav. Served in 10th Cavalry, 1898; remained in U.S. during war with Spain. SOURCE: Cashin, *Under Fire with the Tenth Cavalry*, 350.

WILLIAMS, Wilson; Private; E/25th Inf. Drowned in the Philippines; body recovered. SOURCE: *ANJ* 39 (8 Feb 1902): 577.

WILLIAMS, York; Private; B/9th Cav. Veteran of Philippine Insurrection; at Ft D. A. Russell, WY, in 1910. SOURCE: *Illustrated Review: Ninth Cavalry*.

WILLIAMSON, Alexander; D/10th Cav. Original member of 10th Cavalry; in troop when organized, Ft Leavenworth, KS, 1 Jun 1867. SOURCE: McMiller, "Buffalo Soldiers," 71.

WILLIAMSON, Benny; Private; C/49th Inf. Slightly wounded in head, San Pablo, Luzon, Philippines. SOURCE: *ANJ* 38 (9 Feb 1901): 579.

WILLIAMSON, Cornelius C.; Private; B/9th Cav. At Ft D. A. Russell, WY, in 1910; sharpshooter. SOURCE: *Illustrated Review: Ninth Cavalry*.

WILLIAMSON, David; Corporal; I/9th Cav. Appointed corporal as of 13 Oct 1892. SOURCE: Roster, 9 Cav.

Led troops against insurgents, Taytay, Philippines, Jan 1901. SOURCE: Manila *Times*, 1 Feb 1901.

Led twelve-man detachment against insurgents, 30 Jan–1 Feb 1901. SOURCE: Regt Returns, 9 Cav, Feb 1901.

WILLIAMSON, James; Private; B/9th Cav. At Ft D. A. Russell, WY, in 1910. SOURCE: *Illustrated Review: Ninth Cavalry*.

WILLINGHAM, Ephraim M.; Private; Band/24th Inf. Born Tuscaloosa, AL; occupation minister; Ht 5'10"; black eyes and hair, mulatto complexion; enlisted Ft Gibson, Indian Territory, age 28, 4 Dec 1888; assigned to F/24th Infantry, 9 Dec 1888; on detached service in Band/24th Infantry, learning music, 7 Feb–22 Mar 1889, then transferred to band; died of consumption in post hospital, Ft Bayard, NM, 7 Sep 1889, character excellent, single, clothing $10.32. SOURCE: Descriptive Book, 24 Inf NCS & Band.

WILLINGHAM, Walter E.; Corporal; K/10th Cav. Wounded in action, left calf, Parral, Mexico, 12 Apr 1916. SOURCE: Wharfield, *10th Cavalry and Border Fights*, 92.

WILLINGHAM, William; Private; M/25th Inf. Drowned, Iba, Luzon, Philippines, 10 Aug 1901; body recovered. SOURCE: *ANJ* 39 (12 Oct 1901): 140.

WILLIS; Private; D/24th Inf. At Cabanatuan, Philippines, 1901. *See* **STEVENS**, Samuel, Private, D/24th Infantry

WILLIS, Alex; Private; L/9th Cav. On detached service in field, New Mexico, 21 Jan–24 Feb 1881. SOURCE: Regt Returns, 9 Cav, Feb 1881.

WILLIS, Arthur; 1st Sgt; I/25th Cav. At San Antonio, TX, 1878; best marksman in company and tied for sixth in regiment. SOURCE: 25 Inf, Scrapbook, I.

WILLIS, Cupid; Private; A/10th Cav. Served in 10th Cavalry in Cuba, 1898. SOURCE: Cashin, *Under Fire with the Tenth Cavalry*, 336.

At Ft Robinson, NE, commander asks remission of unexecuted part of his court-martial sentence. SOURCE: CO, A/10, to CO, Ft Robinson, 13 Feb 1903, Register of LS, Ft Robinson.

WILLIS, Dorsie W.; Private; D/25th Inf. Dishonorable discharge, Brownsville. SOURCE: SO 266, AGO, 9 Nov 1906.

After discharge worked as porter and shoeshine man, Northwestern Bank Building barber shop, Minneapolis, since 1913; quit Sep 1972; son is 65; wife Olive is 55; completed sixth grade in Oklahoma Territory; now 86. SOURCE: *New York Times*, 31 Dec 1972.

Voted $25,000 payment by House of Representatives; Senate action not completed; last known survivor of Brownsville raid. SOURCE: New York *Times*, 18 Nov 1973.

Paid $25,000 compensation by government at Minneapolis ceremony; received honorable discharge on 87th birthday, 11 Feb 1973; will use money to repair his house and save the rest. SOURCE: Fargo-Moorhead (MN) *Forum*, 10 Jan 1974.

WILLIS, Frederick; Private; K/10th Cav. Served in 10th Cavalry, 1898; remained in U.S. during war with Spain. SOURCE: Cashin, *Under Fire with the Tenth Cavalry*, 350.

WILLIS, George; Private; F/9th Cav. At Ft D. A. Russell, WY, in 1910; resident of Monroe Co., VA. SOURCE: *Illustrated Review: Ninth Cavalry*, with picture.

WILLIS, George B.; Private; K/10th Cav. Served in 10th Cavalry, 1898; remained in U.S. during war with Spain. SOURCE: Cashin, *Under Fire with the Tenth Cavalry*, 350.

WILLIS, James H.; Trumpeter; H/9th Cav. Born Washington, DC; Ht 5'7"; served in C/9th Cavalry, 1882–87, character very good; in 10th Cavalry, 1887–92, character good; enlisted, Ft Myer, VA, 26 Dec 1892; transferred from K/9th Cavalry to Band/9th Cavalry, 1 Jan 1895, married; six summary court and general court convictions, Ft Robinson, NE, Feb 1896–Mar 1897. SOURCE: Descriptive Book, H/9 Cav.

Private, B/10th Cavalry, at Ft Apache, AZ, 1890, subscribed $.50 to testimonial to General Grierson. SOURCE: List of subscriptions, 23 Apr 1890, 10th Cavalry papers, MHI.

Transfer from A/9th Cavalry to Hospital Corps disapproved by letter, Adjutant General's Office, 26 Feb 1896.

Arrived at Ft Robinson from furlough, sick in quarters since 17 Aug 1898 due to disease and wound in war with Spain. SOURCE: Regt Returns, 9 Cav, Aug 1898.

Relates experience in shooting Spanish sniper in Cuba. SOURCE: Young, *Reminiscences*, 234.

WILLIS, John R.; Recruit; Colored Detachment/ General Service. Convicted by general court martial, Jefferson Barracks, MO, of desertion, 29 Jun–5 Nov 1886; sentenced to dishonorable discharge and four years. SOURCE: GCMO 108, AGO, 30 Dec 1886.

WILLIS, Joseph; Private; C/9th Cav. At Ft D. A. Russell, WY, in 1910; resident of Coatesville, PA. SOURCE: *Illustrated Review: Ninth Cavalry*, with picture.

WILLIS, William; Private; H/24th Inf. Enlisted Harrisburg, PA, 12 Nov 1895. SOURCE: Muster Roll, H/24 Inf, May–Jun 1898.

Absent, sick, since 14 Sep 1898, disease contracted in line of duty. SOURCE: Muster Roll, H/24 Inf, Sep–Oct 1898.

Sick until 10 Nov 1898; discharged, end of term, Ft Douglas, UT, 11 Nov 1898, character excellent, single; clothing $2.11, deposits $123.75; reenlisted in company, Ft Douglas, 12 Nov 1898. SOURCE: Muster Roll, H/24 Inf, Nov–Dec 1898.

WILLOUGHBY, S. J.; A/10th Cav. Letter from Manzanillo, Cuba, notes good relations with Cubans and comments on 10th Cavalry Y.M.C.A. activities. SOURCE: Indianapolis *Freeman*, 19 Jul 1902.

WILLOUGHBY, Thomas; Private; B/25th Inf. Deserted from Santa Mora hospital, Manila, Philippines, 18 Nov 1899. SOURCE: Regt Returns, 25 Inf, Dec 1899.

WILLS, Frank; L/10th Cav. Original member of 10th Cavalry; in troop when organized, Ft Riley, KS, 21 Sep 1867. SOURCE: McMiller, "Buffalo Soldiers," 78.

WILLS, James; K/10th Cav. Original member of 10th Cavalry; in troop when organized, Ft Riley, KS, 1 Sep 1867. SOURCE: McMiller, "Buffalo Soldiers," 77.

WILMORE, Leonard; Private; M/25th Inf. Deserted from military prison, Iba, Philippines, 19 Oct 1900, while awaiting trial for murder. SOURCE: Regt Returns, 25 Inf, Oct 1900.

Musician Wilmore, L/25th Infantry, slayer of Private Weakly, I/25th Infantry, at Iba last August "made escape a short time ago and it is presumed went to the enemy." SOURCE: Richmond *Planet*, 12 Jan 1901.

1st Lt. Carl H. Martin, Adjutant, 25th Infantry, Iba, Mar 1901, "prefers charges against Leonard Wilmore, Company M, 25th Inf, for desertion, treason, violation of the laws of war." SOURCE: LR, 25 Inf, 1901.

Sentence of death commuted by President Roosevelt, in accordance with department commander's recommendation of clemency, to life in prison at Presidio de Manila. SOURCE: *ANJ* 39 (11 Jan 1902): 467.

WILSON, Alfred; Private; E/9th Cav. Relieved from extra duty as laborer, Subsistence Department, Ft Robinson, NE. SOURCE: Special Order 90, 20 Aug 1896, Post Orders, Ft Robinson.

Wounded in action at San Juan, Cuba, 1 Jul 1898. SOURCE: *Illustrated Review: Ninth Cavalry*.

WILSON, Alonzo; Private; I/9th Cav. At Ft D. A. Russell, WY, in 1910; resident of Lafayette, IN. SOURCE: *Illustrated Review: Ninth Cavalry*.

WILSON, Amos; Private; D/9th Cav. Born and resided in North Carolina; prisoner No. 125, U.S. Military Prison, Leavenworth, KS, died 29 Aug 1877 of consumption, age 28, single. SOURCE: Certificates of Disability, DivMo, 1875–87.

WILSON, Arthur; 25th Inf. Born Charleston, SC; enlisted in 25th Infantry, Charleston, 1866; discharged from Jackson Barracks, LA, 1868; went as part of crew of eighty colored waiters and forty-two colored chambermaids to San Francisco, where opened Palace Hotel; worked there three years; five years with Fletchheime and Gooskine wholesale warehouse; five years as porter with Pullman Car Company; twenty-five years as private car porter, Southern Pacific Railroad; retired and lived three years; died of heart trouble; second wife was youngest daughter of Reverend Sanderson; trustee of 15th Street African Methodist Episcopal Church, Oakland, CA. SOURCE: Beasley, *Negro Trailblazers*, 299.

WILSON, Arthur; Private; I/9th Cav. At Ft D. A. Russell, WY, in 1910; resident of Atlanta. SOURCE: *Illustrated Review: Ninth Cavalry*, with picture.

WILSON, Augustus; Sergeant; A/10th Cav. Led scout from Ft Larned, KS, and killed two Indians, Nov 1868. SOURCE: Leckie, *The Buffalo Soldiers*, 43.

WILSON, Broslon; H/10th Cav. Original member of 10th Cavalry; in troop when organized, Ft Leavenworth, KS, 21 Jul 1867. SOURCE: McMiller, "Buffalo Soldiers," 75.

WILSON, Charles; Private; 10th Cav. Relieved from duty with Quartermaster Department. SOURCE: SO 14, Det 10 Cav, Camp near Ft Dodge, KS, 9 Apr 1869, Orders, Det 10 Cav, 1868–69.

WILSON, Charles; Private; H/24th Inf. Enlisted New York City, 6 Jul 1898; joined company 16 Sep 1898; due U.S. for ordnance (cartridge belt, fork, knife) $1.12. SOURCE: Muster Roll, H/24 Inf, Sep–Oct 1898.

Discharged, end of term, 29 Jan 1899, character good, single; due U.S. for clothing $49.69; reenlisted, Ft Douglas, UT, 30 Jan 1899. SOURCE: Muster Roll, H/24 Inf, Jan–Feb 1899.

Wounded in action, scalp, slight, Naguilan, Philippines, 7 Dec 1899. SOURCE: *ANJ* 37 (10 Mar 1900): 659; Muller, *The Twenty Fourth Infantry*, 35.

Fined $10 by summary court, San Isidro, Philippines, for disrespect to noncommissioned officer, 18 Nov 1901, first conviction. SOURCE: Register of Summary Court, San Isidro.

WILSON, Charles; Private; B/9th Cav. Veteran of Philippine Insurrection; at Ft D. A. Russell, WY, in 1910; sharpshooter. SOURCE: *Illustrated Review: Ninth Cavalry*.

WILSON, Charley; Private; F/10th Cav. Served in 10th Cavalry in Cuba, 1898. SOURCE: Cashin, *Under Fire with the Tenth Cavalry*, 344.

WILSON, Edward; L/10th Cav. Mentioned as Indian war survivor. SOURCE: *Winners of the West* 3 (Jun 1926): 7.

WILSON, Ernst; Private; 24th Inf. Sentenced to seven years for part in Houston riot. SOURCE: *Cleveland Gazette*, 5 Jan 1918.

WILSON, Frank; Private; H/10th Cav. Caught and arrested, Hays City, KS, trying to board eastbound train; caught by Mr. Warren with help of Sergeant Johnson, I/10th Cavalry, and Pvt. Dock Burks, I/10th Cavalry, 25 May 1868. SOURCE: LR, Det 10 Cav, 1868–69.

Commander's request of 19 May 1869 for remission of rest of his sentence and his discharge disapproved by assistant adjutant general, Department of the Missouri, 26 May 1869; Wilson had been convicted of desertion and persuading others to do the same and had been sentenced in accordance with General Order 74, Department of the Missouri, 1868, to confinement for remaining portion of his enlistment. SOURCE: LR, Det 10 Cav, 1868–69.

WILSON, Frederick; Private; E/10th Cav. Honorable mention for skill in successful pursuit of raiding parties in Arizona, 1888. SOURCE: Baker, Roster.

At Ft Apache, AZ, 1890, subscribed $.50 to testimonial to General Grierson. SOURCE: List of subscriptions, 23 Apr 1890, 10th Cavalry papers, MHI.

WILSON, George; G/10th Cav. Original member of 10th Cavalry; in troop when organized, Ft Leavenworth, KS, 5 Jul 1867. SOURCE: McMiller, "Buffalo Soldiers," 74.

WILSON, George; 1st Sgt; M/9th Cav. Enlisted, age 22, 1873; retired as first sergeant, M/9th Cavalry, 1903.

Private, recently enlisted; to report to Ft Wingate, NM, and unit. SOURCE: Order 29, 9 Cav, 18 Jun 1879, Regimental Orders.

Sergeant, I/9th Cavalry, appointed sergeant as of 9 May 1888. SOURCE: Roster, 9 Cav.

Private, I/9th Cavalry, relieved of extra duty as overseer, Quartermaster Department, and detailed to extra duty as teamster, Quartermaster Department, Ft Robinson, NE. SOURCE: Special Order 76, 21 Jul 1896, Post Orders, Ft Robinson.

Resided Crawford, NE, with personal property worth $10 and taxed at $1 in 1912 and valued at $22 and taxed at $2 in 1916. SOURCE: Dawes County, NE, tax records.

WILSON, George; Private; C/9th Cav. At Ft McKinney, WY, 1894; authorized furlough in Sheridan, WY, 9–25 Jun 1894. SOURCE: Regt Returns, 9 Cav, Jun 1894.

Military convict, arrived Ft Robinson, NE, 26 Aug 1895; six-month sentence with time off for good behavior expired 22 Jan 1896; discharged. SOURCE: Regt Returns, 9 Cav, Aug 1895–Jan 1896.

WILSON, George; Private; I/10th Cav. Born Nashville, 12 Mar 1873; father George Wilson; occupation laborer; dark complexion; served in 10th Cavalry, 22 Oct 1895–18 Dec 1901; occupation in Cuba mechanic; address in 1938 was c/o American Consul, Antilla, Oriente, Cuba; died Holguin, Cuba, 20 Apr 1950. SOURCE: VA File C 2323163, George Wilson.

Served in 10th Cavalry in Cuba, 1898. SOURCE: Cashin, *Under Fire with the Tenth Cavalry*, 348.

Served with Hotchkiss gun detachment which landed in Cuba, 22 Jun 1898; took part in battle at San Juan; cared for fever patients and got fever; returned to Montauk, NY, then St. Johns Hospital, Brooklyn, NY; discharged Oct 1898; joined troop in Huntsville, AL, for muster out; witnesses: Henry Feason, D/10th Cavalry; Sherman Harris, I/10th Cavalry; William C. Martin, Hospital Corps, all in battle at San Juan. SOURCE: Affidavit, 1933, VA File C2323163, George Wilson.

WILSON, George; Private; G/10th Cav. Reduced from corporal. SOURCE: SO 91, 10 Cav, 9 Dec 1909, Ft Ethan Allen, VT, Misc Records, 10 Cav.

WILSON, Henry; D/10th Cav. Original member of 10th Cavalry; in troop when organized, Ft Leavenworth, KS, 1 Jun 1867. SOURCE: McMiller, "Buffalo Soldiers," 71.

WILSON, Henry; Private; E/9th Cav. Convicted by general court martial, Jefferson Barracks, MO, of desertion, 30 Jun–16 Nov 1885; sentenced to dishonorable discharge and three years. SOURCE: GCMO 3, AGO, 12 Jan 1886.

WILSON, Henry; Private; C/10th Cav. Served in 10th Cavalry, 1898; remained in U.S. during war with Spain. SOURCE: Cashin, *Under Fire with the Tenth Cavalry*, 340.

WILSON, Henry J.; Private; H/10th Cav. Accidentally killed, run over by troop wagon, Ft Mackenzie, WY, 30 Aug 1906. SOURCE: Regt Returns, 10 Cav, Aug 1906.

WILSON, Howard; Private; 10th Cav. Wounded in action, shot through body, Naco, AZ, 4 Oct 1914. SOURCE: Cleveland *Gazette*, 13 May 1916.

WILSON, Isaac; D/40th Inf. Tried by military commission for murder; found guilty of manslaughter and sentenced to ten years. SOURCE: SecWar, *AR 1868*, 368.

WILSON, James; Private; B/10th Cav. Original member of 10th Cavalry; in troop when organized, Ft Leavenworth, KS, 1 Apr 1867. SOURCE: McMiller, "Buffalo Soldiers," 69.

Sick in post hospital, Ft Riley, KS. SOURCE: LR, Det 10 Cav, 1868–69.

WILSON, James; I/10th Cav. Original member of 10th Cavalry; in troop when organized, Ft Riley, KS, 15 Aug 1867. SOURCE: McMiller, "Buffalo Soldiers," 76.

WILSON, James; M/10th Cav. Original member of 10th Cavalry; in troop when organized, Ft Riley, KS, 15 Oct 1867. SOURCE: McMiller, "Buffalo Soldiers," 79.

WILSON, James; Private; B/24th Inf. Murdered, Tayug, Pangasinan, Philippines, by Pvt. William Wynes, I/24th Infantry, 21 Mar 1901. SOURCE: *ANJ* 38 (6 Apr 1901): 767; Manila *Times*, 4 Apr 1901.

WILSON, James E.; Cook; E/10th Cav. Private, at Ft Apache, AZ, 1890, subscribed $.50 to testimonial to General Grierson. SOURCE: List of subscriptions, 23 Apr 1890, 10th Cavalry papers, MHI.

Retires Apr 1901. SOURCE: *ANJ* 38 (27 Apr 1901): 843.

WILSON, James S.; Private; M/24th Inf. Died of typhoid in the Philippines, 26 Nov 1900. SOURCE: *ANJ* 38 (8 Dec 1900): 355.

WILSON, Jasper; Private; F/9th Cav. At Ft D. A. Russell, WY, in 1910; resident of Leasherwood, VA. SOURCE: *Illustrated Review: Ninth Cavalry*, with picture.

WILSON, John; Private; A/10th Cav. Arrived at Ft Leavenworth, KS, from Jefferson Barracks, MO, Oct 1866. SOURCE: LS, 10 Cav, 1866–67.

Original member of 10th Cavalry; in troop when organized, Ft Leavenworth, KS, 18 Feb 1867. SOURCE: McMiller, "Buffalo Soldiers," 68.

WILSON, John; Private; K/9th Cav. Attached to Band/9th Cavalry, for instruction in music. SOURCE: Order 14, 9 Cav, 23 May 1887, Regimental Orders.

WILSON, John; Private; I/10th Cav. Served in 10th Cavalry in Cuba, 1898. SOURCE: Cashin, *Under Fire with the Tenth Cavalry*, 348.

Died of yellow fever complicated by pneumonia in Cuba, 9 Aug 1899. SOURCE: *ANJ* 36 (18 Feb 1899): 590; AG, *Correspondence Regarding the War with Spain*, I:216.

WILSON, John; Private; I/24th Inf. Native of Greensboro, NC; served three years in the Philippines; discharged in the Philippines 1902; resides in Nueva Viscaya Province with Filipino wife Angelita Gerales; has two grown children, Alfred and Isabella; age 95. SOURCE: Thompson, "Veterans Who Never Came Home," 105, with picture.

WILSON, John; Private; H/9th Cav. At Ft D. A. Russell, WY, in 1910; resident of Chicago. SOURCE: *Illustrated Review: Ninth Cavalry*.

WILSON, Joseph L.; Private; B/25th Inf. Dishonorable discharge, Brownsville. SOURCE: SO 266, AGO, 9 Nov 1906.

WILSON, Julius; H/10th Cav. Original member of 10th Cavalry; in troop when organized, Ft Leavenworth, KS, 21 Jul 1867. SOURCE: McMiller, "Buffalo Soldiers," 75.

WILSON, L.; Private; E/9th Cav. On detached service in field, New Mexico, 27 Jan–1 Feb 1881. SOURCE: Regt Returns, 9 Cav, Feb 1881.

WILSON, Leon D.; Private; L/9th Cav. At Ft D. A. Russell, WY, in 1910; resident of Houston. SOURCE: *Illustrated Review: Ninth Cavalry*, with picture.

WILSON, Leon R.; Private; E/9th Cav. Veteran of Philippine Insurrection; at Ft D. A. Russell, WY, in 1910. SOURCE: *Illustrated Review: Ninth Cavalry*, with picture.

WILSON, Morgan; Private; 10th Cav. Enlisted at Helena, AR, 20 Apr 1867. SOURCE: LS, 10 Cav, 1866–67.

WILSON, Percy T.; Private; A/10th Cav. Served in 10th Cavalry in Cuba, 1898. SOURCE: Cashin, *Under Fire with the Tenth Cavalry*, 336.

WILSON, Roy; Private; L/9th Cav. On detached service in field, New Mexico, 21 Jan–24 Feb 1881. SOURCE: Regt Returns, 9 Cav, Feb 1881.

WILSON, Tede; E/10th Cav. Original member of 10th Cavalry; in troop when organized, Ft Leavenworth, KS, 15 Jun 1867. SOURCE: McMiller, "Buffalo Soldiers," 72.

WILSON, Thomas; 10th Cav. Served 1877–91; age 60; subscriber. SOURCE: *Winners of the West* 9 (Apr 1932): 2.

WILSON, Thomas P.; Sergeant; I/24th Inf. Corporal; enlisted Tampa, FL, 10 May 1898, with eleven years' continuous service. SOURCE: Muster Roll, I/24 Inf, Jan–Feb 1899.

Promoted to sergeant, 12 Apr 1899. SOURCE: Muster Roll, I/24 Inf, Mar–Apr 1899.

On detached service at Three Rivers, CA, 3 May–21 Jun 1899; on detached service at Presidio of San Francisco, CA, since 22 Jun 1899. SOURCE: Muster Roll, I/24 Inf, May–Jun 1899.

Rejoined company from detached service. SOURCE: Muster Roll, I/24 Inf, Jul–Aug 1899.

Discharged 31 Dec 1899, character excellent; $31.38 clothing and $624 deposits. SOURCE: Muster Roll, H/24 Inf, May–Jun 1898.

WILSON, Turner; Private; I/10th Cav. Ranked number 417 among rifle experts with 69.00 percent in 1905. SOURCE: GO 101, AGO, 31 May 1906.

WILSON, Walter; Private; H/10th Cav. Served in 10th Cavalry, 1898; remained in U.S. during war with Spain. SOURCE: Cashin, *Under Fire with the Tenth Cavalry*, 347.

WILSON, Will; Private; C/9th Cav. At Ft D. A. Russell, WY, in 1910; resident of 2838 Dearborn St., Chicago. SOURCE: *Illustrated Review: Ninth Cavalry*, with picture.

WILSON, William; Private; L/10th Cav. *See* **PEARCE**, Thomas, Private, L/10th Cavalry

WILSON, William; Private; A/10th Cav. Served in 10th Cavalry, 1898; remained in U.S. during war with Spain. SOURCE: Cashin, *Under Fire with the Tenth Cavalry*, 337.

Died at Ft Robinson, NE, 8 Jun 1905. SOURCE: List of Interments, Ft Robinson.

WILSON, William; Farrier; G/9th Cav. At Ft D. A. Russell, WY, in 1910; resident of Kansas City, MO. SOURCE: *Illustrated Review: Ninth Cavalry*, with picture.

WILSON, William O.; Corporal; I/9th Cav. Born Hagerstown, MD; received Medal of Honor at Ft Robinson, NE, 17 Sep 1891. SOURCE: Lee, *Negro Medal of Honor Men*; Leckie, *The Buffalo Soldiers*, 258.

Cited among men who distinguished themselves in 1890; carried message for help through country occupied by enemy when wagon train under escort of Capt. John Loud attacked by Sioux near Pine Ridge Agency, SD; awarded Medal of Honor. SOURCE: GO 100, AGO, 17 Dec 1898.

Wagon train attacked by hostile Indians on morning of 31 Dec 1890; Corporal Wilson volunteered to ride for help; chased by Indians but succeeded; "such an example of soldier-like conduct is worthy of imitation, and reflects credit not only upon Corpl Wilson but also upon the 9th Cavalry." SOURCE: Order 13, Battalion of 9 Cav, Pine Ridge, 1 Jan 1891, quoted in *ANJ* 28 (17 Jan 1891): 355.

Commissary Department clerk, Ft Robinson; forged checks for $350 drawn on Lt. James Bettens, commissary officer, and deserted with horse and equipment; captured at Chadron, NE, and returned to post. SOURCE: *ANJ* 28 (25 Apr 1891): 593.

Reduced to private for absence without leave, forgery, and borrowing and failing to return Winchester rifle; department commander not satisfied that forgery was proved and remitted dishonorable discharge and hard labor portion of sentence. SOURCE: *ANJ* 28 (18 Jul 1891): 800.

WILSON, Willie; Private; B/10th Cav. Served in 10th Cavalry in Cuba, 1898. SOURCE: Cashin, *Under Fire with the Tenth Cavalry*, 338.

WILSON, Willie; Private; F/48th Inf. Convicted by general court martial, San Fernando, Philippines, of murder and assault and battery with intent to rape; death sentence commuted to thirty years by President McKinley. SOURCE: *ANJ* 38 (12 Jan 1901): 471.

Filed application in federal court for habeas corpus. SOURCE: San Francisco *Chronicle*, 27 Apr 1902.

Released from confinement at Leavenworth in accordance with Supreme Court's Deming decision of 19 May 1902. SOURCE: *ANJ* 39 (7 Jun 1902): 1005.

WILLMORE; Private; B/10th Cav. At Ft Apache, AZ, 1890, subscribed $.50 to testimonial to General Grierson. SOURCE: List of subscriptions, 23 Apr 1890, 10th Cavalry papers, MHI.

WIMBERLY, William; Private; F/48th Inf. Died in Minnesota, SOURCE: Taylor, "Minnesota Black Spanish-American War Veterans."

WIMMS, William M.; K/25th Inf. Has organized Sunday School for company at Castillejos, Philippines, for which men are grateful. SOURCE: Richmond *Planet*, 8 Sep 1900. *See* **WILBURN**, Thomas G., Musician, K/25th Infantry

Officiated at funeral of Pvt. Jesse B. Smith, Jan 1901. SOURCE: Richmond *Planet*, 9 Mar 1901.

To give sermon as semiweekly literary entertainment at Castillejos Y.M.C.A., 17 Mar 1901. SOURCE: Richmond *Planet*, 27 Apr 1901.

WINBURN, A. C.; Sergeant; D/10th Cav. Born in Indiana; private, saddler, corporal, sergeant, H/10th Cavalry, 14 Nov 1888–13 Nov 1893; private, D/10th Cavalry, 17 Nov 1893; corporal, 5 Mar 1897; at Ft Assiniboine, MT, 1897. SOURCE: Baker, Roster.

Served as sergeant, D/10th Cavalry in Cuba, 1898. SOURCE: Cashin, *Under Fire with the Tenth Cavalry*, 341.

Heroism in Cuba noted in unsigned letter from Montauk, NY, 8 Oct 1898. SOURCE: Gatewood, *"Smoked Yankees"*, 80.

WINCHESTER, Lucius; Private; M/10th Cav. Served in 10th Cavalry, 1898; remained in U.S. during war with Spain. SOURCE: Cashin, *Under Fire with the Tenth Cavalry*, 352.

WINCHESTER, Sandy; Sergeant; F/10th Cav. With F/10th Cavalry from 1867 until accidentally shot and killed in Santa Rosa, Mexico, early 1877; "a sore loss." SOURCE: Leckie, *The Buffalo Soldiers*, 152.

WINFIELD; Private; B/10th Cav. At Ft Apache, AZ, 1890, subscribed $.50 to testimonial to General Grierson. SOURCE: List of subscriptions, 23 Apr 1890, 10th Cavalry papers, MHI.

WINFIELD, Arthur; Trumpeter; C/9th Cav. Private, assigned as guard for Fourth of July festivities, Crawford, NE, 1887; assaulted by Pvt. Patrick Fitzgerald, C/8th Infantry, who was finally subdued by Cpl. John Parks, C/9th Cavalry. SOURCE: Post Orders, Ft Robinson.

Trumpeter, in hands of civil authorities, Salt Lake City, 28 Sep 1888. SOURCE: Regt Returns, 9 Cav, Sep 1888.

WINFIELD, Augustus P.; 1st Sgt; I/9th Cav. Sergeant, A/10th Cavalry, at Ft Apache, AZ, 1890, subscribed $.50 to testimonial to General Grierson. SOURCE: List of subscriptions, 23 Apr 1890, 10th Cavalry papers, MHI.

Private, D/9th Cavalry, transferred to Hospital Corps by letter, Adjutant General's Office, 11 Mar 1892.

Reenlistment as private, G/9th Cavalry, authorized by telegram, Adjutant General's Office, 26 Nov 1897.

First sergeant, I/9th Cavalry, stationed at Ft Washakie, WY; sick in post hospital, Ft Robinson, NE, 12 Jul–29 Aug 1896. SOURCE: Regt Returns, 9 Cav, 1896.

WING, James; F/24th Inf. Served 1880–93; subscriber. SOURCE: *Winners of the West* 9 (Oct 1932): 4.

WINGER, William H.; Private; K/10th Cav. Served in 10th Cavalry, 1898; remained in U.S. during war with Spain. SOURCE: Cashin, *Under Fire with the Tenth Cavalry*, 350.

WINN, William; Private; B/10th Cav. Served in 10th Cavalry, 1898; remained in U.S. during war with Spain. SOURCE: Cashin, *Under Fire with the Tenth Cavalry*, 333.

WINROW, William; 1st Sgt; C/10th Cav. Served as sergeant, K/19th Cavalry, 1898; remained in U.S. during war with Spain. SOURCE: Cashin, *Under Fire with the Tenth Cavalry*, 349.

Sergeant, K/10th Cavalry, at Ft Robinson, NE, 1904.

First sergeant, C/10th Cavalry, killed in action at Carrizal, Mexico, 21 Jun 1916; remains not recovered. SOURCE: Wharfield, *10th Cavalry and Border Fights*, 30, 40.

WINSLOW, Arnold; Private; C/10th Cav. Served in 10th Cavalry, 1898; remained in U.S. during war with Spain. SOURCE: Cashin, *Under Fire with the Tenth Cavalry*, 340.

WINSLOW, Oliver; D/10th Cav. Original member of 10th Cavalry; in troop when organized, Ft Leavenworth, KS, 1 Jun 1867. SOURCE: McMiller, "Buffalo Soldiers," 71.

WINSTED, Thomas; Private; B/24th Inf. At Ft McIntosh, TX, 1877. *See* **GRAYSON**, Charles H., Private, G/24th Infantry

WINSTON, Arthur W.; G/10th Cav. Served 1 Dec 1875–1 Dec 1880: "Days and even months we were on the trail of murderous Indian bands, and often we had but little to eat"; resides in Coraopolis, PA. SOURCE: *Winners of the West* 1 (Oct 1924): 19.

WINSTON, George W.; Supply Sgt; C/24th Inf. Won gold medal at rifle competition, Division of the Philippines, 1908. SOURCE: Muller, *The Twenty Fourth Infantry*, 56.

As quartermaster sergeant, B/24th Infantry, ranked number three in Division of Philippines, 1908, and number 11, Division of the Atlantic, 1909; as first sergeant, C/24th Infantry, ranked number four, Department of the Philippines, 1915; distinguished marksman, 1916. SOURCE: AGO, Bulletin 7, 29 Feb 1916.

Supply sergeant, commissioned at Des Moines, IA, training camp from 24th Infantry. SOURCE: Beasley, *Negro Trailblazers*, 285.

WINTERS, Alvin B.; Private; H/48th Inf. Died of variola in the Philippines, 25 May 1900. SOURCE: *ANJ* 37 (2 Jun 1900): 951.

WINTERS, Willie; Private; D/10th Cav. At Ft Robinson, NE, 1904; discharged on certificate of disability with venereal disease, Jul 1904. SOURCE: Certificates of Disability, Ft Robinson; CO, D/9, to CO, Ft Robinson, 9 Jul 1904, Register of LR, Ft Robinson,

WIRLEY, Augustus; F/10th Cav. Original member of 10th Cavalry; in troop when organized, Ft Leavenworth, KS, 21 Jun 1867. SOURCE: McMiller, "Buffalo Soldiers," 73.

WISEMAN, Turner H.; Corporal; K/25th Inf. Private, K/25th Infantry, sang with company's "Imperial Quartette" in the Philippines. SOURCE: Richmond *Planet*, 16 Dec 1899.

Letter from Castillejos, Philippines, 11 Mar 1900, to editor. SOURCE: Indianapolis *Freeman*, 12 May 1900.

Letter from Castillejos, 13 Apr 1900. SOURCE: Gatewood, *"Smoked Yankees"*, 275.

At San Marcelino, Philippines, 14 Aug 1900, signed resolution of condolence to families of Sgt. James Lightfoot, Cpl. William Crawford, Musician Thomas G. Wilburn, and Pvt. Tevis Bronston, all killed in action; other signers were Alexander Jones, Norman Henderson, and Henry E. Johnson; copies of resolution went to families, Richmond *Planet*, Indianapolis *Freeman*, and Augusta (GA) *Baptist*. SOURCE: Richmond *Planet*, 20 Oct 1900.

With Cpl. Thomas Jones took affirmative side in debate, "resolved that whisky is more destructive than war," at K/25th Infantry YMCA, Castillejos, Aug 1900; defeated negative team of Alexander Jones and Lorenzo McCabe; Wiseman is secretary of YMCA and former employee of Indianapolis *Freeman*. SOURCE: Richmond *Planet*, 20 Oct 1900.

At Ft Niobrara, NE, 1902; wife Lottie arrived from San Francisco, Oct 1902. SOURCE: Indianapolis *Freeman*, 15 Nov 1902.

At Ft Niobrara, 1904. SOURCE: Wilson, "History of Fort Niobrara."

WISHER, J. W.; Private; G/9th Cav. On detached service at Ft Craig, NM, 12 Jan–6 Feb 1881. SOURCE: Regt Returns, 9 Cav, Feb 1881.

WITCH, Henry; Private; A/49th Inf. Deserted from Jefferson Barracks, MO, 15 Nov 1899; "was too worthless to be subject to military discipline." SOURCE: Descriptive Book, A/49 Inf.

WITHERS, George; Private; F/9th Cav. At Ft D. A. Russell, WY, in 1910; resident of Tunica Co., VA. SOURCE: *Illustrated Review: Ninth Cavalry*, with picture.

WITHERS, Hamp; Musician; G/49th Inf. Wounded in action above knee, San Ignacio, Philippines, 18 Dec 1900. SOURCE: *ANJ* 38 (29 Dec 1900): 431.

WITHERS, William; Private; G/10th Cav. Served in 10th Cavalry, 1898; remained in U.S. during war with Spain. SOURCE: Cashin, *Under Fire with the Tenth Cavalry*, 346.

WITHERS, William H.; Private; E/9th Cav. Appointed sergeant, F/9th Cavalry, as of 4 Sep 1892. SOURCE: Roster, 9 Cav.

Private, E/9th Cavalry, detailed on special duty as assistant post librarian, Ft Robinson, NE. SOURCE: Special Order 45, 21 Apr 1897, Post Orders, Ft Robinson.

Corporal, E/9th Cavalry, on recruiting duty early 1898. SOURCE: Cashin, *Under Fire with the Tenth Cavalry*, 112.

Private, wounded seriously in action in his hand, near Malabang, Philippines, 27 Dec 1900. SOURCE: *ANJ* 38 (2 Feb 1901): 555; Hamilton, "History of the Ninth Cavalry," 103; *Illustrated Review: Ninth Cavalry*.

WITT, William; Private; M/9th Cav. Veteran of Spanish-American War; at Ft D. A. Russell, WY, in 1910; marksman. SOURCE: *Illustrated Review: Ninth Cavalry*, with picture.

WOLFE, Abraham; L/10th Cav. Original member of 10th Cavalry; in troop when organized, Ft Riley, KS, 21 Sep 1867. SOURCE: McMiller, "Buffalo Soldiers," 78.

WOLLEY, Elbert; Private; Band/24th Inf. Born Shelbyville, TN; occupation waiter; Ht 5'7"; brown eyes, black hair, mulatto; enlisted 2 Aug 1883; joined Band/24th Infantry, age 27, Ft Supply, Indian Territory, 18 Apr 1887; discharged, end of term, Ft Bayard, NM, 1 Aug 1888; character excellent, married, one child; retained $72, clothing $40.11; enlisted Ft Bayard, 2 Aug 1888; fined $5 by garrison court martial, 1889; transferred to K/24th Infantry, 11 Dec 1890, character very good, married, two children; deposits $10. SOURCE: Descriptive Book, 24 Inf NCS & Band.

Resided at 25 South 12th East, Salt Lake City, in 1898. SOURCE: Clark, "A History of the Twenty-fourth," appendix E.

WOOD, Charles W.; Private; G/10th Cav. Served in 10th Cavalry, 1898; remained in U.S. during war with Spain. SOURCE: Cashin, *Under Fire with the Tenth Cavalry*, 346.

WOOD, James T.; Private; E/49th Inf. Wounded in action, leg, in the Philippines, Feb 1901. SOURCE: *ANJ* 38 (23 Feb 1901): 631.

WOOD, John; 49th Inf. Arrested for carrying concealed weapon, San Francisco. SOURCE: San Francisco *Chronicle*, 2 Dec 1899.

WOOD, Manlus; Private; B/10th Cav. Sentenced to dishonorable discharge and confinement, Ft Robinson, NE, Dec 1902, in accordance with Special Order 223, Department of the Missouri, 1903, and released Oct 1903. SOURCE: Regt Returns, 10 Cav, Dec 1902–Oct 1903.

WOOD, Sanders; Private; K/10th Cav. Transferred from I/25th Infantry in accordance with Special Order 174, Adjutant General's Office, 26 Jul 1904.

WOOD, W. R.; Private; C/25th Inf. Ranked number seven among infantry riflemen in Department of Dakota; on department team. SOURCE: *ANJ* 35 (25 Sep 1897): 55.

WOODARD, Larry H.; Private; C/9th Cav. At Ft D. A. Russell, WY, in 1910; resident of Black Creek, NC. SOURCE: *Illustrated Review: Ninth Cavalry*, with picture.

WOODEN, Henry; L/10th Cav. Original member of 10th Cavalry; in troop when organized, Ft Riley, KS, 21 Sep 1867. SOURCE: McMiller, "Buffalo Soldiers," 78.

WOODEN, Joseph; Sergeant; H/10th Cav. Corporal, H/10th Cavalry, served in 10th Cavalry, 1898; remained in U.S. during war with Spain. SOURCE: Cashin, *Under Fire with the Tenth Cavalry*, 346.

Promoted from corporal to sergeant. SOURCE: Special Order 35, Ft Sam Houston, TX, 1 Apr 1899, Special Orders, 10 Cav.

WOODEN, Robert; Private; I/9th Cav. At Ft D. A. Russell, WY, in 1910; resident of Atlanta. SOURCE: *Illustrated Review: Ninth Cavalry*, with picture.

Killed at Ft D. A. Russell, WY, 1910. *See* STRATTON, Robert H., Private, I/9th Cavalry

WOODFIN, Richard; Private; I/10th Cav. Discharged on certificate of disability with gonorrhea from Ft Robinson, NE, 29 Nov 1904. SOURCE: Certificates of Disability, Ft Robinson.

WOODFOLK, Joseph; Private; 25th Inf. Wounded by two escaping insurgents, Castillejos, Philippines, May 1900. SOURCE: Richmond *Planet*, 28 Jul 1900.

WOODFORK, Joseph; Farrier; D/9th Cav. At Ft D. A. Russell, WY, in 1910; resident of Louisville. SOURCE: *Illustrated Review: Ninth Cavalry*, with picture.

WOODLAND, W.; Private; L/9th Cav. On detached service in field, New Mexico, 21 Jan–24 Feb 1881. SOURCE: Regt Returns, 9 Cav, Feb 1881.

WOODS; Private; A/10th Cav. At Ft Apache, AZ, 1890, subscribed $.50 to testimonial to General Grierson. SOURCE: List of subscriptions, 23 Apr 1890, 10th Cavalry papers, MHI.

WOODS; Corporal; E/25th Inf. At Ft Buford, ND, 1893. SOURCE: Nankivell, *History of the Twenty-fifth Infantry*, 50, picture.

WOODS, Brent; Corporal; C/9th Cav. Born Pulaski, KY; enlisted Jan 1879; awarded Medal of Honor as sergeant, B/9th Cavalry, rescuing white cowboys ambushed by Nana in Gavilan Canyon, around fifteen miles from McEver's Ranch, NM, 19 Aug 1881. SOURCE: Carroll, *The Black Military Experience*, 401; Leckie, *The Buffalo Soldiers*, 233; Lee, *Negro Medal of Honor Men*, 76.

Private, B/9th Cavalry, wounded in action in Mimbres Mountains, NM, along with Private Garnett, B/9th Cavalry, 3 Feb 1880. SOURCE: Hamilton, "History of the Ninth Cavalry," 50.

Sergeant, B/9th Cavalry; took charge after commander killed in Apache ambush, Gavilan Canyon, NM, Aug 1881; awarded Medal of Honor. SOURCE: Billington, *New Mexico's Buffalo Soldiers*, 106–7.

First sergeant, E/9th Cavalry, reduced to ranks at own request and transferred to B/9th Cavalry, Ft Duchesne, UT. SOURCE: Order 22, 9 Cav, 1 May 1888, Regimental Orders.

Private, C/9th Cavalry, presented Medal of Honor in front of Ft McKinney, WY, garrison by Maj. E. G. Fechet, 9th Cavalry; Fechet said, "All who know you say that this medal has been worthily bestowed. . . ." SOURCE: *ANJ* 31 (11 Aug 1894): 874–75.

Promoted from lance corporal to corporal, C/9th Cavalry, Ft Robinson, NE. SOURCE: *ANJ* 33 (12 Oct 1895): 87.

Appointed to regimental color guard, Ft Robinson, Mar 1896. SOURCE: *ANJ* 33 (28 Mar 1896): 540.

Authorized to wear knot in lieu of Medal of Honor by letter, Adjutant General's Office, 8 Oct 1897.

WOODS, Charles; H/10th Cav. Resided in Ardmore, Carter Co., OK, in 1912; known by alias George Brown. *See* BARD, Benjamin, Private, H/10th Cavalry

WOODS, Charles; Private; M/49th Inf. Engaged against enemy, Tuao, Cagayan, Philippines, 18 Oct 1900. SOURCE: *ANJ* 38 (11 May 1901): 901.

WOODS, Harry; Private; C/49th Inf. Born East St. Louis, IL, 1867; occupation musician; enlisted at St Louis, 11 Oct 1899, with three years and seven months' prior service in E/9th Cavalry and eighteen days as sergeant major, 7th Volunteer Infantry; battalion sergeant major, 49th Infantry, until reduced to ranks at own request and transferred to C/49th Infantry; resides at 3325 La Salle Street, St. Louis. SOURCE: Descriptive Book, NCS, 49 Inf.

WOODS, Herbert; Private; H/24th Inf. Enlisted New York City, 8 Jul 1898; assigned and joined company, 16 Sep 1898; sick in hospital since 30 Oct 1898, disease contracted in line of duty. SOURCE: Muster Roll, H/24 Inf, Sep–Oct 1898.

Sick in hospital, 30 Oct–2 Nov 1898. SOURCE: Muster Roll, H/24 Inf, Nov–Dec 1898.

Discharged Ft Douglas, UT, 28 Jan 1899, character good, single; deposits $15; due U.S. for clothing $24.47. SOURCE: Muster Roll, H/24 Inf, Jan–Feb 1899.

WOODS, John W.; Private; L/10th Cav. At Ft Stockton, TX, 1879. *See* SIMMONS, William, Trumpeter, L/10th Cavalry

Capt. George A. Armes, 10th Cavalry, tried to coerce Woods into signing affidavit that L/10th Cavalry rations were adequate on scout in field, May 1879, although Armes was previously informed by Woods that such statement was not true; Armes also tried to get such a statement from Pvt. John Thompson, L/10th Cavalry. SOURCE: GCMO 36, AGO, 27 May 1880.

WOODS, Noah; C/10th Cav. Original member of 10th Cavalry; in troop when organized, Ft Leavenworth, KS, 18 Feb 1867. SOURCE: McMiller, "Buffalo Soldiers," 70.

WOODS, Robert Gordon; Captain; I/49th Inf. Born Starkville, MS, 31 Mar 1870; educated at University of Holly Springs, MS; enlisted in 24th Infantry, Memphis, 6 Jul 1889; assigned to G/24th Infantry, San Carlos, AZ, 10 Jan 1890; discharged Ft Bayard, NM, 5 Jul 1894, character excellent; enlisted St. Louis, 23 Jul 1894; clerk in Quartermaster Department, Jul 1895; company clerk, 1 Mar 1896; sergeant and first sergeant, 27 Aug 1896; first sergeant in Cuba and youngest first sergeant in Army; only he, Sgts. J. T. Williams and W. H. Carroll, and Pvt. Samuel Bradshaw in G/24th Infantry did not get yellow fever while stationed at Siboney yellow fever camp; stationed at Ft Douglas, UT, Oct 1898, when commissioned and appointed adjutant, 3rd Battalion, 9th Volunteer Infantry. SOURCE: Coston, *The Spanish-American War Volunteer*, 79, 82.

First sergeant, G/24th Infantry, in Cuba, 1898. SOURCE: Scipio, *Last of the Black Regulars*, 24.

At San Juan Hill, Cuba, 1898. SOURCE: Beasley, *Negro Trailblazers*, 216.

Commissioned second lieutenant, 9th Volunteer Infantry, after Spanish-American War. SOURCE: Cashin, *Under Fire with the Tenth Cavalry*, 360.

Appointed captain, I/49th Infantry, 9 Sep 1899; previous service in G/24th Infantry, 6 Jul 1889–26 Oct 1898, and second lieutenant, 9th Volunteer Infantry, 24 Oct 1898–25 May 1899; on recruiting duty, Little Rock and Pine Bluff, AR, 22 Sep–16 Oct 1899; scouting, 28–31 Oct 1900, and commander, advance guard of expedition, the Philippines, Nov 1900; in emergency notify Mrs. Irene G. Woods, Columbus, MS. SOURCE: Descriptive Book, I/49 Inf.

One of twenty-three officers of 49th Infantry recommended as regular Army second lieutenants. SOURCE: CG, DivPI, Manila, 8 Feb 1901, to AGO, AGO File 355163.

Remained in Manila, Philippines, after discharge to "grow up with the country"; was T. Thomas Fortune's traveling companion, "a man of splendid physique and a military bearing"; had been military governor of Province of Isabella, Philippines. SOURCE: Fortune, "The Filipino," 96, 200, 241, with picture.

Back in U.S. for visit; now chief clerk, Quartermaster Office, Insular Constabulary, Manila, which is his permanent home; believes Philippines an attractive field for "ambitious and energetic young colored men"; reports that "many progressive Afro-Americans" are "making good" there, including Lts. David J. Gilmer, Edward L. Baker, and John E. Green. SOURCE: Indianapolis *Freeman*, 27 Oct 1906.

Chief Clerk, Philippine army, 1937; wrote account of role in battle on San Juan Hill, Cuba, 1898. SOURCE: Woods to AG, USA, 29 Jun 1937, in Scipio, *Last of the Black Regulars*, 29.

WOODS, Thomas; Private; C/10th Cav. Served in 10th Cavalry in Cuba, 1898. SOURCE: Cashin, *Under Fire with the Tenth Cavalry*, 340.

WOODS, West; Trumpeter; K/10th Cav. At Ft Apache, AZ, 1890, subscribed $.50 to testimonial to General Grierson. SOURCE: List of subscriptions, 23 Apr 1890, 10th Cavalry papers, MHI.

WOODS, Willie; Private; C/10th Cav. Served in 10th Cavalry, 1898; remained in U.S. during war with Spain. SOURCE: Cashin, *Under Fire with the Tenth Cavalry*, 340.

WOODS, Woodson; B/10th Cav. Original member of 10th Cavalry; in troop when organized, Ft Leavenworth, KS, 1 Apr 1867. SOURCE: McMiller, "Buffalo Soldiers," 69.

WOODSIDE, John; Saddler; C/9th Cav. At Ft D. A. Russell, WY, in 1910; sharpshooter; resident of Statesville, NC. SOURCE: *Illustrated Review: Ninth Cavalry*, with picture.

WOODSON, James; Private; C/25th Inf. Dishonorable discharge, Brownsville. SOURCE: SO 266, AGO, 9 Nov 1906.

WOODSON, Lee; Cook; C/9th Cav. Served as private, K/10th Cavalry, 1898; remained in U.S. during war with Spain. SOURCE: Cashin, *Under Fire with the Tenth Cavalry*, 350.

Veteran of Spanish-American War and Philippine Insurrection; cook, C/9th Cavalry, at Ft D. A. Russell, WY, in 1910; resident of St. Louis. SOURCE: *Illustrated Review: Ninth Cavalry*, with picture.

WOODWARD; Private; L/9th Cav. Killed in action, 30 Sep 1879. *See* **JOHNSON**, Private, L/9th Cavalry

WOODWARD, Otho J.; QM Sgt; L/10th Cav. Served as private, C/10th Cavalry in Cuba, 1898. SOURCE: Cashin, *Under Fire with the Tenth Cavalry*, 340.

Ranked number 12, Northern Division pistol team, Ft Riley, KS, 1904. SOURCE: GO 167, AGO, 28 Oct 1904.

Thirteenth best pistol shot, Northern Division cavalry, 1904. SOURCE: Glass, *History of the Tenth Cavalry*, 44.

WOODY, C.; Sergeant; C/10th Cav. Stationed in Department of Texas; ranked number 12 on Division of the Missouri rifle team. SOURCE: GO 88, AGO, 13 Dec 1881.

Ranked number seven in rifle competition, Department of Texas, bronze medal, and number 12, Division of the Missouri, silver medal. SOURCE: Baker, Roster.

WOODY, Clayborn; Private; A/9th Cav. In K/9th Cavalry, convicted by garrison court martial, Ft Robinson, NE, of abusive language to employee of post trader and insubordination to 1st Sgt. George Jordan, K/9th Cavalry; sentenced to ten days. SOURCE: Order 238, 2 Dec 1887, Post Orders, Ft Robinson.

Funeral at Ft Robinson, 9 Aug 1891. SOURCE: Order 161, 8 Aug 1891, Post Orders, Ft Robinson.

WOOLEY, Albert; 24th Inf. *See* **WOLLEY**, Elbert, Private, Band/24th Infantry

WOOLEY, William; Band/24th Inf. Defeated John A. Johnson, A/24th Infantry, in boxing match, Ft Bayard, NM, 13 Dec 1889. SOURCE: *ANJ* 27 (28 Dec 1889): 353.

WORKMAN, William; Private; D/24th Inf. Fined $10 at Cabanatuan, Philippines, 19 Dec 1900, for insubordination to Cpl. Squire Williams, D/24th Infantry. SOURCE: Name File, 24 Inf.

At Cabanatuan, 1901. *See* **STONE**, John H., Private, D/24th Infantry

WORLD, William; Sergeant; B/9th Cav. Appointed sergeant as of 27 Jan 1886. SOURCE: Roster, 9 Cav.

WORLEY, George; Private; B/10th Cav. Original member of 10th Cavalry; in troop when organized, Ft Leavenworth, KS, 1 Apr 1867. SOURCE: McMiller, "Buffalo Soldiers," 69.

Mentioned 1873. SOURCE: ES, 10 Cav, 1873–83.

WORMLEY, Fredrick; Corporal; A/38th Inf. At Ft Cummings, NM, 1867–68. SOURCE: Billington, *New Mexico's Buffalo Soldiers*, pp. 29–30.

WORMLEY, James; Corporal; D/10th Cav. Served in 10th Cavalry in Cuba, 1898. SOURCE: Cashin, *Under Fire with the Tenth Cavalry*, 341.

WORMSLEY, William C.; Captain; 49th Inf. In D/9th Cavalry, 12 Mar 1887–11 Mar 1892; first lieutenant and surgeon, 49th Infantry, 9 Sep 1899; captain and surgeon, 8 Jun 1900. SOURCE: Descriptive Book, Field & Staff, 49 Inf.

Private, D/9th Cavalry, at Ft Robinson, NE, for trial for desertion, 26 Oct 1889–22 Jan 1890, and returned to station, Ft McKinney, WY. SOURCE: Regt Returns, 9 Cav, Oct 1889–Jan 1890.

In guardhouse, Ft Robinson, Dec 1889, complained of being worked with prisoners since arrival to stand trial, 20 Oct 1889; still awaiting trial. SOURCE: Report of Inspection, Ft Robinson, 2 Dec 1889, Reports of Inspections, DP, I.

On extra duty as schoolteacher, Ft Robinson, 1 Nov 1891–31 Jan 1892. SOURCE: Reports of Schools, Ft Robinson, 1892–96.

Letter from San Luis, Cuba, 19 May 1899. SOURCE: Gatewood, *"Smoked Yankees"*, 231.

Physician who settled in Tuguegarao, Luzon, Philippines, after discharge; practices medicine, runs drugstore, has several large tobacco plantations. SOURCE: Fortune, "The Filipino," 245.

Mentioned. SOURCE: Beasley, *Negro Trailblazers*, 284.

WORRIOR, Scott; Private; D/10th Cav. Served in 10th Cavalry, 1898; remained in U.S. during war with Spain. SOURCE: Cashin, *Under Fire with the Tenth Cavalry*, 341.

WORTHAM, George W.; Private; K/9th Cav. Died of cholera in the Philippines, 16 Jun 1902. SOURCE: *ANJ* 39 (9 Aug 1902): 1248.

WORTHINGTON, Moses; F/10th Cav. Original member of 10th Cavalry; in troop when organized, Ft Leavenworth, KS, 21 Jun 1867. SOURCE: McMiller, "Buffalo Soldiers," 73.

WRACKS, Charles; Private; B/9th Cav. Sentenced to two months' confinement, Ft Duchesne, UT, for threatening to blow out brains of Dr. R. B. Benham, U.S. Army, because latter refused to excuse him from fatigue duty.

WRIGHT, Aaron; M/10th Cav. Original member of 10th Cavalry; in troop when organized, Ft Riley, KS, 15 Oct 1867. SOURCE: McMiller, "Buffalo Soldiers," 79.

WRIGHT, Albert; Private; I/24th Inf. Involved in Houston riot, 1917: "I will shoot up every white son-of-a-bitch on Washington Street"; confessed to part in riot but refused to testify against comrades. SOURCE: Haynes, *A Night of Violence*, 103, 130, 215.

Sentenced to hang for part in Houston riot. SOURCE: Cleveland *Gazette*, 5 Jan 1918.

WRIGHT, Benjamin; Recruit; D/9th Cav. Convicted by general court martial, Jefferson Barracks, MO, of desertion, 13–22 Nov 1882; sentence of dishonorable discharge and four years reduced to two years by General Sherman. SOURCE: GCMO 83, AGO, 21 Dec 1882.

WRIGHT, Daniel; Sergeant; K/9th Cav. Served at Ft Reno, Indian Territory, 1884, when Rufus Slaughter contracted rheumatism. SOURCE: Wright, Affidavit, [n.d.], VA File XC 2648848, Rufus Slaughter.

WRIGHT, George; Private; K/25th Inf. At Ft Niobrara, NE, 1904. SOURCE: Wilson, "History of Fort Niobrara."

WRIGHT, J. W.; Sergeant; C/25th Inf. Led detachment of eight from station at Ft Stockton, TX, in search of overdue mail stage in vicinity of Pecos Station, TX, Oct 1877. SOURCE: Nankivell, *History of the Twenty-fifth Infantry*, 28.

WRIGHT, James; H/10th Cav. Original member of 10th Cavalry; in troop when organized, Ft Leavenworth, KS, 21 Jul 1867. SOURCE: McMiller, "Buffalo Soldiers," 75.

WRIGHT, James; D/40th Inf. Acquitted of manslaughter by military commission, Aug 1868. SOURCE: SecWar, *AR 1868*, 368.

WRIGHT, James; Private; C/10th Cav. Dishonorably discharged from Ft Griffin, TX, spring 1870. SOURCE: ES, 10 Cav, 1866–71.

WRIGHT, James; Private; D/9th Cav. Veteran of Philippine Insurrection; at Ft D. A. Russell, WY, in 1910; marksman; resident of La Grange, GA. SOURCE: *Illustrated Review: Ninth Cavalry*, with picture.

WRIGHT, James H.; Private; I/9th Cav. Veteran of Philippine Insurrection; at Ft D. A. Russell, WY, in 1910; resident of Plymouth, NC. SOURCE: *Illustrated Review: Ninth Cavalry*, with picture.

WRIGHT, Jerry; 25th Inf. Transferred from Reserve Divisional Hospital, Siboney, Cuba, to U.S. on U.S. Army Transport *Santiago* with yellow fever, 25 Jul 1898. SOURCE: Hospital Papers, Spanish-American War.

WRIGHT, John; Corporal; L/10th Cav. Original member of 10th Cavalry; in troop when organized, Ft Riley, KS, 21 Sep 1867. SOURCE: McMiller, "Buffalo Soldiers," 78.

Escort for convict to Weatherford, TX, Apr 1873. SOURCE: Leckie, *The Buffalo Soldiers*, 73.

WRIGHT, John; Private; C/10th Cav. Served in 10th Cavalry, 1898; remained in U.S. during war with Spain. SOURCE: Cashin, *Under Fire with the Tenth Cavalry*, 340.

WRIGHT, John C.; Private; H/9th Cav. At Ft D. A. Russell, WY, in 1910; resident of Lowell, NC. SOURCE: *Illustrated Review: Ninth Cavalry*, with picture.

WRIGHT, John W.; Sergeant; G/10th Cav. Letter from Ft Grant, AZ, extols opportunity in West. SOURCE: Cleveland *Gazette*, 26 Jan 1889.

At Ft Grant, 1890. *See* **BERRY**, Edward, Sergeant, H/24th Infantry

At Ft Apache, AZ, 1890, subscribed $.50 to testimonial to General Grierson. SOURCE: List of subscriptions, 23 Apr 1890, 10th Cavalry papers, MHI.

WRIGHT, Jonas; I/10th Cav. Original member of 10th Cavalry; in troop when organized, Ft Riley, KS, 15 Aug 1867. SOURCE: McMiller, "Buffalo Soldiers," 76.

WRIGHT, Lincoln; Private; 48th Inf. Sick in the Philippines, Feb 1900. SOURCE: Richmond *Planet*, 14 Apr 1900.

WRIGHT, Marcellous; Corporal; G/10th Cav. Served in 10th Cavalry in Cuba, 1898; wounded in action. SOURCE: Cashin, *Under Fire with the Tenth Cavalry*, 345.

Wounded in action at Santiago, Cuba, 1 Jul 1898. SOURCE: SecWar, *AR 1898*, 324.

WRIGHT, Nealy; 10th Cav. Body transferred from Montauk Point, NY, to national cemetery at Cypress Hills, NY. SOURCE: *ANJ* 37 (21 Jan 1899): 480.

WRIGHT, R. L.; Private; G/24th Inf. Moved to Reserve General Hospital, Siboney, Cuba, with yellow fever, 22 Jun 1898; transferred from Reserve Divisional Hospital to U.S. on U.S. Army Transport *Santiago* with yellow fever, 25 Jul 1898. SOURCE: Hospital Papers, Spanish-American War.

WRIGHT, Samuel; Corporal; D/9th Cav. Killed in action near Ft Lancaster, TX, by Kickapoos, 11 Oct 1867, while escorting Camp Hudson-Ft Stockton, TX, mail along with Pvt. Eldridge T. Jones, D/9th Cavalry. SOURCE: Leckie, *The Buffalo Soldiers*, 84–85; Hamilton, "History of the Ninth Cavalry," 7; Ninth Cavalry, *Historical and Pictorial Review*, 45; *Illustrated Review: Ninth Cavalry*.

WRIGHT, Thomas; A/10th Cav. Original member of 10th Cavalry; in troop when organized, Ft Leavenworth, KS, 18 Feb 1867. SOURCE: McMiller, "Buffalo Soldiers," 68.

WRIGHT, Thomas; B/10th Cav. Original member of 10th Cavalry; in troop when organized, Ft Leavenworth, KS, 1 Apr 1867. SOURCE: McMiller, "Buffalo Soldiers," 69.

WRIGHT, Thomas H.; L/10th Cav. Original member of 10th Cavalry; in troop when organized, Ft Riley, KS, 21 Sep 1867. SOURCE: McMiller, "Buffalo Soldiers," 78.

WRIGHT, Will; Private; D/10th Cav. Served in 10th Cavalry, 1898; remained in U.S. during war with Spain. SOURCE: Cashin, *Under Fire with the Tenth Cavalry*, 341.

WRIGHT, William; Private; 10th Cav. Wright's whereabouts unknown but regimental commander believes pardon from governor of Texas would reclaim him for the service and he so requests. SOURCE: CO, 10 Cav, Ft Concho, TX, to Governor of Texas, 31 Dec 1876, LS, 10 Cav, 1873–83.

WYATT, John; 49th Inf. Arrested for exhibiting deadly weapon. SOURCE: San Francisco *Chronicle*, 2 Dec 1899.

WYATT, Mathew; Private; G/9th Cav. Witness for prosecution in court martial of Sgt. Barney McKay, G/9th Cavalry, Ft Robinson, NE, 1893; claims to have been ostracized in troop since he told commander of McKay's possession of incendiary leaflet; illiterate. SOURCE: Court Martial Records, McKay.

WYATT, Nathan; Trumpeter; A/10th Cav. Served in 10th Cavalry in Cuba, 1898. SOURCE: Cashin, *Under Fire with the Tenth Cavalry*, 336.

Wounded in action at Santiago, Cuba, 1 Jul 1898. SOURCE: SecWar, *AR 1898*, 324.

WYLIE, Daniel; Sergeant; K/9th Cav. Sergeant as of 26 Feb 1883. SOURCE: Roster, 9 Cav.

Vice president of K Troop's Diamond Club, Ft Robinson, NE, 1891. SOURCE: *ANJ* 28 (2 May 1891): 620.

At Ft Robinson, 1895; sergeant since 6 [*sic*] Feb 1883. SOURCE: *ANJ* 33 (7 Dec 1895): 236.

Reenlistment as married soldier authorized by letter, Adjutant General's Office, 6 Nov 1895.

WYLIE, Milton; Private; B/10th Cav. Enlisted Memphis, spring 1867. SOURCE: LS, 10 Cav, 1866–67.

Discharged on certificate of disability, 16 Oct 1867. SOURCE: CO, 10 Cav, to AG, USA, 17 Oct 1867, LS, 10 Cav, 1866–67.

WYNES, William; Private; I/24th Inf. Enlisted Macon, GA, 27 Jun 1899. SOURCE: Muster Roll, I/24 Inf, Jul–Aug 1899.

Allotted $8 per month for six months to Alice Carter. SOURCE: Muster Roll, I/24 Inf, Sep–Oct 1899.

On detached service at Cabanatuan, Philippines, since 30 Dec 1899. SOURCE: Muster Roll, I/24 Inf, Nov–Dec 1899.

Hanged for murder of Pvt. James Wilson, B/24th Infantry, Tayug, Pangasinan, Philippines, 21 Mar 1900. SOURCE: Manila *Times*, 4 and 21 Dec 1901.

WYNN, Alexander; Private; C/9th Cav. Arrived at Ft Robinson, NE, from depot, 1 Mar 1887. SOURCE: Regt Returns, 9 Cav, Mar 1887.

y

YANCEY, Thomas; Private; M/10th Cav. Served in 10th Cavalry, 1898; remained in U.S. during war with Spain. SOURCE: Cashin, *Under Fire with the Tenth Cavalry*, 352.

Died of accidental gunshot wound, Manzanillo, Cuba, 28 Dec 1900. SOURCE: *ANJ* 38 (9 Feb 1901): 579.

YATES, Will; Private; A/9th Cav. At Ft D. A. Russell, WY, in 1910. SOURCE: *Illustrated Review: Ninth Cavalry*, with picture.

YEARGOOD, Evert; Private; H/9th Cav. Died of cholera in the Philippines, 10 Jun 1902. SOURCE: *ANJ* 39 (9 Aug 1902): 1248.

YEATMAN, William; 1st Sgt; A/38th Inf. At Ft Cummings, NM, autumn 1867. SOURCE: Billington, *New Mexico's Buffalo Soldiers*, 39–40, 42.

YELVERTON, Aaron; F/25th Inf. Methodist, stationed at Botolen, Zambales, Philippines, Dec 1900. SOURCE: Steward, *Fifty Years in the Gospel Ministry*, 326.

YERZER, Charles G.; Private; 24th Inf. Drowned at Cabanatuan, Philippines, 27 Nov 1900, while unassigned. SOURCE: Name File, 24 Inf; *ANJ* 38 (12 Jan 1901): 479.

YORK, Edward; 1st Sgt; A/9th Cav. At Ft D. A. Russell, WY, in 1910; sharpshooter. SOURCE: *Illustrated Review: Ninth Cavalry*, with picture.

YOUNG; Private; H/10th Cav. *See* BATTLES, Private, H/10th Cavalry

YOUNG; Sergeant; L/10th Cav. Shot and almost killed by wife near Ft Grant, AZ; she is in jail under $1,000 bond. SOURCE: Cleveland *Gazette*, 15 Jan 1887.

YOUNG; Private; A/10th Cav. At Ft Apache, AZ, 1890, subscribed $.50 to testimonial to General Grierson. SOURCE: List of subscriptions, 23 Apr 1890, 10th Cavalry papers, MHI.

YOUNG; Sergeant; C/10th Cav. Discharged in accordance with Special Order 254, Adjutant General's Office, 29 Oct 1902.

YOUNG, Buford; Private; G/10th Cav. Served in 10th Cavalry, 1898; remained in U.S. during war with Spain. SOURCE: Cashin, *Under Fire with the Tenth Cavalry*, 346.

YOUNG, Charles; Lt Col; U.S. Army. Born in Kentucky, 1868; U.S. Military Academy graduate. SOURCE: *Leslie's Weekly* 87 (25 Aug 1898): 143.

On graduation from military academy, assigned to A/25th Infantry, Ft Custer, MT. SOURCE: *ANJ* 27 (12 Oct 1889): 122.

Second lieutenant, 9th Cavalry; mentioned as 1889 graduate of U.S. Military Academy. SOURCE: Billington, *New Mexico's Buffalo Soldiers*, 190.

"A colored man, graduate of West Point, joined the post [Ft Robinson, NE] for duty." SOURCE: Corliss, Diary, II, 28 Nov 1889.

Arrived at Ft Robinson after graduation leave; assigned to B/9th Cavalry; transferred to Ft Duchesne, UT, with unit. SOURCE: Post Returns, Ft Robinson, Nov 1889–Sep 1890.

Mentioned. SOURCE: *ANJ* 27 (16 Nov 1889) and 27 (18 Jan 1890).

Commander, Ft Robinson, to Young, 5 Apr 1890, complains of his "tactical errors" as officer of the guard. SOURCE: LS, Ft Robinson.

Commander, Ft Robinson, to Young, 28 Apr 1890, reprimands him for neglect of stable duty. SOURCE: LS, Ft Robinson.

Young has had more consideration than any white officer; commander hopes he will improve. SOURCE: CO, Ft Robinson, through AAG, DP, to AG, USA, 7 May 1890, LS, Ft Robinson.

Young required to vacate his quarters; Major Randlett's quarters to be considered two sets when he vacates and Young will be allowed to choose one of them. SOURCE: CO, Ft Robinson, to Post QM, 24 Jun 1890, LS, Ft Robinson.

Granted forty-five days leave from Ft Duchesne. SOURCE: *ANJ* 28 (20 Jun 1891): 732.

Officer-in-charge and teacher, post school, Ft Duchesne, 1 Nov 1892–30 Apr 1893. SOURCE: Reports of Post School, Ft Duchesne.

At Ft Duchesne with 9th Cavalry, then transferred to Wilberforce University as professor of military science, then to L/9th Cavalry. SOURCE: Clark, "A History of the Twenty-fourth," 11–12.

To succeed Lieutenant Alexander as military instructor, Wilberforce University. SOURCE: Cleveland *Gazette*, 26 May 1894.

On detached service from Ft Robinson at Wilberforce University from 1 Sep 1894. SOURCE: Post Returns, Ft Robinson, Sep 1894.

Directed to appear before examination board, Ft Leavenworth, KS, by Special Order 208, Adjutant General's Office, 3 Sep 1896.

In Leavenworth for promotion examination, could not get accommodations in town and had to stay in Kansas City, MO. SOURCE: *ANJ* 34 (19 Sep 1896): 40.

Military instructor at Wilberforce, passed examination at Leavenworth for promotion to first lieutenant; now paid $1,800 per year, "has a handsomely furnished home free, and is only 32 years old." SOURCE: Cleveland *Gazette*, 12 Dec 1896.

Relieved from duty at Wilberforce to command battalion of Ohio colored volunteers; said to be first instance in which colored officer has commanded battalion in Army. SOURCE: Richmond *Planet*, 21 May 1898.

Commander, I/9th Cavalry, Ft Duchesne, as of 31 Dec 1900. SOURCE: Hamilton, "History of the Ninth Cavalry," 102.

Captain, I/9th Cavalry, Nov 1901. SOURCE: *ANJ* 39 (9 Nov 1901): 234.

"The colored officer of the Ninth Cavalry, who will in future be stationed at the Presidio, was a great favorite on the *Sheridan* coming from Manila to San Francisco, and was in great demand. His skin is of the darkest hue of the race, but he is exceedingly clever, a West Point graduate, and a pianist of rare ability." SOURCE: Indianapolis *Freeman*, 27 Dec 1902.

At the Presidio of San Francisco, CA, 1902. *See* **FARRINGTON**, George W., Private, I/9th Cavalry

Lt. B. R. Tillman, son of Benjamin R. Tillman, "the South Carolina Negro hater," gave banquet to number of Army officers, including Captain Young; when asked if he had made a mistake in inviting Young, he said, "No, he is a gentleman and a friend of mine." SOURCE: Indianapolis *Freeman*, 31 Jan 1903.

Biographical article. SOURCE: *Colored American Magazine* 4 (Jan–Feb 1904): 249–50.

Selected for duty as military attaché to Haiti and Santo Domingo. SOURCE: Indianapolis *Freeman*, 4 Jun 1904.

Young's letter from Wilberforce, OH, 29 Jun 1907, solicits funds to build monument to Paul Lawrence Dunbar; $500 collected so far, mostly from whites. SOURCE: Cleveland *Gazette*, 3 Aug 1907.

Captain and commander, I/9th Cavalry, at Ft D. A. Russell, WY, in 1910; veteran of Philippine Insurrection. SOURCE: *Illustrated Review: Ninth Cavalry*, with picture.

On three-officer board investigating vandalism at Ft D. A. Russell. SOURCE: Wyoming *Tribune*, 5 Aug 1911.

To be promoted to major in the autumn; will command third squadron, 9th Cavalry, and have achieved highest rank except for chaplains. SOURCE: Cleveland *Gazette*, 12 Aug 1911.

Went to Liberia with three young men of his choosing to organize and equip the Liberian army, his group including Wilson Ballard, Major, Liberian Defense Forces, who stayed five years; Young replaced in 1916 by John Green, who continued to help government settle its many border disputes. SOURCE: Fletcher, "The Negro Soldier," 172, 178.

Assigned to military attaché duty in Liberia; soon to be major. SOURCE: Cleveland *Gazette*, 6 Jan 1912.

Accompanied to Liberia by three bright young Afro-American college men to organize Liberian constabulary; they have military titles conferred by Liberian government and include Dr. (Capt.) Arthur M. Brown, at $1,600 per year and quarters. SOURCE: Cleveland *Gazette*, 10 Feb 1912.

Just promoted, on duty as military attaché in Liberia; holds highest rank of any Negro in regular Army; graduate of U.S. Military Academy, "quiet, unassuming and very popular." SOURCE: Wyoming *Tribune*, 14 Sep 1912.

Mentioned. SOURCE: Work, *The Negro Year Book, 1912*, 77.

Led successful Liberian effort to suppress revolt of coastal Croo tribe. SOURCE: Cleveland *Gazette*, 15 Feb 1913.

Slightly wounded in action in recent conflict with Liberian natives. SOURCE: Cleveland *Gazette*, 5 Apr 1913.

"An army officer in Washington, D.C., is authority for the following 'tribute' to Young's discretion: 'Army etiquette requires that all officers at a post make a call on a newcomer, an officer, at the earliest possible moment after his arrival. Major Charles Young, who was stationed at a post where I was, waited as long as possible, and then having ascertained beyond a doubt that the new officer was not at home, called and left his card. It goes to show Major Young's appreciation of his position.' RATS!" SOURCE: Cleveland *Gazette*, 11 Apr 1914.

To command Haitian constabulary although he wants to resume command of his battalion of the 10th Cavalry on the Mexican border in Arizona. SOURCE: Cleveland *Gazette*, 12 Feb 1916.

Awarded Spingarn Medal by Governor S. W. McCall of Massachusetts at meeting of the National Association for the Advancement of Colored People; medal for "the Afro-American male or female, who has made the highest achievement during the preceding year in any field of elevated or honorable human endeavor." SOURCE: Cleveland *Gazette*, 26 Feb 1916.

Received Spingarn Medal for work in organizing and training Liberian constabulary. SOURCE: Cleveland *Gazette*, 4 Mar 1916.

"Young Promoted!" to lieutenant colonel. SOURCE: Cleveland *Gazette*, 15 Jul 1916.

Led in fight against Pancho Villa at Aguas Calientes, Chihuahua, Mexico; charged on horseback and routed enemy without fire; led 10th Cavalry to rescue of 13th Cavalry at Santa Cruz de Villegas, Chihuahua, 1916; Maj. Frank Tompkins of 13th said, "By God, Young, I could kiss every black face out there"; Young, unsmiling, responded, "Well, Tompkins, if you want to, you may start with me." SOURCE: Clendenen, *Blood on the Border*, 257, 259.

Camp No. 24, National Indian War Veterans, Washington, D.C., first all-black camp and bears his name, meets at U.S. Soldiers Home but membership drawn from city as well as the Home. SOURCE: *Winners of the West* 6 (May 1929): 1.

Biographical sketch. SOURCE: Logan and Winston, eds., *Dictionary of American Negro Biography*, 677–79.

YOUNG, Charles; Private; C/10th Cav. Served in 10th Cavalry in Cuba, 1898. SOURCE: Cashin, *Under Fire with the Tenth Cavalry*, 340.

YOUNG, Charles; Sergeant; B/9th Cav. Veteran of Spanish-American War and Philippine Insurrection; at Ft D. A. Russell, WY, in 1910; sharpshooter. SOURCE: *Illustrated Review: Ninth Cavalry*, with picture.

YOUNG, Charles H.; Private; C/9th Cav. Fined $5 by garrison court martial, Ft Robinson, NE, for altercation in barracks, 11 Sep 1887. SOURCE: Order 188, 23 Sep 1887, Post Orders, Ft Robinson.

In hands of civil authorities, Crawford, NE, 11–20 Dec 1887, Rock Springs, WY, 1 Jul–Oct 1888, Salt Lake City, 28 Sep 1888. SOURCE: Regt Returns, 9 Cav.

See **HUFF**, Willis, Private, C/9th Cavalry

YOUNG, Clark; Private; M/10th Cav. Killed in action at Cheyenne Agency, Indian Territory, 6 Apr 1875. SOURCE: Leckie, *The Buffalo Soldiers*, 139.

Died of wounds received in action at Cheyenne Agency. SOURCE: CO, 10 Cav, to AG, USA, 18 Jun 1875, ES, 10 Cav, 1873–83.

YOUNG, Clem; Private; H/9th Cav. At Ft D. A. Russell, WY, in 1910; sharpshooter; resident of Grand Chain, IL. SOURCE: *Illustrated Review: Ninth Cavalry*, with picture.

YOUNG, Curley; Private; K/10th Cav. Cook with Lt. John Bigelow in Oct 1885; confined at Ft Grant, AZ, for theft of seven loaves of bread from camp at Clifton, AZ. SOURCE: Bigelow, *On the Bloody Trail of Geronimo*, 86.

YOUNG, David; Private; K/10th Cav. Original member of 10th Cavalry; in troop when organized, Ft Riley, KS, 1 Sep 1867. SOURCE: McMiller, "Buffalo Soldiers," 77.

Detailed teamster. SOURCE: SO 54, HQ, Det 10 Cav, Camp Supply, Indian Territory, 31 Jul 1869, Orders, Det 10 Cav.

Commander, 10th Cavalry, forwards final statement of late Private Young to Adjutant General, 18 Jan 1870. SOURCE: LS, 10 Cav, 1866–67.

YOUNG, David; M/10th Cav. Original member of 10th Cavalry; in troop when organized, Ft Riley, KS, 15 Oct 1867. SOURCE: McMiller, "Buffalo Soldiers," 79.

YOUNG, David; Recruit; 10th Cav. Mentioned Mar 1877 as having enlisted in Jan 1877. SOURCE: ES, 10 Cav, 1873–83.

YOUNG, Frank; Private; K/24th Inf. At Cabanatuan, Philippines, 1901. *See* **MOORE**, Cato, Private, D/24th Infantry

YOUNG, George; Private; K/25th Inf. At Ft Niobrara, NE, 1904. SOURCE: Wilson, "History of Fort Niobrara."

YOUNG, Hartwell; Sergeant; F/25th Cav. Retires from Ft Missoula, MT. SOURCE: *ANJ* 28 (13 Jun 1891): 714.

YOUNG, Jacob; Sergeant; B/10th Cav. Adjutant, 10th Cavalry, Ft Sill, Indian Territory, returns Private Young's complaint of unjust treatment and request for trial, 16 Dec 1870; Young is former first sergeant, H/10th Cavalry, reduced in accordance with law and transferred for sufficient reason; should be thankful he was not tried as would have gotten heavier punishment. SOURCE: ES, 10 Cav, 1866–71.

Request of Sergeant Young, B/10th Cavalry, for transfer disapproved; no reason shown. SOURCE: CO, 10 Cav, to Young, 18 Dec 1875, ES, 10 Cav, 1873–83.

YOUNG, James; Private; E/10th Cav. Original member of 10th Cavalry; in troop when organized, Ft Leavenworth, KS, 15 Jun 1867. SOURCE: McMiller, "Buffalo Soldiers," 72.

Commander, 10th Cavalry, forwards duplicate final statement and inventory of effects of late Private Young to adjutant general, 30 Jun 1870. SOURCE: ES, 10 Cav, 1866–71.

YOUNG, James; Private; K/24th Inf. Mentioned among men who distinguished themselves in 1889; awarded certificate of merit for gallant and meritorious service while escort for Maj. Joseph W. Wham, paymaster, when attacked by band of robbers between Fts Grant and Thomas, AZ; now out of service. SOURCE: GO 18, AGO, 1891.

YOUNG, James; Private; M/10th Cav. Served in 10th Cavalry, 1898; remained in U.S. during war with Spain. SOURCE: Cashin, *Under Fire with the Tenth Cavalry*, 352.

YOUNG, James H.; Private; D/24th Inf. At Cabanatuan, Philippines, 1901. *See* **PRIDE**, Wheeler, Private, D/24th Infantry

YOUNG, James H.; Colonel; 3rd NC Inf. Born slave, Henderson Co., NC; attended Shaw University; served in state legislature before becoming colonel of 3rd North Carolina Infantry. SOURCE: Fletcher, "The Negro Soldier," 237.

Professor C. F. Meserve of Shaw University describes visit with Young. SOURCE: Johnson, *History of Negro Soldiers*, 109–12.

Died in 1921. SOURCE: *Crisis* 22 (Jun 1921): 87.

YOUNG, Jerry; Sergeant; L/10th Cav. Original member of 10th Cavalry; in troop when organized, Ft Riley, KS, 21 Sep 1867. SOURCE: McMiller, "Buffalo Soldiers," 78.

Commander, L/10th Cavalry, forwards final statement of late Sergeant Young to Commander, 10th Cavalry, Dec 1870. SOURCE: ES, 10 Cav, 1866–71.

YOUNG, John W. H.; Private; F/10th Cav. Served in 10th Cavalry in Cuba, 1898. SOURCE: Cashin, *Under Fire with the Tenth Cavalry*, 344.

YOUNG, Joseph; I/10th Cav. Original member of 10th Cavalry; in troop when organized, Ft Riley, KS, 15 Aug 1867. SOURCE: McMiller, "Buffalo Soldiers," 76.

YOUNG, Lee; Private; L/25th Inf. Deserted, cause unknown, Presidio of San Francisco, CA, 22 Oct 1900. SOURCE: Regt Returns, 25 Inf, Dec 1900.

YOUNG, Lewellen; Private; F/9th Cav. Discharged on certificate of disability with "syphilitic mania," from Ft Robinson, NE, and committed to government asylum. SOURCE: Certificates of Disability, Ft Robinson.

To be conducted from Ft Robinson to asylum, Washington, DC, by Saddler Sgt. Robert Benjamin, 9th Cavalry and Pvt. John W. Nicholls, I/8th Infantry. SOURCE: Order 10, 12 Jan 1889, Post Orders, Ft Robinson.

YOUNG, Oscar; Private; D/24th Inf. At Ft Bayard, NM, 1894. SOURCE: *ANJ* 31 (28 Apr 1894): 609.

YOUNG, Risley W.; Private; I/24th Inf. Mutineer, Houston, 1917, who had second thoughts; wrote farewell letter to his family just before 11 Dec 1917 execution. SOURCE: Haynes, *A Night of Violence*, 3, 147.

Hanged at Ft Sam Houston, TX, 13 Dec 1917, for part in Houston riot. SOURCE: Cleveland *Gazette*, 15 Dec 1917.

YOUNG, Robert; Private; K/10th Cav. Original member of 10th Cavalry; in troop when organized, Ft Riley, KS, 1 Sep 1867. SOURCE: McMiller, "Buffalo Soldiers," 77.

Commander, K/10th Cavalry, forwarded duplicate copy of Young's certifcate of disability to commander, detachment of the 10th Cavalry, Ft Lyon, CO, 22 Feb 1869. SOURCE: LR, Det 10 Cav, 1868–69.

YOUNG, Robert; Private; G/10th Cav. Served in 10th Cavalry, 1898; remained in U.S. during war with Spain. SOURCE: Cashin, *Under Fire with the Tenth Cavalry*, 346.

YOUNG, Robert; Private; K/9th Cav. Private, A/9th Cavalry, on special duty at brigade headquarters since 6 Jun 1902. SOURCE: SD List, A/9 Cav, 7 Jun 1902, Nueva Caceres, Philippines.

Veteran of Philippine Insurrection; private, K/9th Cavalry, at Ft D. A. Russell, WY, in 1910; sharpshooter;

resident of Rock Springs, VA. SOURCE: *Illustrated Review: Ninth Cavalry*, with picture.

YOUNG, Roman; Private; A/9th Cav. At Ft D. A. Russell, WY, in 1910. SOURCE: *Illustrated Review: Ninth Cavalry*, with picture.

YOUNG, Seth; Private; M/9th Cav. At Ft D. A. Russell, WY, in 1910; resident of Grand Chain, IL. SOURCE: *Illustrated Review: Ninth Cavalry*, with picture.

YOUNG, Thomas; Private; F/10th Cav. Fined $6 by garrison court martial, Ft Grant, AZ; sentence overturned for administrative errors in process by commander, Department of Arizona; money returned. SOURCE: *ANJ* 24 (16 Jun 1887): 1014.

Served 1882–87; now age 75. SOURCE: *Winners of the West* 13 (Dec 1935): 2.

YOUNG, Thomas; Sergeant; K/10th Cav. Born in Tennessee; private, K/10th Cavalry, 25 Oct 1892; corporal, 16 Oct 1894; at Ft Custer, MT, 1897. SOURCE: Baker, Roster.

Served as sergeant, K/10th Cavalry, 1898; remained in U.S. during war with Spain. SOURCE: Cashin, *Under Fire with the Tenth Cavalry*, 349.

YOUNG, Tom; Private; C/9th Cav. At Ft D. A. Russell, WY, in 1910; resident of 1011 N. 2nd St., East St. Louis. SOURCE: *Illustrated Review: Ninth Cavalry*, with picture.

YOUNG, William; Private; K/10th Cav. *See* **BRANSFORD**, Wesley, Private, K/10th Cavalry

YOUNG, William; Trumpeter; C/10th Cav. Served in 10th Cavalry in Cuba, 1898. SOURCE: Cashin, *Under Fire with the Tenth Cavalry*, 340.

Fined $10 and $5.80 costs for carrying concealed revolver, Crawford, NE, 24 Dec 1903; paid $5.80 and released. SOURCE: Police Court Docket, Crawford.

YOUNG, William; Private; C/9th Cav. At Ft D. A. Russell, WY, in 1910; resident of Sugartown, AL. SOURCE: *Illustrated Review: Ninth Cavalry*, with picture.

YOUNGS, Arthur B.; Staff Sgt; 10th Cav. Retired from Ft Leavenworth, KS, with thirty years' service. SOURCE: *Cavalry Journal* 41 (Jul 1932): 61.

YOURS, Robert; Sergeant; I/25th Inf. At San Isidro, Philippines, 1902. *See* **WILLIAMS**, John, Private, I/25th Infantry

At Ft Niobrara, NE, 1903. *See* **LINAIRE**, Private, I/25th Infantry

Z

ZANEY, John; QM Sgt; A/10th Cav. Born Washington, DC; Ht 5'10"; black complexion; completed first enlistment, I/24th Infantry, 15 Aug 1881; enlisted in A/24th Infantry, 14 Apr 1882; sergeant, 16 Jul 1883; regimental quartermaster sergeant, 6 Jul 1885; discharged, end of term, Ft Supply, Indian Territory, 2 Jan 1887, character excellent, married; retained $72, clothing $75.76. SOURCE: Descriptive Book, 24 Inf NCS & Band.

ZELLARS, John C.; Private; B/24th Inf. Wounded in action in Cuba, 1898. SOURCE: Muller, *The Twenty Fourth Infantry*, 18.

Bibliography

FOR A LARGE PORTION of the works cited in all sections of this bibliography, the biographical entries in the main body of this volume represent an index to all of the references to black soldiers. There are two major exceptions to this effort at inclusion. Among the official military records, only the materials pertaining specifically to the black regiments that are cited from the National Archives' Record Group 391 and some of the Fort Robinson papers in Record Group 393 were combed for all references to individual soldiers. For the *Army and Navy Journal*, the semiofficial weekly military newspaper, only the years 1885 to 1907 are covered comprehensively. Serials and newspapers for which the coverage of long runs is as close to comprehensive as possible are marked with an asterisk (*).

Among these periodicals, the black weekly newspapers are the most important. In the early 1970s, historians studying the experiences of buffalo soldiers discovered a great variety of information in these papers. Reports from soldier-readers at western outposts appeared frequently in newspapers published in cities such as Richmond, Virginia, and Cleveland, Ohio. The newspapers followed the soldiers' activities closely, a clear indication that the men occupied an important place in the black social structure. This high status—conferred by uniform and rifle, regular pay, and, in most cases, the protection of the flag—contrasted dramatically with the low esteem in which soldiers generally were held and resulted, paradoxically enough, in making the black soldier more readily visible and easier to study for historians than his white counterpart.

Next to the black newspapers, the pension files provide the greatest range and variety of information. In many cases, the sixty files listed in this bibliography contain more than routine details of the applicant's military service. They also offer considerable information about the soldier's life before and after his service and about his family and friends. A number of files extend many years beyond the soldier's death to document the lives of widows and children.

Winners of the West, the monthly magazine of the National Indian War Veterans, is useful primarily as a source of two kinds of information. Because the organization that put out the magazine existed to promote pensions for veterans, *Winners of the West* published a number of first-hand accounts of service in the Indian wars, a number of them by buffalo soldiers. It also reported on the activities of local chapters, some of which were black or had black members. In addition, the magazine, which is very rarely, if ever, cited in studies of black soldiers, published letters from soldiers and widows who expressed their appreciation for assistance with pensions.

Other periodicals also contain a wide range of useful material. The *Army and Navy Journal* evolved over the decades after the Civil War into an approximation of a newspaper of record. It contains news of promotions, reductions, awards, and court martials among enlisted men, transfers of units from one station to another, and a variety of stories concerning black soldiers. The Manila *Times* published a surprising amount of information about the black regiments in the Philippines between 1899 and 1902 and did not shy away from publicizing racial conflict. The major black monthlies, starting with the *Colored American Magazine* and *The Voice of the Negro* and later including *Crisis*, the journal of the National Association for the Advancement of Colored People, also contain substantial material on the black regiments; all of these were combed for references to buffalo soldiers.

Overall, the best sources for the study of the lives of individual black soldiers remain the military records. These start with the enlistment registers, which show when a man enlisted, his place of birth, age at enlistment, civilian occupation, physical description, and regiment. Muster rolls, which list all men present for pay and account for those who are absent, are basic documents useful for tracing a soldier's period of service. Both are in Record Group 94 at the National Archives. Moreover, a wide range of records covers the history of individual regiments and forts, and this book draws on a variety of them.

Finally, as a supplement to the above-mentioned literature and the military records, local sources sometimes provide substantial material. My own research in these materials was confined to sources pertaining to Crawford, Nebraska, the town just east of Fort Robinson, but even this limited sample showed the value of city council minutes, police court records, county tax records, and plat maps in drawing a picture of the community of soldiers and veterans and their families.

Books

Alexander, Charles. *The Battles and Victories of Allen Allensworth.* Boston: Sherman, French, and Co., 1914.

Amos, Preston E. *Above and Beyond in the West: Black Medal of Honor Winners, 1870–1890.* Washington, DC: Potomac Corral, 1974.

Armes, George A. *Ups and Downs of an Army Officer.* Washington, DC, 1900.

Beasley, Delilah L. *Negro Trailblazers of California.* Los Angeles: Mirror Printing, 1919.

Bigelow, John, Jr. *On the Bloody Trail of Geronimo.* Los Angeles: Westernlore, 1958.

———. *Reminiscences of the Santiago Campaign.* New York and London, 1899.

Billington, Monroe L. *New Mexico's Buffalo Soldiers, 1866–1900.* Niwot, CO: University of Colorado Press, 1991.

Boris, Joseph J., ed. *Who's Who in Colored America.* New York: Who's Who in Colored America Corp., 1927.

Broadstone, M. A., ed. *History of Greene County, Ohio, Its People, Industries, and Institutions.* Indianapolis: B. F. Brown, 1918.

Carroll, John M., comp. *The Black Military Experience in the American West.* New York: Liveright, 1971.

Carter, William H. *The Life of Lt. General Chaffee.* Chicago: University of Chicago Press, 1917.

Cashin, Herschel V., et al. *Under Fire with the Tenth U.S. Cavalry.* New York: F. Tennyson Neely, 1899.

Clendenen, Clarence C. *Blood on the Border: The United States Army and the Mexican Irregulars.* New York: Macmillan, 1969.

Coston, W. Hilary. *The Spanish-American War Volunteer.* Middletown, PA: Mount Pleasant Printery, 1899.

Coyle, William, ed. *Ohio Authors and Their Books.* Cleveland: The World Publishing Co., 1962.

Cromwell, John W. *The Negro in American History: Men and Women Eminent in the Evolution of the American of African Descent.* Washington, DC: The American Negro Academy, 1914.

Curtis, Mary. *The Black Soldier, or, the Colored Boys of the United States Army*. Washington, DC: Murray Bros., 1918.

Davis, Elizabeth Lindsay. *Lifting as They Climb*. Chicago: National Association of Colored Women, 1933.

Fletcher, Marvin E. *The Black Soldier and Officer in the United States Army, 1891–1917*. Columbia: University of Missouri Press, 1974.

Foner, Jack D. *The United States Soldier between Two Wars: Army Life and Reforms, 1865–1898*. New York: Humanities Press, 1970.

Fowler, Arlen L. *The Black Infantry in the West, 1869–1891*. Westport, CT: Greenwood Publishing Corp., 1971.

Gatewood, Willard B., Jr., comp. *"Smoked Yankees" and the Struggle for Empire: Letters from Negro Soldiers, 1898–1902*. Urbana: University of Illinois Press, 1971.

Glass, Edward L. N. *History of the Tenth Cavalry*. Tucson, AZ: Acme Printing Co., 1921.

Guthrie, James M. *Camp-Fires of the Afro-American, or, the Colored Man as a Patriot*. Philadelphia: Afro-American Publishing Co., 1899.

Hartshorn, William N., ed. *An Era of Progress and Promise, 1863–1910*. Boston: Priscilla Publishing Co., 1910.

Haynes, Robert V. *A Night of Violence: The Houston Riot of 1917*. Baton Rouge: Louisiana State University Press, 1976.

Hine, Darlene C., Elsa Barkley Brown, and Rosalyn Terborg-Penn, eds. *Black Women in America: An Historical Encyclopedia*. Brooklyn, NY: Carlson Publishing Inc., 1993.

Historical and Pictorial Review, Ninth Cavalry Division, United States Army, Camp Funston, Kansas, 1941. N.p.: Army and Navy Publishing Co., [1942].

Illustrated Review: Ninth Cavalry, U.S.A., Fort D. A. Russell, Wyoming, 1910. Denver: Medley and Johnson, 1910.

Johnson, Edward A. *History of Negro Soldiers in the Spanish-American War, and Other Items of Interest*. Raleigh, NC: Capital Printing Co., 1899.

Joiner, William A. *A Half Century of Freedom of the Negro in Ohio*. Xenia, OH: Smith Adv. Co., 1915.

Kelley, William Fitch, comp. and ed. *Pine Ridge, 1890*. San Francisco: Pierre Bovis, 1971.

Koger, A. Briscoe. *The Maryland Negro in Our Wars*. Baltimore: Clarke Press, 1942.

Leckie, William H. *The Buffalo Soldiers: A Narrative of the Negro Cavalry in the West*. Norman: University of Oklahoma Press, 1967.

Lee, Irwin H. *Negro Medal of Honor Men*. New York: Dodd, Mead, 1967.

Logan, Rayford W., and Michael R. Winston, eds. *Dictionary of American Negro Biography*. New York: W. W. Norton and Co., 1982.

Lynk, Miles V. *The Black Troopers, or, the Daring Heroism of the Negro Soldiers in the Spanish-American War*. Jackson, TN: Lynk Publishing Co., 1899.

McGinnis, Frederick A. *A History and an Interpretation of Wilberforce University*. Wilberforce, OH: Brown Publishing Co., 1941.

Morison, Elting B., and John M. Blum, eds. *The Letters of Theodore Roosevelt*. 8 volumes. Cambridge, MA: Harvard University Press, 1951–1954.

Muller, William G. *The Twenty Fourth Infantry: Past and Present*. Fort Collins, CO: Old Army Press, 1972.

Nankivell, John, comp. *History of the Twenty-fifth Regiment, United States Infantry, 1869–1926*. Fort Collins, CO: Old Army Press, 1972.

Northrup, Herbert R. *Organized Labor and the Negro*. New York: Harper and Brothers, 1944.

Payne, Daniel A. *History of the African Methodist Episcopal Church*. Nashville: Publishing House of the African Methodist Episcopal Sunday-School Union, 1891.

Peterson, Robert W. *Only the Ball Was White*. Englewood Cliffs, NJ: Prentice Hall, 1970.

Plummer, Nellie Arnold. *Out of the Depths, or, the Triumph of the Cross*. Hyattsville, MD, 1927.

Reasons, George, and Sam Patrick. *They Had a Dream*. Los Angeles: Times Syndicate, 1969.

Richardson, Clement. *The National Cyclopedia of the Colored Race*. Montgomery, AL: National Publishing Co., 1919.

Richings, George F. *Evidences of Progress among Colored People*. Philadelphia: George S. Ferguson Co., 1897.

Rickey, Don, Jr. *Forty Miles a Day on Beans and Hay: The Enlisted Soldier Fighting the Indian Wars*. Norman: University of Oklahoma Press, 1972.

Schubert, Frank N. *Buffalo Soldiers, Braves, and the Brass: The Story of Fort Robinson, Nebraska*. Shippensburg, PA: White Mane Publishing Co., 1993.

Scipio, L. Albert, II. *Last of the Black Regulars: A History of the 24th Infantry Regiment (1869–1951)*. Silver Spring, MD: Roman Publications, 1983.

Simmons, William J. *Men of Mark: Eminent, Progressive, and Rising*. Cleveland: G. M. Rewell and Co., 1887.

Souvenir Book: Crawford, Nebraska. 75th Year. 1886–1961. Crawford, NE: N.p., 1961.

Spero, Sterling D., and Abram L. Harris. *The Black Worker: The Negro and the Labor Movement*. New York: Columbia University Press, 1931.

Stallard, Patricia Y. *Glittering Misery: Dependents of the Indian Fighting Army*. Fort Collins, CO: Old Army Press, 1978.

Steward, Theophilus G. *Active Service, or, Religious Work among U.S. Soldiers*. New York: U.S. Army Aid Association, 1897.

———. *The Colored Regulars in the United States Army*. Philadelphia: African Methodist Episcopal Book Concern, 1904.

———. *Fifty Years in the Gospel Ministry*. Philadelphia: African Methodist Episcopal Book Concern, 1921.

———, and William Steward. *Gouldtown, a Very Remarkable Settlement of Ancient Date*. Philadelphia: J. B. Lippincott Co., 1913.

Stover, Earl F. *Up from Handymen: The United States Army Chaplaincy, 1865–1920*. Washington, DC: Office of the Chief of Chaplains, Department of the Army, 1977.

Sweeney, W. Allison. *History of the American Negro in the Great War*. N.p.: G. G. Sapp, 1919.

Talbert, Horace. *The Sons of Allen*. Xenia, OH: Aldine Press, 1906.

Taylor, Alrutheus A. *The Negro in South Carolina during the Reconstruction*. Washington, DC: Association for the Study of Negro Life and History, 1924.

Thweatt, Hiram. *What the Newspapers Say of the Negro Soldier in the Spanish-American War*. Thomasville, GA: N.p., n.d.

Weaver, John D. *The Brownsville Raid*. New York: W. W. Norton and Co., 1973.

Wharfield, Harold B. *With Scouts and Cavalry at Fort Apache*. Edited by John A. Carroll. Tucson: Arizona Pioneer Historical Society, 1965.

———. *10th Cavalry and Border Fights*. El Cajon, CA: H. B. Wharfield, 1965.

Williams, C. H. *Sidelights on Negro Soldiers*. Boston: B. J. Brimmer Co., 1923.

Work, Monroe N. *The Negro Year Book, 1912*. Tuskegee, AL: Tuskegee Institute, n.d.

———. *The Negro Yearbook, 1918–1919*. Tuskegee, AL: Tuskegee Institute, n.d.

———. *The Negro Yearbook, 1925–1926*. Tuskegee, AL: Tuskegee Institute, n.d.

———. *The Negro Yearbook, 1931–1932*. Tuskegee, AL: Tuskegee Institute, n.d.

Wright, Richard R., ed. *The Centennial Encyclopedia of the AME Church*. Philadelphia: African Methodist Episcopal Book Concern, 1916.

———, ed. *The Encyclopedia of the African Methodist Episcopal Church*. Philadelphia: African Methodist Episcopal Book Concern, 1947.

Yenser, Thomas, ed. *Who's Who in Colored America, 1933–37*. Brooklyn, NY: Thomas Yenser, 1937.

Young, James Rankin. *Reminiscences and Thrilling Stories of the War by Returned Heroes*. Philadelphia: National Publishing Co., 1899.

Articles

Barrow, Stephen B. "Christmas in the United States Army." *Colored American Magazine* 8 (February 1905).

Billington, Monroe L. "Black Cavalrymen and Apache Indians in New Mexico Territory." *Fort Concho and the South Plains Journal* 22 (Summer 1990).

Clement, Thomas J. "Athletics in the American Army." *Colored American Magazine* 8 (January 1905).

Coffman, Edward M. "Army Life on the Frontier, 1865–1898." *Military Affairs* 20 (1956).

"Colored Doughboy Reprimands Roosevelt." *US Army Recruiting News* 11 (1 August 1929).

Fortune, T. Thomas. "The Filipino." *The Voice of the Negro* 1 (March 1904, May 1904, June 1904).

Frierson, Eugene P. "An Adventure in the Big Horn Mountains, or, the Trials and Tribulations of a Recruit." *Colored American Magazine* 8 (April 1905, May 1905, June 1905).

Gatewood, Willard B., Jr. "Indiana Negroes and the Spanish-American War." *Indiana Magazine of History* 65 (June 1973).

———. "Kansas Negroes and the Spanish-American War." *Kansas Historical Quarterly* 37 (Autumn 1971).

Hunter, John W. "A Negro Trooper of the Ninth Cavalry." *Frontier Times Magazine* 4 (April 1927).

Hutcheson, Grote. "The Ninth Regiment of Cavalry." *Journal of the Military Service Institution of the United States* 8 (1892).

Lemus, Rienzi B. "The Enlisted Man in Action, or, the Colored American Soldier in the Philippines." *Colored American Magazine* 5 (May 1902).

Lowe, Albert S. "Camp Life of the Tenth U.S. Cavalry." *Colored American Magazine* 7 (March 1904).

Miles, Susan. "Fort Concho in 1877." *West Texas Historical Association Yearbook* 35 (October 1959).

Perry, Alexander. "The Ninth U.S. Cavalry in the Sioux Campaign of 1890." *Journal of the United States Cavalry Association* 4 (March 1891).

Remington, Frederick. "Vagabonding with the Tenth." *Cosmopolitan Magazine* 22 (February 1897).

Robinson, Michael C., and Frank N. Schubert. "David Fagen: An Afro-American Rebel in the Philippines, 1899–1901." *Pacific Historical Review* 44 (February 1975).

Schubert, Frank N. "The Fort Robinson Y.M.C.A.: A Social Organization in a Black Regiment." *Nebraska History* 55 (Summer 1974).

———. "The Suggs Affray: The Black Cavalry in the Johnson County War." *Western Historical Quarterly* 4 (January 1973).

———. "The Violent World of Emanuel Stance, Fort Robinson, 1887." *Nebraska History* 55 (Summer 1974).

Simmons, Charlie. "Thanksgiving Day in the Tenth Cavalry." *The Voice of the Negro* 2 (January 1905).

Stover, Earl F. "Chaplain Henry V. Plummer, His Ministry, and His Court Martial." *Nebraska History* 56 (Spring 1975).

Sullivan, Jerry M. "Fort McKavett: A Texas Frontier Post." *Museum Journal* 20 (1981).

Terrell, Mary Church. "A Sketch of Mingo Sanders." *The Voice of the Negro* 4 (March 1904).

Thompson, Era Bell. "Veterans Who Never Came Home." *Ebony* 27 (October 1972).

Villard, Oswald Garrison. "The Negro in the Regular Army." *Atlantic Monthly* 91 (June 1903).
Watson, James W. "Scouting in Arizona." *Journal of the United States Cavalry Association* 10 (June 1897).

Periodicals

Army and Navy Journal, 1879–1916.
Army and Navy Register, 1905.
Army Digest, 1966.
*Cavalry Journal, 1928–1932, 1937–1939, 1942–1945.
**Colored American Magazine*, 1897–1909.
*Crisis, 1910–1931.
The Independent, 1898–1900.
*Infantry Journal, 1904–1930, 1936–1950.
Leslie's Weekly, 1884–1900.
Newsweek, 1972.
9th and 10th Cavalry Association Bulletin, 1972–73.
**The Voice of the Negro*, 1904–1906.
**Winners of the West*, 1923–1939.

Newspapers

(Buffalo, Wyoming) *Big Horn Sentinel*, 1886.
Buffalo (Wyoming) *Bulletin*, 1890.
Cheyenne (Wyoming) *Democratic Leader/Daily Leader/State Leader*, 1887, 1899–1912.
(Cheyenne) *Wyoming State Tribune*, 1898–1912.
Chicago *Broadax*, 1904.
Chicago *Defender*, 1929–1934.
Cleveland *Call & Post*, 1934.
*Cleveland *Gazette*, 1884–1934.
Cleveland *Plain Dealer*, 1934.
*Crawford (Nebraska) *Bulletin*, 1902–1904.
Crawford (Nebraska) *Gazette*, 1894.
*Crawford (Nebraska) *Tribune*, 1897–1916.
Fargo-Moorhead (Minnesota) *Forum*, 1974.
Fremont Clipper (Lander, Wyoming), 1897–1906.
*Indianapolis *Freeman*, 1897–1906.
Lincoln (Nebraska) *Daily State Journal*, 1885.
Louisville (Kentucky) *Courier-Journal*, 1956.
Kansas City (Kansas) *American Citizen*, 1905.
Kearney (Nebraska) *New Era*, 1885.
*Manila (Philippines) *Times*, 1899–1902.
New York *Age*, 1905, 1929–1934.
New York Times, 1972–73.
Omaha *Bee*, 1886–87.
Omaha *Progress*, 1893.
Omaha *World-Herald*, 1992.
Pittsburgh *Courier*, 1929.
*Richmond *Planet*, 1895–1900.

Rock Springs (Wyoming) *Miner*, 1899.
Salt Lake City *Tribune*, 1898.
San Francisco *Chronicle*, 1899–1902.
Sheridan (Wyoming) *Post*, 1904–5.
(Springfield) *Illinois State Register*, 1937.
Toledo *Blade*, 1918.
*Washington *Bee*, 1907–8.
Washington *Colored American*, 1901.
Washington *Post*, 1906–7.
Washington *Star*, 1902–1905, 1929.
*Wichita *Searchlight*, 1900–1902.

U.S. Government Publications and Documents

*Adjutant General, U.S. Army. *Correspondence Regarding the War with Spain.* 2 vols. Washington, DC: Government Printing Office, 1902.
*———. *Bulletins*, 1912–1916.
*———. *Circulars*, 1866–1873, 1875–1878, 1880–81, 1883–1902, 1904–1910, 1912.
*———. *General Court Martial Orders*, 1872, 1874–1894.
*———. *General Orders*, 1866–1910.
———. *Official Army Register*, 1935, 1937.
*———. *American Decorations. Supplement I.* Washington, DC: Government Printing Office, 1937.
Division of the Philippines, U.S. Army. *Alphabetical List of Officers Serving in the Division.* Manila, 1903.
*Secretary of War. *Annual Reports*, 1867–1917.
U.S. Senate. Philippines Committee. *Hearings on Affairs in the Philippine Islands.* 57th Cong., 1st sess., 1902, Senate Document 331.

Unpublished Manuscripts and Documents

Baker, Edward L. Roster of 10th Cavalry Noncommissioned Officers. 1897.
Clark, Michael J. T. "A History of the Twenty-fourth United States Infantry Regiment in Utah, 1896–1900." Ph.D. diss., University of Utah, 1979.
Crawford, Nebraska. Police Court Docket, 1891–1907.
Dawes County (Nebraska). Tax Records, County Treasurer's Office, 1887–1916.
Fletcher, Marvin E. "The Negro Soldier and the United States Army, 1891–1917." Ph.D. diss., University of Wisconsin, 1968.
Hamilton, George F. "History of the Ninth Regiment, U.S. Cavalry." Unpublished manuscript, U.S. Military Academy Library, West Point, New York.
Mann, Simpson. Interview by Don Rickey, Jr. Nebraska State Historical Society, Lincoln, Nebraska.
McMiller, Anita W. "Buffalo Soldiers: The Formation of the Tenth Cavalry Regiment from September 1866 to August 1867." MMAS thesis, U.S. Army Command and General Staff College, Ft Leavenworth, Kansas, 1990.
Ninth Cavalry. "Register of the Commissioned Officers Belonging to the Ninth U.S. Cavalry from Its Organization, July 28, 1866, to July 28, 1893. Also . . . a Complete Roster of Commissioned and Non-Commissioned Officers, Corrected to July 28, 1893." Headquarters, Ninth U.S. Cavalry, Fort Robinson, Nebraska, 1893.
Rickey, Don, Jr. "The Negro Regulars: A Combat Record, 1866–91." Unpublished paper in author's files.

Taylor, David. "Minnesota Black Spanish-American War Veterans." Unpublished paper in author's files.

Thompson, Erwin N. "The Negro Regiments of the U.S. Regular Army, 1866–1900." MA thesis, University of California, Davis, 1966.

Wilson, Charlotte. "History of Fort Niobrara." Unpublished paper, Everett Pitt Wilson Papers, Nebraska State Historical Society, Lincoln, Nebraska.

Archival Collections

Denver Public Library Western History Collection, Denver, Colorado
    Augustus W. Corliss Diary
Rutherford B. Hayes Library, Fremont, Ohio
    Blanche K. Bruce Miscellaneous Manuscripts
    Rutherford B. Hayes Papers
Kansas State Historical Society, Topeka, Kansas
    Frederick Funston Papers
    Kansas State Baptist Convention, Proceedings of Annual Meetings, 1900, 1902
Nebraska State Historical Society, Lincoln, Nebraska
    Isaac Bailey Collection
    E. S. Ricker Tablets
U.S. Army Military History Institute, Carlisle, Pennsylvania
    10th Cavalry Papers

Military Records

Records of the Office of the Quartermaster General. Record Group 92, National Archives
    Quartermaster Consolidated File, Fort Robinson, Nebraska.

Records of the Adjutant General's Office, 1780–1917. Record Group 94, National Archives
    Appointment, commission, and personal files.
        File 4634 ACP 91, Theophilus G. Steward.
        File 3406 PRD 1894, David R. Dillon.
    Carded Records. Voluntary Organizations. Spanish-American War.
    Company Returns, L/49th Infantry, 1900.
    Descriptive Books, 49th Infantry, U.S. Volunteers.
    Document Files, 1890–1917.
    General Orders, Philippine Military Government, 1900.
    General Orders, 49th Infantry, U.S. Volunteers, 1900.
    Hospital Papers, Spanish-American War.
    Letters Sent, 49th Infantry, U.S. Volunteers.
    Medical History, Fort Robinson.
    Muster Rolls, H/24th Infantry, 1898–99.
    Muster Rolls, I/24th Infantry, 1898–99.
    Muster Rolls, L/49th Infantry, U.S. Volunteers, 1900.
    Order Book, F/49th Infantry, U.S. Volunteers.
    Regimental Returns, 9th Cavalry, 1881–1904.
    Regimental Returns, 10th Cavalry, 1898–1906.
    Regimental Returns, 24th Infantry, 1899–1902.

Regimental Returns, 25th Infantry, 1899–1902.
Regimental Returns, 10th Infantry, U.S. Volunteers.
Regimental Returns, 49th Infantry, U.S. Volunteers.
Register of Enlistments.
Special Orders, 1893–1906.

Records of the Office of the Judge Advocate General (Army). Record Group 153, National
    Archives
Proceedings of General Court Martial, David Dillon.
Proceedings of General Court Martial, Herman Hector, Jr.
Proceedings of General Court Martial, Barney McKay.
Proceedings of General Court Martial, Henry V. Plummer.
Proceedings of General Court Martial, Emanuel Stance.

Records of United States Regular Army Mobile Units, 1821–1942. Record Group 391, National
    Archives
Descriptive and Assignment Cards of Recruits, 25th Infantry, 1869–1914.
Descriptive and Assignment Rolls of Recruits, 25th Infantry.
Descriptive Book, H/9th Cavalry, 1885–1906.
Descriptive Book, B/10th Cavalry, 1880–1896.
Descriptive Book, 10th Cavalry Officers and Noncommissioned Officers, 1898–1905.
Descriptive Book, 24th Infantry Noncommissioned Officers and Band, 1885–1896.
Descriptive Book, D/25th Infantry, 1869–1907.
Descriptive Book, F/25th Infantry, 1901–1906.
Endorsements Sent, 10th Cavalry, 1866–1871, 1873–1883.
General Orders, 10th Cavalry, 1915.
General and Special Orders Issued, Detachment of 10th Cavalry, 1868–69.
Letters and Endorsements Sent, 9th Cavalry, 1896–1899.
Letters and Orders Received, 24th Infantry, 1893.
Letters Received, Detachment of 10th Cavalry, 1868–69.
Letters Received, 25th Infantry, 1901.
Letters Sent, C/9th Cavalry, 1883–1886.
Letters Sent, 10th Cavalry, 1866–1871, 1873–1883, and 1889–1904.
Letters Sent, 24th Infantry, 1902.
Letters Sent, 25th Infantry, 1899–1902.
Letters Sent and Orders Issued by the 2nd Squadron, 9th Cavalry, September–November 1900.
Miscellaneous Records, 10th Cavalry, 1869–1918.
Miscellaneous Records, 25th Infantry, 1880–1904.
Muster Roll, Detachment, 9th Cavalry, Ft McKinney, Wyoming, 28 Feb–30 Apr 1891.
Muster Roll, Detachment, 10th Cavalry, 22 Dec 1887–29 Feb 1888.
Muster Rolls, Detachment of Regimental Noncommissioned Staff, 10th Cavalry, Dec 1899–
    Dec 1900.
Muster Rolls, Detachment, Field and Staff, 2nd Squadron, 10th Cavalry, 1902–1905.
Name File, 9th Cavalry, 1867–1898.
Name File, 10th Cavalry, 1866–1868.
Name File, 24th Infantry, 1866–1901.
Press Copies of Letters Sent, 24th Infantry, July–December 1901.
Regimental Orders, 9th Cavalry, 1875–1891.
Register of Summary Court Cases, 1st Battalion, 25th Infantry, 1902.

Scrapbooks, 25th Infantry.
Special Orders, 10th Cavalry, 1898–99, 1902, 1909.
Terrell, First Lieutenant Henry S., Recruiting Officer, Descriptive Book of Recruits, 1907–8.

Records of United States Army Continental Commands, 1821–1920. Record Group 393, National Archives
Certificates of Disability, Division of the Missouri, 1875–1887.
Certificates of Disability, Ft Robinson, Nebraska.
Department of Texas, Annual Report, 1879.
General Court Martial Orders, Department of Texas, 1873.
Investigation of Charges against Chaplain Henry V. Plummer.
Letters Received, Department of the Platte, 1893.
Letters Sent, Department of the Platte.
Letters Sent, Fort Robinson, Nebraska.
Letters Sent, Post Surgeon, Fort Robinson, Nebraska.
List of Interments, Fort Robinson, Nebraska.
Miscellaneous Records, Department of the Missouri, 1904–1912.
Miscellaneous Records, Department of the Platte, 1894–1898.
Miscellaneous Records, Department of Texas, 1870–1912.
Monthly Reports of Post Schools, Department of the Platte.
Post Orders, Fort Robinson, Nebraska.
Post Returns, Fort Robinson, Nebraska.
Register of Correspondence, Fort Robinson, Nebraska, 1887–1894.
Register of Correspondence, Post Surgeon, Fort Robinson, Nebraska, 1887–1904.
Register of Letters Received, Fort Robinson, Nebraska, 1903–4.
Reports of Inspections, Department of the Platte. 2 vols.
Special Orders, Department of the Missouri, 1902–1904.
Summary Court Record, Fort Robinson, Nebraska.

Records of United States Army Overseas Operations and Commands, 1898–1942. Record Group 395, National Archives
Register of Charges and Specifications for Cases Tried by Summary Court, San Isidro, Nueva Ecija, Philippines, December 1899–April 1903.

Veterans Administration Pension Files

VA File XC 2659797, Thomas H. Allsup
VA File SO 1388939, Henry Anderson
VA File C 2579187, John B. Anderson
VA File SC 12244, Louis Anderson
VA File XC 2715800, Edward L. Baker
VA File C 2366152, Wilson C. Ballard
VA File XC 2625176, Benjamin Bard
VA File WC 927337, Robert A. Benjamin
VA File XC 2499129, Caleb Benson
VA File C 2580814, Henry Berryman
VA File SC 258952, Joseph A. Blackburn
VA File XC 876498, Isaac Blake
VA File XC 970422, Joseph Blew

VA File C 2581520, William Branch
VA File SC 11242, Wesley Bransford
VA File C 2349975, Henry Briscoe
VA Invalid Claim 1061386, Preston Brooks
VA File XC 2658566, Richard Bunch
VA File C 2577213, William H. Bush
VA File C 2441072, George Byers
VA File C 2360629, Webb Chatmoun
VA File XC 2643082, Frederick Colbert
VA File XC 921596, Joseph F. M. Counce
VA File XC 2624113, George D. Crockett
VA File XC 2624105, Floyd H. Crumbly
VA File C 2359804, Edward W. Crump
VA File C 2363092, Henry Dent
VA File C 2359453, John Edmonds
VA File C 2577383, Frank Evans, Sr.
VA File C 2580332, George W. Ford
VA File C 2497800, William G. Gardner
VA File C 2583656, James H. Harris
VA File C 2349975, Alex Hatcher
VA File C 2598484, John Henson
VA File C 2326719, Perry Hood
VA File XC 896871, John C. Howerton
VA File C 2555351, James F. Jackson
VA File WC 611769, Jeremiah Jones
VA File XC 2705872, Henry McClain
VA File XC 2659455, Barney McKay
VA File XC 2628090, George F. Mason
VA File C 2493371, John Only
VA File XC 866859, Beverly Perea
VA File WC 17458, Henry V. Plummer
VA File WC 10020, Alfred Pride
VA File C 1392575, George W. Prioleau
VA File XC 2659372, John C. Proctor
VA File XC 2625648, Mingo Sanders
VA File XC 2648848, Rufus Slaughter
VA File C 2410890, Arthur Smith
VA File WC 858864, Thomas Smith
VA File WC 1218572, Augustus Snoten
VA File XC 978555, Peter Snoten
VA File SC 874522, Alex Stepney
VA File XC 2650212, Zekiel Sykes
VA File SC 11405, John Taylor
VA File C 2643745, Archy Wall
VA File WC 894780, William Washington
VA File C 2557169, James C. Williams
VA File C 2323163, George Wilson

Appendix

Black Enlisted Men in the Regular Army, 1867–1916

Year	9th Cav	10th Cav	38th Inf	41st Inf	39th Inf	40th Inf
1867	844	590	1,003	584	669	870
1868	924	1,066	987	783	678	748
					25th Inf	
1869	899	903	919	536	997	
			24th Inf			
1870	**966**	**1,055**	**256**		**477**	
1871	827	937	622		537	
1872	660	618	588		649	
1873	690	729	612		616	
1874	744	951	587		554	
1875	647	658	431		319	
1876	671	772	296		442	
1877	453	953	338		350	
1878	452	804	368		332	
1879	689	722	438		411	
1880	**704**	**728**	**516**		**465**	
1881	716	729	422		443	
1882	707	707	491		478	
1883	735	775	471		472	
1884	759	732	459		453	
1885	747	734	428		423	
1886	622	699	456		419	
1887	663	662	480		478	
1888	729	766	479		454	
1889	752	750	480		451	
1890	**735**	**750**	**497**		**428**	
1891	647	625	438		415	
1892	539	488	475		456	
1893	629	588	453		461	
1894	611	583	486		470	
1895	567	565	517		513	
1896	582	570	522		522	
1897	584	592	512		516	
1898	887	968	576		592	
1899	1,278	1,239	1,379		953	
1900	**1,219**	**1,178**	**1,490**		**1,079**	
1901	789	1,211	1,652		1,716	
1902	1,294	920	964		1,457	
1903	771	804	786		806	
1904	801	787	810		808	
1905	1,052	742	747		767	
1906	992	770	830		799	
1907	686	647	752		840	
1908	923	689	788		810	
1909	734	641	777		944	
1910	**753**	**763**	**808**		**624**	
1911	758	760	680		728	
1912	844	804	1,258		857	
1913	811	780	1,750		1,161	
1914	912	876	1,686		1,796	
1915	1,038	968	1,849		1,808	
1916	940	990	1,646		1,771	

Source: Regimental returns; all data as reported for 30 June.

Ninth Cavalry Sergeants Major

Name	Dates Rank Held
William L. Henderson	[?]–4 Jan 1869
	1 Jul 1869–22 Oct 1871
Joseph Relf	23 Oct 1871–1 Nov 1877
William King	1 Nov 1877–7 May 1880
Benjamin F. Davis	8 May 1880–26 Jan 1885
Jeremiah Jones	12 Feb 1885–5 Jul 1897
John H. Anderson	6 Jul 1897–23 Nov 1899
William H. Brown	24 Nov 1899–14 Dec 1899
Daniel C. Robinson	1 Jun 1900–14 Jun 1901
Alonzo Myers	28 Jun 1901–26 Jun 1904
Horace Cooper	26 Jun 1904–31 Jul 1904
Thomas Goodloe	6 Aug 1904–24 Aug 1904
John A. Logan	[Sep 1904?]–30 Jun 1915*

Source: Regimental returns, supplemented by biographical files.
*Enlisted men accounted for by name only through June 1915.

Tenth Cavalry Sergeants Major

Name	Dates Rank Held
Jacob B. Thomas	1 Oct 1867–11 Feb 1868
Frank Wilson	7 Apr 1868–11 Sep 1870
George Goldsby	12 Sep 1870–11 Sep 1872
Joseph Parker	3 Apr 1873–20 Jan 1882
David Haskins	1 May 1882–1 Sep 1882
George R. Garnett	20 Dec 1882–7 Jan 1891
Henry Briceño	7 Jan 1891–24 Apr 1892
Edward L. Baker, Jr.	25 Apr 1892–5 Aug 1898
	19 Mar 1899–25 Sep 1899
Charles B. Turner	6 Aug 1899–18 Mar 1899
Presley Holliday	1 Oct 1899–1 Sep 1907
	31 Oct 1907–24 Jan 1908
Charles Faulkner	1 Sep 1907–31 Oct 1907
John C. Pendergrass	24 Jan 1908–14 Jul 1910
Eugene Frierson	15 Jul 1910–30 Jun 1915*

Source: Regimental returns, supplemented by biographical files.
*Enlisted men accounted for by name only through June 1915.

Twenty-fourth Infantry Sergeants Major

Name	*Dates Rank Held*
Jacob W. Richardson	31 Nov 1869–9 Mar 1870
James W. Sullivant	15 Aug 1870–7 Oct 1872
	1 Jul 1874–3 Apr 1877
Thomas Lamb	28 Feb 1873–Jun 1874
Edward Davis	1 May 1877–10 Jun 1880
Robert L. Davis	1 Jul 1880–15 Feb 1884
John Sample	1 May 1884–21 Jul 1885
George Lewis	29 Jul 1885–19 Dec 1887
William H. Scroggins	19 Dec 1887–23 Jul 1888
Paschall Conley	5 Oct 1888–1 Feb 1889
James W. Abbott	17 Feb 1889–22 Jun 1897
Benjamin Brown	4 Jul 1897–24 Aug 1898
Walter E. Smith	24 Aug 1898–30 Nov 1898
John R. Green	1 Dec 1898–23 Jul 1901
Walter B. Williams	23 Jul 1901–6 Sep 1906
	21 Mar 1907–30 Jun 1915*
George D. Powell	6 Sep 1906–15 Nov 1906
Mack Stanfield	1 Dec 1906–21 Mar 1907

Source: Regimental returns, supplemented by biographical files.
*Enlisted men accounted for by name only through June 1915.

Twenty-fifth Infantry Sergeants Major

Name	*Dates Rank Held*
Rudolph B. Bagine	20 Apr 1869–5 Nov 1869
Michael Brady	Jan 1870–1 Jul 1871
William L. Russell	1 Sep 1871–15 Feb 1872
William F. King	1 Mar 1872–7 Dec 1874
John Sample	13 May 1875–[Aug 1878?]
James Johnson	[Aug 1878?]–30 Jun 1881
	16 Jul 1888–13 Jun 1894
Richard Craig	10 Nov 1881–19 Mar 1883
	24 Aug 1886–16 Jul 1888
Benjamin Morrell	1 Jul 1883–7 Jun 1885
Frank W. Pullen, Jr.	16 Jul 1894–22 Aug 1898
James P. Dundee	15 Nov 1898–11 Jul 1899
William McBryar	[Jul 1899?]–1 Oct 1899
Anthony A. Marrow	[Oct 1899?]–1 Sep 1903
	1 Feb 1904–30 Nov 1914*
Wyatt Huffman	1 Sep 1903–14 Jan 1904

Source: Regimental returns, supplemented by biographical files.
*Enlisted men accounted for by name only through November 1914.

Buffalo Soldiers Killed in Action, 1867–1916

	9th Cav	*10th Cav*	*24th Inf*	*25th Inf*	*Total*
Indian Wars, 1867–1890	44	17	0	0	61
Apache Campaigns, 1879–1881*	(28)	(9)	(0)	(0)	(37)
Spanish-American War, 1898	3	7	11	8	29
Philippine Insurrection, 1899–1902	2	0	12	9	23
Mexico, 1916	0	7	0	0	7
Totals by Regiment	49	31	23	17	120

Source: Regimental returns, supplemented by biographical files.
*Figures for the Apache campaigns are included in total Indian war figures.

Buffalo Soldier Recipients of the Medal of Honor

Name	Rank and Unit	Campaign or Action
Baker, Edward L., Jr.	Sgt Maj, 10th Cav	Spanish-American War, 1898
Bell, Dennis	Pvt, H/10th Cav	Spanish-American War, 1898
Boyne, Thomas	Sgt, C/9th Cav	Victorio Campaign, 1879
Brown, Benjamin	Sgt, C/24th Inf	Paymaster Escort, 1889
Denny, John	Pvt, C/9th Cav	Victorio Campaign, 1879
Factor, Pompey	Pvt, 24th Inf	Staked Plains Expedition, 1875
Greaves, Clinton	Cpl, C/9th Cav	Apache Campaign, 1877
Johnson, Henry	Sgt, D/9th Cav	Ute Campaign, 1879
Jordan, George	Sgt, K/9th Cav	Victorio Campaign, 1879
Lee, Fitz	Pvt, M/10th Cav	Spanish-American War, 1898
McBryar, William	Sgt, K/10th Cav	Apache Campaign, 1890
Mays, Isaiah	Cpl, B/24th Inf	Paymaster Escort, 1889
Paine, Adam	Pvt, 24th Inf	Comanche Campaign, 1874
Payne, Isaac	Trumpeter, 10th Cav	Staked Plains Expedition, 1875
Shaw, Thomas	Sgt, K/9th Cav	Apache Campaign, 1881
Stance, Emanuel	Sgt, F/9th Cav	Texas Raid, 1870
Thompkins, William H.	Cpl, A/10th Cav	Spanish-American War, 1898
Wally, Augustus	Pvt, I/9th Cav	Apache Campaign, 1881
Wanton, George H.	Pvt, M/10th Cav	Spanish-American War, 1898
Ward, John	Sgt, 24th Inf	Staked Plains Expedition, 1875
Williams, Moses	Sgt, I/9th Cav	Apache Campaign, 1881
Wilson, William O.	Cpl, I/9th Cav	Pine Ridge Campaign, 1890
Woods, Brent	Sgt, B/9th Cav	Apache Campaign, 1881

Source: Amos, *Above and Beyond in the West*, identifies all of the men who received the medal for actions during the period of the Indian wars. Cashin, *Under Fire with the Tenth Cavalry*, identifies recipients in the Cuban campaign.

Ninth Cavalry Regimental Headquarters, 1866–1916

Location	*Dates*
New Orleans, LA	9 Sep 1866–9 Mar 1867
Carrollton, LA	9 Mar 1867–27 Mar 1867
San Antonio, TX	Apr 1867–Jun 1867
Camp Stockton, TX	7 Jul 1867–Apr 1868
San Antonio, TX	Apr 1868–9 Sep 1868
Ft Davis, TX	3 Oct 1868–21 Jan 1871
Ft Stockton, TX	23 Jan 1871–16 Apr 1872
Ft Clark, TX	27 Apr 1872–23 Jan 1873
Ringgold Barracks, TX	7 Feb 1873–10 Jun 1875
Ft Clark, TX	1 Jul 1875–19 Oct 1875
Ft Union, NM	3 Dec 1875–15 Feb 1876
Santa Fe, NM	18 Feb 1876–6 Nov 1881
Ft Riley, KS	8 Nov 1881–14 Jun 1885
Ft McKinney, WY	17 Aug 1885–[?] May 1887
Ft Robinson, NE	16 May 1887–2 Apr 1898
Chickamauga Park, GA	23 Apr 1898–30 Apr 1898
Port Tampa, FL	2 May 1898–13 Jun 1898
Cuba	20 Jun 1898–14 Aug 1898
Camp Wikoff, NY	20 Aug 1898–27 Sep 1898
Ft Grant, AZ	5 Oct 1898–28 Jul 1900
Philippines	6 Oct 1900–20 Sep 1902
Ft Walla Walla, WA	24 Oct 1902–19 Oct 1904
Ft Riley, KS	23 Oct 1904–29 Apr 1907
Philippines	2 Jun 1907–15 May 1909
Ft D. A. Russell, WY	15 Jun 1909–11 Mar 1911
San Antonio, TX	15 Mar 1911–9 Jul 1911
Ft D. A. Russell, WY	14 Jul 1911–9 Sep 1912
Douglas, AZ	13 Sep 1912–25 Dec 1915
Philippines	6 Feb 1916–31 Dec 1916

Source: Regimental returns

Tenth Cavalry Regimental Headquarters, 1866–1916

Location	Dates
Ft Leavenworth, KS	24 Sep 1866–5 Aug 1867
Ft Riley, KS	7 Aug 1867–17 Apr 1868
Ft Gibson, Indian Territory	4 May 1868–31 Mar 1869
Camp Wichita/Ft Sill, Indian Territory	12 Apr 1869–5 Jun 1872
Ft Gibson, Indian Territory	11 Jun 1872–23 Apr 1873
Ft Sill, Indian Territory	4 May 1873–27 Mar 1875
Ft Concho, TX	17 Apr 1875–18 Jul 1882
Ft Davis, TX	29 Jul 1882–11 Apr 1885
Whipple Barracks, AZ	20 May 1885–11 Jul 1886
Ft Grant, AZ	22 Jul 1886–28 Nov 1886
Santa Fe, NM	Nov 1886–6 Dec 1888
Ft Apache, AZ	11 Dec 1888–21 Sep 1890
Ft Grant, AZ	27 Sep 1890–25 Apr 1892
Ft Custer, MT	5 May 1892–Nov 1894
Ft Assiniboine, MT	21 Nov 1894–19 Apr 1898
Chickamauga Park, GA	25 Apr 1898–14 May 1898
Lakeland, FL	16 May 1898–7 Jun 1898
Tampa, FL	7 Jun 1898–14 Jun 1898
Cuba	23 Jun 1898–13 Aug 1898
Camp Wikoff, NY	21 Aug 1898–6 Oct 1898
Camp Forse, AL	11 Oct 1898–29 Jan 1899
Ft Sam Houston, TX	4 Feb 1899–28 Apr 1899
Cuba	7 May 1899–24 Apr 1902
Ft Robinson, NE	4 May 1902–1 Mar 1907
Philippines	3 Apr 1907–15 May 1909
Ft Ethan Allen, VT	28 Jul 1909–5 Dec 1913
Ft Huachuca, AZ	19 Dec 1913–9 Mar 1916

Source: Regimental returns

Twenty-fourth Infantry Regimental Headquarters, 1869–1922

Location	*Dates*
Ft McKavett, TX	1 Nov 1869–7 Aug 1872
Ft Brown, TX	1 Sep 1872–18 Jul 1873
Ft Duncan, TX	1 Aug 1873–15 Oct 1874
Ft Brown, TX	30 Oct 1874–1 Jun 1876
Ft Duncan, TX	19 Sep 1876–14 Dec 1876
Ft Clark, TX	16 Dec 1876–9 Feb 1878
Ft Duncan, TX	11 Feb 1878–13 Mar 1879
Ft Clark, TX	14 Mar 1879–2 Apr 1879
Ft Duncan, TX	3 Apr 1879–29 Apr 1880
Ft Davis, TX	18 Jun 1880–15 Oct 1880
Ft Supply, Indian Territory	16 Dec 1880–5 Oct 1887
Ft Sill, Indian Territory	17 Oct 1887–9 Apr 1888
Ft Supply, Indian Territory	17 Apr 1888–1 Jun 1888
Ft Bayard, NM	4 Jun 1888–19 Oct 1896
Ft Douglas, UT	22 Oct 1896–20 Apr 1898
Chickamauga Park, GA	24 Apr 1898–30 Apr 1898
Tampa, FL	2 May 1898–9 Jun 1898
Cuba	25 Jun 1898–26 Aug 1898
Camp Wikoff, NY	3 Sep 1898–23 Sep 1898
Ft Douglas, UT	1 Oct 1898–5 Apr 1899
Presidio of San Francisco, CA	7 Apr 1899–15 Jul 1899
Philippines	19 Aug 1899–28 Jun 1902
Ft Harrison, MT	16 Aug 1902–23 Dec 1905
Philippines	24 Feb 1906–8 Feb 1908
Madison Barracks, NY	25 Mar 1908–28 Nov 1911
Philippines	1 Jan 1912–14 Sep 1915
San Francisco, CA	14 Nov 1915–25 Feb 1916
Ft D. A. Russell, WY	28 Feb 1916–23 Mar 1916
Mexican Border	26 Mar 1916–5 Oct 1922

Source: Regimental returns

518

Twenty-fifth Infantry Regimental Headquarters, 1869–1918

Location	*Dates*
New Orleans, LA	20 Apr 1869–May 1870
Ft Clark, TX	2 Jul 1870–6 May 1872
Ft Davis, TX	26 May 1872–17 May 1880
Ft Randall, SD	29 Jun 1880–17 Nov 1882
Ft Snelling, MN	20 Nov 1882–23 May 1888
Ft Missoula, MT	26 May 1888–10 Apr 1898
Chickamauga Park, GA	15 Apr 1898–6 May 1898
Tampa, FL	7 May 1898–6 Jun 1898
Cuba	22 Jun 1898–13 Aug 1898
Camp Wikoff, NY	22 Aug 1898–29 Sep 1898
Ft Logan, CO	3 Oct 1898–27 Jun 1899
Philippines	31 Oct 1899–6 Jul 1902
Ft Niobrara, NE	27 Aug 1902–23 Jul 1906
Ft Bliss, TX	28 Jul 1906–12 Jun 1907
Philippines	17 Sep 1907–6 Sep 1909
Ft Lawton, WA	5 Oct 1909–1 Jan 1913
Schofield Barracks, HI	15 Jan 1913–18 Aug 1918

Source: Regimental returns